ROTHM
RUGBY UNION
YEARBOOK
1999-2000

ROTHMANS

EDITORS: MICK CLEARY
AND JOHN GRIFFITHS

HEADLINE

Copyright © 1999 Rothmans Publications Ltd

The right of Mick Cleary and John Griffiths to be identified as the authors
of the Work has been asserted by them in accordance with the
Copyright, Designs and Patents Act 1988.

First published in 1999
by HEADLINE BOOK PUBLISHING

Cover photographs.
Front, L to R: Scotland's captain Gary Armstrong in their win against France in the TSB
Five Nations Championship, Paris, 10 April 1999; Jeremy Guscott beats
Christian Stewart to score England's try against South Africa at Twickenham on
5 December 1998; Scott Quinnell (Wales) and Andre Venter (South Africa)
at Wembley on 14 November 1998.
Back, L to R: Jonny Wilkinson (Newcastle) in the Allied Dunbar Premiership against
Richmond, 5 September 1998; Martin Johnson (England) against France.

All photographs by Colorsport unless otherwise credited.

10 9 8 7 6 5 4 3 2 1

All rights reserved. No part of this publication may be reproduced, stored in a
retrieval system, or transmitted, in any form or by any means without the prior written
permission of the publisher, nor be otherwise circulated in any form of binding or
cover other than that in which it is published and without a similar condition
being imposed on the subsequent purchaser.

ISBN 0 7472 7531 9

Copy-editing by Andrew Kinsman, First Rank Publishing, Brighton

Typeset by Letterpart Limited, Reigate, Surrey

Printed and bound in Great Britain by
Mackays of Chatham plc, Chatham, Kent

HEADLINE BOOK PUBLISHING
A division of the Hodder Headline Group
338 Euston Road
London NW1 3BH

www.headline.co.uk
www.hodderheadline.com

CONTENTS

Abbreviations used in the Yearbook	4
Editorial Preface	5
Viewpoint by Bob Dwyer	6
The International Year	
Review of the 1998-99 Season	9
Rugby World Cup 1999 Preview	17
International Championship 1999	49
Tri-Nations Series 1998	64
Other Major Internationals 1998-99	69
Stop Press Results	73
A International Championship 1999	74
European Cup 1998-99	81
European Shield 1998-99	90
Super-12 Series 1999	93
England	
The 1998-99 Season in England	96
Allied Dunbar Premiership	
1998-99	105
English Leagues 1998-99	107
Tetley's Bitter Cup 1998-99	108
Cheltenham & Gloucester Cup	
1998-99	114
English International Players	115
English International Records	126
English Career Records	130
English Clubs 1998-99	132
Scotland	
The 1998-99 Season in Scotland	169
Scottish Leagues 1998-99	173
Tennents Velvet Tri-Series 1998-99	176
Tennents Velvet Cup 1998-99	177
Scotland to Fiji & Australia 1998	180
Scottish International Players	184
Scottish International Records	194
Scottish Career Records	197
Scottish Clubs 1998-99	199
Ireland	
The 1998-99 Season in Ireland	210
Irish Leagues 1998-99	212
Guinness Inter-Provincial Championship	
1998-99	213
Ireland to South Africa 1998	217
Irish International Players	221
Irish International Records	231
Irish Career Records	234
Irish Clubs 1998-99	236
Wales	
The 1998-99 Season in Wales	245
Welsh Leagues 1998-99	248
SWALEC Cup & Challenge Trophy	
1998-99	251
Wales to Southern Africa 1998	256
Welsh International Players	259
Welsh International Records	269
Welsh Career Records	272
Welsh Clubs 1998-99	274
France	
The 1998-99 Season in France	287
France to Argentina & Fiji 1998	291
French International Players	294
French International Records	304
French Career Records	307
Italy	
The 1998-99 Season in Italy	309
Italian International Records	312
Italian Career Records	314
South Africa	
The 1998 Season in South Africa	316
South Africa to Europe 1998	320
South African International Players	325
South African International Records	331
South African Career Records	334
New Zealand	
The 1998 Season in New Zealand	336
New Zealand Maoris to Britain 1998	339
New Zealand International Players	342
New Zealand International Records	349
New Zealand Career Records	353
Australia	
The 1998 Season in Australia	355
Australia to Europe 1998	358
Australian International Players	361
Australian International Records	369
Australian Career Records	372
International	
Results of International Matches	375
International Honours	409
International Referees 1998-99	410
World International Records	412
Other Rugby 1998-99	418
Obituary 1998-99	431
Fixtures 1999-2000	436

ABBREVIATIONS USED IN THIS YEARBOOK

International Teams

A – Australia; Arg – Argentina; AW – Anglo-Welsh; B – British Forces and Home Unions teams; Bb – Barbarians; Be – Belgium; BI – British Isles teams; Bu – Bulgaria; C – Canada; Cr – Croatia; Cv – New Zealand Cavaliers; Cz – Czechoslovakia; E – England; F – France; Fj – Fiji; Gg – Georgia; H – Netherlands; I – Ireland; It – Italy; Iv – Ivory Coast; J – Japan; K – New Zealand Services; M – Maoris; Mo – Morocco; NAm – North America; Nm – Namibia; NZ – New Zealand; NZA – New Zealand Army; P – President's XV; Po – Poland; Pt – Portugal; R – Romania; Ru – Russia; S – Scotland; SA – South Africa; SAm – South America; SK – South Korea; Sp – Spain; Tg – Tonga; US – United States; W – Wales; Wld – World Invitation XV; WS – Western Samoa; Y – Yugoslavia; Z – Zimbabwe.

Other Abbreviations used in the International Listings

(R) – Replacement or substitute; (t) – temporary replacement; [ ] – Rugby World Cup appearances.

NB: When a series has taken place, figures are used to denote the particular matches in which players have featured. Thus NZ 1,3, would indicate that a player has appeared in the First and Third Tests of the relevant series against New Zealand.

Irish Clubs

CIYMS – Church of Ireland Young Men's Society; KCH – King's College Hospital; NIFC – North of Ireland Football Club.

French Clubs

ASF – Association Sportive Française; BEC – Bordeaux Etudiants Club; CASG – Club Athlétique des Sports Generaux; PUC – Paris Université Club; RCF – Racing Club de France; SB – Stade Bordelais; SBUC – Stade Bordelais Université; SCUF – Sporting Club Universitaire de France; SF – Stade Français; SOE – Stade Olympien des Etudiants; TOEC – Toulouse Olympique Employés Club.

South African Provinces

BB – Blue Bulls; Bol – Boland; Bor – Border; EP – Eastern Province; GL – Gauteng Lions; GW – Griqualand West; N – Natal; NT – Northern Transvaal; OFS – Orange Free State; R – Rhodesia; SET – South-East Transvaal; SWA – South-West Africa; SWD – South-West Districts; Tvl – Transvaal; WP – Western Province; WT – Western Transvaal; Z–R – Zimbabwe–Rhodesia.

Australian States

ACT – Australian Capital Territory; NSW – New South Wales; Q – Queensland; V – Victoria; WA – Western Australia.

EDITORIAL PREFACE

The last major sporting event of the millennium will be the fourth Rugby World Cup to be held in Britain, Ireland and France in October and November 1999. This 28th edition of the *Rothmans Rugby Yearbook*, therefore, devotes a major preview section to a tournament that will culminate in the World Cup final at the Millennium Stadium, Cardiff, on 6th November.

Trying to squeeze a quart into the proverbial pint pot, we have been forced to drop some of the traditional aspects of the Yearbook this season. To give in-depth coverage of the game's leading competitions has meant that the awards section has been abandoned for the time being. It is also with regret that we have had to shelve the sections relating to colts and schools rugby to make way for greater detail and comment on the senior game.

We should therefore like to extend our grateful thanks to the contributors who have striven so hard to provide accurate sections on junior rugby in the past. Thanks, too, go to Sean Diffley, who for the last 20 years has been our man in Ireland. As he sets off to enjoy a well-earned retirement, we welcome in his place Karl Johnston.

Our statisticians in the Home Unions, France and overseas have again worked wonders to ensure that accurate details of the major Test matches are sent to us. Particular thanks go out to Michel Breton in France, Walter Pigatto in Italy, Paul Dobson in South Africa, Matthew Alvarez in Australia and Geoff Miller in New Zealand for confirming facts and figures relating to Tests played in their respective countries.

On the home front David Llewellyn and Chris Rhys gave sterling support supplying much of the copy for this edition of the yearbook, while the production team of Andrew Kinsman and Chris Leggett provided the technical expertise behind the scenes. Our thanks to them all.

Mick Cleary
John Griffiths

NOTE: Statistical sections of the Yearbook are complete up to **30 April 1999**.

WORLD CUP KEEPS ON GETTING BETTER AND BETTER

VIEWPOINT
Bob Dwyer – Coach 1991 World Cup Winners, Australia; now coach at Bristol

We are about to witness the most marvellous World Cup ever held. It will be a raging success. Of that I have no doubt. By the beginning of November the world will once again be forced to sit up and take notice of the sport. That is the impact a World Cup has – on players, on coaches, on spectators and on the public at large. To think that just over 12 years ago we didn't have such a tournament. Those in Britain resisted the idea for the simple reason that they feared that it would lead to professionalism.

Well, they were right; it did. But there was nothing wrong in that. The management of professionalism may have been seriously flawed. In fact, in many instances it has been disastrous. But professionalism itself has been a fantastic thing. Just look at the game on the field itself. The players are that much stronger and faster than even four years ago. The speed and power on view in this World Cup will be way beyond that of South Africa 1995. Skill levels are higher for the simple reason that players have more time to practise.

The World Cup has quickly become a vital fixed point in the calendar for everyone. Coaches spend the four-year cycle working out how to get the decisive edge. Just look at South Africa. They were way behind the eight ball when they came out of isolation in 1992, yet by the time they hosted the World Cup three years later they had not only caught up, they had surpassed all the others. Or they had if you take the winning of the World Cup as the ultimate measuring stick of a country's worth. You can argue that the All Blacks were the best team in 1995. You can argue it, but the record books clearly show, and will do so for ever and a day, that the Springboks were the world champions. New Zealand had that honour in 1987 and Australia in 1991. I'd like to think that there was not much argument that those were the best two teams around at the time. I may be biased but I think I'm right.

And this time? New Zealand and Australia are in the box seats. The All Blacks may have had a sticky time of it last year but even by the end of that season they looked as if they were on the way back. Australia look good to me too. They've done well to get through without the injured trio of captain John Eales as well as Matt Burke and Stephen Larkham in the backs. The arrival of Tiaan Strauss

Bristol coach Bob Dwyer, who led Australia to triumph in the 1991 World Cup.

and Patricio Noriega on to the scene doesn't look too bad a move either. And South Africa? I'm not sure. It looks to me as if coach Nick Mallett is actually using the early season games and even the Tri-Nations to experiment. That's how important the World Cup has become. Mallett won't have been as worried by the loss to Wales as everyone seems to think.

These are my three form horses. No surprise there then. Why are the southern hemisphere consistently better? It's in their culture. They are younger than the other countries and have a desire to prove themselves whenever they can. Sport, and rugby in particular with New Zealand and South Africa, gives them that opportunity. The older cultures are more relaxed, less driven, call it what you will. The difference is a mental one. There's certainly no simply physical reason why they should be better.

For the World Cup, Wales are shaping up well. I'm not certain yet, though, just how good they are. The Springboks were nowhere near their best against them. Still, Wales put together six wins on the trot and that's fair enough in anyone's language. I think Wales will be okay but not great.

Being on home turf will help England enormously. They are a very difficult side to play against and are capable of an upset against anyone. The question is whether they are capable of causing enough upsets to win the entire tournament. Matt Perry has developed well. He's not that big, not that quick and yet beats a lot of tackles. A deceptive player. Jonny Wilkinson looks as if he might be one of the stars of the tournament.

Scotland had an excellent Five Nations. They played a great brand of rugby. I worry about their strength in depth but there's no doubt that they are a first-rate outfit when on song. The mark of a great side is how accurate they are in their execution. Scotland have that quality. The only way you can put an opposition defence under pressure is if you are prepared to put your own attack under pressure. Scotland do just that.

And Ireland? Well, from that quarter-final in Dublin in 1991 when they were so close to beating us, I know all about their potential for causing surprises.

Rugby is in good shape. There have been a few casualties of professionalism but that was inevitable given the appalling management of the changeover. It was never going to be a painless exercise. Market forces will prevail as they do in every thriving economy in the world. We will eventually have a slimmer Premiership, with eight or ten clubs, and so a shorter season. Other sports, like golf or cricket, have an elite tier and a strong amateur base underneath. Rugby will be no different.

The game is unrecognisable from four years ago. And that's a very good thing indeed.

THE AGONY AND THE ECSTASY

REVIEW OF THE 1998-99 SEASON
Mick Cleary

The World Cup is upon us. I have vivid memories of the last World Cup held four years ago in South Africa. Images cluster the mind, of big Jonah on the rampage, of Rob Andrew's drop-goal winner against Australia, of many hours spent travelling the country, most of it good, some of it bad (hands up who got robbed?), of thrilling matches and great competition, of poor Max Brito, of Chester and François and Nelson, symbols all, and of the wonderful mix of colours and races that deliriously saluted the Springboks victory over the All Blacks in the final itself. Great sporting memories, to be repeated in kind (robberies excepted), in just a few weeks' time.

There is another recollection of those days, a fragment tucked away in what seems like the dark and distant recesses. It is of three men sitting at a top table on the eve of the World Cup final at Ellis Park in Johannesburg. They are telling of the new £360 million deal struck between the big three southern hemisphere countries and Rupert Murdoch's Newscorp.

Lies and more lies
'Surely this means the end of amateurism?' came the question from the floor. 'No, it does not,' came the reply. The question was repeated. And then repeated again in another guise. In all, the question was asked 11 times. Back came the same deadbeat reply. I remember it well. I was the bloke asking the question. And getting nowhere.

We were lied to that day. We're still reeling from the consequences north of the equator. The denial of reality has not ceased in four years. Another season passes and with it came more tales of mismanagement and financial hardship. England were thrown out of the Five Nations Championship only to be reinstated 24 hours later; a British league was mooted and backed by many different interests yet failed to come to fruition, the RFU were fined twice over (a total of £80,000 with £50,000 suspended) by the International Board for supposed breaches of regulations and etiquette; Cardiff and Swansea played cross-border friendlies with English clubs rather than against their own in the Welsh Premier League; London Scottish were partly bought out by second division Bristol; and the accumulated debts of all clubs once more rocketed towards £20million.

What else? RFU chairman Cliff Brittle lost out to Brian Baister in the summer of 1998; Will Carling staged a mid-season comeback; West Hartlepool made their entire squad redundant;

Bedford's players came within a few votes of going on strike; the English clubs agreed a £1.8million salary cap for this season; Ian McGeechan left Northampton to take up the coaching reins with Scotland and was replaced by John Steele; Richard Hill was sacked as director of rugby at Gloucester; John Mitchell left Sale to join Wasps; and the Quinnell brothers headed back across the Severn Bridge to Wales.

The Dallaglio saga

And then there was Lawrence Dallaglio. How the heart sank that Sunday morning as the *News of the World* was pushed across the breakfast table. Dallaglio's own heart would have been subterranean by that time too. He had been an utter fool. And he knew it. He had been reckless, indiscreet and had betrayed the confidence of many of those close to him – his parents, partner Alice, and England coach, Clive Woodward. But Dallaglio is not a bad man. His punishment began the moment that story was splashed across five pages of the Sunday tabloid. He suffered publicly. That much was evident from his appearance at a press conference two days after the supposed confessions of drug-taking and drug-pedalling in his youth first appeared. He denied almost everything, only admitting that he had foolishly dabbled with drugs in his teens.

He looked vulnerable that day. As well he might. All that was dear to him, his family and his rugby, was under severe strain. Underneath Twickenham's 'Spirit of Rugby' restaurant, the England players were gathering prior to their departure for the month-long tour to Australia. Dallaglio would not be among them. That would hurt. He resigned his position as captain until at least after the World Cup and perhaps forever. Martin Johnson took over.

And what are we to make of it all? The three man RFU inquiry – headed by Sir John Kay, QC, aided by Bob Rogers and Alan Stevens of the RFU – had to scrutinise all the material. Dallaglio had persuaded a six-man RFU panel on the Monday that he should be given a chance at a fuller hearing. He told them that he had been sucked in by the *News of the World*'s trap, and had, for some unfathomable reason, spun them a complete cock-and-bull story about drug-taking on the Lions tour in 1997.

The six men comprised RFU chief executive, Francis Baron, chairman of the Management Board, Brian Baister, RFU president, Peter Trunkfield, Fran Cotton, chairman of Club England, Bill Beaumont, the RFU's IB representative and Clive Woodward.

It was a sorry tale of foolishness and hubris, Dallaglio clearly overreaching himself. However he is a good man at heart. It's right that he should not be unduly pilloried for a sin of stupidity more than anything else. A six month ban for bringing the game into disrepute would be appropriate.

The controversial former England captain Lawrence Dallaglio breaks through the French defence of Thomas Castaignède and Pascal Giordani in England's 21-10 victory over France at Twickenham.

And now for the good news . . .

The good news was severely rationed, although the arrival of New Zealander Graham Henry was rightly greeted with acclaim. A new eight-year European Cup deal was signed in Paris on 27 March 1999. English clubs will be back in Europe from this season. The agreement was thrashed out over a number of weeks, with former French full-back, Serge Blanco, French Federation president, Bernard Lapasset, IB chairman, Vernon Pugh and Tom Walkinshaw of the English clubs, the key players. The tournament will have 24 teams this season: six from France and England, five from Wales, three from Ireland and two apiece from Scotland and Italy. From the 2001 season the competition will reduce to 20 teams, four from France and England and two each from the other four countries. The other four places will be decided according to the previous year's semi-finals. There will be a maximum of six teams from each country. The European Shield is to feature 32 teams in all.

The deal was good news for all concerned. The projected income for a European Cup side was reckoned to be around £600,000.

. . . In with the new

Two of the front-runners in the professional market in England, Sir John Hall of Newcastle and Ashley Levett of Richmond, cashed their chips. Another, Frank Warren of Bedford, also walked away. Sir John Hall had seen his rugby debts mount to £5million and, in February, one of the hawks of the club scene decided that enough was enough. New backers were on hand, however. The following month a local businessman, Dave Thompson, was announced as the head of the new operation at Newcastle. Thompson, who made his millions from running a management consultancy, has mixed it on the rugby field himself at various levels.

'We can cope with whatever happens,' said Thompson. 'We have thought up some pretty horrendous scenarios just so that we can be ready. I can see a turning point for professional rugby.'

A stab in the back

Try telling that to those at Richmond. Their season ended in turmoil and farce. Their principal backer, Ashley Levett, shocked them in mid-March by withholding a £200,000 payment to the club. The Monaco-based copper-dealer claims that he had given the club repeated warnings that he wanted to significantly reduce his 86% stake in the club. His losses were close to £8million. In the end he pulled the plug without any precise notice. The club was faced with immediate liquidation. They had little option but to apply for administration which they did on March 4th.

Within a week 34 of the staff had been laid off by administrators, Buchler Phillips. Three of those were front-line players, former

French flanker, Laurent Cabannes, ex-Wales fly-half, Adrian Davies and wing Dominic Chapman who had been capped by England only the summer before. There were wage cuts across the board, 10% for those earning less than £50,000 a year, 20% and more for those above that figure.

'I find it impossible to go on funding Richmond when I don't know what I am funding,' said Levett. 'To get Richmond through the next two years, even with a significant reduction in costs, would take £2million and that's far too big a load for one person to carry. I don't know anyone with a sound business sense who would do it.'

Richmond battled on. How cruel and ironic that all this should blow up just after they had delivered their best performance of the season in beating Leicester 15-13 in the quarter-final of the Tetley's Bitter Cup. No sooner had their season reached its peak than the swift descent began. Even so Richmond struggled along, holding on to most of their players as well as their dignity. Scott Quinnell had departed for Llanelli earlier in the year; his wife's homesickness being the principal cause behind the move.

Richmond's directors, Tony Hallett and president, Tony Dorman, made strenuous efforts to bring a consortium together. They felt that they were headed in the right direction when the rug was pulled from under their feet at the end of April. The club had been working towards a deadline of May 31st. Little did they know that English First Division Rugby, the umbrella group of the 14 Premiership clubs, was already taking steps to remove them from the equation. An EFDR board meeting declared that Richmond had forsaken their right to their share in the Premiership the moment they went into administration. EFDR claimed that they were entitled to buy back that share for £1. They actually lodged a £500,000 bid with Richmond's administrators, Buchler Phillips, to facilitate the closure and to preserve the status of Richmond's amateur section.

It was a pre-emptive strike. The administrators themselves called the move 'opportunistic and morally reprehensible'. Two of Richmond's potential backers pulled out of negotiations. 'Our own body is trying to kill us off,' said Tony Dorman. 'They told us that they wanted to reduce the league from 14 to 12 clubs and that, given the situation we were in, we had to go.'

The whole scenario once again threw the sport into desperate relief. The EFDR action was a shoddy ruse. It was poorly planned and miserably executed. EFDR chairman, Tom Walkinshaw, was adamant that the Premiership articles of entry allowed for such action by EFDR.

'We simply need to preserve the financial integrity of the Premiership,' said Walkinshaw. 'Everyone agreed to that at the outset and now Richmond want to change the rules. Were they not, too, one of the first clubs to inflate the transfer market and put a commercial strain on other clubs?'

And so they were. No-one denies that Richmond were ailing and close to meltdown. All they wanted was their allotted time. As it was they didn't get it. There was doubt late in the summer as to whether a merger with London Irish and London Scottish would go ahead. Richmond were suffering a slow death by other means. The players, and who could blame them, were heading for the lifeboats. Craig Quinnell went to Cardiff and Allan Bateman to Northampton.

Politics dominated the agenda once again. They brought out the worst in people. If red and yellow cards had been handed out in the political arena then we would have been rid of many of the monkeys who have been running the game for long stretches.

Players save the day
Thank goodness once again for that lot in jockstraps and studs. (And a bit else besides.) The dreary political sagas, necessary but so draining and self-indulgent, used up so much of our reserves of patience and goodwill, that it was a relief to turn every week to matters on the field. These men did not let us down. They have kept their side of the deal over professionalism. It was another invigorating season on the field. Ulster stunned everyone, perhaps including themselves, by winning the European Cup; Scotland did likewise in taking the last ever Five Nations title. From this season Italy are most welcome additions to the International Championship. Ah, curse it. Another weekend in Rome. Sorry, dear, be back in a few days.

South Africa arrived in the autumn for their Grand Slam tour. The 'Boks were on a roll. They had won the Tri-Nations and, under the shrewd guidance of coach Nick Mallett were fast buffing up their reputations both on and off the field. They had four Tests to play. If they won the lot then they would have won 18 Tests in a row, a new world record. Wales (just), Scotland and Ireland were seen off. South Africa headed to Twickenham in early December. After almost ten months on the road, just one match to go. It proved a match too far. England won, 13-7.

It had been a terrific trip, though, South Africa making friends wherever they went. That has not always been the case. Their captain, Gary Teichmann, may have been a waning force on the field but his influence and stature remain intact. The new kid on the block, back-rower, Bobby Skinstad, gave us tantalising glimpses of what we will see in this World Cup. Nick Mallett was an ambassador for his country and his sport. He returned to London in January to receive the Pat Marshall award from the Rugby Writers' Club, acknowledgement of all his endeavours.

The autumn also saw three World Cup qualifying groups taking place in Scotland, Ireland and Huddersfield in England. None of the groups threw up any surprises, the home nations easing their way through. England, though, were fortunate to get away with a narrow win over Italy in their group match; the Italians having had a perfectly good try disallowed. Holland conceded a century of points to England but conducted themselves with dignity.

The Five Nations Championship has had its critics in recent times. It had been Anglo-French dominated and there was a lobby for casting the Celts off into the wilderness. That lobby is considerably quieter after this year's tournament. There were several fascinating matches, from Ireland's rain-swept one-point defeat to France on the opening day in Dublin to the rout of the French by Scotland in Paris on the closing Saturday. And then, the following day at Wembley, came Scott Gibbs' try. Rarely has the Championship had such a theatrical finale; the Welsh centre crashing over the English try-line in injury-time. A Neil Jenkins conversion put Wales in front 32-31. They won, England lost and Scotland had taken the title for the first time in nine years.

Dallaglio had opted to kick for touch in the closing minutes of the Wembley game rather than asking Jonny Wilkinson to kick for goal. It was seen as an error of judgement. How trivial that oversight seems now in the light of what was later to befall Dallaglio.

On the domestic front Leicester deservedly took the Allied Dunbar Premiership. They were ahead of the pack for most of the season although they did not make sure of the title until a couple of weeks before the league's conclusion. But if anyone doubted that they were not worthy winners then they only had to witness their clinching victory at Newcastle to be disabused. Newcastle had not lost a league match at Kingston Park for three years. Yet Leicester matched them dogged stride for dogged stride, winning 21-12, full-back Tim Stimpson kicking all seven penalties.

Newcastle had a deflating end to the season. They lost 29-19 to Wasps in the final of the Tetley's Bitter Cup and then saw their very outside chance of making it into Europe fade away at Saracens the following Thursday. They were comprehensively beaten 40-26. The six English qualifiers for Europe were Leicester, Northampton, Saracens, Wasps, Harlequins and Bath.

Bedford hung on to their Premiership status by the narrowest of margins, finishing level on points with Rotherham in the play-offs but surviving by dint of having scored more tries over the two matches. How tough it all was for Rotherham. They were only shaded by Bristol for the Second Division title on points difference too. Rotherham will come again.

It was a muted season on the domestic front in Wales. The same could not be said about the international scene, Wales rounding off a heartening season with a first ever victory over the Springboks at the new Millennium Stadium at Cardiff. That made it six wins in a row. The rebel clubs, Cardiff and Swansea, had taken themselves off to play friendlies against the English clubs. And very well they did at it too. Their crowds almost doubled and their results were solid throughout. Interest from the English end inevitably waned. It was good to see some sort of settlement reached with the pair welcomed back into the fold. Arguments still rumbled though as to whether they should both have a European Cup slot. Swansea won the SWALEC Cup, denying Llanelli the double. As well as the league title, Llanelli also won the Challenge Cup. It was heartening to see the famous old club back in good working order on and off the field.

The Scots had a wretched time on the political front. There was little support for the super-district concept. The attendance was pitiful at both the Springbok midweek games against Edinburgh Reivers and Glasgow Caledonians. The clubs were denied access to those players under contract to the Scottish Rugby Union and so their own status faltered. And yet the international side was successful. Step forward, Jim Telfer. What a way to retire from the front-line of coaching. Telfer will continue as director of rugby at Murrayfield.

The Irish scene, in stark contrast, is a model of good housekeeping. Several more players returned back across the water, notably former captain, Paddy Johns, from Saracens. The Inter-Provincial Championship, played home and away, and won by Munster, was a great success. And as for Ulster – their triumph in the European Cup was the story of the season. It was a victory for teamwork and self-belief, all encapsulated in the figure of their coach, Harry Williams. Cork Constitution won the AIB League for the first time since 1991.

And now? All eyes are on the World Cup. They are still working round the clock on the Millennium Stadium. Fingers crossed. It looks as if it will provide a magnificent backdrop. Enjoy the feast.

WORLD CUP GROWS IN STATURE

WORLD CUP PREVIEW
Mick Cleary

During the summer I drifted along to the Concord Oval in Sydney. The Wallabies were training there prior to their match against England. The Oval is not in a great part of town, lying 15kms or so from the centre out on the industrialised Parramatta Road. It's not a bad stadium, open at both ends but with big stands. The ground holds about 16,000 people. At the 1987 World Cup it staged one of the greatest matches in the history of the sport, the semi-final between Australia and France. France won at the death, 30-24, the great Serge Blanco crossing in the corner. The ground was not even full.

Even Mickey Burton in his heyday might not have been able to sell it out. Rugby was simply not that popular. And now? Burton is just one of many corporate moguls licking their lips at the prospect of this fourth World Cup. Each tournament has somehow managed to surpass expectations. Every time the World Cup approaches we state that it surely can't get bigger, more dramatic, more engaging than the last one. And every time we are proven wrong.

In simple terms the fourth World Cup is the biggest. There are 20 teams rather than 16. We welcome the likes of Spain, Uruguay and Namibia. There are fears that we may see mismatches. Those fears are well-founded. Let's hope that there are no serious injuries as a result and that the credibility of the tournament is not undermined either. On the positive side, the game in those countries can only gain in stature as a result of their involvement. Far better, though, in my mind, to have a parallel tournament at the same time for the emerging countries.

There is some disquiet too that four matches are lumped together on each of three days through the qualifiers. Why not stagger the matches in order to spread the appeal through the week? I know that teams need rest periods, but with all due respect Scotland do not need the same preparation time before facing Spain or Uruguay as they do for the Springboks. It's ludicrous too that both semi-finals are to be staged at the same venue, Twickenham.

The competition at the sharp end will be riveting. Wales might be at home to Australia in the quarter-final and who could call that with complete certainty? England might have to travel to Paris to play the Springboks in the quarter-final. This assumes that England have lost to the All Blacks in their pool match and Scotland likewise to South Africa. Neither of those is a foregone conclusion either.

In fact, the only certainty is that it will be a great five weeks. And also that there will be no empty seats at the semi-final. Those days are long gone.

THE TEAMS

POOL A   Scotland, South Africa, Spain, Uruguay

Scotland

Every Scot will be praying that the critics go through the usual routine of writing off Scotland's chances, of belittling their domestic structure and of bemoaning their lack of huge, hulking forwards. We all did it last year, consigning Scotland to the championship dustbin. And what happened? Scotland played the freshest, most vibrant rugby of any team in the Five Nations and deservedly took the last ever championship title. They were sharp and inventive behind the scrum and more than competitive up front. Second row Scott Murray was one of the star turns of the season. True, their front row does lack a bit of poundage while their back row is only workmanlike. However, with coach Jim Telfer putting them through their paces anything is possible. Telfer proved himself a coach apart last season. The backs were the real revelation. The arrival of former Otago centre John Leslie brought stability and direction to the midfield. Gregor Townsend and Alan Tait thrived either side of him. On home turf Scotland could cause several surprises.

South Africa

The champions seemed to be in good order as they began their World Cup season. They had enjoyed their best ever run of form the year before. They had come within 80 minutes of setting a new world record of 18 consecutive Test victories only for England to beat them in the final match of the year. But 1999 began well with thumping victories over beleaguered Italy, who shipped over a 100 points in the second Test of the series. And then came Cardiff. No-one, perhaps not even the most die-hard Welsh supporters, really expected their side to beat the Springboks. They had never managed it before. That defeat will carry through to the tournament. No matter how the 'Boks fared thereafter, the whole world now knows that they are vulnerable. Coach Nick Mallet is under pressure on two fronts. First, to strike the balance between old dependable players like half-backs Joost van der Westhuizen and Henry Honiball and the blooding of fresh talent in the likes of Gaffie du Toit and Breyton Paulse. Mallett is also having to contend with the tricky political issue of positive discrimination by including a quota of black and coloured players.

The Kilted Kiwi. Scotland recruit New Zealand-born John Leslie shows off his skills as he powers through Spain's defences in the World Cup qualifier at Murrayfield.

Spain

There is no doubt that Spain are here for the trip. They must have mixed feelings about what lies in store for them. They qualified through Scotland's group, conceding 85 points to them last December. However, they did enough to just edge ahead of Portugal in the decisive match. Spain are serious in their aspirations to establish the game in their country. The World Cup will at least give context to those ambitions. Their build-up to the World Cup takes in training camps through the summer, a first ever visit by Japan and a tournament in Italy. Several of their players, such as prop Asier Altuna in Dax and wing Rafael Bastide in Colomiers, are based in France. Spain had an unhappy campaign in the European Shield, finishing bottom of their group and going down to hefty defeats to Castres (61-15), Montferrand (88-13) and Bourgoin (55-10). However, they refuse to be bowed by the odds and have targeted the Uruguay match as their chance of World Cup glory.

Uruguay

Uruguay have lived in the shadow of their South American rivals, Argentina, for a long time. This will be their moment to make a mark. It won't be easy. Even though they put up a decent showing in their qualifying group, running the USA close in a 21-16 defeat, they know that the likes of Scotland and South Africa will test their resources to the limit. Uruguay finished bottom of their Americas group and went through to the repêchage where they just came through over two legs against Morocco, 39-24 on aggregate. 33-year-old scrum-half and goal-kicker, Federico Sciarra, kept them on track in the second leg with six penalties in their 21-18 defeat in Casablanca. There are only eight first-class clubs in the country and just 1,200 players. They will turn to the likes of prop Pablo Lemoine for guidance and inspiration. Lemoine is the only front-line professional in the Uruguayan squad and was signed by former Australian coach, Bob Dwyer, to cement the scrum at Bristol. 'Pablo is a great natural talent, as raw as can be imagined, but a player who will develop,' says Dwyer.

Pool B   England, New Zealand, Italy, Tonga

England

Can England break the southern hemisphere hold on the World Cup? Everything that can be done has been done to help achieve that goal. The players have effectively been together for four months, spending five weeks in training camp in Australia followed by regular sessions at different venues in England. And yet the doubts persist. Can England put sides away on a consistent basis? As they showed last year in doing what no-one else managed to do in lowering the Springboks' colours, they have the capability to beat any side on a given day. But can they do it week in week out as they need to do to win the World Cup? And can England finish teams off when opportunity arises? They led Wales in the final match of the championship yet failed to nail down victory. In the summer they had a splendid opening half hour against Australia yet went into the half-time break trailing 10-7, the Wallabies eventually winning 22-15. On the plus side Matt Perry has emerged as a quality full-back, Dan Luger as a threat on the wing with Jonny Wilkinson maturing at fly-half.

New Zealand

We all knew that they had been quiet, too quiet. The All Blacks suffered five defeats in succession last season, one of the worst runs in their history. They didn't tour in their close season so the spotlight moved away. And when it swung back round again it alighted upon a familiar routine as the All Blacks swept aside Samoa and France in their opening internationals, averaging over 60 points. Coach John Hart had failed to change the old guard the season before. He wasn't about to make the same mistake again. A new front row of Carl Hoeft, Anton Oliver and Kees Meeuws has been bedded down while veteran lock Ian Jones (who will be on Gloucester's books after the World Cup) has been eased out of the frontline for the likes of Royce Willis and Norm Maxwell. The midfield was the Blacks' most troublesome area. If Daryl Gibson and Alama Ieremia can continue their early season form then they will solve one of Hart's most pressing problems. The switch of wing Jeff Wilson with full-back Christian Cullen is designed to give the All Blacks more strike-power from the rear. Wilson scored four tries from that position against Samoa as the Blacks ran out 71-13 winners.

Italy

What a tumble. The Italian success story was one of the most encouraging tales of the last decade. They had earned their right to take part in the Five Nations Championship on merit. They had beaten, or run close, all the home countries on a regular basis. There were few dissenting voices when they were brought into the championship from the year 2000. However, the Italians have suffered a severe setback of late. Their year began well with a hugely encouraging show against England in the World Cup qualifier at Huddersfield. England came through 23-15 but Italy were denied a perfectly good try by scrum-half Alessandro Troncon. However, their late season performances were disastrous.

21

Wales put 60 points on them before the Springboks shattered their morale completely with victories by 74-3 and then, on a day of humiliation in Durban, by 101-0.

Tonga

Tonga have been the poor relations of Pacific Islanders rugby. They finished bottom of the pile in the Pacific World Cup qualifying group, their 74-0 defeat by Australia the heaviest of their three losses. Tonga then had to battle through the repêchage to qualify. In the first round they beat Georgia over two legs, a cultural experience if nothing else. The trip to Tbilisi involved four flights over three days. Tonga lost the return leg 28-27 in front of a crowd of 30,000 but went through 64-34 on aggregate. Siua Taumalolo was the star of the return leg, the Tongan full-back scoring three tries. In the final elimination stage Tonga then comfortably beat Korea, 58-26 at home and then 82-15 in Seoul. Flanker Jonny Koloi, who plays for the Falcons in the Currie Cup, proved himself a quality performer at this level. Tonga, as they showed in beating France 20-16 in the summer, have enough raw talent and desire to cause Italy real problems. They drew with Samoa (6-6) and beat Canada (18-10) in the Epson Pacific Cup.

Pool C   France, Canada, Namibia, Fiji

France

France have fallen from grace. The double Grand Slam champions had a desperately poor Five Nations and, as it turned out, only avoided a whitewash by a fluffed last-minute penalty by Ireland in the opening match of the championship. By the end of the tournament France were in disarray, Scotland completely swamping them at the Stade de France, 36-22. That game suggested that France's morale was at an all-time low, a view confirmed by their poor showing in the southern hemisphere during the summer. France lost to Tonga (20-16) and New Zealand A (45-24) and were then blown away by the All Blacks, 54-7. The side lack any power through the middle of the field. Poor Thomas Castaignède, a fiery competitor, was totally out of place in the centre where the All Blacks just lined him up to blast through. French coaches, Jean-Claude Skrela and Pierre Villepreux, have lost their way. The return of Abdel Benazzi is an imperative.

Canada

Has the bubble burst? Canada go into this World Cup with several question marks hanging over them. The side which was the surprise package of the 1991 World Cup and wonderfully competitive four years later, appears to have lost its bite. The Canadians, from the sound base of the early nineties, have not managed to build on those foundations. They had a poor return in the Pacific Rim tournament, losing all five matches to finish bottom of a tournament that they had won for the three previous years. They were also the first team ever to be whitewashed in the competition. Canada, however, were missing several key players. It's far too early to talk of their game being in decline for they still have enough quality in their ranks to go through from this group. Gareth Rees will be contesting his fourth World Cup, a wonderful achievement. He will be backed by other old hands in John Graf and Al Charron.

Namibia

This is Namibia's first World Cup and they are anxious not to leave unnoticed. However, they will have to lift their game from their disappointing summer build-up if they are to seriously trouble the others in the group. They were given a slot in South Africa's Vodacom Cup competition but only managed to win one of their 14 matches, beating North West 22-12. Coach Johan Venter paid the price for such a dismal showing and was replaced by Rudy Joubert, the former manager of coaching at the South African Rugby Football Union. 'We are not going to Wales just to make up the numbers,' said Joubert. Namibia qualified through the Africa group, beating their closest challengers, Morocco, 17-8 in the decisive match.

Fiji

Fiji have made a determined effort to shake off the tag of being no more than dazzling Sevens players. The coach, former All Black Brad Johnstone, has worked hard to bring together a pool of players dedicated to playing the full version of the game. To that end one of the great names of Fijian rugby, Waisale Serevi, was left out of the initial World Cup squad after opting to play at Hong Kong. Fiji finished second in the Pacific qualifier behind Australia. They have been helped in their plans by a $2million loan scheme which has enabled them to bring players together more often. The dividends showed in their Epson Cup campaign where they beat Canada (40-29), Japan (16-9) and Tonga (39-37). Johnstone is pragmatic in his approach: 'I intend to build the side around the front row,' he said . 'You've got to win up front to be able to do the magic at the back.'

Pool D   Wales, Argentina, Japan, Samoa

Wales

Wales have reinvented themselves. They bear no resemblance whatsoever to the shoddy outfit which conceded 96 points to the Springboks in the summer of '98. A year later and the tables were tilted if not quite turned as Wales beat the world champions 29-19 in Cardiff. You don't have to look far to find the reason for the difference – coach Graham Henry. The Aucklander has given Wales pride and self-belief, not to mention a decent scrum. The front row of Peter Rogers, Garin Jenkins and either Ben Evans or David Young, has given Wales a solid base on which to build. Llanelli lock Chris Wyatt has dominated the lineout. One of Henry's former charges from Auckland, full-back Shane Howarth, has been a star turn. Wales became the first British side to win a series 2-0 in Argentina during the summer and then, in beating the Springboks, extended their winning streak to six matches. On home turf they should at least reach the quarter-finals where they will probably meet Australia.

Argentina

Argentina have hit a trough at just the wrong time. Their 2-0 series defeat by Wales, and their lacklustre play over the two matches, led to the removal of coach Jose Luis Imhoff. The coach had completely lost the confidence of his players and it was their stance which led to his demotion. He will remain with the squad but the hands-on coaching role has passed to former All Black, Alex 'Grizz' Wyllie. The problem for Wyllie is that Imhoff had already named a provisional World Cup squad. However, the Pumas do not have huge strength in depth. The current difficulties are due not to a lack of personnel but to a lack of morale. The pack, formidable on its day, has suffered a serious blow with the loss to injury of hooker Federico Mandez. Talented scrum-half, Agustin Pichot, has to learn to trust those outside him. The Pumas have consistently underachieved at World Cups. Now is the time to put that right.

Japan

When the draw was made for the World Cup, Japan were cast as outsiders for this group. No longer. Their victory in the Epson Pacific Rim championship has shown just how tough an opponent they will be. The Japanese have buried any local scruples about the purity of their cause by bringing in outsiders. They have half a dozen former southern hemisphere players in their ranks, notably ex-All Black flanker Jamie Joseph and scrum-half Graeme Bachop. Their captain, centre Andrew McCormick, is also from New

Zealand. He is in no doubt that the Pacific Rim competition, extended this season, has helped to make Japan more streetwise and able to last the distance over 80 minutes. 'The more games you play, the better you get and the more experience you gain,' said McCormick. Coach Seiji Hirao (who played for Japan at the 1987 and 1991 World Cups) has done a good job in marshalling the disparate elements. Japan's only defeat in the Epson Cup was to Fiji (16-9). Fly-half Keiji Hirose scored 90 of his country's 160 points in the competition, including a world record nine penalty goals against Tonga.

Samoa

The presence of the Samoans at the 1991 World Cup was a delight for us all. Well, not all, for their bruising play caused several of their opponents, notably Wales, huge problems. Even so their grace and humility off the field have enhanced the game ever since. Their players are now a regular feature in the English Premiership. The likes of flanker Pat Lam (Northampton), centre Va'aiga Tuigamala (Newcastle) and Junior Paramore (once of Bedford, now at Gloucester) have been hugely influential. There is virtually an entire Samoan XV playing in the UK. Samoa had a decent Pacific Rim, finishing runners-up to Japan who beat them (37-34) in injury-time in Samoa's first match. Far more disturbing, however, was the 71-13 thrashing Samoa received at the hands of the All Blacks in June. Samoa have been quarter-finalists at the last two World Cups.

Pool E   Ireland, Australia, USA, Romania

Ireland

Hopes have been high so often for Ireland only to be dashed, that it's perhaps no bad thing that few people are backing Ireland to really cause trouble at this World Cup. Ireland seem to perform better when under little pressure to do so. They were written up before last season's Five Nations Championship, began reasonably well but tailed off badly. Their summer tour to Australia followed a reverse pattern with a poor show in the opening Test (46-10) followed by a stirring comeback in the second Test (32-26). So where does that leave them? Once again, no-one knows. Consistency has never been an Irish trait. The pack has potential but can so easily fall off the pace. Lions lock Jeremy Davidson needs to recapture the form of two years ago. The back line is short of genuine guile. But Australia know from 1991 that on a wild Dublin day, Ireland can trouble anyone.

Australia

The 1991 champions were the pre-summer favourites of many people. They finished second best to South Africa in the previous year's Tri-Nations but seemed to have moved on from then. They have been beset by injuries – captain and lock John Eales did not play all season while fly-half Stephen Larkham and full-back Matt Burke have had long spells on the sidelines. Even so Australia had enough in reserve to see off both Ireland (twice) and England in June. The forward pack has missed Eales's leadership and athletic presence. The back line, though, has functioned well in the absence of the star names. Tim Horan, switched to fly-half against England, looks as threatening as ever while wingers, Ben Tune and Joe Roff, are dangerous from all parts of the field.

USA

The United States promised so much a decade ago. They looked set to capitalise on their geographical size and commercial clout. Instead they remained grounded, a worthy outfit but one which played second fiddle to their North American neighbours, Canada. Those roles have seemingly been reversed. The USA, who finished bottom last year, enjoyed a good Pacific Rim championship. They narrowly beat Canada, 18-17, but finished comfortably ahead of their great rivals with further wins over Tonga and Fiji. The return to the front-line of Bath back-row forward, Dan Lyle, after 18 months out through injury, brought much-needed drive and direction to the forwards. Former Australian full-back, Roger Gould, has been brought in as technical advisor. The three-match tour of Australia will enable the Americans to hone their new, more enterprising approach. 'We aim to be more adventurous in primary phases,' says head coach, Jack Clark.

Romania

How the Romanians have suffered through the nineties. A decade ago they were the strongest second tier force in European rugby, a real test for all the Five Nations teams. They had annual fixtures against France and recorded a notable victory at Auch in 1990 where they won on French soil for the only time in the 75 years of competition between the two countries. The 1989 Revolution in the country struck hard, two players, Florica Murariu and Radu Durbac, being killed. There was also a considerable player-drain afterwards to France. 'We have lost about 100 or so players to French clubs,' says Romanian coach, Mircea Paraschiv. Romania were without five first choice players for their World Cup qualifying group in Ireland where they lost 53-35 to the hosts and only narrowly beat Georgia, 27-23. A 62-8 defeat to France during the summer confirmed that Romania will find this World Cup taxing. Watch out though for full-back, Mihai Vioreanu, a rising talent.

WORLD CUP FIXTURES: 1999 FINALS

POOL A *(in Scotland)*
Oct	2	Spain v Uruguay (Galashiels)
	3	Scotland v South Africa (Murrayfield)
	8	Scotland v Uruguay (Murrayfield)
	10	South Africa v Spain (Murrayfield)
	15	South Africa v Uruguay (Glasgow)
	16	Scotland v Spain (Murrayfield)

POOL B *(in England)*
Oct	2	England v Italy (Twickenham)
	3	New Zealand v Tonga (Bristol)
	9	England v New Zealand (Twickenham)
	10	Italy v Tonga (Leicester)
	14	New Zealand v Italy (Huddersfield)
	15	England v Tonga (Twickenham)

POOL C *(in France)*
Oct	1	Fiji v Namibia (Béziers)
	2	France v Canada (Béziers)
	8	France v Namibia (Bordeaux)
	9	Fiji v Canada (Bordeaux)
	14	Canada v Namibia (Toulouse)
	16	France v Fiji (Toulouse)

POOL D *(in Wales)*
Oct	1	Wales v Argentina (Cardiff)
	3	Samoa v Japan (Wrexham)
	9	Wales v Japan (Cardiff)
	10	Argentina v Samoa (Llanelli)
	14	Wales v Samoa (Cardiff)
	16	Argentina v Japan (Cardiff)

POOL E *(in Ireland)*
Oct	2	Ireland v USA (Dublin)
	3	Australia v Romania (Belfast)
	9	USA v Romania (Dublin)
	10	Ireland v Australia (Dublin)
	14	Australia v USA (Limerick)
	15	Ireland v Romania (Dublin)

Play-offs
Oct	20	**Runner-up B v Runner-up C (H)** (Twickenham)
	20	**Runner-up A v Runner-up D (G)** (Murrayfield)
	20	**Runner-up E v Best Third in Pools (F)** (Lens)

Quarter-Finals
Oct	23	**Winner D v Winner E (M)** (Cardiff)
	24	**Winner A v Winner H (J)** (Paris)
	24	**Winner B v Winner G (K)** (Murrayfield)
	24	**Winner C v Winner F (L)** (Dublin)

Semi-Finals
Oct	30	**Winner J v Winner M** (Twickenham)
	31	**Winner K v Winner L** (Twickenham)
Nov	4	**Third place play-off** (Cardiff)
Nov	6	**FINAL** (Cardiff)

THE ROAD TO WALES

WORLD CUP QUALIFYING COMPETITIONS 1998-99

The final pieces in the jigsaw of qualifying for the 1999 World Cup fell into place between August and April. Seven week-long tournaments were staged to decide 14 finalists, Wales (as hosts), South Africa, New Zealand and France (the top three finishers in 1995) having automatically qualified. The last two places were decided after a series of repêchages among the best losers from the qualifying competitions.

True, there were few surprises in the tournaments, but as exercises in marrying the younger rugby union nations to their established elders, the RWC organisers could feel proud of their achievements. Geoff Old, the former All Black who coached The Netherlands, perfectly expressed the philosophy of the emerging nations after his side had been hammered by England and Italy. 'Success or failure should not be judged by points on the board,' he said. 'The more matches we have, the better.'

AMERICAS GROUP *Argentina 15-22 August*

FINAL TABLE

	P	W	D	L	F	A	Pts
Argentina	3	3	0	0	161	52	9
Canada	3	2	0	1	97	83	7
USA	3	1	0	2	59	99	5
Uruguay	3	0	0	3	31	114	3

Argentina to Wales Pool; Canada to France Pool; USA to Ireland Pool; Uruguay to the repêchages

This qualifying stage doubled as the Pan American tournament. Argentina, winners of both previous competitions, cantered through their two opening matches to face unbeaten Canada in the final round of games. The Canadians had retained the Pacific Rim tournament two months earlier and were expected to give the Pumas a tight game, but in the event the host union ran out 54-28 winners, their highest-ever score against the Canadians, with fly-half Gonzalo Quesada accumulating 29 points from seven penalties and four conversions in blustery conditions. On the same day, Uruguay gave notice of their rising stock by forcing the USA Eagles to use every inch of their experience to win a tight game by 21-16.

15 August, Buenos Aires Rugby & Cricket Club, Buenos Aires

CANADA 38 (3G 4PG 1T) **URUGUAY 15** (1G 1PG 1T)
CANADA: S Stewart; W Stanley, C Robertson, K Nichols, C Smith; B Ross, J Graf (*capt*); H Toews, A Marshall, R Bice, M James, T Healy, A Charron, M Schmid, D Baugh *Substitutions:* J Tait for Healy (temp 9-15 mins); J Loveday for Smith (temp 35-40 mins); J Hutchinson for Charron (41 mins); J Thiel for Bice (65 mins); G Rees for Stanley (70 mins); J Loveday for Graf (71 mins)
Scorers *Tries:* Stanley, Graf, Baugh, Robertson *Conversions:* Ross (3) *Penalty Goals:* Ross (4)

URUGUAY: A Cardoso; M Ferres, P Vecino, M Mendaro, P Costabile; D Aguirre, F Sciarra; R Sanchez, D Lamelas, P Lemoine, J-C Bado, M Lame, M Panizza, D Ormaechea (*capt*), N Grille *Substitutions:* B Amarillo for Sciarra (47 mins); F de los Santos for Lamelas (47 mins); A Ponce de Leon for Lame (47 mins); G Laffite for Grille (65 mins); C Rodriguez for Cardoso (67 mins); G Storace for Lemione (67 mins)
Scorers *Tries:* Ormaechea, Storace *Conversion:* Aguirre *Penalty Goal:* Aguirre
Referee D R Davies (Wales)

15 August, Buenos Aires Rugby & Cricket Club, Buenos Aires

ARGENTINA 52 (5G 4PG 1T) **USA 24** (1G 4PG 1T)
ARGENTINA: M Contepomi; D Albanese, J Orengo, L Arbizu, F Soler; G Quesada, N Fernandez Miranda; M Reggiardo, F Mendez, O Hasan-Jalil, P Sporleder (*capt*), A Allub, S Phelan, P Camerlinckx, M Ruiz *Substitutions:* R Martin for Phelan (62 mins); M Scelzo for Hasan-Jalil (62 mins); I Fernandez Lobbe for Ruiz (68 mins); E Simone for Orengo (68 mins)
Scorers *Tries:* Soler (2), Mendez, Contepomi, Camerlinckx, penalty try *Conversions:* Quesada (5) *Penalty Goals:* Quesada (4)
USA: K Shuman; A Blom, R Green, M Scharrenberg, S Hiatt; M Williams, B Howard; J McBride, T Billups (*capt*), R Lehner, L Gross, C Vogl, J Holtzman, J Walker, D Gillies *Substitutions:* D Hodges for Gross (63 mins); V Anitoni for Williams (63 mins); J Grobler for Green (72 mins); K Kashigan for Billups (73 mins)
Scorers *Tries:* Blom, Anitoni *Conversion:* Williams *Penalty Goals:* Williams (4)
Referee S Young (Australia)

18 August, San Isidro Athletic Club, Buenos Aires

ARGENTINA 55 (6G 2T 1DG) **URUGUAY 0**
ARGENTINA: F Todeschini; E Jurado, F Garcia, E Simone, M Pfister; J Fernandez Miranda, F del Castillo; M Reggiardo, M Ledesma, M Scelzo, P Sporleder (*capt*), R Perez, R Travaglini, I Fernandez Lobbe, R Martin *Substitutions:* P Bouza for Martin (7 mins); F Mendez for Reggiardo (21 mins); M Ruiz for Lobbe (36 mins)
Scorers *Tries:* Reggiardo, Simone, Bouza, Sporleder, Fernandez Lobbe, Jurado, penalty tries (2) *Conversions:* Todeschini (2), Fernandez Miranda (4) *Dropped Goal:* Fernandez Miranda
URUGUAY: D Aguirre; F Corletto, A Luongo, S Cat, C Rodriguez; S Aguirre, B Amarillo; A Sanabria, F de los Santos, G Storace, A Ponce de Leon, M Lame (*capt*), M Panizza, G Laffite, N Brinoni *Substitutions:* A Chuouldjian for Sanabria (5 mins); L de Olivera for Ponce de Leon (7 mins); M Ferres for D Aguirre (16 mins); N Grille for Panizza (28 mins); M Mendaro for Corletto (32 mins)
Referee C B Muir (Scotland)

18 August, San Isidro Athletic Club, Buenos Aires

CANADA 31 (2G 4PG 1T) **USA 14** (2G)
CANADA: J Pagano; W Stanley, J Hall, S Bryan, D Lougheed; G Rees (*capt*), J Graf; E Evans, P Dunkley, R Snow, M James, C Whittaker, A Charron, I Gordon, J Hutchinson *Substitutions:* B Ross for Lougheed (temp 59-65 mins); R Robson for Hutchinson (67 mins); R Bice for Evans (70 mins); B Ross for Pagano (78 mins)
Scorers *Tries:* Hall, Lougheed, Graf *Conversions:* Rees (2) *Penalty Goals:* Rees (4)
USA: C Morrow; V Anitoni, J Grobler, M Scharrenberg, B Hightower; I Stephens, K Dalzell; G Sucer, T Billups (*capt*), Bill Le Clerc, L Gross, Bob Le Clerc, D Hodges, R Lumkong, F Mounga *Substitutions:* S Paga for Hodges (temp

2-5 mins); J McBride for Bill le Clerc (17 mins); S Hiatt for Morrow (35 mins); J Walker for Mounga (70 mins)
Scorers *Tries:* Hodges, Dalzell *Conversions:* Stephens (2)
Referee C White (England)

22 August, Buenos Aires Rugby & Cricket Club, Buenos Aires

USA 21 (1G 3PG 1T) **URUGUAY 16** (1G 3PG)
USA: A Blom; V Anitoni, J Grobler, M Scharrenberg, B Hightower; M Williams, K Dalzell; J McBride, T Billups (*capt*), G Sucher, L Gross, Bob Le Clerc, D Hodges, R Lumkong, F Mounga *Substitutions:* T Takau for Scharrenberg (63 mins); J Walker for Le Clerc (65 mins); R Lehner for McBride (65 mins)
Scorers *Tries:* Blom, Scharrenberg *Conversion:* Williams *Penalty Goals:* Williams (3)
URUGUAY: A Cardoso; M Ferres, P Vecino, M Mendaro, P Costabile; D Aguirre, F Sciarro; R Sanchez, D Lamelas, P Lemoine, J-C Bado, N Grille, M Panizza, D Ormaechea (*capt*), A Dabo *Substitutions:* M Lame for Dabo (12 mins); B Amarillo for Ferres (60 mins)
Scorers *Try:* Ormaechea *Conversion:* Sciarra *Penalty Goals:* Sciarra (3)
Referee C Spannenberg (South Africa)

22 August, Buenos Aires Rugby & Cricket Club, Buenos Aires

ARGENTINA 54 (4G 7PG 1T) **CANADA 28** (1G 7PG)
ARGENTINA: M Contepomi; D Albanese, E Simone, L Arbizu, F Soler; G Quesada, N Fernandez Miranda; M Reggiardo, F Mendez, O Hasan-Jalil, P Sporleder (*capt*), A Allub, R Travaglini, P Camerlinckx, I Fernandez Lobbe *Substitutions:* Jurado for Soler (17 mins); S Phelan for Travaglini (45 mins); M Scelzo for Hasan-Jalil (52 mins); M Ruiz for Allub (71 mins); J Orengo for Arbizu (75 mins); M Ledesma for Reggiardo (76 mins)
Scorers *Tries:* Albanese, Fernandez Miranda, Simone, Camerlinckx, Scelzo *Conversions:* Quesada (4) *Penalty Goals:* Quesada (7)
CANADA: S Stewart; W Stanley, J Hall, S Bryan, D Lougheed; G Rees (*capt*), J Graf; E Evans, R Snow, R Bice, J Tait, M James, A Charron, M Schmid, J Hutchinson *Substitutions:* I Gordon for Tait (41 mins); P Dunkley for Evans (60 mins); C Whittaker for Schmid (60 mins); D Baugh for Hutchinson (73 mins)
Scorers *Try:* James *Conversion:* Rees *Penalty Goals:* Rees (7)
Referee S Dickinson (Australia)

PACIFIC GROUP *Australia 18-26 September*

FINAL TABLE

	P	W	D	L	F	A	Pts
Australia	3	3	0	0	165	33	9
Fiji	3	2	0	1	78	61	7
Samoa	3	1	0	2	59	109	5
Tonga	3	0	0	3	35	134	3

Australia to Ireland Pool; Fiji to France Pool; Samoa to Wales Pool; Tonga to the repêchages

Full marks to the Australian Rugby Union for taking the tournament away from the traditional rugby union Test centres. The four teams went on the road to play matches in Sydney (at the rugby league stronghold of the Parramatta Stadium) and Canberra (for the first time at Test level), before pitching up in Brisbane for the final matches at Ballymore.

Australia qualified comfortably, though the Samoans made the most capped Wallaby XV of all time struggle in Brisbane on the final day of the tournament. John Eales captained his side admirably and topped the Wallaby points, scoring 35 points from 16 successful goal kicks in the tournament. No forward in the history of international rugby has scored as many points as Eales.

The competition produced an upset in midweek when Fiji turned the tables on Samoa by 26-18. Fiji's coach Brad Johnstone, who had made 14 changes from the side trounced 66-20 by Australia, was delighted. A late corner try by wing Fero Lasagavibau, converted by Waisale Serevi, put the Fijians 19-18 ahead with five minutes to go. They consolidated their lead with a late penalty try also converted by Serevi.

18 September, Parramatta Stadium, Sydney

SAMOA 28 (2G 3PG 1T) **TONGA 20** (1G 1PG 2T)
SAMOA: M T Umaga; A So'oalo, G E Leaupepe, T Fanolua, B P Lima; S J Bachop, S So'oilao; K Faiva'ai, T Leota, F Pala'amo, O Palepoi, L Tone, S Ta'ala, P R Lam (capt), K Toleafoa *Substitutions:* P J Paramore for Tole'afoa; V L Tuigamala for So'oialo
Scorers *Tries:* S So'oialo, Lima, Fanolua *Conversions:* Bachop (2) *Penalty Goals:* Bachop (3)
TONGA: P Hola; S Taupeaafe, S Alatini, S Finau, T Taufahema; B Wooley, S Tu'ipulotu; N Ta'u, F Vunipola (capt), U Fa'a, F Mafi, B H Kivalu, S Koloi, S Latu, H Pohiva *Substitutions:* V Moa for Fa'a; H Fakatou for Pohiva; P Tanginoa for Koloi; F Masila for N Ta'u *Sent off:* S Alatini(75 mins)
Scorers *Tries:* Koloi, Pohiva, Taufahema *Conversion:* Hola *Penalty Goal:* Wooley
Referee T Henning (South Africa)

18 September, Parramatta Stadium, Sydney

AUSTRALIA 66 (9G 1PG) **FIJI 20** (2G 2PG)
AUSTRALIA: J W Roff; J S Little, D J Herbert, T J Horan, D P Smith; S J Larkham, G M Gregan; R L L Harry, P N Kearns, A T Blades, T M Bowman, J A Eales (capt), M J Cockbain, V Ofahengaue, D J Wilson *Substitutions:* O D A Finegan for Cockbain (48 mins); C J Whitaker for Gregan (50 mins); N P Grey for Horan (50 mins); G M Panoho for Blades (65 mins); R S T Kefu for Bowman (65 mins); J A Paul for Kearns (70 mins)
Scorers *Tries:* Smith (2), Larkham (2), Little, Finegan, Roff, Grey, Paul *Conversions:* Eales (9) *Penalty Goal:* Eales
FIJI: O Turuva; M Bari, S C Sorovaki, L Koroi, A Tuilevu; W Serevi, M Rauluni; N Qoro, I Rasila, M Taga, I Tawake (capt), E Katalau, M Tamanitoakula, I Male, W Masirewa *Substitutions:* I Tamanivalu for Tamanitoakula (28 mins); D Rouse for M Taga (temp); S Raiwalui for Tawake (66 mins)
Scorers *Tries:* Sorovaki, Serevi *Conversions:* Serevi (2) *Penalty Goals:* Serevi (2)
Referee A Lewis (Ireland)

22 September, Bruce Stadium, Canberra

SAMOA 18 (1G 2PG 1T) **FIJI 26** (2G 4PG)
SAMOA: M T Umaga; B P Lima, V L Tuigamala, T Fanolua, F Toala; S J Bachop, S So'oilao; K Faiva'ai, T Leota, F Pala'amo, O Palepoi, L Tone, , P R Lam (capt), S Ta'ala, P J Paramore *Substitutions:* F Tipi for Palepoi; B P Reidy for Faiva'ai; T M Vaega for Toala
Scorers *Tries:* Leota, Umaga *Conversion:* Bachop *Penalty Goals:* Bachop (2)
FIJI: J Waqa; F Lasagavibau, A Uluinayau, M Nakauta A Tuilevu; N Little, J Rauluni; D Rouse, G Smith (capt), J Veitayaki, S Raiwalui, A Naevo, I Tamanivalu, A Mocelutu, S Tawake *Substitutions:* E Bose for Tuilevu; W Serevi for Little; E Katalu for Tamanivalu; S C Sorovaki for Nakuta

Scorers *Tries:* Lasagavibau, penalty try *Conversions:* Serevi (2) *Penalty Goals:* Serevi, Little (3)
Referee S Lander (England)

22 September, Bruce Stadium, Canberra

AUSTRALIA 74 (7G 5T) **TONGA 0**
AUSTRALIA: J W Roff; J S Little, D J Herbert, T J Horan, M D Hardy; M H M Edmonds, C J Whitaker; D J Crowley, J A Paul, G M Panoho, J P Welborn, J A Eales (*capt*), O D A Finegan, R S T Kefu, B J Robinson *Substitutions:* S J Larkham for Little (temp 20-26 mins); M J Cockbain for Eales (40 mins); N P Grey for Horan (40 mins); M A Foley for Paul (80 mins)
Scorers *Tries:* Little (4), Edmonds (2), Finegan, Roff, Horan, Paul, Whitaker, Robinson *Conversions:* Eales (2), Edmonds (5)
TONGA: P Hola; P Tanginoa, S Taupeaafe (*capt*), S Ngauamo, T Taufahema; S Tai, S Tu'ipulotu; U Moa, M Pale, N Ta'u, F Mafi, P Latukefu, H Fakatou, B H Kivalu, M Te Pou junior *Substitutions:* D Edwards for Kivalu (34 mins); S Marten for Tu'ipulotu (40 mins); F Masila for Pale (40mins); S Faka'osi'folau for Taupeaafe (temp 30-35 mins) and for Ngauamo (50 mins); U Fa'a for Moa (57 mins); J Sitoa for H Fakatou (71 mins) *Sent off:* J Sitoa (75 mins)
Referee S R Walsh (New Zealand)

26 September, Ballymore Stadium, Brisbane

FIJI 32 (2G 5PG 1DG) **TONGA 15** (1G 1PG 1T)
FIJI: J Waqa; F Lasagavibau, A Uluinayau, S C Sorovaki, M Bari; W Serevi, J Rauluni; D Rouse, G Smith (*capt*), J Veitayaki, S Raiwalui, A Naevo, I Tamanivalu, A Mocelutu, S Tawake
Scorers *Tries:* Naevo, penalty try *Conversions:* Serevi (2) *Penalty Goals:* Serevi (5) *Dropped Goal:* Serevi
TONGA: P Hola; T Taufahema, S Alatini, S Taupeaafe, S Fala'osi'folau; B Wooley, S Marten; N Ta'u, F Vunipola (*capt*), U Fa'a, M Te Pou, P Latukefu, H Pohiva, H Fakatou, S Koloi *Substitution:* U Moa for Fa'a
Scorers *Tries:* Te Pou, Fa'a *Conversion:* Hola *Penalty Goal:* Hola
Referee J Kaplan (South Africa)

26 September, Ballymore, Brisbane

AUSTRALIA 25 (2G 2PG 1T) **SAMOA 13** (1PG 2T)
AUSTRALIA: J W Roff; J S Little, D J Herbert, T J Horan, M D Hardy; S J Larkham, G M Gregan; D J Crowley, P N Kearns, A T Blades, T M Bowman, J A Eales (*capt*), M J Cockbain, V Ofahengaue, D J Wilson *Substitutions:* O D A Finegan for Bowman (temp 3-5 mins; 57 mins); R S T Kefu for V Ofahengaue (57 mins); G M Panoho for Blades (61 mins); A T Blades for Crowley (78 mins)
Scorers *Tries:* Crowley, Ofahengaue, Herbert *Conversions:* Eales (2) *Penalty Goals:* Eales (2)
SAMOA: M T Umaga; B P Lima, G E Leaupepe, T M Vaega, V L Tuigamala; E Va'a, J Clarke; B P Reidy, T Leota, F Pala'amo, S Ta'ala, L Tone, F Tipi, P R Lam (*capt*), P J Paramore *Substitutions:* O Palepoi for Tipi (temp 50-58 mins); A Va'a for Leota (63 mins); K Faiva'ai for Pala'amo (63 mins); K Toleafoa for Paramore (63 mins); T Fanolua for Vaega (68 mins)
Scorers *Tries:* Clarke, Paramore *Penalty Goal:* E Va'a
Referee P J Honiss (New Zealand)

AFRICA GROUP *Morocco 12-19 September*

FINAL TABLE

	P	W	D	L	F	A	Pts
Namibia	3	3	0	0	78	32	9
Morocco	3	2	0	1	29	29	7
Zimbabwe	3	1	0	2	55	54	5
Côte d'Ivoire	3	0	0	3	13	60	3

Namibia to France Pool; Morocco to the repêchages

As in 1994, Casablanca was the scene for the African qualifying tournament. The host nation received a tremendous shot in the arm with its victory on day one by 15-9 against Zimbabwe, who had been Africa's representatives at both the 1987 and 1991 World Cup finals. In their key midweek match, however, the Moroccans were unable to exert their authority over a well-drilled Namibian side. Even so, they held their more experienced opponents at a try apiece and with a decent place-kicker in their ranks could have forced a closer finish. The Namibians thrashed Zimbabwe by six tries to one on the final weekend of the competition and, at their third attempt, thus qualified for the final stages of the World Cup for the first time. 'I am speechless,' Namibia's captain Quin Hough said after the final match. 'This will give rugby in Namibia a great boost.'

12 September, Club Olympique, Casablanca

CÔTE D'IVOIRE 10 (1G 1PG) **NAMIBIA 22** (1G 3T)
CÔTE D'IVOIRE: V K Kouassi; L K Gnogbo, J-B Sathicq (*capt*), L Niakou, D Dogoui Bedel; A Tian Sylvere, F Dupont; D Olivier, E Angoran, P Etenor, J Aka, A Kone, F Legros, E Amapakabo, G Herve *Substitutions:* C N'Gbala for Gnogbo (55 mins); R Y N'Guessan for Kone (63 mins); D Quansah for Aka (45 mins); L N'Drin for Olivier (temp)
Scorers *Try:* Dogoui Bedel *Conversion:* Kouassi *Penalty Goal:* Kouassi
NAMIBIA: L van Dyk; D Farmer, S van Rensburg, L Holtzhousen, A Samuelson; J Zaayman, R Jantjies; E Smith, R van Zyl, J Augustyn, J Theron, H Senekal, S de Beer, Q Hough (*capt*), S van der Merwe *Substitutions:* D Vermark for Zaayman (temp); P Steyn for Theron (45 mins); A Blaauw for Augustyn (49 mins); R Pedro for Jantjies (58 mins); H Lintvelt for S de Beer (73 mins); H Horn for R van Zyl (79 mins)
Scorers *Tries:* Hough (2), Senekal, Samuelson *Conversion:* van Dyk
Referee S Ishiwata (Japan)

12 September, Club Olympique, Casablanca

MOROCCO 15 (1G 1PG 1T) **ZIMBABWE 9** (3PG)
MOROCCO: H Amina; M Oufriche, K El Oula, M Dermouni, A Qaddouri; Y Bouzzedi, F Ferchach; M Gouasmia, N Bouaouali, M Hamdini (*capt*), M Bensoussi, J Hilmi, A Andoh, A Qelai, F Boukanoucha *Substitutions:* S Amzaourou for Gouasmia (temp); K Saadi for Andoh (52 mins); K Chahid for Bouzzedi (75 mins); F Mabrouk for Gouasmia (79 mins)
Scorers *Tries:* El Oula, penalty try *Conversion:* Dermouni *Penalty Goal:* Dermouni
ZIMBABWE: V Olonga; A Roberts, B French, J Eljine, K Mudzamba; K Tsimba (*capt*), N Nortje; R Moore, W Barratt, G Stewart, S Landman, P Georgeou, L Greeff, C McNab, J Putterill *Substitutions:* A Mdehwa for McNab (temp); R Bekker for Nortje (58 mins); G Synder for Moore (58 mins); M Mwerenga for Putterill (temp and 72 mins); B Beattie for Barratt (75 mins)
Scorer *Penalty Goals:* Tsimba (3)
Referee D I Ramage (Scotland)

16 September, Club Olympique, Casablanca

CÔTE D'IVOIRE 0 ZIMBABWE 32 (2G 6PG)
CÔTE D'IVOIRE: V Kouassi; L K Gnogbo, J-B Sathicq (*capt*), L Niakou,
D Dogoui Bedel; A Tian Sylvere, F Dupont; O Diomande, E Angoran,
J F Meslier du Rocan, D Quansah, A Kone, F Legros, M Lebel, E Amapakabo
Substitutions: R Yai for Meslier du Rocan; L Diomade for Sathicq; F D Gneba for
Dupont; N G Koafi for Dogoui Bedel; A A Assigbi for Kouassi; P Etenor for
Quansah
ZIMBABWE: V Olonga; T Manymo, C Brown, J Ewing, T Madamombe;
K Tsimba (*capt*), R Bekker; R Moore, B Beattie, G Stewart, S Landman,
M Mwerenga, L Greeff, B Dawson, C McNab *Substitutions:* K Mazambe for
Manymo; J Putterill for Dawson
Scorers *Tries:* Landman, Olonga *Conversions:* Tsimba (2) *Penalty Goals:* Tsimba
(6)
Referee N Tanaka (Japan)

16 September, Club Olympique, Casablanca

MOROCCO 8 (1PG 1T) **NAMIBIA 17** (4PG 1T)
MOROCCO: H Amina; M Oufriche, M Dermouni, K El Oula, A Quaddouri;
Y Bouzzedi, F Ferchach; M Gouasmia, N Bouaouali, M Hamdini (*capt*),
M Bensoussi, J Hilmi, A Andoh, A Qelai, F Boukanoucha *Substitutions:* I Khalil
for Gouasmia (temp) and for Hamdini
Scorers *Try:* Hamdini *Penalty Goal:* Quaddouri
NAMIBIA: L van Dyk; D Farmer, S van Rensburg, L Holtzhousen, A Samuelson;
J Zaayman, R Jantjies; E Smith, R van Zyl, T Augustyn, J Theron, H Senekal, T
van Rooyen, Q Hough (*capt*), S van der Merwe *Substitutions:* P Steyn for Senekal
(temp); R Pedro for van Rooyen; A Blaauw for Smith; J Nienaber for Samuelson;
H Horn for Theron (temp)
Scorers *Try:* Zaayman *Penalty Goals:* van Dyk (4)
Referee C Giocomel (Italy)

19 September, Club Olympique, Casablanca

ZIMBABWE 14 (3PG 1T) **NAMIBIA 39** (3G 1PG 3T)
ZIMBABWE: V Olonga; K Mudzamba, B French, J Ewing, T Madamombe;
K Tsimba (*capt*), R Bekker; R Moore, B Beattie, G Stewart, S Landman,
M Mwerenga, L Greeff, B Dawson, C McNab *Substitutions:* J Putterill for Leon;
G Synder for Moore; C Brown for French; W Barratt for Beattie; S Williams for
Bekker; J Durand for McNab
Scorers *Try:* Tsimba *Penalty Goals:* Tsimba (3)
NAMIBIA: L van Dyk; D Farmer, L Holtzhousen, J Nienaber, S van Rensburg;
J Zaayman, R Jantjies; E Smith, R van Zyl, T Augustyn, J Theron, P Steyn, T van
Rooyen, Q Hough (*capt*), S van der Merwe *Substitutions:* A Blaauw for Smith;
D Vermaak for Nienaber; A Samuelson for Farmer; S de Beer for van Rooyen
Scorers *Tries:* Augustyn, van Rensburg, Nienaber, Samuelson, Holtzhousen, van
Dyk *Conversions:* van Dyk (3) *Penalty Goal:* van Dyk
Referee D Mené (France)

19 September, Club Olympique, Casablanca

MOROCCO 6 (2PG) **CÔTE D'IVOIRE 3** (1PG)
MOROCCO: H Amina; K El Oula, M Dermouni, Y Bouzzedi, A Qaddouri;
K Chahid, F Ferchach; M Bensoussi, N Bouaouali, M Hamdini (*capt*),
F Mabrouk, J Hilmi, A Andoh, A Qelai, F Boukanoucha *Substitutions:* K Saadi for
Bouaouali; M Oufriche for Bouzzedi; M Gouasmia for Mabrouk; S Amzaourou for

Qaddori; B Hicham for Chahid; S Lahari for Qelai
Scorer *Penalty Goals:* Chahid (2)
CÔTE D'IVOIRE: A A Assigbi; D Dogoui Bedel, C Yapo, L Niakou *(capt)*,
M Sella Koasi; A Tian Sylvere, F D Gneba; L N'Drin, O Diomande, J F Meslier
du Rocan, J Aka, E Dubernard, R Y N'Guessan, M Lebel, E Amapakabo
Substitutions: H Gregoire for N'Guessan; J Dro for Yapo; E Angoran for N'Drin,
A Kone for Dubernard; F Dupont for Gneba; V K Kouassi for Sella Koasi;
J-L Ronan for Dro
Scorer *Penalty Goal:* Assigbi
Referee H A Smith (Ireland)

ASIA GROUP *Singapore 24-31 October*

FINAL TABLE

	P	W	D	L	F	A	Pts
Japan	3	3	0	0	221	25	9
Korea	3	1	0	2	104	81	5
Chinese Taipei	3	1	0	2	57	227	5
Hong Kong	3	1	0	2	39	88	5

Japan to Wales Pool; Korea to the repêchages

Japan, as expected, topped the Asia Group in a competition that doubled as the
biennial Asian Championship. On the way to the title they posted a century of points
on the Chinese Taipei, scoring 20 tries including five by their wing Terunori
Masuho. Qualification depended on a showdown with old rivals Hong Kong on the
final Saturday, but three tries in the opening 12 minutes effectively booked Japan's
passage to Wales. They only conceded three tries in the entire tournament,
prompting Shiggy Konno to say of Japan's prospects for the finals, 'I think we will do
better than we have in the past. Our defence has improved tremendously and I think
this will be a crucial factor.'

The Japanese were captained by New Zealander Andrew McCormick, a name that
will send shudders down the spines of any Welsh supporters over the age of 40. Back
in 1969, his father Fergie kicked 24 points for the All Blacks in a Test against a
Welsh side that included many famous names.

24 October, National Stadium, Singapore

CHINESE TAIPEI 30 (2G 2PG 2T) **HONG KONG 12** (1G 1T)
CHINESE TAIPEI: C-W Chang; C-M Tseng, S-P Kuo, W-C Chen, K-J Lu;
C-S Mai *(capt)*, S-C Wu; Y-H Cheng, C-H Huang, Y-T Lin, C-T Huang,
C-H Cheng, Y-C Tsai, C-L Ho, F-L Lin *Substitution:* Y-L Lin for F-L Lin (50
mins)
Scorers *Tries:* Tseng (2), Ho, Chang *Conversions:* Kuo (2) *Penalty Goals:* Kuo (2)
HONG KONG: C F Ping; M Solomon, J Clark, R McIntosh, A Billington;
R Bredbury, S Kidd *(capt)*; R Grindlay, D Lewis, L Duley, H Bowden, C Scragg,
W Packer, J Hillhild, S Thompson *Substitutions:* J Dunn for Clark (25 mins);
T Bland for Duley (52 mins); T Hall for Scragg (52 mins)
Scorers *Tries:* McIntosh; Billington *Conversion:* Bredbury
Referee P De Luca (Argentina)

24 October, National Stadium, Singapore

KOREA 12 (1G 1T) **JAPAN 40** (5G 1T)
KOREA: C-W Kwan; H-K Kim, S-N Kim, M-S Yoo, H-M Choi; J-S Kim,
C-K No; K-W Kim, Y-H Han, I-S Baek, K-J Kim, D-H Kang *(capt)*, T-I Woo,
J-B Park, S-S Lim *Substitution:* J-H An for Baek

Scorers *Tries:* J-S Park, J-S Kim *Conversion:* J-S Kim
JAPAN: T Matsuda; D Ohata, A McCormick (*capt*), Y Motoki, T Masuho;
K Hirose, W Murata; T Nakamichi, M Kunda, N Nakamura, Y Sakuraba,
H Tanuma, Y Watanabe, T Ito, G Smith
Scorers *Tries:* Watanabe (2), Matsuda (2), Nakamura, Masuho *Conversions:* Hirose
(5)
Referee A Cole (Australia)

---

27 October, National Stadium, Singapore

CHINESE TAIPEI 6 (2PG) **JAPAN 134** (17G 3T)
CHINESE TAIPEI: C-W Chang; C-M Tseng, S-P Kuo, W-C Chen, C-H Chen;
C-S Mai (*capt*), S-C Wu; Y-H Cheng, C-H Huang, Y-T Lin, C-H Cheng,
F-L Lin, Y-C Tsai, C-L Ho, C-T Huang
Scorer *Penalty Goals:* Kuo (2)
JAPAN: T Matsuda; T Masuho, A McCormick (*capt*), O Yatsuhashi, P Tuidraki;
K Hirose, K Ohara; S Hasegawa, M Sakata, N Nakamura, Y Sakuraba,
H Tanuma, K Nakamura, T Ito, Y Watanabe *Substitutions:* K Sawaki for Matsuda
(40 mins); K Iwabuchi for Hirose (40 mins); M Kurokawa for Sakuraba (73 mins)
Scorers *Tries:* Masuho (5), Nakamura (3), Tuidraki (3), Yatsuhashi (3), Sakuraba,
Tanuma, McCormick, Matsuda, Sawaki, Kurokawa *Conversions:* Hirose (10),
Sawaki (7)
Referee S Borsani (Argentina)

---

27 October, National Stadium, Singapore

HONG KONG 20 (2G 2PG) **KOREA 11** (2PG 1T)
HONG KONG: C F Ping; I Tu'ivai, R McIntosh, W Warner, M Solomon;
R Bredbury, S Kidd (*capt*); R Grindlay, D Lewis, T Bland, H Bowden,
R Patterson, W Wild, J Dingley, R Shuttleworth *Substitutions:* T Hall for Bowden
(40 mins); L Duley for Bland (70 mins), S Thompson for Shuttleworth (75 mins)
Scorers *Tries:* Bowden, Solomon *Conversions:* Bredbury, Tu'ivai *Penalty Goals:*
Tu'ivai (2)
KOREA: C-W Kwan; H-K Kim, S-N Kim, M-S Yoo, H-M Choi; J-M Chung,
H-K Sung; K-W Kim, J-H An, I-S Baek, K-J Kim, D-H Kang (*capt*), T-I Woo,
J-B Park, Y-H Han *Substitutions:* J-S Kim for Chung (51 mins); D-S Kim for
D-H Kang (70 mins)
Scorers *Tries:* J-B Park *Penalty Goals:* H-K Sung (2)
Referee S Dickinson (Australia)

---

31 October, National Stadium, Singapore

CHINESE TAIPEI 21 (3G) **KOREA 81** (8G 5T)
CHINESE TAIPEI: C-W Chang; C-M Tseng, W-C Chen, C-W Cheng, C-S Mai
(*capt*); H-L Huang, S-C Wu; Y-H Cheng, S-L Chuang, Y-T Lin, Y-K Lin,
S-K Lin, C-H Cheng, C-L Ho, F-L Lin *Substitution:* C-H Huang for Chuang (40
mins)
Scorers *Tries:* Y-T Lin (2), Ho *Conversions:* H-L Huang (3)
KOREA: C-W Kwan; J-W Lee, Jay-Hyun Kim, M-S Yoo, H-K Kim; J-S Kim,
C-K No; Jim-Heung Kim, Y-H Han, I-S Baek, K-J Kim, D-H Kang (*capt*),
S-S Lim, J-B Park, T-I Woo
Scorers *Tries:* Lee (5), Park (2), Kang (2), Jim-Heung Kim (2), H-K Kim, Lim
Conversions: J-S Kim (6), Jae-Hyun Kim (2)
Referee W J Erickson (Australia)

31 October, National Stadium, Singapore

JAPAN 47 (6G 1T) **HONG KONG** 7 (1G)
JAPAN: T Matsuda; D Ohata, A McCormick (*capt*), Y Motoki, T Masuho;
K Hirose, M Horikoshi; S Hasegawa, M Kunda, N Nakamura, Y Sakuraba,
H Tanuma, Y Watanabe, T Ito, G Smith *Substitutions:* K Nakamura for Watanabe
(40 mins); M Kurokawa for Smith (70 mins); K Iwabuchi for Horikoshi (68 mins);
K Sawaki for Matsuda (68 mins)
Scorers *Tries:* Masuho (2), Ohata (2), Hirose, Motoki, N Nakamura *Conversions:*
Hirose (6)
HONG KONG: C F Ping; M Solomon, W Warner, R McIntosh, I Tu'ivai;
R Bredbury, S Kidd (*capt*); R Grindlay, D Lewis, L Duley, H Bowden,
R Patterson, W Wild, J Dingley, R Shuttleworth *Substitutions:* T Bland for Duley
(40 mins); S Thompson for Shuttleworth (55 mins); A Billington for Solomon (63
mins); R Leung for Lewis (68 mins); T Hall for Bowden (68 mins); D Wigley for
Bredbury (70 mins); J Dunn for McIntosh (75 mins)
Scorers *Try:* Wigley *Conversion:* Wigley
Referee I Hyde-Lay (Canada)

EUROPE GROUP ONE *Ireland 14-21 November*

FINAL TABLE

	P	W	D	L	F	A	Pts
Ireland	2	2	0	0	123	35	6
Romania	2	1	0	1	62	76	4
Georgia	2	0	0	2	23	97	2

Ireland & Romania to Ireland Pool; Georgia to the repêchages

Ireland posted a new national record score in the opening match of the group. They
demolished Georgia by 70-0, passing by ten points their previous highest score and
biggest winning margin set against Romania a dozen years earlier. They also
equalled their record number of tries in an international, scoring five in each half.

The Georgians stretched the Romanians in a lively midweek match. They were
trailing 17-6 before staging a remarkable recovery to pull themselves to within a
point of the Romanians at 17-16, and finally lost an absorbing game by only four
points.

The showdown between Ireland and Romania was watched by a meagre crowd of
13,000. The home side led 19-0 after 25 minutes but lackadaisical defence allowed
the Romanians to get back into the game by scoring 13 points before the interval.
The Romanian backs revealed their flair for attack in a second half of cut and thrust,
scoring three tries to keep the Irish on their toes.

14 November, Lansdowne Road, Dublin

IRELAND 70 (10G) **GEORGIA** 0
IRELAND: C M P O'Shea; J P Bishop, P Duignan, J C Bell, K M Maggs;
E P Elwood, C D McGuinness; P M Clohessy, R P Nesdale, P S Wallace,
P S Johns (*capt*), M E O'Kelly, E R P Miller, V C P Costello, A J Ward
Substitutions: A T H Clarke for Nesdale (29 mins); C J Scally for McGuinness (54
mins); G Dempsey for O'Shea (54 mins); D O'Cuinneagain for Costello (60
mins); J W Davidson for O'Kelly (60 mins); J M Fitzpatrick for Clohessy
Scorers *Tries:* Dempsey (2), P Wallace, Johns, Maggs, O'Shea, Costello, Duignan,
Bell, Scally *Conversions:* Elwood (10)
GEORGIA: V Abachidze; G Bugianachvili, E Dzagnidze, V Katsadze,
A Kavtarachvili; B Tefnadze, C Djanlidze; I Tchikava, L Javelidze, G Chvelidze,
I Zedgenidze, V Nadiradze, A Kobaxidze, K Kobakhidze, G Labadze *Substitutions:*

Z Mtchedlichvili for Labadze (40 mins); M Urdjukachvili for Kobaxidze (40
mins); P Jimcheladze for Dzagnidze (40 mins); L Tsabadze for Tchikava (70 mins)
Referee R G Davies (Wales)

18 November, Lansdowne Road, Dublin

GEORGIA 23 (2G 3PG) **ROMANIA 27** (3G 2PG)
GEORGIA: M Urdjukachvili; A Kavtarachvili, P Jimcheladze, B Khamashuridz,
G Bugianachvili; K Matchitidze, I Giorkhelidze; M Mitiulishvili, I Giorgadze,
L Tsabadze, G Ruskin, Z Mtchedlichvili (*capt*), J Lejava, K Kobakhidze, G Labadze
Substitutions: B Tefnadze for Matchitidze; G Chvelidze for Mitiulishvili; C Djanelidze
for Giorkhelidze; V Nadiradze for Kobakhidze; V Katsadze for Labadze
Scorers *Tries:* Tsabadze, Kavtarachvili *Conversions:* Giorkhelidze, Urdjukachvili
Penalty Goals: Matchitidze, Urdjukachvili, Giorkhelidze
ROMANIA: M Vioreanu; C Hildan, G Brezoianu, R Gontineac, G Solomie;
R Vusec, P Mitu; D Nicolae, R Mavrodin, C Stan, M Dragomir, A Girbu,
A Manta, C Draguceanu (*capt*), F Corodeanu *Substitutions:* F Marioara for Stan;
P Balan for Mavrodin; O Slusariuc for Corodeanu; V Doja for Dragomir;
M Ciolacu for Solomie
Scorers *Tries:* Solomie, Brezoianu, Mitu *Conversions:* Mitu (3)
Penalty Goals: Mitu (2)
Referee J Kaplan (South Africa)

21 November, Lansdowne Road, Dublin

IRELAND 53 (6G 2PG 1T) **ROMANIA 35** (2G 2PG 3T)
IRELAND: C M P O'Shea; J P Bishop, P Duignan, J C Bell, D W O'Mahony;
E P Elwood, C J Scally; P M Clohessy, A T H Clarke, P S Wallace, P S Johns
(*capt*), M E O'Kelly, E R P Miller, V C P Costello, A J Ward *Substitutions:*
K M Maggs for Duignan (40 mins); K G M Wood for Clarke (40 mins);
J W Davidson for Johns (40 mins); D O'Cuinneagain for Miller (40 mins);
J M Fitzpatrick for Wallace (48 mins); D G Humphreys for Elwood (54 mins);
C D McGuinness for Scally (58 mins)
Scorers *Tries:* Bell (2), penalty tries (2) O'Shea, Scally, Ward *Conversions:* Elwood
(3) Humphreys (3) *Penalty Goals:* Elwood (2)
ROMANIA: M Vioreanu; R Fugigi, G Brezoianu, R Gontineac, G Solomie;
R Vusec, P Mitu; D Nicolae, R Mavrodin, F Marioara, M Dragomir, V Doja,
A Manta, C Draguceanu (*capt*), A Girbu *Substitutions:* E Septar for Dragomir (39
mins); C Lupu for Solomie (42 mins); M Ciolacu for Gontineac (61 mins);
O Slusariuc for Girbu (64 mins); P Balan for Mavrodin (76 mins)
Scorers *Tries:* Vioreanu (2), Solomie, Fugigi, Brezoianu *Conversions:* Mitu (2)
Penalty Goals: Mitu(2)
Referee P J Honiss (New Zealand)

EUROPE GROUP TWO *England 14-22 November*

FINAL TABLE

	P	W	D	L	F	A	Pts
England	2	2	0	0	133	15	6
Italy	2	1	0	1	82	30	4
The Netherlands	2	0	0	2	7	177	2

England & Italy to England Pool; Holland to the repêchages

Clive Woodward's England side set several new national records in their overwhelming defeat of the Dutch. It was their highest Test score, their most tries and most

conversions in a Test. Paul Grayson equalled Rob Andrew's mark for most points in a Test by an England player (30) and Neil Back became the first England forward to score four tries in a cap match since 1881.

It was very different eight days later when England struggled to beat Italy on a grey Sunday afternoon in Huddersfield. The *azzurri*, who gave their best display of the season, were unlucky to have a second-half try by their scrum-half, Alessandro Troncon, disallowed by an unsighted referee. England held only a precarious one-point lead as the match entered its last ten minutes and were grateful to Will Greenwood for a 77th minute try that added a touch of respectability to the scoreline.

14 November, Alfred McAlpine Stadium, Huddersfield

ENGLAND 110 (15G 1T) THE NETHERLANDS 0
ENGLAND: M B Perry; D D Luger, W J H Greenwood, J C Guscott, A S Healey; P J Grayson, M J S Dawson; J Leonard, R Cockerill, D J Garforth, G S Archer, M O Johnson (*capt*), B B Clarke, M E Corry, N A Back *Substitutions:* T A K Rodber for Archer (50 mins); G C Rowntree for Garforth (50 mins); R A Hill for Clarke (50 mins); N D Beal for Perry (50 mins)
Scorers *Tries:* Back (4), Guscott (4), penalty try, Greenwood, Cockerill, Corry, Dawson, Luger, Healey, Beal *Conversions:* Grayson (15)
THE NETHERLANDS: A Webber; O Winkels, R van der Walle, G Everts, G Viguurs; B Vervoort, M Marcker (*capt*); J J van der Esch, A Seybel, R Philippo, P Faas, R Donkers, R van der Ven, C Elisara, N Holten *Substitutions:* H Brat for van der Esch (45 mins); S Ramaker for Vervoort (65 mins); R Lips for Marcker (76 mins)
Referee R Duhau (France)

18 November, Alfred McAlpine Stadium, Huddersfield

ITALY 67 (6G 5T) THE NETHERLANDS 7 (1G)
ITALY: M Pini; F Roselli, C Stoica, M Dallan, L Martin; D Dominguez, A Troncon; M Cuttitta, A Moscardi, A Castellani, C Checchinato, S Stocco, M Giovanelli (*capt*), C Caione, M Bergamasco *Substitutions:* G Lanzi for Checchinato (54 mins); S Saviozzi for Moscardi (60 mins); G P de Carli for Cuttitta (66 mins); F Mazzariol for Dominguez (70 mins); G Mazzi for Troncon (70 mins); M Birtig for Caione (75 mins); G Raineri for Stoica (76 mins)
Scorers *Tries:* Checchinato (2), Bergamasco (2), Stoica, Giovanelli, Stocco, Dominguez, Dallan, de Carli, Pini *Conversions:* Dominguez (4), Mazzariol (2)
THE NETHERLANDS: A Webber; R Kofman, R van der Walle, G Everts, B Ossenkoppel; S Rhodes, S Ramaker; D J Vermaas, A Seybel, H Brat, P Faas, R Donkers, R van der Ven, C Elisara (*capt*), N Holten *Substitutions:* T Schumacher for Donkers (54 mins); O Winkels for Rhodes (62 mins); R Lips for Everts (73 mins); R Philippo for Brat (73 mins); P Hudson for van der Ven (77 mins)
Scorers *Try:* Elisara *Conversion:* Everts
Referee P Thomas (France)

22 November, Alfred McAlpine Stadium, Huddersfield

ENGLAND 23 (2G 3PG) ITALY 15 (4PG 1DG)
ENGLAND: M B Perry; A S Healey, W J H Greenwood, J C Guscott, D D Luger; P J Grayson, M J S Dawson; J Leonard, R Cockerill, D J Garforth, M O Johnson (*capt*), G S Archer, B B Clarke, M E Corry, N A Back *Substitutions:* G C Rowntree for Garforth (50 mins); R A Hill for Clarke (50 mins); T A K Rodber for Archer (50 mins);

Martin Johnson leaves the Dutch defenders trailing in his wake in England's 110-0 rout of the Netherlands at the Alfred McAlpine Stadium, Huddersfield.

Scorers *Tries:* Luger, Greenwood *Conversions:* Grayson (2), *Penalty Goals:* Grayson (3)
ITALY: M Pini; F Roselli, C Stoica, M Dallan, L Martin; D Dominguez, A Troncon; M Cuttitta, A Moscardi, G P De Carli, C Checchinato, W Cristofoletto, M Giovanelli *(capt)*, C Caione, M Bergamasco *Substitutions:* O Arancio for Bergamasco (60 mins); G Lanzi for Cristofoletto (84 mins); A Castellani for Cuttitta (84 mins)
Scorer *Penalty Goals:* Dominguez (4) *Dropped Goal:* Dominguez
Referee D Mené (France)

EUROPE GROUP THREE *Scotland 28 November–5 December*

FINAL TABLE

	P	W	D	L	F	A	Pts
Scotland	2	2	0	0	170	14	6
Spain	2	1	0	1	24	102	4
Portugal	2	0	0	2	28	106	2

Scotland & Spain to Scotland Pool; Portugal to the repêchages

Scotland, in contrast to Ireland and England, decided not to award caps for this last round of qualifying matches before the repêchages stage. The hosts showed no sympathy for their visitors, registering 170 points including 26 tries, but the crowds voted with their feet. There were only 6,000 present to see Kenny Logan score five tries against Spain on the final Saturday and the crowds were even smaller for the two matches involving Portugal.

'This bunch of players is as good as any I've worked with,' said Jim Telfer after guiding his men to the final stages. The Spanish coach Alfonso Feijoo reported that coverage of a Real Madrid match had been interrupted to announce the news of his side's qualification for the Rugby World Cup finals.

28 November, Murrayfield, Edinburgh

SCOTLAND 85 (10G 3T) **PORTUGAL 11** (1PG 1DG 1T)
SCOTLAND: G P J Townsend; K M Logan, M J M Mayer, J A Leslie, C A Murray; D W Hodge, B W Redpath *(capt)*; T J Smith, G C Bulloch, D I W Hilton, S Murray, G W Weir, M D Leslie, E W Peters, A C Pountney *Substitutions:* G Armstrong for Redpath (55 mins); A V Tait for J Leslie (58 mins); S J Brotherstone for Bulloch (62 mins); S B Grimes for Weir (66 mins); S L Longstaff for C Murray (72 mins); A P Burnell for Hilton (72 mins); R I Wainwright for Peters (79 mins)
Scorers *Tries:* Mayer (3), J Leslie (2), Townsend (2), Logan (2), C Murray, Bulloch, Peters, Pountney *Conversions:* Hodge (10)
PORTUGAL: J Gomes; F Saldanha, R Hoffman, S Amaral, L Lamas; N Mourao, F Rocha; P Marques, P Silva, J Ferreira *(capt)*, M Melo, M S Ribeiro, M Barbosa, P Castro, M Portela *Substitutions:* J Mota for Amaral (47 mins); A Silva for Marques (56 mins); R Gomes for J Gomes (60 mins)
Scorers *Try:* Hoffman *Penalty Goal:* Mourao *Drop Goal:* Hoffman
Referee G Morandin (Italy)

2 December, Murrayfield, Edinburgh

SPAIN 21 (6PG 1DG) **PORTUGAL 17** (2G 1PG)
SPAIN: F Velasco; M A Frechilla, A Enciso, F Diez, R Bastide; A Kovalenko, J Torres-Morote; J Camps, D Zarzosa, J I Zapatero, J M Villau, L J Martinez, A Malo *(capt)*, A Mata, J Díaz *Substitutions:* D Garcia for Frechilla (40 mins); O Astarloa for Martinez (40 mins); F de la Calle for Zarzosa (65 mins); V Torres

for J Camps (76 mins); C Souto for Villau (76 mins) *Sent off:* J Diáz (25 mins)
Scorers *Penalty Goals:* Kovalenko (6) *Drop Goal:* Diez
PORTUGAL: R Hoffman; R Nuñes, S Amaral, J D Mota, M Portela; T Teixeira,
L Pissarra; N Sa, J Carvalho, J Ferreira *(capt)* P Rogerio, M S Ribeiro,
M Barbosa, M D'O Dias, P Castro *Substitutions:* R Gomes for Rogerio (53 mins);
N Mourao for Teixeira (47 mins)
Scorers *Tries:* Teixeira, Hoffman *Conversions:* Teixeira, Mourao *Penaty Goal:*
Teixeira
Referee S Lander (England)

5 December, Murrayfield, Edinburgh

SCOTLAND 85 (10G 3T) **SPAIN 3** (1PG)
SCOTLAND: G P J Townsend; C A Murray, M J M Mayer, J A Leslie,
K M Logan; D W Hodge, B W Redpath *(capt)*; T J Smith, G C Bulloch,
W A Anderson, S Murray, G W Weir, C Mather, E W Peters, M D Leslie
Substitutions: S B Grimes for S Murray (66 mins); S L Longstaff for Logan (79 mins)
Scorers *Tries:* Logan (5), J Leslie, M Leslie, Smith, Redpath, Townsend,
C Murray, Weir, Longstaff *Conversions:* Hodge (10)
SPAIN: M A Frechilla; D Garcia, A Enciso, F Diez, Alberto Socias; A Kovalenko,
A Gallastegui; J Camps, F de la Calle, A Altuna, L Martinez, S Tuineau, A Malo
(capt), A Mata, O Astarloa *Substitutions:* R Bastide for Diez (40 mins); C Souto for
Malo (56 mins); J Torres-Morote for Gallastegui (56 mins); V Torres for Camps
(56 mins); Antonio Socias for D Garcia (64 mins); O Ripol for Enciso (70 mins);
D Zarzosa for Tuineau (79 mins)
Scorer *Penalty Goal:* Kovalenko
Referee S Young (Australia)

REPÊCHAGE STAGE *6 March-4 May*

Repêchage is the new concept for Rugby World Cup 1999. In the qualifying stages it
gave seven of the nations that did not automatically reach the finals a second bite of
the cherry. Deciders were played over two legs, home and away, with inter-
continental clashes between Asia and the South Seas and, more exotically, Africa
and South America taking place.

Tonga, Uruguay and Korea went through after the first round of repêchages,
Morocco having won a bye to the second stage. The last places in the finals were
eventually earned by Tonga and Uruguay, who will line up in the English and
Scottish pools respectively in October.

ROUND ONE MATCHES

6 March, Nuku'alofa Stadium, Nuku'alofa

TONGA 37 (4G 3PG) **GEORGIA 6** (2PG)
Tonga Scorers *Tries:* E Vunipola (2), Mafi, Tiueti *Conversions:* Tonga (3),
Taumalolo *Penalty Goal:* Taumalolo (3)
Georgia Scorer *Penalty Goals:* Malcmaz (2)
Referee W J Erickson (Australia)

13 March, Carrasco Polo Club, Montevideo

URUGUAY 46 (4G 1PG 3T) **PORTUGAL 9** (3PG)
Uruguay Scorers *Tries:* Lemoine (2), Ormaechea (2), Mendaro, Cardoso,
Lamelas *Conversions:* Sciarra (4) *Penalty Goal:* Sciarra
Portugal Scorer *Penalty Goals:* Texeira (3)
Referee T Henning (South Africa)

14 March, National Rugby Centre, Amsterdam

THE NETHERLANDS 31 (3G 2T) **KOREA 30** (2G 2PG 2T)
Netherlands Scorers *Tries:* Elisara (2), Winkels, van Dalen, van der Loos *Conversions:* Everts (3)
Korea Scorers *Tries:* H-M Yong, H-K Kim, J-H Kim, S-S Lim *Conversions:* J-S Kim (2) *Penalty Goals:* J-S Kim (2)
Referee J Dumé (France)

28 March, National Stadium, Tbilisi

GEORGIA 28 (1G 2PG 3T) **TONGA 27** (1G 4T)
Georgia Scorers *Tries:* Tsabadze, Khekhelashvili, Shvelidze, Kobakhidze *Conversion:* Urjukashvili *Penalty Goals:* Urjukashvili, Kobakhidze
Sent off: Urjukashvili (79 mins)
Tonga Scorers *Tries:* Taumalolo (3), Tiueti, Lutui *Conversion:* Taumalolo
Sent off: S Faka'osifolau (79 mins)
Referee D Mené (France)

3 April, University Grounds, Lisbon

PORTUGAL 24 (3G 1PG) **URUGUAY 33** (3G 4PG)
Portugal Scorers *Tries:* Hoffman, Aguilar, Canha *Conversions:* Mourao (3) *Penalty Goal:* Mourao
Uruguay Scorers *Tries:* Ormaechea, Bado, Sanchez *Conversions:* Sciarra (2), Aguirre *Penalty Goal:* Sciarra (3), Aguirre
Referee B Campsall (England)

4 April, Tongdaemun Stadium, Seoul

KOREA 78 (7G 2PG 1DG 4T) **THE NETHERLANDS 14** (2G)
Korea Scorers *Tries:* H-M Yong (2), J-H Kim (2), M-K Kim (2), J-H No, C-K No, S-S Lim, K-W Kim, K-S Baik *Conversions:* J-S Kim (5), Y-J Choi (2) *Penalty Goals:* J-S Kim (2) *Dropped Goal:* J-S Kim
Netherlands Scorers *Tries:* Elisara, Skyeel *Conversions:* Winkels (2)
Referee W J Erickson (Australia)

Tonga, Uruguay and Korea to Round Two

ROUND TWO MATCHES

16 April, Teufaiva Stadium, Nuku'alofa

TONGA 58 (5G 1PG 4T) **KOREA 26** (3G 1T)
Tonga Scorers *Tries:* Tapueluelu (2), Koloi (2), F Vunipola, Toloke, Tiueti, E Vunipola, Fatani *Conversions:* Tonga (4), Tu'ihalamaka *Penalty Goal:* Tonga
Korea Scorers *Tries:* H-K Kim, H-M Yong, D-S Kim, C-K No *Conversions:* Y-J Choi (3)

18 April, Carrasco Polo Club, Montevideo

URUGUAY 18 (1G 2PG 1T) **MOROCCO 3** (1DG)
Uruguay Scorers *Tries:* Ormaechea, Cardoso *Conversion:* Sciarra *Penalty Goals:* Sciarra (2)
Morocco Scorer *Drop Goal:* Belkhous
Referee S Lander (England)

1 May, Club Olympique, Casablanca

MOROCCO 21 (1G 3PG 1T) **URUGUAY 18** (6PG)
Morocco Scorers *Tries:* El Oula (2) *Conversion:* Belkhous *Penalty Goals:* Belkhous (3)
Uruguay Scorer *Penalty Goals:* Sciarra (6)
Referee A Lewis (Ireland)

4 May, Tongdaemun Stadium, Seoul

KOREA 15 (3T) **TONGA 82** (8G 2PG 4T)
Korea Scorers *Tries:* M-S Yoo, J-W Lee, K-S Baik
Tonga Scorers *Tries:* Koloi (3), Tapueluelu (2), F Vunipola, Fatani, Toloke, S Tuipulotu, Ta'u, Tatafu, penalty try *Conversions:* S Tuipulotu (8) *Penalty Goals:* S Tuipulotu (2)
Referee S Young (Australia)

Tonga to England Pool and Uruguay to Scotland Pool

Matt Dawson attempts to evade the Dutch tacklers during England's World Cup qualifying defeat of The Netherlands.

WORLD CUP RECORDS

1987 IN AUSTRALIA & NEW ZEALAND

Pool 1 Australia 19, England 6; USA 21, Japan 18; England 60, Japan 7; Australia 47, USA 12; England 34, USA 6; Australia 42, Japan 23.
Pool 2 Canada 37, Tonga 4; Wales 13, Ireland 6; Wales 29, Tonga 16; Ireland 46, Canada 19; Wales 40, Canada 9; Ireland 32, Tonga 9.
Pool 3 New Zealand 70, Italy 6; Fiji 28, Argentina 9; New Zealand 74, Fiji 13; Argentina 25, Italy 16; Italy 18, Fiji 15; New Zealand 46, Argentina 15.
Pool 4 Romania 21, Zimbabwe 20; France 20, Scotland 20; France 55, Romania 12; Scotland 60, Zimbabwe 21; France 70, Zimbabwe 12; Scotland 55, Romania 28.
Quarter-finals New Zealand 30, Scotland 3; France 31, Fiji 16; Australia 33, Ireland 15; Wales 16, England 3.
Semi-finals France 30, Australia 24; New Zealand 49, Wales 6.
Third Place match Wales 22, Australia 21.

FINAL NEW ZEALAND 29, FRANCE 9

1991 IN BRITAIN, IRELAND & FRANCE

Pool 1 New Zealand 18, England 12; Italy 30, USA 9; New Zealand 46, USA 6; England 36, Italy 6; England 37, USA 9; New Zealand 31, Italy 21.
Pool 2 Scotland 47, Japan 9; Ireland 55, Zimbabwe 11; Ireland 32, Japan 16; Scotland 51, Zimbabwe 12; Scotland 24, Ireland 15; Japan 52, Zimbabwe 8.
Pool 3 Australia 32, Argentina 19; Western Samoa 16, Wales 13; Australia 9, Western Samoa 3; Wales 16, Argentina 7; Australia 38, Wales 3; Western Samoa 35, Argentina 12.
Pool 4 France 30, Romania 3; Canada 13, Fiji 3; France 33, Fiji 9; Canada 19, Romania 11; Romania 17, Fiji 15; France 19, Canada 13.
Quarter-finals England 19, France 10; Scotland 28, Western Samoa 6; Australia 19, Ireland 18; New Zealand 29, Canada 13.
Semi-finals England 9, Scotland 6; Australia 16, New Zealand 6.
Third Place match New Zealand 13, Scotland 6.

FINAL AUSTRALIA 12, ENGLAND 6

1995 IN SOUTH AFRICA

Pool A South Africa 27, Australia 18; Canada 34, Romania 3; South Africa 21, Romania 8; Australia 27, Canada 11; Australia 42, Romania 3; South Africa 20, Canada 0.
Pool B Western Samoa 42, Italy 18; England 24, Argentina 18; Western Samoa 32, Argentina 26; England 27, Italy 20; Italy 31, Argentina 25; England 44, Western Samoa 22.
Pool C Wales 57, Japan 10; New Zealand 43, Ireland 19; Ireland 50, Japan 28; New Zealand 34, Wales 9; New Zealand 145, Japan 17; Ireland 24, Wales 23.
Pool D Scotland 89, Ivory Coast 0; France 38, Tonga 10; France 54, Ivory Coast 18; Scotland 41, Tonga 5; Tonga 29, Ivory Coast 11; France 22, Scotland 19.
Quarter-finals France 36, Ireland 12; South Africa 42, Western Samoa 14; England 25, Australia 22; New Zealand 48, Scotland 30.
Semi-finals South Africa 19, France 15; New Zealand 45, England 29.
Third Place match France 19, England 9.

FINAL SOUTH AFRICA 15*, NEW ZEALAND 12 (*after extra time; 9-9 after normal time)

The sensation of the last World Cup, Jonah Lomu, evades Tony Underwood's despairing dive on his way to scoring New Zealand's first try in the semi-final victory over England.

COMPETITION RECORDS
(Final stages only)

LEADING SCORERS

MOST POINTS IN THE COMPETITION

126	G J Fox	New Zealand	1987
112	T Lacroix	France	1995
104	A G Hastings	Scotland	1995
84	A P Mehrtens	New Zealand	1995
82	M P Lynagh	Australia	1987

MOST TRIES IN ONE COMPETITION

7	M C G Ellis	New Zealand	1995
7	J T Lomu	New Zealand	1995

MOST CONVERSIONS IN ONE COMPETITION

30	G J Fox	New Zealand	1987
20	S D Culhane	New Zealand	1995
20	M P Lynagh	Australia	1987

MOST PENALTY GOALS IN ONE COMPETITION

26	T Lacroix	France	1995
21	G J Fox	New Zealand	1987
20	C R Andrew	England	1995

MOST DROPPED GOALS IN ONE COMPETITION

3	A P Mehrtens	New Zealand	1995
3	J T Stransky	South Africa	1995
3	C R Andrew	England	1995
3	J Davies	Wales	1987

MOST POINTS IN A MATCH
By a team

145		New Zealand v Japan	1995
89		Scotland v Ivory Coast	1995
74		New Zealand v Fiji	1987
70		New Zealand v Italy	1987
70		France v Zimbabwe	1987

By a player

45	S D Culhane	New Zealand v Japan	1995
44	A G Hastings	Scotland v Ivory Coast	1995
31	A G Hastings	Scotland v Tonga	1995
30	M C G Ellis	New Zealand v Japan	1995
30	D Camberabero	France v Zimbabwe	1987

MOST TRIES IN A MATCH
By a team

21		New Zealand v Japan	1995
13		Scotland v Ivory Coast	1995
13		France v Zimbabwe	1987
12		New Zealand v Italy	1987
12		New Zealand v Fiji	1987

By a player

6	M C G Ellis	New Zealand v Japan	1995
4	A G Hastings	Scotland v Ivory Coast	1995
4	C M Williams	South Africa v Western Samoa	1995
4	J T Lomu	New Zealand v England	1995
4	B F Robinson	Ireland v Zimbabwe	1991
4	I C Evans	Wales v Canada	1987
4	C I Green	New Zealand v Fiji	1987
4	J A Gallagher	New Zealand v Fiji	1987

MOST CONVERSIONS IN A MATCH
By a team

20		New Zealand v Japan	1995
10		New Zealand v Fiji	1987
9		Scotland v Ivory Coast	1995
9		France v Zimbabwe	1987

By a player

20	S D Culhane	New Zealand v Japan	1995
10	G J Fox	New Zealand v Fiji	1987
9	A G Hastings	Scotland v Ivory Coast	1995
9	D Camberabero	France v Zimbabwe	1987

MOST PENALTY GOALS IN A MATCH
By a team

8		Scotland v Tonga	1995
8		France v Ireland	1995

By a player

8	A G Hastings	Scotland v Tonga	1995
8	T Lacroix	France v Ireland	1995

MOST DROPPED GOALS IN A MATCH
By a team

3		Fiji v Romania	1991

By a player

2	J T Stransky	South Africa v New Zealand	1995
2	C R Andrew	England v Argentina	1995
2	T Rabaka	Fiji v Romania	1991
2	L Arbizu	Argentina v Australia	1991
2	J Davies	Wales v Ireland	1981

FAREWELL FIVE NATIONS

THE INTERNATIONAL CHAMPIONSHIP 1999

It was a marvellous championship, full of stunning plot lines and vivid characters. Italy arrive to make up the numbers to six for the 2000 Championship. What a way for the Five Nations to bow out. The fastest try ever scored in international rugby on the opening day by Scotland's John Leslie was neatly bookended by Scott Gibbs's diving injury-time try at Wembley to bring victory to Wales over England on the last afternoon of the tournament. And to think that it almost did not come to pass.

In late January the mood was bleak and the prospects grim. England had been thrown out of the Five Nations Championship over a TV contractual dispute. The absurd face-off lasted no more than 24 hours. It was a poor way to salute the passing of a rich history. Italy are to be admitted to the tournament from this season. And very welcome they are too. They actually played all five countries this season but did not manage a single win. Should we write them off? Only if you were the sort of short-sighted fool who wrote off Scotland before the start of last season's championship. Step forward a short-sighted fool, one of many who did dismiss Scotland's chances. It was a fair call. Their domestic structure was in ruins and their administration riven by in-fighting over the best way forward.

So much for logic. Scotland not only won the last ever Five Nations title, they thoroughly deserved to do so. They played by far the most engaging brand of rugby with their fast, rucking pack delivering quick ball for their back line. That ball was rarely wasted. Indeed if it hadn't been for a couple of fluffed kicks at Twickenham, Scotland would have won the Grand Slam. They scored three tries that afternoon, cutting the supposedly unforgiving English defence to shreds in the process. They put another five tries past the French in Paris. Scotland's points tally – 120 – was exactly the same as the number they conceded in the 1998 championship. What brought about such a dramatic conversion?

The foundation was simple – good selection and good coaching. Jim Telfer was the key man on both fronts. One of his articles of faith is that no matter how good a coach you might be, you can do nothing unless you have some decent material with which to work. He was prepared to shoulder criticism for choosing the New Zealand-born Leslie brothers, John and Martin, to be dubbed the 'Kilted Kiwis', ahead of Scottish-born players. It was a key decision. John Leslie, in particular, transformed the Scottish back line. His steadiness and perception at inside centre were not only admirable traits in their own right; they also drew the best from players around him, notably Gregor Townsend at fly-half. Townsend flourished, so too Alan Tait alongside in the centre. Kenny Logan had his best international season ever on the wing while Glenn Metcalfe showed his promise at full-back.

The Scottish pack also earned its spurs. Bedford lock, Scott Murray, was one of the star turns of the entire championship. There was a great showing, too, from Eric Peters at No.8.

England, of course, were only pipped by points difference. Might they have taken the title if they had struck out with more conviction in some games? Certainly they had a decisive whip hand in matches against Ireland and France; yet they never put the opposition away. The switch of Tim Rodber to the second row was an unqualified success. He was a huge presence in Dublin where the much-trumpeted fire of the Irish pack was snuffed out at source. Martin Johnson proved yet again, if proof were even needed, that few can match him anywhere in the world for work-rate and presence. Occasionally he strayed just the wrong side of the law, picking up yellow cards against Scotland and Ireland.

The confirmation of Jonny Wilkinson, the 19-year-old from Newcastle, as a potential world-class star was a huge bonus for England coach, Clive Woodward. Wilkinson prefers fly-half, but Woodward, deprived of Will Greenwood and Phil de Glanville through injury, played him at inside centre. His tackling was the talk of every town visited.

Wales had a terrible start and a wonderful ending. They performed poorly in Scotland and were loose and reckless in the opening hour against Ireland. But then, as they clawed back a 26-6 deficit, they showed what they can do. Their late rally was not enough to win that day. However, that moment of triumph was not far away. Their one-point win in Paris was one of the highlights of the last decade. It was a stunning reversal of form. The team played with self-belief and imagination, no-one more so than fly-half Neil Jenkins, a man so humiliatingly torn to shreds by the French only 12 months earlier.

And then came Wembley. And then came Scott Gibbs and the boot of Neil Jenkins. The Welsh fly-half finished with 64 points, a new Welsh record for the championship.

Ireland had mixed fortunes, and how often have we written that about them. They were denied victory over France only by a last-minute penalty miss by David Humphreys. Perhaps that might have sent them onward with more confidence. They were well-beaten by England at Lansdowne Road. Their back line is still too one-dimensional although the pack is taking shape.

As for France, they have lost shape entirely. The double Grand Slam champions were very close to a complete whitewash. They lost both their home matches, the first time that has happened since 1957. They had a long list of injuries to contend with but even that does not excuse their feeble lack of heart and resilience.

FINAL TABLE

	P	W	D	L	F	A	Pts
Scotland	4	3	0	1	120	79	6
England	4	3	0	1	103	78	6
Wales	4	2	0	2	109	126	4
Ireland	4	1	0	3	66	90	2
France	4	1	0	3	75	100	2

The final points tally was 473, 28 fewer than the season before and 38 short of the championship record set in 1997.

The points comprised 45 tries (including one penalty try), 34 conversions, 57 penalty goals and three dropped goals. It was the first time since 1996 that more penalty goals than tries were scored in the championship.

The leading individual scorers were: 64 Neil Jenkins (Wales); 60 Jonny Wilkinson (England); 56 David Humphreys (Ireland). Jenkins was three shy of the championship record set by Jonathan Webb in 1992. Alan Tait (five for Scotland), Emile Ntamack (five for France) and Gregor Townsend (four for Scotland, including one in every championship match) were the leading try-scorers.

6 February, Lansdowne Road, Dublin
IRELAND 9 (3PG)   FRANCE 10 (1G 1PG)

There was little need to consult the tea-leaves. Ireland had been down this road so often that every last home supporter packed into Lansdowne Road on a filthy wet afternoon knew that they were destined to lose. Destiny duly delivered the kick in the solar plexus on the stroke of full-time. Thomas Castaignède had just nudged his side into the lead with a penalty awarded for offside against Irish tighthead, Paul Wallace. (That too might have been reversed given that Wallace was punched.) Still, Irish fly-half, David Humphreys had the chance to right the scales of justice himself.

The Ulsterman, who had steered his province to European Cup glory only seven days earlier, had a shot at goal from 30 metres out to the left of the posts. He struck it well, but the wind took the ball across the face of the posts. Victory, in a compelling, at times brutal match belonged to France for the 15th time in succession. For the 11th consecutive season Ireland had opened their Five Nations campaign with a defeat. No such misery for France. After successive Grand Slams, this was their ninth consecutive win in a row in the Five Nations, a new national record.

No wonder Humphreys was to say afterwards: 'I've just lived that old cliché: a week really is a long time in rugby.'

Humphreys, who had been preferred to Eric Elwood, one of four changes in the Irish side, had enjoyed a good all-round game. However, his kicking was off-beam. He converted only three from seven attempts. Ireland deserved better. Their pack, which featured their four Lions for the first time in 18 months, gave them a decent platform. Hooker Keith Wood was as ever to the fore, visibly so in that he looked like a war-clad

Apache after paint from the sponsors' pitch logo became smeared all over face and body.

France did manage to make the most of their limited openings. Full-back Emile Ntamack touched down in the 61st minute after a rumbling maul. Castaignède converted and then delivered the killer blow 18 minutes later.

IRELAND: C M P O'Shea (London Irish); J P Bishop (London Irish), K M Maggs (Bath), J C Bell (Dungannon), G Dempsey (Terenure College); D G Humphreys (Dungannon), C D McGuinness (St Mary's College); P M Clohessy (Young Munster), K G M Wood (Harlequins), P S Wallace (Saracens), P S Johns (Saracens) *(capt)*, J W Davidson (Castres), E R P Miller (Terenure College), V C P Costello (St Mary's College), D O'Cuinneagain (Sale) *Substitutions:* R A J Henderson (Wasps) for Bell (14 mins); J M Fitzpatrick (Dungannon) for Wallace (temp 44-46 mins) and for Clohessy (62 mins); T Brennan (St Mary's College) for Costello (50 mins)
Scorer *Penalty Goals:* Humphreys (3)
FRANCE: E Ntamack (Toulouse); P Bernat-Salles (Biarritz), R Dourthe (Stade Français), F Comba (Stade Français), T Lombard (Stade Français); T Castaignède (Castres), P Carbonneau (Brive); C Califano (Toulouse), R Ibañez (Perpignan) *(capt)*, F Tournaire (Toulouse), O Brouzet (Bègles-Bordeaux), F Pelous (Toulouse), P Benetton (Agen), T Lièvremont (Perpignan), O Magne (Brive) *Substitutions:* S Marconnet (Stade Français) for Califano (40 mins); T Cléda (Pau) for Pelous (68 mins); A Gomès (Stade Français) for Lombard (80 mins)
Scorers *Try:* Ntamack *Conversion:* Castaignède *Penalty Goal:* Castaignède
Referee P L Marshall (Australia)

6 February, Murrayfield
SCOTLAND 33 (2G 3PG 2T)   WALES 20 (2G 2PG)

Pity those Scots who were still guzzling at the bar prior to the kick-off. Pity those, too, who left early to beat the traffic. The bookends of this match contained some fascinating tales. Scottish centre John Leslie scored the fastest try in the history of international rugby, crossing after just nine seconds. But then his team began to tread water. It took a clatter of 18 points in the final 12 minutes to see Scotland home. It was breathless stuff, yielding a record-equalling aggregate of 53 points for the fixture.

Neither side came into the match brimful of confidence, largely owing to their own inexperience. Scotland had four players new to the championship, Wales five. Tellingly, four of those Welsh newcomers were to be found in the front five. There was no Craig Quinnell in the second row nor Dai Young, the tighthead only withdrawing on the eve of the match. There was a strong New Zealand presence on the field with the Leslie brothers and Glenn Metcalfe in Scottish colours, and full-back Shane Howarth and coach Graham Henry on the opposite side. First blood went to the Kilted Kiwis with John Leslie snaffling Duncan Hodge's kick-off from under the nose of Howarth. The nine-second wonder beat the old mark of Leo Price's, set for England against Wales in 1923.

Wales worked their way back. In the 34th minute skipper Robert

Howley tapped and raced away. He chipped, re-gathered and fed wing Dafydd James for a try. Jenkins' two penalty goals to one by Hodge made it 13-8 to Wales at the interval. Then came an opportunist moment from Gregor Townsend, who switched to fly-half when Hodge went off injured shortly after the break. In the 49th minute Townsend intercepted a rushed Welsh pass and sprinted 60 metres for a try.

Back came Wales, Scott Gibbs crossing for a try after great build-up work from lock Chris Wyatt. But then came the final Scottish rush, Townsend creating a try for Alan Tait before lock Scott Murray stretched over two minutes from time. Kenny Logan kicked two penalties in those closing stages.

SCOTLAND: G H Metcalfe (Glasgow Caledonians); C A Murray (Edinburgh Reivers), G P J Townsend (Brive), J A Leslie (Glasgow Caledonians), K M Logan (Wasps); D W Hodge (Edinburgh Reivers), G Armstrong (Newcastle) *(capt)*; T J Smith (Glasgow Caledonians), G C Bulloch (Glasgow Caledonians), A P Burnell (London Scottish), S Murray (Bedford), G W Weir (Newcastle), P Walton (Newcastle), E W Peters (Bath), M D Leslie (Edinburgh Reivers) *Substitutions:* A C Pountney (Northampton) for M Leslie (temp 21-29 mins) and for Walton (67 mins); S B Grimes (Glasgow Caledonians) for Weir (40 mins); A V Tait (Edinburgh Reivers) for Hodge (48 mins); D I W Hilton (Bath) for Burnell (73 mins)
Scorers *Tries:* J Leslie, Townsend, Tait, S Murray *Conversions:* Logan (2) *Penalty Goals:* Logan (2), Hodge
WALES: S P Howarth (Sale); M F D Robinson (Swansea), A G Bateman (Richmond), I S Gibbs (Swansea), D R James (Pontypridd); N R Jenkins (Pontypridd), R Howley (Cardiff) *(capt)*; D R Morris (Swansea), J M Humphreys (Cardiff), C T Anthony (Swansea), I M Gough (Pontypridd), C P Wyatt (Llanelli), C L Charvis (Swansea), L S Quinnell (Llanelli), M E Williams (Pontypridd) *Substitutions:* B H Williams (Richmond) for Humphreys (56 mins); M J Voyle (Llanelli) for Gough (66 mins)
Scorers *Tries:* James, Gibbs *Conversions:* Jenkins (2) *Penalty Goals:* Jenkins (2)
Referee E F Morrison (England)

20 February, Twickenham
ENGLAND 24 (3G 1PG) SCOTLAND 21 (3G)

If there was a certain inevitability in the outcome – this was Scotland's tenth successive defeat by the auld enemy – then there was precious little certainty in the proceedings themselves. Indeed if Kenny Logan had not missed three fairly routine pots at goal, then the Calcutta Cup might well have been heading north of the border. England, who made an emphatic opening during which they scored two tries, tailed away badly. Their pack lost focus, due partly to an injury to Martin Johnson who left the field with a quarter of a hour to go, and their game-plan became predictable and one-eyed.

By contrast Scotland were sharp and inventive. It was they who were hammering away at the England try-line in the final moments, thwarted mainly by the youthful figure of centre Jonny Wilkinson who time and again smashed bigger, and considerably older, men to the ground. The 19-year-old Newcastle centre was making his Five

Nations debut. He kicked all his four attempts at goal.

England opened powerfully, Tim Rodber crossing for a try after seven minutes, Dan Luger following suit 12 minutes later. The winger's try came after he had triggered a counterattack from a Gary Armstrong clearance. Several phases later Neil Back's deft pass put Luger over. And so ended England's best period. Scotland, with the Gregor Townsend-John Leslie axis working well in midfield, began to pull the English defence apart. The first of Alan Tait's two tries came in the 27th minute, Eric Peters teeing it up after snaffling a misguided tap from an English lineout. Tait's second was more creative, the Scottish centre slicing through the middle. England got back in control on the scoreboard in the 67th minute after a powerful run from Nick Beal took him all the way to the try-line.

Scotland were not finished, Townsend harassed Mike Catt into coughing up the ball and raced 40 metres to score. Martin Johnson was lucky to escape with a yellow card after stamping on the throat of John Leslie at a ruck.

ENGLAND: N D Beal (Northampton); D L Rees (Sale), J P Wilkinson (Newcastle), J C Guscott (Bath), D D Luger (Harlequins); M J Catt (Bath), M J S Dawson (Northampton); J Leonard (Harlequins), R Cockerill (Leicester), D J Garforth (Leicester), M O Johnson (Leicester), T A K Rodber (Northampton/Army), L B N Dallaglio (Wasps) *(capt)*, R A Hill (Saracens), N A Back (Leicester) *Substitutions:* D J Grewcock (Saracens) for Johnson (67 mins); K P P Bracken (Saracens) for Dawson (69 mins)
Scorers *Tries:* Rodber, Luger, Beal *Conversions:* Wilkinson (3)
Penalty Goal: Wilkinson
SCOTLAND: G H Metcalfe (Glasgow Caledonians); C A Murray (Edinburgh Reivers), A V Tait (Edinburgh Reivers), J A Leslie (Glasgow Caledonians), K M Logan (Wasps); G P J Townsend (Brive), G Armstrong (Newcastle) *(capt)*; T J Smith (Glasgow Caledonians), G C Bulloch (Glasgow Caledonians), A P Burnell (London Scottish), S Murray (Bedford), S B Grimes (Glasgow Caledonians), P Walton (Newcastle), E W Peters (Bath), M D Leslie (Edinburgh Reivers) *Substitutions:* A C Pountney (Northampton) for Walton (53 mins); D I W Hilton (Bath) for Burnell (68 mins)
Scorers *Tries:* Tait (2), Townsend *Conversions:* Logan (3)
Referee D T M McHugh (Ireland)

20 February, Wembley
WALES 23 (2G 3PG) IRELAND 29 (2G 3PG 2DG)

Irish hooker Keith Wood had waited an awful long time for the moment. He intended to make the most of it. Four years after making his championship debut against England he finally managed to taste victory in the tournament. He played a leading part in bringing about the sweet moment, leading from the front as ever and also crossing the try-line for a theatrical score in the 47th minute, side-stepping Welsh centre Scott Gibbs en route.

That try was converted by David Humphreys who added his fourth penalty of the afternoon three minutes later to put Ireland 26-6 ahead. It was then that the first twinge of anxiety began to cross Wood's face.

Wales stormed back into the match, finding the controlled rage which had eluded them in the first half. With the Quinnell brothers to the fore they scored tries through Craig Quinnell himself in the 52nd minute and then full-back Shane Howarth 13 minutes later following a typical powerful surge from Scott Quinnell. Neil Jenkins converted both tries and added a penalty, his third, in the 68th minute to close the gap to 26-23.

It was invigorating stuff, Wales playing with real passion and direction in the forwards. In the first half they had been reckless, conceding several penalties and good positions through their wild behaviour. It was left to David Humphreys to steady the nerves, the Irish fly-half knocking over his second drop goal with five minutes remaining.

Humphreys finished with 19 points, a new Irish record for the fixture. His was a pivotal role. He charged down his opposite number Neil Jenkins in the 22nd minute to send his centre Kevin Maggs on his way to the try-line. The 52-point match aggregate was also a record for the series. The Irish victory extended their unbeaten away run against Wales to 16 years. In the battle of the New Zealand coaches, it was Warren Gatland who came out on top to record his first win in the championship in five attempts.

WALES: S P Howarth (Sale); M F D Robinson (Swansea), M Taylor (Swansea), I S Gibbs (Swansea), D R James (Pontypridd); N R Jenkins (Pontypridd), R Howley (Cardiff) (*capt*); D R Morris (Swansea), B H Williams (Richmond), D Young (Cardiff, J C Quinnell (Richmond), C P Wyatt (Llanelli), C L Charvis (Swansea), L S Quinnell (Llanelli), M E Williams (Pontypridd)
Substitutions: M J Voyle (Llanelli) for M Williams (temp 27-33 mins); G R Jenkins (Swansea) for B Williams (52 mins); C T Anthony (Swansea) for Young (66 mins)
Scorers *Tries:* C Quinnell, Howarth *Conversions:* N Jenkins (2)
Penalty Goals: N Jenkins (3)
IRELAND: C M P O'Shea (London Irish); J P Bishop (London Irish), K M Maggs (Bath), J C Bell (Dungannon), N K P J Woods (London Irish); D G Humphreys (Dungannon), C D McGuinness (St Mary's College); P M Clohessy (Young Munster), K G M Wood (Harlequins), P S Wallace (Saracens), P S Johns (Saracens) (*capt*), J W Davidson (Castres), D O'Cuinneagain (Sale), E R P Miller (Terenure College), A J Ward (Ballynahinch) *Substitutions:* J M Fitzpatrick (Dungannon) for Clohessy (66 mins); V C P Costello (St Mary's College) for Miller (66 mins); M J Galwey (Shannon) for Johns (80 mins)
Scorers *Tries:* Maggs, Wood *Conversions:* Humphreys (2)
Penalty Goals: Humphreys (3) *Drop Goals:* Humphreys (2)
Referee S Young (Australia)

6 March, Stade de France, St Denis
FRANCE 33 (2G 3PG 2T) WALES 34 (2G 5PG 1T)

Before the match Welsh coach Graham Henry had likened the challenge of achieving victory in Paris to that of scaling Everest. Late on a quite surreal afternoon at the Stade de France the red flag of Wales fluttered at the summit. The fact of winning in Paris for the first time since 1975 was a feat in itself. The manner of victory, and the drama of the closing stages, ensured that this match will go down as one of the championship's greatest ever games. Thomas Castaignède had a kick to win the match in the final minute. He missed.

Wales were expected to arrive cowed and intimidated. Instead they played with brazen belief and assertiveness, none more so than fly-half Neil Jenkins. Jenkins scored 19 points in all, equalling the Welsh record for the most points in a match against France set by Jack Bancroft in 1910.

But it was Jenkins' adventurous play which really caught the eye. In fact his goal-kicking was unusually awry. He missed four in a row at one point.

Wales made four changes, including the entire front row. There was a first cap for Peter Rogers on the loosehead and a first start for Ben Evans on the other side. Former Waikato openside Brett Sinkinson was also called to the colours.

Colin Charvis scored Wales's first try in the eighth minute. France wanted in on the act too, Emile Ntamack following up Franck Comba's chip to score the first of his three tries, the first Frenchman ever to perform the feat against Wales. Ntamack's second try and Castaignède's second penalty of the day put France ahead at 18-16 on the half-hour.

France seemed to have weathered the worst. Not a bit of it. Wales scored two tries in quick succession through Dafydd James and Craig Quinnell to give Wales a ten-point lead 28-18 at the interval.

The second half was tighter but no less dramatic. France drew level with Ntamack's third try and Castaignède's conversion and penalty. Wales came again, Jenkins finally landed a penalty, but France snatched the lead back with a wonderful try from Castaignède. Cue Jenkins again, cue another three points. France had one more chance – but the day belonged to Wales.

FRANCE: E Ntamack (Toulouse); P Bernat-Salles (Biarritz), R Dourthe (Stade Français), F Comba (Stade Français), T Lombard (Stade Français); T Castaignède (Castres), P Carbonneau (Brive); C Califano (Toulouse), R Ibañez (Perpignan) *(capt)*, F Tournaire (Toulouse), O Brouzet (Bègles-Bordeaux), F Pelous (Toulouse), P Benetton (Agen), T Lièvremont (Perpignan), M Raynaud (Narbonne) *Substitutions:* D Aucagne (Pau) for Dourthe (4 mins); S Marconnet (Stade Français) for Tournaire (40 mins); X Garbajosa (Toulouse) for Bernat-Salles (40 mins); R Castel (Béziers) for Benetton (61 mins)
Scorers *Tries:* Ntamack (3), Castaignède *Conversions:* Castaignède (2)
Penalty Goals: Castaignède (3)
WALES: S P Howarth (Sale); M F D Robinson (Swansea), M Taylor (Swansea), I S Gibbs (Swansea), D R James (Pontypridd); N R Jenkins (Pontypridd), R Howley (Cardiff) *(capt)*; P J D Rogers (London Irish), G R Jenkins (Swansea), B R Evans (Swansea), J C Quinnell (Richmond), C P Wyatt (Llanelli), C L Charvis (Swansea), L S Quinnell (Llanelli), B D Sinkinson (Neath) *Substitutions:* G Thomas (Cardiff) for Robinson (51 mins); A L P Lewis (Cardiff) for Rogers (64 mins); D S Llewellyn (Ebbw Vale) for Howley (66 mins)
Scorers *Tries:* Charvis, James, C Quinnell *Conversions:* N Jenkins (2)
Penalty Goals: N Jenkins (5)
Referee J M Fleming (Scotland)

6 March, Lansdowne Road, Dublin
IRELAND 15 (5PG)   ENGLAND 27 (1G 4PG 1DG 1T)

The hype was blowing almost as fiercely as the midweek winds in the fair city. Ireland would match England stride for stride, pounding drive for pounding drive, all over Lansdowne Road. Talk was free and the air was hot. And then the first whistle went. Ireland never managed to raise a real gallop. It may only have been Tim Rodber's injury-time try which put England a comfortable margin ahead on the scoreboard but, in truth, they had been in control for long, long stretches of the match. Even so Ireland might have snatched the spoils only moments before the end, full-back Conor O'Shea being stopped just short.

The England forwards comfortably won the tussle up front with massive performances in particular from Tim Rodber and Martin Johnson in the second row, Johnson's day being spoilt only by his second yellow card of the tournament for supposedly entering a ruck recklessly. In the centre there was real composure to be found in the figure of Jonny Wilkinson who more than tackled his weight. There was much to savour too from full-back Matt Perry, whose delightful try in the 33rd minute was set up by a lovely long pass from Wilkinson.

Ireland made two changes in selection for the match, Girvan Dempsey returning to the wing in place of Niall Woods and Victor Costello being preferred at No.8 to Eric Miller. A dead leg saw Jonathan Bell withdraw to be replaced by Rob Henderson. England made three changes: Kyran Bracken for Matt Dawson, Paul Grayson for Mike Catt at half-back, Matt Perry for Nick Beal at full-back. Lawrence Dallaglio was also switched to No.8 from blindside. There was far more thrust and direction in the English captain's game as a result.

England led 11-9 at the break, Perry's try being supplemented by a penalty from Wilkinson and a dropped goal from Paul Grayson in the 37th minute. Ireland's points came from the boot of David Humphreys. Ireland briefly led when Humphreys put over his fourth penalty shortly after the break. There was to be no revival. The England pack rumbled, Wilkinson kicked three penalties in succession and the crowd was silenced.

IRELAND: C M P O'Shea (London Irish); J P Bishop (London Irish), K M Maggs (Bath), R A J Henderson (Wasps), G Dempsey (Terenure College); D G Humphreys (Dungannon), C D McGuinness (St Mary's College); P M Clohessy (Young Munster), K G M Wood (Harlequins), P S Wallace (Saracens), P S Johns (Saracens) *(capt)*, J W Davidson (Castres), D O'Cuinneagain (Sale), V C P Costello (St Mary's College), A J Ward (Ballynahinch) *Substitutions:* E R P Miller (Terenure College) for Costello (64 mins); J M Fitzpatrick (Dungannon) for Clohessy (65 mins)
Scorer *Penalty Goals:* Humphreys (5)
ENGLAND: M B Perry (Bath); D L Rees (Sale), J P Wilkinson (Newcastle), J C Guscott (Bath), D D Luger (Harlequins); P J Grayson (Northampton), K P P Bracken (Saracens); J Leonard (Harlequins), R Cockerill (Leicester), D J Garforth (Leicester), M O Johnson (Leicester), T A K Rodber

(Northampton/Army), R A Hill (Saracens), L B N Dallaglio (Wasps) *(capt)*,
N A Back (Leicester) *Substitution:* N McCarthy (Gloucester) for Cockerill (temp
66-67 mins)
Scorers *Tries:* Rodber, Perry *Conversion:* Wilkinson *Penalty Goals:* Wilkinson (4)
Dropped Goal: Grayson
Referee P D O'Brien (New Zealand)

20 March, Twickenham
ENGLAND 21 (7PG)   FRANCE 10 (1G 1PG)

This match has so often been the defining moment of recent championships. Well, it defined a few thoughts in our heads once again. It
illustrated quite clearly that France were in a dreadful state, bereft of
self-belief and passion. The double Grand Slam champions had come
to Twickenham intent only on doing a holding job. That they just
about managed, although it was only an injury-time try by Franck
Comba, stemming from a diagonal kick from Philippe Carbonneau,
which gave them any sort of respectability on the scoreboard.

Jonny Wilkinson equalled the Five Nations record for most penalty
goals kicked in a match. Simon Hodgkinson (against Wales in 1991)
and Rob Andrew (against Scotland in 1995) are the only other players
to have kicked seven in a championship game.

France were dreadfully limited in their ambitions. England might
well have put themselves into record-breaking territory if they had
managed to convert the handful of openings that came their way
during this flat, fractured international. Just before half-time Mike
Catt, who had been recalled for the injured Paul Grayson, opted to go
for broke rather than use the two-man overlap. In the 56th minute a
high cross-kick by Jeremy Guscott ricocheted off a pile of leaping
bodies and just away from the grasp of Catt. Guscott himself was
hauled down just short on a couple of other occasions.

France made six changes, one positional, following the home defeat
by Wales. The entire back row was re-shaped while the great Christian
Califano was dropped to the bench for Stade Français loosehead
Sylvain Marconnet. The alterations made little difference. France
might have been reasonably tight in defence but they offered so little in
attack. Only the wonderfully bright and creative Thomas Castaignède
had anything of substance to offer.

Wilkinson had given England a 9-0 lead within 18 minutes. Five
minutes later French wing Xavier Garbajosa almost made the try-line
but was just nudged into touch inches short by a flying tackle from
Matt Perry. France rarely threatened again. Wilkinson kicked his goals
throughout the second half and England ran out very comfortable
winners.

ENGLAND: M B Perry (Bath); D L Rees (Sale), J P Wilkinson (Newcastle),
J C Guscott (Bath), D D Luger (Harlequins); M J Catt (Bath), K P P Bracken
(Saracens); J Leonard (Harlequins), R Cockerill (Leicester), D J Garforth
(Leicester), M O Johnson (Leicester), T A K Rodber (Northampton/Army),
R A Hill (Saracens), L B N Dallaglio (Wasps) *(capt)*, N A Back (Leicester)

Substitutions: M J S Dawson (Northampton) for Bracken (34 mins); M E Corry (Leicester) for Hill ((49 mins); N D Beal (Northampton) for Rees (66 mins); V E Ubogu (Bath) for Garforth (79 mins)
Scorer *Penalty Goals:* Wilkinson (7)
FRANCE: E Ntamack (Toulouse); X Garbajosa (Toulouse), P Giordani (Dax), F Comba (Stade Français), C Dominici (Stade Français); T Castaignède (Castres), P Carbonneau (Brive); S Marconnet (Stade Français), R Ibañez (Perpignan) *(capt)*, F Tournaire (Toulouse), O Brouzet (Bègles-Bordeaux), F Pelous (Toulouse), T Lièvremont (Perpignan), C Juillet (Stade Français), R Castel (Béziers) *Substitutions:* C Califano (Toulouse) for Marconnet (47 mins); D Auradou (Stade Français) for Pelous (65 mins); M Raynaud (Narbonne) for Lièvremont (65 mins)
Scorers *Try:* Comba *Conversion:* Castaignède *Penalty Goal:* Castaignède
Referee C J Hawke (New Zealand) replaced by J M Fleming (Scotland) (39 mins)

20 March, Murrayfield
SCOTLAND 30 (2G 2PG 2T)   IRELAND 13 (1G 2PG)

Murrayfield had become a cold, unappealing place since it was rebuilt. Slowly things are changing. This was Scotland's third consecutive win at the stadium, the first time they have managed such a sequence in six years. The victory was thoroughly deserved too with Scotland once again playing with formidable confidence and imagination. Ireland attempted to hang on to their coat-tails but simply could not match the high-speed accuracy of the Scottish game.

Irish fly-half David Humphreys had another fine match and took his aggregate for the championship to 56 points, a new Irish record. The previous holder was Ollie Campbell who scored 52 points in 1983. Ireland had made two changes, preferring the more mobile Eric Miller in the back row over Victor Costello and restoring Jonathan Bell to the centre after injury in place of Rob Henderson.

The only downbeat note for Scotland came with the injury to prop Tom Smith who broke his leg. The Glasgow loosehead, such a surprise success on the 1997 Lions tour, has had a rough time of it since, missing the entire 1998 season with a groin problem. Elsewhere there were no worries at all for Scotland as they outscored their opponents by four tries to one, the scoring split evenly between the halves. Gregor Townsend was once more on the scoresheet, putting himself within touching distance of becoming only the fifth player in history to score a try in every round of the championship. 'We're playing intelligent, attacking, precise rugby and I'm loving every moment,' said Townsend. 'I can't remember ever having so much fun in a Scottish shirt.'

Welsh referee Derek Bevan extended his world record by taking control of his 37th major international match.

SCOTLAND: G H Metcalfe (Glasgow Caledonians); C A Murray (Edinburgh Reivers), A V Tait (Edinburgh Reivers), J A Leslie (Glasgow Caledonians), K M Logan (Wasps); G P J Townsend (Brive), G Armstrong (Newcastle) *(capt)*; T J Smith (Glasgow Caledonians), G C Bulloch (Glasgow Caledonians), A P Burnell (London Scottish), S Murray (Bedford), S B Grimes (Glasgow

Caledonians), P Walton (Newcastle), E W Peters (Bath), M D Leslie (Edinburgh Reivers) *Substitutions:* D I W Hilton (Bath) for Smith (39 mins); A C Pountney (Northampton) for Walton (66 mins); S L Longstaff (Glasgow Caledonians) for C Murray (76 mins); S J Brotherstone (Edinburgh Reivers) for Bulloch (77 mins); I T Fairley (Edinburgh Reivers) for Armstrong (79 mins)
Scorers *Tries:* C Murray (2), Grimes, Townsend *Conversions:* Logan (2)
Penalty Goals: Logan (2)
IRELAND: C M P O'Shea (London Irish); J P Bishop (London Irish), K M Maggs (Bath), J C Bell (Dungannon), G Dempsey (Terenure College); D G Humphreys (Dungannon), C D McGuinness (St Mary's College); P M Clohessy (Young Munster), K G M Wood (Harlequins), P S Wallace (Saracens), P S Johns (Saracens) *(capt)*, J W Davidson (Castres), D O'Cuinneagain (Sale), E R P Miller (Terenure College), A J Ward (Ballynahinch) *Substitutions:* V C P Costello (St Mary's College) for Miller (16 mins); T Brennan (St Mary's College) for Ward (60 mins); R A J Henderson (Wasps) for Bell (63 mins); C J Scally (UC Dublin) for McGuinness (75 mins)
Scorer *Try:* Penalty try *Conversion:* Humphreys *Penalty Goals:* Humphreys (2)
Referee W D Bevan (Wales)

10 April, Stade de France, St Denis
FRANCE 22 (2G 1PG 1T)   SCOTLAND 36 (4G 1PG 1T)

Paris in springtime has never been billed before as a time when Scotsmen might frolic with gay abandon. This was a role reversal on a massive scale. Scotland made all the running in a quite extraordinary match. There were 55 points scored in a bewildering first half, just three points in the second half. It was the highest half-time aggregate of points ever seen in a Five Nations match.

Scotland actually made a poor start. In the first five minutes they dropped balls, fluffed kicks and could not prevent Emile Ntamack scoring the opening try of the afternoon. That try was triggered by a 50-metre break from Thomas Castaignède. Unfortunately the fly-half injured himself in the process and left the field. From that moment on the day belonged to Scotland. The Scottish attack was sharp and inventive, but the French tackling was woeful.

Scotland posted their highest ever score against France. This was France's second home defeat in the championship, the first time that has happened since 1957.

Gregor Townsend was in sparkling form yet again, galvanising his back line and scoring a try himself in the 13th minute, thus becoming only the fifth player to score a try in all four Five Nations matches in a season. Astonishingly that was Scotland's third try. Martin Leslie had put Scotland on the board in the eighth minute, the Scottish flanker popping up on the end of a sequence involving Kenny Logan, Townsend and Alan Tait. Two minutes later Tait himself scored after a break from defence by full-back, Glenn Metcalfe.

Christophe Juillet wrested back some ground on the scoreboard for France with a try in the 20th minute. It was a brief respite. Back came Scotland. Tait was across the line again in the 22nd minute, then three minutes later it was a second try for Martin Leslie. That made the score 33-12 and the die was cast. Christophe Dominici reduced the

The Scotland captain Gary Armstrong salutes Scotland's remarkable victory over France at the Stade de France. Twenty-four hours later Scotland were celebrating triumph in the last Five Nations tournament.

arrears with a try in the 27th minute to bring an end to the dizzying burst of try-scoring. Aucagne's conversion and penalty on the stroke of the interval brought the first half to an end with the score at 22-33.

The contrast was stark in the second half. Scotland played a tighter game, shutting out any hopes of a French revival. Kenny Logan kicked a penalty in the 51st minute.

FRANCE: E Ntamack (Toulouse); X Garbajosa (Toulouse), P Giordani (Dax), F Comba (Stade Français), C Dominici (Stade Français); T Castaignède (Castres), P Carbonneau (Brive); C Califano (Toulouse), R Ibañez (Perpignan) *(capt)*, F Tournaire (Toulouse), O Brouzet (Bègles-Bordeaux), T Cléda (Pau), R Castel (Béziers), C Juillet (Stade Français), C Labit (Toulouse)
Substitutions: D Aucagne (Pau) for Castaignède (4 mins); C Laussucq (Stade Français) for Carbonneau (38 mins); S Marconnet (Stade Français) for Califano (55 mins); D Auradou (Stade Français) for Cléda (55 mins); P Benetton (Agen) for Castel (55 mins); T Lombard (Stade Français) for Giordani
Scorers *Tries:* Ntamack, Juillet, Dominici *Conversions:* Aucagne (2)
Penalty Goal: Aucagne
SCOTLAND: G H Metcalfe (Glasgow Caledonians); C A Murray (Edinburgh Reivers), A V Tait (Edinburgh Reivers), J A Leslie (Glasgow Caledonians), K M Logan (Wasps); G P J Townsend (Brive), G Armstrong (Newcastle) *(capt)*; D I W Hilton (Bath), G C Bulloch (Glasgow Caledonians), A P Burnell (London Scottish), S Murray (Bedford), S B Grimes (Glasgow Caledonians), A C Pountney (Northampton), S J Reid (Leeds), M D Leslie (Edinburgh Reivers)
Substitutions: G Graham (Newcastle) for Hilton (66 mins); P Walton (Newcastle) for Pountney (73 mins); A I Reed (Wasps) for S Murray (79 mins)
Scorers *Tries:* M Leslie (2), Tait (2), Townsend *Conversions:* Logan (4)
Penalty Goal: Logan
Referee C Thomas (Wales)

11 April, Wembley
WALES 32 (2G 6PG)   ENGLAND 31 (2G 4PG 1T)

Tom Jones and Max Boyce were the warm-up act for Wales' last ever match at Wembley. Who would have thought that a few hours later a patch of turf in north London would be acclaimed as the new green, green grass of home?

Those that were there will never forget the sight of Scott Gibbs crashing past five tacklers to dive across the English try-line in injury-time. Neil Jenkins kicked the conversion and bedlam broke out. The Grand Slam had been within England's grasp. Their reach was not quite long enough.

England had come into the match as warm favourites even though they were fielding an inexperienced back line. There were two new caps, both from Sale. Steve Hanley came in on the wing while there was a late call-up for Barrie-Jon Mather in the centre after Jeremy Guscott cried off injured. Wales were unchanged.

England played some of their best football of the championship and scored three tries in the first half. Dan Luger crossed in the third minute after Matt Perry had opened up the field. In the 20th minute it was Hanley's turn on the other wing, the debutant just holding on to an inside pass from Mike Catt. Then, a minute before half-time, Richard Hill was on hand to take advantage of a terrible mix-up between Shane Howarth and Gareth Thomas. Such accuracy with the line in their sights ought to have put England clear by some distance. But it didn't.

Wales exerted their own pressure and Neil Jenkins was on hand to exact retribution. He knocked over six penalties in the first half to keep the gap to 25-18 at the interval, Jonny Wilkinson having kicked two conversions and two penalties for England. Within two minutes of the restart Wales were level. Neil Back knocked on inside his own 22 with no-one near him. From there Wales worked themselves into position, Jenkins' long pass finding Howarth who touched down. Wilkinson hit two more penalties for England to give them a six-point lead with 25 minutes remaining.

Lawrence Dallaglio opted to go for touch rather than kick for goal with five minutes remaining. It was a costly mistake. Tim Rodber was yellow carded for a high tackle, Wales came downfield and the rest is history.

WALES: S P Howarth (Sale); G Thomas (Cardiff), M Taylor (Swansea), I S Gibbs (Swansea), D R James (Pontypridd); N R Jenkins (Pontypridd), R Howley (Cardiff) *(capt)*; P J D Rogers (London Irish), G R Jenkins (Swansea), B R Evans (Swansea), J C Quinnell (Richmond), C P Wyatt (Llanelli), C L Charvis (Swansea), L S Quinnell (Llanelli), B D Sinkinson (Neath)
Substitutions: N J Walne (Richmond) for Thomas (63 mins); A L P Lewis (Cardiff) for Rogers (68 mins); D Young (Cardiff) for Evans (68 mins)
Scorers *Tries:* Howarth, Gibbs *Conversions:* N Jenkins (2) *Penalty Goals:* N Jenkins (6)
ENGLAND: M B Perry (Bath); D D Luger (Harlequins), J P Wilkinson (Newcastle), B-J Mather (Sale), S M Hanley (Sale); M J Catt (Bath), M J S Dawson (Northampton); J Leonard (Harlequins), R Cockerill (Leicester), D J Garforth (Leicester), M O Johnson (Leicester), T A K Rodber (Northampton/Army), R A Hill (Saracens), L B N Dallaglio (Wasps) *(capt)*, N A Back (Leicester) *Substitution:* V E Ubogu (Bath) for Garforth (68 mins)
Scorers *Tries:* Luger, Hanley, Hill *Conversions:* Wilkinson (2)
Penalty Goals: Wilkinson (4)
Referee A Watson (South Africa)

SPRINGBOKS DISPLACE ALL BLACKS

THE TRI-NATIONS SERIES 1998

There was a new name on the massive Tri-Nations trophy in 1998. New Zealand, who had won all eight of their matches during the first two seasons of the competition, fell from grace and failed to win a single match in 1998, leaving Australia and South Africa to fight it out for the title of 'southern hemisphere champions'.

By August, after six weeks of some of the most absorbing international rugby seen for several years, it was the Springboks who emerged as undisputed winners. In achieving a Grand Slam, Nick Mallett's team showed tactical mastery as well as command of skills. The South Africans proved that they had the ability to subdue and penetrate at the difficult stages of games. That quality was never better demonstrated than in their home tie against the All Blacks in Durban when they overcame a 5-23 deficit to snatch victory from the jaws of defeat.

Australia took plenty of kudos from the tournament. Indeed, they were a trifle unlucky to lose to the Springboks in wet conditions under floodlights in Perth. Their two victories over the All Blacks (which became three by the end of August when they won the additional Bledisloe Cup match) were taken with style and left New Zealand to reflect on their worst Test season since 1949. The New Zealanders lacked conviction and invention and John Hart, their coach, was left with plenty to think about as he began preparations for the 1999 season and World Cup.

FINAL TABLE

	P	W	D	L	F	A	Bonus	Pts
South Africa	4	4	0	0	80	54	1	17
Australia	4	2	0	2	79	82	2	10
New Zealand	4	0	0	4	65	88	2	2

The 224 points scored comprised 22 tries, 12 conversions and 30 penalty goals. Matt Burke was the leading points-scorer with 50. He was also the leading try-scorer in the competition with three.

11 July, Melbourne Cricket Ground
AUSTRALIA 24 (1G 4PG 1T)   NEW ZEALAND 16 (2PG 2T)

First blood to Australia, and well deserved it was too. The New Zealanders lacked cohesion and clearly felt the loss of experienced men such as Zinzan Brooke and Sean Fitzpatrick. Australia, on the other hand, were confident and organised and had a match-winner in Matt Burke. He scored all 24 of their points, the highest by a player in any Test against the All Blacks.

More than 75,000 turned out to see New Zealand lead 8-0 before the Wallabies, inspired by Burke, countered to lead 15-13 by the break.

They never relinquished their advantage as play ebbed from end to end in the second half. At its conclusion, John Eales described the achievement as 'an amazing feeling'. He spoke for Australians every-where – it was their first triumph against the old enemy since 1994.

AUSTRALIA: M Burke (NSW); BN Tune (Queensland), DJ Herbert (Queensland), TJ Horan (Queensland), JWC Roff (ACT); SJ Larkham (ACT), GM Gregan (ACT); RLL Harry (NSW), PN Kearns (NSW), AT Blades (NSW), JA Eales (Queensland) *(capt)*,TM Bowman (NSW), MJ Cockbain (Queensland), RST Kefu (Queensland), DJ Wilson (Queensland) *Substitutions:* DJ Crowley (Queensland) for Harry (16 mins); V Ofahengaue (NSW) for Kefu (47 mins); JA Paul (Canberra & ACT) for Kearns (temp 47-61 mins); ODA Finegan (ACT) for Ofahengaue (76 mins)
Scorers *Tries:* Burke (2) *Conversion:* Burke *Penalty Goals:* Burke (4)
NEW ZEALAND: CM Cullen (Wellington); JW Wilson (Otago), SJ McLeod (Waikato), WK Little (North Harbour), J Vidiri (Counties Manukau); AP Mehrtens (Canterbury), JW Marshall (Canterbury); CW Dowd (Auckland), AD Oliver (Otago), OM Brown (Auckland), ID Jones (North Harbour), RM Brooke (Auckland), MN Jones (Auckland), TC Randell (Otago) *(capt)*, JA Kronfeld (Otago) *Substitutions:* I Maka (Otago) for M Jones (62 mins); JT Lomu (Counties Manukau) for Vidiri (62 mins); CJ Spencer (Auckland) for Mehrtens (temp 47-71 mins) and for McLeod (71 mins)
Scorers *Tries:* Kronfeld, I Jones *Penalty Goals:* Mehrtens, Spencer
Referee C Thomas (Wales)

18 July, Subiaco Oval, Perth
AUSTRALIA 13 (1PG 2T)   SOUTH AFRICA 14 (3PG 1T)

Australia made a promising start to Perth's first rugby union Test when Ben Tune went over in the second minute. Percy Montgomery pulled back three points with a penalty six minutes later before Joost van der Westhuizen caught the Wallabies napping at a penalty and darted in for his 21st Test try, a new Springbok record. Matthew Burke squared the match with a penalty in first-half injury-time.

The steady rain which fell throughout the match detracted from the occasion. George Gregan rounded off the best move of the match with a try 12 minutes after the break to restore Australia's lead. But Montgomery, who had kicked a penalty early in the second half, won the match with a kick from halfway after an hour's play. Thereafter it was a tale of Australian missed chances: Burke fluffed a penalty and in the dying moments Australia failed to take advantage from a scrum on South Africa's line.

AUSTRALIA: M Burke (NSW); BN Tune (Queensland), DJ Herbert (Queensland), TJ Horan (Queensland), JWC Roff (ACT); SJ Larkham (ACT), GM Gregan (ACT); DJ Crowley (Queensland), PN Kearns (NSW), AT Blades (NSW), JA Eales (Queensland) *(capt)*, TM Bowman (NSW), MJ Cockbain (Queensland), RST Kefu (Queensland), DJ Wilson (Queensland)
Substitutions: JA Paul (ACT) for Kearns (temp 20-47 mins); V Ofahengaue (NSW) for Kefu (47 mins); DPP Smith (Queensland) for Tune (50 mins); ODA Finegan (ACT) for Cockbain (temp 50-69 mins)
Scorers *Tries:* Tune, Gregan *Penalty Goal:* Burke

SOUTH AFRICA: PC Montgomery (Western Province); CS Terblanche (Boland), AH Snyman (Blue Bulls), PG Muller (Natal Sharks), PWG Rossouw (Western Province); HW Honiball (Natal), JH van der Westhuizen (Blue Bulls); R Kempson (Natal Sharks), J Dalton (Golden Lions), AC Garvey (Natal Sharks), K Otto (Blue Bulls), MG Andrews (Natal Sharks), JC Erasmus (Free State Cheetahs), GH Teichmann (Natal Sharks) *(capt)*, AG Venter (Free State Cheetahs) *Substitutions:* CM Williams (Western Province) for Montgomery (temp 10-22 mins); AH le Roux (Natal) for Kempson (60 mins)
Scorers *Try:* van der Westhuizen *Penalty Goals:* Montgomery (3)
Referee CJ Hawke (New Zealand)

25 July, Athletic Park, Wellington
NEW ZEALAND 3 (1PG)   SOUTH AFRICA 13 (1G 2PG)

Determined defence and better basic skills were the factors in South Africa's first win on New Zealand soil since 1981. The Springboks, who tackled their hearts out in the first half when the All Blacks threw everything into attack, scored the only points of the spell when Percy Montgomery landed a penalty after 25 minutes.

The only try of this 50th meeting of rugby's great rivals came 11 minutes from no-side when South Africa were ahead 6-3. Pieter Rossouw entered the back line at an attacking scrum and took an inside pass to score under the posts. The closest New Zealand came to a try was when Jeff Wilson just failed to ground the ball before it rolled over the dead-ball-line. Carlos Spencer missed all five of his penalty kicks at goal.

NEW ZEALAND: CM Cullen (Wellington); JW Wilson (Otago), MA Mayerhofler (Canterbury), WK Little (North Harbour), JT Lomu (Counties Manukau); CJ Spencer (Auckland), JW Marshall (Canterbury); CW Dowd (Auckland), AD Oliver (Otago), OM Brown (Auckland), ID Jones (North Harbour), RM Brooke (Auckland), MN Jones (Auckland), TC Randell (Otago) *(capt)*, JA Kronfeld (Otago) *Substitutions:* OFJ Tonu'u (Auckland) for Marshall (28 mins); AP Mehrtens (Canterbury) for Spencer (48 mins); I Maka (Otago) for M Jones (59 mins); SJ McLeod (Waikato) for Mayerhofler (66 mins)
Scorer *Penalty Goal:* Mehrtens
SOUTH AFRICA: PC Montgomery (Western Province); CS Terblanche (Boland), AH Snyman (Blue Bulls), PG Muller (Natal Sharks), PWG Rossouw (Western Province); HW Honiball (Natal), JH van der Westhuizen (Blue Bulls); R Kempson (Natal Sharks), J Dalton (Goldens Lions), AC Garvey (Natal Sharks), K Otto (Blue Bulls), MG Andrews (Natal Sharks), AD Aitken (Western Province), GH Teichmann (Natal Sharks) *(capt)*, AG Venter (Free State Cheetahs) *Substitutions:* CM Williams (Western Province) for Rossouw (temp 14-21 mins); PF Smith (Blue Bulls) for Snyman (40 mins); AH le Roux (Natal) for Kempson (52 mins); RB Skinstad (Western Province) for Andrews (52 mins)
Scorers *Try:* Rossouw *Conversion:* Montgomery *Penalty Goals:* Montgomery (2)
Referee EF Morrison (England)

1 August, Jade Stadium, Christchurch
NEW ZEALAND 23 (2G 3PG)   AUSTRALIA 27 (2G 1PG 2T)

Australia turned on the style against a New Zealand side that lacked ideas. The Wallabies scored two tries to lead 10-3 at the interval and were safe at 27-9 when there were only ten minutes left for play. True, New Zealand did seize the initiative to add respectability to the scoreline with two late converted tries, but make no mistake about it, the Australians were outstanding.

Their forwards ran and handled like threequarters and Stephen Larkham came of age as a fly-half of genuine class. He took the game by the scruff of its neck in the first hour and dictated events with rare vision. New Zealand crashed to their third successive Test defeat – a playing record that their followers had not had to contemplate for nearly 50 years.

NEW ZEALAND: CM Cullen (Wellington); JW Wilson (Otago), MA Mayerhofler (Canterbury), WK Little (North Harbour), JT Lomu (Counties Manukau); AP Mehrtens (Canterbury), JW Marshall (Canterbury); CW Dowd (Auckland), AD Oliver (Otago), OM Brown (Auckland), ID Jones (North Harbour), RM Brooke (Auckland), MN Jones (Auckland), TC Randell (Otago) (capt), MP Carter (Auckland) *Substitutions:* CH Hoeft (Otago) for Dowd (41 mins); SM Robertson (Canterbury) for Carter (63 mins)
Scorers *Tries:* Cullen, Lomu *Conversions:* Mehrtens (2)
Penalty Goals: Mehrtens (3)
AUSTRALIA: M Burke (NSW); JS Little (Queensland), DJ Herbert (Queensland), TJ Horan (Queensland), JWC Roff (ACT); SJ Larkham (ACT), GM Gregan (ACT); DJ Crowley (Queensland), PN Kearns (NSW), AT Blades (NSW), JA Eales (Queensland) (capt), TM Bowman (NSW), MJ Cockbain (Queensland), RST Kefu (Queensland), DJ Wilson (Queensland) *Substitution:* V Ofahengaue (NSW) for Kefu (67 mins)
Scorers *Tries:* Bowman, Burke, Little, Larkham *Conversions:* Eales (2)
Penalty Goal: Burke
Referee WD Bevan (Wales)

15 August, King's Park, Durban
SOUTH AFRICA 24 (2G 2T)   NEW ZEALAND 23 (2G 3PG)

Stefan Terblanche gave South Africa the lead in the third minute but New Zealand, determined to put the disasters of the previous month behind them, played confidently and appeared to be coasting to victory when they led 23-5 with only 15 minutes to go. South Africa then staged arguably the most remarkable recovery of Test history. The team played with a collective will to produce three tries, edging home by a point with an injury-time try scored by James Dalton.

The result tied the series at 24 wins apiece on the day Mark Andrews passed James Small's appearance record of 47 Tests to become South Africa's most-capped player.

SOUTH AFRICA: PC Montgomery (Western Province); CS Terblanche (Boland), AH Snyman (Blue Bulls), PG Muller (Natal Sharks), PWG Rossouw (Western Province); HW Honiball (Natal), JH van der Westhuizen (Blue Bulls); R Kempson (Natal Sharks), J Dalton (Golden Lions), AC Garvey (Natal Sharks), K Otto (Blue Bulls), MG Andrews (Natal Sharks), JC Erasmus (Free State Cheetahs), GH Teichmann (Natal Sharks) (capt), AG Venter (Free State Cheetahs) *Substitutions:* RB Skinstad (Western Province) for Otto (40 mins); AH le Roux (Natal) for Garvey (52 mins); PF Smith (Blue Bulls) for Snyman (65

mins); AD Aitken (Western Province) for Erasmus (65 mins); Otto for Andrews (70 mins)
Scorers *Tries:* Terblanche, van der Westhuizen, Skinstad, Dalton *Conversions:* Montgomery (2)
NEW ZEALAND: CM Cullen (Wellington); JW Wilson (Otago), E Clarke (Auckland), MA Mayerhofler (Canterbury), JT Lomu (Counties Manukau); AP Mehrtens (Canterbury), JW Marshall (Canterbury); CH Hoeft (Otago), AD Oliver (Otago), OM Brown (Auckland), RK Willis (Waikato), RM Brooke (Auckland), TC Randell (Otago) *(capt)*, I Maka (Otago), JA Kronfeld (Otago) *Substitutions:* SM Robertson (Canterbury) for Maka (49 mins); NR Berryman (Northland) for Clarke (62 mins)
Scorers *Tries:* Marshall, Randell *Conversions:* Mehrtens (2) *Penalty Goals:* Mehrtens (3)
Referee PL Marshall (Australia)

22 August, Ellis Park, Johannesburg
SOUTH AFRICA 29 (2G 5PG)   AUSTRALIA 15 (5PG)

South Africa completed a clean sweep of the Tri-Nations with a win in front of 62,308 spectators at Ellis Park. The Australians gave them a good run for their money and there were only four points between the teams at the pause. Percy Montgomery's kicking – altogether he landed seven goals from eight attempts – gave the Springboks a 22-15 lead with only ten minutes left. Then Bobby Skinstad, one of the finds of the Tri-Nations, sealed the match with a try that was converted by Montgomery.

After the match Gary Teichmann, who had equalled François Pienaar's record for most South African Tests as captain, apologised to the Wallabies for the unacceptable behaviour of a section of the crowd who had thrown bottles onto the pitch during the game.

SOUTH AFRICA: PC Montgomery (Western Province); CS Terblanche (Boland), AH Snyman (Blue Bulls), PG Muller (Natal Sharks), PWG Rossouw (Western Province); HW Honiball (Natal), JH van der Westhuizen (Blue Bulls); R Kempson (Natal Sharks), J Dalton (Golden Lions), AC Garvey (Natal Sharks), K Otto (Blue Bulls), MG Andrews (Natal Sharks), JC Erasmus (Free State Cheetahs), GH Teichmann (Natal Sharks) *(capt)*, AG Venter (Free State Cheetahs) *Substitutions:* AH le Roux (Natal) for Kempson (51 mins); RB Skinstad (Western Province) for Andrews (56 mins); AD Aitken (Western Province) for Erasmus (75 mins); PF Smith (Blue Bulls) for Snyman (85 mins)
Scorers *Tries:* Garvey, Skinstad *Conversions:* Montgomery (2)
Penalty Goals: Montgomery (5)
AUSTRALIA: M Burke (NSW); BN Tune (Queensland), DJ Herbert (Queensland), TJ Horan (Queensland), JWC Roff (ACT); SJ Larkham (ACT), GM Gregan (ACT); DJ Crowley (Queensland), PN Kearns (NSW), AT Blades (NSW), TM Bowman (NSW), JA Eales (Queensland) *(capt)*, MJ Cockbain (Queensland), RST Kefu (Queensland), DJ Wilson (Queensland) *Substitutions:* JS Little (Queensland) for Herbert (7 mins); V Ofahengaue (NSW) for Kefu (53 mins); ODA Finegan (ACT) for Cockbain (58 mins); GM Panoho (Queensland) for A Blades (73 mins); NP Grey (NSW) for Tune (84 mins); C Whitaker (NSW) for Larkham (84 mins)
Scorer *Penalty Goals:* Burke (5)
Referee JM Fleming (Scotland)

OTHER MAJOR INTERNATIONAL MATCHES 1998-99

29 August, Sydney Football Stadium (Bledisloe Cup)
AUSTRALIA 19 (1G 4PG) **NEW ZEALAND 14** (2PG 1DG 1T)

AUSTRALIA: M Burke (NSW); BN Tune (Queensland), JS Little (Queensland), TJ Horan (Queensland), JWC Roff (ACT); SJ Larkham (ACT), GM Gregan (ACT); DJ Crowley (Queensland), PN Kearns (NSW), AT Blades (NSW), TM Bowman (NSW), JA Eales (Queensland) *(capt)*, MJ Cockbain (Queensland), RST Kefu (Queensland), DJ Wilson (Queensland) *Substitutions:* V Ofahengaue (NSW) for Kefu (53 mins); GM Panoho (Queensland) for A Blades (58 mins); ODA Finegan (ACT) for Cockbain (71 mins); DPP Smith (Queensland) for Burke (73 mins)
Scorers *Try:* Burke *Conversion:* Eales *Penalty Goals:* Eales (4)
NEW ZEALAND: CM Cullen (Wellington); JW Wilson (Otago), E Clarke (Auckland), MA Mayerhofler (Canterbury), JT Lomu (Counties Manukau); AP Mehrtens (Canterbury), JW Marshall (Canterbury); CH Hoeft (Otago), AD Oliver (Otago), KJ Meeuws (Otago), RK Willis (Waikato), RM Brooke (Auckland), TC Randell (Otago) *(capt)*, XJ Rush (Auckland), JA Kronfeld (Otago) *Substitutions:* ID Jones (North Harbour) for Brooke (51 mins); SM Robertson (Canterbury) for Kronfeld (61 mins); CJ Spencer (Auckland) for Mehrtens (68 mins); CW Dowd (Auckland) for Hoeft (76 mins)
Scorers *Try:* Cullen *Penalty Goals:* Mehrtens (2) *Dropped Goal:* Mehrtens
Referee DTM McHugh (Ireland)

7 November, Stadio Garilli, Piacenza
ITALY 23 (2G 3PG) **ARGENTINA 19** (1G 4PG)

ITALY: P Vaccari (Calvisano); F Roselli (Rome), A-C Stoica (Narbonne, France), F Mazzariol (Treviso), Marcello Cuttitta (Calvisano); D Dominguez (Stade Français, France), A Troncon (Treviso); G P de Carli (Rome), A Moscardi (Treviso), F Properzi-Curti (Treviso), W Cristofoletto (Treviso), C Checchinato (Treviso), M Giovanelli (Narbonne, France) *(capt)*, C Caione (L'Aquila), O Arancio (Treviso) *Substitutions:* M Dallan (Treviso) for Marcello Cuttitta (15 mins); G Lanzi (Calvisano) for Cristofoletto (temp); Massimo Cuttitta (Calvisano) for Properzi-Curti (70 mins)
Scorers *Tries:* Moscardi, Checchinato *Conversions:* Dominguez (2) *Penalty Goals:* Dominguez (3)
ARGENTINA: M Contepomi (Newman); D L Albanese (San Isidro), E Simone (Liceo Naval), L Arbizu (Brive, France), F Soler (Tala); G Quesada (Hindú), A Pichot (Richmond, England); R D Grau (Saracens, England), F E Méndez (Northampton, England), M Reggiardo (Castres, France), P L Sporleder (Curupayti) *(capt)*, A Allub (Jockey Club, Rosario), S Phelan (San Isidro), C I Fernandez-Lobbe (Liceo Naval), R A Martin (San Isidro) *Substitutions:* O J Hasan-Jalil (Wellington, NZ) for Reggiardo (18 mins); M Durand (Champagnat) for Phelan (46 mins); M A Ruiz (Teqüe) for Martin (46 mins); E Jurado (Jockey Club, Rosario) for Soler (51 mins); J Fernandez-Miranda (Hindú) for Quesada (60 mins); N Fernandez-Miranda (Hindú) for Pichot (60 mins)
Scorers *Try:* penalty try *Conversion:* J Fernandez-Miranda *Penalty Goals:* Quesada (3), J Fernandez-Miranda
Referee C White (England)

14 November, Stade de la Beaujoire, Nantes
FRANCE 34 (3G 1PG 2T)   ARGENTINA 14 (3PG 1T)

FRANCE: A Gomès (Stade Français); E Ntamack (Toulouse), F Comba (Stade Français), S Glas (Bourgoin), T Lombard (Stade Français); D Aucagne (Pau), P Carbonneau (Brive); S Marconnet (Stade Français), R Ibañez (Perpignan) (*capt*), F Tournaire (Toulouse), F Pelous (Toulouse), O Brouzet (Bègles-Bordeaux), M Lièvremont (Stade Français), T Lièvremont (Perpignan), O Magne (Dax) *Substitutions:* P Bernat-Salles (Biarritz) for Ntamack (40 mins); R Castel (Béziers) for M Lièvremont (80 mins); T Cléda (Pau) for Pelous (83 mins); C Lamaison (Brive) for Lombard (85 mins)
Scorers *Tries:* Glas (2), Carbonneau, Comba, Bernat-Salles *Conversions:* Aucagne (3) *Penalty Goal:* Aucagne
ARGENTINA: M Contepomi (Newman); D L Albanese (San Isidro), E Simone (Liceo Naval), J Orengo (Atlético Rosario), I Corleto (CU Buenos Aires); L Arbizu (Brive, France), A Pichot (Richmond, England); R D Grau (Saracens, England), F E Méndez (Northampton, England), O J Hasan-Jalil (Wellington, NZ), P L Sporleder (Curupayti) (*capt*), A Allub (Jockey Club, Rosario), M Durand (Champagnat), P J Camerlinckx (Regatas Bella Vista), M A Ruiz (Teqüe) *Substitutions:* M Scelzo (Hindú) for Hasan-Jalil (44 mins); M Ledesma (Curupayti) for Grau (54 mins); F Contepomi (Newman) for Simone (73 mins); C I Fernandez-Lobbe (Liceo Naval) for Allub (77 mins)
Scorers *Try:* Camerlinckx *Penalty Goals:* Arbizu (3)
Referee A Cole (Australia)

21 November, Stradey Park, Llanelli
WALES 43 (4G 5PG)   ARGENTINA 30 (2G 2PG 2T)

WALES: SP Howarth (Sale); G Thomas (Cardiff), M Taylor (Swansea), IS Gibbs (Swansea), DR James (Pontypridd); NR Jenkins (Pontypridd), R Howley (Cardiff) (*capt*); ALP Lewis (Cardiff), JM Humphreys (Cardiff), CT Anthony (Swansea), JC Quinnell (Richmond), CP Wyatt (Llanelli), CL Charvis (Swansea), LS Quinnell (Llanelli), ME Williams (Pontypridd) *Substitutions:* M J Voyle (Llanelli) for S Quinnell (43 mins); B H Williams (Richmond) for M Williams (72 mins)
Scorers *Tries:* Charvis (2), Taylor, James *Conversions:* Jenkins (4)
Penalty Goals: Jenkins (5)
ARGENTINA: M Contepomi (Newman); I Corleto (CU Buenos Aires), J Orengo (Atlético Rosario), L Arbizu (Brive, France), F Soler (Tala); F Contepomi (Newman), A Pichot (Richmond, England); M Reggiardo (Castres, France), F E Méndez (Northampton, England), O J Hasan-Jalil (Wellington, NZ), P L Sporleder (Curupayti) (*capt*), A Allub (Jockey Club, Rosario), M Durand (Champagnat), P J Camerlinckx (Regatas Bella Vista), M A Ruiz (Teqüe) *Substitutions:* R A Martin (San Isidro) for Durand (60 mins); E Simone (Liceo Naval) for Orengo (65 mins); M Ledesma (Curupayti) for Reggiardo (70 mins); D L Albanese (San Isidro) for Soler (73 mins)
Scorers *Tries:* Pichot, F Contepomi, penalty try, Sporleder
Conversions: F Contepomi (2) *Penalty Goals:* F Contepomi (2)
Referee A Lewis (Ireland)

30 January, Stadio Ferraris, Genoa
ITALY 24 (3G 1PG)   FRANCE XV 49 (4G 2PG 3T)

FRANCE XV: E Ntamack (Toulouse); X Garbajosa (Toulouse), F Comba (Stade Français), R Dourthe (Stade Français), A Gomès (Stade Français); T Castaignède (Castres), C Laussucq (Stade Français) (*capt*); P Collazo (Bègles-Bordeaux), R Ibañez (Perpignan), A Galasso (Toulon), H Miorin (Toulouse), T Cléda (Pau),

P Benetton (Agen), C Juillet (Stade Français), S Betsen (Biarritz) *Substitutions:* Y Delaigue (Toulouse) for Dourthe (temp 34-38 mins) and for Castaignède (58 mins); M Lièvremont (Stade Français) for Betsen (40 mins); C Califano (Toulouse) for Galasso (40 mins); P Giordani (Dax) for Comba (45 mins); Y Bru (Toulouse) for Ibañez (54 mins); H Chaffardon (Stade Français) for Cléda (58 mins); P Mignoni (Béziers) for Laussucq (68 mins)
Scorers *Tries:* Gomès (3), Laussucq, Collazo, Juillet, Califano *Conversions:* Castaignède (3), Dourthe *Penalty Goals:* Castaignède (2)
ITALY: M Pini (Richmond, England); M Baroni (Padua), D Dallan (Treviso), L Martin (Bègles-Bordeaux, France), Marcello Cuttitta (Calvisano); D Dominguez (Stade Français, France), A Troncon (Treviso); Massimo Cuttitta (Calvisano) *(capt)*, A Moscardi (Treviso), G P de Carli (Rome), W Cristofoletto (Treviso), C Checchinato (Treviso), M Birtig (Padua), C Caione (L'Aquila), O Arancio (Treviso) *Substitutions:* A Castellani (Rome) for de Carli (11 mins); F Roselli (Rome) for Marcello Cuttitta (40 mins); A Sgorlon (Treviso) for Birtig (74 mins); F Mazzariol (Treviso) for Dallan (80 mins)
Scorers *Tries:* Troncon (2), Moscardi *Conversions:* Dominguez (3)
Penalty Goal: Dominguez
Referee D I Ramage (Scotland)
Only the Italians awarded caps for this match. The FFR had originally planned to give the match Test status, but with European calls denying the national side first-choice players, the title of the team was given as a French Selection.

6 March, Murrayfield
SCOTLAND 30 (3G 3PG)   ITALY 12 (1G 1T)

SCOTLAND: G H Metcalfe (Glasgow Caledonians); C A Murray (Edinburgh Reivers), A V Tait (Edinburgh Reivers), J A Leslie (Glasgow Caledonians), K M Logan (Wasps); G P J Townsend (Brive), I T Fairley (Edinburgh Reivers); T J Smith (Glasgow Caledonians), G C Bulloch (Glasgow Caledonians), A P Burnell (London Scottish), S Murray (Bedford), S B Grimes (Glasgow Caledonians), P Walton (Newcastle), E W Peters (Bath) *(capt)*, M D Leslie (Edinburgh Reivers) *Substitutions:* A C Pountney (Northampton) for M Leslie (temp 28-37 mins) and for Peters (73 mins); G G Burns (Edinburgh Reivers) for Fairley (42 mins); S L Longstaff (Glasgow Caledonians) for Tait (73 mins); A I Reed (Wasps) for Grimes (79 mins); D I W Hilton (Bath) for Smith (81 mins)
Scorers *Tries:* C Murray, Logan, Townsend *Conversions:* Logan (3)
Penalty Goals: Logan (3)
ITALY: J-A Pertile (Rome); F Roselli (Rome), A-C Stoica (Narbonne, France), L Martin (Bègles-Bordeaux, France), D Dallan (Treviso); D Dominguez (Stade Français, France), A Troncon (Treviso); Massimo Cuttitta (Calvisano), A Moscardi (Treviso), F Properzi-Curti (Treviso), W Cristofoletto (Treviso), M Giacheri (West Hartlepool, England), M Giovanelli (Narbonne, France) *(capt)*, C Checchinato (Treviso), A Sgorlon (Treviso) *Substitutions:* C Caione (Rome) for Checchinato (46 mins); S Stocco (Padua) for Cristofoletto (76 mins)
Scorers *Tries:* Martin (2) *Conversion:* Dominguez
Referee R G Davies (Wales)

20 March, Stadio Communale di Monigo, Treviso
ITALY 21 (1G 3PG 1T)   WALES 60 (5G 5PG 2T)

ITALY: J-A Pertile (Rome); F Roselli (Rome), A-C Stoica (Narbonne, France), L Martin (Bègles-Bordeaux, France), D Dallan (Treviso); D Dominguez (Stade Français, France), A Troncon (Treviso); Massimo Cuttitta (Calvisano), A Moscardi (Treviso), F Properzi-Curti (Treviso), W Cristofoletto (Treviso), M Giacheri (West Hartlepool, England), M Giovanelli (Narbonne, France) *(capt)*,

D Scaglia (Treviso), A Sgorlon (Treviso) *Substitutions:* M Baroni (Padua) for
Stoica (22 mins); O Arancio (Treviso) for Cristofoletto (49 mins); A Castellani
(Rome) for Properzi-Curti (53 mins); S Saviozzi (Treviso) for Sgorlon (68 mins);
Properzi-Curti for Castellani (75 mins)
Scorers *Tries:* Martin, Scaglia *Conversion:* Dominguez
Penalty Goals: Dominguez (3)
WALES: S P Howarth (Sale); G Thomas (Cardiff), M Taylor (Swansea),
I S Gibbs (Swansea), D R James (Pontypridd); N R Jenkins (Pontypridd),
R Howley (Cardiff) *(capt)*; P J D Rogers (London Irish), G R Jenkins (Swansea),
B R Evans (Swansea), J C Quinnell (Richmond), C P Wyatt (Llanelli),
C L Charvis (Swansea), L S Quinnell (Llanelli), B D Sinkinson (Neath)
Substitutions: D R Morris (Swansea) for Rogers (57 mins); B H Williams
(Richmond) for G Jenkins (68 mins); N Boobyer (Llanelli) for Taylor (68 mins);
M J Voyle (Llanelli) for C Quinnell (70 mins); N J Walne (Richmond) for James
(70 mins); D S Llewellyn (Ebbw Vale) for Howley (75 mins); G Lewis
(Pontypridd) for Charvis (75 mins)
Scorers *Tries:* Thomas (4), C Quinnell, N Jenkins, Howley *Conversions:* N Jenkins
(5) *Penalty Goals:* N Jenkins (5)
Referee R Dickson (Scotland)

10 April, Lansdowne Road, Dublin
IRELAND 39 (1G 4PG 4T)   ITALY 30 (3G 1PG 2DG)

IRELAND: C M P O'Shea (London Irish); J P Bishop (London Irish),
K M Maggs (Bath), R A J Henderson (Wasps), G Dempsey (Terenure College);
E P Elwood (Galwegians), C J Scally (UC Dublin); J M Fitzpatrick (Dungannon),
R P Nesdale (Newcastle), P M Clohessy (Young Munster), P S Johns (Saracens)
(capt), J W Davidson (Castres), T Brennan (St Mary's College), V C P Costello
(St Mary's College), D O'Cuinneagain (Sale) *Substitutions:* J C Bell (Dungannon)
for Henderson (38 mins); A J Ward (Ballynahinch) for Costello (41 mins);
K G M Wood (Harlequins) for Nesdale (55 mins); P S Wallace (Saracens) for
Fitzpatrick (55 mins)
Scorers *Tries:* O'Shea (2), Bishop, Dempsey, Johns *Conversion:* Elwood
Penalty Goals: Elwood (4)
ITALY: J-A Pertile (Rome); F Roselli (Rome), G Preo (Milan), L Martin
(Bègles-Bordeaux, France), M Baroni (Padua); D Dominguez (Stade Français,
France), A Troncon (Treviso); G P de Carli (Rome), A Moscardi (Treviso),
F Properzi-Curti (Treviso), W Cristofoletto (Treviso), M Giacheri (West
Hartlepool, England), M Giovanelli (Narbonne, France) *(capt)*, O Arancio
(Treviso), S Saviozzi (Treviso) *Substitutions:* W Visser (Treviso) for Giacheri (7
mins); S Stocco (Padua) for Cristofoletto (64 mins); R Rampazzo (Padua) for
Arancio (64 mins)
Scorers *Tries:* Cristofoletto, Baroni, Roselli *Conversions:* Dominguez (3)
Penalty Goal: Dominguez *Dropped Goals:* Dominguez (2)
Referee D Gillet (France)

STOP PRESS RESULTS

MAJOR INTERNATIONAL MATCHES UP TO START OF 1999 TRI-NATIONS TOURNAMENT

3 June France 62, Romania 8

5 June Argentina 26, Wales 36

12 June Australia 46, Ireland 10

12 June South Africa 74, Italy 3

12 June Argentina 16, Wales 23

12 June Samoa 22, France 39

16 June Tonga 20, France 16

18 June New Zealand 71, Samoa 13

19 June Australia 32, Ireland 26

19 June South Africa, 101 Italy 0

19 June New Zealand 54, France 7

26 June Australia 22, England 15

26 June Wales 29, South Africa 19

PACIFIC RIM MATCHES 1999 FOR THE EPSON CUP

1 May Japan 23, Canada 21

8 May Japan 44, Tonga 17

15 May USA 30, Tonga 10

15 May Canada 29, Fiji 40

22 May Japan 37, Samoa 34

22 May USA 25, Fiji 14

29 May Canada 13, Samoa 17

5 June Samoa 6, Tonga 6

5 June Fiji 16, Japan 9

12 June USA 31, Japan 47

19 June Canada 17, USA 18

26 June Tonga 37, Fiji 39

26 June Samoa 27, USA 20

3 July Tonga 18, Canada 10

3 July Fiji 15, Samoa 27

A INTERNATIONAL CHAMPIONSHIP 1999

Wales followed Scotland as winners of the Grand Slam for the shadow international sides. But it was a close thing. England A mounted a strong challenge for the title in only the second year of a full round-robin of matches among the Five Nations. The Welsh, for whom Arwel Thomas picked up 77 points, were pushed to the wire by an England side who, like their senior counterparts, were denied the Grand Slam in the final match of the season.

FINAL TABLE

	P	W	D	L	F	A	Pts
Wales	4	4	0	0	112	79	8
England	4	3	0	1	104	90	6
France	4	1	0	3	86	86	2
Scotland	4	1	0	3	71	91	2
Ireland	4	1	0	3	97	124	2

5 February, Donnybrook, Dublin
IRELAND A 26 (2G 3PG 1DG)   **FRANCE A 25** (1G 1PG 3T)

Niall Woods, the London Irish wing, was the man-of-the-match. His haul of 13 points helped the Irish overtake a visiting side who led 17-3 at one stage during the first half. Earlier Woods had created a memorable try for Killian Keane before France ran in three tries in eight minutes. Woods pulled Ireland level with a penalty after 35 minutes and it was 20-all at the break. Poor place-kicking by Stéphane Prosper and a string of penalties against their forwards let the French down after the interval.

IRELAND A: G D'Arcy (Lansdowne); J P J McWeeney (St Mary's College), S P Horgan (Lansdowne), K P Keane (Garryowen), N K P J Woods (London Irish); B G Everitt (Lansdowne), G Easterby (London Scottish); R Corrigan (Lansdowne), A T H Clarke (Dungannon) *(capt)*, A J W McKeen (Lansdowne), M Blair (Ballymena), G M Fulcher (Lansdowne), A Quinlan (Shannon), A G Foley (Shannon), E O Halvey (Shannon) *Substitutions:* R Weir (Portadown) for Clarke (40 mins); D S Corkery (Cork Const) for Halvey (40 mins); J Duffy (Galwegians) for Blair (56 mins); E Byrne (St Mary's College) for McKeen (78 mins); T A Tierney (Garryowen) for Easterby (80 mins)
Scorers *Tries:* Halvey, Keane *Conversions:* Woods (2) *Penalty Goals:* Woods (3) *Dropped Goal:* Everitt
FRANCE A: N Brusque (Pau); X Garbajosa (Toulouse), F Ribeyrolles (Montferrand), P Giordani (Dax), J-V Bertrand (Agen); S Prosper (Agen), P Mignoni (Béziers); P Collazo (Bègles-Bordeaux), Y Bru (Toulouse), A Galasso (Toulon), D Auradou (Stade Français), H Miorin (Toulouse), S Betsen (Biarritz), C Juillet (Stade Français) *(capt)*, R Sonnes (Agen) *Substitutions:* J-B Rué (Auch) for Galasso (67 mins); R Peillard (Perpignan) for Bru (67 mins); J-P Versailles (Biarritz) for Auradou (67 mins)
Scorers *Tries:* Prosper, Mignoni, Garbajosa, Bertrand *Conversion:* Prosper *Penalty Goal:* Prosper
Referee S W Piercy (England)

5 February, Myreside, Edinburgh
SCOTLAND A 8 (1PG 1T) WALES A 20 (5PG 1T)

Scotland A's hopes of retaining the Grand Slam disappeared in their opening match of the tournament. Arwel Thomas provided the Welsh selectors with a reminder of his kicking accuracy, landing five goals. The highlight of the night, however, was a flowing move involving five players which culminated in a corner try by Nick Walne.

SCOTLAND A: H R Gilmour (Edinburgh Reivers); A G Stanger (Edinburgh Reivers), D G Officer (Harlequins), J McLaren (Bourgoin-Jallieu), C C Moir (Northampton); C M Chalmers (Edinburgh Reivers), G G Burns (Edinburgh Reivers); G Graham (Newcastle), K D McKenzie (Glasgow Caledonians), M J Stewart (Northampton), C Mather (Edinburgh Reivers), R Metcalfe (Northampton), R I Wainwright (Glasgow Caledonians), S J Reid (Leeds), S D Holmes (London Scottish) *(capt) Substitutions:* R Hunter (London Scottish) for Wainwright (temp 23-27 mins); I McAusland (London Scottish) for Gilmour (75 mins); I C Jardine (Edinburgh Reivers) for McLaren (53 mins); G Scott (Glasgow Caledonians) for McKenzie (67 mins); W Anderson (Glasgow Caledonians) for Stewart (73 mins)
Scorers *Try:* Burns *Penalty Goal:* Chalmers
WALES A: D J Weatherley (Swansea); A Sullivan (St Helens RL), L B Davies (Cardiff), J Lewis (Pontypridd), N J Walne (Richmond); A C Thomas (Swansea), P John (Pontypridd) *(capt)*; P J D Rogers (London Irish), G R Jenkins (Swansea), B R Evans (Swansea), S J Moore (Cardiff), A P Moore (Swansea), O Williams (Cardiff), R K Arnold (Newcastle), B D Sinkinson (Neath)
Substitutions: B I Hayward (Llanelli) for Lewis (69 mins); A Griffiths (Pontypridd) for Rogers (48 mins); L Jones (Swansea) for Arnold (66 mins)
Scorers *Try:* Walne *Penalty Goals:* Thomas (5)
Referee J Jutge (France)

19 February, Headingley, Leeds
ENGLAND A 27 (3G 2PG) SCOTLAND A 16 (1G 3PG)

The first international staged at Headingley for 106 years resulted in a hard-earned win for England A. A tight first half ended with the home side nursing a slender 13-10 lead after Scotland A's Jamie Mayer and David Officer had been a constant problem to their opponents. England raised their game after the break with teenager Steve Hanley scoring a try that Mark Mapletoft converted for a 20-10 margin. Ally Donaldson brought the Scots back into contention with two penalties before Jamie Williams's late try sealed the match.

ENGLAND A: J Williams (Harlequins); S P Brown (Richmond), J A Ewens (Bedford), S Hanley (Sale), L D Lloyd (Leicester); M S Mapletoft (Gloucester), S Benton (Gloucester); T J Woodman (Gloucester), G Chuter (Saracens), W R Green (Wasps), G S Archer (Newcastle), R J Fidler (Gloucester), B B Clarke (Richmond), A J Diprose (Saracens) *(capt)*, A Vander (Richmond)
Substitutions: B-J Mather (Sale) for Ewens (61 mins); N P J Walshe (Harlequins) for Benton (72 mins); V E Ubogu (Bath) for Green (62 mins); M J Cornwell (Gloucester) for Archer (72 mins)
Scorers *Tries:* Ewens, Vander, Williams *Conversions:* Mapletoft (3)
Penalty Goals: Mapletoft (2)
SCOTLAND A: S D Lang (Edinburgh Reivers); C C Moir (Northampton), M J M Mayer (Edinburgh Reivers), B R S Eriksson (London Scottish), D G Officer (Harlequins); A Donaldson (Currie), G G Burns (Edinburgh

Reivers); G Graham (Newcastle), G Scott (Glasgow Caledonians), M C Proudfoot (Edinburgh Reivers), R Metcalfe (Northampton), S J Campbell (Glasgow Caledonians), C Mather (Edinburgh Reivers), S J Reid (Leeds) *(capt)*, I Sinclair (Edinburgh Reivers) *Substitutions:* K Milligan (London Scottish) for Officer (63 mins); R R Russell (Edinburgh Reivers) for Scott (69 mins); W Anderson (Glasgow Caledonians) for Graham (74 mins)
Scorers *Try:* Reid *Conversion:* Donaldson *Penalty Goals:* Donaldson (3)
Referee M Whyte (Ireland)

19 February, Eugene Cross Park, Ebbw Vale
WALES A 40 (2G 7PG 1T)   IRELAND A 29 (1G 4PG 2T)

The sides were all-square on tries, but once again it was the pin-point accuracy of Arwel Thomas that steered the Wales A team to a comfortable victory. He kicked 25 points and gave a timely reminder to senior coach Graham Henry that he could also pose a threat as an attacking spearhead. Twice Thomas made searing breaks that left the Irish defence in tatters, and with Nick Walne showing good finishing powers on the wing Wales never looked vulnerable during a final quarter in which they added 23 points.

WALES A: D J Weatherley (Swansea); A Sullivan (St Helens RL), J Lewis (Pontypridd), S Winn (Bridgend), N J Walne (Richmond); A C Thomas (Swansea), P John (Pontypridd) *(capt)*; P J D Rogers (London Irish), A E H Lamerton (Pontypridd), B R Evans (Swansea), S J Moore (Cardiff), A P Moore (Swansea), O Williams (Cardiff), R K Arnold (Newcastle), B D Sinkinson (Neath) *Substitutions:* L Jones (Swansea) for Williams (52 mins); R C McBryde (Llanelli) for Lamerton (61 mins); C Billen (Ebbw Vale) for S Moore (67 mins)
Scorers *Tries:* Walne (2), Lewis *Conversions:* Thomas (2) *Penalty Goals:* Thomas (7)
IRELAND A: G D'Arcy (Lansdowne); J P J McWeeney (St Mary's College), S P Horgan (Lansdowne), K P Keane (Garryowen), D W O'Mahony (Bedford); B G Everitt (Lansdowne), G Easterby (London Scottish); R Corrigan (Lansdowne), A T H Clarke (Dungannon) *(capt)*, A J W McKeen (Lansdowne), M Blair (Ballymena), G W Longwell (Ballymena), D Wallace (Garryowen), A G Foley (Shannon), A Quinlan (Shannon) *Substitutions:* J Hayes (Shannon) for Corrigan (16 mins); S J P Mason (Ballymena) for D'Arcy (30 mins); P Duignan (Galwegians) for McWeeney (40 mins); G M Fulcher (Lansdowne) for Longwell (65 mins)
Scorers *Tries:* McWeeney, O'Mahony, Blair *Conversion:* Keane *Penalty Goals:* Keane (2), Mason (2)
Referee A Rowden (England)

5 March, Donnybrook, Dublin
IRELAND A 21 (3G)   ENGLAND A 28 (4G)

Niall Woods scored in the second minute before England A, skilfully marshalled by Mark Mapletoft who contributed 18 points, effectively won the match during a first-half purple patch that yielded three tries. The visitors were impressive and threatened to sweep all before them. Even so, typical Irish fire in the second half made for an exciting climax and only resolute tackling by the entire England side protected a four tries to three lead in a match devoid of penalty goals.

IRELAND A: S J P Mason (Ballymena); J P J McWeeney (St Mary's College), M P Murphy (Galwegians), S P Horgan (Lansdowne), N K P J Woods (London Irish); B G Everitt (Lansdowne), T A Tierney (Garryowen); J Screen (Buccaneers), A T H Clarke (Dungannon) *(capt)*, A J W McKeen (Lansdowne), G M Fulcher (Lansdowne), G W Longwell (Ballymena), T Brennan (St Mary's College), A G Foley (Shannon), E O Halvey (Shannon) *Substitutions:* P Duignan (Galwegians) for McWeeney (34 mins); G Easterby (London Scottish) for Tierney (69 mins); D S Corkery (Cork Const) for Brennan (69 mins); M Blair (Ballymena) for Longwell (76 mins)
Scorers *Tries:* Woods, Fulcher, Horgan *Conversions:* Mason (3)
ENGLAND A: C E Catling (Gloucester); S Hanley (Sale), J A Ewens (Bedford), B-J Mather (Sale), S P Brown (Richmond); M S Mapletoft (Gloucester), N P J Walshe (Harlequins); T J Woodman (Gloucester), G Chuter (Saracens), A Deacon (Gloucester), G S Archer (Newcastle), R J Fidler (Gloucester), B B Clarke (Richmond), A J Diprose (Saracens) *(capt)*, A Vander (Richmond) *Substitutions:* N P Burrows (London Irish) for Hanley (3 mins); N Hatley (London Irish) for Woodman (40 mins); M J Cornwell (Gloucester) for Fidler (60 mins); R P Kirke (London Irish) for Chuter (66 mins); G L Seely (Northampton) for Clarke (68 mins)
Scorers *Tries:* Mapletoft (2), Clarke, Catling *Conversions:* Mapletoft (4)
Referee N Williams (Wales)

5 March, Périgueux
FRANCE A 17 (2G 1PG)　WALES A 20 (5PG 1T)

Wales trailed 6-14 at half-time after Thierry Cléda and Pascal Giordani had scored tries for France A. But another important contribution by Arwel Thomas, who landed five penalty goals, and a crucial try 15 minutes from the end scored by Newcastle Falcon Richard Arnold kept Wales A on course for the second-XV Grand Slam.

FRANCE A: C Heymans (Agen); C Dominici (Stade-Français), S Roque (Colomiers), P Giordani (Dax), J-V Bertrand (Agen); Y Delaigue (Toulouse), P Mignoni (Béziers); P Collazo (Bègles-Bordeaux), J-B Rué (Auch), S De Besombes (Perpignan), T Cléda (Pau), F Belot (Toulouse) *(capt)*, Mathieu Lièvremont (Toulouse), R Sonnes (Agen), G Le Corvec (Toulon) *Substitutions:* A Costes (Montferrand) for Lièvremont (40 mins); J-P Versailles (Biarritz) for Costes (52 mins); P Bomati (Brive) for Bertrand (70 mins)
Scorers *Tries:* Cléda, Giordani *Conversions:* Delaigue (2) *Penalty Goal:* Delaigue
WALES A: B I Hayward (Llanelli); A Sullivan (St Helens RL), J Lewis (Pontypridd), S Winn (Bridgend), N J Walne (Richmond); A C Thomas (Swansea), P John (Pontypridd) *(capt)*; D R Morris (Swansea), A E H Lamerton (Pontypridd), A Metcalfe (Ebbw Vale), S J Moore (Cardiff), A P Moore (Swansea), G P Lewis (Pontypridd), R K Arnold (Newcastle), M E Williams (Pontypridd) *Substitutions:* I M Gough (Pontypridd) for S Moore (46 mins); R C McBryde (Llanelli) for Lamerton (56 mins)
Scorers *Try:* Arnold *Penalty Goals:* Thomas (5)
Referee G P Hughes (England)

19 March, Myreside, Edinburgh
SCOTLAND A 31 (2G 4PG 1T)　IRELAND A 21 (1G 3PG 1T)

Scotland A won their first match of the championship with an entertaining display of running rugby. They led 28-14 at the break and when Ally Donaldson, the only amateur in the Scottish side, banged over his fourth penalty early in the second half the home side were home and dry.

SCOTLAND A: S D Lang (Edinburgh Reivers); C C Moir (Northampton), M J M Mayer (Edinburgh Reivers), D G Officer (Harlequins), C A Joiner (Leicester); A Donaldson (Currie), G G Burns (Edinburgh Reivers); G Graham (Newcastle), R R Russell (Edinburgh Reivers), M C Proudfoot (Edinburgh Reivers), S J Campbell (Glasgow Caledonians), I A Fullarton (Edinburgh Reivers), C Mather (Edinburgh Reivers), S J Reid (Leeds) *(capt)*, S D Holmes (London Scottish) *Substitutions:* R J S Shepherd (Edinburgh Reivers) for Mayer (temp 18-22 mins) and for Officer (65 mins); K Milligan (London Scottish) for Shepherd (68 mins); W Anderson (Glasgow Caledonians) for Proudfoot (65 mins); C D Hogg (Edinburgh Reivers) for Campbell (77 mins); G N Flockhart (Glasgow Caledonians) for Holmes (65 mins)

Scorers *Tries:* Graham, Mather, Mayer *Conversions:* Donaldson (2) *Penalty Goals:* Donaldson (4)

IRELAND A: S J P Mason (Ballymena); P Duignan (Galwegians), S P Horgan (Lansdowne), Cian Mahony (Dolphin), D W O'Mahony (Bedford); K P Keane (Garryowen), B T O'Meara (Cork Const); J Screen (Buccaneers), A T H Clarke (Dungannon) *(capt)*, J Hayes (Shannon), G M Fulcher (Lansdowne), M Blair (Ballymena), D S Corkery (Cork Const), A G Foley (Shannon), E O Halvey (Shannon) *Substitutions:* F Sheehan (Cork Const) for Clarke (49 mins); D A Hickie (St Mary's College) for Duignan (59 mins); B G Everitt (Lansdowne) for Mahony (59 mins); M Cahill (Bohemians) for Hayes (59 mins)

Scorers *Tries:* Mason, O'Mahony *Conversion:* Mason *Penalty Goals:* Mason (3)

Referee G Simmonds (Wales)

19 March, Redruth
ENGLAND A 24 (1G 4PG 1T)   **FRANCE A 21** (3G)

Nearly 9,000 packed into the Redruth ground to see England A snatch victory in the 83rd minute. France scored three tries to England's two, but Mark Mapletoft's late penalty kept alive the home team's hopes of achieving the Grand Slam at this level.

ENGLAND A: C E Catling (Gloucester); L D Lloyd (Leicester), N P Burrows (London Irish), P Mensah (Harlequins), T Underwood (Newcastle); M S Mapletoft (Gloucester), S Benton (Gloucester); G C Rowntree (Leicester), G Chuter (Saracens), D E Crompton (Richmond), M J Cornwell (Gloucester), R J Fidler (Gloucester), B B Clarke (Richmond), A J Diprose (Saracens) *(capt)*, A Vander (Richmond) *Substitutions:* S O Ojomoh (Gloucester) for Vander (35 mins); S D Shaw (Wasps) for Fidler (40 mins); M P Regan (Bath) for Chuter (57 mins); T J Woodman (Gloucester) for Rowntree (73 mins)

Scorers *Tries:* Benton, Diprose *Conversion:* Mapletoft *Penalty Goals:* Mapletoft (4)

FRANCE A: J-L Sadourny (Colomiers); J-V Bertrand (Agen), L Lafforgue (Agen), P Arlettaz (Narbonne), L Arbo (Pau); S Prosper (Agen), F Galthié (Colomiers) *(capt)*; P Collazo (Bègles-Bordeaux), M Dal Maso (Colomiers), S de Besombes (Perpignan), T Cléda (Pau), F Belot (Toulouse), C Labit (Toulouse), R Sonnes (Agen), P Benetton (Agen) *Substitutions:* H Miorin (Toulouse) for Belot (40 mins); S Betsen (Biarritz) for Sonnes (60 mins); A Tolofua (Grenoble) for de Besombes (73 mins); Y Bru (Toulouse) for Miorin (79 mins)

Scorers *Tries:* Cléda (2), Lafforgue *Conversions:* Prosper (3)

Referee P Adams (Wales)

9 April, Bourges
FRANCE A 23 (1PG 4T)   SCOTLAND A 16 (1G 3PG)

France A recalled Abdel Benazzi, who like Jean-Luc Sadourny had been sidelined through injury for a part of the season. But it was another recent Grand Slam reject, Philippe Bernat-Salles, who paved the way for France A's first win of the championship, scoring two tries. The French led 13-3 at the interval and were made to work hard by a makeshift Scottish XV in the second half.

FRANCE A: J-L Sadourny (Colomiers); P Bernat-Salles (Biarritz), D Douy (Toulon), G Delmotte (Toulon), A Gomès (Stade-Français); G Merceron (Montferrand), F Galthié (Colomiers) *(capt)*; O Milloud (Bourgoin), M de Rougemont (Bègles-Bordeaux), S de Besombes (Perpignan), A Benazzi (Agen), Y Manhès (Brive), L Mallier (Brive), E Gouloumet (Brive), N Bacqué (Pau) *Substitutions:* P Collazo (Bègles-Bordeaux) for Milloud (52 mins); M Felkaoui (Grenoble) for Bacqué (64 mins); J Marlu (Montferrand) for Sadourny (74 mins); O Olibeau (Perpignan) for Gouloumet (79 mins)
Scorers *Tries:* Bernat-Salles (2), Benazzi, Galthié *Penalty Goal:* Merceron
SCOTLAND A: S D Lang (Edinburgh Reivers); C C Moir (Northampton), M J M Mayer (Edinburgh Reivers), R J S Shepherd (Edinburgh Reivers) *(capt)*, C A Joiner (Leicester); A Donaldson (Currie), G G Burns (Edinburgh Reivers); W Anderson (Glasgow Caledonians), R R Russell (Edinburgh Reivers), M C Proudfoot (Edinburgh Reivers), S J Campbell (Glasgow Caledonians), I A Fullarton (Edinburgh Reivers), C Mather (Edinburgh Reivers), R S Hunter (London Scottish), S D Holmes (London Scottish) *Substitutions:* B D Stewart (Northampton) for Anderson (56 mins); G Beveridge (Glasgow Caledonians) for Burns (64 mins); C D Hogg (Edinburgh Reivers) for Mather (71 mins); G N Flockhart (Glasgow Caledonians) for Holmes (72 mins)
Scorers *Try:* Mather *Conversion:* Donaldson *Penalty Goals:* Donaldson (3)
Referee A Watson (Ireland)

9 April, Racecourse Ground, Wrexham
WALES A 32 (2G 6PG)   ENGLAND A 25 (1G 6PG)

Wales A wrapped up the Grand Slam with a win against a hitherto unbeaten England side. Arwel Thomas kicked two conversions and six penalties – just as his counterpart Neil Jenkins did against England two days later – to steer Wales home. There was a flurry of 39 points for the 8,000 crowd to enjoy in the first half as the home side rattled up a 23-16 lead. England, however, recovered lost ground through three Alex King penalties before Wales made certain of their victory with two penalty goals late in the second half.

WALES A: K A Morgan (Pontypridd); M F D Robinson (Swansea), J Lewis (Pontypridd), L B Davies (Cardiff), R Rees (Swansea); A C Thomas (Swansea), P John (Pontypridd) *(capt)*; D R Morris (Swansea), R C McBryde (Llanelli), C T Anthony (Swansea), I M Gough (Pontypridd), A P Moore (Swansea), G Lewis (Pontypridd), R K Arnold (Newcastle), M E Williams (Pontypridd) *Substitutions:* R Jones (Swansea) for John (48 mins); A Griffiths (Pontypridd) for Morris (57 mins); C Billen (Ebbw Vale) for Gough (70 mins)
Scorers *Tries:* Robinson, Williams *Conversions:* Thomas (2)
Penalty Goals: Thomas (6)
ENGLAND A: C E Catling (Gloucester); J Williams (Harlequins), F Waters (Wasps), P Mensah (Harlequins), S P Brown (Richmond); M S Mapletoft (Gloucester), S Benton (Gloucester); T J Woodman (Gloucester), M P Regan

(Bath), D E Crompton (Richmond), M J Cornwell (Gloucester), R J Fidler (Gloucester), S O Ojomoh (Gloucester), A J Diprose (Saracens) *(capt)*, R J Pool-Jones (Stade-Français) *Substitutions:* A D King (Wasps) for Mapletoft (40 mins); W R Green (Wasps) for Woodman (53 mins); S D Shaw (Wasps) for Cornwell (53 mins); P Volley (Wasps) for Pool-Jones (64 mins)
Scorers *Try:* Mensah *Conversion:* Mapletoft *Penalty Goals:* Mapletoft (3), King (3)
Referee D I Ramage (Scotland)

OTHER A INTERNATIONALS IN 1998-99

3 November, Viterbo
ITALY A 9 (3PG)   ARGENTINIANS 31 (2G 4PG 1T)

Italy A Scorer *Penalty Goals:* Mazzariol (3)
Argentinian Scorers *Tries:* Soler, Fernandez-Lobbe, Orengo
Conversions: Quesada, J Fernandez Miranda *Penalty Goals:* Quesada (4)

5 March, Netherdale, Gala
SCOTLAND A 61 (6G 3PG 2T)   ITALY A 6 (2PG)

Scotland A Scorers *Tries:* Mayer (2), Moir (2), Beveridge, Campbell, Lang, Russell *Conversions:* Donaldson (6) *Penalty Goals:* Donaldson (3)
Italy A Scorer *Penalty Goals:* Pilat (2)

19 March, Rovigo
ITALY A 24 (1G 4PG 1T)   WALES A 23 (6PG 1T)

Italy A Scorers *Tries:* De Rossi, Pilat *Conversion:* Preo *Penalty Goals:* Preo (4)
Wales A Scorers *Try:* G Wyatt *Penalty Goals:* A Thomas (6)

9 April, Donnybrook, Dublin
IRELAND A 73 (7G 3PG 3T)   ITALY A 17 (2G 1PG)

Ireland A Scorers *Tries:* Mostyn (2), Hickie (2), Foley, Galwey, McDonald, Staunton, Mullins, Mason *Conversions:* Mason (7) *Penalty Goals:* Mason (3)
Italy A Scorers *Tries:* Pavin, Grangetto *Conversions:* Grangetto (2) *Penalty Goal:* Grangetto

ULSTER FLY THE FLAG FOR IRELAND IN EUROPE

EUROPEAN CUP 1998-99

There was talk of miracles, of divine intervention on the back of a million prayers, of outlandish feats in the country of tall tales. And yet perhaps we do Ulster a disservice by labelling their achievements in such a manner. True, they were unexpected winners of the European Cup. True, too, they were a side of relatively unknown and unheralded players. Only two of their team – flanker Andy Ward and fly-half David Humphreys could lay claim to a regular slot on the international front. But what Ulster did have, and had in spades, was a deep-rooted belief in themselves and in each other.

They also had the reassuring, deft hand of coach Harry Williams to guide them, to keep them calm when bedlam was all around, to fire their bellies with passion and self-belief when the odds towered above them. Ulster's triumph was, above all else, a triumph of teamwork. And, given that we are forever banging on about rugby union being the ultimate team game, then we should salute Ulster for managing to bring together all the different parts to such stunning effect.

Would they have scaled the same heights if the English clubs had not boycotted the tournament? Who knows and who cares? The English clubs made their stand and it cost them dear. They may argue 'til the day the bailiffs come knocking that their case was worth fighting for. However, it cost each of them several hundred thousand pounds, not to mention several riveting sessions on the field of play itself.

The English clubs are back in the fold for this coming season. A deal thrashed out late one Friday night at the end of March in Paris means that the competition is restored to its full standing. The agreement is for eight years. From the 1999-2000 season the tournament will feature 24 teams in six pools of four. There will be six French and English sides, five from Wales, three from Ireland and two each from Scotland and Italy.

For this season Ulster beat what was put before them. In sport that is all that matters. Anything else is usually hokum or sour grapes. Of course it helped that they had two home ties in succession in the knock-out stages against Toulouse and Stade Français. The final itself was in Ireland, too. French commentators spoke of a Celtic conspiracy before the final in that referee Clayton Thomas was a Welshman. It may have slipped their minds that Ulstermen have never been too keen on crossing the border to head south – in fact, wasn't that one of the very reasons that the border was set up in the first place – and, moreover, these miserly critics happened to overlook the fact that Bath had triumphed the year before against Brive, a match staged in France with 30,000 Brive supporters descending on Bordeaux.

Ulster were magnificently served by their home support. There is no doubt that the victories in the quarter-final against Toulouse and then again in the semi-final against Stade Français owed much to the fervent, intimidating backdrop provided by Ravenhill.

For the quarter-final it was dark, cold and windy in the skies above; red-hot and raucous down below. The Frenchmen did not want to be there. It showed from the moment that they took to the field. They still had their chances to win the match but lacked any composure whatsoever. Ulster held on to win 15-13, with the kickers, Simon Mason who hit three penalties, and David Humphreys with two sweet drop goals, seeing them home.

The semi-final could not have provided a sharper contrast in conditions. It was afternoon, the skies were clear, the pitch dry. The only common denominator was the crowd. Same contingent, same noise, same end product. Ulster were in the final.

It was the result the competition needed. Suddenly there was a story, a shaft of the unexpected. There had been a real possibility that all four semi-finalists might have come from France. In the other quarter-finals Stade Français hammered Pontypridd 71-14, Colomiers comfortably saw off Munster 23-9, with Perpignan doing a similar number on Llanelli, 34-17.

The group matches had not set the pulse racing in anything like the same fashion as the previous year. That was the time of wild days and night in Brive, of fair and foul play on an equal footing. This time around the script was much tamer and far more predictable. Leinster were reasonably well set from Pool A but then went down 34-27 in their final home match against Llanelli, so losing out to the Welsh side for the quarter-final place.

Perpignan and Munster ruled the roost in Pool B. They were rarely in trouble against either Padova or Neath, both qualifying with something to spare.

Ulster's group was much different. There was an upset lurking round every corner. Just ask Toulouse. The French side gave one of the tournament's most accomplished ever performances in putting 108 points on Ebbw Vale. Then came the return leg. It appeared a formality for Toulouse. Victory would bring home advantage with it for the quarter-final. And what happened? From somewhere Ebbw Vale produced the goods, winning 19-11. The defeat was to cost Toulouse dear. Ulster also managed to beat them, winning 29-24 at Ravenhill.

Pool D was notable for the encouraging showing of Benetton

Treviso. The Italian side came so close to qualifying, losing out in the end only on points difference to Pontypridd, a team they had beaten home and away in the group matches.

FINAL
30 January 1999, Lansdowne Road, Dublin
Ulster 21 (6PG 1DG)   Colomiers 6 (2PG)

It was party time at Lansdowne Road. The game itself may not have lived up to much, but you would not have found anyone in Dublin complaining. They had poured across the border all weekend. They came by road, by rail and even by sea. The capacity crowd of 49,000 was a record for the competition. This was far more than a mere rugby match. It was an occasion on a grand scale.

Sport has tossed us some fairy tales in its time. Surely the sight of 40,000 Ulstermen celebrating arm-in-arm with southern cousins (and, sad to relate, often enemies) is a story to rival any. At the final whistle they streamed on to the pitch to salute their heroes. Their heroes were only too happy to salute them in return. Everyone was in on this particular act.

Ulster knew the game plan down to the last syllable. They knew that they had to squeeze Colomiers in the middle of the field in order to prevent them from playing it wide. They also chased every hanging kick that went up into the Dublin skies with the fervour of the snarling underdog. It was not fancy. But then, no-one was requesting anything fancy. It was good enough to do for Colomiers.

In the pack the unsung second-row combination of Mark Blair and Gary Longwell had another immensely productive afternoon at the coal-face. In the backs the pick of a noble bunch was centre Jonathan Bell who time and again clattered his man with thumping efficiency. Alongside him, his captain, David Humphreys, was once again a calm figure of authority. It would have been so easy to snatch at this golden opportunity. Humphreys made sure that his men stayed focused.

In the first half the prevailing noise was of hearty songs from the terraces interspersed with the thump of Simon Mason's boot. He knocked over four penalty goals with a penalty by Laurent Labit the only reply for Colomiers.

A dropped goal from Humphreys shortly after the restart settled his side into the second-half groove. More of the same, vicar. And that is how it unfolded. Mason hit two more penalty goals in the 51st and 67th minute to finish as the tournament's top points-scorer with 144 points. Michel Carre got three points back for Colomiers in the 59th minute but no-one noticed. The black stuff was already flowing.

Ulster: S Mason; S Coulter, J Cunningham, J Bell, A Park; D Humphreys *(capt)*, A Matchett; J Fitzpatrick, A Clarke, R Irwin, M Blair, G Longwell, S McKinty,

Irish delight, French despair. The Ulster captain David Humphreys raises the European Cup in triumph after Ulster's 21-6 defeat of Colomiers in Dublin.

A Ward, T McWhirter *Substitutions:* S McDowell for Cunningham (40 mins);
G Leslie for Irwin (72 mins); D Topping for McWhirter (75 mins)
Scorers *Penalty Goals:* Mason (6) *Dropped Goal:* Humphreys
Colomiers: J-L Sadourny; M Biboulet, S Roque, J Sieurac, B Lhande; L Labit,
F Galthie; S Delpuech, M Dal Maso, S Graou, J-M Lorenzi, G Moro, B de
Giusti, P Tabacco, S Peysson *Substitutions:* D Skrela for Lhande (19 mins);
M Carre for Labit (53 mins); P Pueyo for Peysson (67 mins)
Scorers *Penalty Goals:* Labit, Carre
Referee C Thomas (Wales)

SEMI-FINALS
9 January, Colomiers
Colomiers 10 (1G 1PG) Perpignan 6 (2PG)

And on they pressed. But Colomiers left it late enough this time to
have their own supporters trembling at the prospect of defeat.
Benoit Bellot had nosed Perpignan in front with a couple of penalty
goals.

Laurent Labit had replied with one for the hard-pressed
Colomiers, but he left the action after an hour or so, one of a
number of substitutions by an increasingly desperate team. It
needed half-time replacement David Skrela, son of France coach
Jean-Claude Skrela, to save the day. Skrela junior, who normally
plays at full-back or on the wing, had come on at half-time for
Michael Carre in the centre.

The powerfully built 19-year-old – Skrela stands 6ft 3in and
weighs a hefty 15 stones – managed to find a way through late in
the game and then kicked the conversion for good measure.

Colomiers: J-L Sadourny; M Biboulet, M Carre, J Sieurac, B Lhande; L Labit,
F Galthie; S Delpuech, M Dal Maso, S Graou, J-P Revallier, G Moro, B de
Giusti, P Tabacco, S Peysson *Substitutions:* D Skrela for Carre (40 mins); S Milhas
for Galthie (41 mins); P Pueyo for de Giusti (58 mins); R Nones for Delpuech (63
mins); R Bastide for Labit (63 mins)
Scorers *Try:* Skrela *Conversion:* Skrela *Penalty Goal:* Labit
Perpignan: G Arandiga; A Joubert, D Plana, N Martin, H Laporte; B Bellot,
M Barrau; S De Besombes, M Koniekiewicz, R Peillard, O Olibeau, P Furet,
S Deroeux, B Goutta, T Lièvremont *(capt) Substitutions:* E Champagnac for
Goutta (68 mins); D Camberabero for Bellot (70 mins)
Scorers *Penalty Goals:* Bellot (2)
Referee J Dume (France)

9 January, Ravenhill
Ulster 33 (1G 5PG 2DG 1T) Stade Français 27 (3G 2PG)

So Stade Français would take some beating, would they? Well Neil
Jenkins was absolutely right. They did. This was some beating. So
David Humphreys just stuck the ball in the air to get the crowd
going, did he? Well he succeeded. So did the Ulster team. They had
20,000 baying Irishmen at their backs willing them to win from
start to nerve-tingling finish. And the beauty of it all was that

although the much vaunted French side were renowned for their flair and style it was the Irish who played the superior and finer rugby on the day. Richard Pool-Jones, an Englishman on the Paris team, admitted that they prepared for the foullest of weather and, '. . . What did we find? . . . perfect rugby conditions . . . but how can you complain when the better side wins?' And they did. Simon Mason again did his stuff with the boot and Humphreys scored a cracking try. A great day.

Ulster: S Mason; S Coulter, J Cunningham, J Bell, A Park; D Humphreys *(capt)*, A Matchett; J Fitzpatrick, A Clarke, R Irwin, M Blair, G Longwell, S McKinty, A Ward, T McWhirter *Substitutions:* D Topping for McWhirter (33 mins); G Leslie for Irwin (54 mins)
Scorers *Tries:* McKinty, Humphreys *Conversion:* Mason *Penalty Goals:* Mason (5) *Dropped Goals:* Mason (2)
Stade Français: S Viars; A Gomes, R Dourthe, C Mytton, T Lombard; D Dominguez (capt), C Laussucq; S Marconnet, L Pedrosa, P de Villiers, H Chaffardon, D George, C Moni, R Pool-Jones, C Juillet *Substitutions:* S Simon for Marconnet (50 mins); V Moscato for Pedrosa (50 mins); M Lièvremont for Pool-Jones (50 mins)
Scorers *Tries:* Juillet (2), Lièvremont *Conversions:* Dominguez (3) *Penalty Goals:* Dominguez (2)
Referee J Fleming (Scotland)

QUARTER-FINALS
11 December, Ravenhill
Ulster 15 (3PG 2DG) Toulouse 13 (1G 2PG)

For Toulouse, the former champions, cricked necks and broken hearts. For Ulster another historic step and a performance as gutsy as any they have witnessed at Ravenhill. The Ulster tactics were basic.

Hoof it high or hoof it higher still. Captain David Humphreys added another peril to that most fragile of entities the ozone layer, each Garryowen he executed came down with snow on it and the Ulster pack not far behind. And when he was not thumping the ball heavenwards Humphreys was knocking over a brace of drop goals. Michel Marfaing's solitary attempt in injury-time had the whole of the province holding its breath, but he did not have the laser sighting of the Ulster fly-half. And of course there was full-back Simon Mason with three useful penalties. As close as Toulouse got, they were not destined to get any closer.

Ulster: S Mason; S Coulter, S McDowell, J Bell, J Cunningham; D Humphreys *(capt)*, A Matchett; J Fitzpatrick, A Clarke, R Irwin, M Blair, G Longwell, S McKinty, A Ward, T McWhirter *Substitutions:* A Park for McDowell (10 mins); D Topping for McKinty (temp 42-44 mins) and for Ward (49 mins); G Leslie for Irwin (56 mins); R Weir for Clarke (65 mins); B Cunningham for Humphreys (83 mins)
Scorers *Penalty Goals:* S Mason (3) *Dropped Goals:* D Humphreys (2)

Toulouse: S Ougier; X Garbajosa, R Paillet, L Stensness, M Marfaing;
Y Delaigue, J Cazalbou; C Califano, Y Bru, J-L Jordana, F Pelous, F Belot,
S Dispagne, C Labit, D Lacroix *Substitutions:* H Miorin for Lacroix (53 mins);
M Lièvremont for Dispagne (69 mins)
Scorers *Try:* Pelous *Conversion:* Ougier *Penalty Goals:* Delaigue (2).
Referee B Campsall (England)

12 December, Perpignan
Perpignan 34 (2G 5PG 1T)   Llanelli 17 (4PG 1T)

A classic tale of three halves. Llanelli had led briefly in the first when
they scored all their points, then on came a replacement fly-half
Benoit Bellot for the injured Didier Camberabero, and in the second
half the replacement destroyed the Scarlets. Bellot had been out of
action for seven months due to a career-threatening knee injury. He
landed three second-half penalties and scored a late try, Perpignan's
third, to clinch a comprehensive victory. Llanelli had conceded an
eighth-minute try but were eventually able to sneak into the lead
when two Steve Jones second and third penalties were added to a
Darril Williams breakaway try. But with a pack that was totally
outplayed and Bellot's boot earning the French side position time
and again there was nothing the Scarlets were able to do.

Perpignan: G Arandiga; A Joubert, D Plana, N Martin, H Laporte;
D Camberabero, M Barrau; R Peillard *(capt)*, R Ibanez, S de Besombes,
O Olibeau, P Furet, S Deroeux, B Goutta, T Lièvremont *Substitutions:* B Bellot for
Camberabero (38 mins); G Majoral for Goutta (72mins)
Scorers *Tries:* Laporte, Joubert, Bellot *Conversions:* D Camberabero, G Arandiga
Penalty Goals: Bellot (3), Camberabero (2)
Llanelli: D Williams; W Proctor, N Davies, R Boobyer, G Evans; S Jones,
R Moon; P Booth, R McBryde *(capt)*, M Madden, V Cooper, M Voyle,
D Hodges, I Boobyer, C Wyatt. *Substitution:* S Gale for Booth (55 mins)
Scorers *Try:* Williams *Penalty Goals:* Jones (4)
Referee A Lewis (Ireland)

12 December, Paris
Stade Français 71 (9G 1PG 1T)   Pontypridd 14 (2G)

Shell-shocked and well beaten, there was little Pontypridd could say
after a ten-try demolition. Injury was added to insult for good
measure when they lost their influential captain and points machine
Neil Jenkins at half-time. The Welsh club's pack just could not
handle the rampant Stade Français forwards and held out for only
half an hour before being engulfed in a floodtide of tries. They had
fought back well after conceding a fourth-minute try to scrum-half
Christophe Laussucq, countering with a superb touchdown
through Gareth Wyatt after Dafydd James had knifed through the
French side's defence to leave it flapping open. Thereafter though it
was one-way traffic, except for a minor hiccup when flanker Geraint
Lewis sneaked over for their second try. Diego Dominguez finished
with 31 points.

Stade Français: S Viars; A Gomes, R Dourthe, C Mytton, T Lombard;
D Dominguez *(capt)*, C Laussucq; S Marconnet, L Pedrosa, P de Villiers,
H Chaffardon, D George, C Moni, R Pool-Jones, C Juillet *Substitutions:* L Loustan
for Laussucq (66 mins); V Moscato for Pedrosa (56 mins); T Malet for de Villiers
(75 mins); S Keith for Moni (75 mins); D Auradou for George (56 mins).
Scorers *Tries:* Dominguez (2), Laussucq, Mytton, Pool-Jones, George, Gomez, de
Villiers, Loustau, Moscato *Conversions:* Dominguez (9) *Penalty Goal:* Dominguez
Pontypridd: K Morgan; G Wyatt, J Lewis, D James, G O Lewis; N Jenkins
(capt), P John; A Griffiths, A Lamerton, N Tau, G Prosser, I Gough, G P Lewis,
M Williams, D McIntosh *Substitutions:* S Lewis for J Lewis (44 mins); S Enoch for
Jenkins (40 mins); M Taylor for P John (70 mins); M Griffiths for A Griffiths (75
mins); N Eynon for Tau (75 mins); A Freeman for G Prosser (57 mins); M Lloyd
for McIntosh (75 mins)
Scorers *Tries:* Wyatt, G P Lewis *Conversions:* Jenkins, Wyatt
Referee C Muir (Scotland)

13 December, Colomiers
Colomiers 23 (2G 3PG)   Munster 9 (3PG)

Given the competition's record, it was probably only a matter of
time before there was an outbreak of violence. The match ended on
a sad and low note when one of Wales's top officials Nigel
Whitehouse had to be escorted off the field with a massive majority
of the 8,000 crowd screaming for blood – and that was after a
French victory. With all the points coming in the first half that left
only punches for the second. Referee Whitehouse showed yellow
cards to Stephane Delpuech, Frederic Pedoussaint and Des
Clohessy. It took the gloss off what was an impressive performance
by the previous season's Conference champions, whose fly-half
Laurent Labit picked up 13 points. Stephane Peysson scored a try
after 60 seconds and Bernard de Giusti was driven over for the
second 25 minutes later.

Colomiers: D Skrela; B Lhande, M Carre, S Roque, M Biboulet; L Labit,
S Milhas; S Delpuech, M Dalmaso, S Graou, G Moro, J-M Lorenzi, B de Giusti,
P Tabacco, S Peysson *Substitutions:* R Tremoulet for Dalmaso (61 mins);
R Rysman for Moro (68 mins); F Pedoussaut for Milhas (69 mins)
Scorers *Tries:* Peysson, de Giusti *Conversions:* Labit (2) *Penalty Goals:* Labit (3).
Munster: B Roche; J O'Neill, K Keane, R Ellison, M Lynch; B Everitt,
P Stringer; P Clohessy, M McDermott, J Hayes, M Galwey *(capt)*, M O'Driscoll,
D Corkery, E Halvey, A Foley *Substitutions:* D Clohessay for Hayes (41 mins);
T Tierney for Stringer (57 mins); D Wallace for Corkery (65 mins); S Leahy for
O'Driscoll (74 mins)
Scorers *Penalty Goals:* Keane (3)
Referee N Whitehouse (Wales)

PREVIOUS FINALS

1996 Toulouse 21, Cardiff 18 (Cardiff)
1997 Brive 28, Leicester 9 (Cardiff)
1998 Bath 19, Brive 18 (Bordeaux)

POOL MATCHES

Pool A	P	W	D	L	F	A	Pts
Stade Français	6	5	0	1	219	117	10
Llanelli	6	3	0	3	113	180	6
Begles-Bordeaux	6	2	0	4	141	124	4
Leinster	6	2	0	4	127	179	4

Results: Llanelli 27, Leinster 33; Begles-Bordeaux 28, Stade Français 39; Llanelli 22, Begles-Bordeaux 10; Leinster 17, Stade Français 28; Leinster 9, Begles-Bordeaux 3; Stade Français 49, Llanelli 3; Stade Français 56, Leinster 31; Begles-Bordeaux 48, Llanelli 10; Begles-Bordeaux 31, Leinster 10; Llanelli 17, Stade Français 13; Leinster 27, Llanelli 34; Stade Français 34, Begles-Bordeaux 21

Pool B	P	W	D	L	F	A	Pts
Perpignan	6	5	0	1	238	108	10
Munster	6	4	1	1	144	108	9
Neath	6	1	1	4	118	194	3
Padova	6	1	0	5	79	169	2

Results: Munster 20, Padova 13; Neath 33, Perpignan 51; Munster 34, Neath 10; Perpignan 67, Padova 8; Padova 28, Neath 17; Perpignan 41, Munster 24; Padova 6, Perpignan 14; Neath 18, Munster 18; Neath 16, Padova 3; Munster 13, Perpignan 5; Perpignan 60, Neath 24; Padova 21, Munster 35

Pool C	P	W	D	L	F	A	Pts
Ulster	6	4	1	1	197	168	9
Toulouse	6	4	0	2	234	103	8
Edinburgh Reivers	6	2	1	3	179	146	5
Ebbw Vale	6	1	0	5	114	307	2

Results: Ulster 38, Edinburgh Reivers 38; Toulouse 108, Ebbw Vale 16; Toulouse 39, Ulster 3; Edinburgh Reivers 41, Ebbw Vale 17; Ebbw Vale 28, Ulster 61, Edinburgh Reivers 25, Toulouse 29; Ebbw Vale 16, Edinburgh Reivers 43; Ulster 29, Toulouse 24; Ulster 43, Ebbw Vale 18; Toulouse 23, Edinburgh Reivers 11; Ebbw Vale 19, Toulouse 11; Edinburgh Reivers 21, Ulster 23

Pool D	P	W	D	L	F	A	Pts
Colomiers	6	4	0	2	176	121	8
Pontypridd	6	3	0	3	160	141	6
Benetton Treviso	6	3	0	3	142	150	6
Glasgow Caledonians	6	2	0	4	121	187	4

Results: Benetton Treviso 19, Colomiers 22; Glasgow Caledonians 21, Pontypridd 43; Pontypridd 32, Colomiers 27; Benetton Treviso 34, Glasgow Caledonians 15; Pontypridd 13, Benetton Treviso 22; Colomiers 34, Glasgow Caledonians 16; Colomiers 35, Pontypridd 21; Glasgow Caledonians 40, Benetton Treviso 27; Colomiers 41, Benetton Treviso 7; Glasgow Caledonians 26, Colomiers 17; Benetton Treviso 33, Pontypridd 19; Pontypridd 32, Glasgow Caledonians 3

A FRENCH MONOPOLY

EUROPEAN SHIELD 1998-1999
David Llewellyn

The European Shield competition began with what might be termed an all-embracing cast list, were it not for the fact that the English clubs had also boycotted this competition. But the national sides of Spain and Portugal were also included in the starting line-up. Sadly they did not get past the round-robin stage, but it was a beginning, and as Mao Tse Tung once said, 'The journey of a thousand miles begins with the first step.' There were also sides from Romania (Bucharest), Italy (Roma and Rovigo), Wales (Aberavon, Bridgend, Caerphilly and Newport), Ireland (Connacht) with the balance of 10 coming from France. Not surprisingly then the quarter-finals were dominated by French clubs. The sole foreigner was Caerphilly, who had the misfortune to be drawn at Brive and went down 43-12. The semi-finals, held on the same weekend as the European Cup final because snow had caused the ties to be postponed from their original date, saw Bourgoin pip Brive by three points and Narbonne go down 21-27 to Montferrand. With English clubs back in the fray next season, it is to be hoped that the French will not be allowed to monopolise the tournament quite so thoroughly in future.

FINAL
28 February, Stade Gerland, Lyon
Bourgoin 16 (1G 3PG)   Montferrand 35 (1G 6PG 2T)

So a month later than scheduled (because of the weather-hit semi-finals having to be put back) the final of another French-dominated competition finally reached its denouement. An impressive crowd was there to witness what was ultimately a one-sided game; 31,986 people drifted down to Lyon to watch Montferrand book a ticket to next season's European Cup. And they did so in style.

Bourgoin may have been winners of the inaugural tournament two years ago when it went under the title of the European Conference, but they had no answer to the firepower of Montferrand, and in particular to their remarkably consistent goal-kicker Gerald Merceron. The fly-half landed a conversion and half a dozen penalty goals as his side took control of this tie and never lost their grip on matters.

And nor did they rely solely on Merceron for their points, as three tries bear witness. One of the touchdowns came courtesy of a moment of ill-advised action by Bourgoin full-back Nigel Geany, who held back wing Jimmy Marlu and international referee Joel Dume had no hesitation in awarding a penalty try.

Bourgoin managed to stay in touch thanks to three penalties from the boot of Benjamin Boyet, but after the interval Montferrand pulled clear. First Merceron knocked over three more penalties for them and then came the try of the tie. Man-of-the-match Stephane Castaignède made a sniping break from the base of a scrum near the halfway line and took the ball up. Marlu took it on, his power and pace making him unstoppable over the last 35 metres as he left the defence floundering in his wake.

Bourgoin did hit back with a stunning try of their own through their outside centre Jimmy McLaren with a quarter of an hour still on the clock, but the die was cast. A final penalty from Merceron restored the balance of control and a run down the touchline by replacement scrum-half Christophe Larrue which culminated in another unconverted try ensured Montferrand the prize of a European Cup place for the millennium season.

Bourgoin: N Geany; L Saunier, J McLaren, E Tuni, L Giolitti; B Boyet, E Galon; O Milloud, J-F Martin-Cullet, P Peyron, M Cecillon, J Daude, L Nallet, J-F Tordo, P Raschi *(capt) Substitutions:* A Peclier for Tuni (43 mins); R Magellan for Peyron (50 mins); A Studer for Daude (66 mins)
Scorers *Try:* J McLaren *Conversion:* B Boyet *Penalty Goals:* B Boyet (3)
Montferrand: N Nadau; J Marlu, F Ribeyrolles *(capt)*, F Azema, D Bory; G Merceron, S Castaignède; E Menieu, O Azam, F Heyer, D Barrier, C Sarraute, A Costes, J-M Lhermet, E Lecomte *Substitutions:* J Morante for Ribeyrolles (temp 26-29 mins and 33-37 mins); C Larrue for Castaignède (72 mins); L Gunter for Sarraute (79 mins); G Allison for Lhermet (79 mins)
Scorers *Tries:* J Marlu, Larrue, penalty try *Conversion:* G Merceron *Penalty Goals:* G Merceron (6)
Referee J Dume (France)

EARLY ROUNDS

Quarter-finals
Narbonne 30, Pau 13
Brive 43, Caerphilly 12
Bourgoin 29, Agen 19
Montferrand 66, Dax 13

Semi-finals
Bourgoin 26, Brive 23
Montferrand 27, Narbonne 21

Final
Montferrand 35, Bourgoin 16

Previous finals
1997 Bourgoin 18, Castres 9 (Béziers)
1998 Colomiers 43, Agen 5 (Toulouse)

POOL MATCHES

Pool A	P	W	D	L	F	A	Pts
Narbonne	6	6	0	0	228	98	12
Caerphilly	6	4	0	2	167	154	8
Perigueux	6	3	0	3	168	119	6
Connacht	6	3	0	3	129	156	6
Racing CF	6	3	0	3	127	184	6
Rovigo	6	1	0	5	108	156	2
Newport	6	1	0	5	123	183	2

Results: Narbonne 41, Rovigo 17; Caerphilly 31, Perigueux 28; Racing CF 37, Newport 21; Perigueux 40, Racing CF 18; Newport 12, Connacht 31; Rovigo 34, Caerphilly 14; Connacht 29, Perigueux 28; Racing CF 28, Rovigo 12; Caerphilly 17, Narbonne 34; Narbonne 66, Racing CF 5; Rovigo 20, Connacht 21; Perigueux 31, Newport 16; Newport 27, Rovigo 18; Racing CF 20, Caerphilly 31; Connacht 26, Narbonne 38; Rovigo 7, Perigueux 25; Narbonne 31, Newport 17; Caerphilly 39, Connacht 8; Perigueux 16, Narbonne 18; Newport 30, Caerphilly 35; Connacht 14, Racing CF 19

Pool B	P	W	D	L	F	A	Pts
Montferrand	6	5	0	1	303	86	10
Bourgoin	6	5	0	1	222	86	10
Dax	6	5	0	1	163	124	10
Castres	6	3	0	3	229	101	6
Roma	6	2	0	4	117	213	4
Aberavon	6	1	0	5	86	287	2
Spain	6	0	0	6	65	288	0

Results: Bourgoin 55, Spain 10; Castres 87, Aberavon 10; Roma 18, Dax 25; Spain 15, Castres 61; Aberavon 12, Roma 30; Dax 24, Montferrand 22; Roma 25, Spain 21; Montferrand 97, Aberavon 13; Castres 9, Bourgoin 30; Spain 13, Montferrand 88; Aberavon 28, Dax 41; Bourgoin 50, Roma 22; Dax 41, Spain 0; Roma 15, Castres 48; Montferrand 23, Bourgoin 14; Spain 6, Aberavon 18; Bourgoin 47, Dax 17; Castres 15, Montferrand 16; Aberavon 5, Bourgoin 26; Dax 15, Castres 9; Montferrand 57, Roma 7

Pool C	P	W	D	L	F	A	Pts
Brive	6	5	0	1	241	102	10
Agen	6	4	0	2	231	93	8
Pau	6	4	0	2	211	87	8
Biarritz	6	4	0	2	187	124	8
Bridgend	6	2	0	4	158	206	4
Dinamo Bucharest	6	2	0	4	131	246	4
Portugal	6	0	0	6	73	374	0

Results: Dinamo Bucharest 22, Pau 31; Brive 31, Biarritz 22; Bridgend 17, Agen 32; Pau 37, Biarritz 3; Portugal 7, Brive 85; Dinamo Bucharest 45, Bridgend 43; Biarritz 10, Agen 9; Brive 26, Pau 9; Bridgend 45, Portugal 24; Pau 45, Bridgend 21; Portugal 18, Dinamo Bucharest 23; Agen 34, Brive 35; Agen 15, Pau 11; Biarritz 62, Portugal 11; Brive 49, Dinamo Bucharest 10; Pau 78, Portugal 0; Agen 60, Dinamo Bucharest 7; Biarritz 45, Bridgend 12; Portugal 13, Agen 81; Dinamo Bucharest 24, Biarritz 45; Bridgend 20, Brive 15

NEW ZEALAND'S TIMELY REMINDER

THE SUPER-12 SERIES 1999

Just when everyone had written off New Zealand's chances of lifting the 1999 World Cup, the Super-12s proved that the land of the long black cloud was still a considerable rugby force to be reckoned with.

True, the early season form in the round-robin pointed to a likely Australian winner of the tournament. Week in, week out the Queensland Reds showed a depth of all-round strength which suggested that they would mount a serious challenge to New Zealand dominance of the Super-12s. The New Zealand teams, by contrast, began the tournament slowly. The Crusaders, who had lifted the title in 1998, were comprehensively defeated by the Reds in Christchurch by 36-23 in late March, and won only two of their first four games. Another surprise of the tournament was the dismal form of the once invincible Auckland Blues. They were unable to find any rhythm to their play and finished ninth with only four wins from their 11 matches, easily their worst return since the Super-12s began.

The Queensland Reds finished the preliminary stages of the tournament at the top of the table on superior points difference to the Western Stormers. That meant that the two New Zealand teams who finished in the top four were drawn away for the semi-finals. Yet both travelled well. The Crusaders were in commanding form at Ballymore against the Reds. They were ahead 15-6 by half-time and finished with a convincing win by four tries to one. The Otago Highlanders did not have quite such an easy passage in Cape Town, where the Western Stormers began confidently to rattle up an 11-0 lead in as many minutes. Taine Randell's side showed considerable resolve to overhaul their hosts and led 22-18 by the break before scoring 11 further points without reply in the second half.

FINAL
30 May, Carisbrook, Dunedin
Otago Highlanders 19 (2PG 1DG 2T) Canterbury Crusaders 24 (1G 3PG 1DG 1T)

The Highlanders, with first use of the wind, led 14-9 at the break, but the truth was that they needed at least a ten-point cushion to enter the second half with confidence. The Crusaders had defended with their customary mix of aggression and science up to that stage and, as the teams changed ends, many felt that there was an inevitability that the holders would come from behind to claim the title.

During a 20-minute purple patch midway through the second

period, Canterbury duly lived up to that promise. In the 51st minute, Andrew Mehrtens opened the Highlanders' defence to send Daryl Gibson over. Mehrtens, whose tactical control was a significant factor in the Crusaders' win, took his side ahead with the conversion of this try. Then came the moment of the match when Samoan wing Afato So'oalo veered outside Brian Lima, kicked on and raced ahead of Jeff Wilson to touch down. Mehrtens hammered the last nail in Otago's coffin with a sweet dropped goal from a lineout, 11 minutes from time.

The Highlanders mustered one last effort in the dying minutes when Isitolo Maka barnstormed over for a try from a tapped penalty, but by then Taine Randell was already preparing the losers' speech. 'They're a great side,' he conceded afterwards. 'We thought we had one more big match in us but, today, just didn't have enough.'

Otago Highlanders: J Wilson; B Laney, R Ropati, P Alatini, B Lima; T Brown, B Kelleher; C Hoeft, A Oliver, K Meeuws, B Timmins, J Blaikie, T Randell (*capt*), I Maka, J Kronfeld *Substitution:* S Maling for Timmins (67 mins)
Scorers *Tries:* Lima, Maka *Penalty Goals:* Brown (2) *Dropped Goal:* Laney
Canterbury Crusaders: L Macdonald; A So'oalo, N Berryman, D Gibson, C Ralph; A Mehrtens, J Marshall; G Feek, M Hammett, G Somerville, T Blackadder (*capt*), N Maxwell, R Thorne, S Surridge, A Gardiner
Substitutions: D Lilley for Macdonald (18 mins); S Robertson for Gardiner (40 mins); S Lancaster for Maxwell (58 mins); N Mauger for Berryman (66 mins); A Flynn for Gibson (73 mins); C Barrell for Somerville (77 mins)
Scorers *Tries:* So'oalo, Gibson *Conversion:* Mehrtens *Penalty Goals:* Mehrtens (3) *Dropped Goal:* Mehrtens
Referee A Watson (South Africa)

SEMI-FINALS
22 May, Ballymore Park, Brisbane
Queensland Reds 22 (1G 5PG) Canterbury Crusaders 28 (1G 2PG 3T)

Queensland Reds: C Latham; B Tune, D Herbert, T J Horan (*capt*), D Smith; N Spooner, J Rauluni; D Crowley, M Foley, G Panoho, W Waugh, M Connors, M Cockbain, T Kefu, M Murray *Substitution:* N Williams for Tune (74 mins)
Scorers *Try:* Horan *Conversion:* Spooner *Penalty Goals:* Spooner (5)
Canterbury Crusaders: L Macdonald; A So'oalo, N Berryman, D Gibson, C Ralph; A Mehrtens, J Marshall; G Feek, M Hammett, G Somerville, T Blackadder (*capt*), N Maxwell, R Thorne, S Surridge, A Gardiner
Substitutions: S Robertson for Gardiner (40 mins); C Barrell for Somerville (79 mins)
Scorers *Tries:* Feek, Ralph, Macdonald, Robertson *Conversion:* Mehrtens *Penalty Goals:* Mehrtens (2)
Referee A Watson (South Africa)

22 May, Newlands, Cape Town
Western Stormers 18 (1G 2PG 1T) Otago Highlanders 33 (2G 3PG 2T)

Western Stormers: P Montgomery; B Paulse, R Fleck, A Marinos, P Rossouw; B van Straaten, D van Zyl; R Kempson, C Marais, C Visagie, S Boome, J Trytsman, C Krige (*capt*), A Leonard, R Brink *Substitutions:* C Roux for Trytsman (49 mins); A van der Linde for Kempson (71 mins)

Scorers *Tries:* Paulse, Marais *Conversion:* van Straaten *Penalty Goals:* van Straaten (2)
Otago Highlanders: J Wilson; B Laney, R Ropati, P Alatini, B Lima; T Brown,
B Kelleher; C Hoeft, A Oliver, K Meeuws, B Timmins, J Blaikie, T Randell *(capt)*,
I Maka, J Kronfeld *Substitutions:* J McDonnell for Maka (temp 55-65 mins);
S Maling for Timmins (75 mins)
Scorers *Tries:* Lima, Kelleher, Ropati, Randell *Conversions:* Brown (2)
Penalty Goals: Brown (3)
Referee P L Marshall (Australia)

ROUND-ROBIN SUMMARY

26 Feb: Crusaders 48, Chiefs 3 *(Christchurch)*; 26 Feb: Golden Cats 33, Brumbies 22 *(Johannesburg)*; 27 Feb:
Highlanders 19, Blues 13 *(Dunedin)*; 27 Feb: Reds 11, Hurricanes 0 *(Brisbane)*; 27 Feb: Coastal Sharks 13,
Waratahs 13 *(Durban)*; 27 Feb: Stormers 42, Highlanders 22 *(Pretoria)*; 5 Mar: Crusaders 22, Blues 16
(Auckland); 5 Mar: Coastal Sharks 21, Brumbies 16 *(Port Elizabeth)*; 6 Mar: Highlanders 65, Northern Bulls
23 *(Invercargill)*; 6 Mar: Reds 19, Chiefs 17 *(Hamilton)*; 7 Mar: Waratahs 39, Golden Cats 10 *(Bloemfontein)*; 7
Mar: Stormers 24, Hurricanes 22 *(Wellington)*; 12 Mar: Highlanders 46, Stormers 14 *(Dunedin)*; 12 Mar:
Reds 19, Brumbies 18 *(Brisbane)*; 13 Mar: Hurricanes 37, Northern Bulls 18 *(Palmerston North)*; 13 Mar:
Waratahs 36, Chiefs 30 *(Sydney)*; 13 Mar: Coastal Sharks 36,Golden Cats 20 *(Johannesburg)*; 19 Mar:
Crusaders 18, Hurricanes 18 *(Christchurch)*; 19 Mar: Brumbies 39, Stormers 15 *(Canberra)*; 20 Mar: Waratahs
39, Northern Bulls 23 *(Sydney)*; 20 Mar: Blues 12, Reds 12 *(Albany)*; 20 Mar: Highlanders 29, Golden Cats
28 *(Johannesburg)*; 26 Mar: Coastal Sharks 32, Highlanders 8 *(Durban)*; 26 Mar: Stormers 28, Waratahs 18
(Sydney); 27 Mar: Blues 29, Chiefs 18 *(Hamilton)*; 27 Mar: Reds 36, Crusaders 23 *(Christchurch)*; 27 Mar:
Brumbies 73, Northern Bulls 9 *(Canberra)*; 27 Mar: Golden Cats 43, Hurricanes 27 *(Bloemfontein)*; 2 Apr:
Crusaders 28, Brumbies 21 *(Canberra)*; 3 Apr: Golden Cats 57, Northern Bulls 24 *(Johannesburg)*; 3 Apr:
Highlanders 27, Chiefs 10 *(Rotorua)*; 3 Apr: Blues 21, Waratahs 20 *(Sydney)*; 3 Apr: Hurricanes 34, Coastal
Sharks 18 *(East London)*; 3 Apr: Stormers 35, Reds 14 *(Cape Town)*; 9 Apr: Highlanders 23, Crusaders 6
(Dunedin); 9 Apr: Reds 17, Northern Bulls 7 *(Brakpan)*; 10 Apr: Blues 23, Hurricanes 7 *(Auckland)*; 10 Apr:
Chiefs 16, Brumbies 13 *(Canberra)*; 10 Apr: Stormers 35, Coastal Sharks 19 *(Cape Town)*; 16 Apr: Chiefs 24,
Hurricanes 21 *(New Plymouth)*; 17 Apr: Coastal Sharks 29, Northern Bulls 0 *(Durban)*; 17 Apr: Highlanders
20, Reds 19 *(Brisbane)*; 17 Apr: Blues 24, Golden Cats 11 *(Auckland)*; 17 Apr: Brumbies 27, Waratahs 16
(Canberra); 18 Apr: Stormers 28, Crusaders 19 *(Cape Town)*; 23 Apr: Waratahs 23, Highlanders 15 *(Dunedin)*;
24 Apr: Crusaders 30, Northern Bulls 28 *(Pretoria)*; 24 Apr: Chiefs 44, Golden Cats 42 *(Pukekohe)*; 24 Apr:
Coastal Sharks 12, Blues 6 *(Auckland)*; 25 Apr: Brumbies 21, Hurricanes 13 *(Wellington)*; 30 Apr: Chiefs 32,
Coastal Sharks 19 *(Hamilton)*; 1 May: Stormers 37, Blues 23 *(Cape Town)*; 1 May: Highlanders 9, Brumbies 8
(Dunedin); 1 May: Reds 30, Waratahs 13 *(Sydney)*; 2 May: Crusaders 58, Golden Cats 38 *(Nelson)*; 7 May:
Hurricanes 13, Waratahs 7 *(Napier)*; 8 May: Crusaders 34, Coastal Sharks 29 *(Christchurch)*; 8 May: Reds 22,
Golden Cats 12 *(Brisbane)*; 8 May: Northern Bulls 21, Blues 19 *(Witbank)*; 8 May: Stormers 16, Chiefs 9
(Cape Town); 14 May: Brumbies 22, Blues 16 *(Auckland)*; 14 May: Reds 34, Coastal Sharks 13 *(Brisbane)*;
14 May: Chiefs 39, Northern Bulls 31 *(Pretoria)*; 15 May: Crusaders 38, Waratahs 22 *(Sydney)*; 15 May:
Golden Cats 18, Stormers 16 *(Cape Town)*; 15 May: Hurricanes 21, Highlanders 19 *(Wellington)*

FINAL TABLE 1999

	P	W	D	L	F	A	Bonus	Pts
Queensland Reds	11	8	1	2	233	170	2	36
Western Stormers	11	8	0	3	290	244	4	36
Otago Highlanders	11	8	0	3	280	203	3	35
Canterbury Crusaders	11	7	1	3	322	262	3	33
ACT Brumbies	11	5	0	6	278	195	8	28
Waikato Chiefs	11	5	0	6	248	301	6	26
Coastal Sharks	11	5	1	5	241	232	3	25
NSW Waratahs	11	4	1	6	246	246	6	24
Auckland Blues	11	4	1	6	202	201	5	23
Wellington Hurricanes	11	4	1	6	213	226	4	22
Golden Cats	11	4	0	7	312	341	6	22
Northern Bulls	11	1	0	10	203	447	3	7

*The leading scorers in the round-robin were: 170 Andrew Mehrtens (Canterbury Crusaders); 144 Braam van Straaten
(Western Stormers); 131 Nathan Spooner (Queensland Reds); 118 Adrian Cashmore (Auckland Blues). The top
try-scorers in the round-robin were: 8 Conrad Stoltz (Golden Cats), Joe Roff (ACT Brumbies); 7 Afato So'oalo
(Canterbury Crusaders) and Pieter Rossouw (Western Stormers).*

Auckland Blues have won the Super-12s twice (1996 and 1997) and Canterbury Crusaders twice (1998 and
1999).

POLITICS TO THE FORE

THE 1998-1999 SEASON IN ENGLAND
David Llewellyn

It is not surprising, given all the monkeying around with clubs' very existence and players' and coaches' livelihoods, not to mention fixture lists and numbers of teams in Allied Dunbar Premiership One, that one significant – yet ultimately trivial – trouble of a very troubled season was sorted out over a pie and a pint in The Drum and Monkey, a Glasgow pub. It has become a tiresome trait, but England were yet again expelled from the Five Nations shortly after the New Year and not long before the start of the final Five Nations tournament. The exile lasted some 18 hours before old-fashioned reason prevailed, when Messrs Allan Hosie, chairman of the Five Nations, Brian Baister, chairman of the Rugby Football Union, and Bill Beaumont, RFU negotiator and former England captain, got around a pub table and, rather in the spirit of the good old, bad old days, sorted things out over a jar of ale. And with ruffled feathers and dented pride smoothed out, everything was apparently sweetness and light once more.

That, though, was just about the last glimpse anyone had of the old-style amateur ethos prevailing. Thereafter the season blundered through the new age of professionalism, applying what those in charge insisted were the correct commercial standards to the game to bring it in line with the rest of the world and in so doing the heart and soul of the body of the game was cut out. Ruthless does not begin to describe the callous shedding of founder RFU members Richmond, or their erstwhile groundshare neighbours London Scottish. Both were ostensibly swallowed up in a merger with London Irish. In reality, however, they were wiped out of professional existence to suit the rest of their cannibalistic colleagues who had wanted to trim Premiership One from the 14 clubs they had elected for the last season, to what they now decided would be a more manageable and realistic figure: a nice, round, 12 – rugby's own Dirty Dozen as they could be called after the act of genocide they have committed.

The RFU gave their approval to the tripartite merger subject to certain conditions and guarantees being met. London Irish, who were keen on retaining their name (although alternatives such as Richmond Celts and Richmond Exiles were considered) then had the unpleasant task of informing around 50 players from the two clubs that they were out of work and unwanted. But throughout the Premiership, clubs (West Hartlepool and Sale among them) were shedding players as if they were defunct machinery. Sale themselves

The England squad against Scotland at Twickenham on 20th February. L-R back row: D J Grewcock (replacement), M E Corry (replacement), D L Rees, R A Hill, T A K Rodber, M O Johnson, N D Beal, D J Garforth, D D Luger, D J Cockerill, J Leonard; front row: P J Grayson (replacement), M B Perry (replacement), J P Wilkinson, M J Catt, J C Guscott, L B N Dallaglio (captain), N A Back, M J S Dawson, G C Rowntree (replacement), N McCarthy (replacement), K P P Bracken (replacement).

were being discussed in the early summer as a possible takeover target by Worcester, who were keen to get into the top flight; indeed behaved as if it were their right almost, with their owner Cecil Duckworth rumoured to have threatened to reduce his investment if they missed promotion. They missed it, and instead his reaction was to seek to buy his way to the top. Where is the sporting excellence in that? Where is the old ethos of the game?

The truth is that when it comes down to it, professional rugby is all about money from top to bottom. Why else would the International Board resort to fining the Rugby Football Union as a means of punishment for not taking any action in preventing their member clubs from playing unauthorised Anglo-Welsh matches? The RFU promised to fight the fine of £60,000 imposed by what Twickenham insisted was an improperly constituted disciplinary panel chaired by Tim Gresson of New Zealand, in Dublin in December.

The glib talk of improved playing standards and the provision of a broad playing base from which top clubs and England can benefit, was hoofed out of the door at the first sign of perceived financial failure. The 'professionals', the money men, stated at the outset, when they first got their hands on the fruits of a lot of hard labour by lovers of the game, amateurs who had nurtured for a century or more clubs which embodied all that is good in sport, that they were doing everything in the best interests of the game. They also claimed that they had done their research and had calculated just what was needed to turn the clubs into professional outfits. Some way down the line that research looks like an unfounded claim, as the demise of Richmond and London Scottish bears witness. The big money backers did not invest anywhere near enough in the clubs. The now laughable sums of money suggested to take the game into the 21st Century – £2.5 million – turned out to be the amount needed to sustain any club for a single season. What was needed was a bold input of serious money, say around £20 to £25 million, which when invested would provide the clubs with serious working capital for the year; and would then be supplemented by sponsorship, marketing and television monies.

More and more, rugby resembled professional soccer. Coaches, managers, call them what you will, became scapegoats for perceived lack of success. Gloucester got rid of Richard Hill; Geoff Cooke and Paul Turner quit Bedford; while Saracens marketing guru Peter Deakin returned to his first love, rugby league. Ian McGeechan stunned Northampton after taking them into Europe by accepting an offer to coach Scotland – the only job he would have left Saints for – and John Kingston walked out of Richmond when his players were put on the transfer market by the administrator whom the club had invited in to sort out their financial problems. Those problems had been caused by Ashley Levett, the club's backer, pulling the plug on any more financial support, taking Sir John Hall's lead up at Newcastle. The north-east club was eventually bought out by a consortium of businessmen who also involved Rob Andrew, the Falcons director of rugby, on the business side of things.

Amidst all the goings of clubs and personnel there was a second coming, that of Will Carling, who popped up at Harlequins again after 13 months out of the game. The former England captain played in half a dozen Premiership matches and did not, as they say in cricket circles, trouble the scorers. Although he announced on his return in February that he wanted to play into the millennium, he later amended that, stating that he would reconsider his career over the summer.

Strangely enough there were some sensible things to emerge from the season, including wage caps; clubs will be fined if they exceed the agreed £1.8 million. Still, off the field there were swingeing changes to the RFU's management board which saw Fran Cotton moving into a position of more influence and Bill Beaumont joining Malcolm Phillips as the RFU's International Board representatives. Francis Baron was appointed chief executive and wielded the axe at Twickenham where a sizeable number of jobs were made redundant, including Don Rutherford's post as technical director and Roger Uttley's as part-time manager of England. There were also changes within English First Division rugby, where Doug Ash stepped down as chief executive to be replaced by Howard Thomas.

Politics and in-fighting had forced a ludicrous situation with Allied Dunbar Premiership One fixtures agreed only for the first five weeks as the RFU tried to dig in over the unsanctioned Anglo-Welsh series, which was a commercial success and was won by Cardiff, who along with Swansea had been driven out of the Welsh domestic league because of their refusal to sign a 10-year loyalty contract with their union. There was even a point at which the RFU decided not to appoint qualified referees for two sanctioned matches in the Premiership at Sale and West Hartlepool, although that course of action was not followed through. In the end it was decided that the RFU would not allow any of their referees to officiate in Anglo-Welsh matches taking place in England and that saw the re-emergence of an old favourite, Fred Howard, for a handful of matches. It had been suggested that the Anglo-Welsh matches take place in midweek, fulfilling the role of friendly fixtures, but the clubs insisted that they be staged on a Premiership weekend. The clubs had their way and things looked settled, until the Five Nations fiasco. The other Home Unions were unhappy with the share-out of the TV spoils, though thankfully common sense did prevail, as it did when the RFU attempted to change the frequency of British Lions tours from every four years to a six-year cycle. The Home Unions committee came down hard on that one and Twickenham relented, but the seemingly unending little tests and thrusts into the sensitive underbelly of the game's fragile structure really began to pall.

At least the English clubs boycott of the European Cup is over. They decided to participate in the tournament in 1999-2000, too late for Bath to defend their hard-won title of the previous season, but at least they are back. There had been all sorts of rumours flying around before the decision to return; talk of a rival European competition involving the best of France and England and any other takers (Cardiff and Swansea would have been interested), and the possibility of introducing a British League was also discussed.

Remarkably all this while the players had managed to turn up for fixtures and there was actually action on the field. Clive Woodward began to assert himself as coach, re-appointing Lawrence Dallaglio as captain, a role that he was expected to retain until after the World Cup. Sadly the allegations about drug taking and even drug pushing which were levelled at Dallaglio on the eve of the squad's departure for the southern hemisphere forced the Wasps back-row forward to step down as captain and to pull out of the tour (altogether a wise move under the circumstances), the player opting to stay at home to try to sort everything out. Back in the autumn he had been forced to miss England's two World Cup qualifiers against Holland and Italy, but for less dramatic reasons – injury ruled him out. His replacement back then was the same man who took over for the summer tour, Leicester captain Martin Johnson. He led the side admirably. There had been question marks over Johnson's self-discipline since he did seem to be on the receiving end of a number of yellow and white cards, but it did begin to look as if he were a man more sinned against than sinner; targeted for punitive action when lesser referees wanted to make an example of someone prominent (and Johnson physically is most definitely that) to regain what vestiges of control they may have had in the game. The question of refereeing standards was addressed to a certain extent by the appointment of three full-time professionals, Steve Lander, Ed Morrison and Chris White. There were supposed to be a further three in the New Year but that decision was put on hold by the governing body because of a lack of funding. Plans are in place however to end up with a total of nine, once sponsorship has been found.

If the persistent and pesky politicking was irritating, it was sadder still to witness or read of acts of gratuitous violence. England scrum-half Austin Healey was found guilty of a particularly unpleasant piece of illegal footwork on his London Irish counter-part Kevin Putt, which was committed in front of a few million television viewers. Leicester suspended him for a risible three weeks after the Exiles cited him, but the RFU then stepped in and extended that ban by a further five weeks. Bath's Kevin Yates, still swearing his innocence over the infamous ear-biting affair of the previous season, was found guilty of stamping on Wasps' Paul Volley and was handed a sentence which was half that of Healey's. And ear-biting was not a thing of the past. A player from the Gloucestershire club Matson was found guilty of using his teeth and was banned for 33 months. Domestic rugby involving Premiership teams saw the introduction of white triangular cards, to be used dismiss players to the sin bin for 10 minutes for technical offences. The white card though became something of a cop-out and professional fouls and punches were also deemed sin-binnable by certain referees.

The World Cup matches – both of which were played at Huddersfield's McAlpine Stadium, were not the unqualified success that had been expected. True the Dutch were ditched with barely a backward glance as England ran up an impressive 110 points without reply, but Italy, who were on the threshold of turning the Five Nations into Six, were a different proposition. That England won was down to a late Will Greenwood score (and a lot of luck) as the Italians dominated in ruck, maul and around the fringes. Woodward felt that French referee Didier Mene had been too ready to whistle the moment boots and bodies came into contact; the truth was that England just did not get it right on the day. They might even have lost had scrum-half Alessandro Troncon been awarded the try that he and his team-mates clearly felt he had completed. M Mene, fortunately for England, thought differently.

Just a week later it was back to Twickenham and back to normal, well almost; Dallaglio was fit again and back in charge and England lost to Australia. That is the statistic. The scoreline showed a solitary point in favour of the Wallabies and, had Mike Catt converted Jeremy Guscott's try, a magical and well-worked score, that difference would have been in England's favour. England were undone by the boot of Australian lock John Eales. The man was a marvel. The winning penalty (his fourth of the game) was kicked four minutes from time, a nerveless, 46-metre effort that prompted Woodward to say afterwards: 'The bugger never even looked like missing.' Overall there was little drama in the match; that was not to say that it did not have its moments, just that there were not a whole heap of them for fans on either side to celebrate. Australia certainly did not look invincible, but England were just not sharp enough to cut their defences open.

And so another week and it was the turn of the World Champions South Africa. They were on the brink of breaking New Zealand's previously unparalleled run of 17 Test wins in a row. They were also looking to become the first side to complete a Grand Slam of wins over the Home Unions since the Wallabies achieved the feat in 1984. It was tight, but so were the Springboks. So tight that their minds appeared to be on the records and not the reality of the match. England turned in an encouragingly superb all-round performance, with yet another try for Guscott and some phenomenal tackling. There was a high error count, but in a high octane match that was only understandable. Fortunately it was South Africa who committed most mistakes and were made to pay for them either in points, lost territorial advantage or lost opportunities. England triumphed 13-7 and all looked set fair for the Five Nations.

In particular it looked good for Jonny, Wilkinson that is – the boy-man everyone, except Woodward and Rob Andrew, his boss at Newcastle, wanted to see at fly-half. His full debut was at centre against Scotland. Unfortunately it was not the free-flowing match that had been hoped for. What was perceived by many as fussy refereeing by Ireland's David McHugh meant that there were more whistles than cheers, but Wilkinson did his stuff, landing three conversions and a penalty. Dublin produced more tries and more points from Wilkinson's boot as Ireland were brushed aside. There was a suggestion that England hooker Richard Cockerill had abused spectators at Lansdowne Road, running down the touchline giving what he called a 'routine victory gesture', but the matter was not taken any further and, after a thoroughly professional performance by England, Ireland were left applauding their conquerors. Then it was back to Twickenham for the showdown with France. Jonny excelled again. He landed seven penalties to equal the English record originally set by Simon Hodgkinson and subsequently matched by Wilkinson's mentor, Andrew, and England won. A Grand Slam beckoned. So did Wales, playing their farewell match at Wembley, their temporary home in North-West London. It was a thunderous occasion and the tightest of matches, Wales skipping home by a point thanks to a late, late try by Scott Gibbs, converted by another points machine, Neil Jenkins. It was a savage blow, although one not nearly as cruel as that which robbed them of their inspirational leader for the summer tour Down Under.

Meanwhile the Allied Dunbar Premiership One had got under way and, though not a foregone conclusion until late in the season, was nevertheless turning into a fairly straightforward scrap between perhaps half a dozen clubs with latterly Leicester and Northampton pulling away from the pack. The fact that there were places in Europe up for grabs – the top half dozen being rewarded for a good finish with some glamorous fixtures next season – added a distinct edge to proceedings. Saints unfortunately could not sustain their fine run of form and not even a stylish and exhilarating approach to their matches could prevent a home defeat against the Tigers. Losing to London Irish and Saracens at the turn of the year at

Franklin's Gardens did not help their cause, although they did bounce back by trouncing the defending champions, Newcastle, sticking more than fifty points on the Falcons and conceding very few, but the damage had been done. The Tigers slipped away and, although manager Dean Richards maintained a cautious approach as to the destiny of the title, by mid-March, with an eight-point cushion, it was all over bar the fat lady singing.

Bath looked out of the running for a European Cup place until the very last match of the season when they thrashed London Scottish in a 12-try romp, four of those being scored by Jeremy Guscott. It meant that Newcastle had to come away from Saracens not just with victory, but with a margin of 30 points. It all proved too much and they lost. The question of relegation was never in doubt either. That was always going to be West Hartlepool, who remained on the bottom of the table from the start to finish. Their supporters had to wait until the middle of December before they recorded their first win, a surprise victory over fellow strugglers Bedford. They followed that with a stunning result over Wasps, beating them 21-17 at home in the New Year, and produced another rugby rabbit out of the hat with a close verdict over the Premiership's worst travellers Gloucester, but in the end they were token wins. West were too often everyone else's whipping boys; they conceded fifty or more points on no fewer than five occasions and their points conceded was an unprecedented and shameful 1,007. Richmond finished with a flourish, running up a Premiership record of 106 points at Bedford's Goldington Road ground. There were hat-tricks for Brian Cusack and Mel Deane in the 16-try rout. Bedford went on to win a tight play-off with Premiership Two side Rotherham to earn the right to stay up with the 'haves', but the consortium who took over from Frank Warren were not promising a great deal in the way of making cash available for bringing in new players and doubts clouded their future well into the close season. Bristol, who began the takeover trend with their deal to buy out London Scottish in the event of their not gaining promotion from Premiership Two, made it back into the top flight after one season out, on their own rugby recognisance, to all-round relief. The prospect of them purchasing a place in Premiership One by taking over the Exiles slot, in other words, buying success, would have been anathema to most decent-minded sports people. Rotherham will not be kept down for long though, and if they do not fill in for any late fallers from the summer, there is no doubt that they will dominate the Second Division in the new season.

There was cause to mourn the passing of another founder member of the RFU, Blackheath, who slipped out of the Premiership along with Fylde, making way for the thrusting Manchester and Henley from Jewson National League One.

The enlarged Tetley's Bitter Cup embraced a huge cross-section of rugby, with more than 100 clubs taking part, and captured the sort of romance that has made football's FA Cup such a stunning success. For example there was Jeff Probyn, the former England prop, turning out for Barking, the club he coaches, up at Leicester in the fourth round, Sedgley Park entertaining Wasps at the same stage and Henley reaching the fifth round by beating Bedford. Richmond's final weeks of existence saw them go farther than they had ever been in the competition when they beat Leicester at the Madejski Stadium in the quarter-final. Sadly they could not reproduce the spirit or the verve of that performance when they entertained Newcastle in the semi-final and they subsided. The romantic momentum was maintained right up to the final when the knockout cup's perpetual bridesmaids Wasps finally got their names on the winners' register with a comprehensive defeat of Newcastle. It also helped them consign to history their humiliating thumping at the hands of Saracens in the previous year's final. Trelawney's Army watched Cornwall march off with the County Championship title after beating Gloucestershire at Twickenham; Yorkshire lifted the under-21 trophy, beating Cornwall; Cambridge made it five wins in a row with victory over Oxford in the Varsity match for the Bowring Bowl again at Twickenham; Aldwinians won the NPI Cup and Billericay the Tetley's Vase. Gloucester and Bedford met in a repeat of last year's Cheltenham and Gloucester Cup final and again the West Country club emerged victorious. In the Scottish Amicable Trophy – replacing the Sanyo Cup – Leicester were soundly beaten by a Barbarians XV bristling with big names and big men, from Thomas Castaignède, Walter Little and Frank Bunce to du Randt, Zinzan Brooke and François Pienaar. Penguins waddled off with the Middlesex Sevens title, beating Saracens in the final.

TIGERS ROAR THROUGH

ALLIED DUNBAR PREMIERSHIP 1998-99
David Llewellyn

Leicester's emphatic title triumph was the only certainty of another Allied Dunbar Premiership season which was scarred with doubt. Premiership One had been increased to 14 sides for this season, a short-lived move as things turned out. It is back to a dozen for the new season, thanks to the convenience of the London Irish takeover of Richmond and London Scottish. These last two will be sorely missed as will the raft of players who were left with nowhere to go.

The Tigers never really looked anything but championship material from the outset when they crushed Harlequins in the opening match of the season, which thankfully had resorted to a September start. True the Tigers were not always at the head of the pack, but the point about them was that they stayed there or thereabouts, which is more than can said of the defending champions Newcastle, who ended up not even qualifying for Europe.

The surprise of the season was Northampton, who proved dogged rivals. It was not until the beginning of February that Saints' march was halted, when Saracens edged them out narrowly at Franklin's Gardens. Losing their next game – again at home – this time, significantly, to Leicester in a classic four-pointer really put the seal on the fate of the title. Leicester's manager Dean Richards may have demurred at this point, but even a whopping fifty-pointer over Newcastle was too late for Northampton to rectify matters. And furthermore the Tigers by now had enough of a cushion between them and second-placed Saints to allow them the occasional slip-up; hence the defeat at Bath was insignificant. It was also Tigers' fourth and final one. Mathematics precluded premature partying but the title was in the bag.

Europe kept interest going until the very end when Bath, Wasps, Saracens and Harlequins emerged to join Leicester and Northampton in Europe. Bath's chances were looking distinctly dodgy right up to their last match, then in a 12-try spectacular (Jeremy Guscott scoring four of them) against London Scottish they left Newcastle needing to beat Saracens by a clear 30 points in the very last match of the campaign. It proved way beyond the Falcons, who lost at Watford.

The two promoted candidates from the previous season, Bedford and West Hartlepool, struggled from the outset and had settled in the bottom two places very early on. Bedford were caught up in Frank Warren's boxing wrangle for much of the season, and it was something close to a miracle that Bedford strung together quite as many victories – half a dozen – as they did. Among those were two notable scalps. Harlequins were turned over in October at Golding-ton Road when the home side scored two tries in injury-time; then in February came Wasps and, like their London neighbours, they left the ground losers by two points, with Bedford having to endure eight minutes of injury-time before they were able to celebrate what was their first victory since the Harlequins game. Gloucester too stumbled at Bedford, but then their away form for the last two seasons has been appalling. It took Richmond, who ran up the first century in Premiership One, to show their betters how it should be done. That Bedford managed to get into double figures themselves was quite an achievement, considering how little they had the ball, and indeed how infrequently they had it when a score was on. Richmond scored a total of 16 tries, with hat-tricks for Brian Cusack and Mel Deane, and the points glut meant that they finished the last season of their independent existence on something of a high note and with a points difference in their favour. For Bedford the season did not end with the Richmond match. They had already done enough under the astute coaching of Straeuli to reach the play-offs, where they ran up against those seasoned campaigners Rotherham.

The Second Division side just lost out on points difference (10 to be precise) to Bristol in the title race and its concomitant automatic promotion, so, as they had last year, Rotherham had to pit themselves against the stragglers of the top flight. It was all the more galling for Rotherham because they had done the league double over Bristol, but they had not done enough in other matches. As against London Irish last year, the Yorkshire club acquitted themselves well, this time going one better by winning the first leg, but Bedford centre Alistair Murdoch's second-half try in the second meeting ensured survival on a try-count after the two sides finished level on aggregate points. Bristol at one point had looked as if they would have to purchase a place in Premiership One and had lined up troubled London Scottish for a takeover in the event of them not winning automatic promotion from Premier-ship Two. They did not need it. Worcester, the only other threat, lost two points for naming an unregistered player – hooker Tom Robinson from Bath – on the bench for the match at Wakefield. In the end they finished far below the leaders, not as far as Blackheath and Fylde though. They will be replaced in Allied Dunbar Premier-ship Two, which remains a 14-team league going into the millen-nium – by Henley and Manchester, champions and runners-up in Jewson National League One.

ENGLISH LEAGUES 1998–99

ALLIED DUNBAR PREMIERSHIP

Allied Dunbar One

	P	W	D	L	F	A	Pts
Leicester Tigers	26	22	0	4	771	423	44
Northampton	26	19	0	7	754	556	38
Saracens	26	16	1	9	748	583	33
NEC Harlequins	26	16	1	9	687	653	33
Wasps	26	15	1	10	717	506	31
Bath	26	15	0	11	698	574	30
London Irish	26	15	0	11	703	607	30
Newcastle Falcs	26	14	0	12	719	639	28
Richmond	26	11	2	13	720	715	22*
Gloucester	26	9	1	16	554	640	19
Manchester Sale	26	9	1	16	604	731	19
London Scottish	26	8	0	18	491	734	16
Bedford	26	6	0	20	541	840	12
West Hartlepool	26	3	1	22	501	1007	7

Following the Play-offs Bedford remain in Allied Dunbar Premiership 1 for Season 1999/2000.

Allied Dunbar Two

	P	W	D	L	F	A	Pts
Bristol	26	22	0	4	848	418	44
Rotherham	26	22	0	4	756	336	44
Worcester	26	18	0	8	716	409	34*
London Welsh	26	17	0	9	662	552	34
Exeter	26	14	1	11	591	598	29
Leeds	26	16	0	10	713	367	28*
Coventry	26	14	0	12	652	560	28
Orrell	26	12	0	14	566	483	24
Waterloo	26	12	0	14	419	634	24
Moseley	26	10	0	16	498	633	20
Rugby Lions	26	9	0	17	425	660	18
Wakefield	26	6	0	20	469	812	12
Blackheath	26	5	0	21	419	842	10
Fylde	26	4	1	21	375	805	9

Following the Play-offs Rotherham remain in Allied Dunbar Premiership 2 for Season 1999/2000.

* denotes points deducted.

Previous champions

1988 Leicester
1989 Bath
1990 Wasps
1991 Bath
1992 Bath
1993 Bath
1994 Bath
1995 Leicester
1996 Bath
1997 Wasps
1998 Newcastle

JEWSON NATIONAL LEAGUE

Jewson One

	P	W	D	L	F	A	Pts
Henley	26	22	1	3	642	299	45
Manchester	26	20	1	5	758	372	41
Rosslyn Park	26	17	1	8	588	371	35
Nottingham	26	16	0	10	590	467	32
Otley	26	15	1	10	508	416	31
Newbury	26	14	1	11	552	476	29
Wharfedale	26	13	1	12	477	421	27
Lydney	26	11	2	13	438	482	24
Camberley	26	10	1	15	529	661	21
Reading	26	10	0	16	468	635	20
Birmingham S	26	9	0	17	422	521	18
Harrogate	26	8	2	16	309	461	18
Morley	26	7	1	18	468	643	15
Liverpool St Hel.	26	4	0	22	335	859	8

Jewson Two North

	P	W	D	L	F	A	Pts
Preston Grass	26	23	0	3	822	341	46
Stourbridge	26	22	0	4	895	413	44
New Brighton	26	20	0	6	703	329	40
Kendal	26	18	0	8	635	347	36
Nuneaton	26	14	2	10	597	533	30
Sheffield	26	15	0	11	496	455	30
Sandal	26	13	0	13	697	611	26
Sedgley Park	26	12	1	13	710	553	25
Walsall	26	10	1	15	515	720	21
Aspatria	26	10	0	16	578	675	20
Whitchurch	26	9	1	16	450	599	19
Hinckley	26	7	1	18	445	733	15
Lichfield	26	3	0	23	371	950	6
Winnington Park	26	3	0	23	310	965	6

Jewson Two South

	P	W	D	L	F	A	Pts
Bracknell	26	23	1	2	631	317	47
Esher	26	23	0	3	864	308	46
North Walsham	26	22	0	4	630	306	44
Barking	26	19	1	6	644	327	39
Met. Police	26	14	1	11	470	545	29
Norwich	26	11	0	15	383	429	22
Clifton	26	10	1	15	415	483	21
Tabard	26	9	1	16	461	501	19
Weston-S-Mare	26	9	1	16	417	588	19
Bridgwater & A	26	8	2	16	462	624	18
Redruth	26	8	1	17	503	657	17
Plymouth Albion	26	7	1	18	457	666	15
Cheltenham	26	7	0	19	335	608	14
Havant	26	7	0	19	361	674	14

NO MORE THE BRIDESMAID

TETLEY'S BITTER CUP 1998-99
Mick Cleary and David Llewellyn

15 May 1999, Twickenham
Wasps 29 (2G 4PG 1DG) **Newcastle 19** (1G 4PG)

They had been here too often before. They knew the ritual by heart – expectation, nervousness, frantic activity and then crushing disappointment. Four times they had been through the agonies. Four times they had nurtured hope in their hearts. And four times they had had to cope with failure.

On this occasion there was to be no mistake. Wasps won the cup at the fifth attempt and they did so with a calculating and disciplined performance. They had done their homework on Newcastle, who had twice won the cup in their previous incarnations as Gosforth. Wasps knew that Va'aiga Tuigamala was the rallying point of the Newcastle attack. The great Samoan was the club's top try-scorer coming into the match with 19 tries in 31 matches. He had single-handedly done for Richmond in the Tetley's semi-final. But more than his mere try-scoring feats (considerable though they were) was his ability to create space for those around him and to inspire his teammates with his own prodigious work-rate. Stop Inga and you stop Newcastle.

Wasps' winger, Josh Lewsey, was one man who managed it more often and more dramatically than any other. Just before the hour mark, Tuigamala intercepted a pass on half-way from Wasps lock Simon Shaw, who was trying to find Lawrence Dallaglio on the outside. Tuigamala set off for the try-line. Lewsey made up ground and in a super claw-back tackle managed to halt Tuigamala just a few metres short.

Tuigamala injured his shoulder in the process but played on. It was a crucial moment. A converted try at that stage – and even though we had already witnessed the extraordinary sight of Jonny Wilkinson actually missing a kick at Twickenham there was little reason to suspect that he would not have added the two points – would have made the score 19-16.

But it was not to be. Wasps composed themselves, kept Newcastle at bay on the gain-line, continued to forage with real appetite in the loose and put themselves en route to the winners' rostrum with Lewsey's try in the 77th minute.

Once again Tuigamala was involved. He tried to find Legg on the outside, Lewsey nipped in, snaffled the ball and raced 40 metres to the line. Three minutes later, with the final whistle poised in Steve

One swallow dive makes a season. Wasps fly-half Alex King beats Newcastle captain Gary Armstrong to score the opening try for his side in their 29-19 Tetley's Bitter Cup final success.

Lander's lips, Tuigamala had a minor moment of consolation when he snatched the ball from Lewsey and ran in the try.

The match itself was rather fractured and flat. It had its moments and there was no lack of effort on both sides. But Twickenham was only two-thirds full, the 50,000 crowd being the lowest attendance for ten years.

A few players were not about to waste the platform they had been given. For Wasps fly-half Alex King the final was a great opportunity to showcase his talents. And in the 26th minute most were on view in one movement. King took a pass from a scrum position in midfield. Nothing much seemed on. A decoy run from Mark Denney, however, tugged the Newcastle defence inside. King saw the gap and set off. Only Newcastle full-back Stuart Legg stood between him and the goal-line. Round him or over him? King went for the aerial route. He chipped and chased, winning the touch-down in theatrical swallow-diving fashion, ahead of Newcastle's Gary Armstrong.

Add in a sweet drop goal just three minutes after the interval and it wasn't a bad day at the office for Alex King. He held the whip hand on his opposite number, Jonny Wilkinson. The 19-year-old is ahead of him in the England rankings; both were to depart for England's summer tour to Australia shortly after this match.

Wilkinson had a tough time of it. Mind you, his pack were held in check and Newcastle were never able to generate the pace and momentum achieved by the Wasps back row. Wasps openside, Joe Worsley, 21, was named man of the match and showed in his bristling play just why he had been called-up to Clive Woodward's 36-man tour squad.

There were good times to savour too for Wasps full-back, Gareth Rees. He played in the 1986 Cup final for Wasps against Bath as an 18-year-old schoolboy at Harrow. Since then he has appeared in three World Cup finals. He had had a mixed season through injury and lack of form and was only guaranteed a slot here when wing Kenny Logan's troublesome ankle reduced him to a role on the bench. Rees took his chance, scoring 16 points from four penalties and two conversions to equal the individual record for a Cup final.

Wilkinson hit four penalties and a conversion for Newcastle. But they were always in the slipstream of Wasps.

Newcastle: S Legg; J Naylor, M Shaw, T May, V Tuigamala; J Wilkinson, G Armstrong (*capt*); G Graham, R Nesdale, M Hurter, G Archer, G Weir, P Walton, R Beattie, R Arnold *Substitutions:* T Underwood for Naylor (40 mins); I Peel for Hurter (69 mins)
Scorers *Try:* Tuigamala *Conversion:* Wilkinson *Penalty Goals:* Wilkinson (4)
Wasps: G Rees; J Lewsey, F Waters, M Denney, P Sampson; A King, A Gomarsall; D Molloy, T Leota, W Green, M Weedon (*capt*), S Shaw,

L Dallaglio, P Scrivener, J Worsley *Substitutions:* K Logan for Sampson (46 mins); M Friday for Gomarsall (48 mins); R Henderson for Denney (66 mins)
Scorers *Tries:* King, Lewsey *Conversions:* Rees (2) *Penalty Goals:* Rees (4) *Dropped Goal:* King
Referee S Lander (Liverpool)

Earlier Rounds

As a hard core of self-styled and so-called professionals attempt to make life tough for everyone, it is refreshing to know that the age of rugby romance is not yet dead. The sponsors of the knock-out competition are a reminder that there is still room and time for some of the old-fashioned values, beer bellies and bloody good shows. There was no better illustration of the amateur ethos than at Hull Ionians. They battled through three rounds, starting with the preliminary, where they accounted for a famous rugby name from the ancient times, Broughton Park, at the beginning of September. They then blitzed Egremont in the first round proper, which, like the preliminary round had been regionalised, before accounting for Macclesfield.

The brush with the big-time resulted in Newbury sweeping them aside in the third round, but at least the opportunity had been there. Barking, who entered at the first round, also managed three wins, the third at Swanage earning them a trip into the Tigers' den. Jeff Probyn, the former England and Wasps tighthead prop and now director of rugby at the Essex club, could not resist it, coming out of retirement from the big-time to play for the full 80 minutes and contribute mightily to a respectable fourth-round show. Lydney of Jewson National One went one better, beating Second Division Moseley at The Reddings by a solitary point, while Henley, promoted from the same division, recorded a convincing win over Premiership One side Bedford at Goldington Road. Bedford were in distinguished company as far as fourth-round casualties went; Bath, 10-times winners of the competition, were also knocked out up at Newcastle. The highest score of the first four rounds was recorded by Henley who stuck 100 on Havant in the second.

The hard-tilting yards of the fifth round quickly dispelled the last vestiges of romanticism, however, with Henley and Lydney crashing out, although not by a cricket score in either case, so respectability was maintained. But the First Division sides were just too strong and well organised and so the cup campaigns of Exeter, Waterloo and Leeds also came to a shuddering halt. The only surprises were London Irish's comfortable win at Northampton and the difficult time Harlequins had in disposing of struggling London Scottish, while Newcastle did not have things all their own way at North-East neighbours West Hartlepool.

The quarter-finals were a different matter. Richmond, the focus of attention for all the wrong reasons in the latter stages of the season, turned in a superhuman performance to dump Leicester out of the competition and dash the dreams of a league and cup double for another year. The tie was not won through the boot either. Richmond reached the semi-finals for the first time in their history with some compelling rugby, matching Leicester try for try and producing a defensive display worthy of a southern hemisphere side. There was an equally dramatic victory for Gloucester at Kingsholm where Mark Mapletoft's fifth penalty of the match in the fifth minute of stoppage time accounted for a spirited Harlequins. There was a degree of disappointment to Newcastle's victory over Saracens at Kingston Park, where a mere 3,496 spectators turned up on a bitterly cold Sunday afternoon to watch their side reach the semi-finals for the first time since 1981, and doing so by beating the holders, Saracens, who it must be said, appeared to freeze in every sense of the word. Wasps sorted out London Irish with little problem in the remaining tie of the round.

In the semi-finals Richmond's dreams of a final appearance were rudely shattered by a high-class performance by Newcastle and in particular fly-half Rob Andrew, who controlled every aspect of the tie. Richmond, probably still reeling from the news that Ashley Levett was pulling out, looked shell-shocked at the end of a game in which they had seen so little of the ball that they probably would have had to have introduced themselves to it in the tunnel afterwards. Wasps turned it on in the other tie the following day. The Loftus Road faithful, whose number was swelled to almost 10,000 by the Cherry and White following, saw their team buzz around scoring four tries to nil, which said it all really. Gloucester had one clear-cut chance, Terry Fanolua crossing for what appeared to be a good try only to have it disallowed, but the outcome would always have been the same.

RESULTS

Preliminary round

Abbey 35, Chinnor 9; Aspull 46, West Hartlepool 13; Barkers Butts 35, Belgrave 26; Bromsgrove 20, Longton 19; Charlton Park 16, Wimbledon 18; Darlington Mowden Park 8, Tynedale 12; Egremont 17, Bridlington 16; Finchley 10, Cheshunt 29; Guilford & Godalming 54, Old Emmanuel 17; Harlow 6, Cambridge 14; Hull Ionians 26, Broughton Park 3; Ipswich 26, Old Albanians 3; Keynsham 15, Launceston 21; Lewes 11, Ruislip 33; Malvern 23, Westleigh 3; Mansfield 13, Bedford Athletic 25; Marlow 10, Penzance/Newlyn 44; Matson 19, Torquay Athletic 27; Morpeth 34, Wigton 16; Nottingham Moderns 0, Scunthorpe 34; Old Colfeians 13, Haywards Heath 10; Slough 0, Maidenhead 25; Spartans 13, Salisbury 9; Stafford 13, Kenilworth 41; Stockport 3, Doncaster 44; Swanage & Wareham 14, Stroud 13; Tiverton 29, Clevedon 34; Warrington 18, Macclesfield 26; Wellingborough 20, Broadstreet 26; Westcombe Park 40, Staines 20; Winchester 32, Jersey 8; Woodrush 8, Banbury 53

First round

Aspatria 17, Bedford Athletic 32; Banbury 15, Scunthorpe 17; Barkers Butts 17, Macclesfield 27; Bromsgrove 10, Sedgley Park 34; Cheshunt 33, Morpeth 26; Clevedon 7, Barking 32; Clifton 3, Esher 60; Doncaster 30, Walsall 19; Guildford & Godalming 18, Bridgewater & Albion 28; Hinckley 20, Nuneaton 24; Hull Ionians 59, Egremont; Kendal 13, Broadstreet 12; Launceston 32, North Walsham 18;

Malvern 14, Sandal 52; Metropolitan Police 34, Cheltenham 8; New Brighton 38, Lichfield 8; Norwich 15, Winchester 23; Penzance & Newlyn 32, Cambridge 13; Plymouth Albion 32, Redruth 18; Preston Grasshoppers 43, Kenilworth 6; Ruislip 9, Old Colfeians 43; Spartans 10, Havant 24; Stourbridge 32, Sheffield 6; Swanage & Wareham 44, Abbey 7; Tabard 26, Wimbledon 23; Torquay Athletic 15, Maidenhead 29; Tynedale 47, Winnington Park 10; Westcombe Park 14, Bracknell 21; Weston Super Mare 26, Ipswich 24; Whitchurch 32, Aspull 10

Second round

Bridgewater & Albion 15, Rosslyn Park 49; Esher 41, Tabard 3; Henley 100, Havant 19; Hull Ionians 13, Macclesfield 3; Kendal 20, Liverpool St Helens 7; Lydney 44, Camberley 34; Maidenhead 22, Launceston 21; Metropolitan Police 25, Winchester 14; New Brighton 25, Nuneaton 10; Newbury 37, Cheshunt 13; Nottingham 50, Preston Grasshoppers 3; Old Colfeians 23, Swanage & Wareham 32; Otley 18, Morley 20; Plymouth Albion 13, Barking 18; Reading 21, Penzance Newlyn 5; Sandal 6, Doncaster 3; Scunthorpe 0, Harrogate 29; Sedgley Park 20, Manchester 17; Tynedale 22, Stourbridge 30; Weston Super Mare 15, Bracknell 43; Wharfedale 27, Birmingham Solihull 5; Whitchurch 23, Bedford Athletic 15

Third round

Blackheath 21, Sedgley Park 22; Bracknell 13, Metropolitan Police 6; Bristol 55, Sandal 0; Coventry 26, Worcester 36; Esher 42, Harrogate 17; Exeter 81, Whitchurch 11; Hull Ionians 7, Newbury 31; Lydney 44, Stourbridge 5; Morley 39, Maidenhead 25; Moseley 22, Fylde 15; Nottingham 27, Wharfedale 17; Reading 12, Orrell 23; Rosslyn Park 12, Henley 16; Rotherham 8, London Welsh 6; Rugby 7, Leeds 68; Swanage & Wareham 6, Barking 36; Wakefield 8, Kendal 16; Waterloo 34, New Brighton 23

Fourth round

Bedford 22, Henley 29; Bristol 19, London Irish 43; Gloucester 31, Worcester 17; Harlequins 46, Esher 10; Kendal 20, London Scottish 25; Leicester 65, Barking 6; Manchester Sale 31, Northampton 47; Morley 8, Saracens 76; Moseley 24, Lydney 25; Newcastle 25, Bath 22; Nottingham 8, Exeter 24; Richmond 46, Newbury 12; Rotherham 24, Leeds 27; Sedgley Park 3, Wasps 53; Waterloo 18, Orrell 11; West Hartlepool 34, Bracknell 14

Fifth round

Gloucester 31, Henley 9; Leicester 49, Leeds 0; London Scottish 33, Harlequins 37; Lydney 0, Saracens 40; Northampton 6, London Irish 21; Richmond 37, Exeter 10; Wasps 27, Waterloo 10; West Hartlepool 21, Newcastle 32

Quarter-finals

Gloucester 15, Harlequins 13; Newcastle 15, Saracens 0; Richmond 15, Leicester 13; Wasps 19, London Irish 3

Semi-finals

Richmond 3, Newcastle 20; Wasps 35, Gloucester 21

Final *(at Twickenham)*

Wasps 29, Newcastle 19

Previous finals *(all at Twickenham)*

1972 Gloucester 17, Moseley 6
1973 Coventry 27, Bristol 15
1974 Coventry 26, London Scottish 6
1975 Bedford 28, Rosslyn Park 12
1976 Gosforth 23, Rosslyn Park 14
1977 Gosforth 27, Waterloo 11
1978 Gloucester 6, Leicester 3
1979 Leicester 15, Moseley 12
1980 Leicester 21, London Irish 9
1981 Leicester 22, Gosforth 15
1982 Gloucester 12, Moseley 12
      (title shared)
1983 Bristol 28, Leicester 22
1984 Bath 10, Bristol 9
1985 Bath 24, London Welsh 15
1986 Bath 25, Wasps 17
1987 Bath 19, Wasps 12
1988 Harlequins 28, Bristol 22
1989 Bath 10, Leicester 6
1990 Bath 48, Gloucester 6
1991 Harlequins 25, Northampton 13
      (aet)
1992 Bath 15, Harlequins 12 *(aet)*
1993 Leicester 23, Harlequins 16
1994 Bath 21, Leicester 9
1995 Bath 36, Wasps 16
1996 Bath 16, Leicester 15
1997 Leicester 9, Sale 3
1998 Saracens 48, Wasps 18

GLOUCESTER'S REPEAT PERFORMANCE

CHELTENHAM & GLOUCESTER CUP 1998-99

9 April 1999, Franklin's Gardens, Northampton
Gloucester 24 (2G 2T) **Bedford 9** (3PG)

There was a touch of *déjà vu* to the second Cheltenham and Gloucester Cup final. Apart from the fact that the match was staged at Northampton again, the organisers saw the same two sides contest the final, Gloucester repeating their 1998 triumph.

The competition embracing the clubs from the two senior divisions took place on the weekends when England were involved in international matches. As expected, four of the premier's sides came through the early rounds to reach the semi-finals. Gloucester beat Sale 45-37 at Kingsholm and there was an exciting 27-all tie between Bedford and Newcastle at Goldington Road, the home side going forward to the final on the strength of a superior try tally.

With nine of their side called up for England or England A duty on the weekend of the final, Gloucester wisely stuck to simple tactics. Their forwards were all-conquering. Ed Pearce was credited with two tries from pushovers, there was a penalty try and Dave Sims completed the scoring with a charge from short range. Bedford, who trailed 6-14 at the break, were unable to break the deadlock imposed by the Gloucester pack in the second half and their only addition to the score was a third penalty goal kicked by outside-half Tony Yapp. Phil Vickery, making his first appearance since October in the senior side, spent ten minutes in the sin-bin for a dangerous tackle on Bedford's Charlie Harrison.

Gloucester: A Lumsden; B Johnson, R Greenslade-Jones, R Tombs, T Beim; M Kimber, L Beck; T Windo, C Fortey, P Vickery, R Ward, D Sims (*capt*), A Eustace, E Pearce, N Carter *Substitutions:* A Deacon for Eustace (55 mins); A Harris for Ward (66 mins); R Stott for Deacon (66 mins)
Scorers *Tries:* Pearce (2), Sims, pen try *Conversions:* Kimber (2)
Bedford: S Howard; B Whetstone, D Harris, J Ewens, A Murdoch (*capt*); A Yapp, C Harrison; A Ozdemir, A Davis, A Olver, A Codling, A Duke, P Elphick, R Winters, J Forster *Substitutions:* V Hartland for Ozdemir (19 mins); P Hewitt for Codling (35 mins); R Underwood for Howard (51 mins); R Elliott for Harrison (73 mins)
Scorers *Penalty Goal:* Yapp (3)
Referee R Goodliffe

ENGLISH INTERNATIONAL PLAYERS
(up to 30 April 1999)

Note: Years given for Five Nations' matches are for second half of season; eg 1972 means season 1971-72. Years for all other matches refer to the actual year of the match. When a series has taken place, figures have been used to denote the particular matches in which players have featured. Thus 1984 *SA* 2 indicates that a player appeared in the second Test of the series.

Aarvold, C D (Cambridge U, W Hartlepool, Headingley, Blackheath) 1928 *A, W, I, F, S*, 1929 *W, I, F*, 1931 *W, S, F*, 1932 *SA, W, I, S*, 1933 *W*
Ackford, P J (Harlequins) 1988 *A*, 1989 *S, I, F, W, R, Fj*, 1990 *I, F, W, S, Arg* 3, 1991 *W, S, I, F, A, [NZ, It, F, S, A]*
Adams, A A (London Hospital) 1910 *F*
Adams, F R (Richmond) 1875 *I, S*, 1876 *S*, 1877 *I*, 1878 *S*, 1879 *S, I*
Adebayo, A A (Bath) 1996, *It*, 1997 *Arg* 1,2, *A* 2, *NZ* 1, 1998 *S*
Adey, G J (Leicester) 1976 *I, F*
Adkins, S J (Coventry) 1950 *I, F, S*, 1953 *W, I, F, S*
Agar, A E (Harlequins) 1952 *SA, W, S, I, F*, 1953 *W, I*
Alcock, A (Guy's Hospital) 1906 *SA*
Alderson, F H R (Hartlepool R) 1891 *W, I, S*, 1892 *W, S*, 1893 *W*
Alexander, H (Richmond) 1900 *I, S*, 1901 *W, I, S*, 1902 *W, I*
Alexander, W (Northern) 1927 *F*
Allison, D F (Coventry) 1956 *W, I, S, F*, 1957 *W*, 1958 *W, S*
Allport, A (Blackheath) 1892 *W*, 1893 *I*, 1894 *W, I, S*
Anderson, S (Rockcliff) 1899 *I*
Anderson, W F (Orrell) 1973 *NZ* 1
Anderton, C (Manchester FW) 1889 *M*
Andrew, C R (Cambridge U, Nottingham, Wasps, Toulouse, Newcastle) 1985 *R, F, S, I, W*, 1986 *W, S, I, F*, 1987 *I, F, W, [J (R), US]*, 1988 *S, I* 1,2, *A* 1,2, *Fj, A*, 1989 *S, I, F, W, R, Fj*, 1990 *I, F, W, S, Arg* 3, 1991 *W, S, I, F, Fj, A, [NZ, It, US, F, S, A]*, 1992 *S, I, F, W, C, SA*, 1993 *F, W, NZ*, 1994 *S, I, F, W, SA* 1,2, *R, C*, 1995 *F, W, S, [Arg, It, A, NZ, F]*, 1997 *W*(R)
Archer, G S (Bristol, Army, Newcastle) 1996 *S, I*, 1997 *A* 2, *NZ* 1, *SA, NZ* 2, 1998 *F, W, S, I, A* 1, *NZ* 1, *H, It*
Archer, H (Bridgwater A) 1909 *W, F, I*
Armstrong, R (Northern) 1925 *W*
Arthur, T G (Wasps) 1966 *W, I*
Ashby, R C (Wasps) 1966 *I, F*, 1967 *A*
Ashcroft, A (Waterloo) 1956 *W, I, S, F*, 1957 *W, I, F, S*, 1958 *W, A, I, F, S*, 1959 *I, F, S*
Ashcroft, A H (Birkenhead Park) 1909 *A*
Ashford, W (Richmond) 1897 *W, I*, 1898 *S, W*
Ashworth, A (Oldham) 1892 *I*
Askew, J G (Cambridge U) 1930 *W, I, F*
Aslett, A R (Richmond) 1926 *W, I, F, S*, 1929 *S, F*
Assinder, E W (O Edwardians) 1909 *A, W*
Aston, R L (Blackheath) 1890 *S, I*
Auty, J R (Headingley) 1935 *S*

Back, N A (Leicester) 1994 *S, I*, 1995 *[Arg* (t), *It, WS]*, 1997 *NZ* 1 (R), *SA, NZ* 2, 1998 *F, W, S, I, H, It, A* 2, *SA* 2, 1999 *S, I, F, W*
Bailey, M D (Cambridge U, Wasps) 1984 *SA* 1,2, 1987 *[US]*, 1989 *Fj*, 1990 *I, F, S* (R)
Bainbridge, S (Gosforth, Fylde) 1982 *F, W*, 1983 *F, W, S, I, NZ*, 1984 *S, I, F, W*, 1985 *NZ* 1,2, 1987 *F, W, S, [J, US]*
Baker, D G S (OMTs) 1955 *W, I, F, S*
Baker, E M (Moseley) 1895 *W, I, S*, 1896 *W, I, S*, 1897 *W*
Baker, H C (Clifton) 1887 *W*
Bance, J F (Bedford) 1954 *S*
Barley, B (Wakefield) 1984 *I, F, W, A*, 1988 *A* 1,2, *Fj*
Barnes, S (Bristol, Bath) 1984 *A*, 1985 *R* (R), *NZ* 1,2, 1986 *S* (R), *F* (R), 1987 *I* (R), 1988 *Fj*, 1993 *S, I*
Barr, R J (Leicester) 1932 *SA, W, I*
Barrett, E I M (Lennox) 1903 *S*
Barrington, T J M (Bristol) 1931 *W, I*
Barrington-Ward, L E (Edinburgh U) 1910 *W, I, F, S*
Barron, J H (Bingley) 1896 *S*, 1897 *W, I*
Bartlett, J T (Waterloo) 1951 *W*
Bartlett, R M (Harlequins) 1957 *W, I, F, S*, 1958 *I, F, S*
Barton, J (Coventry) 1967 *I, F, W*, 1972 *F*

Batchelor, T B (Oxford U) 1907 *F*
Bates, S M (Wasps) 1989 *R*
Bateson, A H (Otley) 1930 *W, I, F, S*
Bateson, H D (Liverpool) 1879 *I*
Batson, T (Blackheath) 1872 *S*, 1874 *S*, 1875 *I*
Batten, J M (Cambridge U) 1874 *S*
Baume, J L (Northern) 1950 *S*
Baxendell, J J N (Sale) 1998 *NZ* 2, *SA* 1
Baxter, J (Birkenhead Park) 1900 *W, I, S*
Bayfield, M C (Northampton) 1991 *Fj, A*, 1992 *S, I, F, W, C, SA*, 1993 *F, W, S, I*, 1994 *S, I, SA* 1,2, *R, C*, 1995 *I, F, W, S, [Arg, It, A, NZ, F]*, *SA, WS*, 1996 *F, W*
Bazley, R C (Waterloo) 1952 *I, F*, 1953 *W, I, F, S*, 1955 *W, I, F, S*
Beal, N D (Northampton) 1996 *Arg*, 1997 *A* 1, 1998 *NZ* 1,2, *SA* 1, *H* (R), *SA* 2, 1999 *S, F* (R)
Beaumont, W B (Fylde) 1975 *I, A* 1(R),2, 1976 *A, W, S, I, F*, 1977 *S, I, F, W*, 1978 *F, W, S, I, NZ*, 1979 *S, I, F, W, NZ*, 1980 *I, F, W, S*, 1981 *W, S, I, F, Arg* 1,2, 1982 *A, S*
Bedford, H (Morley) 1889 *M*, 1890 *S, I*
Bedford, L L (Headingley) 1931 *W, I*
Beer, I D S (Harlequins) 1955 *F, S*
Beese, M C (Liverpool) 1972 *W, I, F*
Beim, T D (Sale) 1998 *NZ* 1(R),2
Bell, F J (Northern) 1900 *W*
Bell, H (New Brighton) 1884 *I*
Bell, J L (Darlington) 1878 *I*
Bell, P J (Blackheath) 1968 *W, I, F, S*
Bell, R W (Northern) 1900 *W, I, S*
Bendon, G J (Wasps) 1959 *W, I, F, S*
Bennett, N O (St Mary's Hospital, Waterloo) 1947 *W, S, F*, 1948 *A, W, I, S*
Bennett, W N (Bedford, London Welsh) 1975 *S, A*1, 1976 *S* (R), 1979 *S, I, F, W*
Bennetts, B B (Penzance) 1909 *A, W*
Bentley, J (Sale, Newcastle) 1988 *I* 2, *A* 1, 1997 *A* 1, *SA*
Bentley, J E (Gipsies) 1871 *S*, 1872 *S*
Benton, S (Gloucester) 1998 *A* 1
Berridge, M J (Northampton) 1949 *W, I*
Berry, H (Gloucester) 1910 *W, I, F, S*
Berry, J (Tyldesley) 1891 *W, I, S*
Berry, J (T W (Leicester) 1939 *W, I, S*
Beswick, E (Swinton) 1882 *I, S*
Biggs, J M (UCH) 1878 *S*, 1879 *I*
Birkett, J G G (Harlequins) 1906 *S, F, SA*, 1907 *F, W, S*, 1908 *F, W,I , S*, 1910 *W, I, S*, 1911 *W, F, I , S*, 1912 *W, I , S, F*
Birkett, L (Clapham R) 1875 *S*, 1877 *I, S*
Birkett, R H (Clapham R) 1871 *S*, 1875 *S*, 1876 *S*, 1877 *I*
Bishop, C C (Blackheath) 1927 *F*
Black, B H (Blackheath) 1930 *W, I, F, S*, 1931 *W, I, S, F*, 1932 *S*, 1933 *W*
Blacklock, J H (Aspatria) 1898 *I*, 1899 *I*
Blakeway, P J (Gloucester) 1980 *I, F, W, S*, 1981 *W, S, I, F*, 1982 *I, F, W*, 1984 *I, F, W, SA* 1, 1985 *R, F, S, I*
Blakiston, A F (Northampton) 1920 *S*, 1921 *W, I, S, F*, 1922 *W*, 1923 *S, F*, 1924 *W, I, F, S*, 1925 *NZ, W, I, S, F*
Blatherwick, T (Manchester) 1878 *I*
Body, J A (Gipsies) 1872 *S*, 1873 *S*
Bolton, C A (United Services) 1909 *F*
Bolton, R (Harlequins) 1933 *W*, 1936 *S*, 1937 *S*, 1938 *W, I*
Bolton, W N (Blackheath) 1882 *I, S*, 1883 *W, I, S*, 1884 *W, I, S*, 1885 *I*, 1887 *I, S*
Bonaventura, M S (Blackheath) 1931 *W*
Bond, A M (Sale) 1978 *NZ*, 1979 *S, I, NZ*, 1980 *I*, 1982 *I*
Bonham-Carter, E (Oxford U) 1891 *S*
Bonsor, F (Bradford) 1886 *W, I, S*, 1887 *W, S*, 1889 *M*
Boobbyer, B (Rosslyn Park) 1950 *W, I, F, S*, 1951 *W, F*, 1952 *S, I, F*
Booth, L A (Headingley) 1933 *W, I, S*, 1934 *S*, 1935 *W, I, S*
Botting, I J (Oxford U) 1950 *W, I*

115

Boughton, H J (Gloucester) 1935 *W, I, S*
Boyle, C W (Oxford U) 1873 *S*
Boyle, S B (Gloucester) 1983 *W, S, I*
Boylen, F (Hartlepool R) 1908 *F, W, I, S*
Bracken, K P P (Bristol, Saracens) 1993 *NZ*, 1994 *S, I, C*, 1995 *I, F, W, S, [It, WS* (t)], *SA*, 1996 *It* (R), 1997 *Arg* 1,2, *A* 2, *NZ* 1,2, 1998 *F, W*, 1999 *S*(R), *I, F*
Bradby, M S (United Services) 1922 *I, F*
Bradley, R (W Hartlepool) 1903 *W*
Bradshaw, H (Bramley) 1892 *S*, 1893 *W, I, S*, 1894 *W, I, S*
Brain, S E (Coventry) 1984 *SA* 2, *A* (R), 1985 *R, F, S, I, W, NZ* 1,2, 1986 *W, S, I, F*
Braithwaite, J (Leicester) 1905 *NZ*
Braithwaite-Exley, B (Headingley) 1949 *W*
Brettargh, A T (Liverpool OB) 1900 *W*, 1903 *I, S*, 1904 *W, I, S*, 1905 *I, S*
Brewer, J (Gipsies) 1876 *I*
Briggs, A (Bradford) 1892 *W, I, S*
Brinn, A (Gloucester) 1972 *W, I, S*
Broadley, T (Bingley) 1893 *W, S*, 1894 *W, I, S*, 1896 *S*
Bromet, W E (Richmond) 1891 *W, I*, 1892 *W, I, S*, 1893 *W, I, S*, 1895 *W, I, S*, 1896 *I*
Brook, P W P (Harlequins) 1930 *S*, 1931 *F*, 1936 *S*
Brooke, T J (Richmond) 1968 *F, S*
Brooks, F G (Bedford) 1906 *SA*
Brooks, M J (Oxford U) 1874 *S*
Brophy, T J (Liverpool) 1964 *I, F, S*, 1965 *W, I*, 1966 *W, I, F*
Brough, J W (Silloth) 1925 *NZ, W*
Brougham, H (Harlequins) 1912 *W, I, S, F*
Brown, A A (Exeter) 1938 *S*
Brown, L G (Oxford U, Blackheath) 1911 *W, F, I, S*, 1913 *SA, W, F, I, S*, 1914 *W, I, S, F*, 1921 *W, I, S, F*, 1922 *W*
Brown S P (Richmond) 1998 *A* 1, *SA* 1
Brown, T W (Bristol) 1928 *S*, 1929 *W, I, S, F*, 1932 *S*, 1933 *W, I, S*
Brunton, J (N Durham) 1914 *W, I, S*
Brutton, E B (Cambridge U) 1886 *S*
Bryden, C C (Clapham R) 1876 *I*, 1877 *S*
Bryden, H A (Clapham R) 1874 *S*
Buckingham, R A (Leicester) 1927 *F*
Bucknall, A L (Richmond) 1969 *SA*, 1970 *I, W, S, F*, 1971 *W, I, F, S* (2[1C])
Buckton, J R D (Saracens) 1988 *A* (R), 1990 *Arg* 1,2
Budd, A (Blackheath) 1878 *I*, 1879 *S, I*, 1881 *W, S*
Budworth, R T D (Blackheath) 1890 *W*, 1891 *W, S*
Bull, A G (Northampton) 1914 *W*
Bullough, E (Wigan) 1892 *W, I, S*
Bulpitt, M P (Blackheath) 1970 *S*
Bulteel, A J (Manchester) 1876 *I*
Bunting, W L (Moseley) 1897 *I, S*, 1898 *I, S, W*, 1899 *S*, 1900 *S*, 1901 *I, S*
Burland, D W (Bristol) 1931 *W, I, F*, 1932 *I, S*, 1933 *W, I, S*
Burns, B H (Blackheath) 1871 *S*
Burton, G W (Blackheath) 1879 *S, I*, 1880 *S, I*, 1881 *I, W, S*
Burton, H C (Richmond) 1926 *W*
Burton, M A (Gloucester) 1972 *W, I, F, S, SA*, 1974 *F, W*, 1975 *S, A* 1,2, 1976 *A, W, S, I, F*, 1978 *F, W*
Bush, J A (Clifton) 1872 *S*, 1873 *S*, 1875 *S*, 1876 *I, S*
Butcher, C J S (Harlequins) 1984 *SA* 1,2, *A*
Butcher, W V (Streatham) 1903 *S*, 1904 *W, I, S*, 1905 *W, I, S*
Butler, A G (Harlequins) 1937 *W, I*
Butler, P E (Gloucester) 1975 *A* 1, 1976 *F*
Butterfield, J (Northampton) 1953 *F, S*, 1954 *W, NZ, I, S, F*, 1955 *W, I, F, S*, 1956 *W, I, S, F*, 1957 *W, I, F, S*, 1958 *W, A, I, F, S*, 1959 *W, I, F, S*
Byrne, F A (Moseley) 1897 *W*
Byrne, J F (Moseley) 1894 *W, I, S*, 1895 *I, S*, 1896 *I*, 1897 *W, I, S*, 1898 *I, S, W*, 1899 *I*

Cain, J J (Waterloo) 1950 *W*
Callard, J E B (Bath) 1993 *NZ*, 1994 *S, I*, 1995 *[WS], SA*
Campbell, D A (Cambridge U) 1937 *W, I*
Candler, P L (St Bart's Hospital) 1935 *W*, 1936 *NZ, W, I, S*, 1937 *W, I, S*, 1938 *W, S*
Cannell, L B (Oxford U, St Mary's Hospital) 1948 *F*, 1949 *W, I, F, S*, 1950 *W, I, F, S*, 1952 *SA, W*, 1953 *W, I, F*, 1956 *I, S, F*, 1957 *W, I*
Caplan, D W N (Headingley) 1978 *S, I*
Cardus, R M (Roundhay) 1979 *F, W*
Carey, G M (Blackheath) 1895 *W, I, S*, 1896 *W, I*

Carleton, J (Orrell) 1979 *NZ*, 1980 *I, F, W, S*, 1981 *W, S, I, F, Arg* 1,2, 1982 *A, S, I, F, W*, 1983 *F, W, S, I, NZ*, 1984 *S, I, F, W, A*
Carling, W D C (Durham U, Harlequins) 1988 *F, W, S, I* 1,2, *A2, Fj, A*, 1989 *S, I, F, W, Fj*, 1990 *I, F, W, S, Arg* 1,2,3, 1991 *W, S, I, F, Fj, A, [NZ, It, US, F, S, A]*, 1992 *S, I, F, W, C, SA*, 1993 *F, W, S, I, NZ*, 1994 *S, I, F, W, SA* 1,2, *R, C*, 1995 *I, F, W, S, [Arg, WS, A, NZ, F], SA, WS*, 1996 *F, W, S, I, It, Arg*
Carpenter, A D (Gloucester) 1932 *SA*
Carr, R S L (Manchester) 1939 *W, I, S*
Cartwright, V H (Nottingham) 1903 *W, I, S*, 1904 *W, S*, 1905 *W, I, S, NZ*, 1906 *W, I, S, F, SA*
Catcheside, H C (Percy Park) 1924 *W, I, F, S*, 1926 *W, I*, 1927 *I, S*
Catt, M J (Bath) 1994 *W* (R), *C* (R), 1995 *I, F, W, S, [Arg, It, WS, A, NZ, F], SA, WS*, 1996 *F, W, S, I, It, Arg*, 1997 *W, Arg* 1, *A* 1,2, *NZ* 1, *SA*, 1998 *F, W* (R), *I, A* 2(R), *SA* 2, 1999 *S, F, W*
Cattell, R H B (Blackheath) 1895 *W, I, S*, 1896 *W, I, S*, 1900 *W*
Cave, J W (Richmond) 1889 *M*
Cave, W T C (Blackheath) 1905 *W*
Challis, R (Bristol) 1957 *I, F, S*
Chambers, E L (Bedford) 1908 *F*, 1910 *W, I*
Chantrill, B S (Bristol) 1924 *W, I, F, S*
Chapman, C E (Cambridge U) 1884 *W*
Chapman D E (Richmond) 1998 *A* 1(R)
Chapman, F E (Hartlepool) 1910 *W, I, F, S*, 1912 *W*, 1914 *W, I*
Cheesman, W I (OMTs) 1913 *SA, W, F, I*
Cheston, E C (Richmond) 1873 *S*, 1874 *S*, 1875 *I, S*, 1876 *S*
Chilcott, G J (Bath) 1984 *A*, 1986 *I, F*, 1987 *F* (R), *W, [J, US, W* (R)], 1988 *I* 2 (R), *Fj*, 1989 *I* (R), *F, W, R*
Christopherson, P (Blackheath) 1891 *W, S*
Clark, C W H (Liverpool) 1876 *I*
Clarke, A J (Coventry) 1935 *W, I, S*, 1936 *NZ, W, I*
Clarke, B B (Bath, Richmond) 1992 *SA*, 1993 *F, W, S, I, NZ*, 1994 *S, F, W, SA* 1,2, *R, C*, 1995 *I, F, W, S, [Arg, It, A, NZ, F], SA, WS*, 1996 *F, W, S, I, Arg* (R), 1997 *W, Arg* 1,2, *A* 1 (R), 1998 *A* 1(t),*NZ* 1,2, *SA* 1, *H, It*
Clarke, S J S (Cambridge U, Blackheath) 1963 *W, I, F, S, NZ* 1,2, *A*, 1964 *NZ, W, I*, 1965 *I, F, S*
Clayton, J H (Liverpool) 1871 *S*
Clements, J W (O Cranleighans) 1959 *I, F, S*
Cleveland, C R (Blackheath) 1887 *W, S*
Clibborn, W G (Richmond) 1886 *W, I, S*, 1887 *W, I, S*
Clough, F J (Cambridge U, Orrell) 1986 *I, F*, 1987 *[J* (R), *US]*
Coates, C H (Yorkshire W) 1880 *S*, 1881 *S*, 1882 *S*
Coates, V H M (Bath) 1913 *SA, W, F, I, S*
Cobby, W (Hull) 1900 *W*
Cockerham, A (Bradford Olicana) 1900 *W*
Cockerill, R (Leicester) 1997 *Arg* 1 (R), 2, *A* 2 (t + R), *NZ* 1, *SA, NZ* 2, 1998 *W, S, I, A* 1, *NZ* 1,2, *SA* 1, *H, It, A* 2, *SA* 2, 1999 *S, I, F, W*
Colclough, M J (Angoulême, Wasps, Swansea) 1978 *S, I*, 1979 *NZ*, 1980 *F, W, S*, 1981 *W, S, I, F*, 1982 *A, S, I, F, W*, 1983 *F, NZ*, 1984 *S, I, F, W*, 1986 *W, S, I, F*
Coley, E (Northampton) 1929 *F*, 1932 *W*
Collins, P J (Camborne) 1952 *S, I, F*
Collins, W E (O Cheltonians) 1874 *S*, 1875 *I, S*, 1876 *I, S*
Considine, S G U (Bath) 1925 *F*
Conway, G S (Cambridge U, Rugby, Manchester) 1920 *F, I, S*, 1921 *F*, 1922 *W, I, F, S*, 1923 *W, I, S, F*, 1924 *W, I, F, S*, 1925 *NZ*, 1927 *W*
Cook, J G (Bedford) 1937 *S*
Cook, P W (Richmond) 1965 *I, F*
Cooke, D A (Harlequins) 1976 *W, S, I, F*
Cooke, D H (Harlequins) 1981 *W, S, I, F*, 1984 *I*, 1985 *R, F, S, I, W, NZ* 1,2
Cooke, P (Richmond) 1939 *W, I*
Coop, T (Leigh) 1892 *S*
Cooper, J G (Moseley) 1909 *A, W*
Cooper, M J (Moseley) 1973 *F, S, NZ* 2 (R), 1975 *F, W*, 1976 *A, W*, 1977 *S, I, F, W*
Coopper, S F (Blackheath) 1900 *W*, 1902 *W, I*, 1905 *W, I, S*, 1907 *W*
Corbett, L J (Bristol) 1921 *F*, 1923 *W, I*, 1924 *W, I, F, S*, 1925 *NZ, W, I, S, F*, 1927 *W, I, S, F*
Corless, B J (Coventry, Moseley) 1976 *A, I* (R), 1977 *S, I, F, W*, 1978 *F, W, S, I*

Corry, M E (Bristol, Leicester) 1997 *Arg* 1,2, 1998 *H, It, SA* 2(t), 1999 *F*(R)
Cotton, F E (Loughborough Colls, Coventry, Sale) 1971 *S* (2[1C]), *P,* 1973 *W, I, F, S, NZ* 2, *A,* 1974 *S, I,* 1975 *I, F, W,* 1976 *A, W, S, I, F,* 1977 *S, I, F, W,* 1978 *S, I,* 1979 *NZ,* 1980 *I, F, W, S,* 1981 *W*
Coulman, M J (Moseley) 1967 *A, I, F, S, W,* 1968 *W, I, F, S*
Coulson, T J (Coventry) 1927 *W,* 1928 *A, W*
Court, E D (Blackheath) 1885 *W*
Coverdale, H (Blackheath) 1910 *F,* 1912 *I, F,* 1920 *W*
Cove-Smith, R (OMTs) 1921 *S, F,* 1922 *I, F, S,* 1923 *W, I, S, F,* 1924 *W, I, S, F,* 1925 *NZ, W, I, S, F,* 1927 *W, I, S, F,* 1928 *A, W, I, F, S,* 1929 *W, I*
Cowling, R J (Leicester) 1977 *S, I, F, W,* 1978 *F, NZ,* 1979 *S, I*
Cowman, A R (Loughborough Colls, Coventry) 1971 *S* (2[1C]), *P,* 1973 *W, I*
Cox, N S (Sunderland) 1901 *S*
Cranmer, P (Richmond, Moseley) 1934 *W, I, S,* 1935 *W, I, S,* 1936 *NZ, W, I, S,* 1937 *W, I, S,* 1938 *W, I, S*
Creed, R N (Coventry) 1971 *P*
Cridlan, A G (Blackheath) 1935 *W, I, S*
Crompton, C A (Blackheath) 1871 *S*
Crosse, C W (Oxford U) 1874 *S,* 1875 *I*
Cumberlege, B S (Blackheath) 1920 *W, I, S,* 1921 *W, I, S, F,* 1922 *W*
Cumming, D C (Blackheath) 1925 *S, F*
Cunliffe, F L (RMA) 1874 *S*
Currey, F I (Marlborough N) 1872 *S*
Currie, J D (Oxford U, Harlequins, Bristol) 1956 *W, I, S, F,* 1957 *W, I, F, S,* 1958 *W, A, I, F, S,* 1959 *W, I, F, S,* 1960 *W, I, F, S,* 1961 *SA,* 1962 *W, I, F*
Cusani, D A (Orrell) 1987 *I*
Cusworth, L (Leicester) 1979 *NZ,* 1982 *F, W,* 1983 *F, W, NZ,* 1984 *S, I, F, W,* 1988 *F, W*

D'Aguilar, F B G (Royal Engineers) 1872 *S*
Dallaglio, L B N (Wasps) 1995 *SA* (R), *WS,* 1996 *F, W, S, I, It, Arg,* 1997 *S, I, F,* 1998 *F, W, A* 1,2, *NZ* 1, *SA, NZ* 2, 1998 *F, W, S, I, A* 2, *SA* 2, 1999 *S, I, F, W*
Dalton, T J (Coventry) 1969 *S*(R)
Danby, T (Harlequins) 1949 *W*
Daniell, J (Richmond) 1899 *W,* 1900 *I, S,* 1902 *I, S,* 1904 *I, S*
Darby, A J L (Birkenhead Park) 1899 *I*
Davenport, A (Ravenscourt Park) 1871 *S*
Davey, J (Redruth) 1908 *S,* 1909 *W*
Davey, R F (Teignmouth) 1931 *W*
Davidson, Jas (Aspatria) 1897 *S,* 1898 *S, W,* 1899 *I, S*
Davidson, Jos (Aspatria) 1899 *W, S*
Davies, G H (Cambridge U, Coventry, Wasps) 1981 *S, I, F, Arg* 1,2, 1982 *A, S, I,* 1983 *F, W, S,* 1984 *S, SA* 1,2, 1985 *R* (R), *NZ* 1,2, 1986 *W, S, I, F*
Davies, P H (Sale) 1927 *I*
Davies, V G (Harlequins) 1922 *W,* 1925 *NZ*
Davies, W J A (United Services, RN) 1913 *SA, W, F, I, S,* 1914 *I, S, F,* 1920 *F, I, S,* 1921 *W, I, S, F,* 1922 *I, F, S,* 1923 *W, I, S, F*
Davies, W P C (Harlequins) 1953 *S,* 1954 *NZ, I,* 1955 *W, I, F, S,* 1956 *W,* 1957 *F, S,* 1958 *W*
Davis, A M (Torquay Ath, Harlequins) 1963 *W, I, S, NZ* 1,2, 1964 *NZ, W, I, F, S,* 1966 *W,* 1967 *A,* 1969 *SA,* 1970 *I, W, S*
Dawe, R G R (Bath) 1987 *I, F, W, [US],* 1995 *[WS]*
Dawson, E F (RIEC) 1878 *I*
Dawson, M J S (Northampton) 1995 *WS,* 1996 *F, W, S, I,* 1997 *A* 1, *SA, NZ* 2 (R), 1998 *W* (R), *S, I, NZ* 1,2, *SA* 1, *H, It, A* 2, *SA* 2, 1999 *S, F*(R),
Day, H L V (Leicester) 1920 *W,* 1922 *W, F,* 1926 *S*
Dean, G J (Harlequins) 1931 *I*
Dee, J M (Hartlepool R) 1962 *S,* 1963 *NZ* 1
Devitt, Sir T G (Blackheath) 1926 *I, F,* 1928 *A, W*
Dewhurst, J H (Richmond) 1887 *W, I, S,* 1890 *W*
De Glanville, P R (Bath) 1992 *SA* (R), 1993 *W* (R), *NZ,* 1994 *S, I, F, W, SA* 1,2, *C* (R), 1995 *[Arg* (R), *It, WS],* *SA* (R), 1996 *W* (R), *I* (R), *It,* 1997 *S, I, F, W, Arg* 1,2, *A* 1,2, *NZ* 1,2, 1998 *W* (R), *S* (R), *I* (R), *A* 2, *SA* 2
De Winton, R F C (Marlborough N) 1893 *W*
Dibble, R (Bridgwater A) 1906 *S, F, SA,* 1908 *F, W, I, S,* 1909 *A, W, F, I, S,* 1910 *S, 1911 *W, F, S,* 1912 *W, I, S*
Dicks, J (Northampton) 1934 *W, I, S,* 1935 *W, I, S,* 1936 *S,* 1937 *I*
Dillon, E W (Blackheath) 1904 *W, I, S,* 1905 *W*
Dingle, A J (Hartlepool R) 1913 *I,* 1914 *S, F*

Diprose, A J (Saracens) 1997 *Arg* 1,2, *A* 2, *NZ* 1, 1998 *W* (R), *S* (R), *I, A* 1, *NZ* 2, *SA* 1
Dixon, P J (Harlequins, Gosforth) 1971 *P,* 1972 *W, I, F, S,* 1973 *I, F, S,* 1974 *S, I, F, W,* 1975 *I,* 1976 *F,* 1977 *S, I, F, W,* 1978 *F, S, I, NZ*
Dobbs, G E B (Devonport A) 1906 *W, I*
Doble, S A (Moseley) 1972 *SA,* 1973 *NZ* 1, *W*
Dobson, D D (Newton Abbot) 1902 *W, I, S,* 1903 *W, I, S*
Dobson, T H (Bradford) 1895 *S*
Dodge, P W (Leicester) 1978 *W, S, I, NZ,* 1979 *S, I, F, W,* 1980 *W, S,* 1981 *W, S, I, F, Arg* 1,2, 1982 *A, S, F, W,* 1983 *F, W, S, I, NZ,* 1985 *R, F, S, I, W, NZ* 1,2
Donnelly, M P (Oxford U) 1947 *I*
Dooley, W A (Preston Grasshoppers, Fylde) 1985 *R, F, S, I, W, NZ* 2 (R), 1986 *W, S, I, F,* 1987 *F, W, [A, US, W],* 1988 *F, W, S, I* 1,2, *A* 1,2, *Fj, A,* 1989 *S, I, F, W, R, Fj,* 1990 *I, F, W, S, Arg* 1,2,3, 1991 *W, S, I, F, [NZ, US, F, S, A],* 1992 *S, I, F, W, C, SA,* 1993 *W, S, I*
Dovey, B A (Rosslyn Park) 1963 *W, I*
Down, P J (Bristol) 1909 *A*
Dowson, A O (Moseley) 1899 *S*
Drake-Lee, N J (Cambridge U, Leicester) 1963 *W, I, F, S,* 1964 *NZ, W, I,* 1965 *W*
Duckett, H (Bradford) 1893 *I, S*
Duckham, D J (Coventry) 1969 *I, F, S, W, SA,* 1970 *I, W, S, F,* 1971 *W, I, F, S* (2[1C]), *P,* 1972 *W, I, F, S,* 1973 *NZ* 1, *W, I, F, S, NZ* 2, *A,* 1974 *S, I, F, W,* 1975 *I, F, W,* 1976 *A, W, S*
Dudgeon, H W (Richmond) 1897 *S,* 1898 *I, S, W,* 1899 *W, I, S*
Dugdale, J M (Ravenscourt Park) 1871 *S*
Dun, A F (Wasps) 1984 *W*
Duncan, R F H (Guy's Hospital) 1922 *I, F, S*
Dunkley, P E (Harlequins) 1931 *I, S,* 1936 *NZ, W, I, S*
Duthie, J (W Hartlepool) 1903 *W*
Dyson, J W (Huddersfield) 1890 *S,* 1892 *S,* 1893 *I, S*

Ebdon, P J (Wellington) 1897 *W, I*
Eddison, J H (Headingley) 1912 *W, I, S, F*
Edgar, C S (Birkenhead Park) 1901 *S*
Edwards, R (Newport) 1921 *W, I, S, F,* 1922 *W, F,* 1923 *W,* 1924 *W, F, S,* 1925 *NZ*
Egerton, D W (Bath) 1988 *I* 2, *A* 1, *Fj* (R), *A,* 1989 *Fj,* 1990 *I, Arg* 2 (R)
Elliot, C H (Sunderland) 1886 *W*
Elliot, E W (Sunderland) 1901 *W, I, S,* 1904 *W*
Elliot, W (United Services, RN) 1932 *I, S,* 1933 *W, I, S,* 1934 *W, I*
Elliott, A E (St Thomas's Hospital) 1894 *S*
Ellis, J (Wakefield) 1939 *S*
Ellis, S S (Queen's House) 1880 *I*
Emmott, C (Bradford) 1892 *W*
Enthoven, H J (Richmond) 1878 *I*
Estcourt, N S D (Blackheath) 1955 *S*
Evans, B J (Leicester) 1988 *A* 2, *Fj*
Evans, E (Sale) 1948 *A,* 1950 *W,* 1951 *I, F, S,* 1952 *SA, W, S, I, F,* 1953 *I, F, S,* 1954 *W, NZ, I, F,* 1956 *W, I, S, F,* 1957 *W, I, F, S,* 1958 *W, A, I, F, S*
Evans, G W (Coventry) 1972 *S,* 1973 *W* (R), *F, S, NZ* 2, 1974 *S, I, F, W*
Evans, N L (RNEC) 1932 *W, I, S,* 1933 *W, I*
Evanson, A M (Richmond) 1883 *W, I, S,* 1884 *S*
Evanson, W A D (Richmond) 1875 *S,* 1877 *S,* 1878 *S,* 1879 *S, I*
Evershed, F (Blackheath) 1889 *M,* 1890 *W, S, I,* 1892 *W, I, S,* 1893 *W, I, S*
Eyres, W C T (Richmond) 1927 *I*

Fagan, A R St L (Richmond) 1887 *I*
Fairbrother, K E (Coventry) 1969 *I, F, S, W, SA,* 1970 *I, W, S, F,* 1971 *W, I, F*
Faithfull, C K T (Harlequins) 1924 *I,* 1926 *F, S*
Fallas, H (Wakefield T) 1884 *I*
Fegan, J H C (Blackheath) 1895 *W, I, S*
Fernandes, C W L (Leeds) 1881 *I, W, S*
Fidler, J H (Gloucester) 1981 *Arg* 1,2, 1984 *SA* 1,2
Fidler, R J (Gloucester) 1998 *NZ* 2, *SA* 1
Field, E (Middlesex W) 1893 *W, I*
Fielding, K J (Moseley, Loughborough Colls) 1969 *I, F, S, SA,* 1970 *I, F,* 1972 *W, I, F, S*
Finch, R T (Cambridge U) 1880 *S*
Finlan, J F (Moseley) 1967 *I, F, S, W, NZ,* 1968 *W, I, 1969 *I, F, S, W,* 1970 *F,* 1973 *NZ* 1
Finlinson, H W (Blackheath) 1895 *W, I, S*

Finney, S (RIE Coll) 1872 *S*, 1873 *S*
Firth, F (Halifax) 1894 *W, I, S*
Fletcher, N C (OMTs) 1901 *W, I, S*, 1903 *S*
Fletcher, T (Seaton) 1897 *W*
Fletcher, W R B (Marlborough N) 1873 *S*, 1875 *S*
Fookes, E F (Sowerby Bridge) 1896 *W, I, S*, 1897 *W, I, S*, 1898 *I, W*, 1899 *I, S*
Ford, P J (Gloucester) 1964 *W, I, F, S*
Forrest, J W (United Services, RN) 1930 *W, I, F, S*, 1931 *W, I, S, F*, 1934 *I, S*
Forrest, R (Wellington) 1899 *W*, 1900 *S*, 1902 *I, S*, 1903 *I, S*
Foulds, R T (Waterloo) 1929 *W, I*
Fowler, F D (Manchester) 1878 *S*, 1879 *S*
Fowler, H (Oxford U) 1878 *S*, 1881 *W, S*
Fowler, R H (Leeds) 1877 *I*
Fox, F H (Wellington) 1890 *W, S*
Francis, T E S (Cambridge U) 1926 *W, I, F, S*
Frankcom, G P (Cambridge U, Bedford) 1965 *W, I, F, S*
Fraser, E C (Blackheath) 1875 *I*
Fraser, G (Richmond) 1902 *W, I, S*, 1903 *W, I*
Freakes, H D (Oxford U) 1938 *W*, 1939 *W, I*
Freeman, H (Marlborough N) 1872 *S*, 1873 *S*, 1874 *S*
French, R J (St Helens) 1961 *W, I, F, S*
Fry, H A (Liverpool) 1934 *W, I, S*
Fry, T W (Queen's House) 1880 *I, S*, 1881 *W*
Fuller, H G (Cambridge U) 1882 *I, S*, 1883 *W, I, S*, 1884 *W*

Gadney, B C (Leicester, Headingley) 1932 *I, S*, 1933 *I, S*, 1934 *W, I, S*, 1935 *I, S*, 1936 *NZ, W, I, S*, 1937 *S*, 1938 *W*
Gamlin, H T (Blackheath) 1899 *W, S*, 1900 *W, I, S*, 1901 *S*, 1902 *W, I, S*, 1903 *W, I, S*, 1904 *W, I, S*
Gardner, E R (Devonport Services) 1921 *W, I, S*, 1922 *W, I, F*, 1923 *W, I, S, F*
Gardner, H P (Richmond) 1878 *I*
Garforth, D J (Leicester) 1997 *W* (R), *Arg* 1,2, *A* 1, *NZ* 1, *SA, NZ* 2, 1998 *F, W* (R), *S, I, H, It, A* 2, *SA* 2, 1999 *S, I, F, W*
Garnett, H W T (Bradford) 1877 *S*
Gavins, M N (Leicester) 1961 *W*
Gay, D J (Bath) 1968 *W, I, F, S*
Gent, D R (Gloucester) 1905 *NZ*, 1906 *W, I*, 1910 *W, I*
Genth, J S M (Manchester) 1874 *S*, 1875 *S*
George, J T (Falmouth) 1947 *S, F*, 1949 *I*
Gerrard, R A (Bath) 1932 *SA, W, I, S*, 1933 *W, I, S*, 1934 *W, I, S*, 1936 *NZ, W, I, S*
Gibbs, G A (Bristol) 1947 *F*, 1948 *I*
Gibbs, J C (Harlequins) 1925 *NZ, W*, 1926 *F*, 1927 *W, I, S, F*
Gibbs, N (Harlequins) 1954 *S, F*
Giblin, L F (Blackheath) 1896 *W, I*, 1897 *S*
Gibson, A S (Manchester) 1871 *S*
Gibson, C O P (Northern) 1901 *W*
Gibson, G R (Northern) 1899 *W*, 1901 *S*
Gibson, T A (Northern) 1905 *W, S*
Gilbert, F G (Devonport Services) 1923 *W, I*
Gilbert, R (Devonport A) 1908 *W, I, S*
Giles, J L (Coventry) 1935 *W, I*, 1937 *W, I*, 1938 *I, S*
Gittings, W J (Coventry) 1967 *NZ*
Glover, P B (Bath) 1967 *A*, 1971 *F, P*
Godfray, R E (Richmond) 1905 *NZ*
Godwin, H O (Coventry) 1959 *F, S*, 1963 *S, NZ* 1,2, *A*, 1964 *NZ, I, F, S*, 1967 *NZ*
Gomarsall, A C T (Wasps) 1996 *It, Arg*, 1997 *S, I, F, Arg* 2 (R)
Gordon-Smith, G W (Blackheath) 1900 *W, I, S*
Gotley, A L H (Oxford U) 1910 *F, S*, 1911 *W, F, I, S*
Graham, D (Aspatria) 1901 *W*
Graham, H J (Wimbledon H) 1875 *I, S*, 1876 *I, S*
Graham, J D G (Wimbledon H) 1876 *I*
Gray, A (Otley) 1947 *W, I, S*
Grayson, P J (Northampton) 1995 *WS*, 1996 *F, W, S, I*, 1997 *S, I, F, A* 2 (t), *SA* (R), *NZ* 2, 1998 *F, W, S, I, H, It, A* 2, 1999 *I*
Green, J (Skipton) 1905 *I*, 1906 *S, F, SA*, 1907 *F, W, I, S*
Green, J F (West Kent) 1871 *S*
Green, W R (Wasps) 1997 *A* 2, 1998 *NZ* 1(t+R)
Greening, P B T (Gloucester) 1996 *It* (R), 1997 *W* (R), *Arg* 1 1998 *NZ* 1(R),2(R)
Greenstock, N J J (Wasps) 1997 *Arg* 1,2, *A* 1, *SA*
Greenwell, J R (Rockcliff) 1893 *W, I*
Greenwood, J E (Cambridge U, Leicester) 1912 *F*, 1913 *SA, W, F, I, S*, 1914 *W, S, F*, 1920 *W, F, I, S*
Greenwood, J R H (Waterloo) 1966 *I, F, S*, 1967 *A*, 1969 *I*

Greenwood, W J H (Leicester) 1997 *A* 2, *NZ* 1, *SA, NZ* 2, 1998 *F, W, S, I, H, It*
Greg, W (Manchester) 1876 *I, S*
Gregory, G G (Bristol) 1931 *I, S, F*, 1932 *SA, W, I, S*, 1933 *W, I, S*, 1934 *W, I, S*
Gregory, J A (Blackheath) 1949 *W*
Grewcock, D J (Coventry, Saracens) 1997 *Arg* 2, *SA*, 1998 *W* (R), *S* (R), *I* (R), *A* 1, *NZ* 1, *SA* 2(R), 1999 *S*(R)
Grylls, W M (Redruth) 1905 *I*
Guest, R H (Waterloo) 1939 *W, I, S*, 1947 *W, I, S, F*, 1948 *A, W, I, S*, 1949 *F, S*
Guillemard, A G (West Kent) 1871 *S*, 1872 *S*
Gummer, C H A (Plymouth A) 1929 *F*
Gunner, C R (Marlborough N) 1876 *I*
Gurdon, C (Richmond) 1880 *I, S*, 1881 *I, W, S*, 1882 *I, S*, 1883 *S*, 1884 *W, S*, 1885 *I*, 1886 *W, I, S*
Gurdon, E T (Richmond) 1878 *S*, 1879 *I*, 1880 *S*, 1881 *I, W, S*, 1882 *I, S*, 1883 *W, I, S*, 1884 *W, I, S*, 1885 *W, I*, 1886 *S*
Guscott, J C (Bath) 1989 *R, Fj*, 1990 *I, F, W, S, Arg* 3, 1991 *W, S, I, F, Fj, A*, [*NZ, It, F, S, A*], 1992 *S, I, F, W, C, SA*, 1993 *F, W, S, I*, 1994 *R, C*, 1995 *I, F, W, S*, [*Arg, It, A, NZ, F*], *SA, WS*, 1996 *F, W, S, I, Arg*, 1997 *I* (R), *W* (R), 1998 *F, W, S, I, H, It, A* 2, *SA* 2, 1999 *S, I, F*

Haag, M (Bath) 1997 *Arg* 1,2
Haigh, L (Manchester) 1910 *W, I, S*, 1911 *W, F, I, S*
Hale, P M (Moseley) 1969 *SA*, 1970 *I, W*
Hall, C (Gloucester) 1901 *I, S*
Hall, J (N Durham) 1894 *W, I, S*
Hall, J P (Bath) 1984 *S* (R), *I, F, SA* 1,2, *A*, 1985 *R, F, S, I, W, NZ* 1,2, 1986 *W, S*, 1987 *I, F, W, S*, 1990 *Arg* 3, 1994 *S*
Hall, N M (Richmond) 1947 *W, I, S, F*, 1949 *W, I*, 1952 *SA, W, S, I, F*, 1953 *W, I, F, S*, 1955 *W, I*
Halliday, S J (Bath, Harlequins) 1986 *W, S*, 1987 *S*, 1988 *S, I* 1,2, *A* 1, *A*, 1989 *S, I, F, W, R, Fj* (R), 1990 *W, S*, 1991 [*US, S, A*], 1992 *S, I, F, W*
Hamersley, A St G (Marlborough N) 1871 *S*, 1872 *S*, 1873 *S*, 1874 *S*
Hamilton-Hill, E A (Harlequins) 1936 *NZ, W, I*
Hamilton-Wickes, R H (Cambridge U) 1924 *I*, 1925 *NZ, W, I, S, F*, 1926 *W, I, S*, 1927 *W*
Hammett, E D G (Newport) 1920 *W, F, S*, 1921 *W, I, S, F*, 1922 *W*
Hammond, C E L (Harlequins) 1905 *S, NZ*, 1906 *W, I, S, F*, 1908 *W, I*
Hancock, A W (Northampton) 1965 *F, S*, 1966 *F*
Hancock, G E (Birkenhead Park) 1939 *W, I, S*
Hancock, J H (Newport) 1955 *W, I*
Hancock, P F (Blackheath) 1886 *W, I*, 1890 *W*
Hancock, P S (Richmond) 1904 *W, I, S*
Handford, F G (Manchester) 1909 *W, F, I, S*
Hands, R H M (Blackheath) 1910 *F, S*
Hanley, J (Plymouth A) 1927 *W, S, F*, 1928 *W, I, F, S*
Hanley, S M (Sale) 1999 *W*
Hannaford, R C (Bristol) 1971 *W, I, F*
Hanvey, R J (Aspatria) 1926 *W, I, F, S*
Harding, E H (Devonport Services) 1931 *I*
Harding, R M (Bristol) 1985 *R, F, S*, 1987 *S*, [*A, J, W*], 1988 *I* 1 (R),2, *A* 1,2, *Fj*
Harding, V S J (Saracens) 1961 *S*, 1962 *W, I, F, S*
Hardwick, P F (Percy Park) 1902 *I, S*, 1903 *W, I, S*, 1904 *W, I, S*
Hardwick, R J K (Coventry) 1996 *It* (R)
Hardy, E M P (Blackheath) 1951 *I, F, S*
Hare, W H (Nottingham, Leicester) 1974 *W*, 1978 *F, NZ*, 1979 *NZ*, 1980 *I, F, W, S*, 1981 *W, S, Arg* 1,2, 1982 *F, W*, 1983 *F, W, S, I, NZ*, 1984 *I, F, W, SA* 1,2
Harper, C H (Exeter) 1899 *W*
Harriman, A T (Harlequins) 1988 *A*
Harris, S W (Blackheath) 1920 *I, S*
Harris, T W (Northampton) 1929 *S*, 1932 *I*
Harrison, A C (Hartlepool R) 1931 *I, S*
Harrison, A L (United Services, RN) 1914 *I, F*
Harrison, G (Hull) 1877 *I, S*, 1879 *S, I*, 1880 *S*, 1885 *W, I*
Harrison, H C (United Services, RN) 1909 *S*, 1914 *I, S, F*
Harrison, M E (Wakefield) 1985 *NZ* 1,2, 1986 *S, I, F*, 1987 *I, F, W, S*, [*A, J, US, W*], 1988 *F, W*
Hartley, B C (Blackheath) 1901 *S*, 1902 *S*
Haslett, L W (Birkenhead Park) 1926 *I, F*
Hastings, G W D (Gloucester) 1955 *W, I, F, S*, 1957 *W, I, F, S*, 1958 *W, A, I, F, S*
Havelock, H (Hartlepool R) 1908 *F, W, I*
Hawcridge, J J (Bradford) 1885 *W, I*
Hayward, L W (Cheltenham) 1910 *I*

Hazell, D St G (Leicester) 1955 *W, I, F, S*
Healey, A S (Leicester) 1997 *I* (R), *W, A* 1 (R), 2 (R), *NZ* 1 (R), *SA* (R), *NZ* 2, 1998 *F, W, S, I, A* 1, *NZ* 1,2, *H, It, A* 2, *SA* 2(R)
Hearn, R D (Bedford) 1966 *F, S,* 1967 *I, F, S, W*
Heath, A H (Oxford U) 1876 *S*
Heaton, J (Waterloo) 1935 *W, I, S,* 1939 *W, I, S,* 1947 *I, S, F*
Henderson, A P (Edinburgh Wands) 1947 *W, I, S, F,* 1948 *I, S, F,* 1949 *W, I*
Henderson, R S F (Blackheath) 1883 *W, S,* 1884 *W, S,* 1885 *W*
Heppell, W G (Devonport A) 1903 *I*
Herbert, A J (Wasps) 1958 *F, S,* 1959 *W, I, F, S*
Hesford, R (Bristol) 1981 *S* (R), 1982 *A, S, F* (R), 1983 *F* (R), 1985 *R, F, S, I, W*
Heslop, N J (Orrell) 1990 *Arg* 1,2,3, 1991 *W, S, I, F, [US, F],* 1992 *W* (R)
Hetherington, J G G (Northampton) 1958 *A, I,* 1959 *W, I, F, S*
Hewitt, E N (Coventry) 1951 *W, I, F*
Hewitt, W W (Queen's House) 1881 *I, W, S,* 1882 *I*
Hickson, J L (Bradford) 1887 *W, I, S,* 1890 *W, S, I*
Higgins, R (Liverpool) 1954 *W, NZ, I, S,* 1955 *W, I, F, S,* 1957 *W, I, F, S,* 1959 *W*
Hignell, A J (Cambridge U, Bristol) 1975 *A* 2, 1976 *A, W, S, I,* 1977 *S, I, F, W,* 1978 *W,* 1979 *S, I, F, W*
Hill, B A (Blackheath) 1903 *I, S,* 1904 *W, I,* 1905 *W, NZ,* 1906 *SA,* 1907 *F, W*
Hill, R A (Saracens) 1997 *S, I, F, W, A* 1,2, *NZ* 1, *SA, NZ* 2, 1998 *F, W, H* (R), *It* (R), *A* 2, *SA* 2, 1999 *S, I, F, W*
Hill, R J (Bath) 1984 *SA* 1,2, 1985 *I* (R), *NZ* 2 (R), 1986 *F* (R), 1987 *I, F, W, [US],* 1989 *Fj,* 1990 *I, F, W, S, Arg* 1,2,3, 1991 *W, S, I, F, Fj, A, [NZ, It, US, F, S, A]*
Hillard, R J (Oxford U) 1925 *NZ*
Hiller, R (Harlequins) 1968 *W, I, F, S,* 1969 *I, F, S, W, SA,* 1970 *I, W, S,* 1971 *I, F, S* (2[1C]), *P,* 1972 *W, I*
Hind, A E (Leicester) 1905 *NZ,* 1906 *W*
Hind, G R (Blackheath) 1910 *S,* 1911 *I*
Hobbs, R F A (Blackheath) 1899 *S,* 1903 *W*
Hobbs, R G S (Richmond) 1932 *SA, W, I, S*
Hodges, H A (Nottingham) 1906 *W, I*
Hodgkinson, S D (Nottingham) 1989 *R, Fj,* 1990 *I, F, W, S, Arg* 1,2,3, 1991 *W, S, I, F, [US]*
Hodgson, J McD (Northern) 1932 *SA, W, I, S,* 1934 *W, I,* 1936 *I*
Hodgson, S A M (Durham City) 1960 *W, I, F, S,* 1961 *SA, W,* 1962 *W, I, F, S,* 1964 *W*
Hofmeyr, M B (Oxford U) 1950 *W, F, S*
Hogarth, T B (Hartlepool R) 1906 *F*
Holford, G (Gloucester) 1920 *W, F*
Holland, D (Devonport A) 1912 *W, I, S*
Holliday, T E (Aspatria) 1923 *S, F,* 1925 *I, S, F,* 1926 *F, S*
Holmes, C B (Manchester) 1947 *S,* 1948 *I, F*
Holmes, E (Manningham) 1890 *S, I*
Holmes, W A (Nuneaton) 1950 *W, I, F, S,* 1951 *W, I, F, S,* 1952 *SA, S, I, F,* 1953 *W, I, F, S*
Holmes, W B (Cambridge U) 1949 *W, I, F, S*
Hook, W G (Gloucester) 1951 *S,* 1952 *SA, W*
Hooper, C A (Middlesex W) 1894 *W, I, S*
Hopley, D P (Wasps) 1995 *[WS* (R)]*, SA, WS*
Hopley, F J V (Blackheath) 1907 *F, W,* 1908 *I*
Hordern, P C (Gloucester) 1931 *I, S, F,* 1934 *W*
Horley, C H (Swinton) 1885 *I*
Hornby, A N (Manchester) 1877 *I, S,* 1878 *S, I,* 1880 *I,* 1881 *I, S,* 1882 *I, S*
Horrocks-Taylor, J P (Cambridge U, Leicester, Middlesbrough) 1958 *W, A,* 1961 *S,* 1962 *S,* 1963 *NZ* 1,2, *A,* 1964 *NZ, W*
Horsfall, E L (Harlequins) 1949 *W*
Horton, A L (Blackheath) 1965 *W, I, F, S,* 1966 *F, S,* 1967 *NZ*
Horton, J P (Bath) 1978 *W, S, I, NZ,* 1980 *I, F, W, S,* 1981 *W,* 1983 *S, I,* 1984 *SA* 1,2
Horton, N E (Moseley, Toulouse) 1969 *I, F, S, W,* 1971 *I, F, S,* 1974 *S,* 1975 *W,* 1977 *S, I, F, W,* 1978 *F, W,* 1979 *S, I, F, W,* 1980 *I*
Hosen, R W (Bristol, Northampton) 1963 *NZ* 1,2, *A,* 1964 *F, S,* 1967 *A, I, F, S, W*
Hosking, G R d'A (Devonport Services) 1949 *W, I, F, S,* 1950 *W*
Houghton, S (Runcorn) 1892 *I,* 1896 *W*
Howard, P D (O Millhillians) 1930 *W, I, F, S,* 1931 *W, I, S, F*

Hubbard, G C (Blackheath) 1892 *W, I*
Hubbard, J C (Harlequins) 1930 *S*
Hudson, A (Gloucester) 1906 *W, I, F,* 1908 *F, W, I, S,* 1910 *F*
Hughes, G E (Barrow) 1896 *S*
Hull, P A (Bristol, RAF) 1994 *SA* 1,2, *R, C*
Hulme, F C (Birkenhead Park) 1903 *W, I,* 1905 *W, I*
Hunt, J T (Manchester) 1882 *I, S,* 1884 *W*
Hunt, R (Manchester) 1880 *I,* 1881 *W, S,* 1882 *I*
Hunt, W H (Manchester) 1876 *S,* 1877 *I, S,* 1878 *I*
Hunter, I (Northampton) 1992 *C,* 1993 *F, W,* 1994 *F, W,* 1995 *[WS, F]*
Huntsman, R P (Headingley) 1985 *NZ* 1,2
Hurst, A C B (Wasps) 1962 *S*
Huskisson, T F (OMTs) 1937 *W, I, S,* 1938 *W, I,* 1939 *W, I, S*
Hutchinson, F (Headingley) 1909 *F, I, S*
Hutchinson, J E (Durham City) 1906 *I*
Hutchinson, W C (RIE Coll) 1876 *S,* 1877 *I*
Hutchinson, W H H (Hull) 1875 *I,* 1876 *I*
Huth, H (Huddersfield) 1879 *S*
Hyde, J P (Northampton) 1950 *F, S*
Hynes, W B (United Services, RN) 1912 *F*

Ibbitson, E D (Headingley) 1909 *W, F, I, S*
Imrie, H M (Durham City) 1906 *NZ,* 1907 *I*
Inglis, R E (Blackheath) 1886 *W, I, S*
Irvin, S H (Devonport A) 1905 *W*
Isherwood, F W (Ravenscourt Park) 1872 *S*

Jackett, E J (Leicester, Falmouth) 1905 *NZ,* 1906 *W, I, S, F, SA,* 1907 *W, I, S,* 1909 *W, F, I, S*
Jackson, A H (Blackheath) 1878 *I,* 1880 *I*
Jackson, B S (Broughton Park) 1970 *S* (R), *F*
Jackson, P B (Coventry) 1956 *W, I, F,* 1957 *W, I, F, S,* 1958 *W, A, F, S,* 1959 *W, I, F, S,* 1961 *S,* 1963 *W, I, F, S*
Jackson, W J (Halifax) 1894 *S*
Jacob, F (Cambridge U) 1897 *W, I, S,* 1898 *I, S, W,* 1899 *W, I*
Jacob, H P (Blackheath) 1924 *W, I, F, S,* 1930 *F*
Jacob, P G (Blackheath) 1898 *I*
Jacobs, C R (Northampton) 1956 *W, I, S, F,* 1957 *W, I, F, S,* 1958 *W, A, I, F, S,* 1960 *W, I, F, S,* 1961 *SA, W, I, F, S,* 1963 *NZ* 1,2, *A,* 1964 *W, I, F, S*
Jago, R A (Devonport A) 1906 *W, I, SA,* 1907 *W, I*
Janion, J P A G (Bedford) 1971 *W, I, F, S* (2[1C]), *P,* 1972 *W, S, SA,* 1973 *A,* 1975 *A* 1,2
Jarman, J W (Bristol) 1900 *W*
Jeavons, N C (Moseley) 1981 *S, I, F, Arg* 1,2, 1982 *A, S, I, F, W,* 1983 *F, W, S, I*
Jeeps, R E G (Northampton) 1956 *W,* 1957 *W, I, F, S,* 1958 *W, A, I, F, S,* 1959 *I,* 1960 *W, I, F, S,* 1961 *SA, W, I, F, S,* 1962 *W, I, F, S*
Jeffery, G L (Blackheath) 1886 *W, I, S,* 1887 *W, I, S*
Jennins, C R (Waterloo) 1967 *A, I, F*
Jewitt, J (Hartlepool R) 1902 *W*
Johns, W A (Gloucester) 1909 *W, F, I, S,* 1910 *W, I, F*
Johnson, M O (Leicester) 1993 *F, NZ,* 1994 *S, I, F, W, R, C,* 1995 *I, F, W, S, [Arg, It, WS, A, NZ, F], SA, WS,* 1996 *F, W, S, I, It, Arg,* 1997 *S, I, F, W, A* 2, *NZ* 1,2, 1998 *F, W, S, I, H, It, A* 2, *SA* 2, 1999 *S, I, F, W*
Johnston, W R (Bristol) 1910 *W, I, S,* 1912 *W, I, S, F,* 1913 *SA, W, F, I, S,* 1914 *W, I, S, F*
Jones, F P (New Brighton) 1893 *S*
Jones, H A (Barnstaple) 1950 *W, I, F*
Jorden, A M (Cambridge U, Blackheath, Bedford) 1970 *F,* 1973 *I, F, S,* 1974 *F,* 1975 *W, S*
Jowett, D (Heckmondwike) 1889 *M,* 1890 *S, I,* 1891 *W, I, S*
Judd, P E (Coventry) 1962 *W, I, F, S,* 1963 *S, NZ* 1,2, *A,* 1964 *NZ,* 1965 *I, F, S,* 1966 *W, I, F, S,* 1967 *A, I, F, S, W, NZ*

Kayll, H E (Sunderland) 1878 *S*
Keeling, J H (Guy's Hospital) 1948 *A, W*
Keen, B W (Newcastle U) 1968 *W, I, F, S*
Keeton, G H (Leicester) 1904 *W, I, S*
Kelly, G A (Bedford) 1947 *W, I, S,* 1948 *W*
Kelly, T S (London Devonians) 1906 *W, I, S, F, SA,* 1907 *F, W, I, S,* 1908 *F, I, S*
Kemble, A T (Liverpool) 1885 *W, I,* 1887 *I*
Kemp, D T (Blackheath) 1935 *W*
Kemp, T A (Richmond) 1937 *W, I,* 1939 *S,* 1948 *A, W*
Kendall, P D (Birkenhead Park) 1901 *S,* 1902 *W,* 1903 *S*

Kendall-Carpenter, J MacG K (Oxford U, Bath) 1949 *I, F, S,* 1950 *W, I, F, S,* 1951 *I, F, S,* 1952 *SA, W, S, I, F,* 1953 *W, I, F, S,* 1954 *W, NZ, I, F*
Kendrew, D A (Leicester) 1930 *W, I,* 1933 *I, S,* 1934 *S,* 1935 *W, I,* 1936 *NZ, W, I*
Kennedy, R D (Camborne S of M) 1949 *I, F, S*
Kent, C P (Rosslyn Park) 1977 *S, I, F, W,* 1978 *F* (R)
Kent, T (Salford) 1891 *W, I, S,* 1892 *W, I, S*
Kershaw, C A (United Services, RN) 1920 *W, F, I, S,* 1921 *W, I, S, F,* 1922 *W, I, F, S,* 1923 *W, I, S, F*
Kewley, E (Liverpool) 1874 *S,* 1875 *S,* 1876 *I, S,* 1877 *I, S,* 1878 *S*
Kewney, A L (Leicester) 1906 *W, I, S, F,* 1909 *A, W, F, I, S,* 1911 *W, F, I, S,* 1912 *I, S,* 1913 *SA*
Key, A (O Cranleighans) 1930 *I,* 1933 *W*
Keyworth, M (Swansea) 1976 *A, W, S, I*
Kilner, B (Wakefield T) 1880 *I*
Kindersley, R S (Exeter) 1883 *W,* 1884 *S,* 1885 *W*
King, A D (Wasps) 1997 *Arg* 2 (R), 1998 *SA* 2 (R)
King, I (Harrogate) 1954 *W, NZ, I*
King, J A (Headingley) 1911 *W, F, I, S,* 1912 *W, I, S,* 1913 *SA, W, F, I, S*
King, Q E M A (Army) 1921 *S*
Kingston, P (Gloucester) 1975 *A* 1,2, 1979 *I, F, W*
Kitching, A E (Blackheath) 1913 *I*
Kittermaster, H J (Harlequins) 1925 *NZ, W, I,* 1926 *W, I, F, S*
Knight, F (Plymouth) 1909 *A*
Knight, P M (Bristol) 1972 *F, S, SA*
Knowles, E (Millom) 1896 *S,* 1897 *S*
Knowles, T C (Birkenhead Park) 1931 *S*
Krige, J A (Guy's Hospital) 1920 *W*

Labuschagne, N A (Harlequins, Guy's Hospital) 1953 *W,* 1955 *W, I, F, S*
Lagden, R O (Richmond) 1911 *S*
Laird, H C C (Harlequins) 1927 *W, I, S,* 1928 *A, W, I, F, S,* 1929 *W, I*
Lambert, D (Harlequins) 1907 *F,* 1908 *F, W, S,* 1911 *W, F, I*
Lampkowski, M S (Headingley) 1976 *A, W, S, I*
Lapage, W N (United Services, RN) 1908 *F, W, I, S*
Larter, P J (Northampton, RAF) 1967 *A, NZ,* 1968 *W, I, F, S,* 1969 *I, F, S, W, SA,* 1970 *I, W, F, S,* 1971 *W, I, F, S* (2[1C]), *P,* 1972 *SA,* 1973 *NZ* 1, *W*
Law, A F (Richmond) 1877 *S*
Law, D E (Birkenhead Park) 1927 *I*
Lawrence, Hon H A (Richmond) 1873 *S,* 1874 *S,* 1875 *I, S*
Lawrie, P W (Leicester) 1910 *S,* 1911 *S*
Lawson, R G (Workington) 1925 *I*
Lawson, T M (Workington) 1928 *A, W*
Leadbetter, M M (Broughton Park) 1970 *F*
Leadbetter, V H (Edinburgh Wands) 1954 *S, F*
Leake, W R M (Harlequins) 1891 *W, I, S*
Leather, G (Liverpool) 1907 *I*
Lee, F H (Marlborough N) 1876 *S,* 1877 *I*
Lee, H (Blackheath) 1907 *F*
Le Fleming, J (Blackheath) 1887 *W*
Leonard, J (Saracens, Harlequins) 1990 *Arg* 1,2,3, 1991 *W, S, I, F, Fj, A,* [*NZ, It, US, F, S, A*], 1992 *S, I, F, W, C, SA,* 1993 *F, W, S, I, NZ,* 1994 *S, I, F, W, SA* 1,2, *R, C,* 1995 *I, F, W, S,* [*Arg, It, A, NZ, F*], *SA, WS,* 1996 *F, W, S, I, It, Arg,* 1997 *S, I, F, W, A* 2, *NZ* 1, *SA, NZ* 2, 1998 *F, W, S, I, H, It, A* 2 *SA* 2, 1999 *S, I, F, W*
Leslie-Jones, F A (Richmond) 1895 *W, I*
Lewis, A O (Bath) 1952 *SA, W, S, I, F,* 1953 *W, I, F, S,* 1954 *F*
Lewsey, O J (Wasps) 1998 *NZ* 1,2, *SA* 1
Leyland, R (Waterloo) 1935 *W, I, S*
Linnett, M S (Moseley) 1989 *Fj*
Livesay, R O'H (Blackheath) 1898 *W,* 1899 *W*
Lloyd, R H (Harlequins) 1967 *NZ,* 1968 *W, I, F, S*
Locke, H M (Birkenhead Park) 1923 *S, F,* 1924 *W, F, S,* 1925 *W, I, S, F,* 1927 *W, I, S*
Lockwood, R E (Heckmondwike) 1887 *W, I, S,* 1889 *M,* 1891 *W, I, S,* 1892 *W, I, S,* 1893 *W, I,* 1894 *W, I*
Login, S H M (RN Coll) 1876 *I*
Lohden, F C (Blackheath) 1893 *W*
Long, A E (Bath) 1997 *A* 2
Longland, R J (Northampton) 1932 *S,* 1933 *W, S,* 1934 *W, I, S,* 1935 *W, I, S,* 1936 *NZ, W, I, S,* 1937 *W, I, S,* 1938 *W, I, S*

Lowe, C N (Cambridge U, Blackheath) 1913 *SA, W, F, I, S,* 1914 *W, I, S, F,* 1920 *W, F, I, S,* 1921 *W, I, S, F,* 1922 *W, I, F, S,* 1923 *W, I, S, F*
Lowrie, F (Wakefield T) 1889 *M,* 1890 *W*
Lowry, W M (Birkenhead Park) 1920 *F*
Lozowski, R A P (Wasps) 1984 *A*
Luddington, W G E (Devonport Services) 1923 *W, I, S, F,* 1924 *W, I, F, S,* 1925 *W, I, S, F,* 1926 *W*
Luger, D D (Harlequins) 1998 *H, It, SA* 2, 1999 *S, I, F, W*
Luscombe, F (Gipsies) 1872 *S,* 1873 *S,* 1875 *I, S,* 1876 *I, S*
Luscombe, J H (Gipsies) 1871 *S*
Luxmoore, A F C C (Richmond) 1900 *S,* 1901 *W*
Luya, H F (Waterloo, Headingley) 1948 *W, I, S, F,* 1949 *W*
Lyon, A (Liverpool) 1871 *S*
Lyon, G H d'O (United Services, RN) 1908 *S,* 1909 *A*

McCanlis, M A (Gloucester) 1931 *W, I*
McCarthy, N (Gloucester) 1999 *I* (t)
McFadyean, C W (Moseley) 1966 *I, F, S,* 1967 *A, I, F, S, W, NZ,* 1968 *W, I*
MacIlwaine, A H (United Services, Hull & E Riding) 1912 *W, I, S, F,* 1920 *I*
Mackie, O G (Wakefield T, Cambridge U) 1897 *S,* 1898 *I*
Mackinlay, J E H (St George's Hospital) 1872 *S,* 1873 *S,* 1875 *I*
MacLaren, W (Manchester) 1871 *S*
MacLennan, R R F (OMTs) 1925 *I, S, F*
McLeod, N F (RIE Coll) 1879 *S, I*
Madge, R J P (Exeter) 1948 *A, W, I, S*
Malir, F W S (Otley) 1930 *W, I, S*
Mallett, J A (Bath) 1995 [*WS* (R)]
Mallinder, J (Sale) 1997 *Arg* 1,2
Mangles, R H (Richmond) 1897 *W, I*
Manley, D C (Exeter) 1963 *W, I, F, S*
Mann, W E (United Services, Army) 1911 *W, F, I*
Mantell, N D (Rosslyn Park) 1975 *A* 1
Mapletoft, M S (Gloucester) 1997 *Arg* 2
Markendale, E T (Manchester R) 1880 *I*
Marques, R W D (Cambridge U, Harlequins) 1956 *W, I, S, F,* 1957 *W, I, F, S,* 1958 *W, A, I, F, S,* 1959 *W, I, F, S,* 1960 *W, I, F, S,* 1961 *SA, W*
Marquis, J C (Birkenhead Park) 1900 *I, S*
Marriott, C J B (Blackheath) 1884 *W, I, S,* 1886 *W, I, S,* 1887 *I*
Marriott, E E (Manchester) 1876 *I*
Marriott, V R (Harlequins) 1963 *NZ* 1,2, *A,* 1964 *NZ*
Marsden, G H (Morley) 1900 *W, I, S*
Marsh, H (RIE Coll) 1873 *S*
Marsh, J (Swinton) 1892 *I*
Marshall, H (Blackheath) 1893 *W*
Marshall, M W (Blackheath) 1873 *S,* 1874 *S,* 1875 *I, S,* 1876 *I, S,* 1877 *I, S,* 1878 *S, I*
Marshall, R M (Oxford U) 1938 *I, S,* 1939 *W, I, S*
Martin, C R (Bath) 1985 *F, S, I, W*
Martin, N O (Harlequins) 1972 *F* (R)
Martindale, S A (Kendal) 1929 *F*
Massey, E J (Leicester) 1925 *W, I, S*
Mather, B-J (Sale) 1999 *W*
Mathias, J L (Bristol) 1905 *W, I, S, NZ*
Matters, J C (RNE Coll) 1899 *S*
Matthews, J R C (Harlequins) 1949 *F, S,* 1950 *I, F, S,* 1952 *SA, W, S, I, F*
Maud, P (Blackheath) 1893 *W, I*
Maxwell, A W (New Brighton, Headingley) 1975 *A* 1, 1976 *A, W, S, I, F,* 1978 *F*
Maxwell-Hyslop, J E (Oxford U) 1922 *I, F, S*
Maynard, A F (Cambridge U) 1914 *W, I, S*
Meikle, G W C (Waterloo) 1934 *W, I, S*
Meikle, S S C (Waterloo) 1929 *S*
Mellish, F W (Blackheath) 1920 *W, F, I, S,* 1921 *W, I*
Melville, N D (Wasps) 1984 *A,* 1985 *I, W, NZ* 1,2, 1986 *W, S, I, F,* 1988 *F, W, S, I* 1
Merriam, L P B (Blackheath) 1920 *W, F*
Michell, A T (Oxford U) 1875 *I, S,* 1876 *I*
Middleton, B B (Birkenhead Park) 1882 *I,* 1883 *I*
Middleton, J A (Richmond) 1922 *S*
Miles, J H (Leicester) 1903 *W*
Millett, H (Richmond) 1920 *F*
Mills, F W (Marlborough N) 1872 *S,* 1873 *S*
Mills, S G F (Gloucester) 1981 *Arg* 1,2, 1983 *W,* 1984 *SA* 1, *A*
Mills, W A (Devonport A) 1906 *W, I, S, F, SA,* 1907 *F, W, I, S,* 1908 *F, W*
Milman, D L K (Bedford) 1937 *W,* 1938 *W, I, S*

Milton, C H (Camborne S of M) 1906 *I*
Milton, J G (Camborne S of M) 1904 *W, I, S*, 1905 *S*, 1907 *I*
Milton, W H (Marlborough N) 1874 *S*, 1875 *I*
Mitchell, F (Blackheath) 1895 *W, I, S*, 1896 *W, I, S*
Mitchell, W G (Richmond) 1890 *W, S, I*, 1891 *W, I, S*, 1893 *S*
Mobbs, E R (Northampton) 1909 *A, W, F, I, S*, 1910 *I, F*
Moberley, W O (Ravenscourt Park) 1872 *S*
Moore, B C (Nottingham, Harlequins) 1987 *S, [A, J, W]*, 1988 *F, W, S, I* 1,2, *A* 1, 2, *Fj, A*, 1989 *S, I, F, W, R, Fj*, 1990 *I, F, W, S, Arg* 1,2, 1991 *W, S, I, F, Fj, A, [NZ, It, F, S, A]*, 1992 *S, I, F, W, SA*, 1993 *F, W, S, I, NZ*, 1994 *S, I, F, W, SA* 1,2, *R, C*, 1995 *I, F, W, S, [Arg, It, WS* (R), *A, NZ, F]*
Moore, E J (Blackheath) 1883 *I, S*
Moore, N J N H (Bristol) 1904 *W, I, S*
Moore, P B C (Blackheath) 1951 *S*
Moore, W K T (Leicester) 1947 *W, I*, 1949 *F, S*, 1950 *I, F, S*
Mordell, R J (Rosslyn Park) 1978 *W*
Morfitt, S (W Hartlepool) 1894 *W, I, S*, 1896 *W, I, S*
Morgan, J R (Hawick) 1920 *W*
Morgan, W G D (Medicals, Newcastle) 1960 *W, I, F, S*, 1961 *SA, W, I, F, S*
Morley, A J (Bristol) 1972 *SA*, 1973 *NZ* 1, *W, I*, 1975 *S, A* 1,2
Morris, A D W (United Services, RN) 1909 *A, W, F*
Morris, C D (Liverpool St Helens, Orrell) 1988 *A*, 1989 *S, I, F, W*, 1992 *S, I, F, W, C, SA*, 1993 *F, W, S, I*, 1994 *F, W, SA* 1,2, *R*, 1995 *S* (t), *[Arg, WS, A, NZ, F]*
Morrison, P H (Cambridge U) 1890 *W, S, I*, 1891 *I*
Morse, S (Marlborough N) 1873 *S*, 1874 *S*, 1875 *S*
Mortimer, W (Marlborough N) 1899 *W*
Morton, H J S (Blackheath) 1909 *I, S*, 1910 *W, I*
Moss, F (Broughton) 1885 *W, I*, 1886 *W*
Mullins, A R (Harlequins) 1989 *Fj*
Mycock, J (Sale) 1947 *W, I, S, F*, 1948 *A*
Myers, E (Bradford) 1920 *I, S*, 1921 *W, I*, 1922 *W, I, F, S*, 1923 *W, I, S, F*, 1924 *W, I, F, S*, 1925 *S, F*
Myers, H (Keighley) 1898 *I*

Nanson, W M B (Carlisle) 1907 *F, W*
Nash, E H (Richmond) 1875 *I*
Neale, B A (Rosslyn Park) 1951 *I, F, S*
Neale, M E (Blackheath) 1912 *F*
Neame, S (O Cheltonians) 1879 *S, I*, 1880 *I, S*
Neary, A (Broughton Park) 1971 *W, I, F, S* (2[1C]), *P*, 1972 *W, I, F, S, SA*, 1973 *NZ* 1, *W, I, F, S, NZ* 2, *A*, 1974 *S, I, F, W*, 1975 *I, F, W, S, A* 1, 1976 *A, W, S, I, F*, 1977 *I*, 1978 *F* (R), 1979 *S, I, F, W, NZ*, 1980 *I, F, W, S*
Nelmes, B G (Cardiff) 1975 *A* 1,2, 1978 *W, S, I, NZ*
Newbold, C J (Blackheath) 1904 *W, I, S*, 1905 *W, I, S*
Newman, S C (Oxford U) 1947 *I, F*, 1948 *A, W*
Newton, A W (Blackheath) 1907 *S*
Newton, P A (Blackheath) 1882 *S*
Newton-Thompson, J O (Oxford U) 1947 *S, F*
Nichol, W (Brighouse R) 1892 *W, S*
Nicholas, P L (Exeter) 1902 *W*
Nicholson, B E (Harlequins) 1938 *W, I*
Nicholson, E S (Leicester) 1935 *W, I, S*, 1936 *NZ, W*
Nicholson, E T (Birkenhead Park) 1900 *W, I*
Nicholson, T (Rockcliff) 1893 *I*
Ninnes, B F (Coventry) 1971 *W*
Norman, D J (Leicester) 1932 *SA, W*
North, E H G (Blackheath) 1891 *W, I, S*
Northmore, S (Millom) 1897 *I*
Novak, M J (Harlequins) 1970 *W, S, F*
Novis, A L (Blackheath) 1929 *S, F*, 1930 *W, I, F*, 1933 *I, S*

Oakeley, F E (United Services, RN) 1913 *S*, 1914 *I, S, F*
Oakes, R F (Hartlepool R) 1897 *W, I, S*, 1898 *I, S, W*, 1899 *W, S*
Oakley, L F L (Bedford) 1951 *W*
Obolensky, A (Oxford U) 1936 *NZ, W, I, S*
Ojomoh, S O (Bath, Gloucester) 1994 *I, F, SA* 1 (R), 2, *R*, 1995 *S* (R), *[Arg, WS, A* (t), *F]*, 1996 *F*, 1998 *NZ* 1
Old, A G B (Middlesbrough, Leicester, Sheffield) 1972 *W, I, F, S, SA*, 1973 *NZ* 2, *A*, 1974 *S, I, F, W*, 1975 *I, A* 2, 1976 *S, I*, 1978 *F*
Oldham, W L (Coventry) 1908 *S*, 1909 *A*
Olver, C J (Northampton) 1990 *Arg* 3, 1991 *[US]*, 1992 *C*
O'Neill, A (Teignmouth, Torquay A) 1901 *W, I, S*
Openshaw, W E (Manchester) 1879 *I*

Orwin, J (Gloucester, RAF, Bedford) 1985 *R, F, S, I, W, NZ* 1,2, 1988 *F, W, S, I* 1,2, *A* 1,2
Osborne, R R (Manchester) 1871 *S*
Osborne, S H (Oxford U) 1905 *S*
Oti, C (Cambridge U, Nottingham, Wasps) 1988 *S, I* 1, 1989 *S, I, F, W, R*, 1990 *Arg* 1,2, 1991 *Fj, A*, *[NZ, It]*
Oughtred, B (Hartlepool R) 1901 *S*, 1902 *W, I, S*, 1903 *W, I*
Owen, J E (Coventry) 1963 *W, I, F, S, A*, 1964 *NZ*, 1965 *W, I, F, S*, 1966 *I, F, S*, 1967 *NZ*
Owen-Smith, H G O (St Mary's Hospital) 1934 *W, I, S*, 1936 *NZ, W, I, S*, 1937 *W, I, S*

Page, J J (Bedford, Northampton) 1971 *W, I, F, S*, 1975 *S*
Pallant, J N (Notts) 1967 *I, F, S*
Palmer, A C (London Hospital) 1909 *I, S*
Palmer, F H (Richmond) 1905 *W*
Palmer, G V (Richmond) 1928 *I, F, S*
Palmer, J A (Bath) 1984 *SA* 1,2, 1986 *I* (R)
Pargetter, T A (Coventry) 1962 *S*, 1963 *F, NZ* 1
Parker, G W (Gloucester) 1938 *I, S*
Parker, Hon S (Liverpool) 1874 *S*, 1875 *S*
Parsons, E I (RAF) 1939 *S*
Parsons, M J (Northampton) 1968 *W, I, F, S*
Patterson, W M (Sale) 1961 *SA, S*
Pattisson, R M (Blackheath) 1883 *I, S*
Paul, J E (RIE Coll) 1875 *S*
Payne, A T (Bristol) 1935 *I, S*
Payne, C M (Harlequins) 1964 *I, F, S*, 1965 *I, F, S*, 1966 *W, I, F, S*
Payne, J H (Broughton) 1882 *S*, 1883 *W, I, S*, 1884 *I*, 1885 *W, I*
Pearce, G S (Northampton) 1979 *S, I, F, W*, 1981 *Arg* 1,2, 1982 *A, S*, 1983 *F, W, S, I, NZ*, 1984 *S, SA* 2, *A*, 1985 *R, F, S, I, W, NZ* 1,2, 1986 *W, S, I, F*, 1987 *I, F, W, S, [A, US, W]*, 1988 *Fj*, 1991 *[US]*
Pears, D (Harlequins) 1990 *Arg* 1,2, 1992 *F* (R), 1994 *F*
Pearson, A W (Blackheath) 1875 *I, S*, 1876 *I, S*, 1877 *S*, 1878 *S, I*
Peart, T G A H (Hartlepool R) 1964 *F, S*
Pease, F E (Hartlepool R) 1887 *I*
Penny, S H (Leicester) 1909 *A*
Penny, W J (United Hospitals) 1878 *I*, 1879 *S, I*
Percival, L J (Rugby) 1891 *I*, 1892 *I*, 1893 *S*
Periton, H G (Waterloo) 1925 *W*, 1926 *W, I, F, S*, 1927 *W, I, S, F*, 1928 *A, I, F, S*, 1929 *W, I, S, F*, 1930 *W, I, F, S*
Perrott, E S (O Cheltonians) 1875 *I*
Perry, D G (Bedford) 1963 *F, S, NZ* 1,2, *A* 1964 *NZ, W, I*, 1965 *W, I, F, S*, 1966 *W, I, F*
Perry, M B (Bath) 1997 *A* 2, *NZ* 1, *SA, NZ* 2, 1998 *W, S, I, A* 1, *NZ* 1,2, *SA* 1, *H, A* 2, 1999 *I, F, W*
Perry, S V (Cambridge U, Waterloo) 1947 *W, I*, 1948 *A, W, I, S, F*
Peters, J (Plymouth) 1906 *S, F*, 1907 *I, S*, 1908 *W*
Phillips, C (Birkenhead Park) 1880 *S*, 1881 *I, S*
Phillips, M S (Fylde) 1958 *A, I, F, S*, 1959 *W, I, F, S*, 1960 *W, I, F, S*, 1961 *W*, 1963 *W, I, F, S, NZ* 1,2, *A*, 1964 *NZ, W, I, F, S*
Pickering, A S (Harrogate) 1907 *I*
Pickering, R D A (Bradford) 1967 *I, F, S, W*, 1968 *F, S*
Pickles, R C W (Bristol) 1922 *I, F*
Pierce, R (Liverpool) 1898 *I*, 1903 *S*
Pilkington, W N (Cambridge U) 1898 *S*
Pillman, C H (Blackheath) 1910 *W, I, F, S*, 1911 *W, F, I, S*, 1912 *W, F*, 1913 *SA, W, F, I, S*, 1914 *W, I, S*
Pillman, R L (Blackheath) 1914 *F*
Pinch, J (Lancaster) 1896 *W, I*, 1897 *S*
Pinching, W W (Guy's Hospital) 1872 *S*
Pitman, I J (Oxford U) 1922 *S*
Plummer, K C (Bristol) 1969 *W*, 1976 *S, I, F*
Pool-Jones, R J (Stade Francais) 1998 *A* 1
Poole, F O (Oxford U) 1895 *W, I, S*
Poole, R W (Hartlepool R) 1896 *S*
Pope, E B (Blackheath) 1931 *W, S, F*
Portus, G V (Blackheath) 1908 *F, I*
Potter, S (Leicester) 1998 *A* 1 (t)
Poulton, R W (later Poulton Palmer) (Oxford U, Harlequins, Liverpool) 1909 *F, I, S*, 1910 *W*, 1911 *S*, 1912 *W, I, S*, 1913 *SA, W, F, I, S*, 1914 *W, I, S, F*
Powell, D L (Northampton) 1966 *W, I*, 1969 *I, F, S, W*, 1971 *W, I, F, S* (2[1C])
Pratten, W E (Blackheath) 1927 *S, F*
Preece, I (Coventry) 1948 *I, S, F*, 1949 *F, S*, 1950 *W, I, F, S*, 1951 *W, I, F*

Preece, P S (Coventry) 1972 *SA*, 1973 *NZ* 1, *W, I, F, S, NZ* 2, 1975 *I, F, W, A* 2, 1976 *W* (R)
Preedy, M (Gloucester) 1984 *SA* 1
Prentice, F D (Leicester) 1928 *I, F, S*
Prescott, R E (Harlequins) 1937 *W, I*, 1938 *I*, 1939 *W, I, S*
Preston, N J (Richmond) 1979 *NZ*, 1980 *I, F*
Price, H L (Harlequins) 1922 *I, S*, 1923 *W, I*
Price, J (Coventry) 1961 *I*
Price, P L A (RIE Coll) 1877 *I, S*, 1878 *S*
Price, T W (Cheltenham) 1948 *S, F*, 1949 *W, I, F, S*
Probyn, J A (Wasps, Askeans) 1988 *F, W, S, I* 1,2, *A* 1, 2, *A*, 1989 *S, I, R* (R), 1990 *I, F, W, S, Arg* 1,2,3, 1991 *W, S, I, F, Fj, A, [NZ, It, F, S, A]*, 1992 *S, I, F, W*, 1993 *F, W, S, I*
Prout, D H (Northampton) 1968 *W, I*
Pullin, J V (Bristol) 1966 *W*, 1968 *W, I, F, S*, 1969 *I, F, S, W, SA*, 1970 *I, W, S, F*, 1971 *W, I, F, S* (2[1C]), *P*, 1972 *W, I, F, S, SA*, 1973 *NZ* 1, *W, I, F, S, NZ* 2, *A*, 1974 *S, I, F, W*, 1975 *I, W* (R), *S, A* 1,2, 1976 *F*
Purdy, S J (Rugby) 1962 *S*
Pyke, J (St Helens Recreation) 1892 *W*
Pym, J A (Blackheath) 1912 *W, I, S, F*

Quinn, J P (New Brighton) 1954 *W, NZ, I, S, F*

Rafter, M (Bristol) 1977 *S, F, W*, 1978 *F, W, S, I, NZ*, 1979 *S, I, F, W, NZ*, 1980 *W*(R), 1981 *W, Arg* 1,2
Ralston, C W (Richmond) 1971 *S* (C), *P*, 1972 *W, I, F, S, SA*, 1973 *NZ* 1, *W, I, F, S, NZ* 2, *A*, 1974 *S, I, F, W*, 1975 *I, F, W, S*
Ramsden, H E (Bingley) 1898 *W, S*
Ranson, J M (Rosslyn Park) 1963 *NZ* 1,2, *A*, 1964 *W, I, F, S*
Raphael, J E (OMTs) 1902 *W, I, S*, 1905 *W, S, NZ*, 1906 *W, S, F*
Ravenscroft, J (Birkenhead Park) 1881 *I*
Ravenscroft, S C W (Saracens) 1998 *A* 1, *NZ* 2 (R)
Rawlinson, W C W (Blackheath) 1876 *S*
Redfern, S (Leicester) 1984 *I* (R)
Redman, N C (Bath) 1984 *A*, 1986 *S* (R), 1987 *I, S, [A, J, W]*, 1988 *Fj*, 1990 *Arg* 1,2, 1991 *Fj, [It, US]*, 1993 *NZ*, 1994 *F, W, SA* 1,2, 1997 *Arg* 1, *A* 1
Redmond, G F (Cambridge U) 1970 *F*
Redwood, B W (Bristol) 1968 *W, I*
Rees, D L (Sale) 1997 *A* 2, *NZ* 1, *SA, NZ* 2, 1998 *F, W, SA* 2 (R), 1999 *S, I, F*
Rees, G W (Nottingham) 1984 *SA* 2 (R), *A*, 1986 *I, F*, 1987 *F, W, S, [A, J, US, W]*, 1988 *S* (R), *I* 1,2, *A* 1,2, *Fj*, 1989 *W* (R), *R* (R), *Fj* (R), 1990 *Arg* 3 (R), 1991 *Fj, [US]*
Reeve, J S R (Harlequins) 1929 *F*, 1930 *W, I, F, S*, 1931 *W, I, S*
Regan, M (Liverpool) 1953 *W, I, F, S*, 1954 *W, NZ, I, S, F*, 1956 *I, F*
Regan, M P (Bristol, Bath) 1995 *SA, WS*, 1996 *F, W, S, I, It, Arg*, 1997 *S, I, F, W, A* 1, *NZ* 2 (R), 1998 *F*
Rendall, P A G (Wasps, Askeans) 1984 *W, SA* 2, 1986 *W, S*, 1987 *I, F, S, [A, J, W]*, 1988 *F, W, S, I* 1,2, *A* 1,2, *A*, 1989 *S, I, F, W, R*, 1990 *I, F, W, S*, 1991 *[It* (R)]
Rew, H (Blackheath) 1929 *S, F*, 1930 *F, S*, 1931 *W, S, F*, 1934 *W, I, S*
Reynolds, F J (O Cranleighans) 1937 *S*, 1938 *I, S*
Reynolds, S (Richmond) 1900 *W, I, S*, 1901 *I*
Rhodes, J (Castleford) 1896 *W, I, S*
Richards, D (Leicester) 1986 *I, F*, 1987 *S, [A, J, US, W]*, 1988 *F, W, S, I* 1, *A* 1,2, *Fj, A*, 1989 *S, I, F, W, R*, 1990 *Arg* 3, 1991 *W, S, I, F, Fj, A, [NZ, It, US]*, 1992 *S* (R), *F, W, C*, 1993 *NZ*, 1994 *W, SA* 1, *C*, 1995 *I, F, W, S, [WS, A, NZ]*, 1996 *F* (t), *S, I*
Richards, E E (Plymouth A) 1929 *S, F*
Richards, J (Bradford) 1891 *W, I, S*
Richards, S B (Richmond) 1965 *W, I, F, S*, 1967 *A, I, F, S, W*
Richardson, J V (Birkenhead Park) 1928 *A, W, I, F, S*
Richardson, W R (Manchester) 1881 *I*
Rickards, C H (Gipsies) 1873 *S*
Rimmer, G (Waterloo) 1949 *W, I*, 1950 *W*, 1951 *W, I, F*, 1952 *SA, W*, 1954 *W, NZ, I, S*
Rimmer, L I (Bath) 1961 *SA, W, I, F, S*
Ripley, A G (Rosslyn Park) 1972 *W, I, F, S, SA*, 1973 *NZ* 1, *W, I, F, S, NZ* 2, *A*, 1974 *S, I, F, W*, 1975 *I, F, S, A* 1,2, 1976 *A, W, S*
Risman, A B W (Loughborough Coll) 1959 *W, I, F, S*, 1961 *SA, W, I, F*
Ritson, J A S (Northern) 1910 *F, S*, 1912 *F*, 1913 *SA, W, F, I, S*

Rittson-Thomas, G C (Oxford U) 1951 *W, I, F*
Robbins, G L (Coventry) 1986 *W, S*
Robbins, P G D (Oxford U, Moseley, Coventry) 1956 *W, I, S, F*, 1957 *W, I, F, S*, 1958 *W, A, I, S*, 1960 *W, I, F, S*, 1961 *SA, W*, 1962 *S*
Roberts, A D (Northern) 1911 *W, F, I, S*, 1912 *I, S, F*, 1914 *I*
Roberts, E W (RNE Coll) 1901 *W, I*, 1905 *NZ*, 1906 *W, I*, 1907 *S*
Roberts, G D (Harlequins) 1907 *S*, 1908 *F, W*
Roberts, J (Sale) 1960 *W, I, F, S*, 1961 *SA, W, I, F, S*, 1962 *W, I, F, S*, 1963 *W, I, F, S*, 1964 *NZ*
Roberts, R S (Coventry) 1932 *I*
Roberts, S (Swinton) 1887 *W, I*
Roberts, V G (Penryn, Harlequins) 1947 *F*, 1949 *W, I, F, S*, 1950 *I, F, S*, 1951 *W, I, F, S*, 1956 *W, I, S, F*
Robertshaw, A R (Bradford) 1886 *W, I, S*, 1887 *W, S*
Robinson, A (Blackheath) 1889 *M*, 1890 *W, S, I*
Robinson, E T (Coventry) 1954 *S*, 1961 *I, F, S*
Robinson, G C (Percy Park) 1897 *I, S*, 1898 *I*, 1899 *W*, 1900 *I, S*, 1901 *I, S*
Robinson, J J (Headingley) 1893 *S*, 1902 *W, I, S*
Robinson, R A (Bath) 1988 *A* 2, *Fj, A*, 1989 *S, I, F, W*, 1995 *SA*
Robson, A (Northern) 1924 *W, I, F, S*, 1926 *W*
Robson, M (Oxford U) 1930 *W, I, F, S*
Rodber, T A K (Army, Northampton) 1992 *S, I*, 1993 *NZ*, 1994 *I, F, W, SA* 1,2, *R, C*, 1995 *I, F, W, S, [Arg, It, WS* (R), *A, NZ, F]*, *SA, WS*, 1996 *W, S* (R), *I* (t), *It, Arg*, 1997 *S, I, F, W, A* 1, 1998 *H* (R), *It* (R), *A* 2, *SA* 2, 1999 *S, I, F, W*
Rogers, D P (Bedford) 1961 *I, F, S*, 1962 *W, I, F*, 1963 *W, I, F, S, NZ* 1,2, *A*, 1964 *NZ, W, I, F, S*, 1965 *W, I, F, S*, 1966 *W, I, F, S*, 1967 *A, S, W, NZ*, 1969 *I, F, S, W*
Rogers, J H (Moseley) 1890 *W, S, I*, 1891 *S*
Rogers, W L Y (Blackheath) 1905 *W, I*
Rollitt, D M (Bristol) 1967 *I, F, S, W*, 1969 *I, F, S, W*, 1975 *S, A* 1,2
Roncoroni, A D S (West Herts, Richmond) 1933 *W, I, S*
Rose, W M H (Cambridge U, Coventry, Harlequins) 1981 *I, F*, 1982 *A, S, I*, 1987 *I, F, W, S, [A]*
Rossborough, P A (Coventry) 1971 *W*, 1973 *NZ* 2, *A*, 1974 *S, I*, 1975 *I, F*
Rosser, D W A (Wasps) 1965 *W, I, F, S*, 1966 *W*
Rotherham, Alan (Richmond) 1883 *W, S*, 1884 *W, S*, 1885 *W, I*, 1886 *W, I, S*, 1887 *W, I, S*
Rotherham, Arthur (Richmond) 1898 *S, W*, 1899 *W, I, S*
Roughley, D (Liverpool) 1973 *A*, 1974 *S, I*
Rowell, R E (Leicester) 1964 *W*, 1965 *W*
Rowley, A J (Coventry) 1932 *SA*
Rowley, H C (Manchester) 1879 *S, I*, 1880 *I, S*, 1881 *I, W, S*, 1882 *I, S*
Rowntree, G C (Leicester) 1995 *S* (t), *[It, WS]*, *WS*, 1996 *F, W, S, I, It, Arg*, 1997 *S, I, F, W, A* 1, 1998 *A* 1, *NZ* 1, 2, *SA* 1, *H* (R), *It* (R)
Royds, P M R (Blackheath) 1898 *S, W*, 1899 *W*
Royle, A V (Broughton R) 1889 *M*
Rudd, E L (Liverpool) 1965 *W, I, S*, 1966 *W, I, S*
Russell, R F (Leicester) 1905 *NZ*
Rutherford, D (Percy Park, Gloucester) 1960 *W, I, F, S*, 1961 *SA*, 1965 *W, I, F, S*, 1966 *W, I, F, S*, 1967 *NZ*
Ryalls, H J (New Brighton) 1885 *W, I*
Ryan, D (Wasps, Newcastle) 1990 *Arg* 1,2, 1992 *C*, 1998 *S*
Ryan, P H (Richmond) 1955 *W, I*

Sadler, E H (Army) 1933 *I, S*
Sagar, J W (Cambridge U) 1901 *W, I*
Salmon, J L B (Harlequins) 1985 *NZ* 1,2, 1986 *W, S*, 1987 *I, F, W, S, [A, J, US, W]*
Sample, C H (Cambridge U) 1884 *I*, 1885 *I*, 1886 *S*
Sampson, P C (Wasps) 1998 *SA* 1
Sanders, D L (Harlequins) 1954 *W, NZ, I, S, F*, 1956 *W, I, S, F*
Sanders, F W (Plymouth A) 1923 *I, S, F*
Sanderson, P H (Sale) 1998 *NZ* 1,2, *SA* 1
Sandford, J R P (Marlborough N) 1906 *I*
Sangwin, R D (Hull and E Riding) 1964 *NZ, W*
Sargent, G A F (Gloucester) 1981 *I* (R)
Savage, K F (Northampton) 1966 *W, I, F, S*, 1967 *A, I, F, S, W, NZ*, 1968 *W, F, S*
Sawyer, C M (Broughton) 1880 *S*, 1881 *I*
Saxby, L E (Gloucester) 1932 *SA, W*
Schofield, J W (Manchester) 1880 *I*

Scholfield, J A (Preston Grasshoppers) 1911 *W*
Schwarz, R O (Richmond) 1899 *S*, 1901 *W, I*
Scorfield, E S (Percy Park) 1910 *F*
Scott, C T (Blackheath) 1900 *W, I*, 1901 *W, I*
Scott, E K (St Mary's Hospital, Redruth) 1947 *W*, 1948 *A, W, I, S*
Scott, F S (Bristol) 1907 *W*
Scott, H (Manchester) 1955 *F*
Scott, J P (Rosslyn Park, Cardiff) 1978 *F, W, S, I, NZ,* 1979 *S* (R), *I, F, W, NZ,* 1980 *I, F, W, S,* 1981 *W, S, I, F, Arg* 1,2, 1982 *I, F, W,* 1983 *F, W, S, I, NZ,* 1984 *S, I, F, W, SA* 1,2
Scott, J S M (Oxford U) 1958 *F*
Scott, M T (Cambridge U) 1887 *I*, 1890 *S, I*
Scott, W M (Cambridge U) 1889 *M*
Seddon, R L (Broughton R) 1887 *W, I, S*
Sellar, K A (United Services, RN) 1927 *W, I, S,* 1928 *A, W, I, F*
Sever, H S (Sale) 1936 *NZ, W, I, S,* 1937 *W, I, S,* 1938 *W, I, S*
Shackleton, I R (Cambridge U) 1969 *SA,* 1970 *I, W, S*
Sharp, R A W (Oxford U, Wasps, Redruth) 1960 *W, I, F, S,* 1961 *I, F,* 1962 *W, I, F,* 1963 *W, I, F, S,* 1967 *A*
Shaw, C H (Moseley) 1906 *S, SA,* 1907 *F, W, I, S*
Shaw, F (Cleckheaton) 1898 *I*
Shaw, J F (RNE Coll) 1898 *S, W*
Shaw, S D (Bristol, Wasps) 1996 *It, Arg,* 1997 *S, I, F, W, A* 1, *SA* (R)
Sheasby, C M A (Wasps) 1996 *It, Arg,* 1997 *W* (R), *Arg* 1 (R), 2 (R), *SA* (R), *NZ* 2 (t)
Sheppard, A (Bristol) 1981 *W* (R), 1985 *W*
Sherrard, C W (Blackheath) 1871 *S,* 1872 *S*
Sherriff, G A (Saracens) 1966 *S,* 1967 *A, NZ*
Shewring, H E (Bristol) 1905 *I, NZ,* 1906 *W, S, F, SA,* 1907 *F, W, I, S*
Shooter, J H (Morley) 1899 *I, S,* 1900 *I, S*
Shuttleworth, D W (Headingley) 1951 *S,* 1953 *S*
Sibree, H J H (Harlequins) 1908 *F,* 1909 *I, S*
Silk, N (Harlequins) 1965 *W, I, F, S*
Simms, K G (Cambridge U, Liverpool, Wasps) 1985 *R, F, S, I, W,* 1986 *I, F,* 1987 *I, F, W,* [*A, I, W*], 1988 *F, W*
Simpson, C P (Harlequins) 1965 *W*
Simpson, P D (Bath) 1983 *NZ,* 1984 *S,* 1987 *I*
Simpson, T (Rockcliff) 1902 *S,* 1903 *W, I, S,* 1904 *I, S,* 1905 *I, S,* 1906 *S, SA,* 1909 *F*
Sims, D (Gloucester) 1998 *NZ* 1 (R),2, *SA* 1
Skinner, M G (Harlequins) 1988 *F, W, S, I* 1,2, 1989 *Fj,* 1990 *I, F, W, S, Arg* 1,2, 1991 *Fj* (R), [*US, F, S, A*], 1992 *S, I, F, W*
Sladen, G M (United Services, RN) 1929 *W, I, S*
Sleightholme, J M (Bath) 1996 *F, W, S, I, It, Arg,* 1997 *S, I, F, W, Arg* 1,2
Slemen, M A C (Liverpool) 1976 *I, F,* 1977 *S, I, F, W,* 1978 *F, W, S, I, NZ,* 1979 *S, I, F, W, NZ,* 1980 *I, F, W, S,* 1981 *W, S, I, F,* 1982 *A, S, I, F, W,* 1983 *NZ,* 1984 *S*
Slocock, L A N (Liverpool) 1907 *F, W, I, S,* 1908 *F, W, I, S*
Slow, C F (Leicester) 1934 *S*
Small, H D (Oxford U) 1950 *W, I, F, S*
Smallwood, A M (Leicester) 1920 *F, I,* 1921 *W, I, S, F,* 1922 *I, S,* 1923 *W, I, S, F,* 1925 *I, S*
Smart, C E (Newport) 1979 *F, W, NZ,* 1981 *S, I, F, Arg* 1,2, 1982 *A, S, I, F, W,* 1983 *F, W, S, I*
Smart, S E J (Gloucester) 1913 *SA, W, F, I, S,* 1914 *W, I, S, F,* 1920 *W, I, S*
Smeddle, R W (Cambridge U) 1929 *W, I, S,* 1931 *F*
Smith, C C (Gloucester) 1901 *W*
Smith, D F (Richmond) 1910 *W*
Smith, J V (Cambridge U, Rosslyn Park) 1950 *W, I, F, S*
Smith, K (Roundhay) 1974 *F, W,* 1975 *W, S*
Smith, M J K (Oxford U) 1956 *W*
Smith, S J (Sale) 1973 *I, F, S, A,* 1974 *I, F,* 1975 *W* (R), 1976 *F,* 1977 *F* (R), 1979 *NZ,* 1980 *I, F, W, S,* 1981 *W, S, I, F, Arg* 1,2, 1982 *A, S, I, F, W,* 1983 *F, W, S*
Smith, S R (Richmond) 1959 *W, F, S,* 1964 *F, S*
Smith, S T (Wasps) 1985 *R, F, S, I, W, NZ* 1,2, 1986 *W, S*
Smith, T H (Northampton) 1951 *W*
Soane, F (Bath) 1893 *S,* 1894 *W, S*
Sobey, W H (O Millhillians) 1930 *W, F, S,* 1932 *SA, W*
Solomon, B (Redruth) 1910 *W*
Sparks, R H W (Plymouth A) 1928 *I, F, S,* 1929 *W, I, S,* 1931 *I, S, F*
Speed, H (Castleford) 1894 *W, I, S,* 1896 *S*
Spence, F W (Birkenhead Park) 1890 *I*
Spencer, J (Harlequins) 1966 *W*

Spencer, J S (Cambridge U, Headingley) 1969 *I, F, S, W, SA,* 1970 *I, W, S, F,* 1971 *W, I, S* (2[1C]), *P*
Spong, R S (O Millhillians) 1929 *F,* 1930 *W, I, F, S,* 1931 *F,* 1932 *SA, W*
Spooner, R H (Liverpool) 1903 *W*
Springman, H H (Liverpool) 1879 *S,* 1887 *S*
Spurling, A (Blackheath) 1882 *I*
Spurling, N (Blackheath) 1886 *I, S,* 1887 *W*
Squires, P J (Harrogate) 1973 *F, S, NZ* 2, *A,* 1974 *S, I, F, W,* 1975 *I, F, S, W, A* 1,2, 1976 *A, W,* 1977 *S, I, F, W,* 1978 *F, W, S, I, NZ,* 1979 *S, I, F, W*
Stafford R C (Bedford) 1912 *W, I, S, F*
Stafford, W F H (RE) 1874 *S*
Stanbury, E (Plymouth A) 1926 *W, I, S,* 1927 *W, I, S, F,* 1928 *A, W, I, F, S,* 1929 *W, I, S, F*
Standing, G (Blackheath) 1883 *W, I*
Stanger-Leathes, C F (Northern) 1905 *I*
Stark, K J (O Alleynians) 1927 *W, I, S, F,* 1928 *A, W, I, F, S*
Starks, A (Castleford) 1896 *W, I*
Starmer-Smith, N C (Harlequins) 1969 *SA,* 1970 *I, W, S, F,* 1971 *S* (C), *P*
Start, S P (United Services, RN) 1907 *S*
Steeds, J H (Saracens) 1949 *F, S,* 1950 *I, F, S*
Steele-Bodger, M R (Cambridge U) 1947 *W, I, S, F,* 1948 *A, W, I, S, F*
Steinthal, F E (Ilkley) 1913 *W, F*
Stevens, C B (Penzance-Newlyn, Harlequins) 1969 *SA,* 1970 *I, W, S,* 1971 *P,* 1972 *W, I, F, S, SA,* 1973 *NZ* 1, *W, I, F, S, NZ* 2, *A,* 1974 *S, I, F, W,* 1975 *I, F, W, S*
Still, E R (Oxford U, Ravenscourt P) 1873 *S*
Stimpson, T R G (Newcastle) 1996 *It,* 1997 *S, I, F, W, A* 1, *NZ* 2 (t + R), 1998 *A* 1, *NZ* 1,2 (R), *SA* 1 (R)
Stirling, R V (Leicester, RAF, Wasps) 1951 *W, I, F, S,* 1952 *SA, W, S, I, F,* 1953 *W, I, F, S,* 1954 *W, NZ, I, S, F*
Stoddart, A E (Blackheath) 1885 *W, I,* 1886 *W, I, S,* 1889 *M,* 1890 *W, I,* 1893 *W, S*
Stoddart, W B (Liverpool) 1897 *W, I, S*
Stokes, F (Blackheath) 1871 *S,* 1872 *S,* 1873 *S*
Stokes, L (Blackheath) 1875 *I,* 1876 *S,* 1877 *I, S,* 1878 *S,* 1879 *S, I,* 1880 *I, S,* 1881 *I, W, S*
Stone, F le S (Blackheath) 1914 *F*
Stoop, A D (Harlequins) 1905 *S,* 1906 *S, F, SA,* 1907 *F, W,* 1910 *W, I, S,* 1911 *W, F, I, S,* 1912 *W, S*
Stoop, F M (Harlequins) 1910 *S,* 1911 *F, I,* 1913 *SA*
Stout, F M (Richmond) 1897 *W, I,* 1898 *I, S, W,* 1899 *I, S,* 1903 *S,* 1904 *W, I, S,* 1905 *W, I, S*
Stout, P W (Richmond) 1898 *S, W,* 1899 *W, I, S*
Stringer, N C (Wasps) 1982 *A* (R), 1983 *NZ* (R), 1984 *SA* 1 (R), *A,* 1985 *R*
Strong, E L (Oxford U) 1884 *W, I, S*
Sturnham B (Saracens) 1998 *A* 1, *NZ* 1 (t),2 (t)
Summerscales, G E (Durham City) 1905 *NZ*
Sutcliffe, J W (Heckmondwike) 1889 *M*
Swarbrick, D W (Oxford U) 1947 *W, I, F,* 1948 *A, W,* 1949 *I*
Swayne, D H (Oxford U) 1931 *W*
Swayne, J W R (Bridgwater) 1929 *W*
Swift, A H (Swansea) 1981 *Arg* 1,2, 1983 *F, W, S,* 1984 *SA* 2
Syddall, J P (Waterloo) 1982 *I,* 1984 *A*
Sykes, A R V (Blackheath) 1914 *F*
Sykes, F D (Northampton) 1955 *F, S,* 1963 *NZ* 2, *A*
Sykes, P W (Wasps) 1948 *F,* 1952 *S, I, F,* 1953 *W, I, F*
Syrett, R E (Wasps) 1958 *W, A, I, F,* 1960 *W, I, F, S,* 1962 *W, I, F*

Tallent, J A (Cambridge U, Blackheath) 1931 *S, F,* 1932 *SA, W,* 1935 *I*
Tanner, C C (Cambridge U, Gloucester) 1930 *S,* 1932 *SA, W, I, S*
Tarr, F N (Leicester) 1909 *A, W, F,* 1913 *S*
Tatham, W M (Oxford U) 1882 *S,* 1883 *W, I, S,* 1884 *W, I, S*
Taylor, A S (Blackheath) 1883 *W, I,* 1886 *W, I*
Taylor, E W (Rockcliff) 1892 *I,* 1893 *I,* 1894 *W, I, S,* 1895 *W, I, S,* 1896 *W, I,* 1897 *W, I, S,* 1899 *I*
Taylor, F (Leicester) 1920 *F, I*
Taylor, F M (Leicester) 1914 *W*
Taylor, H H (Blackheath) 1879 *S,* 1880 *S,* 1881 *I, W,* 1882 *S*
Taylor, J T (W Hartlepool) 1897 *I,* 1899 *I,* 1900 *I,* 1901 *W, I,* 1902 *W, I, S,* 1903 *W, I,* 1905 *S*
Taylor, P J (Northampton) 1955 *W, I,* 1962 *W, I, F, S*
Taylor, R B (Northampton) 1966 *W,* 1967 *I, F, S, W, NZ,* 1969 *F, S, W, SA,* 1970 *I, W, S, F,* 1971 *S* (2[1C])

Taylor, W J (Blackheath) 1928 *A, W, I, F, S*
Teague, M C (Gloucester, Moseley) 1985 *F* (R), *NZ* 1, 2, 1989 *S, I, F, W, R,* 1990 *F, W, S,* 1991 *W, S, I, F, Fj, A,* [*NZ, It, F, S, A*], 1992 *SA,* 1993 *F, W, S, I*
Teden, D E (Richmond) 1939 *W, I, S*
Teggin, A (Broughton R) 1884 *I,* 1885 *W,* 1886 *I, S,* 1887 *I, S*
Tetley, T S (Bradford) 1876 *S*
Thomas, C (Barnstaple) 1895 *W, I, S,* 1899 *I*
Thompson, P H (Headingley, Waterloo) 1956 *W, I, S, F,* 1957 *W, I, F, S,* 1958 *W, A, I, F, S,* 1959 *W, I, F, S*
Thomson, G T (Halifax) 1878 *S,* 1882 *I, S,* 1883 *W, I, S,* 1884 *I, S,* 1885 *I*
Thomson, W B (Blackheath) 1892 *W,* 1895 *W, I, S*
Thorne, J D (Bristol) 1963 *W, I, F*
Tindall, V R (Liverpool U) 1951 *W, I, F, S*
Tobin, F (Liverpool) 1871 *S*
Todd, A F (Blackheath) 1900 *I, S*
Todd, R (Manchester) 1877 *S*
Toft, H B (Waterloo) 1936 *S,* 1937 *W, I, S,* 1938 *W, I, S,* 1939 *W, I, S*
Toothill, J T (Bradford) 1890 *S, I,* 1891 *W, I,* 1892 *W, I, S,* 1893 *W, I, S,* 1894 *W, I*
Tosswill, L R (Exeter) 1902 *W, I, S*
Touzel, C J C (Liverpool) 1877 *I, S*
Towell, A C (Bedford) 1948 *F,* 1951 *S*
Travers, B H (Harlequins) 1947 *W, I,* 1948 *A, W,* 1949 *F, S*
Treadwell, W T (Wasps) 1966 *I, F, S*
Trick, D M (Bath) 1983 *I,* 1984 *SA* 1
Tristram, H B (Oxford U) 1883 *S,* 1884 *W, S,* 1885 *W,* 1887 *S*
Troop, C L (Aldershot S) 1933 *I, S*
Tucker, J S (Bristol) 1922 *W,* 1925 *NZ, W, I, S, F,* 1926 *W, I, F, S,* 1927 *W, I, S, F,* 1928 *A, W, I, F, S,* 1929 *W, I, F,* 1930 *W, I, F, S,* 1931 *W*
Tucker, W E (Blackheath) 1894 *W, I,* 1895 *W, I, S*
Tucker, W E (Blackheath) 1926 *I,* 1930 *W, I*
Turner, D P (Richmond) 1871 *S,* 1872 *S,* 1873 *S,* 1874 *S,* 1875 *I, S*
Turner, E B (St George's Hospital) 1876 *I,* 1877 *I,* 1878 *I*
Turner, G R (St George's Hospital) 1876 *S*
Turner, H J C (Manchester) 1871 *S*
Turner, M F (Blackheath) 1948 *S, F*
Turquand-Young, D (Richmond) 1928 *A, W,* 1929 *I, S, F*
Twynam, H T (Richmond) 1879 *I,* 1880 *I,* 1881 *W,* 1882 *I,* 1883 *I,* 1884 *W, I, S*

Ubogu, V E (Bath) 1992 *C, SA,* 1993 *NZ,* 1994 *S, I, F, W, SA* 1,2, *R, C,* 1995 *I, F, W, S,* [*Arg, WS, A, NZ, F*], *SA,* 1999 *F* (R), *W* (R)
Underwood, A M (Exeter) 1962 *W, I, F, S,* 1964 *I*
Underwood, R (Leicester, RAF) 1984 *I, F, W, A,* 1985 *R, F, S, I, W,* 1986 *W, I, F,* 1987 *I, F, W, S,* [*A, J, W*], 1988 *F, W, S, I* 1,2, *A* 1,2, *A,* 1989 *S, I, F, W, R, Fj,* 1990 *I, F, W, S, Arg* 3, 1991 *W, S, I, F, Fj, A,* [*NZ, It, US, F, S, A*], 1992 *S, I, F, W, SA,* 1993 *F, W, S, I, NZ,* 1994 *S, I, F, W, SA* 1,2, *R, C,* 1995 *I, F, W, S,* [*Arg, It, WS, A, NZ*], 1996 *F, W, S, I*
Underwood, T (Leicester, Newcastle) 1992 *C, SA,* 1993 *S, I, NZ,* 1994 *S, I, W, SA* 1,2, *R, C,* 1995 *I, F, W, S,* [*Arg, It, A, NZ*], 1996 *Arg,* 1997 *S, I, F, W,* 1998 *A* 2, *SA* 2
Unwin, E J (Rosslyn Park, Army) 1937 *S,* 1938 *W, I, S*
Unwin, G T (Blackheath) 1898 *S*
Uren, R (Waterloo) 1948 *I, S, F,* 1950 *I*
Uttley, R M (Gosforth) 1973 *I, F, S, NZ* 2, *A,* 1974 *I, F, W,* 1975 *F, W, S, A* 1,2, 1977 *S, I, F, W,* 1978 *NZ* 1979 *S,* 1980 *I, F, W, S*

Valentine J (Swinton) 1890 *W,* 1896 *W, I, S*
Vanderspar, C H R (Richmond) 1873 *S*
Van Ryneveld, C B (Oxford U) 1949 *W, I, F, S*
Varley, H (Liversedge) 1892 *S*
Vassall, H (Blackheath) 1881 *W, S,* 1882 *I, S,* 1883 *W*
Vassall, H H (Blackheath) 1908 *I*
Vaughan, D B (Headingley) 1948 *A, W, I, S,* 1949 *I, F, S,* 1950 *W*
Vaughan-Jones, A (Army) 1932 *I, S,* 1933 *W*
Verelst, C L (Liverpool) 1876 I, 1878 *I*
Vernon, G F (Blackheath) 1878 *S, I,* 1880 *I, S,* 1881 *I*
Vickery, G (Aberavon) 1905 *I*
Vickery, P J (Gloucester) 1998 *W, A* 1, *NZ* 1,2, *SA* 1
Vivyan, E J (Devonport A) 1901 *W,* 1904 *W, I, S*

Voyce, A T (Gloucester) 1920 *I, S,* 1921 *W, I, S, F,* 1922 *W, I, F, S,* 1923 *W, I, S, F,* 1924 *W, I, F, S,* 1925 *NZ, W, I, S, F,* 1926 *W, I, F, S*

Wackett, J A S (Rosslyn Park) 1959 *W, I*
Wade, C G (Richmond) 1883 *W, I, S,* 1884 *W, S,* 1885 *W,* 1886 *W, I*
Wade, M R (Cambridge U) 1962 *W, I, F*
Wakefield, W W (Harlequins) 1920 *W, F, I, S,* 1921 *W, I, S, F,* 1922 *W, I, F, S,* 1923 *W, I, S, F,* 1924 *W, I, F, S,* 1925 *NZ, W, I, S, F,* 1926 *W, I, F, S,* 1927 *S, F*
Walker, G A (Blackheath) 1939 *W, I*
Walker, H W (Coventry) 1947 *W, I, S, F,* 1948 *A, W, I, S, F*
Walker, R (Manchester) 1874 *S,* 1875 *I,* 1876 *S,* 1879 *S,* 1880 *S*
Wallens, J N S (Waterloo) 1927 *F*
Walton, E J (Castleford) 1901 *W, I,* 1902 *I, S*
Walton, W (Castleford) 1894 *S*
Ward, G (Leicester) 1913 *W, F, S,* 1914 *W, I, S*
Ward, H (Bradford) 1895 *W*
Ward, J I (Richmond) 1881 *I,* 1882 *I*
Ward, J W (Castleford) 1896 *W, I, S*
Wardlow, C S (Northampton) 1969 *SA* (R), 1971 *W, I, F, S* (2[1C])
Warfield, P J (Rosslyn Park, Durham U) 1973 *NZ* 1, *W, I,* 1975 *I, F, S*
Warr, A L (Oxford U) 1934 *W, I*
Watkins, J A (Gloucester) 1972 *SA,* 1973 *NZ* 1, *W, NZ* 2, *A,* 1975 *F, W*
Watkins, J K (United Services, RN) 1939 *W, I, S*
Watson, F B (United Services, RN) 1908 *S,* 1909 *S*
Watson, J H D (Blackheath) 1914 *W, S, F*
Watt, D E J (Bristol) 1967 *I, F, S, W*
Webb, C S H (Devonport Services, RN) 1932 *SA, W, I, S,* 1933 *W, I, S,* 1935 *S,* 1936 *NZ, W, I, S*
Webb, J M (Bristol, Bath) 1987 [*A* (R), *J, US, W*], 1988 *F, W, S, I* 1,2, *A* 1,2, *A,* 1989 *S, I, F, W,* 1991 *Fj, A,* [*NZ, It, F, S, A*], 1992 *S, I, F, W, C, SA,* 1993 *F, W, S, I*
Webb, J W G (Northampton) 1926 *F, S,* 1929 *S*
Webb, R E (Coventry) 1967 *S, W, NZ,* 1968 *I, F, S,* 1969 *I, F, S, W,* 1972 *I, F*
Webb, St L H (Bedford) 1959 *W, I, F, S*
Webster, J G (Moseley) 1972 *W, I, SA,* 1973 *NZ* 1, *W, NZ* 2, 1974 *S, W,* 1975 *I, F, W*
Wedge, T G (St Ives) 1907 *F,* 1909 *W*
Weighill, R H G (RAF, Harlequins) 1947 *S, F,* 1948 *S, F*
Wells, C M (Cambridge U, Harlequins) 1893 *S,* 1894 *W, S,* 1896 *S,* 1897 *W, S*
West, B R (Loughborough Colls, Northampton) 1968 *W, I, F, S,* 1969 *SA,* 1970 *I, W, S*
West, D E (Leicester) 1998 *F* (R), *S* (R)
West, R (Gloucester) 1995 [*WS*]
Weston, H T F (Northampton) 1901 *S*
Weston, L E (W of Scotland) 1972 *F, S*
Weston, M P (Richmond, Durham City) 1960 *W, I, F, S,* 1961 *SA, W, I, F, S,* 1962 *W, I, F,* 1963 *W, I, F, S, NZ* 1,2, *A,* 1964 *NZ, W, I, F, S,* 1965 *F, S,* 1966 *S,* 1968 *F, S*
Weston, W H (Northampton) 1933 *I, S,* 1934 *I, S,* 1935 *W, I, S,* 1936 *NZ, W, S,* 1937 *W, I, S,* 1938 *W, I, S*
Wheatley, A A (Coventry) 1937 *W, I, S,* 1938 *W, S*
Wheatley, H F (Coventry) 1936 *I,* 1937 *S,* 1938 *W, S,* 1939 *W, I, S*
Wheeler, P J (Leicester) 1975 *F, W,* 1976 *A, W, S, I,* 1977 *S, I, F, W,* 1978 *F, W, S, I, NZ,* 1979 *S, I, F, W, NZ,* 1980 *I, F, W, S,* 1981 *W, S, I, F,* 1982 *A, S, I, F, W,* 1983 *F, S, I, NZ,* 1984 *S, I, F, W*
White, C (Gosforth) 1983 *NZ,* 1984 *S, I, F*
White, D F (Northampton) 1947 *W, I, S,* 1948 *I, F,* 1951 *S,* 1952 *SA, W, S, I, F,* 1953 *W, I, S*
Whiteley, E C P (O Alleynians) 1931 *S, F*
Whiteley, W (Bramley) 1896 *W*
Whitely, H (Northern) 1929 *W*
Wightman, B J (Moseley, Coventry) 1959 *W,* 1963 *W, I, NZ* 2, *A*
Wigglesworth, H J (Thornes) 1884 *I*
Wilkins, D T (United Services, RN, Roundhay) 1951 *W, I, F, S,* 1952 *SA, W, S, I, F,* 1953 *W, I, F, S*
Wilkinson, E (Bradford) 1886 *W, I, S,* 1887 *W, S*
Wilkinson, H (Halifax) 1929 *W, I, S,* 1930 *F*
Wilkinson, H J (Halifax) 1889 *M*
Wilkinson, J P (Newcastle) 1998 *I* (R), *A* 1, *NZ* 1, 1999 *S, I, F, W*
Wilkinson, P (Law Club) 1872 *S*
Wilkinson, R M (Bedford) 1975 *A* 2, 1976 *A, W, S, I, F*

Willcocks, T J (Plymouth) 1902 *W*
Willcox, J G (Oxford U, Harlequins) 1961 *I, F, S,* 1962 *W, I, F, S,* 1963 *W, I, F, S,* 1964 *NZ, W, I, F, S*
William-Powlett, P B R W (United Services, RN) 1922 *S*
Williams, C G (Gloucester, RAF) 1976 *F*
Williams, C S (Manchester) 1910 *F*
Williams, J E (O Millhillians, Sale) 1954 *F,* 1955 *W, I, F, S,* 1956 *I, S, F,* 1965 *W*
Williams, J M (Penzance-Newlyn) 1951 *I, S*
Williams, P N (Orrell) 1987 *S, [A, J, W]*
Williams, S G (Devonport A) 1902 *W, I, S,* 1903 *I, S,* 1907 *I, S*
Williams, S H (Newport) 1911 *W, F, I, S*
Williamson, R H (Oxford U) 1908 *W, I, S,* 1909 *A, F*
Wilson, A J (Camborne S of M) 1909 *I*
Wilson, C E (Blackheath) 1898 *I*
Wilson, C P (Cambridge U, Marlborough N) 1881 *W*
Wilson, D S (Met Police, Harlequins) 1953 *F,* 1954 *W, NZ, I, S, F,* 1955 *F, S*
Wilson, G S (Tyldesley) 1929 *W, I*
Wilson, K J (Gloucester) 1963 *F*
Wilson, R P (Liverpool OB) 1891 *W, I, S*
Wilson, W C (Richmond) 1907 *I, S*
Winn, C E (Rosslyn Park) 1952 *SA, W, S, I, F,* 1954 *W, S, F*
Winterbottom, P J (Headingley, Harlequins) 1982 *A, S, I, F, W,* 1983 *F, W, S, I, NZ,* 1984 *S, F, W, SA 1,2,* 1986 *W, S, I, F,* 1987 *I, F, W, [A, J, US, W],* 1988 *F, W, S,* 1989 *R, Fj,* 1990 *I, F, W, S, Arg 1,2,3,* 1991 *W, S, I, F, A, [NZ, It, F, S, A],* 1992 *S, I, F, W, C, SA,* 1993 *F, W, S, I*
Wintle, T C (Northampton) 1966 *S,* 1969 *I, F, S, W*
Wodehouse, N A (United Services, RN) 1910 *F,* 1911 *W, F, I, S,* 1912 *W, I, S, F,* 1913 *SA, W, F, I, S*
Wood, A (Halifax) 1884 *I*
Wood, A E (Gloucester, Cheltenham) 1908 *F, W, I*
Wood, G W (Leicester) 1914 *W*
Wood, R (Liversedge) 1894 *I*
Wood, R D (Liverpool OB) 1901 *I,* 1903 *W, I*
Woodgate, E E (Paignton) 1952 *W*

Woodhead, E (Huddersfield) 1880 *I*
Woodruff, C G (Harlequins) 1951 *W, I, F, S*
Woods, S M J (Cambridge U, Wellington) 1890 *W, S, I,* 1891 *W, I, S,* 1892 *I, S,* 1893 *W, I,* 1895 *W, I, S*
Woods, T (Bridgwater) 1908 *S*
Woods, T (United Services, RN) 1920 *S,* 1921 *W, I, S, F*
Woodward, C R (Leicester) 1980 *I (R), F, W, S,* 1981 *W, S, I, F, Arg 1,2,* 1982 *A, S, I, F, W,* 1983 *I, NZ,* 1984 *S, I, F, W*
Woodward, J E (Wasps) 1952 *SA, W, S,* 1953 *W, I, F, S,* 1954 *W, NZ, I, S, F,* 1955 *W, I,* 1956 *S*
Wooldridge, C S (Oxford U, Blackheath) 1883 *W, I, S,* 1884 *W, I, S,* 1885 *I*
Wordsworth, A J (Cambridge U) 1975 *A 1 (R)*
Worton, J R B (Harlequins, Army) 1926 *W,* 1927 *W*
Wrench, D F B (Harlequins) 1964 *F, S*
Wright, C C G (Cambridge U, Blackheath) 1909 *I, S*
Wright, F T (Edinburgh Acady, Manchester) 1881 *S*
Wright, I D (Northampton) 1971 *W, I, F, S (R)*
Wright. J C (Met Police) 1934 *W*
Wright, J F (Bradford) 1890 *W*
Wright, T P (Blackheath) 1960 *W, I, F, S,* 1961 *SA, W, I, F, S,* 1962 *W, I, F, S*
Wright, W H G (Plymouth) 1920 *W, F*
Wyatt, D M (Bedford) 1976 *S (R)*

Yarranton, P G (RAF, Wasps) 1954 *W, NZ, I,* 1955 *F, S*
Yates, K P (Bath) 1997 *Arg 1,2*
Yiend, W (Hartlepool R, Gloucester) 1889 *M,* 1892 *W, I, S,* 1893 *I, S*
Young, A T (Cambridge U, Blackheath, Army) 1924 *W, I, F, S,* 1925 *NZ, F,* 1926 *I, F, S,* 1927 *I, S, F,* 1928 *A, W, I, F, S,* 1929 *I*
Young, J R C (Oxford U, Harlequins) 1958 *I,* 1960 *W, I, F, S,* 1961 *SA, W, I, F*
Young, M (Gosforth) 1977 *S, I, F, W,* 1978 *F, W, S, I, NZ,* 1979 *S*
Young, P D (Dublin Wands) 1954 *W, NZ, I, S, F,* 1955 *W, I, F, S*
Youngs, N G (Leicester) 1983 *I, NZ,* 1984 *S, I, F, W*

Kick-starting England. The rising star of English rugby Jonny Wilkinson finally settled into the pivotal role of fly-half on England's summer tour.

ENGLISH INTERNATIONAL RECORDS
(*up to 30 April 1999*)

MATCH RECORDS

MOST CONSECUTIVE TEST WINS

10 1882 *W*, 1883 *I, S*, 1884 *W, I, S*, 1885 *W, I*, 1886 *W, I*

10 1994 *R, C*, 1995 *I, F, W, S, Arg, It, WS, A*

MOST CONSECUTIVE TESTS WITHOUT DEFEAT

P	W	D	Period
12	10	2	1882–87
11	10	1	1922–24
10	6	4	1878–82
10	10	0	1994–95

MOST POINTS IN A MATCH
by the team

Pts	Opp	Venue	Year
110	H	Huddersfield	1998
60	J	Sydney	1987
60	C	Twickenham	1994
60	W	Twickenham	1998
58	R	Bucharest	1989
58	Fj	Twickenham	1989

by a player

30 by C R Andrew v Canada at Twickenham 1994
30 by P J Grayson v Holland at Huddersfield 1998
27 by C R Andrew v South Africa at Pretoria 1994
24 by J M Webb v Italy at Twickenham 1991
24 by C R Andrew v Romania at Twickenham 1994
24 by C R Andrew v Scotland at Twickenham 1995
24 by C R Andrew v Argentina at Durban 1995

MOST TRIES IN A MATCH
by the team

T	Opp	Venue	Year
16	H	Huddersfield	1998
13	W	Blackheath	1881
10	J	Sydney	1987
10	Fj	Twickenham	1989
9	F	Paris	1906
9	F	Richmond	1907
9	F	Paris	1914
9	R	Bucharest	1989

by a player

5 by D Lambert v France at Richmond 1907
5 by R Underwood v Fiji at Twickenham 1989
4 by G W Burton v Wales at Blackheath 1881
4 by A Hudson v France at Paris 1906
4 by R W Poulton v France at Paris 1914
4 by C Oti v Romania at Bucharest 1989
4 by J C Guscott v Holland at Huddersfield 1998
4 by N A Back v Holland at Huddersfield 1998

MOST CONVERSIONS IN A MATCH
by the team

C	Opp	Venue	Year
15	H	Huddersfield	1998
8	R	Bucharest	1989
7	W	Blackheath	1881
7	J	Sydney	1987
7	Arg	Twickenham	1990
7	W	Twickenham	1998

by a player

15 by P J Grayson v Holland at Huddersfield 1998
8 by S D Hodgkinson v Romania at Bucharest 1989
7 by J M Webb v Japan at Sydney 1987
7 by S D Hodgkinson v Argentina at Twickenham 1990
7 by P J Grayson v Wales at Twickenham 1998

MOST PENALTY GOALS IN A MATCH
by the team

P	Opp	Venue	Year
7	W	Cardiff	1991
7	S	Twickenham	1995
7	F	Twickenham	1999
6	W	Twickenham	1986
6	C	Twickenham	1994
6	Arg	Durban	1995
6	S	Murrayfield	1996
6	I	Twickenham	1996

by a player

7 by S D Hodgkinson v Wales at
Cardiff — 1991
7 by C R Andrew v Scotland at
Twickenham — 1995
7 by J P Wilkinson v France at
Twickenham — 1999
6 by C R Andrew v Wales at
Twickenhan — 1986
6 by C R Andrew v Canada at
Twickenham — 1994
6 by C R Andrew v Argentina at
Durban — 1995
6 by P J Grayson v Scotland at
Murrayfield — 1996
6 by P J Grayson v Ireland at
Twickenham — 1996

MOST DROPPED GOALS IN A MATCH

by the team

D	Opp	Venue	Year
2	I	Twickenham	1970
2	F	Paris	1978
2	F	Paris	1980
2	R	Twickenham	1985
2	Fj	Suva	1991
2	Arg	Durban	1995
2	F	Paris	1996

by a player

2 by R Hiller v Ireland at
Twickenham — 1970
2 by A G B Old v France at Paris — 1978
2 by J P Horton v France at Paris — 1980
2 by C R Andrew v Romania at
Twickenham — 1985
2 by C R Andrew v Fiji at Suva — 1991
2 by C R Andrew v Argentina at
Durban — 1995
2 by P J Grayson v France at Paris — 1996

CAREER RECORDS

MOST CAPPED PLAYERS

Caps	Player	Career
85	R Underwood	1984–96
72	W D C Carling	1988–97
71	C R Andrew	1985–97
71	J Leonard	1990–99
64	B C Moore	1987–95
59	J C Guscott	1989–99
58	P J Winterbottom	1982–93
55	W A Dooley	1985–93
48	D Richards	1986–96
45	M O Johnson	1993–99

MOST CONSECUTIVE TESTS

Tests	Player	Span
44	W D C Carling	1989–95
40	J Leonard	1990–95
36	J V Pullin	1968–75
33	W B Beaumont	1975–82
30	R Underwood	1992–96

MOST TESTS AS CAPTAIN

Tests	Captain	Span
59	W D C Carling	1988–96
21	W B Beaumont	1978–82
14	L B N Dallaglio	1997–99
13	W W Wakefield	1924–26
13	N M Hall	1949–55
13	R E G Jeeps	1960–62
13	J V Pullin	1972–75

MOST TESTS IN INDIVIDUAL POSITIONS

Full-back J M Webb		33	1987–93
Wing R Underwood		85	1984–96
Centre W D C Carling		72	1988–97
Fly-half C R Andrew		70	1985–97
Scrum-half R J Hill		29	1984–91
Prop J Leonard		71	1990–99
Hooker B C Moore		63★	1987–95
Lock W A Dooley		55	1985–93
Flanker P J Winterbottom		58	1982–93
No. 8 D Richards		47★	1986–96

★ *excludes an appearance as a temporary replacement*

MOST POINTS IN TESTS

Pts	Player	Tests	Career
396	C R Andrew	71	1985–97
296	J M Webb	33	1987–93
256	P J Grayson	19	1995–99
240	W H Hare	25	1974–84
210	R Underwood	85	1984–96

MOST TRIES IN TESTS

Tries	Player	Tests	Career
49	R Underwood	85	1984–96
24	J C Guscott	59	1989–99
18	C N Lowe	25	1913–23
13	T Underwood	27	1992–98
12	W D C Carling	72	1988–97

MOST CONVERSIONS IN TESTS

Cons	Player	Tests	Career
41	J M Webb	33	1987–93
40	P J Grayson	19	1995–99
35	S D Hodgkinson	14	1989–91

33	C R Andrew	71	1985–97
17	L Stokes	12	1875–81

MOST PENALTY GOALS IN TESTS

Pens	Player	Tests	Career
86	C R Andrew	71	1985–97
67	W H Hare	25	1974–84
66	J M Webb	33	1987–93
51	P J Grayson	19	1995–99

43	S D Hodgkinson	14	1989–91

MOST DROPPED GOALS IN TESTS

Drops	Player	Tests	Career
21	C R Andrew	71	1985–97
6	P J Grayson	19	1995–99
4	J P Horton	13	1978–84

INTERNATIONAL CHAMPIONSHIP RECORDS

Record	Detail		Set
Most points in season	146	in four matches	1998
Most tries in season	20	in four matches	1914
Highest score	60	60–26 v Wales	1998
Biggest win	40	46–6 v Ireland	1997
Highest score conceded	37	12–37 v France	1972
Biggest defeat	27	6–33 v Scotland	1986
Most appearances	50	R Underwood	1984–96
Most points in matches	185	C R Andrew	1985–97
	185	P J Grayson	1996–99
Most points in season	67	J M Webb	1992
Most points in match	24	C R Andrew	v Scotland, 1995
Most tries in matches	18	C N Lowe	1913–23
	18	R Underwood	1984–96
Most tries in season	8	C N Lowe	1914
Most tries in match	4	R W Poulton	v France, 1914
Most cons in matches	21	P J Grayson	1996–99
Most cons in season	14	P J Grayson	1998
Most cons in match	7	P J Grayson	v Wales, 1998
Most pens in matches	50	W H Hare	1974–84
Most pens in season	18	S D Hodgkinson	1991
Most pens in match	7	S D Hodgkinson	v Wales, 1991
	7	C R Andrew	v Scotland, 1995
	7	J P Wilkinson	v France, 1999
Most drops in matches	9	C R Andrew	1985–97
Most drops in season	3	P J Grayson	1996
Most drops in match	2	R Hiller	v Ireland, 1970
	2	A G B Old	v France, 1978
	2	J P Horton	v France, 1980
	2	P J Grayson	v France, 1996

MAJOR TOUR RECORDS

Record	Detail	Year	Place
Most individual points	58 by C R Andrew	1994	South Africa
Most points in match	36 by W N Bennett	1975 v W Australia	Perth
Most tries in match	4 by A J Morley	1975 v W Australia	Perth
	4 by P S Preece	1975 v NSW	Sydney

MISCELLANEOUS RECORDS

Record	Holder	Detail
Longest Test career	G S Pearce	14 seasons, 1978–79 to 1991–92
Youngest Test cap	H C C Laird	18 yrs 134 days in 1927
Oldest Test cap	F Gilbert	38 yrs in 1923

Paul Grayson lines up a kick in the England-Netherlands World Cup qualifier in November 1998, a match in which he recorded an English record 15 conversions.

ENGLISH INTERNATIONAL CAREER RECORDS *(up to 30 April 1999)*

Player	Debut	Caps since last season	Caps	T	C	PG	DG	Pts
T R G Stimpson	1996 v It	1998 *A* 1, *NZ* 1,2(R), *SA* 1(R)	11	1	2	2	0	15
N D Beal	1996 v Arg	1998 *NZ* 1,2, *SA* 1, *H*(R), *SA* 2, 1999 *S*, *F*(R)	9	2	0	0	0	10
M B Perry	1997 v A	1998 *A* 1, *NZ* 1,2, *SA* 1, *H*, *It*, *A* 2, 1999 *I*, *F*, *W*	17	2	0	0	0	10
D L Rees	1997 v A	1998 *SA* 2(R), 1999 *S*, *I*, *F*	10	3	0	0	0	15
S P Brown	1998 v A	1998 *A* 1, *SA* 1	2	0	0	0	0	0
T D Beim	1998 v NZ	1998 *NZ* 1(R),2	2	1	0	0	0	5
S M Hanley	1999 v W	1999 *W*	1	1	0	0	0	5
D E Chapman	1998 v A	1998 *A* 1(R)	1	0	0	0	0	0
P C Sampson	1998 v SA	1998 *SA* 1	1	0	0	0	0	0
T Underwood	1992 v C	1998 *A* 2, *SA* 2	27	13	0	0	0	65
D D Luger	1998 v H	1998 *H*, *It*, *SA*2, 1999 *S*, *I*, *F*, *W*	7	4	0	0	0	20
J C Guscott	1989 v R	1998 *H*, *It*, *A* 2, *SA* 2, 1999 *S*, *I*, *F*	59	24	0	0	2	113
B-J Mather	1999 v W	1999 *W*	1	0	0	0	0	0
S C W Ravenscroft	1998 v A	1998 *A* 1, *NZ* 2(R)	2	0	0	0	0	0
J J N Baxendell	1998 v NZ	1998 *NZ* 2, *SA* 1	2	0	0	0	0	0
W J H Greenwood	1997 v A	1998 *H*, *It*	10	3	0	0	0	15
P R de Glanville	1992 v SA	1998 *A* 2, *SA* 2	32	5	0	0	0	25
S Potter	1998 v A	1998 *A* 1(t)	1	0	0	0	0	0
J P Wilkinson	1998 v I	1998 *A* 1, *NZ* 1, 1999 *S*, *I*, *F*, *W*	7	0	6	16	0	60
O J Lewsey	1998 v NZ	1998 *NZ* 1,2, *SA* 1	3	0	0	0	0	0
M J Catt	1994 v W	1998 *A* 2(R), *SA* 2, 1999 *S*, *F*, *W*	34	4	14	22	2	120
P J Grayson	1995 v WS	1998 *H*, *It*, *A* 2, 1999 *I*	19	1	40	51	6	256
A D King	1997 v Arg	1998 *SA* 2(R)	2	1	0	0	0	5
M J S Dawson	1995 v WS	1998 *NZ* 1,2, *SA* 1, *H*, *It*, *A* 2, *SA* 2, 1999 *S*, *F*(R), *W*	21	5	2	3	0	38
S Benton	1998 v A	1998 *A* 1	1	0	0	0	0	0
A S Healey	1997 v I	1998 *A* 1, *NZ* 1,2, *H*, *It*, *A* 2, *SA* 2(R)	18	3	0	0	0	15
K P P Bracken	1993 v NZ	1999 *S*(R), *I*, *F*	22	2	0	0	0	10
R Cockerill	1997 v Arg	1998 *A* 1, *NZ* 1,2, *SA* 1, *H*, *It*, *A* 2, *SA* 2, 1999 *S*, *I*, *F*, *W*	21	3	0	0	0	15
N McCarthy	1999 v I	1999 *I*(t)	1	0	0	0	0	0
P B T Greening	1996 v It	1998 *NZ* 1(R),2(R)	5	0	0	0	0	0
W R Green	1997 v A	1998 *NZ* 1(t&R)	2	0	0	0	0	0
D J Garforth	1997 v W	1998 *H*, *It*, *A* 2, *SA* 2, 1999 *S*, *I*, *F*, *W*	19	0	0	0	0	0
J Leonard	1990 v Arg	1998 *H*, *It*, *A* 2, *SA* 2, 1999 *S*, *I*, *F*, *W*	71	1	0	0	0	5

V E Ubogu	1992 v C	1999 *F*(R), *W*(R)	23	1	0	0	0	5
P J Vickery	1998 v W	1998 *A* 1, *NZ* 1,2, *SA* 1	5	0	0	0	0	0
G C Rowntree	1995 v S	1998 *A* 1, *NZ* 1,2, *SA* 1, *H*(R), *It*(R)	21	0	0	0	0	0
G S Archer	1996 v S	1998 *A* 1, *NZ* 1, *H*, *It*	14	0	0	0	0	0
D J Grewcock	1997 v Arg	1998 *A* 1, *NZ* 1, *SA* 2(R), 1999 *S*(R)	9	1	0	0	0	5
D Sims	1998 v NZ	1998 *NZ* 1(R),2, *SA* 1	3	0	0	0	0	0
R J Fidler	1998 v NZ	1998 *NZ* 2, *SA* 1	2	0	0	0	0	0
M O Johnson	1993 v F	1998 *H*, *It*, *A* 2, *SA* 2, 1999 *S*, *I*, *F*, *W*	45	1	0	0	0	5
S D Shaw	1996 v It		8	0	0	0	0	0
R A Hill	1997 v S	1998 *H*(R), *It*(R), *A* 2, *SA* 2, 1999 *S*, *I*, *F*, *W*	19	4	0	0	0	20
L B N Dallaglio	1995 v SA	1998 *A* 2, *SA* 2, 1999 *S*, *I*, *F*, *W*	26	5	0	0	0	25
B Sturnham	1998 v A	1998 *A* 1, *NZ* 1(t),2(t)	3	0	0	0	0	0
T A K Rodber	1992 v S	1998 *H*(R), *It*(R), *A* 2, *SA* 2, 1999 *S*, *I*, *F*, *W*	40	5	0	0	0	25
M E Corry	1997 v Arg	1998 *H*, *It*, *SA* 2(t), 1999 *F*(R)	6	1	0	0	0	5
N A Back	1994 v S	1998 *H*, *It*, *A* 2, *SA* 2, 1999 *S*, *I*, *F*, *W*	20	7	0	0	0	35
R J Pool Jones	1998 v A	1998 *A* 1	1	0	0	0	0	0
P H Sanderson	1998 v NZ	1998 *NZ* 1,2, *SA* 1	3	0	0	0	0	0
B B Clarke	1992 v SA	1998 *A* 1(t), *NZ* 1,2, *SA* 1, *H*, *It*	39	3	0	0	0	15
S O Ojomoh	1994 v I	1998 *NZ* 1	12	0	0	0	0	0
A J Diprose	1997 v Arg	1998 *A* 1, *NZ* 2, *SA* 1	10	1	0	0	0	5
C M A Sheasby	1996 v It		7	1	0	0	0	5

ENGLISH CLUBS 1998-99

Bath

Year of formation 1865
Ground Recreation Ground, London Road, Bath BA2 6PW Tel: Bath (01225) 325200
Web site http://www.bathrugby.co.uk/
Colours Blue, white and black hoops; royal blue shorts
Captain 1998-99 R E Webster
Allied Dunbar Leagues 1998-99 Div 1 6th
Tetley's Bitter Cup 1998-99 Lost 22-25 to Newcastle (4th round)

Given the season they had, a place in Europe next year must have come as a welcome relief for a much troubled club. They had all sorts of problems and changes to contend with even before the new campaign began: Tony Swift stepped down as chief executive and reverted to the role of non-executive chairman, this after they had signed the All Black utility half-back Jon Preston of whom great things were expected. He played for some 27 minutes at the Stoop Memorial Ground in the defeat against Harlequins before coming off with an Achilles tendon injury, never to play again. Then Phil de Glanville suffered a dislocated shoulder and Matt Perry a concussion against South Africa and Australia respectively in doing their bit for their country, while captain Richard Webster suffered a fractured eye socket. What with those injuries, Victor Ubogu's sending-off in an Anglo-Welsh match at Cardiff and Kevin Yates' four week ban for stamping against Wasps, not to mention Jeremy Guscott's court case which hung over the England centre during the last few weeks of the season, they could be forgiven for thinking it just was not their year.

Swift resigned at Christmas from the non-executive post; according to rumour Jack Rowell rejected an offer to return as chief executive and David Jenkins left to take up that very role with Cardiff. The departures did not stop there either. Andy Nicol, the Scotland scrum-half, decided that he had had enough of playing second fiddle to the very ordinary Steve Hatley and joined Glasgow Caledonians. Nigel Redman ended a 16-year association with the club when he left to take up a coaching position with Basingstoke, and Yates signed up with New Zealand side Wellington in the hope of gaining some Super-12s experience. Ben Clarke returned to the fold from Richmond, while former Wallaby lock, Warwick Waugh, also arrived.

There was on-field disappointment as well. The only consistency they showed was when they strung together six Allied Dunbar Premiership defeats on the trot, their longest losing sequence in the league and, having clawed their way out of that run with a narrow win at Sale, promptly crashed out of the Tetley's Bitter Cup in the fourth round up at Newcastle.

League Record 1998-99

Date	Venue	Opponents	Result	Scorers
5 Sep	H	Wasps	36-27	*T:* Guscott 2, Peters *C:* Catt 3 *P:* Catt 5
12 Sep	A	Newcastle	17-19	*T:* Adebayo *P:* Catt 4
19 Sep	H	Richmond	36-14	*T:* Guscott 2, Adebayo, Nicol *C:* Catt 2 *P:* Catt 4
26 Sep	H	Gloucester	21-16	*T:* Adebayo, Long *C:* Catt *P:* Catt 3
3 Oct	H	Bedford	57-19	*T:* Guscott 2, Webster 2, Balshaw, Hatley, Perry *C:* Catt 5 *P:* Catt 4
10 Oct	H	London Irish	23-20	*T:* Sturnham 2, Balshaw *C:* Catt *P:* Catt 2
17 Oct	A	West Hartlepool	50-20	*T:* Guscott 2, Hatley 2, Balshaw, Catt, Earnshaw *C:* Catt 6 *P:* Catt
24 Oct	H	Sale	27-3	*T:* Nicol, penalty try, Webster *C:* Catt 3 *P:* Catt 2
31 Oct	A	London Scottish	11-13	*T:* Nicol *P:* Catt 2

7 Nov	A	Leicester	13-36	*T:* Guscott *C:* Catt *P:* Catt 2
21 Nov	A	Harlequins	31-43	*T:* Balshaw, Nicol, Regan *C:* Callard 2
				P: Callard 3, Preston
12 Dec	H	Northampton	9-15	*P:* Catt 3
19 Dec	H	Saracens	11-19	*T:* Balshaw *P:* Catt 2
2 Jan	A	Gloucester	7-23	*T:* Adebayo *C:* Callard
5 Jan	A	Sale	32-30	*T:* Guscott, Catt, Adebayo, Hilton *C:* Catt 3
				P: Perry 2
16 Jan	H	Newcastle	16-11	*T:* Catt *C:* Catt *P:* Catt 3
23 Jan	A	Bedford	30-17	*T:* Adebayo, Balshaw, penalty try *C:* Catt 3
				P: Catt 3
7 Feb	A	Wasps	0-35	
13 Mar	A	Richmond	30-23	*T:* Adebayo, Perry *C:* Catt *P:* Catt 6
28 Mar	A	Saracens	33-14	*T:* Balshaw 3, Cooper, Peters *C:* Catt 4
3 Apr	H	Leicester	24-16	*T:* Balshaw, penalty try *C:* Catt *P:* Catt 4
17 Apr	A	London Irish	22-47	*T:* Catt, Regan, Tindall *C:* Catt 2 *P:* Catt
24 Apr	H	West Hartlepool	56-24	*T:* Balshaw 2, Perry 2, Cooper, Maggs, Regan,
				Tindall *C:* Catt 5 *P:* Catt 2
1 May	A	Northampton	17-40	*T:* Tindall, Catt, Earnshaw *C:* Perry
8 May	H	Harlequins	13-17	*T:* Earnshaw *C:* Perry *P:* Perry 2
15 May	H	London Scottish	76-13	*T:* Guscott 4, Catt 2, Perry 2, Balshaw, Cooper,
				Regan, Hilton *C:* Catt 8

Bedford

Year of formation 1886
Ground Goldington Road, Bedford MK40 3NF Tel: Bedford (01234) 347980
Web site http://www.bedfordrugby.co.uk/
Colours Oxford and Cambridge blue hoops; navy blue shorts
Captain 1998-99 R Straeuli
Allied Dunbar Leagues 1998-99 Div 1 13th; *Won Division 1/2 play-off* against Rotherham on
more tries rule after drawing 38-all on aggregate
Tetley's Bitter Cup 1998-99 Lost 22-29 to Henley (4th round)

As their miserable season receded, rumours lingered that Bedford were still not out
of the financial mire. Frank Warren's legal battle with American boxing promoter
Don King left the rugby club – innocent bystanders in all the wranglings – financially
knackered as a High Court ruling froze all of Warren's assets including Bedford.
Players went without pay and the future did not even stretch to Christmas at one
point. That they even made it to the end of the season, retaining their Premiership
One status in the process, was little short of miraculous. They played some
marvellous rugby despite the trials and tribulations. If they had shown a little more
consistency and a lot more staying power in the hard games then they might have
avoided the play-offs. As it was they scraped through against Rotherham courtesy of
Alistair Murdoch's try in the second leg, having lost the first leg. Murdoch's
touchdown brought their try count to four in the two matches, compared to
Rotherham's three, and so Bedford survived.

   But what an up and downer of a season it was. Director of Rugby and Chief
Executive Geoff Cooke hung in there for a long time, adopting a hands-on coaching
role after the sudden departure of Paul Turner, but eventually it all became too
much even for the seasoned old campaigner. They lost Junior Paramore to
Gloucester and lock Scott Murray to Saracens. Former England coach Cooke left at
the beginning of December and Rudi Straeuli took over his responsibilities, the
South African having announced his retirement as a player because of injury. He had
to undergo five Premiership defeats and the humiliating fourth round Tetley's Cup
defeat at home to Henley before the team recorded their first win. It was well worth
the wait though, a victory over Wasps. They had already beaten Harlequins in
October, but winter had been particularly unkind to them and after a hiccup at
home to Sale further wins followed at London Scottish and at home to Gloucester.

The decision to field a Second XV against Richmond, a match in which they conceded the highest score in the history of the league, was perhaps ill-judged, but Straeuli had not wanted to risk injury to any of the players in the run-up to the crucial play-offs.

League Record 1998-99

Date	Venue	Opponents	Result	Scorers
12 Sep	A	Sale	21-39	*T:* Howard, O'Mahony *C:* Howard *P:* Howard 3
19 Sep	H	London Scottish	24-16	*T:* Underwood, Yapp *C:* Howard *P:* Howard 3 *D:* Yapp
26 Sep	H	Leicester	23-32	*T:* Forster, Murdoch *C:* Howard 2 *P:* Howard 3
3 Oct	A	Bath	19-57	*T:* Howard, O'Mahony 2 *C:* Howard 2
10 Oct	H	Harlequins	35-33	*T:* Ewens 2, O'Mahony 2 *C:* Howard 3 *P:* Howard 2 *D:* Yapp
17 Oct	A	Northampton	29-34	*T:* Underwood 2, Cockle, Ewens *C:* Howard 3 *P:* Howard
21 Oct	A	Wasps	19-35	*T:* Forster *C:* Howard *P:* Howard 3 *D:* Yapp
24 Oct	H	Newcastle	22-29	*T:* Paramore *C:* Yapp *P:* Yapp 5
1 Nov	A	Richmond	32-38	*T:* O'Mahony 3, Paramore *C:* Howard 3 *P:* Howard 2
7 Nov	A	Gloucester	21-31	*T:* Richards, Yapp, Zaltzman *C:* Howard 3
15 Nov	H	Saracens	20-25	*T:* Underwood, Paramore *C:* Howard 2 *P:* Howard 2
21 Nov	A	London Irish	19-30	*T:* Underwood, Whetstone, Ewens *C:* Howard 2
12 Dec	H	West Hartlepool	10-23	*T:* Ewens, Howard
26 Dec	A	Leicester	0-26	
3 Jan	A	Saracens	13-44	*T:* Paramore *C:* Yapp *P:* Yapp 2
5 Jan	A	Newcastle	23-34	*T:* Underwood 2, Forster *C:* Yapp *P:* Yapp *D:* Yapp
23 Jan	H	Bath	17-30	*T:* Elliott, Murdoch, Zaltzman *C:* Howard
13 Feb	H	Wasps	25-23	*T:* Underwood, Richards, Stewart *C:* Howard 2 *P:* Howard *D:* Howard
27 Feb	H	Sale	7-18	*T:* Paramore *C:* Howard
13 Mar	A	London Scottish	24-15	*T:* Underwood, Forster *C:* Yapp *P:* Yapp 4
27 Mar	H	Gloucester	19-15	*T:* Davies *C:* Yapp *P:* Yapp 4
17 Apr	A	Harlequins	16-29	*T:* Underwood *C:* Yapp *P:* Yapp 3
24 Apr	H	Northampton	31-42	*T:* Ewens, Forster, Murdoch, O'Mahony, Olver *C:* Yapp 2, Stewart
2 May	A	West Hartlepool	39-0	*T:* O'Mahony 3, Ewens, Zaltzman *C:* Yapp 4 *P:* Yapp *D:* Yapp
8 May	H	London Irish	21-36	*T:* Harrison, Underwood, Yapp *C:* Yapp 3
16 May	H	Richmond	12-106	*T:* Cook 2 *C:* Howard
Play-offs				
20 May	A	Rotherham	11-19	*T:* Forster *P:* Yapp 2
26 May	H	Rotherham	27-19	*T:* Forster, Murdoch, O'Mahony *C:* Yapp 3 *P:* Yapp *D:* Yapp

Blackheath

Year of formation 1858
Ground Rectory Field, Charlton Road, Blackheath, London SE3 8SR Tel: 0181 293 0853
Web site http://www.users.globalnet.co.uk/bheath/
Colours Red and black hoops with blue lines; black shorts
Captain 1998-99 C Wilkins
Allied Dunbar Leagues 1998-99 Div 2 13th
Tetley's Bitter Cup 1998-99 Lost 21-22 to Sedgley Park (3rd round)

This season saw an end to Premiership rugby at the Rectory Field after an unhappy couple of years. The playing strength was just not there. How they needed to have hung on to John Schuster. Their loss was Harlequins gain. That they finished their league programme on a winning note is scant consolation, especially since that away victory was gained against Fylde, the club who finished below them in Premiership Two. Indeed it had been against Fylde in the home match that they had finally recorded their first victory of the season after a straight 12 defeats from the start. The most notable of their five victories in the Second Division was against Orrell. They conceded 50 points or more on no fewer than five occasions so there was little wonder that they had the worst defensive record in the division. The 842 points that were scored against them was 30 more than the next worst, Wakefield.

League Record 1998-99

Date	Venue	Opponents	Result	Scorers
5 Sep	A	Rugby	12-18	*P:* Aitken 4
13 Sep	H	London Welsh	16-20	*T:* Kardooni *C:* Aitken *P:* Aitken 3
20 Sep	A	Leeds	6-60	*P:* Aitken 2
26 Sep	A	Orrell	3-60	*P:* Aitken
3 Oct	H	Bristol	9-41	*P:* Aitken 3
10 Oct	A	Rotherham	3-46	*P:* Aitken
17 Oct	H	Coventry	18-30	*T:* Griffiths, Howe *C:* Aitken *P:* Aitken 2
24 Oct	A	Wakefield	9-19	*P:* Aitken 3
31 Oct	H	Moseley	14-18	*T:* Merlin, Wilkins *C:* Aitken 2
7 Nov	A	Worcester	9-21	*P:* Aitken 3
21 Nov	A	Waterloo	18-24	*T:* Jennings, Razak *C:* Aitken *P:* Aitken 2
12 Dec	A	Exeter	7-26	*T:* Clarke *C:* Braithwaite
19 Dec	H	Fylde	24-17	*T:* Clarke 2, Razak *C:* Braithwaite 3 *P:* Braithwaite
2 Jan	A	Waterloo	25-31	*T:* Fitzgerald, Sangster, Braithwaite, Smith *C:* Braithwaite *P:* Braithwaite
16 Jan	H	Worcester	3-51	*P:* Braithwaite
23 Jan	A	Moseley	16-22	*T:* Fitzgerald *C:* Amor *P:* Amor 3
6 Feb	H	Wakefield	28-20	*T:* Clarke 2, Sangster, Griffiths *C:* Amor *P:* Amor 2
13 Feb	A	Coventry	8-35	*T:* Pawson *P:* Amor
28 Feb	H	Rotherham	19-29	*T:* Sangster *C:* Amor *P:* Amor 4
13 Mar	A	Bristol	17-50	*T:* Clarke, Pawson *C:* Amor, Aitken *P:* Amor
27 Mar	H	Orrell	15-9	*T:* Clarke, Aitken *C:* Amor *P:* Aitken
3 Apr	H	Leeds	22-37	*T:* Clarke, Aitken, Booth *C:* Amor, Aitken *P:* Aitken
10 Apr	H	Exeter	26-41	*T:* Clarke, Griffiths, Fitzgerald, Sangster *C:* Amor 3
17 Apr	A	London Welsh	22-71	*T:* Clarke, Merlin, Percival *C:* Amor 2 *P:* Amor
24 Apr	H	Rugby	43-20	*T:* Clarke, Fitzgerald, James, Razak, Wilson *C:* Amor 3 *P:* Amor 3 *D:* Amor
1 May	A	Fylde	27-26	*T:* Ririnui, Clarke, Sangster, Braithwaite *C:* Amor 2 *P:* Amor

Bristol

Year of formation 1888
Ground Memorial Ground, Filton Avenue, Horfield, Bristol BS7 0AQ
Tel: Bristol (0117) 908 5500
Web site http://www.bristolrugby.co.uk/
Colours Navy blue and white stripes
Captain 1998-99 J Evans
Allied Dunbar Leagues 1998-99 Div 2 *Winners – promoted*
Tetley's Bitter Cup 1998-99 Lost 19-43 to London Irish (4th round)

February was a worrying month. For the first time in the season Bristol lost the leadership of Allied Dunbar Premiership Two and had to watch their closest challengers Worcester take over. Order was restored by the start of March though and despite a strong challenge by Rotherham, superior points difference won the day. They must have had a premonition of how close things would turn out, however, because it was back in January that they first mooted the idea of a takeover, with London Scottish as the target. Such a deal was being seen as the best way to bring back top-flight rugby to the fallen giants of the game if they failed to win outright promotion. In fact right up to the end of the season there was an option for Bristol to go ahead with it, thankfully it was not necessary. The coaching staff was boosted halfway through the season when Dean Ryan joined them as player-coach. Top players arrived in droves. Garath Archer followed Ryan down from Newcastle at the end of the season and Bob Dwyer also secured the services of South African outside-half Henry Honiball as well as Argentine scrum-half Agustin Pichot, hooker Barrie Williams and prop Darren Crompton all from Richmond, and Matthew Back from Swansea.

League Record 1998-99

Date	Venue	Opponents	Result	Scorers
5 Sep	A	Exeter	22-15	*T:* Breeze, Charron, J Evans *C:* Hull 2 *P:* Hull
12 Sep	H	Fylde	55-14	*T:* Marsden 3, Charron, Brownrigg, Adams, Dewdney, C Evans, Hull *C:* Hull 5
19 Sep	A	Rugby	30-20	*T:* Dewdney 2, Bennett, Pritchard *C:* Hull 2 *P:* Hull 2
26 Sep	H	London Welsh	37-3	*T:* Breeze, Barlow, Hull, Larkin *C:* Hull 4 *P:* Hull 3
3 Oct	A	Blackheath	41-9	*T:* Larkin 3, Eagle, Martin, Wring *C:* Hull 4 *P:* Hull
10 Oct	H	Orrell	29-19	*T:* Dewdney, Marsden, Nissen *C:* Martin *P:* Hull 2, Martin 2
17 Oct	A	Leeds	16-13	*T:* Davey *C:* Hull *P:* Hull 3
24 Oct	A	Rotherham	5-16	*T:* Martin
30 Oct	H	Coventry	14-12	*T:* Larkin *P:* Knox 3
7 Nov	A	Wakefield	46-15	*T:* Larkin 2, Breeze 2, C Evans, Missen, Wring *C:* Knox 4 *P:* Knox
22 Nov	H	Moseley	58-18	*T:* Misson 2,Gabey, Baber, Barnard, Breeze, Giles, Short, Larkin *C:* Knox 4, Larkin *P:* Knox
13 Dec	A	Worcester	9-20	*P:* Hull 3
19 Dec	H	Waterloo	36-8	*T:* Larkin 2, Hull, Hassan, Gabey, Bennett *C:* Martin 3
2 Jan	A	Moseley	43-6	*T:* Misson 2, Larkin 2, Martin, Baber, Marsden *C:* Hull 4
16 Jan	H	Wakefield	35-19	*T:* Baber, Gabey, Lemoine, penalty try *C:* Knox 3 *P:* Knox 3
6 Feb	H	Rotherham	31-36	*T:* Baber, Pritchard, Gabey, penalty try *C:* Knox 4 *P:* Knox
13 Feb	H	Leeds	20-5	*T:* J Evans *P:* Knox 3, Hull *D:* Knox
21 Feb	A	Coventry	19-22	*T:* Misson, Gabey, penalty try *C:* Knox 2
27 Feb	A	Orrell	34-32	*T:* Lemoine 2, Baber, J Evans, Lines *C:* Knox 3 *P:* Knox
13 Mar	H	Bristol	50-17	*T:* Nabaro 5, Gabey, Hassan, Tamati *C:* Hull 4, Hassan
27 Mar	A	London Welsh	25-6	*T:* Nabaro 2, Robinson *C:* Hull 2 *P:* Hull 2
3 Apr	H	Rugby	49-13	*T:* Nabaro 3, Baber 2, Gabey, Hull, Charron *C:* Hull 3 *P:* Hull

17 Apr	A	Fylde	43-39	*T:* Nabaro 2, Robinson 2, Nissen, Hull, C Evans *C:* Hull *P:* Hull 2
24 Apr	H	Exeter	36-17	*T:* Baber, Eagle, Larkin, Leaupepe, Pritchard, Robinson *C:* Hull 3
1 May	A	Waterloo	44-13	*T:* Nabaro, Baber, Gabey, Bennett, Evans *C:* Horak 4, Hull *P:* Hull 2, Horak
9 May	H	Worcester	21-11	*T:* Eagle, C Evans *C:* Horak *P:* Horak 3

Coventry

Year of formation 1874
Ground Barker Butts Lane, Coundon Road, Coventry CV6 1DU
Tel: Coventry (01203) 601174
Web site N/A
Colours Navy blue and white stripes; blue shorts
Captain 1998-99 J Horrobin
Allied Dunbar Leagues 1998-99 Div 2 7th
Tetley's Bitter Cup 1998-99 Lost 26-36 to Worcester (3rd round)

In one of the more curious moves of an at times bizarre rugby season Coventry persuaded American boxing promoter Don King to come on board as a patron, not that his presence did much for their season. It was more of a publicity stunt, with King invited to spectate when Bedford, then owned by his erstwhile partner Frank Warren, visited them in the Cheltenham & Gloucester Cup. When Keith Richardson took over the coaching it was enough to persuade Derek Eves that a return to Bristol was a sensible move and he took Scotland international prop Alan Sharp back with him. There was a further connection with Bristol, although not a terribly savoury one, when Mark Gabey claimed that he had been racially abused by an unnamed Coventry player. That player was subsequently reprimanded and the focus returned to the playing field, not that there was much to shout about.

After a promising start Coventry fell away badly, slipping as low as ninth after having been in third place in October. They finally finished in seventh position. Too often it appeared that they allowed themselves to be caught out by lesser teams. They still rattled up some big wins notably against Fylde and London Welsh. But however prolific and threatening their attack, their defence leaked too much too easily, something which Richardson will no doubt have worked on in the summer months.

League Record 1998-99

Date	Venue	Opponents	Result	Scorers
5 Sep	A	Worcester	7-22	*T:* Smallwood *C:* Gough
12 Sep	H	Waterloo	21-15	*T:* Eves, Fountain *C:* Gough *P:* Gough 3
19 Sep	A	Exeter	25-31	*T:* Eves, Gallagher, Whitley *C:* Gough 2 *P:* Gough 2
26 Sep	H	Fylde	64-9	*T:* Kilford 3, Smallwood 2, Crane, Crofts, Gallagher, Gough *C:* Gough 8 *P:* Gough
4 Oct	A	Rugby	20-17	*T:* Horrobin *P:* Gough 4 *D:* Criscuolo
10 Oct	H	London Welsh	63-19	*T:* Gough 3, Kilford 2, Criscuolo, Curtis, Crofts *C:* Gough 5, Criscuolo 2 *P:* Gough 3
17 Oct	A	Blackheath	30-18	*T:* Robinson 2, Eves, Horrobin *C:* Gough 2 *P:* Gough 2
24 Oct	H	Orrell	26-14	*T:* Robinson, penalty try *C:* Gough 2 *P:* Gough 4
30 Oct	A	Bristol	12-14	*P:* Gough 4
7 Nov	H	Rotherham	22-12	*T:* Gallagher, Gough, Smallwood *C:* Gough 2 *P:* Gough
22 Nov	A	Leeds	12-36	*T:* Robinson, Smallwood *C:* Criscuolo
12 Dec	A	Wakefield	18-10	*T:* Eves, Minshull *C:* Gough *P:* Gough 2

20 Dec	H	Moseley	21-46	*T:* Crofts, penalty try, Horrobin *C:* Gough 3
3 Jan	H	Leeds	27-33	*T:* Mafi 2, penalty try *C:* Gough 3 *P:* Gough 2
16 Jan	A	Rotherham	12-19	*P:* Gough 4
6 Feb	A	Orrell	0-31	
13 Feb	H	Blackheath	35-8	*T:* Whitley, Gallagher, Smallwood, Watkins *C:* Gallagher 3 *P:* Gallagher 2 *D:* Criscuolo
21 Feb	H	Bristol	22-19	*T:* Whitley, Robinson, Gough *C:* Gough 2 *P:* Gough
27 Feb	A	London Welsh	34-42	*T:* Addleton, Horrobin, Smallwood *C:* Gough 2 *P:* Gough 4 *D:* Criscuolo
13 Mar	H	Rugby	19-21	*T:* Gough *C:* Gough *P:* Gough 4
27 Mar	A	Fylde	22-27	*T:* Gough, Kerr, Smallwood *C:* Gough 2 *P:* Gough
3 Apr	H	Exeter	20-13	*T:* Crofts, Curtis *C:* Gough 2 *P:* Gough 2
17 Apr	A	Waterloo	25-24	*T:* Dawson, Gough, Smallwood *C:* Gough 2 *P:* Gough 2
24 Apr	H	Worcester	26-17	*T:* Smallwood 2 *C:* Gough 2 *P:* Gough 4
1 May	A	Moseley	29-30	*T:* Horrobin, Crane, Watkins, Salisbury *C:* Gough 3 *P:* Gough
8 May	H	Wakefield	40-13	*T:* Smallwood 4, Mafi, Houston *C:* Gough 2 *P:* Gough 2

Exeter

Year of formation 1872
Ground County Ground, Church Road, St Thomas, Exeter, Devon EX2 9BQ
Tel: Exeter (01392) 278759
Web site N/A
Colours Black; black shorts
Captain 1998-99 Robert Baxter
Allied Dunbar Leagues 1998-99 Div 2 6th
Tetley's Bitter Cup 1998-99 Lost 10-37 to Richmond (5th round)

It was the Tetley's Bitter Cup which caught the imagination in Devon. Having pulverised Whitchurch in the third round – Exeter's point of entry into the competition – when they ran in 13 tries, they travelled up to Nottingham in the fourth round in January and recorded a satisfying victory there and a place in the fifth round. That was where they ground to a halt. They were drawn away at Richmond and, perhaps it was the imposing Madejski Stadium, perhaps they just froze at the thought of how far they had gone; whatever, they were never in the tie even though Richmond were far from their best. Still after that their concentration on the league saw them inflict defeats on Waterloo, Worcester and Wakefield and a final forty-point flourish against Orrell secured sixth place in the table.

League Record 1998-99

Date	Venue	Opponents	Result	Scorers
5 Sep	H	Bristol	15-22	*P:* Easson 5
12 Sep	A	Rotherham	17-28	*T:* Alvis, Turner *C:* Easson 2 *P:* Easson
19 Sep	H	Coventry	31-25	*T:* Alvis, Armstrong, Easson *C:* Easson 2 *P:* Easson 4
26 Sep	A	Wakefield	27-19	*T:* Barrow, Fabian, Webber *P:* Easson 4
3 Oct	H	Moseley	20-8	*T:* Fabian, Thomas, Woodman *C:* Easson *P:* Easson
10 Oct	A	Worcester	15-40	*T:* Alvis, John *C:* Easson *P:* Easson
17 Oct	H	Waterloo	41-14	*T:* Fabian 4, Baxter, John, Wall *C:* Easson 3
25 Oct	H	Leeds	13-11	*T:* penalty try *C:* Easson *P:* Easson 2
31 Oct	A	Fylde	26-26	*T:* Alvis, Hutchinson *C:* Easson 2 P: Easson 4

7 Nov	H	Rugby	7-23	T: Alvis C: Easson
21 Nov	A	London Welsh	27-62	T: Beatty, John, Reed, Willis, Woodman C: Easson
12 Dec	H	Blackheath	26-7	T: Hargreaves, John, Sluman C: Easson P: Easson 3
19 Dec	A	Orrell	23-21	T: Willis, Armstrong C: Easson 2 P: Easson 3
2 Jan	H	London Welsh	16-17	T: Woodman C: Easson P: Easson 3
23 Jan	H	Fylde	42-10	T: Rich Baxter 3, Laity, penalty try, Woodman C: Easson 3 P: Easson 2
7 Feb	A	Leeds	7-44	T: Barrow C: Easson
13 Feb	A	Waterloo	13-11	T: Rob Baxter C: Easson P: Easson 2
27 Feb	H	Worcester	27-23	T: Beattie, Webber, Willis C: Easson 3 P: Easson 2
13 Mar	A	Moseley	15-12	T: Alvis, Woodman C: Easson P: Easson
21 Mar	A	Rugby	9-13	P: Easson 3
27 Mar	H	Wakefield	37-13	T: Willis 2, Woodman 2, Webber C: Easson 3 P: Easson 2
3 Apr	A	Coventry	13-20	T: Willis, Rose P: Easson
10 Apr	A	Blackheath	41-26	T: Armstrong, Woodman, Webber, John, Rose, Sluman, Easson C: Easson 3
17 Apr	H	Rotherham	24-35	T: Armstrong, Woodman C: Easson P: Easson 4
24 Apr	A	Bristol	17-36	T: Wall 2, Barrow C: Easson
1 May	H	Orrell	42-32	T: Reed 3, Laity, Wall C: Easson 4 P: Easson 3

Fylde

Year of formation 1919
Ground Woodlands Memorial Ground, Blackpool Road, Ansdell, Lytham St Annes, Lancashire FY8 4EL Tel: Lytham (01253) 739137
Web site http://www.cyberscape.net/users/fylderugby/
Colours Claret, white and gold hoops; white shorts
Captain 1998-99 I Barclay
Allied Dunbar Leagues 1998-99 Div 2 14th *relegated*
Tetley's Bitter Cup 1998-99 Lost 15-22 to Moseley (3rd round)

They may have missed out on relegation last season through a technicality, when the clubs decided that a reshuffle was in order to ensure the appropriate size fixture list so necessary these days for the game to survive, but this time around there was no escape. Fylde were very quickly marked out as the whipping boys of the division with Coventry, Bristol and Worcester all piling on half centuries. Indeed it is remarkable that Bristol were forced to wait until injury-time of the return match at the Woodlands Memorial Ground for the two scores necessary for victory and as for beating Coventry, it was as clear cut as it gets: a five-point margin and proof that they could compete with the bigger sides. They also beat Moseley convincingly but just could not sustain any kind of a winning run. They failed to get into double figures because Fylde could only draw against Exeter back in the autumn. Still for a squad that was built and sustained on fairly meagre rations they acquitted themselves with a certain amount of pride.

League Record 1998-99

Date	Venue	Opponents	Result	Scorers
5 Sep	H	Orrell	6-20	P: Peacock 2
12 Sep	A	Bristol	14-55	T: Preston, Wappett C: Barclay, Tanner
26 Sep	A	Coventry	9-64	P: Tanner 3
3 Oct	H	Wakefield	20-18	T: Barclay, Rae, Wappett C: Barclay P: Barclay

10 Oct	A	Moseley	22-44	*T:* Barclay, Tanner, Whitehead *C:* Tanner 2
				P: Tanner
17 Oct	H	Worcester	8-17	*T:* Anderton *P:* Smaje
24 Oct	A	Waterloo	6-27	*P:* Peacock 2
31 Oct	H	Exeter	26-26	*T:* Evans, Preston *C:* Peacock 2
				P: Peacock 4
7 Nov	H	Leeds	6-26	*P:* Peacock 2
21 Nov	A	Rugby	16-30	*T:* Barclay *C:* Peacock *P:* Peacock 2
				D: Tetlow
12 Dec	A	London Welsh	15-36	*T:* Lavin, Smaje *C:* Tanner *P:* Tanner
19 Dec	A	Blackheath	17-24	*T:* Tetlow, Booth *C:* Peacock 2 *P:* Peacock
2 Jan	H	Rugby	6-14	*P:* Peacock 2
17 Jan	A	Leeds	0-48	
23 Jan	A	Exeter	10-42	*T:* O'Toole *C:* Peacock *P:* Peacock
6 Feb	H	Waterloo	24-5	*T:* Scott, Evans, Anderton, Rigby *C:* Peacock 2
13 Feb	A	Worcester	0-56	
20 Feb	H	Rotherham	5-34	*T:* O'Grady
27 Feb	H	Moseley	17-8	*T:* Evans, Lavin, Taylor *C:* Peacock
13 Mar	A	Wakefield	11-27	*T:* Evans *P:* Peacock 2
27 Mar	H	Coventry	27-22	*T:* Scott, Lavin, Anderton, Ireland
				C: Loxton 2 *P:* Loxton
3 Apr	A	Rotherham	16-43	*T:* O'Toole *C:* Loxton *P:* Loxton 3
17 Apr	H	Bristol	39-43	*T:* Evans 2, Ireland, Loxton, Tetlow
				C: Loxton 4 *P:* Loxton 2
24 Apr	A	Orrell	18-28	*T:* Lavin, Tetlow *C:* Loxton *P:* Loxton 2
1 May	H	Blackheath	26-27	*T:* Anderton 2, Lavin, Barlow *C:* Loxton 3
8 May	H	London Welsh	11-21	*T:* Rae *P:* Loxton 2

Gloucester

Year of formation 1873
Ground Kingsholm, Kingsholm Road, Gloucester GL1 3AX Tel: Gloucester (01452) 381087
Web site http://www.kingsholm-chronicle.org.uk/
Colours Cherry and white stripes; black shorts
Captain 1998-99 D Sims
Allied Dunbar Leagues 1998-99 Div 1 10th
Tetley's Bitter Cup 1998-99 Lost 21-35 to Wasps (semi-final)

Even the dismissal of Richard Hill and the handing over of the reins to former France international wing Philippe Saint-Andre could not supply the missing ingredient that would get Gloucester into Europe. They were in ninth place in Allied Dunbar Premiership One when Hill was sacked and finished up a frustrating season a place lower. Sacking was the name of the game at Kingsholm; Keith Richardson had been brought back in as forwards coach, only to part company with the club again 53 days later. There was a real problem with their away form, something that had manifested itself the season before. In fact even given the fact that there were four more matches in the Premiership's second season, their away record was abysmal: 12 defeats as compared with eight the season before. Short of Electro Convulsive Therapy there would seem to be no cure for the collective homesickness suffered by the Gloucester players, unsurprisingly they left in droves at the end of the season. Sadly there were a couple of home-grown boys among them, including erstwhile club captain Dave Sims and hooker Phil Greening, the latter went up to Sale, while Scott Benton joined Leeds.

There had been rumours of problems with Sims from the New Year but things had apparently been sorted out between player and management; clearly that was not the case. Sims went to Worcester along with prop Tony Windo, flanker Nathan Carter and hooker Chris Hall. Into Kingsholm came Ebbw Vale flanker Kingsley Jones, Dave Hinkins from Bristol, while Tom Beim the prodigal returned from Sale as well as the

Cheshire club's threequarter Chris Yates. In the summer manager John Fidler flew out to New Zealand to sign All Black lock Ian Jones.

Terry Fanolua, the darling of the shed, had an unhappy time; he was in trouble for making a late return from World Cup duty with Samoa, then he was found guilty of an assault charge and fined £1,000. England prop Phil Vickery lasted just 15 minutes of his attempted comeback after a career-threatening neck injury and all in all, had it not been for the two knock-out competitions Gloucester would have had nothing to shout about. They made it to the semi-finals of the Tetley's Bitter Cup and went on to retain the Cheltenham & Gloucester Cup, beating Bedford in a repeat of last year's final.

League Record 1998-99

Date	Venue	Opponents	Result	Scorers
5 Sep	H	London Irish	29-22	T: penalty try, Mapletoft C: Mapletoft 2 P: Mapletoft 5
12 Sep	A	Richmond	25-22	T: Mapletoft 2, P St-André C: Mapletoft 2 P: Mapletoft 2
20 Sep	H	West Hartlepool	36-3	T: Tombs 2, Catling, Ojomoh, P St-André C: Mapletoft 4 P: Mapletoft
26 Sep	A	Bath	16-21	T: Mannix, P St-André P: Mapletoft D: Mapletoft
3 Oct	H	Wasps	12-13	P: Mapletoft 4
17 Oct	H	Newcastle	41-32	T: Catling 3, Lumsden, P St-André C: Mannix 2 P: Mannix 4
20 Oct	A	Harlequins	7-39	T: penalty try C: Mannix
25 Oct	H	London Scottish	29-16	T: Dawling, P St-André C: Mannix 2 P: Mannix 5
31 Oct	A	Northampton	8-22	T: Lumsden P: Mannix
7 Nov	H	Bedford	31-21	T: Catling, Fortey, Ojomoh C: Mapletoft 2 P: Mapletoft 4
21 Nov	H	Saracens	28-27	T: Tombs 2, Fanolua C: Mannix 2 P: Mannix 3
12 Dec	A	Sale	10-26	T: P St-André C: Mannix P: Mannix
19 Dec	H	Leicester	18-23	T: Johnson, Mapletoft C: Mapletoft P: Mapletoft 2
27 Dec	A	Wasps	9-23	P: Mapletoft 2, Fanolua
2 Jan	H	Bath	23-7	T: Catling 2, Fanolua C: Mapletoft P: Mapletoft 2
5 Jan	A	London Scottish	13-24	T: Mapletoft C: Mapletoft P: Mapletoft 2
16 Jan	H	Richmond	24-24	T: Benton, penalty try C: Mapletoft P: Mapletoft 4
23 Jan	A	Leicester	16-23	T: Tombs C: Mapletoft P: Mapletoft 3
7 Feb	A	London Irish	20-42	T: Carter, St-André, Benton C: Mapletoft P: Mapletoft
13 Feb	H	Harlequins	20-31	T: Beim, penalty try C: Mapletoft 2 P: Mapletoft 2
14 Mar	A	West Hartlepool	32-33	T: Beim, penalty try, Carter, Ojomoh, Mapletoft C: Mapletoft 2 P: Mapletoft
27 Mar	A	Bedford	15-19	T: Cornwell, St-André C: Mannix P: Mannix
25 Apr	A	Newcastle	15-39	T: Beim, Davis C: Mannix P: Mapletoft
1 May	H	Sale	24-34	T: Woodman, Tombs C: Mapletoft P: Mapletoft 4
7 May	A	Saracens	10-26	T: Eustace C: S Ward P: S Ward
16 May	H	Northampton	43-31	T: Catling, Mannix, Tombs, Carter C: Mannix 4 P: Mannix 5

Harlequins

Year of formation 1866
Ground Stoop Memorial Ground, Langhorn Drive, Twickenham, Middlesex, TW2 7SX
Tel: 0181 410 6000
Web site http://www.quins.co.uk/main-frame.html
Colours Light blue, magenta, chocolate, French grey, black and light green; white shorts
Captain 1998-99 Z V Brooke
Allied Dunbar Leagues 1998-99 Div 1 4th
Tetley's Bitter Cup 1998-99 Lost 13-15 to Gloucester (quarter-final)

It was nip and tuck for a while but Harlequins did eventually cruise into Europe with a little to spare. But even before Will Carling's second coming this was a far better overall performance than the previous season. They were always on the fringe of a vital top six place and proved well capable of travelling anywhere and winning; witness their victories at Saracens, Richmond and Bath on the run-in, not to mention a remarkable win over Gloucester at Kingsholm. The slip at Newcastle proved immaterial and anyway they finished with something of a flourish beating Wasps at The Stoop in the last Allied Dunbar Premiership One match of the season.

But for all their improvement there was still room for more. They lost unexpectedly and there were frequent echoes of flabby past performances, London Scottish for example ran them very close at the beginning of October at The Stoop, but when it came to the return match – away on the same ground since the two clubs had become temporary bedfellows – they won with something to spare. Bedford beat them at Goldington Road, edging home by a couple of points, and they could only manage a home draw with Richmond, although they then won away in the rearranged match. They were able to boast well-deserved doubles over Wasps, Saracens and Bath, an achievement not to be sneezed at, but there is still a need for them to strive for more consistency of performance and purpose.

Carling's reincarnation was something out of left field. He turned up at the beginning of February, saying how much he had missed the dressing room camaraderie, the smell of the crowd, the cries of the horse liniment. He denied that he was motivated by a need and desire for publicity or cash; it was simply that he loved the game. The cynics were silenced after he made a fist of his comeback, beginning with eight minutes or so as a replacement at home to Leicester, followed by a further half-dozen matches. He did not score a try but he certainly proved his worth in defence.

League Record 1998-99

Date	Venue	Opponents	Result	Scorers
5 Sep	A	Leicester	15-49	*P:* Schuster 5
12 Sep	A	Northampton	6-25	*P:* Schuster 2
26 Sep	A	Sale	34-44	*T:* Luger 2, Ridgeway *C:* Schuster 2
				P: Schuster 5
3 Oct	H	London Scottish	22-20	*T:* Luger *C:* Schuster *P:* Schuster 5
10 Oct	A	Bedford	33-35	*T:* Luger, Jenkins, Schuster *C:* Schuster 3
				P: Schuster 4
17 Oct	H	Saracens	41-28	*T:* Jenkins, O'Leary, Williams, Wood
				C: Schuster 3 *P:* Schuster 5
20 Oct	H	Gloucester	39-7	*T:* O'Leary 2, Luger, Wright *C:* Schuster 2
				P: Schuster 5
24 Oct	H	West Hartlepool	25-10	*T:* Harries, Luger, Ngauamo *C:* Schuster 2
				P: Schuster 2
1 Nov	A	Wasps	22-21	*T:* Officer *C:* Schuster *P:* Schuster 4
				D: Schuster
7 Nov	H	Newcastle	25-20	*T:* Luger *C:* Schuster *P:* Schuster 6
21 Nov	H	Bath	43-31	*T:* Keyter 2, Schuster 2, Morgan *C:* Schuster 3
				P: Schuster 4

19 Dec	A	London Irish	16-20	*T:* Wood *C:* Schuster *P:* Schuster 3
27 Dec	H	Sale	17-15	*T:* Williams *P:* Schuster 4
2 Jan	A	London Scottish	35-24	*T:* Harries, Brooke, Halpin *C:* Schuster *P:* Schuster 6
16 Jan	H	Northampton	17-24	*T:* penalty try, Schuster *C:* Schuster 2 *D:* Wood
23 Jan	H	London Irish	17-22	*T:* Mensah, O'Leary *C:* Schuster 2 *P:* Schuster
6 Feb	H	Leicester	9-34	*P:* Schuster 3
13 Feb	A	Gloucester	31-20	*T:* O'Leary, Wright, Llewellyn *C:* Schuster 2 *P:* Schuster 4
27 Mar	H	Richmond	32-32	*T:* Lacroix 2, Schuster, Halpin *C:* Schuster 3 *P:* Schuster 2
17 Apr	H	Bedford	29-16	*T:* Luger, O'Leary, Williams *C:* Schuster *P:* Schuster 4
21 Apr	A	West Hartlepool	47-37	*T:* Jenkins, Luger, Liley, Mensah, O'Leary *C:* Schuster 5 *P:* Schuster 3, Liley
25 Apr	A	Saracens	38-30	*T:* Murphy, Luger, Sheasby, O'Leary *C:* Liley 2, Lacroix *P:* Lacroix 2, Liley 2
3 May	A	Richmond	30-23	*T:* Lacroix , Keyter, Morgan *C:* Lacroix 3 *P:* Lacroix 2 *D:* Lacroix
8 May	A	Bath	17-13	*T:* Luger, Mensah, Williams *C:* Schuster
11 May	A	Newcastle	23-22	*T:* Keyter, Williams *C:* Lacroix 2 *P:* Lacroix 2 *D:* Lacroix
19 May	H	Wasps	27-20	*T:* Harries, Lacroix, Sheasby *C:* Lacroix 3 *P:* Lacroix *D:* Lacroix

Leeds

Year of formation 1992 (on amalgamation of the Headingley and Roundhay clubs whose years of formation were 1877 and 1923 respectively)
Ground Headingley Stadium, St Michael's Lane, Headingley, Leeds LS6 3BR
Tel: Leeds (0113) 278 6181
Web site http://www.leedsrugby.co.uk/
Colours Blue with white and gold stripes; blue shorts
Captain 1998-99 S Tuipulotu / S J Reid
Allied Dunbar Leagues 1998-99 Div 2 5th
Tetley's Bitter Cup 1998-99 Lost 0-49 to Leicester (5th round)

It was a case of Hello Sailor, and goodbye. The arrival of Wendell Sailor, the Australian rugby league wing, in a joint deal with the Leeds Rhinos RL side was designed to give the union team a higher profile and a more competitive cutting edge to their attack. They certainly got the higher profile. Sailor's debut in the win against Rotherham in November provoked an argument over his registration, which eventually led to the club being docked four points. It was deemed by the RFU that Sailor did not qualify for a Home Office work permit to play rugby union professionally. Leeds ignored warnings not to select him against Rotherham, claiming that they were playing him as an amateur. However, he was eventually registered and played in five Premiership Two matches in which he scored four tries. His Tetley's Bitter Cup debut was a memorable one: he ran in five tries against hapless Rugby, although he failed to score when they crashed out of the competition in the fifth round against Leicester, at which point his secondment to the union club ended. Leeds' season rather tailed away after that. Enthusiasm for the club seemed to have waned and at the end owner Paul Caddick sanctioned only part-time contracts for the coming campaign. Stuart Reid and Tongan Sateki Tuipulotu became the first internationals to represent the amalgam of Headingley and Roundhay, although both left in the summer: Scotland No.8 and Leeds captain Reid going to Narbonne. In the summer they signed scrum-half Scott Benton from Gloucester.

League Record 1998-99

Date	Venue	Opponents	Result	Scorers
6 Sep	H	London Welsh	18-20	T: Cawthorne, Easterby C: Tuipulotu P: Tuipulotu 2
12 Sep	A	Moseley	22-27	T: Kirkby, Lancaster, Shelley C: Tuipulotu 2 P: Tuipulotu
20 Sep	H	Blackheath	60-6	T: Kirkby 2, Feeley 2, Easterby, Hawthorn, Reid, Swarbrigg, Tuipulotu C: Tuipulotu 6 P: Tuipulotu
27 Sep	A	Worcester	19-24	T: penalty try C: Tuipulotu P: Tuipulotu 4
3 Oct	A	Orrell	13-11	T: Fourie C: Tuipulotu P: Tuipulotu D: Duncombe
10 Oct	A	Waterloo	12-13	P: Tuipulotu 4
17 Oct	H	Bristol	13-16	T: Tuipulotu C: Tuipulotu P: Tuipulotu 2
25 Oct	A	Exeter	11-13	T: Emmerson P: Tuipulotu 2
1 Nov	H	Rotherham	15-10	P: Tuipulotu 5
7 Nov	A	Fylde	26-6	T: Fourie, O'Hare, Sailor C: Tuipulotu P: Tuipulotu 3
22 Nov	H	Coventry	36-12	T: Fourie 2, Edwards, Sailor C: Tuipulotu 2 P: Tuipulotu 4
13 Dec	A	Rugby	18-9	T: Saverimutto, Sailor C: Tuipulotu P: Tuipulotu 2
20 Dec	H	Wakefield	38-0	T: Sailor, Rhodes, Tuipulotu, Middleton, Saverimutto, Denham C: Tuipulotu 4
3 Jan	A	Coventry	33-27	T: Sailor, Saverimutto C: Tuipulotu P: Tuipulotu 7
17 Jan	H	Fylde	48-0	T: Sailor 3, Fourie, James, O'Hare, Scales, Shelley C: James 4
23 Jan	A	Rotherham	10-25	T: penalty try C: James P: James
7 Feb	H	Exeter	44-7	T: Scales 4, Easterby, Edwards, Emmerson C: Tuipulotu 2, Rhodes P: Tuipulotu
13 Feb	A	Bristol	5-20	T: Denham
28 Feb	H	Waterloo	9-10	P: Tuipulotu 3
14 Mar	H	Orrell	20-7	T: Middleston 2 C: Tuipulotu 2 P: Tuipulotu 2
28 Mar	H	Worcester	26-16	T: Middleton, Shelley C: Tuipulotu 2 P: Tuipulotu 4
3 Apr	A	Blackheath	37-22	T: Scales, Easterby, Fourie, James, Middleton, O'Hare C: Tuipulotu 2 P: Tuipulotu
18 Apr	H	Moseley	50-8	T: Saverimutto, Easterby 2, Denham, Fourie, Middleton, Scales C: Tuipulotu 5
25 Apr	A	London Welsh	17-24	T: Middleton P: Tuipulotu 4
2 May	A	Wakefield	51-13	T: Scales 2, Fourie 2, Easterby, Shelley, Jones, Middleton, Feeley C: James 3
9 May	H	Rugby	64-21	T: Middleton 2, O'Hare, Easterby, Cawthorn, Saverimutto, Jones, Palmer, Feeley, Scales C: Tuipulotu 5, James 2

Leicester

Year of formation 1880
Ground Welford Road, Aylestone Road, Leicester LE2 7LF Tel: Leicester (0116) 254 1607
Web site http://www.tigers.co.uk/
Colours Scarlet, green and white stripes; white shorts
Captain 1998-99 M O Johnson
Allied Dunbar Leagues 1998-99 Div 1 *Winners*
Tetley's Bitter Cup 1998-99 Lost 13-15 to Richmond (quarter-final)

There was a misconception that Leicester played one-dimensional rugby, showing not the least inclination to spin the ball wide. While the forwards, in particular Neil

ALLIED DUNBAR
PREMIERSHIP ONE
CHAMPIONS

ALLIED
DUNBAR
PREMIERSHIP

Their cup runneth over. New champions Leicester celebrate success in the Allied Dunbar Premiership after their final game, a 72-37 demolition of West Hartlepool.

145

Back, his back-row colleagues and members of the ABC front-row club, were frequently included on the scoresheet, such a perception overlooked the contribution by wings Leon Lloyd and Nnamdi Ezulike, outside-half Joel Stransky and, until he was struck down with a chronic groin injury, Will Greenwood. Leicester were worthy winners of the Allied Dunbar Premiership title because they produced a balanced blend of rugby. They knew when to keep it tight and how to open up defences to let in their potent backs. They scored 86 tries in the Premiership, six more than Bath and four more than second-placed Northampton, two sides regarded as playing a more expansive, imaginative game. Leicester did so when the situation allowed, but they were not trotting out merely to entertain, they wanted to win as well.

And they did. There were blips at Saracens, London Irish, Wasps and Bath, but that was it. They remained unbeaten at home, a record which goes back to December 1997 when Newcastle slipped away with both points. They had led the table for just about the whole season and by mid-February had opened up a gap of half a dozen points between themselves and Northampton, which increased briefly to eight before dropping back again. It was as emphatic a march to the championship title as there has been.

League Record 1998-99

Date	Venue	Opponents	Result	Scorers
5 Sep	H	Harlequins	49-15	T: Lloyd 2, Back, Cockerill, Ezulike, Healey, Stransky C: Stransky 4 P: Stransky 2
12 Sep	A	London Scottish	38-3	T: Ezulike, Gustard, Stimpson, Stransky C: Stransky 3 P: Stransky 4
19 Sep	H	Northampton	35-25	T: Ezulike, Back, Stimpson, Healey C: Stransky 3 P: Stransky 3
26 Sep	A	Bedford	32-23	T: Ezulike, Back, penalty try , Potter C: Stransky 2, Stimpson P: Stransky, Stimpson
11 Oct	A	Saracens	10-22	T: Lloyd C: Stransky P: Stransky
17 Oct	H	Sale	31-15	T: Back 2, Gustard C: Stransky 2 P: Stransky 4
20 Oct	A	London Irish	23-24	T: Healey, Lloyd C: Stransky 2 P: Stransky 3
24 Oct	H	Richmond	27-0	T: Back, Garforth, Stransky C: Stransky 3 P: Stransky 2
1 Nov	A	West Hartlepool	45-15	T: Murphy 2, Overend 2, Stransky C: Stransky 4 P: Stransky 3, Murphy
7 Nov	H	Bath	36-13	T: Greenwood 2, Gustard, Overend, Stransky C: Stransky 4 P: Stransky
15 Nov	A	Wasps	17-45	T: Gustard, Murphy C: Stransky 2 P: Stransky
12 Dec	H	Newcastle	31-18	T: Back 2, Stuart C: Murphy 2 P: Murphy 2, Stimpson 2
19 Dec	A	Gloucester	23-18	T: Lougheed P: Stimpson 6
26 Dec	H	Bedford	26-0	T: Lougheed, Cockerill, Back C: Stimpson P: Stimpson 3
16 Jan	H	London Scottish	24-12	T: van Heerden 2, Lloyd P: Murphy 2, Stimpson
23 Jan	H	Gloucester	23-16	T: Lougheed 2, Stransky C: Stimpson P: Stimpson 2
26 Jan	A	Richmond	23-11	T: Lougheed, M Johnson, Jelley C: Stransky P: Stimpson 2
6 Feb	A	Harlequins	34-9	T: Lloyd 2, Moody, Back, Stransky C: Stransky 3 P: Stransky
13 Feb	H	London Irish	31-10	T: Lougheed, Lloyd P: Stransky 7
13 Mar	A	Northampton	22-15	T: Corry, Joiner, penalty try C: Stimpson 2 P: Stimpson
27 Mar	H	Wasps	16-6	T: Back C: Stimpson P: Stimpson 3
3 Apr	A	Bath	16-24	T: penalty try C: Howard P: Stimpson 3

17 Apr	H	Saracens	25-18	*T:* Corry *C:* Stimpson *P:* Stimpson 6
24 Apr	A	Sale	41-17	*T:* Back 2, Corry, Healey, Lougheed *C:* Stimpson 2 *P:* Stimpson 4
2 May	A	Newcastle	21-12	*P:* Stimpson 7
16 May	H	West Hartlepool	72-37	*T:* Back 3, Murphy 2, Healey 2, Lougheed, Joiner, Howard, Corry, Gustard *C:* Stimpson 5, Murphy

London Irish

Year of formation 1898
Ground The Avenue, Sunbury-on-Thames, Middlesex TW16 5EQ
Tel: Sunbury (01932) 783034
Web site http://212.158.20.26/
Colours Emerald green; white shorts
Captain 1998-99 C M P O'Shea
Allied Dunbar Leagues 1998-99 Div 1 7th
Tetley's Bitter Cup 1998-99 Lost 3-19 to Wasps (quarter-final)

Events of an exciting, if ultimately disappointing season, were overtaken in the late spring by the takeover of London Scottish and Richmond; a deal that met with RFU approval in principle in June. There was talk that the club would keep their name, then that they would change it to Richmond Exiles, or Richmond Celts, but at the start of the Allied Dunbar Premiership campaign there were those who felt that Antipodean Exiles might have been a more apposite title. In fact Dick Best reckoned that his trawl of the southern hemisphere for some truly great players had left the club with more English and Irish qualified players than many. By qualified he meant in terms of talent as well as passport. There was no doubt that Kevin Putt and Steve Bachop added a hardened edge to the attack. This half-back pairing was one of the most potent in the Premiership. And just outside them was probably the outstanding centre-playmaker in the country, Brendan Venter. The Free State back was inspirational and his vision and split-second assessment of each and every situation was a lesson to every aspiring youngster. In fact videos of the Exiles' matches featuring Venter should become compulsory viewing in schools and colleges.

Up front they had Peter Rogers, a Welshman by way of Maidenhead and South Africa who beefed up the front row no end. The likes of Australian lock Nick Harvey, Western Samoan Isaac Fea'unati and his back-row colleague, Jake Boer, complemented the existing playing staff. Irish were cruelly robbed of the brilliant Ireland second row Malcolm O'Kelly through injury. Sadly he then decided his future lay in his home country and he was lost to them altogether. Still they get to keep their brilliant captain Conor O'Shea. His do-or-die trail-blazing upfield left defences dazed and hanging open.

League Record 1998-99

Date	Venue	Opponents	Result	Scorers
5 Sep	A	Gloucester	22-29	*T:* Jones *C:* Woods *P:* Woods 5
13 Sep	A	West Hartlepool	44-20	*T:* Bishop, O'Shea, Richards, Venter, Woods *C:* Woods 5 *P:* Woods 3
19 Sep	H	Wasps	24-36	*T:* Venter, Woods *C:* Woods *P:* Woods 3, O'Shea
27 Sep	A	Newcastle	23-21	*T:* Campbell, O'Shea *C:* Woods, O'Shea *P:* Woods, O'Shea 2
3 Oct	H	Richmond	29-33	*T:* Todd, O'Kelly *C:* Woods 2 *P:* Woods 5
10 Oct	A	Bath	20-23	*T:* Woods 2, O'Shea *C:* Woods *P:* Woods
20 Oct	H	Leicester	24-23	*T:* O'Kelly, O'Shea *C:* Woods *P:* Woods 3 *D:* O'Shea
24 Oct	H	Northampton	10-26	*T:* Woods *C:* Woods *P:* Woods
7 Nov	H	Sale	25-31	*T:* Burrows 2, Harvey *C:* Woods 2 *P:* Woods 2

14 Nov	A	London Scottish	23-17	*T:* Bachop, Woods *C:* Cunningham, Woods *P:* Woods 2, Cunningham
21 Nov	H	Bedford	30-19	*T:* Burrows 2, Berridge *C:* Woods, Cunningham 2 *P:* Cunningham 2, Woods
13 Dec	A	Saracens	26-40	*T:* Boer, Kirke *C:* Cunningham 2 *P:* Cunningham 4
19 Dec	H	Harlequins	20-16	*T:* Bachop, penalty try *C:* Cunningham 2 *P:* Cunningham 2
26 Dec	A	Richmond	25-13	*T:* Gallagher *C:* Cunningham *P:* Cunningham 6
2 Jan	A	Newcastle	16-14	*T:* Bishop *C:* Cunningham *P:* Cunningham 3
5 Jan	A	Northampton	32-8	*T:* Woods 4, Burrows *C:* Woods 2 *P:* Woods
16 Jan	H	West Hartlepool	43-21	*T:* Kirke 3, Burrows 2, Bachop, Boer *C:* Cunningham 4
23 Jan	A	Harlequins	22-17	*T:* O'Shea 2, Bishop *C:* Woods 2 *P:* Woods
7 Feb	H	Gloucester	42-30	*T:* Berridge 2, Woods, Feaunati, Hatley, Cunningham *C:* Cunningham 2, Woods *P:* Cunningham *D:* Bachop
13 Feb	A	Leicester	10-31	*T:* Venter *C:* Woods *P:* Woods
14 Mar	A	Wasps	27-38	*T:* Bishop, Burrows, Venter *C:* Cunningham 2,Woods *P:*Woods 2
27 Mar	H	London Scottish	35-12	*T:* Gallagher, Kirke *C:* Cunningham, O'Shea *P:* Cunningham 5, O'Shea 2
3 Apr	A	Sale	27-30	*T:* Gallagher, Harvey, O'Shea *C:* Cunningham 3 *P:* Cunningham 2
17 Apr	H	Bath	47-22	*T:* Todd 3, Berridge, Burrows, Hardwick, O'Shea *C:* O'Shea 3 *P:* O'Shea 2
1 May	H	Saracens	21-26	*T:* Dawson, Harvey *C:* Woods *P:* Woods 3
8 May	A	Bedford	36-21	*T:* Bachop, O'Shea, Woods, Cunningham *C:* Cunningham 2 *P:* Cunningham 4

London Scottish

Year of formation 1878
Ground Stoop Memorial Ground, Langhorn Drive, Twickenham, Middlesex TW2 7SX
Tel: 0181 410 6002
Web site N/A
Colours Blue jersey with red lion crest; blue shorts
Captain 1998-99 R Hunter
Allied Dunbar Leagues 1998-99 Div 1 12th
Tetley's Bitter Cup 1998-99 Lost 33-37 to Harlequins (5th round)

At least they were a success on the field, even if off it there was too tangled a skein to unravel. Limited by budget constraints and injuries their director of coaching John Steele did sterling work with his squad. Against all expectation they did not just survive in the top flight but also avoided the play-offs, finishing four clear points ahead of Bedford. One of their most famous victories early on had to be against Bath, a 13-11 triumph at The Stoop, but there were further successes at home against Gloucester and Newcastle; but the win of their season had to be the overturning of Saracens in late December, when they outscored the fancy dans and favourites by three tries to one.

So what a shame that they have now been swallowed up in a three-way merger, which looks more like a takeover. There was not enough money, that they acknowledge, and it was particularly disappointing for them that there were no Scottish businessmen or consortia eager to come in with a rescue package. Sure there was talk of them being moved locker room, squad and concept north of the border, but that was a non-starter. Then there was the Bristol takeover, a very real prospect, but not one that delighted die-hard Exiles' supporters. Scottish, like Irish and Welsh, are more than mere rugby clubs; they are cultural centres, oases of familiarity in a metropolis in a different country. They creak with tradition and history and now it is all to go. Like Richmond they will retain their membership of the Rugby Football Union as amateurs, but that is not the same as playing top flight rugby, where they deserve to be.

They had their ups and downs throughout the season without all the financial shenanigans. Mick Watson's injudicious shove of the fourth official after being sin-binned at Gloucester, however inadvertent, earned the player a fine from the club's authorities. They also introduced Jannie de Beer, a man with prodigious kicking powers and a fair amount of pace, not to mention a useful footballing brain.

League Record 1998-99

Date	Venue	Opponents	Result	Scorers
5 Sep	H	Sale	25-20	*T:* Milligan *C:* McAusland *P:* McAusland 6
12 Sep	H	Leicester	3-38	*P:* McAusland
19 Sep	A	Bedford	16-24	*T:* Sharman *C:* McAusland *P:* McAusland 3
26 Sep	H	Saracens	20-58	*T:* Milligan 2, Bonney *C:* McAusland *P:* McAusland
3 Oct	A	Harlequins	20-22	*T:* Jones *P:* McAusland 5
10 Oct	H	Northampton	22-33	*T:* Jones *C:* McAusland *P:* McAusland 5
25 Oct	A	Gloucester	16-29	*T:* Holmes *C:* McAusland *P:* McAusland 3
31 Oct	H	Bath	13-11	*T:* Sharman *C:* McAusland *P:* McAusland 2
14 Nov	H	London Irish	17-23	*T:* Holmes, Easterby *C:* de Beer 2 *P:* de Beer
22 Nov	A	West Hartlepool	37-7	*T:* Hunter 2, Easterby, Fenn, Forrest *C:* de Beer 3 *P:* de Beer 2
12 Dec	H	Wasps	9-17	*P:* de Beer 3
19 Dec	H	Richmond	16-28	*T:* Easterby *C:* de Beer *P:* de Beer 3
27 Dec	A	Saracens	24-7	*T:* Milligan, Irving, Watson *C:* McAusland 3 *P:* McAusland
2 Jan	H	Harlequins	24-35	*T:* Milligan, Hunter *C:* Forrest *P:* McAusland 3, Forrest
5 Jan	H	Gloucester	24-13	*T:* Easterby, Johnstone *C:* de Beer *P:* de Beer 3 *D:* de Beer
16 Jan	A	Leicester	12-24	*P:* de Beer 3 *D:* de Beer
23 Jan	A	Richmond	22-40	*T:* Hunter *C:* de Beer *P:* de Beer 4 *D:* de Beer
6 Feb	A	Sale	23-7	*T:* T Davies, Easterby *C:* de Beer 2 *P:* de Beer 3
13 Feb	H	Newcastle	27-17	*T:* Fenn, Johnstone, Easterby, Holmes *C:* de Beer 2 *P:* de Beer
13 Mar	H	Bedford	15-24	*T:* Bonney, M Watson *C:* de Beer *P:* de Beer
27 Mar	A	London Irish	12-35	*P:* de Beer 3 *D:* de Beer
31 Mar	A	Newcastle	20-43	*T:* de Beer, Easterby *C:* de Beer 2 *P:* de Beer *D:* de Beer
17 Apr	A	Northampton	13-44	*T:* McAusland *C:* de Beer *P:* de Beer 2
2 May	A	Wasps	22-45	*T:* Sharman *C:* McAusland *P:* de Beer, McAusland 3 *D:* de Beer
8 May	H	West Hartlepool	26-14	*T:* Sharman 2 *C:* de Beer 2 *P:* de Beer 4
15 May	A	Bath	13-76	*T:* Holmes *C:* McAusland *P:* de Beer 2

London Welsh

Year of formation 1885
Ground Old Deer Park, Kew Road, Richmond, Surrey TW9 2AZ Tel: 0181 940 2368
Web site http://www.london-welsh.co.uk/
Colours Red with black stripe; black shorts
Captain 1998-99 R D Phillips
Allied Dunbar Leagues 1998-99 Div 2 4th
Tetley's Bitter Cup 1998-99 Lost 6-8 to Rotherham (3rd round)

They did not quite have what it would have taken to challenge Bristol and Rotherham, but they had a good go and there was never any danger of London Welsh struggling in Allied Dunbar Premiership Two. They did not have the surest of starts, although their opening two matches, away to Leeds and Blackheath followed by a home game against Orrell, left them with a 100 per cent record and must have raised intemperate hopes and conjured up images of Premiership One rugby at Old Deer Park. They were brought down to earth with a bump at Bristol in the very next match, Rotherham then turned them over at home and an unhappy treble was completed when they travelled up to Coventry, who stuck 63 points on them. They did manage to show their own ruthless streak with a storming victory over strugglers Blackheath, piling on 71 points in an 11-try rout. But the fact that they lost to all three sides who finished above them, home and away, indicated that fourth place was a more realistic finish. It was still a commendable performance – consolidation of their status with plenty of room for improvement and development and at least they retained their independent Exile status. They had the briefest of flirtations with the Tetley's Bitter Cup, departing at the first opportunity, losing by two points in a low-scoring tie at Rotherham.

League Record 1998-99

Date	Venue	Opponents	Result	Scorers
6 Sep	A	Leeds	20-18	*T:* Currier, L Jones, C Langley *C:* Pearce *P:* Pearce
13 Sep	A	Blackheath	20-16	*T:* Buckett, Pearce *C:* Pearce 2 *P:* Pearce 2
19 Sep	H	Orrell	24-17	*T:* Shaw, Pearce *C:* Pearce *P:* Pearce, Hewlett 2 *D:* Currier
26 Sep	A	Bristol	3-37	*P:* Hewlett
3 Oct	H	Rotherham	13-27	*T:* Shaw *C:* Pearce *P:* Pearce 2
10 Oct	A	Coventry	19-63	*T:* Shaw, White, Whittaker *C:* Pearce, Pilgrim
17 Oct	H	Wakefield	45-21	*T:* White 3, Phillips 2, Giraud, Storey *C:* Pearce 2 *P:* Pearce 2
24 Oct	A	Moseley	31-16	*T:* penalty try, Phillips, Shaw, Storey *C:* Pearce 4 *P:* Pearce
31 Oct	H	Worcester	14-22	*T:* Lee *P:* Pearce 3
7 Nov	A	Waterloo	10-12	*T:* Currier *C:* Pearce *P:* Pearce
21 Nov	H	Exeter	62-27	*T:* Currier 3, Giraud 2, Shanklin 2, Shaw, Edwards, Phillips *C:* Lee 6
12 Dec	H	Fylde	36-15	*T:* Woodard 3, Currier, Edwards, Phillips *C:* Lee 3
19 Dec	H	Rugby	11-7	*T:* Woodard *P:* Lee 2
2 Jan	A	Exeter	17-16	*T:* Woodard, Storey *C:* Lee 2 *P:* Lee
16 Jan	H	Waterloo	49-17	*T:* Jones 2, Storey 2, White 2, Woodard, Edwards *C:* Lee 3 *P:* Lee
23 Jan	A	Worcester	12-14	*T:* Currier, Roskell *C:* Lee
6 Feb	H	Moseley	26-24	*T:* Giraud 2, Currier *C:* Lee *P:* Lee 2, Raymond
13 Feb	A	Wakefield	30-16	*T:* Giraud, Currier, Edwards *C:* Lee 3 *P:* Lee 3
27 Feb	H	Coventry	42-34	*T:* Currier 3, Alexander, Edwards, White *C:* Lee 3 *P:* Lee 2
13 Mar	A	Rotherham	8-28	*T:* Currier *P:* Lee
27 Mar	H	Bristol	6-25	*P:* Lee 2
3 Apr	A	Orrell	15-18	*T:* Lurie, Phillips, Shanklin
17 Apr	H	Blackheath	71-22	*T:* Woodard 4, Mardon 3, Currier, Carr, Millward, Storey *C:* Raymond 8
25 Apr	H	Leeds	24-17	*T:* Woodard 2, Currier *C:* Raymond 3 *P:* Raymond
1 May	A	Rugby	33-12	*T:* Woodard 2, Storey 2, penalty try *C:* Lee 4
8 May	A	Fylde	21-11	*T:* Mardon, Raymond, Storey *C:* Raymond 3

Manchester Sale

Year of formation 1861
Ground Heywood Road, Brooklands, Sale, Cheshire M33 3WB Tel: 0161 283 1861
Web site http://www.salerugby.co.uk/
Colours Royal blue and white; blue shorts
Captain 1998-99 J Mallinder
Allied Dunbar Leagues 1998-99 Div 1 11th
Tetley's Bitter Cup 1998-99 Lost 31-47 to Northampton (4th round)

The gloomier among the Sale faithful pinpoint the fateful cup final appearance as being the start of all the troubles. Whenever it all started to go wrong, there is no doubt that last season had to be the worst in the grand old club's 138-year history. And even after the season had ended the problems did not go away. The very virtue of having survived in Allied Dunbar Premiership One suddenly became a double-edged sword. As the game has blundered deeper into professional waters, so places in Premiership One have come to resemble commodities; items to be bought and sold to those who can afford it. Thus it was that Worcester began sniffing around the possibility of buying their way into the top flight by taking over Sale.

Coach John Mitchell left, disillusioned with the underachievement of his players, although there had been a clash between him and his squad when he had threatened to put the whole team on the transfer list after a poor show against Bath. That brought a rebuke from the directors, but eventually Mitchell had had enough and so had the players. Their vote of no confidence in him triggered his departure and Adrian Hadley and long-serving full-back Jim Mallinder took over the coaching duties.

Sale finished in 10th place in Premiership One, their lowest position since getting into the First Division in 1995. There was a touch of irony at the end of the season when Adrian Hadley put, if not quite the whole squad on the transfer list, then the cream of them, including Barrie-Jon Mather who had earlier in the season made his England debut. But this wholesale off-loading was forced on Hadley because he had to cut down the wage bill; the club's backers, having ploughed in more than £3 million over a period of two years, were becoming increasingly concerned at falling gates. There were other departures too, chief executive Howard Thomas left in December, Tom Beim returned to Gloucester and Dion O'Cuinneagain, the South African Irishman, also left the club, while Graham Dawe was relieved of his duties as Second XV coach.

League Record 1998-99

Date	Venue	Opponents	Result	Scorers
5 Sep	A	London Scottish	20-25	*T:* R Smith 2, Moore *C:* Howarth *P:* Howarth
12 Sep	H	Bedford	39-21	*T:* Moore 2, Beim, Machacek, Yates *C:* Howarth 4 *P:* Howarth 2
20 Sep	A	Saracens	26-43	*T:* Moore, Beim, Machacek, R Smith *C:* Howarth 3
26 Sep	H	Harlequins	44-34	*T:* R Smith, Beim, Winstanley, Yates *C:* Howarth 3 *P:* Howarth 6
3 Oct	A	Northampton	17-37	*T:* Howarth, Machacek *C:* Howarth 2 *P:* Howarth
17 Oct	A	Leicester	15-31	*T:* Howarth, R Smith *C:* Howarth *P:* Howarth
24 Oct	A	Bath	3-27	*P:* Howarth
28 Oct	H	Richmond	10-39	*T:* Machacek *C:* Howarth *P:* Howarth
7 Nov	A	London Irish	31-25	*T:* Beim, O'Cuinneagain, penalty try *C:* Howarth 2 *P:* Howarth 4
13 Nov	H	West Hartlepool	42-26	*T:* Ellis 2, Davidson, Baldwin, penalty try *C:* Davidson 4 *P:* Davidson 3

151

22 Nov	A	Wasps	19-32	T: Davidson 2, Yates C: Davidson 2
12 Dec	H	Gloucester	26-10	T: Hanley 2, Howarth, Mallinder C: Howarth 3
20 Dec	A	Newcastle	15-30	T: Hanley, Howarth C: Howarth P: Howarth
27 Dec	A	Harlequins	15-17	T: Hanley, Yates C: Howarth P: Howarth
2 Jan	H	Northampton	24-39	T: Hanley 2, Machacek, Moore C: Howarth 2
5 Jan	H	Bath	30-32	T: Moore 2, Hanley, Williamson C: Howarth 2 P: Howarth 2
23 Jan	H	Newcastle	20-28	T: Hanley, Davidson, O'Cuinneagain C: Howarth P: Howarth
6 Feb	H	London Scottish	7-23	T: Mather C: Shaw
14 Feb	A	Richmond	24-29	T: Hanley 2, Howarth, Mather C: Howarth 2
27 Feb	A	Bedford	18-7	T: Hanley 2 C: Howarth P: Howarth 2
13 Mar	H	Saracens	32-24	T: Baxendell, Raiwalui, Yates C: Howarth P: Howarth 5
28 Mar	A	West Hartlepool	33-33	T: Baxendell, Moore, O'Cuinneagain C: Howarth 3 P: Howarth 4
3 Apr	H	London Irish	30-27	T: Ellis, Greening, Howarth C: Howarth 3 P: Howarth 2 D: Howarth
24 Apr	H	Leicester	17-41	T: Baxendell, Howarth, Mather C: Howarth
1 May	A	Gloucester	34-24	T: Howarth 2, Smith, Moore C: Howarth 4 P: Howarth D: Howarth
8 May	H	Wasps	13-27	T: Moore, Mather P: Howarth

Moseley

Year of formation 1873
Ground The Reddings, Reddings Road, Moseley, Birmingham B13 8LW Tel: 0121 499 2149
Web site http://www.moseleyrugby.co.uk/moseley/default.asp
Colours Red and black; black shorts
Captain 1998-99 M Chudleigh
Allied Dunbar Leagues 1998-99 Div 2 10th
Tetley's Bitter Cup 1998-99 Lost 24-25 to Lydney (4th round)

Yet another transitional season at The Reddings. Moseley were bought out of administration two months before the start of the season by a new consortium, which included John White, a former captain, coach and chairman. He took over as director of rugby and with just seven contracted players, had to pick up what few pieces were left and turn it into a competitive outfit. Ambitions were, of necessity, limited – as were resources. But the fact that they secured their place in Allied Dunbar Premiership Two by early March has to be regarded as a remarkable achievement. White worked wonders with his young squad; on occasion the team's average age was less than 23 and featured several members of the team which won the National Colts Cup two seasons ago, including lock Andrew Hall, Alan Hubbleday, Scott Bemand the scrum-half and No.8 Peter Short. Sadly this last moved to Leicester in the close season. Lock Tony Healy, who had won 14 Canadian caps when he joined the club, was capped as a Moseley player during the season. Ian Smith's career was ended by knee injury and, although he stayed on to help out with the coaching of the forwards, he moved on in the close season to Newport to fill a similar role with the Welsh club. The signing of centre Simon Brading from Bedford in February had a big impact on the team. They capped their season by completing a double over rivals Coventry.

League Record 1998-99

Date	Venue	Opponents	Result	Scorers
5 Sep	H	Wakefield	32-33	T: Patten, penalty try, Smart, Simpson C: Smart 3 P: Smart 2

12 Sep	H	Leeds	27-22	T: Chudleigh, Cook, Eason, Gregory
				C: Binns 2 P: Binns
19 Sep	A	Worcester	8-23	T: Simpson P: Binns
26 Sep	H	Waterloo	13-15	T: White, Gregory P: Binns
3 Oct	A	Exeter	8-20	T: Martin P: Binns
10 Oct	H	Fylde	44-22	T: Ayeb, Chudleigh, Buxton, Martin, Simpson
				C: Binns 5 P: Binns 3
18 Oct	A	Rugby	8-30	T: Mellors P: Binns
24 Oct	H	London Welsh	16-31	T: Buxton C: Smart P: Smart 3
31 Oct	A	Blackheath	18-14	T: Cook, Mellors C: Sparkes P: Sparkes
				D: Sparkes
7 Nov	H	Orrell	25-3	T: Jones 2, Cook, Mellors C: Jones P: Jones
22 Nov	A	Bristol	18-58	T: Martin, Simpson C: Smart P: Smart
				D: Smart
12 Dec	H	Rotherham	6-16	P: Jones 2
20 Dec	A	Coventry	46-21	T: Ayeb, Gregory, McKinnon, Buxton, Healy,
				Mitchell C: Jones 5 P: Jones 2
2 Jan	H	Bristol	6-43	P: Jones 2
16 Jan	A	Orrell	14-20	T: Mellors P: Jones 3
23 Jan	H	Blackheath	22-16	T: Cook, Patten, Simpson C: Smart 2
				P: Jones
6 Feb	A	London Welsh	24-26	T: Cook, Mitchell C: Binns P: Jones 4
13 Feb	H	Rugby	35-20	T: Simpson, Martin, Binns, Mellors C: Jones 3
				P: Jones 3
27 Feb	A	Fylde	8-17	T: Roberts P: Jones
13 Mar	H	Exeter	12-15	P: Binns 4
27 Mar	A	Waterloo	32-8	T: Roberts 2, Cook, Drake-Lee, Protherough
				C: Binns 2 P: Binns
3 Apr	H	Worcester	18-16	T: Brading, Martin C: Binns P: Binns 2
18 Apr	A	Leeds	8-50	T: Brading P: Binns
24 Apr	A	Wakefield	20-38	T: Cook 2, Buxton C: Binns P: Binns
1 May	H	Coventry	30-29	T: Binns, Ayeb, Cook, Martin C: Smart 2
				P: Smart D: Smart
8 May	A	Rotherham	0-27	

Newcastle

Year of formation 1877, reformed in 1995
Ground Kingston Park, Brunton Road, Kenton Bank Foot, Newcastle upon Tyne NE13 8AF
Tel: Newcastle (0191) 214 5588
Web site N/A
Colours Black and white stripes; black shorts
Captain 1998-99 D Ryan / C R Andrew
Allied Dunbar Leagues 1998-99 Div 1 8th
Tetley's Bitter Cup 1998-99 Lost 19-29 to Wasps (final)

This was one club that survived being ditched by its owner. In fact Sir John Hall did at least have the patience to wait for a serious buyer, David Thompson, who brought Director of Rugby Rob Andrew on board, and there were few alarums or excursions as a smooth transition was made. Before the takeover the club finally conceded that the move to the Gateshead Stadium was little short of a failure and they moved back to Kingston Park after the match against Saracens.

They had a snag or two in meeting the due payment to Wigan for Va'aiga Tuigamala. It needed the threat of a winding-up order from the rugby league club to prompt them into finding the cash. That small disaster averted, they found themselves struggling on the injury front. Dean Ryan, their inspirational captain was discovered to need an operation on his neck that would keep him out of action for more than two months. During his recuperation period Ryan was tempted away by

Bristol and took up the role of player and forwards coach under Bob Dwyer. At the end of the season Bristol also secured the signature of Garath Archer, who had had one attempt at settling in the West Country a few years before. Back on the injury front scrum-half Gary Armstrong suffered a broken thumb. It was originally thought that he would be sidelined for between four and six weeks, however they breed them hard in the Borders; he was back after two weeks. They had lost their Goliath of a lock Richard Metcalfe, the 7ft 1in second row joining Northampton in the close season and there was another blow not long after the start of the new campaign when their fitness guru Steve Black was snaffled by Wales, having impressed the national coach Graham Henry.

It did not augur well for their defence of the Allied Dunbar Premiership One and so it proved. They only ever really hovered around on the fringes of the top six, never quite able to string together enough wins to put pressure on the leading bunch. They could not in the end even secure the sixth and final place in Europe.

League Record 1998-99

Date	Venue	Opponents	Result	Scorers
5 Sep	A	Richmond	29-41	T: Walton, Tuigamala, Naylor, Weir C: Andrew 2, Wilkinson P: Wilkinson
12 Sep	H	Bath	19-17	T: Ryan C: Wilkinson P: Wilkinson 4
27 Sep	H	London Irish	21-23	T: penalty try, Underwood C: Wilkinson P: Wilkinson 3
4 Oct	A	West Hartlepool	24-19	T: Walton, Tuigamala, Weir C: Wilkinson 3 P: Wilkinson
11 Oct	H	Wasps	27-19	T: Armstrong, Underwood C: Wilkinson P: Wilkinson 5
17 Oct	A	Gloucester	32-41	T: Walton, Wilkinson, Naylor, Weir C: Wilkinson 3 P: Wilkinson 2
24 Oct	A	Bedford	29-22	T: Tuigamala, Naylor, Armstrong, Underwood C: Andrew 2, Wilkinson P: Wilkinson
31 Oct	H	Saracens	43-12	T: Underwood 3, Horton, Shaw, Armstrong C: Wilkinson 4, Andrew P: Wilkinson
7 Nov	A	Harlequins	20-25	T: Armstrong, Naylor, Underwood C: Wilkinson P: Wilkinson
15 Nov	H	Northampton	45-35	T: Wilkinson 2, Armstrong, Arnold, Tuigamala, Walton C: Wilkinson 6 P: Wilkinson
12 Dec	A	Leicester	18-31	T: Andrew, Legg C: Wilkinson P: Wilkinson 2
20 Dec	H	Sale	30-15	T: Legg 2, Armstrong, Shaw, Archer C: Wilkinson P: Wilkinson
27 Dec	H	West Hartlepool	29-13	T: Wilkinson, Beattie, Charlton, Tuigamala C: Wilkinson 3 P: Wilkinson
2 Jan	A	London Irish	14-16	T: Tuigamala, Armstrong C: Wilkinson 2
5 Jan	H	Bedford	34-23	T: Tuigamala 2, Wilkinson, Cartmell, Shaw C: Wilkinson 3 P: Wilkinson
16 Jan	A	Bath	11-16	T: Naylor P: Wilkinson 2
23 Jan	A	Sale	28-20	T: Graham, Underwood, Vyvyan C: Wilkinson 2 P: Wilkinson 3
13 Feb	A	London Scottish	17-27	T: Shaw, Legg C: Wilkinson 2 P: Wilkinson
27 Mar	A	Northampton	16-57	T: Charlton C: Andrew P: Andrew 3
31 Mar	H	London Scottish	43-20	T: Legg, Cartmell, Graham, Walton, Wilkinson C: Wilkinson 3 P: Wilkinson 4
18 Apr	A	Wasps	33-34	T: Tuigamala 2, Wilkinson C: Wilkinson 3 P: Wilkinson 4
21 Apr	H	Richmond	47-14	T: Armstrong 3, Beattie, Graham, Naylor, Wilkinson C: Legg 6
25 Apr	H	Gloucester	39-15	T: Armstrong 2, Graham, Legg, Wood C: Wilkinson 4 P: Wilkinson 2

2 May	H	Leicester	12-21	*P:* Wilkinson 4
11 May	H	Harlequins	33-22	*T:* Tuigamala 2, Cartmell *C:* Wilkinson 3
				P: Wilkinson 4
20 May	A	Saracens	26-40	*T:* Shaw, Wilkinson *C:* Wilkinson 2
				P: Wilkinson 4

Northampton

Year of formation 1880
Ground Franklins Gardens, Weedon Road, St James', Northampton NN5 5BG
Tel: Northampton (01604) 751543
Web site http://www.northamptonsaints.co.uk/
Colours Black, green and gold bands; black shorts
Captain 1998-99 T A K Rodber
Allied Dunbar Leagues 1998-99 Div 1 2nd
Tetley's Bitter Cup 1998-99 Lost 6-21 to London Irish (5th round)

The jubilation which engulfed the club after one of their most successful seasons was quickly dispelled when it was learned that the man who had masterminded their successful Allied Dunbar Premiership One campaign would not be there to plot their approach to their debut season in the European Cup. Ian McGeechan left the Saints for the only job he could not refuse, to become Scotland's coach. Whether the Saints will have recovered from this shattering news in time for the start of the new season remains to be seen. Still McGeechan's legacy is a generous one. A structured development system which is producing plenty of promising talent and a belief and indeed knowledge that they can compete with the best.

If they started the Premiership season shakily, things soon picked up. After defeats at Saracens and Leicester in September they did not lose another match until November up at Newcastle and they kept the pressure on Leicester, making second place theirs from very early on. If they had managed to remain focused against London Irish at Franklin's Gardens at the beginning of January and again at home to Saracens a month later then the Tigers might have found the leadership stakes a trifle tougher. Saints' defeats in those matches effectively turned the Premiership title challenge into a race of one. Thankfully they had opened up enough of a gap between themselves and the scrapping pack to be able to sustain their losses without slipping down the table. Not even a last day defeat at Kingsholm could spoil things.

The playing strength had been added to with the signing of 7ft 1in lock Richard Metcalfe from Newcastle and David Dantiacq from Pau; Ian Hunter retired, finally giving up the war against injuries after losing his most recent battle. They had a scare over one of their players of the season, Freddy Mendez. The Argentine front row had a hankering for the green, green grass of the Pampas and was considering not returning for the millennium season. Fortunately he was persuaded to sign again.

League Record 1998-99

Date	Venue	Opponents	Result	Scorers
6 Sep	A	Saracens	7-34	*T:* Dawson *C:* Grayson
12 Sep	H	Harlequins	25-6	*T:* Seely 2, Dantiacq, Pountney *C:* Grayson
				P: Grayson
19 Sep	A	Leicester	25-35	*T:* Pountney *C:* A Hepher *P:* Grayson 6
3 Oct	H	Sale	37-17	*T:* M Allen, Dantiacq, penalty try, Moir
				C: Grayson 4 *P:* Grayson 3
10 Oct	A	London Scottish	33-22	*T:* M Allen, A Hepher, MacKinnon, Lam
				C: Grayson 2 *P:* Grayson 3
17 Oct	H	Bedford	34-29	*T:* Beal, Lam, Pagel, Sleightholme
				C: A Hepher *P:* Grayson 2, A Hepher 2
24 Oct	A	London Irish	26-10	*T:* A Hepher, Lam, Pountney *C:* A Hepher
				P: A Hepher 3

31 Oct	H	Gloucester	22-8	T: penalty try C: A Hepher P: A Hepher 4, Grayson
7 Nov	H	Wasps	26-21	T: Beal, Mackinnon C: Grayson 2 P: Grayson 4
15 Nov	A	Newcastle	35-45	T: Pagel 2, Malone, Metcalfe C: A Hepher 3 P: A Hepher 3
21 Nov	H	Richmond	44-27	T: Pagel, penalty try, Seely, M Allen, C Allan C: A Hepher 5 P: A Hepher 3
12 Nov	A	Bath	15-9	T: Dawson, Pountney C: Grayson P: Grayson
20 Dec	A	West Hartlepool	33-9	T: Dawson 2, Lam 2, Pountney C: Grayson 4
2 Jan	A	Sale	39-24	T: Lam 3, M Allen, Malone C: Grayson 4 P: Grayson 2
5 Jan	H	London Irish	8-32	T: Blyth P: Grayson
16 Jan	A	Harlequins	24-17	T: Grayson, Lam, Pagel C: Grayson 3 P: Grayson
23 Jan	H	West Hartlepool	19-14	T: Lam C: Grayson P: Grayson 4
6 Feb	H	Saracens	18-21	P: Grayson 6
13 Mar	H	Leicester	15-22	P: Dawson 5
27 Mar	H	Newcastle	57-16	T: Cohen 2, Mendez 2, M Allen, Beal, Dawson, Metcalfe, Pountney C: Dawson 6
13 Apr	A	Wasps	24-15	T: Beal, Lam C: A Hepher P: A Hepher 4
17 Apr	H	London Scottish	44-13	T: Pountney 2, Beal, Lam, Moir, Dawson C: A Hepher 4 P: A Hepher 2
24 Apr	A	Bedford	42-31	T: Lam 2, Cohen, Seely, penalty try C: A Hepher 4 P: A Hepher 3
1 May	H	Bath	40-17	T: Seely 2, Pountney, Mendez C: Dawson 4 P: A Hepher 2, Dawson 2
8 May	A	Richmond	31-19	T: Malone 2, Phillips, Seely C: Dawson 4 P: Dawson
16 May	A	Gloucester	31-43	T: S Hepher 2, Malone, Dantiacq, Moir C: Dawson 3

Orrell

Year of formation 1927
Ground Edge Hall Road, Orrell, Wigan, Lancashire WN5 8TL
Tel: Upholland (01695) 623193
Web site N/A
Colours Black and amber; black shorts
Captain 1998-99 D Lyon
Allied Dunbar Leagues 1998-99 Div 2 8th
Tetley's Bitter Cup 1998-99 Lost 11-18 to Waterloo (4th round)

It was not just Richmond who went into administration. With debts of more than £500,000 Orrell faced up to a few financial facts of life and voluntarily took the plunge. Meanwhile as negotiations went on into the summer for likely partners, Wigan Rugby League club emerged as favourites in the would-be venture. A cost-cutting exercise had seen the departure of Ged Glynn, the England under-21 coach, as well as the cancellation of a number of other full-time contracts. On the field things were not all doom and gloom. They set off in fine style, winning at Fylde and then beating Rugby; London Welsh put a little spanner in the works, but a 60-point thrashing of the Allied Dunbar Premiership Two's whipping boys Blackheath restored the feelgood factor. Notable scalps thereafter included Rotherham, Coventry and London Welsh (all at home) and they completed the double over Waterloo, although that could have been turned into a treble if they had managed to beat them in extra-time of the fourth round Tetley's Bitter Cup tie at Blundellsands. Simon Verbickas scored 221 points in the Premiership, the fourth highest scorer in the Second Division, while David Slemen, son of Mike, emerged as an outside-half of great promise and was included in the England under-21 party to tour Argentina.

League Record 1998-99

Date	Venue	Opponents	Result	Scorers
5 Sep	A	Fylde	20-6	T: Liptrot, Lyon, M Oliver C: Verbickas P: Verbickas
12 Sep	H	Rugby	32-3	T: Liptrot, penalty try, M Oliver, Wynn C: Verbickas 3 P: Verbickas 2
19 Sep	A	London Welsh	17-24	T: Russell, M Oliver C: Verbickas, Liptrot P: Verbickas
26 Sep	H	Blackheath	60-3	T: Liptrot 2, Kelly 2, Lyon 2, Manley, Moffat C: Hamer 7 P: Hamer 2
3 Oct	H	Leeds	11-13	T: Liptrot P: Hamer 2
10 Oct	A	Bristol	19-29	T: Bell, Cundick, Lyon C: Bell, Hamer
17 Oct	H	Rotherham	19-12	T: Russell, Warr P: Verbickas 2 D: Ryan
24 Oct	A	Coventry	14-28	T: Johnson P: Verbickas 3
31 Oct	H	Wakefield	24-5	T: Slemen 2, Lyon P: Slemen 3
7 Nov	A	Moseley	3-25	P: Verbickas
21 Nov	H	Worcester	9-13	P: Verbickas 2 D: Ryan
12 Dec	A	Waterloo	17-10	T: Wynn P: Verbickas 3 D: Ryan
19 Dec	H	Exeter	21-23	T: Johnson 2, Kelly P: Verbickas 2
2 Jan	A	Worcester	0-17	
16 Jan	H	Moseley	20-14	T: Lacey, Verbickas C: Verbickas 2 P: Verbickas 2
23 Jan	A	Wakefield	13-25	T: Slemen C: Verbickas P: Verbickas 2
6 Feb	H	Coventry	31-0	T: Hope, Wynn, Slemen, Verbickas C: Verbickas 4 P: Verbickas
13 Feb	A	Rotherham	10-47	T: Hope, Johnson
27 Feb	H	Bristol	32-34	T: Johnson 3, Verbickas C: Verbickas 3 P: Verbickas 2
14 Mar	A	Leeds	7-20	T: Verbickas C: Verbickas
27 Mar	A	Blackheath	9-15	P: Verbickas 3
3 Apr	H	London Welsh	18-15	T: Johnson, Lacey C: Verbickas P: Verbickas 2
17 Apr	A	Rugby	41-29	T: Verbickas 2, Wynn 2, Newton, Ryan, Warr C: Verbickas 3
24 Apr	H	Fylde	28-18	T: Verbickas 2, Rees C: Verbickas 2 P: Verbickas 2 D: Wynn
1 May	A	Exeter	32-42	T: Verbickas 2, Newton, Brown C: Verbickas 3 P: Verbickas 2
8 May	H	Waterloo	59-15	T: Verbickas 3, Johnson 2, Grainey, Hitchmough, Kelly, Wynn C: Verbickas 6, Slemen

Richmond

Year of formation 1861
Ground Madejski Stadium, Reading Tel: Reading (0118) 975 7400 or 0181 332 7112 (club office)
Web site http://richmondrugby.uk.oracle.com/
Colours Old gold, red and black; black shorts
Captain 1998-99 B B Clarke
Allied Dunbar Leagues 1998-99 Div 1 9th
Tetley's Bitter Cup 1998-99 Lost 3-20 to Newcastle (semi-final)

However sound (for financial and fixture purposes) the decision might have been to ditch one of the founding members of the Rugby Football Union – and make no mistake, maintaining the name of the amateur club in the constituent body of the union is little more than a sop; the club is extinct to all intents and purposes – the sense of betrayal is not confined to the vicinity of the Athletic Ground. Having been let down, as they might see it, by their big-money backer Ashley Levett, they were then dumped on by the fellow Premiership One clubs. Levett's departure prompted a, possibly naïve, decision to go into administration. It was a voluntary thing, but perhaps they should have taken a leaf out of the conscripts' book; in the Army they say 'Never volunteer for anything'.

Anyway 'tis done. And at least they enjoyed one of their better seasons even if those players so carefully garnered and gathered together by the admirable John Kingston to be moulded into what turned out to be a more than useful force – although perhaps a little too inconsistent for any lasting success – are now scattered to the four winds.

Their finest hour had to be in the quarter-final of the Tetley's Bitter Cup when they overcame Leicester at the Madejski Stadium, matching the Tigers try for try and exceeding them in guts and sheer bloody-mindedness. The only disappointment of that victory, which took them into the semi-finals for the first time, was the size of the crowd, 7,088. There were just about 3,000 more to witness their anticlimactic exit in the next round at the same venue against Newcastle. The Allied Dunbar Premiership was a serious let-down. They lost their last five home matches – four of them on the trot in the run-in; the win at West Hartlepool was by a point and that followed a high-scoring draw at Harlequins.

League Record 1998-99

Date	Venue	Opponents	Result	Scorers
5 Sep	H	Newcastle	41-29	T: R Hutton 2, Clarke, Pichot, Brown, Bateman C: A Davies 4 P: A Davies
12 Sep	H	Gloucester	22-25	T: Bateman, Cuthbert, C Quinnell C: A Davies 2 P: A Davies
19 Sep	A	Bath	14-36	T: Deane, Williams C: A Davies 2
3 Oct	A	London Irish	33-29	T: Brown 2, S Quinnell, Va'a, C: Va'a 2 P: A Davies, Pini, Va'a
10 Oct	H	West Hartlepool	41-23	T: Pichot 2, Best 2, S Quinnell 2, Walne C: Va'a 3
18 Oct	A	Wasps	27-22	T: Brown, Clarke, Pini, Va'a C: Va'a 2 P: Pini
24 Oct	A	Leicester	0-27	
28 Oct	A	Sale	39-10	T: Pichot, C Quinnell, S Quinnell, Clarke, Bateman, Brown C: Va'a 3 P: Va'a
1 Nov	H	Bedford	38-32	T: C Quinnell 2, Va'a, Williams, Vander C: Va'a 2 P: Va'a 3
8 Nov	A	Saracens	17-33	T: penalty try, Va'a C: Butland 2 P: Butland
21 Nov	A	Northampton	27-44	T: Walne 2, Brown, Va'a C: Va'a 2 P: Va'a
19 Dec	A	London Scottish	28-16	T: Vander 2, Va'a C: Va'a 2 P: Va'a 3
26 Dec	H	London Irish	13-25	T: Pichot, Pini P: Va'a
16 Jan	A	Gloucester	24-24	T: Clarke, Brown C: Va'a P: Va'a 4
23 Jan	H	London Scottish	40-22	T: Bateman 2, Hutton, C Quinnell, Vander, Walne C: Va'a 5
26 Jan	H	Leicester	11-23	T: Walne P: Va'a 2
14 Feb	H	Sale	29-24	T: Pichot, Clarke, Brown C: Va'a P: Va'a 4
13 Mar	H	Bath	23-30	T: Hutton, Vander C: Va'a 2 P: Va'a 3
27 Mar	A	Harlequins	32-32	T: Clarke, Hutton, Dixon, Va'a C: Va'a 3 P: Va'a 2
18 Apr	A	West Hartlepool	36-35	T: Best, Williams, Wright C: Va'a 3 P: Va'a 5
21 Apr	A	Newcastle	14-47	T: Williams P: Butland 3
25 Apr	H	Wasps	5-29	T: Pichot
3 May	H	Harlequins	23-30	T: Bateman 2, Clarke,Walne P: Va'a
8 May	H	Northampton	19-31	T: Vander 2, C Quinnell C: Va'a 2
12 May	H	Saracens	18-25	T: Wright, Va'a C: Va'a P: Va'a 2
16 May	A	Bedford	106-12	T: Cusack 3, Deane 3, C Quinnell 2, Wright 2, Bateman, Vander, Walne, Shelbourne, Whitford, Williams C: Butland 13

Rotherham

Year of formation 1923
Ground Clifton Lane Grounds, Badsley Moor Lane, Rotherham, South Yorkshire S65 2PH
Tel: Rotherham (01709) 370763
Web site N/A
Colours Maroon, sky blue and navy blue stripes; black shorts
Captain 1998-99 M Schmid
Allied Dunbar Leagues 1998-99 Div 2 2nd; Lost Division 1/2 play-off against Bedford on try-scoring rule after drawing 38-all on aggregate
Tetley's Bitter Cup 1998-99 Lost 24-27 to Leeds (4th round)

For the second season running Rotherham earned themselves a play-off. Having beaten Bedford in the first leg, they fought themselves to a standstill down at Goldington Road, but with the aggregate scores level they found themselves stuck, in a kind of groundhog day, in Allied Dunbar Premiership Two because they had scored fewer tries over the two matches. Rotherham were remarkably consistent throughout their league campaign, taking over third place shortly before Christmas and moving up to second place, where they remained, in March, having won 17 games on the trot. Unsurprisingly they remained unbeaten at home in the league. They were pipped on points difference by Bristol and fully deserved to make the grade; and on this showing it can only be a matter of time. They completed home and away doubles over Bristol and Worcester and the only time they lost at Clifton Lane was in the fourth round of the Tetley's Bitter Cup against Leeds.

They have developed into an entertaining team, wing Dean Lax was the leading try-scorer with 18, with wing forward Ben Wade a close second on 16. The shrewd recruiting policy came up trumps with the likes of outside-half Jake Niarchos, a colt from Loughborough University, and Glen Kenworthy, a lock from Hawke's Bay New Zealand, making a big impression.

League Record 1998-99

Date	Venue	Opponents	Result	Scorers
5 Sep	A	Waterloo	7-22	*T:* Dudley *C:* Trivella
12 Sep	H	Exeter	28-17	*T:* Austin 2, Buzza *C:* Trivella 2 *P:* Trivella 3
26 Sep	H	Rugby	44-0	*T:* Austin, Harper, Hassan, Schmid, Trivella, Wade *C:* Trivella 4 *P:* Trivella 2
3 Oct	A	London Welsh	27-13	*T:* Austin, Dudley, Schmid, Trivella *C:* Trivella 2 *P:* Trivella
10 Oct	H	Blackheath	46-3	*T:* Wade 2, Harper, Lax, Schmid, Trivella *C:* Trivella 5 *P:* Trivella 2
17 Oct	A	Orrell	12-19	*T:* Wade, Lax *C:* Trivella
24 Oct	H	Bristol	16-5	*T:* Trivella *C:* Trivella *P:* Trivella 3
1 Nov	A	Leeds	10-15	*T:* Thorpe *C:* Scully *P:* Scully
7 Nov	A	Coventry	12-22	*T:* Scully, Wade *C:* Scully
21 Nov	H	Wakefield	34-7	*T:* Garnett, Hall, penalty try, Umaga, Wade *C:* Niarchos 2, Scully *P:* Scully
12 Dec	A	Moseley	16-6	*T:* Austin *C:* Niarchos *P:* Niarchos 3
19 Dec	H	Worcester	29-19	*T:* Austin 2, Walker, Umaga *C:* Niarchos 3 *P:* Niarchos
2 Jan	A	Wakefield	40-13	*T:* Walker 2, Austin, Scully, Wade, Schmid *C:* Niarchos 2 *P:* Niarchos 2
16 Jan	H	Coventry	19-12	*T:* Harper *C:* Niarchos *P:* Niarchos 4
23 Jan	H	Leeds	25-10	*T:* Wade 3, Lax, Parr
6 Feb	A	Bristol	36-31	*T:* Lax, Spence, Wade, Umaga, *C:* Trivella 2 *P:* Trivella 4
13 Feb	H	Orrell	47-10	*T:* Lax 4, Dudley, Scully, Kenworthy *C:* Trivella 2, Niarchos *P:* Trivella 2

20 Feb	A	Fylde	34-5	*T:* Schmid 2, Lax, Scully, Wade *C:* Niarchos 3 *P:* Niarchos
28 Feb	A	Blackheath	29-19	*T:* Lax, Scully, Shepherd, Umaga, Walker *C:* Niarchos 2
13 Mar	H	London Welsh	28-8	*T:* Dudley, McIntyre, Niarchos, Wade *C:* Trivella 4
27 Mar	A	Rugby	33-10	*T:* Lax 2, Dudley, Umaga. Wade *C:* Trivella *P:* Trivella 2
3 Apr	H	Fylde	43-16	*T:* Lax, Parr, Schmid, Shepherd, West, Sinclair, Wade *C:* Niarchos 4
17 Apr	A	Exeter	35-24	*T:* Lax, Parr, Trivella, Umaga, Wade *C:* Trivella 2 *P:* Trivella 2
24 Apr	H	Waterloo	44-3	*T:* Lax 3, Austin, Dudley, Hall, West *C:* Niarchos 3 *P:* Niarchos
1 May	A	Worcester	35-27	*T:* Walker 3, Austin *C:* Niarchos 3 *P:* Niarchos 3
8 May	H	Moseley	27-0	*T:* Garnett, Lax, Umaga, Webster *C:* Niarchos, Trivella *P:* Niarchos
Play-offs				
20 May	H	Bedford	19-11	*T:* Umaga *C:* Niarchos *P:* Niarchos 4
26 May	A	Bedford	19-27	*T:* Lax, Scully *P:* Niarchos 3

Rugby

Year of formation 1873
Ground Webb Ellis Road, Rugby CV22 7AU Tel: Rugby (01788) 334466
Web site http://www.the-rugby-fc.com/
Colours White with red lion crest; blue shorts
Captain 1998-99 M Ellis
Allied Dunbar Leagues 1998-99 Div 2 11th
Tetley's Bitter Cup 1998-99 Lost 7-68 to Leeds (3rd round)

There were a few wobbles on the way, especially a run of four defeats after their opening victory over Blackheath, and there were premature and, as things turned out, unfounded fears of a disastrous season, but Rugby rallied well and were comfortably clear of the danger zone by the end of a season which had seen them win what was, for them, the big one against local rivals Coventry, at Coundon Road in mid-March. The arrival of No.8 Chris Tarbuck from London Scottish and the fiercely competitive lock Richard Kinsey from Wasps made a big difference to the performance up front, while in the centre the veteran Samoan To'o Vaega, who played in the 1987 World Cup and could well make it into the 1999 tournament, had real pace and tackled like a tanker in midfield, despite his slight build. Whether they can afford to hang on to him is debatable; Vaega was rumoured to be earning £30,000 and with whispers of players being switched to pay for play contracts, he may need more financial security than that.

League Record 1998-99

Date	Venue	Opponents	Result	Scorers
5 Sep	H	Blackheath	18-12	*T:* Rees, Withers *C:* Hopkins
12 Sep	A	Orrell	3-32	*P:* D Evans
19 Sep	H	Bristol	20-30	*T:* Saunders, Wingham *C:* M Davies 2 *P:* M Davies 2
26 Sep	A	Rotherham	0-44	
4 Oct	H	Coventry	17-20	*T:* Bale *P:* M Davies 3 *D:* Morgan
10 Oct	A	Wakefield	26-22	*T:* Gillooly, Thompson, Bale *C:* M Davies *P:* M Davies 2 *D:* Morgan
18 Oct	H	Moseley	30-8	*T:* Bale, A Davies, Vaega *C:* M Davies 3 *P:* M Davies 3

24 Oct	A	Worcester	6-29	P: Morgan D: Morgan
31 Oct	H	Waterloo	20-9	T: Bale, penalty try C: M Davies 2 P: M Davies 2
7 Nov	A	Exeter	23-7	T: Morgan 2, Saunders C: M Davies P: M Davies 2
21 Nov	H	Fylde	30-16	T: Ellis, Field, Saunders, Tarbuck C: M Davies 2 P: M Davies 2
13 Dec	H	Leeds	9-18	P: M Davies 3
19 Dec	A	London Welsh	7-11	T: Gallagher C: M Davies
2 Jan	A	Fylde	14-6	T: Saunders P: M Davies 3
23 Jan	A	Waterloo	3-11	P: M Davies
6 Feb	H	Worcester	23-36	T: M Davies, Saunders C: M Davies 2 P: M Davies 3
13 Feb	A	Moseley	20-35	T: Saunders 2, Ellis C: D Evans P: M Davies
27 Feb	H	Wakefield	17-23	T: Field, Tarbuck C: M Davies 2 P: M Davies
13 Mar	A	Coventry	21-19	T: Hopkins, Tarbuck C: M Davies P: M Davies 3
21 Mar	H	Exeter	13-9	T: Milner, Vaega P: M Davies
27 Mar	H	Rotherham	10-33	T: M Davies C: M Davies P: M Davies
3 Apr	A	Bristol	13-49	T: Bale C: M Davies P: M Davies 2
17 Apr	H	Orrell	29-41	T: Bale, M Davies, Vaega, Tarbuck, Withers C: M Davies 2
24 Apr	A	Blackheath	20-43	T: M Davies, Harrison C: M Davies 2 P: M Davies 2
1 May	H	London Welsh	12-33	P: M Davies 4
9 May	A	Leeds	21-64	T: Docherty, S Evans, Bailey C: D Evans 2, Bedden

Saracens

Year of formation 1876
Ground Vicarage Road Stadium, Watford, Hertfordshire WD1 8ER
Tel: Watford (01923) 496200
Web site http://www.saracens.net/
Colours Black with red and white hoops on sleeve; black shorts
Captain 1998-99 A J Diprose / J F Pienaar
Allied Dunbar Leagues 1998-99 Div 1 3rd
Tetley's Bitter Cup 1998-99 Lost 0-15 to Newcastle (quarter-final)

Not perhaps the finish that they were looking for; an improvement on last season's second place in the Allied Dunbar Premiership would have been the logical expectation. But at least they did not disgrace themselves. They face a demanding, but exciting, debut in the European Cup as the reward for finishing third in Premiership One and if nothing else they managed to consolidate their standing in the Watford community. Crowds were good; several times the magic figure of 10,000 was topped and for the visit of Leicester there were more than 17,000 people in the Vicarage Road stadium. Unfortunately the genius behind the crowd-pulling and marketing of the club, Peter Deakin, was lured back to his first love, rugby league, just a couple of months after agreeing a five-year contract with Nigel Wray. Deakin had laid a lot of solid foundations though and if he is missed, Saracens are perfectly capable of picking up where he left off.

There were other departures, Chief Executive Mike Smith went not long after the start of the season. Alain Penaud, although a success, decided at the end of the season that he needed to return to France with his family, who were homesick. Ireland lock Paddy Johns also went home, joining the growing exodus of Irishmen to respond to the siren call of the Irish Rugby Union. He left at the end of the season to play for Ulster. Wing Brendon Daniel also departed, heading a little further south to join Harlequins. And having obtained the services of Paul Turner to lend a hand with the backs' coaching they parted company with him at the end of the season.

Tony Diprose lost the captaincy to Francois Pienaar following the narrow defeat against Gloucester at Kingsholm. After one victory under new leadership they lost at home in the shock result of their season to strugglers London Scottish. They went on to play out the first draw in the Premiership against Wasps at Loftus Road. Having slipped as low as eighth in the league, their campaign was completed in a flourish with a convincing victory over last season's champions Newcastle, which denied Rob Andrew's side a place in Europe.

League Record 1998-99

Date	Venue	Opponents	Result	Scorers
6 Sep	H	Northampton	34-7	*T:* Coker, Johnson, Penaud, Thomson *C:* Johnson 4　*P:* Johnson 2
20 Sep	H	Sale	43-26	*T:* Daniel 2, Constable, penalty try, Singer *C:* Johnson 3　*P:* Johnson 4
26 Sep	A	London Scottish	58-20	*T:* Daniel 2, Johnson 2, Constable, Chuter, Singer, P Wallace　*C:* Johnson 6　*P:* Johnson 2
11 Oct	H	Leicester	22-10	*T:* Constable　*C:* Johnson　*P:* Johnson 3, Penaud 2
17 Oct	A	Harlequins	28-41	*T:* Daniel, P Wallace, Ravenscroft, Penaud *C:* Penaud 4
20 Oct	A	West Hartlepool	52-3	*T:* R Wallace, Bracken, penalty try, Sorrell, Diprose, Hill, Pienaar　*C:* Penaud 3, Lee *P:* Penaud 3
25 Oct	H	Wasps	17-31	*T:* Daniel, Johnson　*C:* Johnson 2　*P:* Johnson
31 Oct	A	Newcastle	12-43	*T:* Hill, Johnson　*C:* Johnson
8 Nov	H	Richmond	33-17	*T:* Ravenscroft 2, Johnson　*C:* Johnson 3 *P:* Johnson 4
15 Nov	A	Bedford	25-20	*T:* Coker, de Jonge, R Wallace　*C:* Johnson 2 *P:* Johnson 2
21 Nov	A	Gloucester	27-28	*T:* Ravenscroft, Pienaar, Sorrell　*C:* Johnson 3 *P:* Johnson 2
13 Dec	H	London Irish	40-26	*T:* Pienaar 2, Free, Flatman　*C:* Johnson 4 *P:* Johnson 4
19 Dec	A	Bath	19-11	*T:* Ravenscroft　*C:* Johnson　*P:* Johnson 3 *D:* Penaud
27 Dec	H	London Scottish	7-24	*T:* Daniel　*C:* Johnson
3 Jan	H	Bedford	44-13	*T:* Grewcock 2, R Wallace, Johns, Daniel, Olsen　*C:* Johnson 4　*P:* Johnson 2
6 Jan	A	Wasps	15-15	*P:* Johnson 5
6 Feb	A	Northampton	21-18	*T:* Daniel, Ravenscroft　*C:* Johnson *P:* Johnson 3
14 Feb	H	West Hartlepool	48-27	*T:* Diprose 3, Penaud, Bracken, Thirlby, Grewcock　*C:* Johnson 4, Thirlby　*P:* Johnson
13 Mar	A	Sale	24-32	*T:* Hill, Penaud　*C:* Thirlby　*P:* Thirlby 3 *D:* Penaud
28 Mar	H	Bath	14-33	*T:* Grau, Hill　*C:* Thirlby 2
17 Apr	A	Leicester	18-25	*P:* Johnson 6
25 Apr	H	Harlequins	30-38	*T:* Daniel 2, penalty try　*C:* Johnson 3 *P:* Johnson 3
1 May	A	London Irish	26-21	*T:* Diprose, Johnson　*C:* Johnson 2 *P:* Johnson 3　*D:* Penaud
7 May	H	Gloucester	26-10	*T:* Daniel , Bracken, Cole　*C:* Johnson *P:* Johnson 3
12 May	A	Richmond	25-18	*T:* Penaud, Johnson, Sorrell　*C:* Johnson 2 *P:* Johnson 2
20 May	H	Newcastle	40-26	*T:* Diprose, Bracken, Chuter, Constable *C:* Johnson 4　*P:* Johnson 3　*D:* Penaud

Wakefield

Year of formation 1901
Ground Pinderfields Road, College Grove, Wakefield WF1 3RR
Tel: Wakefield (01924) 374801
Web site http://www.rugbysupporters.co.uk/
Colours Black and gold quarters; black shorts
Captain 1998-99 N Summers
Allied Dunbar Leagues 1998-99 Div 2 12th
Tetley's Bitter Cup 1998-99 Lost 8-16 to Kendal (3rd round)

A Groundhog Day of a season for a club which did not look to have taken itself anywhere. Wakefield finished third from bottom, a repeat of last season's effort, having won the same number of matches – six – but having conceded the second highest total of points, 812, in the division. And even though they played four more matches, their overall performance has to be regarded as a step backwards, finishing as they did just a couple of points clear of relegation. Even the recruitment of former England manager Geoff Cooke to attempt a rescue operation merely served to consolidate their league position. They remained resolutely in 12th place even after Cooke's arrival in mid-February, which was only a temporary move. At least they gained something from Cooke's appointment. He was shrewd enough to sign Rob Ashforth, the Cambridge Blue, on loan from Cooke's previous club Bedford, and the outside-half went on to play a crucial role in Wakefield's survival.

League Record 1998-99

Date	Venue	Opponents	Result	Scorers
5 Sep	A	Moseley	33-32	*T:* Birkby 2, Elisara *C:* Ure 3 *P:* Ure 4
12 Sep	H	Worcester	22-48	*T:* Hitchmough, Maynard, Simpson-Daniel *C:* Ure 2 *P:* Ure
19 Sep	A	Waterloo	25-36	*T:* Elisara, Flint, McKenzie *C:* Ure 2 *P:* Ure 2
26 Sep	H	Exeter	19-27	*T:* Hitchmough, Simpson-Daniel *P:* Ure 3
3 Oct	A	Fylde	18-20	*T:* Flint, McKenzie *C:* Ure *P:* Ure, Maynard
10 Oct	H	Rugby	22-26	*T:* Birkby, McKenzie, Wilson *C:* Ure 2 *P:* Ure
17 Oct	A	London Welsh	21-45	*T:* Elisara, McKenzie, Flint *C:* Ure 3
24 Oct	H	Blackheath	19-9	*T:* Dixon, McKenzie *P:* Ure 3
31 Oct	A	Orrell	5-24	*T:* Plevey
7 Nov	H	Bristol	15-46	*T:* Flint, Simpson-Daniel, Summers
21 Nov	A	Rotherham	7-34	*T:* Flint *C:* Ure
12 Dec	H	Coventry	10-18	*T:* Wilson *C:* Edwards *P:* Edwards
20 Dec	A	Leeds	0-38	
2 Jan	H	Rotherham	13-40	*T:* White *C:* Dixon *P:* Dixon 2
16 Jan	A	Bristol	19-35	*T:* Breheny *C:* Dixon *P:* Dixon 4
23 Jan	H	Orrell	25-13	*T:* Shine 2, Flint, Lloyd *C:* Dixon *P:* Dixon
6 Feb	A	Blackheath	20-28	*T:* Breheny, Simpson-Daniel *C:* Dixon 2 *P:* Dixon 2
13 Feb	H	London Welsh	16-30	*T:* Summers, Elisara *P:* Dixon 2
27 Feb	A	Rugby	23-17	*T:* Breheny, Summers, Yates *C:* Ashforth *P:* Ashforth 2
13 Mar	H	Fylde	27-11	*T:* Edwards 2, Flint *P:* Ashforth 4
27 Mar	A	Exeter	13-37	*T:* Summers *C:* Ashforth *P:* Ashforth, Dixon
3 Apr	H	Waterloo	14-20	*T:* Breheny *P:* Ashforth 3
17 Apr	A	Worcester	19-67	*T:* Dixon, Shine, Summers *C:* Ashforth 2
24 Apr	H	Moseley	38-20	*T:* Breheny 4, Ashworth, Dixon *C:* Dixon *P:* Ashforth 2
2 May	H	Leeds	13-51	*T:* Breheny, Skurr *P:* Ashforth
8 May	A	Coventry	13-40	*T:* Breheny, Edwards *P:* Dixon

Wasps

Year of formation 1867
Grounds Loftus Road Stadium, South Africa Road, Shepherds Bush, London W12 7PA
Tel: 0181 743 0262
Web site http://www.wasps.co.uk/
Colours Black with gold wasp on left breast; black shorts
Captain 1998-99 M Weedon
Allied Dunbar Leagues 1998-99 Div 1 5th
Tetley's Bitter Cup 1998-99 *Winners* -beat Newcastle 29-19 (final)

A glorious season, with silverware and a place in Europe secured, was overshadowed by allegations of drug taking against their former captain Lawrence Dallaglio, the England No.8, a matter which became the subject of an independent and a club inquiry during the summer months. Whatever the outcome of all that there was no doubt as to the way their season had gone. The crowning moment came at Twickenham in May, where, at the fifth attempt, Wasps finally won the Tetley's Bitter Cup with an emphatic victory over Newcastle. Fly-half Alex King gave a commanding performance. Gareth Rees, who had played in his first final for the club aged 18, turned in a perfect performance at full-back, from where he shouldered the responsibilities of the kicking duties. Josh Lewsey, who has turned out at stand-off and at full-back, now had a bash on the wing in place of the injured Kenny Logan and made a fist of it. He scored a fine try to wrap the match up in the 77th minute when he intercepted a Va'aiga Tuigamala pass; but more importantly he had earlier prevented a Newcastle score when he chased, and caught, the luckless Samoan man mountain Tuigamala. Victory was all the sweeter for helping to put last season's cup final humiliation at the hands of Saracens out of mind.

If the Allied Dunbar Premiership was a disappointment it could only be because of their propensity to lose games they shouldn't. An early example was the defeat at home to Richmond, followed three weeks later by another reverse at Loftus Road against Harlequins; as for the performance up at West Hartlepool in the New Year, that must remain one of the mysteries of the Allied Dunbar Premiership. The setbacks were countered with some excellent results, not least the thrashing of Leicester at home, and in February they also became the first side in the history of league rugby to prevent Bath from scoring a single point.

League Record 1998-99

Date	Venue	Opponents	Result	Scorers
5 Sep	A	Bath	27-36	*T:* Leota, Logan, Worsley *P:* Rees 4
19 Sep	A	London Irish	36-24	*T:* Roiser, Logan, Scrase, Volley *C:* Logan 2 *P:* Logan 4
27 Sep	H	West Hartlepool	71-14	*T:* Roiser 2, Volley 2, Dallaglio, Greenstock, King, Logan, Shaw, Worsley *C:* Logan 6 *P:* Logan 3
3 Oct	A	Gloucester	13-12	*T:* Green *C:* Logan *P:* Logan 2
11 Oct	A	Newcastle	19-27	*T:* Roiser, Dallaglio, Leota *C:* Logan 2
18 Oct	H	Richmond	22-27	*T:* Leota *C:* Logan *P:* Logan 5
21 Oct	H	Bedford	35-19	*T:* Rossigneux, Dallaglio, Friday *C:* Logan *P:* Logan 6
25 Oct	A	Saracens	31-17	*T:* Henderson, King, Lewsey, Logan *C:* Logan *P:* Logan 3
1 Nov	H	Harlequins	21-22	*T:* Greenstock, Scrase *C:* Logan *P:* Logan 3
7 Nov	A	Northampton	21-26	*T:* Volley, Logan *C:* Logan *P:* Logan 3
15 Nov	H	Leicester	45-17	*T:* Leota 2, Volley 2, Logan, Roiser *C:* Logan 3 *P:* Logan 3
22 Nov	H	Sale	32-19	*T:* Leota, Roiser, Rollitt, Weedon *C:* King 3 *P:* King *D:* King
12 Dec	A	London Scottish	17-9	*T:* penalty try, Lewsey *C:* Logan 2 *P:* Logan

27 Dec	H	Gloucester	23-9	*T:* Le Chevalier, Sampson *C:* Logan 2
				P: Logan 3
3 Jan	A	West Hartlepool	17-21	*T:* Alexopoulos, Greenstock, Scrivener
				C: Logan
6 Jan	H	Saracens	15-15	*P:* Logan 5
7 Feb	H	Bath	35-0	*T:* Scrivener 2, Wood 2, Weedon *C:* King 2
				P: King 2
13 Feb	A	Bedford	23-25	*T:* Reed, King, Dallaglio *C:* King *P:* King 2
14 Mar	H	London Irish	38-27	*T:* Scrivener 2, Sampson, Weedon *C:* Logan 3
				P: Logan 4
27 Mar	A	Leicester	6-16	*P:* Logan *D:* King
13 Apr	H	Northampton	15-24	*P:* King 5
18 Apr	H	Newcastle	34-33	*T:* Lewsey, Molloy, Wood *C:* King 2
				P: King 4 *D:* King
25 Apr	A	Richmond	29-5	*T:* Denney, Sampson, Logan, Ufton
				C: Logan 2, King *P:* King
2 May	H	London Scottish	45-22	*T:* Lewsey, Sampson, Volley, Waters, Denney,
				penalty try *C:* Logan 3 *P:* Logan 3
8 May	A	Sale	27-13	*T:* Dallaglio, Sampson, Logan *C:* Logan 3
				P: Logan 2
19 May	A	Harlequins	20-27	*T:* Henderson, Rees *C:* Rees 2 *P:* Rees 2

Waterloo

Year of formation 1882
Grounds St Anthony's Road, Blundellsands, Liverpool L23 8TW Tel: 0151 924 4552
Web site N/A
Colours Green, red and white hoops; green shorts
Captain 1998-99 P White
Allied Dunbar Leagues 1998-99 Div 2 9th
Tetley's Bitter Cup 1998-99 Lost 10-27 to Wasps (5th round)

It was a grim finish to their Allied Dunbar Premiership Two campaign, conceding more than 50 points to Orrell, especially after such a bright opening when they beat a powerful Rotherham side. At that point they had styled themselves The Drummers and proceeded to beat Worcester and Leeds in those early weeks of the season when they reached the heady heights of third place in Premiership Two. They also ran Coventry close and remained in or around the top five through the winter months, but in March things began to go wrong and other sides began to beat them. The Drummers fell into disuse as they slipped too many times to be able to save their season. Ninth place was enough to convince Tony Russ, who had joined as director of rugby in 1996, to give up the job after the Orrell debacle and instead go off and run a hotel in Keswick.

Waterloo had a reasonable run in the Tetley's Bitter Cup, coming through a gruelling tie against Orrell, which went into extra-time before it was settled. They eventually lost a far from one-sided fifth round tie at Wasps. Outside-half Lyndon Griffiths topped 200 points in the season, 198 of those coming in the Premiership, to make him fifth highest scorer in the Second Division.

League Record 1998-99

Date	Venue	Opponents	Result	Scorers
5 Sep	H	Rotherham	22-7	*T:* Davies *C:* Griffiths *P:* Griffiths 5
12 Sep	A	Coventry	15-21	*T:* La Rue, O'Reilly *C:* Griffiths *P:* Griffiths
19 Sep	H	Wakefield	36-25	*T:* La Rue, Mullins, O'Reilly, Woof
				C: Griffiths 2 *P:* Griffiths 4
26 Sep	A	Moseley	15-13	*T:* Beckett, Mullins *C:* Griffiths *P:* Griffiths
3 Oct	H	Worcester	31-26	*T:* Stewart, White, Woof *C:* Griffiths 2
				P: Griffiths 4

10 Oct	H	Leeds	13-12	*T:* Woof *C:* Griffiths *P:* Griffiths 2
17 Oct	A	Exeter	14-41	*T:* Hill, Mullins *C:* Griffiths 2
24 Oct	H	Fylde	27-6	*T:* Griffiths, La Rue *C:* Griffiths
				P: Griffiths 5
31 Oct	A	Rugby	9-20	*P:* Griffiths 3
7 Nov	H	London Welsh	12-10	*P:* Griffiths 4
21 Nov	A	Blackheath	24-18	*T:* Hackney 2, Graham *C:* Griffiths 3
				P: Griffiths
12 Dec	H	Orrell	10-17	*T:* La Rue *C:* Griffiths *P:* Griffiths
19 Dec	A	Bristol	8-36	*T:* Griffiths *P:* Griffiths
2 Jan	H	Blackheath	31-25	*T:* Woof, Holt, Wands *C:* Griffiths 2
				P: Griffiths 3 *D:* Handley
23 Jan	H	Rugby	11-3	*T:* Hackney *P:* Griffiths 2
6 Feb	A	Fylde	5-24	*T:* Beckett
13 Feb	H	Exeter	11-13	*T:* Graham *P:* Griffiths 2
28 Feb	A	Leeds	10-9	*T:* Morris *C:* Griffiths *D:* Handley
13 Mar	A	Worcester	15-41	*T:* Graham, Swetman *C:* Griffiths
				P: Griffiths
27 Mar	H	Moseley	8-32	*T:* Swetman *P:* Griffiths
3 Apr	A	Wakefield	20-14	*T:* Stewart, Holt *C:* Griffiths 2 *P:* Griffiths 2
17 Apr	H	Coventry	24-25	*T:* Morris 2, Holt *C:* Griffiths 3 *P:* Griffiths
24 Apr	A	Rotherham	3-44	*P:* Griffiths
1 May	H	Bristol	13-44	*T:* Wolfenden, Wood *P:* Swetman
8 May	A	Orrell	15-59	*T:* Morris 2 *C:* Griffiths *P:* Griffiths

West Hartlepool

Year of formation 1881
Grounds Victoria Park, Clarence Road, Hartlepool TS24 8BZ
Tel: Hartlepool (01429) 233149
Web site http://www.west-rugby.org.uk/
Colours Red, white and green; white and green shorts
Captain 1998-99 T Nu'uali'itia / P Farner
Allied Dunbar Leagues 1998-99 Div 1 14th *relegated*
Tetley's Bitter Cup 1998-99 Lost 21-32 to Newcastle (5th round)

There was a feeling of inevitability about West's season. Two days after losing to Bedford at the beginning of May, a result which confirmed what everyone knew was inevitable, that they were not good enough to stay in Allied Dunbar Premiership One, the club's directors applied to go into company voluntary arrangement as they attempted to sort out the financial mess that has saddled them with more than £400,000 in debts. That was followed by West giving all 24 of their full-time professionals, including coach Mike Brewer, the former All Black, and their office staff, their redundancy notices. In Premiership Two they will be staffed by part-timers. The writing had been on the clubhouse wall long before that though. West had sold their Brierton Lane headquarters the previous July in order to help clear debts then of more than £1 million. They moved to Victoria Park, the Town's football club, but that arrangement has now been terminated. Just as well since it alienated many of their supporters who chose not to watch their club play at a soccer ground. They were due to discuss the possibility of sharing junior club Hartlepool Rovers' ground for the new season.

The first cuts were not that deep, they did ditch the Second XV and put half a dozen or so players on pay-if-you-play contracts, but to judge by their first 11 matches – all of which they lost – it did not seem as if anyone was playing. They were most definitely the First Division's whipping boys. Wasps stuck 71 points on them, a score bettered by Leicester by one point in the final match of a miserable season. Bath managed a half century each time and Saracens also scored fifty. There was a feeling bordering on disbelief when West broke their duck, beating Bedford at

Goldington Road. Brewer's mid-season recruiting campaign paid some modest dividends and three weeks later, in the New Year, came the high point of their season when they beat Wasps at home. They triumphed, again at home, over Gloucester (no difficult task given the West Country side's appalling away form), albeit by a solitary point, and there was a high-scoring draw with Sale. That was followed by the narrowest of defeats at home to Richmond, but the seal had been set with their lack of early season form and the outcome was never in doubt.

League Record 1998-99

Date	Venue	Opponents	Result	Scorers
13 Sep	H	London Irish	20-44	*T:* S John 2 *C:* Belgian 2 *P:* Vile 2
20 Sep	A	Gloucester	3-36	*P:* Belgian
27 Sep	A	Wasps	14-71	*T:* penalty try, Vile *C:* Vile 2
4 Oct	H	Newcastle	19-24	*T:* Farrell, Benson *P:* Vile 3
11 Oct	A	Richmond	23-41	*T:* S John, Benson *C:* Vile 2 *P:* Vile 3
17 Oct	H	Bath	20-50	*T:* penalty try, Farrell *C:* Vile 2 *P:* Vile 2
20 Oct	H	Saracens	3-52	*P:* Vile
24 Oct	A	Harlequins	10-25	*T:* Connolly *C:* Vile *P:* Vile
1 Nov	H	Leicester	15-45	*T:* penalty try, Nu'uali'itia *C:* Benson *P:* Benson
13 Nov	A	Sale	26-42	*T:* penalty try, S John *C:* Vile, Benson *P:* Vile 3, Benson
22 Nov	H	London Scottish	7-37	*T:* Lough *C:* Vile
12 Dec	A	Bedford	23-10	*T:* Brewer, Farrell *C:* Vile 2 *P:* Vile 3
20 Dec	H	Northampton	9-33	*P:* Vile 3
27 Dec	A	Newcastle	13-29	*T:* S John, McDonald *P:* Vile
3 Jan	H	Wasps	21-17	*T:* Handley, Ponton *C:* Vile *P:* Vile 2 *D:* Farrell
16 Jan	A	London Irish	21-43	*T:* Nu'uali'itia 2, McDonald *C:* Vile 3
23 Jan	A	Northampton	14-19	*T:* Tanginoa, Vile *C:* Vile 2
14 Feb	A	Saracens	27-48	*T:* S John, Tanginoa *C:* Vile *P:* Vile 5
14 Mar	H	Gloucester	33-32	*T:* Monkley, Vile *C:* Vile *P:* Vile 6 *D:* Vile
28 Mar	H	Sale	33-33	*T:* Farner, Mullins, Ponton, Vile *C:* Vile 2 *P:* Vile 3
18 Apr	H	Richmond	35-36	*T:* Mullins, Vile *C:* Vile 2 *P:* Vile 7
21 Apr	H	Harlequins	37-47	*T:* Fourie 2, Hyde, Benson *C:* Vile 4 *P:* Vile 3
24 Apr	A	Bath	24-56	*T:* Farrell, Greaves *C:* Vile *P:* Vile 4
2 May	H	Bedford	0-39	
8 May	A	London Scottish	14-26	*T:* Hyde, Greaves *C:* Benson 2
16 May	A	Leicester	37-72	*T:* McClure 2, Farrell, Beale, Brewer *C:* Benson 3 *P:* Benson 2

Worcester

Year of formation 1871
Ground Sixways, Pershore Lane, Hindlip, Worcester WR3 8ZE
Tel: Worcester (01905) 454183
Web site http://www.wrfc.co.uk/
Colours Old gold with navy blue stripes; navy shorts
Captain 1998-99 B Fenley
Allied Dunbar Leagues 1998-99 Div 2 3rd
Tetley's Bitter Cup 1998-99 Lost 17-31 to Gloucester (4th round)

The frustration of missing out on first promotion then the play-off place was offset somewhat by the news that owner Cecil Duckworth was trying to persuade the Rugby Football Union to give the go-ahead to a merger with Sale, which would bring Allied Dunbar Premiership One rugby to Sixways. The news emanating from

Twickenham in mid-summer was not encouraging, however. The RFU did not approve of the merger in principle according to reports. Frankly, the harsh fact of the matter was that Worcester are perfectly capable of reaching the top flight without having to buy their way into it. They overcame the docking of two precious points in the autumn for playing hooker Tim Beddow for four minutes as a replacement against Rugby and eventually took over the leadership of Allied Dunbar Premiership Two from their close rivals Bristol. But at the end of February they began the disastrous run of form that was to cost them their dream. They lost at Exeter and suffered defeats in a further five matches, winning only two of their last eight.

League Record 1998-99

Date	Venue	Opponents	Result	Scorers
5 Sep	H	Coventry	22-7	T: Baxter, Denhardt, Fenley, Tomlinson C: Le Bas
12 Sep	A	Wakefield	48-22	T: Myler 3, Hughes 2, Linnett, Smith C: Le Bas 5 P: Le Bas
19 Sep	H	Moseley	23-8	T: Denhardt 2, penalty try C: Le Bas P: Le Bas 2
27 Sep	H	Leeds	24-19	T: Hughes, Baxter C: Le Bas P: Le Bas 4
3 Oct	A	Waterloo	26-31	T: Jenner, Linnett C: Le Bas 2 P: Le Bas 4
10 Oct	H	Exeter	40-15	T: Baxter, Hilton-Jones, Hughes, Le Bas C: Le Bas 4 P: Le Bas 4
17 Oct	A	Fylde	17-8	T: Fenley, Le Bas C: Liley 2 P: Le Bas
24 Oct	H	Rugby	29-6	T: Hughes, Holford C: Liley 2 P: Liley 5
31 Oct	A	London Welsh	22-14	T: Myler 2 P: Liley 4
7 Nov	H	Blackheath	21-9	T: Baxter, Holford C: Liley P: Liley 3
21 Nov	A	Orrell	13-9	T: Richardson C: Liley P: Liley 2
13 Dec	H	Bristol	20-9	T: Jenner P: Liley 5
19 Dec	A	Rotherham	19-29	T: McLaughlin C: Liley P: Liley 4
2 Jan	H	Orrell	17-0	T: McLaughlin P: Liley 4
16 Jan	A	Blackheath	51-3	T: Devereux 2, Fenley, Jenner, Liley, Malone, Morris, Myler C: Malone 2, Liley 2 P: Liley
23 Jan	H	London Welsh	14-12	T: Myler P: Liley 3
6 Feb	A	Rugby	36-23	T: Myler, Lyman, Hilton-Jones, Lenner C: Le Bas 2 P: Le Bas 4
13 Feb	H	Fylde	56-0	T: Morris 2, Le Bas, Jenner, Powell, Holford, McLaughlin, penalty try C: Malone, Le Bas 4 P: Le Bas 2
27 Feb	A	Exeter	23-27	T: Le Bas, penalty try C: Le Bas 2 P: Le Bas 3
13 Mar	H	Waterloo	41-15	T: Baxter 2, Fenley, Holford, Linnett, Morris C: Lofthouse 3, Le Bas P: Le Bas
28 Mar	A	Leeds	16-26	T: Harvey C: Liley P: Liley 2, Lofthouse
3 Apr	A	Moseley	16-18	T: Goodwin C: Liley P: Liley 3
17 Apr	H	Wakefield	67-19	T: Baxter 3, McLaughlin 2, Crisp, Goodwin, Harvey, Liley, Lloyd, Turner C: Lofthouse 6
24 Apr	A	Coventry	17-26	T: Baxter P: Lofthouse 4
1 May	H	Rotherham	27-35	T: Baxter 2, Hilton-Jones C: Le Bas 3 P: Le Bas 2
9 May	A	Bristol	11-21	T: Baxter P: Le Bas 2

A YEAR OF CONTRASTS

THE 1998-99 SEASON IN SCOTLAND
Bill McMurtrie

Scottish rugby in 1998-99 had a season of marked contrasts on the international field. Results and performances in Murrayfield's four autumn matches, even with substantial victories in the World Cup qualifying games, revealed no portents that Scotland would become the winners of the last Five Nations Championship.

A 24-8 defeat by New Zealand Maori in November was followed a week later by a 35-10 loss to South Africa. At least it was less severe than the 68-10 hammering by the same opponents a year earlier. Runaway wins followed against Portugal and Spain. Margins less than the respective 85-11 and 85-3 would have been totally unacceptable to Scottish rugby.

When the Five Nations Championship started, with Wales visiting Murrayfield in February, a win by any margin would have been enough to satisfy the Scots. After all, Scotland had won only one international in each of the two previous seasons – both against Ireland. Moreover, all three Tests on the 1998 summer tour had produced defeats – 51-26 by Fiji, and 45-3 and 33-11 by Australia. However, the opening of the Scotland vs. Wales match could hardly have been more startling; John Leslie scoring a try from the kick-off to send the home team on their way to a 33-20 victory. True, Scotland had twice to come from behind. Wales led 13-8 at half-time and 20-15 with just over an hour gone.

Hopes were high for the Calcutta Cup match at Twickenham, but, as has happened so often in the past, Scotland failed there. The margin, though, was narrow, 24-21. A Jonny Wilkinson penalty goal was the tie-breaker between three converted tries apiece.

A 30-12 victory over Italy, avenging defeat in Treviso the previous year, kept Scotland ticking over before the ramparts of 'Fortress Murrayfield' were further strengthened by the annual victory against Ireland. Scotland were not put off by an Irish penalty try after only two minutes – they struck back to win by 30-13, scoring four tries, as they had done against Wales.

Eleven Scottish tries had been recorded in three championship internationals. Yet that strike rate was incredibly surpassed when the Scots visited Paris to play at Stade de France for the first time. Scotland reacted to Emile Ntamack's early try by scoring five of their own – two each by Alan Tait and Martin Leslie, and one by Gregor Townsend. The Scots led 33-22 at the interval, but the splendour of the first half could not be maintained as the only score

The Scotland squad that faced France in Paris on 10th April in Paris. L-R back row: S L Longstaff (replacement), P Walton (replacement), C M Chalmers (replacement), A I Reed (replacement), J A Leslie, D I W Hilton, M D Leslie, S Murray, S B Grimes, A C Pountney, G H Metcalfe, S J Brotherstone (replacement), G Graham (replacement), I T Fairley (replacement); front row: A P Burnell, K M Logan, A V Tait, G Armstrong (captain), G P J Townsend, S J Reid, G C Bulloch, C A Murray.

of the second was a Kenny Logan penalty goal. Scotland then had to wait for Wales to beat England in a dramatic finale at Wembley.

Townsend scored a try in every one of those five internationals from February to April. He thus became only the second Scot to achieve such a personal 'set of four' in the Five Nations Championship, emulating the feat of Johnnie Wallace in the 1925 Grand Slam.

Yet five months earlier Townsend was far from the most popular of Scottish players with the national selectors and the public. He was off his game at stand-off in the Maori match; and he was dropped to the bench for the international against South Africa, though he was soon back on the field as replacement full-back when Derrick Lee was injured, and Townsend remained in that role for the two World Cup qualifiers.

Even for the game against Wales, Townsend was denied his favoured role. Instead, the selectors opted for Duncan Hodge at stand-off, with Townsend at outside centre. However, Hodge's leg fracture allowed Townsend to switch to outside-half, and it was an opportunity that was not wasted on the Brive stand-off. He went on to have his best championship, not just by scoring in every international – he had full control of his game throughout.

However, Scotland's success was certainly not a one-man show. Townsend was part of a team effort. Fore and aft, he had a strong liaison with Gary Armstrong, captaining the team from scrum-half, and John Leslie, the Otago centre who quickly established himself in Scottish rugby only days after his arrival from New Zealand to enlist with his paternal grandfather's native country. Alan Tait found another lease of life at outside centre, Glenn Metcalfe took literally and metaphorically long strides in his development as an international full-back, Cammie Murray flourished on the right wing, and Kenny Logan, despite costly lapses against England, relished the additional role of goal-kicker after Hodge's injury.

Hodge was not the only injury victim. Doddie Weir also was removed from the frame in the game against Wales, whereas injuries to Tom Smith and Eric Peters against Ireland ruled them out of the Paris match. Yet Scotland had strength enough in depth to ride out those troubles, especially where Stuart Grimes, taking over from Weir, joined in a profitable pairing with Scott Murray at lock. Elsewhere in the pack, Gordon Bulloch continued to develop his all-round game as hooker, Paul Burnell played the best rugby of his career of 48 internationals, and Martin Leslie confirmed his pre-arrival reports as a versatile breakaway forward. Indeed, even in Peters's absence, Leslie's presence allowed the Scottish selectors the flexibility for the Paris match to change Peter Walton from starting blindside flanker to being an impact replacement for the second half.

Scotland A fell short of the benchmark the previous season's team had set as 'Grand Slam' champions at that level. They won only their games against Italy (61-6) and Ireland (31-21), both at home.

Neither of the Scottish representatives in the European Cup, Edinburgh Reivers and Glasgow Caledonians, reached the knock-out stages of the competition, though the former were only a score away from the quarter-finals. However, a late interception try by Stephen Coulter snatched a 23-21 victory for Ulster at Myreside in a head-to-head decider to qualify for the quarter-finals – Ulster then went on to win the European Cup.

Reivers' only European wins were against Ebbw Vale, home and away, though they had opened their campaign with a 38-all draw with Ulster at Ravenhill. Glasgow Caledonians also won just two European matches, their home games against Colomiers and Treviso.

Reivers defeated Caledonians 2-1 in a three-match domestic series. The Edinburgh team were also the more successful when the SuperTeams competed in the Welsh Rugby Union Challenge Trophy competition in January, Reivers reaching the third-place play-off before they suffered their first defeat in the tournament, beaten 25-23 by Bridgend at the Brewery Field.

Reivers and Caledonians were the offspring of a Scottish Rugby Union decision to combine the four districts into two SuperTeams. The innovation was not unanimously accepted within Scottish rugby, with senior clubs leading the strongest opposition because of their losses to the professional ranks and their consequent need to rely on younger, less experienced players. Yet Heriot's FP, with a mainly young team, emerged as the top club for the first time in 20 years, taking the SRU Tennent's Velvet Premiership trophy.

Gala took the Scottish Cup as well as the Second Division championship and the prestigious Melrose sevens trophy. For their part Melrose won the Bank of Scotland Border League title and also the Kings of the Sevens trophy as overall champions in the Borders' seven-a-side circuit.

Because of the advent of the SuperTeams and their three-match domestic contest, the inter-district championship was not held, though the ancient inter-city series between Edinburgh and Glasgow was continued with teams confined to non-contracted players. Edinburgh won the late-season match by 42-15 at Prestonpans and took a 60-40 lead in the series, which was first contested in 1872.

Scotland's only victory in the under-21 international programme was against Italy by 54-0 at Old Anniesland, Glasgow. The under-19 team suffered an initial setback in the IRB/FIRA World Junior Championship in Wales, beaten 21-10 by France, but they recovered with wins against Uruguay by 37-12, England 18-13, and

Chile 45-0, finishing ninth in the competition. Two days after the win over England, Scotland had another age-group victory against the Auld Enemy – 21-6 at Whitecraigs, near Glasgow, in the opening match of the inaugural Four Nations Under-18 Tournament. The Scots, however, lost their two other matches in that competition.

With the introduction of the SuperTeams, the only inter-district championships were contested by the age-group teams. The Borders took the under-21 and under-18 titles whereas Glasgow were under-19 champions for the first time.

SRU TENNENT'S VELVET PREMIERSHIP AND NATIONAL LEAGUE REVIEW 1998-99

Heriot's ended 20 barren years by winning the SRU Tennent's Velvet Premier title, and they did it with a style befitting champions. In their 18 league matches they ran in no fewer than 75 tries – a striking rate of more than four per game.

Their success was all the more creditable in that they did not have to rely heavily on well-seasoned, long-established campaigners . . . apart from their 36-year-old captain and loose-head prop, Jock Bryce. The champions were well blessed with talented youngsters who responded to Bryce's admirable lead.

Gordon Ross, the 21-year-old stand-off, scored 265 of Heriot's points, including four tries, and, as a measure of the club's running rugby, he kicked more conversions (49) than penalty goals (47). Stewart Walker and Charlie Keenan on the wings moreover provided the champions with exceptional pace. Walker ran in 16 tries, including four in Heriot's 68-16 demolition of Stirling County at Goldenacre in October. In a highly mobile pack none made more of an impression than the 20-year-old Simon Taylor, a back-row forward with an undoubtedly bright future – he was not born when Heriot's last won the title in 1979.

Heriot's lost four matches on the way to the championship, including both games against Melrose. The first of those, a 23-20 defeat at home in September, knocked Heriot's from the top of the table, leaving Currie out on their own in the lead. However, Currie slipped up in their next two matches, beaten by Glasgow Hawks and Heriot's. That left Heriot's back in front, with Melrose and Hawks leading the chase. By the time Heriot's suffered their next defeat, losing 22-17 at home against Hawks, they had enough in hand to stay at the top.

Heriot's lost away matches in January against Melrose and Currie, failing to record a try in either game. However, they finished in full flight, scoring five tries at Hawick, five more at home against Boroughmuir, and 10 at Stirling to round off their championship campaign. Melrose hung on at Heriot's heels to finish as runners-up for the second successive year, edging Hawks into second place with a better haul of bonus points.

Stirling, failing to win a league game, and Boroughmuir were relegated. It was the first time in the championship's 26 seasons that Boroughmuir had dropped from the top flight, though they only narrowly failed to survive, edged out by West of Scotland on a slender points difference of eight. West hung on to their First Division place only by picking up a bonus point with a fourth try at Currie in injury-time of their last match.

Gala and Kelso returned to the top echelon as respective champions and runners-up in the Second Division. The title was decided in a head-to-head finale between those two Border clubs, Gala winning 24-14 at home, a victory they were to repeat against Kelso in the national cup final four weeks later.

Another Border club, Peebles, won the Third Division and stepped up along with East Kilbride, who were promoted for the second successive season. Ross High and Helensburgh, as respective champions of the National League's Second and Fifth Divisions, were promoted for the fourth year in a row.

Perthshire and Strathendrick were the only championship clubs to win all of their matches. The former, though penalised four league points for fielding an ineligible player, had plenty in hand to win National Division 3 whereas Strathendrick, Glasgow and District League champions the previous season, sailed through the Seventh Division to become the first club to record 1,000 points in a championship season.

SRU TENNENTS PREMIERSHIP

Division 1	P	W	D	L	F	A	B	Pts
Heriot's FP	18	14	0	4	621	322	13	69
Melrose	18	13	0	5	491	300	11	63
Glasgow Hks	18	13	1	4	437	273	7	61
Currie	18	12	0	6	434	343	8	56
Hawick	18	9	0	9	338	460	5	41
Watsonians	18	7	2	9	396	428	6	38
Jed-Forest	18	7	2	9	356	449	3	35
W of Scotland	18	6	0	12	355	419	10	34
Boroughmuir	18	6	0	12	382	454	10	34
Stirling Cty	18	0	1	17	300	662	6	8

Hawick have won the Scottish championship 10 times, 1973-74 to 1977-78, 1981-82, 1983-84 to 1986-87; **Melrose** six times, 1989-90, 1991-92 to 1993-94, 1995-96 and 1996-97; **Gala** three times, 1979-80, 1980-81 and 1982-83; **Kelso** twice, 1987-88 and 1988-89; **Heriot's FP** twice, 1978-79 and 1998-99; **Boroughmuir** 1990-91; **Stirling County** 1994-95 and **Watsonians** 1997-98 once.

Division 2	P	W	D	L	F	A	B	Pts
Gala	18	14	0	4	523	242	14	70
Kelso	18	14	1	3	436	235	8	66
Kirkcaldy	18	11	0	7	372	298	12	56
Dun'ee HSFP*	18	8	1	9	446	431	8	38
Biggar	18	8	1	9	249	341	4	38
Ab'deen GSFP	18	6	2	10	299	343	8	36
Selkirk*	18	8	1	9	279	340	6	36
Musselburgh	18	7	0	11	379	472	6	34
Kilmarnock	18	6	0	12	326	475	7	31
Edinburgh A	18	5	0	13	283	415	8	28

Division 3	P	W	D	L	F	A	B	Pts
Peebles	18	14	0	4	398	294	6	62
East Kilbride	18	12	1	5	364	250	7	57
Preston Lodge	18	12	0	6	378	243	8	56
Berwick	18	11	0	7	360	271	6	50
Gordonians	18	9	2	7	445	267	8	48
Grangemouth	18	10	1	7	310	269	5	47
Ayr	18	8	1	9	291	277	8	42
Stewart's Melv	18	4	1	13	358	470	9	27
Glenrothes	18	4	0	14	217	491	4	20
Glasgow Sthn	18	3	0	15	210	499	2	14

SRU TENNENTS NATIONAL LEAGUE

Division 1

	P	W	D	L	F	A	B	Pts
Hutch'sons'/Al	18	12	1	5	483	252	12	62
Hillhead/Jhill*	18	14	0	4	465	235	9	61
Langholm	18	11	0	7	313	313	6	50
Duns	18	9	0	9	413	357	12	48
Stewartry	18	8	1	9	328	314	6	40
Annan	18	8	1	9	289	350	6	40
Corstorphine	18	8	0	10	264	455	6	38
Livingston	18	7	0	11	296	315	7	35
Haddington	18	6	1	11	207	317	5	31
Trinity Acads	18	5	0	13	280	430	8	28

Division 2

	P	W	D	L	F	A	B	Pts
Ross High	18	13	2	3	379	203	7	63
Murrayfield W	18	14	0	4	406	212	6	62
Dalziel	18	11	0	7	315	291	5	49
Linlithgow	18	10	0	8	316	356	9	49
St Boswells	18	9	0	9	336	274	11	47
Edinburgh U	18	9	0	9	324	259	9	45
Royal High	18	7	1	10	244	381	3	33
Dunfermline	18	5	2	11	245	312	5	29
Cambuslang	18	6	0	12	249	409	5	29
Portobello FP	18	3	1	14	216	333	7	21

Division 3

	P	W	D	L	F	A	B	Pts
Perthshire*	18	18	0	0	748	130	11	79
Cartha QP	18	14	0	4	535	217	10	66
Madras FP	18	11	1	6	442	281	8	54
Garnock	18	9	1	8	373	289	5	43
Allan Glen's*	18	10	1	7	369	254	4	42
Alloa	18	9	0	9	292	334	6	42
Howe o' Fife*	18	7	1	10	322	377	7	33
Morgan FP	18	5	1	12	318	332	7	29
Dumfries	18	4	1	13	254	490	4	22
Wigtowns're*	18	0	0	18	99	1048	1	-3

Division 4

	P	W	D	L	F	A	B	Pts
Aberdeenshire	18	15	0	3	548	151	9	69
Highland	18	14	0	4	603	211	10	66
Clydebank	18	11	0	7	357	304	8	52
Ardrossan	18	11	1	6	248	191	5	51
Waysiders/Dr	18	9	0	9	315	198	11	47
Lismore	18	9	1	8	459	251	7	45
Lochaber	18	10	0	8	343	328	5	45
Cumbernauld	18	7	2	9	219	329	2	34
Penicuik	18	1	0	17	147	594	4	8
Paisley*	18	1	0	17	114	796	3	3

Division 5

	P	W	D	L	F	A	B	Pts
Helensburgh	16	13	0	3	375	116	11	63
Greenock W	16	12	0	4	423	177	7	55
Carnoustie FP	16	11	0	5	423	170	9	53
Hillfoots	16	10	0	6	284	160	5	45
Whitecraigs	16	8	0	8	329	219	8	40
Lenzie	16	8	0	8	322	300	5	37
Leith Acads	16	5	0	11	186	399	5	25
Lasswade	16	4	0	12	188	404	4	20
North Berwick*	16	1	0	15	109	694	1	1

(Aberdeen University disqualified from Division 5)

Division 6

	P	W	D	L	F	A	B	Pts
Cumnock	16	13	0	3	450	151	12	64
RAF L'mouth	16	12	1	3	511	248	12	62
Hamilton	16	13	0	3	368	140	7	59
Forrester FP	16	10	0	6	365	242	6	46
Falkirk	16	6	1	9	248	317	7	33
Earlston	16	6	0	10	254	375	4	28
Moray*	16	4	1	11	223	361	4	18
Marr*	16	4	1	11	270	442	4	18
RAF Kinloss	16	1	2	13	127	540	2	10

(Dunbar disqualified from Division 6)

Division 7

	P	W	D	L	F	A	B	Pts
Strathendrick	18	18	0	0	1003	163	16	88
Irvine	18	11	0	7	367	232	9	53
Heriot-W. U*	18	12	0	6	339	453	6	50
Brough FP*	18	7	2	9	328	368	9	37
St And. U	18	7	1	10	266	424	7	37
Newton Stew	18	7	0	11	311	332	8	36
Walkerburn*	18	9	0	9	259	404	4	36
Orkney	18	5	2	11	455	371	10	34
Dalkeith*	18	6	1	11	262	508	5	27
Panmure*	18	5	0	13	206	541	3	19

(Four points for a win, two for a draw, and a bonus for scoring four tries and/or losing by seven points or less)
(* Clubs deducted four championship points)
Divisions 5-7 to be recast into four regional divisions for season 1999-2000.

BANK OF SCOTLAND BORDER LEAGUE

	P	W	D	L	F	A	B	Pts
Melrose	14	12	0	2	566	230	21	59
Gala	13	8	0	5	295	207	8	37
Kelso	11	7	0	4	250	197	6	31
Jed-Forest	13	6	0	7	261	263	4	29
Selkirk	12	4	0	8	201	314	3	23
Hawick	9	5	0	4	215	224	3	22
Peebles	10	1	0	9	78	256	0	12
Langholm	6	1	0	5	58	233	0	8

TENNENTS VELVET TRI-SERIES 1998-99

13 September, Easter Road, Edinburgh

Edinburgh Reivers 17 (2G 1PG) **Glasgow Caledonians 19** (1G 4PG)
Edinburgh Reivers: H R Gilmour; A G Stanger, M J M Mayer, A G Shiel, C A Murray; D W Hodge,
I T Fairley; B D Stewart, S J Brotherstone, M C Proudfoot, D G Burns, I A Fullarton, T A McVie,
B L Renwick (*capt*), A G Roxburgh *Substitutions:* P H Wright for Proudfoot (temp 16-22 mins); R B McNulty
for Stewart (temp 18-22 mins); G G Burns for Fairley (31-34 mins); McNulty for Brotherstone (47 mins);
G N Hayter for Fullarton (48 mins); A V Tait for Shiel (56 mins); Wright for Proudfoot (67 mins);
G J McCallum for Renwick (78 mins)
Scorers *Tries:* Fairley, Gilmour *Conversions:* Hodge (2) *Penalty Goal:* Hodge
Glasgow Caledonians: R J S Shepherd (*capt*); D A Stark, C T Simmers, A J Collins, J M Craig; T Hayes,
F H Stott; T J Smith, K D McKenzie, W Anderson, S B Grimes, S J Campbell, J P R White, G T Mackay,
J Shaw *Substitutions:* S L Longstaff for Collins (40 mins); G R McIlwham for Anderson (47 mins);
R I Wainwright for Grimes (65 mins); G C Bulloch for McKenzie (68 mins); G N Flockhart for Shaw (75
mins); A J Bulloch for Simmers (77 mins)
Scorers *Try:* Shepherd *Conversion:* Hayes *Penalty Goals:* Hayes (4)
Referee A Watson (Ireland)

25 October, Rubislaw, Aberdeen

Glasgow Caledonians 10 (1G 1PG) **Edinburgh Reivers 47** (3G 2PG 4T)
Glasgow Caledonians: G H Metcalfe; J M Craig, I C Jardine, R J S Shepherd (*capt*), S L Longstaff; T Hayes,
F H Stott; T J Smith, K D McKenzie, W Anderson, S B Grimes, S J Campbell, J P R White, I R Wainwright,
M Waite *Substitutions:* A J Bulloch for Metcalfe (32 mins); D A Stark for Shepherd (48 mins); G R McIlwham
for Anderson (62 mins); G C Perrett for Campbell (62 mins); J Shaw for Waite (74 mins)
Scorer *Try:* Hayes *Conversion:* Hayes *Penalty Goal:* Hayes
Edinburgh Reivers: S D Lang; A G Stanger, M J M Mayer, A V Tait, C A Murray; C M Chalmers,
B W Redpath; R B McNulty, G McKelvey, B D Stewart, D G Burns, I A Fullarton, C G Mather,
B L Renwick (*capt*), I W Sinclair *Substitutions:* M D Leslie for Renwick (41 mins); D W Hodge for Chalmers
(57 mins); H R Gilmour for Lang (64 mins); S J Brotherstone for McKelvey (64 mins); P H Wright for
McNulty (69 mins); A G Roxburgh for Sinclair (69 mins); I T Fairley for Tait (71 mins)
Scorers *Tries:* Stanger (2), Tait (2), Hodge, Leslie, Murray *Conversions:* Chalmers (2), Hodge
Penalty Goals: Chalmers (2)
Referee D Mené (France)

3 January, Netherdale, Galashiels

Edinburgh Reivers 33 (3G 4PG) **Glasgow Caledonians 3** (1PG)
Edinburgh Reivers: S Hastings; A G Stanger, A V Tait (*capt*), C M Chalmers, C A Murray; D W Hodge,
I T Fairley; R B McNulty, S J Brotherstone, B D Stewart, D G Burns, I A Fullarton, C G Mather,
M D Leslie, I W Sinclair *Substitutions:* G McKelvey for Brotherstone (64 mins); C D Hogg for D Burns (66
mins); A G Roxburgh for Sinclair (72 mins); J A Kerr for Chalmers (74 mins); P H Wright for McNulty (77
mins); G G Burns for Fairley (78 mins)
Scorers *Tries:* Mather, Hodge, Kerr *Conversions:* Hodge (3) *Penalty Goals:* Hodge (4)
Glasgow Caledonians: T Hayes; S L Longstaff, I C Jardine (*capt*), J A Leslie, D A Stark; L Smith,
F H Stott; G R McIlwham, G C Bulloch, W Anderson, S B Grimes, S J Campbell, G N Flockhart, M Waite,
J Shaw *Substitutions:* K D McKenzie for Bulloch (temp 22-26 mins); G Simpson for Shaw (51 mins),
A J Kittle for Anderson (62 mins), J M Petrie for Flockhart (62 mins), C T Simmers for Jardine (66 mins)
Scorer *Penalty Goal:* Smith
Referee C Thomas (Wales)

119th INTER-CITY MATCH

8 May, Pennypit Park, Prestonpans

Edinburgh 42 (4G 2PG 1DG 1T) **Glasgow 15** (1G 1PG 1T)
Edinburgh: G J M Lawson (Heriot's FP); G D Caldwell (Currie), G J Kiddie (Boroughmuir), L J A Graham
(Boroughmuir), C H Keenan (Heriot's FP); G Ross (Heriot's FP) (*capt*), C H Black (Edinburgh
Academicals); A F Jacobsen (Preston Lodge FP), J W C Taylor (Heriot's FP), A D G Binnie (Heriot's FP),
A K Dall (Heriot's FP), G J McCallum (Boroughmuir), T A McVie (Heriot's FP), S M Taylor (Heriot's FP),
G N Hayter (Watsonians) *Substitutions:* C E Macdonald (Boroughmuir) for Dall (54 mins); S K Paris
(Watsonians) for Binnie (57 mins); C Capaldi (Stewart's Melville FP) for Hayter (63 mins); D G Cunningham
(Boroughmuir) for J Taylor (66 mins); N A Barrett (Currie) for Graham (72 mins); G Tait (Currie) for Black
(74 mins)
Scorers *Tries:* Kiddie (2), Caldwell, Dall, Lawson *Conversions:* Ross (4) *Penalty Goals:* Ross (2)
Dropped Goal: Ross

Glasgow: P Harris (Glasgow Hawks); R C Kerr (West of Scotland), I R McInroy (West of Scotland), D Wilson (Glasgow Hawks) (*capt*), T G R Mathewson (Glasgow Hawks); C J Duck (West of Scotland), K Sinclair (Kilmarnock); K Horton (Glasgow Hawks), C A di Ciacca (West of Scotland), R Balmer (West of Scotland), B S Irvine (Glasgow Hawks), S Hutton (Glasgow Hawks), R A McKay (Glasgow Hawks), C Houston (West of Scotland), T Wright (Kilmarnock) *Substitutions:* J McCormick (Hillhead/Jordanhill) for Wright (40 mins); C C Murdoch (Ayr) for Harris (48 mins); G P Blackburn (Glasgow Hawks) for Balmer (51 mins); D W H Hall (Hillhead/Jordanhill) for di Ciacca (51 mins); A Gibbon (West of Scotland) for Wilson (54 mins); E A Murray (Glasgow Southern) for Horton (63 mins)
Scorers *Tries:* Mathewson (2) *Conversion:* Murdoch *Penalty Goal:* Murdoch
Referee J C Hogg (Hawick)

SRU TENNENTS VELVET CUP 1998-99

24 April 1999, Murrayfield
Gala 8 (1DG 1T) Kelso 3 (1PG)

Gala snatched victory from Kelso in the dying minutes of the final to add the SRU Tennent's Velvet Cup to the Premiership Second Division title that they had won only three weeks earlier. In doing so, they emulated Glasgow Hawks, who had achieved the same double the previous season, also completing it with victory over Kelso in the cup final.

It was the second successive cup final contested by two Second Division clubs. It was, too, the second time in four weeks that Gala had beaten Kelso for a trophy as the Second Division championship had been decided in a head-to-head contest between those two.

Kelso should have had the final sewn up long before Chris Paterson slipped through for Gala's winning score with less than five minutes left. Paterson then added a drop goal that hammered yet another nail in the Kelso coffin.

Kelso took the lead after only three minutes, when Graeme Aitchison slotted a penalty goal, and thereafter they had so much domination that they seemed certain to make up for the previous cup final defeat. However, Aitchison missed a couple of penalties that would have given Kelso a better cushion, and their game plan was limited as they preferred to rely too heavily on their forwards. Even overlaps were ignored as backs sought to take the ball back into the forwards.

It was perhaps an understandable policy when the Kelso forwards were so much on top, with Stewart Bennet providing an exemplary lead. In addition, Kelso lost a potential match-winner when full-back Kosie Alberts retired after only 13 minutes because of a knee injury that had made him doubtful throughout the pre-final week. Whatever the reason, the Kelso policy played into the hands of Gala, whose sterling defence twice denied Bennet as he was going over.

Not only was a close, hard, physical contest dictated by Kelso's game. It was also a match of too many handling errors and turnovers. Only rarely did it expand, and twice it was Gala who broke the pattern set by the forwards. First, Davie Gray cut through to tear upfield, though he then misfired what would have been a scoring pass to Kevin Amos, and midway through the second half Paterson weaved up the left touchline before he was denied by Stevie Ross close to the Kelso line.

With less than five minutes left, Gary Parker, Gala's player-coach, opted to kick for touch instead of going for the penalty goal that would have tied the scores and probably sent the final into extra-time. Captain Richie Gray won the lineout in the Kelso 22, John Amos induced a ruck in front of the posts, and as Kelso drifted too far wide, perhaps to cover Parker's threat on the wing, Paterson saw the gap to cut through for the try. His subsequent drop goal left no doubt that he be awarded the man of the match trophy which had earlier seemed destined for Bennet's hands.

Gala: M Dods; G A Parker, C G B Townsend, D R Gray, K A Amos; C D Paterson, D A Boland; A R W Johnston, S Scott, E M Johnstone, R J Gray (*capt*), N J Hines, G Brown, D T Weir, J P Amos *Substitutions:* G H Robson for Boland (55 mins); B M Easson for Johnstone (63 mins); P Harrison for Brown (70 mins)
Scorer *Try:* Paterson *Drop Goal:* Paterson
Kelso: J B Alberts; S A Ross, G Laing, K Utterson, D J Baird; G J Aitchison, G Cowe (*capt*); R J Hogarth, K D Thomson, D D Howlett, S C M Rowley, C Rutherford, S Bennet, S I Forsyth, D Rankin *Substitutions:* J Fleming for Alberts (14 mins); S Laing for Rutherford (27 mins)
Scorer *Penalty Goal:* Aitchison
Referee J R Dickson (Madras College FP)

Earlier Rounds

Both finalists saw off former cup-holders on the way to Murrayfield. Gala edged out 1997 winners Melrose by 28-22 in a home semi-final, with Gary Parker scoring 23 points to counter his former club's 3-2 try-count, and Kelso won by an even narrower margin, 13-10, in the fifth round, when they visited Glasgow Hawks, the defending cup-holders.

Hawick, the first winners of the trophy in 1996, also dropped out at the fifth-round stage, beaten at home by Boroughmuir by 16-8. It was the third successive year in which Hawick have been ousted from the cup by that Edinburgh club, who went on to reach the semi-finals before losing at home to Kelso by 15-40, Kosie Alberts scoring three of the winners' five tries.

Gala and Kelso set out on the road to the Murrayfield final with overwhelming wins in the third round, each running up more than 70 points in their respective matches against Gordonians and Lenzie. Gala then successively beat Ayr at home by 32-7, Langholm away by 39-16, and Stewartry by 35-19, also away. Kelso went on win by 23-7 on a sixth-round visit to Biggar, the club now coached by Eric Paxton, the former Poynder Park favourite. Between the visits to Hawks and Boroughmuir, Kelso had a home win over Preston Lodge by 38-10.

Yet even at the third-round stage, when the heavyweights entered the competition, two First Division clubs fell by the wayside. Stirling County lost by 8-15 on their visit to Linlithgow, from National

League Division 2, and Jed-Forest succumbed by 25-27 at home against Preston Lodge, who went through two more rounds before falling to Kelso in a quarter-final. Cumnock, from National League Division 6, also were among the giant-killers with a home win by 20-14 against a Premiership Division 3 club, Stewart's Melville.

Boroughmuir, Ayr, and Kilmarnock all knocked up centuries in the third round. However, Ayr then ran up against the champions-to-be. Kilmarnock, compensating for a dismal league season in which they were relegated from the Premier Second Division, went on to the quarter-finals before falling to Melrose by 13-42 on a visit to the Greenyards whereas Boroughmuir, also belying their league form, successively beat Edinburgh Academicals, Hawick, and Heriot's, who were to win the Premiership title.

Jed, though eliminated in the third round, still picked up a Murrayfield prize, beating Gordonians by 35-23 to win the shield, the second event of finals day. Duns, opening that day of Border domination, beat Garnock 34-17 in the bowl final.

RESULTS

Third round

Alloa 17, Strathmore 7; Ayr 109, Carrick 5; Biggar 47, Annan 16; Boroughmuir 117, Howe of Fife 8; Cumnock 20, Stewart's Melville FP 14; Dalziel 12, Kirkcaldy 46; Dunfermline 6, Langholm 17; East Kilbride 28, Selkirk 18; Gala 76, Gordonians 19; Glasgow Southern 17, Glasgow Hawks 71; Greenock Wanderers 10, Melrose 99; Haddington 19, Ross High 17; Hawick 40, Berwick 18; Hawick Linden 7, Edinburgh Academicals 17; Heriot's FP 73, Glenrothes 11; Hillhead/Jordanhill 13, St Boswells 6; Hutchesons'/Aloysians 72, Allan Glen's 0; Irvine 8, Stewartry 21; Jed-Forest 25, Preston Lodge FP 27; Kelso 73, Lenzie 5; Kilmarnock 109, Hyndland FP 0; Linlithgow 15, Stirling County 8; Morgan Academy FP 20, Ellon 8; Murrayfield Wanderers 43, Cartha Queen's Park 12; Musselburgh 24, Grangemouth 9; Peebles 50, Livingston 5; Perthshire 47, Royal (Dick) Veterinary College 3; Portobello 0, Currie 66; Strathaven 12, Watsonians 64; Trinity Academicals 7, Dundee HSFP 60; Waysiders/Drumpellier 6, Aberdeen GSFP 31; West of Scotland 53, Cambuslang 10

Fourth round

Alloa 3, Stewartry 13; Biggar 7, Kelso 23; Edinburgh Academicals 6, Boroughmuir 39; Gala 32, Ayr 7; Glasgow Hawks 50, Dundee HSFP 12; Hawick 19, Currie 13; Kilmarnock 18, East Kilbride 12; Kirkcaldy 13, Aberdeen GSFP 10; Langholm 20, Linlithgow 15; Melrose 45, Hillhead/Jordanhill 7; Morgan Academy FP 0, Heriot's FP 70; Musselburgh 23, West of Scotland 17; Peebles 16, Haddington 9; Perthshire 17, Murrayfield Wanderers 7; Preston Lodge FP 44, Cumnock 6; Watsonians 44, Hutchesons'/Aloysians 9

Fifth round

Glasgow Hawks 10, Kelso 13; Hawick 8, Boroughmuir 16; Heriot's FP 45, Perthshire 10; Kilmarnock 12, Musselburgh 10; Langholm 16, Gala 39; Preston Lodge FP 33, Peebles 23; Stewartry 25, Kirkcaldy 22; Watsonians 0, Melrose 33

Quarter-finals

Boroughmuir 16, Heriot's FP 15; Kelso 38, Preston Lodge FP 10; Melrose 42, Kilmarnock 13; Stewartry 19, Gala 35

Semi-finals

Boroughmuir 15, Kelso 40; Gala 28, Melrose 22

Final (at Murrayfield)

Gala 8, Kelso 3

Previous finals (all at Murrayfield)

1996 Hawick 17, Watsonians 15
1997 Melrose 31, Boroughmuir 23
1998 Glasgow Hawks 36, Kelso 14

SCOTLAND TO FIJI & AUSTRALIA 1998

THE TOURING PARTY

Manager A B Hastie **Coach** J W Telfer **Captain** R I Wainwright

Full-backs: D J Lee (London Scottish), G H Metcalfe (Glasgow Hawks)

Threequarters: A J Bulloch (West of Scotland), H R Gilmour (Heriot's FP), I C Jardine (Stirling County), C A Joiner (Leicester), S L Longstaff (Dundee HSFP), M J M Mayer (Watsonians), C A Murray (Hawick), D G Officer (Harlequins), R J S Shepherd (Melrose)

Half-backs: G G Burns (Watsonians), I T Fairley (Kelso), D W Hodge (Watsonians), B W Redpath (Melrose), G P J Townsend (Brive)

Forwards: S J Brotherstone (Melrose), G C Bulloch (West of Scotland), S J Campbell (Dundee HSFP), S B Grimes (Watsonians), D I W Hilton (Bath), S D Holmes (London Scottish), C G Mather (Watsonians), G R McIlwham (Glasgow Hawks), K D McKenzie (Stirling County), R Metcalfe (Newcastle), S Murray (Bedford), E W Peters (Bath), M C Proudfoot (Melrose), S J Reid (Boroughmuir), A G Roxburgh (Kelso), *G W Scott (Dundee HSFP), G L Simpson (Kirkcaldy), M J Stewart (Northampton), R I Wainwright (Dundee HSFP), P H Wright (West of Scotland)

* *Replacement during tour*

TOUR RECORD

All matches   Played 8   Won 3   Lost 5   Points for 206   Against 231
International matches   Played 2   Won 0   Lost 2   Points for 14   Against 78

SCORING DETAILS

All matches					International matches			
For:	24T	16C	18PG	206 Pts	For:	1T	3PG	14 Pts
Against:	30T	18C	15PG	231 Pts	Against:	9T	6C	7PG	78 Pts

MATCH DETAILS

1998	OPPONENTS	VENUE	RESULT
26 May	FIJI	Suva	L 26-51
30 May	Victoria	Melbourne	W 42-13
2 June	New South Wales Country	Bathurst	W 34-13
6 June	New South Wales	Sydney	W 34-10
9 June	Australian Barbarians	Penrith	L 34-39
13 June	AUSTRALIA	Sydney	L 3-45
16 June	Queensland	Brisbane	L 22-27
20 June	AUSTRALIA	Brisbane	L 11-33

MATCH 1 26 May, National Stadium, Suva   Test Match
FIJI 51 (5G 2PG 2T) SCOTLAND 26 (2G 4PG)

FIJI: J Waqa; F Lasagavibau, M Nakauta, S Sorovaki (*capt*), A Tuilevu; N Little, S Rabaka; J Veitayaki, I Rasila, M Taga, S Raiwalui, E Katalau, A Naevo, M Tamanitoakula, A Mocelutu. *Substitutions:* W Serevi for Little (50 mins); S Saumaisue for Tamanitoakula (50 mins); I Tawake for Mocelutu (62 mins); J Raulini for Rabaka (79 mins)
Scorers *Tries:* Tuilevu (3), Lasagavibau, Naevo, Veitayaki, Waqa *Conversions:* Little, Serevi (4) *Penalty Goals:* Little, Serevi
SCOTLAND: Lee; Gilmour, C Murray, Jardine, Longstaff; Townsend, Redpath; McIlwham, Bulloch, Proudfoot, Grimes, S Murray, Wainwright (*capt*), Peters, Roxburgh *Substitutions:* Shepherd for Jardine (temp 22-33 mins); Stewart for Proudfoot (60 mins); Campbell for S Murray (70 mins)
Scorers *Tries:* Bulloch, Gilmour *Conversions:* Lee (2) *Penalty Goals:* Lee (4)
Referee P J Honiss (New Zealand)

MATCH 2   30 May, Olympic Park, Melbourne

Victoria 13 (1G 2PG) **Scotland XV** 42 (3G 2PG 3T)
Victoria: A Pili; D Snaddon, M Nasalio, J Goodman, A Bolavatonaki; J Berger, S Brown (*capt*); L Oxenham, D Thompson, I Naituku, B Parsons, S Becker, C Frater, R Pale, J Ross *Substitutions:* L Hardley for Pali (40 mins); K Tora for Pili (61 mins); D Rutene for Parsons (61 mins); J Iosefu for Naituku (64 mins); N Higgins for Berger (65 mins); C Smith for Thompson (69 mins); Parsons for Becker (69 mins)
Scorers *Try:* Frater *Conversion:* Goodman *Penalty Goals:* Goodman (2)
Scotland XV: G Metcalfe; A Bulloch, Officer, Shepherd, Joiner; Hodge, Burns; Wright, Brotherstone, Stewart, R Metcalfe, Grimes, Mather, Reid (*capt*), Simpson *Substitutions:* McKenzie for Brotherstone (57 mins); Campbell for Grimes (67 mins); Mayer for Shepherd (75 mins); Hilton for Stewart (78 mins)
Scorers *Tries:* G Metcalfe (2), A Bulloch, Hodge, Mather, Shepherd *Conversions:* Hodge (3) *Penalty Goals:* Hodge (2)
Referee G Ayoub (New South Wales)

MATCH 3   3 June, Carrington Park, Bathurst

New South Wales Country 13 (1PG 2T) **Scotland XV** 34 (3G 1PG 2T)
New South Wales Country: B Whare; E Needham, N Friis, G Condon (*capt*), L Job; A Harding, S Merrick; D Nolan, C Frankin, W Petty, M Mitchell, J Quinn, S Fava, A Hurdley, J Whittle *Substitutions:* A Scott for Petty (23 mins); S Davies for Frankin (temp 45-52 mins); M Alexander for Whare (49 mins); M Greatbach for Whittle (63 mins)
Scorers *Tries:* Hurdley (2) *Penalty Goal:* Friis
Scotland XV: Lee; Gilmour, C Murray, Shepherd, Longstaff; Townsend, Burns; McIlwham, McKenzie, Stewart, S Murray, Campbell, Wainwright (*capt*), Simpson, Roxburgh *Substitutions:* R Metcalfe for S Murray (66 mins); Reid for Simpson (66 mins); Hodge for Townsend (67 mins); Officer for Shepherd (70 mins); Hilton for Stewart (70 mins); Fairley for Burns (73 mins)
Scorers *Tries:* Burns, McIlwham, Shepherd, Townsend, penalty try *Conversions:* Lee (3) *Penalty Goal:* Lee
Referee L Bray (New South Wales)

MATCH 4   6 June, Sydney Football Ground

New South Wales 10 (2T) **Scotland XV 34** (4G 2PG)
New South Wales: S Staniforth; M Dowling, J Jones-Hughes, C Warner, G Bond; M Edmonds, T Hall; W De Jong, T Tavalea, C Blades, J Welborn, S Domoni, M Brial (*capt*), S Pinkerton, C Strauss *Substitutions:* B Williams for Staniforth (40 mins); M Crick for Tavalea (40 mins); J Hart for Domoni (58 mins); J Shelley for De Jong (67 mins); S Devine for Hall (73 mins); K Gleeson for Strauss (73 mins); M Stcherbina for Edmonds (74 mins)
Scorers *Tries:* Dowling, Williams
Scotland XV: G Metcalfe; Joiner, C Murray, Shepherd, Longstaff; Townsend, Redpath; Hilton, G Bulloch, Proudfoot, S Murray, Grimes, Wainwright (*capt*), Peters, Simpson *Substitutions:* Hodge for Shepherd (71 mins); Lee for C Murray (78 mins); Campbell for Grimes (78 mins)
Scorers *Tries:* Joiner, Longstaff, G Metcalfe, S Murray *Conversions:* Shepherd (4) *Penalty Goals:* Shepherd (2)
Referee S Young (New South Wales)

MATCH 5   9 June, Penrith Stadium, Sydney

Australian Barbarians 39 (3G 1PG 3T) **Scotland XV 34** (3G 1PG 2T)
Australian Barbarians: M Bartholomeusz; R Nalatu, J Jones-Hughes, E Flatley, D Smith; P Howard (*capt*), S Cordingley; B Young, B Cannon, G Panoho, J Langford, N Sharpe, I Fenukitau, P Besseling, K Gleeson *Substitutions:* S Drahm for Flatley (40 mins); S Webster for Panoho (41 mins); C Latham for Bartholomeusz (53 mins); G Morgan for Langford (55 mins); B Johnstone for Cordingley (67 mins); T Jaques for Fenukitau (70 mins); M Crick for Nalatu (76 mins)
Scorers *Tries:* Nalatu (2), Drahm, Fenukitau, Howard, Langford *Conversions:* Drahm (2), Flatley *Penalty Goal:* Flatley
Scotland XV: Lee; Gilmour, Mayer, Jardine, A Bulloch; Hodge, Burns; McIlwham, Brotherstone, Stewart, Campbell, R Metcalfe, Roxburgh, Reid (*capt*), Holmes *Substitutions:* Wright for Stewart (72 mins); McKenzie for Brotherstone (75 mins); Mather for Holmes (75 mins); Officer for Jardine (75 mins)
Scorers *Tries:* Lee (2), Jardine, Mayer, Roxburgh *Conversions:* Hodge (3) *Penalty Goal:* Hodge
Referee W Erickson (New South Wales)

MATCH 6   13 June, Sydney Football Ground   1st Test

AUSTRALIA 45 (4G 4PG 1T) **SCOTLAND 3** (1PG)

AUSTRALIA: M Burke; B N Tune, D J Herbert, T J Horan, J W Roff; S J Larkham, G M Gregan; R L L Harry, P N Kearns, A T Blades, T M Bowman, J A Eales (*capt*), M Cockbain, R S T Kefu, D J Wilson *Substitutions:* V Ofahengaue for Kefu (49 mins); O D A Finegan for Cockbain (53 mins); D J Crowley for Harry (66 mins); J A Paul for Kearns (71 mins)
Scorers *Tries:* Burke, Horan, Roff, Tune, Wilson *Conversions:* Burke (4) *Penalty Goals:* Burke (4)
SCOTLAND: G Metcalfe; Lee, C Murray, Shepherd, Longstaff; Townsend, Redpath; Hilton, Bulloch, Proudfoot, S Murray, Grimes, Wainwright (*capt*), Peters, Simpson *Substitutions:* McKenzie for Bulloch (5 mins); Roxburgh for Simpson (77 mins)
Scorer *Penalty Goal:* Lee
Referee A Watson (South Africa)

Match 7   16 June, Ballymore, Brisbane

Queensland 27 (3G 2PG) **Scotland XV 22** (1G 5PG)
Queensland: N Williams; T Lough, J Little (*capt*), E Flatley, D Smith; S Drahm, J Raulini; S Webster, M Foley, A Heath, B Cockbain, N Sharpe, M Gabey, M Connors, M Murray *Substitutions:* L Hammond for Cockbain (63 mins); B Johnstone for Raulini (64 mins)
Scorers *Tries:* Flatley, Little, Williams *Conversions:* Drahm (3) *Penalty Goals:* Drahm (2)
Scotland XV: Lee; Joiner, Mayer, Officer, A Bulloch; Hodge, Burns; McIlwham, Brotherstone, Stewart, R Metcalfe, Campbell, Mather, Reid (*capt*), Roxburgh *Substitutions:* Gilmour for Lee (40 mins); S Murray for Metcalfe (52 mins); Jardine for Officer (63 mins); Wright for Stewart (63 mins); Fairley for Burns (77 mins)
Scorers *Try:* Brotherstone *Conversion:* Hodge *Penalty Goals:* Hodge (5)
Referee S Dickinson (New South Wales)

MATCH 8   20 June, Ballymore, Brisbane   2nd Test
AUSTRALIA 33 (2G 3PG 2T) SCOTLAND 11 (2PG 1T)

AUSTRALIA: M Burke; B N Tune, D J Herbert, T J Horan, J W Roff; S J Larkham, G M Gregan; R L L Harry, P N Kearns, A T Blades, T M Bowman, J A Eales (*capt*), M Cockbain, R S T Kefu, D J Wilson *Substitutions:* O D A Finegan for Cockbain (temp 23-31 mins); V Ofahengaue for Kefu (40 mins); D J Crowley for Blades (60 mins); J S Little for Tune (62 mins); Finegan for Cockbain (71 mins); N P Grey for Horan (74 mins)
Scorers *Tries:* Grey, Larkham, Ofahengaue, Tune *Conversions:* Burke (2) *Penalty Goals:* Burke (3)
SCOTLAND: G Metcalfe; Lee, C Murray, Shepherd, Longstaff; Townsend, Redpath; Hilton, McKenzie, Proudfoot, S Murray, Grimes, Wainwright (*capt*), Peters, Simpson *Substitutions:* Joiner for C Murray (59 mins); McIlwham for Hilton (62 mins); Hodge for Metcalfe (66 mins); Campbell for Grimes (75 mins); Roxburgh for Simpson (75 mins)
Scorers *Try:* Hodge *Penalty Goals:* Lee (2)
Referee B Campsall (England)

SCOTTISH INTERNATIONAL PLAYERS
(*up to 30 April 1999*)

Note: Years given for Five Nations' matches are for second half of season; eg 1972 means season 1971-72. Years for all other matches refer to the actual year of the match. When a series has taken place, figures have been used to denote the particular matches in which players have featured. Thus 1981 *NZ* 1,2 indicates that a player appeared in the first and second Tests of the series. The abandoned game with Ireland at Belfast in 1885 is now included as a cap match.

Abercrombie, C H (United Services) 1910 *I, E,* 1911 *F, W,* 1913 *F, W*
Abercrombie, J G (Edinburgh U) 1949 *F, W, I,* 1950 *F, W, I, E*
Agnew, W C C (Stewart's Coll FP) 1930 *W, I*
Ainslie, R (Edinburgh Inst FP) 1879 *I, E,* 1880 *I, E,* 1881 *E,* 1882 *I, E*
Ainslie, T (Edinburgh Inst FP) 1881 *E,* 1882 *I, E,* 1883 *W, I, E,* 1884 *W, I, E,* 1885 *W, I* 1,2
Aitchison, G R (Edinburgh Wands) 1883 *I*
Aitchison, T G (Gala) 1929 *W, I, E*
Aitken, A I (Edinburgh Inst FP) 1889 *I*
Aitken, G G (Oxford U) 1924 *W, I, E,* 1925 *F, W, I, E,* 1929 *F*
Aitken, J (Gala) 1977 *E, I, F,* 1981 *F, W, E, I, NZ* 1,2, *R, A,* 1982 *E, I, F, W,* 1983 *I, F, W, E, NZ,* 1984 *W, E, I, F, R*
Aitken, R (London Scottish) 1947 *W*
Allan, B (Glasgow Acads) 1881 *I*
Allan, J (Edinburgh Acads) 1990 *NZ* 1, 1991, *W, I, R,* [*J, I, WS, E, NZ*]
Allan, J L (Melrose) 1952 *F, W, I,* 1953 *W*
Allan, J L F (Cambridge U) 1957 *I, E*
Allan, J W (Melrose) 1927 *F,* 1928 *I,* 1929 *F, W, I, E,* 1930 *F, E,* 1931 *F, W, I, E,* 1932 *SA, W, I,* 1934 *I, E*
Allan, R C (Hutchesons' GSFP) 1969 *I*
Allardice, W D (Aberdeen GSFP) 1947 *A,* 1948 *F, W, I,* 1949 *F, W, I, E*
Allen, H W (Glasgow Acads) 1873 *E*
Anderson, A H (Glasgow Acads) 1894 *I*
Anderson, D G (London Scottish) 1889 *I,* 1890 *W, I, E,* 1891 *W, E,* 1892 *W, E*
Anderson, E (Stewart's Coll FP) 1947 *I, E*
Anderson, J W (W of Scotland) 1872 *E*
Anderson, T (Merchiston) 1882 *I*
Angus, A W (Watsonians) 1909 *W,* 1910 *F, W, E,* 1911 *W, I,* 1912 *F, W, I, E, SA,* 1913 *F, W,* 1914 *E,* 1920 *F, W, I, E*
Anton, P A (St Andrew's U) 1873 *E*
Armstrong, G (Jedforest, Newcastle) 1988 *A,* 1989 *W, E, I, F, Fj, R,* 1990 *I, F, W, E, NZ* 1,2, *Arg,* 1991 *F, W, E, I, R,* [*J, I, WS, E, NZ*], 1993 *I, F, W, E,* 1994 *E, I,* 1996 *NZ,* 1,2, *A,* 1997 *W, SA* (R), 1998 *It, I, F, W, E, SA* (R), 1999 *W, E, I, F*
Arneil, R J (Edinburgh Acads, Leicester and Northampton) 1968 *I, E, A,* 1969 *F, W, I, E, SA,* 1970 *F, W, I, E, A,* 1971 *F, W, I, E* (2[1C]), 1972 *F, W, E, NZ*
Arthur, A (Glasgow Acads) 1875 *E,* 1876 *E*
Arthur, J W (Glasgow Acads) 1871 *E,* 1872 *E*
Asher, A G G (Oxford U) 1882 *I,* 1884 *W, I, E,* 1885 *W,* 1886 *I, E*
Auld, W (W of Scotland) 1889 *W,* 1890 *W*
Auldjo, L J (Abertay) 1878 *E*

Bain, D McL (Oxford U) 1911 *E,* 1912 *F, W, E, SA,* 1913 *F, W, I, E,* 1914 *W, I*
Baird, G R T (Kelso) 1981 *A,* 1982 *E, I, F, W, A* 1,2, 1983 *I, F, W, E, NZ,* 1984 *W, E, I, F, A,* 1985 *I, W, E,* 1986 *F, W, E, I, R,* 1987 *E,* 1988 *I*
Balfour, A (Watsonians) 1896 *W, I, E,* 1897 *E*
Balfour, L M (Edinburgh Acads) 1872 *E*
Bannerman, E M (Edinburgh Acads) 1872 *E,* 1873 *E*
Bannerman, J M (Glasgow HSFP) 1921 *F, W, I, E,* 1922 *F, W, I, E,* 1923 *F, W, I, E,* 1924 *F, W, I, E,* 1925 *F, W, I, E,* 1926 *F, W, I, E,* 1927 *F, W, I, E, A,* 1928 *F, W, I, E,* 1929 *F, W, I, E*
Barnes, I A (Hawick) 1972 *W,* 1974 *F* (R), 1975 *E* (R), *NZ,* 1977 *I, F, W*
Barrie, R W (Hawick) 1936 *E*
Bearne, K R F (Cambridge U, London Scottish) 1960 *F, W*

Beattie, J A (Hawick) 1929 *F, W,* 1930 *W,* 1931 *F, W, I, E,* 1932 *SA, W, I, E,* 1933 *W, E, I,* 1934 *I, E,* 1935 *W, I, E, NZ,* 1936 *W, I, E*
Beattie, J R (Glasgow Acads) 1980 *I, F, W, E,* 1981 *F, W, E, I,* 1983 *F, W, E, NZ,* 1984 *E* (R), *R, A,* 1985 *I,* 1986 *F, W, E, I, R,* 1987 *I, F, W, E*
Bedell-Sivright, D R (Cambridge U, Edinburgh U) 1900 *W,* 1901 *W, I, E,* 1902 *W, I, E,* 1903 *W, I,* 1904 *W, I, E,* 1905 *NZ,* 1906 *W, I, E, SA,* 1907 *W, I, E,* 1908 *W, I*
Bedell-Sivright, J V (Cambridge U) 1902 *W*
Begbie, T A (Edinburgh Wands) 1881 *I, E*
Bell, D L (Watsonians) 1975 *I, F, W, E*
Bell, J A (Clydesdale) 1901 *W, I, E,* 1902 *W, I, E*
Bell, L H I (Edinburgh Acads) 1900 *E,* 1904 *W, I*
Berkeley, W V (Oxford U) 1926 *F,* 1929 *F, W, I*
Berry, C W (Fettesian-Lorettonians) 1884 *I, E,* 1885 *W, I* 1, 1887 *I, W, E,* 1888 *W, I*
Bertram, D M (Watsonians) 1922 *F, W, I, E,* 1923 *F, W, I, E,* 1924 *W, I, E*
Biggar, A G (London Scottish) 1969 *SA,* 1970 *F, I, E, A,* 1971 *F, W, I, E* (2[1C]), 1972 *F, W*
Biggar, M A (London Scottish) 1975 *I, F, W, E,* 1976 *W, E, I,* 1977 *I, F, W,* 1978 *I, F, W, E, NZ,* 1979 *W, E, I, F, NZ,* 1980 *I, F, W, E*
Birkett, G A (Harlequins, London Scottish) 1975 *NZ*
Bishop, J M (Glasgow Acads) 1893 *I*
Bisset, A A (RIE Coll) 1904 *W*
Black, A W (Edinburgh U) 1947 *F, W,* 1948 *E,* 1950 *W, I, E*
Black, W P (Glasgow HSFP) 1948 *F, W, I, E,* 1951 *E*
Blackadder, W F (W of Scotland) 1938 *E*
Blaikie, C F (Heriot's FP) 1963 *I, E,* 1966 *E,* 1968 *A,* 1969 *F, W, I, E*
Blair, P C B (Cambridge U) 1912 *SA,* 1913 *F, W, I, E*
Bolton, W H (W of Scotland) 1876 *E*
Borthwick, J B (Stewart's Coll FP) 1938 *W, I*
Bos, F H ten (Oxford U, London Scottish) 1959 *E,* 1960 *F, W, SA,* 1961 *F, SA, W, I, E,* 1962 *F, W, I, E,* 1963 *F, W, I, E*
Boswell, J D (W of Scotland) 1889 *W, I, E,* 1891 *W, I, E,* 1892 *W, I, E,* 1893 *I, E,* 1894 *I, E*
Bowie, T C (Watsonians) 1913 *I, E,* 1914 *I, E*
Boyd, G M (Glasgow HSFP) 1926 *E*
Boyd, J L (United Services) 1912 *E, SA*
Boyle, A C W (London Scottish) 1963 *F, W, I*
Boyle, A H W (St Thomas's Hospital, London Scottish) 1966 *A,* 1967 *F, NZ,* 1968 *F, W, I*
Brash, J C (Cambridge U) 1961 *E*
Breakey, R W (Gosforth) 1978 *E*
Brewis, N T (Edinburgh Inst FP) 1876 *E,* 1878 *E,* 1879 *I, E,* 1880 *I, E*
Brewster, A K (Stewart's-Melville FP) 1977 *E,* 1980 *I, F,* 1986 *E, I, R*
Brotherstone, S J (Melrose) 1999 *I* (R)
Brown, A H (Heriot's FP) 1928 *E,* 1929 *F, W*
Brown, A R (Gala) 1971 *E* (2[1C]), 1972 *F, W, E*
Brown, C H C (Dunfermline) 1929 *E*
Brown, D I (Cambridge U) 1933 *W, E, I*
Brown, G L (W of Scotland) 1969 *SA,* 1970 *F, W* (R), *I, E, A,* 1971 *F, W, I, E* (2[1C]), 1972 *F, W, E, NZ,* 1973 *E* (R), *P,* 1974 *W, E, I, F,* 1975 *I, F, W, E, A,* 1976 *F, W, E, I*
Brown, J A (Glasgow Acads) 1908 *W, I*
Brown, J B (Glasgow Acads) 1879 *I, E,* 1880 *I, E,* 1881 *I, E,* 1882 *I, E,* 1883 *W, I, E,* 1884 *W, I, E,* 1885 *I* 1,2, 1886 *W, I, E*
Brown, P C (W of Scotland, Gala) 1964 *F, NZ, W, I, E,* 1965 *I, E, SA,* 1966 *A,* 1969 *I, E,* 1970 *W, E,* 1971 *F, W, I, E* (2[1C]), 1972 *F, W, E, NZ,* 1973 *F, W, I, E, P*
Brown, T G (Heriot's FP) 1929 *W*
Brown, W D (Glasgow Acads) 1871 *E,* 1872 *E,* 1873 *E,* 1874 *E,* 1875 *E*

Brown, W S (Edinburgh Inst FP) 1880 *I, E*, 1882 *I, E*, 1883 *W, E*
Browning, A (Glasgow HSFP) 1920 *I*, 1922 *F, W, I*, 1923 *W, I, E*
Bruce, C R (Glasgow Acads) 1947 *F, W, I, E*, 1949 *F, W, I, E*
Bruce, N S (Blackheath, Army and London Scottish) 1958 *F, A, I, E*, 1959 *F, W, I, E*, 1960 *F, W, I, E, SA*, 1961 *F, SA, W, I, E*, 1962 *F, W, I, E*, 1963 *F, W, I, E*, 1964 *F, NZ, W, I, E*
Bruce, R M (Gordonians) 1947 *A*, 1948 *F, W, I*
Bruce-Lockhart, J H (London Scottish) 1913 *W*, 1920 *E*
Bruce-Lockhart, L (London Scottish) 1948 *E*, 1950 *F, W*, 1953 *I, E*
Bruce-Lockhart, R B (Cambridge U and London Scottish) 1937 *I*, 1939 *I, E*
Bryce, C C (Glasgow Acads) 1873 *E*, 1874 *E*
Bryce, R D H (W of Scotland) 1973 *I* (R)
Bryce, W E (Selkirk) 1922 *W, I, E*, 1923 *F, W, I, E*, 1924 *F, W, I, E*
Brydon, W R C (Heriot's FP) 1939 *W*
Buchanan, A (Royal HSFP) 1871 *E*
Buchanan, F G (Kelvinside Acads and Oxford U) 1910 *F*, 1911 *F, W*
Buchanan, J C R (Stewart's Coll FP) 1921 *W, I, E*, 1922 *W, I, E*, 1923 *F, W, I, E*, 1924 *F, W, I, E*, 1925 *F, I*
Buchanan-Smith, G A E (London Scottish, Heriot's FP) 1989 *Fj* (R), 1990 *Arg*
Bucher, A M (Edinburgh Acads) 1897 *E*
Budge, G M (Edinburgh Wands) 1950 *F, W, I, E*
Bullmore, H H (Edinburgh U) 1902 *I*
Bulloch, G C (West of Scotland) 1997 *SA*, 1998 *It, I, F, W, E, Fj, A 1, SA*, 1999 *W, E, It, I, F*
Burnet, P J (London Scottish and Edinburgh Acads) 1960 *SA*
Burnet, W (Hawick) 1912 *E*
Burnet, W A (W of Scotland) 1934 *W*, 1935 *W, I, E, NZ*, 1936 *W, I, E*
Burnett, J N (Heriot's FP) 1980 *I, F, W, E*
Burns, G G (Watsonians) 1999 *I* (R)
Burrell, G (Gala) 1950 *F, W, I*, 1951 *SA*

Cairns, A G (Watsonians) 1903 *W, I, E*, 1904 *W, I, E*, 1905 *W, I, E*, 1906 *W, I, E*
Calder, F (Stewart's-Melville FP) 1986 *F, W, E, I, R*, 1987 *I, F, W, E*, [*F, Z, R, NZ*], 1988 *I, F, W, E*, 1989 *W, E, I, F, R*, 1990 *I, F, W, E, NZ 1,2*, 1991 *R*, [*J, I, WS, E, NZ*]
Calder, J H (Stewart's-Melville FP) 1981 *F, W, E, I, NZ 1,2, R, A*, 1982 *I, F, W, A 1,2*, 1983 *I, F, W, E, NZ*, 1984 *W, E, I, F, A*, 1985 *I, F, W*
Callander, G J (Kelso) 1984 *R*, 1988 *I, F, W, E, A*
Cameron, A (Glasgow HSFP) 1948 *W*, 1950 *I, E*, 1951 *F, W, I, E, SA*, 1953 *I, E*, 1955 *F, W, I, E*, 1956 *F, W, I, E*
Cameron, A D (Hillhead HSFP) 1951 *F*, 1954 *F, W*
Cameron, A W (Watsonians) 1887 *W*, 1893 *W*, 1894 *I*
Cameron, D (Glasgow HSFP) 1953 *I, E*, 1954 *F, NZ, I, E*
Cameron, N W (Glasgow U) 1952 *E*, 1953 *F, W*
Campbell, A J (Hawick) 1984 *I, F, R*, 1985 *I, F, W, E*, 1986 *F, W, E, I, R*, 1988 *F, W, A*
Campbell, G T (London Scottish) 1892 *W, I, E*, 1893 *I*, 1894 *W, I, E*, 1895 *W, I, E*, 1896 *W, I, E*, 1897 *I*, 1899 *I*, 1900 *E*
Campbell, H H (Cambridge U, London Scottish) 1947 *I, E*, 1948 *I, E*
Campbell, J A (W of Scotland) 1878 *E*, 1879 *I, E*, 1881 *I, E*
Campbell, J A (Cambridge U) 1900 *I*
Campbell, N M (London Scottish) 1956 *F, W*
Campbell, S J (Dundee HSFP) 1995 *C, I, F, W, E, R*, [*Iv, NZ* (R)], WS (t), 1996 *I, F, W, E*, 1997 *A, SA*, 1998 *Fj* (R), *A 2* (R)
Campbell-Lamerton, J R E (London Scottish) 1986 *F*, 1987 [*Z, R*(R)]
Campbell-Lamerton, M J (Halifax, Army, London Scottish) 1961 *F, SA, W, I*, 1962 *F, W, I, E*, 1963 *F, W, I, E*, 1964 *I, E*, 1965 *F, W, I, E, SA*, 1966 *F, W, I, E*

Carmichael, A B (W of Scotland) 1967 *I, NZ*, 1968 *F, W, I, E, A*, 1969 *F, W, I, E, SA*, 1970 *F, W, I, E, A*, 1971 *F, W, I, E* (2[1C]), 1972 *F, W, E, NZ*, 1973 *F, W, I, E, P*, 1974 *W, E, I, F*, 1975 *I, F, W, E, NZ, A*, 1976 *F, W, E, I*, 1977 *E, I* (R), *F, W*, 1978 *I*
Carmichael, J H (Watsonians) 1921 *F, W, I*
Carrick, J S (Glasgow Acads) 1876 *E*, 1877 *E*
Cassels, D Y (W of Scotland) 1880 *E*, 1881 *I*, 1882 *I, E*, 1883 *W, I, E*
Cathcart, C W (Edinburgh U) 1872 *E*, 1873 *E*, 1876 *E*
Cawkwell, G L (Oxford U) 1947 *F*
Chalmers, C M (Melrose) 1989 *W, E, I, F, Fj*, 1990 *I, F, W, E, NZ 1,2, Arg*, 1991 *F, W, E, I, R*, [*J, Z*(R)], *I, WS, E, NZ*], 1992 *E, I, F, W, A 1,2*, 1993 *I, F, W, E, NZ*, 1994 *W, SA*, 1995 *C, I, F, W, E, R*, [*Iv, Tg, F, NZ*], WS, 1996 *A, It*, 1997 *W, I, F, A*), *SA*, 1998 *It, I, F, W, E*
Chalmers, T (Glasgow Acads) 1871 *E*, 1872 *E*, 1873 *E*, 1874 *E*, 1875 *E*, 1876 *E*
Chambers, H F T (Edinburgh U) 1888 *W, I*, 1889 *W, I*
Charters, R G (Hawick) 1955 *W, I, E*
Chisholm, D H (Melrose) 1964 *I, E*, 1965 *E, SA*, 1966 *F, I, E, A*, 1967 *F, W, NZ*, 1968 *F, W, I*
Chisholm, R W T (Melrose) 1955 *I, E*, 1956 *F, W, I, E*, 1958 *F, W, A, I*, 1960 *SA*
Church, W C (Glasgow Acads) 1906 *W*
Clark, R L (Edinburgh Wands, Royal Navy) 1972 *F, W, E, NZ*, 1973 *F, W, I, E, P*
Clauss, P R A (Oxford U) 1891 *W, I, E*, 1892 *W, E*, 1895 *I*
Clay, A T (Edinburgh Acads) 1886 *W, I, E*, 1887 *I, W, E*, 1888 *W*
Clunies-Ross, A (St Andrew's U) 1871 *E*
Coltman, S (Hawick) 1948 *I*, 1949 *F, W, I, E*
Colville, A G (Merchistonians, Blackheath) 1871 *E*, 1872 *E*
Connell, G C (Trinity Acads and London Scottish) 1968 *E, A*, 1969 *F, E*, 1970 *F*
Cooper, M McG (Oxford U) 1936 *W, I*
Corcoran, I (Gala) 1992 *A 1*(R)
Cordial, I F (Edinburgh Wands) 1952 *F, W, I, E*
Cotter, J L (Hillhead HSFP) 1934 *I, E*
Cottington, G S (Kelso) 1934 *I, E*, 1935 *W, I*, 1936 *F, W*
Coughtrie, S (Edinburgh Acads) 1959 *F, W, I, E*, 1962 *W, I, E*, 1963 *F, W, I, E, P*
Couper, J H (W of Scotland) 1896 *W, I*, 1899 *I*
Coutts, F H (Melrose, Army) 1947 *W, I, E*
Coutts, I D F (Old Alleynians) 1951 *F*, 1952 *E*
Cowan, R C (Selkirk) 1961 *F*, 1962 *F, W, I, E*
Cowie, W L K (Edinburgh Wands) 1953 *E*
Cownie, W B (Watsonians) 1893 *W, I, E*, 1894 *W, I, E*, 1895 *W, I, E*
Crabbie, G E (Edinburgh Acads) 1904 *W*
Crabbie, J E (Edinburgh Acads, Oxford U) 1900 *W*, 1902 *I*, 1903 *W, I*, 1904 *E*, 1905 *W*
Craig, J B (Heriot's FP) 1939 *W*
Craig, J M (West of Scotland) 1997 *A*
Cramb, R I (Harlequins) 1987 [*R*(R)], 1988 *I, F, A*
Cranston, A G (Hawick) 1976 *W, E, I*, 1977 *E, W*, 1978 *F* (R), *W, E, NZ*, 1981 *NZ 1,2*
Crawford, J A (Army, London Scottish) 1934 *I*
Crawford, W H (United Services, RN) 1938 *W, I, E*, 1939 *W, E*
Crichton-Miller, D (Gloucester) 1931 *W, I, E*
Crole, G B (Oxford U) 1920 *F, W, I, E*
Cronin, D F (Bath, London Scottish, Bourges, Wasps) 1988 *I, F, W, E, A*, 1989 *W, E, I, F, Fj, R*, 1990 *I, F, W, E, NZ 1,2*, 1991 *F, W, E, I, R*, [*Z*], 1992 *A 2*, 1993 *I, F, W, E, NZ*, 1995 *C, I, F*, [*Tg, F, NZ*], WS, 1996 *NZ 1,2, A, It*, 1997 *F* (R), 1998 *I, F, W, E*
Cross, M (Merchistonians) 1875 *E*, 1876 *E*, 1877 *I, E*, 1878 *E*, 1879 *I, E*, 1880 *I, E*
Cross, W (Merchistonians) 1871 *E*, 1872 *E*
Cumming, R S (Aberdeen U) 1921 *F, W*
Cunningham, G (Oxford U) 1908 *W, I*, 1909 *W, E*, 1910 *F, I, E*, 1911 *E*
Cunningham, R F (Gala) 1978 *NZ*, 1979 *W, E*
Currie, L R (Dunfermline) 1947 *A*, 1948 *F, W, I*, 1949 *F, W, I, E*
Cuthbertson, W (Kilmarnock, Harlequins) 1980 *I*, 1981 *W, E, I, NZ 1,2, R, A*, 1982 *E, I, F, W, A 1,2*, 1983 *I, F, W, NZ*, 1984 *W, E, A*

Dalgleish, A (Gala) 1890 *W, E*, 1891 *W, I*, 1892 *W*, 1893 *W*, 1894 *W, I*

Dalgleish, K J (Edinburgh Wands, Cambridge U) 1951 *I, E*, 1953 *F, W*
Dallas, J D (Watsonians) 1903 *E*
Davidson, J A (London Scottish, Edinburgh Wands) 1959 *E*, 1960 *I, E*
Davidson, J N G (Edinburgh U) 1952 *F, W, I, E*, 1953 *F, W*, 1954 *F*
Davidson, J P (RIE Coll) 1873 *E*, 1874 *E*
Davidson, R S (Royal HSFP) 1893 *E*
Davies, D S (Hawick) 1922 *F, W, I, E*, 1923 *F, W, I, E*, 1924 *F, E*, 1925 *W, I, E*, 1926 *F, W, I, E*, 1927 *F, W, I*
Dawson, J C (Glasgow Acads) 1947 *A*, 1948 *F, W*, 1949 *F, W, I*, 1950 *F, W, I, E*, 1951 *F, W, I, E, SA*, 1952 *F, W, I, E*, 1953 *E*
Deans, C T (Hawick) 1978 *F, W, E, NZ*, 1979 *W, E, I, F, NZ*, 1980 *I, F*, 1981 *F, W, E, I, NZ* 1,2, *R, A*, 1982 *E, I, F, W, A* 1,2, 1983 *I, F, W, E, NZ*, 1984 *W, E, I, F, A*, 1985 *I, F, W, E*, 1986 *F, W, E, I, R*, 1987 *I, F, W, E, [F, Z, R, NZ]*
Deans, D T (Hawick) 1968 *E*
Deas, D W (Heriot's FP) 1947 *F, W*
Dick, L G (Loughborough Colls, Jordanhill, Swansea) 1972 *W* (R), *E*, 1974 *W, E, I, F*, 1975 *I, F, W, E, NZ, A*, 1976 *F*, 1977 *E*
Dick, R C S (Cambridge U, Guy's Hospital) 1934 *W, I, E*, 1935 *W, I, E, NZ*, 1936 *W, I, E*, 1937 *W*, 1938 *W, I, E*
Dickson, G (Gala) 1978 *NZ*, 1979 *W, E, I, F, NZ*, 1980 *W*, 1981 *F*, 1982 *W* (R)
Dickson, M R (Edinburgh U) 1905 *I*
Dickson, W M (Blackheath, Oxford U) 1912 *F, W, E, SA*, 1913 *F, W, I*
Dobson, J (Glasgow Acads) 1911 *E*, 1912 *F, W, I, E, SA*
Dobson, J D (Glasgow Acads) 1910 *I*
Dobson, W G (Heriot's FP) 1922 *W, I, E*
Docherty, J T (Glasgow HSFP) 1955 *F, W*, 1956 *E*, 1958 *F, W, A, I, E*
Dods, F P (Edinburgh Acads) 1901 *I*
Dods, J H (Edinburgh Acads) 1895 *W, I, E*, 1896 *W, I, E*, 1897 *I, E*
Dods, M (Gala, Northampton) 1994 *I* (t), *Arg* 1,2, 1995 *WS*, 1996 *I, F, W, E*
Dods, P W (Gala) 1983 *I, F, W, E, NZ*, 1984 *W, E, I, F, R, A*, 1985 *I, F, W, E*, 1989 *W, E, I, F*, 1991 *I* (R), *R, [Z, NZ* (R)]
Donald, D G (Oxford U) 1914 *W, I*
Donald, R L H (Glasgow HSFP) 1921 *W, I, E*
Donaldson, W P (Oxford U, W of Scotland) 1893 *I*, 1894 *I*, 1895 *E*, 1896 *I, E*, 1899 *I*
Don-Wauchope, A R (Fettesian-Lorettonians) 1881 *E*, 1882 *E*, 1883 *W*, 1884 *W, I, E*, 1885 *W, I* 1,2, 1886 *W, I, E*, 1888 *I*
Don-Wauchope, P H (Fettesian-Lorettonians) 1885 *I* 1,2, 1886 *W*, 1887 *I, W, E*
Dorward, A F (Cambridge U, Gala) 1950 *F*, 1951 *SA*, 1952 *W, I, E*, 1953 *F, W, E*, 1955 *F*, 1956 *I, E*, 1957 *F, W, I, E*
Dorward, T F (Gala) 1938 *W, I, E*, 1939 *I, E*
Douglas, G (Jedforest) 1921 *W*
Douglas, J (Stewart's Coll FP) 1961 *F, SA, W, I, E*, 1962 *F, W, I, E*, 1963 *F, W, I*
Douty, P S (London Scottish) 1927 *A*, 1928 *F, W*
Drew, D (Glasgow Acads) 1871 *E*, 1876 *E*
Druitt, W A H (London Scottish) 1936 *W, I, E*
Drummond, A H (Kelvinside Acads) 1938 *W, I*
Drummond, C W (Melrose) 1947 *F, W, I, E*, 1948 *F, I, E*, 1950 *F, W, I, E*
Drybrough, A S (Edinburgh Wands, Merchistonians) 1902 *I*, 1903 *I*
Dryden, R H (Watsonians) 1937 *E*
Drysdale, D (Heriot's FP) 1923 *F, W, I, E*, 1924 *F, W, I, E*, 1925 *F, W, I, E*, 1926 *F, W, I, E*, 1927 *F, W, I, E, A*, 1928 *F, W, I, E*, 1929 *E*
Duff, P L (Glasgow Acads) 1936 *W, I*, 1938 *W, I, E*, 1939 *W*
Duffy, H (Jedforest) 1955 *F*
Duke, A (Royal HSFP) 1888 *W, I*, 1889 *W, I*, 1890 *W, I*
Duncan, A W (Edinburgh U) 1901 *W, I, E*, 1902 *W, I, E*
Duncan, D D (Oxford U) 1920 *F, W, I, E*
Duncan, M D F (W of Scotland) 1986 *F, W, E, R*, 1987 *I, F, W, E, [F, Z, R, NZ]*, 1988 *I, F, W, E, A*, 1989 *W*
Duncan, M M (Fettesian-Lorettonians) 1888 *W*
Dunlop, J W (W of Scotland) 1875 *E*
Dunlop, Q (W of Scotland) 1971 *E* (2[1C])
Dykes, A S (Glasgow Acads) 1932 *E*

Dykes, J C (Glasgow Acads) 1922 *F, E*, 1924 *I*, 1925 *F, W, I*, 1926 *F, W, I, E*, 1927 *F, W, I, E, A*, 1928 *F, I*, 1929 *F, W, I*
Dykes, J M (Clydesdale, Glasgow HSFP) 1898 *I, E*, 1899 *W, E*, 1900 *W, I*, 1901 *W, I, E*, 1902 *E*

Edwards, D B (Heriot's FP) 1960 *I, E, SA*
Edwards, N G B (Harlequins, Northampton) 1992 *E, I, F, W, A* 1, 1994 *W*
Elgie, M K (London Scottish) 1954 *NZ, I, E, W*, 1955 *F, W, I, E*
Elliot, C (Langholm) 1958 *E*, 1959 *F*, 1960 *F*, 1963 *E*, 1964 *F, NZ, W, I, E*, 1965 *F, W, I*
Elliot, M (Hawick) 1895 *W*, 1896 *E*, 1897 *I, E*, 1898 *I, E*
Elliot, T (Gala) 1905 *E*
Elliot, T (Gala) 1955 *W, I, E*, 1956 *F, W, I, E*, 1957 *F, W, I, E*, 1958 *W, A, I*
Elliot, T G (Langholm) 1968 *W, A*, 1969 *F, W*, 1970 *F, E*
Elliot, W I D (Edinburgh Acads) 1947 *F, W, E, A*, 1948 *F, W, I, E*, 1949 *F, W, I, E*, 1950 *F, W, I, E*, 1951 *F, W, I, E*, *SA*, 1952 *F, W, I, E*, 1954 *NZ, I, E, W*
Ellis, D G (Currie) 1997 *W, E, I, F*
Emslie, W D (Royal HSFP) 1930 *F*, 1932 *I*
Eriksson, B R S (London Scottish) 1996 *NZ* 1, *A*, 1997 *E*
Evans, H L (Edinburgh U) 1885 *I* 1,2
Ewart, E N (Glasgow Acads) 1879 *E*, 1880 *I, E*

Fahmy, Dr E C (Abertillery) 1920 *F, W, I, E*
Fairley, I T (Kelso) 1999 *It, I* (R)
Fasson, F H (London Scottish, Edinburgh Wands) 1900 *W*, 1901 *W, I*, 1902 *W, E*
Fell, A N (Edinburgh U) 1901 *W, I, E*, 1902 *W, E*, 1903 *W, E*
Ferguson, J H (Gala) 1928 *W*
Ferguson, W G (Royal HSFP) 1927 *A*, 1928 *F, W, I, E*
Fergusson, E A J (Oxford U) 1954 *F, NZ, I, E, W*
Finlay, A B (Edinburgh Acads) 1875 *E*
Finlay, J F (Edinburgh Acads) 1871 *E*, 1872 *E*, 1874 *E*, 1875 *E*
Finlay, N J (Edinburgh Acads) 1875 *E*, 1876 *E*, 1878 *E*, 1879 *I, E*, 1880 *I, E*, 1881 *I, E*
Finlay, R (Watsonians) 1948 *E*
Fisher, A T (Waterloo, Watsonians) 1947 *I, E*
Fisher, C D (Waterloo) 1975 *NZ, A*, 1976 *W, E, I*
Fisher, D (W of Scotland) 1893 *I*
Fisher, J P (Royal HSFP, London Scottish) 1963 *E*, 1964 *F, NZ, W, I, E*, 1965 *F, W, I, E, SA*, 1966 *F, W, I, E, A*, 1967 *F, W, I, E, NZ*, 1968 *F, W, I, E*
Fleming, C J N (Edinburgh Wands) 1896 *I, E*, 1897 *I*
Fleming, G R (Glasgow Acads) 1875 *E*, 1876 *E*
Fletcher, H N (Edinburgh U) 1904 *E*, 1905 *W*
Flett, A B (Edinburgh U) 1901 *W, I, E*, 1902 *W, I*
Forbes, J L (Watsonians) 1905 *W*, 1906 *I, E*
Ford, D St C (United Services, RN) 1930 *I, E*, 1931 *E*, 1932 *W, I*
Ford, J R (Gala) 1893 *I*
Forrest, J E (Glasgow Acads) 1932 *SA*, 1935 *E, NZ*
Forrest, J G S (Cambridge U) 1938 *W, I, E*
Forrest, W T (Hawick) 1903 *W, I, E*, 1904 *W, I, E*, 1905 *W, I*
Forsayth, H H (Oxford U) 1921 *F, W, I, E*, 1922 *W, I, E*
Forsyth, I W (Stewart's Coll FP) 1972 *NZ*, 1973 *F, W, I, E, P*
Forsyth, J (Edinburgh U) 1871 *E*
Foster, R A (Hawick) 1930 *W*, 1932 *SA, I, E*
Fox, J (Gala) 1952 *F, W, I, E*
Frame, J N M (Edinburgh U, Gala) 1967 *NZ*, 1968 *F, W, I, E*, 1969 *W, I, E, SA*, 1970 *F, W, I, E, A*, 1971 *F, W, I, E* (2[1C]), 1972 *F, W, E*, 1973 *P* (R)
France, C (Kelvinside Acads) 1903 *I*
Fraser, C F P (Glasgow U) 1888 *W*, 1889 *W*
Fraser, J W (Edinburgh Inst FP) 1881 *E*
Fraser, R (Cambridge U) 1911 *F, W, I, E*
French, J (Glasgow Acads) 1886 *W*, 1887 *I, W, E*
Frew, A (Edinburgh U) 1901 *W, I, E*
Frew, G M (Glasgow HSFP) 1906 *SA*, 1907 *W, I, E*, 1908 *W, I, E*, 1909 *W, I, E*, 1910 *F, W, I*, 1911 *I, E*
Friebe, J P (Glasgow HSFP) 1952 *E*
Fulton, A K (Edinburgh U, Dollar Acads) 1952 *F*, 1954 *F*
Fyfe, K C (Cambridge U, Sale, London Scottish) 1933 *W, E*, 1934 *E*, 1935 *W, I, E, NZ*, 1936 *W, E*, 1939 *I*

Gallie, G H (Edinburgh Acads) 1939 *W*
Gallie, R A (Glasgow Acads) 1920 *F, W, I, E,* 1921 *F, W, I, E*
Gammell, W B B (Edinburgh Wands) 1977 *I, F, W,* 1978 *W, E*
Geddes, I C (London Scottish) 1906 *SA,* 1907 *W, I, E,* 1908 *W, E*
Geddes, K I (London Scottish) 1947 *F, W, I, E*
Gedge, H T S (Oxford U, London Scottish, Edinburgh Wands) 1894 *W, I, E,* 1896 *E,* 1899 *W, E*
Gedge, P M S (Edinburgh Wands) 1933 *I*
Gemmill, R (Glasgow HSFP) 1950 *F, W, I, E,* 1951 *F, W, I*
Gibson, W R (Royal HSFP) 1891 *I, E,* 1892 *W, I, E,* 1893 *W, I, E,* 1894 *W, I, E,* 1895 *W, I, E*
Gilbert-Smith, D S (London Scottish) 1952 *E*
Gilchrist, J (Glasgow Acads) 1925 *F*
Gill, A D (Gala) 1973 *P,* 1974 *W, E, I, F*
Gillespie, J I (Edinburgh Acads) 1899 *E,* 1900 *W, E,* 1901 *W, I, E,* 1902 *W, I,* 1904 *I, E*
Gillies, A C (Watsonians) 1924 *W, I, E,* 1925 *F, W, E,* 1926 *F, W,* 1927 *F, W, I, E*
Gilmour, H R (Heriot's FP) 1998 *Fj*
Gilray, C M (Oxford U, London Scottish) 1908 *E,* 1909 *W, E,* 1912 *I*
Glasgow, I C (Heriot's FP) 1997 *F* (R)
Glasgow, R J C (Dunfermline) 1962 *F, W, I, E,* 1963 *I, E,* 1964 *I, E,* 1965 *W, I*
Glen, W S (Edinburgh Wands) 1955 *W*
Gloag, L G (Cambridge U) 1949 *F, W, I, E*
Goodfellow, J (Langholm) 1928 *W, I, E*
Goodhue, F W J (London Scottish) 1890 *W, I, E,* 1891 *W, I, E,* 1892 *W, I, E*
Gordon, R (Edinburgh Wands) 1951 *W,* 1952 *F, W, I, E,* 1953 *W*
Gordon, R E (Royal Artillery) 1913 *F, W, I*
Gordon, R J (London Scottish) 1982 *A 1,2*
Gore, A C (London Scottish) 1882 *I*
Gossman, B M (W of Scotland) 1980 *W,* 1983 *F, W*
Gossman, J S (W of Scotland) 1980 *E (R)*
Gowans, J J (Cambridge U, London Scottish) 1893 *W,* 1894 *W, E,* 1895 *W, I, E,* 1896 *I, E*
Gowland, G C (London Scottish) 1908 *W,* 1909 *W, E,* 1910 *F, W, I, E*
Gracie, A L (Harlequins) 1921 *F, W, I, E,* 1922 *F, W, I, E,* 1923 *W, I, E,* 1924 *F*
Graham, G (Newcastle) 1997 *A* (R), *SA* (R), 1998 *I, F* (R), *W* (R), 1999 *F* (R)
Graham, I N (Edinburgh Acads) 1939 *I, E*
Graham, J (Kelso) 1926 *I, E,* 1927 *F, W, I, E, A,* 1928 *F, W, I, E,* 1930 *I, E,* 1932 *SA, W*
Graham, J H S (Edinburgh Acads) 1876 *E,* 1877 *I, E,* 1878 *E,* 1879 *I, E,* 1880 *I, E,* 1881 *I, E*
Grant, D (Hawick) 1965 *F, E, SA,* 1966 *F, W, I, E, A,* 1967 *F, W, I, E, NZ,* 1968 *F*
Grant, D M (East Midlands) 1911 *W, I*
Grant, M L (Harlequins) 1955 *F,* 1956 *F, W,* 1957 *F*
Grant, T O (Hawick) 1960 *I, E, SA,* 1964 *F, NZ, W*
Grant, W St C (Craigmount) 1873 *E,* 1874 *E*
Gray, C A (Nottingham) 1989 *W, E, I, F, Fj, R,* 1990 *I, F, W, E, NZ 1,2, Arg,* 1991 *F, W, E, I, [J, I, WS, E, NZ]*
Gray, D (W of Scotland) 1978 *E,* 1979 *I, F, NZ,* 1980 *I, F, W, E,* 1981 *F*
Gray, G L (Gala) 1935 *NZ,* 1937 *W, I, E*
Gray, T (Northampton, Heriot's FP) 1950 *E,* 1951 *F, E*
Greenlees, H D (Leicester) 1927 *A,* 1928 *F, W,* 1929 *I, E,* 1930 *E*
Greenlees, J R C (Cambridge U, Kelvinside Acads) 1900 *I,* 1902 *W, I, E,* 1903 *W, I, E*
Greenwood, J T (Dunfermline and Perthshire Acads) 1952 *F,* 1955 *F, W, I, E,* 1956 *F, W, I, E,* 1957 *F, W, E,* 1958 *F, W, A, I, E,* 1959 *F, W, I*
Greig, A (Glasgow HSFP) 1911 *I*
Greig, L L (Glasgow Acads, United Services) 1905 *NZ,* 1906 *SA,* 1907 *W,* 1908 *W, I*
Greig, R C (Glasgow Acads) 1893 *W,* 1897 *I*
Grieve, C F (Oxford U) 1935 *W,* 1936 *E*
Grieve, R M (Kelso) 1935 *W, I, E, NZ,* 1936 *W, I, E*
Grimes, S B (Watsonians) 1997 *A* (t + R), 1998 *I* (R), *F* (R), *W* (R), *E* (R), *Fj, A 1, 2,* 1999 *W, E, It, I, F*
Gunn, A W (Royal HSFP) 1912 *F, W, I, SA,* 1913 *F*

Hamilton, A S (Headingley) 1914 *W,* 1920 *F*
Hamilton, H M (W of Scotland) 1874 *E,* 1875 *E*
Hannah, R S M (W of Scotland) 1971 *I*

Harrower, P R (London Scottish) 1885 *W*
Hart, J G M (London Scottish) 1951 *SA*
Hart, T M (Glasgow U) 1930 *W, I*
Hart, W (Melrose) 1960 *SA*
Harvey, L (Greenock Wands) 1899 *I*
Hastie, A J (Melrose) 1961 *W, I, E,* 1964 *I, E,* 1965 *E, SA,* 1966 *W, I, E, A,* 1967 *F, W, I, NZ,* 1968 *F, W*
Hastie, I R (Kelso) 1955 *F,* 1958 *F, E,* 1959 *F, W, I*
Hastie, J D H (Melrose) 1938 *W, I, E*
Hastings, A G (Cambridge U, Watsonians, London Scottish) 1986 *F, W, E, I, R,* 1987 *I, F, W, [F, Z, R, NZ],* 1988 *I, F, W, E, A,* 1989 *Fj, R,* 1990 *I, F, W, E, NZ 1,2, Arg,* 1991 *F, W, E, I, [J, I, WS, E, NZ],* 1992 *E, I, F, W, A 1,* 1993 *I, F, W, E, NZ,* 1994 *W, E, I, F, SA,* 1995 *C, I, F, W, E, R, [Iv, Tg, F, NZ]*
Hastings, S (Watsonians) 1986 *F, W, E, I, R,* 1987 *I, F, W, [R],* 1988 *I, F, W, A,* 1989 *W, E, I, F, Fj, R,* 1990 *I, F, W, E, NZ 1,2, Arg,* 1991 *F, W, E, I, [J, Z, I, WS, E, NZ],* 1992 *E, I, F, W, A 1,2,* 1993 *I, F, W, E, NZ,* 1994 *E, I, F, SA,* 1995 *W, E, R* (R), *[Tg, F, NZ],* 1996 *I, F, W, E, NZ 2, It,* 1997 *W, E* (R)
Hay, B H (Boroughmuir) 1975 *NZ, A,* 1976 *F,* 1978 *I, F, W, E, NZ,* 1979 *W, E, I, F, NZ,* 1980 *I, F, W, E,* 1981 *F, W, E, I, NZ 1,2*
Hay, J A (Hawick) 1995 *WS*
Hay-Gordon, J R (Edinburgh Acads) 1875 *E,* 1877 *I, E*
Hegarty, C B (Hawick) 1978 *I, F, W, E*
Hegarty, J J (Hawick) 1951 *F,* 1953 *F, W, I, E,* 1955 *F*
Henderson, B C (Edinburgh Wands) 1963 *E,* 1964 *F, I, E,* 1965 *F, W, I, E,* 1966 *F, W, I, E*
Henderson, F W (London Scottish) 1900 *W, I*
Henderson, I C (Edinburgh Acads) 1939 *I, E,* 1947 *F, W, E, A,* 1948 *I, E*
Henderson, J H (Oxford U, Richmond) 1953 *F, W, I, E,* 1954 *F, NZ, I, E, W*
Henderson, J M (Edinburgh Acads) 1933 *W, E, I*
Henderson, J Y M (Watsonians) 1911 *E*
Henderson, M M (Dunfermline) 1937 *W, I, E*
Henderson, N F (London Scottish) 1892 *I*
Henderson, R G (Newcastle Northern) 1924 *I, E*
Hendrie, K G P (Heriot's FP) 1924 *F, W, I*
Hendry, T L (Clydesdale) 1893 *W, I, E,* 1895 *I*
Henriksen, E H (Royal HSFP) 1953 *I*
Hepburn, D P (Woodford) 1947 *A,* 1948 *F, W, I, E,* 1949 *F, W, I, E*
Heron, G (Glasgow Acads) 1874 *E,* 1875 *E*
Hill, C C P (St Andrew's U) 1912 *F, I*
Hilton, D I W (Bath) 1995 *C, I, F, W, E, R, [Tg, F, NZ], WS,* 1996 *I, F, W, E, NZ 1,2, A, It,* 1997 *W, A, SA,* 1998 *It, I* (R), *F, W, E, A 1,2, SA* (R), 1999 *W* (R), *E* (R), *It* (R), (R), *F*
Hinshelwood, A J W (London Scottish) 1966 *F, W, I, E, A,* 1967 *F, W, I, E, NZ,* 1968 *F, W, I, E, A,* 1969 *F, W, I, SA,* 1970 *F, W*
Hodge D W (Watsonians) 1997 *F* (R), *A, SA* (t + R), 1998 *A 2* (R), *SA,* 1999 *W*
Hodgson, C G (London Scottish) 1968 *I, E*
Hogg, C D (Melrose) 1992 *A 1,2,* 1993 *NZ* (R), 1994 *Arg 1,2*
Hogg, C G (Boroughmuir) 1978 *F* (R), *W* (R)
Holmes, S D (London Scottish) 1998 *It, I, F*
Holms, W F (RIE Coll) 1886 *W, E,* 1887 *I, E,* 1889 *W, I*
Horsburgh, G B (London Scottish) 1937 *W, I, E,* 1938 *W, I, E,* 1939 *W, I, E*
Howie, D D (Kirkcaldy) 1912 *F, W, I, E, SA,* 1913 *F, W*
Howie, R A (Kirkcaldy) 1924 *F, W, I, E,* 1925 *W, I, E*
Hoyer-Millar, G C (Oxford U) 1953 *F*
Huggan, J L (London Scottish) 1914 *E*
Hume, J (Royal HSFP) 1912 *F,* 1920 *F,* 1921 *F, W, I, E,* 1922 *F*
Hume, J W G (Oxford U, Edinburgh Wands) 1928 *I,* 1930 *F*
Hunter, F (Edinburgh U) 1882 *I*
Hunter, I G (Selkirk) 1984 *I* (R), 1985 *F* (R), *W, E*
Hunter, J M (Cambridge U) 1947 *F*
Hunter, M D (Glasgow High) 1974 *F*
Hunter, W J (Hawick) 1964 *F, NZ, W,* 1967 *F, W, I, E*
Hutchison, W R (Glasgow HSFP) 1911 *E*
Hutton, A H M (Dunfermline) 1932 *I*
Hutton, J E (Harlequins) 1930 *E,* 1931 *F*

Inglis, H M (Edinburgh Acads) 1951 *F, W, I, E, SA,* 1952 *W, I*
Inglis, J M (Selkirk) 1952 *E*

Inglis, W M (Cambridge U, Royal Engineers) 1937 *W, I, E*, 1938 *W, I, E*
Innes, J R S (Aberdeen GSFP) 1939 *W, I, E*, 1947 *A*, 1948 *F, W, I, E*
Ireland, J C H (Glasgow HSFP) 1925 *W, I, E*, 1926 *F, W, I, E*, 1927 *F, W, I, E*
Irvine, A R (Heriot's FP) 1972 *NZ*, 1973 *F, W, I, E, P*, 1974 *W, E, I, F*, 1975 *I, F, W, E, NZ, A*, 1976 *F, W, E, I*, 1977 *E, I, F, W*, 1978 *I, F, E, NZ*, 1979 *W, E, I, NZ*, 1980 *I, F, W, E*, 1981 *F, W, E, I, NZ* 1,2, *R, A*, 1982 *E, I, F, W, A* 1,2
Irvine, D R (Edinburgh Acads) 1878 *E*, 1879 *I, E*
Irvine, R W (Edinburgh Acads) 1871 *E*, 1872 *E*, 1873 *E*, 1874 *E*, 1875 *E*, 1876 *E*, 1877 *I, E*, 1878 *E*, 1879 *I, E*, 1880 *I, E*
Irvine T W (Edinburgh Acads) 1885 *I* 1,2, 1886 *W, I, E*, 1887 *I, W, E*, 1888 *W, I*, 1889 *I*

Jackson, K L T (Oxford U) 1933 *W, E, I*, 1934 *W*
Jackson, T G H (Army) 1947 *F, W, E, A*, 1948 *F, W, I, E*, 1949 *F, W, I, E*
Jackson, W D (Hawick) 1964 *I*, 1965 *E, SA*, 1968 *A*, 1969 *F, W, I, E*
Jamieson, J (W of Scotland) 1883 *W, I, E*, 1884 *W, I, E*, 1885 *W, I* 1,2
Jardine, I C (Stirling County) 1993 *NZ*, 1994 *W, E* (R), *Arg* 1,2, 1995 *C, I, F*, [*Tg, F* (t & R), *NZ* (R)], 1996 *I, F, W, E, NZ* 1,2, 1998 *Fj*
Jeffrey, J (Kelso) 1984 *A*, 1985 *I, E*, 1986 *F, W, E, I, R*, 1987 *I, F, W, E*, [*F, Z, R*], 1988 *I, W, A*, 1989 *W, E, I, F, Fj, R*, 1990 *I, F, W, E, NZ* 1,2, *Arg*, 1991 *F, W, E, I*, [*J, I, WS, E, NZ*]
Johnston, D I (Watsonians) 1979 *NZ*, 1980 *I, F, W, E*, 1981 *R, A*, 1982 *E, I, F, W, A* 1,2, 1983 *I, F, W, NZ*, 1984 *W, E, I, F, R*, 1986 *F, W, E, I, R*
Johnston, H H (Edinburgh Collegian FP) 1877 *I, E*
Johnston, J (Melrose) 1951 *SA*, 1952 *F, W, I, E*
Johnston, W C (Glasgow HSFP) 1922 *F*
Johnston, W G S (Cambridge U) 1935 *W, I*, 1937 *W, I, E*
Joiner, C A (Melrose, Leicester) 1994 *Arg* 1,2, 1995 *C, I, F, W, E, R*, [*Iv, Tg, F, NZ*], 1996 *I, F, W, E, NZ* 1, 1997 *SA*, 1998 *It, I, A* 2 (R)
Jones, P M (Gloucester) 1992 *W* (R)
Junor, J E (Glasgow Acads) 1876 *E*, 1877 *I, E*, 1878 *E*, 1879 *E*, 1881 *I*

Keddie, R R (Watsonians) 1967 *NZ*
Keith, G J (Wasps) 1968 *F, W*
Keller, D H (London Scottish) 1949 *F, W, I, E*, 1950 *F, W, I*
Kelly, R F (Watsonians) 1927 *A*, 1928 *F, W, E*
Kemp, J W Y (Glasgow HSFP) 1954 *W*, 1955 *F, W, I, E*, 1956 *F, W, I, E*, 1957 *F, W, I, E*, 1958 *F, W, A, I, E*, 1959 *F, W, I, E*, 1960 *F, W, I, E*
Kennedy, A E (Watsonians) 1983 *NZ*, 1984 *W, E, A*
Kennedy, F (Stewart's Coll FP) 1920 *F, W, I, E*, 1921 *E*
Kennedy, N (W of Scotland) 1903 *W, I, E*
Ker, A B M (Kelso) 1988 *W, E*
Ker, H T (Glasgow Acads) 1887 *I, W, E*, 1888 *I*, 1889 *W*, 1890 *I, E*
Kerr, D S (Heriot's FP) 1923 *F, W*, 1924 *F*, 1926 *I, E*, 1927 *W, E*, 1928 *I, E*
Kerr, G C (Old Dunelmians, Edinburgh Wands) 1898 *I, E*, 1899 *I, W, E*, 1900 *W, I, E*
Kerr, J M (Heriot's FP) 1935 *NZ*, 1936 *I, E*, 1937 *W, I*
Kerr, W (London Scottish) 1953 *E*
Kidston, D W (Glasgow Acads) 1883 *W, E*
Kidston, W H (W of Scotland) 1874 *E*
Kilgour, I J (RMC Sandhurst) 1921 *F*
King, J H F (Selkirk) 1953 *F, W, E*, 1954 *E*
Kininmonth, P W (Oxford U, Richmond) 1949 *F, W, I, E*, 1950 *F, W, I, E*, 1951 *F, W, I, E, SA*, 1952 *F, W, I*, 1954 *F, NZ, I, E, W*
Kinnear, R M (Heriot's FP) 1926 *F, W, I*
Knox, J (Kelvinside Acads) 1903 *W, I, E*
Kyle, W E (Hawick) 1902 *W, I, E*, 1903 *W, I, E*, 1904 *W, I, E*, 1905 *W, I, E, NZ*, 1906 *W, I, E*, 1908 *E*, 1909 *W, I, E*, 1910 *W*

Laidlaw, A S (Hawick) 1897 *I*
Laidlaw, F A L (Melrose) 1965 *F, W, I, E, SA*, 1966 *F, W, I, E, A*, 1967 *F, W, I, E, NZ*, 1968 *F, W, I, A*, 1969 *F, W, I, E, SA*, 1970 *F, W, I, E, A*, 1971 *F, W, I*

Laidlaw, R J (Jedforest) 1980 *I, F, W, E*, 1981 *F, W, E, I, NZ* 1,2, *R, A*, 1982 *E, I, F, W, A* 1,2, 1983 *I, F, W, E, NZ*, 1984 *W, E, I, F, R, A*, 1985 *I, F*, 1986 *F, W, E, I, R*, 1987 *I, F, W, E*, [*F, R, NZ*], 1988 *I, F, W, E*
Laing, A D (Royal HSFP) 1914 *W, I, E*, 1920 *F, W, I*, 1921 *F*
Lambie, I K (Watsonians) 1978 *NZ* (R), 1979 *W, E, NZ*
Lambie, L B (Glasgow HSFP) 1934 *W, I, E*, 1935 *W, I, E, NZ*
Lamond, G A W (Kelvinside Acads) 1899 *W, E*, 1905 *E*
Lang, D (Paisley) 1876 *E*, 1877 *I*
Langrish, R W (London Scottish) 1930 *F*, 1931 *F, W, I*
Lauder, W (Neath) 1969 *I, E, SA*, 1970 *F, W, I, A*, 1973 *F*, 1974 *W, E, I, F*, 1975 *I, F, NZ, A*, 1976 *F*, 1977 *E*
Laughland, I H P (London Scottish) 1959 *F*, 1960 *F, W, I, E*, 1961 *SA, W, I, E*, 1962 *F, W, I, E*, 1963 *F, W, I*, 1964 *F, NZ, W, I, E*, 1965 *F, W, I, E, SA*, 1966 *F, W, I, E*, 1967 *E*
Lawrie, J R (Melrose) 1922 *F, W, I, E*, 1923 *F, W, I, E*, 1924 *W, I, E*
Lawrie, K G (Gala) 1980 *F* (R), *W, E*
Lawson, A J M (Edinburgh Wands, London Scottish) 1972 *F* (R), *E*, 1973 *F*, 1974 *W, E*, 1976 *E, I*, 1977 *E*, 1978 *NZ*, 1979 *W, E, I, F, NZ*, 1980 *W* (R)
Lawther, T H B (Old Millhillians) 1932 *SA, W*
Ledingham, G A (Aberdeen GSFP) 1913 *F*
Lee, D J (London Scottish) 1998 *I* (R), *F, W, E, Fj, A* 1,2, *SA*
Lees, J B (Gala) 1947 *I, A*, 1948 *F, W, E*
Leggatt, H T O (Watsonians) 1891 *W, I, E*, 1892 *W, I*, 1893 *W, E*, 1894 *I, E*
Lely, W G (Cambridge U, London Scottish) 1909 *I*
Leslie, D G (Dundee HSFP, W of Scotland, Gala) 1975 *I, F, W, E, NZ, A*, 1976 *F, W, E, I*, 1978 *NZ*, 1980 *E*, 1981 *W, E, I, NZ* 1,2, *R, A*, 1982 *E*, 1983 *I, F, W, E*, 1984 *W, E, I, F, R*, 1985 *F, W, E*
Leslie, J A (Glasgow Caledonians) 1998 *SA*, 1999 *W, E, It, I, F*
Leslie, M D (Glasgow Caledonians) 1998 *SA* (R), 1999 *W, E, It, I, F*
Liddell, E H (Edinburgh U) 1922 *F, W, I*, 1923 *F, W, I, E*
Lind, H (Dunfermline) 1928 *I*, 1931 *F, W, I, E*, 1932 *SA, W, E*, 1933 *W, E, I*, 1934 *W, I, E*, 1935 *I*, 1936 *E*
Lindsay, A B (London Hospital) 1910 *I*, 1911 *I*
Lindsay, G C (London Scottish) 1884 *W*, 1885 *I* 1, 1887 *W, E*
Lindsay-Watson, R H (Hawick) 1909 *I*
Lineen, S R P (Boroughmuir) 1989 *W, E, I, F, Fj, R*, 1990 *I, F, W, E, NZ* 1,2, *Arg*, 1991 *F, W, E, I, R*, [*J, Z, I, E, NZ*], 1992 *E, I, F, W, A* 1,2
Little, A W (Hawick) 1905 *W*
Logan, K M (Stirling County, Wasps) 1992 *A* 2, 1993 *E* (R), *NZ* (t), 1994 *W, E, I, F, Arg* 1,2, *SA*, 1995 *C, I, F, W, E, R*, [*Iv, Tg, F, NZ*], *WS*, 1996 *W* (R), *NZ* 1,2, *A, It*, 1997 *W, E, I, F, A*, 1998 *I, F, SA* (R), 1999 *W, E, It, I, F*
Logan, W R (Edinburgh U, Edinburgh Wands) 1931 *E*, 1932 *SA, W, I*, 1933 *W, E, I*, 1934 *W, I, E*, 1935 *W, I, E, NZ*, 1936 *W, I, E*, 1937 *W, I, E*
Longstaff, S L (Dundee HSFP) 1998 *F* (R), *W, E, Fj, A* 1,2 1999 *It* (R), *I* (R)
Lorraine, H D B (Oxford U) 1933 *W, E, I*
Loudoun-Shand, E G (Oxford U) 1913 *E*
Lowe, J D (Heriot's FP) 1934 *W*
Lumsden, I J M (Bath, Watsonians) 1947 *F, W, A*, 1949 *F, W, I, E*
Lyall, G G (Gala) 1947 *A*, 1948 *F, W, I, E*
Lyall, W J C (Edinburgh Acads) 1871 *E*

Mabon, J T (Jedforest) 1898 *I, E*, 1899 *I*, 1900 *I*
Macarthur, J P (Waterloo) 1932 *E*
MacCallum, J C (Watsonians) 1905 *E, NZ*, 1906 *W, I, E, SA*, 1907 *W, I, E*, 1908 *W, I, E*, 1909 *W, I, E*, 1910 *F, W, I, E*, 1911 *F, I, E*, 1912 *F, W, I, E*
McClung, T (Edinburgh Acads) 1956 *I, E*, 1957 *W, I, E*, 1959 *F, W, I*, 1960 *W*
McClure, G B (W of Scotland) 1873 *E*
McClure, J H (W of Scotland) 1872 *E*
McCowan, D (W of Scotland) 1880 *I, E*, 1881 *I, E*, 1882 *I, E*, 1883 *I, E*, 1884 *I, E*
McCowat, R H (Glasgow Acads) 1905 *I*
McCrae, I G (Gordonians) 1967 *E*, 1968 *I*, 1969 *F* (R), *W*, 1972 *F, NZ*
McCrow, J W S (Edinburgh Acads) 1921 *I*
Macdonald, A E D (Heriot's FP) 1993 *NZ*
McDonald, C (Jedforest) 1947 *A*

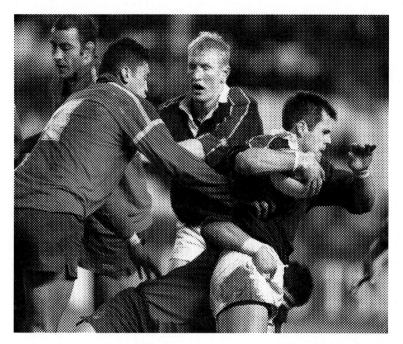

Down but not out. Scotland wing Kenny Logan is felled by the Spanish defence during the World Cup qualifier at Murrayfield in December 1998. The SRU elected not to award caps for the matches against Spain and Portugal.

Macdonald, D C (Edinburgh U) 1953 *F, W,* 1958 *I, E*
Macdonald, D S M (Oxford U, London Scottish, W of Scotland) 1977 *E, I, F, W,* 1978 *I, W, E*
Macdonald, J D (London Scottish, Army) 1966 *F, W, I, E,* 1967 *F, W, I, E*
Macdonald, J M (Edinburgh Wands) 1911 *W*
Macdonald, J S (Edinburgh U) 1903 *E,* 1904 *W, I, E,* 1905 *W*
Macdonald, K R (Stewart's Coll FP) 1956 *F, W, I,* 1957 *W, I, E*
Macdonald, R (Edinburgh U) 1950 *F, W, I, E*
McDonald, W A (Glasgow U) 1889 *W,* 1892 *I, E*
Macdonald, W G (London Scottish) 1969 *I* (R)
Macdougall, J B (Greenock Wands, Wakefield) 1913 *F,* 1914 *I,* 1921 *F, I, E*
McEwan, M C (Edinburgh Acads) 1886 *E,* 1887 *I, W, E,* 1888 *W, I,* 1889 *W, I,* 1890 *W, I, E,* 1891 *W, I, E,* 1892 *E*
MacEwan, N A (Gala, Highland) 1971 *F, W, I, E* (2[1C]), 1972 *F, W, E, NZ,* 1973 *F, W, I, E, P,* 1974 *W, E, I, F,* 1975 *W, E*
McEwan, W M C (Edinburgh Acads) 1894 *W, E,* 1895 *W, E,* 1896 *W, I, E,* 1897 *I, E,* 1898 *I, E,* 1899 *I, W, E,* 1900 *W, E*
MacEwen, R K G (Cambridge U, London Scottish) 1954 *F, NZ, I, W,* 1956 *F, W, I, E,* 1957 *F, W, I, E,* 1958 *W*
Macfarlan, D J (London Scottish) 1883 *W,* 1884 *W, I, E,* 1886 *W, I,* 1887 *I,* 1888 *I*
McFarlane, J L H (Edinburgh U) 1871 *E,* 1872 *E,* 1873 *E*
McGaughey, S K (Hawick) 1984 *R*
McGeechan, I R (Headingley) 1972 *NZ,* 1973 *F, W, I, E, P,* 1974 *F, I,* 1975 *I, F, W, E, NZ, A,* 1976 *F, W, E, I,* 1977 *E, I, F, W,* 1978 *I, F, W, NZ,* 1979 *W, E, I, F*
McGlashan, T P L (Royal HSFP) 1947 *F, I, E,* 1954 *F, NZ, I, E, W*

MacGregor, D G (Watsonians, Pontypridd) 1907 *W, I, E*
MacGregor, G (Cambridge U) 1890 *W, I, E,* 1891 *W, I, E,* 1893 *W, I, E,* 1894 *W, I, E,* 1896 *E*
MacGregor, I A A (Hillhead HSFP, Llanelli) 1955 *I, E,* 1956 *F, W, I, E,* 1957 *F, W, I*
MacGregor, J R (Edinburgh U) 1909 *I*
McGuinness, G M (W of Scotland) 1982 *A* 1,2, 1983 *I,* 1985 *I, F, W, E*
McHarg, A F (W of Scotland, London Scottish) 1968 *I, E, A,* 1969 *F, W, I, E,* 1971 *F, W, I, E* (2[1C]), 1972 *F, E, NZ,* 1973 *F, W, I, E, P,* 1974 *W, E, I, F,* 1975 *I, F, W, E, NZ, A,* 1976 *F, W, E, I,* 1977 *E, I, F, W,* 1978 *I, F, W, NZ,* 1979 *W, E*
McIlwham, G R (Glasgow Hawks) 1998 *Fj, A* 2 (R)
McIndoe, F (Glasgow Acads) 1886 *W, I*
MacIntyre, I (Edinburgh Wands) 1890 *W, I, E,* 1891 *W, I, E*
McIvor, D J (Edinburgh Acads) 1992 *E, I, F, W,* 1993 *NZ,* 1994 *SA*
Mackay, E B (Glasgow Acads) 1920 *W,* 1922 *E*
McKeating, E (Heriot's FP) 1957 *F, W,* 1961 *SA, W, I, E*
McKelvey, G (Watsonians) 1997 *A*
McKendrick, J G (W of Scotland) 1889 *I*
Mackenzie, A D G (Selkirk) 1984 *A*
Mackenzie, C J G (United Services) 1921 *E*
Mackenzie, D D (Edinburgh U) 1947 *W, I, E,* 1948 *F, W, I*
Mackenzie, D K A (Edinburgh Wands) 1939 *I, E*
Mackenzie, J M (Edinburgh U) 1905 *NZ,* 1909 *W, I, E,* 1910 *W, I, E,* 1911 *W, I*
McKenzie, K D (Stirling County) 1994 *Arg* 1,2, 1995 *R,* [*Iv*], 1996 *I, F, W, E, NZ* 1,2, *A, It,* 1998 *A* 1(R), 2
Mackenzie, R C (Glasgow Acads) 1877 *I, E,* 1881 *I, E*
Mackie, G Y (Highland) 1975 *A,* 1976 *F, W,* 1978 *F*

189

MacKinnon, A (London Scottish) 1898 *I, E,* 1899 *I, W, E,* 1900 *E*
Mackintosh, C E W C (London Scottish) 1924 *F*
Mackintosh, H S (Glasgow U, W of Scotland) 1929 *F, W, I, E,* 1930 *F, W, I, E,* 1931 *F, W, I, E,* 1932 *SA, W, I, E*
MacLachlan, L P (Oxford U, London Scottish) 1954 *NZ, I, E, W*
Maclagan, W E (Edinburgh Acads) 1878 *E,* 1879 *I, E,* 1880 *I, E,* 1881 *I, E,* 1882 *I, E,* 1883 *W, I, E,* 1884 *W, I, E,* 1885 *W, I 1;2,* 1887 *I, W, E,* 1888 *W, I,* 1890 *W, I, E*
McLaren, A (Durham County) 1931 *F*
McLaren, E (London Scottish, Royal HSFP) 1923 *F, W, I, E,* 1924 *F*
McLauchlan, J (Jordanhill) 1969 *E, SA,* 1970 *F, W,* 1971 *F, W, I, E* (2[1C]), 1972 *F, W, E, NZ,* 1973 *F, W, I, E, P,* 1974 *W, E, I, F,* 1975 *I, F, W, E, NZ, A,* 1976 *F, W, E, I,* 1977 *W,* 1978 *I, F, W, E, NZ,* 1979 *W, E, I, F, NZ*
McLean, D I (Royal HSFP) 1947 *I, E*
Maclennan, W D (Watsonians) 1947 *F, I*
MacLeod, D A (Glasgow U) 1886 *I, E*
MacLeod, G (Edinburgh Acads) 1878 *E,* 1882 *I*
McLeod, H F (Hawick) 1954 *F, NZ, I, E, W,* 1955 *F, W, I, E,* 1956 *F, W, I, E,* 1957 *F, W, I, E,* 1958 *F, W, A, I, E,* 1959 *F, W, I, E,* 1960 *F, W, I, E, SA,* 1961 *F, SA, W, I, E,* 1962 *F, W, I, E*
MacLeod, K G (Cambridge U) 1905 *NZ,* 1906 *W, I, E, SA,* 1907 *W, I, E,* 1908 *I, E*
MacLeod, L M (Cambridge U) 1904 *W, I, E,* 1905 *W, I, NZ*
Macleod, W M (Fettesian-Lorettonians, Edinburgh Wands) 1886 *W, I*
McMillan, K H D (Sale) 1953 *F, W, I, E*
MacMillan, R G (London Scottish) 1887 *W, I, E,* 1890 *W, I, E,* 1891 *W, E,* 1892 *W, I, E,* 1893 *W, E,* 1894 *W, I, E,* 1895 *W, I, E,* 1897 *I, E*
MacMyn, D J (Cambridge U, London Scottish) 1925 *F, W, I, E,* 1926 *F, W, I, E,* 1927 *E, A,* 1928 *F*
McNeil, A S B (Watsonians) 1935 *I*
McPartlin, J J (Harlequins, Oxford U) 1960 *F, W,* 1962 *F, W, I, E*
Macphail, J A R (Edinburgh Acads) 1949 *E,* 1951 *SA*
Macpherson, D G (London Hospital) 1910 *I, E*
Macpherson, G P S (Oxford U, Edinburgh Acads) 1922 *F, W, I, E,* 1924 *W, E,* 1925 *F, W, E,* 1927 *F, W, I, E,* 1928 *F, W, E,* 1929 *I, E,* 1930 *F, W, I, E,* 1931 *W, E,* 1932 *SA, E*
Macpherson, N C (Newport) 1920 *W, I, E,* 1921 *F, E,* 1923 *I, E*
McQueen, S B (Waterloo) 1923 *F, W, I, E*
Macrae, D J (St Andrew's U) 1937 *W, I, E,* 1938 *W, I, E,* 1939 *W, I, E*
Madsen, D F (Gosforth) 1974 *W, E, I, F,* 1975 *I, F, W, E,* 1976 *F,* 1977 *E, I, F, W,* 1978 *I*
Mair, N G R (Edinburgh U) 1951 *F, W, I, E*
Maitland, G (Edinburgh Inst FP) 1885 *W, I 2*
Maitland, R (Edinburgh Inst FP) 1881 *E,* 1882 *I, E,* 1884 *W,* 1885 *W*
Maitland, R P (Royal Artillery) 1872 *E*
Malcolm, A G (Glasgow U) 1888 *I*
Manson, J J (Dundee HSFP) 1995 *E* (R)
Marsh, J (Edinburgh Inst FP) 1889 *W, I*
Marshall, A (Edinburgh Acads) 1875 *E*
Marshall, G R (Selkirk) 1988 *A* (R), 1989 *Fj,* 1990 *Arg,* 1991 [*Z*]
Marshall, J C (London Scottish) 1954 *F, NZ, I, E, W*
Marshall, K W (Edinburgh Acads) 1934 *W, I, E,* 1935 *W, I, E,* 1936 *W,* 1937 *E*
Marshall, T R (Edinburgh Inst FP) 1871 *E,* 1872 *E,* 1873 *E,* 1874 *E*
Marshall, W (Edinburgh Acads) 1872 *E*
Martin, H (Edinburgh Acads, Oxford U) 1908 *W, I, E,* 1909 *W, E*
Masters, W H (Edinburgh Inst FP) 1879 *I,* 1880 *I, E*
Maxwell, F T (Royal Engineers) 1872 *E*
Maxwell, G H H P (Edinburgh Acads, RAF, London Scottish) 1913 *I, E,* 1914 *W, I, E,* 1920 *W, E,* 1921 *F, W, I, E,* 1922 *F, E*
Maxwell, J M (Langholm) 1957 *I*
Mayer, M J M (Watsonians) 1998 *SA*
Mein, J (Edinburgh Acads) 1871 *E,* 1872 *E,* 1873 *E,* 1874 *E,* 1875 *E*
Melville, C L (Army) 1937 *W, I, E*
Menzies, H F (W of Scotland) 1893 *W, I,* 1894 *W, E*
Metcalfe, G H (Glasgow Hawks) 1998 *A 1,2,* 1999 *W, E, It, I, E*

Methuen, A (London Scottish) 1889 *W, I*
Michie, E J S (Aberdeen U, Aberdeen GSFP) 1954 *F, NZ, I, E,* 1955 *W, I, E,* 1956 *F, W, I, E,* 1957 *F, W, I, E*
Millar, J N (W of Scotland) 1892 *W, I, E,* 1893 *W,* 1895 *I, E*
Millar, R K (London Scottish) 1924 *I*
Millican, J G (Edinburgh U) 1973 *W, I, E*
Milne, C J B (Fettesian-Lorettonians, W of Scotland) 1886 *W, I, E*
Milne, D F (Heriot's FP) 1991 [*J*(R)]
Milne, I G (Heriot's FP, Harlequins) 1979 *I, F, NZ,* 1980 *I, F,* 1981 *NZ 1,2, R, A,* 1982 *E, I, F, W, A 1,2,* 1983 *I, F, W, E, NZ,* 1984 *W, E, I, F, A,* 1985 *F, W, E,* 1986 *F, W, E, I, R,* 1987 *I, F, W, E,* [*F, Z, NZ*], 1988 *A,* 1989 *W,* 1990 *NZ 1,2*
Milne, K S (Heriot's FP) 1989 *W, E, I, F, Fj, R,* 1990 *I, F, W, E, NZ 2, Arg,* 1991 *F, W* (R), *E,* [*Z*], 1992 *E, I, F, W, A 1,* 1993 *I, F, W, E, NZ,* 1994 *W, E, I, F, SA,* 1995 *C, I, F, W, E,* [*Tg, F, NZ*]
Milne, W M (Glasgow Acads) 1904 *I, E,* 1905 *W, I*
Milroy, E (Watsonians) 1910 *W,* 1911 *E,* 1912 *W, I, E, SA,* 1913 *F, W, I, E,* 1914 *I, E*
Mitchell, G W E (Edinburgh Wands) 1967 *NZ,* 1968 *F, W*
Mitchell, J G (W of Scotland) 1885 *W, I 1,2*
Moncreiff, F J (Edinburgh Acads) 1871 *E,* 1872 *E,* 1873 *E*
Monteith, H G (Cambridge U, London Scottish) 1905 *E,* 1906 *W, I, E, SA,* 1907 *W, I,* 1908 *E*
Monypenny, D B (London Scottish) 1899 *I, W, E*
Moodie, A R (St Andrew's U) 1909 *E,* 1910 *F,* 1911 *F*
Moore, A (Edinburgh Acads) 1990 *NZ 2, Arg,* 1991 *F, W, E*
Morgan, D W (Stewart's-Melville FP) 1973 *W, I, E, P,* 1974 *I, F,* 1975 *I, F, W, E, NZ, A,* 1976 *F, W,* 1977 *I, F, W,* 1978 *I, F, W, E*
Morrison, I R (London Scottish) 1993 *I, F, W, E,* 1994 *W, SA,* 1995 *C, I, F, W, E, R,* [*Tg, F, NZ*]
Morrison, M C (Royal HSFP) 1896 *W, I, E,* 1897 *I, E,* 1898 *I, E,* 1899 *I, W, E,* 1900 *W, E,* 1901 *W, I, E,* 1902 *W, I, E,* 1903 *W, I,* 1904 *W, I, E*
Morrison, R H (Edinburgh U) 1886 *W, I, E*
Morrison, W H (Edinburgh Acads) 1900 *W*
Morton, D S (W of Scotland) 1887 *I, W, E,* 1888 *W, I,* 1889 *W, I,* 1890 *I, E*
Mowat, J G (Glasgow Acads) 1883 *W, E*
Muir, D E (Heriot's FP) 1950 *F, W, I, E,* 1952 *W, I, E*
Munnoch, N M (Watsonians) 1952 *F, W, I*
Munro, D S (Glasgow High Kelvinside) 1994 *W, E, I, F, Arg 1,2,* 1997 *W* (R)
Munro, P (Oxford U, London Scottish) 1905 *W, I, E, NZ,* 1906 *W, I, E, SA,* 1907 *I, E,* 1911 *F, W, I*
Munro, R (St Andrew's U) 1871 *E*
Munro, S (Ayr, W of Scotland) 1980 *I, F,* 1981 *F, W, E, I, NZ 1,2, R,* 1984 *W*
Munro, W H (Glasgow HSFP) 1947 *I, E*
Murdoch, W C W (Hillhead HSFP) 1935 *E, NZ,* 1936 *W, I,* 1939 *E,* 1948 *F, W, I, E*
Murray, C A (Hawick) 1998 *E* (R), *Fj, A 1,2, SA,* 1999 *W, E, It, I, F*
Murray, G M (Glasgow Acads) 1921 *I,* 1926 *W*
Murray, H M (Glasgow U) 1936 *W, I*
Murray, K T (Hawick) 1985 *I, F, W*
Murray, R O (Cambridge U) 1935 *W, E*
Murray, S (Bedford) 1997 *A, SA,* 1998 *It, Fj, A 1,2, SA,* 1999 *W, E, It, I, F*
Murray, W A K (London Scottish) 1920 *F, I,* 1921 *F*

Napier, H M (W of Scotland) 1877 *I, E,* 1878 *E,* 1879 *I, E,* 1965 *F*
Neill, J B (Edinburgh Acads) 1963 *E,* 1964 *F, NZ, W, I, E,* 1965 *F*
Neill, R M (Edinburgh Acads) 1901 *E,* 1902 *I*
Neilson, G T (W of Scotland) 1891 *W, I, E,* 1892 *W, E,* 1893 *W,* 1894 *W, I,* 1895 *W, I, E,* 1896 *W, I, E*
Neilson, J A (Glasgow Acads) 1878 *E,* 1879 *E*
Neilson, R T (W of Scotland) 1898 *I, E,* 1899 *I, W,* 1900 *I, E*
Neilson, T (W of Scotland) 1874 *E*
Neilson, W (Merchiston, Cambridge U, London Scottish) 1891 *W, E,* 1892 *W, I, E,* 1893 *I, E,* 1894 *E,* 1895 *W, I, E,* 1896 *I,* 1897 *I, E*
Neilson, W G (Merchistonians) 1894 *E*
Nelson, J B (Glasgow Acads) 1925 *F, W, I, E,* 1926 *F, W, I, E,* 1927 *F, W, I, E,* 1928 *I, E,* 1929 *F, W, I, E,* 1930 *F, W, I, E,* 1931 *F, W, I*
Nelson, T A (Oxford U) 1898 *E*
Nichol, J A (Royal HSFP) 1955 *W, I, E*

Nichol, S A (Selkirk) 1994 *Arg* 2 (R)
Nicol, A D (Dundee HSFP, Bath) 1992 *E, I, F, W, A* 1,2, 1993 *NZ,* 1994 *W,* 1997 *A, SA*
Nimmo, C S (Watsonians) 1920 *E*

Ogilvy, C (Hawick) 1911 *I, E,* 1912 *I*
Oliver, G H (Hawick) 1987 [*Z*], 1990 *NZ* 2 (R), 1991 [*Z*]
Oliver, G K (Gala) 1970 *A*
Orr, C E (W of Scotland) 1887 *I, E, W,* 1888 *W, I,* 1889 *W, I,* 1890 *W, I, E,* 1891 *W, I, E,* 1892 *W, I, E*
Orr, H J (London Scottish) 1903 *W, I, E,* 1904 *W, I*
Orr, J E (W of Scotland) 1889 *I,* 1890 *W, I, E,* 1891 *W, I, E,* 1892 *W, I, E,* 1893 *I, E*
Orr, J H (Edinburgh City Police) 1947 *F, W*
Osler, F L (Edinburgh U) 1911 *F, W*

Park, J (Royal HSFP) 1934 *W*
Paterson, D S (Gala) 1969 *SA,* 1970 *I, E, A,* 1971 *F, W, I, E* (2[1C]), 1972 *W*
Paterson, G Q (Edinburgh Acads) 1876 *E*
Paterson, J R (Birkenhead Park) 1925 *F, W, I, E,* 1926 *F, W, I, E,* 1927 *F, W, I, E, A,* 1928 *F, W, I, E,* 1929 *F, W, I, E*
Patterson, D (Hawick) 1896 *W*
Patterson, D W (West Hartlepool) 1994 *SA,* 1995 [*Tg*]
Pattullo, G L (Panmure) 1920 *F, W, I, E*
Paxton, I A M (Selkirk) 1981 *NZ* 1,2, *R, A,* 1982 *E, I, F, W, A* 1,2, 1983 *I, E, NZ,* 1984 *W, E, I, F,* 1985 *I* (R), *F, W, E,* 1986 *W, E, I, R,* 1987 *I, F, W, E,* [*F, Z, R, NZ*], 1988 *I, E, A*
Paxton, R E (Kelso) 1982 *I, A* 2 (R)
Pearson, J (Watsonians) 1909 *I, E,* 1910 *F, W, I, E,* 1911 *F,* 1912 *F, W, SA,* 1913 *I, E*
Pender, I M (London Scottish) 1914 *E*
Pender, N E K (Hawick) 1977 *I,* 1978 *F, W, E*
Penman, W M (RAF) 1939 *I*
Peterkin, W A (Edinburgh U) 1881 *E,* 1883 *I,* 1884 *W, I, E,* 1885 *W, I* 1,2
Peters, E W (Bath) 1995 *C, I, F, W, E, R,* [*Tg, F, NZ*], 1996 *I, F, W, E, NZ* 1,2, *A, It,* 1997 *A, SA,* 1998 *W, E, Fj, A* 1,2, *SA,* 1999 *W, E, It, I*
Petrie, A G (Royal HSFP) 1873 *E,* 1874 *E,* 1875 *E,* 1876 *E,* 1877 *I, E,* 1878 *E,* 1879 *I, E,* 1880 *I, E*
Philp, A (Edinburgh Inst FP) 1882 *E*
Pocock, E I (Edinburgh Wands) 1877 *I, E*
Pollock, J A (Gosforth) 1982 *W,* 1983 *E, NZ,* 1984 *E* (R), *I, F, R,* 1985 *F*
Polson, A H (Gala) 1930 *E*
Pountney, A C (Northampton) 1998 *SA,* 1999 *W* (t + R), *E* (R), *It* (t + R), *I* (R), *F*
Proudfoot, M C (Melrose) 1998 *Fj, A* 1,2
Purdie, W (Jedforest) 1939 *W, I, E*
Purves, A B H L (London Scottish) 1906 *W, I, E, SA,* 1907 *W, I, E,* 1908 *W, I, E*
Purves, W D C L (London Scottish) 1912 *F, W, I, SA,* 1913 *I, E*

Rea, C W W (W of Scotland, Headingley) 1968 *A,* 1969 *W, I, SA,* 1970 *F, W, I, A,* 1971 *F, W, E* (2[1C])
Redpath, B W (Melrose) 1993 *NZ* (t), 1994 *E* (t), *F, Arg* 1,2, 1995 *C, I, F, W, E, R,* [*Iv, F, NZ*], *WS,* 1996 *I, F, W, E, A* (R), *It,* 1997 *E, I, F,* 1998 *Fj, A* 1,2, *SA*
Reed, A I (Bath, Wasps) 1993 *I, F, W, E,* 1994 *E, I, F, Arg* 1,2, *SA,* 1996 *It,* 1997 *W, E, I, F,* 1999 *It* (R), *F* (R)
Reid, C (Edinburgh Acads) 1881 *I, E,* 1882 *I, E,* 1883 *W, I, E,* 1884 *W, I, E,* 1885 *W, I* 1,2, 1886 *W, I, E,* 1887 *I, W, E,* 1888 *W, I*
Reid, J (Edinburgh Wands) 1874 *E,* 1875 *E,* 1876 *E,* 1877 *I, E*
Reid, J M (Edinburgh Acads) 1898 *I, E,* 1899 *I*
Reid, M F (Loretto) 1883 *I, E*
Reid, S J (Boroughmuir, Leeds) 1995 *WS,* 1999 *F*
Reid-Kerr, J (Greenock Wand) 1909 *E*
Relph, W K L (Stewart's Coll FP) 1955 *F, W, I, E*
Renny-Tailyour, H W (Royal Engineers) 1872 *E*
Renwick, J M (Hawick) 1972 *F, W, E, NZ,* 1973 *F,* 1974 *W, E, I, F,* 1975 *I, F, W, E, NZ, A,* 1976 *F, W, E* (R), 1977 *I, F, W,* 1978 *I, F, W, E, NZ,* 1979 *W, E, I, F, NZ,* 1980 *I, F, W, E,* 1981 *F, W, E, I, NZ* 1,2, *R, A,* 1982 *E, I, F, W,* 1983 *I, F, W, E,* 1984 *R*
Renwick, W L (London Scottish) 1989 *R*
Renwick, W N (London Scottish, Edinburgh Wands) 1938 *E,* 1939 *W*
Richardson, J F (Edinburgh Acads) 1994 *SA*
Ritchie, G (Merchistonians) 1871 *E*

Ritchie, G F (Dundee HSFP) 1932 *E*
Ritchie, J M (Watsonians) 1933 *W, E, I,* 1934 *W, I, E*
Ritchie, W T (Cambridge U) 1905 *I, E*
Robb, G H (Glasgow U) 1881 *I,* 1885 *W*
Roberts, G (Watsonians) 1938 *W, I, E,* 1939 *W, E*
Robertson, A H (W of Scotland) 1871 *E*
Robertson, A W (Edinburgh Acads) 1897 *E*
Robertson, D (Edinburgh Acads) 1875 *E*
Robertson, D D (Cambridge U) 1893 *W*
Robertson, I (London Scottish, Watsonians) 1968 *E,* 1969 *E, SA,* 1970 *F, W, I, E, A*
Robertson, I P M (Watsonians) 1910 *F*
Robertson, J (Clydesdale) 1908 *E*
Robertson, K W (Melrose) 1978 *NZ,* 1979 *W, E, I, F, NZ,* 1980 *W, E, I, R, A,* 1982 *E, I, F, A* 1,2, 1983 *I, F, W, E,* 1984 *E, I, F, R, A,* 1985 *I, F, W, E,* 1986 *I,* 1987 *F* (R), *W, E,* [*F, Z, NZ*], 1988 *E, A,* 1989 *E, I, F*
Robertson, L (London Scottish United Services) 1908 *E,* 1911 *W,* 1912 *W, I, E, SA,* 1913 *W, I, E*
Robertson, M A (Gala) 1958 *F*
Robertson, R D (London Scottish) 1912 *F*
Robson, A (Hawick) 1954 *F,* 1955 *F, W, I, E,* 1956 *F, W, I, E,* 1957 *F, W, I, E,* 1958 *W, A, I, E,* 1959 *F, W, I, E,* 1960 *F*
Rodd, J A T (United Services, RN, London Scottish) 1958 *F, W, A, I, E,* 1960 *F, W,* 1962 *F,* 1964 *F, NZ, W,* 1965 *F, W, I*
Rogerson, J (Kelvinside Acads) 1894 *W*
Roland, E T (Edinburgh Acads) 1884 *I, E*
Rollo, D M D (Howe of Fife) 1959 *E,* 1960 *F, W, I, E, SA,* 1961 *F, SA, W, I, E,* 1962 *F, W, E,* 1963 *F, W, I, E,* 1964 *F, NZ, W, I, E,* 1965 *F, W, I, E, SA,* 1966 *F, W, I, E, A,* 1967 *F, W, E, NZ,* 1968 *F, W, I*
Rose, D M (Jedforest) 1951 *F, W, I, E, SA,* 1953 *F, W*
Ross, A (Kilmarnock) 1924 *F, W*
Ross, A (Royal HSFP) 1905 *W, I, E,* 1909 *W, I*
Ross, A R (Edinburgh U) 1911 *W,* 1914 *W, I, E*
Ross, E J (London Scottish) 1904 *W*
Ross, G T (Watsonians) 1954 *NZ, I, E, W*
Ross, I A (Hillhead HSFP) 1951 *F, W, I, E*
Ross, J (London Scottish) 1901 *W, I, E,* 1902 *W,* 1903 *E*
Ross, K I (Boroughmuir FP) 1961 *SA, W, I, E,* 1962 *F, W, I, E,* 1963 *F, W, E*
Ross, W A (Hillhead HSFP) 1937 *W, E*
Rottenburg, H (Cambridge U, London Scottish) 1899 *W, E,* 1900 *W, I, E*
Roughead, W N (Edinburgh Acads, London Scottish) 1927 *A,* 1928 *F, W, I, E,* 1930 *I, E,* 1931 *F, W, I, E,* 1932 *W*
Rowan, N A (Boroughmuir) 1980 *W, E,* 1981 *F, W, E, I,* 1984 *R,* 1985 *I,* 1987 [*R*], 1988 *I, F, W, E*
Rowand, R (Glasgow HSFP) 1930 *F, W,* 1932 *E,* 1933 *W, E, I,* 1934 *W*
Roxburgh, A J (Kelso) 1997 *A,* 1998 *It, F* (R), *W, E, Fj, A* 1 (R),2 (R)
Roy, A (Waterloo) 1938 *W, I, E,* 1939 *W, I, E*
Russell, W L (Glasgow Acads) 1905 *NZ,* 1906 *W, I, E*
Rutherford, J Y (Selkirk) 1979 *F, W, E, I, NZ,* 1980 *I, F, E,* 1981 *F, W, E, I, NZ* 1,2, *A,* 1982 *E, I, F, W, A* 1,2, 1983 *E, NZ,* 1984 *W, E, I, F, R,* 1985 *I, F, W, E,* 1986 *F, W, E, I, R,* 1987 *I, F, W, E,* [*F*]

Sampson, R W F (London Scottish) 1939 *W,* 1947 *E*
Sanderson, G A (Royal HSFP) 1907 *W, I, E,* 1908 *I*
Sanderson, J L P (Edinburgh Acads) 1873 *E*
Schulze, D G (London Scottish) 1905 *E,* 1907 *I, E,* 1908 *W, I, E,* 1909 *W, I, E,* 1910 *W, I, E,* 1911 *W, I*
Scobie, R M (Royal Military Coll) 1914 *W, I, E*
Scotland, K J F (Heriot's FP, Cambridge U, Leicester) 1957 *F, W, I, E,* 1958 *E,* 1959 *F, W, I, E,* 1960 *F, W, I, E,* 1961 *F, SA, W, I, E,* 1962 *F, W, I, E,* 1963 *F, W, I, E,* 1965 *F*
Scott, D M (Langholm, Watsonians) 1950 *I, E,* 1951 *W, I, E, SA,* 1952 *F, W, I,* 1953 *F*
Scott, J M B (Edinburgh Acads) 1907 *E,* 1908 *W, I, E,* 1909 *W, I, E,* 1910 *F, W, I, E,* 1911 *F, W, I,* 1912 *W, I, E, SA,* 1913 *W, I, E*
Scott, J S (St Andrew's U) 1950 *E*
Scott, J W (Stewart's Coll FP) 1925 *F, W, I, E,* 1926 *F, W, I, E,* 1927 *F, W, I, E, A,* 1928 *F, W, E,* 1929 *E,* 1930 *F*
Scott, M (Dunfermline) 1992 *A* 2
Scott, R (Hawick) 1898 *I,* 1900 *I, E*
Scott, T (Langholm, Hawick) 1896 *W,* 1897 *I, E,* 1898 *I, E,* 1899 *I, E,* 1900 *W, I, E*
Scott, T M (Hawick) 1893 *E,* 1895 *W, I, E,* 1896 *W, E,* 1897 *I, E,* 1898 *I, E,* 1900 *W, I*

Scott, W P (W of Scotland) 1900 *I, E,* 1902 *I, E,* 1903 *W, I, E,* 1904 *W, I, E,* 1905 *W, I, E, NZ,* 1906 *W, I, E, SA,* 1907 *W, I, E*
Scoular, J G (Cambridge U) 1905 *NZ,* 1906 *W, I, E, SA*
Selby, J A R (Watsonians) 1920 *W, I*
Shackleton, J A P (London Scottish) 1959 *E,* 1963 *F, W,* 1964 *NZ, W,* 1965 *I, SA*
Sharp, A V (Bristol) 1994 *E, I, F, Arg* 1,2 *SA*
Sharp, J (Stewart's FP, Army) 1960 *F,* 1964 *F, NZ, W*
Shaw, G D (Sale) 1935 *NZ,* 1936 *W,* 1937 *W, I, E,* 1939 *I*
Shaw, I (Glasgow HSFP) 1937 *I*
Shaw, J N (Edinburgh Acads) 1921 *W, I*
Shaw, R W (Glasgow HSFP) 1934 *W, I, E,* 1935 *W, I, E, NZ,* 1936 *W, I, E,* 1937 *W, I, E,* 1938 *W, I, E,* 1939 *W, I, E*
Shedden, D (W of Scotland) 1972 *NZ,* 1973 *F, W, I, E, P,* 1976 *W, E, I,* 1977 *I, F, W,* 1978 *I, F, W*
Shepherd, R J S (Melrose) 1995 *WS,* 1996 *I, F, W, E, NZ* 1,2, *A, It,* 1997 *W, E, I, F, SA,* 1998 *It, I, W* (R), *Fj* (t), *A* 1,2
Shiel, A G (Melrose) 1991 *[I* (R), *WS],* 1993 *I, F, W, E, NZ,* 1994 *Arg* 1,2, *SA,* 1995 *R, [Iv, F, NZ], WS*
Shillinglaw, R B (Gala, Army) 1960 *I, E, SA,* 1961 *F, SA*
Simmers, B M (Glasgow Acads) 1965 *F, W,* 1966 *A,* 1967 *F, W, I,* 1971 *F* (R)
Simmers, W M (Glasgow Acads) 1926 *W, I, E,* 1927 *F, W, I, E, A,* 1928 *F, W, I, E,* 1929 *F, W, I, E,* 1930 *F, W, I, E,* 1931 *F, W, I, E,* 1932 *SA, W, I, E*
Simpson, G L (Kirkcaldy) 1998 *A* 1,2
Simpson, J W (Royal HSFP) 1893 *I, E,* 1894 *W, I, E,* 1895 *W, I, E,* 1896 *W, I,* 1897 *E,* 1899 *W, E*
Simpson, R S (Glasgow Acads) 1923 *I*
Simson, E D (Edinburgh U, London Scottish) 1902 *E,* 1903 *W, I, E,* 1904 *W, I, E,* 1905 *W, I, E, NZ,* 1906 *W, I, E,* 1907 *W, I, E*
Simson, J T (Watsonians) 1905 *NZ,* 1909 *W, I, E,* 1910 *F, W,* 1911 *I*
Simson, R F (London Scottish) 1911 *E*
Sloan, A T (Edinburgh Acads) 1914 *W,* 1920 *F, W, I, E,* 1921 *F, W, I, E*
Sloan, D A (Edinburgh Acads, London Scottish) 1950 *F, W, E,* 1951 *W, I, E,* 1953 *F*
Sloan, T (Glasgow Acads, Oxford U) 1905 *NZ,* 1906 *W, SA,* 1907 *W, E,* 1908 *W,* 1909 *I*
Smeaton, P W (Edinburgh Acads) 1881 *I,* 1883 *I, E*
Smith, A R (Oxford U) 1895 *W, I, E,* 1896 *W, I,* 1897 *I, E,* 1898 *I, E,* 1900 *I, E*
Smith, A R (Cambridge U, Gosforth, Ebbw Vale, Edinburgh Wands) 1955 *W, I, E,* 1956 *F, W, I, E,* 1957 *F, W, I, E,* 1958 *F, W, I, E,* 1959 *F, W, I, E,* 1960 *F, W, I, E, SA,* 1961 *F, SA, W, I, E,* 1962 *F, W, I, E*
Smith, D W C (London Scottish) 1949 *F, W, I, E,* 1950 *F, W, I,* 1953 *I*
Smith, E R (Edinburgh Acads) 1879 *I*
Smith, G K (Kelso) 1957 *I, E,* 1958 *F, W, A,* 1959 *F, W, I, E,* 1960 *F, W, I, E,* 1961 *F, SA, W, I, E*
Smith, H O (Watsonians) 1895 *W,* 1896 *W, I, E,* 1898 *I, E,* 1899 *W, I, E,* 1900 *E,* 1902 *E*
Smith, I R (Gloucester, Moseley) 1992 *E, I, W, A* 1,2, 1994 *E* (R), *I, F, Arg* 1,2, 1995 *[Iv], WS,* 1996 *I, F, W, E, NZ* 1,2, *A, It,* 1997 *E, I, F, A, SA*
Smith, I S (Oxford U, Edinburgh U) 1924 *W, I, E,* 1925 *F, W, I, E,* 1926 *F, W, I, E,* 1927 *F, I, E,* 1929 *F, W, I, E,* 1930 *F, W, I,* 1931 *F, W, I, E,* 1932 *SA, W, I, E,* 1933 *W, E, I*
Smith I S G (London Scottish) 1969 *SA,* 1970 *F, W, I, E,* 1971 *F, W, I*
Smith, M A (London Scottish) 1970 *W, I, E, A*
Smith, R T (Kelso) 1929 *F, W, I, E,* 1930 *F, W, I*
Smith, S H (Glasgow Acads) 1877 *I,* 1878 *E*
Smith, T J (Gala) 1983 *E, NZ,* 1985 *I, F*
Smith T J (Watsonians, Dundee HSFP) 1997 *E, I, F,* 1998 *SA,* 1999 *W, E, It, I*
Sole, D M B (Bath, Edinburgh Acads) 1986 *F, W,* 1987 *I, F, W, E, [F, Z, R, NZ],* 1988 *I, F, W, E, A,* 1989 *W, E, I, F, Fj, R,* 1990 *I, F, W, E, NZ* 1,2, *Arg,* 1991 *F, W, E, I, R, [J, I, WS, E, NZ],* 1992 *E, I, F, W, A* 1,2
Somerville, D (Edinburgh Inst FP) 1879 *I,* 1882 *I,* 1883 *W, I, E,* 1884 *W*
Speirs, L M (Watsonians) 1906 *SA,* 1907 *W, I, E,* 1908 *W, I, E,* 1910 *F, W, E*
Spence, K M (Oxford U) 1953 *I*
Spencer, E (Clydesdale) 1898 *I*
Stagg, P K (Sale) 1965 *F, W, E, SA,* 1966 *F, W, I, E, A,* 1967 *F, W, I, E, NZ,* 1968 *F, W, I, E, A,* 1969 *F, W, I* (R), *SA,* 1970 *F, W, I, E, A*

Stanger, A G (Hawick) 1989 *Fj, R,* 1990 *I, F, W, E, NZ* 1,2, *Arg,* 1991 *F, W, E, I, R, [J, Z, I, WS, E, NZ],* 1992 *E, I, F, W, A* 1,2, 1993 *I, F, W, E, NZ,* 1994 *W, E, I, F, SA,* 1995 *R, [Iv],* 1996 *NZ* 2, *A, It,* 1997 *W, E, I, F, A, SA,* 1998 *It, I* (R), *F, W, E*
Stark, D A (Boroughmuir, Melrose, Glasgow Hawks) 1993 *I, F, W, E,* 1996 *NZ* 2(R), *It* (R), 1997 *W* (R), *E, SA*
Steele, W C C (Langholm, Bedford, RAF, London Scottish) 1969 *E,* 1971 *F, W, I, E* (2[1C]), 1972 *F, W, E, NZ,* 1973 *F, W, I, E,* 1975 *I, F, W, E, NZ* (R), 1976 *W, E, I,* 1977 *E*
Stephen, A E (W of Scotland) 1885 *W,* 1886 *I*
Steven, P D (Heriot's FP) 1984 *A,* 1985 *F, W, E*
Steven, R (Edinburgh Wands) 1962 *I*
Stevenson, A K (Glasgow Acads) 1922 *F,* 1923 *F, W, E*
Stevenson, A M (Glasgow U) 1911 *F*
Stevenson, G D (Hawick) 1956 *E,* 1957 *F,* 1958 *F, W, A, I, E,* 1959 *W, I, E,* 1960 *W, I, E, SA,* 1961 *F, SA, W, I, E,* 1963 *F, W, I,* 1964 *E,* 1965 *F*
Stevenson, H J (Edinburgh Acads) 1888 *W, I,* 1889 *W, I,* 1890 *W, I, E,* 1891 *W, I, E,* 1892 *W, I, E,* 1893 *I, E*
Stevenson, L E (Edinburgh U) 1888 *W*
Stevenson, R C (London Scottish) 1897 *I, E,* 1898 *E,* 1899 *I, W, E*
Stevenson, R C (St Andrew's U) 1910 *F, I, E,* 1911 *F, W, I*
Stevenson, W H (Glasgow Acads) 1925 *F*
Stewart, A K (Edinburgh U) 1874 *E,* 1876 *E*
Stewart, A M (Edinburgh Acads) 1914 *W*
Stewart, B D (Edinburgh Acads) 1996 *NZ* 2, *A*
Stewart, C A R (W of Scotland) 1880 *I, E*
Stewart, C E B (Kelso) 1960 *W,* 1961 *F*
Stewart, J (Glasgow HSFP) 1930 *F*
Stewart, J L (Edinburgh Acads) 1921 *I*
Stewart M J (Northampton) 1996 *It,* 1997 *W, E, I, F, A, SA,* 1998 *It, I, F, W, Fj* (R)
Stewart, M S (Stewart's Coll FP) 1932 *SA, W, I,* 1933 *W, E, I,* 1934 *W, I, E*
Stewart, W A (London Hospital) 1913 *F, W, I,* 1914 *W*
Steyn, S S L (Oxford U) 1911 *E,* 1912 *I*
Strachan, G M (Jordanhill) 1971 *E* (C) (R), 1973 *W, I, E, P*
Stronach, R S (Glasgow Acads) 1901 *W, E,* 1905 *W, I, E*
Stuart, C D (W of Scotland) 1909 *I,* 1910 *F, W, I, E,* 1911 *I, E*
Stuart, L M (Glasgow HSFP) 1923 *F, W, I, E,* 1924 *F,* 1928 *E,* 1930 *F, E*
Suddon, N (Hawick) 1965 *W, I, E, SA,* 1966 *A,* 1968 *E, A,* 1969 *F, W, I,* 1970 *I, E, A*
Sutherland, W R (Hawick) 1910 *W, E,* 1911 *F, E,* 1912 *F, W, E, SA,* 1913 *F, W, I, E,* 1914 *W*
Swan, J S (Army, London Scottish, Leicester) 1953 *E,* 1954 *F, NZ, I, E, W,* 1955 *F, W, I, E,* 1956 *F, W, I, E,* 1957 *F, W,* 1958 *F*
Swan, M W (Oxford U, London Scottish) 1958 *F, W, A, I, E,* 1959 *F, W, I*
Sweet, J B (Glasgow HSFP) 1913 *E,* 1914 *I*
Symington, A W (Cambridge U) 1914 *W, E*

Tait, A V (Kelso, Newcastle) 1987 *[F(R), Z, R, NZ],* 1988 *I, F, W, E,* 1997 *I, F, A, SA,* 1998 *It, I, F, W, E, SA,* 1999 *W* (R), *E, It, I, F*
Tait, J G (Edinburgh Acads) 1880 *I,* 1885 *I* 2
Tait, P W (Royal HSFP) 1935 *E*
Taylor, E G (Oxford U) 1927 *W, A*
Taylor, R C (Kelvinside-West) 1951 *W, I, E, SA*
Telfer, C M (Hawick) 1968 *A,* 1969 *F, W, I, E,* 1972 *F, W, E,* 1973 *W, I, E, P,* 1974 *W, E, I,* 1975 *A,* 1976 *F*
Telfer, J W (Melrose) 1964 *F, NZ, W, I, E,* 1965 *F, W, I,* 1966 *F, W, I, E,* 1967 *W, I, E,* 1968 *E, A,* 1969 *F, W, I, E, SA,* 1970 *F, W, I*
Tennent, J M (W of Scotland) 1909 *W, I, E,* 1910 *F, W, E*
Thom, D A (London Scottish) 1934 *W,* 1935 *W, I, E, NZ*
Thom, G (Kirkcaldy) 1920 *F, W, I, E*
Thom, J R (Watsonians) 1933 *W, E, I*
Thomson, A E (United Services) 1921 *F, W, E*
Thomson, A M (St Andrew's U) 1949 *I*
Thomson, B E (Oxford U) 1953 *F, W, I*
Thomson, I H M (Heriot's FP, Army) 1951 *W, I,* 1952 *F, W, I,* 1953 *I, E*
Thomson, J S (Glasgow Acads) 1871 *E*
Thomson, R H (London Scottish, PUC) 1960 *I, E, SA,* 1961 *F, SA, W, I, E,* 1963 *F, W, I, E,* 1964 *F, NZ, W*
Thomson, W H (W of Scotland) 1906 *SA*
Thomson, W J (W of Scotland) 1899 *W, E,* 1900 *W*

Timms, A B (Edinburgh U, Edinburgh Wands) 1896 *W*, 1900 *W, I*, 1901 *W, I, E*, 1902 *W, E*, 1903 *W, E*, 1904 *I, E*, 1905 *I, E*
Tod, H B (Gala) 1911 *F*
Tod, J (Watsonians) 1884 *W, I, E*, 1885 *W, I* 1,2, 1886 *W, I, E*
Todd, J K (Glasgow Acads) 1874 *E*, 1875 *E*
Tolmie, J M (Glasgow HSFP) 1922 *E*
Tomes, A J (Hawick) 1976 *E, I*, 1977 *E*, 1978 *I, F, W, E, NZ*, 1979 *W, E, I, F, NZ*, 1980 *F, W, E*, 1981 *F, W, E, I, NZ* 1,2, *R, A*, 1982 *E, I, F, W, A* 1,2, 1983 *I, F, W*, 1984 *W, E, I, F, R, A*, 1985 *W, E*, 1987 *I, F, E* (R), *[F, Z, R, NZ]*
Torrie, T J (Edinburgh Acads) 1877 *E*
Townsend, G P J (Gala, Northampton, Brive) 1993 *E* (R), 1994 *W, E, I, F, Arg* 1,2, 1995 *C, I, F, W, E, WS*, 1996 *I, F, W, E, NZ* 1,2, *A, It*, 1997 *W, E, I, F, A, SA*, 1998 *It, I, F, W, E, Fj, A* 1,2, *SA* (R), 1999 *W, E, It, I, F*
Tukalo, I (Selkirk) 1985 *I*, 1987 *I, F, W, E*, *[F, Z, R, NZ]*, 1988 *F, W, E, A*, 1989 *W, E, I, F, Fj*, 1990 *I, F, W, E, NZ* 1, 1991 *I, R*, *[J, Z, I, WS, E, NZ]*, 1992 *E, I, F, W, A* 1,2
Turk, A S (Langholm) 1971 *E* (R)
Turnbull, D J (Hawick) 1987 *[NZ]*, 1988 *F, E*, 1990 *E* (R), 1991 *F, W, E, I, R*, *[Z]*, 1993 *I, F, W, E*, 1994 *W*
Turnbull, F O (Kelso) 1951 *F, SA*
Turnbull, G O (W of Scotland) 1896 *I, E*, 1897 *I, E*, 1904 *W*
Turnbull, P (Edinburgh Acads) 1901 *W, I, E*, 1902 *W, I, E*
Turner, F H (Oxford U, Liverpool) 1911 *F, W, I, E*, 1912 *F, W, I, E, SA*, 1913 *F, W, I, E*, 1914 *I, E*
Turner, J W C (Gala) 1966 *W, A*, 1967 *F, W, I, E, NZ*, 1968 *F, W, I, E, A*, 1969 *F, W*, 1970 *A*, 1971 *F, W, I, E* (2[1C])

Usher, C M (United Services, Edinburgh Wands) 1912 *E*, 1913 *F, W, I, E*, 1914 *E*, 1920 *F, W, I, E*, 1921 *W, E*, 1922 *F, W, I, E*

Valentine, A R (RNAS, Anthorn) 1953 *F, W, I*
Valentine, D D (Hawick) 1947 *I, E*
Veitch, J P (Royal HSFP) 1882 *E*, 1883 *I*, 1884 *W, I, E*, 1885 *I* 1,2, 1886 *E*
Villar, C (Edinburgh Wands) 1876 *E*, 1877 *I, E*

Waddell, G H (London Scottish, Cambridge U) 1957 *E*, 1958 *F, W, A, I, E*, 1959 *F, W, I, E*, 1960 *I, E, SA*, 1961 *F*, 1962 *F, W, I, E*
Waddell, H (Glasgow Acads) 1924 *F, W, I, E*, 1925 *I, E*, 1926 *F, W, I, E*, 1927 *F, W, I, E*, 1930 *W*
Wade, A L (London Scottish) 1908 *E*
Wainwright, R I (Edinburgh Acads, West Hartlepool, Watsonians, Army, Dundee HSFP) 1992 *I* (R), *F, A* 1,2, 1993 *NZ*, 1994 *W, E*, 1995 *C, I, F, W, E, R*, *[Iv, Tg, F, NZ]*, *WS*, 1996 *I, F, W, E, NZ* 1,2, 1997 *W, E, I, F, SA*, 1998 *It, I, F, W, E, Fj, A* 1,2
Walker, A (W of Scotland) 1881 *I*, 1882 *E*, 1883 *W, I, E*
Walker, A W (Cambridge U, Birkenhead Park) 1931 *F, W, I, E*, 1932 *I*
Walker, J G (W of Scotland) 1882 *E*, 1883 *W*
Walker, M (Oxford U) 1952 *F*
Wallace, A C (Oxford U) 1923 *F*, 1924 *F, W, E*, 1925 *F, W, I, E*, 1926 *F*
Wallace, W M (Cambridge U) 1913 *E*, 1914 *W, I, E*
Wallace, M I (Glasgow High Kelvinside) 1996 *A, It*, 1997 *W*
Walls, W A (Glasgow Acads) 1882 *E*, 1883 *W, I, E*, 1884 *W, I, E*, 1886 *W, I, E*
Walter, M W (London Scottish) 1906 *I, E, SA*, 1907 *W, I*, 1908 *W, I*, 1910 *I*
Walton, P (Northampton, Newcastle) 1994 *E, I, F, Arg* 1,2, 1995 *[Iv]*, 1997 *W, E, I, F, SA* (R), 1998 *I, F, SA*, 1999 *W, E, It, I, F* (R)
Warren, J R (Glasgow Acads) 1914 *I*
Warren, R C (Glasgow Acads) 1922 *W, I*, 1930 *W, I, E*
Waters, F H (Cambridge U, London Scottish) 1930 *F, W, I, E*, 1932 *SA, W, I*
Waters, J A (Selkirk) 1933 *W, E, I*, 1934 *W, I, E*, 1935 *W, I, E, NZ*, 1936 *W, I, E*, 1937 *W, I, E*
Waters, J B (Cambridge U) 1904 *I, E*

Watherston, J G (Edinburgh Wands) 1934 *I, E*
Watherston, W R A (London Scottish) 1963 *F, W, I*
Watson, D H (Glasgow Acads) 1876 *E*, 1877 *I, E*
Watson, W S (Boroughmuir) 1974 *W, E, I, F*, 1975 *NZ*, 1977 *I, F, W*, 1979 *I, F*
Watt, A G J (Glasgow High Kelvinside) 1991 *[Z]*, 1993 *I, NZ*, 1994 *Arg* 2 (t & R)
Watt, A G M (Edinburgh Acads) 1947 *F, W, I, A*, 1948 *F, W*
Weatherstone, T G (Stewart's Coll FP) 1952 *E*, 1953 *I, E*, 1954 *F, NZ, I, E, W*, 1955 *F*, 1958 *W, A, I, E*, 1959 *W, I, E*
Weir, G W (Melrose, Newcastle) 1990 *Arg*, 1991 *R*, *[J, Z, I, WS, E, NZ]*, 1992 *E, I, F, W, A* 1,2, 1993 *I, F, W, E, NZ*, 1994 *W* (R), *E, I, F, SA*, 1995 *F* (R), *W, E, R*, *[Iv, Tg, F, NZ]*, *WS*, 1996 *I, F, W, E, NZ* 1,2, *A, It* (R), 1997 *W, E, I, F*, 1998 *It, I, F, W, E, SA*, 1999 *W*
Welsh, R (Watsonians) 1895 *W, I, E*, 1896 *W*
Welsh, R B (Hawick) 1967 *I, E*
Welsh, W B (Hawick) 1927 *A*, 1928 *F, W, I*, 1929 *I, E*, 1930 *F, W, I, E*, 1931 *F, W, I, E*, 1932 *SA, W, I, E*, 1933 *W, E, I*
Welsh, W H (Edinburgh U) 1900 *I, E*, 1901 *W, I, E*, 1902 *W, I, E*
Wemyss, A (Gala, Edinburgh Wands) 1914 *W, I*, 1920 *F, E*, 1922 *F, W, I*
West, L (Edinburgh U, West Hartlepool) 1903 *W, I, E*, 1905 *I, E, NZ*, 1906 *W, I, E*
Weston, V G (Kelvinside Acads) 1936 *I, E*
White, D B (Gala, London Scottish) 1982 *F, W, A* 1,2, 1987 *W, E*, *[F, R, NZ]*, 1988 *I, F, W, E, A*, 1989 *W, E, I, F, Fj, R*, 1990 *I, F, W, E, NZ* 1,2, 1991 *W, E, I, R*, *[J, Z, I, WS, E, NZ]*, 1992 *E, I, F, W*
White, D M (Kelvinside Acads) 1963 *F, W, I, E*
White, T B (Edinburgh Acads) 1888 *W, I*, 1889 *W*
Whittington, T P (Merchistonians) 1873 *E*
Whitworth, R J E (London Scottish) 1936 *I*
Whyte, D J (Edinburgh Wands) 1965 *W, I, E, SA*, 1966 *F, W, I, E, A*, 1967 *W, I, E*
Will, J G (Cambridge U) 1912 *F, W, I, E*, 1914 *W, I, E*
Wilson, A W (Dunfermline) 1931 *F, I, E*
Wilson, G A (Oxford U) 1949 *F, W, E*
Wilson, G R (Royal HSFP) 1886 *E*, 1890 *W, I, E*, 1891 *I*
Wilson, J H (Watsonians) 1953 *I*
Wilson, J S (St Andrew's U) 1931 *F, W, I, E*, 1932 *E*
Wilson, J S (United Services, London Scottish) 1908 *I*, 1909 *W*
Wilson, R (London Scottish) 1976 *E, I*, 1977 *E, I, F*, 1978 *I, F*, 1981 *R*, 1983 *I*
Wilson, R L (Gala) 1951 *F, W, I, E, SA*, 1953 *F, W, E*
Wilson, R W (W of Scotland) 1873 *E*, 1874 *E*
Wilson, S (Oxford U, London Scottish) 1964 *F, NZ, W, I, E*, 1965 *W, I, E, SA*, 1966 *F, W, I, A*, 1967 *W, I, E, NZ*, 1968 *F, W, I, E*
Wood, A (Royal HSFP) 1873 *E*, 1874 *E*, 1875 *E*
Wood, G (Gala) 1931 *W, I*, 1932 *W, I, E*
Woodburn, J C (Kelvinside Acads) 1892 *I*
Woodrow, A N (Glasgow Acads) 1887 *I, W, E*
Wotherspoon, W (W of Scotland) 1891 *I*, 1892 *I*, 1893 *W, E*, 1894 *W, I, E*
Wright, F A (Edinburgh Acads) 1932 *E*
Wright, H B (Watsonians) 1894 *W*
Wright, K M (London Scottish) 1929 *F, W, I, E*
Wright, P H (Boroughmuir) 1992 *A* 1,2, 1993 *F, W, E*, 1994 *W*, 1995 *C, I, F, W, E, R*, *[Iv, Tg, F, NZ]*, 1996 *W, E, NZ* 1
Wright, R W J (Edinburgh Wands) 1973 *F*
Wright, S T H (Stewart's Coll FP) 1949 *E*
Wright, T (Hawick) 1947 *A*
Wyllie, D S (Stewart's-Melville FP) 1984 *A*, 1985 *W* (R), *E*, 1987 *I, F*, *[F, Z, R, NZ]*, 1989 *R*, 1991 *R*, *[J* (R), *Z]*, 1993 *NZ* (R), 1994 *W* (R), *E, I, F*

Young, A H (Edinburgh Acads) 1874 *E*
Young, E T (Glasgow Acads) 1914 *E*
Young, R G (Watsonians) 1970 *W*
Young, T E B (Durham) 1911 *F*
Young, W B (Cambridge U, London Scottish) 1937 *W, I, E*, 1938 *W, I, E*, 1939 *W, I, E*, 1948 *E*

SCOTTISH INTERNATIONAL RECORDS (*up to 30 April 1999*)

MATCH RECORDS

MOST CONSECUTIVE TEST WINS

6 1925 *F, W, I, E,* 1926 *F, W*
6 1989 *Fj, R,* 1990 *I, F, W, E*

MOST CONSECUTIVE TESTS WITHOUT DEFEAT

P	W	D	Period
9	6*	3	1885–87
6	6	0	1925–26
6	6	0	1989–90
6	4	2	1877–80
6	5	1	1983–84

* includes an abandoned match

MOST POINTS IN A MATCH
by the team

Pts	Opp	Venue	Year
89	Iv	Rustenburg	1995
60	Z	Wellington	1987
55	R	Dunedin	1987
51	Z	Murrayfield	1991
49	A	Murrayfield	1990
49	R	Murrayfield	1995

by a player
44 by A G Hastings v Ivory Coast at Rustenburg — 1995
31 by A G Hastings v Tonga at Pretoria — 1995
27 by A G Hastings v Romania at Dunedin — 1987
21 by A G Hastings v England at Murrayfield — 1986
21 by A G Hastings v Romania at Bucharest — 1986

MOST TRIES IN A MATCH
by the team

T	Opp	Venue	Year
13	Iv	Rustenburg	1995
12	W	Raeburn Place	1887
11	Z	Wellington	1987
9	R	Dunedin	1987
9	Arg	Murrayfield	1990

by a player
5 by G C Lindsay v Wales at Raeburn Place — 1887
4 by W A Stewart v Ireland at Inverleith — 1913

4 by I S Smith v France at Inverleith — 1925
4 by I S Smith v Wales at Swansea — 1925
4 by A G Hastings v Ivory Coast at Rustenburg — 1995

MOST CONVERSIONS IN A MATCH
by the team

C	Opp	Venue	Year
9	Iv	Rustenburg	1995
8	Z	Wellington	1987
8	R	Dunedin	1987

by a player
9 by A G Hastings v Ivory Coast at Rustenburg — 1995
8 by A G Hastings v Zimbabwe at Wellington — 1987
8 by A G Hastings v Romania at Dunedin — 1987

MOST PENALTY GOALS IN A MATCH
by the team

P	Opp	Venue	Year
8	Tg	Pretoria	1995
6	F	Murrayfield	1986

by a player
8 by A G Hastings v Tonga at Pretoria — 1995
6 by A G Hastings v France at Murrayfield — 1986

MOST DROPPED GOALS IN A MATCH
by the team

D	Opp	Venue	Year
3	I	Murrayfield	1973
2	several instances		

by a player
2 by R C MacKenzie v Ireland at Belfast — 1877
2 by N J Finlay v Ireland at Glasgow — 1880
2 by B M Simmers v Wales at Murrayfield — 1965
2 by D W Morgan v Ireland at Murrayfield — 1973
2 by B M Gossman v France at Parc des Princes — 1983

2 by J Y Rutherford v New Zealand at Murrayfield	1983
2 by J Y Rutherford v Wales at Murrayfield	1985
2 by J Y Rutherford v Ireland at Murrayfield	1987
2 by C M Chalmers v England at Twickenham	1995

Lock A J Tomes	48	1976–87
Flanker J Jeffrey	40	1984–91
No. 8 D B White	29	1982–92
E W Peters	29	1995–99

CAREER RECORDS

MOST CAPPED PLAYERS

Caps	Player	Career
65	S Hastings	1986–97
61	A G Hastings	1986–95
59	C M Chalmers	1989–98
52	J M Renwick	1972–84
52	C T Deans	1978–87
52	A G Stanger	1989–98
52	G W Weir	1990–99
51	A R Irvine	1972–82
50	A B Carmichael	1967–78
48	A J Tomes	1976–87
48	A P Burnell	1989–99

MOST CONSECUTIVE TESTS

Tests	Player	Span
49	A B Carmichael	1967–78
40	H F McLeod	1954–62
37	J M Bannerman	1921–29
35	A G Stanger	1989–94

MOST TESTS AS CAPTAIN

Tests	Captain	Span
25	D M B Sole	1989–92
20	A G Hastings	1993–95
19	J McLauchlan	1973–79
16	R I Wainright	1995–98
15	M C Morrison	1899–1904
15	A R Smith	1957–62
15	A R Irvine	1980–82

MOST TESTS IN INDIVIDUAL POSITIONS

Full-back A G Hastings	61	1986–95
Wing A G Stanger	47	1989–98
Centre S Hastings	63	1986–97
Fly-half C M Chalmers	55	1989–98
Scrum-half R J Laidlaw	47	1980–88
Prop A B Carmichael	50	1967–78
Hooker C T Deans	52	1978–87

MOST POINTS IN TESTS

Pts	Player	Tests	Career
667	A G Hastings	61	1986–95
273	A R Irvine	51	1972–82
210	P W Dods	23	1983–91
166	C M Chalmers	59	1989–98
106	A G Stanger	52	1989–98

MOST TRIES IN TESTS

Tries	Player	Tests	Career
24	I S Smith	32	1924–33
24	A G Stanger	52	1989–98
17	A G Hastings	61	1986–95
15	I Tukalo	37	1985–92
14	A V Tait	22	1987–99

MOST CONVERSIONS IN TESTS

Cons	Player	Tests	Career
86	A G Hastings	61	1986–95
26	P W Dods	23	1983–91
25	A R Irvine	51	1972–82
19	D Drysdale	26	1923–29
14	F H Turner	15	1911–14
14	R J S Shepherd	20	1995–98
14	K M Logan	39	1992–99

MOST PENALTY GOALS IN TESTS

Pens	Player	Tests	Career
140	A G Hastings	61	1986–95
61	A R Irvine	51	1972–82
50	P W Dods	23	1983–91
32	C M Chalmers	59	1989–98
21	M Dods	8	1994–96
21	R J S Shepherd	20	1995–98

MOST DROPPED GOALS IN TESTS

Drops	Player	Tests	Career
12	J Y Rutherford	42	1979–87
9	C M Chalmers	59	1989–98
7	I R McGeechan	32	1972–79
6	D W Morgan	21	1973–78
5	H Waddell	15	1924–30

INTERNATIONAL CHAMPIONSHIP RECORDS

Record	Detail	Holder	Set
Most points in season	120	in four matches	1999
Most tries in season	17	in four matches	1925
Highest score	38	38–10 v Ireland	1997
Biggest win	28	31–3 v France	1912
	28	38–10 v Ireland	1997
Highest score conceded	51	16–51 v France	1998
Biggest defeat	35	16–51 v France	1998
Most appearances	42	J M Renwick	1972–83
Most points in matches	288	A G Hastings	1986–95
Most points in season	56	A G Hastings	1995
Most points in match	21	A G Hastings	v England, 1986
Most tries in matches	24	I S Smith	1924–33
Most tries in season	8	I S Smith	1925
Most tries in match	5	G C Lindsay	v Wales, 1887
Most cons in matches	20	A G Hastings	1986–95
Most cons in season	11	K M Logan	1999
Most cons in match	5	F H Turner	v France, 1912
	5	J W Allan	v England, 1931
	5	R J S Shepherd	v Ireland, 1997
Most pens in matches	77	A G Hastings	1986–95
Most pens in season	14	A G Hastings	1986
Most pens in match	6	A G Hastings	v France, 1986
Most drops in matches	8	J Y Rutherford	1979–87
	8	C M Chalmers	1989–98
Most drops in season	3	J Y Rutherford	1987
Most drops in match	2	on several occasions	

MAJOR TOUR RECORDS

Record	Detail	Year	Place
Most individual points	69 by R J S Shepherd	1996	New Zealand
Most points in match	24 by D W Morgan	1975 v Wellington	Wellington (NZ
	24 by A R Irvine	1981 v King Country	Taumarunui (N
	24 by A R Irvine	1981 v Wairarapa/ Bush	Masterton (NZ
Most tries in match	3 by A R Smith	1960 v E Transvaal	Springs (SA)
	3 by D A Stark	1996 v Bay of Plenty	Rotorua (NZ)

MISCELLANEOUS RECORDS

Record	Holder	Detail
Longest Test career	W C W Murdoch	14 seasons, 1934–35 to 1947–48
Youngest Test cap	N J Finlay	17 yrs 36 days in 1875*
Oldest Test cap	J McLauchlan	37 yrs 210 days in 1979

* C Reid, also 17 yrs 36 days on debut in 1881, was a day *older* than Finlay, having lived through an extra leap-year day.

SCOTTISH INTERNATIONAL CAREER RECORDS (*up to 30 April 1999*)

Player	Debut	Caps since last season	Caps	T	C	PG	DG	Pts
R J S Shepherd	1995 v WS	1998 *Fj*(t), *A* 1,2	20	2	14	21	1	104
D J Lee	1998 v I	1998 *Fj*, *A* 1,2, *SA*	8	0	4	7	0	29
G H Metcalfe	1998 v A	1998 *A* 1,2, 1999 *W*, *E*, *It*, *I*, *F*	7	0	0	0	0	0
S L Longstaff	1998 v F	1998 *Fj*, *A* 1,2, 1999 *It*(R), *I*(R)	8	1	0	0	0	5
C A Joiner	1994 v Arg	1998 *A* 2(R)	21	3	0	0	0	15
H R Gilmour	1998 v Fj	1998 *Fj*	1	1	0	0	0	5
K M Logan	1992 v A	1998 *SA*(R), 1999 *W*, *E*, *It*, *I*, *F*	39	8	14	8	0	92
M J M Mayer	1998 v SA	1998 *SA*	1	0	0	0	0	0
J A Leslie	1998 v SA	1998 *SA*, 1999 *W*, *E*, *It*, *I*, *F*	6	1	0	0	0	5
C A Murray	1998 v E	1998 *Fj*, *A* 1,2,*SA*, 1999 *W*, *E*, *It*, *I*, *F*	10	3	0	0	0	15
I C Jardine	1993 v NZ	1998 *Fj*	18	0	0	0	0	0
A V Tait	1987 v F	1998 *SA*, 1999 *W*(R), *E*, *It*, *I*, *F*	22	14	0	0	0	66
G P J Townsend	1993 v E	1998 *Fj*, *A* 1,2, *SA*(R), 1999 *W*, *E*, *It*, *I*, *F*	41	10	0	0	3	59
C M Chalmers	1989 v W		59	5	11	32	9	166
D W Hodge	1997 v F	1998 *A* 2(R), *SA*, 1999 *W*	6	2	1	3	0	21
G G Burns	1999 v It	1999 *It*(R)	1	0	0	0	0	0
G Armstrong	1988 v A	1998 *SA*(R), 1999 *W*, *E*, *I*, *F*	45	4	0	0	0	16
I T Fairley	1999 v It	1999 *It*, *I*(R)	2	0	0	0	0	0
B W Redpath	1993 v NZ	1998 *Fj*, *A* 1,2, *SA*	28	0	0	0	0	0
G C Bulloch	1997 v SA	1998 *Fj*, *A* 1, *SA*, 1999 *W*, *E*, *It*, *I*, *F*	14	1	0	0	0	5
S J Brotherstone	1999 v I	1999 *I*(R)	1	0	0	0	0	0
K D McKenzie	1994 v Arg	1998 *A* 1(R),2	14	1	0	0	0	5
G Graham	1997 v A	1999 *F*(R)	6	0	0	0	0	0
G R McIlwham	1998 v Fj	1998 *Fj*, *A* 2(R)	2	0	0	0	0	0
M C Proudfoot	1998 v Fj	1998 *Fj*, *A* 1,2	3	0	0	0	0	0
T J Smith	1997 v E	1998 *SA*, 1999 *W*, *E*, *It*, *I*	8	0	0	0	0	0
D I W Hilton	1995 v C	1998 *A* 1,2, *SA*(R), 1999 *W*(R), *E*(R), *It*(R), *I*(R), *F*	34	1	0	0	0	5
M J Stewart	1996 v It	1998 *Fj*(R)	12	0	0	0	0	0
A P Burnell	1989 v E	1998 *SA*, 1999 *W*, *E*, *It*, *I*, *F*	48	1	0	0	0	5
G W Weir	1990 v Arg	1998 *SA*, 1999 *W*	52	4	0	0	0	19
S Murray	1997 v A	1998 *Fj*, *A* 1,2, *SA*, 1999 *W*, *E*, *It*, *I*, *F*	12	2	0	0	0	10
A I Reed	1993 v I	1999 *It*(R), *F*(R)	17	0	0	0	0	0
S J Campbell	1995 v C	1998 *Fj*(R), *A* 2(R)	17	0	0	0	0	0

M D Leslie	1998 v SA	1998 *SA*(R), 1999 *W*, *E*, *It*, *I*, *F*	6	2	0	0	0	10
R I Wainwright	1992 v I	1998 *Fj*, *A* 1,2	37	3	0	0	0	14
P Walton	1994 v E	1998 *SA*, 1999 *W*, *E*, *It*, *I*, *F*(R)	19	3	0	0	0	15
A J Roxburgh	1997 v A	1998 *Fj*, *A* 1(R),2(R)	8	0	0	0	0	0
G L Simpson	1998 v A	1998 *A* 1,2	2	0	0	0	0	0
A C Pountney	1998 v SA	1998 *SA*, 1999 *W*(t&R), *E*(R), *It*(t&R), *I*(R), *F*	6	0	0	0	0	0
S D Holmes	1998 v It		3	0	0	0	0	0
S B Grimes	1997 v A	1998 *Fj*, *A* 1,2, 1999 *W*(R), *E*, *It*, *I*, *F*	13	1	0	0	0	5
E W Peters	1995 v C	1998 *Fj*, *A* 1,2, *SA*, 1999 *W*, *E*, *It*, *I*	29	5	0	0	0	25
S J Reid	1995 v WS	1999 *F*	2	0	0	0	0	0

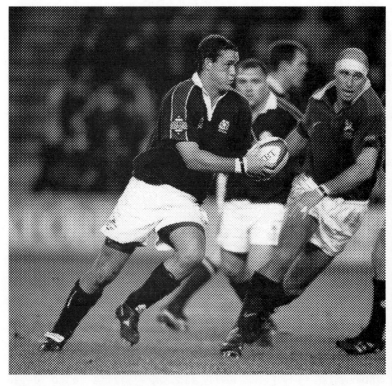

Like father, like son. Martin Leslie, son of former All Black captain Andy, displays typical family fervour in taking on the Springbok defence during Scotland's 35-10 defeat at Murrayfield in November 1998.

SCOTTISH CLUBS 1998-99

Boroughmuir

Year of formation 1919 (Boroughmuir FP until 1974)
Ground Meggetland, Colinton Road, Edinburgh EH14 1AS Tel: (0131) 443 7571
Web site http://www.boroughmuirrfc.co.uk/
Colours Blue and green quarters
Captain 1998-99 A Knight
SRU Tennent's Velvet Championship 1998-99 Div 1 9th (relegated)
SRU Tennent's Velvet Cup 1998-99 Lost 15-40 to Kelso (semi-finals)

Boroughmuir, though coached by two former international players, Sean Lineen and
Iain Paxton, lost their proud record of never having been relegated after 25 years in
the First Division. Their poor record in the first half of the league was a severe
handicap from which they could not recover – their only win in that time was at
home against Stirling County by 36-24. Boroughmuir halted the losing run with a
second victory over Stirling and followed that up with a 33-18 home win over
championship contenders Glasgow Hawks. However, not even a strong finish, with
three wins in four games, could save Boroughmuir. Their fate was sealed when West
of Scotland picked up a bonus point in injury-time at Currie on the same day that
Kelso eliminated Boroughmuir from the cup with a 40-15 win at Meggetland.

League Record 1998-99

Date	Venue	Opponents	Result	Scorers
5 Sep	A	Currie	24-37	*T:* Kiddie, McLean 2, McKinley *C:* Kiddie 2
12 Sep	H	Stirling County	36-24	*T:* Couper, Finnie 2, Kiddie, Lightoller, McKinlay *C:* Kiddie 3
19 Sep	A	Glasgow Hawks	17-38	*T:* Jackson, Rutherford *C:* Kiddie 2 *PG:* Kiddie
26 Sep	H	Jed-Forest	13-17	*T:* Couper, Cadzow *PG:* Kiddie
3 Oct	A	Watsonians	12-22	*T:* Couper 2 *C:* Kiddie
10 Oct	H	Melrose	12-38	*T:* Kiddie, Roberts *C:* Kiddie
17 Oct	A	West of Scotland	13-20	*T:* Cadzow, Clapperton *PG:* Kiddie
24 Oct	H	Heriot's FP	11-31	*T:* Kiddie *PG:* Kiddie 2
31 Oct	A	Hawick	15-33	*T:* Graham 2 *C:* Reekie *PG:* Reekie
12 Dec	A	Stirling County	56-13	*T:* Clapperton, Fitzgerald, Graham, Henwood, Howarth, Knight, McLean 2 *C:* Howarth 5 *PG:* Howarth 2
19 Dec	H	Glasgow Hawks	33-18	*T:* Cunningham, Graham, Martyn 2, McLean *C:* Howarth 4
16 Jan	A	Jed-Forest	19-23	*T:* Kiddie, McLean *PG:* Howarth 3
23 Jan	H	Watsonians	6-16	*PG:* Howarth 2
30 Jan	A	Melrose	17-18	*T:* Kiddie 2 *C:* Howarth 2 *PG:* Howarth
27 Feb	H	West of Scotland	25-24	*T:* Fitzgerald, Graham, Kiddie, Murray *C:* Howarth *PG:* Howarth
13 Mar	A	Heriot's FP	13-42	*T:* Couper *C:* Howarth *PG:* Howarth 2
21 Mar	H	Currie	22-17	*T:* Howarth 2, Murray *C:* Howarth 2 *PG:* Howarth
27 Mar	H	Hawick	38-23	*T:* Clapperton, Knight, Macdonald 2 *C:* Howarth 3 *PG:* Howarth 4

Currie

Year of formation 1970
Ground Malleny Park, Balerno, Edinburgh EH14 5HA Tel: (0131) 449 2432
Colours Amber and black
Captain 1998-99 D Rogerson

SRU Tennent's Velvet Championship 1998-99 Div 1 4th
SRU Tennent's Velvet Cup 1998-99 Lost 13-19 to Hawick (4th round)

Currie were among the championship contenders until well into the latter half of the league season despite two defeats by Glasgow Hawks. The first loss to Hawks was immediately followed by a 31-28 defeat away to Heriot's, the ultimate champions, but it was a home setback against Jed-Forest that finally knocked Currie out of the title race. It was the narrowest of defeats by Jed, Chris Richards kicking an injury-time penalty goal in a 21-20 win for the Borderers, who only eight days earlier had lost their home league match to Currie by 27-55. Ally Donaldson was once again Currie's leading points-scorer, with 155 points.

League Record 1998-99

Date	Venue	Opponents	Result	Scorers
5 Sep	H	Boroughmuir	37-24	T: Craig, Hardie, Reed, Ward, Watt C: Donaldson 3 PG: Donaldson 2
12 Sep	A	Melrose	17-8	T: Craig, Reed C: Donaldson 2 PG: Donaldson
19 Sep	H	Stirling County	27-17	T: Blackie, Bowie, Rogerson C: Donaldson 3 PG: Donaldson 2
26 Sep	A	West of Scotland	23-8	T: Caldwell 2, Tonkin C: Donaldson PG: Donaldson DG: Donaldson
3 Oct	H	Glasgow Hawks	21-31	T: Caldwell, Reed C: Donaldson PG: Donaldson 3
10 Oct	A	Heriot's FP	28-31	T: Caldwell, Plumb, Reed C: Donaldson 2 PG: Donaldson 3
24 Oct	H	Hawick	31-22	T: Black, Caldwell, Reed, Russell C: Donaldson 4 PG: Donaldson
31 Oct	A	Watsonians	24-18	T: Caldwell, Reed C: Donaldson PG: Donaldson 4
12 Dec	H	Melrose	19-18	T: Donaldson C: Donaldson PG: Donaldson 4
19 Dec	A	Stirling County	18-10	T: Laugerson, penalty try C: Donaldson PG: Donaldson 2
23 Jan	A	Glasgow Hawks	8-26	T: Rogerson PG: Donaldson
30 Jan	H	Heriot's FP	9-3	PG: Donaldson 3
27 Feb	A	Jed-Forest	55-27	T: Armstrong, Bowie, Caldwell, Reedie 3, Thomson C: Donaldson 7 PG: Donaldson 2
7 Mar	H	Jed-Forest	20-21	T: Bowie 2 C: Donaldson 2 PG: Donaldson 2
13 Mar	A	Hawick	35-7	T: Barrett, Clark, Thomson 2 C: Barrett 3 PG: Barrett 3
21 Mar	A	Boroughmuir	17-22	T: Clark 2, Watt C: Barrett
3 Apr	H	West of Scotland	10-29	T: Reed 2
17 Apr	H	Watsonians	35-21	T: Armstrong, Barrett, Bowie, Caldwell, Sneddon C: Barrett 5

Gala

Year of formation 1875
Ground Netherdale, Nether Road, Galashiels TD1 3HE Tel: (01896) 755145
Colours Maroon
Captain 1998-99 R J Gray
SRU Tennent's Velvet Championship 1998-99 Div 2 *Winners*
SRU Tennent's Velvet Cup 1998-99 *Winners* – beat Kelso 8-3 (final)

Gala had a highly successful season, not only returning to the top flight as Second Division champions but also winning the Scottish Cup and the prestigious Melrose Sevens trophy. The style of rugby engendered by player-coach Gary Parker was adventurous and profitable and they earned enough bonus points to compensate for having a slightly inferior playing record than Kelso, the eventual runners-up. A mid-season stumble, with away defeats by Kelso and Aberdeen Grammar, hauled Gala back to a share of the lead with Kelso, and a further flow of success was interrupted only by a home defeat by Kirkcaldy. That result set up a head-to-head decider for the title between Gala and Kelso at Netherdale, a match that the home team won 24-14. Parker was a major contributor to the team's success with 152 points, including eight tries. Chris Paterson, the Scotland under-21 stand-off and cup final match-winner, also ran in eight tries in a tally of 126 points.

League Record 1998-99

Date	Venue	Opponents	Result	Scorers
5 Sep	H	Aberdeen GSFP	32-14	*T:* Parker, penalty try *C:* C Paterson 2 *PG:* Parker 2, C Paterson 4
12 Sep	A	Biggar	21-22	*T:* Boland, McCorkindale *C:* Parker *PG:* Parker 2 *DG:* C Paterson
19 Sep	A	Selkirk	34-13	*T:* Boland, D Gray, Hines, Parker *C:* Parker *PG:* Parker 4
26 Sep	H	Dundee HSFP	31-22	*T:* Dalziel *C:* Parker *PG:* Parker 8
3 Oct	A	Edinburgh Acads	43-13	*T:* K Amos, Andrew, Boland, Parker, Harrison, Hines *C:* Parker 5 *PG:* Parker
10 Oct	H	Kilmarnock	38-3	*T:* K Amos, Dalziel 2, Hines, Parker, Robson *C:* Parker 4
17 Oct	A	Kirkcaldy	34-24	*T:* J Amos 2, Parker, C Paterson *C:* Parker 4 *PG:* Parker *DG:* C Paterson
24 Oct	H	Musselburgh	38-3	*T:* K Amos, Hines, Parker 2, Townsend 2 *C:* Parker 4
31 Oct	A	Kelso	10-14	*T:* K Amos *C:* Parker *DG:* C Paterson
7 Nov	A	Aberdeen GSFP	12-16	*PG:* Parker 4
12 Dec	H	Biggar	31-5	*T:* Boland, Changleng 2, Dods *C:* C Paterson *PG:* C Paterson 3
19 Dec	H	Selkirk	34-3	*T:* Changleng, C Paterson 2, Weir, penalty try *C:* C Paterson 3 *PG:* C Paterson
16 Jan	A	Dundee HSFP	36-12	*T:* Boland, Dods, Hines, C Paterson, Townsend *C:* C Paterson 4 *PG:* C Paterson
23 Jan	H	Edinburgh Acads	30-0	*T:* J Amos 2, Dods, C Paterson *C:* C Paterson 2 *PG:* Paterson 2
30 Jan	A	Kilmarnock	25-12	*T:* Boland, Brown, C Paterson *C:* C Paterson 2 *PG:* C Paterson *DG:* C Paterson
27 Feb	H	Kirkcaldy	18-34	*T:* R Scott, Townsend 2 *PG:* C Paterson
13 Mar	A	Musselburgh	32-18	*T:* Dods, Hines, C Paterson 2, Robson *C:* C Paterson 2 *PG:* C Paterson
27 Mar	H	Kelso	24-14	*T:* J Amos, Parker, Shepherd, Townsend *C:* Parker 2

Glasgow Hawks

Year of formation 1997 (association of Glasgow Academicals and GHK, the latter a 1982 amalgamation of Glasgow High RFC and Kelvinside Academicals)
Grounds New Anniesland, Helensburgh Drive, Glasgow Tel: (0141) 959 4569 Old Anniesland, 637 Crow Road, Glasgow Tel: (0141) 959 1154
Web site http://www.glasgowhawks.com/
Colours Red, white and back bands divided by narrow green stripes
Captain 1998-99 D Wilson
SRU Tennent's Velvet Championship 1998-99 Div 1 3rd
SRU Tennent's Velvet Cup 1998-99 Lost 10-13 to Kelso (5th round)

Despite a home defeat by Heriot's on the league's opening day, Glasgow Hawks stayed on in the championship race until the final strides, finishing third behind Heriot's and Melrose. They avenged the opening defeat when they visited Goldenacre and won 22-17, picking up a bonus point as well, but Hawks' cause was severely handicapped by two December defeats – at home against Hawick by only 13-12, and then by 33-18 away to Boroughmuir, who were to be relegated to the Second Division. Hawks could have taken the lead in the table had they done better than a 9-9 draw with Watsonians at Myreside in February, and it was only a 32-15 defeat at Melrose that eventually removed the Glasgow challengers from contention. New Zealander Eugene Martin kicked 139 of Hawks' league points.

League Record 1998-99

Date	Venue	Opponents	Result	Scorers
5 Sep	H	Heriot's FP	13-31	*T:* Little, Wilson *PG:* Harris
12 Sep	A	Hawick	25-19	*T:* Hawkes 2, Mathewson *C:* Martin 2 *PG:* Martin 2
19 Sep	H	Boroughmuir	38-17	*T:* Dunlop, Hawkes, Mathewson, Plastow, F Wallace, Wilson *C:* Martin 4
26 Sep	A	Stirling County	21-16	*T:* Dunlop 2, Hutton *PG:* Martin 2
3 Oct	A	Currie	31-21	*T:* Hutton, Wilson, penalty try *C:* Martin 2 *PG:* Harris, Martin 3
10 Oct	H	Jed-Forest	28-7	*T:* Harris, Little 2, Ness *C:* Martin 4
24 Oct	H	Melrose	20-8	*T:* Ness *PG:* Martin 5
31 Oct	A	West of Scotland	51-0	*T:* Dunlop, Harris, Hawkes 2, McGrandles, Plastow 2, F Wallace, Wilson *C:* Martin 3
7 Nov	A	Heriot's FP	22-17	*T:* Afuakwah, Hawkes, Little, M Wallace *C:* Martin
12 Dec	H	Hawick	12-13	*T:* Dunlop, Horton *C:* Harris
19 Dec	A	Boroughmuir	18-33	*T:* McFarlane, penalty try *C:* Harris *PG:* Harris 2
16 Jan	H	Stirling County	41-6	*T:* Harris, Mathewson, Ness 2, Plastow *C:* Martin 5 *PG:* Martin 2
23 Jan	H	Currie	26-8	*T:* Mathewson, M Wallace *C:* Martin 2 *PG:* Martin 4
30 Jan	A	Jed-Forest	15-10	*T:* Plastow 2 *C:* Martin *PG:* Martin
13 Feb	A	Watsonians	9-9	*PG:* Martin 3
27 Feb	H	Watsonians	30-10	*T:* Bassi, Docherty, Mathewson, Plastow *C:* Martin 2 *PG:* Martin 2
13 Mar	A	Melrose	15-32	*T:* Hawkes 2 *C:* Martin *PG:* Martin
27 Mar	H	West of Scotland	22-16	*T:* Harris, Mathewson, M Wallace *C:* Martin 2 *PG:* Martin

Hawick

Year of formation 1873
Ground Mansfield Park, Mansfield Road, Hawick Tel: (01450) 737429
Colours Green
Captain 1998-99 G Sharp
SRU Tennent's Velvet Championship 1998-99 Div 1 5th
SRU Tennent's Velvet Cup 1998-99 Lost 8-16 to Boroughmuir (5th round)

Hawick had a strangely inconsistent league season in which six successive wins, four by less than five points, were sandwiched by a slow start and a slack finish. They won only two of their first seven matches, but by the time they edged West of Scotland by 26-25 on their visit to Burnbrae in late January, with Gary Murdie kicking six penalty goals, it seemed that Hawick might be surging through for a late challenge. However, their only other success was to complete a double over Stirling County. West were the only other club whom Hawick beat twice. Conversely, Hawick lost twice to both Heriot's FP, the eventual champions, and Melrose. Murdie was Hawick's leading scorer in the league programme with 126 points whereas Ross Cook, the Scotland under-19 international wing, topped the try list with eight.

League Record 1998-99

Date	Venue	Opponents	Result	Scorers
12 Sep	H	Glasgow Hawks	19-25	*T:* D Landels, Reid *PG:* Murdie 2, Sharp
19 Sep	A	Jed-Forest	13-28	*T:* Murray *C:* Sharp *PG:* Murray *DG:* Sharp
26 Sep	H	Watsonians	15-6	*T:* D Landels, Murray *C:* Sharp *PG:* Murray
3 Oct	A	Melrose	10-51	*T:* Murray *C:* Murray *DG:* McCrae
10 Oct	H	West of Scotland	9-7	*PG:* Murdie 3
17 Oct	A	Heriot's FP	22-29	*T:* Stevenson *C:* Murdie *PG:* Murdie 5
24 Oct	A	Currie	22-31	*T:* Cook, McCrae, Reid *C:* Murdie 2 *PG:* Murdie
31 Oct	H	Boroughmuir	33-15	*T:* Cook 2, Douglas, M Landels, Murdie *C:* Murdie *PG:* Murdie 2
7 Nov	H	Stirling County	29-15	*T:* Cook 2, Douglas, Keown, Murdie *C:* Murdie 2
12 Dec	A	Glasgow Hawks	13-12	*T:* Cook *C:* Murdie *PG:* Murdie 2
19 Dec	H	Jed-Forest	25-21	*T:* Cook, Robbards *PG:* Murdie 5
23 Jan	H	Melrose	27-25	*T:* Cook, Douglas 3, penalty try *C:* Murdie
30 Jan	A	West of Scotland	26-25	*T:* Sharp *PG:* Murdie 6 *DG:* McCrae
27 Feb	H	Heriot's FP	21-47	*T:* Cranston 2, Gray *PG:* Murdie 2
7 Mar	A	Stirling County	24-14	*T:* Cranston, Suddon, Turnbull *C:* Murdie 2, Sharp *PG:* Sharp
13 Mar	H	Currie	7-35	*T:* Suddon *C:* Murdie
27 Mar	A	Boroughmuir	23-38	*T:* Cranston, Imray *C:* Murdie 2 *PG:* Murdie 2 *DG:* McCrae
3 Apr	A	Watsonians	0-31	

Heriot's FP

Year of formation 1890
Ground Goldenacre, Bangholm Terrace, Edinburgh EH3 5QN Tel: (0131) 552 5925
Colours Blue with white horizontal stripes
Captain 1998-99 J Bryce
SRU Tennent's Velvet Championship 1998-99 Div 1 *Winners*
SRU Tennent's Velvet Cup 1998-99 Lost 15-16 to Boroughmuir (quarter-finals)

A mainly young Heriot's team responded to the 37-year-old Jock Bryce's lead to win the national club championship for the second time, 20 years after their first success. They lost four matches on the way to the title, including both games against Melrose. The first of those, a 23-20 defeat at home in September, knocked Heriot's from the top of the table, but by the next time they were beaten, 22-17 at home against Hawks, they had enough in hand to stay at the top. Gordon Ross, the Scotland under-21 stand-off, scored 265 of their points with four tries, 49 conversions, 47 penalty goals and two dropped goals. Heriot's had exceptional pace on the wings with Stewart Walker and Charlie Keenan. Walker ran in 16 tries, including four in Heriot's 68-16 demolition of Stirling County at Goldenacre in October. In a highly mobile pack none made more of an impression than the 20-year-old Simon Taylor.

League Record 1998-99

Date	Venue	Opponents	Result	Scorers
5 Sep	A	Glasgow Hawks	31-13	*T:* Binnie, Keenan 2, Lawson *C:* Ross *PG:* Ross 3

12 Sep	H	Jed-Forest	44-17	*T:* Lawrie, Smith, S Taylor, Walker 2 *C:* Ross 5 *PG:* Ross 3
19 Sep	A	Watsonians	44-19	*T:* Smith, Stent, S Taylor, Walker *C:* Ross 3 *PG:* Ross 6
26 Sep	H	Melrose	23-30	*T:* A Dall, Rutherford 2 *C:* Ross *PG:* Ross 2
3 Oct	A	West of Scotland	45-14	*T:* Keenan, McVie 2, Proctor, Short, Walker *C:* Ross 3 *PG:* Ross 3
10 Oct	H	Currie	31-28	*T:* Proctor, Short, S Taylor *C:* Ross 2 *PG:* Ross 4
17 Oct	H	Hawick	29-22	*T:* McVie, Proctor, S Taylor, Walker *C:* Ross 3 *PG:* Ross
24 Oct	A	Boroughmuir	31-11	*T:* Lawson, Ross, J Taylor *C:* Ross 2 *PG:* Ross 3 *DG:* Ross
31 Oct	H	Stirling County	68-16	*T:* Lawson, Proctor, Ross, Stent 2, J Taylor, S Taylor, Walker 4 *C:* Ross 5 *PG:* Ross
7 Nov	H	Glasgow Hawks	17-22	*T:* Bryce, Stent *C:* Ross 2 *DG:* Ross
12 Dec	A	Jed-Forest	32-9	*T:* Boswell, Ross, S Taylor 2 *C:* Ross 3 *PG:* Ross 2
19 Dec	H	Watsonians	32-19	*T:* Keenan, Melvin, Walker *C:* Ross *PG:* Ross 5
16 Jan	A	Melrose	3-22	*PG:* Ross
23 Jan	H	West of Scotland	23-12	*T:* Keenan, Ross, Walker *C:* Ross *PG:* Ross 2
30 Jan	A	Currie	3-9	*PG:* Ross
27 Feb	A	Hawick	47-21	*T:* Short, Smith, Walker 3 *C:* Ross 5 *PG:* Ross 4
13 Mar	H	Boroughmuir	42-13	*T:* G Dall, Keenan, J Taylor, Walker 2 *C:* Ross 4 *PG:* Ross 3
27 Mar	A	Stirling County	75-25	*T:* A Dall, G Dall, Keenan 3, Lawson, McVie, Melvin, Turnbull, penalty try *C:* Ross 8 *PG:* Ross 3

Jed-Forest

Year of formation 1884
Ground Riverside Park, Jedburgh Tel: (01835) 862 855 and (01835) 862 232
Colours Royal blue
Captain 1998-99 Calum K Brown
SRU Tennent's Velvet Championship 1998-99 Div 1 7th
SRU Tennent's Velvet Cup 1998-99 Lost 25-27 to Preston Lodge FP (3rd round)

Jed-Forest made a strong start to their league programme, with wins against West of Scotland, Hawick, Boroughmuir, and Stirling County interrupted by only a defeat on the visit to Heriot's, the eventual champions. Away defeats by Glasgow Hawks and Melrose removed Jed from the championship race, and though they went on to complete doubles against West, Boroughmuir, and Stirling they finished seventh, only one point clear of relegated Boroughmuir. A crucial result in avoiding relegation was their away win against Currie by 21-20, albeit with an injury-time penalty goal by Chris Richards, only a week after they had conceded a half-century against the same opponents. Richards topped the points list with 173, whereas Kevin Liddle, the long-serving back-row forward, led the try-scoring with 10. Jed disappointed in the Scottish Cup, eliminated by Third Division Preston Lodge, though they had some compensation with victory in the Tennent's Velvet Shield final.

League Record 1998-99

Date	Venue	Opponents	Result	Scorers
5 Sep	H	West of Scotland	31-15	*T:* Dunnet, Hotson, Szkudro *C:* Richards 2 *PG:* Richards 4

12 Sep	A	Heriot's FP	17-44	T: Dungait, Scott C: Richards 2 PG: Richards
19 Sep	H	Hawick	28-13	T: Hill, Liddle, Lofthagen C: Hill, Richards PG: Hill, Richards DG: C Laidlaw
26 Sep	A	Boroughmuir	17-13	T: Liddle 2 C: Richards 2 PG: Richards
3 Oct	H	Stirling County	21-21	T: Liddle, Richards, Szkudro PG: Richards 2
10 Oct	A	Glasgow Hawks	7-28	T: Chapman C: Richards
24 Oct	H	Watsonians	22-22	T: C J Brown 2, Scott C: Richards 2 PG: Richards
31 Oct	A	Melrose	24-32	T: Liddle, Richards, Scott C: Richards 3 PG: Richards
7 Nov	A	West of Scotland	24-23	T: Dunnet, Renwick C: Richards PG: Richards 4
12 Dec	H	Heriot's FP	9-32	PG: Richards 3
19 Dec	A	Hawick	21-25	T: Hill, Liddle C: Richards PG: Richards 3
16 Jan	H	Boroughmuir	23-19	T: Lofthagen, penalty try C: Richards 2 PG: Richards 3
23 Jan	A	Stirling County	26-20	T: Elder, Goodfellow, Liddle, Richards C: Richards 3
30 Jan	H	Glasgow Hawks	10-15	T: Richards C: Richards PG: Richards
27 Feb	H	Currie	27-55	T: C Laidlaw, Liddle 2 C: Richards 3 PG: Richards 2
7 Mar	A	Currie	21-20	T: C Laidlaw, Liddle C: Richards PG: Richards 3
13 Mar	A	Watsonians	18-31	T: C J Brown, Renwick C: Richards PG: Richards 2
27 Mar	H	Melrose	10-21	T: S Laidlaw C: Richards PG: Richards

Kelso

Year of formation 1876
Ground Poynder Park, Bowmont Street, Kelso Tel: (01573) 224300 (club) and (01573) 223773 (committee room)
Colours Black and white
Captain 1998-99 G Cowe
SRU Tennent's Velvet Championship 1998-99 Div 2 2nd (promoted)
SRU Tennent's Velvet Cup 1998-99 Lost 3-8 to Gala (final)

Kelso lost their opening league match, 10-28 at Dundee, but they suffered only two more defeats, finishing with the best won-drawn-lost record in the second division. However, they were edged out for the title by Gala's superior tally of bonus points. A 10-3 defeat away to lowly Edinburgh Academicals was a crucially poor result. A week later they had a close call at home to Kilmarnock, winning by 20-19 even though the visitors scored three tries to one, and Kelso stumbled on the run-in with a 15-15 draw on a visit to Biggar. However, that result guaranteed promotion for Kelso and set up a head-to-head decider for the title, a match that they lost 14-24 to Gala at Netherdale. Graeme Aitchison was once again Kelso's leading scorer, registering more than half the club's league points with 223 out of 436, his tally comprising seven tries, 34 conversions, and 40 penalty goals. Three times Aitchison scored more than 20 points in a match.

League Record 1998-99

Date	Venue	Opponents	Result	Scorers
5 Sep	A	Dundee HSFP	10-28	T: Bennet C: Aitchison PG: Aitchison
12 Sep	H	Edinburgh Acads	33-10	T: G Laing, Murray, K Thomson, Utterson C: Aitchison 2 PG: Aitchison 3
19 Sep	A	Kilmarnock	38-24	T: Aitchison 2, Rankin, Ross, Utterson C: Aitchison 5 PG: Aitchison

26 Sep	H	Kirkcaldy	16-9	*T:* Mannion *C:* Aitchison *PG:* Aitchison 3
3 Oct	A	Musselburgh	39-22	*T:* Baird, S Laing, Murray, Ross 2
				C: Aitchison 4 *PG:* Aitchison 2
10 Oct	H	Selkirk	30-9	*T:* Bennet, Mannion, Rankin *C:* Aitchison 3
				PG: Aitchison 3
17 Oct	H	Aberdeen GSFP	25-13	*T:* Bennet, Utterson 2 *C:* Aitchison 2
				PG: Aitchison 2
24 Oct	H	Gala	14-10	*T:* Ross *PG:* Aitchison 2 *DG:* Mannion
7 Nov	H	Dundee HSFP	43-10	*T:* Alberts 3, Aitchison, Bennet, James
				A Thomson, Utterson *C:* Aitchison 4
20 Nov	H	Biggar	34-5	*T:* Aitchison 2, Forsyth, S Laing
				C: Aitchison 4 *PG:* Aitchison 2
12 Dec	A	Edinburgh Acads	3-10	*PG:* Aitchison
19 Dec	H	Kilmarnock	20-19	*T:* Utterson *PG:* Aitchison 5
16 Jan	A	Kirkcaldy	10-8	*T:* Rowley *C:* Aitchison *PG:* Aitchison
23 Jan	H	Musselburgh	43-5	*T:* Alberts 2, Fleming, S Laing, Rankin, Ross
				C: Aitchison 2 *PG:* Aitchison 3
30 Jan	A	Selkirk	31-3	*T:* Aitchison 2, Alberts, Bennet
				C: Aitchison 4 *PG:* Aitchison
27 Feb	A	Aberdeen GSFP	18-11	*T:* Baird 2 *C:* Aitchison *PG:* Aitchison 2
13 Mar	A	Biggar	15-15	*PG:* Aitchison 5
27 Mar	A	Gala	14-24	*T:* Utterson *PG:* Aitchison 3

Melrose

Year of formation 1877
Ground The Greenyards, Melrose, Roxburghshire TD6 9SA Tel: (01896) 822 993 (office) and (01896) 822 559 (clubrooms) Fax: (01896) 822 993
Web site http://www.melrose.bordernet.co.uk/traders/rfc/index.htm
Colours Yellow and black
Captain 1998-99 R R Brown
SRU Tennent's Velvet Championship 1998-99 Div 1 2nd
SRU Tennent's Velvet Cup 1998-99 Lost 22-28 to Gala (semi-final)

Melrose, Scottish title-winners six times in the eight years up to 1997, opened the Premiership programme with a hefty win over Watsonians, the defending champions. The Greenyards club also inflicted defeats on Heriot's in both league matches against the eventual champions. However, Melrose lost twice to Currie as well as the away matches against Glasgow Hawks, West of Scotland and Hawick. December and January were not good months for Melrose. A 24-0 defeat on the visit to West of Scotland was followed by a home win against Heriot's to start the new year, but the immediate loss to Hawick at Mansfield Park proved too much of a handicap to carry them through the run-in for the title as Melrose eventually finished six points behind the champions. Alex Morris attained a three-figure league haul with 103 points, whereas Scott Nichol was leading try-scorer with eight. Melrose regained the Border League title as well as winning the Kings of the Sevens trophy in the abbreviated game's Border circuit.

League Record 1998-99

Date	Venue	Opponents	Result	Scorers
5 Sep	A	Watsonians	50-11	*T:* Aitken, R R Brown, Clark, Laurie 2, Nichol,
				C Redpath, Thom *C:* Morris 5
12 Sep	H	Currie	8-17	*T:* Thom *PG:* Morris
19 Sep	H	West of Scotland	23-17	*T:* Laurie, Morris *C:* Morris 2 *PG:* Morris 3
26 Sep	A	Heriot's FP	30-23	*T:* R R Brown, M Browne, Purves, Thom
				C: Morris 2 *PG:* Morris 2
3 Oct	H	Hawick	51-10	*T:* R R Brown, Clark, Graham, Nichol, Purves,
				B Ruthven, Thom, Thomson *C:* Morris 4
				PG: Morris

10 Oct	A	Boroughmuir	38-12	*T:* R R Brown 2, Clark, Nichol, C Redpath, B Ruthven *C:* Morris 4
17 Oct	H	Stirling County	35-11	*T:* Griffith, Moncreiff, B Ruthven, Smith 2 *C:* Morris 2 *PG:* Morris 2
24 Oct	A	Glasgow Hawks	8-20	*T:* Nichol *PG:* Morris
31 Oct	H	Jed-Forest	32-24	*T:* Nichol, S Ruthven 2, Thom *C:* S Ruthven 3 *PG:* S Ruthven 2
7 Nov	H	Watsonians	39-11	*T:* Aitken, R R Brown, S Ruthven, Thom, Thomson *C:* S Ruthven 4 *PG:* S Ruthven *DG:* S Ruthven
12 Dec	A	Currie	18-19	*T:* Smith, Watt *C:* S Ruthven *PG:* S Ruthven 2
19 Dec	A	West of Scotland	0-24	
16 Jan	H	Heriot's FP	22-3	*T:* Aitken, Laurie *PG:* Morris 4
23 Jan	A	Hawick	25-27	*T:* Henderson, Mitchell, Nichol *C:* Morris 2 *PG:* Morris 2
30 Jan	H	Boroughmuir	18-17	*T:* Nichol 2 *C:* Morris *PG:* Morris 2
27 Feb	A	Stirling County	41-29	*T:* M Browne, Henderson 2, Laurie, Purves, B Ruthven, penalty try *C:* McGarva 3
13 Mar	H	Glasgow Hawks	32-15	*T:* R R Brown, Clark, Griffith, Purves *C:* McGarva 3 *PG:* McGarva 2
27 Mar	A	Jed-Forest	21-10	*T:* B Ruthven 2 *C:* McGarva *PG:* McGarva 3

Stirling County

Year of formation 1904
Ground Bridgehaugh, Causewayhead Road, Stirling Tel: (01786) 474827 (clubhouse) and (01786) 478866 (office) Fax: (01786) 447767
Colours Red, white and black
Captain 1998-99 J Henderson
SRU Tennent's Velvet Championship 1998-99 Div 1 10th (relegated)
SRU Tennent's Velvet Cup 1998-99 Lost 8-15 to Linlithgow (3rd round)

Stirling County, Scottish champions only four years earlier, slid out of the First Division without winning a match. Only a 21-all draw away to Jed-Forest saved them from a whitewash, and to add to their dismal season they were eliminated from the Scottish Cup on a third-round visit to Linlithgow, a club four divisions below them. Before the end of the season, County parted company with their New Zealand coach, Paul McKeany. Robbie Mailer was their leading scorer in league matches, missing a century by only two points. Prop David Jamieson scored five tries, only one fewer than two backs, Murray Fraser and Wayne Barr.

League Record 1998-99

Date	Venue	Opponents	Result	Scorers
12 Sep	A	Boroughmuir	24-36	*T:* Fraser, Jamieson 2, McKillop *C:* Mailer 2
19 Sep	A	Currie	17-27	*T:* Jamieson, Mailer *C:* Mailer 2 *PG:* Mailer
26 Sep	H	Glasgow Hawks	16-21	*T:* Mailer *C:* Mailer *PG:* Mailer 3
3 Oct	A	Jed-Forest	21-21	*T:* Hogg, Jamieson *C:* Mailer *PG:* Mailer 3
10 Oct	H	Watsonians	11-47	*T:* Barr *PG:* Mailer 2
17 Oct	A	Melrose	11-35	*T:* Barr *PG:* Mailer 2
31 Oct	A	Heriot's FP	16-68	*T:* Fraser *C:* Mailer *PG:* Mailer 3
7 Nov	A	Hawick	15-29	*T:* Hogg, Reid *C:* Adamson *PG:* Adamson
12 Dec	H	Boroughmuir	13-56	*T:* Hogg, Jamieson *PG:* Adamson
19 Dec	H	Currie	10-18	*T:* Barr *C:* Adamson *PG:* Adamson
16 Jan	A	Glasgow Hawks	6-41	*PG:* Adamson 2
23 Jan	H	Jed-Forest	20-26	*T:* Barr, Leslie, McAllister *C:* Adamson *PG:* Adamson

30 Jan	A	Watsonians	23-34	*T:* Fraser 2 *C:* McKillop 2 *PG:* Leslie 2 *DG:* Adamson
27 Feb	H	Melrose	29-41	*T:* D Dunsire, Fraser, Lewis, Mailer *C:* Mailer 3 *PG:* Mailer
7 Mar	H	Hawick	14-24	*T:* Fraser, Wyllie *C:* Mailer 2
13 Mar	A	West of Scotland	10-39	*T:* Barr, Imrie
21 Mar	H	West of Scotland	19-24	*T:* Barr, Lewis *PG:* Mailer 3
27 Mar	H	Heriot's FP	25-75	*T:* Allan, Kennedy, McKillop 2 *C:* Mailer *PG:* Mailer

Watsonians

Year of formation 1875
Ground Myreside, Myreside Road, Edinburgh EH10 5DB Tel: (0131) 447 5200 (office) and (0131) 447 9261 (clubroom)
Colours Maroon and white
Captain 1998-99 N Penny
SRU Tennent's Velvet Championship 1998-99 Div 1 6th
SRU Tennent's Velvet Cup 1998-99 Lost 0-33 to Melrose (5th round)

Watsonians, the previous season's champions, slipped to sixth in the First Division table, winning only seven matches, four of those against Boroughmuir and Stirling County, the clubs who were to be relegated. When Watsonians lost to Heriot's in December they themselves were threatened with relegation, but the return of Scott Hastings, released from his SRU contract, helped to change the club's fortunes. Bruce Aitchison's goal-kicking was invaluable as he scored 82 points in Watsonians' final eight games.

League Record 1998-99

Date	Venue	Opponents	Result	Scorers
5 Sep	H	Melrose	11-50	*T:* Hills *PG:* Smith 2
12 Sep	A	West of Scotland	45-31	*T:* di Rollo, Garry, Hills, Smith, Weston *C:* Guest 4 *PG:* Guest 4
19 Sep	H	Heriot's FP	19-44	*T:* di Rollo, Osborne, Smith *C:* Smith 2
26 Sep	A	Hawick	6-15	*PG:* Guest 2
3 Oct	H	Boroughmuir	22-12	*T:* di Rollo 2, Smith, Weston *C:* Threadgall
10 Oct	A	Stirling County	47-11	*T:* di Rollo 2, Elliott 2, Guest, Hills, Weston *C:* Guest 3 *PG:* Guest 2
24 Oct	A	Jed-Forest	22-22	*T:* di Rollo 2, Hayter *C:* Guest 2 *DG:* Guest
31 Oct	H	Currie	18-24	*T:* Scott, Weston *C:* Guest *PG:* Guest 2
7 Nov	A	Melrose	11-39	*T:* Reed *PG:* Threadgall 2
12 Dec	H	West of Scotland	19-27	*T:* di Rollo, Mallinson, penalty try *C:* Threadgall 2
19 Dec	A	Heriot's FP	19-32	*T:* Reynolds *C:* Aitchison *PG:* Aitchison 4
23 Jan	A	Boroughmuir	16-6	*T:* penalty try *C:* Aitchison *PG:* Aitchison 3
30 Jan	H	Stirling County	34-23	*T:* Hastings 2, Hayter 2, Taylor *C:* Aitchison 3 *PG:* Aitchison
13 Feb	H	Glasgow Hawks	9-9	*PG:* Aitchison 3
27 Feb	A	Glasgow Hawks	10-30	*T:* Garry *C:* Aitchison *PG:* Aitchison
13 Mar	H	Jed-Forest	31-18	*T:* Crawford 2, Raeburn *C:* Aitchison 2 *PG:* Aitchison 4
3 Apr	H	Hawick	31-0	*T:* Dickson, Hastings, Raeburn, Wilson *C:* Aitchison *PG:* Aitchison 3
17 Apr	A	Currie	21-35	*T:* Hastings 2 *C:* Aitchison *PG:* Aitchison 3

West of Scotland

Year of formation 1865
Ground Burnbrae, Glasgow Road, Milngavie, Glasgow G62 6HX Tel: (0141) 956 3116
Colours Red and yellow hoops
Captain 1998-99 G Curtis
SRU Tennent's Velvet Championship 1998-99 Div 1 8th
SRU Tennent's Velvet Cup 1998-99 Lost 17-23 to Musselburgh (4th round)

West of Scotland survived in the First Division, though they left it agonisingly late. Not only did they win their final match, beating Currie 29-10 at Malleny Park, but it was five minutes into injury-time before Ian McInroy's second try secured the bonus point that West needed to edge past Boroughmuir on points difference. In a slow start, West suffered six successive defeats before they beat Boroughmuir 20-13 at home. New Zealander Guy Curtis was West's principal contributor to the league points tally – 195 out of 355 – and he enjoyed a phenomenal run by scoring at least one try in seven successive matches. He was surrounded by a mainly young squad, with no fewer than 13 West players making representative appearances for Glasgow's under-21 team.

League Record 1998-99

Date	Venue	Opponents	Result	Scorers
5 Sep	A	Jed-Forest	15-31	*PG:* Curtis 5
12 Sep	H	Watsonians	31-45	*T:* N Craig, McKechnie, Pope, Sheridan *C:* Curtis *PG:* Curtis 3
19 Sep	A	Melrose	17-23	*T:* Bryce, MacLeod *C:* Curtis 2 *PG:* Curtis
26 Sep	H	Currie	8-23	*T:* Curtis *PG:* Curtis
3 Oct	H	Heriot's FP	14-45	*T:* McInroy, MacLeod *C:* Curtis 2
10 Oct	A	Hawick	7-9	*T:* Pope *C:* Curtis
17 Oct	H	Boroughmuir	20-13	*T:* Bryce, Kerr *C:* Curtis 2 *PG:* Curtis 2
31 Oct	H	Glasgow Hawks	0-51	
7 Nov	H	Jed-Forest	23-24	*T:* Curtis, MacLeod *C:* Curtis 2 *PG:* Curtis 3
12 Dec	A	Watsonians	27-19	*T:* Curtis 2, Duck *C:* Curtis 3 *PG:* Curtis 2
19 Dec	H	Melrose	24-0	*T:* Curtis 2, Kerr *C:* Curtis 3 *PG:* Curtis
23 Jan	A	Heriot's FP	12-23	*T:* Curtis, Hamilton *C:* Curtis
30 Jan	H	Hawick	25-26	*T:* Curtis, Howieson 2 *C:* Curtis 2 *PG:* Curtis 2
27 Feb	H	Boroughmuir	24-25	*T:* Curtis, Kerr, Pope 2 *C:* Curtis 2
13 Mar	H	Stirling County	39-10	*T:* N Craig 2, Curtis, di Ciacca 2 *C:* Curtis 4 *PG:* Curtis 2
21 Mar	A	Stirling County	24-19	*T:* N Craig, Henderson, Williamson *C:* Curtis 3 *PG:* Curtis
27 Mar	A	Glasgow Hawks	16-22	*T:* Howieson *C:* Curtis *PG:* Curtis 3
3 Apr	A	Currie	29-10	*T:* Curtis, McInroy 2, MacLeod *C:* Curtis 3 *PG:* Curtis

EXPECTATION TAKES ANOTHER BATTERING

THE 1998-99 SEASON IN IRELAND
Karl Johnston Editor, *Irish Rugby Review*

Ireland's rugby followers have every reason to be exasperated; a state of mind, be it said, to which they are by now well accustomed. An international season that began in hope and expectation ended in bitter disappointment with yet another trouncing at Murrayfield. That dismal trend continued through the summer. Ireland lost the First Test to Australia in Brisbane by a record margin for matches between the two countries, although there was a sterling revival in the Second Test.

The return from England of leading players like David Humphreys, Mark McCall, Allen Clarke and Jonathan Bell not only reversed the trend which had started with the advent of professionalism, but was also obviously a boost to the domestic game, as well as being good for the morale at representative level. For the first time, the Guinness Inter-Provincial Championship was played on a home and away basis. The Super-12 bonus points system was introduced and the result was the competition's best ever campaign, with Munster emerging narrow, but worthy winners.

There were some good displays by the provinces in the European Cup and Shield, though the challenges of Leinster, Munster and Connacht eventually petered out. A largely contrived drugs 'controversy' also faded away, though at its height the ham-fisted handling of the situation by the Irish Rugby Football Union didn't help.

National squad sessions, under the efficient three-man management of Warren Gatland, Philip Danaher and Donal Lenihan, were well organised. And the fact that they were staged at different locations throughout the country, where big attendances of school children turned up, was a good idea, both in terms of promotion of the game in areas outside the capital and the morale of the players.

But hopes of a renaissance at international level began to subside somewhat after Ireland's indifferent form in the World Cup qualifying matches against Georgia and Romania; victories were achieved on successive Saturdays in November, but hardly in the most convincing manner. A week on, Ireland faced South Africa; doing well in the first half, only to be effectively killed off soon after the resumption. Three days before, the Springboks had overrun the Combined Provinces in Cork, and three days later, the tourists trounced a very strong Ireland A team in Belfast.

Ulster's European Cup victory, followed by the one-point defeat

The Ireland team that played France at Lansdowne Road on 6th February. L-R back row: R A J Henderson (replacement), T Brennan (replacement), K G M Wood, E R P Miller, D O'Cuinneagain, J W Davidson, V C P Costello, G Dempsey, P S Wallace, J C Bell, M J Galwey (replacement) ; front row: J P Bishop, K M Maggs, C M P O'Shea, P S Johns (captain), N A A Murphy (president IRFU), mascot, P M Clohessy, C D McGuinness, D G Humphreys.

211

by France and success over Wales at Wembley suggested a change in Five Nations Championship fortunes. But Ireland's international season ended, as usual, in disappointment, and a modest win against Italy was scant consolation.

As in the past, the national sides at schools and underage level fared infinitely better. But just how to nurture this talent through to the top continues to be a major problem.

On the domestic front, Munster clubs continued to dominate the AIB League, with Cork Constitution winning the title for the second time by defeating Garryowen, who had headed the Division 1 table, in a final that was a repeat of the play-off in the competition's inaugural season in 1990/91. Shannon failed in their bid for a fifth successive title; but the real success at club level was Buccaneers, who reached the semi-finals in their first year in Division 1.

'Buccs', born of the amalgamation of the Athlone and Ballinasloe clubs, drew capacity attendances to their home matches in the previously rugby-impoverished midlands. Struggling Irish clubs – and they are many – might usefully take notice.

This was the longest Irish rugby season ever, and did not end until 29 May when Cork Constitution and Garryowen met again in the final of the Munster Senior Cup, with the Limerick club successful on this occasion. Next season, the four provincial branches will play their Senior Cup competitions between 25 September and 25 October, while a national under-20 club competition will also be introduced.

AIB LEAGUE TABLES

Division 1	P	W	D	L	F	A	Pts
Garryowen	11	8	0	3	237	140	16
Cork Const	11	8	0	3	265	170	16
Buccaneers	11	8	0	3	196	202	16
St Mary's Coll	11	7	0	4	215	117	14
Lansdowne	11	7	0	4	189	184	14
Shannon	11	6	0	5	224	164	12
Young Munster	11	4	1	6	134	135	9
Terenure Coll	11	4	1	6	175	182	9
Ballymena	11	4	0	7	190	224	8
Clontarf	11	4	0	7	198	246	8
Blackrock Coll	11	4	0	7	180	232	8
Galwegians	11	1	0	10	117	264	2

Division 2	P	W	D	L	F	A	Pts
Dungannon	15	13	0	2	479	259	26
DLSP	15	10	2	3	284	211	22
Wanderers	15	10	0	5	342	293	20
Old Belvedere	15	9	1	5	276	212	19
Malone	15	9	1	5	233	206	19
Bective Rangers	15	8	2	5	240	269	18
Portadown	15	8	1	6	250	268	17
Greystones	15	8	0	7	334	313	16

	P	W	D	L	F	A	Pts
Old Crescent	15	7	1	7	305	236	15
Sunday's Well	15	7	0	8	270	246	14
City of Derry	15	7	0	8	284	293	14
UCC	15	5	4	6	248	303	14
Dolphin	15	5	1	9	218	256	11
Skerries	15	3	1	11	199	262	7
Old Wesley	15	2	2	11	181	315	6
Ballynahinch	15	1	0	14	171	372	2

Division 3 Section A	P	W	D	L	F	A	Pts
UCD	13	10	0	3	362	176	20
NIFC	13	9	0	4	246	186	18
Monkstown	13	8	0	5	209	238	16
Instonians	13	7	1	5	277	178	15
Bohemians	13	6	0	7	179	225	12
Section B	P	W	D	L	F	A	Pts
Richmond	13	7	0	6	156	208	14
County Carlow	13	6	0	7	212	208	12
Corinthians	13	5	1	7	256	223	11
Dublin Univ	13	4	0	9	193	253	8
Highfield	13	2	0	11	130	325	4

Division 4	P	W	D	L	F	A	Pts
Midleton	10	7	1	2	194	83	15
Ballina	10	7	1	2	167	96	15
Banbridge	10	7	0	3	161	129	14
Waterpark	10	5	0	5	155	121	10
Omagh Acad	10	5	0	5	142	123	10
Suttonians	10	5	0	5	161	146	10
Queen's Univ	10	5	0	5	152	226	10
Bangor	10	4	1	5	113	153	9
Ards	10	4	0	6	134	153	8
Collegians	10	3	1	6	150	159	7
CIYMS	10	1	0	9	55	195	2

AIB League Division 1 Semi-final
Garryowen 19, St Mary's College 17 (Dooradoyle, Limerick); Cork Constitution 32, Buccaneers 20 (Temple Hill, Cork)

Final
Cork Constitution 14, Garryowen 11 (Lansdowne Road, Dublin)

WINNERS OF PROVINCIAL TOURNAMENTS

CONNACHT
Senior Cup: Buccaneers
Senior League: Buccaneers

MUNSTER
Senior Cup: Garryowen
Senior League: Garryowen

LEINSTER
Senior Cup: Clontarf
Senior League: Terenure College

ULSTER
Senior Cup: Instonians
Senior League: Ballymena

GUINNESS INTER-PROVINCIAL CHAMPIONSHIP

14 August, Donnybrook, Dublin

Leinster 14 (2G) **Ulster 34** (4G 2PG)
Leinster: K Nowlan (St Mary's College); J McWeeney (St Mary's College), S Horgan (Lansdowne) B Carey (Blackrock College), G Dempsey (Terenure College); A McGowan (Blackrock College), D O'Mahony (Lansdowen); E Byrne (St Mary's College), S Byrne (Blackrock College), A McKeen (Lansdowne), P Holden (Terenure College), G Fulcher (Lansdowne) *(capt)*, D O'Brien (Clontarf), B Gibney (Blackrock College), V Costello (St Mary's College) *Substitutions:* D Hegarty (Terenure College) for O'Mahony; C Brownlie (Clontarf) for Gibney; H Hurley (Clontarf) for E Byrne; M Ridge (Wanderers) for Carey
Scorers *Tries:* Horgan, Nowlan *Conversions:* McGowan (2)
Ulster: S Mason (Ballymena); J Cunningham (Ballymena), S McDowell (Ballymena), M McCall (Dungannon) *(capt)*, A Park (Ballymena); D Humphreys (Dungannon), S Bell (Dungannon); J Fitzpatrick (Dungannon), A Clarke (Dungannon), G Leslie (Dungannon), M Rea (Malone), G Longwell (Ballymena), S McKinty (Bangor), A Ward (Ballynahinch), T McWhirter (Ballymena) *Substitutions:* A Matchett (Ballymena) for Bell; D Macartney (Ballymena) for McWhirter; S Duncan (Malone) for McKinty
Scorers *Tries:* McWhirter, Ward (2), McDowell *Conversions:* Mason (4)
Penalty Goals: Mason (2)
Referee B Smith

15 August, Sports Ground, Galway

Connacht 13 (1G 2PG) **Munster 18** (1G 2PG 1T)
Connacht: W Ruane (Galwegians); N Carolan (Galwegians), P Duignan (Galwegians), M Murphy (Buccaneers), A Reddan (Galwegians); E Elwood (Galwegians) *(capt)*, D Reddan (Galwegians); J Screene (Buccaneers), B Mulcahy (Skerries), M Cahill (Buccaneers), J Cullen (Galwegians), J Duffy (Galwegians), J Charlie (Galwegians), S McEntee (Lansdowne), B Gavin (Galwegians) *Substitutions:* B Jackman (Clontarf) for Mulcahy; J Maher (St Mary's College) for Screene
Scorers *Try:* Ruane *Conversion:* Elwood *Penalty Goals:* Elwood (2)
Munster: D Crotty (Garryowen); J Lacey (Shannon), M Lynch (Young Munster), R Ellison (Shannon), A Horgan (Cork Constitution); K Keane (Garryowen), B O'Meara (Cork Constitution); I Murray (Cork Constitution), M McDermott (Shannon), P Clohessy (Young Munster), M Galwey (Shannon) *(capt)*, S Leahy (Garryowen), U O'Callaghan (Cork Constitution), E Halvey (Shannon), A Foley (Shannon) *Substitution:* B Walsh (Cork Constitution) for Ellison
Scorers *Tries:* Lacey, Keane *Conversion:* Keane *Penalty Goals:* Keane (2)
Referee A Lewis

21 August, Dooradoyle, Limerick

Munster 18 (1G 2PG 1T) **Leinster 24** (1G 4PG 1T)
Munster: D Crotty (Garryowen); J Lacey (Shannon), B Walsh (Cork Constitution), M Lynch (Young Munster), A Horgan (Cork Constitution); K Keane (Garryowen), B O'Meara (Cork Constitution); I Murray

(Cork Constitution), M McDermott (Shannon), P Clohessy (Young Munster), M Galwey (Shannon) *(capt)*, S Leahy (Garryowen), U O'Callaghan (Cork Constitution), E Halvey (Shannon), A Foley (Shannon) *Substitutions:* T Tierney (Garryowen) for O'Meara; F Sheahan (Cork Constitution) for McDermott; D Clohessy (Young Munster) for Murray; D Wallace (Garryowen) for O'Callaghan
Scorers *Tries:* Horgan, Walsh *Conversion:* Keane *Penalty Goals:* Keane (2)
Leinster: K Nowlan (St Mary's College); J McWeeney (St Mary's College), S Horgan (Lansdowne), M Ridge (Wanderers), G Dempsey (Terenure College); A McGowan (Blackrock College), D O'Mahony (Lansdowne); E Byrne (St Mary's College), S Byrne (Blackrock College), A McKeen (Lansdowne), P Holden (St Mary's College), G Fulcher (Lansdowne) *(capt)*, T Brennan (St Mary's College), C Brownlie (Clontarf), V Costello (St Mary's College) *Substitutions:* B Carey (Blackrock College) for Horgan; H Hurley (Clontarf) for E Byrne
Scorers *Tries:* Dempsey, Nowlan *Conversion:* McGowan *Penalty Goals:* McGowan (4)
Referee W Watson

---

22 August, Sports Ground, Galway

Connacht 21 (3G) **Ulster 18** (1G 2PG 1T)
Connacht: W Ruane (Galwegians); N Carolan (Galwegians), P Duignan (Galwegians), M Murphy (Galwegians), A Reddan (Galwegians); E Elwood (Galwegians), D Reddan (Galwegians); J Screene (Buccaneers), B Mulcahy (Skerries), M Cahill (Buccaneers), J Cullen (Galwegians), J Duffy (Galwegians), J Casserley (Galwegians), S McEntee (Lansdowne), B Gavin (Galwegians) *Substitution:* I Dillon (Bohemians) for Casserley
Scorers *Tries:* Duignan (2), Murphy *Conversions:* Elwood (3)
Ulster: S Mason (Ballymena); J Cunningham (Ballymena), S McDowell (Ballymena), M McCall (Dungannon) *(capt)*, A Park (Ballymena); D Humphreys (Dungannon), S Bell (Dungannon); J Fitzpatrick (Dungannon), A Clarke (Dungannon), G Leslie (Dungannon), M Rea (Malone), G Longwell (Ballymena), S McKinty (Bangor), A Ward (Ballynahinch), T McWhirter (Ballymena)
Scorers *Tries:* Cunningham, Ward *Conversion:* Mason *Penalty Goals:* Mason (2)

---

28 August, Donnybrook, Dublin

Leinster 29 (2G 5PG) **Connacht 24** (2G 2T)
Leinster: K Nowlan (St Mary's College); J McWeeney (St Mary's College), S Horgan (Lansdowne), M Ridge (Wanderers), G Dempsey (Terenure College); A McGowan (Blackrock College), D O'Mahony (Lansdowne); E Byrne (St Mary's College), S Byrne (Blackrock College), A McKeen (Lansdowne), P Holden (Terenure College), G Fulcher (Lansdowne) *(capt)*, D O'Brien, C Brownlie (Clontarf), V Costello (St Mary's College) *Substitution:* B Carey (Blackrock College) for Ridge (temp)
Scorers *Tries:* Dempsey, Costello *Conversions:* McGowan (2) *Penalty Goals:* McGowan (5)
Connacht: W Raune (Galwegians); R Southam (Buccaneers), P Duignan (Galwegians), M Murphy (Galwegians), A Reddan (Galwegians); E Elwood (Galwegians) *(capt)*, D Reddan (Galwegians); J Screene (Buccaneers), B Mulcahy (Skerries), M Cahill (Buccaneers), J Cullen (Galwegians), J Duffy (Galwegians), S McEntee (Lansdowne), I Dillon (Bohemians), B Gavin (Galwegians)
Substitutions: B Jackman (Clontarf) for Mulcahy; S Allnutt (Buccaneers) for Elwood; J Maher (St Mary's College) for Cahill; G Heaslip (Galwegians) for Duffy; D Mescal (Galwegians) for D Reddan; N Carolan (Galwegians) for A Reddan
Scorers *Tries:* Gavin, Murphy, Duignan, Screene *Conversions:* Allnutt (2)
Referee S Landers

---

4 September, Ravenhill, Belfast

Ulster 29 (2G 5PG) **Munster 12** (4PG)
Ulster: S Mason (Ballymena); J Davis (Dungannon), J Bell (Dungannon), J Cunningham (Ballymena), A Park (Ballymena); D Humphreys (Dungannon), A Matchett (Ballymena); J Fitzpatrick (Dungannon), A Clarke (Dungannon), G Leslie (Dungannon), M Rea (Malone), G Longwell (Ballymena), D Macartney (Ballymena) *(capt)*, A Ward (Ballynahinch), T McWhirter (Ballymena) *Substitutions:* S Duncan (Malone) for Macartney; R Irwin (Ballymena) for Leslie
Scorers *Tries:* Cunningham, Rea *Conversions:* Mason (2) *Penalty Goals:* Mason (5)
Munster: D Crotty (Garryowen); A Horgan (Cork Constitution), K Keane (Garryowen), M Lynch (Young Munster), J Kelly (Cork Constitution); R O'Gara (Cork Constitution), B O'Meara (Cork Constitution); D Clohessy (Young Munster), F Sheahan (Cork Constitution), P Clohessy (Young Munster), M Galwey (Shannon) *(capt)*, D O'Callaghan (Cork Constitution), D Wallace (Garryowen), J Murray (Cork Constitution), A Foley (Shannon) *Substitutions:* I Murray (Cork Constitution) for D Clohessy (temp); D Corkery (Cork Constitution) for Murray (temp); M McDermott (Shannon) for Sheahan (temp)
Scorers *Penalty Goals:* Keane (4)
Referee A Lewis

---

11 September, Ravenhill, Belfast

Ulster 11 (2PG 1T) **Leinster 35** (2G 2PG 3T)
Ulster: S Mason (Ballymena); J Davis (Dungannon); J Bell (Dungannon), J Cunningham (Ballymena), A Park (Ballymena); D Humphreys (Dungannon), A Matchett (Ballymena); J Fitzpatrick (Dungannon),

A Clarke (Dungannon), G Leslie (Dungannon), M Rea (Malone), G Longwell (Ballymena), D Macartney (Ballymena) *(capt)*, A Ward (Ballynahinch), T McWhirter (Ballymena) *Substitutions:* B Cunningham (Bective Rangers) for Humphreys; S McKinty (Bangor) for Macartney; S Coulter (Ballymena) for Davis; R Irwin (Ballymena) for Fitzpatrick; S Duncan (Malone) for McWhirter; S Bell (Dungannon) for Matchett
Scorers Try: Rea *Penalty Goals:* Mason (2)

Leinster: K Nowlan (St Mary's College); G Dempsey (Terenure College), S Horgan (Lansdowne), M Ridge (Wanderers), D Hickie (St Mary's College); A McGowan (Blackrock College), D Hegarty (Terenure College); H Hurley (Clontarf), S Byrne (Blackrock College), E Byrne (S Mary's College), P Holden (Terenure College), G Fulcher (Lansdowne) *(capt)*,T Brennan (St Mary's College), C Brownlie (Clontarf), V Costello (St Mary's College) *Substitution:* D O'Brien (Clontarf) for Brennan
Scorers *Tries:* Nowlan (2), Holden, Hegarty, Hickie *Conversions:* McGowan (2) *Penalty Goals:* McGowan (2)
Referee D McHugh

---

12 September, Dooradoyle, Limerick

Munster 21 (1G 3PG 1T) Connacht 7 (1G)
Munster: D Crotty (Garryowen); J Lacey (Shannon), B Walsh (Cork Constitution), M Lynch (Young Munster), A Horgan (Cork Constitution); K Keane (Garryowen), T Tierney (Garryowen); P Clohessy (Young Munster), M McDermott (Shannon), J Hayes (Shannon), M Galwey (Shannon) *(capt)*, S Leahy (Garryowen), A Quinlan (Shannon), E Halvey (Shannon), A Foley (Shannon) *Substitutions:* I Murray (Cork Constitution) for Clohessy; D Corkery (Cork Constitution) for Quinlan; D Wallace (Garryowen) for Foley
Scorers *Tries:* Quinlan, Lacey *Conversion:* Keane *Penalty Goals:* Keane (3)
Connacht: W Ruane (Galwegians); A Reddan (Galwegians), P Duignan (Galwegians), M Murphy (Galwegians) *(capt)*, N Carolan (Galwegians); S Allnutt (Buccaneers), C McGuinness (St Mary's College); J Maher (St Mary's College), J McVeigh (Buccaneers), J Screene (Buccaneers), G Heaslip (Galwegians), J Duffy (Galwegians), I Dillon (Bohemians), S McEntee (Lansdowne), J Charlie (Galwegians) *Substitutions:* D Reddan (Galwegians) for McGuinness (temp); B Jackman (Clontarf) for McVeigh; N Culliton (Galwegians) for Dillon
Scorers *Try:* Heaslip *Conversion:* Allnutt
Referee B Stirling

---

3 October, Musgrave Park, Cork

Munster 31 (1G 3PG 3T) Ulster 9 (1DG 2PG)
Munster: B Roche (Shannon); J Lacey (Shannon), M Lynch (Young Munster), J Kelly (Cork Constitution), A Horgan (Cork Constitution); B Everitt (Lansdowne), B O'Meara (Cork Constitution); P Clohessy (Young Munster), M McDermott (Shannon), J Hayes (Shannon), M Galwey (Shannon) *(capt)*, M O'Driscoll (UCC), A Quinlan (Shannon), E Halvey (Shannon), A Foley (Shannon) *Substitutions:* P Stringer (UCC) for O'Meara; S Leahy (Garryowen) for O'Driscoll; I Murray (Cork Constitution) for Hayes; F Sheahan (Cork Constitution) for McDermott
Scorers *Tries:* Lacey, Horgan, Foley, Galwey *Conversion:* Lynch *Penalty Goals:* Lynch (3)
Ulster: S Mason (Ballymena); S Coulter (Ballymena), J Bell (Dungannon), C Van Rensburg (Ballymena), S McDowell (Ballymena); D Humphreys (Dungannon) *(capt)*, A Matchett (Ballymena); J Fitzpatrick (Dungannon), A Clarke (Dungannon), G Leslie (Dungannon), M Rea (Malone), G Longwell (Ballymena), S McKinty (Bangor), A Ward (Ballynahinch), D Macartney *Substitutions:* A Park (Ballymena) for McDowell; R Irwin (Ballymena) for Leslie; T McWhirter (Ballymena) for McKinty (temp); S Duncan (Malone) for McKinty; R Weir (Portadown) for Clarke
Scorers *Dropped Goal:* Humphreys *Penalty Goals:* Mason (2)

---

3 October, Sports Ground, Galway

Connacht 24 (3G 1PG) Leinster 23 (2G 3PG)
Connacht: W Ruane (Galwegians); R Southam (Buccaneers), P Duignan (Galwegians), M Murphy (Galwegians) *(capt)*, A Reddan (Galwegians); S Allnutt (Buccaneers), C McGuinness (St Mary's College); J Screene (Buccaneers), B Mulcahy (Skerries), M Cahill (Buccaneers), G Heaslip (Galwegians), J Duffy (Galwegians), J Charlie (Galwegians), S McEntee (Lansdowne), B Gavin (Galwegians) *Substitutions:* N Carolan (Galwegians) for Southam; M Finlay (Galwegians) for Screene (temp); I Dillon (Bohemians) for McEntee
Scorers *Tries:* Mulcahy, Reddan, Allnutt *Conversions:* Allnutt (3) *Penalty Goal:* Allnutt
Leinster: K Nowlan (St Mary's College); G D'Arcy (Lansdowne), S Horgan (Lansdowne), B Carey (Blackrock College), G Dempsey (Terenure College); A McGowan (Blackrock College), D Hegarty (Terenure College); E Byrne (St Mary's College), S Byrne (Blackrock College), A McKeen (Lansdowne), P Holden (Terenure College), G Fulcher (Lansdowne) *(capt)*, T Brennan (St Mary's College), C Brownlie (Clontarf), V Costello (St Mary's College) *Substitutions:* C Scally (UCD) for Hegarty; H Hurley (Clontarf) for E Byrne; P Smyth (St Mary's College) for S Byrne; D O'Brien (Clontarf) for Brennan; L Cullen (Blackrock College) for Costello
Scorers *Tries:* Nowlan, Dempsey *Conversions:* McGowan (2) *Penalty Goals:* McGowan (3)
Referee D McHugh

23 October, Ravenhill, Belfast

Ulster 36 (4G 1PG 1T) **Connacht 6** (2PG)
Ulster: S Mason (Ballymena); J Topping (Ballymena), J Bell (Dungannon), C Van Rensburg (Ballymena), J Cunningham (Ballymena); D Humphreys (Dungannon) *(capt)*, S Bell (Dungannon); J Fitzpatrick (Dungannon), A Clarke (Dungannon), R Irwin (Ballymena), M Blair (Ballymena), G Longwell (Ballymena), S McKinty (Bangor), A Ward (Ballynahinch), E Miller (Terenure College) *Substitutions:* G Leslie (Dungannon) for Irwin; T McWhirter (Ballymena) for McKinty; R Weir (Portadown) for Clarke; S Coulter (Ballymena) for Cunningham
Scorers *Tries:* Ward, McKinty, Topping, Clarke, Mason *Conversions:* Mason (4) *Penalty Goal:* Mason
Connacht: W Ruane (Galwegians); N Carolan (Galwegians), P Duignan (Galwegians), M Murphy (Galwegians) *(capt)*, A Reddan (Galwegians); S Allnutt (Buccaneers), C McGuinness (St Mary's College); J Screene (Buccaneers), B Mulcahy (Skerries), M Cahill (Buccaneers), G Heaslip (Galwegians), J Duffy (Galwegians), J Charlie (Galwegians), I Dillon (Bohemians), B Gavin (Galwegians) *Substitutions:* J Maher (St Mary's College) for Cahill; J Casserley (Galwegians), N Culliton (Wanderers) for Dillon
Scorers *Penalty Goals:* Allnutt (2)
Referee D McHugh

23 October, Donnybrook, Dublin

Leinster 10 (1G 1PG) **Munster 25** (1G 2DG 4PG)
Leinster: K Nowlan (St Mary's College); J McWeeney (St Mary's College), S Horgan (Lansdowne), B Carey (Blackrock College), G Dempsey (Terenure College); A McGowan (Blackrock College), D Hegarty (Terenure College); E Byrne (St Mary's College), S Byrne (Blackrock College), A McKeen (Lansdowne), P Holden (Terenure College), G Fulcher (Lansdowne) *(capt)*, T Brennan (St Mary's College), C Brownlie (Clontarf), V Costello (St Mary's College) *Substitutions:* D Hickie (St Mary's College) for Carey; C Scally (UCD) for McWeeney; R Corrigan (Lansdowne) for E Byrne; D O'Brien (Clontarf) for Brennan; R Murphy (Clontarf) for Hegarty; P Smyth (St Mary's College) for S Byrne; L Cullen (Blackrock College) for Costello
Scorers *Try:* Scally *Conversion:* McGowan *Penalty Goal:* McGowan
Munster: B Roche (Shannon); J Kelly (Cork Constitution), K Keane (Garryowen), R Ellison (Shannon), A Horgan (Cork Constitution); B Everitt (Lansdowne), P Stringer (UCC); P Clohessy (Young Munster), M McDermott (Shannon), J Hayes (Shannon), M Galwey (Shannon) *(capt)*, M O'Driscoll UCC), A Quinlan (Shannon), E Halvey (Shannon), A Foley (Shannon) *Substitutions:* B Walsh (Cork Constitution) for Roche; S Leahy (Garryowen) for O'Driscoll; D Clohessy (Young Munster) for Hayes; D Corkery (Cork Constitution) for Quinlan; F Sheahan (Cork Constitution) for McDermott
Scorers *Try:* Kelly *Conversion:* Keane *Dropped Goals:* Everitt (2) *Penalty Goals:* Keane (4)
Referee C White

FINAL TABLE

	P	W	D	L	F	A	Bonus	Pts
Munster	6	4	0	2	125	92	2	18
Ulster	6	4	0	2	137	119	3	15
Leinster	6	3	0	3	135	136	2	14
Connacht	6	2	0	4	95	145	3	11

IRELAND TO SOUTH AFRICA 1998

THE TOURING PARTY

Manager DG Lenihan   **Coach** WD Gatland
Assistant Coach PPA Danaher   **Captain** PS Johns

Full-backs: CMP O'Shea (London Irish), CP Clarke (Terenure College)

Threequarters: DA Hickie (St Mary's College), RM Wallace (Saracens), JA Topping (Ballymena), RAJ Henderson (Wasps), MC McCall (London Irish), KM Maggs (Bristol), JC Bell (Northampton), KP Keane (Garryowen), *JP Bishop (London Irish)

Half-backs: EP Elwood (Galwegians), DG Humphreys (London Irish), CD McGuinness (St Mary's College), BT O'Meara (Cork Constitution), DJ Hegarty (Terenure College)

Forwards: R Corrigan (Greystones), JM Fitzpatrick (London Irish), PS Wallace (Saracens), PM Clohessy (Young Munster), JJ Hayes (Shannon), KGM Wood (Harlequins), ATH Clarke (Northampton), B Jackman (Clontarf), PS Johns (Saracens), MJ Galwey (Shannon), GM Fulcher (London Irish), ME O'Kelly (London Irish), DS Corkery (Bristol), T Brennan (St Mary's College), AJ Ward (Ballynahinch), D O'Cuinneagain (Sale), VCP Costello (St Mary's College), AG Foley (Shannon), DP Wallace (Garryowen), *D Clohessy (Young Munster)

* *Replacements on tour*

TOUR RECORD

All matches   Played 7   Won 2   Lost 5   Points for 126   Against 214
International matches   Played 2   Lost 2   Points for 13   Against 70

SCORING DETAILS

All matches				International matches			
For:	11T 7C 19PG		= 126 pts	For:	1T 1C 2PG	= 13 pts	
Against:	26T 21C 13PG 1DG		= 214 pts	Against:	10T 7C 2PG	= 70 pts	

MATCH DETAILS

1998	OPPONENTS	VENUE	RESULT
30 May	Boland	Wellington	W 48-35
3 June	South West Districts	George	L 20-27
6 June	Western Province	Cape Town	L 6-12
9 June	Griqualand West	Kimberley	L 13-52
13 June	SOUTH AFRICA	Bloemfontein	L 13-37
16 June	North West	Potchefstroom	W 26-18
20 June	SOUTH AFRICA	Pretoria	L 0-33

MATCH 1   30 May, Boland Stadium, Wellington

Boland 35 (5G)   **Ireland XV 48** (6G 2PG)
Boland: M Goosen; J Daniels, R Lubbe, E Wolfaardt, M Hendricks; P O'Neill, P Roux; P Marais, D Santon, T Laubscher, C Holwill, C Swanepoel, J Coetzee, F Bleuler (*capt*), H de Kock *Substitutions:* N du Toit for Laubscher (49 mins); C Lotter for Roux (60 mins); A Moolman for Wolfaardt (70 mins); H Caradie for de Kock (74 mins); R Julies for Holwill (79 mins); A Williams for Coetzee (79 mins)
Scorers *Tries:* Bleuler (2), Santon, Hendricks, Goosen *Conversions:* O'Neill (5)

Ireland XV: O'Shea; Topping, Bell, McCall, Hickie; Elwood, McGuinness; Corrigan, Clarke, P Clohessy, Johns (*capt*), Fulcher, O'Cuinneagain, Costello, Ward *Substitutions:* Maggs for Topping (37 mins); Keane for Bell (40 mins); Hayes for Corrigan (40 mins); Jackman for Clarke (69 mins); Brennan for Costello (69 mins)
Scorers *Tries:* Topping (2), O'Cuinneagain, Hickie, O'Shea, McGuinness *Conversions:* Elwood (6) *Penalty Goals:* Elwood (2)
Referee C Spannenberg (Western Province)

MATCH 2   3 June, George

South West Districts 27 (1G 4PG 1DG 1T)   **Ireland XV 20** (5PG 1T)
South West Districts: T van Rensburg; B Vorster, C Stoltz, C Korff, M du Toit; J Benade (*capt*), F Roberts; S Wagner, T Webb, J Espag, T Stoltz, J Capp, D Frans, L Hattingh, F van Zyl *Substitutions:* M Bosman for van Zyl (49 mins); J Human for Wagner (69 mins); R Nel for Korff (74 mins); K Meyer for Stoltz (80 mins)
Scorers *Tries:* C Stoltz, Roberts *Conversion:* Benade *Penalty Goals:* Benade (4) *Dropped Goal:* Benade
Ireland XV: Clarke; R Wallace, Keane, Henderson, Maggs; Humphreys, O'Meara; Fitzpatrick, Jackman, P Clohessy, O'Kelly, Fulcher, Brennan, D Wallace, Foley (*capt*) *Substitutions:* Hayes for P Clohessy (66 mins); Corkery for Brennan (66 mins); Bishop for Clarke (69 mins); Johns for Foley (80 mins)
Scorers *Try:* Foley *Penalty Goals:* Humphreys (5)
Referee M Lawrence (Mpumalanga)

MATCH 3   6 June, Newlands, Cape Town

Western Province 12 (4PG)   **Ireland XV 6** (2PG)
Western Province : J Swart; B Paulse, R Fleck, C Stewart, C Williams; L Koen, J Adlam; A van der Linde, J van Wyk, C Visagie, S Boome, H Louw, R Brink, A Aitken (*capt*), R Skinstad *Substitutions:* C Marais for van Wyk (38 mins); M Hurter for Visagie (50 mins); L Blom for Louw (59 mins); M Kirsten for Adlam (63 mins)
Scorer *Penalty Goals:* Koen (4)
Ireland XV: O'Shea; Bishop, Maggs, McCall, Hickie; Humphreys, McGuinness; Fitzpatrick, Clarke, P Wallace, Johns (*capt*), O'Kelly, Corkery, O'Cuinneagain, Ward *Substitutions:* Costello for Corkery (56 mins); P Clohessy for Fitzpatrick (70 mins)
Scorer *Penalty Goals:* Humphreys (2)
Referee J Kaplan (Natal)

MATCH 4   9 June, Hoffepark, Kimberley

Griqualand West 52 (7G 1PG)   **Ireland XV 13** (1PG 2T)
Griqualand West: A Vermeulen; S Scholtz, L Venter, E Lubbe, H Bosman; H Markram, H Husselman; DW Venter, B de Coning, D Theron, A van der Berg, P Smit, B Krause, G Watts, F Engelbrecht (*capt*) *Substitutions:* J de Jager for Markram (44 mins); D Vermeulen for Engelbrecht (60 mins); V Venter for Smit (60 mins); J Brand for DW Venter (60 mins); A Skinner for de Coning (60 mins); D von Hoesslin for Husselman (64 mins); W October for Scholtz (65 mins)
Scorers *Tries:* L Venter (2), Markram, A Vermeulen, Lubbe, Bosman, October *Conversions:* de Coning (5), Bosman, October *Penalty Goal:* de Coning
Ireland XV: Clarke; R Wallace, Keane, Henderson, Bishop; Humphreys, Hegarty; D Clohessy, Jackman, P Clohessy, Galwey, Fulcher, Brennan, D Wallace, Foley (*capt*)

Substitutions: McCall for Humphreys (44 mins); Costello for Foley (46 mins); Wood for Jackman (47 mins); O'Cuinneagain for Fulcher (49 mins); Hayes for Brennan (56 mins); O'Shea for Clarke (72 mins)
Scorers *Tries:* Foley, O'Shea *Penalty Goal:* Humphreys
Referee T Henning (Northern Transvaal)

MATCH 5   13 June, Free State Stadium, Bloemfontein   1st Test
SOUTH AFRICA 37 (3G 2PG 2T)   IRELAND 13 (1G 2PG)

SOUTH AFRICA: PC Montgomery (Western Province); CS Terblanche (Boland), AH Snyman (Blue Bulls), PG Muller (Natal Sharks), PWG Rossouw (Western Province); GS du Toit (Griqualand West), JH van der Westhuizen (Blue Bulls); AH le Roux (Natal), J Dalton (Goldens Lions), AC Garvey (Natal Sharks), K Otto (Blue Bulls), MG Andrews (Natal Sharks), JC Erasmus (Free State Cheetahs), GH Teichmann (Natal Sharks) *(capt)*, AG Venter (Free State Cheetahs) *Substitution:* PF Smith (Blue Bulls) for du Toit (temp 6-14 mins)
Scorers *Tries:* Terblanche (4), Andrews *Conversions:* du Toit (3)
Penalty Goals: du Toit (2)
IRELAND: O'Shea; Bishop, Maggs, McCall, Hickie; Elwood, McGuinness; Fitzpatrick, Wood, P Wallace, Johns *(capt)*, O'Kelly, O'Cuinneagain, Costello, Ward *Substitutions:* Henderson for Hickie (66 mins); Brennan for Costello (67 mins); Fulcher for Johns (71 mins)
Scorers *Try:* Bishop *Conversion:* Elwood *Penalty Goals:* Elwood (2)
Referee EF Morrison (England)

MATCH 6   16 June, Olenpark, Potchefstroom

North West 18 (1G 2PG 1T)   **Ireland XV 26** (7PG 1T)
North West: E Bouwer; J van den Berg, AJ de Jager, T Joubert, JB van den Berg; AC Prinsloo, B Koetze; H Human, D de Waal, S van Wyk, K Tromp, W Lessing, K Dreyer, B Pool, M van Greunen *(capt)* *Substitutions:* B Christiaan for Human (65 mins); D du Preez for Joubert (68 mins); N Saunders for Koetze (72 mins)
Scorers *Tries:* Bouwer, Prinsloo *Conversion:* JB van den Berg *Penalty Goals:* JB Van den Berg (2)
Ireland XV: Clarke; R Wallace, Keane, Henderson, Hickie; Humphreys, O'Meara; D Clohessy, Clarke, Hayes, Galwey, Fulcher, Brennan, D Wallace, Corkery *Substitutions:* Hegarty for O'Meara (50 mins); P Clohessy for Hayes (50 mins); Ward for Corkery (57 mins)
Scorers *Try:* R Wallace *Penalty Goals:* Humphreys (7)
Referee M Wiles (Zimbabwe)

MATCH 7   20 June, Loftus Versfeld, Pretoria   2nd Test
SOUTH AFRICA 33 (4G 1T)   IRELAND 0

SOUTH AFRICA: PC Montgomery (Western Province); CS Terblanche (Boland), AH Snyman (Blue Bulls), PG Muller (Natal Sharks), PWG Rossouw (Western Province); PF Smith (Blue Bulls), JH van der Westhuizen (Blue Bulls); AH le Roux (Natal), J Dalton (Goldens Lions), AC Garvey (Natal Sharks), K Otto (Blue Bulls), MG Andrews (Natal Sharks), JC Erasmus (Free State Cheetahs), GH Teichmann (Natal Sharks) *(capt)*, AG Venter (Free State Cheetahs) *Substitutions:* M Hendricks (Boland) for Terblanche (43 mins); R Kempson (Natal Sharks) for le Roux (55 mins); AE Drotské (Free State Cheetahs) for Dalton (62 mins); W Swanepoel (Free State Cheetahs) for van der Westhuizen (75 mins); AD Aitken (Western Province) for Erasmus (75 mins)

Scorers *Tries:* van der Westhuizen, Erasmus, Dalton, Teichmann, Rossouw
Conversions: Montgomery (4)
IRELAND: O'Shea; Bishop, Maggs, McCall, Hickie; Elwood, McGuinness;
Fitzpatrick, Wood, P Wallace, Johns (*capt*), O'Kelly, O'Cuinneagain, Costello,
Ward *Substitutions:* Henderson for Hickie (41 mins); Humphreys for Elwood (temp
21-23 mins; 38-42 mins and 53 mins); Brennan for Costello (54 mins); P Clohessy
for Fitzpatrick (63 mins)
Referee J Dumé (France)

*Andy Ward tries to evade the challenge of Gary Teichmann in Ireland's 27-13 loss to South
Africa at Lansdowne Road in November 1998.*

IRISH INTERNATIONAL PLAYERS
(*up to 30 April 1999*)

Note: Years given for Five Nations' matches are for second half of season; eg 1972 means season 1971-72. Years for all other matches refer to the actual year of the match. When a series has taken place, figures have been used to denote the particular matches in which players have featured. Thus 1981 *SA* 2 indicates that a player appeared in the second Test of the series. The abandoned game with Scotland at Belfast in 1885 is now included as a cap match.

NB – The second of Ireland's two matches against France in 1972 was a non-championship match.

Abraham, M (Bective Rangers) 1912 *E, S, W, SA*, 1914 *W*

Adams, C (Old Wesley), 1908 *E*, 1909 *E, F*, 1910 *F*, 1911 *E, S, W, F*, 1912 *S, W, SA*, 1913 *W, F*, 1914 *F, E, S*

Agar, R D (Malone) 1947 *F, E, S, W*, 1948 *F*, 1949 *S, W*, 1950 *F, E, W*

Agnew, P J (CIYMS) 1974 *F* (R), 1976 *A*

Ahearne, T (Queen's Coll, Cork) 1899 *E*

Aherne, L F P (Dolphin, Lansdowne) 1988 *E* 2, *WS, It*, 1989 *F, W, E, S, NZ*, 1990 *E, S, F, W* (R), 1992 *E, S, F, A*

Alexander, R (NIFC, Police Union) 1936 *E, S, W*, 1937 *E, S, W*, 1938 *E, S*, 1939 *E, S, W*

Allen, C E (Derry, Liverpool) 1900 *E, S, W*, 1901 *E, S, W*, 1903 *S, W*, 1904 *E, S, W*, 1905 *E, S, W, NZ*, 1906 *E, S, W, SA*, 1907 *S, W*

Allen, G G (Derry, Liverpool) 1896 *E, S, W*, 1897 *E, S*, 1898 *E, S*, 1899 *E, W*

Allen, T C (NIFC) 1885 *E, S* 1

Allen, W S (Wanderers) 1875 *E*

Allison, J B (Edinburgh U) 1899 *E, S*, 1900 *E, S, W*, 1901 *E, S, W*, 1902 *E, S, W*, 1903 *S*

Anderson, F E (Queen's U, Belfast, NIFC) 1953 *F, E, S, W*, 1954 *NZ, F, E, S, W*, 1955 *F, E, S, W*

Anderson, H J (Old Wesley) 1903 *E, S*, 1906 *E, S*

Anderson, W A (Dungannon) 1984 *A*, 1985 *S, F, W, E*, 1986 *F, S, R*, 1987 *E, S, F, W, [W, C, Tg, A]*, 1988 *S, F, W, E* 1,2, 1989 *F, W, E, NZ*, 1990 *E, S*

Andrews, G (NIFC) 1875 *E*, 1876 *E*

Andrews, H W (NIFC) 1888 *M*, 1889 *S, W*

Archer, A M (Dublin U, NIFC) 1879 *S*

Arigho, J E (Lansdowne) 1928 *F, E, W*, 1929 *F, E, S, W*, 1930 *F, E, S, W*, 1931 *F, E, S, W, SA*

Armstrong, W K (NIFC) 1960 *SA*, 1961 *E*

Arnott, D T (Lansdowne) 1876 *E*

Ash, W H (NIFC) 1875 *E*, 1876 *E*, 1877 *S*

Aston, H R (Dublin U) 1908 *E, W*

Atkins, A P (Bective Rangers) 1924 *F*

Atkinson, J M (NIFC) 1927 *F, A*

Atkinson, J R (Dublin U) 1882 *W, S*

Bagot, J C (Dublin U, Lansdowne) 1879 *S, E*, 1880 *E, S*, 1881 *S*

Bailey, A H (UC Dublin, Lansdowne) 1934 *W*, 1935 *E, S, W, NZ*, 1936 *E, S, W*, 1937 *E, S, W*, 1938 *E, S*

Bailey, N (Northampton) 1952 *E*

Bardon, M E (Bohemians) 1934 *E*

Barlow, M (Wanderers) 1875 *E*

Barnes, R J (Dublin U, Armagh) 1933 *W*

Barr, A (Methodist Coll, Belfast) 1898 *W*, 1899 *S*, 1901 *E, S*

Barry, N J (Garryowen) 1991 *Nm* 2 (R)

Beamish, C E St J (RAF, Leicester) 1933 *W, S*, 1934 *S, W*, 1935 *E, S, W, NZ*, 1936 *E, S, W*, 1938 *W*

Beamish, G R (RAF, Leicester) 1925 *E, S, W*, 1928 *F, E, S, W*, 1929 *F, E, S, W*, 1930 *F, S, W*, 1931 *F, E, S, W, SA*, 1932 *E, S, W*, 1933 *E, W, S*

Beatty, W J (NIFC, Richmond) 1910 *F*, 1912 *F, W*

Becker, V A (Lansdowne) 1974 *F, W*

Beckett, G G P (Dublin U) 1908 *E, S, W*

Bell, J C (Ballymena, Northampton, Dungannon) 1994 *A* 1,2, *US*, 1995 *S, It, [NZ, W, F], Fj*, 1996 *US, S, F, W, E, WS, A*, 1997 *It* 1, *F, W, E, S*, 1998 *Gg, R, SA* 3, 1999 *F, S It* (R)

Bell, R J (NIFC) 1875 *E*, 1876 *E*

Bell, W E (Belfast Collegians) 1953 *F, E, S, W*

Bennett, F (Belfast Collegians) 1913 *S*

Bent, G C (Dublin U) 1882 *W, E*

Berkery, P J (Lansdowne) 1954 *W*, 1955 *W*, 1956 *S, W*, 1957 *F, E, S, W*, 1958 *A, E, S*

Bermingham, J J C (Blackrock Coll) 1921 *E, S, W, F*

Bishop, J P (London Irish) 1998 *SA, 1,2, Gg, R, SA* 3, 1999 *F, W, E, S, It*

Blackham, J C (Queen's Coll, Cork) 1909 *S, W, F*, 1910 *E, S, W*

Blake-Knox, S E F (NIFC) 1976 *E, S*, 1977 *F* (R)

Blayney, J J (Wanderers) 1950 *S*

Bond, A T W (Derry) 1894 *S, W*

Bornemann, W W (Wanderers) 1960 *E, S, W, SA*

Bowen, D St J (Cork Const) 1977 *W, E, S*

Boyd, C A (Dublin U) 1900 *S*, 1901 *S, W*

Boyle, C V (Dublin U) 1935 *NZ*, 1936 *E, S, W*, 1937 *E, S, W*, 1938 *W*, 1939 *W*

Brabazon, H M (Dublin U) 1884 *E*, 1885 *S* 1, 1886 *E*

Bradley, M J (Dolphin) 1920 *W, F*, 1922 *E, S, W, F*, 1923 *E, S, W, F*, 1925 *F, S, W*, 1926 *F, E, S, W*, 1927 *F, W*

Bradley, M T (Cork Constitution) 1984 *A*, 1985 *S, F, W, E*, 1986 *F, W, E, S, R*, 1987 *E, S, F, W, [W, C, Tg, A]*, 1988 *S, F, W, E* 1, 1990 *W*, 1992 *NZ* 1,2, 1993 *S, F, W, E, R*, 1994 *F, W, E, S, A* 1,2, *US*, 1995 *S, F, [NZ]*

Bradshaw, G (Belfast Collegians) 1903 *W*

Bradshaw, R M (Wanderers) 1885 *E, S* 1,2

Brady, A M (UC Dublin, Malone) 1966 *S*, 1968 *E, S, W*

Brady, J A (Wanderers) 1976 *E, S*

Brady, J R (CIYMS) 1951 *E, S, W*, 1953 *E, S, W*, 1954 *W*, 1956 *W*, 1957 *F, E, S, W*

Bramwell, T (NIFC) 1928 *F*

Brand, T N (NIFC) 1924 *NZ*

Brennan, J I (CIYMS) 1957 *S, W*

Brennan, T (St Mary's Coll) 1998 *SA* 1 (R),2 (R), 1999 *F* (R), *S* (R), *It*

Bresnihan, F P K (UC Dublin, Lansdowne, London Irish) 1966 *E, W*, 1967 *A* 1, *E, S, W, F*, 1968 *F, E, S, W, A*, 1969 *F, E, S, W*, 1970 *SA, F, E, S, W*, 1971 *F, E, S, W*

Brett, J T (Monkstown) 1914 *W*

Bristow, J R (NIFC) 1879 *E*

Brophy, N H (Blackrock Coll, UC Dublin, London Irish) 1957 *F, E*, 1959 *E, S, W, F*, 1960 *F, SA*, 1961 *S, W*, 1962 *E, S, W*, 1963 *E, W*, 1967 *E, S, W, F, A* 2

Brown, E L (Instonians) 1958 *F*

Brown, G S (Monkstown, United Services) 1912 *S, W, SA*

Brown, H (Windsor) 1877 *E*

Brown, T (Windsor) 1877 *E, S*

Brown, W H (Dublin U) 1899 *E*

Brown, W J (Malone) 1970 *SA, F, S, W*

Brown, W S (Dublin U) 1893 *S, W*, 1894 *E, S, W*

Browne, A W (Dublin U) 1951 *SA*

Browne, D (Blackrock Coll) 1920 *F*

Browne, H C (United Services and RN) 1929 *E, S, W*

Browne, W F (United Services and Army) 1925 *E, S, W*, 1926 *S, W*, 1927 *E, S, F, W, A*, 1928 *E, S*

Browning, D R (Wanderers) 1881 *E, S*

Bruce, S A M (NIFC) 1883 *E, S*, 1884 *E*

Brunker, A A (Lansdowne) 1895 *E, W*

Bryant, C H (Cardiff) 1920 *E, S*

Buchanan, A McM (Dublin U) 1926 *E, S, W*, 1927 *S, W, A*

Buchanan, J W B (Dublin U) 1882 *S*, 1884 *E, S*

Buckley, J H (Sunday's Well) 1973 *E, S*

Bulger, L Q (Lansdowne) 1896 *E, S, W*, 1897 *E, S*, 1898 *E, S, W*

Bulger, M J (Dublin U) 1888 *M*

Burges, J H (Rosslyn Park) 1950 *F, E*

Burgess, R B (Dublin U) 1912 *SA*

Burke, P A (Cork Constitution, Bristol) 1995 *E, S, W* (R), *It, [J], Fj*, 1996 *US* (R), *A*, 1997 *It* 1, *S* (R)

Burkitt, J C S (Queen's Coll, Cork) 1881 *E*

Burns, I J (Wanderers) 1980 *E* (R)

Butler, L G (Blackrock Coll) 1960 *W*

221

Butler, N (Bective Rangers) 1920 *E*
Byers, R M (NIFC) 1928 *S, W,* 1929 *E, S, W*
Byrne, E M J (Blackrock Coll) 1977 *S, F,* 1978 *F, W, E, NZ*
Byrne, N F (UC Dublin) 1962 *F*
Byrne, S J (UC Dublin, Lansdowne) 1953 *S, W,* 1955 *F*
Byron, W G (NIFC) 1896 *E, S, W,* 1897 *E, S, W,* 1898 *E, S, W,* 1899 *E, S, W*

Caddell, E D (Dublin U, Wanderers) 1904 *S,* 1905 *E, S, W, NZ,* 1906 *E, S, W, SA,* 1907 *E, S,* 1908 *S, W*
Cagney, S J (London Irish) 1925 *W,* 1926 *F, E, S, W,* 1927 *F,* 1928 *E, S, W,* 1929 *F, E, S, W*
Callan, C P (Lansdowne) 1947 *F, E, S, W,* 1948 *F, E, S, W,* 1949 *F, E*
Cameron, E D (Bective Rangers) 1891 *S, W*
Campbell, C E (Old Wesley) 1970 *SA*
Campbell, E F (Monkstown) 1899 *S, W,* 1900 *E, W*
Campbell, S B B (Derry) 1911 *E, S, W, F,* 1912 *F, E, S, W, SA,* 1913 *E, S, F*
Campbell, S O (Old Belvedere) 1976 *A,* 1979 *A 1,2, 1980 E, S, F, W,* 1981 *F, W, E, S, SA 1,* 1982 *W, E, S, F,* 1983 *S, F, W, E,* 1984 *F, W*
Canniffe, D M (Lansdowne) 1976 *W, E*
Cantrell, J L (UC Dublin, Blackrock Coll) 1976 *A, F, W, E, S,* 1981 *S, SA 1,2, A*
Carey, R W (Dungannon) 1992 *NZ 1,2*
Carpendale, M J (Monkstown) 1886 *S,* 1887 *W,* 1888 *W, S*
Carr, N J (Ards) 1985 *S, F, W, E,* 1986 *W, E, S, R,* 1987 *E, S, W*
Carroll, C (Bective Rangers) 1930 *F*
Carroll, R (Lansdowne) 1947 *F,* 1950 *S, W*
Casement, B N (Dublin U) 1875 *E,* 1876 *E,* 1879 *E*
Casement, F (Dublin U) 1906 *E, S, W*
Casey, J C (Young Munster) 1930 *S,* 1932 *E*
Casey, P J (UC Dublin, Lansdowne) 1963 *F, E, S, W, NZ,* 1964 *E, S, W, F,* 1965 *F, E, S*
Chambers, J (Dublin U) 1886 *E, S,* 1887 *E, S, W*
Chambers, R R (Instonians) 1951 *F, E, S, W,* 1952 *F, W*
Clancy, T P J (Lansdowne) 1988 *W, E* 1,2, *WS, It,* 1989 *F, W, E, S*
Clarke, A T H (Northampton, Dungannon) 1995 *Fj* (R), 1996 *W, E, WS,* 1997 *F* (R), *It 2* (R), 1998 *Gg* (R), *R*
Clarke, C P (Terenure Coll) 1993 *F, W, E,* 1998 *W, E*
Clarke, D J (Dolphin) 1991 *W, Nm* 1,2, *[J, A],* 1992 *NZ* 2(R)
Clarke, J A B (Bective Rangers) 1922 *S, W, F,* 1923 *F,* 1924 *F, S, W*
Clegg, R J (Bangor) 1973 *F,* 1975 *E, S, F, W*
Clifford, J T (Young Munster) 1949 *F, E, S, W,* 1950 *F, E, S, W,* 1951 *F, E, SA,* 1952 *F, S, W*
Clinch, A D (Dublin U, Wanderers) 1892 *S,* 1893 *W,* 1895 *E, S, W,* 1896 *E, S, W,* 1897 *E, S*
Clinch, J D (Wanderers, Dublin U) 1923 *W,* 1924 *F, E, S, W, NZ,* 1925 *F, E, S,* 1926 *E, S, W,* 1927 *F,* 1928 *F, E, S, W,* 1929 *F, E, S, W,* 1930 *F, E, S, W,* 1931 *F, E, S, W, SA*
Clohessy, P M (Young Munster) 1993 *F, W, E,* 1994 *F, W, E, S, A* 1,2, *US,* 1995 *E, S, F, W,* 1996 *S, F,* 1997 *It* 2, 1998 *F* (R), *W* (R), *SA* 2 (R), *Gg, R, SA* 3, 1999 *F, W, E, S, It*
Clune, J J (Blackrock Coll) 1912 *SA,* 1913 *W, F,* 1914 *F, E, W*
Coffey, J J (Lansdowne) 1900 *E,* 1901 *W,* 1902 *E, S, W,* 1903 *E, S, W,* 1905 *E, S, W, NZ,* 1906 *E, S, W, SA,* 1907 *E,* 1908 *W,* 1910 *F*
Cogan, W St J (Queen's Coll, Cork) 1907 *E, S*
Collier, S R (Queen's Coll, Belfast) 1883 *S*
Collins, P C (Lansdowne, London Irish) 1987 *[C],* 1990 *S* (R)
Collis, W R F (KCH, Harlequins) 1924 *F, W, NZ,* 1925 *F, E, S,* 1926 *F*
Collis, W S (Wanderers) 1884 *W*
Collopy, G (Bective Rangers) 1891 *S,* 1892 *S*
Collopy, R (Bective Rangers) 1923 *E, S, W, F,* 1924 *F, E, S, W, NZ,* 1925 *F, E, S, W*
Collopy, W P (Bective Rangers) 1914 *F, E, S, W,* 1921 *E, S, W, F,* 1922 *E, S, W, F,* 1923 *S, W, F,* 1924 *F, E, S, W*
Combe, A (NIFC) 1875 *E*
Condon, H C (London Irish) 1984 *S* (R)
Cook, H G (Lansdowne) 1884 *W*
Coote, P B (RAF, Leicester) 1933 *S*
Corcoran, J C (London Irish) 1947 *A,* 1948 *F*
Corken, T S (Belfast Collegians) 1937 *E, S, W*

Corkery, D S (Cork Constitution, Bristol) 1994 *A* 1,2, *US,* 1995 *E, [NZ, J, W, F], Fj,* 1996 *US, S, F, W, E, WS, A,* 1997 *It* 1, *F, W, E, S,* 1998 *S, F, W, E*
Corley, H H (Dublin U, Wanderers) 1902 *E, S, W,* 1903 *E, S, W,* 1904 *E, S*
Cormac, H S T (Clontarf) 1921 *E, S, W*
Corrigan, R (Greystones) 1997 *C* (R), *It* 2, 1998 *S, F, W, E, SA* 3 (R)
Costello, P (Bective Rangers) 1960 *F*
Costello, R A (Garryowen) 1993 *S*
Costello, V C P (St Mary's Coll, London Irish) 1996 *US, F, W, E, WS* (R), 1997 *C, It* 2 (R), 1998 *S* (R), *F, W, E, SA* 1,2, *Gg, R, SA* 3, 1999 *F, W* (R), *E, S* (R), *It*
Cotton, J (Wanderers) 1889 *W*
Coulter, H H (Queen's U, Belfast) 1920 *E, S, W*
Courtney, A W (UC Dublin) 1920 *S, W, F,* 1921 *E, S, W, F*
Cox, H L (Dublin U) 1875 *E,* 1876 *E,* 1877 *E, S*
Craig, R G (Queen's U, Belfast) 1938 *S, W*
Crawford, E C (Dublin U) 1885 *E, S* 1
Crawford, W E (Lansdowne) 1920 *E, S, W, F,* 1921 *E, S, W, F,* 1922 *E, S,* 1923 *E, S, W, F,* 1924 *F, E, W, NZ,* 1925 *F, E, S, W,* 1926 *F, E, S, W,* 1927 *F, E, S, W*
Crean, T J (Wanderers) 1894 *E, S, W,* 1895 *E, S, W,* 1896 *E, S, W*
Crichton, R Y (Dublin U) 1920 *E, S, W, F,* 1921 *F,* 1922 *E,* 1923 *W, F,* 1924 *F, E, S, W, NZ,* 1925 *E, S*
Croker, E W D (Limerick) 1878 *E*
Cromey, G E (Queen's U, Belfast) 1937 *E, S, W,* 1938 *E, S, W,* 1939 *E, S, W*
Cronin, B M (Garryowen) 1995 *S,* 1997 *S*
Cronyn, A P (Dublin U, Lansdowne) 1875 *E,* 1876 *E,* 1880 *S*
Crossan, K D (Instonians) 1982 *S,* 1984 *F, W, E, S,* 1985 *S, F, W, E,* 1986 *E, S, R,* 1987 *E, S, F, W, [W, C, Tg, A],* 1988 *S, F, W, E* 1, *WS, It,* 1989 *W, S, NZ,* 1990 *E, S, F, W, Arg,* 1991 *E, S, Nm* 2 *[Z, J, S],* 1992 *W*
Crotty, D J (Garryowen) 1996 *A,* 1997 *It* 1, *F, W*
Crowe, J F (UC Dublin) 1974 *NZ*
Crowe, L (Old Belvedere) 1950 *E, S, W*
Crowe, M P (Lansdowne) 1929 *W,* 1930 *E, S, W,* 1931 *F, S, W, SA,* 1932 *S, W,* 1933 *W, S,* 1934 *E*
Crowe, P M (Blackrock Coll) 1935 *E,* 1938 *E*
Cullen, T J (UC Dublin) 1949 *F*
Cullen, W J (Monkstown and Manchester) 1920 *E*
Culliton, M G (Wanderers) 1959 *E, S, W, F,* 1960 *E, S, W, F, SA,* 1961 *E, S, W, F,* 1962 *S, F,* 1964 *E, S, W, F*
Cummins, W E A (Queen's Coll, Cork) 1879 *S,* 1881 *E,* 1882 *E*
Cunningham, D McC (NIFC) 1923 *E, S, W,* 1925 *F, E, W*
Cunningham, M J (UC Cork) 1955 *F, E, S, W,* 1956 *F, S, W*
Cunningham, V J G (St Mary's Coll) 1988 *E* 2, *It,* 1990 *Arg* (R), 1991 *Nm* 1,2, *[Z, J(R)],* 1992 *NZ* 1,2, *A,* 1993 *S, F, W, E,* 1994 *F*
Cunningham, W A (Lansdowne) 1920 *W,* 1921 *E, S, W, F,* 1922 *E,* 1923 *S, W*
Cuppaidge, J L (Dublin U) 1879 *E,* 1880 *E, S*
Currell, J (NIFC) 1877 *S*
Curtis, A B (Oxford U) 1950 *F, E, S*
Curtis, D M (London Irish) 1991 *W, E, S, Nm* 1,2, *[Z, J, S, A],* 1992 *W, E, S* (R), *F*
Cuscaden, W A (Dublin U, Bray) 1876 *E*
Cussen, D J (Dublin U) 1921 *E, S, W, F,* 1922 *E,* 1923 *E, S, W, F,* 1926 *F, E, S, W,* 1927 *F, E*

Daly, J C (London Irish) 1947 *F, E, S, W,* 1948 *E, S, W*
Daly, M J (Harlequins) 1938 *E*
Danaher, P P A (Lansdowne, Garryowen) 1988 *S, F, W, WS, It,* 1989 *F, NZ* (R), 1990 *F,* 1992 *S, F, NZ* 1, *A,* 1993 *S, F, W, E, R,* 1994 *F, W, E, S, A* 1,2, *US,* 1995 *E, S, F, W*
Dargan, M J (Old Belvedere) 1952 *S, W*
Davidson, C T (NIFC) 1921 *F*
Davidson, I G (NIFC) 1899 *E,* 1900 *S, W,* 1901 *E, S, W,* 1902 *E, S, W*
Davidson, J C (Dungannon) 1969 *F, E, S, W,* 1973 *NZ,* 1976 *NZ*
Davidson, J W (Dungannon, London Irish, Castres) 1995 *Fj,* 1996 *S, F, W, E, WS, A,* 1997 *It* 1, *F, W, E, S,* 1998 *Gg* (R), *R* (R), *SA* 3 (R), 1999 *F, W, E, S, It*
Davies, F E (Lansdowne) 1892 *S, W,* 1893 *E, S, W*
Davis, J L (Monkstown) 1898 *E, S*
Davis, W J N (Edinburgh U, Bessbrook) 1890 *S, W, E,* 1891 *E, S, W,* 1892 *E, S,* 1895 *S*
Davison, W (Belfast Academy) 1887 *W*

Davy, E O'D (UC Dublin, Lansdowne) 1925 *W*, 1926 *F, E, S, W*, 1927 *F, E, S, W, A*, 1928 *F, E, S, W*, 1929 *F, E, S, W*, 1930 *F, E, S, W*, 1931 *F, E, S, W, SA*, 1932 *E, S, W*, 1933 *E, W, S*, 1934 *E*
Dawson, A R (Wanderers) 1958 *A, E, S, W, F*, 1959 *E, S, W, F*, 1960 *F, SA*, 1961 *E, S, W, F, SA*, 1962 *S, F, W*, 1963 *F, E, S, W, NZ*, 1964 *E, S, F*
Dawson, K (London Irish) 1997 *NZ, C*, 1998 *S*
Dean, P M (St Mary's Coll) 1981 *SA* 1,2, *A*, 1982 *W, E, S, F*, 1984 *A*, 1985 *S, F, W, E*, 1986 *F, W, R*, 1987 *E, S, F, W*, [*W, A*], 1988 *S, F, W, E* 1,2, *WS, It*, 1989 *F, W, E, S*
Deane, E C (Monkstown) 1909 *E*
Deering, M J (Bective Rangers) 1929 *W*
Deering, S J (Bective Rangers) 1935 *E, S, W, NZ*, 1936 *E, S, W*, 1937 *E, S*
Deering, S M (Garryowen, St Mary's Coll) 1974 *W*, 1976 *F, W, E, S*, 1977 *W, E*, 1978 *NZ*
de Lacy, F H (Harlequins) 1948 *E, S*
Delany, M G (Bective Rangers) 1895 *W*
Dempsey, G (Terenure Coll) 1998 *Gg* (R). *SA* 3, 1999 *F, E, S, It*
Dennison, S P (Garryowen) 1973 *F*, 1975 *E, S*
Dick, C J (Ballymena) 1961 *W, F, SA*, 1962 *W*, 1963 *F, E, S, W*
Dick, J S (Queen's U, Belfast) 1962 *E*
Dick, J S (Queen's U, Cork) 1887 *E, S, W*
Dickson, J A N (Dublin U) 1920 *E, W, F*
Doherty, A E (Old Wesley) 1974 *P* (R)
Doherty, W D (Guy's Hospital) 1920 *E, S, W*, 1921 *E, S, W, F*
Donaldson, J A (Belfast Collegians) 1958 *A, E, S, W*
Donovan, T M (Queen's Coll, Cork) 1889 *S*
Dooley, J F (Galwegians) 1959 *E, S, W*
Doran, B R W (Lansdowne) 1900 *S, W*, 1901 *E, S, W*, 1902 *E, S, W*
Doran, E F (Lansdowne) 1890 *S, W*
Doran, G P (Lansdowne) 1899 *S, W*, 1900 *E, S*, 1902 *S, W*, 1903 *W*, 1904 *E*
Douglas, A C (Instonians) 1923 *F*, 1924 *E, S*, 1927 *A*, 1928 *S*
Downing, A J (Dublin U) 1882 *W*
Dowse, J C A (Monkstown) 1914 *F, S, W*
Doyle, J A P (Greystones) 1984 *E, S*
Doyle, J T (Bective Rangers) 1935 *W*
Doyle, M G (Blackrock Coll, UC Dublin, Cambridge U, Edinburgh Wands) 1965 *F, E, S, W, SA*, 1966 *F, E, S, W*, 1967 *A* 1, *E, S, W, F, A* 2, 1968 *F, E, S, W, A*
Doyle, T J (Wanderers) 1968 *E, S, W*
Duggan, A T A (Lansdowne) 1963 *NZ*, 1964 *F*, 1966 *W*, 1967 *A* 1, *S, W, A* 2, 1968 *F, E, S, W*, 1969 *F, E, S, W*, 1970 *SA, F, E, S, W*, 1971 *F, E, S, W*, 1972 *F* 2
Duggan, W (UC Cork) 1920 *S, W*
Duggan, W P (Blackrock Coll) 1975 *E, S, F, W*, 1976 *A, F, W, S, NZ*, 1977 *W, E, S, F*, 1978 *S, F, W, E, NZ*, 1979 *E, S, A* 1,2, 1980 *E*, 1981 *F, W, E, S, SA* 1,2, *A*, 1982 *W, E, S*, 1983 *S, F, W, E*, 1984 *F, W, E, S*
Duignan, P (Galwegians) 1998 *Gg, R*
Duncan, W R (Malone) 1984 *W, E*
Dunlea, F J (Lansdowne) 1989 *W, E, S*
Dunlop, R (Dublin U) 1889 *W*, 1890 *S, W, E*, 1891 *E, S, W*, 1892 *E, S*, 1893 *W*, 1894 *W*
Dunn, P E F (Bective Rangers) 1923 *S*
Dunn, T B (NIFC) 1935 *NZ*
Dunne, M J (Lansdowne) 1929 *F, E, S*, 1930 *F, E, S, W*, 1932 *E, S, W*, 1933 *E, W, S*, 1934 *E, S, W*
Dwyer, P J (UC Dublin) 1962 *W*, 1963 *F, NZ*, 1964 *S, W*

Edwards, H G (Dublin U) 1877 *E*, 1878 *E*
Edwards, R W (Malone) 1904 *W*
Edwards, T (Lansdowne) 1888 *M*, 1890 *S, W, E*, 1892 *W*, 1893 *E*
Edwards, W V (Malone) 1912 *F, E*
Egan, J D (Bective Rangers) 1922 *S*
Egan, J T (Cork Constitution) 1931 *F, E, SA*
Egan, M S (Garryowen) 1893 *E*, 1895 *S*
Ekin, W (Queen's Coll, Belfast) 1888 *W, S*
Elliott, W R J (Bangor) 1979 *S*
Elwood, E P (Lansdowne, Galwegians) 1993 *W, E, R*, 1994 *F, W, E, S, A* 1,2, 1995 *F, W*, [*NZ, W, F*], 1996 *US, S*, 1997 *F, W, E, NZ, C, It* 2 (R), 1998 *F, W, E, SA* 1,2, *Gg, R, SA* 3, 1999 *It*

English, M A F (Lansdowne, Limerick Bohemians) 1958 *W, F*, 1959 *E, S, F*, 1960 *E, S*, 1961 *S, W, F*, 1962 *F, W*, 1963 *E, S, W, NZ*
Ennis, F N G (Wanderers) 1979 *A* 1 (R)
Ensor, A H (Wanderers) 1973 *W, F*, 1974 *F, W, E, S, P, NZ*, 1975 *E, S, F, W*, 1976 *A, F, W, E, NZ*, 1977 *E*, 1978 *S, F, W, E*
Entrican, J C (Queen's U, Belfast) 1931 *S*
Erskine, D J (Sale) 1997 *NZ* (R), *C, It* 2

Fagan, G L (Kingstown School) 1878 *E*
Fagan, W B C (Wanderers) 1956 *F, E, S*
Farrell, J L (Bective Rangers) 1926 *F, E, S, W*, 1927 *F, E, S, W, A*, 1928 *F, E, S, W*, 1929 *F, E, S, W*, 1930 *F, E, S, W*, 1931 *F, E, S, W, SA*, 1932 *E, S, W*
Feddis, N (Lansdowne) 1956 *E*
Feighery, C F P (Lansdowne) 1972 *F* 1, *E, F* 2
Feighery, T A O (St Mary's Coll) 1977 *W, E*
Ferris, H H (Queen's Coll, Belfast) 1901 *W*
Ferris, J H (Queen's Coll, Belfast) 1900 *E, S, W*
Field, M J (Malone) 1994 *E, S, A* 1 (R), 1995 *F* (R), *W* (t), *It* (R), [*NZ*(t + R), *J*], *Fj*, 1996 *F* (R), *W, E, A* (R), 1997 *F, W, E, S*
Finlay, J E (Queen's Coll, Belfast) 1913 *E, S, W*, 1920 *E, S, W*
Finlay, J E (NIFC) 1876 *E*, 1877 *E, S*, 1878 *E*, 1879 *S, E*, 1880 *S*, 1882 *S*
Finn, M C (UC Cork, Cork Constitution) 1979 *E*, 1982 *W, E, S, F*, 1983 *S, F, W, E*, 1984 *E, S, A*, 1986 *F, W*
Finn, R G A (UC Dublin) 1977 *F*
Fitzgerald, C C (Glasgow U, Dungannon) 1902 *E*, 1903 *E, S*
Fitzgerald, C F (St Mary's Coll) 1979 *A* 1,2, 1980 *E, S, F, W*, 1982 *W, E, S, F*, 1983 *S, F, W, E*, 1984 *F, W, A*, 1985 *S, F, W, E*, 1986 *F, W, E, S*
Fitzgerald, D C (Lansdowne, De La Salle Palmerston) 1984 *E, S*, 1986 *W, E, S, R*, 1987 *E, S, F, W*, [*W, C, A*], 1988 *S, F, W, E* 1, 1989 *NZ* (R), 1990 *E, S, F, W, Arg*, 1991 *F, W, E, S, Nm* 1,2, [*Z, S, A*], 1992 *W, S* (R)
Fitzgerald, J (Wanderers) 1884 *W*
Fitzgerald, J J (Young Munster) 1988 *S, F*, 1990 *S, F, W*, 1991 *F, W, E, S*, [*J*], 1994 *A* 1,2
Fitzgibbon, M J J (Shannon) 1992 *W, E, S, F, NZ* 1,2
Fitzpatrick, J M (Dungannon) 1998 *SA* 1,2 *Gg* (R), *R* (R), *SA* 3, 1999 *F* (R), *W* (R), *E* (R), *It*
Fitzpatrick, M P (Wanderers) 1978 *S*, 1980 *S, F, W*, 1981 *F, W, E, S*, 1985 *F* (R)
Flavin, P (Blackrock Coll) 1997 *F* (R), *S*
Fletcher, W W (Kingstown) 1882 *W, S*, 1883 *E*
Flood, R S (Dublin U) 1925 *W*
Flynn, M K (Wanderers) 1959 *F*, 1960 *F*, 1962 *E, S, F, W*, 1964 *E, S, W, F*, 1965 *F, E, S, W, SA*, 1966 *F, E, S*, 1972 *F* 1, *E, F* 2, 1973 *NZ*
Fogarty, T (Garryowen) 1891 *W*
Foley, A G (Shannon) 1995 *E, S, F, W, It*, [*J*(t + R)], 1996 *A*, 1997 *It* 1, *E* (R)
Foley, B O (Shannon) 1976 *F, E*, 1977 *W* (R), 1980 *F, W*, 1981 *F, E, S, SA* 1,2, *A*
Forbes, R E (Malone) 1907 *E*
Forrest, A J (Wanderers) 1880 *E, S*, 1881 *E, S*, 1882 *W, E*, 1883 *E*, 1885 *S* 2
Forrest, E G (Wanderers) 1888 *M*, 1889 *S, W*, 1890 *S, E*, 1891 *E*, 1893 *S, W*, 1894 *E, S, W*, 1895 *W*, 1897 *E, S*
Forrest, H (Wanderers) 1893 *S, W*
Fortune, J J (Clontarf) 1963 *NZ*, 1964 *E*
Foster, A R (Derry) 1910 *E, S, F*, 1911 *E, S, W, F*, 1912 *F, E, S, W*, 1914 *E, S, W*, 1921 *E, S, W*
Francis, N P J (Blackrock Coll, London Irish, Old Belvedere) 1987 [*Tg, A*], 1988 *WS, It*, 1989 *S*, 1990 *E, F, W*, 1991 *E, S, Nm* 1,2, [*Z, J, S, A*], 1992 *W, E, S*, 1993 *F, R*, 1994 *F, W, E, S, A* 1,2, *US*, 1995 *E*, [*NZ, J, W, F*], *Fj*, 1996 *US, S*
Franks, J G (Dublin U) 1898 *E, S, W*
Frazer, E F (Bective Rangers) 1891 *S*, 1892 *S*
Freer, A E (Lansdowne) 1901 *E, S, W*
Fulcher, G M (Cork Constitution, London Irish) 1994 *A* 2, *US*, 1995 *E* (R), *S, F, W, It*, [*NZ, W, F*], *Fj*, 1996 *US, S, F, W, E, A*, 1997 *It* 1, *W* (R), 1998 *SA* 1 (R)
Fulton, J (NIFC) 1895 *S, W*, 1896 *E*, 1897 *E*, 1898 *W*, 1899 *E*, 1900 *W*, 1901 *E*, 1902 *E, S, W*, 1903 *E, S, W*, 1904 *E, S*
Furlong, J N (UC Galway) 1992 *NZ* 1,2

Gaffikin, W (Windsor) 1875 *E*
Gage, J H (Queen's U, Belfast) 1926 *S, W,* 1927 *S, W*
Galbraith, E (Dublin U) 1875 *E*
Galbraith, H T (Belfast Acad) 1890 *W*
Galbraith, R (Dublin U) 1875 *E,* 1876 *E,* 1877 *E*
Galwey, M J (Shannon) 1991 *F, W, Nm* 2 (R), *[J],* 1992 *E, S, F, NZ* 1,2, *A,* 1993 *F, W, E, R,* 1994 *F, W, E, S, A* 1, *US* (R), 1995 *E,* 1996 *WS,* 1998 *F* (R), 1999 *W* (R)
Ganly, J B (Monkstown) 1927 *F, E, S, W, A,* 1928 *F, E, S, W,* 1929 *F, S,* 1930 *F*
Gardiner, F (NIFC) 1900 *E, S,* 1901 *E, W,* 1902 *E, S, W,* 1903 *E, W,* 1904 *E, S, W,* 1906 *E, S, W,* 1907 *S, W,* 1908 *S, W,* 1909 *E, S, F*
Gardiner, J B (NIFC) 1923 *E, S, W, F,* 1924 *F, E, S, W, NZ,* 1925 *F, E, S, W*
Gardiner, S (Belfast Albion) 1893 *E, S*
Gardiner, W (NIFC) 1892 *E, S,* 1893 *E, S, W,* 1894 *E, S, W,* 1895 *E, S, W,* 1896 *E, S, W,* 1897 *E, S,* 1898 *W*
Garry, M G (Bective Rangers) 1909 *E, S, W, F,* 1911 *E, S, W*
Gaston, J T (Dublin U) 1954 *NZ, F, E, S, W,* 1955 *W* 1956 *F, E*
Gavin, T J (Moseley, London Irish) 1949 *F, E*
Geoghegan, S P (London Irish, Bath) 1991 *F, W, E, S, Nm* 1, *[Z, S, A],* 1992 *E, S, F, A,* 1993 *S, F, W, E,* 1994 *F, W, E, S, A* 1,2, *US,* 1995 *E, S, F, W, [NZ, J, W, F], Fj,* 1996 *US, S, W, E*
Gibson, C M H (Cambridge U, NIFC) 1964 *E, S, W, F,* 1965 *F, E, S, W, SA,* 1966 *F, E, S, W,* 1967 *A* 1, *E, S, W, F, A* 2, 1968 *E, S, W, A,* 1969 *E, S, W,* 1970 *SA, F, E, S, W,* 1971 *F, E, S, W,* 1972 *F* 1, *E, F* 2, 1973 *NZ, E, S, W, F,* 1974 *F, W, E, S, P,* 1975 *E, S, F, W,* 1976 *A, F, W, E, S, NZ,* 1977 *W, E, S, F,* 1978 *F, W, E, NZ,* 1979 *S, A* 1,2
Gibson, M E (Lansdowne, London Irish) 1979 *F, W, E, S,* 1981 *W* (R), 1986 *R,* 1988 *S, F, W, E* 2
Gifford, H P (Wanderers) 1890 *S*
Gillespie, J C (Dublin U) 1922 *W, F*
Gilpin, F G (Queen's U, Belfast) 1962 *E, S, F*
Glass, D C (Belfast Collegians) 1958 *F,* 1960 *W,* 1961 *W, SA*
Glennon, B T (Lansdowne) 1993 *F* (R)
Glennon, J J (Skerries) 1980 *E, S,* 1987 *E, S, F, [W* (R)]
Godfrey, R P (UC Dublin) 1954 *S, W*
Goodall, K G (City of Derry, Newcastle U) 1967 *A* 1, *E, S, W, F, A* 2, 1968 *F, E, S, W, A,* 1969 *F, E, S,* 1970 *SA, F, E, S, W*
Gordon, A (Dublin U) 1884 *S*
Gordon, T G (NIFC) 1877 *E, S,* 1878 *E*
Gotto, R P C (NIFC) 1906 *SA*
Goulding, W J (Cork) 1879 *S*
Grace, T O (UC Dublin, St Mary's Coll) 1972 *F* 1, *E,* 1973 *NZ, E, S, W,* 1974 *E, S, P, NZ,* 1975 *E, S, F, W,* 1976 *A, F, W, E, S, NZ,* 1977 *W, E, S, F,* 1978 *S*
Graham, R I (Dublin U) 1911 *F*
Grant, E L (CIYMS) 1971 *F, E, S, W*
Grant, P J (Bective Rangers) 1894 *S, W*
Graves, C R A (Wanderers) 1934 *E, S, W,* 1935 *E, S, W, NZ,* 1936 *E, S, W,* 1937 *E, S,* 1938 *E, S, W*
Gray, R D (Old Wesley) 1923 *E, S,* 1925 *F,* 1926 *F*
Greene, E H (Dublin U, Kingstown) 1882 *W,* 1884 *W,* 1885 *E, S* 2, 1886 *F*
Greer, R (Kingstown) 1876 *E*
Greeves, T J (NIFC) 1907 *E, S, W,* 1909 *W, F*
Gregg, R J (Queen's U, Belfast) 1953 *F, E, S, W,* 1954 *F, E, S*
Griffin, C S (London Irish) 1951 *F, E*
Griffin, J L (Wanderers) 1949 *S, W*
Griffiths, W (Limerick) 1878 *E*
Grimshaw, C (Queen's U, Belfast) 1969 *E* (R)
Guerin, B N (Galwegians) 1956 *S*
Gwynn, A P (Dublin U) 1895 *W*
Gwynn, L H (Dublin U) 1893 *S,* 1894 *E, S, W,* 1897 *S,* 1898 *E, S*

Hakin, R F (CIYMS) 1976 *W, S, NZ,* 1977 *W, E, F*
Hall, R O N (Dublin U) 1884 *W*
Hall, W H (Instonians) 1923 *E, S, W, F,* 1924 *F, S*
Hallaran, C F G T (Royal Navy) 1921 *E, S, W,* 1922 *E, S, W,* 1923 *E, F,* 1924 *F, E, S, W,* 1925 *F,* 1926 *F, E*
Halpin, G F (Wanderers, London Irish) 1990 *E,* 1991 *[J],* 1992 *E, S, F,* 1993 *R,* 1994 *F* (R), 1995 *It, [NZ, W, F]*
Halpin, T (Garryowen) 1909 *S, W, F,* 1910 *E, S, W,* 1911 *E, S, W, F,* 1912 *F, E, S*

Halvey, E O (Shannon) 1995 *F, W, It, [J, W* (t), *F* (R)], 1997 *NZ, C* (R)
Hamilton, A J (Lansdowne) 1884 *W*
Hamilton, G F (NIFC) 1991 *F, W, E, S, Nm* 2, *[Z, J, S, A],* 1992 *A*
Hamilton, R L (NIFC) 1926 *F*
Hamilton, R W (Wanderers) 1893 *W*
Hamilton, W J (Dublin U) 1877 *E*
Hamlet, G T (Old Wesley) 1902 *E, S, W,* 1903 *E, S, W,* 1904 *S, W,* 1905 *E, S, W, NZ,* 1906 *SA,* 1907 *E, S, W,* 1908 *E, S, W,* 1909 *E, S, W, F,* 1910 *E, S, F,* 1911 *E, S, W, F*
Hanrahan, C J (Dolphin) 1926 *S, W,* 1927 *E, S, W, A,* 1928 *F, E, S,* 1929 *F, E, S, W,* 1930 *F, E, S, W,* 1931 *F,* 1932 *S, W*
Harbison, H T (Bective Rangers) 1984 *W* (R), *E, S,* 1986 *R,* 1987 *E, S, F, W*
Hardy, G G (Bective Rangers) 1962 *S*
Harman, G R A (Dublin U) 1899 *E, W*
Harper, J (Instonians) 1947 *F, E, S*
Harpur, T G (Dublin U) 1908 *E, S, W*
Harrison, T (Cork) 1879 *S,* 1880 *S,* 1881 *E*
Harvey, F M W (Wanderers) 1907 *W,* 1911 *F*
Harvey, G A D (Wanderers) 1903 *E, S,* 1904 *W,* 1905 *E, S, W,* 1903 *E, W*
Harvey, T A (Dublin U) 1900 *W,* 1901 *S, W,* 1902 *E, S, W,* 1903 *E, W*
Haycock, P P (Terenure Coll) 1989 *E*
Headon, T A (UC Dublin) 1939 *S, W*
Healey, P (Limerick) 1901 *E, S, W,* 1902 *E, S, W,* 1903 *E, S, W,* 1904 *S*
Heffernan, M R (Cork Constitution) 1911 *E, S, W, F*
Hemphill, R (Dublin U) 1912 *F, E, S, W*
Henderson, N J (Queen's U, Belfast, NIFC) 1949 *S, W,* 1950 *F,* 1951 *F, E, S, W, SA,* 1952 *F, S, W, E,* 1953 *F, E, S, W,* 1954 *NZ, F, E, S, W,* 1955 *F, E, S, W,* 1956 *S, W,* 1957 *F, E, S, W,* 1958 *A, E, S, W, F,* 1959 *E, S, W, F*
Henderson R A J (London Irish, Wasps) 1996 *WS,* 1997 *NZ, C,* 1998 *F, W, SA* 1 (R),2 (R), 1999 *F* (R), *E, S* (R), *It*
Henebrey, G J (Garryowen) 1906 *E, S, W, SA,* 1909 *W, F*
Heron, A G (Queen's Coll, Belfast) 1901 *E*
Heron, J (NIFC) 1877 *S,* 1879 *E*
Heron, W T (NIFC) 1880 *E, S*
Herrick, R W (Dublin U) 1886 *S*
Heuston, F S (Kingstown) 1882 *W,* 1883 *E, S*
Hewitt, D (Queen's U, Belfast, Instonians) 1958 *A, E, S, F,* 1959 *S, W, F,* 1960 *E, S, W, F,* 1961 *E, S, W, F,* 1962 *S, F,* 1965 *W*
Hewitt, F S (Instonians) 1924 *W, NZ,* 1925 *F, E, S,* 1926 *E,* 1927 *E, S, W*
Hewitt, J A (NIFC) 1981 *SA* 1 (R), 2 (R)
Hewitt, T R (Queen's U, Belfast) 1924 *W, NZ,* 1925 *F, E, S,* 1926 *F, E, S, W*
Hewitt, V A (Instonians) 1935 *S, W, NZ,* 1936 *E, S, W*
Hewitt, W J (Instonians) 1954 *E,* 1956 *S,* 1959 *W,* 1961 *SA*
Hewson, F T (Wanderers) 1875 *E*
Hickie, D A (St Mary's Coll) 1997 *W, E, S, NZ, C, It* 2, 1998 *S, F, W, E, SA* 1,2
Hickie, D J (St Mary's Coll) 1971 *F, E, S, W,* 1972 *F* 1, *E*
Higgins, J A D (Civil Service) 1947 *S, W, A,* 1948 *F, S, W*
Higgins, W W (NIFC) 1884 *E, S*
Hillary, M F (UC Dublin) 1952 *E*
Hingerty, D J (UC Dublin) 1947 *F, E, S, W*
Hinton, W P (Old Wesley) 1907 *W,* 1908 *E, S, W,* 1909 *E, S,* 1910 *E, S, W, F,* 1911 *E, S, W,* 1912 *F, E, W*
Hipwell, M L (Terenure Coll) 1962 *E, S,* 1968 *F, A,* 1969 *F* (R), *S* (R), *W,* 1971 *F, E, S, W,* 1972 *F* 2
Hobbs, T H M (Dublin U) 1884 *S,* 1885 *E*
Hobson, E W (Dublin U) 1876 *E*
Hogan, N A (Terenure Coll, London Irish) 1995 *E, W, [J, W, F],* 1996 *F, W, E, WS,* 1997 *F, W, E, It* 2
Hogan, P (Garryowen) 1992 *F*
Hogg, W (Dublin U) 1885 *S* 2
Holland, J J (Wanderers) 1981 *SA* 1,2, 1986 *W*
Holmes, G W (Dublin U) 1912 *SA,* 1913 *E, S*
Holmes, L J (Lisburn) 1889 *S, W*
Hooks, K J (Queen's U, Belfast, Ards, Bangor) 1981 *S,* 1989 *NZ,* 1990 *F, W, Arg,* 1991 *F*
Horan, A K (Blackheath) 1920 *E, W*
Houston, K J (Oxford U, London Irish) 1961 *SA,* 1964 *S, W,* 1965 *F, E, SA*
Hughes, R W (NIFC) 1878 *E,* 1880 *E, S,* 1881 *S,* 1882 *E, S,* 1883 *E, S,* 1884 *E, S,* 1885 *E,* 1886 *E*
Humphreys, D G (London Irish, Dungannon) 1996 *F, W, E, WS,* 1997 *E* (R), *S, It* 2, 1998 *S, E* (R), *SA* 2 (t + R), *R* (R), 1999 *F, W, E, S*

Hunt, E W F de Vere (Army, Rosslyn Park) 1930 *F*, 1932 *E, S, W*, 1933 *E*
Hunter, D V (Dublin U) 1885 *S 2*
Hunter, L (Civil Service) 1968 *W, A*
Hunter, W R (CIYMS) 1962 *E, S, W, F*, 1963 *F, E, S*, 1966 *F, E, S*
Hurley, H D (Old Wesley, Moseley) 1995 *Fj* (t), 1996 *WS*
Hutton, S A (Malone) 1967 *S, W, F, A 2*

Ireland, J (Windsor) 1876 *E*, 1877 *E*
Irvine, H A S (Collegians) 1901 *S*
Irwin, D G (Queen's U, Belfast, Instonians) 1980 *F, W*, 1981 *F, W, E, S, SA* 1,2, *A*, 1982 *W*, 1983 *S, F, W, E*, 1984 *F, W*, 1987 [*Tg, A* (R)], 1989 *F, W, E, S, NZ*, 1990 *E, S*
Irwin, J W S (NIFC) 1938 *E, S*, 1939 *E, S, W*
Irwin, S T (Queen's Coll, Belfast) 1900 *E, S, W*, 1901 *E, W*, 1902 *E, S, W*, 1903 *S*

Jack, H W (UC Cork) 1914 *S, W*, 1921 *W*
Jackson, A R V (Wanderers) 1911 *E, S, W, F*, 1913 *W, F*, 1914 *F, E, S, W*
Jackson, F (NIFC) 1923 *E*
Jackson, H W (Dublin U) 1877 *E*
Jameson, J S (Lansdowne) 1888 *M*, 1889 *S, W*, 1891 *W*, 1892 *E, W*, 1893 *S*
Jeffares, E W (Wanderers) 1913 *E, S*
Johns, P S (Dublin U, Dungannon, Saracens) 1990 *Arg*, 1992 *NZ* 1,2, *A*, 1993 *S, F, W, E, R*, 1994 *F, W, E, S, A* 1,2, *US*, 1995 *E, S, W, It*, [*NZ, J, W, F*], *Fj*, 1996 *US, S, F, WS*, 1997 *It* 1 (R), *F, W, E, S, NZ, C, It* 2, 1998 *S, F, W, E, SA* 1,2, *Gg, R, SA* 3, 1999 *F, W, E, S, It*
Johnston, J (Belfast Acad) 1881 *S*, 1882 *S*, 1884 *S*, 1885 *S* 1,2, 1886 *E*, 1887 *E, S, W*
Johnston, M (Dublin U) 1880 *E, S*, 1881 *E, S*, 1882 *E*, 1884 *E, S*, 1886 *E*
Johnston, R (Wanderers) 1893 *E, W*
Johnston, R W (Dublin U) 1890 *S, W, E*
Johnston, T J (Queen's Coll, Belfast) 1892 *E, S, W*, 1893 *E, S*, 1895 *E*
Johnstone, W E (Dublin U) 1884 *W*
Johnstone-Smyth, T R (Lansdowne) 1882 *E*

Kavanagh, J R (UC Dublin, Wanderers) 1953 *F, E, S, W*, 1954 *NZ, S, W*, 1955 *F, E*, 1956 *E, S, W*, 1957 *F, E, S, W*, 1958 *A, E, S, W*, 1959 *S, W, F*, 1960 *E, S, W, F, SA*, 1961 *E, S, W, F, SA*, 1962 *F*
Kavanagh, P J (UC Dublin, Wanderers) 1952 *E*, 1955 *W*
Keane, K P (Garryowen) 1998 *E* (R)
Keane, M I (Lansdowne) 1974 *F, W, E, S, P, NZ*, 1975 *E, S, F, W*, 1976 *A, F, W, E, S, NZ*, 1977 *W, E, S, F*, 1978 *S, F, W, E, NZ*, 1979 *F, W, E, S, A* 1,2, 1980 *E, S, F, W*, 1981 *F, W, E, S*, 1982 *W, E, S, F*, 1983 *S, F, W, E*, 1984 *F, W, E, S*
Kearney, R K (Wanderers) 1982 *F*, 1984 *A*, 1986 *F, W*
Keeffe, E (Sunday's Well) 1947 *F, E, S, W, A*, 1948 *F*
Kelly, H C (NIFC) 1877 *E, S*, 1878 *E*, 1879 *S*, 1880 *E, S*
Kelly, J C (UC Dublin) 1962 *F, W*, 1963 *F, E, S, W, NZ*, 1964 *E, S, W, F*
Kelly, S (Lansdowne) 1954 *S, W*, 1955 *S*, 1960 *W, F*
Kelly, W (Wanderers) 1884 *S*
Kennedy, A G (Belfast Collegians) 1956 *F*
Kennedy, A P (London Irish) 1986 *W, E*
Kennedy, F (Wanderers) 1880 *E*, 1881 *E*, 1882 *W*
Kennedy, F A (Wanderers) 1904 *E, W*
Kennedy, H (Bradford) 1938 *S, W*
Kennedy, J M (Wanderers) 1882 *W*, 1884 *W*
Kennedy, K W (Queen's U, Belfast, London Irish) 1965 *F, E, S, W, SA*, 1966 *F, E, S, W*, 1967 *A* 1, *E, S, W, F, A* 2, 1968 *F, A*, 1969 *F, E, S, W*, 1970 *SA, F, E, S, W*, 1971 *F, E, S, W*, 1972 *F* 1, *E, F* 2, 1973 *NZ, E, S, W, F*, 1974 *F, W, E, S, P, NZ*, 1975 *F, W*
Kennedy, T J (St Mary's Coll) 1978 *NZ*, 1979 *F, W, E* (R), *A* 1,2, 1980 *E, S, F, W*, 1981 *SA* 1,2, *A*
Kenny, P (Wanderers) 1992 *NZ* 2 (R)
Keogh, F S (Bective Rangers) 1964 *W, F*
Keon, J J (Limerick) 1879 *E*
Keyes, R P (Cork Constitution) 1986 *E*, 1991 [*Z, J, S, A*], 1992 *W, E, S*
Kidd, F W (Dublin U, Lansdowne) 1877 *E, S*, 1878 *E*
Kiely, M D (Lansdowne) 1962 *W*, 1963 *F, E, S, W*
Kiernan, M J (Dolphin, Lansdowne) 1982 *W* (R), *E, S, F*, 1983 *S, F, W, E*, 1984 *E, S, A*, 1985 *S, F, W, E*, 1986 *F, W, E, S, R*, 1987 *E, S, F, W*, [*W, C, A*], 1988 *S, F, W, E* 1,2, *WS*, 1989 *F, W, E, S*, 1990 *E, S, F, W, Arg*, 1991 *F*

Kiernan, T J (UC Cork, Cork Const) 1960 *E, S, W, F, SA*, 1961 *E, S, W, F, SA*, 1962 *E, W*, 1963 *F, S, W, NZ*, 1964 *E, S*, 1965 *F, E, S, W, SA*, 1966 *F, E, S, W*, 1967 *A* 1, *E, S, W, F, A* 2, 1968 *F, E, S, W, A*, 1969 *F, E, S, W*, 1970 *SA, F, E, S, W*, 1971 *F* 1, *E, F* 2, 1973 *NZ, E, S*
Killeen, G V (Garryowen) 1912 *E, S, W*, 1913 *E, S, W, F*, 1914 *E, S, W*
King, H (Dublin U) 1883 *E, S*
Kingston, T J (Dolphin) 1987 [*W, Tg, A*], 1988 *S, F, W, E* 1, 1990 *F, W*, 1991 [*J*], 1993 *F, W, E, R*, 1994 *F, W, E, S*, 1995 *F, W, It*, [*NZ, J* (R), *W, F*], *Fj*, 1996 *US, S, F*
Knox, J H (Dublin U, Lansdowne) 1904 *W*, 1905 *E, S, W, NZ*, 1906 *E, S, W*, 1907 *W*, 1908 *S*
Kyle, J W (Queen's U, Belfast, NIFC) 1947 *F, E, S, W, A*, 1948 *F, E, S, W*, 1949 *F, E, S, W*, 1950 *F, E, S, W*, 1951 *F, E, S, W, SA*, 1952 *F, S, W, E*, 1953 *F, E, S, W*, 1954 *NZ, F*, 1955 *F, E, W*, 1956 *F, E, S, W*, 1957 *F, E, S, W*, 1958 *A, E, S*

Lambert, N H (Lansdowne) 1934 *S, W*
Lamont, R A (Instonians) 1965 *F, E, SA*, 1966 *F, E, S, W*, 1970 *SA, F, E, S, W*
Landers, M F (Cork Const) 1904 *W*, 1905 *E, S, W, NZ*
Lane, D (UC Cork) 1934 *S, W*, 1935 *E, S*
Lane, M F (UC Cork) 1947 *W*, 1949 *F, E, S, W*, 1950 *F, E, S, W*, 1951 *F, E, S, W, SA*, 1952 *F, S*, 1953 *F, E*
Lane, P (Old Crescent) 1964 *W*
Langan, D J (Clontarf) 1934 *W*
Langbroek, J A (Blackrock Coll) 1987 [*Tg*]
Lavery, P (London Irish) 1974 *W*, 1976 *W*
Lawlor, P J (Clontarf) 1951 *S, SA*, 1952 *F, S, W, E*, 1953 *F*, 1954 *NZ, E, S*, 1956 *F, E*
Lawlor, P J (Bective Rangers) 1935 *E, S, W*, 1937 *E, S, W*
Lawlor, P J (Bective Rangers) 1990 *Arg*, 1992 *A*, 1993 *S*
Leahy, K T (Wanderers) 1992 *NZ* 1
Leahy, M W (UC Cork) 1964 *W*
Lee, S (NIFC) 1891 *E, S, W*, 1892 *E, S, W*, 1893 *E, S, W*, 1894 *E, S, W*, 1895 *E, W*, 1896 *E, S, W*, 1897 *E*, 1898 *E*
Le Fanu, V C (Cambridge U, Lansdowne) 1886 *E, S*, 1887 *E, W*, 1888 *S*, 1889 *W*, 1890 *E*, 1891 *E*, 1892 *E, S, W*
Lenihan, D G (UC Cork, Cork Const) 1981 *A*, 1982 *W, E, S, F*, 1983 *S, F, W, E*, 1984 *F, W, E, S, A*, 1985 *S, F, W, E*, 1986 *F, W, E, S, R*, 1987 *E, S, F, W*, [*W, C, Tg, A*], 1988 *S, F, W, E* 1,2, *WS, It*, 1989 *F, W, E, S, NZ*, 1990 *S, F, W, Arg*, 1991 *Nm* 2, [*Z, S, A*], 1992 *W*
L'Estrange, L P F (Dublin U) 1962 *E*
Levis, F H (Wanderers) 1884 *E*
Lightfoot, E J (Lansdowne) 1931 *F, E, S, W, SA*, 1932 *E, S, W*, 1933 *E, W, S*
Lindsay, H (Dublin U, Armagh) 1893 *E, S, W*, 1894 *E, S, W*, 1895 *E*, 1896 *E, S, W*, 1898 *E, S, W*
Little, T J (Bective Rangers) 1898 *W*, 1899 *S, W*, 1900 *S, W*, 1901 *E, S*
Lloyd, R A (Dublin U, Liverpool) 1910 *E, S*, 1911 *E, S, W, F*, 1912 *F, E, S, W, SA*, 1913 *E, S, W, F*, 1914 *F, E*, 1920 *E, F*
Lydon, C T J (Galwegians) 1956 *S*
Lyle, R K (Dublin U) 1910 *W, F*
Lyle, T R (Dublin U) 1885 *E, S* 1,2, 1886 *E*, 1887 *E, S*
Lynch, J F (St Mary's Coll) 1971 *F, E, S, W*, 1972 *F* 1, *E, F* 2, 1973 *NZ, E, S, W*, 1974 *F, W, E, S, P, NZ*
Lynch, L (Lansdowne) 1956 *S*
Lytle, J H (NIFC) 1894 *E, S, W*, 1895 *W*, 1896 *E, S, W*, 1897 *E, S*, 1898 *E, S*, 1899 *S*
Lytle, J N (NIFC) 1888 *M*, 1889 *W*, 1890 *E*, 1891 *E, S*, 1894 *E, S, W*
Lyttle, V J (Collegians, Bedford) 1938 *E*, 1939 *E, S*

McAleese, D R (Ballymena) 1992 *F*
McAllan, G H (Dungannon) 1896 *S, W*
Macauley, J (Limerick) 1887 *E, S*
McBride, W D (Malone) 1988 *W, E* 1, *WS, It*, 1989 *S*, 1990 *F, W, Arg*, 1993 *S, F, W, E, R*, 1994 *W, E, S, A* 1, 1995 *F, E*, [*NZ, W, F*], *Fj* (R), 1996 *W, WS, A*, 1997 *It* 1 (R), *F, W, E, S*
McBride, W J (Ballymena) 1962 *E, S, F, W*, 1963 *F, E, S, W, NZ*, 1964 *E, S, F*, 1965 *F, E, S, W, SA*, 1966 *F, E, S*, 1967 *A* 1, *E, S, W, F, A* 2, 1968 *F, E, S, W, A*, 1969 *F, E, S, W*, 1970 *SA, F, E, S, W*, 1971 *F, E, S, W*, 1972 *F* 1, *E, F* 2, 1973 *NZ, E, S, W, F*, 1974 *F, W, E, S, P, NZ*, 1975 *E, S, F, W*
McCahill, S A (Sunday's Well) 1995 *Fj* (t)
McCall, B W (London Irish) 1985 *F* (R), 1986 *E, S*

McCall, M C (Bangor, Dungannon, London Irish) 1992
NZ 1 (R), 2, 1994 *W*, 1996 *E* (R), *A*, 1997 *It* 1, *NZ, C, It*
2, 1998 *S, E, SA* 1,2
McCallan, B (Ballymena) 1960 *E, S*
McCarten, R J (London Irish) 1961 *E, W, F*
McCarthy, E A (Kingstown) 1882 *W*
McCarthy, J S (Dolphin) 1948 *F, E, S, W*, 1949 *F, E, S,
W*, 1950 *W*, 1951 *F, E, S, W, SA*, 1952 *F, S, W, E*, 1953 *F,
E, S*, 1954 *NZ, F, E, S, W*, 1955 *F, E*
McCarthy, P D (Cork Const) 1992 *NZ* 1,2, *A*, 1993 *S, R*
(R)
MacCarthy, St G (Dublin U) 1882 *W*
McCarthy, T (Cork) 1898 *W*
McClelland, T A (Queen's U, Belfast) 1921 *E, S, W, F*,
1922 *E, W, F*, 1923 *E, S, W, F*, 1924 *F, E, S, W, NZ*
McClenahan, R O (Instonians) 1923 *E, S, W*
McClinton, A N (NIFC) 1910 *W, F*
McCombe, W McM (Dublin U, Bangor) 1968 *F*, 1975
E, S, F, W
McConnell, A A (Collegians) 1947 *A*, 1948 *F, E, S, W*,
1949 *F, E*
McConnell, G (Derry, Edinburgh U) 1912 *F, E*, 1913 *W, F*
McConnell, J W (Lansdowne) 1913 *S*
McCormac, F M (Wanderers) 1909 *W*, 1910 *W, F*
McCormick, W J (Wanderers) 1930 *E*
McCoull, H C (Belfast Albion) 1895 *E, S, W*, 1899 *E*
McCourt, D (Queen's U, Belfast) 1947 *A*
McCoy, J J (Dungannon, Bangor, Ballymena) 1984 *W,
A*, 1985 *S, F, W, E*, 1986 *F*, 1987 *[Tg]*, 1988 *E* 2, *WS, S*,
1989 *F, W, E, S, NZ*
McCracken, H (NIFC) 1954 *W*
McDermott, S J (London Irish) 1955 *S, W*
Macdonald, J A (Methodist Coll, Belfast) 1875 *E*, 1876
E, 1877 *S*, 1878 *E*, 1879 *S*, 1880 *E*, 1881 *S*, 1882 *E, S*,
1883 *E, S*, 1884 *E, S*
McDonald, J P (Malone) 1987 *[C]*, 1990 *E* (R), *S, Arg*
McDonnell, A C (Dublin U) 1889 *W*, 1890 *S, W*, 1891 *E*
McDowell, J C (Instonians) 1924 *F, NZ*
McFarland, B A T (Derry) 1920 *S, W, F*, 1922 *W*
McGann, B J (Lansdowne) 1969 *F, E, S, W*, 1970 *SA, F,
E, S, W*, 1971 *F, E, S, W*, 1972 *F* 1, *E, F* 2, 1973 *NZ, E, S,
W*, 1976 *F, W, E, S, NZ*
McGowan, A N (Blackrock Coll) 1994 *US*
McGown, T M W (NIFC) 1899 *E, S*, 1901 *S*
McGrath, D G (UC Dublin, Cork Const) 1984 *S*, 1987
[W, C, Tg, A]
McGrath, N F (Oxford U, London Irish) 1934 *W*
McGrath, P J (UC Cork) 1965 *E, S, W, SA*, 1966 *F, E, S,
W*, 1967 *A* 1, *A* 2
McGrath, R J M (Wanderers) 1977 *W, E, F* (R), 1981
SA 1,2, *A*, 1982 *W, E, S, F*, 1983 *S, F, W, E*, 1984 *F, W*
McGrath, T (Garryowen) 1956 *W*, 1958 *F*, 1960 *E, S, W,
F*, 1961 *SA*
McGuinness, C D (St Mary's Coll) 1997 *NZ, C*, 1998 *F,
W, E, SA* 1,2, *Gg, R* (R), *SA* 3, 1999 *F, W, E, S*
McGuire, E P (UC Galway) 1963 *E, S, W, NZ*, 1964 *E,
S, W, F*
MacHale, S (Lansdowne) 1965 *F, E, S, W, SA*, 1966 *F, E,
S, W*, 1967 *S, W, F*
McIldowie, G (Malone) 1906 *SA*, 1910 *E, S, W*
McIlrath, J A (Ballymena) 1976 *A, F, NZ*, 1977 *W, E*
McIlwaine, E H (NIFC) 1895 *S, W*
McIlwaine, E N (NIFC) 1875 *E*, 1876 *E*
McIlwaine, J E (NIFC) 1897 *E, S*, 1898 *E, S, W*, 1899 *E, W*
McIntosh, L M (Dublin U) 1884 *W*
MacIvor, C V (Dublin U) 1912 *F, E, S, W*, 1913 *E, S, F*
McIvor, S C (Garryowen) 1996 *A*, 1997 *It* 1, *S* (R)
McKay, J W (Queen's U, Belfast) 1947 *F, E, S, W, A*,
1948 *F, E, S, W*, 1949 *F, E, S, W*, 1950 *F, E, S, W*, 1951 *F,
E, S, W, SA*, 1952 *F*
McKee, W D (NIFC) 1947 *A*, 1948 *F, E, S, W*, 1949 *F, E,
S, W*, 1950 *F, E*, 1951 *SA*
McKelvey, J M (Queen's U, Belfast) 1956 *F, E*
McKibbin, A R (Instonians, London Irish) 1977 *W, E, S*,
1978 *S, F, W, E, NZ*, 1979 *F, W, E, S*, 1980 *E, S*
McKibbin, C H (Instonians) 1976 *S* (R)
McKibbin, D (Instonians) 1950 *F, E, S, W*, 1951 *F, E, S, W*
McKibbin, H R (Queen's U, Belfast) 1938 *W*, 1939 *E, S, W*
McKinney, S A (Dungannon) 1972 *F* 1, *E, F* 2, 1973 *W,
F*, 1974 *F, E, S, P, NZ*, 1975 *E, S*, 1976 *A, F, W, E, S, NZ*,
1977 *W, E, S*, 1978 *S* (R), *F, W, E*
McLaughlin, J H (Derry) 1887 *E, S*, 1888 *W, S*
McLean, R E (Dublin U) 1881 *S*, 1882 *W, E, S*, 1883 *E,
S*, 1884 *E, S*, 1885 *E, S* 1

Maclear, B (Cork County, Monkstown) 1905 *E, S, W,
NZ*, 1906 *E, S, W, SA*, 1907 *E, S, W*
McLennan, A C (Wanderers) 1977 *F*, 1978 *S, F, W, E,
NZ*, 1979 *F, W, E, S*, 1980 *E, F*, 1981 *F, W, E, S, SA* 1,2
McLoughlin, F M (Northern) 1976 *A*
McLoughlin, G A J (Shannon) 1979 *F, W, E, S, A* 1,2,
1980 *E*, 1981 *SA* 1,2, 1982 *W, E, S, F*, 1983 *S, F, W, E*,
1984 *F*
McLoughlin, R J (UC Dublin, Blackrock Coll, Gosforth)
1962 *E, S, F*, 1963 *E, S, W, NZ*, 1964 *E, S*, 1965 *F, E, S, W,
SA*, 1966 *F, E, S, W*, 1971 *F, E, S, W*, 1972 *F* 1, *E, F* 2, 1973
NZ, E, S, W, F, 1974 *F, W, E, S, P, NZ*, 1975 *E, S, F, W*
McMahon, L B (Blackrock Coll, UC Dublin) 1931 *E, SA*,
1933 *E*, 1934 *E*, 1936 *E, S, W*, 1937 *E, S, W*, 1938 *E, S*
McMaster, A W (Ballymena) 1972 *F* 1, *E, F* 2, 1973 *NZ,
E, S, W, F*, 1974 *F, E, S, P*, 1975 *F, W*, 1976 *A, F, W, NZ*
McMordie, J (Queen's Coll, Belfast) 1886 *S*
McMorrow, A (Garryowen) 1951 *W*
McMullen, A R (Cork) 1881 *E, S*
McNamara, V (UC Cork) 1914 *E, S, W*
McNaughton, P P (Greystones) 1978 *S, F, W, E*, 1979 *F,
W, E, S, A* 1,2, 1980 *E, S, F, W*, 1981 *F*
MacNeill, H P (Dublin U, Oxford U, Blackrock Coll,
London Irish) 1981 *F, W, E, S, A*, 1982 *W, E, S, F*, 1983 *S,
F, W, E*, 1984 *F, W, E, A*, 1985 *S, F, W, E*, 1986 *F, W, E, S,
R*, 1987 *E, S, F, W, [W, C, Tg, A]*, 1988 *S* (R), *E* 1,2
McQuilkin, K P (Bective Rangers, Lansdowne) 1996
US, S, F, 1997 *F* (t & R), *S*
MacSweeney, D A (Blackrock Coll) 1955 *S*
McVicker, H (Army, Richmond) 1927 *E, S, W, A*, 1928 *F*
McVicker, J (Collegians) 1924 *F, E, S, W, NZ*, 1925 *F, E,
S, W*, 1926 *F, E, S, W*, 1927 *F, E, S, W, A*, 1928 *W*, 1930 *F*
McVicker, S (Queen's U, Belfast) 1922 *E, S, W, F*
McWeeney, J P J (St Mary's Coll) 1997 *NZ*
Madden, M N (Sunday's Well) 1955 *E, S, W*
Magee, J T (Bective Rangers) 1895 *E, S*
Magee, A M (Louis) (Bective Rangers, London Irish)
1895 *E, S, W*, 1896 *E, S, W*, 1897 *E, S*, 1898 *E, S, W*,
1899 *E, S, W*, 1900 *E, S, W*, 1901 *E, S, W*, 1902 *E, S, W*,
1903 *E, S, W*, 1904 *W*
Maggs, K M (Bristol, Bath) 1997 *NZ* (R), *C*, *It* 2, 1998
S, F, W, E, SA 1,2, *Gg, R* (R), *SA* 3, 1999 *F, W, E, S, It*
Maginiss, R M (Dublin U) 1875 *E*, 1876 *E*
Magrath, R M (Cork Constitution) 1909 *S*
Maguire, J F (Cork) 1884 *S*
Mahoney, J (Dolphin) 1923 *E*
Malcolmson, G L (RAF, NIFC) 1935 *NZ*, 1936 *E, S, W*,
1937 *E, S, W*
Malone, N G (Oxford U, Leicester) 1993 *S, F*, 1994 *US*
(R)
Mannion, N P (Corinthians, Lansdowne, Wanderers)
1988 *WS, It*, 1989 *F, W, E, S, NZ*, 1990 *E, S, F, W, Arg*,
1991 *Nm* 1 (R), 2, *[J]*, 1993 *S*
Marshall, B D E (Queen's U, Belfast) 1963 *E*
Mason, S J P (Orrell, Richmond) 1996 *W, E, WS*
Massey-Westropp, R H (Limerick, Monkstown) 1886 *E*
Matier, R N (NIFC) 1878 *E*, 1879 *S*
Matthews, P M (Ards, Wanderers) 1984 *A*, 1985 *S, F, W,
E*, 1986 *R*, 1987 *E, S, F, W, [W, Tg, A]*, 1988 *S, F, W, E*
1,2, *WS, It*, 1989 *F, W, E, S, NZ*, 1990 *E, S*, 1991 *F, W, E,
S, Nm* 1 [*Z, S, A*], 1992 *W, E, S*
Mattsson, J (Wanderers) 1948 *E*
Mayne, R B (Queen's U, Belfast) 1937 *W*, 1938 *E, W*,
1939 *E, S, W*
Mayne, R H (Belfast Academy) 1888 *W, S*
Mayne, T (NIFC) 1921 *E, S, F*
Mays, K M A (UC Dublin) 1973 *NZ, E, S, W*
Meares, A W D (Dublin U) 1899 *S, W*, 1900 *E, W*
Megaw, J (Richmond, Instonians) 1934 *W*, 1938 *E*
Millar, A (Kingstown) 1880 *S*, 1883 *E*
Millar, H J (Monkstown) 1904 *W*, 1905 *E, S, W*
Millar, S (Ballymena) 1958 *F*, 1959 *E, S, W, F*, 1960 *E,
S, W, F, SA*, 1961 *E, S, W, F, SA*, 1962 *E, S, F*, 1963 *F, E,
S, W*, 1964 *F, E, S, W, A*, 1969 *F, E, S, W*, 1970
SA, F, E, S, W
Millar, W H J (Queen's U, Belfast) 1951 *E, S, W*, 1952 *S, W*
Miller, E R P (Leicester, Tererure Coll) 1997 *It* 1, *F, W,
E, NZ, It* 2, 1998 *S, W* (R), *Gg, R*, 1999 *F, W, E* (R), *S*
Miller, F H (Wanderers) 1886 *S*
Milliken, R A (Bangor) 1973 *E, S, W, F*, 1974 *F, W, E, S,
P, NZ*, 1975 *E, S, F, W*
Millin, T J (Dublin U) 1925 *W*
Minch, J B (Bective Rangers) 1912 *SA*, 1913 *E, S*, 1914
E, S

Moffat, J (Belfast Academy) 1888 *W, S, M*, 1889 *S*, 1890 *S, W*, 1891 *S*
Moffatt, J E (Old Wesley) 1904 *S*, 1905 *E, S, W*
Moffett, J W (Ballymena) 1961 *E, S*
Molloy, M G (UC Galway, London Irish) 1966 *F, E*, 1967 *A* 1*, E, S, W, F, A* 2, 1968 *F, E, S, W, A*, 1969 *F, E, S, W*, 1970 *F, E, S, W*, 1971 *F, E, S, W*, 1973 *F*, 1976 *A*
Moloney, J J (St Mary's Coll) 1972 *F* 1*, E, F* 2, 1973 *NZ, E, S, W, F*, 1974 *F, W, E, S, P, NZ*, 1975 *E, S, F, W*, 1976 *S*, 1978 *S, F, W, E*, 1979 *A* 1,2, 1980 *S, W, NZ*
Moloney, L A (Garryowen) 1976 *W* (R)*, S*, 1978 *S* (R)*, NZ*
Molony, J U (UC Dublin) 1950 *S*
Monteith, J D E (Queen's U, Belfast) 1947 *E, S, W*
Montgomery, A (NIFC) 1895 *S*
Montgomery, F P (Queen's U, Belfast) 1914 *E, S, W*
Montgomery, R (Cambridge U) 1887 *E, S, W*, 1891 *E*, 1892 *W*
Moore, C M (Dublin U) 1887 *S*, 1888 *W, S*
Moore, D F (Wanderers) 1883 *E, S*, 1884 *E, W*
Moore, F W (Wanderers) 1884 *W*, 1885 *E, S* 2, 1886 *S*
Moore, H (Windsor) 1876 *E*, 1877 *S*
Moore, H (Queen's U, Belfast) 1910 *S*, 1911 *W, F*, 1912 *F, E, S, W, SA*
Moore, T A P (Highfield) 1967 *A* 2, 1973 *NZ, E, S, W, F*, 1974 *F, W, E, S, P, NZ*
Moore, W D (Queen's Coll, Belfast) 1878 *E*
Moran, F G (Clontarf) 1936 *E*, 1937 *E, S, W*, 1938 *S, W*, 1939 *E, S, W*
Morell, H B (Dublin U) 1881 *E, S*, 1882 *W, E*
Morgan, G J (Clontarf) 1934 *E, S, W*, 1935 *E, S, W, NZ*, 1936 *E, S, W*, 1937 *E, S, W*, 1938 *E, S, W*, 1939 *E, S, W*
Moriarty, C C H (Monkstown) 1899 *W*
Moroney, J C M (Garryowen) 1968 *W, A*, 1969 *F, E, S, W*
Moroney, R J M (Lansdowne) 1984 *F, W*, 1985 *F*
Moroney, T A (UC Dublin) 1964 *W*, 1967 *A* 1*, E*
Morphy, E McG (Dublin U) 1908 *E*
Morris, D P (Bective Rangers) 1931 *W*, 1932 *E*, 1935 *E, S, W, NZ*
Morrow, J W R (Queen's Coll, Belfast) 1882 *S*, 1883 *E, S*, 1884 *E, W*, 1885 *S* 1,2, 1886 *E, S*, 1888 *S*
Morrow, R D (Bangor) 1986 *F, E, S*
Mortell, M (Bective Rangers, Dolphin) 1953 *F, E, S, W*, 1954 *NZ, F, E, S, W*
Morton, W A (Dublin U) 1888 *S*
Moyers, L W (Dublin U) 1884 *W*
Moylett, M M F (Shannon) 1988 *E* 1
Mulcahy, W A (UC Dublin, Bective Rangers, Bohemians) 1958 *A, E, S, W, F*, 1959 *E, S, W, F*, 1960 *E, S, W, SA*, 1961 *E, S, W, SA*, 1962 *E, S, F, W*, 1963 *F, E, S, W, NZ*, 1964 *E, S, W, F*, 1965 *F, E, S, W, SA*
Mullan, B (Clontarf) 1947 *F, E, S, W*, 1948 *F, E, S, W*
Mullane, J P (Limerick Bohemians) 1928 *W*, 1929 *F*
Mullen, K D (Old Belvedere) 1947 *F, E, S, W, A*, 1948 *F, E, S, W*, 1949 *F, E, S, W*, 1950 *F, E, S, W*, 1951 *F, E, S, W, SA*, 1952 *F, S, W*
Mulligan, A A (Wanderers) 1956 *F, E*, 1957 *F, E, S, W*, 1958 *A, E, S, F*, 1959 *E, S, W, F*, 1960 *E, S, W, F, SA*, 1961 *W, F, SA*
Mullin, B J (Dublin U, Oxford U, Blackrock Coll, London Irish) 1984 *A*, 1985 *S, W, E*, 1986 *F, W, E, S, R*, 1987 *E, S, F, W,* [*W, C, Tg, A*], 1988 *S, F, W, E* 1,2, *WS, It*, 1989 *F, W, E, S, NZ*, 1990 *E, S, W, Arg*, 1991 *F, W, E, S, Nm* 1,2, [*J, S, A*], 1992 *W, E, S*, 1994 *US*, 1995 *E, S, F, W, It*, [*NZ, J, W, F*]
Murphy, C J (Lansdowne) 1939 *E, S, W*, 1947 *F, E*
Murphy, J G M W (London Irish) 1951 *SA*, 1952 *S, W, E*, 1954 *NZ*, 1958 *W*
Murphy, J J (Greystones) 1981 *SA* 1, 1982 *W* (R), 1984 *S*
Murphy, J N (Greystones) 1992 *A*
Murphy, K J (Cork Constitution) 1990 *E, S, F, W, Arg*, 1991 *F, W* (R)*, S* (R), 1992 *S, F, NZ* 2 (R)
Murphy, N A A (Cork Constitution) 1958 *A, E, S, W, F*, 1959 *E, S, W, F*, 1960 *E, S, W, F, SA*, 1961 *E, S, W*, 1962 *E, S, W, F*, 1963 *NZ*, 1964 *E, S, W, F*, 1965 *F, E, S, W, SA*, 1966 *F, E, S, W*, 1967 *A* 1*, E, S, W, F*, 1969 *F, E, S, W*
Murphy, N F (Cork Constitution) 1930 *E, W*, 1931 *F, E, S, W, SA*, 1932 *E, S, W*, 1933 *E*
Murphy-O'Connor, J (Bective Rangers) 1954 *E*
Murray, H W (Dublin U) 1877 *S*, 1878 *E*, 1879 *E*
Murray, J B (UC Dublin) 1963 *F*
Murray, P F (Wanderers) 1927 *F*, 1929 *F, E, S*, 1930 *F, E, S, W*, 1931 *F, E, S, W, SA*, 1932 *E, S, W*, 1933 *E, W, S*
Murtagh, C W (Portadown) 1977 *S*

Myles, J (Dublin U) 1875 *E*

Nash, L C (Queen's Coll, Cork) 1889 *S*, 1890 *W, E*, 1891 *E, S, W*
Neely, M R (Collegians) 1947 *F, E, S, W*
Neill, H J (NIFC) 1885 *E, S* 1,2, 1886 *S*, 1887 *E, S, W*, 1888 *W, S*
Neill, J McF (Instonians) 1926 *F*
Nelson, J E (Malone) 1947 *A*, 1948 *E, S, W*, 1949 *F, E, S, W*, 1950 *F, E, S, W*, 1951 *F, E, W*, 1954 *F*
Nelson, R (Queen's Coll, Belfast) 1882 *E, S*, 1883 *S*, 1886 *S*
Nesdale, R P (Newcastle) 1997 *W, E, S, NZ* (R)*, C*, 1998 *F* (R)*, W* (R)*, Gg, SA* 3 (R), 1999 *It*
Nesdale, T J (Garryowen) 1961 *F*
Neville, W C (Dublin U) 1879 *S, E*
Nicholson, P C (Dublin U) 1900 *E, S, W*
Norton, G W (Bective Rangers) 1949 *F, E, S, W*, 1950 *F, E, S, W*, 1951 *F, E, S*
Notley, J R (Wanderers) 1952 *F, S*
Nowlan, K W (St Mary's Coll) 1997 *NZ, C, It* 2

O'Brien, B (Derry) 1893 *S, W*
O'Brien, B A P (Shannon) 1968 *F, E, S*
O'Brien, D J (London Irish, Cardiff, Old Belvedere) 1948 *E, S, W*, 1949 *F, E, S, W*, 1950 *F, E, S, W*, 1951 *F, E, S, W, SA*, 1952 *F, S, W, E*
O'Brien, K A (Broughton Park) 1980 *E*, 1981 *SA* 1 (R), 2
O'Brien-Butler, P E (Monkstown) 1897 *S*, 1898 *E, S*, 1899 *S, W*, 1900 *E*
O'Callaghan, C T (Carlow) 1910 *W, F*, 1911 *E, S, W, F*, 1912 *F*
O'Callaghan, M P (Sunday's Well) 1962 *W*, 1964 *E, F*
O'Callaghan, P (Dolphin) 1967 *A* 1*, E, A* 2, 1968 *F, E, S, W*, 1969 *F, E, S, W*, 1970 *SA, F, E, S, W*, 1976 *F, W, E, S, NZ*
O'Connell, K D (Sunday's Well) 1994 *F, E* (t)
O'Connell, P (Bective Rangers) 1913 *W, F*, 1914 *F, E, S, W*
O'Connell, W J (Lansdowne) 1955 *F*
O'Connor, H S (Dublin U) 1957 *F, E, S, W*
O'Connor, J (Garryowen) 1895 *S*
O'Connor, J H (Bective Rangers) 1888 *M*, 1890 *S, W, E*, 1891 *E, S*, 1892 *E, W*, 1893 *E, S*, 1894 *E, S, W*, 1895 *E*, 1896 *E, S, W*
O'Connor, J J (Garryowen) 1909 *F*
O'Connor, J J (UC Cork) 1933 *S*, 1934 *E, S, W*, 1935 *E, S, W, NZ*, 1936 *S, W*, 1938 *S*
O'Connor, P J (Lansdowne) 1887 *W*
O'Cuinneagain, D (Sale) 1998 *SA* 1,2, *Gg* (R)*, R* (R)*, SA* 3, 1999 *F, W, E, S, It*
Odbert, R V M (RAF) 1928 *F*
O'Donnell, R C (St Mary's Coll) 1979 *A* 1,2, 1980 *S, F, W*
O'Donoghue, P J (Bective Rangers) 1955 *F, E, S, W*, 1956 *W*, 1957 *F, E*, 1958 *A, E, S, W*
O'Donnell, R (Manchester) 1971 *F* (R)*, E, S, W*
O'Driscoll, B G (Manchester) 1971 *F* (R)*, E, S, W*
O'Driscoll, J B (London Irish, Manchester) 1978 *S*, 1979 *A* 1,2, 1980 *E, S, F, W*, 1981 *F, W, E, S, SA* 1,2, *A*, 1982 *W, E, S, F*, 1983 *S, F, W, E*, 1984 *F, W, E, S*
O'Flanagan, K P (London Irish) 1947 *A*
O'Flanagan, M (Lansdowne) 1948 *S*
O'Grady, D (Sale) 1997 *It* 2
O'Hanlon, B (Dolphin) 1947 *E, S, W*, 1948 *F, E, S, W*, 1949 *F, E, S, W*, 1950 *F*
O'Hara, P T J (Sunday's Well, Cork Const) 1988 *WS* (R), 1989 *F, W, E, NZ*, 1990 *E, S, F, W*, 1991 *Nm* 1, [*J*], 1993 *F, W, E*, 1994 *US*
O'Kelly, M E (London Irish) 1997 *NZ, C, It* 2, 1998 *S, F, W, E, SA* 1,2, *Gg, R, SA* 3
O'Leary, A (Cork Constitution) 1952 *S, W, E*
O'Loughlin, D B (UC Cork) 1938 *E, S, W*, 1939 *E, S, W*
O'Mahony, D W (UC Dublin, Moseley, Bedford) 1995 *It*, [*F*], 1997 *It* 2, 1998 *R*
O'Mahony, David (Cork Constitution) 1995 *It*
O'Meara, B T (Cork Constitution) 1997 *E* (R)*, S, NZ* (R), 1998 *S*
O'Meara, J A (UC Cork, Dolphin) 1951 *F, E, S, W, SA*, 1952 *F, S, W, E*, 1953 *F, E, S, W*, 1954 *NZ, F, E, S*, 1955 *F, E*, 1956 *S, W*, 1958 *W*
O'Neill, H O'H (Queen's U, Belfast, UC Cork) 1930 *E, S, W*, 1933 *E, S, W*
O'Neill, J B (Queen's U, Belfast) 1920 *S*
O'Neill, W A (UC Dublin, Wanderers) 1952 *E*, 1953 *F, E, S, W*, 1954 *NZ*

227

O'Reilly, A J F (Old Belvedere, Leicester) 1955 *F, E, S, W,* 1956 *F, E, S, W,* 1957 *F, E, S, W,* 1958 *A, E, S, W, F,* 1959 *E, S, W, F,* 1960 *E,* 1961 *E, F, SA,* 1963 *F, S, W,* 1970 *E*
Orr, P A (Old Wesley) 1976 *F, W, E, S, NZ,* 1977 *W, E, S, F,* 1978 *E, W, E, NZ,* 1979 *W, E, S, A* 1,2, 1980 *E, S, F, W,* 1981 *F, W, E, S, SA* 1,2, *A,* 1982 *W, E, S, F,* 1983 *S, F, W, E,* 1984 *F, W, E, S, A,* 1985 *S, F, W, E,* 1986 *F, S, R,* 1987 *E, S, F, W,* [*W, C, A*]
O'Shea, C M P (Lansdowne, London Irish) 1993 *R,* 1994 *F, W, E, S, A* 1,2, *US,* 1995 *E, S,* [*J, W, F*], 1997 *It* 1, *F, S* (R), 1998 *S, F, SA* 1,2, *Gg, R, SA* 3, 1999 *F, W, E, S, It*
O'Sullivan, A C (Dublin U) 1882 *S*
O'Sullivan, J M (Limerick) 1884 *S,* 1887 *S*
O'Sullivan, P J A (Galwegians) 1957 *F, E, S, W,* 1959 *E, S, W, F,* 1960 *SA,* 1961 *E, S,* 1962 *F, W,* 1963 *F, NZ*
O'Sullivan, W (Queen's Coll, Cork) 1895 *S*
Owens, R H (Dublin U) 1922 *E, S*

Parfrey, P (UC Cork) 1974 *NZ*
Parke, J C (Monkstown) 1903 *W,* 1904 *E, S, W,* 1905 *W, NZ,* 1906 *E, S, W, SA,* 1907 *E, S, W,* 1908 *E, S, W,* 1909 *E, S, W, F*
Parr, J S (Wanderers) 1914 *F, E, S, W*
Patterson, C S (Instonians) 1978 *NZ,* 1979 *F, W, E, S, A* 1,2, 1980 *E, S, F, W*
Patterson, R d'A (Wanderers) 1912 *F, S, W, SA,* 1913 *E, S, W, F*
Payne, C T (NIFC) 1926 *E,* 1927 *F, E, S, A,* 1928 *F, E, S, W,* 1929 *F, E, W,* 1930 *F, E, S, W*
Pedlow, A C (CIYMS) 1953 *W,* 1954 *NZ, F, E,* 1955 *F, E, S, W,* 1956 *F, E, S, W,* 1957 *F, E, S, W,* 1958 *A, E, S, W, F,* 1959 *E, S, W, F, SA,* 1961 *S,* 1962 *W,* 1963 *F*
Pedlow, J (Bessbrook) 1882 *S,* 1884 *W*
Pedlow, R (Bessbrook) 1891 *W*
Pedlow, T B (Queen's Coll, Belfast) 1889 *S, W*
Peel, T (Limerick) 1892 *E, S, W*
Peirce, W (Cork) 1881 *E*
Phipps, G C (Army) 1950 *E, W,* 1952 *F, W, E*
Pike, T O (Lansdowne) 1927 *E, S, W, A,* 1928 *F, E, S, W*
Pike, V J (Lansdowne) 1931 *E, S, W, SA,* 1932 *E, S, W,* 1933 *E, S, W,* 1934 *E, S, W*
Pike, W W (Kingstown) 1879 *E,* 1881 *E, S,* 1882 *E,* 1883 *S*
Pinion, G (Belfast Collegians) 1909 *E, S, W, F*
Piper, O J S (Cork Constitution) 1909 *E, S, W, F,* 1910 *E, S, W, F*
Polden, S E (Clontarf) 1913 *W, F,* 1914 *F,* 1920 *F*
Popham, I (Cork Constitution) 1922 *S, W, F,* 1923 *F*
Popplewell, N J (Greystones, Wasps, Newcastle) 1989 *NZ,* 1990 *Arg,* 1991 *Nm* 1,2, [*Z, S, A*], 1992 *W, E, S, F, NZ* 1,2, *A,* 1993 *S, F, W, E, R,* 1994 *F, W, E, S, US,* 1995 *E, S, F, W, It,* [*NZ, J, W, F*], *Fj,* 1996 *US, S, F, W, E, A,* 1997 *It* 1, *F, W, E, NZ, C,* 1998 *S* (t), *F* (R)
Potterton, H N (Wanderers) 1920 *W*
Pratt, R H (Dublin U) 1933 *E, W, S,* 1934 *E, S*
Price, A H (Dublin U) 1920 *S, F*
Pringle, J C (NIFC) 1902 *S, W*
Purcell, N M (Lansdowne) 1921 *E, S, W, F*
Purdon, H (NIFC) 1879 *S, E,* 1880 *E,* 1881 *E, S*
Purdon, W B (Queen's Coll, Belfast) 1906 *E, S, W*
Purser, F C (Dublin U) 1898 *E, S, W*

Quinlan, S V J (Blackrock Coll) 1956 *F, E, W,* 1958 *W*
Quinn, B T (Old Belvedere) 1947 *F*
Quinn, F P (Old Belvedere) 1981 *F, W, E*
Quinn, J P (Dublin U) 1910 *E, S,* 1911 *E, S, W, F,* 1912 *E, S, W,* 1913 *E, W, F,* 1914 *F, E, S*
Quinn, K (Old Belvedere) 1947 *F, A,* 1953 *F, E, S*
Quinn, M A M (Lansdowne) 1973 *F,* 1974 *F, W, E, S, P, NZ,* 1977 *S, F,* 1981 *SA* 2
Quirke, J M T (Blackrock Coll) 1962 *E, S,* 1968 *S*

Rainey, P I (Ballymena) 1989 *NZ*
Rambaut, D F (Dublin U) 1887 *E, S, W,* 1888 *W*
Rea, H H (Edinburgh U) 1967 *A* 1, 1969 *F*
Read, H M (Dublin U) 1910 *E, S,* 1911 *E, S, W, F,* 1912 *F, E, S, W, SA,* 1913 *E, S*
Reardon, J V (Cork Constitution) 1934 *E, S*
Reid, C (NIFC) 1899 *S, W,* 1900 *E,* 1903 *W*
Reid, J L (Richmond) 1934 *S, W*
Reid, P J (Garryowen) 1947 *A,* 1948 *F, E, W*
Reid, T E (Garryowen) 1953 *E, S, W,* 1954 *NZ, F,* 1955 *E, S,* 1956 *F, E,* 1957 *F, E, S, W*

Reidy, C J (London Irish) 1937 *W*
Reidy, G F (Dolphin, Lansdowne) 1953 *W,* 1954 *F, E, S, W*
Richey, H A (Dublin U) 1889 *W,* 1890 *S*
Ridgeway, E C (Wanderers) 1932 *S, W,* 1935 *E, S, W*
Rigney, B J (Greystones) 1991 *F, W, E, S, Nm* 1, 1992 *F, NZ* 1 (R), 2
Ringland, T M (Queen's U, Belfast, Ballymena) 1981 *A,* 1982 *W, E, F,* 1983 *S, F, W, E,* 1984 *F, W, E, S, A,* 1985 *S, F, W, E,* 1986 *F, W, E, S, R,* 1987 *E, S, F, W,* [*W, C, Tg, A*], 1988 *S, F, W, E* 1
Riordan, W F (Cork Constitution) 1910 *E*
Ritchie, J S (London Irish) 1956 *F, E*
Robb, C G (Queen's Coll, Belfast) 1904 *E, S, W,* 1905 *NZ,* 1906 *S*
Robbie, J C (Dublin U, Greystones) 1976 *A, F, NZ,* 1977 *S, F,* 1981 *F, W, E, S*
Robinson, B F (Ballymena, London Irish) 1991 *F, W, E, S, Nm* 1,2, [*Z, S, A*], 1992 *W, E, S, F, NZ* 1,2, *A,* 1993 *W, E, R,* 1994 *F, W, E, S, A* 1,2
Robinson, T T H (Wanderers) 1904 *E, S,* 1905 *E, S, W, NZ,* 1906 *SA,* 1907 *E, S, W*
Roche, J (Wanderers) 1890 *S, W, E,* 1891 *E, S, W,* 1892 *W*
Roche, R E (UC Galway) 1955 *E, S,* 1957 *S, W*
Roche, W J (UC Cork) 1920 *E, S, F*
Roddy, P J (Bective Rangers) 1920 *S, F*
Roe, R (Lansdowne) 1952 *E,* 1953 *F, E, S, W,* 1954 *F, E, S, W,* 1955 *F, E, S, W,* 1956 *F, E, S, W,* 1957 *F, E, S, W*
Rolland, A C (Blackrock Coll) 1990 *Arg,* 1994 *US* (R), 1995 *It* (R)
Rooke, C V (Dublin U) 1891 *E, W,* 1892 *E, S, W,* 1893 *E, S, W,* 1894 *E, S, W,* 1895 *E, S, W,* 1896 *E, S, W,* 1897 *E, S, W,* 1898 *E, S, W*
Ross, D J (Belfast Academy) 1884 *E,* 1885 *S* 1,2, 1886 *E, S*
Ross, G R P (CIYMS) 1955 *W*
Ross, J F (NIFC) 1886 *S*
Ross, J P (Lansdowne) 1885 *E, S* 1,2, 1886 *E, S*
Ross, N G (Malone) 1927 *F, E*
Ross, W McC (Queen's U, Belfast) 1932 *E, S, W,* 1933 *E, W, S,* 1934 *E, S,* 1935 *NZ*
Russell, J (UC Cork) 1931 *F, E, S, W, SA,* 1933 *E, W, S,* 1934 *E, S, W,* 1935 *E, S, W,* 1936 *E, S, W,* 1937 *E, S*
Russell, P (Instonians) 1990 *E,* 1992 *NZ* 1,2, *A*
Rutherford, W G (Tipperary) 1884 *E, S,* 1885 *E, S* 1, 1886 *E,* 1888 *W*
Ryan, E (Dolphin) 1937 *W,* 1938 *E, S*
Ryan, J (Rockwell Coll) 1897 *E,* 1898 *E, S, W,* 1899 *E, S, W,* 1900 *S, W,* 1901 *E, S, W,* 1902 *E,* 1904 *E*
Ryan, J G (UC Dublin) 1939 *E, S, W*
Ryan, M (Rockwell Coll) 1897 *E, S,* 1898 *E, S, W,* 1899 *E, S, W,* 1900 *E, S, W,* 1901 *E, S, W,* 1903 *E,* 1904 *E, S*

Saunders, R (London Irish) 1991 *F, W, E, S, Nm* 1,2, [*Z, J, S, A*], 1992 *W,* 1994 *F* (t)
Saverimutto, C (Sale) 1995 *Fj,* 1996 *US, S*
Sayers, H J M (Lansdowne) 1935 *E, S, W,* 1936 *E, S, W,* 1938 *W,* 1939 *E, S, W*
Scally, C J (U C Dublin) 1998 *Gg* (R), *R,* 1999 *S* (R), *It*
Schute, F (Wanderers) 1878 *E,* 1879 *E*
Schute, F G (Dublin U) 1912 *SA,* 1913 *E, S*
Scott, D (Malone) 1961 *F, SA,* 1962 *S*
Scott, R D (Queen's U, Belfast) 1967 *E, F,* 1968 *F, E, S*
Scovell, R H (Kingstown) 1883 *E,* 1884 *E*
Scriven, G (Dublin U) 1879 *S, E,* 1880 *E, S,* 1881 *E,* 1882 *S,* 1883 *E, S*
Sealy, J (Dublin U) 1896 *E, S, W,* 1897 *S,* 1899 *E, S, W,* 1900 *E, S*
Sexton, J F (Dublin U, Lansdowne) 1988 *E* 2, *WS, It,* 1989 *F*
Sexton, W J (Garryowen) 1984 *A,* 1988 *S, E* 2
Shanahan, T (Lansdowne) 1885 *E, S* 1,2, 1886 *E,* 1888 *S, W*
Shaw, G M (Windsor) 1877 *S*
Sheehan, M D (London Irish) 1932 *E*
Sherry, B F (Terenure Coll) 1967 *A* 1, *E, S, A* 2, 1968 *F, E*
Sherry, M J A (Lansdowne) 1975 *F, W*
Siggins, J A E (Belfast Collegians) 1931 *F, E, S, W, SA,* 1932 *E, S, W,* 1933 *E, W, S,* 1934 *E, S, W,* 1935 *E, S, W, NZ,* 1936 *E, S, W,* 1937 *E, S, W*
Slattery, J F (UC Dublin, Blackrock Coll) 1970 *SA, F, E, S, W,* 1971 *F, E, S, W,* 1972 *F* 1, *E, F* 2, 1973 *NZ, E, S, W, F,* 1974 *F, W, E, S, P, NZ,* 1975 *E, S, F, W,* 1976 *A,* 1977 *S, F,* 1978 *S, F, W, E, NZ,* 1979 *F, W, E, S, A* 1,2, 1980 *E, S, F, W,* 1981 *F, W, E, S, SA* 1,2, *A,* 1982 *W, E, S, F,* 1983 *S, F, W, E,* 1984 *F*
Smartt, F N B (Dublin U) 1908 *E, S,* 1909 *E*

Smith, B A (Oxford U, Leicester) 1989 *NZ*, 1990 *S, F, W, Arg*, 1991 *F, W, E, S*
Smith, J H (London Irish) 1951 *F, E, S, W, SA*, 1952 *F, S, W, E*, 1954 *NZ, W, F*
Smith, R E (Lansdowne) 1892 *E*
Smith, S J (Ballymena) 1988 *E* 2, *WS, It*, 1989 *F, W, E, S, NZ*, 1990 *E, 1991 F, W, E, S, Nm* 1,2, [*Z, S, A*], 1992 *W, E, S, F, NZ* 1,2, 1993 *S*
Smithwick, F F S (Monkstown) 1898 *S, W*
Smyth, J T (Queen's U, Belfast) 1920 *F*
Smyth, P J (Belfast Collegians) 1911 *E, S, F*
Smyth, R S (Dublin U) 1903 *E, S*, 1904 *E*
Smyth, T (Malone, Newport) 1908 *E, S, W*, 1909 *E, S, W*, 1910 *E, S, W, F*, 1911 *E, S, W*, 1912 *E*
Smyth, W S (Belfast Collegians) 1910 *W, F*, 1920 *E*
Solomons, B A H (Dublin U) 1908 *E, S, W*, 1909 *E, S, W, F*, 1910 *E, S, W*
Spain, A W (UC Dublin) 1924 *NZ*
Sparrow, W (Dublin U) 1893 *W*, 1894 *E*
Spillane, B J (Bohemians) 1985 *S, F, W, E*, 1986 *F, W, E*, 1987 *F, W*, [*W, C, A* (R)], 1989 *E* (R)
Spring, D E (Dublin U) 1978 *S, NZ*, 1979 *S*, 1980 *S, F, W*, 1981 *W*
Spring, R M (Lansdowne) 1979 *F, W, E*
Spunner, H F (Wanderers) 1881 *E, S*, 1884 *W*
Stack, C R R (Dublin U) 1889 *S*
Stack, G H (Dublin U) 1875 *E*
Staples, J E (London Irish, Harlequins) 1991 *W, E, S, Nm* 1,2, [*Z, J, S, A*], 1992 *W, E, NZ* 1,2, *A*, 1995 *F, W, It*, [*NZ*], *Fj*, 1996 *US, S, F, A*, 1997 *W, E, S*
Steele, H W (Ballymena) 1976 *F*, 1977 *F*, 1978 *F, W, E*, 1979 *F, W, E, A* 1,2
Stephenson, G V (Queen's U, Belfast, London Hosp) 1920 *F*, 1921 *E, S, W, F*, 1922 *E, S, W, F*, 1923 *E, S, W, F*, 1924 *F, E, S, W, NZ*, 1925 *F, E, S, W*, 1926 *F, E, S, W*, 1927 *F, E, S, W, A*, 1928 *F, E, S, W*, 1929 *F, E, W*, 1930 *F, E, S, W*
Stephenson, H W V (United Services) 1922 *S, W, F*, 1924 *F, E, S, W, NZ*, 1925 *F, E, S, W*, 1927 *A*, 1928 *F*
Stevenson, J (Dungannon) 1888 *M*, 1889 *S*
Stevenson, J B (Instonians) 1958 *A, E, S, W, F*
Stevenson, R (Dungannon) 1887 *E, S, W*, 1888 *M*, 1889 *S, W*, 1890 *S, W*, 1891 *W*, 1892 *W*, 1893 *E, S, W*
Stevenson, T H (Belfast Acad) 1895 *E, W*, 1896 *E, S, W*, 1897 *E, S*
Stewart, A L (NIFC) 1913 *W, F*, 1914 *F*
Stewart, W J (Queen's U, Belfast, NIFC) 1922 *F*, 1924 *S*, 1928 *F, E, S, W*, 1929 *F, E, S, W*
Stoker, E W (Wanderers) 1888 *W, S*
Stoker, F O (Wanderers) 1886 *S*, 1888 *W, M*, 1889 *S*, 1891 *W*
Stokes, O S (Cork Bankers) 1882 *E*, 1884 *E*
Stokes, P (Garryowen) 1913 *E, S*, 1914 *F*, 1920 *E, S, W, F*, 1921 *E, S, F*, 1922 *W, F*
Stokes, R D (Queen's Coll, Cork) 1891 *S, W*
Strathdee, E (Queen's U, Belfast) 1947 *E, S, W, A*, 1948 *W, F*, 1949 *E, S, W*
Stuart, C P (Clontarf) 1912 *SA*
Stuart, I M B (Dublin U) 1924 *E, S*
Sugars, H S (Dublin U) 1905 *NZ*, 1906 *SA*, 1907 *S*
Sugden, M (Wanderers) 1925 *F, E, S, W*, 1926 *F, E, S, W*, 1927 *E, S, W, A*, 1928 *F, E, S, W*, 1929 *F, E, S, W*, 1930 *F, E, S, W*, 1931 *F, E, S, W*
Sullivan, D B (UC Dublin) 1922 *E, S, W, F*
Sweeney, J A (Blackrock Coll) 1907 *E, S, W*
Symes, G R (Monkstown) 1895 *E*
Synge, J S (Lansdowne) 1929 *S*

Taggart, T (Dublin U) 1887 *W*
Taylor, A S (Queen's Coll, Belfast) 1910 *E, S, W*, 1912 *F*
Taylor, D R (Queen's Coll, Belfast) 1903 *E*
Taylor, J (Belfast Collegians) 1914 *E, S, W*
Taylor, J W (NIFC) 1879 *S*, 1880 *E, S*, 1881 *S*, 1882 *E, S*, 1883 *E, S*
Tector, W R (Wanderers) 1955 *F, E, S*
Tedford, A (Malone) 1902 *E, S, W*, 1903 *E, S, W*, 1904 *E, S, W*, 1905 *E, S, W, NZ*, 1906 *E, S, W, SA*, 1907 *E, S, W*, 1908 *E, S, W*
Teehan, C (UC Cork) 1939 *E, S, W*
Thompson, C (Belfast Collegians) 1907 *E, S*, 1908 *E, S, W*, 1909 *E, S, W, F*, 1910 *E, S, W, F*
Thompson, J A (Queen's Coll, Belfast) 1885 *S* 1,2
Thompson, J K S (Dublin U) 1921 *W*, 1922 *E, S, F*, 1923 *E, S, W, F*
Thompson, R G (Lansdowne) 1882 *W*

Thompson, R H (Instonians) 1951 *SA*, 1952 *F*, 1954 *NZ, F, E, S, W*, 1955 *F, S, W*, 1956 *W*
Thornhill, T (Wanderers) 1892 *E, S, W*, 1893 *E*
Thrift, H (Dublin U) 1904 *W*, 1905 *E, S, W, NZ*, 1906 *E, W, SA*, 1907 *E, S, W*, 1908 *E, S, W*, 1909 *E, S, W, F*
Tierney, D (UC Cork) 1938 *S, W*, 1939 *E*
Tillie, C R (Dublin U) 1887 *E, S*, 1888 *W, S*
Todd, A W P (Dublin U) 1913 *W, F*, 1914 *F*
Topping, J A (Ballymena) 1996 *WS, A*, 1997 *It* 1, *F, E*
Torrens, J D (Bohemians) 1938 *W*, 1939 *E, S, W*
Tucker, C C (Shannon) 1979 *F, W*, 1980 *F* (R)
Tuke, B B (Bective Rangers) 1890 *E*, 1891 *E, S*, 1892 *E*, 1894 *E, S, W*, 1895 *E, S*
Turley, N (Blackrock Coll) 1962 *E*
Tweed, D A (Ballymena) 1995 *F, W, It*, [*J*]
Tydings, J J (Young Munster) 1968 *A*
Tyrrell, W (Queen's U, Belfast) 1910 *F*, 1913 *E, S, W, F*, 1914 *F, E, S, W*

Uprichard, R J H (Harlequins, RAF) 1950 *S, W*

Waide, S L (Oxford U, NIFC) 1932 *E, S, W*, 1933 *E, W*
Waites, J (Bective Rangers) 1886 *S*, 1888 *M*, 1889 *W*, 1890 *S, W, E*, 1891 *E*
Waldron, O C (Oxford U, London Irish) 1966 *S, W*, 1968 *A*
Walker, S (Instonians) 1934 *E, S*, 1935 *E, S, W, NZ*, 1936 *E, S, W*, 1937 *E, S, W*, 1938 *E, S, W*
Walkington, D B (NIFC) 1887 *E, W*, 1888 *W*, 1890 *W, E*, 1891 *E, S, W*
Walkington, R B (NIFC) 1875 *E*, 1876 *E*, 1877 *E, S*, 1878 *E*, 1879 *S*, 1880 *E, S*, 1882 *E, S*
Wall, H (Dolphin) 1965 *S, W*
Wallace, Jas (Wanderers) 1904 *E, S*
Wallace, Jos (Wanderers) 1903 *S, W*, 1904 *E, S, W*, 1905 *E, S, W, NZ*, 1906 *W*
Wallace, P S (Blackrock Coll, Saracens) 1995 [*J*], *Fj*, 1996 *US, W, E, WS, A*, 1997 *It* 1, *F, W, E, S, NZ, C*, 1998 *S, F, W, E, SA* 1,2, *Gg, R*, 1999 *F, W, E, S, It* (R)
Wallace, R M (Garryowen, Saracens) 1991 *Nm* 1 (R), 1992 *W, E, S, F, A*, 1993 *S, F, W, E, R*, 1994 *F, W, E, S*, 1995 *W, It*, [*NZ, J, W*], *Fj*, 1996 *US, S, F, WS*, 1998 *S, F, W, E*
Wallace, T H (Cardiff) 1920 *E, S, W*
Wallis, A K (Wanderers) 1892 *E, S, W*, 1893 *E, W*
Wallis, C O'N (Old Cranleighans, Wanderers) 1935 *NZ*
Wallis, T G (Wanderers) 1921 *F*, 1922 *E, S, W, F*
Wallis, W A (Wanderers) 1880 *S*, 1881 *E, S*, 1882 *W*, 1883 *S*
Walmsley, G (Bective Rangers) 1894 *E*
Walpole, A (Dublin U) 1888 *S, M*
Walsh, E J (Lansdowne) 1887 *E, S, W*, 1892 *E, S, W*, 1893 *E*
Walsh, H D (Dublin U) 1875 *E*, 1876 *E*
Walsh, J C (UC Cork, Sunday's Well) 1960 *S, SA*, 1961 *E, S, F, SA*, 1963 *E, S, W, NZ*, 1964 *E, S, W, F*, 1965 *F, S, W, SA*, 1966 *F, S, W*, 1967 *E, S, W, F, A* 2
Ward, A J (Ballynahinch) 1998 *F, W, E, SA* 1,2, *Gg, R, SA* 3, 1999 *W, E, S, It* (R)
Ward, A J P (Garryowen, St Mary's Coll, Greystones) 1978 *S, F, W, E, NZ*, 1979 *F, W, E*, 1981 *W, E, S, A*, 1983 *E* (R), 1984 *E, S*, 1986 *S*, 1987 [*C, Tg*]
Warren, J P (Kingstown) 1883 *E*
Warren, R G (Lansdowne) 1884 *W*, 1885 *E, S* 1,2, 1886 *E*, 1887 *E, S, W*, 1888 *W, S, M*, 1889 *S, W*, 1890 *S, W, E*
Watson, R (Wanderers) 1912 *SA*
Wells, H G (Bective Rangers) 1891 *S, W*, 1894 *E, S*
Westby, A J (Dublin U) 1876 *E*
Wheeler, G H (Queen's Coll, Belfast) 1884 *S*, 1885 *E*
Wheeler, J R (Queen's U, Belfast) 1922 *E, S, W, F*, 1924 *E*
Whelan, P C (Garryowen) 1975 *E, S*, 1976 *NZ*, 1977 *W, E, S, F*, 1978 *S, F, W, E, NZ*, 1979 *F, W, E, S*, 1981 *F, W, E*
White, M (Queen's Coll, Cork) 1906 *E, S, W, SA*, 1907 *E, W*
Whitestone, A M (Dublin U) 1877 *E*, 1879 *S, E*, 1880 *E*, 1883 *S*
Whittle, D (Bangor) 1988 *F*
Wilkinson, C R (Malone) 1993 *S*
Wilkinson, R W (Wanderers) 1947 *A*
Williamson, F W (Dolphin) 1930 *E, S, W*
Willis, W J (Lansdowne) 1879 *E*
Wilson, F (CIYMS) 1977 *W, E, S*

Wilson, H G (Glasgow U, Malone) 1905 *E, S, W, NZ,* 1906 *E, S, W, SA,* 1907 *E, S, W,* 1908 *E, S, W,* 1909 *E, S, W,* 1910 *W*
Wilson, W H (Bray) 1877 *E, S*
Withers, H H C (Army, Blackheath) 1931 *F, E, S, W, SA*
Wolfe, E J (Armagh) 1882 *E*
Wood, G H (Dublin U) 1913 *W,* 1914 *F*
Wood, B G M (Garryowen) 1954 *E, S,* 1956 *F, E, S, W,* 1957 *F, E, S, W,* 1958 *A, E, S, W, F,* 1959 *E, S, W, F,* 1960 *E, S, W, F, SA,* 1961 *E, S, W, F, SA*
Wood, K G M (Garryowen, Harlequins) 1994 *A* 1,2, *US,* 1995 *E, S,* [*J*], 1996 *A,* 1997 *It* 1, *F,* 1997 *NZ, It* 2, 1998 *S, F, W, E, SA* 1,2, *R* (R), *SA* 3, 1999 *F, W, E, S, It* (R)

Woods, D C (Bessbrook) 1888 *M,* 1889 *S*
Woods, N K P J (Blackrock Coll, London Irish) 1994 *A* 1,2, 1995 *E, F,* 1996 *F, W, E,* 1999 *W*
Wright, R A (Monkstown) 1912 *S*

Yeates, R A (Dublin U) 1889 *S, W*
Young, G (UC Cork) 1913 *E*
Young, R M (Collegians) 1965 *F, E, S, W, SA,* 1966 *F, E, S, W,* 1967 *W, F,* 1968 *W, A,* 1969 *F, E, S, W,* 1970 *SA, F, E, S, W,* 1971 *F, E, S, W*

Hooker Keith Wood in a rare quiet moment during Ireland's World Cup match qualifier against Romania in November 1998.

IRISH INTERNATIONAL RECORDS
(*up to 30 April 1999*)

MATCH RECORDS

MOST CONSECUTIVE TEST WINS
6 1968 *S, W, A,* 1969 *F, E, S*

MOST CONSECUTIVE TESTS WITHOUT DEFEAT

P	W	D	Period
7	6	1	1968–69
5	4	1	1972–73

MOST POINTS IN A MATCH
by the team

Pts	Opp	Venue	Year
70	Gg	Dublin	1998
60	R	Dublin	1986
55	Z	Dublin	1991
53	R	Dublin	1998
50	J	Bloemfontein	1995

by a player
24 by P A Burke v Italy at Dublin 1997
23 by R P Keyes v Zimbabwe at
Dublin 1991
21 by S O Campbell v Scotland at
Dublin 1982
21 by S O Campbell v England at
Dublin 1983
20 by M J Kiernan v Romania at
Dublin 1986
20 by E P Elwood v Romania at
Dublin 1993
20 by S J P Mason v Western Samoa
at Dublin 1996
20 by E P Elwood v Georgia
at Dublin 1998

MOST TRIES IN A MATCH
by the team

T	Opp	Venue	Year
10	R	Dublin	1986
10	Gg	Dublin	1998
8	WS	Dublin	1988
8	Z	Dublin	1991
7	J	Bloemfontein	1995
7	R	Dublin	1998

by a player
4 by B F Robinson v Zimbabwe at
Dublin 1991
3 by R Montgomery v Wales at
Birkenhead 1887
3 by J P Quinn v France at Cork 1913

3 by E O'D Davy v Scotland at
Murrayfield 1930
3 by S J Byrne v Scotland at
Murrayfield 1953
3 by K D Crossan v Romania at
Dublin 1986
3 by B J Mullin v Tonga at
Brisbane 1987

MOST CONVERSIONS IN A MATCH
by the team

C	Opp	Venue	Year
10	Gg	Dublin	1998
7	R	Dublin	1986
6	J	Bloemfontein	1995
6	R	Dublin	1998
5	C	Dunedin	1987

by a player
10 by E P Elwood v Georgia at
Dublin 1998
7 by M J Kiernan v Romania at
Dublin 1986
6 by P A Burke v Japan at
Bloemfontein 1995
5 by M J Kiernan v Canada at
Dunedin 1987

MOST PENALTY GOALS IN A MATCH
by the team

P	Opp	Venue	Year
8	It	Dublin	1997
6	S	Dublin	1982
6	R	Dublin	1993
6	US	Atlanta	1996
6	WS	Dublin	1996

by a player
8 by P A Burke v Italy at Dublin 1997
6 by S O Campbell v Scotland at
Dublin 1982
6 by EP Elwood v Romania at
Dublin 1993
6 by S J P Mason v Western Samoa
at Dublin 1996

MOST DROPPED GOALS IN A MATCH
by the team

D	Opp	Venue	Year
2	A	Dublin	1967
2	F	Dublin	1975
2	A	Sydney	1979
2	E	Dublin	1981
2	C	Dunedin	1987
2	E	Dublin	1993
2	W	Wembley	1999

by a player

2 by C M H Gibson v Australia at Dublin	1967
2 by W M McCombe v France at Dublin	1975
2 by S O Campbell v Australia at Sydney	1979
2 by E P Elwood v England at Dublin	1993
2 by D G Humphreys v Wales at Wembley	1999

CAREER RECORDS

MOST CAPPED PLAYERS

Caps	Player	Career
69	C M H Gibson	1964–79
63	W J McBride	1962–75
61	J F Slattery	1970–84
58	P A Orr	1976–87
55	B J Mullin	1984–95
54	T J Kiernan	1960–73
52	D G Lenihan	1981–92
51	M I Keane	1974–84
51	P S Johns	1990–99
48	N J Popplewell	1989–98

MOST CONSECUTIVE TESTS

Tests	Player	Span
52	W J McBride	1964–75
49	P A Orr	1976–86
43	D G Lenihan	1981–89
39	M I Keane	1974–81
37	G V Stephenson	1920–29

MOST TESTS AS CAPTAIN

Tests	Captain	Span
24	T J Kiernan	1963–73
19	C F Fitzgerald	1982–86
17	J F Slattery	1979–81
17	D G Lenihan	1986–90

MOST TESTS IN INDIVIDUAL POSITIONS

Full-back T J Kiernan	54	1960–73
Wing K D Crossan	41	1982–92
Centre B J Mullin	55	1984–95
Fly-half J W Kyle	46	1947–58
Scrum-half M T Bradley	40	1984–95
Prop P A Orr	58	1976–87
Hooker K W Kennedy	45	1965–75
Lock W J McBride	63	1962–75
Flanker J F Slattery	61	1970–84
No. 8 W P Duggan	39	1975–84

MOST POINTS IN TESTS

Pts	Player	Tests	Career
308	M J Kiernan	43	1982–91
276	E P Elwood	31	1993–99
217	S O Campbell	22	1976–84
158	T J Kiernan	54	1960–73
113	A J P Ward	19	1978–87

MOST TRIES IN TESTS

Tries	Player	Tests	Career
17	B J Mullin	55	1984–95
14	G V Stephenson	42	1920–30
12	K D Crossan	41	1982–92
11	A T A Duggan	25	1963–72
11	S P Geoghegan	37	1991–96

MOST CONVERSIONS IN TESTS

Cons	Player	Tests	Career
40	M J Kiernan	43	1982–91
36	E P Elwood	31	1993–99
26	T J Kiernan	54	1960–73
16	R A Lloyd	19	1910–20
15	S O Campbell	22	1976–84

MOST PENALTY GOALS IN TESTS

Pens	Player	Tests	Career
66	E P Elwood	31	1993–99
62	M J Kiernan	43	1982–91
54	S O Campbell	22	1976–84
31	T J Kiernan	54	1960–73
29	A J P Ward	19	1978–87

MOST DROPPED GOALS IN TESTS

Drops	Player	Tests	Career
7	R A Lloyd	19	1910–20
7	S O Campbell	22	1976–84
6	C M H Gibson	69	1964–79
6	B J McGann	25	1969–76
6	M J Kiernan	43	1982–91

INTERNATIONAL CHAMPIONSHIP RECORDS

Record	Detail		Set
Most points in seaon	71	in four matches	1983
Most tries in season	12	in four matches	1928 & 1953
Highest score	30	30–17 v Wales	1996
Biggest win	24	24–0 v France	1913
Highest score conceded	46	6–46 v England	1997
Biggest defeat	40	6–46 v England	1997
Most appearances	56	C M H Gibson	1964–79
Most points in matches	207	M J Kiernan	1982–91
Most points in season	56	D G Humphreys	1999
Most points in match	21	S O Campbell	v Scotland, 1982
	21	S O Campbell	v England, 1983
Most tries in matches	14	G V Stephenson	1920–30
Most tries in season	5	J E Arigho	1928
Most tries in match	3	R Montgomery	v Wales, 1887
	3	J P Quinn	v France, 1913
	3	E O'D Davy	v Scotland, 1930
	3	S J Byrne	v Scotland, 1953
Most cons in matches	21	M J Kiernan	1982–91
Most cons in season	7	R A Lloyd	1913
Most cons in match	4	P F Murray	v Scotland, 1932
	4	R J Gregg	v Scotland, 1953
Most pens in matches	48	S O Campbell	1980–84
Most pens in season	14	S O Campbell	1983
	14	E P Elwood	1994
Most pens in match	6	S O Campbell	v Scotland, 1982
Most drops in matches	7	R A Lloyd	1910–20
Most drops in season	2	on several occasions	
Most drops in match	2	W M McCombe	v France, 1975
	2	E P Elwood	v England, 1993
	2	D G Humphreys	v Wales, 1999

MAJOR TOUR RECORDS

Record	Detail	Year	Place
Most individual points	60 by S O Campbell	1979	Australia
Most points in match	21 by D G Humphreys	1998 v North-West,	Potchefstroom (SA)
Most tries in match	3 by A T A Duggan	1967 v Victoria	Melbourne
	3 by J F Slattery	1981 v SA President's XV	East London (SA)
	3 by M J Kiernan	1981 v Gold Cup XV	Oudtshoorn (SA)
	3 by M J Field	1994 v W Australia	Perth

MISCELLANEOUS RECORDS

Record	Holder	Detail
Longest Test career	A J F O'Reilly	16 seasons, 1954–55 to 1969–70
	C M H Gibson	16 seasons, 1963–64 to 1979
Youngest Test cap	F S Hewitt	17 yrs 157 days in 1924
Oldest Test cap	C M H Gibson	36 yrs 195 days in 1979

IRISH INTERNATIONAL CAREER RECORDS (*up to 30 April 1999*)

Player	Debut	Caps since last season	Caps	T	C	PG	DG	Pts
C M P O'Shea	1993 v R	1998 *SA* 1,2, *Gg, R, SA* 3, 1999 *F, W, E, S, It*	28	4	1	3	1	34
S J P Mason	1996 v W		3	0	3	12	0	42
G Dempsey	1998 v Gg	1998 *Gg*(R), *SA* 3, 1999 *F, E, S, It*	6	3	0	0	0	15
J P Bishop	1998 v SA	1998 *SA* 1,2, *Gg, R, SA* 3, 1999 *F, W, E, S, It*	10	2	0	0	0	10
K M Maggs	1997 v NZ	1998 *SA* 1,2, *Gg, R*(R), *SA* 3, 1999 *F, W, E, S, It*	17	3	0	0	0	15
D A Hickie	1997 v W	1998 *SA* 1,2	12	5	0	0	0	25
N K P J Woods	1994 v A	1999 *W*	8	1	0	0	0	5
P Duignan	1998 v Gg	1998 *Gg, R*	2	1	0	0	0	5
M C McCall	1992 v NZ	1998 *SA* 1,2	13	0	0	0	0	0
K P Keane	1998 v E		1	0	0	0	0	0
J C Bell	1994 v A	1998 *Gg, R, SA* 3, 1999 *F, W, S, It*(R)	28	6	0	0	0	30
R A J Henderson	1996 v WS	1998 *SA* 1(R),2(R), 1999 *F*(R), *E, S*(R), *It*	11	0	0	0	0	0
D W O'Mahony	1995 v It	1998 *R*	4	1	0	0	0	5
D G Humphreys	1996 v F	1998 *SA* 2(t&R), *R*(R), 1999 *F, W, E, S*	15	1	9	21	4	98
P A Burke	1995 v E		10	0	11	26	1	103
E P Elwood	1993 v W	1998 *SA*1,2, *Gg, R, SA* 3, 1999 *It*	31	0	36	66	2	276
C J Scally	1998 v Gg	1998 *Gg*(R), *R*, 1999 *S*(R), *It*	4	2	0	0	0	10
C D McGuinness	1997 v NZ	1998 *SA* 1,2, *Gg, R*(R), *SA* 3, 1999 *F, W, E, S*	14	1	0	0	0	5
A T H Clarke	1995 v Fj	1998 *Gg*(R), *R*	8	0	0	0	0	0
R P Nesdale	1997 v W	1998 *Gg, SA* 3(R), 1999 *It*	10	0	0	0	0	0
K G M Wood	1994 v A	1998 *SA* 1,2, *R*(R), *SA* 3, 1999 *F, W, E, S, It*(R)	24	4	0	0	0	20
R Corrigan	1997 v C	1998 *SA* 3(R)	7	0	0	0	0	0
J M Fitzpatrick	1998 v SA	1998 *SA* 1,2, *Gg*(R), *R*(R), *SA* 3, 1999 *F*(R), *W*(R), *E*(R), *It*	9	0	0	0	0	0
P S Wallace	1995 v J	1998 *SA* 1,2, *Gg, R*, 1999 *F, W, E, S, It*(R)	27	3	0	0	0	15
P M Clohessy	1993 v F	1998 *SA* 2(R), *Gg, R, SA* 3, 1999 *F, W, E, S, It*	28	2	0	0	0	10
G M Fulcher	1994 v A	1998 *SA* 1(R)	20	1	0	0	0	5

234

J W Davidson	1995 v Fj	1998 *Gg*(R), *R*(R), *SA* 3(R) , 1999 *F, W, E, S, It*	20	0	0	0	0	0
M E O'Kelly	1997 v NZ	1998 *SA* 1,2, *Gg, R, SA* 3	12	0	0	0	0	0
P S Johns	1990 v Arg	1998 *SA* 1,2, *Gg, R, SA* 3, 1999 *F, W, E, S, It*	51	4	0	0	0	20
M J Galwey	1991 v F	1999 *W*(R)	24	1	0	0	0	5
A J Ward	1998 v F	1998 *SA* 1,2, *Gg, R, SA* 3, 1999 *W, E ,S, It*(R)	12	2	0	0	0	10
D O'Cuinneagain	1998 v SA	1998 *SA* 1,2, *Gg*(R), *R*(R), *SA* 3, 1999 *F, W, E, S, It*	10	0	0	0	0	0
T Brennan	1998 v SA	1998 *SA* 1(R),2(R), 1999 *F*(R), *S*(R), *It*	5	0	0	0	0	0
D S Corkery	1994 v A		25	3	0	0	0	15
V C P Costello	1996 v US	1998 *SA* 1,2, *Gg, R, SA* 3, 1999 *F, W*(R), *E, S*(R), *It*	21	3	0	0	0	15
E R P Miller	1997 v It	1998 *Gg, R*, 1999 *F, W, E*(R), *S*	14	1	0	0	0	5

Ireland's new record-holder for most penalty goals in Tests, Eric Elwood, who was as reliable as ever with the boot.

IRISH CLUBS 1998-99

Ballymena

Year of formation 1922
Ground Eaton Park, Raceview Road, Ballymena Tel: Ballymena 656746
Web site http://www.ballymena.rfc.mcmail.com/Mainmenu.html
Colours Black
Captain 1998-99 D McCartney
Insurance Corporation League Div 1 9th

Ultimately Ballymena were lucky to escape the drop to Division Two in what was, again, a disappointing season for the Ulster club. Their situation was not helped by the presence of 10 of their players in the successful Ulster European Cup squad. As a result of Ulster's run in the tournament, their fixtures became truncated and the players found it difficult to perform at a high level after the euphoria of the European success. Many would argue that the selections of South African coach André Bester did not help. He continually played flankers Derek Topping and Dean McCartney at centre and wing respectively and on occasion former Irish full-back Simon Mason lined up at fly-half. Often they gained their usual forward domination but failed to put teams away, such as against Garryowen when although 13 points ahead they lost 18-13. Top points-scorer Mason had joined from Richmond, but they missed injured international winger James Topping for much of the season. Mason, Gary Longwell and Mark Blair all made appearances for Ireland A during the season, but they may again struggle next season, having lost at least six of their Ulster squad players.

League Record 1998-99

Date	Venue	Opponents	Result	Scorers
5 Dec	H	Shannon	23-3	*T:* Blair, McKearnan *C:* Mason 2 *PG:* Mason 3
19 Dec	H	St Mary's College	23-13	*T:* Mason, Graham *C:* Mason 2 *PG:* Mason 3
2 Jan	A	Clontarf	40-17	*T:* pen try 2, Irwin, Coulter *C:* Mason 4 *PG:* Mason 4
23 Jan	A	Young Munster	0-36	
13 Feb	H	Buccaneers	16-34	*T:* Stewart, Machett *PG:* Mason 2
27 Feb	H	Garryowen	13-19	*T:* McWhirter *C:* Mason *PG:* Mason 2
13 Mar	A	Lansdowne	24-25	*T:* Irwin, J Topping *C:* Mason *PG:* Mason 3 *DG:* Mason
27 Mar	H	Terenure College	13-20	*T:* McDowell *C:* Mason *PG:* Mason 2
3 Apr	A	Cork Constitution	12-21	*PG:* Mason 4
11 Apr	A	Galwegians	13-3	*T:* Blair *C:* Mason *PG:* Mason 2
17 Apr	A	Blackrock College	13-33	*T:* Stewart *C:* Mason *PG:* Mason 2

Blackrock College

Year of formation 1882
Ground Stradbrook Road, Blackrock, Dublin Tel: Dublin 2805967
Colours Royal blue and white hoops
Captain 1998-99 S Byrne
Insurance Corporation League Div 1 11th (relegated)

Before Christmas the club had high hopes that newly appointed coach, New Zealander Kevin West, was confounding the doubters and setting Blackrock up for a challenge at the top of the table. However, wins over Terenure and Galwegians and a narrow defeat against reigning champions Shannon proved to be a false dawn. The season turned in January when they suffered four successive defeats and, despite some enterprising attacking play from the likes of Aidan Guinan and Alan McGowan, the team were guilty of several defensive lapses. Yet again McGowan was the main contributor of points and captain Shane Byrne did his utmost to bring out the best from the forwards. Among the pack youngster Robert Casey was excellent, and after achieving international under-21 honours he was rewarded with a place on the full Ireland squad in Australia. Eventually their fate was sealed on the final Saturday when, despite a 33-13 win over Ballymena, they finished behind Clontarf on points difference.

League Record 1998-99

Date	Venue	Opponents	Result	Scorers
5 Dec	H	Terenure College	22-16	*T:* Roche *C:* McGowan *PG:* McGowan 5
12 Dec	A	Galwegians	16-9	*T:* Guinan, Boyd *PG:* McGowan 2
19 Dec	H	Shannon	24-26	*T:* McGowan, Robinson *C:* McGowan *PG:* McGowan 4
2 Jan	A	Cork Constitution	17-26	*T:* Guinan, McLoughlin, Roche *C:* McGowan
9 Jan	H	Clontarf	15-28	*T:* Guinan, Carey *C:* Carey *PG:* Carey
16 Jan	A	St Mary's College	11-34	*T:* Guinin *PG:* Carey 2
23 Jan	A	Lansdowne	22-41	*T:* Assaf, Wheeler, pen try *C:* Quinlan 2 *DG:* O'Donovan
13 Feb	H	Young Munster	10-3	*T:* Casey *C:* Carey *PG:* Carey
27 Feb	H	Buccaneers	10-14	*T:* Carey, Jordan
13 Mar	A	Garryowen	0-22	
17 Apr	H	Ballymena	33-13	*T:* Jackson, Wheelar, Guinnan, Jordan *C:* Carey 2 *PG:* Carey *DG:* O'Donovan 2

Buccaneers

Year of formation 1994
Ground Keane Park, Athlone Tel: Athlone 75582
Colours Black navy amber and white
Captain 1998-99 B Rigney
Insurance Corporation League Div 1 3rd (lost in play-off semi-final)

Buccaneers were by far the biggest surprise of the season in Irish rugby. Promoted along with Galwegians to become the first Connacht clubs in the top flight, they were particularly well drilled by coach Eddie O'Sullivan and had former international Brian Rigney as an inspirational captain. They forced their way into play-off contention with tremendous wins over St Mary's and especially Garryowen, when Stephen Allnutt, their top points-scorer of the season, scored all 16 points. Their place in the play-offs was secured on the final Saturday with a close win over fellow contenders Lansdowne at the smaller Ballinasloe ground where they were to finish the season unbeaten. The final win over Lansdowne caused O'Sullivan to describe the season as a 'ridiculous achievement' – only two seasons ago the club were in Division Three. Despite losing their semi-final encounter with Constitution, they had every right to be proud of their overall performance. With the addition of players like John Maher (returning from Lansdowne) and new Ireland winger Matt Mostyn (from Bègles-Bordeaux) they will again challenge for top honours next season.

League Record 1998-99

Date	Venue	Opponents	Result	Scorers
5 Dec	H	Galwegians	21-14	*T:* Rigney, pen try 2 *C:* Allnutt 3
12 Dec	A	Clontarf	16-34	*T:* pen try *C:* Allnutt *PG:* Allnutt 3
19 Dec	H	Terenure College	21-16	*T:* Lee, Devine *C:* Allnutt *PG:* Allnutt 2 *DG:* Allnutt
9 Jan	H	St Mary's College	11-10	*T:* Rigney *PG:* Allnutt 2

16 Jan	A	Cork Constitution	25-32	*T:* Rigney 2, Brennan *C:* Allnutt 2 *PG:* Allnutt 2
23 Jan	H	Garryowen	16-10	*T:* Allnutt *C:* Allnutt *PG:* Allnutt 3
13 Feb	A	Ballymena	34-16	*T:* McVeigh, Lee, Steffort, Devine *C:* Allnutt 4 *PG:* Allnutt 2
27 Feb	A	Blackrock College	14-10	*T:* Cahill, Steferet *C:* Allnutt 2
13 Mar	H	Young Munster	21-13	*PG:* Allnutt 7
27 Mar	A	Shannon	3-36	*PG:* Allnutt
17 Apr	H	Lansdowne	14-11	*T:* Lee *PG:* Allnutt 3

League Play-off semi-final:

25 Apr	A	Cork Constitution	20-32	*T:* Brennan, Devine *C:* Allnutt 2 *PG:* Allnutt 2

Clontarf

Year of formation 1876
Ground Castle Avenue, Clontarf, Dublin Tel: Dublin 8332621
Colours Scarlet and royal blue hoops
Captain 1998-99 B Jackman
Insurance Corporation League Div 1 10th

After last season's promising campaign this year failed to live up to expectations. Relegation was avoided only by points difference on the final day. Predicted as being a fringe team for the play-offs, Clontarf were never in this category despite an early season win over Buccaneers. Their season became focused on a relegation battle with Blackrock and Ballymena and their ultimate survival was decided in mid-March when they lost to eventual play-off finalists Constitution by only one point. On the same day Blackrock lost to Garryowen by 22 points, allowing Clontarf to establish the better points difference. Although they have attracted Alan Reddan from Galwegians and Rob Casey from Old Wesley for next season, they have lost their New Zealand coach Brent Pope, who has returned to St Mary's.

League Record 1998-99

Date	Venue	Opponents	Result	Scorers
5 Dec	A	Garryowen	15-22	*PG:* Murphy 5
12 Dec	H	Buccaneers	34-16	*T:* O'Brien, Winchester, Smyth *C:* Murphy 2 *PG:* Murphy 3, Woods *DG:* Woods
19 Dec	A	Lansdowne	3-15	*PG:* Murphy
2 Jan	H	Ballymena	17-40	*T:* Vaster 2, Moore *C:* Murphy
9 Jan	A	Blackrock College	28-15	*T:* Winchester, Moore, Brownlie *C:* Murphy 2 *PG:* Murphy 3
16 Jan	H	Young Munster	6-3	*PG:* Murphy 2
23 Jan	H	St Mary's College	17-46	*T:* Woods, Moore *C:* Murphy 2 *DG:* Murphy
13 Feb	A	Galwegians	21-30	*T:* Meagher, Barry *C:* Murphy *PG:* Murphy 3
27 Feb	H	Shannon	9-24	*PG:* Murphy 2 *DG:* Berti
13 Mar	H	Cork Constitution	16-17	*T:* Winchester *C:* Murphy *PG:* Murphy 3
17 Apr	A	Terenure College	32-18	*T:* Noble 2, McQuillan *C:* Murphy *PG:* Murphy 4 *DG:* Murphy

Cork Constitution

Year of formation 1892
Ground Temple Hill, Ballintemple, Cork Tel: Cork 292563
Colours White
Captain 1998-99 P Soden
Insurance Corporation League Div 1 winners (won play-off final)

Cork Constitution only managed one win from their first four games before producing some sizzling form to wrestle the title from Shannon. David Corkery, signed from Bristol, and half-backs Ronan O'Gara and Brian O'Meara were in excellent form throughout the season and made significant contributions to the club's success. Constitution's early loss to Lansdowne was at a time when five of their players were injured, but by the turn of the year they were at full strength and, with coaches Pat Derham and former Irish scrum-half Michael Bradley pulling the strings, produced some first-rate performances. Despite finishing second in the league table to Garryowen on points difference, they overcame Buccaneers in the semi-final and went on to secure the title at Lansdowne Road with an extra-time penalty to overcome Garryowen.

League Record 1998-99

Date	Venue	Opponents	Result	Scorers
5 Dec	A	Lansdowne	17-24	*T:* O'Brien *PG:* O'Gara 4
19 Dec	A	Young Munster	11-17	*T:* Walsh *PG:* O'Gara 2
2 Jan	H	Blackrock College	26-17	*T:* Horgan, Walsh, Corkery, O'Mera *PG:* O'Gara 2
9 Jan	A	Garryowen	22-24	*T:* Kelly, O'Callaghan, Mahoney *C:* O'Gara 2 *PG:* O'Gara
16 Jan	H	Buccaneers	32-25	*T:* Kiernan 2, Walsh *C:* O'Gara *PG:* O'Gara 5
23 Jan	H	Galwegians	41-8	*T:* O'Brien 3, Mahony 2, Sheehan *C:* O'Gara 4 *PG:* O'Gara
13 Feb	A	Terenure College	14-8	*T:* Corkery *PG:* O'Gara 3
27 Feb	H	St. Mary's College	38-0	*T:* O'Meara, Kelly, O'Gara, Murphy, Byrne *C:* O'Gara 2 *PG:* O'Gara 3
13 Mar	A	Clontarf	17-16	*T:* Walsh *PG:* O'Gara 4
3 Apr	H	Ballymena	21-12	*T:* O'Gara, Murray *C:* O'Gara *PG:* O'Gara 2 *DG:* O'Mera
17 Apr	H	Shannon	26-19	*T:* Walsh, Kelly, O'Gara *C:* O'Gara *PG:* O'Gara 3

League Play-off semi-final:

25 Apr	H	Buccaneers	32-20	*T:* O'Driscoll, Kelly, O'Brien *C:* O'Gara *PG:* O'Gara 5

League Play-off final:

1 May		Garryowen	14-11	*T:* Horgan *PG:* O'Gara 3

Galwegians

Year of formation 1922
Ground Crowley Park, Glenina, Galway Tel: Galway 753435
Colours Sky blue
Captain 1998-99 E Elwood
Insurance Corporation League Div 1 12th (Relegated)

Even with Connacht players Pat Duignan, Mervyn Murphy and Ireland outside-half Eric Elwood in the back line, this was never going to be an easy season for Galwegians. The bookies' favourites to go straight back down to Division Two, they duly obliged with only one win all season. Despite some heavy defeats they also managed a few creditable performances, most notably their narrow defeats at Lansdowne and against St Mary's. George Hook took over the coaching duties in February from John Healey and immediately saw his side get their only win, over Clontarf. Duignan and Willie Ruane produced some fine defensive displays while Elwood, predictably, was consistent with the boot. Yet it was never going to be enough and they finished six points adrift at the bottom of the table.

League Record 1998-99

Date	Venue	Opponents	Result	Scorers
5 Dec	A	Buccaneers	14-21	*T:* Murphy, Elwood *C:* Elwood 2
12 Dec	H	Blackrock College	9-16	*PG:* Elwood 3
19 Dec	A	Garryowen	0-46	
2 Jan	H	Young Munster	3-6	*PG:* Elwood
9 Jan	A	Lansdowne	22-26	*T:* Elwood 2, Gavin *C:* Elwood 2
				PG: Elwood
23 Jan	A	Cork Constitution	8-41	*T:* Casserley *PG:* Elwood
13 Feb	H	Clontarf	30-21	*T:* Carolan, Duignan, Reddan *C:* Elwood 3
				PG: Elwood 3
27 Feb	A	Terenure College	15-26	*T:* Elwood, Duignan *C:* Elwood *PG:* Elwood
13 Mar	A	Shannon	3-31	*PG:* Elwood
11 Apr	H	Ballymena	3-13	*PG:* Elwood
17 Apr	H	St. Mary's College	10-17	*T:* Reddan *C:* Elwood *PG:* Elwood

Garryowen

Year of formation 1884
Ground Dooradoyle, Limerick Tel: Limerick 303099
Colours Light blue with white five pointed star
Captain 1998-99 K Keane
Insurance Corporation League Div 1 2nd (lost play-off final)

Garryowen, who were coached for the first time by former Bath and England flanker John Hall, became the escape artists of the division and finally finished on top of the league table with the help of some narrow wins and some impressive victories away from Dooradoyle. An example was their 19-13 win at Ballymena. They were 13-0 down with 10 minutes left and looked dead and buried but managed to fight back and ended with a Tom Tierney try securing the win in the last minute. This luck carried into their play-off matches, when they faced St Mary's in the semi-finals. Hall had forecast a close match against 'the best team we faced all season'. But when 17 points adrift, and with Kieran Ronan sent off, they looked doomed. Yet they staged an amazing comeback to snatch the match with a Killian Keane penalty from 47 metres in the last minute. The following week they nearly did it again against Cork Constitution when they tied the match with a Jack Clarke try in the final minutes of a tense final. Although they could not quite pull off one final escape, they finished a very promising season as league runners-up.

League Record 1998-99

Date	Venue	Opponents	Result	Scorers
5 Dec	H	Clontarf	22-15	*T:* Cronin *C:* Keane *PG:* Keane 5
19 Dec	H	Galwegians	46-0	*T:* Keane, Varley 2, Wallace, McNamara, Ronan pen try *C:* Keane 4 *PG:* Keane
2 Jan	A	St Mary's College	7-18	*T:* Ronan *C:* Keane
9 Jan	H	Cork Constitution	24-22	*T:* Staunton, Keane, pen try *C:* Keane 3 *PG:* Keane
16 Jan	A	Terenure College	20-6	*T:* Wallace, O'Riordan *C:* Keane 2 *PG:* Keane 2
23 Jan	A	Buccaneers	10-16	*T:* Brooks *C:* Keane *PG:* Keane
31 Jan	A	Shannon	23-20	*T:* Cunningham, Laffan *C:* Keane 2 *PG:* Keane 3
13 Feb	H	Lansdowne	15-17	*PG:* Keane 5
27 Feb	A	Ballymena	19-13	*T:* O'Riordan, Keane, Tierney *C:* Keane 2
13 Mar	H	Blackrock College	22-0	*T:* O'Riordan 2, Crotty *C:* Keane 2 *PG:* Feane
17 Apr	A	Young Munster	29-13	*T:* McNamara, O'Riordan, Crotty, Hogan, Staunton *C:* Staunton 2

League Play-off semi-final:
24 Apr   H   St Mary's College   19-17   *T:* pen try   *C:* Keane   *PG:* Keane 4
League Play-off final:
 1 May   H   Cork Constitution   11-14   *T:* Clarke   *PG:* Keane 2

Lansdowne

Year of formation 1872
Ground Lansdowne Road, Dublin Tel: Dublin 6689300
Colours Red, yellow and black
Captain 1998-99 K McQuilkin
Insurance Corporation League Div 1 5th

The arrival of established club players such as Barry Everitt and Liam Toland and internationals Reggie Corrigan from Greystones and Gabriel Fulcher from London Irish gave coach Mick Cosgrove ample material on which to build a creditable league challenge. Injuries to several players, however, ultimately robbed Lansdowne of a play-off place. They set the early pace in the league, sitting on top at the Christmas break, but faced a difficult time in the New Year with Corrigan, Angus McKeen and Gordon D'Arcy all carrying injuries sustained while playing for Ireland A. The final game against Buccaneers decided which of the two teams were to make the top four and on a wet day in Ballinasloe, Lansdowne were unable to play their preferred running game. Cosgrove wryly observed after the match, 'I don't think they would have lived with us if it had stayed dry.' With the majority of the squad available next season, there is every chance that the Dublin club will be able to take a step nearer to wresting the title from the dominant Munster clubs.

League Record 1998-99

Date	Venue	Opponents	Result	Scorers
5 Dec	H	Cork Constitution	24-17	*T:* Gunne, Dillon, Everitt, Bohan *C:* Kearns 2
12 Dec	A	St Mary's College	20-10	*T:* McEntee *PG:* Kearns 4 *DG:* McQuilkin
19 Dec	H	Clontarf	15-3	*PG:* Kearns 5
2 Jan	A	Terenure College	7-14	*T:* Glennon *C:* Kearns
9 Jan	H	Galwegians	26-22	*T:* Kearns, McEntee *C:* Kearns 2 *PG:* Kearns 3 *DG:* Everitt
16 Jan	A	Shannon	0-35	
23 Jan	H	Blackrock College	41-22	*T:* D'Arcy 2, McEntee, Gunne, pen try *C:* Kearns 5 *PG:* Kearns 2
13 Feb	A	Garryowen	17-15	*T:* D'Arcy *PG:* Kearns 4
27 Feb	A	Young Munster	3-8	*PG:* Kearns
13 Mar	H	Ballymena	25-24	*T:* Dillon, Kearns, Ennis *C:* Kearns 2 *PG:* Kearns *DG:* Everitt
17 Apr	A	Buccaneers	11-14	*T:* Dillon *PG:* Kearns 2

St Mary's College

Year of formation 1900
Ground Templeville Road, Templeogue, Dublin Tel: Dublin 4900440
Web site http://www.angelfire.com/me/StMarys/
Colours Royal Blue with five-pointed white star
Captain 1998-99 C McGuinness
Insurance Corporation League Div 1 4th (Lost in play-off Semi-Final)

Once again St Mary's were genuine title contenders throughout the season and played their best rugby in dry conditions. They missed centre Gareth Gannon (injured) but were still able to field the most potent back line in the league, with Irish international Conor McGuinness controlling matters from scrum-half. As usual the evergreen Steve Jameson was a colossal presence in the pack where they were also able to field two internationals in the back row, Victor Costello and Trevor Brennan. Former player Brent Pope will coach next season while the pack will be bolstered by the arrival of Ireland player Malcolm O'Kelly from London Irish. St Mary's hopes of topping the league were shattered by a late-season injury crisis and, against Cork Constitution when they suffered one of their heaviest ever league defeats, they were without six regular first-team players, including internationals John McWeeney, Kevin Nowlan, Brennan and Costello. However, they bounced back to secure a top four finish with their first ever league win over Terenure on the final Saturday. Despite the heavy league defeat against Constitution they were in positive form in the semi-final and raced into a 17-point lead. Yet from that point they crumbled and the season finished in the worst possible fashion when they lost the game to a last-minute penalty. Coach Steve Hennessy was distraught after the game but should reflect on an excellent season in which St Mary's ended as Dublin's top club.

League Record 1998-99

Date	Venue	Opponents	Result	Scorers
5 Dec	A	Young Munster	31-15	T: McGuinness, McWeeney, McIlreavey, pen try C: Ormond 4 PG: Ormond
12 Dec	H	Lansdowne	10-20	T: Costello C: Ormond PG: Ormond
19 Dec	A	Ballymena	13-23	T: McGuinness C: Ormond PG: Ormond 2
2 Jan	H	Garryowen	18-7	T: Cuddihy, Jameson C: Campion PG: Campion 2
9 Jan	A	Buccaneers	10-11	T: Nowlan C: Campion PG: Campion
16 Jan	H	Blackrock College	34-11	T: Costello 2, Cuddihy, Lane, McKenna, pen try C: Campion 2
23 Jan	A	Clontarf	46-17	T: McWeeney 2, McKenna, Coyle, McIlreavy, Campion C: Campion 5 PG: Campion DG: Smyth
13 Feb	H	Shannon	17-12	T: Brennan PG: Campion 3 DG; Campion
27 Feb	A	Cork Constitution	0-38	
13 Mar	H	Terenure College	19-13	T: McKenna C: Campion PG: Campion 2 DG: Campion, McIlreavy
17 Apr	A	Galwegians	17-10	T: Costello PG: Campion 4
League Play-off semi-final:				
24 Apr	A	Garryowen	17-19	T: McWeeney, McKenna C: Campion 2 PG: Campion

Shannon

Year of formation 1884
Ground Thomond Park, Limerick Tel: Limerick 452350
Colours Black and blue hoops
Captain 1998-99 A Foley
Insurance Corporation League Div 1 6th

This was the season that Shannon's All Ireland League bubble finally burst. After four years as champions they were unable to make even the play-offs this time. Although their form had taken a dip from their previously extremely high standards, there was no less heart in the squad and they fought to the end. Despite winning only six of their 11 games they still returned a points difference of +60 (bettered only by the top two), but crucially could only beat one of the top four sides. Coach Pat Murray felt that their poor early season form was in part due to the demands of the Ireland A squad, with four of the pack playing at that level on the Tuesday before the first league match. The high point of the season was their great win over Lansdowne, who were the league's pacesetters at the time. With pack domination leading to overall control Shannon showed their old style, but it was a short lived return to the past as in the next match Terenure became the first side to win a league game at Shannon for nearly five years. Mick Galwey was a vital part of the pack and

Rhys Ellison in the centre also had a fine season. It is a measure of Shannon's expectations that this was considered such a poor season, yet they ended just one win away from a play-off place.

League Record 1998-99

Date	Venue	Opponents	Result	Scorers
5 Dec	A	Ballymena	3-23	*PG:* Thompson
19 Dec	A	Blackrock College	26-24	*T:* Horan, McMahon *C:* Thompson 2 *PG:* Thompson 4
10 Jan	A	Young Munster	10-9	*T:* McMahon *C:* Thompson *PG:* Burke
16 Jan	H	Lansdowne	35-0	*T:* Hayes, McMahon, McDermott 2, Lacey 2 *C:* Thompson *PG:* Thompson
23 Jan	H	Terenure College	8-27	*T:* Lacey *PG:* Thompson
31 Jan	H	Garryowen	20-23	*T:* Horan, Lacey *C:* Thompson 2 *PG:* Thompson 2
13 Feb	A	St Mary's College	12-17	*PG:* Thompson 2 *DG:* Gavin 2
27 Feb	A	Clontarf	24-9	*T:* Roache, Hayes, Thompson *C:* Thompson 3 *PG:* Thompson
13 Mar	H	Galwegians	31-3	*T:* Halvey, Hayes, O'Shea, Horan, Foley *C:* Thompson 3
27 Mar	H	Buccaneers	36-3	*T:* Horan 2, McNamara, Foley *C:* Thompson 2 *PG:* Thompson 4
17 Apr	A	Cork Constitution	19-26	*T:* Galwey, McMahon, Galvin *C:* Thompson 2

Terenure College

Year of formation 1940
Ground Lakelands Park, Greenlea, Terenure, Dublin Tel: Dublin 4907572
Web site http://ireland.iol.ie/~tcrfc/
Colours Purple, black and white
Captain 1998-99 J Blaney
Insurance Corporation League Div 1 8th

For a second season Terenure finished in mid-table and never threatened to mount a serious challenge for anything higher. Indeed, it was only on the penultimate Saturday of league action that they secured their place in the division. A relatively comfortable win away to a disjointed Ballymena side guaranteed their safety, despite losing their last game against fellow strugglers Clontarf. The high point of the season was the splendid win at Shannon, the first home defeat suffered by the former champions in more than four years. They also won against Dublin rivals Lansdowne when Niall Hogan, who had returned to the club from London Irish, had a splendid game. International back row Eric Miller had also joined on his return home from Leicester, but injury robbed him of the chance to play any major role in the league season. With Miller undergoing ankle surgery in the close season he should be able to take a fuller part in the action next season, and this may be the catalyst that Terenure need to push themselves into the top flight.

League Record 1998-99

Date	Venue	Opponents	Result	Scorers
5 Dec	A	Blackrock College	16-22	*T:* Clarke *C:* Fitzpatrick *PG:* Fitzpatrick 3
19 Dec	A	Buccaneers	16-21	*T:* Blaney *C:* Tracey *PG:* Treacy, Hill 2
2 Jan	H	Lansdowne	14-7	*T:* Hogan *PG:* Fitzpatrick, Treacy 2
16 Jan	H	Garryowen	6-20	*PG:* Lynagh 2
23 Jan	A	Shannon	27-8	*T:* Dempsey, Hogan *C:* Fitzpatrick *PG:* Fitzpatrick 4 *DG:* Treacy
31 Jan	H	Young Munster	11-11	*T:* Blaney *PG:* Fitzpatrick 2
13 Feb	H	Cork Constitution	8-14	*T:* Coleman *PG:* Fitzpatrick
27 Feb	H	Galwegians	26-15	*T:* Dempsey 2, Treacy, Smith *PG:* Treacy 2

13 Mar	A	St. Mary's College	13-19	*T:* Smyth *C:* Fitzpatrick *PG:* Fitzpatrick 2
27 Mar	A	Ballymena	20-13	*T:* Tracey, Cullen *C:* Lynagh 2 *PG:* Lynagh 2
17 Apr	H	Clontarf	18-32	*T:* Smith, Dempsey *C:* Treacy *PG:* Treacy 2

Young Munster

Year of formation 1895
Ground Tom Clifford Park, Greenfields, Limerick Tel: Limerick 228433
Web site http://www.angelfire.com/on/youngmunster/
Colours Black and amber hoops
Captain 1998-99 P Clohessy
Insurance Corporation League Div 1 7th

Young Munster had high hopes for a very productive season. After finishing third last season they strengthened their squad with New Zealand back row Matt Webber and Dolphin wing Dennis O'Dowd. But two wins from their first five games ensured that they were going to struggle to reach the levels of the previous campaign. A comprehensive win over Ballymena was tempered by the fact that the Ulster club had rested all of their European Cup squad members and after that win the Munster's managed to pick up only three more points. Despite this poor form, a victory over Lansdowne left the Limerick side with the opportunity to reach the play-offs if they could beat title-chasing Buccaneers and Garryowen in the last two games. They were unable to win either and ultimately finished five points adrift of a top four place. Although new Irish player Mike Mullins is set to join from West Hartlepool, they have lost five first-team players including leading points-scorers Aidan O'Halloran and Mick Lynch.

League Record 1998-99

Date	Venue	Opponents	Result	Scorers
5 Dec	H	St Mary's College	15-31	*T:* McChill, Clohessy *C:* O'Halloran *PG:* O'Halloran
19 Dec	H	Cork Constitution	17-11	*T:* Earls 2, Buckley *C:* O'Halloran
2 Jan	A	Galwegians	6-3	*PG:* O'Halloran 2
10 Jan	H	Shannon	9-10	*PG:* Lynch 2 *DG:* Lynch
16 Jan	A	Clontarf	3-6	*PG:* O'Halloran
23 Jan	H	Ballymena	36-0	*T:* O'Dowd 2, Tobin, O'Mera, Clohessy *C:* Lynch 4 *PG:* Lynch
31 Jan	A	Terenure College	11-11	*T:* Tobin *PG:* Lynch 2
13 Feb	A	Blackrock College	3-10	*PG:* O'Halloran
27 Feb	H	Lansdowne	8-3	*T:* Prendergast *PG:* Lynch
13 Mar	A	Buccaneers	13-21	*T:* O'Dowd *C:* Lynch *PG:* Lynch 2
17 Apr	H	Garryowen	13-29	*T:* O'Dowd *C:* O'Halloran *PG:* O'Halloran *DG:* Prendergast

WALES FIND THEIR INSPIRATION

THE 1998-99 SEASON IN WALES
John Billot

Once it was overheard at Sandhurst, 'The Welsh make damned fine soldiers – with white officers.' Well, the WRU went to the other side of the world to find the man to lick the natives into shape. Although he cost an arm and a leg, they were of the opinion that he was worth it. New Zealander Graham Henry, aged 52, was appointed national coaching supremo at the end of July on a five-year contract worth around £250,000 a year. The former Auckland schoolmaster had enjoyed an impressive coaching record, inspiring Auckland to 86 victories in 108 matches between 1992 and 1998, and collecting three national provincial championships and 22 Ranfurly Shield victories. He also directed Auckland to the Super-12 series title in 1996 and 1997. So, after spending three months on their global search, the WRU were well pleased with their capture.

But could he bring about a regeneration after the unhappy demise of the Welsh game? First, he induced a spirited performance to frighten the Springboks when Wales stole an amazing 14-0 lead just five months after being whipped by 96-13 in Pretoria. He galvanised the Quinnell brothers from unfit plodders into dramatic ball-carriers. That certainly shocked South Africa. So Henry was hailed, despite defeat by 28-20, as the 'Great Redeemer', who could lift Wales off the life-support machine and bring back at least a semblance of the glory days.

However, Scotland and Ireland then threw hefty spanners into the works and it was a humbled Henry who took fresh stock. Doubters re-emerged from nooks and crannies. Wales had failed against the two countries they had expected to defeat and now faced the two most difficult games. What transpired could have been scripted by Scheherazade! Wales had not won in Paris for 24 years and had lost to France by 51-0 at Wembley the previous season. This time it was a case of the 'Taming of the Blues'. The French forwards were transformed from the wild bunch into the mild bunch and Wales, dubbed 'the 20 minutes team', waded through the full 80 minutes for that long-awaited success. 'This was pay-back time,' sighed happy captain Rob Howley after one of the all-time great Five Nations matches. It was a case of 'don't dare blink or you'll miss something thrilling'. One point was enough for victory – and one point was sufficient a second time with England the astonished victims.

England were up for the Grand Slam and coach Henry offered the opinion that Welsh chances were less than favourable. He is ever

New dawn in Wales? At long last the game on and off the field appears to be coming together in Wales. Here the Welsh team line up at the Millennium Stadium before their stunning first ever victory over South Africa.

the pragmatist and remarked afterwards, 'England were the better team, but we hung on in there.' To snatch victory by a whisker at 32-31 through Scott Gibbs's wonder-try in the second minute of injury-time, which Neil Jenkins converted, was a near-miracle. Wales had left it agonisingly late to embrace the elusive essence of success. For England it was the torment of Tantalus.

Coach Henry expresses vehement views. 'The structure of Welsh rugby is a shambles,' he insists. 'There is a need for administrators and clubs to get together. We should lock the door and throw away the key until they have organised a new structure.' On the standards of play in the lower divisions he comments, 'My grandmother could play in some of the leagues here! And I don't think she would expect to be paid. Over here, everyone thinks that if they play rugby they are professionals. The sooner the decision is made to make the game amateur below the Premier Division the better. We should have a semi-pro Premier Division, then three or four professional teams above that playing in a Super-12 type competition.'

The unaccommodating reality of the club scene was that the absence of Cardiff and Swansea, who were playing friendly fixtures against the major English clubs, meant a diminution of quality in the Premier Division. Newport were reprieved from relegation while Caerphilly and Aberavon were promoted from Division One to replace the 'truants'. Cardiff and Swansea considered that they were driven out by the WRU demand to sign a 10-year loyalty contract. A Premier Division without them stripped the league of much of its charisma, though they offered to compete in the cup competition and were accepted by the WRU.

If Welsh rugby is to leave a powerful imprint on the game it needs Cardiff and Swansea. They were fined £150,000 each by the WRU: £60,000 for playing cross-border games without permission; £60,000 for negotiating their own television deals; and a further £30,000 for using unsanctioned referees. Many in Wales considered both clubs to be rebels with a cause and that their stand would hasten the formation of a much-needed British League. Rebels or freedom fighters, the pair stimulated interest with their English club fixtures and home attendances trebled for a time.

Many clubs endured financial crises: Ebbw Vale put leading players up for sale, the Bridgend players accepted a pay cut and Llanelli and Neath needed urgent aid from the WRU. Neath were on the point of folding, with debts of around £645,000, but were saved by a WRU take-over of management control. Maesteg players announced that they were withdrawing their services after being asked to back a wage cut and one match was postponed. The professional game is still a disturbing influence in Wales.

CARDIFF AND SWANSEA OPT OUT

WRU NATIONAL LEAGUE 1998-99

Imagine a Premier Division in the Football League without Manchester United or Arsenal? The equivalent occurred in Welsh rugby: Cardiff and Swansea took no part in the WRU top division, which then was shorn of much of its glamour and excitement. It was like Holmes without Watson, Laurel without Hardy or Morse without Lewis. Consequently we had a two-horse race. Llanelli and Pontypridd were vastly superior to the other teams and, although Ebbw Vale and Neath had their moments, no-one was going to prevent the Scarlets and Ponty dominating the scene.

Actually, Pontypridd were fortunate that they built a commanding lead in second place before the new play-off stage was enacted. Without captain Neil Jenkins, recovering from a shoulder operation, Ponty managed to win just one of their six play-off fixtures. A worried Jenkins admitted that his team lacked strength in depth and stressed that they had urgent need to recruit during the summer if they were to continue to compete with teams possessing more powerful squads.

Llanelli remained unbeaten at home in league matches and proved worthy champions, bringing the title back to Stradey after a six-year wait. They clinched the prize in their fourth play-off game when they defeated Neath by 37-11 and, with two games left, could not be overhauled. Neath had surprised the Stradey men by 32-17 at the Gnoll in the opening play-off; but that was Llanelli's only failure, though an anxious 23-all draw with Ebbw Vale at Stradey came as a surprise, probably to both sides!

Cynics claim, and with every justification, that there was little to bother the two top teams, and the return of Swansea and Cardiff is essential to revitalise a division that limped through a worrying season with cash crises around every corner. After Neath, Llanelli and Bridgend fell victims to serious financial problems, Ebbw Vale were compelled to release leading players to cut costs. Some teams' players accepted a reduction in pay, but Maesteg's players briefly went on strike when they were asked to take a cut. Division One clubs warned the WRU that it could be 'disastrous' for some of them unless more funding were made available. They pointed out that Premier Division clubs received £500,000 from the WRU annually, while Division One received only £75,000 a club.

Neath made an astounding recovery from a desperate situation. They went bust in August 1998 and the WRU put in a financial adviser. Some 13 players left for other clubs; yet Neath regrouped, reorganised and could claim home victories against league leaders Llanelli and Pontypridd on the way to edging out Ebbw Vale for third place in the division. Call it Black Magic! The Blacks certainly bounced back from the pit with gusto.

Ebbw Vale faded after a promising start that brought six victories in their opening seven league fixtures, but they won only two of their last seven games and skipper Kingsley Jones joined Gloucester, while star kicker Byron Hayward transferred to Llanelli to ease the financial plight. Caerphilly's part-time professionals were an example to others. They enjoyed a successful season with five victories over Newport (including the European Shield match) and Brett Davey broke the scoring record he had set for them the previous season with a new tally of 384 points.

Aberavon found a bright young star in Cerith Rees, an accomplished goal-kicker and tactical controller at outside-half, but finished bottom of the division with just two victories (against Bridgend and Newport). Division One saw enterprising Dunvant as top team with Bonymaen runners-up, while Division Two honours went to Abercynon in a tight finish with Llanharan.

WRU LEAGUES 1998-99

Premier Div.	P	W	D	L	T	B	F	A	Pts
Llanelli	20	15	1	4	104	18	768	341	64
Pontypridd	20	12	0	8	80	10	646	468	46
Neath	20	12	0	8	68	8	568	491	44
Ebbw Vale	20	12	1	7	58	7	541	468	44
Caerphilly	20	10	2	8	63	5	550	562	37
Bridgend	20	9	2	9	61	5	522	597	34
Newport	20	5	0	15	63	8	499	629	23
Aberavon	20	2	0	18	51	4	391	929	10

Brett Davey (Caerphilly) was the season's leading points-scorer with 257; Wayne Proctor (Llanelli) scored most tries (16).

Swansea have won the Welsh League title three times, 1991-92, 1993-94 and 1997-98; **Neath** twice, 1990-91 and 1995-96; **Llanelli** twice, 1992-93 and 1998-99; **Cardiff** 1994-95; **Pontypridd** 1996-97.

Division 1	P	W	D	L	T	B	F	A	Pts
Dunvant	30	24	1	5	151	24	1046	503	97
Bonymaen	30	22	2	6	120	23	827	392	91
Pontypool	30	23	0	7	101	11	766	494	80
Treorchy	30	16	2	12	113	14	808	567	64
Cross Keys	30	18	1	11	88	7	725	603	62
Merthyr	30	16	2	12	87	9	643	624	59
Llandovery	30	15	2	13	104	9	771	688	56
Tredegar	30	16	1	13	84	6	676	620	55
Rumney	30	12	1	17	92	14	626	753	51
Newbridge	30	14	0	16	71	6	628	611	48
Abertillery	30	12	2	16	69	10	565	615	48
UWIC	30	12	1	17	74	5	585	719	42
Blackwood	30	11	0	19	87	9	570	707	40
Tondu	30	10	1	19	68	7	502	673	38
S W Police	30	9	1	20	71	1	503	864	29
Maesteg	30	2	0	20	45	2	363	1171	8

Division 2	P	W	D	L	T	B	F	A	Pts
Abercynon	26	20	0	6	114	20	802	344	80
Llanharan	26	19	0	7	119	22	807	360	79
Ystradgynlais	26	18	2	6	121	21	820	367	77
Whitland	26	21	0	5	98	12	691	338	75
Tenby Utd	26	17	0	9	105	15	717	456	66
Rhymney	26	16	0	10	89	11	598	451	59
Mountain A.	26	15	0	11	55	5	540	470	50
Llantrisant	26	12	1	13	68	11	501	473	48
Narberth	26	13	0	13	65	5	500	512	44
Oakdale	26	8	0	18	63	10	516	560	34

St Peter's	26	8	0	18	73	9	545	676	33
Wrexham	25	9	1	15	52	3	412	715	31
Kenfig Hill	26	3	0	23	48	2	342	1162	11
Pyle	25	0	0	25	28	1	224	1131	-5

Division 3 E	P	W	D	L	T	B	F	A	Pts
Glamorgan W.	26	21	0	5	112	16	772	306	79
Bedwas	26	19	2	5	102	14	676	320	73
Risca	26	18	0	8	83	7	661	515	61
Gilfach Goch	26	16	0	10	87	13	577	455	61
Treherbert	26	15	0	11	60	8	469	420	53
Builth Wells	26	14	0	12	79	11	572	443	53
Brynmawr	26	12	1	13	58	5	455	453	42
Ystrad Rhond.	26	11	1	14	78	8	532	474	42
Abergavenny	26	11	0	15	62	9	487	525	42
Penygraig	26	11	0	15	75	7	526	497	40
Garndiffaith	26	11	0	15	74	6	542	617	39
Hirwaun	26	10	0	16	53	6	503	695	36
Blaina	26	9	0	17	53	5	449	617	32
Penarth	26	2	0	24	41	1	312	1196	7

Division 3 W	P	W	D	L	T	B	F	A	Pts
Carmarthen Q.	26	25	0	1	128	21	879	299	96
Carmarthen A.	26	21	0	5	93	18	655	310	81
Resolven	26	19	0	7	90	13	708	387	70
Tonmawr	26	15	0	11	71	10	514	504	55
Aberavon Q.	26	13	0	13	88	12	598	508	51
Seven Sisters	26	13	0	13	62	10	504	406	49
Vardre	26	14	1	11	54	5	473	417	48
Llangennech	26	13	0	13	63	7	526	503	46
Cardigan	26	12	0	14	60	7	436	523	43
Felinfoel	26	10	1	15	75	6	562	715	37
Pencoed	26	10	0	16	53	3	432	567	33
Glynneath	26	9	2	15	49	1	441	714	30
Kidwelly	26	4	0	22	42	2	293	696	14
Tumble	26	2	0	24	28	1	264	736	7

Other Winners

Division 4 East: Tonyrefail
Division 4 West: Cwmllynfell
Division 5 East: Croesyceiliog
Division 5 Central: Ystalyfera
Division 5 West: Mumbles
Division 5 North: Bethesda
Division 6 East: Caldicot
Division 6 Central: Cwmavon
Division 6 West: Penclawdd
Division 7 East: Abercwmboi
Division 7 Central: Blaengarw
Division 7 West: Loughor

VICTORY FOR THE REBELS

SWALEC CUP 1998-99

15 May, Ninian Park, Cardiff
Swansea 37 (4G 1PG 2DG) **Llanelli 10** (1G 1PG)

Llanelli's hopes of a unique treble – WRU Challenge Trophy, Premier Division title and SWALEC Cup – were unequivocally shattered by a record margin for a Welsh Cup final. No team had ever raised 37 points in the tourney's 28 years, but Llanelli, in their 14th final, had no complaints. Swansea were always in command with arch-schemer Arwel Thomas voted outstanding player to win the Lloyd Lewis Memorial Award for his 15 goal points, a salvo of shrewd tactical kicks and a wickedly delicious little dummy that set up South African Tyrone Maullin's try. It was the turning point just before half-time to establish a 24-10 lead with no way back for the subdued Scarlets.

'I don't think we played at our best, but it proved enough,' reflected Scott Gibbs, who recovered from a chest injury in time to lead his side. 'We knew if we kept the ball we would win.' His forwards did this for him with dominating impact. They always had the squeeze on Robin McBryde's pack and few chances materialised for the Llanelli backs, though Wayne Proctor was put into space smoothly for their only try.

On the morning of the match, Colin Charvis, who had not played since suffering a fractured cheekbone against England five weeks earlier, decided to risk a canter – and obligingly scored the first two tries. Arwel fed on under pressure to Mark Taylor and Charvis was in close support to cross; next, Taylor's thunderbolt burst again found Charvis loping along for the final pass. Cheers for Charvis, but the bell toiled for Llanelli ambitions of a record 11th cup. The final Swansea try came during injury-time, snapped up by Dean Thomas, one of a crop of substitutes who came flooding on near the end.

Most of the excitement and presentation of skills occurred during the opening half for the delectation of a sell-out attendance of 14,500 and Arwel's two dropped goals were glittering gems that helped decorate events. Both sides started with 12 internationals in their ranks and it was previewed as a battle between the Llanelli loyalists and Swansea rebels. Doubtless, those whose sympathies often are with the rebels of life were satisfied by the outcome.

Swansea: D J Weatherley; R Rees, M Taylor, I S Gibbs (*capt*), M F D Robinson; A C Thomas, R Jones; D R Morris, G R Jenkins, B R Evans, T Maullin, A P Moore, W P Moriarty, L Jones, C L Charvis *Substitutions:* J Griffiths for Moore (61 mins); D Thomas for Moriarty (70 mins); C T Anthony for Evans (72 mins); L Davies for A C Thomas (79 mins); C Wells for Jenkins (79 mins); A Booth for R Jones (79 mins); C van Rensburg for Gibbs (79 mins)
Scorers *Tries:* Charvis (2), Maullin, D Thomas *Conversions:* A C Thomas (3), L Davies *Penalty Goal:* A C Thomas *Dropped Goals:* A C Thomas (2)
Llanelli: B I Hayward; W T Proctor, S Finau, N G Davies, G Evans; S Jones, R H StJ B Moon; M Madden, R C McBryde (*capt*), J D Davies, M J Voyle,

Keeping it in the family. Swansea's Rhodri Jones is tackled by his namesake Stephen Jones in the SWALEC Cup final victory over Llanelli at Ninian Park.

C P Wyatt, H Jenkins, L S Quinnell, I Boobyer *Substitutions:* M Thomas for Boobyer (temp 35-45 mins); A H Copsey for Jenkins (72 mins); P Booth for Madden (72 mins); V Cooper for Voyle (72 mins); A Thomas for Moon (79 mins); I Jones for Boobyer (79 mins); C Warlow for N G Davies (79 mins)
Scorers *Try:* Proctor *Conversion:* Hayward *Penalty Goal:* Hayward
Referee R G Davies (Dunvant)

Earlier Rounds

Invariably there is an undercurrent of apprehension when Llanelli supporters find their team drawn against Cardiff. The Arms Park side had won six of their previous cup meetings, but the Stradey faithful need not have felt any concern this time; not even when Cardiff established a 10-0 lead after 15 minutes in the semi-final tie at the Brewery Field. The cup-holders were biding their time. When Llanelli turned up the volume it blew Cardiff apart. A dynamic display by the forwards produced victory by 39-10 and one of Cardiff's most dismal efforts of the season. Llanelli possessed passion and purpose; Cardiff were afflicted by an amazing apathy. Byron Hayward kicked 24 points, Mike Voyle and Scott Quinnell crossed for tries and there was a penalty try. For Cardiff, Lee Jarvis converted Craig Morgan's try and fired over a penalty.

Swansea's pace devastated Cross Keys by 60-3 in the other semi-final at Sardis Road, Pontypridd with Matthew Robinson a slippery customer who sprinted for three tries. Other tries were added by Richard Rees (two), Mark Taylor, Tyrone Maullin and Dean Thomas. There was also a smoothly-struck drop-shot from David Rees, the Cross Keys player/coach at outside-half.

Swansea and Cardiff had to enter the competition in the second round because they were not accorded seeded status, having opted out of the National League. Swansea raised their highest cup tally by 100-7 with 16 tries (three by Simon Davies) at Amman Utd. Then they put out Crynant by 48-0 with three tries by third-choice scrum-half Ed Lewsey. Scott Gibbs was another three-try scorer as Swansea won by 57-8 at Risca; and next it was Richard Rees who crossed for three tries against his former club as Swansea accounted for Newport by 60-38. Arwel Thomas's 16 points helped knock out Bridgend by 43-16 before Ebbw Vale, the previous season's defeated finalists, failed by 42-14 at Swansea. This time Arwel's 17 points ensured that Swansea avenged their cup exit of a year earlier.

Llanelli's 16 tries (three by hooker Marcus Thomas on his debut) saw Llanelli complete their record cup score by 100-0 against Ynysybwl before the referee called a halt some seven minutes early. It was almost another century as Llanhilleth went out by 91-0 with Wayne Proctor obtaining four of the 15 tries at Stradey. Pontypridd captain Neil Jenkins spent 10 minutes in the sin-bin for dissent and Llanelli were winners by 22-17 at Sardis Road.

RESULTS

Third round

Abercwmboi 21, Pill Harriers 7; Betws 21, Llangennech 20; Blaengarw 20, Penclawdd 19; Blaina 14, Rhymney 18; Bridgend Ath 6, Ynysybwl 14; Cardiff 84, Seven Sisters 10; Carmarthen Quins 50, BP Llandarcy 3; Cefn Coed 0, Bedwas 60; Cowbridge 5, Whitland 22; Crynant 0, Swansea 48; Cwmavon 16, Tumble 13; Gilfach Goch 12, Builth Wells 34; Glyncoch 12, Nantymoel 34; Glynneath 14, Fairwater 12; Gorseinon 3, Aberavon Quins 28; Heol-y-Cyw 47, Pembroke Dock Quins 10; Hirwaun 31, Skewen 6; Llanharan 90, Gowerton 0; Llanhilleth 27, Cardigan 20; Monmouth 29, Tycroes 14; Morriston 11, Ystradgynlais 18; Narberth 52, Ogmore Vale 17; Oakdale 27, Canton 11; Pencoed 34, Abercynon 21; Penygraig 21, Tenby Utd 8; Pontyclun 22, Cwmgwrach 13; Risca 23, Resolven 21; St Peter's 18, Pontypool Utd 19; Treherbert 23, Abergavenny 7; Trimsaran 16, Llantrisant 10; Vardre Utd 37, Llantwit Fardre 15; Wrexham 31, Glamorgan Wanderers 22

Fourth round

Aberavon 49, Carmarthen Quins 22; Abercwmboi 5, Maesteg 29; Beddau 0, Whitland 35; Betws 3, Blackwood 15; Blaengarw 10, Ynysybwl 10 (won on away team rule); Bonymaen 51, Newbridge 12; Bridgend 29, Treorchy 24; Builth Wells 5, Rumney 26; Cross Keys 25, Dunvant 14; Cwmavon 17, Bedwas 21; Cwmllynfell 13, Taffs Well 7; Dinas Powys 5, Pontypool Utd 16; Ebbw Vale 73, Treherbert 15; Glynneath 10, Trimsaran 25; Heol-y-Cyw 10, Tondu 27; Hirwaun 19, Kidwelly 9; Llandovery 22, Cardiff 40; Llanharan 19, Newport 25; Monmouth 11, Llanhilleth 20; Narberth 19, Caerphilly 29; Oakdale 7, UWIC 12; Pencoed 11, Abertillery 25; Penygraig 10, Rhymney 8; Pontyclun 0, Llanelli 80; Pontypool 64, Rhigos 6; Pontypridd 71, Aberavon Quins 15; Risca 8, Swansea 57; Talywain 9, Nantymoel 14; Tredegar 20, Merthyr 16; Wrexham 15, Neath 46; Ystradgynlais 32, Vardre 20; Ystrad Rhondda 19, SW Police 13

Fifth round

Bonymaen 82, UWIC 19; Caerphilly 53, Bedwas 10; Cardiff 33, Abertillery 3; Cross Keys 38, Trimsaran 7; Cwmllynfell 0, Pontypridd 41; Hirwaun 13, Tondu 36; Llanelli 100, Ynysybwl 0; Llanhilleth 26, Ystradgynlais 19; Maesteg 8, Blackwood 31; Nantymoel 0, Bridgend 29; Penygraig 3, Neath 47; Pontypool Utd 3, Ebbw Vale 61; Swansea 60, Newport 38; Tredegar 35, Rumney 14; Whitland 13, Pontypool 15; Ystrad Rhondda 7, Aberavon 37

Sixth round

Aberavon 12, Cardiff 20; Blackwood 9, Tredegar 12 (aet); Bridgend 16, Swansea 43; Caerphilly 15, Ebbw Vale 20; Cross Keys 39, Tondu 11; Llanelli 91, Llanhilleth 0; Pontypool 15, Neath 14; Pontypridd 47, Bonymaen 12

Quarter-finals

Pontypool 26, Cardiff 52; Pontypridd 17, Llanelli 22; Swansea 42, Ebbw Vale 14; Tredegar 12, Cross Keys 17

Semi-finals

Llanelli 39, Cardiff 10 (at Bridgend); Swansea 60, Cross Keys 3 (at Pontypridd)

Final (at Ninian Park, Cardiff)

Swansea 37, Llanelli 10

Previous finals

1972	Neath 15, Llanelli 9
1973	Llanelli 30, Cardiff 7
1974	Llanelli 12, Aberavon 10
1975	Llanelli 15, Aberavon 6
1976	Llanelli 16, Swansea 4
1977	Newport 16, Cardiff 15
1978	Swansea 13, Newport 9
1979	Bridgend 18, Pontypridd 12
1980	Bridgend 15, Swansea 9
1981	Cardiff 14, Bridgend 6
1982*	Cardiff 12, Bridgend 12
1983	Pontypool 18, Swansea 6
1984	Cardiff 24, Neath 19
1985	Llanelli 15, Cardiff 14
1986	Cardiff 28, Newport 21
1987	Cardiff 16, Swansea 15
1988	Llanelli 28, Neath 13
1989	Neath 14, Llanelli 13
1990	Neath 16, Bridgend 10
1991	Llanelli 24, Pontypool 9
1992	Llanelli 16, Swansea 7
1993	Llanelli 21, Neath 18
1994	Cardiff 15, Llanelli 8
1995	Swansea 17, Pontypridd 12
1996	Pontypridd 29, Neath 22
1997	Cardiff 33, Swansea 26
1998	Llanelli 19, Ebbw Vale 12

* Winners on 'most tries' rule

STEPHEN'S DECISIVE 31 POINTS

WRU CHALLENGE TROPHY 1998-99

30 January, Stradey Park, Llanelli
Llanelli 41 (3G 5PG 1T) **Pontypridd 18** (1G 2PG 1T)

Pontypridd, holders of the trophy, which was launched the previous season, were well and truly undone by Stephen Jones on his home ground. The Llanelli youngster, this time operating in the centre, collected 31 points with two tries, three conversions and five penalty goals in the final. It seemed that he could almost have walked on water, though he owed a debt of gratitude to Byron Hayward, who initiated both his tries. Ponty were without six leading players, including Neil Jenkins, because of Wales squad requirements, while Llanelli had three first-choice forwards absent for the same reason. Pontypridd borrowed Robert Morgan and Gavin Owen from Treorchy and two Romanians.

The competition was restructured so that no Welsh clubs met in the pool games and the overseas contingent could reach the final, which was denied them previously. Stronger development teams from the guest countries brought five successes against home clubs compared with just one the previous year. Natal Wildebeests defeated Neath (36-18) and Caerphilly (37-32); Rugby Canada enjoyed successes against Aberavon (10-0) and Neath (14-11); while Northern Transvaal Bulls gained a 39-24 verdict at Newport.

Llanelli's progress to the final brought victims in the shape of the Bulls (23-10), Gauteng Falcons (36-15), Glasgow Caledonians (21-19) and Romania (57-12). Pontypridd's fixture with Edinburgh Reivers was cancelled, each team taking one point, but Neil Jenkins's side still reached the final by marching through Georgia by 69-7. Ponty had defeated the Wildebeests by 37-14 and Rugby Canada by 52-10, with 22 points from skipper Jenkins. Bridgend won the third-place play-off against Edinburgh Reivers by 25-23.

Llanelli: D Williams; W T Proctor (*capt*), S Finau, S Jones, G Evans; B I Hayward, R H StJ B Moon; P Booth, J Hyatt, M Madden, V Cooper, A H Copsey, D Hodges, H Jenkins, I Boobyer *Substitutions:* J D Davies for Madden; I Jones for Boobyer
Scorers *Tries:* S Jones (2), Williams, Finau *Conversions:* S Jones (3) *Penalty Goals:* S Jones (5)
Pontypridd: R Morgan; R Shorney, J Lewis, A Barnard, S Enoch; G Wyatt, P John; A Griffiths, A E Lamerton, N T'au, G Prosser, A Freeman, M Lloyd, D L M McIntosh (*capt*), G Owen *Substitutions:* M Vioreanu for Morgan; R Appleyard for Owen; S Mordan for Enoch; H Whitfield for Prosser
Scorers *Tries:* Lamerton, Shorney *Conversion:* Wyatt *Penalty Goals:* Wyatt (2)
Referee P L Marshall (Australia)

WALES TO ZIMBABWE & SOUTH AFRICA 1998

THE TOURING PARTY

Managers D Jones & T James **Coach** D John **Assistant Coach** L Howells
Captain R Howley

Full-backs: DJ Weatherley (Swansea), D Williams (Llanelli), *Geraint Evans
(Neath)

Threequarters: R Rees (Swansea), L Woodard (Ebbw Vale), Garan R Evans
(Llanelli), DR James (Pontypridd), WT Proctor (Llanelli), M Taylor (Swansea),
LB Davies (Cardiff), JS Funnell (Ebbw Vale), *S Jones (Llanelli)

Half-backs: BI Hayward (Ebbw Vale), AC Thomas (Swansea), R Howley (Cardiff),
Paul John (Pontypridd), *DS Llewellyn (Ebbw Vale)

Forwards: BR Evans (Neath), DR Morris (Neath), JD Davies (Richmond),
M Griffiths (Pontypridd), BH Williams (Richmond), GR Jenkins (Swansea),
MA Jones (Ebbw Vale), IM Gough (Newport), P Arnold (Swansea), CP Wyatt
(Llanelli), AP Moore (Swansea), N Thomas (Bath), ME Williams (Pontypridd),
RC Appleyard (Swansea), CL Charvis (Swansea), LS Quinnell (Richmond),
*G Lewis (Pontypridd), *KP Jones (Ebbw Vale), *D Thomas (Swansea),
*C Stephens (Bridgend)

* *Replacements on tour*

TOUR RECORD

All matches Played 6 Won 1 Lost 5 Points for 143 Against 235
International matches Played 2 Won 1 Lost 1 Points for 62 Against 107

SCORING DETAILS

All matches						International matches					
For:	17T	11C	12PG	=	143pts	For:	9T	4C	3PG	=	62pts
Against:	33T	17C	12PG	=	235pts	Against:	16T	9C	3PG	=	107pts

MATCH DETAILS

1998	OPPONENTS	VENUE	RESULT
6 June	ZIMBABWE	Harare	W 49-11
12 June	Emerging Springboks	Secunda	L 13-35
16 June	Border	East London	L 8-24
19 June	Natal Sharks	Durban	L 23-30
23 June	Gauteng Falcons	Vanderbijlpark	L 37-39
27 June	SOUTH AFRICA	Pretoria	L 13-96

MATCH 1   6 June, National Stadium, Harare   Test Match

ZIMBABWE 11 (2PG 1T)   **WALES 49** (3G 1PG 5T)

ZIMBABWE: V Olonga (High); G Campbell (Harare Sports Club), J Ewing
(Harare Sports Club), B French (Old Hararians), R Karimazondo (Old
Georgians); K Tsimba (Bath, England), R Bekker (Old Georgians); G Snyder
(Harare Sports Club), W Barratt (Harare Sports Club), G Stewart (Old
Georgians), B Catterall (Old Hararians), S Landman (Harare Sports Club),
L Greeff (Old Hararians), B Dawson (Old Miltonians)(*capt*), M Mwerenga

(Old Hararains) *Substitutions:* C McNab (Old Miltonians) for Mwerenga (30 mins); D Walters (Old Miltonians) for Karimazondo (49 mins); D Trivella (Orrell, England) for Tsimba (60 mins); N Nortje (Harare Sports Club) for Bekker (70 mins); I Neilson (Old Hararians) for Barratt (72 mins)
Scorers *Try:* Bekker *Penalty Goals:* Tsimba (2)
WALES: Weatherley; Proctor, James, Taylor, Rees; A Thomas, Howley (*capt*); Morris, G Jenkins, J Davies, M Jones, A Moore, N Thomas, S Quinnell, M Williams *Substitutions:* Funnell for Taylor (27 mins); Hayward for Weatherley (31 mins); B Williams for G Jenkins (56 mins); Charvis for Quinnell (56 mins); Wyatt for M Jones (71 mins); John for Howley (78 mins)
Scorers *Tries:* Hayward (3), Rees (2), A Thomas (2), Proctor
Conversions: A Thomas (3) *Penalty Goal:* A Thomas
Referee J Meuwesen (Namibia)

MATCH 2   12 June, Secunda Stadium, Witbank

Emerging Springboks 35 (2G 2PG 3T)   **Wales XV 13** (1G 2PG)
Emerging Springboks: M Goosen; J Davies, D Kayer, R Fleck, L Venter; L Koen, H Husselman; S Wagner, O Nkumane, E Fynne, S Boome, B Thorne, P Krause, A Vos (*capt*), A Venter *Substitutions:* DR du Preez for Fynne (55 mins); C Stolz for L Venter (64 mins); C Alcock for Husselman (64 mins); N Trytsman for Thorne (64 mins); J van Wyk for Nkumane (67 mins); D Frans for Krause (72 mins)
Scorers *Tries:* Daniels (3), Fleck, L Venter *Conversions:* Koen (2)
Penalty Goals: Koen (2)
Wales XV: D Williams; Woodard, L Davies, Funnell, Garan Evans; Hayward, John (*capt*); Griffiths, B Williams, B Evans, Arnold, Gough, Appleyard, Wyatt, Charvis *Substitutions:* N Thomas for Appleyard (40 mins); James for Funnell (65 mins); M Jones for Arnold (65 mins)
Scorers *Try:* James *Conversion:* Hayward *Penalty Goals:* Hayward (2)
Referee J Kaplan (Natal)

MATCH 3   16 June, Basil Kenyon Stadium, East London

Border 24 (1G 4PG 1T)   **Wales XV 8** (1PG 1T)
Border: D Heidtmann; D Maidza, G Gelderbloom (*capt*), K van der Merwe, K Molotana; W Weyer, J Bradbrook; H Kok, D du Preez, R Swanepoel, B Holtzhausen, A Fox, B Jacobs, M van der Walt, A Botha
Scorers *Tries:* Heidtmann, van der Walt *Conversion:* Bradbrook
Penalty Goals: Bradbrook (4)
Wales XV: D Williams; Rees, Taylor, Geraint Evans, Garan Evans; A Thomas, John; Griffiths, G Jenkins (*capt*), B Evans, Arnold, Wyatt, G Lewis, N Thomas, M Williams *Substitutions:* A Moore for G Lewis (52 mins); M Jones for Arnold (59 mins)
Scorers *Try:* Rees *Penalty Goal:* A Thomas
Referee T Henning (Northern Transvaal)

MATCH 4   19 June, King's Park, Durban

Natal Sharks 30 (2G 2PG 2T)   **Wales XV 23** (2G 3PG)
Natal Sharks: A Joubert; S Sayne, J Thomson, T van der Mescht, S Brink; J van der Westhuyzen, K Putt; D Morkel, M Visser, J Smit, J Slade, S Atherton (*capt*), D Kriese, W Brosnihan, B McLeod-Henderson *Substitutions:* D Strydom for Thomson (32 mins); R Bennett for Strydom (72 mins); H Martens for Putt (62 mins); N Wegner for Slade (62 mins); C McIntosh for Brosnihan (63 mins)
Scorers *Tries:* Brink (3), Joubert *Conversions:* Joubert (2) *Penalty Goals:* Joubert (2)

Wales XV: Hayward; Proctor, James, Taylor, Garan Evans; A Thomas, Howley (*capt*); Morris, B Williams, J Davies, Gough, A Moore, M Williams, Charvis, K Jones *Substitutions:* D Williams for Proctor (19 mins); Wyatt for A Moore (62 mins)
Scorers *Tries:* A Thomas, Hayward *Conversions:* A Thomas (2)
Penalty Goals: A Thomas (3)
Referee A Watson (Eastern Transvaal)

MATCH 5 23 June, Isak Steyl Stadium, Vanderbijlpark, Brakpan

Gauteng Falcons 39 (3G 1PG 3T) **Wales XV 37** (4G 3PG)
Gauteng Falcons: P Matthys; W Geyer, W Lourens, E Meyer (*capt*), L van Riet; B van Straaten, D de Kock; G Williamson, G van der Walt, J le Roux, R Schroeder, W Boardman, D Strydom, N Rossouw, B Volschenk
Substitutions: B Moyle for le Roux (45 mins); J Booysen for Strydom (45 mins); J Gurnun for van Riet (65 mins); R van As for van Straaten (70 mins)
Scorers *Tries:* Geyer (2), Strydom, Lourens, Moyle, Booysen *Conversions:* van Straaten (2), van As *Penalty Goal:* van Straaten
Wales XV: D Williams; Woodard, Geraint Evans, Funnell, Rees; Hayward, John; Morris, G Jenkins (*capt*), B Evans, Arnold, Stephens, G Lewis, Wyatt, D Thomas
Substitutions: Griffiths for Morris (40 mins); Taylor for Geraint Evans (57 mins); S Jones for Rees (57 mins)
Scorers *Tries:* Funnell, Arnold, Woodard, Taylor *Conversions:* Hayward (4)
Penalty Goals: Hayward (3)
Referee C Spannenberg (Western Province)

MATCH 6 27 June, Loftus Versfeld, Pretoria Test Match
SOUTH AFRICA 96 (9G 1PG 6T) WALES 13 (1G 2PG)

SOUTH AFRICA: PC Montgomery (Western Province); CS Terblanche (Boland), AH Snyman (Blue Bulls), PG Muller (Natal Sharks), PWG Rossouw (Western Province); PF Smith (Blue Bulls), JH van der Westhuizen (Blue Bulls); RJ Kempson (Natal Sharks), J Dalton (Goldens Lions), AC Garvey (Natal Sharks), K Otto (Blue Bulls), MG Andrews (Natal Sharks), JC Erasmus (Free State Cheetahs), GH Teichmann (Natal Sharks) (*capt*), AG Venter (Free State Cheetahs) *Substitutions:* HW Honiball (Natal) for Muller (40 mins); RB Skinstad (Western Province) for Andrews (55 mins); W Swanepoel (Free State Cheetahs) for van der Westhuizen (45 mins); M Hendricks (Boland) for Terblanche (47 mins); AD Aitken (Western Province) for Teichmann (58 mins); AE Drotské (Free State University & Free State Cheetahs) for Dalton (60 mins); AH le Roux (Natal) for Garvey (66 mins)
Scorers *Tries:* Rossouw (3), Montgomery (2), Terblanche (2), Venter (2), van der Westhuizen, Otto, Smith, Erasmus, Skinstad, Hendricks *Conversions:* Montgomery (9) *Penalty Goal:* Montgomery
WALES: Hayward; Garan Evans, Taylor, Funnell, James; A Thomas, John; Griffiths, B Williams, J Davies, Gough, A Moore, N Thomas, Charvis, K Jones (*capt*) *Substitutions:* Wyatt for K Jones (40 mins); D Williams for Hayward (48 mins); S Jones for Funnell (50 mins); Morris for J Davies (60 mins); G Jenkins for B Williams (66 mins); G Lewis for Charvis (73 mins); Llewellyn for John (79 mins)
Scorer *Try:* A Thomas *Conversion:* A Thomas *Penalty Goals:* A Thomas (2)
Referee PD O'Brien (New Zealand)

WELSH INTERNATIONAL PLAYERS
(*up to 30 April 1999*)

Note: Years given for Five Nations' matches are for second half of season; eg 1972 means season 1971-72. Years for all other matches refer to the actual year of the match. When a series has taken place, figures have been used to denote the particular matches in which players have featured. Thus 1969 *NZ* 2 indicates that a player appeared in the second Test of the series.

Ackerman, R A (Newport, London Welsh) 1980 *NZ*, 1981 *E, S, A,* 1982 *I, F, E, S,* 1983 *S, I, F, R,* 1984 *S, I, F, E, A,* 1985 *S, I, F, E, Fj*
Alexander, E P (Llandovery Coll, Cambridge U) 1885 *S,* 1886 *E, S,* 1887 *E, I*
Alexander, W H (Llwynypia) 1898 *I, E,* 1899 *E, S, I,* 1901 *S, I*
Allen, A G (Newbridge) 1990 *F, E, I*
Allen, C P (Oxford U, Beaumaris) 1884 *E, S*
Andrews, F (Pontypool) 1912 *SA,* 1913 *E, S, I*
Andrews, F G (Swansea) 1884 *E, S*
Andrews, G E (Newport) 1926 *E, S,* 1927 *E, F, I*
Anthony, C T (Swansea) 1997 *US* 1 (R), 2 (R), *C* (R), *Tg* (R), 1998 *SA* 2, *Arg,* 1999 *S, I* (R)
Anthony, L (Neath) 1948 *E, S, F*
Appleyard, R C (Swansea) 1997 *C, R, Tg, NZ,* 1998 *It, E* (R), *S, I, F*
Arnold, P (Swansea) 1990 *Nm* 1, 2, *Bb,* 1991 *E, S, I, F* 1, *A,* [*Arg, A*], 1993 *F* (R), *Z* 2, 1994 *Sp, Fj,* 1995 *SA,* 1996 *Bb* (R)
Arnold, W R (Swansea) 1903 *S*
Arthur, C S (Cardiff) 1888 *I, M,* 1891 *E*
Arthur, T (Neath) 1927 *S, F, I,* 1929 *E, S, F, I,* 1930 *E, S, I, F,* 1931 *E, S, F, I, SA,* 1933 *E, S*
Ashton, C (Aberavon) 1959 *E, S, I,* 1960 *E, S, I,* 1962 *I*
Attewell, S L (Newport) 1921 *E, S, F*

Back, M J (Bridgend) 1995 *F* (R), *E* (R), *S, I*
Badger, O (Llanelli) 1895 *E, S, I,* 1896 *E*
Baker, A (Neath) 1921 *I,* 1923 *E, S, F, I*
Baker, A M (Newport) 1909 *S, F,* 1910 *S*
Bancroft, J (Swansea) 1909 *E, S, F, I,* 1910 *F, E, S, I,* 1911 *E, F, I,* 1912 *E, S, I,* 1913 *I,* 1914 *E, S, F*
Bancroft, W J (Swansea) 1890 *S, E, I,* 1891 *E, S, I,* 1892 *E, S, I,* 1893 *E, S, I,* 1894 *E, S, I,* 1895 *E, S, I,* 1896 *E, S, I,* 1897 *E,* 1898 *I, E,* 1899 *E, S, I,* 1900 *E, S, I,* 1901 *E, S, I*
Barlow, T M (Cardiff) 1884 *I*
Barrell, R J (Cardiff) 1929 *S, F, I,* 1933 *I*
Bartlett, J D (Llanelli) 1927 *S,* 1928 *E, S*
Bassett, A (Cardiff) 1934 *I,* 1935 *E, S, I,* 1938 *E, S*
Bassett, J A (Penarth) 1929 *E, S, F, I,* 1930 *E, S, I,* 1931 *E, S, F, I, SA,* 1932 *E, S, I*
Bateman, A G (Neath, Richmond) 1990 *S, I, Nm* 1,2, 1996 *SA,* 1997 *US, S, F, E, R, NZ,* 1998 *It, E, S, I,* 1999 *S*
Bayliss, G (Pontypool) 1933 *S*
Bebb, D I E (Carmarthen TC, Swansea) 1959 *E, S, I, F,* 1960 *E, S, I, F, SA,* 1961 *E, S, I, F,* 1962 *E, S, F, I,* 1963 *E, F, NZ,* 1964 *E, S, F, SA,* 1965 *E, S, I, F,* 1966 *F, A,* 1967 *S, I, F, E*
Beckingham, G (Cardiff) 1953 *E, S,* 1958 *F*
Bennett, A M (Cardiff) 1995 [*NZ*] *SA, Fj*
Bennett, I (Aberavon) 1937 *I*
Bennett, P (Cardiff Harlequins) 1891 *E, S,* 1892 *S, I*
Bennett, P (Llanelli) 1969 *F* (R), 1970 *SA, S, F,* 1972 *S* (R), *NZ,* 1973 *E, S, I, F, A,* 1974 *S, I, E, F,* 1975 *S* (R), *I,* 1976 *E, S, I, F,* 1977 *I, F, E, S,* 1978 *E, S, I, F*
Bergiers, R T E (Cardiff Coll of Ed, Llanelli) 1972 *E, S, F, NZ,* 1973 *E, S, I, F, A,* 1974 *E,* 1975 *I*
Bevan, G W (Llanelli) 1947 *E*
Bevan, J A (Cambridge U) 1881 *E*
Bevan, J C (Cardiff, Cardiff Coll of Ed) 1971 *E, S, I, F,* 1972 *E, S, F, NZ,* 1973 *E, S*
Bevan, J D (Aberavon) 1975 *F, E, S, A*
Bevan, S (Swansea) 1904 *I*
Beynon, B (Swansea) 1920 *E, S*
Beynon, G E (Swansea) 1925 *F, I*
Bidgood, R A (Newport) 1992 *S,* 1993 *Z* 1,2, *Nm, J* (R)
Biggs, N W (Cardiff) 1888 *M,* 1889 *I,* 1892 *I,* 1893 *E, S, I,* 1894 *E, I*
Biggs, S H (Cardiff) 1895 *E, S,* 1896 *S,* 1897 *E,* 1898 *I, E,* 1899 *S, I,* 1900 *I*

Birch, J (Neath) 1911 *S, F*
Birt, F W (Newport) 1911 *E, S,* 1912 *E, S, I, SA,* 1913 *E*
Bishop, D J (Pontypool) 1984 *A*
Bishop, E H (Swansea) 1889 *S*
Blackmore, J H (Abertillery) 1909 *E*
Blackmore, S W (Cardiff) 1987 *I,* [*Tg* (R), *C, A*]
Blake, J (Cardiff) 1899 *E, S, I,* 1900 *E, S, I,* 1901 *E, S, I*
Blakemore, R E (Newport) 1947 *E*
Bland, A F (Cardiff) 1887 *E, S, I,* 1888 *S, I, M,* 1890 *S, E, I*
Blyth, L (Swansea) 1951 *SA,* 1952 *E, S*
Blyth, W R (Swansea) 1974 *E,* 1975 *S* (R), 1980 *F, E, S, I*
Boobyer, N (Llanelli) 1993 *Z* 1 (R), 2, *Nm,* 1994 *Fj, Tg,* 1998 *F,* 1999 *It* (R)
Boon, R W (Cardiff) 1930 *S, F,* 1931 *E, S, F, I, SA,* 1932 *E, S, I,* 1933 *E, I*
Booth, J (Pontymister) 1898 *I*
Boots, J G (Newport) 1898 *I, E,* 1899 *I,* 1900 *E, S, I,* 1901 *E, S, I,* 1902 *E, S, I,* 1903 *E, S, I,* 1904 *E*
Boucher, A W (Newport) 1892 *E, S, I,* 1893 *E, S, I,* 1894 *E, S, I,* 1895 *E, S, I,* 1896 *E, I,* 1897 *E*
Bowcott, H M (Cardiff, Cambridge U) 1929 *S, F, I,* 1930 *E, S, I,* 1931 *E, S, I,* 1933 *E, I*
Bowdler, F A (Cross Keys) 1927 *A,* 1928 *E, S, I, F,* 1929 *E, S, F, I,* 1930 *E,* 1931 *SA,* 1932 *E, S, I,* 1933 *I*
Bowen, B (S Wales Police, Swansea) 1983 *R,* 1984 *S, I, F, E,* 1985 *Fj,* 1986 *E, S, I, F, Fj, Tg, WS,* 1987 [*C, E, NZ*], *US,* 1988 *E, S, I, F, WS,* 1989 *S, I*
Bowen, C A (Llanelli) 1896 *E, S, I,* 1897 *E*
Bowen, D H (Llanelli) 1883 *E,* 1886 *E, S,* 1887 *E*
Bowen, G E (Swansea) 1887 *S, I,* 1888 *S, I*
Bowen, W (Swansea) 1921 *S, F,* 1922 *E, S, I, F*
Bowen, Wm A (Swansea) 1886 *E, S,* 1887 *E, S, I,* 1888 *M,* 1889 *S, I,* 1890 *S, E, I,* 1891 *E, S*
Brace, D O (Llanelli, Oxford U) 1956 *E, S, I, F,* 1957 *E,* 1960 *S, I, F,* 1961 *I*
Braddock, K J (Newbridge) 1966 *A,* 1967 *S, I*
Bradshaw, K (Bridgend) 1964 *E, S, I, F, SA,* 1966 *E, S, I, F*
Brewer, T J (Newport) 1950 *E,* 1955 *E, S*
Brice, A B (Aberavon) 1899 *E, S, I,* 1900 *E, S, I,* 1901 *E, S, I,* 1902 *E, S, I,* 1903 *E, S, I,* 1904 *E, S, I*
Bridges, C J (Neath) 1990 *Nm* 1,2, *Bb,* 1991 *E* (R), *I, F* 1, *A*
Bridie, R H (Newport) 1882 *I*
Britton, G R (Newport) 1961 *S*
Broughton, A S (Treorchy) 1927 *A,* 1929 *S*
Brown, A (Newport) 1921 *I*
Brown, J (Cardiff) 1925 *I*
Brown, J A (Cardiff) 1907 *E, S, I,* 1908 *E, S, F,* 1909 *E*
Brown, M (Pontypool) 1983 *R,* 1986 *E, S, Fj* (R), *Tg, WS*
Bryant, D J (Bridgend) 1988 *NZ* 1,2, *WS, R,* 1989 *S, I, F, E*
Buchanan, A (Llanelli) 1987 [*Tg, E, NZ, A*], 1988 *I*
Buckett, I M (Swansea) 1994 *Tg,* 1997 *US* 2, *C*
Burcher, D H (Newport) 1977 *I, F, E, S*
Burgess, R C (Ebbw Vale) 1977 *I, F, E, S,* 1981 *I, F,* 1982 *F, E, S*
Burnett, R (Newport) 1953 *E*
Burns, J (Cardiff) 1927 *F, I*
Bush, P F (Cardiff) 1905 *NZ,* 1906 *E, SA,* 1907 *I,* 1908 *E, S,* 1910 *S, I*
Butler, E T (Pontypool) 1980 *F, E, S, I, NZ* (R), 1982 *S,* 1983 *E, S, I, F, R,* 1984 *S, I, F, E, A*

Cale, W R (Newbridge, Pontypool) 1949 *E, S, I,* 1950 *E, S, I, F*
Carter, A J (Newport) 1991 *E, S*
Cattell, A (Llanelli) 1883 *E, S*
Challinor, C (Neath) 1939 *E*

Charvis, C L (Swansea) 1996 *A* 3(R), *SA*, 1997 *US, S, I, F*, 1998 *It* (R), *E, S, I, F, Z* (R), *SA* 1,2, *Arg*, 1999 *S, I, F, It, E*

Clapp, T J S (Newport) 1882 *I*, 1883 *E, S*, 1884 *E, S, I*, 1885 *E, S*, 1886 *S*, 1887 *E, S, I*, 1888 *S, I*

Clare, J (Cardiff) 1883 *E*

Clark, S S (Neath) 1882 *I*, 1887 *I*

Cleaver, W B (Cardiff) 1947 *E, S, F, I, A*, 1948 *E, S, F, I*, 1949 *I*, 1950 *E, S, I, F*

Clegg, B G (Swansea) 1979 *F*

Clement, A (Swansea) 1987 *US* (R), 1988 *E, NZ* 1, *WS* (R), *R*, 1989 *NZ*, 1990 *S* (R), *I* (R), *Nm* 1,2, 1991 *S* (R), *F* 2, [*WS, A*], 1992 *I, F, E, S*, 1993 *I* (R), *F, J, C*, 1994 *S, I, F, Sp, C* (R), *Tg, WS, It, SA*, 1995 *F, E*, [*J, NZ, I*]

Clement, W H (Llanelli) 1937 *E, S, I*, 1938 *E, S, I*

Cobner, T J (Pontypool) 1974 *S, I, F, E*, 1975 *F, E, S, I, A*, 1976 *E, S*, 1977 *F, E, S*, 1978 *E, S, I, F, A* 1

Coldrick, A P (Newport) 1911 *E, S, I*, 1912 *E, S, F*

Coleman, E (Newport) 1949 *E, S, I*

Coles, F C (Pontypool) 1960 *S, I, F*

Collins, J (Aberavon) 1958 *A, E, S, F*, 1959 *E, S, I, F*, 1960 *E*, 1961 *I*

Collins, R G (S Wales Police, Cardiff, Pontypridd) 1987 *E* (R), *I*, [*I, E, NZ*], *US*, 1988 *E, S, I, F, R*, 1990 *E, S, I*, 1991 *A, F* 2, [*WS*], 1994 *C, Fj, Tg, WS, R, It, SA*, 1995 *F, E, S, I*

Collins, T (Mountain Ash) 1923 *I*

Conway-Rees, J (Llanelli) 1892 *S*, 1893 *E*, 1894 *E*

Cook, T (Cardiff) 1949 *S, I*

Cope, W (Cardiff, Blackheath) 1896 *S*

Copsey, A H (Llanelli) 1992 *I, F, E, S, A*, 1993 *E, S, I, J, C*, 1994 *E* (R), *Pt, Sp* (R), *Fj, Tg, WS* (R)

Cornish, F H (Cardiff) 1897 *E*, 1898 *I, E*, 1899 *I*

Cornish, R A (Cardiff) 1923 *E, S*, 1924 *E*, 1925 *E, S, F*, 1926 *E, S, I, F*

Coslett, K (Aberavon) 1962 *E, S, F*

Cowey, B T V (Welch Regt, Newport) 1934 *E, S, I*, 1935 *E*

Cresswell, B (Newport) 1960 *E, S, I, F*

Cummins, W (Treorchy) 1922 *E, S, I, F*

Cunningham, L J (Aberavon) 1960 *E, S, I, F*, 1962 *E, S, F, I*, 1963 *NZ*, 1964 *E, S, I, F, SA*

Dacey, M (Swansea) 1983 *E, S, I, F, R*, 1984 *S, I, F, E, A*, 1986 *Fj, Tg, WS*, 1987 *F* (R), [*Tg*]

Daniel, D J (Llanelli) 1891 *S*, 1894 *E, S, I*, 1898 *I, E*, 1899 *E, I*

Daniel, L T D (Newport) 1970 *S*

Daniels, P C T (Cardiff) 1981 *A*, 1982 *I*

Darbishire, G (Bangor) 1881 *E*

Dauncey, F H (Newport) 1896 *E, S, I*

Davey, C (Swansea) 1930 *F*, 1931 *E, S, F, I, SA*, 1932 *E, S, I*, 1933 *E, S*, 1934 *E, S, I*, 1935 *E, S, I, NZ*, 1936 *S*, 1937 *E, I*, 1938 *E, I*

David, R J (Cardiff) 1907 *I*

David, T P (Llanelli, Pontypridd) 1973 *F, A*, 1976 *I, F*

Davidge, G D (Newport) 1959 *F*, 1960 *S, I, F, SA*, 1961 *E, S, I*, 1962 *F*

Davies, A (Cambridge U, Neath, Cardiff) 1990 *Bb* (R), 1991 *A*, 1993 *Z* 1,2, *J, C*, 1994 *Fj*, 1995 [*J, I*]

Davies, A C (London Welsh) 1889 *I*

Davies, A E (Llanelli) 1984 *A*

Davies, B (Llanelli) 1895 *E*, 1896 *E*

Davies, C (Cardiff) 1947 *S, F, I, A*, 1948 *E, S, F, I*, 1949 *F*, 1950 *E, S, I, F*, 1951 *E, S, I*

Davies, C (Llanelli) 1988 *WS*, 1989 *S, I* (R), *F*

Davies, C H A (Llanelli, Cardiff) 1957 *I*, 1958 *A, E, S, I*, 1960 *SA*, 1961 *E*

Davies, C L (Cardiff) 1956 *E, S, I*

Davies, C R (Bedford, RAF) 1934 *E*

Davies, D (Bridgend) 1921 *I*, 1925 *I*

Davies, D B (Llanelli) 1907 *E*

Davies, D B (Llanelli) 1962 *I*, 1963 *E, S*

Davies, D G (Cardiff) 1923 *E, S*

Davies, D H (Neath) 1904 *S*

Davies, D H (Aberavon) 1924 *E*

Davies, D J (Swansea) 1939 *E*

Davies, D J (Neath) 1962 *I*

Davies, D M (Somerset Police) 1950 *E, S, I, F*, 1951 *E, S, I, F, SA*, 1952 *E, S, I, F*, 1953 *I, F, NZ*, 1954 *E*

Davies, E (Aberavon) 1947 *A*, 1948 *I*

Davies, E (Maesteg) 1919 *NZA*

Davies, E G (Cardiff) 1912 *E, F*

Davies, E G (Cardiff) 1928 *F*, 1929 *E*, 1930 *S*

Davies, G (Swansea) 1900 *E, S, I*, 1901 *E, S, I*, 1905 *E, S, I*

Davies, G (Cambridge U, Pontypridd) 1947 *S, A*, 1948 *E, S, F, I*, 1949 *E, S, F*, 1951 *E, S*

Davies, G (Llanelli) 1921 *F, I*, 1925 *F*

Davies, H (Swansea) 1898 *I, E*, 1901 *S, I*

Davies, H (Swansea, Llanelli) 1939 *S, I*, 1947 *E, S, F, I*

Davies, H (Neath) 1912 *E, S*

Davies, H (Bridgend) 1984 *S, I, F, E*

Davies, H J (Cambridge U, Aberavon) 1959 *E, S*

Davies, H J (Newport) 1924 *S*

Davies, I T (Llanelli) 1914 *S, F, I*

Davies, J (Neath, Llanelli, Cardiff) 1985 *E, Fj*, 1986 *E, S, I, F, Fj, Tg, WS*, 1987 *F, E, S, I*, [*I, Tg* (R), *C, E, NZ, A*], 1988 *E, S, I, F, NZ* 1,2, *WS, R*, 1996 *A* 3, 1997 *US* (t), *S* (R), *F* (R), *E*

Davies, J H (Aberavon) 1923 *I*

Davies, L (Swansea) 1939 *S, I*

Davies, L (Bridgend) 1966 *E, S, I*

Davies, L B (Neath, Cardiff) 1996 *It, E, S, I, F* 1, *A* 1, *Bb, F* 2, *It* (R), 1997 *US* 1,2, *C, R, Tg, NZ* (R), 1998 *E* (R), *I, F*

Davies, L M (Llanelli) 1954 *F, S*, 1955 *I*

Davies, M (Swansea) 1981 *A*, 1982 *I*, 1985 *Fj*

Davies, M J (Blackheath) 1939 *S, I*

Davies, N G (London Welsh) 1955 *E*

Davies, N G (Llanelli) 1988 *NZ* 2, *WS*, 1989 *S, I*, 1993 *F*, 1994 *S, I, E, Pt, Sp, C, Fj, Tg* (R), *WS, R, It*, 1995 *E, S, I, Fj*, 1996 *E, S, I, F* 1, *A* 1,2, *Bb, F* 2, 1997 *E*

Davies, P T (Llanelli) 1985 *E, Fj*, 1986 *E, S, I, F, Fj, Tg, WS*, 1987 *F, E, I*, [*Tg, C, NZ*], 1988 *WS, R*, 1989 *S, I, F, E, NZ*, 1990 *F, E, S*, 1991 *I, F* 1, *A, F* 2, [*WS, Arg, A*], 1993 *F, Z* 1, *Nm*, 1994 *S, I, F, E, C, Fj* (R), *WS, R, It*, 1995 *F, I*

Davies, R H (Oxford U, London Welsh) 1957 *S, I, F*, 1958 *A*, 1962 *E, S*

Davies, S (Treherbert) 1923 *I*

Davies, S (Swansea) 1992 *I, F, E, S, A*, 1993 *E, S, I, Z* 1 (R), 2, *Nm, J*, 1995 *F*, [*J, I*], 1998 *I* (R), *F*

Davies, T G R (Cardiff, London Welsh) 1966 *A*, 1967 *S, I, F, E*, 1968 *E, S*, 1969 *S, I, F, NZ* 1,2, *A*, 1971 *E, S, I, F*, 1972 *E, S, F, NZ*, 1973 *E, S, I, F, A*, 1974 *S, F, E*, 1975 *F, E, S, I*, 1976 *E, S, I, F*, 1977 *I, F, E, S*, 1978 *E, S, I, A* 1,2

Davies, T J (Devonport Services, Swansea, Llanelli) 1953 *E, S, I, F*, 1957 *E, S, I, F*, 1958 *A, E, S, F*, 1959 *E, S, I, F*, 1960 *SA*, 1961 *E, S, F*

Davies, T M (London Welsh, Swansea) 1969 *S, I, F, E, NZ* 1,2, *A*, 1970 *SA, S, E, I, F*, 1971 *E, S, I, F*, 1972 *E, S, F, NZ*, 1973 *E, S, I, F, A*, 1974 *S, I, F, E*, 1975 *F, E, S, I, A*, 1976 *E, S, I, F*

Davies, W (Cardiff) 1896 *S*

Davies, W (Swansea) 1931 *SA*, 1932 *E, S, I*

Davies, W A (Aberavon) 1912 *S, I*

Davies, W G (Cardiff) 1978 *A* 1,2, *NZ*, 1979 *S, I, F, E*, 1980 *F, E, S, NZ*, 1981 *E, S, A*, 1982 *E, S, F*, 1985 *S, I, F*

Davies, W T H (Swansea) 1936 *I*, 1937 *E, I*, 1939 *E, S, I*

Davis, C E (Newbridge) 1978 *A* 2, 1981 *E, S*

Davis, M (Newport) 1991 *A*

Davis, W E N (Cardiff) 1939 *E, S, I*

Dawes, S J (London Welsh) 1964 *I, F, SA*, 1965 *E, S, I, F*, 1966 *A*, 1968 *I, F*, 1969 *E, NZ* 2, *A*, 1970 *SA, S, E, I, F*, 1971 *E, S, I, F*

Day, H C (Newport) 1930 *S, I, F*, 1931 *E, S*

Day, H T (Newport) 1892 *I*, 1893 *E, S*, 1894 *S, I*

Day, T B (Swansea) 1931 *E, S, F, I, SA*, 1932 *E, S, I*, 1934 *S, I*, 1935 *E, S, I*

Deacon, J T (Swansea) 1891 *I*, 1892 *E, S, I*

Delahay, W J (Bridgend) 1922 *E, S, I, F*, 1923 *E, S, F, I*, 1924 *NZ*, 1925 *E, S, F, I*, 1926 *E, S, I, F*, 1927 *S*

Delaney, L (Llanelli) 1989 *I, F, E*, 1990 *E*, 1991 *F* 2, [*WS, Arg, A*], 1992 *I, F, E*

Devereux, D (Neath) 1958 *A, E, S*

Devereux, J A (S Glamorgan Inst, Bridgend) 1986 *E, S, I, F, Fj, Tg, WS*, 1987 *F, E, S, I*, [*I, C, E, NZ, A*], 1988 *NZ* 1,2, *R*, 1989 *S, I*

Diplock, R (Bridgend) 1988 *R*

Dobson, G (Cardiff) 1900 *S*

Dobson, T (Cardiff) 1898 *I, E*, 1899 *E, S*

Donovan, A J (Swansea) 1978 *A* 2, 1981 *I* (R), *A*, 1982 *E, S*
Donovan, R (S Wales Police) 1983 *F* (R)
Douglas, M H J (Llanelli) 1984 *S, I, F*
Douglas, W M (Cardiff) 1886 *E, S*, 1887 *E, S*
Dowell, W H (Newport) 1907 *E, S, I*, 1908 *E, S, F, I*
Dyke, J C M (Penarth) 1906 *SA*
Dyke, L M (Penarth, Cardiff) 1910 *I*, 1911 *S, F, I*

Edmunds, D A (Neath) 1990 *I* (R), *Bb*
Edwards, A B (London Welsh, Army) 1955 *E, S*
Edwards, B O (Newport) 1951 *I*
Edwards, D (Glynneath) 1921 *E*
Edwards, G O (Cardiff, Cardiff Coll of Ed) 1967 *F, E, NZ*, 1968 *E, S, I, F*, 1969 *S, I, F, E, NZ* 1,2, 1970 *SA, S, E, I, F*, 1971 *E, S, I, F*, 1972 *E, S, F, NZ*, 1973 *E, S, I, F, A*, 1974 *S, I, F, E*, 1975 *F, E, S, I, A*, 1976 *E, S, I, F*, 1977 *I, F, E, S*, 1978 *E, S, I, F*
Eidman, I H (Cardiff) 1983 *S, R*, 1984 *I, F, E, A*, 1985 *S, I, Fj*, 1986 *E, S, I, F*
Elliott, J E (Cardiff) 1894 *I*, 1898 *I, E*
Elsey, W J (Cardiff) 1895 *E*
Emyr, Arthur (Swansea) 1989 *E, NZ*, 1990 *F, E, S, I, Nm* 1,2, 1991 *F* 1,2, [*WS, Arg, A*]
Evans, A (Pontypool) 1924 *E, I, F*
Evans, B (Swansea) 1933 *S*
Evans, B (Llanelli) 1933 *E, S*, 1936 *E, S, I*, 1937 *E*
Evans, B R (Swansea) 1998 *SA* 2 (R), 1999 *F, It, E*
Evans, B S (Llanelli) 1920 *E*, 1922 *E, S, I, F*
Evans, C (Pontypool) 1960 *E*
Evans, D (Penygraig) 1896 *S, I*, 1897 *E*, 1898 *E*
Evans, D B (Swansea) 1926 *E*
Evans, D D (Cheshire, Cardiff U) 1934 *E*
Evans, D P (Llanelli) 1960 *SA*
Evans, D W (Cardiff) 1889 *S, I*, 1890 *E, I*, 1891 *E*
Evans, D W (Oxford U, Cardiff, Treorchy) 1989 *F, E, NZ*, 1990 *F, E, S, I, Bb*, 1991 *A* (R), *F* 2 (R), [*A* (R)], 1995 [*J* (R)]
Evans, E (Llanelli) 1937 *E*, 1939 *S, I*
Evans, F (Llanelli) 1921 *S*
Evans, G (Cardiff) 1947 *E, S, F, I, A*, 1948 *E, S, F, I*, 1949 *E, S, I*
Evans, G (Maesteg) 1981 *S* (R), *I, F, A*, 1982 *I, F, E, S*, 1983 *F, R*
Evans, G L (Newport) 1977 *F* (R), 1978 *F, A* 2 (R)
Evans, G R (Llanelli) 1998 *SA* 1
Evans, I (London Welsh) 1934 *S, I*
Evans, I (Swansea) 1922 *E, S, I, F*
Evans, I C (Llanelli, Bath) 1987 *F, E, S, I*, [*I, C, E, NZ, A*], 1988 *E, S, I, F, NZ* 1,2, 1989 *I, F, E*, 1991 *E, S, I, F* 1, *A, F* 2, [*WS, Arg, A*], 1992 *I, F, E, S, A*, 1993 *E, S, I, F, J, C*, 1994 *S, I, E, Pt, Sp, C, Fj, Tg, WS, R*, 1995 *E, S, I*, [*J, NZ, I*], *SA, Fj*, 1996 *It, E, S, I, F* 1, *A* 1,2, *Bb, F* 2, *A* 3, *SA*, 1997 *US, S, I, F*, 1998 *It*
Evans, I L (Llanelli) 1991 *F* 2 (R)
Evans, J (Llanelli) 1896 *S, I*, 1897 *E*
Evans, J (Blaina) 1904 *E*
Evans, J (Pontypool) 1907 *E, S, I*
Evans, J D (Cardiff) 1958 *I, F*
Evans, J E (Llanelli) 1924 *S*
Evans, J R (Newport) 1934 *E*
Evans, O J (Cardiff) 1887 *E, S*, 1888 *S, I*
Evans, P D (Llanelli) 1951 *E, F*
Evans, R (Cardiff) 1889 *S*
Evans, R (Bridgend) 1963 *S, I, F*
Evans, R L (Llanelli) 1993 *E, S, I, F*, 1994 *S, I, F, E, Pt, Sp, C, Fj, WS, R, It, SA*, 1995 *F*, [*NZ, I* (R)]
Evans, R T (Newport) 1947 *F, I*, 1950 *E, S, I, F*, 1951 *E, S, I, F*
Evans, S (Swansea, Neath) 1985 *F, E*, 1986 *Fj, Tg, WS*, 1987 *F, E*, [*I, Tg*]
Evans, T (Swansea) 1924 *I*
Evans, T G (London Welsh) 1970 *SA, S, E, I*, 1972 *E, S, F*
Evans, T H (Llanelli) 1906 *I*, 1907 *E, S, I*, 1908 *I, A*, 1909 *E, S, F, I*, 1910 *F, E, S, I*, 1911 *E, S, F, I*
Evans, T P (Swansea) 1975 *F, E, S, I, A*, 1976 *E, S, I, F*, 1977 *I*
Evans, V (Neath) 1954 *I, F, S*
Evans, W (Llanelli) 1958 *A*
Evans, W F (Rhymney) 1882 *I*, 1883 *S*
Evans, W G (Brynmawr) 1911 *I*
Evans, W H (Llwynypia) 1914 *E, S, F, I*
Evans, W J (Pontypool) 1947 *S*

Evans, W R (Bridgend) 1958 *A, E, S, I, F*, 1960 *SA*, 1961 *E, S, I, F*, 1962 *E, S, I*
Everson, W A (Newport) 1926 *S*

Faulkner, A G (Pontypool) 1975 *F, E, S, I, A*, 1976 *E, S, I, F*, 1978 *E, S, I, F, A* 1,2, *NZ*, 1979 *S, I, F*
Faull, J (Swansea) 1957 *I, F*, 1958 *A, E, S, I, F*, 1959 *E, S, I*, 1960 *E, F*
Fauvel, T J (Aberavon) 1988 *NZ* 1 (R)
Fear, A G (Newport) 1934 *S, I*, 1935 *S, I*
Fender, N H (Cardiff) 1930 *I, F*, 1931 *E, S, F, I*
Fenwick, S P (Bridgend) 1975 *F, E, S, A*, 1976 *E, S, I, F*, 1977 *I, F, E, S*, 1978 *E, S, I, F, A* 1,2, *NZ*, 1979 *S, I, F, E*, 1980 *F, E, S, I, NZ*, 1981 *E, S*
Finch, E (Llanelli) 1924 *F, NZ*, 1925 *F, I*, 1926 *F*, 1927 *A*, 1928 *I*
Finlayson, A A J (Cardiff) 1974 *I, F, E*
Fitzgerald, D (Cardiff) 1894 *S, I*
Ford, F J V (Welch Regt, Newport) 1939 *E*
Ford, I (Newport) 1959 *E, S*
Ford, S P (Cardiff) 1990 *I, Nm* 1,2, *Bb*, 1991 *E, S, I, A*
Forward, A (Pontypool, Mon Police) 1951 *S, SA*, 1952 *E, S, I, F*
Fowler, I J (Llanelli) 1919 *NZA*
Francis, D G (Llanelli) 1919 *NZA*, 1924 *S*
Francis, P (Maesteg) 1987 *S*
Funnell, J S (Ebbw Vale) 1998 *Z* (R), *SA* 1

Gabe, R T (Cardiff, Llanelli) 1901 *I*, 1902 *E, S, I*, 1903 *E, S, I*, 1904 *E, S, I*, 1905 *E, S, I, NZ*, 1906 *E, I, SA*, 1907 *E, S, I*, 1908 *E, S, F, I*
Gale, N R (Swansea, Llanelli) 1960 *I*, 1963 *E, S, I, NZ*, 1964 *E, S, I, F, SA*, 1965 *E, S, I, F*, 1966 *E, S, I, F, A*, 1967 *E, NZ*, 1968 *E*, 1969 *NZ* 1 (R), 2, *A*
Gallacher, I S (Llanelli) 1970 *F*
Garrett, R M (Penarth) 1888 *M*, 1889 *S*, 1890 *S, E, I*, 1891 *S, I*, 1892 *E*
Geen, W P (Oxford U, Newport) 1912 *SA*, 1913 *E, I*
George, E E (Pontypridd, Cardiff) 1895 *S, I*, 1896 *E*
George, G M (Newport) 1991 *E, S*
Gething, G I (Neath) 1913 *F*
Gibbs, A (Newbridge) 1995 *I, SA*, 1996 *A* 2, 1997 *US* 1,2, *C*
Gibbs, I S (Neath, Swansea) 1991 *E, S, I, F* 1, *A, F* 2, [*WS, Arg, A*], 1992 *I, F, E, S, A*, 1993 *E, S, I, F, J, C*, 1996 *It, A* 3, *SA*, 1997 *US, S, I, F, Tg, NZ*, 1998 *It, E, S, SA* 2, *Arg*, 1999 *S, I, F, It, E*
Gibbs, R A (Cardiff) 1906 *S, I*, 1907 *E, S*, 1908 *E, S, F, I*, 1910 *F, E, S, I*, 1911 *E, S, F, I*
Giles, R (Aberavon) 1983 *R*, 1985 *Fj* (R), 1987 [*C*]
Girling, B E (Cardiff) 1881 *E*
Goldsworthy, S J (Swansea) 1884 *I*, 1885 *E, S*
Gore, J H (Blaina) 1924 *I, F, NZ*, 1925 *E*
Gore, W (Newbridge) 1947 *S, F, I*
Gough, I M (Newport, Pontypridd) 1998 *SA* 1, 1999 *S*
Gould, A J (Newport) 1885 *E, S*, 1886 *E, S*, 1887 *E, S, I*, 1888 *S*, 1889 *I*, 1890 *S, E, I*, 1892 *E, S, I*, 1893 *E, S, I*, 1894 *E, S*, 1895 *E, S, I*, 1896 *E, S, I*, 1897 *E*
Gould, G H (Newport) 1892 *I*, 1893 *S, I*
Gould, R (Newport) 1882 *I*, 1883 *E, S*, 1884 *E, S, I*, 1885 *E, S*, 1886 *E*, 1887 *E, S*
Graham, T C (Newport) 1890 *I*, 1891 *S, I*, 1892 *E, S*, 1893 *E, S, I*, 1894 *E, S*, 1895 *E, S*
Gravell, R W R (Llanelli) 1975 *F, E, S, I, A*, 1976 *E, S, I, F*, 1978 *E, S, I, F, A* 1,2, *NZ*, 1979 *S, I*, 1981 *I, F*, 1982 *F, E, S*
Gray, A J (London Welsh) 1968 *E, S*
Greenslade, D (Newport) 1962 *S*
Greville, H G (Llanelli) 1947 *A*
Griffin, Dr J (Edinburgh U) 1883 *S*
Griffiths, C (Llanelli) 1979 *E* (R)
Griffiths, D (Llanelli) 1888 *M*, 1889 *I*
Griffiths, G (Llanelli) 1889 *I*
Griffiths, G M (Cardiff) 1953 *E, S, I, F, NZ*, 1954 *I, F, S*, 1955 *I, F*, 1957 *E, S*
Griffiths, J L (Llanelli) 1988 *NZ* 2, 1989 *S*
Griffiths, M (Bridgend, Cardiff, Pontypridd) 1988 *WS, R*, 1989 *S, I, F, E, NZ*, 1990 *F, E, Nm* 1,2, *Bb*, 1991 *I, F* 1,2, [*WS, Arg, A*], 1992 *I, F, E, S, A*, 1993 *Z* 1,2, *Nm, J, C*, 1995 *F* (R), *E, S, I*, [*J, I*], 1998 *SA* 1
Griffiths, V M (Newport) 1924 *S, I, F*
Gronow, B (Bridgend) 1910 *F, E, S, I*

The Welsh battleship Scott Gibbs evades the challenge of Martin Johnson in the Wales-England match at Wembley. A last-minute try by Gibbs gave Wales victory and cost England the Five Nations Championship.

Gwilliam, J A (Cambridge U, Newport) 1947 A, 1948 I, 1949 E, S, I, F, 1950 E, S, I, F, 1951 E, S, I, SA, 1952 E, S, I, F, 1953 E, I, F, NZ, 1954 E
Gwynn, D (Swansea) 1883 E, 1887 S, 1890 E, I, 1891 E, S
Gwynn, W H (Swansea) 1884 E, S, I, 1885 E, S

Hadley, A M (Cardiff) 1983 R, 1984 S, I, F, E, 1985 F, E, Fj, 1986 E, S, I, F, Fj, Tg, 1987 S (R), I, [I, Tg, C, E, NZ, A], US, 1988 E, S, I, F
Hall, I (Aberavon) 1967 NZ, 1970 SA, S, E, 1971 S, 1974 S, I, F
Hall, M R (Cambridge U, Bridgend, Cardiff) 1988 NZ 1 (R), 2, WS, R, 1989 S, I, F, E, NZ, 1990 F, E, S, 1991 A, F 2, [WS, Arg, A], 1992 I, F, E, S, A, 1993 E, S, I, 1994 S, I, F, E, Pt, Sp, C, Tg, R, It, SA, 1995 F, S, I, [J, NZ, I]
Hall, W H (Bridgend) 1988 WS
Hancock, F E (Cardiff) 1884 I, 1885 E, S, 1886 S
Hannan, J (Newport) 1888 M, 1889 S, I, 1890 S, E, I, 1891 E, 1892 E, S, I, 1893 E, S, I, 1894 E, S, I, 1895 E, S, I
Harding, A F (London Welsh) 1902 E, S, I, 1903 E, S, I, 1904 E, S, I, 1905 E, S, I, NZ, 1906 E, S, I, SA, 1907 I, 1908 E, S
Harding, G F (Newport) 1881 E, 1882 I, 1883 E, S
Harding, R (Swansea, Cambridge U) 1923 E, S, F, I, 1924 I, F, NZ, 1925 F, I, 1926 E, I, F, 1927 E, S, F, I, 1928 E
Harding, T (Newport) 1888 M, 1889 S, I
Harris, D J E (Pontypridd, Cardiff) 1959 I, F, 1960 S, I, F, SA, 1961 E, S
Harris, T (Aberavon) 1927 A
Hathway, G F (Newport) 1924 I, F
Havard, Rev W T (Llanelli) 1919 NZA
Hawkins, F (Pontypridd) 1912 I, F
Hayward, B I (Ebbw Vale) 1998 Z (R), SA 1
Hayward, D (Newbridge) 1949 E, F, 1950 E, S, I, F, 1951 E, S, I, F, SA, 1952 E, S, I, F
Hayward, D J (Cardiff) 1963 E, NZ, 1964 S, I, F, SA
Hayward, G (Swansea) 1908 S, F, I, A, 1909 E
Hellings, R (Llwynypia) 1897 E, 1898 I, E, 1899 S, I, 1900 E, I, 1901 E, S
Herrerá, R C (Cross Keys) 1925 S, F, I, 1926 E, S, I, F, 1927 E
Hiams, H (Swansea) 1912 I, F
Hickman, A (Neath) 1930 E, 1933 S
Hiddlestone, D D (Neath) 1922 E, S, I, F, 1924 NZ
Hill, A F (Cardiff) 1885 S, 1886 E, S, 1888 S, I, M, 1889 S, 1890 S, I, 1893 E, S, I, 1894 E, S, I
Hill, S D (Cardiff) 1993 Z 1,2, Nm, 1994 I (R), F, SA, 1995 F, SA, 1996 A 2, F 2(R), It, 1997 E
Hinam, S (Cardiff) 1925 I, 1926 E, S, I, F
Hinton, J T (Cardiff) 1884 I
Hirst, G L (Newport) 1912 S, 1913 S, 1914 E, S, F, I
Hodder, W (Pontypool) 1921 E, S, F
Hodges, J J (Newport) 1899 E, S, I, 1900 E, S, I, 1901 E, S, 1902 E, S, I, 1903 E, S, I, 1904 E, S, 1905 E, S, I, NZ, 1906 E, S, I
Hodgson, G T R (Neath) 1962 I, 1963 E, S, I, F, NZ, 1964 E, S, I, F, SA, 1966 S, I, F, 1967 I
Hollingdale, H (Swansea) 1912 SA, 1913 E
Hollingdale, T H (Neath) 1927 A, 1928 E, S, I, F, 1930 E
Holmes, T D (Cardiff) 1978 A 2, NZ, 1979 S, I, F, E, 1980 F, E, S, I, NZ, 1981 A, 1982 I, F, E, 1983 E, S, I, F, 1984 E, 1985 S, I, F, E, Fj
Hopkin, W H (Newport) 1937 S
Hopkins, K (Cardiff, Swansea) 1985 E, 1987 F, E, S, [Tg, C (R)], US
Hopkins, P L (Swansea) 1908 A, 1909 E, I, 1910 E
Hopkins, R (Maesteg) 1970 E (R)
Hopkins, T (Swansea) 1926 E, S, I, F
Hopkins, W J (Aberavon) 1925 E, S
Howarth, S P (Sale) 1998 SA 2, Arg, 1999 S, I, F, It, E
Howells, B (Llanelli) 1934 E
Howells, W G (Llanelli) 1957 E, S, I, F
Howells, W H (Swansea) 1888 S, I
Howley, R (Bridgend, Cardiff) 1996 E, S, I, F 1, A 1,2, Bb, F 2, It, A 3, SA, 1997 US, S, I, F, E, Tg (R), NZ, 1998 It, E, S, I, F, Z, SA 2, Arg, 1999 S, I, F, It, E
Hughes, D (Newbridge) 1967 NZ, 1969 NZ 2, 1970 SA, S, E, I
Hughes, G (Penarth) 1934 E, S, I
Hughes, H (Cardiff) 1887 S, 1889 S
Hughes, K (Cambridge U, London Welsh) 1970 I, 1973 A, 1974 S
Hullin, W (Cardiff) 1967 S

Humphreys, J M (Cardiff) 1995 [NZ, I], SA, Fj, 1996 It, E, S, I, F 1, A 1,2, Bb, It, A 3, SA, 1997 S, I, F, E, Tg (R), NZ (R), 1998 It (R), E (R), S (R), I (R), F (R), SA 2, Arg, 1999 S
Hurrell, J (Newport) 1959 F
Hutchinson, F (Neath) 1894 I, 1896 S, I
Huxtable, R (Swansea) 1920 F, I
Huzzey, H V P (Cardiff) 1898 I, E, 1899 E, S, I
Hybart, A J (Cardiff) 1887 E

Ingledew, H M (Cardiff) 1890 I, 1891 E, S
Isaacs, I (Cardiff) 1933 E, S

Jackson, T H (Swansea) 1895 E
James, B (Bridgend) 1968 E
James, C R (Llanelli) 1958 A, F
James, D (Swansea) 1891 I, 1892 S, I, 1899 E
James, D R (Treorchy) 1931 F, I
James, D R (Bridgend, Pontypridd) 1996 A 2(R), It, A 3, SA, 1997 I, Tg (R), 1998 F (R), Z, SA 1,2, Arg, 1999 S, I, F, It, E
James, E (Swansea) 1890 S, 1891 I, 1892 S, I, 1899 E
James, M (Cardiff) 1947 A, 1948 E, S, F, I
James, T O (Aberavon) 1935 I, 1937 S
James, W J (Aberavon) 1983 E, S, I, F, R, 1984 S, 1985 S, I, F, E, Fj, 1986 E, S, I, F, Fj, Tg, WS, 1987 E, S, I
James, W P (Aberavon) 1925 E, S
Jarman, H (Newport) 1910 E, S, I, 1911 E
Jarrett, K S (Newport) 1967 E, 1968 E, S, 1969 S, I, F, E, NZ 1,2, A
Jarvis, L (Cardiff) 1997 R (R)
Jeffery, J J (Cardiff Coll of Ed, Newport) 1967 NZ
Jenkin, A M (Swansea) 1895 I, 1896 E
Jenkins, A (Llanelli) 1920 E, S, F, I, 1921 S, F, 1922 F, 1923 E, S, F, I, 1924 NZ, 1928 S, I
Jenkins, D M (Treorchy) 1926 E, S, I, F
Jenkins, D R (Swansea) 1927 A, 1929 E
Jenkins, E (Newport) 1910 S, I
Jenkins, E M (Aberavon) 1927 S, F, I, A, 1928 E, S, I, F, 1929 F, 1930 E, S, I, F, 1931 E, S, F, I, SA, 1932 E, S, I
Jenkins, G R (Pontypool, Swansea) 1991 F 2, [WS (R), Arg, A], 1992 I, F, E, S, A, 1993 C, 1994 S, I, F, Pt, Sp, C, Tg, WS, R, It, SA, 1995 F, E, S, I, [J], SA (R), Fj (t), 1996 E (R), 1997 US, US 1, C, 1998 S, I, F, Z, SA 1 (R), 1999 I (R), F, It, E
Jenkins, J C (London Welsh) 1906 SA
Jenkins, J L (Aberavon) 1923 S, F
Jenkins, L H (Mon TC, Newport) 1954 I, 1956 E, S, I, F
Jenkins, N R (Pontypridd) 1991 E, S, I, F 1, 1992 I, F, E, S, 1993 E, S, I, F Z 1,2, Nm, J, C, 1994 S, I, F, E, Pt, Sp, C, Tg, WS, R, It, SA, 1995 F, E, S, I, [J, NZ, I], SA, Fj, 1996 F 1, A 1,2, Bb, F 2, It, A 3(R), SA, 1997 S, I, F, E, Tg, NZ, 1998 It, E, S, I, F, SA 2, Arg, 1999 S, I, F, It, E
Jenkins, V G J (Oxford U, Bridgend, London Welsh) 1933 E, I, 1934 S, I, 1935 E, S, NZ, 1936 E, S, I, 1937 E, 1938 E, S, 1939 E
Jenkins, W (Cardiff) 1912 I, F, 1913 S, I
John, B (Llanelli, Cardiff) 1966 A, 1967 S, NZ, 1968 E, S, I, F, 1969 S, I, F, E, NZ 1,2, A, 1970 SA, S, E, I, 1971 E, S, I, F, 1972 E, S, F
John, D A (Llanelli) 1925 I, 1928 E, S, I
John, D E (Llanelli) 1923 F, I, 1928 E, S, I
John, E R (Neath) 1950 E, S, I, F, 1951 E, S, I, F, SA, 1952 E, S, I, F, 1953 E, S, I, F, NZ, 1954 E
John G (St Luke's Coll, Exeter) 1954 E, F
John, J H (Swansea) 1926 E, S, I, F, 1927 E, S, F, I
John, P (Pontypridd) 1994 Tg, 1996 Bb (t), 1997 US (R), US 1,2, C, R, Tg, 1998 Z (R), SA 1
John, S C (Llanelli, Cardiff) 1995 S, I, 1997 E (R), Tg, NZ (R)
Johnson, T A (Cardiff) 1921 E, F, I, 1923 E, S, F, 1924 E, S, NZ, 1925 E, S, F
Johnson, W D (Swansea) 1953 E
Jones, A H (Cardiff) 1933 E, S
Jones, B (Abertillery) 1914 E, S, F, I
Jones, Bert (Llanelli) 1934 S, I
Jones, Bob (Llwynypia) 1901 I
Jones, B J (Newport) 1960 I, F
Jones, B Lewis (Devonport Services, Llanelli) 1950 E, S, I, F, 1951 E, S, SA, 1952 E, S, I, F
Jones, C W (Cambridge U, Cardiff) 1934 E, S, I, 1935 E, S, I, NZ, 1936 E, S, I, 1938 E, S, I
Jones, C W (Bridgend) 1920 E, S, F
Jones, D (Neath) 1927 A

263

Jones, D (Aberavon) 1897 *E*
Jones, D (Swansea) 1947 *E, F, I*, 1949 *E, S, I, F*
Jones, D (Treherbert) 1902 *E, S, I*, 1903 *E, S, I*, 1905 *E, S, I, NZ*, 1906 *E, S, SA*
Jones, D (Newport) 1926 *E, S, I, F*, 1927 *E*
Jones, D (Llanelli) 1948 *E*
Jones, D (Cardiff) 1994 *SA*, 1995 *F, E, S, [J, NZ, I]*, *SA, Fj*, 1996 *It, E, S, I, F* 1, *A* 1,2, *Bb, It, A* 3
Jones, D K (Llanelli, Cardiff) 1962 *E, S, F, I*, 1963 *E, F, NZ*, 1964 *E, S, SA*, 1966 *E, S, I, F*
Jones, D P (Pontypool) 1907 *I*
Jones, E H (Neath) 1929 *E, S*
Jones, E L (Llanelli) 1930 *F*, 1933 *E, S, I*, 1935 *E*
Jones, Elvet L (Llanelli) 1939 *S*
Jones, G (Ebbw Vale) 1963 *S, I, F*
Jones, G (Llanelli) 1988 *NZ* 2, 1989 *F, E, NZ*, 1990 *F*
Jones, G G (Cardiff) 1930 *S*, 1933 *I*
Jones, G H (Bridgend) 1995 *SA*
Jones, H (Penygraig) 1902 *S, I*
Jones, H (Neath) 1904 *I*
Jones, H (Swansea) 1930 *I, F*
Jones, Iorwerth (Llanelli) 1927 *A*, 1928 *E, S, I, F*
Jones, I C (London Welsh) 1968 *I*
Jones, Ivor E (Llanelli) 1924 *E, S*, 1927 *S, F, I, A*, 1928 *E, S, I, F*, 1929 *E, S, F, I*, 1930 *E, S*
Jones, J (Aberavon) 1901 *E*
Jones, J (Swansea) 1924 *F*
Jones, Jim (Aberavon) 1919 *NZA*, 1920 *E, S*, 1921 *S, F, I*
Jones, J A (Cardiff) 1883 *S*
Jones, J P (Tuan) (Pontypool) 1913 *S*
Jones, J P (Pontypool) 1908 *A*, 1909 *E, S, F, I*, 1910 *F, E*, 1912 *E, F*, 1913 *F, I*, 1920 *F, I*, 1921 *E*
Jones, K D (Cardiff) 1960 *SA*, 1961 *E, S, I*, 1962 *E, F*, 1963 *E, S, I, NZ*
Jones, K J (Newport) 1947 *E, S, F, I, A*, 1948 *E, S, F, I*, 1949 *E, S, I, F*, 1950 *E, S, I, F*, 1951 *E, S, I, F, SA*, 1952 *E, S, I, F*, 1953 *E, S, I, F, NZ*, 1954 *E, I, F, S*, 1955 *E, S, I, F*, 1956 *E, S, I, F*, 1957 *S*
Jones, K P (Ebbw Vale) 1996 *Bb, F* 2, *It, A* 3, 1997 *I* (R), *E*, 1998 *S, I, F* (R), *SA* 1
Jones, K W J (Oxford U, London Welsh) 1934 *E*
Jones, M A (Neath, Ebbw Vale) 1987 *S*, 1988 *NZ* 2 (R), 1989 *E, S, I, F, E, NZ*, 1990 *F, E, S, I, Nm* 1,2, *Bb*, 1998 *Z*
Jones, P (Newport) 1912 *SA*, 1913 *E, S, F*, 1914 *E, S, F, I*
Jones, P B (Newport) 1921 *S*
Jones, R (Swansea) 1901 *I*, 1902 *E*, 1904 *E, S, I*, 1905 *E*, 1908 *F, I, A*, 1909 *E, S, F, I*, 1910 *F, E*
Jones, R (London Welsh) 1929 *E*
Jones, R (Northampton) 1926 *E, S, F*
Jones, R (Swansea) 1927 *A*, 1928 *F*
Jones, R B (Cambridge U) 1933 *E, S*
Jones, R E (Coventry) 1967 *F, E*, 1968 *S, I, F*
Jones, R G (Llanelli, Cardiff) 1996 *It, E, S, I, F* 1, *A* 1, 1997 *US* (R), *S* (R), *US* 1,2, *R, Tg, NZ*
Jones, R L (Llanelli) 1993 *Z* 1,2, *Nm, J, C*
Jones, R N (Swansea) 1986 *E, S, I, F, Fj, Tg, WS*, 1987 *F, E, S, I, [I, Tg, E, NZ, A], US*, 1988 *E, S, I, F, NZ* 1, *WS, R*, 1989 *I, F, E, NZ*, 1990 *F, E, S, I*, 1991 *E, S, F* 2, *[WS, Arg, A]*, 1992 *I, F, E, S, A*, 1993 *E, S, I*, 1994 *I* (R), *Pt*, 1995 *F, E, S, I, [NZ, I]*
Jones, S (Llanelli) 1998 *SA* 1 (R)
Jones, S T (Pontypool) 1983 *S, I, F, R*, 1984 *S*, 1988 *E, S, F, NZ* 1,2
Jones, Tom (Newport) 1922 *E, S, I, F*, 1924 *E, S*
Jones, T B (Newport) 1882 *I*, 1883 *E, S*, 1884 *S*, 1885 *E, S*
Jones, W (Cardiff) 1898 *I, E*
Jones, W (Mountain Ash) 1905 *I*
Jones, W I (Llanelli, Cambridge U) 1925 *E, S, F, I*
Jones, W J (Llanelli) 1924 *I*
Jones, W K (Cardiff) 1967 *NZ*, 1968 *E, S, I, F*
Jones-Davies, T E (London Welsh) 1930 *E, I*, 1931 *E, S*
Jordan, H M (Newport) 1885 *E, S*, 1889 *S*
Joseph, W (Swansea) 1902 *E, S, I*, 1903 *E, S, I*, 1904 *E, S*, 1905 *E, S, I, NZ*, 1906 *E, S, I, SA*
Jowett, W F (Swansea) 1903 *E*
Judd, S (Cardiff) 1953 *E, S, I, F, NZ*, 1954 *E, F, S*, 1955 *E, S*
Judson, J H (Llanelli) 1883 *E, S*

Kedzlie, Q D (Cardiff) 1888 *S, I*
Keen, L (Aberavon) 1980 *F, E, S, I*
Knight, P (Pontypridd) 1990 *Nm* 1,2, *Bb* (R), 1991 *E, S*
Knill, F M D (Cardiff) 1976 *F* (R)

Lamerton, A E H (Llanelli) 1993 *F, Z* 1,2, *Nm, J*
Lane, S M (Cardiff) 1978 *A* 1 (R), 2, 1979 *I* (R), 1980 *S, I*
Lang, J (Llanelli) 1931 *F, I*, 1934 *S, I*, 1935 *E, S, I, NZ*, 1936 *E, S, I*, 1937 *E*
Lawrence, S (Bridgend) 1925 *S, I*, 1926 *S, I, F*, 1927 *E*
Law, V J (Newport) 1939 *I*
Legge, W S G (Newport) 1937 *I*, 1938 *I*
Leleu, J (London Welsh, Swansea) 1959 *E, S*, 1960 *F, SA*
Lemon, A (Neath) 1929 *I*, 1930 *S, I, F*, 1931 *E, S, F, I, SA*, 1932 *E, S, I*, 1933 *I*
Lewis, A J L (Ebbw Vale) 1970 *F*, 1971 *E, I, F*, 1972 *E, S, F*, 1973 *E, S, I, F*
Lewis, A L P (Cardiff) 1996 *It, E, S, I, A* 2(t), 1998 *It, E, S, I, F, SA* 2, *Arg*, 1999 *F* (R), *E* (R)
Lewis, A R (Abertillery) 1966 *E, S, I, F, A*, 1967 *I*
Lewis, B R (Swansea, Cambridge U) 1912 *I*, 1913 *I*
Lewis, C P (Llandovery Coll) 1882 *I*, 1883 *E, S*, 1884 *E, S*
Lewis, D H (Cardiff) 1886 *E, S*
Lewis, E J (Llandovery) 1881 *E*
Lewis, E W (Llanelli, Cardiff) 1991 *I, F* 1, *A, F* 2, *[WS, Arg, A]*, 1992 *I, F, S, A*, 1993 *E, S, I, F, Z* 1,2, *Nm, J, C*, 1994 *S, I, F, E, Pt, Sp, Fj, WS, R, It, SA*, 1995 *E, S, I, [J, I]*, 1996 *It, E, S, I, F* 1
Lewis, G (Pontypridd) 1998 *SA* 1 (R), 1999 *It* (R)
Lewis, G W (Richmond) 1960 *E, S*
Lewis, H (Swansea) 1913 *S, F, I*, 1914 *E*
Lewis, J G (Llanelli) 1887 *I*
Lewis, J M C (Cardiff, Cambridge U) 1912 *E*, 1913 *S, F, I*, 1914 *E, S, F, I*, 1921 *I*, 1923 *E, S*
Lewis, J R (S Glam Inst, Cardiff) 1981 *E, S, I, F*, 1982 *F, E, S*
Lewis, M (Treorchy) 1913 *F*
Lewis, P I (Llanelli) 1984 *A*, 1985 *S, I, F, E*, 1986 *E, S, I*
Lewis, T W (Cardiff) 1926 *E*, 1927 *E, S*
Lewis, W (Llanelli) 1925 *F*
Lewis, W H (London Welsh, Cambridge U) 1926 *I*, 1927 *E, F, I, A*, 1928 *F*
Llewellyn, D B (Newport, Llanelli) 1970 *SA, S, E, I, F*, 1971 *E, S, I, F*, 1972 *E, S, F, NZ*
Llewellyn, D S (Ebbw Vale) 1998 *SA* 1 (R), 1999 *F* (R), *It* (R)
Llewellyn, G D (Neath) 1990 *Nm* 1,2, *Bb*, 1991 *E, S, I, F* 1, *A, F* 2
Llewellyn, G O (Neath, Harlequins) 1989 *NZ*, 1990 *E, S, I*, 1991 *E, S, A* (R), 1992 *I, F, E, S, A*, 1993 *E, S, I, F, Z* 1,2, *Nm, J, C*, 1994 *S, I, F, E, Pt, Sp, C, Tg, WS, R, It, SA*, 1995 *F, E, S, I, [J, NZ, I]*, 1996 *It, E, S, I, F* 1, *A* 1,2, *Bb, F* 2, *It, A* 3, *SA*, 1997 *US, S, I, F, E, US* 1,2, *NZ*, 1998 *It, E*
Llewellyn, P D (Swansea) 1973 *I, F, A*, 1974 *S, E*
Llewellyn, W (Llwynypia) 1899 *E, S, I*, 1900 *E, S, I*, 1901 *E, S, I*, 1902 *E, S, I*, 1903 *I*, 1904 *E, S, I*, 1905 *E, S, I, NZ*
Lloyd, D J (Bridgend) 1966 *E, S, I, F, A*, 1967 *S, I, F, E*, 1968 *S, I, F*, 1969 *S, I, F, E, NZ* 1, *A*, 1970 *F*, 1972 *E, S, F*, 1973 *E, S*
Lloyd, E (Llanelli) 1895 *S*
Lloyd, G L (Newport) 1896 *I*, 1899 *S, I*, 1900 *E, S*, 1901 *E, S*, 1902 *S, I*, 1903 *E, S, I*
Lloyd, P (Llanelli) 1890 *S, E*, 1891 *E, I*
Lloyd, R A (Pontypool) 1913 *S, F, I*, 1914 *E, S, F, I*
Lloyd, T (Maesteg) 1953 *I, F*
Lloyd, T C (Neath) 1909 *F*, 1913 *F, I*, 1914 *E, S, F, I*
Loader, C D (Swansea) 1995 *SA, Fj*, 1996 *F* 1, *A* 1,2, *Bb, F* 2, *It, A* 3, *SA*, 1997 *US, S, I, F, E, US* 1, *R, Tg, NZ*
Lockwood, T W (Newport) 1887 *E, S, I*
Long, E C (Swansea) 1936 *E, S, I*, 1937 *E, S*, 1939 *S, I*
Lyne, H S (Newport) 1883 *S*, 1884 *E, S, I*, 1885 *E*

McBryde, R C (Swansea, Llanelli) 1994 *Fj, SA* (t), 1997 *US* 2
McCall, B E W (Welch Regt, Newport) 1936 *E, S, I*
McCarley, A (Neath) 1938 *E, S, I*
McCutcheon, W M (Swansea) 1891 *S*, 1892 *E, S*, 1893 *E, S, I*, 1894 *E*
McIntosh, D L M (Pontypridd) 1996 *SA*, 1997 *E* (R)
Maddock, H T (London Welsh) 1906 *E, S, I*, 1907 *E, S*, 1910 *F*
Maddocks, K (Neath) 1957 *E*
Main, D R (London Welsh) 1959 *E, S, I, F*
Mainwaring, H J (Swansea) 1961 *F*
Mainwaring, W T (Aberavon) 1967 *S, I, F, E, NZ*, 1968 *E*
Major, W C (Maesteg) 1949 *F*, 1950 *S*

Male, B O (Cardiff) 1921 *F*, 1923 *S*, 1924 *S, I*, 1927 *E, S, F, I*, 1928 *S, I, F*
Manfield, L (Mountain Ash, Cardiff) 1939 *S, I*, 1947 *A*, 1948 *E, S, F, I*
Mann, B B (Cardiff) 1881 *E*
Mantle, J T (Loughborough Colls, Newport) 1964 *E, SA*
Margrave, F L (Llanelli) 1884 *E, S*
Marsden-Jones, D (Cardiff) 1921 *E*, 1924 *NZ*
Martin, A J (Aberavon) 1973 *A*, 1974 *S, I*, 1975 *F, E, S, I, A*, 1976 *E, S, I, F*, 1977 *I, F, E, S*, 1978 *E, S, I, F, A* 1,2, *NZ*, 1979 *S, I, F, E*, 1980 *F, E, S, I, NZ*, 1981 *I, F*
Martin, W J (Newport) 1912 *I, F*, 1919 *NZA*
Mason, J (Pontypridd) 1988 *NZ* 2 (R)
Mathews, Rev A A (Lampeter) 1886 *S*
Mathias, R (Llanelli) 1970 *F*
Matthews, C (Bridgend) 1939 *I*
Matthews, J (Cardiff), 1947 *E, A*, 1948 *E, S, F*, 1949 *E, S, I, F*, 1950 *E, S, I, F*, 1951 *E, S, I, F*
May, P S (Llanelli) 1988 *E, S, I, F, NZ* 1,2, 1991 *[WS]*
Meek, N N (Pontypool) 1993 *E, S, I*
Meredith, A (Devonport Services) 1949 *E, S, I*
Meredith, B V (St Luke's Coll, London Welsh, Newport) 1954 *I, F, S*, 1955 *E, S, I, F*, 1956 *E, S, I, F*, 1957 *E, S, I, F*, 1958 *A, E, S, I*, 1959 *E, S, I, F*, 1960 *E, S, F, SA*, 1961 *E, S, I*, 1962 *E, S, F, I*
Meredith, C C (Neath) 1953 *S, NZ*, 1954 *E, I, F, S*, 1955 *E, S, I, F*, 1956 *S, I*, 1957 *E, S*
Meredith, J (Swansea) 1888 *S, I*, 1890 *S, E*
Merry, A E (Pill Harriers) 1912 *I, F*
Michael, G (Swansea) 1923 *E, S, F*
Michaelson, R C B (Aberavon, Cambridge U) 1963 *E*
Miller, F (Mountain Ash) 1896 *I*, 1900 *E, S, I*, 1901 *E, S, I*
Mills, F M (Swansea, Cardiff) 1892 *E, S, I*, 1893 *E, S, I*, 1894 *E, S, I*, 1895 *E, S, I*, 1896 *E*
Moon, R H StJ B (Llanelli) 1993 *F, Z* 1,2, *Nm, J, C*, 1994 *S, I, F, E, Sp, C, Fj, WS, R, It, SA*, 1995 *E* (R)
Moore, A P (Cardiff) 1995 *[J], SA, Fj*, 1996 *It*
Moore, A P (Swansea) 1995 *SA* (R), *Fj*, 1998 *S, I, F, Z, SA* 1
Moore, S J (Swansea, Moseley) 1997 *C, R, Tg*
Moore, W J (Bridgend) 1933 *I*
Morgan, C H (Llanelli) 1957 *I, F*
Morgan, C I (Cardiff) 1951 *I, F, SA*, 1952 *E, S, I*, 1953 *S, I, F, NZ*, 1954 *E, I, S*, 1955 *E, S, I, F*, 1956 *S, I, F*, 1957 *E, S, I, F*, 1958 *E, S, I, F*
Morgan, D (Swansea) 1885 *S*, 1886 *E, S*, 1887 *E, S, I*, 1889 *I*
Morgan, D (Llanelli) 1895 *I*, 1896 *E*
Morgan, D R R (Llanelli) 1962 *E, S, F, I*, 1963 *E, S, I, F, NZ*
Morgan, E (Llanelli) 1920 *I*, 1921 *E, S, F*
Morgan, Edgar (Swansea) 1914 *E, S, F, I*
Morgan, E T (London Welsh) 1902 *E, S, I*, 1903 *I*, 1904 *E, S, I*, 1905 *E, S, I, NZ*, 1906 *E, S, I, SA*, 1908 *F*
Morgan, F L (Llanelli) 1938 *E, S, I*, 1939 *E*
Morgan, H J (Abertillery) 1958 *E, S, I, F*, 1959 *I, F*, 1960 *E*, 1961 *E, S, I, F*, 1962 *E, S, F, I*, 1963 *S, I, F*, 1965 *E, S, I, F*, 1966 *E, S, I, F, A*
Morgan, H P (Newport) 1956 *E, S, I, F*
Morgan, I (Swansea) 1908 *A*, 1909 *E, S, I, F*, 1910 *F, E, S, I*, 1911 *E, F, I*, 1912 *S*
Morgan, J L (Llanelli) 1912 *SA*, 1913 *E*
Morgan, K A (Pontypridd) 1997 *US* 1,2, *C, R, NZ*, 1998 *S, I, F*
Morgan, M E (Swansea) 1938 *E, S, I*, 1939 *E*
Morgan, N (Newport) 1960 *S, I, F*
Morgan, P E J (Aberavon) 1961 *E, S, F*
Morgan, P J (Llanelli) 1980 *S* (R), *I, NZ* 1981 *I*
Morgan, R (Newport) 1984 *S*
Morgan, T (Llanelli) 1889 *I*
Morgan, W G (Cambridge U) 1927 *F, I*, 1929 *E, S, F, I*, 1930 *I, F*
Morgan, W L (Cardiff) 1910 *S*
Moriarty, R D (Swansea) 1981 *A*, 1982 *I, F, E, S*, 1983 *E*, 1984 *S, I, F, E*, 1985 *S, I, F*, 1986 *Fj, Tg, WS*, 1987 *[I, Tg, C] E, NZ, A]*
Moriarty, W P (Swansea) 1986 *I, F, Fj, Tg, WS*, 1987 *F, E, S, I, [I, Tg, C, E, NZ, A]*, *US*, 1988 *E, S, I, F, NZ* 1
Morley, J C (Newport) 1929 *E, S, F, I*, 1930 *E, I*, 1931 *E, S, F, I, SA*, 1932 *E, S, I*
Morris, D R (Neath, Swansea) 1998 *Z, SA* 1 (R),2 (R), 1999 *S, I, It* (R)
Morris, G L (Swansea) 1882 *I*, 1883 *E, S*, 1884 *E, S*
Morris, H T (Cardiff) 1951 *F*, 1955 *I, F*

Morris, J I T (Swansea) 1924 *E, S*
Morris, M S (S Wales Police, Neath) 1985 *S, I, F*, 1990 *I, Nm* 1,2, *Bb*, 1991 *I, F* 1, [*WS* (R)], 1992 *E*
Morris, R R (Swansea, Bristol) 1933 *S*, 1937 *S*
Morris, S (Cross Keys) 1920 *E, S, F, I*, 1922 *E, S, I, F*, 1923 *E, S, F, I*, 1924 *E, S, F, NZ*, 1925 *E, S, F*
Morris, W (Abertillery) 1919 *NZA*, 1920 *F*, 1921 *I*
Morris, W (Llanelli) 1896 *S, I*, 1897 *E*
Morris, W D (Neath) 1967 *F, E*, 1968 *E, S, I, F*, 1969 *S, I, F, E, NZ* 1,2, *A*, 1970 *SA, S, E, I, F*, 1971 *E, S, I, F*, 1972 *E, S, F, NZ*, 1973 *E, S, I, A*, 1974 *S, I, F, E*
Morris, W J (Newport) 1965 *S*, 1966 *F*
Morris, W J (Pontypool) 1963 *S, I*
Moseley, K (Pontypool, Newport) 1988 *NZ* 2, *R*, 1989 *S, I*, 1990 *F*, 1991 *F* 2, [*WS, Arg, A*]
Murphy, C D (Cross Keys) 1935 *E, S, I*
Mustoe, L (Cardiff) 1995 *Fj*, 1996 *A* 1 (R), 2, 1997 *US* 1,2, *C, R* (R), 1998 *E* (R), *I* (R), *F* (R)

Nash, D (Ebbw Vale) 1960 *SA*, 1961 *E, S, I, F*, 1962 *F*
Newman, C H (Newport) 1881 *E*, 1882 *I*, 1883 *E, S*, 1884 *E, S*, 1885 *E, S*, 1886 *E*, 1887 *E*
Nicholas, D L (Llanelli) 1981 *E, S, I, F*
Nicholas, T J (Cardiff) 1919 *NZA*
Nicholl, C B (Cambridge U, Llanelli) 1891 *I*, 1892 *E, S, I*, 1893 *E, S, I*, 1894 *E, S*, 1895 *E, S, I*, 1896 *E, S, I*
Nicholl, D W (Llanelli) 1894 *I*
Nicholls, E G (Cardiff) 1896 *S, I*, 1897 *E*, 1898 *I, E*, 1899 *E, S, I*, 1900 *S, I*, 1901 *E, S, I*, 1902 *E, S, I*, 1903 *I*, 1904 *E*, 1905 *I, NZ*, 1906 *E, S, I, SA*
Nicholls, F E (Cardiff Harlequins) 1892 *I*
Nicholls, H (Cardiff) 1958 *I*
Nicholls, S H (Cardiff) 1888 *M*, 1889 *S, I*, 1891 *S*
Norris, C H (Cardiff) 1963 *F*, 1966 *F*
Norster, R L (Cardiff) 1982 *S*, 1983 *E, S, I, F*, 1984 *S, I, F, E, A*, 1985 *S, I, F, E, Fj*, 1986 *Fj, Tg, WS*, 1987 *F, E, S, I, [I, C, E], US*, 1988 *E, S, I, F, NZ* 1, *WS*, 1989 *F, E*
Norton, W B (Cardiff) 1882 *I*, 1883 *E, S*, 1884 *E, S, I*

O'Connor, A (Aberavon) 1960 *SA*, 1961 *E, S*, 1962 *F, I*
O'Connor, R (Aberavon) 1957 *E*
O'Neill, W (Cardiff) 1904 *S, I*, 1905 *E, S, I*, 1907 *E, I*, 1908 *E, S, F, I*
O'Shea, J P (Cardiff) 1967 *S, I*, 1968 *S, I, F*
Oliver, G (Pontypool) 1920 *E, S, F, I*
Osborne, W T (Mountain Ash) 1902 *E, S, I*, 1903 *E, S, I*
Ould, W J (Cardiff) 1924 *E, S*
Owen, A (Swansea) 1924 *E*
Owen, G D (Newport) 1955 *I, F*, 1956 *E, S, I, F*
Owen, R M (Swansea) 1901 *I*, 1902 *E, S, I*, 1903 *E, S, I*, 1904 *E, S, I*, 1905 *E, S, I, NZ*, 1906 *E, S, I, SA*, 1907 *E, S*, 1908 *F, I, A*, 1909 *E, S, F, I*, 1910 *F, E, S, I*, 1911 *E, S, F, I*, 1912 *E, S*

Packer, H (Newport) 1891 *E*, 1895 *S, I*, 1896 *E, S, I*, 1897 *E*
Palmer, F (Swansea) 1922 *E, S, I*
Parfitt, F C (Newport) 1893 *E, S, I*, 1894 *E, S, I*, 1895 *S*, 1896 *S, I*
Parfitt, S A (Swansea) 1990 *Nm* 1 (R), *Bb*
Parker, D S (Swansea) 1924 *I, F, NZ*, 1925 *E, S, F, I*, 1929 *F, I*, 1930 *E*
Parker, T (Swansea) 1919 *NZA*, 1920 *E, S, I*, 1921 *E, S, F, I*, 1922 *E, S, I, F*, 1923 *E, S, F*
Parker, W (Swansea) 1899 *E, S*
Parsons, G W (Newport) 1947 *E*
Pascoe, D (Bridgend) 1923 *F, I*
Pask, A E I (Abertillery) 1961 *F*, 1962 *E, S, F, I*, 1963 *E, S, I, F, NZ*, 1964 *E, S, I, F, SA*, 1965 *E, S, I, F*, 1966 *E, S, I, F, A*, 1967 *S, I*
Payne, G W (Army, Pontypridd) 1960 *E, S, I*
Payne, H (Swansea) 1935 *NZ*
Peacock, H (Newport) 1929 *S, F, I*, 1930 *S, I, F*
Peake, E (Chepstow) 1881 *E*
Pearce, G P (Bridgend) 1981 *I, F*, 1982 *I* (R)
Pearson, T W (Cardiff, Newport) 1891 *E, I*, 1892 *E, S*, 1894 *S, I*, 1895 *E, S, I*, 1897 *E*, 1898 *I, E*, 1903 *E*
Pegge, E V (Neath) 1891 *E*
Perego, M A (Llanelli) 1990 *S*, 1993 *F, Z* 1, *Nm* (R), 1994 *S, I, F, E, Sp*
Perkins, S J (Pontypool) 1983 *S, I, F, R*, 1984 *S, I, F, E, A*, 1985 *S, I, F, E, Fj*, 1986 *E, S, I, F*
Perrett, F L (Neath) 1912 *SA*, 1913 *E, S, F, I*
Perrins, V C (Newport) 1970 *SA, S*

Perry, W (Neath) 1911 *E*
Phillips, A J (Cardiff) 1979 *E*, 1980 *F, E, S, I, NZ*, 1981 *E, S, I, F, A*, 1982 *I, F, E, S*, 1987 *[C, E, A]*
Phillips, B (Aberavon) 1925 *E, S, F, I*, 1926 *E*
Phillips, D H (Swansea) 1952 *F*
Phillips, H P (Newport) 1892 *E*, 1893 *E, S, I*, 1894 *E, S*
Phillips, H T (Newport) 1927 *E, S, F, I, A*, 1928 *E, S, I, F*
Phillips, K H (Neath) 1987 *F, [I, Tg, NZ]*, *US*, 1988 *E, NZ* 1, 1989 *NZ*, 1990 *F, E, S, I, Nm* 1,2, *Bb*, 1991 *E, S, I, F* 1, *A*
Phillips, L A (Newport) 1900 *E, S, I*, 1901 *S*
Phillips, R (Neath) 1987 *US*, 1988 *E, S, I, F, NZ* 1,2, *WS*, 1989 *S, I*
Phillips, W D (Cardiff) 1881 *E*, 1882 *I*, 1884 *E, S, I*
Pickering, D F (Llanelli) 1983 *E, S, I, F, R*, 1984 *S, I, F, E, A*, 1985 *S, I, F, E, Fj*, 1986 *E, S, I, F, Fj*, 1987 *F, E*
Plummer, R C S (Newport) 1912 *S, I, F, SA*, 1913 *E*
Pook, T (Newport) 1895 *S*
Powell, G (Ebbw Vale) 1957 *I, F*
Powell, J (Cardiff) 1906 *I*
Powell, J (Cardiff) 1923 *I*
Powell, R W (Newport) 1888 *S, I*
Powell, W C (London Welsh) 1926 *S, I, F*, 1927 *E, F, I*, 1928 *S, I, F*, 1929 *E, S, F, I*, 1930 *S, I, F*, 1931 *E, S, F, I, SA*, 1932 *E, S, I*, 1935 *E, S, I*
Powell, W J (Cardiff) 1920 *E, S, F, I*
Price, B (Newport) 1961 *I, F*, 1962 *E, S*, 1963 *E, S, F, NZ*, 1964 *E, S, I, F, SA*, 1965 *E, S, I, F*, 1966 *E, S, I, F, A*, 1967 *S, I, F, E*, 1969 *S, I, F, NZ* 1,2, *A*
Price, G (Pontypool) 1975 *F, E, S, I, A*, 1976 *E, S, I, F*, 1977 *I, F, E, S*, 1978 *E, S, I, F, A* 1,2, *NZ*, 1979 *S, I, F, E*, 1980 *F, E, S, I, NZ*, 1981 *E, S, I, F, A*, 1982 *I, F, E, S*, 1983 *E, I, F*
Price, M J (Pontypool, RAF) 1959 *E, S, I, F*, 1960 *E, S, I, F*, 1962 *E*
Price, R E (Weston-s-Mare) 1939 *S, I*
Price, T G (Llanelli) 1965 *E, S, I, F*, 1966 *E, A*, 1967 *S, F*
Priday, A J (Cardiff) 1958 *I*, 1961 *I*
Pritchard, C (Pontypool) 1928 *E, S, I, F*, 1929 *E, S, F, I*
Pritchard, C C (Newport, Pontypool) 1904 *S, I*, 1905 *NZ*, 1906 *E, S*
Pritchard, C M (Newport) 1904 *I*, 1905 *E, S, NZ*, 1906 *E, S, I, SA*, 1907 *E, S, I*, 1908 *E*, 1910 *F, E, A* 1,2, *Bb, F* 2, *It, A* 3, 1997 *E* (R)
Proctor, W T (Llanelli) 1992 *A*, 1993 *E, S, Z* 1,2, *Nm, C*, 1994 *I, C, Fj, WS, R, It, SA*, 1995 *S, I, [NZ], Fj*, 1996 *It, E, S, I, A* 1,2, *Bb, F* 2, *It, A* 3, 1997 *E*(R), *US* 1,2, *C, R*, 1998 *E* (R), *S, I, F, Z*
Prosser, D R (Neath) 1934 *S, I*
Prosser, G (Neath) 1934 *E, S, I*, 1935 *NZ*
Prosser, G (Pontypridd) 1995 *[NZ]*
Prosser, J (Cardiff) 1921 *I*
Prosser, T R (Pontypool) 1956 *S, F*, 1957 *E, S, I, F*, 1958 *A, E, S, I, F*, 1959 *S, I, F*, 1960 *E, S, I, F, SA*, 1961 *I, F*
Prothero, G J (Bridgend) 1964 *S, I, F*, 1965 *E, S, I, F*, 1966 *E, S, I, F*
Pryce-Jenkins, T J (London Welsh) 1888 *S, I*
Pugh, C (Maesteg) 1924 *E, S, I, F, NZ*, 1925 *E, S*
Pugh, J D (Neath) 1987 *US*, 1988 *S* (R), 1990 *S*
Pugh, P (Neath) 1989 *NZ*
Pugsley, J (Cardiff) 1910 *E, S, I*, 1911 *E, S, F, I*
Pullman, J J (Neath) 1910 *F*
Purdon, F T (Newport) 1881 *E*, 1882 *I*, 1883 *E, S*

Quinnell, D L (Llanelli) 1972 *F* (R), *NZ*, 1973 *E, S, A*, 1974 *S, F*, 1975 *E* (R), 1977 *I* (R), *F, E, S*, 1978 *E, S, I, F, A* 1, *NZ*, 1979 *S, I, F, E*, 1980 *NZ*
Quinnell, J C (Llanelli, Richmond) 1995 *Fj*, 1996 *A* 3(R), 1997 *US* (R), *S* (R), *I* (R), *E* (R), 1998 *SA* 2, *Arg*, 1999 *I, F, It, E*
Quinnell, L S (Llanelli, Richmond) 1993 *C*, 1994 *S, I, F, E, Pt, Sp, C, WS*, 1997 *US, S, I, F, E*, 1998 *It, E, S* (R), *SA* 2, *Arg*, 1999 *S, I, F, It, E*

Radford, W J (Newport) 1923 *I*
Ralph, A R (Newport) 1931 *F, I, SA*, 1932 *E, S, I*
Ramsey, S H (Treorchy) 1896 *E*, 1904 *E*
Randell, A (Aberavon) 1924 *I, F*
Raybould, W H (London Welsh, Cambridge U, Newport) 1967 *S, I, F, E, NZ*, 1968 *I, F*, 1970 *SA, E, I, F* (R)
Rayer, M A (Cardiff) 1991 *[WS* (R), *Arg, A* (R)], 1992 *E* (R), *A*, 1993 *E, S, I, Z* 1, *Nm, J* (R), 1994 *S* (R), *I* (R), *F, E, Pt, C, Fj, WS, R, It*

Rees, Aaron (Maesteg) 1919 *NZA*
Rees, Alan (Maesteg) 1962 *E, S, F*
Rees, A M (London Welsh) 1934 *E*, 1935 *E, S, I, NZ*, 1936 *E, S, I*, 1937 *E, S, I*, 1938 *E, S*
Rees, B I (London Welsh) 1967 *S, I, F*
Rees, C F W (London Welsh) 1974 *I*, 1975 *A*, 1978 *NZ*, 1981 *F, A*, 1982 *I, F, E, S*, 1983 *E, S, I, F*
Rees, D (Swansea) 1968 *S, I, F*
Rees, Dan (Swansea) 1900 *E*, 1903 *E, S*, 1905 *E, S*
Rees, E B (Swansea) 1919 *NZA*
Rees, H (Cardiff) 1937 *S, I*, 1938 *E, S, I*
Rees, H E (Neath) 1979 *S, I, F, E*, 1980 *F, E, S, I, NZ*, 1983 *E, S, I, F*
Rees, J (Swansea) 1920 *E, S, F, I*, 1921 *E, S, I*, 1922 *E, 1923 *E, S, F, I*, 1924 *E*
Rees, J I (Swansea) 1934 *E, S, I*, 1935 *S, NZ*, 1936 *E, S, I*, 1937 *E, S, I*, 1938 *E, S, I*
Rees, L M (Cardiff) 1933 *I*
Rees, P (Llanelli) 1947 *E, F*
Rees, P M (Newport) 1961 *E, S, I*, 1964 *I*
Rees, R (Swansea) 1998 *Z*
Rees, T (Newport) 1935 *S, I, NZ*, 1936 *E, S, I*, 1937 *E, S*
Rees, T A (Llandovery) 1881 *E*
Rees, T E (London Welsh) 1926 *I, F*, 1927 *A*, 1928 *E*
Rees-Jones, G R (Oxford U, London Welsh) 1934 *E, S*, 1935 *I, NZ*, 1936 *E*
Reeves, F (Cross Keys) 1920 *F, I*, 1921 *E*
Reynolds, A (Swansea) 1990 *Nm* 1,2 (R), 1992 *A* (R)
Rhapps, J (Penygraig) 1897 *E*
Rice-Evans, W (Swansea) 1890 *S*, 1891 *E, S*
Richards, B (Swansea)1960 *F*
Richards, C (Pontypool) 1922 *E, S, I, F*, 1924 *I*
Richards, D S (Swansea) 1979 *F, E*, 1980 *F, E, S, I, NZ*, 1981 *E, S, I, F*, 1982 *I, F*, 1983 *E, S, I, R* (R)
Richards, E G (Cardiff) 1927 *S*
Richards, E S (Swansea) 1885 *E*, 1887 *S*
Richards, H D (Neath) 1986 *Tg* (R), 1987 *[Tg, E* (R), *NZ]*
Richards, I (Cardiff) 1925 *E, S, F*
Richards, K H L (Bridgend) 1960 *SA*, 1961 *E, S, I, F*
Richards, M C R (Cardiff) 1968 *I, F*, 1969 *S, I, F, E, NZ* 1,2, *A*
Richards, R (Aberavon) 1913 *S, F, I*
Richards, R (Cross Keys) 1956 *F*
Richards, T L (Maesteg) 1923 *I*
Richardson, S J (Aberavon) 1978 *A* 2 (R), 1979 *E*
Rickards, A R (Cardiff) 1924 *F*
Ring, J (Aberavon) 1921 *E*
Ring, M G (Cardiff, Pontypool) 1983 *E*, 1984 *A*, 1985 *S, I, F*, 1987 *I, [I, Tg, A]*, *US*, 1988 *E, S, I, F, NZ* 1,2, 1989 *NZ*, 1990 *F, E, S, I, Nm* 1,2, *Bb*, 1991 *E, S, I, F* 1,2, *[WS, Arg, A]*
Ringer, P (Ebbw Vale, Llanelli) 1978 *NZ*, 1979 *S, I, F, E*, 1980 *F, E, NZ*
Roberts, C (Neath) 1958 *I, F*
Roberts, D E A (London Welsh) 1930 *E*
Roberts, E (Llanelli) 1886 *E*, 1887 *I*
Roberts, E J (Llanelli) 1888 *S, I*, 1889 *I*
Roberts, G J (Cardiff) 1985 *F* (R), 1987 *[I, Tg, C, E, A]*
Roberts, H M (Cardiff) 1960 *SA*, 1961 *E, S, I, F*, 1962 *S, F*, 1963 *I*
Roberts, J (Cardiff) 1927 *E, S, F, I, A*, 1928 *E, S, I, F*, 1929 *E, S, F, I*
Roberts, M G (London Welsh) 1971 *E, S, I, F*, 1973 *I, F*, 1975 *S*, 1979 *E*
Roberts, T (Newport, Risca) 1921 *S, F, I*, 1922 *E, S, I, F*, 1923 *E, S*
Roberts, W (Cardiff) 1929 *E*
Robins, J D (Birkenhead Park) 1950 *E, S, I, F*, 1951 *E, S, I, F*, 1953 *E, I, F*
Robins, R J (Pontypridd) 1953 *S*, 1954 *F, S*, 1955 *E, S, I, F*, 1956 *E, F*, 1957 *E, S, I, F*
Robinson, I R (Cardiff) 1974 *F, E*
Robinson, M F D (Swansea) 1999 *S, I, F*
Rocyn-Jones, D N (Cambridge U) 1925 *I*
Roderick, W B (Llanelli) 1884 *I*
Rogers, P J D (London Irish) 1999 *F, It, E*
Rosser, M A (Penarth) 1924 *S, F*
Rowland, E M (Lampeter) 1885 *E*
Rowlands, C F (Aberavon) 1926 *I*
Rowlands, D C T (Pontypool) 1963 *E, S, I, F, NZ*, 1964 *E, S, I, F, SA*, 1965 *E, S, I, F*
Rowlands, G (RAF, Cardiff) 1953 *NZ*, 1954 *E, F*, 1956 *F*

Rowlands, K A (Cardiff) 1962 *F, I*, 1963 *I*, 1965 *I, F*
Rowles, G R (Penarth) 1892 *E*
Rowley, M (Pontypridd) 1996 *SA*, 1997 *US, S, I, F, R*
Roy, W S (Cardiff) 1995 *[J (R)]*
Russell, S (London Welsh) 1987 *US*

Samuel, D (Swansea) 1891 *I*, 1893 *I*
Samuel, F (Mountain Ash) 1922 *S, I, F*
Samuel, J (Swansea) 1891 *I*
Scourfield, T (Torquay) 1930 *F*
Scrine, G F (Swansea) 1899 *E, S*, 1901 *I*
Shanklin, J L (London Welsh) 1970 *F*, 1972 *NZ*, 1973 *I, F*
Shaw, G (Neath) 1972 *NZ*, 1973 *E, S, I, F, A*, 1974 *S, I, F, E*, 1977 *I, F*
Shaw, T W (Newbridge) 1983 *R*
Shea, J (Newport) 1919 *NZA*, 1920 *E, S*, 1921 *E*
Shell, R C (Aberavon) 1973 *A* (R)
Simpson, H J (Cardiff) 1884 *E, S, I*
Sinkinson, B D (Neath) 1999 *F, It, E*
Skrimshire, R T (Newport) 1899 *E, S, I*
Skym, A (Llanelli) 1928 *E, S, I, F*, 1930 *E, S, I, F*, 1931 *E, S, F, I, SA*, 1932 *E, S, I*, 1933 *E, S, I*, 1935 *E*
Smith, J S (Cardiff) 1884 *E, I*, 1885 *E*
Sparks, B (Neath) 1954 *I*, 1955 *E, F*, 1956 *E, S, I*, 1957 *S*
Spiller, W J (Cardiff) 1910 *S, I*, 1911 *E, S, F, I*, 1912 *E, F, SA*, 1913 *E*
Squire, J (Newport, Pontypool) 1977 *I, F*, 1978 *E, S, I, F, A* 1, *NZ*, 1979 *S, I, F, E*, 1980 *F, E, S, I, NZ*, 1981 *E, S, I, F, A*, 1982 *I, F, E*, 1983 *E, S, I, F*
Stadden, W J W (Cardiff) 1884 *I*, 1886 *E, S*, 1887 *I*, 1888 *S, M*, 1890 *S, E*
Stephens, C (Bridgend) 1998 *E* (R)
Stephens, C J (Llanelli) 1992 *I, F, E, A*
Stephens, G (Neath) 1912 *E, S, I, F, SA*, 1913 *E, S, F, I*, 1919 *NZA*
Stephens, I (Bridgend) 1981 *E, S, I, F, A*, 1982 *I, F, E, S*, 1984 *I, F, E, A*
Stephens, Rev J G (Llanelli) 1922 *E, S, I, F*
Stephens, J R G (Neath) 1947 *E, S, F, I*, 1948 *I*, 1949 *S, I, F*, 1951 *F, SA*, 1952 *E, S, I, F*, 1953 *E, S, I, F, NZ*, 1954 *E, I*, 1955 *E, S, I, F*, 1956 *S, I, F*, 1957 *E, S, I, F*
Stock, A (Newport) 1924 *F, NZ*, 1926 *E, S*
Stone, P (Llanelli) 1949 *F*
Strand-Jones, J (Llanelli) 1902 *E, S, I*, 1903 *E, S*
Summers, R H B (Haverfordwest) 1881 *E*
Sutton, S (Pontypool, S Wales Police) 1982 *F, E*, 1987 *F, E, S, I, [C, NZ (R), A]*
Sweet-Escott, R B (Cardiff) 1891 *S*, 1894 *I*, 1895 *I*

Tamplin, W E (Cardiff) 1947 *S, F, I, A*, 1948 *E, S, F*
Tanner, H (Swansea, Cardiff) 1935 *NZ*, 1936 *E, S, I*, 1937 *E, S, I*, 1938 *E, S, I*, 1939 *E, S, I*, 1947 *E, S, F, I*, 1948 *E, S, F, I*, 1949 *E, S, I, F*
Tarr, D J (Swansea, Royal Navy) 1935 *NZ*
Taylor, A R (Cross Keys) 1937 *I*, 1938 *I*, 1939 *E*
Taylor, C G (Ruabon) 1884 *E, S, I*, 1885 *E, S*, 1886 *E, S*, 1887 *E, I*
Taylor, H T (Cardiff) 1994 *Pt, C, Fj, Tg, WS* (R), *R, It, SA*, 1995 *E, S, [J, NZ, I]*, *SA, Fj*, 1996 *It, E, S, I, F* 1, *A* 1,2, *It, A* 3
Taylor, J (London Welsh) 1967 *S, I, F, E, NZ*, 1968 *I, F*, 1969 *S, I, F, E, NZ* 1, *A*, 1970 *F*, 1971 *S, I, F*, 1972 *E, S, F, NZ*, 1973 *E, S, I, F*
Taylor, M (Pontypool, Swansea) 1994 *SA*, 1995 *F, E, SA* (R), 1998 *Z, SA* 1,2, *Arg*, 1999 *I, F, It, E*
Thomas, A (Newport) 1963 *NZ*, 1964 *F*
Thomas, A C (Bristol, Swansea) 1996 *It, E, S, I, F* 2(R), *SA*, 1997 *US, S, I, F, US* 1,2, *C, R, NZ* (t), 1998 *It, E, S* (R), *Z, SA* 1
Thomas, A G (Swansea, Cardiff) 1952 *E, S, I, F*, 1953 *S, I, F*, 1954 *E, I, F*, 1955 *S, I, F*
Thomas, Bob (Swansea) 1900 *E, S, I*, 1901 *E*
Thomas, Brian (Neath, Cambridge U) 1963 *E, S, I, F, NZ*, 1964 *E, S, I, F, SA*, 1965 *E, I*, 1966 *E, S, I*, 1967 *NZ*, 1969 *S, I, F, E, NZ* 1,2
Thomas, C (Bridgend) 1925 *E, S*
Thomas, C J (Newport) 1888 *I, M*, 1889 *S, I*, 1890 *S, E, I*, 1891 *E, I*
Thomas, D (Aberavon) 1961 *I*
Thomas, D (Llanelli) 1954 *I*
Thomas, Dick (Mountain Ash) 1906 *SA*, 1908 *F, I*, 1909 *S*
Thomas, D J (Swansea) 1904 *E*, 1908 *A*, 1910 *E, S, I*, 1911 *E, S, F, I*, 1912 *E*

Thomas, D J (Swansea) 1930 *S, I*, 1932 *E, S, I*, 1933 *E, S*, 1934 *E*, 1935 *E, S, I*
Thomas, D L (Neath) 1937 *E*
Thomas, E (Newport) 1904 *S, I*, 1909 *S, F, I*, 1910 *F*
Thomas, G (Llanelli) 1923 *E, S, F, I*
Thomas, G (Newport) 1888 *M*, 1890 *I*, 1891 *S*
Thomas, G (Bridgend, Cardiff) 1995 *[J, NZ, I]*, *SA, Fj*, 1996 *F* 1, *A* 1,2, *Bb, F* 2, *It, A* 3, 1997 *US, S, I, F, E, US* 1,2, *C, R, Tg, NZ*, 1998 *It, E, S, I, F, SA* 2, *Arg*, 1999 *F* (R), *It, E*
Thomas, H (Llanelli) 1912 *F*
Thomas, H (Neath) 1936 *E, S, I*, 1937 *E, S, I*
Thomas, H W (Swansea) 1912 *SA*, 1913 *E*
Thomas, I (Bryncethin) 1924 *E*
Thomas, L C (Cardiff) 1885 *E, S*
Thomas, M C (Newport, Devonport Services) 1949 *F*, 1950 *E, S, I, F*, 1951 *E, S, I, F, SA*, 1952 *E, S, I, F*, 1953 *E*, 1956 *E, S, I, F*, 1957 *E, S*, 1958 *E, S, I, F*, 1959 *I, F*
Thomas, M G (St Bart's Hospital) 1919 *NZA*, 1921 *S, F, I*, 1923 *F*, 1924 *E*
Thomas, N (Bath) 1996 *SA* (R), 1997 *US* 1 (R), 2, *C* (R), *R, Tg, NZ*, 1998 *Z, SA* 1
Thomas, R (Pontypool) 1909 *F, I*, 1911 *S, F*, 1912 *E, S, SA*, 1913 *E*
Thomas, R C C (Swansea) 1949 *F*, 1952 *I, F*, 1953 *S, I, F, NZ*, 1954 *I, F, S*, 1955 *S, I*, 1956 *E, S, I*, 1957 *E*, 1958 *A, E, S, I, F*, 1959 *E, S, I, F*
Thomas, R L (London Welsh) 1889 *S, I*, 1890 *I*, 1891 *E, S, I*, 1892 *E*
Thomas, S (Llanelli) 1890 *S, E*, 1891 *I*
Thomas, W D (Llanelli) 1966 *A*, 1968 *S, I, F*, 1969 *E, NZ* 2, *A*, 1970 *SA, E, I, F*, 1971 *E, S, I, F*, 1972 *E, S, F, NZ*, 1973 *E, S, I, F*, 1974 *E*
Thomas, W G (Llanelli, Waterloo, Swansea) 1927 *E, S, F, I*, 1929 *E, S*, 1931 *E, S, SA*, 1932 *E, S, I*, 1933 *E, S, I*
Thomas, W H (Llandovery Coll, Cambridge U) 1885 *S*, 1886 *E, S*, 1887 *E, S*, 1888 *S, I*, 1890 *E, I*, 1891 *S, I*
Thomas, W J (Cardiff) 1961 *F*, 1963 *F*
Thomas, W J L (Llanelli, Cardiff) 1995 *SA, Fj*, 1996 *It, E, S, I, F* 1, 1996 *Bb* (R), 1997 *US*
Thomas, W L (Newport) 1894 *S*, 1895 *E, I*
Thomas, W T (Abertillery) 1930 *E*
Thompson, J F (Cross Keys) 1923 *E*
Thorburn, P H (Neath) 1985 *F, E, Fj*, 1986 *E, S, I, F*, 1987 *F, [I, Tg, C, E, NZ, A]*, *US*, 1988 *S, I, F, WS, R* (R), 1989 *S, I, F, E, NZ*, 1990 *F, E, S, I, Nm* 1,2, *Bb*, 1991 *E, S, I, F* 1, *A*
Titley, M H (Bridgend, Swansea) 1983 *E, M*, 1984 *S, I, F, E, A*, 1985 *S, I, Fj*, 1986 *F, Fj, Tg, WS*, 1990 *F, E*
Towers, W H (Swansea) 1887 *I*, 1888 *M*
Travers, G (Pill Harriers) 1903 *E, S, I*, 1905 *E, S, I, NZ*, 1906 *E, S, I, SA*, 1907 *E, S, I*, 1908 *E, S, F, I, A*, 1909 *E, S, I*, 1911 *S, F, I*
Travers, W H (Newport) 1937 *S, I*, 1938 *E, S, I*, 1939 *E, S, I*, 1949 *E, S, I, F*
Treharne, E (Pontypridd) 1881 *E*, 1883 *E*
Trew, W J (Swansea) 1900 *E, S, I*, 1901 *E, S*, 1903 *S*, 1905 *S*, 1906 *S*, 1907 *E, S*, 1908 *E, S, F, I, A*, 1909 *E, S*, *F, I*, 1910 *F, E, S*, 1911 *E, S, F, I*, 1912 *S, F*, 1913 *S, F*
Trott, R F (Cardiff) 1948 *E, S, F, I*, 1949 *E, S, I, F*
Truman, W H (Llanelli) 1934 *E*, 1935 *E*
Trump, L C (Newport) 1912 *E, S, I, F*
Turnbull, B R (Cardiff) 1925 *I*, 1927 *E, S*, 1928 *E, F*, 1930 *S*
Turnbull, M J L (Cardiff) 1933 *E, I*
Turner, P (Newbridge) 1989 *I* (R), *F, E*

Uzzell, H (Newport) 1912 *E, S, I, F*, 1913 *S, F, I*, 1914 *E, S, F, I*, 1920 *E, S, F, I*
Uzzell, J R (Newport) 1963 *NZ*, 1965 *E, S, I, F*

Vickery, W E (Aberavon) 1938 *E, S, I*, 1939 *E*
Vile, T H (Newport) 1908 *E, S*, 1910 *I*, 1912 *I, F, SA*, 1913 *E*, 1921 *S*
Vincent, H C (Bangor) 1882 *I*
Voyle, M J (Newport, Llanelli) 1996 *A* 1(t), *F* 2, 1997 *E, US* 1,2, *C, Tg, NZ*, 1998 *It, E, S, I, F, Arg* (R), 1999 *S* (R), *I* (t), *It* (R)

Wakeford, J D M (S Wales Police) 1988 *WS, R*
Waldron, R (Neath) 1965 *E, S, I, F*
Walker, N (Cardiff) 1993 *I, F, J*, 1994 *S, F, E, Pt, Sp*, 1995 *F, E*, 1997 *US* 1,2, *C, R* (R), *Tg, NZ*, 1998 *E*
Waller, P D (Newport) 1908 *A*, 1909 *E, S, F, I*, 1910 *F*

Walne, N J (Richmond) 1999 *It* (R), *E* (R)
Walters, N (Llanelli) 1902 *E*
Wanbon, R (Aberavon) 1968 *E*
Ward, W S (Cross Keys) 1934 *S, I*
Warlow, J (Llanelli) 1962 *I*
Waters, D R (Newport) 1986 *E, S, I, F*
Waters, K (Newbridge) 1991 [*WS*]
Watkins, D (Newport) 1963 *E, S, I, F, NZ,* 1964 *E, S, I, F, SA,* 1965 *E, S, I, F,* 1966 *E, S, I, F,* 1967 *I, F, E*
Watkins, E (Neath) 1924 *E, S, I, F*
Watkins, E (Blaina) 1926 *S, I, F*
Watkins, E (Cardiff) 1935 *NZ,* 1937 *S, I,* 1938 *E, S, I,* 1939 *E, S*
Watkins, H (Llanelli) 1904 *S, I,* 1905 *E, S, I,* 1906 *E*
Watkins, I J (Ebbw Vale) 1988 *E* (R), *S, I, F, NZ* 2, *R,* 1989 *S, I, F, E*
Watkins, L (Oxford U, Llandaff) 1881 *E*
Watkins, M J (Newport) 1984 *I, F, E, A*
Watkins, S J (Newport, Cardiff) 1964 *S, I, F,* 1965 *E, S, I, F,* 1966 *E, S, I, F, A,* 1967 *S, I, F, E, NZ,* 1968 *E, S,* 1969 *S, I, F, E, NZ* 1, 1970 *E, I*
Watkins, W R (Newport) 1959 *F*
Watts, D (Maesteg) 1914 *E, S, F, I*
Watts, J (Llanelli) 1907 *E, S, I,* 1908 *E, S, F, I, A,* 1909 *S, F, I*
Watts, W (Llanelli) 1914 *E*
Watts, W H (Newport) 1892 *E, S, I,* 1893 *E, S, I,* 1894 *E, S, I,* 1895 *E, I,* 1896 *E*
Weatherley, D J (Swansea) 1998 *Z*
Weaver, D (Swansea) 1964 *E*
Webb, J (Abertillery) 1907 *S,* 1908 *E, S, F, I, A,* 1909 *E, S, F, I,* 1910 *F, E, S, I,* 1911 *E, S, F, I,* 1912 *E, S*
Webb, J E (Newport) 1888 *M,* 1889 *S*
Webbe, G M C (Bridgend) 1986 *Tg* (R), *WS,* 1987 *F, E, S,* [*Tg*], *US,* 1988 *F* (R), *NZ* 1, *R*
Webster, R E (Swansea) 1987 [*A*], 1990 *Bb,* 1991 [*Arg, A*], 1992 *I, F, E, S, A,* 1993 *E, S, I, F*
Wells, G T (Cardiff) 1955 *E, S,* 1957 *I, F,* 1958 *A, E, S*
Westacott, D (Cardiff) 1906 *I*
Wetter, H (Newport) 1912 *SA,* 1913 *E*
Wetter, J J (Newport) 1914 *S, F, I,* 1920 *E, S, F, I,* 1921 *E,* 1924 *I, NZ*
Wheel, G A D (Swansea) 1974 *I, E* (R), 1975 *F, E, I, A,* 1976 *E, S, I, F,* 1977 *I, F, E,* 1978 *E, S, I, F, A* 1,2, *NZ,* 1979 *S, I,* 1980 *F, E, S, I,* 1981 *E, S, I, F, A,* 1982 *I*
Wheeler, P J (Aberavon) 1967 *NZ,* 1968 *E*
Whitefoot, J (Cardiff) 1984 *A* (R), 1985 *S, I, F, E, Fj,* 1986 *E, S, I, F, Fj, Tg, WS,* 1987 *F, E, S, I,* [*I, C*]
Whitfield, J (Newport) 1919 *NZA,* 1920 *E, S, F, I,* 1921 *E,* 1922 *E, S, I, F,* 1924 *S, I*
Whitson, G K (Newport) 1956 *F,* 1960 *S, I*
Wilkins, G (Bridgend) 1994 *Tg*
Williams, A (Bridgend, Swansea) 1990 *Nm* 2 (R), 1995 *Fj* (R)
Williams, B (Llanelli) 1920 *S, F, I*
Williams, B H (Neath, Richmond) 1996 *F* 2, 1997 *R, Tg, NZ,* 1998 *It, E, Z* (R), *SA* 1, *Arg* (R), 1999 *S* (R), *I, It* (R)
Williams, B L (Cardiff) 1947 *E, S, F, I, A,* 1948 *E, S, F, I,* 1949 *E, S, I,* 1951 *I, SA,* 1952 *S,* 1953 *E, S, I, F, NZ,* 1954 *S,* 1955 *E*
Williams, B R (Neath) 1990 *S, I, Bb,* 1991 *E, S*
Williams, C (Llanelli) 1924 *NZ,* 1925 *E*
Williams, C (Aberavon, Swansea) 1977 *E, S,* 1980 *F, E, S, I, NZ,* 1983 *E*
Williams, C D (Cardiff, Neath) 1955 *F,* 1956 *F*
Williams, D (Llanelli) 1998 *SA* 1 (R)
Williams, D (Ebbw Vale) 1963 *E, S, I, F,* 1964 *E, S, I, F, SA,* 1965 *E, S, I, F,* 1966 *E, S, I, A,* 1967 *F, E, NZ,* 1968 *E,* 1969 *S, I, F, E, NZ* 1,2, *A,* 1970 *SA, S, E, I,* 1971 *E, S, I, F*
Williams, D B (Newport, Swansea) 1978 *A* 1, 1981 *E, S*
Williams, E (Neath) 1924 *NZ,* 1925 *F*
Williams, E (Aberavon) 1925 *E, S*
Williams, F L (Cardiff) 1929 *S, F, I,* 1930 *E, S, I, F,* 1931 *F, I, SA,* 1932 *E, S, I,* 1933 *I*
Williams, G (Aberavon) 1936 *E, S, I*
Williams, G (London Welsh) 1950 *I, F,* 1951 *E, S, I, F, SA,* 1952 *E, S, I, F,* 1953 *NZ,* 1954 *E*
Williams, G (Bridgend) 1981 *I, F,* 1982 *E* (R), *S*

Williams, G P (Bridgend) 1980 *NZ,* 1981 *E, S, A,* 1982 *I*
Williams, J (Blaina) 1920 *E, S, F, I,* 1921 *S, F, I*
Williams, J F (London Welsh) 1905 *I, NZ,* 1906 *S, SA*
Williams, J J (Llanelli) 1973 *F* (R), *A,* 1974 *S, I, F, E,* 1975 *F, E, S, I, A,* 1976 *E, S, I, F,* 1977 *I, F, E, S,* 1978 *E, S, I, F, A* 1,2, *NZ,* 1979 *S, I, F, E*
Williams, J L (Cardiff) 1906 *SA,* 1907 *E, S, I,* 1908 *E, S, I, A,* 1909 *E, S, F, I,* 1910 *I,* 1911 *E, S, F, I*
Williams, J P R (London Welsh, Bridgend) 1969 *S, I, F, E, NZ* 1,2, *A,* 1970 *SA, S, E, I, F,* 1971 *E, S, I, F,* 1972 *E, S, F, NZ,* 1973 *E, S, I, F, A,* 1974 *S, I, F,* 1975 *F, E, S, I, A,* 1976 *E, S, I, F,* 1977 *I, F, E, S,* 1978 *E, S, I, F, A* 1,2, *NZ,* 1979 *S, I, F, E,* 1980 *NZ,* 1981 *E, S*
Williams, L (Llanelli, Cardiff) 1947 *E, S, F, I, A,* 1948 *I,* 1949 *E*
Williams, L H (Cardiff) 1957 *S, I, F,* 1958 *E, S, I, F,* 1959 *E, S, I,* 1961 *F,* 1962 *E, S*
Williams, M (Newport) 1923 *F*
Williams, M E (Pontypridd) 1996 *Bb, F* 2, *It* (t), 1998 *It, E, Z, SA* 2, *Arg,* 1999 *S, I*
Williams, O (Bridgend) 1990 *Nm* 2
Williams, O (Llanelli) 1947 *E, S, A,* 1948 *E, S, F, I*
Williams, R (Llanelli) 1954 *S,* 1957 *F,* 1958 *A*
Williams, R D G (Newport) 1881 *E*
Williams, R F (Cardiff) 1912 *SA,* 1913 *E, S,* 1914 *I*
Williams, R H (Llanelli) 1954 *I, F, S,* 1955 *S, I, F,* 1956 *E, S, I,* 1957 *E, S, I, F,* 1958 *A, E, S, I, F,* 1959 *E, S, I, F,* 1960 *E*
Williams, S (Llanelli) 1947 *E, S, F, I,* 1948 *S, F*
Williams, S A (Aberavon) 1939 *E, S, I*
Williams, S M (Neath, Cardiff) 1994 *Tg,* 1996 *E* (t), *A* 1,2, *Bb, F* 2, *It, A* 3, *SA,* 1997 *US, S, I, F, E, US* 1,2 (R), *C, R* (R), *Tg* (R), *NZ* (t + R)
Williams, T (Pontypridd) 1882 *I*
Williams, T (Swansea) 1888 *S, I*
Williams, T (Swansea) 1912 *I,* 1913 *F,* 1914 *E, S, F, I*
Williams, Tudor (Swansea) 1921 *F*
Williams, T G (Cross Keys) 1935 *S, I, NZ,* 1936 *E, S, I,* 1937 *S, I*
Williams, W A (Crumlin) 1927 *E, S, F, I*
Williams, W A (Newport) 1952 *I, F,* 1953 *E*
Williams, W E O (Cardiff) 1887 *S, I,* 1889 *S,* 1890 *S, E*
Williams, W H (Pontymister) 1900 *E, S, I,* 1901 *E*
Williams, W O G (Swansea, Devonport Services) 1951 *F, SA,* 1952 *E, S, I, F,* 1953 *E, S, I, F, NZ,* 1954 *E, I, F, S,* 1955 *E, S, I, F,* 1956 *E, S, I*
Williams, W P J (Neath) 1974 *I, F*
Williams-Jones, H (S Wales Police, Llanelli) 1989 *S* (R), 1990 *F* (R), *I,* 1991 *A,* 1992 *S, A,* 1993 *E, S, I, F, Z* 1, *Nm,* 1994 *Fj, Tg, WS* (R), *It* (t), 1995 *E* (R)
Willis, W R (Cardiff) 1950 *E, S, I, F,* 1951 *E, S, I, F, SA,* 1952 *E, S,* 1953 *S, NZ,* 1954 *E, I, F, S,* 1955 *E, S, I, F*
Wiltshire, M L (Aberavon) 1967 *NZ,* 1968 *E, S, F*
Windsor, R W (Pontypool) 1973 *A,* 1974 *S, I, F, E,* 1975 *F, E, S, I, A,* 1976 *E, S, I, F,* 1977 *I, F, E, S,* 1978 *E, S, I, F, A* 1,2, *NZ,* 1979 *S, I, F*
Winfield, H B (Cardiff) 1903 *I,* 1904 *E, S, I,* 1905 *NZ,* 1906 *E, S, I,* 1907 *S, I,* 1908 *E, S, F, I, A*
Winmill, S (Cross Keys) 1921 *E, S, F, I*
Wintle, M E (Llanelli) 1996 *It*
Wintle, R V (London Welsh) 1988 *WS* (R)
Wooller, W (Sale, Cambridge U, Cardiff) 1933 *E, S, I,* 1935 *E, S, I, NZ,* 1936 *E, S, I,* 1937 *E, S, I,* 1938 *S, I,* 1939 *E, S, I*
Wyatt, C P (Llanelli) 1998 *Z* (R), *SA* 1 (R),2, *Arg,* 1999 *S, I, F, It, E*
Wyatt, D (Pontypridd) 1997 *Tg*
Wyatt, M A (Swansea) 1983 *E, S, I, F,* 1984 *A,* 1985 *S, I,* 1987 *E, S, I*

Young, D (Swansea, Cardiff) 1987 [*E, NZ*], *US,* 1988 *E, S, I, F, NZ* 1,2, *WS, R,* 1989 *S, NZ,* 1990 *F,* 1996 *A* 3, *SA,* 1997 *US, S, I, F, E, R, NZ,* 1998 *It, E, S, I, F,* 1999 *I, E* (R)
Young, G A (Cardiff) 1886 *E, S*
Young, J (Harrogate, RAF, London Welsh) 1968 *S, I, F,* 1969 *S, I, F, E, NZ* 1, 1970 *E, I, F,* 1971 *E, S, I, F,* 1972 *E, S, F, NZ,* 1973 *E, S, I, F*

WELSH INTERNATIONAL RECORDS
(up to 30 April 1999)

MATCH RECORDS

MOST CONSECUTIVE TEST WINS

11 1907 *I*, 1908 *E, S, F, I, A*, 1909 *E, S, F, I*, 1910 *F*

8 1970 *F*, 1971 *E, S, I, F*, 1972 *E, S, F*

MOST CONSECUTIVE TESTS WITHOUT DEFEAT

P	W	D	Period
11	11	0	1907–10
8	8	0	1970–72

MOST POINTS IN A MATCH
by the team

Pts	Opp	Venue	Year
102	Pt	Lisbon	1994
70	R	Wrexham	1997
60	It	Treviso	1999
57	J	Bloemfontein	1995
55	J	Cardiff	1993

by a player

30 by N R Jenkins v Italy at Treviso 1999
24 by N R Jenkins v Canada at Cardiff 1993
24 by N R Jenkins v Italy at Cardiff 1994
23 by A C Thomas v Romania at Wrexham 1997
23 by N R Jenkins v Argentina at Llanelli 1998
22 by N R Jenkins v Portugal at Lisbon 1994
22 by N R Jenkins v Japan at Bloemfontein 1995
22 by N R Jenkins v England at Wembley 1999

MOST TRIES IN A MATCH
by the team

T	Opp	Venue	Year
16	Pt	Lisbon	1994
11	F	Paris	1909
11	R	Wrexham	1997
10	F	Swansea	1910
9	F	Cardiff	1908
9	J	Cardiff	1993

by a player

4 by W Llewellyn v England at Swansea 1899

4 by R A Gibbs v France at Cardiff 1908
4 by M C R Richards v England at Cardiff 1969
4 by I C Evans v Canada at Invercargill 1987
4 by N Walker v Portugal at Lisbon 1994
4 by G Thomas v Italy at Treviso 1999

MOST CONVERSIONS IN A MATCH
by the team

C	Opp	Venue	Year
11	Pt	Lisbon	1994
8	F	Swansea	1910
7	F	Paris	1909

by a player

11 by N R Jenkins v Portugal at Lisbon 1994
8 by J Bancroft v France at Swansea 1910
6 by J Bancroft v France at Paris 1909

MOST PENALTY GOALS IN A MATCH
by the team

P	Opp	Venue	Year
8	C	Cardiff	1993
7	It	Cardiff	1994
6	F	Cardiff	1982
6	Tg	Nuku'alofa	1994
6	E	Wembley	1999

by a player

8 by N R Jenkins v Canada at Cardiff 1993
7 by N R Jenkins v Italy at Cardiff 1994
6 by G Evans v France at Cardiff 1982
6 by N R Jenkins v Tonga at Nuku'alofa 1994
6 by N R Jenkins v England at Wembley 1999

MOST DROPPED GOALS IN A MATCH
by the team

D	Opp	Venue	Year
2	S	Swansea	1912
2	S	Cardiff	1914

2	E	Swansea	1920
2	S	Swansea	1921
2	F	Paris	1930
2	E	Cardiff	1971
2	F	Cardiff	1978
2	E	Twick-enham	1984
2	I	Wellngtn	1987
2	S	Cardiff	1988

by a player

2 by J Shea v England at Swansea	1920
2 by A Jenkins v Scotland at Swansea	1921
2 by B John v England at Cardiff	1971
2 by M Dacey v England at Twickenham	1984
2 by J Davies v Ireland at Wellington	1987
2 by J Davies v Scotland at Cardiff	1988

CAREER RECORDS

MOST CAPPED PLAYERS

Caps	Player	Career
72	I C Evans	1987–98
64	N R Jenkins	1991–99
62	G O Llewellyn	1989–98
57	N R Jenkins	1991–98
55	J P R Williams	1969–81
54	R N Jones	1986–95
53	G O Edwards	1967–78
46	T G R Davies	1966–78
46	P T Davies	1985–95
44	K J Jones	1947–57
42	M R Hall	1988–95
42	G R Jenkins	1991–99

MOST CONSECUTIVE TESTS

Tests	Player	Span
53	G O Edwards	1967–78
43	K J Jones	1947–56
39	G Price	1975–83
38	T M Davies	1969–76
33	W J Bancroft	1890–1901

MOST TESTS AS CAPTAIN

Tests	Captain	Span
28	I C Evans	1991–95
18	A J Gould	1889–97
17	J M Humphreys	1995–97
14	D C T Rowlands	1963–65
14	W J Trew	1907–13

MOST TESTS IN INDIVIDUAL POSITIONS

Full-back J P R Williams	54	1969–81
Wing I C Evans	72	1987–98
Centre I S Gibbs	39	1991–99
Fly-half N R Jenkins	47	1991–99
Scrum-half { G O Edwards	53	1967–78
{ R N Jones	53	1986–95
Prop G Price	41	1975–83
Hooker G R Jenkins	41	1991–99
Lock G O Llewellyn	61	1989–98
Flanker W D Morris	32	1967–74
No. 8 T M Davies	38	1969–76

MOST POINTS IN TESTS

Pts	Player	Tests	Career
726	N R Jenkins	64	1991–99
304	P H Thorburn	37	1985–91
173	A C Thomas	20	1996–98
166	P Bennett	29	1969–78
157	I C Evans	72	1987–98

MOST TRIES IN TESTS

Tries	Player	Tests	Career
33	I C Evans	72	1987–98
20	G O Edwards	53	1967–78
20	T G R Davies	46	1966–78
18	G Thomas	33	1995–99
17	R A Gibbs	16	1906–11
17	J L Williams	17	1906–11
17	K J Jones	44	1947–57

MOST CONVERSIONS IN TESTS

Cons	Player	Tests	Career
93	N R Jenkins	64	1991–99
43	P H Thorburn	37	1985–91
38	J Bancroft	18	1909–14
24	A C Thomas	20	1996–98
20	W J Bancroft	33	1890–1901

MOST PENALTY GOALS IN TESTS

Pens	Player	Tests	Career
164	N R Jenkins	64	1991–99
70	P H Thorburn	37	1985–91
36	P Bennett	29	1969–78
35	S P Fenwick	30	1975–81
25	A C Thomas	20	1996–98

MOST DROPPED GOALS IN TESTS

Drops	Player	Tests	Career
13	J Davies	32	1985–97
8	B John	25	1966–72
7	W G Davies	21	1978–85

INTERNATIONAL CHAMPIONSHIP RECORDS

Record	Detail		Set
Most points in season	109	in four matches	1999
Most tries in season	21	in four matches	1910
Highest score	49	49–14 v France	1910
Biggest win	35	49–14 v France	1910
Highest score conceded	60	26–60 v England	1998
Biggest defeat	51	0–51 v France	1998
Most appearances	45	G O Edwards	1967–78
Most points in matches	284	N R Jenkins	1991–99
Most points in season	64	N R Jenkins	1999
Most points in match	22	N R Jenkins	v England, 1999
Most tries in matches	18	G O Edwards	1967–78
Most tries in season	6	M C R Richards	1969
Most tries in match	4	W Llewellyn	v England, 1899
	4	M C R Richards	v England, 1969
Most cons in matches	32	J Bancroft	1909–1914
Most cons in season	9	J Bancroft	1910
	9	J A Bassett	1931
Most cons in match	8	J Bancroft	v France, 1910
Most pens in matches	68	N R Jenkins	1991–99
Most pens in season	16	P H Thorburn	1986
	16	N R Jenkins	1999
Most pens in match	6	G Evans	v France, 1982
	6	N R Jenkins	v England, 1999
Most drops in matches	8	J Davies	1985–97
Most drops in season	4	J Davies	1988
Most drops in match	2	J Shea	v England, 1920
	2	A Jenkins	v Scotland, 1921
	2	B John	v England, 1971
	2	M Dacey	v England, 1984
	2	J Davies	v Scotland, 1988

MAJOR TOUR RECORDS

Record	Detail	Year	Place
Most individual points	89 by N R Jenkins	1993	Africa
Most points in match	34 by L Jarvis	1997 v Southern RFU USA	Namibia
Most tries in match	5 by G Thomas	1996 v W Australia	Perth

MISCELLANEOUS RECORDS

Record	Holder	Detail
Longest Test career	W J Trew	14 seasons, 1899–1900 to 1912–13
	T H Vile	14 seasons, 1907–08 to 1920–21
	H Tanner	14 seasons, 1935–36 to 1948–49
Youngest Test cap	N Biggs	18 yrs 49 days in 1888
Oldest Test cap	T H Vile	38 yrs 152 days in 1921

WELSH INTERNATIONAL CAREER RECORDS *(up to 30 April 1999)*

Player	Debut	Caps since last season	Caps	T	C	PG	DG	Pts
K A Morgan	1997 v US		8	2	0	0	0	10
D J Weatherley	1998 v Z	1998 Z	1	0	0	0	0	0
S P Howarth	1998 v SA	1998 SA 2, Arg, 1999 S, I, F, It, E	7	2	0	0	0	10
B I Hayward	1998 v Z	1998 Z(R), SA 1	2	3	0	0	0	15
D Williams	1998 v SA	1998 SA 1(R)	1	0	0	0	0	0
G R Evans	1998 v SA	1998 SA 1	1	0	0	0	0	0
M F D Robinson	1999 v S	1999 S, I, F	3	0	0	0	0	0
R Rees	1998 v Z	1998 Z	1	2	0	0	0	10
N J Walne	1999 v It	1999 It(R), E(R)	2	0	0	0	0	0
W T Proctor	1992 v A	1998 Z	38	11	0	0	0	55
D R James	1996 v A	1998 Z, SA 1,2, Arg, 1999 S, I, F, It, E	16	4	0	0	0	20
S Jones	1998 v SA	1998 SA 1(R)	1	0	0	0	0	0
G Thomas	1995 v J	1998 SA 2, Arg, 1999 F(R), It, E	33	18	0	0	0	90
N Boobyer	1993 v Z	1999 It(R)	7	0	0	0	0	0
J S Funnell	1998 v Z	1998 Z(R), SA 1	2	0	0	0	0	0
A G Bateman	1990 v S	1999 S	16	6	0	0	0	30
L B Davies	1996 v It		18	4	0	0	0	20
I S Gibbs	1991 v E	1998 SA 2, Arg, 1999 S, I, F, It, E	39	6	0	0	0	30
M Taylor	1994 v SA	1998 Z, SA 1,2, Arg, 1999 I, F, It, E	12	1	0	0	0	5
N R Jenkins	1991 v E	1998 SA 2, Arg, 1999 S, I, F, It, E	64	8	93	164	3	726
A C Thomas	1996 v It	1998 Z, SA 1	20	10	24	25	0	173
L Jarvis	1997 v R		1	0	1	0	0	2
Paul John	1994 v Tg	1998 Z(R), SA 1	10	1	0	0	0	5
R Howley	1996 v E	1998 Z, SA 2, Arg, 1999 S, I, F, It, E	31	6	0	0	0	30
D S Llewellyn	1998 v SA	1998 SA 1(R), 1999 F(R), It(R)	3	0	0	0	0	0
G R Jenkins	1991 v F	1998 Z, SA 1(R), 1999 I(R), F, It, E	42	1	0	0	0	5
J M Humphreys	1995 v NZ	1998 SA 2, Arg, 1999 S	29	2	0	0	0	10
B H Williams	1996 v F	1998 Z(R), SA 1, Arg(R), 1999 S(R), I, It(R)	12	2	0	0	0	10
P J D Rogers	1999 v F	1999 F, It, E	3	0	0	0	0	0
S C John	1995 v S		5	0	0	0	0	0
D R Morris	1998 v Z	1998 Z, SA 1(R),2(R), 1999 S, I, It(R)	6	0	0	0	0	0
A L P Lewis	1996 v It	1998 SA 2, Arg, 1999 F(R), E(R)	14	0	0	0	0	0
B R Evans	1998 v SA	1998 SA 2(R), 1999 F, It, E	4	0	0	0	0	0
M Griffiths	1988 v WS	1998 SA 1	35	0	0	0	0	0
D Young	1987 v E	1999 I, E(R)	30	1	0	0	0	4

C T Anthony	1997 v US	1998 *SA* 2, *Arg*, 1999 *S*, *I*(R)	8	1	0	0	0	5
J D Davies	1991 v I	1998 *Z*, *SA* 1	34	1	0	0	0	0
I M Gough	1998 v SA	1998 *SA* 1, 1999 *S*	2	0	0	0	0	0
C P Wyatt	1998 v Z	1998 *Z*(R), *SA* 1(R),2, *Arg*, 1999 *S*, *I*, *F*, *It*, *E*	9	0	0	0	0	0
G O Llewellyn	1989 v NZ		62	5	0	0	0	24
C Stephens	1998 v E		1	0	0	0	0	0
M A Jones	1987 v S	1998 *Z*	15	2	0	0	0	8
A P Moore	1995 v SA	1998 *Z*, *SA* 1	7	0	0	0	0	0
S J Moore	1997 v C		3	0	0	0	0	0
M J Voyle	1996 v A	1998 *Arg*(R), 1999 *S*(R), *I*(t), *It*(R)	17	0	0	0	0	0
N Thomas	1996 v SA	1998 *Z*, *SA* 1	9	0	0	0	0	0
J C Quinnell	1995 v Fj	1998 *SA* 2, *Arg*, 1999 *I*, *F*, *It*, *E*	12	3	0	0	0	15
K P Jones	1996 v Bb	1998 *SA* 1	10	0	0	0	0	0
M E Williams	1996 v Bb	1998 *Z*, *SA* 2, *Arg*, 1999 *S*, *I*	10	0	0	0	0	0
B D Sinkinson	1999 v F	1999 *F*, *It*, *E*	3	0	0	0	0	0
C L Charvis	1996 v A	1998 *Z*(R), *SA* 1,2, *Arg*, 1999 *S*, *I*, *F*, *It*, *E*	20	3	0	0	0	15
R C Appleyard	1997 v C		9	0	0	0	0	0
S M Williams	1994 v Tg		20	1	0	0	0	5
G Lewis	1998 v SA	1998 *SA* 1(R), 1999 *It*(R)	2	0	0	0	0	0
L S Quinnell	1993 v C	1998 *Z*, *SA* 2, *Arg*, 1999 *S*, *I*, *F*, *It*, *E*	25	5	0	0	0	25

Howarth's way. The exciting new Welsh recruit, former All Black Shane Howarth, brought direction and thrust to the Welsh back line throughout the season.

WELSH CLUBS 1998-99

Aberavon

Year of formation 1876
Ground Talbot Athletic Ground, Manor Street, Port Talbot, West Glamorgan Tel: Port Talbot (01639) 886038 and 882427
Colours Red and black hoops
Captain 1998-99 I Greenslade / J Hughes
WRU Leagues 1998-99 Div 1 8th
SWALEC Cup 1998-99 Lost 12-20 to Cardiff (6th round)

Promotion brought much heartache for the Wizards. They secured just two victories in League One (home fixtures against Bridgend and Newport) to finish bottom of the division. Llanelli gobbled them up by 83-10 at Stradey and there were six scores over the half-century mark against them in league matches alone. More disasters engulfed them in the European Shield, where the only success came by 18-6 against Spain at El Ferol. Aberavon lost by 87-10 at Castres and by 97-13 at Montferrand; but they gave visitors Cardiff a fright in the SWALEC Cup before going out, many thought unluckily, by 20-12. Head coach Glen Ball stood down and Steve Brown joined in that role from Bridgend. Cerith Rees, aged 20, a highly-talented fly-half, proved the Wizards' outstanding performer. Among the signings were New Zealander Aaron Hamilton, from Hawke's Bay, who had been in the side that defeated the Lions in 1993; centre Gary Schofield, who played a record 46 rugby league Tests for Great Britain (13 as captain) from 1984 to 1994; Crispin Cormack (from Pontypridd); and Justin Burnell and Paul Owen (from Bridgend).

League Record 1998-99

Date	Venue	Opponents	Result	Scorers
29 Aug	A	Bridgend	10-45	*T:* S McIntosh *C:* C Cormack *PG:* C Cormack
5 Sep	H	Newport	5-47	*T:* R Lewis
8 Sep	H	Ebbw Vale	5-29	*T:* N Stork
12 Sep	A	Pontypridd	28-64	*T:* J Hughes, E Lewsey, R Morris, D Neill *C:* C Cormack 2, N Stork 2
3 Oct	H	Neath	27-37	*T:* R Lewis 2, M Evans *C:* N Stork 3 *PG:* N Stork 2
21 Nov	A	Caerphilly	19-49	*T:* D Griffiths 2, G Schofield *C:* P Roberts 2
28 Nov	H	Llanelli	12-48	*T:* C Rees, penalty try *C:* C Rees
5 Dec	A	Newport	16-36	*T:* H Merrett *C:* C Rees *PG:* C Rees 3
12 Dec	H	Bridgend	16-6	*T:* N Stork *C:* C Rees *PG:* C Rees 3
2 Jan	H	Pontypridd	21-49	*T:* A Hamilton, D Neill, B Shenton *C:* C Rees 3
13 Feb	A	Neath	24-63	*T:* A Jacobs, P Jones, N Stork *C:* C Rees 3 *PG:* C Rees
9 Mar	A	Ebbw Vale	17-52	*T:* C Rees 2 *C:* C Rees 2 *PG:* C Rees
13 Mar	H	Caerphilly	24-27	*T:* D Griffiths, R Lewis, R Morris, C Rees *C:* C Rees 2
3 Apr	A	Llanelli	10-83	*T:* C Rees *C:* C Rees *PG:* C Rees
Play-off phase				
24 Apr	A	Newport	19-57	*T:* D Griffiths, D Neill, C Rees *C:* C Rees 2
28 Apr	H	Bridgend	26-68	*T:* D Griffiths, C Rees, T Green, A Jacobs *C:* C Rees 3
1 May	A	Caerphilly	13-65	*T:* P Roberts *C:* C Rees *PG:* C Rees 2
5 May	H	Newport	40-38	*T:* D Griffiths, C Rees, P Roberts, H Merrett, A Jacobs *C:* C Rees 3 *PG:* C Rees 3

8 May	A	Bridgend	33-37	*T:* C Rees, P Roberts, T Green, I Strang
				C: C Rees 2 *PG:* C Rees 2 *DG:* C Rees
12 May	H	Caerphilly	26-29	*T:* C Rees 2, T Green, A Jacobs *C:* C Rees 3

Bridgend

Year of formation 1878
Ground Brewery Field, Tondu Road, Bridgend, Mid Glamorgan Tel: Bridgend (01656) 652707 and 659032
Colours Blue and white hoops
Captain 1998-99 C Stephens
WRU Leagues 1998-99 Div 1 6th
SWALEC Cup 1998-99 Lost 16-43 to Swansea (6th round)

A disappointing season ended with considerable encouragement when local businessman Leighton Samuel injected £1m into the club, so new director of rugby Brian Powell could look forward to better days. Chris Stephens, aged 21, was the new captain and the legendary JPR Williams took over as team manager. 'The club's future is in the balance,' warned chairman Derrick King when financial problems loomed. They owed the taxman more than £100,000 and the players' wage bill was a staggering £842,793. Centre Gareth Jones returned from Cardiff, who also released scrum-half Steve Wake to the Brewery Field team. Chris Higgs and Steve Pearce joined from Bristol, Phil Thomas from Pontypridd, Peter Roberts from UWIC and Cliff Vogl resumed after a spell with London Welsh. Bridgend won all their WRU Challenge Trophy matches, including the third-place play-off by 25-23 against Edinburgh Reivers. A notable success came by 20-15 against Brive in the European Shield, but Bridgend were distinctly unfortunate to lose by 45-43 in Bucharest. Six victories in the six Premier Division play-offs saw Bridgend finish in sixth spot. Durbar Lawrie, who had been secretary for 42 years, died aged 84.

League Record 1998-99

Date	Venue	Opponents	Result	Scorers
29 Aug	H	Aberavon	45-10	*T:* G Cull, G Bowen, G Jones, B Roach, G Wilkins, P Roberts, A Williams *C:* G Cull 5
5 Sep	A	Ebbw Vale	20-23	*T:* C Stephens *PG:* G Cull 5
9 Sep	H	Pontypridd	24-52	*T:* G Jones, S Pearce, C Stephens *C:* G Bowen 2, G Cull *PG:* G Cull
12 Sep	A	Neath	9-38	*PG:* G Bowen 3
3 Oct	H	Caerphilly	24-24	*T:* B Roach, O Thomas, S Winn *C:* G Cull 3 *PG:* G Cull
28 Nov	H	Newport	30-24	*T:* O Thomas 3, A Durston *C:* G Bowen 2 *PG:* G Bowen 2
5 Dec	H	Ebbw Vale	23-13	*T:* S Greenaway, S Winn *C:* M Lewis 2 *PG:* G Cull 3
12 Dec	A	Aberavon	6-16	*PG:* M Lewis 2
2 Jan	H	Neath	17-20	*T:* S Pearce, S Wake *C:* G Cull 2 *PG:* G Bowen
9 Mar	A	Llanelli	11-47	*T:* S Ford *PG:* L Thomas 2
13 Mar	H	Llanelli	17-32	*T:* A Durston, A Joy *C:* G Cull 2 *PG:* G Cull
23 Mar	A	Pontypridd	14-73	*T:* A Durston, S Pearce *C:* G Bowen 2
3 Apr	A	Newport	0-33	
15 Apr	A	Caerphilly	31-31	*T:* C Higgs 2, A Durston *C:* G Cull 2 *PG:* G Cull 4
Play-off phase				
24 Apr	H	Caerphilly	31-25	T: A Williams *C:* G Cull *PG:* G Cull 8

28 Apr	A	Aberavon	68-26	*T:* S Greenaway 3, C Davies 2, C Higgs, L Davies, G Cull, G Jones, S Wake *C:* G Cull 9
1 May	A	Newport	28-18	*T:* G Jones 2, S Wake *C:* G Cull 2 *PG:* G Cull 3
5 May	A	Caerphilly	32-30	*T:* L Manning 2, G Jones, S Ford *C:* G Cull 3 *PG:* G Cull 2
8 May	H	Aberavon	37-33	*T:* S Ford 2, A Williams, A Joy, G Thomas *C:* G Cull 3 *PG:* G Cull 2
12 May	H	Newport	55-29	*T:* G Jones 2, C Davies, G Bowen, A Jenkins, L Manning, S Wake, A Williams *C:* G Cull 5, G Bowen *PG:* G Cull

Caerphilly

Year of formation 1886
Ground Virginia Park, Pontygwindy Road, Caerphilly Tel: Caerphilly (01222) 882573
Colours Green and white hoops
Captain 1998-99 N Jones
WRU Leagues 1998-99 Div 1 5th
SWALEC Cup 1998-99 Lost 15-20 to Ebbw Vale (6th round)

Another noteworthy season for the Greens. Led by Nathan Jones they possessed a regular match-winner in Brett Davey, an accomplished full-back who kicked goals with amazing accuracy to finish the season with a tally of 384 points. Among the recruits were outside-half Paul Williams (from Cardiff), scrum-half Chris Bridges, Adam Palfrey, Chris John (all from Neath), Ben Watkins (from Tredegar), John Wakeford (from SW Police), and Danzi Niblo and Richard Wintle (from Swansea). They released distinguished veteran David Phillips, who joined Bedwas as player/coach. Their most notable landmark was five victories over Newport (including the European Shield match), while there were also four league successes against Aberavon. The Greens defeated Neath home and away and a notable success was their 31-20 away defeat of Racing Club de France in the European Shield, where they reached the quarter-final before losing 43-12 at Brive. Chief coach Chris Davey built an impressive reputation with his team of part-time professionals.

League Record 1998-99

Date	Venue	Opponents	Result	Scorers
29 Aug	H	Pontypridd	3-23	*PG:* B Davey
5 Sep	A	Neath	21-18	*T:* J Hooper, S Marshall, R Wintle *PG:* B Davey 2
9 Sep	A	Newport	28-20	*T:* C Murphy, P Williams, R Wintle *C:* B Davey 2 *PG:* B Davey 2 *DG:* B Davey
12 Sep	H	Llanelli	20-51	*T:* R Bidgood, B Davey, S Marshall *C:* B Davey *PG:* B Davey
3 Oct	A	Bridgend	24-24	*T:* N Berbillion, B Watkins *C:* B Davey *PG:* B Davey 4
21 Nov	H	Aberavon	49-19	*T:* C Brown 2, M Wilson 2, N Berbillion, R Wintle *C:* B Davey 5 *PG:* B Davey 3
28 Nov	A	Ebbw Vale	19-24	*T:* J Hooper *C:* B Davey *PG:* B Davey 4
1 Dec	A	Pontypridd	15-55	*T:* S Marshall, M Wilson *C:* P Phillips *PG:* P Phillips
5 Dec	H	Neath	33-22	*T:* C Ferris, penalty try, R Bidgood *C:* B Davey 3 *PG:* B Davey 4
2 Jan	A	Llanelli	7-62	*T:* W Bray *C:* B Davey
13 Mar	A	Aberavon	27-24	*T:* R Wintle 2, N Berbillion, B Davey *C:* B Davey 2 *PG:* B Davey
27 Mar	H	Newport	40-25	*T:* C Brown 2, J Hooper, C John *C:* B Davey 4 *PG:* B Davey 4

3 Apr	H	Ebbw Vale	13-24	*T:* R Wintle *C:* B Davey *PG:* B Davey 2
15 Apr	H	Bridgend	31-31	*T:* C John 2, N Jones *C:* B Davey 2
				PG: B Davey 4

Play-off phase

24 Apr	A	Bridgend	25-31	*T:* C Bridges 2, J Hooper, J Savastano
				C: B Davey *PG:* B Davey
28 Apr	A	Newport	35-16	*T:* S Marshall 2, B Davey, C John
				C: B Davey 3 *PG:* B Davey 3
1 May	H	Aberavon	65-13	*T:* R Bidgood 3, B Davey 2, P Williams 2,
				C Ferris *C:* B Davey 8 *PG:* B Davey 3
5 May	H	Bridgend	30-32	*T:* R Boobyer, penalty try *C:* B Davey
				PG: B Davey 6
8 May	H	Newport	36-22	*T:* R Bidgood, B Davey, G Jones, J Savastano,
				R Wintle *C:* B Davey 4 *PG:* B Davey
12 May	A	Aberavon	29-26	*T:* R Bidgood 3, C Bridges *C:* B Davey 3
				DG: C John

Cardiff

Year of formation 1876
Ground Cardiff Arms Park, Westgate Street, Cardiff CF1 1JA Tel: Cardiff (01222) 383546
Web site http://www.cardiffrfc.com/english/front_door.html
Colours Cambridge blue and black
Captain 1998-99 D Young
WRU Leagues 1998-99 Did not enter
SWALEC Cup 1998-99 Lost 10-39 to Llanelli (semi-final)

Together with Swansea, Cardiff were rebels who took no part in the WRU League structure. They opted for friendly fixtures with major English clubs, although competing in the SWALEC Cup. The WRU imposed £150,000 of fines on both clubs. Chief executive Gareth Davies resigned before the end of the season to take over from former Glamorgan CCC captain Ossie Wheatley as chairman of the Sports Council for Wales. Cardiff's millionaire chairman Peter Thomas said that though the club lost more than £2.5m in 13 months to 31 May 1998, the friendly fixtures with Allied Dunbar clubs had brought big crowds back to home matches. On more than one Saturday, Cardiff's attendance exceeded the total figures for the entire WRU Premier Division. Terry Holmes replaced Australian Alec Evans as chief coach for the start of the season, but six days after the dismal SWALEC Cup defeat by Llanelli, Holmes decided to quit. David Young became new captain. Nigel Walker was forced to retire through shoulder injury, Mike Hall because of knee problems and Tony Rees with neck trouble. Great Britain rugby league wing Anthony Sullivan played on three months' loan from St Helens. Recruits included scrum-half Robert Jones (from Bristol), Ireland outside-half Paul Burke, Canada flanker Dan Baugh and former Swansea lock Steve Moore (from Moseley). Cardiff were unbeaten at home, but lost nine away games.

Anglo-Welsh Friendlies 1998-99

Date	Venue	Opponents	Result	Scorers
5 Sep	A	Bedford	27-10	*T:* J Humphreys, D Kacala, M Wintle
				C: L Jarvis 3 *PG:* L Jarvis 2
12 Sep	H	Saracens	40-19	*T:* S Hill, R Howley, M Wintle *C:* L Jarvis 2
				PG: L Jarvis 6 *DG:* L Jarvis
19 Sep	A	Harlequins	27-24	*T:* S Hill, M Hall, L Jarvis *C:* L Jarvis 3
				PG: L Jarvis 2
26 Sep	H	Northampton	30-19	*T:* R Howley, M Hall, L Davies
				C: L Jarvis 3 *PG:* L Jarvis 3
2 Oct	A	Leicester	35-20	*T:* S Hill 2, O Williams, M Wintle,
				J Humphreys *C:* L Jarvis 2 *PG:* L Jarvis 2

10 Oct	A	Sale	25-34	*T:* L Botham 2, P Burke, S Hill *C:* P Burke *PG:* P Burke
17 Oct	H	London Scottish	38-15	*T:* L Botham 2, P Burke, D Baugh, E Lewis, G Thomas *C:* P Burke 4
20 Oct	H	Bath	24-3	*T:* R Howley, M Rayer, G Thomas *C:* L Jarvis 3 *PG:* L Jarvis
7 Nov	H	West Hartlepool	40-17	*T:* G Thomas, L Jarvis, M Rayer, R Jones, A Sullivan, S Williams *C:* L Jarvis 5
14 Nov	H	Gloucester	17-9	*T:* G Kacala, C Morgan, M Wintle *C:* P Burke
22 Nov	A	Newcastle	16-36	*T:* C Morgan *C:* L Jarvis *PG:* L Jarvis 3
5 Dec	A	Swansea	15-31	*T:* D Baugh, C Morgan *C:* P Burke *PG:* P Burke
12 Dec	A	Richmond	28-35	*T:* L Davies, D Baugh, A Sullivan *C:* P Burke 2 *PG:* P Burke 3
20 Dec	A	Wasps	24-28	*T:* L Jarvis, J Humphreys *C:* L Jarvis *PG:* L Jarvis 4
26 Dec	A	Northampton	10-38	*T:* M Hall *C:* P Burke *PG:* P Burke
2 Jan	H	Leicester	29-13	*T:* R Howley 2, C Morgan, A Sullivan *C:* L Jarvis 3 *PG:* L Jarvis
9 Jan	H	Swansea	40-19	*T:* A Sullivan, S Hill, penalty try, M Wintle, S Moore *C:* L Jarvis 3 *PG:* L Jarvis 3
17 Jan	A	Saracens	20-36	*T:* L Botham, C Morgan, O Williams *C:* L Jarvis *PG:* L Jarvis
23 Jan	H	Wasps	14-10	*T:* L Davies *PG:* L Jarvis 2 *DG:* L Jarvis
7 Feb	H	Bedford	57-14	*T:* L Botham 4, S Hill 2, E Lewis, M Rayer, R Williams *C:* P Burke 6
13 Feb	A	Bath	32-44	*T:* L Botham 2, M Hall, L Jarvis *C:* L Jarvis 3 *PG:* L Jarvis 2
13 Mar	H	Harlequins	48-20	*T:* G Thomas 2, S Hill 2, R Jones, J Thomas, D Young *C:* L Jarvis 3, M Rayer 2 *PG:* L Jarvis
17 Mar	A	Gloucester	30-25	*T:* P Burke, S John, M Rayer, P Young *C:* P Burke 2 *PG:* P Burke 2
4 Apr	A	West Hartlepool	50-26	*T:* C Morgan 3, L Botham, L Jarvis, R Jones *C:* L Jarvis 2, L Botham 2 *PG:* L Jarvis 4
7 Apr	H	Sale	42-5	*T:* L Botham 2, P Burke, M Wintle, D Baugh, J Ringer *C:* P Burke 6
21 Apr	H	London Irish	53-20	*T:* J Ringer 2, L Botham, R Howley, R Jones, G Thomas, O Williams, J Robinson *C:* P Burke 4, L Jarvis *PG:* P Burke
24 Apr	H	London Scottish	34-15	*T:* L Botham, G Thomas, M Wintle J Robinson *C:* L Jarvis 4 *PG:* L Jarvis 2
1 May	H	Richmond	96-28	*T:* C Morgan 4, S Hill 3, L Botham 2, D Kacala 2, Wheeler 2, D Geraghty, J Robinson, M Wintle *C:* L Botham 5, M Rayer 3
8 May	H	Newcastle	70-20	*T:* J Robinson 4, S Hill 3, D Baugh, L Botham, E Lewis, M Rayer *C:* M Rayer 6 *PG:* M Rayer
16 May	A	London Irish	40-50	*T:* L Botham, R Jones, C Morgan, S Williams *C:* M Rayer 3 *PG:* M Rayer 2 *DG:* M Rayer

Ebbw Vale

Year of formation 1880
Ground Eugene Cross Park, Ebbw Vale, Gwent Tel: Ebbw Vale (01495) 302995
Colours Red, white and green
Captain 1998-99 K P Jones / M A Jones
WRU Leagues 1998-99 Div 1 4th
SWALEC Cup 1998-99 Lost 14-42 to Swansea (quarter-final)

Supporters were dismayed in November when several leading players were released to cut £175,000 off the wage bill. So captain Kingsley Jones went to Gloucester, Byron Hayward, outstanding goal-kicker, to Llanelli and Lennie Woodard, exciting wing, to London Welsh. Ex-Gloucester coach Richard Hill joined as assistant coach in March, Mark Jones assumed the captaincy and recruits included wing David Manley and forwards Andrew Metcalfe and Mark Spiller (all from Pontypridd). Mark Jones was suspended for one match after being cited by Llanelli for an off-the-ball incident during the 1998 SWALEC Cup final. He was ordered off again against Pontypridd at Ebbw Vale after flooring jumper Ian Gough, who needed an operation on his right eye-socket. Banned for three matches, Jones revealed that he was seeking 'outside help' for his on-the-field attitude. 'I realise I have a problem I have to correct,' he said. He wrote to Gough and the WRU saying, 'I would sincerely like to apologise for a thoughtless, stupid and violent act.' Ebbw won home league games against leaders Llanelli and Pontypridd. They were hammered by 108-16 at Toulouse in the European Cup, but remarkably won the return 19-11, which upset the French visitors, who were fined £2,600 in costs at a disciplinary hearing and strongly reprimanded for unacceptable behaviour.

League Record 1998-99

Date	Venue	Opponents	Result	Scorers
29 Aug	A	Llanelli	18-35	T: A Harries 2 C: B Hayward PG: B Hayward 2
5 Sep	H	Bridgend	23-20	T: D Llewellyn PG: B Hayward 5 DG: B Hayward
8 Sep	A	Aberavon	29-5	T: A Harries 2, K Jones, penalty try C: B Hayward 3 PG: B Hayward
12 Sep	H	Newport	57-17	T: B Hayward 3, A Harries, R Collins, D Manley, M Jones, J Strange, S Taumalolo C: B Hayward 6
3 Oct	H	Pontypridd	24-23	T: C Billen, D Manley C: B Hayward PG: B Hayward 4
28 Nov	H	Caerphilly	24-19	T: S Taumalolo, L Olsen, penalty try C: J Strange 3 PG: J Strange
1 Dec	H	Llanelli	24-20	T: D Llewellyn, J Strange C: J Strange PG: J Strange 4
5 Dec	A	Bridgend	13-23	T: G Green, R Collins PG: J Strange
2 Jan	A	Newport	29-30	T: D Llewellyn, L Olsen C: J Strange 2 PG: J Strange 5
23 Feb	A	Neath	22-20	T: penalty try C: J Strange PG: J Strange 5
9 Mar	H	Aberavon	52-17	T: K Faletau 2, J Hawker 2, R Jones, D Manley, A Metcalfe, L Olsen C: J Strange 6
13 Mar	H	Neath	25-24	T: N Budgett, J Hawker, D Llewellyn C: J Strange 2 PG: J Strange 2
3 Apr	A	Caerphilly	24-13	T: A Harries, D Llewellyn C: J Strange PG: J Strange 3 DG: J Strange
16 Apr	A	Pontypridd	9-21	PG: J Strange 3
Play-off phase				
20 Apr	H	Pontypridd	36-23	T: M Jones, N Budgett, penalty try C: J Strange 3 PG: J Strange 5
24 Apr	H	Llanelli	3-42	PG: J Strange
28 Apr	A	Neath	39-43	T: S Taumalolo 2, J Hawker, D Manley, J Williams, G Williams C: J Williams 3 PG: J Williams
1 May	A	Pontypridd	29-34	T: R Jones, penalty try C: J Strange 2 PG: J Strange 4 DG: J Strange
4 May	A	Llanelli	23-23	T: D Llewellyn, G Williams C: A Harries 2 PG: A Harries 3
7 May	H	Neath	38-16	T: M Jones, C Billen, D Manley, N Budgett C: J Strange 3 PG: J Strange 4

Llanelli

Year of formation 1872
Ground Stradey Park, Llanelli, Dyfed SA15 4BT Tel: Llanelli (01554) 774060 and 0891 660221
Web site http://www.scarlets.co.uk/
Colours Scarlet and white
Captain 1998-99 R C McBryde
WRU Leagues 1998-99 Div 1 – *Winners*
SWALEC Cup 1998-99 Lost 10-37 to Swansea (final)

Though they failed to crown an eminently successful season with what would have been a record 11th cup triumph in their 14th final (they lost the SWALEC Cup final by 37-10 to Swansea), Llanelli had every reason for satisfaction. They won the WRU Challenge Trophy, defeating holders Pontypridd by 41-18 at Stradey, and became champions of the Premier Division (with only four defeats) after a six-year wait. Robin McBryde was retained as captain and significant signings included John Davies and Scott Quinnell (from Richmond), centre Salesi Finau (from Tonga), Byron Hayward (from Ebbw Vale), Tony Copsey (from Saracens), who took over as commercial manager, Marcus Thomas (from Pontrypridd), Phil Booth (from Cardiff), Martyn Madden (from Penzance/Newlyn) and Ian Boobyer (from Neath) to join his two brothers Roddy and Neil. Released were Andrew Gibbs (to Newport), Matthew Wintle (to Cardiff) and Paul Jones (to Leeds). No league team won at Stradey, though Ebbw Vale drew there 23-all in the play-off stage. Stephen Jones scored 324 points in all matches and Hayward 193. Wayne Proctor obtained 29 tries. Saracens, as England's cup-holders, and Llanelli, as Welsh cup-holders, met in a showpiece at Stradey in August 1998 with Saracens winners by 55-9.

League Record 1998-99

Date	Venue	Opponents	Result	Scorers
29 Aug	H	Ebbw Vale	35-18	*T:* D Williams, W Proctor, P Booth, D Hodges *C:* S Jones 3 *PG:* S Jones 2 *DG:* S Jones
5 Sep	A	Pontypridd	15-22	*PG:* S Jones 5
9 Sep	H	Neath	30-20	*T:* S Jones 2, W Proctor 2, G Evans *C:* S Jones *PG:* S Jones
12 Sep	A	Caerphilly	51-20	*T:* N Boobyer 2, I Boobyer, A Copsey, G Evans, R McBryde, W Proctor, H Jenkins, D Rogers *C:* S Jones 3
3 Oct	H	Newport	68-26	*T:* W Proctor 2, N Boobyer, S Jones, M Madden, I Jones, R Boobyer, G John, R Moon, C Wyatt *C:* S Jones 9
28 Nov	A	Aberavon	48-12	*T:* R Boobyer, W Proctor, J Hyatt, J Barrell, I Jones, D Hodges, G Evans, C Wyatt *C:* S Jones 4
1 Dec	A	Ebbw Vale	20-24	*T:* S Finau *PG:* S Jones 5
5 Dec	H	Pontypridd	24-16	*PG:* B Hayward 8
2 Jan	H	Caerphilly	62-7	*T:* C Wyatt 3, D Williams 2, S Finau, D Morris, D Rogers, S Quinnell, M Voyle *C:* S Jones 6
10 Feb	A	Neath	21-24	*T:* W Proctor 2 *C:* S Jones *PG:* S Jones 3
9 Mar	H	Bridgend	47-11	*T:* N Boobyer 3, P Booth, G Evans, B Hayward, M Voyle *C:* S Jones 3 *PG:* S Jones 2
13 Mar	A	Bridgend	32-17	*T:* J Davies, M Madden, D Williams, W Proctor, C Wyatt *C:* S Jones 2 *PG:* S Jones
23 Mar	A	Newport	30-11	*T:* R Moon, G Evans, penalty try *C:* B Hayward 3 *PG:* B Hayward 3
3 Apr	H	Aberavon	83-10	*T:* W Proctor 3, S Finau 2, I Boobyer, P Booth, J Davies, D Hodges, H Jenkins, M Thomas, M Voyle, C Warlow *C:* S Jones 6, B Hayward 3

Play-off phase

21 Apr	A	Neath	17-32	*T:* W Proctor 2, R Moon *C:* S Jones
24 Apr	A	Ebbw Vale	42-3	*T:* S Finau 2, B Hayward, D Hodges, H Jenkins *C:* B Hayward 4 *PG:* B Hayward 2 *DG:* B Hayward
28 Apr	A	Pontypridd	42-12	*T:* C Wyatt 2, S Finau, H Jenkins, M Thomas *C:* B Hayward 4 *PG:* B Hayward 3
1 May	H	Neath	37-11	*T:* C Wyatt, R Moon, H Jenkins, C Warlow *C:* B Hayward *PG:* B Hayward 5
4 May	H	Ebbw Vale	23-23	*T:* G Evans, W Proctor, S Finau, *C:* B Hayward *PG:* B Hayward 2
8 May	H	Pontypridd	41-22	*T:* S Finau 2, A Copsey, M Jones, R McBryde, D Rogers, C Wyatt *C:* B Hayward 3

Neath

Year of formation 1871
Ground The Gnoll, Gnoll Park Road, Neath, West Glamorgan Tel: Neath (01639) 636547
Colours All black with white Maltese cross
Captain 1998-99 P Horgan
WRU Leagues 1998-99 Div 1 3rd
SWALEC Cup 1998-99 Lost 14-15 to Pontypool (6th round)

The club was in danger of going to the wall with debts of around £645,000 in the late summer of 1998. Thirteen players left and the WRU put an administrator in to begin reorganisation, though no extra WRU money was made available. Late in the season, the WRU relinquished control and a new board of directors was set up. Some former players were taking legal action against a number of ex-committeemen, claiming loss of earnings. Against such an unpromising background, Neath battled back to finish third in the Premier Division, winning five of their last seven fixtures, including victories over champions Llanelli and runners-up Pontypridd. All this was unimaginable when the season started. Inspiring work by coach Lyn Jones produced a remarkable transformation. Wing Shane Williams proved an important signing from Amman Utd, while Brett Sinkinson, from Waikato Chiefs, won a place in the Wales team on the strength of Welsh grandparents. Tongan David Tiueti also impressed with Delme Williams another sharp attacker. Matthew Pearce kicked 144 points.

League Record 1998-99

Date	Venue	Opponents	Result	Scorers
29 Aug	A	Newport	36-8	*T:* D Case, J Colderley, M Davies, G Evans, D Tiueti, B Sinkinson *C:* D Case 3
5 Sep	H	Caerphilly	18-21	*T:* S Eggar 2, P Horgan *PG:* D Case
9 Sep	A	Llanelli	20-30	*T:* S Eggar 2 *C:* D Case 2 *PG:* D Case 2
12 Sep	H	Bridgend	38-9	*T:* G Evans, D Tiueti, D Williams, L Gerrard *C:* L Richards 3 *PG:* L Richards 4
3 Oct	A	Aberavon	37-27	*T:* S Eggar, I Jones, S Jenkins, L Richards *C:* L Richards 4 *PG:* L Richards 2 *DG:* L Richards
28 Nov	A	Pontypridd	7-44	*T:* M Morgan *C:* M McCarthy
5 Dec	A	Caerphilly	22-33	*T:* D Case *C:* D Case *PG:* D Case 5
12 Dec	H	Newport	30-13	*T:* D Tiueti, T Davies, M Davies, B Sinkinson *C:* D Case 2 *PG:* D Case 2
2 Jan	A	Bridgend	20-17	*T:* D Tiueti, D Case, S van Rensburg *C:* D Case *PG:* D Case
10 Feb	H	Llanelli	24-21	*T:* M Turner 2 *C:* M Pearce *PG:* M Pearce 3 *DG:* M Pearce

13 Feb	H	Aberavon	63-24	*T:* D Williams 3, B Sinkinson 2, G Evans, L Gerrard, D Jones, S Williams *C:* M Pearce 6 *PG:* M Pearce 2
23 Feb	H	Ebbw Vale	20-22	*T:* R Davies 2, D Williams *C:* M Pearce *PG:* M Pearce
13 Mar	A	Ebbw Vale	24-25	*T:* S Williams 2, R Johnson *C:* M Pearce 3 *PG:* M Pearce
3 Apr	H	Pontypridd	53-31	*T:* penalty tries 2, S Williams, G Evans, J Colderley, L Gerrard *C:* M Pearce 4 *PG:* M Pearce 4 *DG:* M Pearce

Play-off phase

21 Apr	H	Llanelli	32-17	T: penalty try, D Williams, D Tiueti *C:* M Pearce *PG:* M Pearce 5
24 Apr	H	Pontypridd	33-21	*T:* S Williams 3 *C:* M Pearce 3 *PG:* M Pearce 4
28 Apr	H	Ebbw Vale	43-39	*T:* S Williams 2, D Williams 2, D Case, D Tiueti *C:* M Pearce 5 *PG:* M Pearce
1 May	A	Llanelli	11-37	*T:* A Jackson *PG:* M Pearce *DG:* M Pearce
4 May	A	Pontypridd	21-14	*T:* Martin Davies 2, Mark Davies *PG:* M Pearce *DG:* M Pearce
7 May	A	Ebbw Vale	16-38	*T:* S Martin *C:* M Pearce *PG:* M Pearce 2 *DG:* M Pearce

Newport

Year of formation 1874
Ground Rodney Parade, Newport, Gwent NP9 0UU Tel: Newport (01633) 258193 or 267410
Colours Black and amber
Captain 1998-99 S Cronk
WRU Leagues 1998-99 Div 1 7th
SWALEC Cup 1998-99 Lost 38-60 to Swansea (5th round)

The club became a limited company in July 1998, aiming to raise £500,000 to fight its way back to prominence, but it proved another disappointing season. There were only five league victories, all against Bridgend and bottom team Aberavon, and just one success in their six European Shield games: 27-18 against Rovigo. There was a club record win by 104-3 against Trinant in the Ben Francis Cup first round with Shaun Connor setting a club record by scoring 34 points to pass the 33 by Canadian Gareth Rees against Abertillery in 1995. Newport pulled out of the Ben Francis Cup at the semi-final stage. Allan Lewis, formerly of Llanelli, joined as coaching director from Moseley. Prop Sven Cronk was captain and signings included Andrew Gibbs (from Llanelli), full-back Matt Cardey (from North Harbour) and Canada centre Kyle Nicholls. But Ian Gough was lost to Pontypridd and Jan Machacek to Sale. Wales under-21 back-row stars Alix Popham and Nathan Bonner-Evans were highly promising players for the future.

League Record 1998-99

Date	Venue	Opponents	Result	Scorers
29 Aug	H	Neath	8-36	*T:* R Snow *PG:* S Connor
5 Sep	A	Aberavon	47-5	*T:* G King 2, N Lloyd 2, G Hicks, M Llewellyn, R Snow *C:* S Connor 6
9 Sep	H	Caerphilly	20-28	*T:* D Burn, G King, M Watkins *C:* S Connor *PG:* S Connor
12 Sep	A	Ebbw Vale	17-57	*T:* N McKim, S Mitchell *C:* S Connor 2 *PG:* S Connor
3 Oct	A	Llanelli	26-68	*T:* D Gray 2, A Harris, M Watkins *C:* S Mitchell 3

28 Nov	A	Bridgend	24-30	*T:* M Watkins, D Burn, S Connor
				C: S Connor 2, S Mitchell *PG:* S Connor
5 Dec	H	Aberavon	36-16	*T:* M Cardy, A Harris, S Connor, M Watkins
				C: S Connor 2 *PG:* S Mitchell 3, S Connor
12 Dec	A	Neath	13-30	*T:* A Popham *C:* S Connor *PG:* S Connor 2
2 Jan	H	Ebbw Vale	30-29	*T:* M Llewellyn, S Moore, K Nicholls
				C: S Connor 3 *PG:* S Connor 2
				DG: S Connor
13 Mar	A	Pontypridd	16-31	*T:* C Jones, B Clark *PG:* S Mitchell 2
23 Mar	H	Llanelli	11-30	*T:* G Hicks *PG:* S Mitchell 2
27 Mar	A	Caerphilly	25-40	*T:* D Smith, M Watkins, G Hicks
				C: S Mitchell 2 *PG:* S Mitchell 2
31 Mar	H	Pontypridd	13-16	*T:* M Cardey *C:* S Connor *PG:* S Connor 2
3 Apr	H	Bridgend	33-0	*T:* R Snow, M Watkins, D Smith, D Gray,
				A Popham *C:* S Mitchell 4

Play-off phase

24 Apr	H	Aberavon	57-19	T: M Cardey 2, S Connor 2, R Snow,
				S Mitchell, M Watkins, S Moore
				C: S Mitchell 7 *PG:* S Mitchell
28 Apr	H	Caerphilly	16-35	*T:* M Watkins *C:* S Mitchell
				PG: S Mitchell 3
1 May	H	Bridgend	18-28	*T:* N Lloyd, M Llewellyn *C:* S Mitchell
				PG: S Mitchell 2
5 May	A	Aberavon	38-40	*T:* S Mitchell 2, M Watkins, G Taylor,
				A Popham *C:* S Mitchell 5 *PG:* S Mitchell
8 May	A	Caerphilly	22-36	*T:* G Chapman, M Llewellyn, N McKim
				C: S Mitchell 2 *PG:* S Mitchell
12 May	A	Bridgend	29-55	*T:* A Harris, M Watkins, N McKim, penalty
				try *C:* S Mitchell 3 *PG:* S Mitchell

Pontypridd

Year of formation 1876
Ground Sardis Road Ground, Pwllgwaun, Pontypridd Tel: Pontypridd (01443) 405006 and 407170
Web site http://www.pontypriddrfc.co.uk/
Colours Black and white hoops
Captain 1998-99 N R Jenkins
WRU Leagues 1998-99 Div 1 2nd
SWALEC Cup 1998-99 Lost 17-22 to Llanelli (quarter-final)

Though they lost eight league games (twice as many as the previous season), Pontypridd finished runners-up to Llanelli. There was a club record defeat by 71-14 in Paris against Stade Français in the European Cup quarter-final and only one of six play-off fixtures brought success at the end of the season. So Ponty under-achieved by their standards. Only Llanelli and Neath won at Sardis Road in the league, and that was at the play-off stage when an injury-hit side were without captain Neil Jenkins, who was recovering from a shoulder operation. As holders of the WRU Challenge Trophy, they had expectations of repeating the success, but this time they did not enjoy home advantage and lost the final by 41-18 at Llanelli. They signed Ian Gough (from Newport), USA Eagles hooker Tom Billups, speedy wing Rhys Shorney (from UWIC), Tonga tight-head Ngalu T'au and Jason Forster (from Bedford). Among those released were familiar faces David Manley, Crispin Cormack, Phil John, Stuart Roy, Mark Rowley, Phil Thomas and Phil Ford. Neil Jenkins was linked with Cardiff at the end of the season, but insisted that he would see out the remaining four years of his contract with Ponty. He scored 325 points.

League Record 1998-99

Date	Venue	Opponents	Result	Scorers
29 Aug	A	Caerphilly	23-3	*T:* J Lewis, S Enoch *C:* N Jenkins 2 *PG:* N Jenkins 3
5 Sep	H	Llanelli	22-15	*T:* R Shorney, M Williams *PG:* N Jenkins 4
9 Sep	A	Bridgend	52-24	*T:* G O Lewis 2, G P Lewis 2, G Prosser, R Shorney *C:* N Jenkins 5 *PG:* N Jenkins 4
12 Sep	H	Aberavon	64-28	*T:* R Shorney 7, N Jenkins, J Lewis, A Lamerton *C:* N Jenkins 7
3 Oct	A	Ebbw Vale	23-24	*T:* R Shorney, G Wyatt *C:* N Jenkins 2 *PG:* N Jenkins 3
28 Nov	H	Neath	44-7	*T:* K Morgan 2, M Lloyd 2, D McIntosh, G Wyatt *C:* N Jenkins 4 *PG:* N Jenkins 2
1 Dec	H	Caerphilly	55-15	*T:* G Wyatt 3, K Morgan, A Lamerton, G O Lewis, A Freeman, D James *C:* N Jenkins 6 *PG:* N Jenkins
5 Dec	A	Llanelli	16-24	*T:* K Morgan *C:* N Jenkins *PG:* N Jenkins 3
2 Jan	A	Aberavon	49-21	*T:* R Shorney 2, G O Lewis, M Lloyd, K Morgan, G Prosser, M Williams *C:* G Wyatt 4 *PG:* G Wyatt 2
13 Mar	H	Newport	31-16	*T:* K Morgan 2, N Jenkins *C:* N Jenkins 2 *PG:* N Jenkins 4
23 Mar	H	Bridgend	73-14	*T:* K Morgan 3, N Ta'u 2, D McIntosh, G Wyatt, Paul John, J Lewis, G P Lewis, N Jenkins *C:* N Jenkins 9
31 Mar	A	Newport	16-13	*T:* K Morgan, N T'au *PG:* G Wyatt 2
3 Apr	A	Neath	31-53	*T:* M Williams, G O Lewis, Paul John, A Griffiths, K Morgan *C:* G Wyatt 3
16 Apr	H	Ebbw Vale	21-9	*T:* M Williams, N T'au *C:* C Sweeney *PG:* C Sweeney 3
Play-off phase				
20 Apr	A	Ebbw Vale	23-36	T: D James, K Morgan *C:* G Wyatt, C Sweeney *PG:* C Sweeney 3
24 Apr	A	Neath	21-33	*T:* J Lewis, R Shorney *C:* G Wyatt *PG:* G Wyatt 3
28 Apr	H	Llanelli	12-42	*PG:* Paul John 4
1 May	H	Ebbw Vale	34-29	*T:* G O Lewis 2, G P Lewis, N T'au, G Wyatt *C:* G Wyatt 3 *PG:* G Wyatt
4 May	H	Neath	14-21	*T:* G Wyatt *PG:* G Wyatt 2 *DG:* G Wyatt
8 May	A	Llanelli	22-41	*T:* J Bryant, S Enoch, R Sidoli *C:* C Sweeney 2 *PG:* C Sweeney

Swansea

Year of formation 1873
Ground St Helen's Ground, Bryn Road, Swansea, West Glamorgan SA2 0AR Tel: Swansea (01792) 466593
Colours All white
Captain 1998-99 I S Gibbs
WRU Leagues 1998-99 Did not enter
SWALEC Cup 1998-99 *Winners* — beat Llanelli 37-10 (Final)

Swansea won the SWALEC Cup final by 37-10 to foil Llanelli's aim of securing a notable treble. Swansea and Cardiff took no part in the WRU League structure. Instead, they played friendly fixtures against England's premier clubs and enjoyed vastly improved home attendances. Scott Gibbs was the new captain and the capture of props Darren Morris, Ben Evans and Lee Jones (from Neath), and Natal B centre Clinton van Rensburg strengthened the squad. No.8 Stuart Davies was forced to retire in October on medical advice with neck trouble. Arwel Thomas, the man-of-the-match in the Cup final, brought the invention of his game to the fore on numerous occasions, despite being dogged by injuries. His immeasurable zest meant variety and enterprise in the back division. Only Saracens and London Scottish won in friendly games at St Helen's and there was a thumping victory by 100-7 at Amman Utd in the second round of the SWALEC Cup. Lee Davies scored 233 points and Arwel Thomas 211.

Anglo-Welsh Friendlies 1998-99

Date	Venue	Opponents	Result	Scorers
5 Sep	H	West Hartlepool	32-26	*T:* Simon Davies 2, P Moriarty, penalty try *C:* L Davies 3 *PG:* L Davies 2
13 Sep	A	Wasps	28-18	*T:* P Moriarty, R Rees, M Taylor *C:* L Davies 2 *PG:* L Davies 3
19 Sep	H	Newcastle	26-14	*T:* A Booth *PG:* A Thomas 6 *DG:* A Thomas
26 Sep	A	Richmond	13-28	*T:* P Moriarty *C:* L Davies *PG:* A Thomas 2
3 Oct	H	Saracens	25-32	*T:* C Charvis, M Taylor, D Thomas *C:* L Davies 2 *PG:* L Davies 2
10 Oct	H	Gloucester	27-16	*T:* M Back, L Davies, M Taylor *C:* L Davies 3 *PG:* L Davies 2
17 Oct	A	London Irish	38-20	*T:* M Robinson 2, G Jenkins, M Taylor *C:* L Davies 3 *PG:* L Davies 4
20 Oct	A	Northampton	34-18	*T:* L Jones 2, M Robinson, Rhodri Jones, M Taylor *C:* L Davies 3 *DG:* L Davies
31 Oct	A	Sale	22-24	*T:* S Gibbs 2, penalty try *C:* L Davies 2 *PG:* L Davies
7 Nov	H	London Scottish	76-5	*T:* S Gibbs 3, C Charvis 2, D Morris, G Jenkins, L Davies, A Moore, M Robinson, M Morgan, Robbie Jones *C:* L Davies 8
13 Nov	A	Bath	7-34	*T:* Rhodri Jones *C:* L Davies
20 Nov	A	Leicester	20-7	*T:* C van Rensburg, D Weatherley *C:* L Davies 2 *PG:* L Davies 2
5 Dec	H	Cardiff	31-15	*T:* M Robinson 2, S Gibbs, L Davies *C:* L Davies *PG:* L Davies 3
12 Dec	H	Harlequins	32-18	*T:* R Rees 2, M Robinson *C:* A Thomas *PG:* A Thomas 4 *DG:* A Thomas
20 Dec	A	Bedford	28-14	*T:* L Jones, S Gibbs, C Charvis, D Thomas *C:* A Thomas 4
26 Dec	H	Bath	50-17	*T:* M Robinson 2, C Charvis, P Arnold, G Jenkins, penalty try *C:* A Thomas 4 *PG:* A Thomas 4
2 Jan	H	Richmond	57-3	*T:* G Jenkins 2, Rhodri Jones 2, P Arnold, C Charvis, S Gibbs, L Jones, A Lawson *C:* M Back 6
9 Jan	A	Cardiff	19-40	*T:* R Rees *C:* A Thomas *PG:* A Thomas 4
16 Jan	H	Wasps	27-13	*T:* Simon Davies, Rhodri Jones, S Mills *C:* A Thomas 3 *PG:* A Thomas 2
24 Jan	A	Saracens	29-59	*T:* M Robinson, D Weatherley, penalty try *C:* L Davies *PG:* L Davies 4
7 Feb	A	West Hartlepool	28-27	*T:* R Rees 2, Rhodri Jones, Noble *C:* L Davies *PG:* L Davies 2
13 Feb	H	Northampton	58-24	*T:* M Taylor 2, A Thomas 2, D Weatherley 2, L Davies, C Loader, R Rees *C:* A Thomas 5 *PG:* A Thomas
14 Mar	A	Newcastle	25-43	*T:* M Back, D Morris, penalty try *C:* L Davies 2 *PG:* L Davies 2
3 Apr	H	London Scottish	12-27	*T:* penalty try, Simon Davies *C:* M Back
20 Apr	H	Bedford	46-31	*T:* A Lawson 2, A Booth, D Thomas, C Wells, S Davies, L Davies *C:* L Davies 4 *PG:* L Davies

24 Apr	H	London Irish	34-31	*T:* penalty tries 2, S Gibbs, T Maullin, R Rees
				C: L Davies 3 *PG:* L Davies
4 May	A	Gloucester	10-37	*T:* J Griffiths *C:* L Davies *PG:* L Davies
8 May	H	Leicester	34-22	*T:* L Jones, Rhodri Jones, M Taylor,
				M Robinson *C:* A Thomas 4
				PG: A Thomas 2

Swansea's away match at Harlequins and home match with Sale were cancelled.

Rebels with a cause. Swansea's Andrew Booth sets the backs in motion during the Anglo-Welsh friendly game against Wasps at Loftus Road in September 1998, one of the series of matches played by dissident Welsh clubs Swansea and Cardiff throughout the season.

FRANCE PERFORM TO TYPE AND MYSTIFY EVERYONE

THE 1998-99 SEASON IN FRANCE
Bob Donahue *International Herald Tribune*

A calamitous French international season ended with Jim Telfer of Scotland saying that he would not be surprised if France reached the 1999 World Cup final. Telfer presumably would not be surprised, either, if France did not reach the World Cup final. In other words, the old cliché about the French being 'unpredictable' looked apt for once.

The question remained: Why did they fall apart in the International Championship? A simple answer would be that a dramatically improved Wales side caught confident France napping and it was downhill from here. A fuller answer would point to injuries, a lightweight midfield, a disjointed club championship and tactical ineptitude suggestive of jadedness. In the view of Bernard Lapasset, president of the Fédération Française de Rugby, France played 'like zombies' against Scotland in April. Lapasset continued to back Jean-Claude Skrela and Pierre Villepreux, whose cerebral coaching was not to everyone's taste.

Supporters had to wonder, too, whether it was a matter of the current crop of top players not simply being good enough. World Cup performance would tell. Optimists recalled how worries about talent and coaching had preceded France's World Cup soccer triumph in July 1998.

There could be no denying that a more or less world-class national rugby squad, winners of the Grand Slam in 1997 and 1998, turned spiritless in 1999. From inside the squad came this anonymous criticism: 'The guys are hoping to make it to the World Cup without injury. They're not giving their all at every outing.'

Before the 1998-99 season, a June tour to Argentina and Fiji produced three comfortable Test victories but not much of the 'enthusiasm' that Skrela said he was looking for. Thomas Castaignède had said before departure: 'We're setting out tired. We're not machines!' The press wondered aloud whether it would not have been better to give the players a rest.

Lapasset was re-elected unopposed. Serge Blanco, later to play a major role in bringing English clubs back to the European Cup for 1999-2000, now emerged as president of a grouping of the major clubs called the Ligue Nationale du Rugby (which translates, interestingly, as National Rugby League).

Club competition began in mid-August, and European Cup play

a month later. Argentina turned up in November for the usual defeat. At this point, Raphael Ibañez, hooker and captain since the start of the 1998 International Championship, had eight victories under his belt. But now came Australia. Said Skrela, 'This is simply the moment of truth.' The truth turned out to be failure, 21-32. This was France's eighth consecutive loss to the three major southern hemisphere nations going back to the autumn of 1995.

The next bad news was Ulster eliminating Toulouse and then Stade Français, and finally winning the European Cup final in Dublin against Colomiers. Dublin was where France would now start the International Championship — and where, probably, it would play a World Cup quarter-final.

Good fortune saw France through against the Irish in February. The weather was awful. The match, said Richard Dourthe, was the hardest that he had ever played in. The French, it was felt, had shown character and defended well. Another Grand Slam was still on offer.

Common sense, which can be dangerous, saw England at Twickenham as the big match, and Wales and Scotland at the glorious Stade de France as lesser problems. When Wales trotted out, the crowd of some 79,000 was even bigger than the one that had seen France beat Brazil in the World Cup final.

Well, the home pack were outplayed. The Welsh attacked out wide twice as often as the French. When Dourthe went off injured after five minutes, the French midfield defence collapsed. Castaignède could still have won the match with a penalty goal at the end, but it would have been an injustice. Wales had knocked the French back on their heels, and there they were to stay.

Suddenly the Twickenham objective was mainly to restore the team's credibility by tightening the defence and the scrum. That was achieved. Defeat was accepted with scarcely a murmur, rather as if the concern were to get this cursed season over with. The worst remained, though.

In April it was Castaignède's turn to limp off early, and lo and behold Scotland scored five tries in 18 minutes. 'Pitiful,' the press called France. Scotland were 'radiant, wonderful'. It was observed that Gregor Townsend, who played for Brive in the French club championship, did not look jaded at all.

Time to get out the record book. France finish last for the first time since 1969 (which was also a year preceded by two years in which France were top of the table). France lose both home matches for the first time since 1957. Nine French tries were scored in 1999 after 18 tries in 1998. The penalty goal balance of minus 10 (six for, 16 against) is France's worst in the history of the championship. A wit is heard to say mournfully that the Tricolours finished last in the first Five Nations tournament, in 1910, and

The French squad for the match against Ireland in Dublin on 6th February. L-R back row: J M Fleming (touch-judge), S Young (touch-judge), T Cléda (replacement), S Marconnet (replacement), M Dal Maso (replacement), C Califano, F Tournaire, M Raynaud (replacement), T Lièvremont, P Benetton, O Magne, F Pelous, O Brouzet, P L Marshall (referee); front row: R Dourthe, C Laussucq (replacement), T Castaignède, F Comba, R Ibañez (captain), P Carbonneau, P Bernat-Salles, E Ntamack, A Gomès (replacement), T Lombard, D Aucagne (replacement).

should be credited with elegant symmetry for doing likewise in the final one.

Skrela had argued in 1998 that the northern hemisphere urgently needed a Celtic revival. A year later, he reassured his own men that the revival of Scotland and Wales showed what could be done.

In the club championship, a tedious initial phase of three groups of eight ended in February, followed by a cut-throat 'Top 16' phase with better rugby and bigger crowds. Eight clubs survived for a knockout phase starting in mid-May.

In June, a 62-8 defeat of Romania was notable for the successful return to the national side of former captain Abdelatif Benazzi. He was among the 30 men who set out that month for Western Samoa, Tonga and New Zealand. Only 10 of these tourists had gone to Argentina and Fiji a year before.

FRENCH CLUB CHAMPIONSHIP FINAL

29 May, Stade de France (Saint-Denis)
TOULOUSE 15 (1G 1PG 1T) MONTFERRAND 11 (2PG 1T)

Toulouse took the Brennus Shield for the 15th time, and the fifth time in six years (they had lost it to Stade Français in 1998), in France's 100th club championship. They had eliminated Stade Français and Bourgoin in the knockout phase, while Montferrand were ousting Castres and Grenoble. The other quarter-finalists were Bègles and Colomiers.

A former All Black, Lee Stensness, now wearing No.10 for Toulouse, was the man of the match, scoring his side's first try and making the second to put them ahead 15-6 after 12 minutes of the second half.

Toulouse: S Ougier; X Garbajosa, C Desbrosse, E Ntamack, M Marfaing; L Stensness, J Cazalbou; C Califano, Y Bru, F Tournaire, F Pelous, F Belot *(capt)*, D Lacroix, S Dispagne, C Labit *Substitutions:* H Miorin for Dispagne (38 mins); P Bondouy for Garbajosa (71 mins); J-L Jordana for Tournaire (71 mins); Matthieu Lièvremont for Labit (76 mins)
Scorers *Tries:* Stensness, Desbrosse *Conversion:* Marfaing *Penalty Goal:* Marfaing
Montferrand: N Nadau; J Marlu, J Morante, T Marsh, D Bory; G Merceron, S Castaignède; E Ménieu, O Azam, F Heyer, D Barrier, C Sarraute, A Costes, D Courteix, J-M Lhermet *(capt) Substitutions:* O Merle for Sarraute (57 mins); E Nicol for Morante (66 mins); J Bonvoisin for Lhermet (66 mins); P Laurent-Varange for Azam (66 mins); O Toulouze for Nadau (71 mins); C Duchêne for Ménieu (80 mins); C Larrue for Castaignède (80 mins)
Scorers *Try:* Nadau *Penalty Goals:* Merceron (2)
Referee G Borreani (Côte d'Azur)

FRANCE TO ARGENTINA & FIJI 1998

THE TOURING PARTY

Manager J Maso   **Coach** J-C Skrela
Assistant Coaches P Villepreux & M Godemet   **Captain** R Ibañez

Full-back: A Gomès (Stade Français)

Threequarters: P Bernat-Salles (Pau), C Dominici (Stade Français), X Garbajosa (Stade Français), D Plana (Perpignan), F Comba (Stade Français), S Glas (Bourgoin-Jallieu), J Marlu (Montferrand), J-M Aué (Castres)

Half-backs: T Castaignède (Castres), D Aucagne (Pau), P Carbonneau (Brive), F Galthié (Colomiers)

Forwards: R Ibañez (Dax), M Dal Maso (Agen), C Soulette (Béziers), F Tournaire (Narbonne), S de Besombes (Perpignan), P Collazo (Bègles-Bordeaux), O Brouzet (Bègles-Bordeaux), T Cléda (Pau), F Pelous (Toulouse), F Belot (Toulouse), P Benetton (Agen), M Lièvremont (Stade Français), R Castel (Béziers), O Magne (Brive), T Lièvremont (Perpignan)

TOUR RECORD

All matches   Played 5   Won 4   Lost 1   Points for 164   Against 107
International matches   Played 3   Won 3   Points for 106   Against 39

SCORING DETAILS

All matches				International matches			
For:	22T 18C 6PG	= 164pts	For:	14T 12C 4PG	= 106pts
Against:	11T 5C 13PG 1DG	= 107pts	Against:	2T 1C 8PG 1DG	= 39pts

MATCH DETAILS

1998	OPPONENTS	VENUE	RESULT
13 June	ARGENTINA	Buenos Aires	W 35-18
16 June	Buenos Aires	Buenos Aires	L 22-36
20 June	ARGENTINA	Buenos Aires	W 37-12
24 June	Fijian Barbarians	Sigatoka, Nadi	W 36-32
27 June	FIJI	Suva	W 34-9

MATCH 1   13 June, Vélez Sarsfield Stadium, Buenos Aires
1st Test

ARGENTINA 18 (1G 2PG 1T)   FRANCE 35 (5G)

ARGENTINA: EH Jurado (Jockey Club, Rosario); DL Albanese (San Isidro Club), E Simone (Liceo Naval), J Orengo (Atletico Rosario), F Soler (Tala, Cordoba); L Arbizu (Brive, France) *(capt)*, A Pichot (Richmond, England); RD Grau (Saracens, England), FE Mendez (Bath, England), M Reggiardo (Castres, France), A Allub (Jockey Club, Rosario), GA Llanes (Bath, England), RA Martin (Richmond, England), F Rossi (Rosario), MA Ruiz (Teque, Cuyo)
Substitutions: S Phelan (CA San Isidro) for Martin (41 mins); O Hasan-Jalil (ACT, Australia) for Grau (41 mins); CI Fernandez-Lobbe (Liceo Naval) for Allub (41 mins); D Giannantonio (Cordoba) for Jurado (54 mins); M Ledesma (Curupayti) for Mendez (65 mins)
Scorers *Tries:* Orengo, Soler *Conversion:* Arbizu *Penalty Goals:* Arbizu (2)

France: Gomès; Bernat-Salles, Comba, Glas, Dominici; Castaignède, Carbonneau; Soulette, Ibañez (*capt*), Tournaire, Brouzet, Pelous, M Lièvremont, T Lièvremont, Magne *Substitutions:* Dal Maso for Ibañez (temp 38-46 mins); Benetton for Magne (54 mins); De Besombes for Tournaire (75 mins); Cléda for Pelous (78 mins)
Scorers *Tries:* M Lièvremont (2), Dominici, Dal Maso, Castaignède
Conversions: Castaignède (5)
Referee S R Walsh (New Zealand)

MATCH 2   16 June, Buenos Aires

Buenos Aires XV 36 (2G 4PG 2T)   **France XV 22** (2G 1PG 1T)
Buenos Aires XV: M Contepomi (Newman); T Solari (Hindu), FL Garcia (Alumni), JC Fernandez-Miranda (Hindu), O Bartolucci (Rosario Athletic); JL Cilley (San Isidro Club) (*capt*), N Fernandez-Miranda (Hindu); J Guateria (Hindu), C Villar (Hindu), M Scelzo (Banco Hipotecario), B Anthony (Hindu), G Ugartemendia (Los Matreros), G Longo Elia (San Isidro Club), R Travaglini (CASI), C Viel (Newman)
Scorers *Tries:* Anthony, Bartolucci, Contepomi, Garcia *Conversions:* Cilley (2) *Penalty Goals:* Cilley (4)
France XV: Gomès; Garbajosa, Plana, Aué, Marlu; Aucagne, Galthié (*capt*); Collazo, Dal Maso, De Besombes, Belot, Cléda, Castel, Benetton, Magne
Substitutions: Glas for Gomès (49 mins); M Lièvremont for Magne (62 mins)
Scorers *Tries:* Marlu (2), penalty try *Conversions:* Aucagne (2)
Penalty Goal: Aucagne
Referee: AG Riley (New Zealand)

MATCH 3   20 June, Vélez Sarsfield Stadium, Buenos Aires
2nd Test

ARGENTINA 12 (3PG 1DG)   FRANCE 37 (3G 2PG 2T)

ARGENTINA: D Giannantonio (Cordoba); DL Albanese (San Isidro Club), E Simone (Liceo Naval), J Orengo (Atletico Rosario), F Soler (Tala, Cordoba); L Arbizu (Brive, France), A Pichot (Richmond, England); M Reggiardo (Castres, France), M Ledesma (Curupayti), O Hasan-Jalil (ACT, Australia), A Allub (Jockey Club, Rosario), PL Sporleder (Curupayti) (*capt*), S Phelan (CA San Isidro), CI Fernandez-Lobbe (Liceo Naval), RA Martin (Richmond, England)
Substitutions: G Quesada (Hindu) for Arbizu (temp 29-33 mins); FE Mendez (Bath, England) for Reggiardo (39 mins); MA Ruiz (Teque, Cuyo) for Martin (54 mins); M Scelzo (Banco Hipoticario) for Hasan (61 mins)
Scorer *Penalty Goals:* Arbizu (3) *Dropped Goal:* Arbizu
France: Gomès; Bernat-Salles, Comba, Glas, Domenici; Castaignède, Carbonneau; Soulette, Ibañez (*capt*), Tournaire, Brouzet, Pelous, M Lièvremont, T Lièvremont, Magne *Substitutions:* Garbajosa for Bernat-Salles (18 mins); Benetton for Magne (43 mins); Aucagne for Castaignède (78 mins)
Scorers *Tries:* Soulette (2), Dominici, Garbajosa, Brouzet
Conversions: Castaignède (3) *Penalty Goals:* Castaignède (2)
Referee PJ Honiss (New Zealand)

MATCH 4   24 June, Sigatoka, Nadi

Fiji Barbarians 32 (2G 1PG 3T)   **France XV 36** (4G 1PG 1T)
Fiji Barbarians: A Uluinayau (Suntory, Japan); M Bari (Nadroga & Otago, NZ), L Koroi (Suva), E Nauga (Suva), L Duvuduvukula (Suva); W Serevi (Leicester, England), J Rauluni (Easts, Queensland); N Qoro (Lautoka), L Nyholt

(Suva),VB Cavubati (Wellington, NZ), I Tawake (Nadroga) (*capt*), T Waqavolavola (Nadroga), IT Tabua (Brothers & Queensland), M Olsson (Suntory, Japan), M Korovou (Nadi) *Substitutions:* S Nasau (Lautoka) for Nyholt (53 mins); M Nakauta (Manly, NSW) for Waqavolavola (60 mins); S Rabaka (Nadi) for Rauluni (71 mins)
Scorers *Tries:* Bari (2), Uluinayau, Duvuduvulula, Serevi *Conversions:* Serevi (2) *Penalty Goal:* Serevi
France XV: Garbajosa; Dominici, Plana, Aué, Marlu; Aucagne, Galthié (*capt*); Collazo, Dal Maso, De Besombes, Cléda, Belot, Benetton, T Lièvremont, Castel *Substitutions:* M Lièvremont for T Lièvremont (64 mins); Tournaire for Collazo (80 mins)
Scorers *Tries:* T Lièvremont, Castel, Aué, Dominici, M Lièvremont *Conversions:* Aucagne (4) *Penalty Goal:* Aucagne
Referee G Ayoub (Australia)

MATCH 5   27 June, National Stadium, Suva   Test Match

FIJI 9 (3PG)   FRANCE 34 (4G 2PG 1DG)

FIJI: J Waqa (Nadroga); A Tuilevu (Waikato, NZ), SC Sorovaki (Kintetsu, Japan) (*capt*), M Nakauta (Manly, NSW), FT Lasagavibau (Nadroga); NT Little (North Harbour, NZ), J Rauluni (Easts, Queensland); J Veitayaki (Northland, NZ), I Rasila (Nadroga), M Taga (Wellington, NZ), S Raiwalui (Saracens, England), E Katalau (North Harbour), A Naevo (Counties, NZ), IT Tabua (Brothers, Queensland), S Saumaisue (Powerhouse, Victoria) *Substitutions:* VB Cavubati (Wellington, NZ) for Taga (45 mins); A Uluinayau (Suntory, Japan) for Tuilevu (49 mins); W Serevi (Leicester, England) for Little (63 mins); I Tawake (Nadroga) for Tabua (63 mins); M Tamanitoakila (Tailevu) for Saumaisue (temp 68-73 mins)
Scorer *Penalty Goals:* N Little (3)
FRANCE: Gomès; Bernat-Salles, Comba, Glas, Garbajosa; Castaignède, Carbonneau; Soulette, Ibañez (*capt*), Tournaire, Brouzet, Pelous, M Lièvremont, T Lièvremont, Magne *Substitutions:* Cléda for Pelous (45 mins); Benetton for T Lièvremont (63 mins); De Besombes for Soulette (67 mins); Marlu for Garbajosa (68 mins); Dal Maso for Ibañez (75 mins); Galthié for Carbonneau (75 mins); Aucagne for Glas (75 mins)
Scorers *Tries:* T Lièvremont, Gomès, Bernat-Salles, Aucagne *Conversions:* Castaignède (4) *Penalty Goal:* Castaignède *Dropped Goal:* Castaignède
Referee A Cole (Australia)

FRENCH INTERNATIONAL PLAYERS
(up to 30 April 1999)

Note: Years given for Five Nations matches are for second half of season, eg 1972 refers to season 1971-72. Years for all other matches refer to the actual year of the match. When a series has taken place, or more than one match has been played against a country in the same year, figures have been used to denote the particular matches in which players have featured. Thus 1967 *SA* 2,4 indicates that a player appeared in the second and fourth Tests of the 1967 series against South Africa. This list includes only those players who have appeared in FFR International Matches *'donnant droit au titre d'international'*.

Abadie, A (Pau) 1964 *I*
Abadie, A (Graulhet) 1965 *R*, 1967 *SA* 1, 3, 4, *NZ*, 1968 *S, I*
Abadie, L (Tarbes) 1963 *R*
Accoceberry, G (Bègles) 1994 *NZ* 1,2, *C* 2, 1995 *W, E, S, I, R* 1, [*Iv, S*], *It*, 1996 *I, W* 1, *R, Arg* 1, *W* 2(R), *SA* 2, 1997 *S, It* 1
Aguerre, R (Biarritz O) 1979 *S*
Aguilar, D (Pau) 1937 *G*
Aguirre, J-M (Bagnères) 1971 *A* 2, 1972 *S*, 1973 *W, I, J, R*, 1974 *I, W, Arg* 2, *R, SA* 1, 1976 *W* (R), *E, US, A* 2, *R*, 1977 *W, E, S, I, Arg* 1,2, *NZ* 1,2, *R*, 1978 *E, S, I, W, R*, 1979 *I, W, E, S, NZ* 1,2, *R*, 1980 *W, I*
Ainciart, E (Bayonne) 1933 *G*, 1934 *G*, 1935 *G*, 1937 *G, It*, 1938 *G* 1
Albaladejo, P (Dax) 1954 *E, It*, 1960 *W, I, It, R*, 1961 *S, SA, E, W, I, NZ* 1,2, *A*, 1962 *S, E, W, I*, 1963 *S, I, E, W, It*, 1964 *S, NZ, W, It, I, SA, Fj*
Alvarez, A-J (Tyrosse) 1945 *B2*, 1946 *B, I, K, W*, 1947 *S, I, W, E*, 1948 *I, A, S, W, E*, 1949 *I, E, W*, 1951 *S, E, W*
Amand, H (SF) 1906 *NZ*
Ambert, A (Toulouse) 1930 *S, I, E, G, W*
Amestoy, J-B (Mont-de-Marsan) 1964 *NZ, E*
André, G (RCF) 1913 *SA, E, W, I*, 1914 *I, W, E*
Andrieu, M (Nîmes) 1986 *Arg* 2, *NZ* 1, *R* 2, *NZ* 2, 1987 [*R, Z*], *R*, 1988 *E, S, I, W, Arg* 1,2,3,4, *R*, 1989 *I, W, E, S, NZ* 2, *B, A* 2, 1990 *W, E, I* (R)
Anduran, J (SCUF) 1910 *W*
Araou, R (Narbonne) 1924 *R*
Arcalis, R (Brive) 1950 *S, I*, 1951 *I, E, W*
Arino, M (Agen) 1962 *R*
Aristouy, P (Pau) 1948 *S*, 1949 *Arg* 2, 1950 *S, I, E, W*
Arlettaz, P (Perpignan) 1995 *R* 2
Armary, L (Lourdes) 1987 [*R*], *R*, 1988 *S, I, W, Arg* 3,4, *R*, 1989 *W, S, A* 1,2, 1990 *W, E, S, I, A* 1,2,3, *NZ* 1, 1991 *W* 2, 1992 *S, I, R, Arg* 1,2, *SA* 1, 2, *Arg*, 1993 *E, S, I, W, SA* 1,2, *R* 2, *A* 1,2, 1994 *I, W, NZ* 1 (t), 2 (t), 1995 *I, R* 1 [*Tg, I, SA*]
Arnal, J-M (RCF) 1914 *I, W*
Arnaudet, M (Lourdes) 1964 *I*, 1967 *It, W*
Arotca, R (Bayonne) 1938 *R*
Arrieta, J (SF) 1953 *E, W*
Arthapignet, P (see Harislur-Arthapignet)
Astre, R (Béziers) 1971 *R*, 1972 *I* 1, 1973 *E* (R), 1975 *E, S, I, SA* 1,2, 1974 *A* 2, 1976 *A* 2, *R*
Aucagne, D (Pau) 1997 *W* (R), *S, It* 1, *R* 1 (R), *A* 1, *R* 2 (R), *SA* 2 (R), 1998 *S* (R), *W* (R), *Arg* 2 (R), *Fj* (R), *Arg* 3, *A*, 1999 *W* (R), *S* (R)
Aué, J-M (Castres) 1998 *W* (R)
Augé, J (Dax) 1929 *S, W*
Augras-Fabre, L (Agen) 1931 *I, S, W*
Auradou, D (SF) 1999 *E* (R), *S* (R)
Averous, J-L (La Voulte) 1975 *S, I, SA* 1,2, 1976 *I, W, E, US, A* 1,2, *R*, 1977 *W, E, S, I, Arg* 1, *R*, 1978 *E, S, I*, 1979 *NZ* 1,2, 1980 *S, I*, 1981 *A* 2
Azam, O (Montferrand) 1995 *R* 2, *Arg* (R)
Azarete, J-L (Dax, St Jean-de-Luz) 1969 *W, R*, 1970 *S, I, W, R*, 1971 *S, I, E, SA* 1,2, *A* 1, 1972 *E, W, I* 2, *A* 1, *R*, 1973 *NZ, W, I, R*, 1974 *I, R, SA* 1,2, 1975 *W*

Bacqué, N (Pau) 1997 *R* 2
Bader, E (Primevères) 1926 *M*, 1927 *I, S*
Badin, C (Chalon) 1973 *W, I*, 1975 *Arg* 1
Baillette, M (Perpignan) 1925 *I, NZ, S*, 1926 *W, M*, 1927 *I, W, G* 2, 1929 *G*, 1930 *S, I, E, G*, 1931 *I, S, E*, 1932 *G*
Baladie, G (Agen) 1945 *B* 1,2, *W*, 1946 *B, I, K*
Ballarin, J (Tarbes) 1924 *E*, 1925 *NZ, S*
Baquey, J (Toulouse) 1921 *I*
Barbazanges, A (Roanne) 1932 *G*, 1933 *G*

Barrau, M (Beaumont, Toulouse) 1971 *S, E, W*, 1972 *E, W, A* 1,2, 1973 *S, NZ, E, I, J, R*, 1974 *I, S*
Barrère, P (Toulon) 1929 *G*, 1931 *W*
Barrière, R (Béziers) 1960 *R*
Barthe, E (SBUC) 1925 *W, E*
Barthe, J (Lourdes) 1954 *Arg* 1,2, 1955 *S*, 1956 *I, W, It, E, Cz*, 1957 *S, I, E, W, R* 1,2, 1958 *S, E, A, W, It, I, SA* 1,2, 1959 *S, E, It, W*
Basauri, R (Albi) 1954 *Arg* 1
Bascou, P (Bayonne) 1914 *E*
Basquet, G (Agen) 1945 *W*, 1946 *B, I, K, W*, 1947 *S, I, W, E*, 1948 *I, A, S, W, E*, 1949 *S, I, E, W, Arg* 1, 1950 *S, I, E, W*, 1951 *S, I, E, W*, 1952 *S, I, SA, W, E, It*
Bastiat, J-P (Dax) 1969 *R*, 1970 *S, I, W*, 1971 *S, I, SA* 2, 1972 *S, A* 1, 1973 *E*, 1974 *Arg* 1,2, *SA* 2, 1975 *W, Arg* 1,2, *R*, 1976 *S, I, W, E, A* 1,2, *R*, 1977 *W, E, S, I*, 1978 *E, S, I, W*
Baudry, N (Montferrand) 1949 *S, I, W, Arg* 1,2
Baulon, R (Vienne, Bayonne) 1954 *S, NZ, W, E, It*, 1955 *S, I, W, It*, 1956 *S, I, W, It, E, Cz*, 1957 *S, I, It*
Baux, J-P (Lannemezan) 1968 *NZ* 1,2, *SA* 1,2
Bavozet, J (Lyon) 1911 *S, E, W*
Bayard, J (Toulouse) 1923 *S, W, E*, 1924 *W, R, US*
Bayardon, J (Chalon) 1964 *S, NZ, E*
Beaurin-Gressier, C (SF) 1907 *E*, 1908 *E*
Bégu, D (Dax) 1982 *Arg* 2 (R), 1984 *E, S*
Béguerie, C (Agen) 1979 *NZ* 1
Beguet, L (RCF) 1922 *I*, 1923 *S, W, E, I*, 1924 *S, I, E, R, US*
Behoteguy, A (Bayonne, Cognac) 1923 *E*, 1924 *S, I, E, W, R, US*, 1926 *E*, 1927 *E, G* 1,2, 1928 *A, I, E, G, W*, 1929 *S, W, E*
Behoteguy, H (RCF, Cognac) 1923 *W*, 1928 *A, I, E, G, W*
Belascain, C (Bayonne) 1977 *R*, 1978 *E, S, I, W, R*, 1979 *I, W, E, S*, 1982 *W, E, S, I*, 1983 *E, S, I, W*
Belletante, G (Nantes) 1951 *I, E, W*
Benazzi, A (Agen) 1990 *A* 1,2,3, *NZ* 1,2, 1991 *E, US* 1 (R), 2, [*R, Fj, C*], 1992 *SA* 1 (R), 2, *Arg*, 1993 *E, S, I, W, A* 1,2, 1994 *S, S, C* 1, *NZ* 1,2, *C* 2, 1995 *W, E, S, I*, [*Tg, Iv, S, I, SA, E*], *NZ* 1,2, 1996 *E, S, I, W* 1, *Arg* 1,2, *SA* 2, 1997 *I, W, E, S, R* 1, *A* 1,2, *It* 2, *R* 2 (R), *Arg, SA* 1,2
Bénésis, R (Narbonne) 1969 *W, R*, 1970 *S, I, W, E, R*, 1971 *S, I, E, W, A* 2, *R*, 1972 *S, I* 1, *E, W, I* 2, *A* 1, *R*, 1973 *NZ, E, W, I, R*, 1974 *I, R, SA* 1,2, 1975 *W*
Benetière, J (Roanne) 1954 *It, Arg* 1
Benetton, P (Agen) 1989 *B*, 1990 *NZ* 2, 1991 *US* 2, 1992 *Arg* 1,2 (R), *SA* 1 (R), 2, *Arg*, 1993 *E, S, I, W, SA* 1,2, *R* 2, *A* 1,2, 1994 *I, W, E, S, C* 1, *NZ* 1,2, *C* 2, 1995 *W, E, S, I*, [*Tg, Iv* (R), *S*], *It*, *R* 2 (R), *Arg, NZ* 1, 2
Benezech, L (RCF) 1994 *E, S, C* 1, *NZ* 1,2, *C* 2, 1995 *W, E*, [*Iv, S, E*], *R* 2, *Arg, NZ* 1, 2
Berbizier, P (Lourdes, Agen) 1981 *S, I, W, E, NZ* 1,2, 1982 *I, R*, 1983 *S, I*, 1984 *S* (R), *NZ* 1,2, 1985 *Arg* 1,2, 1986 *S, I, W, E, R* 1, *Arg* 1, *A, NZ* 1, *R* 2, *NZ* 2,3, 1987 *W, E, S, I*, [*S, R, Fj, A, NZ*], *R*, 1988 *E, S, I, W, Arg* 1,2, 1989 *I, W, E, S, NZ* 1,2, *B, A* 1, 1990 *W, E*, 1991 *S, I, W, I, E*
Berejnoi, J-C (Tulle) 1963 *R*, 1964 *S, W, It, I, SA, Fj, R*, 1965 *S, I, E, W, It, R*, 1966 *S, I, E, W, It, R*, 1967 *S, A, E, It, W, I, R*
Berges, B (Toulouse) 1926 *I*
Berges-Cau, R (Lourdes) 1976 *E* (R)
Bergese, F (Bayonne) 1936 *G* 2, 1937 *G, It*, 1938 *G* 1, *R*, *G* 2
Bergougnan, Y (Toulouse) 1945 *B* 1, *W*, 1946 *B, I, K, W*, 1947 *S, I, W, E*, 1948 *S, W, E*, 1949 *S, E, Arg* 1,2
Bernard, R (Bergerac) 1951 *S, I, E, W*

Bernat-Salles, P (Pau, Bègles-Bordeaux, Biarritz) 1992 *Arg*, 1993 *R* 1, *SA* 1,2, *R* 2, *A* 1,2, 1994 *I*, 1995 *E, S*, 1996 *E* (R), 1997 *R* 1, *A* 1,2, 1998 *E, S, I, W, Arg* 1,2, *Fj, Arg* 3 (R), *A* 1999 *I, W*
Bernon, J (Lourdes) 1922 *I*, 1923 *S*
Bérot, J-L (Toulouse) 1968 *NZ* 3, *A*, 1969 *S, I*, 1970 *E, R*, 1971 *S, I, E, W, SA* 1,2, *A* 1,2, *R*, 1972 *S, I* 1, *E, W, A* 1, 1974 *I*
Bérot, P (Agen) 1986 *R* 2, *NZ* 2, 3, 1987 *W, E, S, I, R*, 1988 *E, S, I, Arg* 1, 2, 3, 4, *R*, 1989 *S, NZ* 1, 2
Bertrand, P (Bourg) 1951 *I, E, W*, 1953 *S, I, E, W, It*
Bertranne, R (Bagnères) 1971 *E, W, SA* 2, *A* 1,2, 1972 *S, I* 1, 1973 *NZ, E, J, R*, 1974 *I, W, E, S, Arg* 1,2, *R, SA* 1,2, 1975 *W, E, S, I, SA* 1,2, *Arg* 1,2, *R*, 1976 *S, I, W, E, US, A* 1,2, *R*, 1977 *W, E, S, I, Arg* 1,2, *NZ* 1,2, *R*, 1978 *E, S, I, W, R*, 1979 *I, W, E, S, R*, 1980 *W, E, S, I, SA, R*, 1981 *S, I, W, E, R, NZ* 1,2
Berty, D (Toulouse) 1990 *NZ* 2, 1992 *R* (R), 1993 *R* 2, 1995 *NZ* 1 (R), 1996 *W* 2(R), *SA* 1
Besset, E (Grenoble) 1924 *S*
Besset, L (SCUF) 1914 *W, E*
Besson, M (CASG) 1924 *I*, 1925 *I, E*, 1926 *S, W*, 1927 *I*
Besson, P (Brive) 1963 *S, I, E*, 1965 *R*, 1968 *SA* 1
Betsen, S (Biarritz) 1997 *It* 1 (R)
Bianchi, J (Toulon) 1986 *Arg* 1
Bichindaritz, J (Biarritz O) 1954 *It, Arg* 1,2
Bidart, L (La Rochelle) 1953 *W*
Biemouret, P (Agen) 1969 *E, W*, 1970 *I, W, E*, 1971 *W, SA* 1,2, *A* 1, 1972 *E, W, I* 2, *A* 2, *R*, 1973 *S, NZ, E, W, I*
Biénès, R (Cognac) 1950 *S, I, E, W*, 1951 *S, I, E, W*, 1952 *S, I, SA, W, E, It*, 1953 *S, I, E*, 1954 *S, I, NZ, W, E, Arg* 1,2, 1956 *S, I, W, It, E*
Bigot, C (Quillan) 1930 *S, E*, 1931 *I, S*
Bilbao, L (St Jean-de-Luz) 1978 *I*, 1979 *I*
Billac, E (Bayonne) 1920 *S, E, W, I, US*, 1921 *S, W*, 1922 *W*, 1923 *E*
Billière, M (Toulouse) 1968 *NZ* 3
Bioussa, A (Toulouse) 1924 *W, US*, 1925 *I, NZ, S, E*, 1926 *S, I, E*, 1928 *E, G, W*, 1929 *I, S, W, E*, 1930 *S, I, E, G, W*
Bioussa, C (Toulouse) 1913 *W, I*, 1914 *I*
Biraben, M (Dax) 1920 *W, I, US*, 1921 *S, W, E, I*, 1922 *S, E, I*
Blain, A (Carcassonne) 1934 *G*
Blanco, S (Biarritz O) 1980 *SA, R*, 1981 *S, W, E, A* 1,2, *R, NZ* 1,2, 1982 *W, E, S, I, R, Arg* 1,2, 1983 *E, S, I, W*, 1984 *I, W, E, S, NZ* 1,2, *R*, 1985 *E, S, I, W, Arg* 1,2, 1986 *S, I, W, E, R* 1, *Arg* 2, *A, NZ* 1, *R* 2, *NZ* 2,3, 1987 *W, E, S, I*, [*S, R, Fj, A, NZ*], *R*, 1988 *E, S, I, W, Arg* 1,2,3,4, *R*, 1989 *I, W, E, S, NZ* 1,2, *B, A* 1, 1990 *E, S, I, R, A* 1,2,3, *NZ* 1,2, 1991 *S, I, W* 1, *E, R*, 1992 *S, I, W* 2, [*R, Fj, C, E*]
Blond, J (SF) 1935 *G*, 1936 *G* 2, 1937 *G*, 1938 *G* 1, *R, G* 2
Blond, X (RCF) 1990 *A* 3, 1991 *S, I, W* 1, *E*, 1994 *NZ* 2 (R)
Boffelli, V (Aurillac) 1971 *A* 2, *R*, 1972 *S, I* 1, 1973 *J, R*, 1974 *I, W, E, S, Arg* 1,2, *R, SA* 1,2, 1975 *W, S, I*
Bonal, J-M (Toulouse) 1968 *E, W, Cz, NZ* 2,3, *SA* 1,2, *R*, 1969 *S, I, E, R*, 1970 *W, E*
Bonamy, R (SB) 1928 *A, I*
Bondouy, P (Narbonne) 1997 *S* (R), *It* 1, *A* 2 (R), *R* 2
Boniface, A (Mont-de-Marsan) 1954 *I, NZ, W, E, It, Arg* 1,2, 1955 *S, I*, 1956 *S, I, W, It, Cz*, 1957 *S, I, W, R* 2, 1958 *S, E*, 1959 *E*, 1961 *NZ* 1,3, *A, R*, 1962 *E, W, I, It, R*, 1963 *S, I, E, W, It, R*, 1964 *S, NZ, E, W, It*, 1965 *W, It, R*, 1966 *S, I, E, W*
Boniface, G (Mont-de-Marsan) 1960 *W, I, It, R, Arg* 1,2,3, 1961 *S, SA, E, W, It, I, NZ* 1,2,3, *R*, 1962 *R*, 1963 *S, I, E, W, It, R*, 1964 *S*, 1965 *S, I, E, W*, 1966 *S, I, E, W*
Bonnes, E (Narbonne) 1924 *W, R, US*
Bonneval, E (Toulouse) 1984 *NZ* 2 (R), 1985 *W, Arg* 1, 1986 *W, E, R* 1, *Arg* 1,2, *A, R* 2, *NZ* 2,3, 1987 *W, E, S, I*, [*Z*], 1988 *E*
Bonnus, F (Toulon) 1950 *S, I, E, W*
Bonnus, M (Toulon) 1937 *It*, 1938 *G* 1, *R, G* 2, 1940 *B*
Bontemps, D (La Rochelle) 1968 *SA* 2
Borchard, G (RCF) 1908 *E*, 1909 *E, W, I*, 1911 *I*
Borde, F (RCF) 1920 *I, US*, 1921 *S, W, E*, 1922 *S, W*, 1923 *S, I*, 1924 *E*, 1925 *I, E*
Bordenave, L (Toulon) 1948 *A, S, W, E*, 1949 *S*
Boubée, J (Tarbes) 1921 *S, E, I*, 1922 *E, W*, 1923 *E, I*, 1925 *NZ, S*
Boudreaux, R (SCUF) 1910 *W, S*
Bouet, D (Dax) 1989 *NZ* 1,2, *B, A* 2, 1990 *A* 3

Bouguyon, G (Grenoble) 1961 *SA, E, W, It, I, NZ* 1,2,3, *A*
Bouic, G (Agen) 1996 *SA* 1
Boujet, C (Grenoble) 1968 *NZ* 2, *A* (R), *SA* 1
Bouquet, J (Bourgoin, Vienne) 1954 *S*, 1955 *E*, 1956 *S, I, W, It, E, Cz*, 1957 *S, E, W, R* 2, 1958 *S, E*, 1959 *S, It, W, I*, 1960 *S, E, W, I, R*, 1961 *S, SA, E, W, It, I, R*, 1962 *S, E, W, I*
Bourdeu, J R (Lourdes) 1952 *S, I, SA, W, E, It*, 1953 *S, I, E*
Bourgarel, R (Toulouse) 1969 *R*, 1970 *S, I, E, R*, 1971 *W, SA* 1,2, 1973 *S*
Bourguignon, G (Narbonne) 1988 *Arg* 3, 1989 *I, E, B, A* 1, 1990 *R*
Bousquet, A (Béziers) 1921 *E, I*, 1924 *R*
Bousquet, R (Albi) 1926 *M*, 1927 *I, S, W, E, G* 1, 1929 *W, E*, 1930 *W*
Boyau, M (SBUC) 1912 *I, S, W, E*, 1913 *W, I*
Boyer, P (Toulon) 1935 *G*
Branca, G (SF) 1928 *S*, 1929 *I, S*
Branlat, A (RCF) 1906 *NZ, E*, 1908 *W*
Brejassou, R (Tarbes) 1952 *S, I, SA, W, E*, 1953 *W, E*, 1954 *S, I, NZ*, 1955 *S, I, E, W, It*
Brethes, R (St Sever) 1960 *Arg* 2
Bringeon, A (Biarritz O) 1925 *W*
Brouzet, O (Grenoble, Bègles) 1994 *S, NZ* 2 (R), 1995 *E, S, I, R* 1, [*Tg, Iv, E* (t)], *It, Arg* (R), 1996 *W* 1 (R), 1997 *R* 1, *A* 1,2, *It* 2, *Arg, SA* 1,2, 1998 *E, S, I, W, Arg* 1,2, *Fj, Arg* 3, *A*, 1999 *I, W, E, S*
Brun, G (Vienne) 1950 *E, W*, 1951 *S, E, W*, 1952 *S, I, SA, W, E, It*, 1953 *E, W, It*
Bruneau, M (SBUC) 1910 *W, E*, 1913 *SA, E*
Brunet, Y (Perpignan) 1975 *SA* 1, 1977 *Arg* 1
Brusque, N (Pau) 1997 *R* 2 (R)
Buchet, E (Nice) 1980 *R*, 1982 *E, R* (R), *Arg* 1,2
Buisson, H (see Empereur-Buisson)
Buonomo, Y (Béziers) 1971 *A* 2, *R*, 1972 *I* 1
Burgun, M (RCF) 1909 *I*, 1910 *W, S, I*, 1911 *S, E*, 1912 *I, S*, 1913 *S, E*, 1914 *E*
Bustaffa, D (Carcassonne) 1977 *Arg* 1,2, *NZ* 1,2, 1978 *W, R*, 1980 *E, S, SA, R*
Buzy, C-E (Lourdes) 1946 *K, W*, 1947 *S, I, W, E*, 1948 *I, A, S, W, E*, 1949 *S, I, E, W, Arg* 1,2

Cabanier, J-M (Montauban) 1963 *R*, 1964 *S, Fj*, 1965 *S, I, W, It, R*, 1966 *S, I, E, W, It, R*, 1967 *S, A, E, It, W, I, SA* 1,3, *NZ, R*, 1968 *S, I*
Cabannes, L (RCF, Harlequins) 1990 *NZ* 2 (R), 1991 *S, I, W* 1, *E, US* 2, *W* 2, [*R, Fj, C, E*], 1992 *W, E, S, I, R, Arg* 2, *SA* 1,2, 1993 *E, S, I, W, R* 1, *SA* 1,2, 1994 *E, S, C* 1, *NZ* 1,2, 1995 *W, E, S, R* 1, [*Tg* (R), *Iv, S, I, SA, E*], 1996 *E, S, I, W* 1, 1997 *It* 2, *Arg, SA* 1,2
Cabrol, H (Béziers) 1972 *A* 1 (R), 2, 1973 *J*, 1974 *SA* 2
Cadenat, J (SCUF) 1910 *S, E*, 1911 *W, I*, 1912 *W, E*, 1913 *I*
Cadieu, J-M (Toulouse) 1991 *R, US* 1, [*R, Fj, C, E*], 1992 *W, I, R, Arg* 1,2, *SA* 1
Cahuc, F (St Girons) 1922 *S*
Califano, C (Toulouse) 1994 *NZ* 1,2, *C* 2, 1995 *W, E, S, I*, [*Iv, S, I, SA, E*], *It, Arg, NZ* 1, 2, 1996 *E, S, I, W* 1, *R, Arg* 1,2, *SA* 1,2, 1997 *I, W, E, A* 1,2, *It* 2, *R* 2 (R), *Arg, SA* 1,2, 1998 *E, S, I, W*, 1999 *I, W, E* (R), *S*
Cals, R (RCF) 1938 *G* 1
Calvo, G (Lourdes) 1961 *NZ* 1,3
Camberabero, D (La Voulte, Béziers) 1982 *R, Arg* 1,2, 1983 *E, W*, 1987 [*R* (R), *Z, Fj* (R), *A, NZ*], 1988 *I*, 1989 *B, A* 1, 1990 *W, S, I, R, A* 1,2,3, *NZ* 1,2, 1991 *S, I, W* 1, *E, R, US* 1,2, *W* 2, [*R, Fj, C*], 1993 *E, S, I*
Camberabero, G (La Voulte) 1961 *NZ* 3, 1962 *R*, 1964 *R*, 1967 *A, E, It, W, I, SA* 1,3,4, 1968 *S, E, W*
Camberabero, L (La Voulte) 1964 *R*, 1965 *S, I*, 1966 *E, W*, 1967 *A, E, It, W, I*, 1968 *S, E, W*
Cambré, T (Oloron) 1920 *E, W, I, US*
Camel, A (Toulouse) 1928 *S, A, I, E, G, W*, 1929 *W, E, G*, 1930 *S, I, E, G, W*, 1935 *G*
Camel, M (Toulouse) 1929 *S, W, E*
Camicas, F (Tarbes) 1927 *G* 2, 1928 *S, I, E, G, W*, 1929 *I, S, W, E*
Camo, E (Villeneuve) 1931 *I, S, W, E, G*, 1932 *G*
Campaes, A (Lourdes) 1965 *W*, 1967 *NZ*, 1968 *S, I, E, W, Cz, NZ* 1,2, *A*, 1969 *S, W*, 1972 *R*, 1973 *NZ*
Campan, O (Agen) 1993 *SA* 1 (R), 2 (R), *R* 2 (R), 1996 *I, W, I, R*
Cantoni, J (Béziers) 1970 *W, R*, 1971 *S, I, E, W, SA* 1,2, *A* 1, *R*, 1972 *S, I* 1, 1973 *S, NZ, W, I*, 1975 *W* (R)

Capdouze, J (Pau) 1964 *SA, Fj, R*, 1965 *S, I, E*
Capendeguy, J-M (Bègles) 1967 *NZ, R*
Capitani, P (Toulon) 1954 *Arg* 1,2
Capmau, J-L (Toulouse) 1914 *E*
Carabignac, G (Agen) 1951 *S, I*, 1952 *SA, W, E*, 1953 *S, I*
Carbonne, J (Perpignan) 1927 *W*
Carbonneau, P (Toulouse, Brive) 1995 *R* 2, *Arg, NZ* 1, 2, 1996 *E, S, R* (R), *Arg* 2, *W* 2, *SA* 1, 1997 *I* (R), *W, E, S* (R), *R* 1 (R), *A* 1,2, 1998 *E, S, I, W, Arg* 1,2, *Fj, Arg* 3, *A*, 1999 *I, W, E, S*
Carminati, A (Béziers, Brive) 1986 *R* 2, *NZ* 2, 1987 *[R, Z]*, 1988 *I, W, Arg* 1,2, 1989 *I, W, S, NZ* 1 (R), 2, *A* 2, 1990 *S*, 1995 *It, R* 2, *Arg, NZ* 1, 2
Caron, L (Lyon O, Castres) 1947 *E*, 1948 *I, A, W, E*, 1949 *S, I, E, W, Arg* 1
Carpentier, M (Lourdes) 1980 *E, SA, R*, 1981 *S, I, A* 1, 1982 *E, S*
Carrère, C (Toulon) 1966 *R*, 1967 *S, A, E, W, I, SA* 1,3,4, *NZ, R*, 1968 *S, I, E, W, Cz, NZ* 3, *A, R*, 1969 *S, I*, 1970 *S, I, W, E*, 1971 *E, W*
Carrère, J (Vichy, Toulon) 1956 *S*, 1957 *E, W, R* 2, 1958 *S, SA* 1,2, 1959 *I*
Carrère, R (Mont-de-Marsan) 1953 *E, It*
Casadei, D (Brive) 1997 *S, R* 1, *SA* 2 (R)
Casaux, L (Tarbes) 1959 *I, It*, 1962 *S*
Cassagne, P (Pau) 1957 *It*
Cassayet-Armagnac, A (Tarbes, Narbonne) 1920 *S, E, W, US*, 1921 *W, E, I*, 1922 *S, E, W, I*, 1923 *S, W, E, I*, 1924 *S, E, W, R, US*, 1925 *I, NZ, S, W*, 1926 *S, I, E, W, M*, 1927 *I, S, W*
Cassiède, M (Dax) 1961 *NZ* 3, *A, R*
Castaignède, T (Toulouse, Castres) 1995 *R* 2, *Arg, NZ* 1, 2, 1996 *E, S, I, W* 1, *Arg* 1,2, 1997 *I, A* 1,2, *It* 2, 1998 *E, S, I, W, Arg* 1,2, *Fj*, 1999 *I, W, E, S*
Castel, R (Toulouse, Béziers) 1996 *I, W* 1, *W* 2, *SA* 1(R),2, 1997 *I* (R), *W, E* (R), *S* (R), *A* 1 (R), 1998 *Arg* 3 (R), *A* (R), 1999 *W* (R), *E, S*
Castets, J (Toulon) 1923 *W, E, I*
Caujolle, J (Tarbes) 1909 *E*, 1913 *SA, E*, 1914 *W, E*
Caunègre, R (SB) 1938 *R, G* 2
Caussade, A (Lourdes) 1978 *R*, 1979 *I, W, E, NZ* 1,2, *R*, 1980 *W, E, S*, 1981 *S* (R), *I*
Caussarieu, G (Pau) 1929 *I*
Cayrefourcq, E (Tarbes) 1921 *E*
Cazalbou, J (Toulouse) 1997 *It* 2 (R), *R* 2, *Arg, SA* 2 (R)
Cazals, P (Mont-de-Marsan) 1961 *NZ* 1, *A, R*
Cazenave, A (Pau) 1927 *E, G* 1, 1928 *S, A, G*
Cazenave, F (RCF) 1950 *E*, 1952 *S*, 1954 *I, NZ, W, E*
Cecillon, M (Bourgoin) 1988 *I, W, Arg* 2,3,4, *R*, 1989 *I, E, NZ* 1,2, *A* 1, 1991 *S, I, E* (R), *R, US* 1, *W* 2, *[E]*, 1992 *W, E, S, I, R, Arg* 1,2, *SA* 1,2, 1993 *E, S, I, W, R* 1, *SA* 1,2, *R* 2, *A* 1,2, 1994 *I, W, NZ* 1 (R), 1995 *I, R* 1, *[Tg, S* (R), *I, SA]*
Celaya, M (Biarritz O, SBUC) 1953 *E, W, It*, 1954 *I, E, It, Arg* 1,2, 1955 *S, I, E, W, It*, 1956 *S, I, W, It, E, Cz* 1957 *S, I, E, W, R* 2, 1958 *S, E, A, W, It*, 1959 *S, E, I, W, R, Arg* 1,2,3, 1961 *S, SA, E, W, It, I, NZ* 1,2,3, *A, R*
Celhay, M (Bayonne) 1935 *G*, 1936 *G* 1, 1937 *G, It*, 1938 *G* 1, 1940 *B*
Cessieux, N (Lyon) 1906 *NZ*
Cester, E (TOEC, Valence) 1966 *S, I, E*, 1967 *W*, 1968 *S, I, E, W, Cz, NZ* 1,3, *A, SA* 1,2, *R*, 1969 *S, I, E, W*, 1970 *S, I, W, E*, 1971 *A* 1, 1972 *R*, 1973 *S, NZ, W, I, J, R*, 1974 *I, W, E, S*
Chaban-Delmas, J (CASG) 1945 *B* 2
Chabowski, H (Nice, Bourgoin) 1985 *Arg* 2, 1986 *R* 2, *NZ* 2, 1989 *B* (R)
Chadebech, P (Brive) 1982 *R, Arg* 1,2, 1986 *S, I*
Champ, E (Toulon) 1985 *Arg* 1,2, 1986 *I, W, E, R* 1, *Arg* 1,2, *A, NZ* 1, *R* 2, *NZ* 2,3, 1987 *W, E, S, I, [S, R, Fj, A, NZ]*, 1988 *E, S, Arg* 1,3,4, *R*, 1989 *W, S, A* 1,2, 1990 *W, E, NZ* 1, 1991 *R, US* 1, *[R, Fj, C, E]*
Chapuy, L (SF) 1926 *S*
Charpentier, G (SF) 1911 *E*, 1912 *W, E*
Charton, P (Montferrand) 1940 *B*
Charvet, D (Toulouse) 1986 *W, E, R* 1, *Arg* 1, *A, NZ* 1,3, 1987 *W, E, S, I, [S, R, Z, Fj, A, NZ]*, *R*, 1989 *E* (R), 1990 *W, E*, 1991 *S, I*
Chassagne, J (Montferrand) 1938 *G* 1
Chatau, A (Bayonne) 1913 *SA*
Chaud, E (Toulon) 1932 *G*, 1934 *G*, 1935 *G*
Chenevay, C (Grenoble) 1968 *SA* 1

Chevallier, B (Montferrand) 1952 *S, I, SA, W, E*, 1953 *E, W, It*, 1954 *S, I, NZ, W, Arg* 1, 1955 *S, I, E, W, It*, 1956 *S, I, W, It, E, Cz*, 1957 *S*
Chiberry, J (Chambéry) 1955 *It*
Chilo, A (RCF) 1920 *S, W*, 1925 *I, NZ*
Cholley, G (Castres) 1975 *E, S, I, SA* 1,2, *Arg* 1,2, *R*, 1976 *S, I, W, E, A* 1,2, *R*, 1977 *W, E, S, I, Arg* 1,2, *NZ* 1,2, *R*, 1978 *E, S, I, W, R*, 1979 *I, S*
Choy J (Narbonne) 1930 *S, I, E, G, W*, 1931 *I*, 1933 *G*, 1934 *G*, 1935 *G*, 1936 *G* 2
Cigagna, A (Toulouse) 1995 *[E]*
Cimarosti, J (Castres) 1976 *US* (R)
Clady, A (Lezignan) 1929 *G*, 1931 *I, S, E, G*
Clarac, H (St Girons) 1938 *G* 1
Claudel, R (Lyon) 1932 *G*, 1934 *G*
Clauzel, F (Béziers) 1924 *E, W*, 1925 *W*
Clavé, J (Agen) 1936 *G* 2, 1938 *R, G* 2
Claverie, H (Lourdes) 1954 *NZ, W*
Cléda, T (Pau) 1998 *E* (R), *S* (R), *I* (R), *W* (R), *Arg* 1 (R), *Fj* (R), *Arg* 3 (R), 1999 *I* (R), *S*
Clément, G (RCF) 1931 *W*
Clément, J (RCF) 1921 *S, W, E*, 1922 *S, E, W, I*, 1923 *S, W, I*
Clemente, M (Oloron) 1978 *R*, 1980 *S, I*
Cluchague, L (Biarritz O) 1924 *S*, 1925 *E*
Coderc, J (Chalon) 1932 *G*, 1933 *G*, 1934 *G*, 1935 *G*, 1936 *G* 1
Codorniou, D (Narbonne) 1979 *NZ* 1,2, *R*, 1980 *W, E, S, I*, 1981 *S, W, E, A* 2, 1983 *E, S, I, W, A* 1,2, *R*, 1984 *I, W, E, S, NZ* 1,2, *R*, 1985 *E, S, I, W, Arg* 1,2
Coeurveille, C (Agen) 1992 *Arg* 1 (R), 2
Cognet, L (Montferrand) 1932 *G*, 1936 *G* 1,2, 1937 *G, It*
Colombier, J (St Junien) 1952 *SA, W, E*
Colomine, G (Narbonne) 1979 *NZ* 1
Comba, F (SF) 1998 *Arg* 1,2, *Fj, Arg* 3, 1999 *I, W, E, S*
Combe, J (SF) 1910 *S, E, I*, 1911 *S*
Combes, G (Fumel) 1945 *B* 2
Communeau, M (SF) 1906 *NZ, E*, 1907 *E*, 1908 *E, W*, 1909 *E, W, I*, 1910 *S, E, I*, 1911 *S, E, I*, 1912 *I, S, W, E*, 1913 *SA, E, W*
Condom, J (Boucau, Biarritz O) 1982 *R*, 1983 *E, S, I, W, A* 1,2, *R*, 1984 *I, W, E, S, NZ* 1,2, *R*, 1985 *E, S, I, W, Arg* 1,2, 1986 *S, I, W, E, R* 1, *Arg* 1,2, *NZ* 1, *R* 2, *NZ* 2,3, 1987 *W, E, S, I, [S, R, Z, A, NZ]*, *R*, 1988 *E, S, W, Arg* 1,2,3,4, *R*, 1989 *I, W, E, S, NZ* 1,2, *A* 1, 1990 *I, R, A* 2,3 (R)
Conilh de Beyssac, J-J (SBUC) 1912 *I, S*, 1914 *I, W, E*
Constant, G (Perpignan) 1920 *W*
Coscolla, G (Béziers) 1921 *S, W*
Costantino, J (Montferrand) 1973 *R*
Costes, A (Montferrand) 1994 *C* 2, 1995 *R* 1, *[Iv]*, 1997 *It* 1
Costes, F (Montferrand) 1979 *E, S, NZ* 1,2, *R*, 1980 *W, I*
Couffignal, H (Colomiers) 1993 *R* 1
Coulon, E (Grenoble) 1928 *S*
Courtiols, M (Bègles) 1991 *R, US* 1, *W* 2
Crabos, R (RCF) 1920 *S, E, W, I, US*, 1921 *S, W, E, I*, 1922 *S, W, I*, 1923 *S, I*, 1924 *S, I*
Crampagne, J (Bègles) 1967 *SA* 4
Crancee, R (Lourdes) 1960 *Arg* 3, 1961 *S*
Crauste, M (RCF, Lourdes) 1957 *R* 1,2, 1958 *S, E, A, W, It, I*, 1959 *E, It, W, I*, 1960 *S, E, W, I, R, Arg* 1,3, 1961 *S, SA, E, W, It, I, NZ* 1,2,3, *A, R*, 1962 *S, E, W, I, It, R*, 1963 *S, I, E, W, It, R*, 1964 *S, NZ, E, W, It, I, SA, Fj, R*, 1965 *S, I, E, W, It, R*, 1966 *S, I, E, W, It*
Cremaschi, M (Lourdes) 1980 *R*, 1981 *R, NZ* 1,2, 1982 *W, S*, 1983 *A* 1,2, *R*, 1984 *I, W*
Crenca, J-J (Agen) 1996 *SA* 2(R)
Crichton, W H (Le Havre) 1906 *NZ, E*
Cristina, J (Montferrand) 1979 *R*
Cussac, P (Biarritz O) 1934 *G*
Cutzach, A (Quillan) 1929 *G*

Daguerre, F (Biarritz O) 1936 *G* 1
Daguerre, J (CASG) 1933 *G*
Dal Maso, M (Mont-de-Marsan, Agen) 1988 *R* (R), 1990 *NZ* 2, 1996 *SA* 1(R),2, 1997 *I, W, E, S, It* 1, *R* 1 (R), *A* 1,2, *It* 2, *Arg, SA* 1,2, 1998 *W* (R), *Arg* 1 (t), *Fj* (R)
Danion, J (Toulon) 1924 *I*
Danos, P (Toulon, Béziers) 1954 *Arg* 1,2, 1957 *R* 2, 1958 *S, E, W, It, I, SA* 1,2, 1959 *S, E, It, W, I*, 1960 *S, E*
Dantiacq, D (Pau) 1997 *R* 1
Darbos, P (Dax) 1969 *R*
Darracq, R (Dax) 1957 *It*
Darrieussecq, A (Biarritz O) 1973 *E*

Thomas Castaignède, whose last-minute penalty miss cost his side dear, breaks into the open field during the thrilling Five Nations encounter between France and Wales at the Stade de France.

Darrieussecq, J (Mont-de-Marsan) 1953 *It*
Darrouy, C (Mont-de-Marsan) 1957 *I, E, W, It, R* 1, 1959 *E*, 1961 *R*, 1963 *S, I, E, W, It*, 1964 *NZ, E, W, It, I, SA, Fj, R*, 1965 *S, I, E, It, R*, 1966 *S, I, E, W, It, R*, 1967 *S, A, E, It, W, I, SA* 1, 2, 4
Daudignon, G (SF) 1928 *S*
Dauga, B (Mont-de-Marsan) 1964 *S, NZ, E, W, It, I, SA, Fj, R*, 1965 *S, I, E, W, It, R*, 1966 *S, I, E, W, It, R*, 1967 *S, A, E, It, W, I, SA* 1,2,3,4, *NZ, R*, 1968 *S, I, NZ* 1,2,3, *A, SA* 1,2, *R*, 1969 *S, I, E, W*, 1970 *S, I, W, E, R*, 1971 *S, I, E, W, SA* 1,2, *A* 1,2, *R*, 1972 *S, I* 1, *W*
Dauger, J (Bayonne) 1945 *B* 1,2, 1953 *S*
Daulouede, P (Tyrosse) 1937 *G, It*, 1938 *G* 1, 1940 *B*
De Besombes, S (Perpignan) 1998 *Arg* 1 (R), *Fj* (R)
Decamps, P (RCF) 1911 *S*
Dedet, J (SF) 1910 *S, E, I*, 1911 *W, I*, 1912 *S*, 1913 *E, I*
Dedeyn, P (RCF) 1906 *NZ*
Dedieu, P (Béziers) 1963 *E, It*, 1964 *W, It, I, SA, Fj, R*, 1965 *S, I, E, W*
De Gregorio, J (Grenoble) 1960 *S, E, W, I, It, R, Arg* 1,2, 1961 *S, SA, E, W, It, I*, 1962 *S, E, W*, 1963 *S, W, It*, 1964 *NZ, E*
Dehez, J-L (Agen) 1967 *SA* 2, 1969 *R*
De Jouvencel, E (SF) 1909 *W, I*
De Laborderie, M (RCF) 1921 *I*, 1922 *I*, 1925 *W, E*
Delage, C (Agen) 1983 *S, I*
De Malherbe, H (CASG) 1932 *G*, 1933 *G*
De Malmann, R (RCF) 1908 *E, W*, 1909 *E, W, I*, 1910 *E, I*
De Muizon, J J (SF) 1910 *I*
Delaigue, G (Toulon) 1973 *J, R*
Delaigue, Y (Toulon) 1994 *S, NZ* 2 (R), *C* 2, 1995 *I, R* 1, [*Tg, Iv*], *It, R* 2 (R), 1997 *It* 1
Delque, A (Toulouse) 1937 *It*, 1938 *G* 1, *R, G* 2
De Rougemont, M (Toulon) 1995 *E* (t), *R* 1 (t), [*Iv*], *NZ* 1, 2, 1996 *I* (R), *Arg* 1,2, *W* 2, *SA* 1, 1997 *E* (R), *S* (R), *It* 1
Descamps, P (SB) 1927 *G* 2
Desclaux, F (RCF) 1949 *Arg* 1,2, 1953 *It*
Desclaux, J (Perpignan) 1934 *G*, 1935 *G*, 1936 *G* 1,2, 1937 *G, It*, 1938 *G* 1, *R, G* 2, 1945 *B* 1
Deslandes, C (RCF) 1990 *A* 1, *NZ* 2, 1991 *W* 1, 1992 *R, Arg* 1,2
Desnoyer, L (Brive) 1974 *R*
Destarac, L (Tarbes) 1926 *S, I, E, W, M*, 1927 *W, E, G* 1,2
Desvouges, R (SF) 1914 *W*
Detrez, P-E (Nîmes) 1983 *A* 2 (R), 1986 *Arg* 1 (R), 2, *A* (R), *NZ*1
Devergie, T (Nîmes) 1988 *R*, 1989 *NZ* 1,2, *B, A* 2, 1990 *W, E, S, I, R, A* 1,2,3, 1991 *US* 2, *W* 2, 1992 *R* (R), *Arg* 2 (R)
Deygas, M (Vienne) 1937 *It*
Deylaud, C (Toulouse) 1992 *R, Arg* 1,2, *SA* 1, 1994 *C* 1, *NZ* 1,2, 1995 *W, E, S*, [*Iv* (R), *S, I, SA*], *It, Arg*
Dintrans, P (Tarbes) 1979 *NZ* 1,2, *R*, 1980 *E, S, I, SA, R*, 1981 *S, I, W, E, A* 1,2, *R, NZ* 1,2, 1982 *W, E, S, I, R, Arg* 1,2, 1983 *E, W, A* 1,2, *R*, 1984 *I, W, E, S*, 1985 *E, S, I, W, Arg* 1,2, 1987 [*R*], 1988 *Arg* 1,2,3, 1989 *W, E, S*, 1990 *R*
Dispagne, S (Toulouse) 1996 *I* (R), *W* 1
Dizabo, P (Tyrosse) 1948 *A, S, E*, 1949 *S, I, E, W, Arg* 2, 1950 *S, I*, 1960 *Arg* 1,2,3
Domec, A (Carcassonne) 1929 *W*
Domec, H (Lourdes) 1953 *W, It*, 1954 *S, I, NZ, W, E, It*, 1955 *S, I, E, W*, 1956 *I, W, It*, 1958 *E, A, W, It, I*
Domenech, A (Vichy, Brive) 1954 *W, E, It*, 1955 *S, I, E, W*, 1956 *S, I, W, It, E, Cz*, 1957 *S, I, E, W, It, R* 1,2, 1958 *S, E, It*, 1959 *It*, 1960 *S, E, W, I, It, R, Arg* 1,2,3, 1961 *S, SA, E, W, It, I, NZ* 1,2,3, *A, R*, 1962 *S, E, W, I, It, R*, 1963 *W, It*
Domercq, J (Bayonne) 1912 *I, S*
Dominici, C (SF) 1998 *E, S, Arg* 1,2, 1999 *E, S*
Dorot, J (RCF) 1935 *G*
Dospital, P (Bayonne) 1977 *R*, 1980 *I*, 1981 *S, I, W, E*, 1982 *I, R, Arg* 1,2, 1983 *E, S, I, W*, 1984 *E, S, NZ* 1,2, *R*, 1985 *E, S, I, W, Arg* 1
Dourthe, C (Dax) 1966 *R*, 1967 *S, A, E, W, I, SA* 1,2,3, *NZ*, 1968 *W, NZ* 3, *SA* 1,2, 1969 *W*, 1971 *SA* 2 (R), *R*, 1972 *I* 1,2, *A* 1,2, *R*, 1973 *S, NZ, E*, 1974 *I, Arg* 1,2, *SA* 1,2, 1975 *W, E, S*
Dourthe, R (Dax, SF) 1995 *R* 2, *Arg, NZ* 1, 2, 1996 *E, R*, 1996 *Arg* 1,2, *W* 2, *SA* 1,2, 1997 *W, A* 1, 1999 *I, W*
Doussau, E (Angoulême) 1938 *R*

Droitecourt, M (Montferrand) 1972 *R*, 1973 *NZ* (R), *E*, 1974 *E, S, Arg* 1, *SA* 2, 1975 *SA* 1,2, *Arg* 1,2, *R*, 1976 *S, I, W, A* 1, 1977 *Arg* 2
Dubertrand, A (Montferrand) 1971 *A* 2, *R*, 1972 *I* 2, 1974 *I, W, E, S*, 1975 *Arg* 1,2, *R*, 1976 *S, US*
Dubois, D (Bègles) 1971 *S*
Dubroca, D (Agen) 1979 *NZ* 2, 1981 *NZ* 2 (R), 1982 *E, S*, 1984 *W, E, S*, 1985 *Arg* 2, 1986 *S, I, W, E, R* 1, *Arg* 2, *A, NZ* 1, *R* 2, *NZ* 2,3, 1987 *W, E, S, I*, [*S, Z, Fj, A, NZ*], *R*, 1988 *E, S, I, W*
Duché, A (Limoges) 1929 *G*
Duclos, A (Lourdes) 1931 *S*
Ducousso, J (Tarbes) 1925 *S, W, E*
Dufau, G (RCF) 1948 *I, A*, 1949 *I, W*, 1950 *S, E, W*, 1951 *S, I, W*, 1952 *SA, W*, 1953 *S, I, E, W*, 1954 *S, I, NZ, W, E, It*, 1955 *S, I, E, W, It*, 1956 *S, I, W, It*, 1957 *S, I, E, W, It, R* 1
Dufau, J (Biarritz) 1912 *I, S, W, E*
Duffaut, Y (Agen) 1954 *Arg* 1,2
Duffour, R (Tarbes) 1911 *W*
Dufourcq, J (SBUC) 1906 *NZ, E*, 1907 *E*, 1908 *W*
Duhard, Y (Bagnères) 1980 *E*
Duhau, J (SF) 1928 *I*,1930 *I, G*, 1931 *I, S, W*, 1933 *G*
Dulaurens, C (Toulouse) 1926 *I*, 1928 *S*, 1929 *W*
Duluc, A (Béziers) 1934 *G*
Du Manoir, Y le P (RCF) 1925 *I, NZ, S, W, E*, 1926 *S*, 1927 *I, S*
Dupont, C (Lourdes) 1923 *S, W, I*, 1924 *S, I, W, R, US*, 1925 *S*, 1927 *E, G* 1,2, 1928 *A, G, W*, 1929 *I*
Dupont, J-L (Agen) 1983 *S*
Dupont, L (RCF) 1934 *G*, 1935 *G*, 1936 *G* 1,2, 1938 *R, G* 2
Dupouy, A (SB) 1924 *W, R*
Duprat, B (Bayonne) 1966 *E, W, It, R*, 1967 *S, A, E, SA* 2,3, 1968 *S, I, 1972 *E, W, I* 2, *A* 1
Dupré, P (RCF) 1909 *W*
Dupuy, J (Tarbes) 1956 *S, I, W, It, E, Cz*, 1957 *S, I, E, W, It, R* 2, 1958 *S, E, SA* 1,2, 1959 *S, E, It, W, I*, 1960 *W, I, It, Arg* 1,3, 1961 *S, SA, E, NZ* 2, *R*, 1962 *S, E, W, I, It*, 1963 *W, It, R*, 1964 *S*
Du Souich, C J (see Judas du Souich)
Dutin, B (Mont-de-Marsan) 1968 *NZ* 2, *A, SA* 2, *R*
Dutour, F X (Toulouse) 1911 *E, I*, 1912 *S, W, E*, 1913 *S*
Dutrain, H (Toulouse) 1945 *W*, 1946 *B, I*, 1947 *E*, 1949 *I, E, W, Arg* 1
Dutrey, J (Lourdes) 1940 *B*
Duval, R (SF) 1908 *E, W*, 1909 *E*, 1911 *E, W, I*

Echavé, L (Agen) 1961 *S*
Elissalde, E (Bayonne) 1936 *G* 2, 1940 *B*
Elissalde, J-P (La Rochelle) 1980 *SA, R*, 1981 *A* 1,2, *R*
Empereur-Buisson, H (Béziers) 1931 *E, G*
Erbani, D (Agen) 1981 *A* 1,2, *NZ* 1,2, 1982 *Arg* 1,2, 1983 *S* (R), *A* 1,2, *R*, 1984 *W, E, R*, 1985 *E, W* (R), *Arg* 2, 1986 *S, I, W, E, R* 1, *Arg* 2, *NZ* 1,2 (R), 3, 1987 *W, E, S, I*, [*S, R, Fj, A, NZ*], 1988 *E, S*, 1989 *I* (R), *W, E, S, NZ* 1, *A* 2, 1990 *W, E*
Escaffre, P (Narbonne) 1933 *G*, 1934 *G*
Escommier, M (Montelimar) 1955 *It*
Esponda, J-M (RCF) 1967 *SA* 1,2, *R*, 1968 *NZ* 1,2, *SA* 2, *R*, 1969 *S, I* (R), *E*
Estève, A (Béziers) 1971 *SA* 1, 1972 *I* 1, *E, W, I* 2, *A* 2, *R*, 1973 *S, NZ, E, I*, 1974 *I, W, E, S, A* 1,2, 1975 *W, E*
Estève, P (Narbonne, Lavelanet) 1982 *R, Arg* 1,2, 1983 *E, S, I, W, A* 1,2, *R*, 1984 *I, W, E, S, NZ* 1,2, *R*, 1985 *E, S, I, W*, 1986 *S, I*, 1987 [*S, Z*]
Etcheberry, J (Rochefort, Cognac) 1923 *W, I*, 1924 *S, I, E, W, R, US*, 1926 *S, I, E, M*, 1927 *I, S, W, E* 2
Etchenique, J-M (Biarritz O) 1974 *R, SA* 1, 1975 *E, Arg* 2
Etchepare, A (Bayonne) 1922 *I*
Etcheverry, M (Pau) 1971 *S, I*
Eutrope, A (SCUF) 1913 *I*

Fabre, E (Toulouse) 1937 *It*, 1938 *G* 1,2
Fabre, J (Toulouse) 1963 *S, I, E, W, It*, 1964 *S, NZ, E*
Fabre, L (Lezignan) 1930 *G*
Fabre, M (Béziers) 1981 *A* 1, *R, NZ* 1,2, 1982 *I, R*
Failliot, P (RCF) 1911 *S, W, I*, 1912 *I, S, E*, 1913 *E, W*
Fargues, G (Dax) 1923 *I*
Fauré, F (Tarbes) 1914 *I, W, E*
Fauvel, J-P (Tulle) 1980 *R*
Favre, M (Lyon) 1913 *E, W*
Ferrand, L (Chalon) 1940 *B*
Ferrien, R (Tarbes) 1950 *S, I, E, W*

Finat, R (CASG) 1932 *G*, 1933 *G*
Fite, R (Brive) 1963 *W, It*
Forestier, J (SCUF) 1912 *W*
Forgues, F (Bayonne) 1911 *S, E, W*, 1912 *I, W, E*, 1913 *S, SA, W*, 1914 *I, E*
Fort, J (Agen) 1967 *It, W, I, SA* 1,2,3,4
Fourcade, G (BEC) 1909 *E, W*
Foures, H (Toulouse) 1951 *S, I, E, W*
Fournet, F (Montferrand) 1950 *W*
Fouroux, J (La Voulte) 1972 *I* 2, *R*, 1974 *W, E, Arg* 1,2, *R, SA* 1,2, 1975 *W, Arg* 1, *R*, 1976 *S, I, W, E, US, A* 1, 1977 *W, E, S, I, Arg* 1,2, *NZ* 1,2, *R*
Francquenelle, A (Vaugirard) 1911 *S*, 1913 *W, I*
Furcade, R (Perpignan) 1952 *S*

Gabernet, S (Toulouse) 1980 *E, S*, 1981 *S, I, W, E, A* 1,2, *R, NZ* 1,2, 1982 *I*, 1983 *A* 2, *R*
Gachassin, J (Lourdes) 1961 *S, I*, 1963 *R*, 1964 *S, NZ, E, W, It, I, SA, Fj, R*, 1965 *S, I, E, W, It, R*, 1966 *S, I, E, W*, 1967 *S, A, It, W, I, NZ*, 1968 *I, E*, 1969 *S, I*
Galau, H (Toulouse) 1924 *S, I, E, W, US*
Galia, J (Quillan) 1927 *E, G* 1,2, 1928 *S, A, I, E, W*, 1929 *I, E, G*, 1930 *S, I, E, G, W*, 1931 *S, W, E, G*
Gallart, P (Béziers) 1990 *R, A* 1,2 (R), 3, 1992 *S, I, R, Arg* 1,2, *SA* 1,2, *Arg*, 1994 *I, W, E*, 1995 *I* (t), *R* 1, *[Tg]*
Gallion, J (Toulon) 1978 *E, S, I, W*, 1979 *I, W, E, S, NZ* 2, *R*, 1980 *W, E, S, I*, 1983 *A* 1,2, *R*, 1984 *I, W, E, S, R*, 1985 *E, S, I, W*, 1986 *Arg* 2
Galthié, F (Colomiers) 1991 *R, US* 1, *[R, Fj, C, E]*, 1992 *W, E, S, R, Arg*, 1994 *I, W, E*, 1995 *[SA, E]*, 1996 *W* 1(R), 1997 *I, It* 2, *SA* 1,2, 1998 *W* (R), *Fj* (R)
Galy, J (Perpignan) 1953 *W*
Garbajosa, X (Toulouse) 1998 *I, W, Arg* 2 (R), *Fj*, 1999 *W* (R), *E, S*
Garuet-Lempirou, J-P (Lourdes) 1983 *A* 1,2, *R*, 1984 *I, NZ* 1,2, *R*, 1985 *E, S, I, W, Arg* 1, 1986 *S, I, W, E, R* 1, *Arg* 1, *NZ* 1, *R* 2, *NZ* 2,3, 1987 *W, E, S, I, [S, R, Fj, A, NZ]*, 1988 *E, S, Arg* 1,2, *R*, 1989 *E* (R), *S, NZ* 1,2, 1990 *W, E*
Gasc, J (Graulhet) 1977 *NZ* 2
Gasparotto, G (Montferrand) 1976 *A* 2, *R*
Gauby, G (Perpignan) 1956 *Cz*
Gaudermen, P (RCF) 1906 *E*
Gayraud, W (Toulouse) 1920 *I*
Geneste, R (BEC) 1945 *B* 1, 1949 *Arg* 2
Genet, J-P (RCF) 1992 *S, I, R*
Gensane, R (Béziers) 1962 *S, E, W, I, It, R*, 1963 *S*
Gerald, G (RCF) 1927 *E, G* 2, 1928 *S*, 1929 *I, S, W, E, G*, 1930 *S, I, E, G, W*, 1931 *I, S, E, G*
Gerintes, G (CASG) 1924 *R*, 1925 *I*, 1926 *W*
Geschwind, P (RCF) 1936 *G* 1,2
Giacardy, M (SBUC) 1907 *E*
Gimbert, P (Bègles) 1991 *R, US* 1, 1992 *W, E*
Giordani, P (Dax) 1999 *E, S*
Glas, S (Bourgoin) 1996 *S* (t), *I* (R), *W* 1, *R, Arg* 2(R), *W* 2, *SA* 1,2, 1997 *I, W, E, S, It* 2 (R), *R* 2, *Arg, SA* 1,2, 1998 *E, S, I, W, Arg* 1,2, *Fj, Arg* 3, *A*
Gomès, A (SF) 1998 *Arg* 1,2, *Fj, Arg* 3, *A*, 1999 *I* (R)
Gommes, J (RCF) 1909 *I*
Gonnet, C-A (Albi) 1921 *E, I*, 1922 *E, W*, 1924 *S, E*, 1926 *S, I, E, W, M*, 1927 *I, S, W, E, G* 1
Gonzalez, J-M (Bayonne) 1992 *Arg* 1,2, *SA* 1,2, *Arg*, 1993 *R* 1, *SA* 1,2, *R* 2, *A* 1,2, 1994 *I, W, E, S, C* 1, *NZ* 1,2, *C* 2, 1995 *W, E, S, I, R* 1, *[Tg, S, I, SA, E]*, *It, Arg*, 1996 *E, S, I, W* 1
Got, R (Perpignan) 1920 *I, US*, 1921 *S, W*, 1922 *S, E, W, I*, 1924 *I, E, W, R, US*
Gourdon, J-F (RCF, Bagnères) 1974 *S, Arg* 1, 2, *R, SA* 1, 2, 1975 *W, E, S, I, R*, 1976 *S, I, W, E*, 1978 *E, S*, 1979 *W, E, S, R*, 1980 *I*
Gourragne, J-F (Béziers) 1990 *NZ* 2, 1991 *W* 1
Goyard, A (Lyon U) 1936 *W, G* 1,2, 1937 *G, It*, 1938 *G* 1, *R, G* 2
Graciet, R (SBUC) 1926 *I, W*, 1927 *S, G* 1, 1929 *E*, 1930 *W*
Graou, S (Auch, Colomiers) 1992 *Arg* (R), 1993 *SA* 1,2, *R* 2, *A* 2 (R), 1995 *R* 2, *Arg* (t), *NZ* 2 (R)
Gratton, J (Agen) 1984 *NZ* 2, *R*, 1985 *E, S, I, W, Arg* 1,2, 1986 *S, NZ* 1
Graule, V (Arl Perpignan) 1926 *I, E, W*, 1927 *S, W*, 1931 *G*
Greffe, M (Grenoble) 1968 *W, Cz, NZ* 1,2, *SA* 1
Griffard, J (Lyon U) 1932 *G*, 1933 *G*, 1934 *G*
Gruarin, A (Toulon) 1964 *W, It, I, SA, Fj, R*, 1965 *S, I, E, W, It*, 1966 *S, I, E, W, It, R*, 1967 *S, A, E, It, W, I, NZ*, 1968 *S, I*

Guelorget, P (RCF) 1931 *E, G*
Guichemerre, A (Dax) 1920 *E*, 1921 *E, I*, 1923 *S*
Guilbert, A (Toulon) 1975 *E, S, I, SA* 1,2, 1976 *A* 1, 1977 *Arg* 1,2, *NZ* 1,2, *R*, 1979 *I, W, E*
Guillemin, P (RCF) 1908 *E, W*, 1909 *E, I*, 1910 *W, S, E, I*, 1911 *S, E, W*
Guilleux, P (Agen) 1952 *SA, It*
Guiral, M (Agen) 1931 *G*, 1932 *G*, 1933 *G*
Guiraud, H (Nîmes) 1996 *R*

Haget, A (PUC) 1953 *E*, 1954 *I, NZ, E, Arg* 2, 1955 *E, W, It*, 1957 *I, E, It, R* 1, 1958 *It, SA* 2
Haget, F (Agen, Biarritz O) 1974 *Arg* 1,2, 1975 *SA* 2, *Arg* 1,2, *R*, 1976 *S*, 1978 *S, I, W, R*, 1979 *I, W, E, S, NZ* 1,2, *R*, 1980 *W, S, I*, 1984 *S, NZ* 1,2, *R*, 1985 *E, S, I*, 1986 *S, I, W, E, R* 1, *Arg* 1, *A, NZ* 1, 1987 *S, I, [R, Fj]*
Haget, H (CASG) 1928 *S*, 1930 *G*
Halet, R (Strasbourg) 1925 *NZ, S, W*
Harislur-Arthapignet, P (Tarbes) 1988 *Arg* 4 (R)
Harize, D (Cahors, Toulouse) 1975 *SA* 1,2, 1976 *A* 1,2, *R*, 1977 *W, E, S, I*
Hauc, J (Toulon) 1928 *E, G*, 1929 *I, S, G*
Hauser, M (Lourdes) 1969 *E*
Hedembaigt, M (Bayonne) 1913 *S, SA*, 1914 *W*
Hericé, D (Bègles) 1950 *I*
Herrero, A (Toulon) 1963 *R*, 1964 *NZ, E, W, It, I, SA, Fj, R*, 1965 *S, I, E, W*, 1966 *W, It, R*, 1967 *S, A, E, It, I, R*
Herrero, B (Nice) 1983 *I*, 1986 *Arg* 1
Heyer, F (Montferrand) 1990 *A* 2
Hiquet, J-C (Agen) 1964 *E*
Hoche, M (PUC) 1957 *I, E, W, It, R* 1
Hondagné-Monge, M (Tarbes) 1988 *Arg* 2 (R)
Hontas, P (Biarritz) 1990 *S, I, R*, 1991 *R*, 1992 *Arg*, 1993 *E, S, I, W*
Hortoland, J-P (Béziers) 1971 *A* 2
Houblain, H (SCUF) 1909 *E*, 1910 *W*
Houdet, R (SF) 1927 *S, W, G* 1, 1928 *G, W*, 1929 *I, S, E*, 1930 *S, E*
Hourdebaigt, A (SBUC) 1909 *I*, 1910 *W, S, E, I*
Hubert, A (ASF) 1906 *E*, 1907 *E*, 1908 *E, W*, 1909 *E, W, I*
Hueber, A (Lourdes, Toulon) 1990 *A* 3, *NZ* 1, 1991 *US* 2, 1992 *I, Arg* 1,2, *SA* 1,2, 1993 *E, S, I, W, R* 1, *SA* 1,2, *R* 2, *A* 1,2, 1995 *[Tg, S* (R)*, I]*
Hutin, R (CASG) 1927 *I, S, W*
Hyardet, A (Castres) 1995 *It, Arg* (R)

Ibanez, R (Dax, Perpignan) 1996 *W* 1(R), 1997 *It* 1 (R), *R* 1, *It* 2 (R), *R* 2, *SA* 2 (R), 1998 *E, S, I, W, Arg* 1,2, *Fj, Arg* 3, *A*, 1999 *I, W, E, S*
Icard, J (SF) 1909 *E, W*
Iguiniz, E (Bayonne) 1914 *E*
Ihingoué, D (BEC) 1912 *I, S*
Imbernon, J-F (Perpignan) 1976 *I, W, E, US, A* 1, 1977 *W, E, S, I, Arg* 1,2, *NZ* 1,2, 1978 *E, R*, 1979 *I*, 1981 *S, I, W, E*, 1982 *I*, 1983 *I, W*
Iraçabal, J (Bayonne) 1968 *NZ* 1,2, *SA* 1, 1969 *S, I, W, R*, 1970 *S, I, W, E, R*, 1971 *W, SA* 1,2, *A* 1, 1972 *E, W, I* 2, *A* 2, *R*, 1973 *S, NZ, E, W, I, J*, 1974 *I, W, E, S, Arg* 1, *SA* 2 (R)
Isaac, H (RCF) 1907 *E*, 1908 *E*
Ithurra, E (Biarritz O) 1936 *G* 1,2, 1937 *G*

Janeczek, T (Tarbes) 1982 *Arg* 1,2, 1990 *R*
Janik, K (Toulouse) 1987 *R*
Jarasse, A (Brive) 1945 *B* 1
Jardel, J (SB) 1928 *I, E*
Jauréguy, A (RCF, Toulouse, SF) 1920 *S, E, W, I, US*, 1922 *S, W*, 1923 *S, W, E, I*, 1924 *S, W, E, R, US*, 1925 *I, NZ*, 1926 *S, E, W, M*, 1927 *I, E*, 1928 *S, A, E, G, W*, 1929 *I, S, E*
Jauréguy, P (Toulouse) 1913 *S, SA, W, I*
Jeangrand, M-H (Tarbes) 1921 *I*
Jeanjean, P (Toulon) 1948 *I*
Jérôme, G (SF) 1906 *NZ, E*
Joinel, J-L (Brive) 1977 *NZ* 1, 1978 *R*, 1979 *I, W, E, S, NZ* 1,2, *R*, 1980 *W, E, S, I, SA*, 1981 *S, I, W, E, R, NZ* 1,2, 1982 *E, S, I, R*, 1983 *E, S, I, W, A* 1, 1984 *I, W, E, S, NZ* 1,2, 1985 *S, I, W, Arg* 1, 1986 *S, I, W, E, R* 1, *Arg* 1,2, 1987 *[Z]*
Jol, M (Biarritz O) 1947 *S, I, W, E*, 1949 *S, I, E, W, Arg* 1,2
Jordana, J-L (Pau, Toulouse) 1996 *R* (R), *Arg* 1(t),2, *W* 2, 1997 *I* (t), *W, S* (R)
Judas du Souich, C (SCUF) 1911 *W, I*
Juillet, C (Montferrand, SF) 1995 *R* 2, *Arg*, 1999 *E, S*

Junquas, L (Tyrosse) 1945 *B* 1,2, *W*, 1946 *B, I, K, W,* 1947 *S, I, W, E,* 1948 *S, W*

Kaczorowski, D (Le Creusot) 1974 *I* (R)
Kaempf, A (St Jean-de-Luz) 1946 *B*

Labadie, P (Bayonne) 1952 *S, I, SA, W, E, It,* 1953 *S, I, It,* 1954 *S, I, NZ, W, E, Arg* 2, 1955 *S, I, E, W,* 1956 *I,* 1957 *I*
Labarthete, R (Pau) 1952 *S*
Labazuy, A (Lourdes) 1952 *I,* 1954 *S, W,* 1956 *E,* 1958 *A, W, I,* 1959 *S, E, It, W*
Labit, C (Toulouse) 1999 *S*
Laborde, C (RCF) 1962 *It, R,* 1963 *R,* 1964 *SA,* 1965 *E*
Labrousse, T (Brive) 1996 *R, SA* 1
Lacans, P (Béziers) 1980 *SA,* 1981 *W, E, A* 2, *R,* 1982 *W*
Lacassagne, H (SBUC) 1906 *NZ,* 1907 *E*
Lacaussade, R (Bègles) 1948 *A, S*
Lacaze, C (Lourdes, Angoulême) 1961 *NZ* 2,3, *A, R,* 1962 *W, I, It,* 1963 *W, R,* 1964 *S, NZ, E,* 1965 *It, R,* 1966 *S, I, E, W, It, R,* 1967 *S, E, SA* 1,3,4, *R,* 1968 *S, E, W, Cz, NZ* 1, 1969 *E*
Lacaze, H (Périgueux) 1928 *I, G, W,* 1929 *I, W*
Lacaze, P (Lourdes) 1958 *SA* 1,2, 1959 *S, E, It, W, I*
Lacazedieu, C (Dax) 1923 *W, I,* 1928 *A, I,* 1929 *S*
Lacombe, B (Agen) 1989 *B,* 1990 *A* 2
Lacome, M (Pau) 1960 *Arg* 2
Lacoste, R (Tarbes) 1914 *I, W, E*
Lacrampe, F (Béziers) 1949 *Arg* 2
Lacroix, P (Mont-de-Marsan, Agen) 1958 *A,* 1960 *W, I, It, R, Arg* 1,2,3, 1961 *S, SA, E, W, I, NZ* 1,2,3, *A, R,* 1962 *S, E, W, I, R,* 1963 *S, I, E, W*
Lacroix, T (Dax, Harlequins) 1989 *A* 1 (R), 2, 1991 *W* 1 (R), 2 (R), [*R, C* (R), *E*], 1992 *SA* 2, 1993 *E, S, I, W, SA* 1,2, *R* 2, *A* 1,2, 1994 *I, W, E, S, C* 1, *NZ* 1,2, *C* 2, 1995 *W, E, S, R* 1, [*Tg, Iv, S, I, SA, E*], 1996 *E, S, I,* 1997 *It* 2, *R* 2, *Arg, SA* 1,2
Lafarge, Y (Montferrand) 1978 *R,* 1979 *NZ* 1, 1981 *I* (R)
Laffitte, R (SCUF) 1910 *W, S*
Laffont, H (Narbonne) 1926 *W*
Lafond, A (Bayonne) 1922 *E*
Lafond, J-B (RCF) 1983 *A* 1, 1985 *Arg* 1,2 1986 *S, I, W, E, R* 1, 1987 *I* (R), 1988 *W,* 1989 *I, W, E,* 1990 *W, A* 3 (R), *NZ* 2, 1991 *S, I, W* 1, *E, R, US* 1, *W* 2, [*R* (R), *Fj, C, E*], 1992 *W, E, S, I* (R), *SA* 2, 1993 *E, S, I, W*
Lagisquet, P (Bayonne) 1983 *A* 1,2, 1984 *I, W, NZ* 1,2, 1986 *R* 1 (R), *Arg* 1,2, *A, NZ* 1, 1987 [*S, R, Fj, A, NZ*], *R,* 1988 *S, I, W, Arg* 1,2,3,4, *R,* 1989 *I, W, E, S, NZ* 1,2, *B, A* 1,2, 1990 *W, E, S, I, A* 1,2,3, 1991 *S, I, US* 2, [*R*]
Lagrange, J-C (RCF) 1966 *It*
Lalande, M (RCF) 1923 *S, W, I*
Lamaison, C (Brive) 1996 *SA* 1(R),2, 1997 *W, E, S, R* 1, *A* 2, *It* 2, *R* 2, *Arg, SA* 1,2, 1998 *E, S, I, W, Arg* 3 (R), *A*
Lane, G (RCF) 1906 *NZ, E,* 1907 *E,* 1908 *E, W,* 1909 *E, W, I,* 1910 *W, E,* 1911 *S, W,* 1912 *I, W, E,* 1913 *S*
Langlade, J-C (Hyères) 1990 *R, A* 1, *NZ* 1
Laperne, D (Dax) 1997 *R* 1 (R)
Laporte, G (Graulhet) 1981 *I, W, E, R, NZ* 1,2, 1986 *S, I, W, E, R* 1, *Arg* 1, *A* (R), 1987 [*R, Z* (R), *Fj*]
Larreguy, P (Bayonne) 1954 *It*
Larribau, J (Périgueux) 1912 *I, S, W, E,* 1913 *S,* 1914 *I, E*
Larrieu, J (Tarbes) 1920 *I, US,* 1921 *W,* 1923 *S, W, E, I*
Larrieux, M (SBUC) 1927 *G* 2
Larrue, H (Carmaux) 1960 *W, I, It, R, Arg* 1,2,3
Lasaosa, P (Dax) 1950 *I,* 1952 *S, I, E, It,* 1955 *It*
Lascubé, G (Agen) 1991 *S, I, W* 1, *E, US* 2, *W* 2, [*R, Fj, C, E*], 1992 *W, E*
Lassegue, J-B (Toulouse) 1946 *W,* 1947 *S, I, W,* 1948 *W,* 1949 *I, E, W, Arg* 1
Lasserre, F (René) (Bayonne, Cognac, Grenoble) 1914 *I,* 1920 *S,* 1921 *S, W, I,* 1922 *S, E, W, I,* 1923 *W, E,* 1924 *S, I, R, US*
Lasserre, J-C (Dax) 1963 *It,* 1964 *S, NZ, E, W, It, I, Fj,* 1965 *W, It, R,* 1966 *R,* 1967 *S*
Lasserre, M (Agen) 1967 *SA* 2,3, 1968 *E, W, Cz, NZ* 3, *A, SA* 1,2, 1969 *S, I, E,* 1970 *E,* 1971 *E, W*
Laterrade, G (Tarbes) 1910 *E, I,* 1911 *S, E, I*
Laudouar, J (Soustons, SBUC) 1961 *NZ* 1,2, *R,* 1962 *I, R*
Lauga, P (Vichy) 1950 *S, I, E, W*
Laurent, A (Biarritz O) 1925 *NZ, S, W, E,* 1926 *W*
Laurent, J (Bayonne) 1920 *S, E, W*
Laurent, M (Auch) 1932 *G,* 1933 *G,* 1934 *G,* 1935 *G,* 1936 *G* 1
Lassucq, C (SF) 1999 *S* (R)

Lavail, G (Perpignan) 1937 *G,* 1940 *B*
Lavaud, R (Carcassonne) 1914 *I, W*
Lavergne, P (Limoges) 1950 *S*
Lavigne, B (Agen) 1984 *R,* 1985 *E*
Lavigne, J (Dax) 1920 *E, W*
Lazies, H (Auch) 1954 *Arg* 2, 1955 *It,* 1956 *E,* 1957 *S*
Le Bourhis, R (La Rochelle) 1961 *R*
Lecointre, M (Nantes) 1952 *It*
Le Droff, J (Auch) 1963 *It, R,* 1964 *S, NZ, E,* 1970 *E, R,* 1971 *S, I*
Lefevre, R (Brive) 1961 *NZ* 2
Leflamand, L (Bourgoin) 1996 *SA* 2, 1997 *W, E, S, It* 2, *Arg, SA* 1,2 (R)
Lefort, J-B (Biarritz O) 1938 *G* 1
Le Goff, R (Métro) 1938 *R, G* 2
Legrain, M (SF) 1909 *I,* 1910 *I,* 1911 *S, E, W, I,* 1913 *S, SA, E, I,* 1914 *I, W*
Lemeur, Y (RCF) 1993 *R* 1
Lenient, J-J (Vichy) 1967 *R*
Lepatey, J (Mazamet) 1954 *It,* 1955 *S, I, E, W*
Lepatey, L (Mazamet) 1924 *S, I, E*
Lescarboura, J-P (Dax) 1982 *W, E, S, I,* 1983 *A* 1,2, *R,* 1984 *I, W, E, S, NZ* 1,2, *R,* 1985 *E, S, I, W, Arg* 1,2, 1986 *Arg* 2, *A, NZ* 1, *R* 2, *NZ* 2, 1988 *S, W,* 1990 *R*
Lesieur, E (SF) 1906 *E,* 1908 *E, W,* 1909 *E, W, I,* 1910 *S, E, I,* 1911 *E, I,* 1912 *W*
Leuvielle, M (SBUC) 1908 *W,* 1913 *S, SA, E, W,* 1914 *W, E*
Levasseur, R (SF) 1925 *W, E*
Levée, H (RCF) 1906 *NZ*
Lewis, E W (Le Havre) 1906 *E*
Lhermet, J-M (Montferrand) 1990 *S, I,* 1993 *R* 1
Libaros, G (Tarbes) 1936 *G* 1, 1940 *B*
Lievremont, M (Perpignan, SF) 1995 *It, R* 2, *Arg* (R), *NZ* 2 (R), 1996 *R, Arg* 1(R), *SA* 2 (R), 1997 *R* 1, *A* 2 (R), 1998 *E* (R), *S, I, W, Arg* 1,2, *Fj, Arg* 3, *A*
Lievremont, T (Perpignan, SF) 1996 *W* 2 (R), 1998 *E, S, I, W, Arg* 1,2, *Fj, Arg* 3, *A,* 1999 *I, W, E*
Lira, M (La Voulte) 1962 *R,* 1963 *I, E, W, It, R,* 1964 *W, It, I, SA,* 1965 *S, I, R*
Llari, R (Carcassonne) 1926 *S*
Lobies, J (RCF) 1921 *S, W, E*
Lombard, F (Narbonne) 1934 *G,* 1937 *It*
Lombard, T (SF) 1998 *Arg* 3, *A,* 1999 *I, W, S* (R)
Lombarteix, R (Montferrand) 1938 *R, G* 2
Londios, J (Montauban) 1967 *SA* 3
Loppy, L (Toulon) 1993 *R* 2
Lorieux, A (Grenoble, Aix) 1981 *A* 1, *R, NZ* 1,2, 1982 *W,* 1983 *A* 2, *R,* 1984 *I, W, E,* 1985 *Arg* 1,2 (R), 1986 *R* 2, *NZ* 2,3, 1987 *W, E,* [*S, Z, Fj, A, NZ*], 1988 *S, I, W, Arg* 1,2,4, 1989 *W, A* 2
Loury, A (RCF) 1927 *E, G* 1,2, 1928 *S, A, I*
Loustau, M (Pau) 1959 *I*
Lubin-Lebrère, M-F (Toulouse) 1914 *I, W, E,* 1920 *S, E, W, I, US,* 1921 *S,* 1922 *S, E, W,* 1924 *W, US,* 1925 *I*
Lubrano, A (Béziers) 1972 *A* 2, 1973 *S*
Lux, J-P (Tyrosse, Dax) 1967 *E, It, W, I, SA* 1,2,4, 1968 *I, E, Cz, NZ* 3, *A, SA* 1,2, 1969 *S, I, E,* 1970 *S, I, W, E, R,* 1971 *S, I, E, W, A* 1,2, 1972 *S, I* 1, *E, W, I* 2, *A* 1,2, *R,* 1973 *S, NZ, E,* 1974 *I, W, E, S, Arg* 1,2, 1975 *W*

Macabiau, A (Perpignan) 1994 *S, C* 1
Maclos, P (SF) 1906 *E,* 1907 *E*
Magne, O (Dax, Brive) 1997 *W* (R), *E, S, R* 1 (R), *A* 1,2, *It* 2 (R), *R* 2, *Arg* (R), 1998 *E, S, I, W, Arg* 1,2, *Fj, Arg* 3, *A,* 1999 *I*
Magnanou, C (RCF) 1923 *E,* 1925 *W, E,* 1926 *S,* 1929 *S, W,* 1930 *S, I, E, W*
Magnol, L (Toulouse) 1928 *S,* 1929 *S, W, E*
Magois, H (La Rochelle) 1968 *SA* 1,2, *R*
Majerus, R (SF) 1928 *W,* 1929 *I, S,* 1930 *S, I, E, G, W*
Malbet, J-C (Agen) 1967 *SA* 2,4
Maleig, A (Oloron) 1979 *W, E, NZ* 2, 1980 *W, E, SA, R*
Malquier, Y (Narbonne) 1979 *S*
Manterola, T (Lourdes) 1955 *It,* 1957 *R* 1
Mantoulan, C (Pau) 1959 *I*
Marcet, J (Albi) 1925 *I, NZ, S, W, E,* 1926 *I, E*
Marchal, J-F (Lourdes) 1979 *S, R,* 1980 *W, S, I*
Marconnet, S (SF) 1998 *Arg* 3, *A,* 1999 *I* (R), *W* (R), *E, S* (R)
Marchand, R (Poitiers) 1920 *S, W*
Marfaing, M (Toulouse) 1992 *R, Arg* 1
Marlu, J (Montferrand) 1998 *Fj* (R)

Marocco, P (Montferrand) 1968 *S, I, W, E, R* 1, *Arg* 1,2, *A*, 1988 *Arg* 4, 1989 *I*, 1990 *E* (R), *NZ* 1 (R), 1991 *S, I, W* 1, *E, US* 2, [*R, Fj, C, E*]
Marot, A (Brive) 1969 *R*, 1970 *S, I, W*, 1971 *SA* 1, 1972 *I* 2, 1976 *A* 1
Marquesuzaa, A (RCF) 1958 *It, SA* 1,2, 1959 *S, E, It, W*, 1960 *S, E, Arg* 1
Marracq, H (Pau) 1961 *R*
Martin, C (Lyon) 1909 *I*, 1910 *W, S*
Martin, H (SBUC) 1907 *E*, 1908 *W*
Martin, J-L (Béziers) 1971 *A* 2, *R*, 1972 *S, I* 1
Martin, L (Pau) 1948 *I, A, S, W, E*, 1950 *S*
Martine, R (Lourdes) 1952 *S, I, It*, 1953 *It*, 1954 *S, I, NZ, W, E, It, Arg* 2, 1955 *S, I, W*, 1958 *A, W, It, I, SA* 1,2, 1960 *S, E, Arg* 3, 1961 *S, It*
Martinez, G (Toulouse) 1982 *W, E, S, Arg* 1,2, 1983 *E, W*
Mas, F (Béziers) 1962 *R*, 1963 *S, I, E, W*
Maso, J (Perpignan, Narbonne) 1966 *It, R*, 1967 *S, R*, 1968 *S, W, Cz, NZ* 1,2,3, *A, R*, 1969 *S, I, W*, 1971 *SA* 1,2, *R*, 1972 *E, W, A* 2, 1973 *W, I, J, R*
Massare, J (PUC) 1945 *B* 1,2, *W*, 1946 *B, I, W*
Massé, A (SBUC) 1908 *W*, 1909 *E, W*, 1910 *W, S, E, I*
Masse, H (Grenoble) 1937 *G*
Matheu-Cambas, J (Agen) 1945 *W*, 1946 *B, I, K, W*, 1947 *S, I, W, E*, 1948 *I, A, S, W, E*, 1949 *S, I, E, W, Arg* 1,2, 1950 *E, W*, 1951 *S, I*
Mauduy, G (Périgueux) 1957 *It, R* 1,2, 1958 *S, E*, 1961 *W, It*
Mauran, J (Castres) 1952 *SA, W, E, It*, 1953 *I, E*
Mauriat, P (Lyon) 1907 *E*, 1908 *E, W*, 1909 *W, I*, 1910 *W, S, E, I*, 1911 *S, E, W, I*, 1912 *I, S*, 1913 *S, SA, W, I*
Maurin, G (ASF) 1906 *E*
Maury, A (Toulouse) 1925 *I, NZ, S, W, E*, 1926 *S, I, E*
Mayssonnié, A (Toulouse) 1908 *E, W*, 1910 *W*
Mazas, L (Colomiers, Biarritz) 1992 *Arg*, 1996 *SA* 1
Melville, E (Toulon) 1990 *I* (R), *A* 1,2,3, *NZ* 1, 1991 *US* 2
Menrath, R (SCUF) 1910 *W*
Menthiller, Y (Romans) 1964 *W, It, SA, R*, 1965 *E*
Meret, F (Tarbes) 1940 *B*
Mericq, S (Agen) 1959 *I*, 1960 *S, E, W*, 1961 *I*
Merle, O (Grenoble, Montferrand) 1993 *SA* 1,2, *R* 2, *A* 1,2, 1994 *I, W, E, S, C* 1, *NZ* 1,2, *C* 2, 1995 *W, I, F, S, I, SA, E*], *It, R* 2, *Arg, NZ* 1, 2, 1996 *E, S, R, Arg* 1,2, *W* 2, *SA* 2, 1997 *I, W, E, S, It* 1, *R* 1, *A* 1,2, *It* 2, *R* 2, *SA* 1 (R), 2
Merquey, J (Toulon)1950 *S, I, E, W*
Mesnel, F (RCF) 1986 *NZ* 2 (R), 3, 1987 *W, E, S, I, [S, Z, Fj, A, NZ]*, *R*, 1988 *E, I, W, Arg* 1,2,3,4, *R*, 1989 *I, W, E, S, NZ* 1, *A* 1,2, 1990 *E, S, I, A* 2,3, *NZ* 1,2, 1991 *S, I, W* 1, *E, R, US* 1,2, *W* 2, [*R, Fj, C, E*], 1992 *W, E, S, I, SA* 1,2, 1993 *E* (R), *W*, 1995 *I, R* 1, [*Iv, E*]
Mesny, P (RCF, Grenoble) 1979 *NZ* 1,2, 1980 *SA, R*, 1981 *I, W* (R), *A* 1,2, *R*, *NZ* 1,2, 1982 *I, Arg* 1,2
Meyer, G-S (Périgueux) 1960 *S, E, It, W*
Meynard, J (Cognac) 1954 *Arg* 1, 1956 *Cz*
Mias, L (Mazamet) 1951 *S, I, E, W*, 1952 *I, SA, W, E, It*, 1953 *S, I, W, It*, 1954 *S, I, NZ, W*, 1957 *R* 2, 1958 *S, E, A, W, I, SA* 1,2, 1959 *S, It, W, I*
Mignoni, P (Béziers) 1997 *R* 2 (R), *Arg* (t)
Milliand, P (Grenoble) 1936 *G* 2, 1937 *G, It*
Minjat, R (Lyon) 1945 *B* 1
Miorin, H (Toulouse) 1996 *R, SA* 1, 1997 *I, W, E, S, It* 1
Mir, J-H (Lourdes) 1967 *R*, 1968 *I*
Mir, J-P (Lourdes) 1967 *A*
Modin, R (Brive) 1987 [*Z*]
Moga, A-M-A (Bègles) 1945 *B* 1,2, *W*, 1946 *B, I, K, W*, 1947 *S, I, W, E*, 1948 *I, A, S, W, E*, 1949 *S, I, E, W, Arg* 1,2
Mola, U (Dax) 1997 *S* (R)
Mommejat, B (Cahors, Albi) 1958 *It, I, SA* 1,2, 1959 *S, E, It, W, I*, 1960 *S, E, I, R*, 1962 *S, E, W, I, It, R*, 1963 *S, I, W*
Moncla, F (RCF, Pau) 1956 *Cz*, 1957 *I, E, W, It, R* 1, 1958 *SA* 1,2, 1959 *S, E, It, W, I*, 1960 *S, E, W, I, It, R, Arg* 1,2,3, 1961 *S, SA, E, W, It, I, NZ* 1,2,3
Moni, C (Nice) 1996 *R*
Monié, R (Perpignan) 1956 *Cz*, 1957 *E*
Monier, R (SBUC) 1911 *I*, 1912 *S*
Monniot, M (RCF) 1912 *W, E*
Montade, A (Perpignan) 1925 *I, NZ, S, W*, 1926 *W*
Montlaur, P (Agen) 1992 *E* (R), 1994 *S* (R)
Moraitis, B (Toulon) 1969 *E, W*
Morel, A (Grenoble) 1954 *Arg* 2
Morere, J (Toulouse) 1927 *E, G* 1, 1928 *S, A*

Moscato, V (Bègles) 1991 *R, US* 1, 1992 *W, E*
Mougeot, C (Bègles) 1992 *W, E, Arg*
Mouniq, P (Toulouse) 1911 *S, E, W, I*,1912 *I, E*, 1913 *S, SA, E*
Moure, H (SCUF) 1908 *E*
Moureu, P (Béziers) 1920 *I, US*, 1921 *W, E, I*, 1922 *S, W, I*, 1923 *S, W, E, I*, 1924 *S, I, E, W*, 1925 *E*
Mournet, A (Bagnères) 1981 *A* 1 (R)
Mouronval, F (SF) 1909 *I*
Muhr, A H (RCF) 1906 *NZ, E*, 1907 *E*
Murillo, G (Dijon) 1954 *It, Arg* 1

Namur, R (Toulon) 1931 *E, G*
Noble, J-C (La Voulte) 1968 *E, W, Cz, NZ* 3, *A, R*
Normand, A (Toulouse) 1957 *R* 1
Novès, G (Toulouse) 1977 *NZ* 1,2, *R*, 1978 *W, R*, 1979 *I, W*
Ntamack, E (Toulouse) 1994 *W, C* 1, *NZ* 1,2, *C* 2, 1995 *W, I, R* 1, [*Tg, S, I, SA, E*], *It, R* 2, *Arg, NZ* 1, 2, 1996 *E, S, I, W* 1, *R* (R), *Arg* 1,2, *W* 2, 1997 *I*, 1998 *Arg* 3, 1999 *I, W, E, S*

Olive, D (Montferrand) 1951 *I*, 1952 *I*
Ondarts, P (Biarritz O) 1986 *NZ* 3, 1987 *W, E, S, I, [S, Z, Fj, A, NZ]*, *R*, 1988 *E, I, W, Arg* 1,2,3,4, *R*, 1989 *I, W, E, NZ* 1,2, *A* 2, 1990 *W, E, S, I, R* (R), *NZ* 1,2, 1991 *S, I, W* 1, *E, US* 2, *W* 2, [*R, Fj, C, E*]
Orso, J-C (Nice, Toulon) 1982 *Arg* 1,2, 1983 *E, S, A* 1, 1984 *E* (R), *S, NZ* 1, 1985 *I* (R), *W*, 1988 *I*
Othats, J (Dax) 1960 *Arg* 2,3
Ougier, S (Toulouse) 1992 *R, Arg* 1, 1993 *E* (R), 1997 *It* 1

Paco, A (Béziers) 1974 *Arg* 1,2, *R, SA* 1,2, 1975 *W, E, Arg* 1,2, *R*, 1976 *S, I, W, E, US, A* 1,2, *R*, 1977 *W, E, S, I, NZ* 1,2, *R*, 1978 *E, S, I, W, R*, 1979 *I, W, E, S*, 1980 *W*
Palat, J (Perpignan) 1938 *G* 2
Palmié, M (Béziers) 1975 *SA* 1,2, *Arg* 1,2, *R*, 1976 *S, I, W, E, US*, 1977 *W, E, S, I, Arg* 1,2, *NZ* 1,2, *R*, 1978 *E, S, I, W*
Paoli, R (see Simonpaoli)
Paparemborde, R (Pau) 1975 *SA* 1,2, *Arg* 1,2, *R*, 1976 *S, I, W, E, US, A* 1,2, *R*, 1977 *W, E, S, I, Arg* 1, *NZ* 1,2, 1978 *E, S, I, W, R*, 1979 *I, W, E, S, NZ* 1,2, *R*, 1980 *W, E, S, SA, R*, 1981 *S, I, W, E, A* 1,2, *R, NZ* 1,2, 1982 *W, I, R, Arg* 1,2 1983 *E, S, I, W*
Pardo, L (Hendaye) 1924 *I, E*
Pardo, L (Bayonne) 1980 *SA, R*, 1981 *S, I, W, E, A* 1, 1982 *W, E, S*, 1983 *A* 1 (R), 1985 *S, I, Arg* 2
Pargade, J-H (Lyon U) 1953 *I*
Paries, L (Biarritz O) 1968 *SA* 2, *R*, 1970 *S, I, W*, 1975 *E, S, I*
Pascalin, P (Mont-de-Marsan) 1950 *I, E, W*, 1951 *S, I, E, W*
Pascarel, J-R (TOEC) 1912 *W, E*, 1913 *S, SA, E, I*
Pascot, J (Perpignan) 1922 *S, E, I*, 1923 *S*, 1926 *I*, 1927 *G* 2
Paul, R (Montferrand) 1940 *B*
Pauthe, G (Graulhet) 1956 *E*
Pebeyre, E-J (Fumel, Brive) 1945 *W*, 1946 *I, K, W*, 1947 *S, I, W, E*
Pebeyre, M (Vichy, Montferrand) 1970 *E, R*, 1971 *I, SA* 1,2, *A* 1, 1973 *W*
Pecune, J (Tarbes) 1974 *W, E, S*, 1975 *Arg* 1,2, *R*, 1976 *I, W, E, US*
Pedeutour, P (Bègles) 1980 *I*
Pellissier, L (RCF) 1928 *A, I, E, G, W*
Pelous, F (Dax, Toulouse) 1995 *R* 2, *Arg, NZ* 1, 2, 1996 *E, S, I, R* (R), *Arg* 1,2, *W* 2, *Arg* 3, 1997 *I, W, E, S, It* 1, *R* 1, *A* 1,2, *It* 2, *R* 2, *Arg, SA* 1,2 (R), 1998 *E, S, I, W, Arg* 1,2, *Fj, Arg* 3, *A*, 1999 *I, W, E*
Penaud, A (Brive) 1992 *W, E, S, I, R, Arg* 1,2, *SA* 1,2, *Arg*, 1993 *R* 1, *SA* 1,2, *R* 2, *A* 1,2, 1994 *I, W, E*, 1995 *NZ* 1, 2, 1996 *S, R, Arg* 1,2, *W* 2, 1997 *I, E, R* 1, *A* 2
Périé, M (Toulon) 1996 *E, S, I* (R)
Peron, P (RCF) 1975 *SA* 1,2
Perrier, P (Bayonne) 1982 *W, E, S, I* (R)
Pesteil, J-P (Béziers) 1975 *SA* 1, 1976 *A* 2, *R*
Petit, C (Lorrain) 1931 *W*
Peyrelade, H (Tarbes) 1940 *B*
Peyroutou, G (Périgueux) 1911 *S, E*
Phliponeau, J-F (Montferrand) 1973 *W, I*
Piazza, A (Montauban) 1968 *NZ* 1, *A*
Picard, T (Montferrand) 1985 *Arg* 2, 1986 *R* 1 (R), *Arg* 2
Pierrot, G (Pau) 1914 *I, W, E*
Pilon, J (Périgueux) 1949 *E*, 1950 *E*

Piqué, J (Pau) 1961 *NZ* 2,3, *A*, 1962 *S, It*, 1964 *NZ, E, W, It, I, SA, Fj, R*, 1965 *S, I, E, W, It*
Piquemal, M (Tarbes) 1927 *I, S*, 1929 *I, G*, 1930 *S, I, E, G, W*
Piquiral, E (RCF) 1924 *S, I, E, W, R, US*, 1925 *E*, 1926 *S, I, E, W, M*, 1927 *I, S, W, E, G* 1,2, 1928 *E*
Piteu, R (Pau) 1921 *S, W, E, I*, 1922 *S, E, W, I*, 1923 *E*, 1924 *E*, 1925 *I, NZ, W, E*, 1926 *E*
Plantefol, A (RCF) 1967 *SA* 2,3,4, *NZ, R*, 1968 *E, W, Cz, NZ* 2, 1969 *E, W*
Plantey, S (RCF) 1961 *A*, 1962 *It*
Podevin, G (SF) 1913 *W, I*
Poeydebasque, F (Bayonne) 1914 *I, W*
Poirier, A (SCUF) 1907 *E*
Pomathios, M (Agen, Lyon U, Bourg) 1948 *I, A, S, W, E*, 1949 *S, I, E, W, Arg* 1,2, 1950 *S, I, W*, 1951 *S, I, E, W*, 1952 *W, E*, 1953 *S, I, W*, 1954 *S*
Pons, P (Toulouse) 1920 *S, E, W*, 1921 *S, W*, 1922 *S*
Porra, M (Lyon) 1931 *I*
Porthault, A (RCF) 1951 *S, E, W*, 1952 *I*, 1953 *S, I, It*
Portolan, C (Toulouse) 1986 *A*, 1989 *I, E*
Potel, A (Begles) 1932 *G*
Prat, J (Lourdes) 1945 *B* 1,2, *W*, 1946 *B, I, K, W*, 1947 *S, I, W, E*, 1948 *I, A, S, W, E*, 1949 *S, I, E, W, Arg* 1,2, 1950 *S, I, E, W*, 1951 *S, E, W*, 1952 *S, I, SA, W, E, It*, 1953 *S, I, E, W, It*, 1954 *S, I, NZ, W, E, It*, 1955 *S, I, E, W, It*
Prat, M (Lourdes) 1951 *I*, 1952 *S, I, SA, W, E*, 1953 *S, I, E*, 1954 *I, NZ, W, E, It*, 1955 *S, I, E, W, It*, 1956 *I, W, It, Cz*, 1957 *S, I, W, It, R* 1, 1958 *A, W, I*
Prevost, A (Albi) 1926 *M*, 1927 *I, S, W*
Prin-Clary, J (Cavaillon, Brive) 1945 *B* 1,2, *W*, 1946 *B, I, K, W*, 1947 *S, I, W*
Puech, L (Toulouse) 1920 *S, E, I*, 1921 *E, I*
Puget, M (Toulouse) 1961 *It*, 1966 *S, I, It*, 1967 *SA* 1,3,4, *NZ*, 1968 *NZ* 1,2, *SA* 1,2, *R*, 1969 *E, R*, 1970 *W*
Puig, A (Perpignan) 1926 *S, E*
Pujol, A (SOE Toulouse) 1906 *NZ*
Pujolle, M (Nice) 1989 *B, A* 1, 1990 *S, I, R, A* 1,2, *NZ* 2

Quaglio, A (Mazamet) 1957 *R* 2, 1958 *S, E, A, W, I, SA* 1,2, 1959 *S, E, It, W, I*
Quilis, A (Narbonne) 1967 *SA* 1,4, *NZ*, 1970 *R*, 1971 *I*

Ramis, R (Perpignan) 1922 *E, I*, 1923 *W*
Rancoule, H (Lourdes, Toulon, Tarbes) 1955 *E, W, It*, 1958 *A, W, It, I, SA* 1, 1959 *S, It, W*, 1960 *I, It, R, Arg* 1,2, 1961 *SA, E, W, It, NZ* 1,2, 1962 *S, E, W, I, It*
Rapin, A (SBUC) 1938 *R*
Raymond, F (Toulouse) 1925 *S*, 1927 *W*, 1928 *I*
Raynal, F (Perpignan) 1935 *G*, 1936 *G* 1,2, 1937 *G, It*
Raynaud, F (Carcassonne) 1933 *G*
Raynaud, M (Narbonne) 1999 *W, E* (R)
Razat, J-P (Agen) 1962 *R*, 1963 *S, I, R*
Rebujent, R (RCF) 1963 *E*
Revailler, D (Graulhet) 1981 *S, I, W, E, A* 1,2, *R, NZ* 1,2, 1982 *W, S, I, R, Arg* 1
Revillon, J (RCF) 1926 *I, E*, 1927 *S*
Ribère, E (Perpignan, Quillan) 1924 *I*, 1925, *I, NZ, S*, 1926 *S, I, W, M*, 1927 *I, S, W, E, G* 1,2, 1928 *S, A, I, E, G, W*, 1929 *I, E, G*, 1930 *S, I, E, W*, 1931 *I, S, W, E, G*, 1932 *G*, 1933 *G*
Rives, J-P (Toulouse, RCF) 1975 *E, S, I, Arg* 1,2, *R*, 1976 *S, I, W, E, US, A* 1,2, *R*, 1977 *W, E, S, I, Arg* 1,2, *R*, 1978 *E, S, I, W, R*, 1979 *W, E, S, NZ* 1,2, *R*, 1980 *W, E, S, I, SA*, 1981 *S, I, W, E, A* 2, 1982 *W, E, S, I, R*, 1983 *E, S, I, W, A* 1,2, *R*, 1984 *I, W, E, S*
Rochon, A (Montferrand) 1936 *G* 1
Rodrigo, M (Mauléon) 1931 *I, W*
Rodriguez, L (Mont-de-Marsan, Montferrand, Dax) 1981 *A* 1,2, *R, NZ* 1,2, 1982 *W, E, S, I, R*, 1983 *E, S*, 1984 *I, NZ* 1,2, *R*, 1985 *E, S, I, W*, 1986 *Arg* 1, *A, R* 2, *NZ* 2,3, 1987 *W, E, S, I, [S, Z, Fj, A, NZ], R*, 1988 *E, S, I, W, Arg* 1,2,3,4, *R*, 1989 *I, E, S, NZ* 1,2, *B, A* 1, 1990 *W, E, S, I, NZ* 1
Rogé, L (Béziers) 1952 *It*, 1953 *E, W, It*, 1954 *S, Arg* 1,2, 1955 *S, I*, 1956 *W, It, E*, 1957 *S*, 1960 *S, E*
Rollet, J (Bayonne) 1960 *Arg* 3, 1961 *NZ* 3, *A*, 1962 *It*, 1963 *I*
Romero, H (Montauban) 1962 *S, E, W, I, It, R*, 1963 *E*
Romeu, J-P (Montferrand) 1972 *R*, 1973 *S, NZ, E, W, I, R*, 1974 *W, E, S, Arg* 1,2, *R, SA* 1,2 (R), 1975 *W, SA* 2, *Arg* 1,2, *R*, 1976 *S, I, W, E, US*, 1977 *W, E, S, I, Arg* 1,2, *NZ* 1,2, *R*

Roques, A (Cahors) 1958 *A, W, It, I, SA* 1,2, 1959 *S, E, W, I*, 1960 *S, E, W, I, It, Arg* 1,2,3, 1961 *S, SA, E, W, It, I*, 1962 *S, E, W, I, It*, 1963 *S*
Roques, J-C (Brive) 1966 *S, I, It, R*
Rossignol, J-C (Brive) 1972 *A* 2
Rouan, J (Narbonne) 1953 *S, I*
Roucaries, G (Perpignan) 1956 *S*
Rouffia, L (Narbonne) 1945 *B* 2, *W*, 1946 *W*, 1948 *I*
Rougerie, J (Montferrand) 1973 *J*
Rougé-Thomas, P (Toulouse) 1989 *NZ* 1,2
Roujas, F (Tarbes) 1910 *I*
Roumat, O (Dax) 1989 *NZ* 2 (R), *B*, 1990 *W, E, S, I, R, A* 1,2,3, *NZ* 1,2, 1991 *S, I, W* 1, *E, R, US* 1, *W* 2, [*R, Fj, C, E*], 1992 *W* (R), *E* (R), *S, I, SA* 1,2, *Arg*, 1993 *E, S, I, W, R* 1, *SA* 1,2, *R* 2, *A* 1,2, 1994 *I, W, E, C* 1, *NZ* 1,2, *C* 2, 1995 *W, E, S*, [*Iv, S, I, SA, E*], 1996 *E, S, I, W* 1, *Arg* 1,2
Rousie, M (Villeneuve) 1931 *S, G*, 1932 *G*, 1933 *G*
Rousset, G (Béziers) 1975 *SA* 1, 1976 *US*
Ruiz, A (Tarbes) 1968 *SA* 2, *R*
Rupert, J-J (Tyrosse) 1963 *R*, 1964 *S, Fj*, 1965 *E, W, It*, 1966 *S, I, E, W, It*, 1967 *It, R*, 1968 *S*

Sadourny, J-L (Colomiers) 1991 *W* 2 (R), [*C* (R)], 1992 *E* (R), *S, I, Arg* 1 (R), 2, *SA* 1,2, 1993 *R* 1, *SA* 1,2, *R* 2, *A* 1,2, 1994 *I, W, E, S, C* 1, *NZ* 1,2, *C* 2, 1995 *W, E, S, I, R* 1, [*Tg, S, I, SA, E*], *It, R* 2, *Arg, NZ* 1, 1996 *E, S, I, W* 1, *Arg* 1, *W* 2, *SA* 1,2, 1997 *I, W, E, S, It* 1, *R* 1, *A* 1,2, *It* 2, *R* 2, *Arg, SA* 1,2, 1998 *E, S, I, W*
Sagot, P (SF) 1906 *NZ*, 1908 *E*, 1909 *W*
Sahuc, A (Métro) 1945 *B* 1,2
Sahuc, F (Toulouse) 1936 *G* 2
Saint-André, P (Montferrand, Gloucester) 1990 *R, A* 3, *NZ* 1,2, 1991 *I* (R), *W* 1, *E, US* 1,2, *W* 2, [*R, Fj, C, E*], 1992 *W, E, S, I, R, Arg* 1,2, *SA* 1,2, 1993 *E, S, I, W, SA* 1,2, *A* 1,2, 1994 *I, W, E, S, C* 1, *NZ* 1,2, *C* 2, 1995 *W, E, S, I, R* 1, [*Tg, Iv, S, I, SA, E*], *It, R* 2, *Arg, NZ* 1, 2, 1996 *E, S, I, W* 1, *R, Arg* 1,2, *W* 2, 1997 *It* 1,2, *R* 2, *Arg, SA* 1,2
Saisset, O (Béziers) 1971 *R*, 1972 *S, I* 1, *A* 1,2, 1973 *S, NZ, E, W, I, J, R*, 1974 *I, Arg* 2, *SA* 1,2, 1975 *W*
Salas, P (Narbonne) 1979 *NZ* 1,2, *R*, 1980 *W, E*, 1981 *A* 1, 1982 *Arg* 2
Salinié, R (Perpignan) 1923 *E*
Sallefranque, M (Dax) 1981 *A* 2, 1982 *W, E, S*
Salut, J (TOEC) 1966 *R*, 1967 *S*, 1968 *I, E, Cz, NZ* 1, 1969 *I*
Samatan, R (Agen) 1930 *S, I, E, G, W*, 1931 *I, S, W, E, G*
Sanac, A (Perpignan) 1952 *It*, 1953 *S, I*, 1954 *E*, 1956 *Cz*, 1957 *S, I, E, W, It*
Sangalli, F (Narbonne) 1975 *I, SA* 1,2, 1976 *S, A* 1,2, *R*, 1977 *W, E, S, I, Arg* 1,2, *NZ* 1,2
Sanz, H (Narbonne) 1988 *Arg* 3,4, *R*, 1989 *A* 2, 1990 *S, I, R, A* 1,2, *NZ* 2, 1991 *W* 2
Sappa, M (Nice) 1973 *J, R*, 1977 *R*
Sarrade, R (Pau) 1929 *I*
Saux, J-P (Pau) 1960 *W, It, Arg* 1,2, 1961 *SA, E, W, It, I, NZ* 1,2,3, *A*, 1962 *S, E, W, I, It*, 1963 *S, I, E, It*
Savitsky, M (La Voulte) 1969 *R*
Savy, M (Montferrand) 1931 *I, S, W, E*, 1936 *G* 1
Sayrou, J (Perpignan) 1926 *W, M*, 1928 *E, G, W*, 1929 *S, W, E, G*
Scohy, R (BEC) 1931 *S, W, E, G*
Sébedio, J (Tarbes) 1913 *S, E*, 1914 *I*, 1920 *S, I, US*, 1922 *S, E*, 1923 *S*
Seguier, N (Béziers) 1973 *J, R*
Seigne, L (Agen, Merignac) 1989 *B, A* 1, 1990 *NZ* 1, 1993 *E, S, I, W, R* 1, *A* 1,2, 1994 *S, C* 1, 1995 *E* (R), *S*
Sella, P (Agen) 1982 *R, Arg* 1,2, 1983 *E, S, I, W, A* 1,2, *R*, 1984 *I, W, E, S, NZ* 1,2, *R*, 1985 *E, S, I, W, Arg* 1,2, 1986 *S, I, W, E, R* 1, *Arg* 1,2, *A, NZ* 1, *R* 2, *NZ* 2,3, 1987 *W, E, S, I*, [*S, R, Z* (R), *Fj, A, NZ*], 1988 *E, S, I, W, Arg* 1,2,3,4, *R*, 1989 *I, W, E, S, NZ* 1,2, *B, A* 1,2, 1990 *W, E, S, I, A* 1,2,3, 1991 *W* 1, *E, R, US* 1,2, *W* 2, [*Fj, C, E*], 1992 *W, E, S, I, Arg*, 1993 *E, S, I, W, R* 1, *SA* 1,2, *R* 2, *A* 1,2, 1994 *I, W, E, S, C* 1, *NZ* 1,2, *C* 2, 1995 *W, E, S, I*, [*Tg, S, I, SA, E*]
Semmartin, J (SCUF) 1913 *W, I*
Senal, G (Béziers) 1974 *Arg* 1,2, *R, SA* 1,2, 1975 *W*
Sentilles, J (Tarbes) 1912 *W, E*, 1913 *S, SA*
Serin, L (Béziers) 1928 *E*, 1929 *W, E, G*, 1930 *S, I, E, G, W*, 1931 *I, W, E*
Serre, P (Perpignan) 1920 *S, E*
Serrière, P (RCF) 1986 *A*, 1987 *R*, 1988 *E*
Servole, L (Toulon) 1931 *I, S, W, E, G*, 1934 *G*, 1935 *G*
Sicart, N (Perpignan) 1922 *I*

Sillières, J (Tarbes) 1968 *R*, 1970 *S, I*, 1971 *S, I, E*, 1972 *E, W*
Siman, M (Montferrand) 1948 *E*, 1949 *S*, 1950 *S, I, E, W*
Simon, S (Bègles) 1991 *R, US* 1
Simonpaoli, R (SF) 1911 *I*, 1912 *I, S*
Sitjar, M (Agen) 1964 *W, It, I, R*, 1965 *It, R*, 1967 *A, E, It, W, I, SA* 1,2
Skrela, J-C (Toulouse) 1971 *SA* 2, *A* 1,2, 1972 *I* 1 (R), *E, W, I* 2, *A* 1, 1973 *W, J, R*, 1974 *W, E, S, Arg* 1, *R*, 1975 *W* (R), *E, S, I, SA* 1,2, *Arg* 1,2, *R*, 1976 *S, I, W, E, US, A* 1,2, *R*, 1977 *W, E, S, I, Arg* 1,2, *NZ* 1,2, *R*, 1978 *E, S, I, W*
Soler, M (Quillan) 1929 *G*
Soro, R (Lourdes, Romans) 1945 *B* 1,2, *W*, 1946 *B, I, K*, 1947 *S, I, W, E*, 1948 *I, A, S, W, E*, 1949 *S, I, E, W, Arg* 1,2
Sorondo, L-M (Montauban) 1946 *K*, 1947 *S, I, W, E*, 1948 *I*
Soulette, C (Béziers) 1997 *R* 2, 1998 *S* (R), *I* (R), *W* (R), *Arg* 1,2, *Fj*
Soulié, E (CASG) 1920 *E, I, US*, 1921 *S, E, I*, 1922 *E, W, I*
Sourgens, J (Bègles) 1926 *M*
Spanghero, C (Narbonne) 1971 *E, W, SA* 1,2, *A* 1,2, *R*, 1972 *S, E, W, I* 2, *A* 1,2, 1974 *I, W, E, S, R, SA* 1, 1975 *E, S, I*
Spanghero, W (Narbonne) 1964 *SA, Fj, R*, 1965 *S, I, E, W, It, R*, 1966 *S, I, E, W, It, R*, 1967 *S, A, E, SA* 1,2,3,4, *NZ*, 1968 *S, I, E, W, NZ* 1,2,3, *A, SA* 1,2, *R*, 1969 *S, I, W*, 1970 *R*, 1971 *E, W, SA* 1, 1972 *E, I* 2, *A* 1,2, *R*, 1973 *S, NZ, E, W, I*
Stener, G (PUC) 1956 *S, I, E*, 1958 *SA* 1,2
Struxiano, P (Toulouse) 1913 *W, I*, 1920 *S, E, W, I, US*
Sutra, G (Narbonne) 1967 *SA* 2, 1969 *W*, 1970 *S, I*
Swierczinski, C (Bègles) 1969 *E*, 1977 *Arg* 2

Tachdjian, M (RCF) 1991 *S, I, E*
Taffary, M (RCF) 1975 *W, E, S, I*
Taillantou, J (Pau) 1930 *I, G, W*
Tarricq, P (Lourdes) 1958 *A, W, It, I*
Tavernier, H (Toulouse) 1913 *I*
Techoueyres, W (SBUC) 1994 *E, S*, 1995 *[Iv]*
Terreau, M-M (Bourg) 1945 *W*, 1946 *B, I, K, W*, 1947 *S, I, W, E*, 1948 *I, A, W, E*, 1949 *S, Arg* 1,2, 1951 *S*
Theuriet, A (SCUF) 1909 *E, W*, 1910 *S*, 1911 *W*, 1913 *E*
Thevenot, M (SCUF) 1910 *W, E, I*
Thierry, R (RCF) 1920 *S, E, W, US*
Thiers, P (Montferrand) 1936 *G* 1,2, 1937 *G, It*, 1938 *G* 1,2, 1940 *B*, 1945 *B*, 1,2
Tignol, P (Toulouse) 1953 *S, I*
Tilh, H (Nantes) 1912 *W, E*, 1913 *S, SA, E, W*
Tolot, J-L (Agen) 1987 *[Z]*
Tordo, J-F (Nice) 1991 *US* 1 (R), 1992 *W, E, S, I, R, Arg* 1,2, *SA* 1, *Arg*, 1993 *E, S, I, W, R* 1
Torossian, F (Pau) 1997 *R* 1
Torreilles, S (Perpignan) 1956 *S*
Tournaire, F (Narbonne, Toulouse) 1995 *It*, 1996 *I, W* 1, *R, Arg* 1,2(R), *W* 2, *SA* 1,2, 1997 *I, E, S, It* 1, *R* 1, *A* 1,2, *It* 2, *R* 2, *Arg, SA* 1,2, 1998 *E, S, I, W, Arg* 1,2, *Fj, Arg* 3, *A*, 1999 *I, W, E, S*
Tourte, R (St Girons) 1940 *B*

Trillo, J (Bègles) 1967 *SA* 3,4, *NZ, R*, 1968 *S, I, NZ* 1,2,3, *A*, 1969 *I, E, W, R*, 1970 *E, R*, 1971 *S, I, SA* 1,2, *A* 1,2, 1972 *S, A* 1,2, *R*, 1973 *S, E*
Triviaux, R (Cognac) 1931 *E, G*
Tucco-Chala, M (PUC) 1940 *B*

Ugartemendia, J-L (St Jean-de-Luz) 1975 *S, I*

Vaills, G (Perpignan) 1928 *A*, 1929 *G*
Vallot, C (SCUF) 1912 *S*
Van Heerden, A (Tarbes) 1992 *E, S*
Vannier, M (RCF, Chalon) 1953 *W*, 1954 *S, I, Arg* 1,2, 1955 *S, I, E, W, It*, 1956 *S, I, W, It, E*, 1957 *S, I, E, W, It, R* 1,2, 1958 *S, E, A, W, It, I*, 1960 *S, E, W, I, It, R, Arg* 1,3, 1961 *SA, E, W, It, I, NZ* 1, *A*
Vaquer, F (Perpignan) 1921 *S, W*, 1922 *W*
Vaquerin, A (Béziers) 1971 *R*, 1972 *S, I* 1, *A* 1, 1973 *S*, 1974 *W, E, S, Arg* 1,2, *R, SA* 1,2, 1975 *W, E, S, I*, 1976 *US, A* 1 (R), 2, *R*, 1977 *Arg* 2, 1979 *W, E*, 1980 *S, I*
Vareilles, C (SF) 1907 *E*, 1908 *E, W*, 1910 *S, E*
Varenne, F (RCF) 1952 *S*
Varvier, T (RCF) 1906 *E*, 1909 *E, W*, 1911 *E, W*, 1912 *I*
Vassal, G (Carcassonne) 1938 *R, G* 2
Vaysse, J (Albi) 1924 *US*, 1926 *M*
Vellat, E (Grenoble) 1927 *I, E, G* 1,2, 1928 *A*
Venditti, D (Bourgoin, Brive) 1996 *R, SA* 1(R),2, 1997 *I, W, E, S, R* 1, *A* 1, *SA* 2
Vergé, L (Bègles) 1993 *R* 1 (R)
Verger, A (SF) 1927 *W, E, G* 1, 1928 *I, E, G, W*
Verges, S-A (SF) 1906 *NZ, E*, 1907 *E*
Viard, G (Narbonne) 1969 *W*, 1970 *S, R*, 1971 *S, I*
Viars, S (Brive) 1992 *W, E, I, R, Arg* 1,2, *SA* 1,2 (R), *Arg*, 1993 *R* 1, 1994 *C* 1 (R), *NZ* 1 (t), 1995 *E* (R), *[Iv]*, 1997 *R* 1 (R), *A* 1 (R), 2
Vigerie, M (Agen) 1931 *W*
Vigier, R (Montferrand) 1956 *S, W, It, E, Cz*, 1957 *S, E, W, It, R* 1,2, 1958 *S, E, A, W, It, I, SA* 1,2, 1959 *S, E, It, W, I*
Vigneau, A (Bayonne) 1935 *G*
Vignes, C (RCF) 1957 *R* 1,2, 1958 *S, E*
Vila, E (Tarbes) 1926 *M*
Vilagra, J (Vienne) 1945 *B* 2
Villepreux, P (Toulouse) 1967 *It, I, SA* 2, *NZ*, 1968 *I, Cz, NZ* 1,2,3, *A*, 1969 *S, I, E, W, R*, 1970 *S, I, W, E, R*, 1971 *S, I, E, W, A* 1,2, *R*, 1972 *I* 1, *A* 1,2
Viviès, B (Agen) 1978 *E, S, I, W*, 1980 *SA, R*, 1981 *S, A* 1, 1983 *A* 1 (R)
Volot, M (SF) 1945 *W*, 1946 *B, I, K, W*

Weller, S (Grenoble) 1989 *A* 1,2, 1990 *A* 1, *NZ* 1
Wolf, J-P (Béziers) 1980 *SA, R*, 1981 *A* 2, 1982 *E*

Yachvili, M (Tulle, Brive) 1968 *E, W, Cz, NZ* 3, *A, R*, 1969 *S, I, R*, 1971 *E, SA* 1,2 *A* 1, 1972 *R*, 1975 *SA* 2

Zago, F (Montauban) 1963 *I, E*

FRENCH INTERNATIONAL RECORDS
(up to 30 April 1999)

MATCH RECORDS

MOST CONSECUTIVE TEST WINS
10 1931 *E, G,* 1932 *G,* 1933 *G,* 1934 *G,*
    1935 *G,* 1936 *G* 1,2, 1937 *G, It*
 8 1998 *E, S, I, W, Arg* 1,2 *Fj, Arg* 3

MOST CONSECUTIVE TESTS WITHOUT DEFEAT

P	W	D	Period
10	10	0	1931–38
10	8	2	1958–59
10	9	1	1986–87

MOST POINTS IN A MATCH
by the team

Pts	Opp	Venue	Year
70	Z	Auckland	1987
64	R	Aurillac	1996
60	It	Toulon	1967
59	R	Paris	1924
55	R	Wellington	1987

by a player
30 by D Camberabero v Zimbabwe
  at Auckland   1987
27 by G Camberabero v Italy at
  Toulon   1967
26 by T Lacroix v Ireland at
  Durban   1995
25 by J-P Romeu v United States
  at Chicago   1976
25 by P Berot v Romania at Agen   1987
25 by T Lacroix v Tonga at
  Pretoria   1995

MOST TRIES IN A MATCH
by the team

T	Opp	Venue	Year
13	R	Paris	1924
13	Z	Auckland	1987
11	It	Toulon	1967
10	R	Aurillac	1996

by a player
4 by A Jauréguy v Romania at
  Paris   1924
4 by M Celhay v Italy at Paris   1937

MOST CONVERSIONS IN A MATCH
by the team

C	Opp	Venue	Year
9	It	Toulon	1967
9	Z	Auckland	1987
8	R	Wellington	1987

by a player
9 by G Camberabero v Italy at
  Toulon   1967
9 by D Camberabero v Zimbabwe
  at Auckland   1987
8 by G Laporte v Romania at
  Wellington   1987

MOST PENALTY GOALS IN A MATCH
by the team

P	Opp	Venue	Year
8	I	Durban	1995
6	Arg	Buenos Aires	1977
6	S	Paris	1997
6	It	Auch	1997

by a player
8 by T Lacroix v Ireland at Durban 1995
6 by J-M Aguirre v Argentina at
  Buenos Aires   1977
6 by C Lamaison v Scotland at
  Paris   1997
6 by C Lamaison v Italy at Auch   1997

MOST DROPPED GOALS IN A MATCH
by the team

D	Opp	Venue	Year
3	I	Paris	1960
3	E	Twickenham	1985
3	NZ	Christchurch	1986
3	A	Sydney	1990
3	S	Paris	1991
3	NZ	Christchurch	1994

by a player
3 by P Albaladejo v Ireland at Paris 1960
3 by J-P Lescarboura v England at
  Twickenham   1985
3 by J-P Lescarboura v New
  Zealand at Christchurch   1986
3 by D Camerabero v Australia at
  Sydney   1990

CAREER RECORDS

MOST CAPPED PLAYERS

Caps	Player	Career
111	P Sella	1982–95
93	S Blanco	1980–91
69	R Bertranne	1971–81
69	P Saint-André	1990–97
64	J-L Sadourny	1991–98
63	M Crauste	1957–66
63	B Dauga	1964–72
61	J Condom	1982–90
61	O Roumat	1989–96
61	A Benazzi	1990–97

MOST CONSECUTIVE TESTS

Tests	Player	Span
46	R Bertranne	1973–79
45	P Sella	1982–87
44	M Crauste	1960–66
35	B Dauga	1964–68

MOST TESTS AS CAPTAIN

Tests	Captain	Span
34	J-P Rives	1978–84
34	P Saint-André	1994–97
25	D Dubroca	1986–88
24	G Basquet	1948–52
22	M Crauste	1961–66

MOST TESTS IN INDIVIDUAL POSITIONS

Full-back S Blanco	81	1980–91
Wing P Saint-André	67	1990–97
Centre P Sella	104	1982–95
Fly-half J-P Romeu	33	1972–77
Scrum-half P Berbizier	56	1981–91
Prop R Paparemborde	55	1975–83
Hooker P Dintrans	50	1979–90
Lock J Condom	61	1982–90
Flanker J-P Rives	59	1975–84
No. 8 G Basquet	33	1945–52

MOST POINTS IN TESTS

Pts	Player	Tests	Career
367	T Lacroix	43	1989–97
354	D Camberabero	36	1982–93
265	J-P Romeu	34	1972–77
233	S Blanco	93	1980–91
200	J-P Lescarboura	28	1982–90

MOST TRIES IN TESTS

Tries	Player	Tests	Career
38	S Blanco	93	1980–91
33	P Saint-André	69	1990–97
30	P Sella	111	1982–95
23	C Darrouy	40	1957–67
22	E Ntamack	32	1994–99

MOST CONVERSIONS IN TESTS

Cons	Player	Tests	Career
48	D Camberabero	36	1982–93
45	M Vannier	43	1953–61
36	T Castaignède	25	1995–99
32	T Lacroix	43	1989–97
29	P Villepreux	34	1967–72

MOST PENALTY GOALS IN TESTS

Pens	Player	Tests	Career
89	T Lacroix	43	1989–97
59	D Camberabero	36	1982–93
56	J-P Romeu	34	1972–77
36	C Lamaison	18	1996–98
33	P Villepreux	34	1967–72
33	P Bérot	19	1986–89

MOST DROPPED GOALS IN TESTS

Drops	Player	Tests	Career
15	J-P Lescarboura	28	1982–90
12	P Albaladejo	30	1954–64
11	G Camberabero	14	1961–68
11	D Camberabero	36	1982–93
9	J-P Romeu	34	1972–77

INTERNATIONAL CHAMPIONSHIP RECORDS

Record	Detail		Set
Most points in season	144	in four matches	1998
Most tries in season	18	in four matches	1998
Highest score	51	51–16 v Scotland	1998
	51	51–0 v Wales	1998
Biggest win	51	51–0 v Wales	1998
Highest score conceded	49	14–49 v Wales	1910
Biggest defeat	37	0–37 v England	1911
Most appearances	50	P Sella	1983–95
Most points in matches	113	D Camberabero	1983–93
Most points in season	54	J-P Lescarboura	1984
Most points in match	24	S Viars	v Ireland, 1992
	24	C Lamaison	v Scotland, 1997
Most tries in matches	14	S Blanco	1981–91
	14	P Sella	1983–95
Most tries in season	5	P Estève	1983
	5	E Bonneval	1987
	5	E Ntamack	1999
Most tries in match	3	M Crauste	v England, 1962
	3	C Darrouy	v Ireland, 1963
	3	E Bonneval	v Scotland, 1987
	3	D Venditti	v Ireland, 1997
	3	E Ntamack	v Wales, 1999
Most cons in matches	18	P Villepreux	1967–72
Most cons in season	9	C Lamaison	1998
Most cons in match	5	P Villepreux	v England, 1972
	5	S Viars	v Ireland, 1992
	5	T Castaignède	v Ireland, 1996
	5	C Lamaison	v Wales, 1998
Most pens in matches	22	T Lacroix	1991–96
Most pens in season	10	J-P Lescarboura	1984
Most pens in match	6	C Lamaison	v Scotland, 1997
Most drops in matches	9	J-P Lescarboura	1982–88
Most drops in season	5	G Camberabero	1967
Most drops in match	3	P Albaladejo	v Ireland, 1960
	3	J-P Lescarboura	v England, 1985

MAJOR TOUR RECORDS

Record	Detail	Year	Place
Most individual points	112 by S Viars	1992	Argentina
Most points in match	28 by P Lagisquet	1988 v Paraguayan XV	Ascunción (Paraguay)
Most tries in match	7 by P Lagisquet	1988 v Paraguayan XV	Ascunción (Paraguay)

MISCELLANEOUS RECORDS

Record	Holder	Detail
Longest Test career	F Haget	14 seasons, 1974 to 1987
Youngest Test cap	C Dourthe	18 yrs 7 days in 1966
Oldest Test cap	A Roques	37 yrs 329 days in 1963

FRENCH INTERNATIONAL CAREER RECORDS (*up to 30 April 1999*)

Player	Debut	Caps since last season	Caps	T	C	PG	DG	Pts
J-L Sadourny	1991 v W		64	14	0	0	4	81
A Gomes	1998 v Arg	1998 *Arg* 1,2, *Fj*, *Arg* 3, *A*, 1999 *I*(R)	6	1	0	0	0	5
J Marlu	1998 v Fj	1998 v *Fj*(R)	1	0	0	0	0	0
P Bernat-Salles	1992 v Arg	1998 *Arg* 1,2, *Fj*, *Arg* 3(R), *A*, 1999 *I*, *W*	25	15	0	0	0	75
C Dominici	1998 v E	1998 *Arg* 1,2, 1999 *E*, *S*	6	4	0	0	0	20
X Garbajosa	1998 v I	1998 *Arg* 2(R), *Fj*, 1999 *W*(R), *E*, *S*	7	3	0	0	0	15
E Ntamack	1994 v W	1998 *Arg* 3, 1999 *I*, *W*, *E*, *S*	32	22	1	1	0	115
D Venditti	1996 v R		10	6	0	0	0	30
T Lombard	1998 v Arg	1998 *Arg* 3, *A*, 1999 *I*, *W*, *S*(R)	5	1	0	0	0	5
F Comba	1998 v Arg	1998 *Arg* 1,2, *Fj*, *Arg* 3, 1999 *I*, *W*, *E*, *S*	8	2	0	0	0	10
S Glas	1996 v S	1998 *Arg* 1,2, *Fj*, *Arg* 3, *A*	26	8	0	0	0	40
R Dourthe	1995 v R	1999 *I*, *W*	15	2	16	15	0	87
P Giordani	1999 v E	1999 *E*, *S*	2	0	0	0	0	0
C Lamaison	1996 v SA	1998 *Arg* 3(R), *A*	18	1	26	36	1	168
T Castaignède	1995 v R	1998 *Arg* 1,2, *Fj*, 1999 *I*, *W*, *E*, *S*	25	9	36	19	4	186
D Aucagne	1997 v W	1998 *Arg* 2(R), *Fj*(R), *Arg* 3, *A*, 1999 *W*(R), *S*(R)	15	1	9	5	0	38
P Carbonneau	1995 v R	1998 *Arg* 1,2, *Fj*, *Arg* 3, *A*, 1999 *I*, *W*, *E*, *S*	30	5	0	0	0	25
C Laussucq	1999 v S	1999 *S*(R)	1	0	0	0	0	0
F Galthié	1991 v R	1998 *Fj*(R)	23	4	0	0	0	19
P Mignoni	1997 v R		2	0	0	0	0	0
M Dal Maso	1988 v R	1998 *Arg* 1(t), *Fj*(R)	19	2	0	0	0	10
R Ibañez	1996 v W	1998 *Arg* 1,2, *Fj*, *Arg* 3, *A*, 1999 *I*, *W*, *E*, *S*	19	2	0	0	0	10
F Tournaire	1995 v It	1998 *Arg* 1,2, *Fj*, *Arg* 3, *A*, 1999 *I*, *W*, *E*, *S*	34	2	0	0	0	10
S Marconnet	1998 v Arg	1998 *Arg* 3, *A*, 1999 *I*(R), *W*(R), *E*, *S*(R)	6	0	0	0	0	0
S de Besombes	1998 v Arg	1998 *Arg* 1(R), *Fj* (R)	2	0	0	0	0	0
C Califano	1994 v NZ	1999 *I*, *W*, *E*(R), *S*	43	6	0	0	0	30
C Soulette	1997 v R	1998 *Arg* 1,2, *Fj*	7	2	0	0	0	10
F Pelous	1995 v R	1998 *Arg* 1,2, *Fj*, *Arg* 3, *A*, 1999 *I*, *W*, *E*	38	2	0	0	0	10
T Cléda	1998 v E	1998 *Arg* 1(R), *Fj*(R), *Arg* 3(R), 1999 *I*(R), *S*	9	0	0	0	0	0
D Auradou	1999 v E	1999 *E*(R), *S*(R)	2	0	0	0	0	0

O Brouzet	1994 v S	1998 *Arg* 1,2, *Fj*, *Arg* 3, *A*, 1999 *I*, *W*, *E*, *S*	32	2	0	0	0	10
T Lièvremont	1996 v W	1998 *Arg* 1,2, *Fj*, *Arg* 3, *A*, 1999 *I*, *W*, *E*	13	2	0	0	0	10
R Castel	1996 v I	1998 *Arg* 3(R), *A*(R), 1999 *W*(R), *E*, *S*	15	2	0	0	0	10
M Raynaud	1999 v W	1999 *W*, *E*(R)	2	0	0	0	0	0
P Benetton	1989 v BL	1998 *Arg* 1(R),2(R), *Fj*(R) , 1999 *I*, *W*, *S*(R)	59	7	0	0	0	34
C Labit	1999 v S	1999 *S*	1	0	0	0	0	0
O Magne	1997 v W	1998 *Arg* 1,2, *Fj*, *Arg* 3, *A*, 1999 *I*	19	1	0	0	0	5
M Lièvremont	1995 v It	1998 *Arg* 1,2, *Fj*, *Arg* 3, *A*	18	5	0	0	0	25
C Juillet	1995 v R	1999 *E*, *S*	4	1	0	0	0	5
A Benazzi	1990 v A		61	7	0	0	0	35

Captain under pressure. The French hooker and skipper Raphael Ibañez finishes the season on a low note as his team are torn apart by Scotland at the Stade de France.

INJURIES CAUSE CONCERN

THE 1998-99 SEASON IN ITALY
Giampaolo Tassinari *Tuttosport*

What should have been the season of Italy's confirmation at the highest level of European rugby became instead a year of big concerns. The *azzurri* went through a two-faced period, earning two wonderful victories over Argentina and Holland before losing all five Tests in a row to France and the Home Unions – the nations they will meet annually from 2000 onwards. True, in the match against England a refereeing decision deprived Italy of a famous win, but the other losses were well deserved.

There were two main causes of Italy's troubles. Georges Coste's men showed a worrying lack of mental strength when facing teams that they had previously beaten. Moreover, a long injury list kept several key players out for long periods. Only Fabio Roselli, Diego Dominguez, Alessandro Troncon and Alessandro Moscardi appeared in all seven Tests while 11 players were new to the national side, among them two promising youngsters in Simone Stocco and Giacomo Preo. At full-back, Matt Pini of Richmond was unable to match the form he had shown for Australia in 1994 and despite Carlo Caione's efforts the No.8 role also caused concern in the wake of Julian Gardner's departure.

To make matters even worse Paolo Vaccari's long-term injury to his right hand sidelined him for almost the whole season and his presence at the World Cup is doubtful. There was satisfaction, however, with the Dominguez-Troncon axis, while there was a good partnership at centre involving Alessandro Stoica and Luca Martin, and Massimo Giovanelli again led by example. But he has a major task ahead to motivate the squad for the upcoming World Cup and inaugural Six Nations.

ITALIAN CLUB CHAMPIONSHIP FINAL

29 May, Stadio Battaglini, Rovigo
Benetton Treviso 23 (2G 3PG) **Petrarca Padova 14** (3PG 1T)

Same finalists, same outcome. That was the story of the 1999 Italian Club Championship. Benetton's eighth title was their third in a row, but the final was a chaotic match full of fouls and was repeatedly interrupted by the referee. As in the previous year, Petrarca lost through an inability to hold passes and failure to kick goals.

Benetton opened the scoring in the third minute when Corrado Pilat crossed for a try that he also converted. Although the Treviso side

The Italian squad against England in the World Cup qualifying match staged at Huddersfield on 22nd November.

remained in front for the rest of the match, the Paduans never allowed their opponents to establish more than a ten-point margin.

The best passages of the match came early in the second half when Benetton struggled to retain their lead, having lost Alessandro Troncon through injury. A Marty Berry try in the 52nd minute brought Petrarca back to 11-13 and an exchange of penalty goals made it 14-16 with only a quarter of an hour to go. Tommaso Visentin then put the seal on Benetton's victory with a try from a counterattack in the 70th minute. At that stage his side had only 14 men on the park; Francesco Mazzariol having been temporarily dispatched to the sin-bin.

Benetton dedicated the victory to the late Ivan Francescato, the centre who had featured prominently in their 1998 success. For Petrarca, their coach Vittorio Munari splendidly summed up his feelings after the match when he said, 'whatever the result, tonight we'll have a big feast together.'

Benetton Treviso: C Pilat; M Perziano, T Visentin, M Dallan, D Dallan; L Pavin, A Troncon (*capt*); G Grespan, A Moscardi, F Properzi-Curti, W Cristofoletto, W Visser, O Arancio, C Checchinato, A Sgorlon *Substitutions:* F Mazzariol for Pilat (26 mins); M Bergamo for Troncon (38 mins); A Gritti for Visser (53 mins); N De Meneghi for Grespan (57 mins); S Saviozzi for Moscardi (71 mins); L Bot for Checchinato (75 mins); G Faliva for Properzi-Curti (78 mins)
Scorers *Tries:* Pilat, Visentin *Conversions:* Pilat, Pavin *Penalty Goals:* Pavin (3)
Petrarca Padova: K Rolleston; V D'Anna, M Piovene, R Salvan, M Baroni; M J Berry, H De Marco; P-G Menapace, A Moretti, A Muraro, A Giacon, S Stocco, R Saetti, M Birtig, A Zulian (*capt*) *Substitutions:* C Covi for Birtig (31 mins); R Rampazzo for Giacon (44 mins); F Gomez for Berry (58 mins); L Pasqualin for Salvan (66 mins); P Vigolo for Menapace (71 mins)
Scorers *Try:* Berry *Penalty Goals:* Rolleston (3)
Referee M Salera (Rome)

ITALIAN INTERNATIONAL RECORDS
(up to 30 April 1999)

MATCH RECORDS

MOST CONSECUTIVE TEST WINS
6 1968 *Pt, G,Y,* 1969 *Bu, Sp, Be*

MOST CONSECUTIVE TESTS WITHOUT DEFEAT

P	W	D	Period
6	6	0	1968-69
5	4	1	1982-83

MOST POINTS IN A MATCH
by the team

Pts	Opp	Venue	Year
104	Cz	Viadana	1994
78	Cr	Perpignan	1993
70	Mo	Carcassonne	1993
67	H	Huddersfield	1998
64	Pt	Lisbon	1996

by a player

29 by S Bettarello v Canada at Toronto — 1983
28 by D Dominguez v Holland at Calvisano — 1994
27 by D Dominguez v Ireland at Bologna — 1997
25 by D Dominguez v Romania at Tarbes — 1997
24 by L Troiani v Spain at Parma — 1994

MOST TRIES IN A MATCH
by the team

T	Opp	Venue	Year
16	Cz	Viadana	1994
11	Cr	Perpignan	1993
11	H	Huddersfield	1998
10	Be	Paris	1937
10	Mo	Carcassonne	1993
10	Pt	Lisbon	1996

by a player

4 by R Cova v Belgium at Paris — 1937
4 by I Francescato v Morocco at Carcassonne — 1993

MOST CONVERSIONS IN A MATCH
by the team

C	Opp	Venue	Year
12	Cz	Viadana	1994
10	Cr	Perpignan	1993
10	Mo	Carcassonne	1993
8	Sp	Parma	1994

by a player

12 by L Troiani v Czech Republic at Viadana — 1994
10 by L Troiani v Croatia at Perpignan — 1993
10 by G Filizzola v Morocco at Carcassonne — 1993
8 by L Troiani v Spain at Parma — 1994

MOST PENALTIES IN A MATCH
by the team

P	Opp	Venue	Year
8	R	Catania	1994
6	S	Rovigo	1993
6	Arg	Lourdes	1997
6	I	Bologna	1997
6	S	Treviso	1998

by a player

8 by D Dominguez v Romania at Catania — 1994
6 by D Dominguez v Scotland at Rovigo — 1993
6 by D Dominguez v Argentina at Lourdes — 1997
6 by D Dominguez v Ireland at Bologna — 1997
6 by D Dominguez v Scotland at Treviso — 1998

CAREER RECORDS

MOST CAPPED PLAYERS

Caps	Player	Career
65	Massimo Cuttitta	1990-99
60	S Ghizzoni	1977-87
55	S Bettarello	1979-88
54	M Mascioletti	1977-90
54	Marcello Cuttitta	1987-99
53	G Pivetta	1979-93

MOST CONSECUTIVE TESTS

Tests	Player	Span
29	M Bollesan	1968-72
27	Massimo Cuttitta	1991-94
25	C Orlandi	1995-98
24	D Dominguez	1995-99

23	A Sgorlon	1995-98
22	S Bettarello	1979-83

MOST TESTS AS CAPTAIN

Tests	Captain	Span
34	M Bollesan	1969-75
30	M Giovanelli	1992-99
22	Massimo Cuttitta	1993-99
20	M Innocenti	1985-88

MOST TESTS IN INDIVIDUAL POSITIONS

Full-back L Troiani	41	1985-95
Wing Marcello Cuttitta	54	1987-99
Centre N Francescato	39	1972-82
Fly-half S Bettarello	55	1979-88
Scrum-half A Troncon	40	1994-99
Prop M Cuttitta	65	1990-99
Hooker C Orlandi	40	1992-98
Lock R Favaro	42	1988-96
Flanker M Giovanelli	50	1989-99
No. 8 C Checchinato	29	1991-99

MOST POINTS IN TESTS

Pts	Player	Tests	Career
687	D Dominguez	50	1991-99
483	S Bettarello	55	1979-88
296	L Troiani	47	1985-95
133	E Ponzi	20	1973-77
110	Marc Cuttitta	54	1987-99

MOST TRIES IN TESTS

Tries	Player	Tests	Career
25	Marc Cuttitta	54	1987-99
21	M Marchetto	43	1972-81
19	P Vaccari	49	1991-98
17	S Ghizzoni	60	1977-87
17	M Mascioletti	54	1977-90

MOST CONVERSIONS IN TESTS

Cons	Player	Tests	Career
95	D Dominguez	50	1991-99
58	L Troiani	47	1985-95
46	S Bettarello	55	1979-88
17	E Ponzi	20	1973-77
16	G Filizzola	12	1993-95

MOST PENALTY GOALS IN TESTS

Pens	Player	Tests	Career
144	D Dominguez	50	1991-99
104	S Bettarello	55	1979-88
57	L Troiani	47	1985-95
31	E Ponzi	20	1973-77

MOST DROPPED GOALS IN TESTS

Drops	Player	Tests	Career
17	S Bettarello	55	1979-88
10	D Dominguez	50	1991-99
5	M Bonomi	34	1988-96
5	O Collodo	15	1977-87

ITALIAN INTERNATIONAL CAREER RECORDS *(up to 30 April 1999)*

Player	Debut	Caps since last season	Caps	T	C	PG	DG	Pts
J A Pertile	1994 v R	1999 S, W, I	13	1	0	0	0	5
M Pini	1998 v H	1998 H, E, 1999 F	3	1	0	0	0	5
C Pilat	1997 v I		3	1	0	0	0	5
F Mazzariol	1995 v F	1998 Arg, H(R), 1999 F(R)	11	1	2	0	0	9
M Ravazzolo	1993 v Cr		23	3	0	0	0	15
F Roselli	1995 v F	1998 Arg, H, E, 1999 F(R), S, W, I	11	3	0	0	0	15
P Vaccari	1991 v Nm	1998 Arg	49	19	0	0	0	92
Marc Cuttitta	1987 v Pt	1998 Arg, 1999 F	54	25	0	0	0	110
G Preo	1999 v I	1999 I	1	0	0	0	0	0
M Baroni	1999 v F	1999 F, W(R), I	3	1	0	0	0	5
G Raineri	1998 v H	1998 H(R)	1	0	0	0	0	0
I Francescato	1990 v R		38	16	0	0	0	77
M Dallan	1997 v Arg	1998 Arg(R), H, E	6	2	0	0	0	10
D Dallan	1999 v F	1999 F, S, W	3	0	0	0	0	0
L Martin	1997 v F	1998 H, E, 1999 F, S, W, I	11	4	0	0	0	20
C-A Stoica	1997 v I	1998 Arg, H, E, 1999 S, W	12	4	0	0	0	20
D Dominguez	1991 v F	1998 Arg, H, E, 1999 F, S, W, I	50	7	95	144	10	687
G Mazzi	1998 v H	1998 H(R)	1	0	0	0	0	0
G L Guidi	1996 v Pt		5	0	0	0	0	0
A Troncon	1994 v Sp	1998 Arg, H, E, 1999 F, S, W, I	40	7	0	0	0	35
G P De Carli	1996 v W	1998 Arg, H(R), E, 1999 F, I	9	2	0	0	0	10
S Saviozzi	1998 v Ru	1998 H(R), 1999 W(R), I	4	0	0	0	0	0
A Moscardi	1993 v Pt	1998 Arg, H, E, 1999 F, S, W, I	10	3	0	0	0	15
A Moretti	1997 v R		2	0	0	0	0	0
C Orlandi	1992 v S		40	4	0	0	0	20
A Castellani	1994 v Cz	1998 H, E(R) , 1999 F(R), W(R)	15	1	0	0	0	5
Mass Cuttitta	1990 v Po	1998 Arg(R), H, E, 1999 F, S, W	65	6	0	0	0	29
F Properzi-Curti	1990 v Po	1998 Arg, 1999 S, W, I	45	3	0	0	0	15
G Lanzi	1998 v Arg	1998 Arg(t), H(R), E(R)	3	0	0	0	0	0
C Caione	1995 v R	1998 Arg, H, E, 1999 F, S(R)	10	0	0	0	0	0
S Stocco	1998 v H	1998 H, 1999 S(R), I(R)	3	1	0	0	0	5
M Giacheri	1992 v R	1999 S, W, I	27	0	0	0	0	0
W Cristofoletto	1992 v R	1998 Arg, E, 1999 F, S, W, I	23	1	0	0	0	5
W Visser	1999 v I	1999 I(R)	1	0	0	0	0	0
D Scaglia	1994 v R	1999 W	6	1	0	0	0	5

G Croci	1990 v Sp		24	3	0	0	0	13
J M Gardner	1992 v R		20	4	0	0	0	20
M Bergamasco	1998 v H	1998 *H, E*	2	2	0	0	0	10
R Piovan	1996 v Pt		2	0	0	0	0	0
R Rampazzo	1996 v W	1999 *I*(R)	2	0	0	0	0	0
M Birtig	1998 v H	1998 *H*(R), 1999 *F*	2	0	0	0	0	0
A Sgorlon	1993 v Pt	1999 *F*(R), *S, W*	37	2	0	0	0	10
M Giovanelli	1989 v Z	1998 *Arg, H, E,* 1999 *S, W, I*	51	4	0	0	0	19
O Arancio	1993 v Ru	1998 *Arg, E*(R) , 1999 *F, W*(R), *I*	31	2	0	0	0	10
C Checchinato	1990 v Sp	1998 *Arg, H, E,* 1999 *F, S*	44	11	0	0	0	55

With a little help from his friends. The Italian forwards place Carlo Checchinato in position at a lineout during the World Cup qualifying game against England at the Alfred McAlpine Stadium, Huddersfield, a match that Italy were unlucky to lose.

A BRIDGE TOO FAR LEADS TO SPRINGBOK COLLAPSE

THE 1998 SEASON IN SOUTH AFRICA
Dan Retief

Gauged by almost any yardstick, 1998 will go down as a halcyon year for South Africa – so why did the Christmas champagne taste so stale and flat? The answer is that Lawrence Dallaglio and his England team spoiled what was meant to be the celebration of a lifetime for Gary Teichmann and his Springbok team. Twickenham on December 5 proved to be a bridge too far and the Springboks were left to rue the fact that they had missed their date with destiny, as they tried to come to terms with a demanding public who treated them as though they had failed.

But I'm getting ahead of the story. Let's reel the spool back a little to put the year in perspective. First there were the fighting Irish. Tempers became frayed and both teams disgraced themselves in the second international at Loftus Versfeld in Pretoria, but the 'Boks ran up a combined winning score of 70 points to 13 over two Tests to see off Paddy Johns and his men.

Next came Wales, also marching to Pretoria. And how this once-proud rugby nation must have wished that they could expunge from the record books the Test they played at Loftus Versfeld on June 27, 1998. The Welsh could take some dubious solace in the fact that South Africa failed to score a century, but only just. The Springboks ran in a record 15 tries in amassing a record total of 96 points, while Percy Montgomery claimed the individual points-scoring record of 31 points from two tries, nine conversions and a penalty goal.

England, too, were beaten – 18-0 in so much mud at Newlands that officials were finally persuaded that the old field needed to be dug up and re-laid – and then it was into the third southern hemisphere Tri-Nations tournament.

After struggling in the Super-12 competition (the Natal Sharks were knocked out by eventual winners Canterbury Crusaders in the semi-final, but the other three new regional teams – the Northern Bulls, the Cats and the Stormers – finished in the bottom four) there was not much confidence that the Springboks would be competitive against either the All Blacks or the Wallabies.

Away from the playing fields, however, dramatic and far-reaching changes were taking place. After a long drawn-out battle in which he had challenged, and succeeded, in getting President Nelson Mandela to appear in court to justify a decision to launch a commission of enquiry into the running of rugby, the SA Rugby Football Union's disputatious president, Louis Luyt, resigned. This brought Silas Nkanunu, a Port Elizabeth lawyer, into the chair as SARFU tried to rid itself of its controversial image. With hindsight it was as though the proverbial cloud had lifted from Springbok rugby.

On the playing front there was a harbinger of things to come when the Wallabies beat the All Blacks 24-16 at the MCG in Melbourne while the Springboks were unpacking in Perth.

Keen to impress a new audience, the Springboks were given the distinction of playing the first ever rugby union international at the 45,000-seater rugby league Subiaco Oval – a decision encouraged in no small way by the presence of thousands of expatriate South Africans in Western Australia.

In poor weather it was a game that neither team could afford to lose; and it showed in the style of play with the Springboks' uncompromising tackling getting them home by a single point. Perth represented South Africa's first away victory in the Tri-Nations and the team was in a buoyant mood as it set off to beard the All Blacks in their Athletic Park den in Wellington. It turned out to be a day to savour as Pieter Rossouw's cleverly-worked scrum-ball try gave the Springboks a 13-3 victory and, with their first win in New Zealand since 1981, new horizons began to reveal themselves.

Two away victories meant that the 'Boks had the inside lane in the race for the Tri-Nations, but when Australia beat the All Blacks in Christchurch it meant the 'Boks would not be able to relax in the return against New Zealand in Durban. And what a game it turned out to be. With 15 minutes to go the Springboks trailed 5-23 but somehow they managed to conjure up tries by Joost van der Westhuizen, Bobby Skinstad and James Dalton to snatch it 24-23 and give Gary Teichmann his first win as captain of the Springboks at his home-ground, King's Park.

And so to Ellis Park with everything to play for in what could well have been described as the second most important test in the annals of South African rugby after the Rugby World Cup final. The 'Boks, however, had saved their best for last and wrote an illustrious chapter into the green-and-gold register with an impressive and confident 29-15 victory. This victory was South Africa's 14th in succession in their triumphal march under Nick Mallett and put them in line to establish a world record if they could win all four internationals on their Grand Slam tour to Britain.

By the time of the tour, however, the players were tired, with the Currie Cup competition also having taken its toll, and the warning bells started to ring right from the start as the 'Boks struggled to suppress a gallant Welsh team, unrecognisable from the rag-tag bunch who had been humiliated earlier in the year, at the Wembley Football Stadium.

With former All Black Shane Howarth at full-back and the Quinnell brothers, Scott and Craig, as well as Scott Gibbs in superb form, Wales led for most of the way and seemed set to spoil Mark Andrews's day as the first Springbok to reach 50 international appearances.

In the end they were unlucky to go down to a dubious penalty try, a piece of Joost van der Westhuizen magic and a stirring Springbok fight-back that led to the winning try by Andre Venter.

It was clear that something would have to be done to right a listing Springbok ship, but no-one expected or anticipated Mallett's measures ... former Canadian international Christian Stewart came in for Franco Smith at inside centre and Bobby Skinstad's exceptional form in the midweek team was rewarded – but the big shock was that the man who had to make room for him was Andre Venter. The Scots brought in two 'kilted Kiwis' in the Leslie brothers, John and Martin, but although they competed well in terms of possession they just could not match the speed and skill of the Springboks.

Crossing the Irish Sea brought a definite tightening of the tension – keener opposition for the midweek team and a re-match, in the Test at Lansdowne Road in Dublin, of two teams who had turned their previous encounter in South Africa into a slugfest. Inspired by Keith Wood, the world's No.1 hooker in 1998, the Irish had the 'Boks rattled until two pieces of pure genius by Skinstad snatched the game away from them and preserved the Springboks' chance to go for the record 18 victories at Twickenham.

But in the end it was not to be as injuries took their toll and a magnificent England pack wrested complete control after South Africa had scored the opening try. Thus a wonderful year ended in disappointment, but perhaps it is apt that South Africa and New Zealand, who have always been inseparable as the great powers of world rugby, remain deadlocked. They have each won as many Tests as they have lost against each other and it seems historically appropriate that they should jointly hold a record – 17 straight Test victories – which Mallett, for one, believes is unlikely to be challenged.

BANKFIN CURRIE CUP 1998

	P	W	D	L	F	A	TF	TA	Bonus	Total
Griqualand West	13	10	0	3	478	216	69	26	10	50
Blue Bulls	13	10	0	3	461	231	65	28	9	49
Natal Sharks	13	9	1	3	410	242	54	25	9	47
Western Province	13	10	0	3	371	247	49	27	7	47
Free State	13	8	1	4	453	314	56	31	9	43
MTN Falcons	13	9	1	3	381	285	48	35	5	43
SWD Eagles	13	7	1	5	378	290	51	38	9	39
Golden Lions	13	7	0	6	389	279	55	37	8	36
Eastern Province	13	5	0	8	345	313	46	45	8	28

Boland	13	5	0	8	253	456	38	67	4	24
Mpumalanga Pumas	13	4	0	9	284	381	37	52	5	21
Border	13	2	0	11	236	472	27	68	5	13
North West	13	2	0	11	236	637	28	100	2	10
Northern FS	13	1	0	12	212	524	27	71	5	9

*The competition was played on the Super-12 format: four points for a win, two points for a draw, one extra point for scoring four tries or more, one point for a defeat by seven points or less.

Semi-finals:
Griqualand West 11, Western Province 27 (Kimberley); Blue Bulls 31, Natal Sharks 17 (Pretoria)

Final:
Blue Bulls 24, Western Province 20 (Pretoria)

VODACOM CUP

Semi-finals:
Golden Lions 31, SWD Eagles 19 (Johannesburg); Griqualand West 47, Natal Wildebeest 28 (Kimberley)

Final:
Griqualand West 57, Golden Lions 0 (Kimberley)

SOUTH AFRICA TO BRITAIN & IRELAND 1998

THE TOURING PARTY

Manager A Petersen **Coach** NVH Mallett **Assistant Coach** A Solomons
Captain GH Teichmann

Full-backs: PC Montgomery (Western Province), GS du Toit (Griqualand West)

Threequarters: CS Terblanche (Boland), PWG Rossouw (Western Province),
BJ Paulse (Western Province), RL Markram (Griqualand West), AH Snyman (Blue
Bulls), C Stewart (Western Province), RF Fleck (Western Province), DJ Kayser
(Eastern Province), SL Venter (Griqualand West)

Half-backs: HW Honiball (Natal Sharks), PF Smith (Blue Bulls), AJJ van Straaten
(Gauteng Falcons), JH van der Westhuizen (Blue Bulls), W Swanepoel (Free State
Cheetahs), CD Alcock (Eastern Province)

Forwards: J Dalton (Golden Lions), AE Drotské (Free State Cheetahs),
O Nkumane (Golden Lions), RB Kempson (Natal Sharks), AC Garvey (Natal
Sharks), AH le Roux (Natal Sharks), W Meyer (Free State Cheetahs), A van der
Linde (Western Province), K Otto (Blue Bulls), MG Andrews (Natal Sharks),
CS Boome (Western Province), J Erasmus (Free State Cheetahs), CPJ Krige
(Western Province), RB Skinstad (Western Province), AG Venter (Free State
Cheetahs), PL Smit (Griqualand West), GH Teichmann (Natal Sharks),
JW Trytsman (Western Province), AN Vos (Golden Lions), *B Moyle (Gauteng
Falcons)

* *Replacement on tour*

TOUR RECORD

All matches   Played 8   Won 7   Lost 1   Points for 290   Against 92
International matches   Played 4   Won 3   Lost 1   Points for 97   Against 56

SCORING DETAILS

All matches					**International matches**				
For:	42T	28C	8PG	= 290pts	For:	12T	8C	7PG	= 97pts
Against:	6T	4C	18PG	= 92pts	Against:	4T	3C	10PG	= 56pts

MATCH DETAILS

1998	OPPONENTS	VENUE	RESULT
10 Nov	Glasgow Caledonians	Glasgow	W 62-9
14 Nov	WALES	Wembley	W 28-20
17 Nov	Edinburgh Reivers	Edinburgh	W 49-3
21 Nov	SCOTLAND	Murrayfield	W 35-10
24 Nov	Combined Provinces	Cork	W 32-5
28 Nov	IRELAND	Dublin	W 27-13
1 Dec	Ireland A	Belfast	W 50-19
5 Dec	ENGLAND	Twickenham	L 7-13

MATCH 1   10 November, Firhill Stadium, Glasgow

Glasgow Caledonians 9 (3PG)   **South Africa XV 62** (6G 4T)
Glasgow Caledonians: T Hayes; J Craig, I Jardine (*capt*), J Leslie, D Stark;
L Smith, D Patterson; G McIlwham, K McKenzie, A Kittle, S Campbell,
G Perrett, J White, G Mackay, J Shaw *Substitutions:* A Bulloch for Craig (55 mins);

G Flockhart for Hayes (60 mins); G Scott for McKenzie (65 mins)
Scorer *Penalty Goals:* Hayes (3)
South Africa XV: du Toit; Paulse, Fleck, Stewart, L Venter; van Straaten, Swanepoel; Meyer, Drotské, le Roux, Boome, Trytsman, Krige, Skinstad (*capt*), Vos *Substitutions:* Smit for Boome (40 mins); van der Linde for le Roux (40 mins); Kayser for L Venter (62 mins); Alcock for Swanepoel (62 mins); Nkumane for Drotske (62 mins)
Scorers *Tries:* Paulse (3), Fleck (2), Boome, L Venter, du Toit, van Straaten, Skinstad *Conversions:* van Straaten (6)
Referee N Whitehouse (Wales)

MATCH 2   14 November, Wembley Stadium   Test Match
WALES 20 (5PG 1T)   SOUTH AFRICA 28 (2G 3PG 1T)

WALES: SP Howarth (Sale); G Thomas (Cardiff), M Taylor (Swansea), IS Gibbs (Swansea), DR James (Pontypridd); NR Jenkins (Pontypridd), R Howley (Cardiff) (*capt*); ALP Lewis (Cardiff), JM Humphreys (Cardiff), CT Anthony (Swansea), JC Quinnell (Richmond), CP Wyatt (Llanelli), CL Charvis (Swansea), LS Quinnell (Llanelli), ME Williams (Pontypridd) *Substitutions:* DR Morris (Swansea) for Lewis (48 mins); BR Evans (Swansea) for Anthony (68 mins)
Scorers *Try:* G Thomas *Penalty Goals:* Jenkins (5)
SOUTH AFRICA: Montgomery; Terblanche, Snyman, Smith, Rossouw; Honiball, van der Westhuizen; Kempson, Dalton, Garvey, Otto, Andrews, Erasmus, Teichmann (*capt*), A Venter *Substitutions:* le Roux for Garvey (47 mins); Skinstad for Andrews (47 mins)
Scorers *Tries:* penalty try, van der Westhuizen, A Venter *Conversions:* Smith (2) *Penalty Goals:* Smith (3)
Referee S Dickinson (Australia)

MATCH 3   17 November, Easter Road, Edinburgh

Edinburgh Reivers 3 (1PG)   South Africa XV 49 (7G)
Edinburgh Reivers: S Lang; H Gilmour, S Hastings, I Fairley, J Kerr; S Welsh, G Burns; R McNulty, S Scott, B Stewart, D Burns, I Fullarton, A Roxburgh, B Renwick (*capt*), I Sinclair *Substitutions:* A Common for Kerr (52 mins); J Hay for Scott (52 mins); P Wright for McNulty (52 mins); C Hogg for D Burns (64 mins); T McVie for Roxburgh (64 mins)
Scorer *Penalty Goal:* Welsh
South Africa XV: Paulse; Markram, Fleck, van Straaten, Kayser; Stewart, Alcock; van der Linde, Nkumane, Meyer, Boome, Smit, Krige, Vos, Skinstad (*capt*) *Substitutions:* Trytsman for Skinstad (40 mins); L Venter for Stewart (47 mins); le Roux for van der Linde (47 mins); Drotské for Nkumane (47 mins); du Toit for Paulse (62 mins); Swanepoel for Alcock (65 mins)
Scorers *Tries:* van der Linde, Vos, Skinstad, le Roux, Meyer, Krige, L Venter *Conversions:* van Straaten (7)
Referee M Whyte (Ireland)

MATCH 4   21 November, Murrayfield   Test Match
SCOTLAND 10 (1G 1PG)   SOUTH AFRICA 35 (2G 2PG 3T)

SCOTLAND: DJ Lee (London Scottish); AV Tait (Edinburgh Reivers), MJM Mayer (Edinburgh Reivers), JA Leslie (Glasgow Caledonians), CA Murray (Edinburgh Reivers); DW Hodge (Edinburgh Reivers), BW Redpath (Edinburgh Reivers) (*capt*); TJ Smith (Glasgow Caledonians), GC Bulloch (Glasgow

Caledonians), AP Burnell (London Scottish), S Murray (Bedford), GW Weir (Newcastle), P Walton (Newcastle), EW Peters (Bath), AC Pountney (Northampton) *Substitutions:* GPJ Townsend (Brive, France) for Lee (15 mins); MD Leslie (Edinburgh Reivers) for Walton (50 mins); DIW Hilton (Bath) for Burnell (57 mins); KM Logan (Wasps) for Tait (70 mins); G Armstrong for Redpath (76 mins)
Scorer *Try:* Hodge *Conversion:* Hodge *Penalty Goal:* Hodge
SOUTH AFRICA: Montgomery; Terblanche, Snyman, Stewart, Rossouw; Honiball, van der Westhuizen; Kempson, Dalton, Garvey, Otto, Andrews, Erasmus, Teichmann (*capt*), Skinstad *Substitutions:* le Roux for Garvey (50 mins); A Venter for Otto (57 mins)
Scorers *Tries:* Terblanche, van der Westhuizen, Snyman, Rossouw, Skinstad *Conversions:* Montgomery (2) *Penalty Goals:* Montgomery (2)
Referee C White (England)

MATCH 5   24 November, Musgrave Park, Cork

Combined Irish Provinces 5 (1T)   **South Africa XV 32** (2G 1PG 3T)
Combined Irish Provinces: C Clarke (Terenure College); J Kelly (Cork Constitution), K Keane (Garryowen), M Murphy (Galwegians), J Cunningham (Ballymena); B Everitt (Lansdowne), S Bell (Dungannon); E Byrne (St Mary's College), A Clarke (Dungannon), J Hayes (Shannon), M Galwey (Shannon) (*capt*), J Duffy (Galwegians), D Wallace (Garryowen), A Foley (Shannon), E Halvey (Shannon) *Substitutions:* D Clohessy (Young Munster) for Hayes (66 mins); S Byrne (Blackrock Coll) for A Clarke (66 mins); D O'Brien (Skerries) for Foley (66 mins); S Mason (Ballymena) for C Clarke (70 mins); G Longwell (Ballymena) for Duffy (75 mins); P Stringer (University College, Cork) for Bell (70 mins)
Scorer *Try:* Halvey
South Africa XV: du Toit; L Venter, Fleck, Smith, Paulse; van Straaten, Swanepoel; van der Linde, Drotské, Meyer, Trytsman, Boome, A Venter, Vos (*capt*), Smit *Substitutions:* le Roux for van der Linde (51 mins); Kayser for Smith (55 mins); Nkumane for Drotské (70 mins); Markram for van Straaten (72 mins); Alcock for Swanepoel (72 mins)
Scorers *Tries:* Paulse (2), A Venter, van Straaten, le Roux *Conversions:* van Straaten (2) *Penalty Goal:* van Straaten
Referee F Maciello (France)

MATCH 6   28 November, Lansdowne Road, Dublin Test Match

IRELAND 13 (1G 2PG)   SOUTH AFRICA 27 (3G 2PG)

IRELAND: CMP O'Shea (London Irish); JP Bishop (London Irish), JC Bell (Dungannon), KM Maggs (Bath), G Dempsey (Terenure College); EP Elwood (Galwegians), CD McGuinness (St Mary's College); JM Fitzpatrick (Dungannon), KGM Wood (Harlequins), PM Clohessy (Young Munster), PS Johns (Saracens) (*capt*), ME O'Kelly (London Irish), D O'Cuinneagain (Sale), VCP Costello (St Mary's College), AJ Ward (Ballynahinch) *Substitutions:* R Corrigan (Greystones) for Fitzpatrick (54 mins); JW Davidson (Castres, France) for O'Kelly (54 mins); RP Nesdale (Newcastle) for Wood (79 mins)
Scorers *Try:* Wood *Conversion:* Elwood *Penalty Goals:* Elwood (2)
SOUTH AFRICA: Montgomery; Terblanche, Snyman, Stewart, Rossouw; Honiball, van der Westhuizen; Kempson, Dalton, Garvey, Otto, Andrews, Erasmus, Teichmann (*capt*), Skinstad *Substitutions:* Drotské for Dalton (12 mins); le Roux for Kempson (50 mins); A Venter for Andrews (50 mins); Kempson for Garvey (80 mins)

Scorers *Tries:* Erasmus, Skinstad, van der Westhuizen
Conversions: Montgomery (3) *Penalty Goals:* Montgomery (2)
Referee C Thomas (Wales)

MATCH 7   1 December, Ravenhill, Belfast

Ireland A 19 (1G 4PG)   **South Africa XV 50** (5G 3T)
Ireland A: G Dempsey (Terenure College); N Woods (London Irish),
R Henderson (Wasps), P Duignan (Galwegians), D O'Mahony (Bedford);
D Humphreys (Dungannon), C Scally (UC Dublin); R Corrigan (Greystones),
R Nesdale (Newcastle), J Hayes (Shannon), M Galwey (Shannon) *(capt)*,
J Davidson (Castres, France), D Corkery (Shannon), A Foley (Shannon),
E Halvey (Shannon) *Substitutions:* D Wallace (Garryowen) for Corkery (30 mins);
S Mason (Ballymena) for Woods (59 mins); E Byrne (St Mary's College) for
Hayes (59 mins); A Clarke (Dungannon) for Nesdale (79 mins); J Duffy
(Galwegians) for Davidson (79 mins)
Scorers *Try:* O'Mahony *Conversion:* Mason *Penalty Goals:* Woods (4)
South Africa XV: du Toit; Kayser, Fleck, Smith, Markram; van Straaten, Alcock;
van der Linde, Nkumane, Moyle, A Venter, Trytsman, Krige, Vos *(capt)*, Smit
Substitutions: le Roux for Nkumane (40 mins); Boome for A Venter (49 mins);
Paulse for Markram (58 mins); L Venter for Smith (58 mins); Swanepoel for
Alcock (68 mins)
Scorers *Tries:* du Toit (2), Fleck, Alcock, Smith, van Straaten, L Venter,
Swanepoel *Conversions:* van Straaten (5)
Referee R Dickson (Scotland)

MATCH 8   5 December, Twickenham   Test Match
ENGLAND 13 (1G 2PG)   SOUTH AFRICA 7 (1G)

ENGLAND: ND Beal (Northampton); T Underwood (Newcastle), PR de
Glanville (Bath), JC Guscott (Bath), DD Luger (Harlequins); MJ Catt (Bath),
MJS Dawson (Northampton); J Leonard (Harlequins), R Cockerill (Leicester),
DJ Garforth (Leicester), MO Johnson (Leicester), TAK Rodber (Northampton),
LBN Dallaglio (Wasps) *(capt)*, RA Hill (Saracens), NA Back (Leicester)
Substitutions: DL Rees (Sale) for Underwood (8 mins); AS Healey (Leicester) for
Rees (22 mins); AD King (Wasps) for Catt (59 mins); ME Corry (Leicester) for
de Glanville (60 mins); Catt for King and King for Corry (62 mins); DJ Grewcock
for Rodber (67 mins)
Scorers *Try:* Guscott *Conversion:* Dawson *Penalty Goals:* Dawson (2)
SOUTH AFRICA: Montgomery; Terblanche, Snyman, Stewart, Rossouw;
Honiball, van der Westhuizen; Kempson, Dalton, Garvey, Otto, Andrews,
Erasmus, Teichmann *(capt)*, Skinstad *Substitutions:* le Roux for Kempson (temp
26-40 mins) and for Garvey (59 mins); A Venter for Andrews (48 mins);
Swanepoel for van der Westhuizen (60 mins)
Scorers *Try:* Rossouw *Conversion:* Montgomery
Referee PD O'Brien (New Zealand)

The South African record-holder for most tries in Tests, Joost van der Westhuizen, in full flight during the England–South Africa match at Twickenham in December.

SOUTH AFRICAN INTERNATIONAL PLAYERS (*up to 30 April 1999*)

Ackermann, D S P (WP) 1955 *BI* 2,3,4, 1956 *A* 1,2, *NZ* 1,3, 1958 *F* 2
Ackermann, J N (NT) 1996 *Fj*, *A* 1, *NZ* 1, *A* 2
Aitken, A D (WP) 1997 *F* 2 (R), *E*, 1998 *I* 2 (R), *W* 1 (R), *NZ* 1,2 (R), *A* 2 (R)
Albertyn, P K (SWD) 1924 *BI* 1,2,3,4
Alexander, F A (GW) 1891 *BI* 1,2
Allan, J (N) 1993 *A* 1 (R), *Arg* 1,2 (R), 1994 *E* 1,2, *NZ* 1,2,3, 1996 *Fj*, *A* 1, *NZ* 1, *A* 2, *NZ* 2
Allen, P B (EP) 1960 *S*
Allport, P H (WP) 1910 *BI* 2,3
Anderson, J W (WP) 1903 *BI* 3
Anderson, J H (WP) 1896 *BI* 1,3,4
Andrew, J B (Tvl) 1896 *BI* 2
Andrews, K S (WP) 1992 *E*, 1993 *F* 1,2, *A* 1 (R), 2,3, *Arg* 1 (R), 2, 1994 *NZ* 3
Andrews, M G (N) 1994 *E* 2, *NZ* 1,2,3, *Arg* 1,2, *S, W*, 1995 *WS*, [*A, WS, F, NZ*], *W, It*, 1996 *Fj*, *A* 1, *NZ* 1, *A* 2, *NZ* 2,3,4,5, *Arg* 1,2, *F* 1,2, *W*, 1997 *Tg* (R), *BI* 1,2, *NZ* 1, *A* 1, *NZ* 2, *A* 2, *It*, *F* 1,2, *E, S*, 1998 *I* 1,2, *W* 1, *E* 1, *A* 1, *NZ* 1,2, *A* 2, *W* 2, *S, I* 3, *E* 2
Antelme, M J G (Tvl) 1960 *NZ* 1,2,3,4, 1961 *F*
Apsey, J T (WP) 1933 *A* 4,5, 1938 *BI* 2
Ashley, S (WP) 1903 *BI* 2
Aston, F T D (Tvl) 1896 *BI* 1,2,3,4
Atherton, S (N) 1993 *Arg* 1,2, 1994 *E* 1,2, *NZ* 1,2,3, 1996 *NZ* 2
Aucamp, J (WT) 1924 *BI* 1,2

Baard, A P (WP) 1960 *I*
Babrow, L (WP) 1937 *A* 1,2, *NZ* 1,2,3
Badenhorst, C (OFS) 1994 *Arg* 2, 1995 *WS* (R)
Barnard, A S (EP) 1984 *S Am* 1,2, 1986 *Cv* 1,2
Barnard, J H (Tvl) 1965 *S*, *A* 1,2, *NZ* 3,4
Barnard, R W (Tvl) 1970 *NZ* 2 (R)
Barnard, W H M (NT) 1949 *NZ* 4, 1951 *W*
Barry, J (WP) 1903 *BI* 1,2,3
Bartmann, W J (Tvl, N) 1986 *Cv* 1,2,3,4, 1992 *NZ*, *A*, *F*, 1,2
Bastard, W E (N) 1937 *A* 1, *NZ* 1,2,3, 1938 *BI* 1,3
Bates, A J (WT) 1969 *E*, 1970 *NZ* 1,2, 1972 *E*
Bayvel, P C R (Tvl) 1974 *BI* 2,4, *F* 1,2, 1975 *F* 1,2, 1976 *NZ* 1,2,3,4
Beck, J J (WP) 1981 *NZ* 2 (R), 3 (R), *US*
Bedford, T P (N) 1963 *A* 1,2,3,4, 1964 *W*, *F*, 1965 *I*, *A* 1,2, 1968 *BI* 1,2,3,4, *F* 1,2, 1969 *A* 1,2,3,4, *S*, *E*, 1970 *I*, *W*, 1971 *F* 1,2
Bekker, H J (WP) 1981 *NZ* 1,3
Bekker, H P J (NT) 1952 *E*, *F*, 1953 *A* 1,2,3,4, 1955 *BI* 2,3,4, 1956 *A* 1,2, *NZ* 1,2,3,4
Bekker, M J (NT) 1960 *S*
Bekker, R P (NT) 1953 *A* 3,4
Bekker, S (NT) 1997 *A* 2 (t)
Bennett, R G (Border) 1997 *Tg* (R), *BI* 1 (R), 3, *NZ* 1, *A* 1, *NZ* 2
Bergh, W F (SWD) 1931 *W*, *I*, 1932 *E*, *S*, 1933 *A* 1,2,3,4,5, 1937 *A* 1,2, *NZ* 1,2,3, 1938 *BI* 1,2,3
Bestbier, A (OFS) 1974 *F* 2 (R)
Bester, J J N (WP) 1924 *BI* 2,4
Bester, J L A (WP) 1938 *BI* 2,3
Beswick, A M (Bor) 1896 *BI* 2,3,4
Bezuidenhoudt, C E (NT) 1962 *BI* 2,3,4
Bezuidenhoudt, N S E (NT) 1972 *E*, 1974 *BI* 2,3,4, *F* 1,2, 1975 *F* 1,2, 1977 *Wld*
Bierman, J N (Tvl) 1931 *I*
Bisset, W M (WP) 1891 *BI* 1,3
Blair, R (WP) 1977 *Wld*
Bosch, G R (Tvl) 1974 *BI* 2, *F* 1,2, 1975 *F* 1,2, 1976 *NZ* 1,2,3,4
Bosman, N J S (Tvl) 1924 *BI* 2,3,4
Botha, D S (NT) 1981 *NZ* 1
Botha, H E (NT) 1980 *S Am* 1,2, *BI* 1,2,3,4, *S Am* 3,4, *F*, 1981 *I* 1,2, *NZ* 1,2,3, *US*, 1982 *S Am* 1,2, 1986 *Cv* 1,2,3,4, 1989 *Wld* 1,2, 1992 *NZ*, *A*, *F* 1,2, *E*
Botha, J A (Tvl) 1903 *BI* 3
Botha, J P F (NT) 1962 *BI* 2,3,4
Botha, P H (Tvl) 1965 *A* 1,2
Boyes, H C (GW) 1891 *BI* 1,2

Brand, G H (WP) 1928 *NZ* 2,3, 1931 *W*, *I*, 1932 *E*, *S*, 1933 *A* 1,2,3,4,5, 1937 *A* 1,2, *NZ* 2,3, 1938 *BI* 1
Bredenkamp, M J (GW) 1896 *BI* 1,3
Breedt, J C (Tvl) 1986 *Cv* 1,2,3,4, 1989 *Wld* 1,2, 1992 *NZ*, *A*
Brewis, J D (NT) 1949 *NZ* 1,2,3,4, 1951 *S*, *I*, *W*, 1952 *E*, *F*, 1953 *A* 1
Briers, T P D (WP) 1955 *BI* 1,2,3,4, 1956 *NZ* 2,3,4
Brink, D J (WP) 1906 *S*, *W*, *E*
Brink, R (WP) 1995 [*R, C*]
Brooks, D (Bor) 1906 *S*
Brosnihan, W (GL) 1997 *A* 2
Brown, C B (WP) 1903 *BI* 1,2,3
Brynard, G S (WP) 1965 *A* 1, *NZ* 1,2,3,4, 1968 *BI* 3,4
Buchler, J U (Tvl) 1951 *S*, *I*, *W*, 1952 *E*, *F*, 1953 *A* 1,2,3,4, 1956 *A* 2
Burdett, A F (WP) 1906 *S*, *I*
Burger, J M (WP) 1989 *Wld* 1,2
Burger, M B (NT) 1980 *BI* 2 (R), *S Am* 3, 1981 *US* (R)
Burger, S W P (WP) 1984 *E* 1,2, 1986 *Cv* 1,2,3,4
Burger, W A G (Bor) 1906 *S*, *I*, *W*, 1910 *BI* 2

Carelse, G (EP) 1964 *W*, *F*, 1965 *I*, *S*, 1967 *F* 1,2,3, 1968 *F* 1,2, 1969 *A* 1,2,3,4, *S*
Carlson, R A (WP) 1972 *E*
Carolin, H W (WP) 1903 *BI* 3, 1906 *S*, *I*
Castens, H H (WP) 1891 *BI* 1
Chignell, T W (WP) 1891 *BI* 3
Cilliers, G D (OFS) 1963 *A* 1,3,4
Cilliers, N V (WP) 1996 *NZ* 3 (t)
Claassen, J T (WT) 1955 *BI* 1,2,3,4, 1956 *A* 1,2, *NZ* 1,2,3,4, 1958 *F* 1,2, 1960 *S*, *NZ* 1,2,3, *W*, *I*, 1961 *E*, *S*, *F*, *I*, *A* 1,2, 1962 *BI* 1,2,3,4
Claassen, W (N) 1981 *I* 1,2, *NZ* 2,3, *US*, 1982 *S Am* 1,2
Clark, W H G (Tvl) 1933 *A* 3
Clarkson, W A (N) 1921 *NZ* 1,2, 1924 *BI* 1
Cloete, H A (WP) 1896 *BI* 4
Cockrell, C H (WP) 1969 *S*, 1970 *I*, *W*
Cockrell, R J (WP) 1974 *F* 1,2, 1975 *F* 1,2, 1976 *NZ* 1,2, 1977 *Wld*, 1981 *NZ* 1,2 (R), 3, *US*
Coetzee, J H H (WP) 1974 *BI* 1, 1975 *F* 2 (R), 1976 *NZ* 1,2,3,4
Cope, D K (Tvl) 1896 *BI* 2
Cotty, W (GW) 1896 *BI* 3
Crampton, G (WP) 1903 *BI* 2
Craven, D H (WP) 1931 *W*, *I*, 1932 *S*, 1933 *A* 1,2,3,4,5, 1937 *A* 1,2, *NZ* 1,2,3, 1938 *BI* 1,2,3,
Cronje, P A (Tvl) 1971 *F* 1,2, *A* 1,2,3, 1974 *BI* 3,4
Crosby, J H (Tvl) 1896 *BI* 2
Crosby, N J (Tvl) 1910 *BI* 1,3
Currie, C (GW) 1903 *BI* 2

D'Alton, G (WP) 1933 *A* 1
Dalton, J (Tvl, GL) 1994 *Arg* 1 (R), 1995 [*A, C*], *W, It*, *E*, 1996 *NZ* 4 (R), 5, *Arg* 1,2, *F* 1,2, *W*, 1997 *Tg* (R), *BI* 3, *NZ* 2, *A* 2, *It*, *F* 1,2, *E*, *S*, 1998 *I* 1,2, *W* 1, *E* 1, *A* 1, *NZ* 1,2, *A* 2, *W* 2, *S*, *I* 3, *E* 2
Daneel, G M (WP) 1928 *NZ* 1,2,3,4, 1931 *W*, *I*, 1932 *E*, *S*
Daneel, H J (WP) 1906 *S*, *I*, *W*, *E*
Davison, P M (EP) 1910 *BI* 1
De Beer, J H (OFS) 1997 *BI* 3, *NZ* 1, *A* 1, *NZ* 2, *A* 2, *F* 2 (R), *S*
De Bruyn, J (OFS) 1974 *BI* 3
De Jongh, H P K (WP) 1928 *NZ* 3
De Klerk, I J (Tvl) 1969 *E*, 1970 *I*, *W*
De Klerk, K B H (Tvl) 1974 *BI* 1,2,3 (R), 1975 *F* 1,2, 1976 *NZ* 2 (R), 3,4, 1980 *S Am* 1,2, *BI* 2, 1981 *I* 1,2
De Kock, A N (GW) 1891 *BI* 2
De Kock, J S (WP) 1921 *NZ* 3, 1924 *BI* 3
Delport, W H (EP) 1951 *S*, *I*, *W*, 1952 *E*, *F*, 1953 *A* 1,2,3,4
De Melker, S C (GW) 1903 *BI* 2, 1906 *E*
Devenish, C E (GW) 1896 *BI* 2
Devenish, G St L (Tvl) 1896 *BI* 2
Devenish, G E (Tvl) 1891 *BI* 1
De Villiers, D I (Tvl) 1910 *BI* 1,2,3

De Villiers, D J (WP, Bol) 1962 *BI* 2,3, 1965 *I, NZ* 1,3,4, 1967 *F* 1,2,3,4, 1968 *BI* 1,2,3,4, *F* 1,2, 1969 *A* 1,4, *E*, 1970 *I, W, NZ* 1,2,3,4
De Villiers, H A (WP) 1906 *S, W, E*
De Villiers, H O (WP) 1967 *F* 1,2,3,4, 1968 *F* 1,2, 1969 *A* 1,2,3,4, *S, E*, 1970 *I, W*
De Villiers, P du P (WP) 1928 *NZ* 1,3,4, 1932 *E*, 1933 *A* 4, 1937 *A* 1,2, *NZ* 1
Devine, D (Tvl) 1924 *BI* 3, 1928 *NZ* 2
De Vos, D J J (WP) 1965 *S*, 1969 *A* 3, *S*
De Waal, A N (WP) 1967 *F* 1,2,3,4
De Waal, P J (WP) 1896 *BI* 4
De Wet, A E (WP) 1969 *A* 3,4, *E*
De Wet, P J (WP) 1938 *BI* 1,2,3
Dinkelmann, E E (NT) 1951 *S, I*, 1952 *E, F*, 1953 *A* 1,2
Dirksen, C W (NT) 1963 *A* 4, 1964 *W*, 1965 *I, S*, 1967 *F* 1,2,3,4, 1968 *BI* 1,2
Dobbin, F J (GW) 1903 *BI* 1,2, 1906 *S, W, E*, 1910 *BI* 1, 1912 *S, I, W*
Dobie, J A R (Tvl) 1928 *NZ* 2
Dormehl, P J (WP) 1896 *BI* 3,4
Douglass, F W (EP) 1896 *BI* 1
Drotské, A E (OFS) 1993 *Arg* 2, 1995 [*WS* (R)], 1996 *A* 1 (R), 1997 *Tg, BI* 1,2,3 (R), *NZ* 1, *A* 1, *NZ* 2 (R), 1998 *I* 2 (R), *W* 1 (R), *I* 3 (R)
Dryburgh, R G (WP) 1955 *BI* 2,3,4, 1956 *A* 2, *NZ* 1,4, 1960 *NZ* 1,2
Duff, B R (WP) 1891 *BI* 1,2,3
Duffy, B A (Bor) 1928 *NZ* 1
Du Plessis, C J (WP) 1982 *S Am* 1,2, 1984 *E* 1,2, *S Am* 1,2, 1986 *Cv* 1,2,3,4, 1989 *Wld* 1,2
Du Plessis, D C (NT) 1977 *Wld*, 1980 *S Am* 2
Du Plessis, F (Tvl) 1949 *NZ* 1,2,3
Du Plessis, M (WP) 1971 *A* 1,2,3, 1974 *BI* 1,2, *F* 1,2, 1975 *F* 1,2, 1976 *NZ* 1,2,3,4, 1977 *Wld*, 1980 *S Am* 1,2, *BI* 1,2,3,4, *S Am* 4, *F*
Du Plessis, M J (WP) 1984 *S Am* 1,2, 1986 *Cv* 1,2,3,4, 1989 *Wld* 1,2
Du Plessis, N J (WT) 1921 *NZ* 2,3, 1924 *BI* 1,2,3
Du Plessis, P G (NT) 1972 *E*
Du Plessis, T D (NT) 1980 *S Am* 1,2
Du Plessis, W (WP) 1980 *S Am* 1,2, *BI* 1,2,3,4, *S Am* 3,4, *F*, 1981 *I* 1,2,3, 1982 *S Am* 1,2
Du Plooy, A J J (EP) 1955 *BI* 1
Du Preez, F C H (NT) 1961 *E, S, A* 1,2, 1962 *BI* 1,2,3, 1963 *A* 1, 1964 *W, F*, 1965 *A* 1,2, *NZ* 1,2,3,4, 1967 *F* 4, 1968 *BI* 1,2,3,4, *F* 1,2, 1969 *A* 1,2, *S*, 1970 *I, W, NZ* 1,2,3,4, 1971 *F* 1,2, *A* 1,2,3
Du Preez, J G H (WP) 1956 *NZ* 1
Du Preez, R J (N) 1992 *NZ, A*, 1993 *F* 1,2, *A* 1,2,3
Du Rand, J A (R, NT) 1949 *NZ* 2,3, 1951 *S, I, W*, 1952 *E, F*, 1953 *A* 1,2,3,4, 1955 *BI* 1,2,3,4, 1956 *A* 1,2, *NZ* 1,2,3,4
Du Randt, J P (OFS) 1994 *Arg* 1,2, *S, W*, 1995 *WS*, [*A, WS, F, NZ*], 1996 *Fj, A* 1, *NZ* 1, *A* 2, *NZ* 2,3,4, 1997 *Tg, BI* 1,2,3, *NZ* 1, *A* 1, *NZ* 2, *A* 2, *It, F* 1,2, *E, S*
Du Toit, A F (WP) 1928 *NZ* 3,4
Du Toit, B A (Tvl) 1938 *BI* 1,2,3
Du Toit, G S (GW) 1998 *I* 1
Du Toit, P A (NT) 1949 *NZ* 2,3,4, 1951 *S, I, W*, 1952 *E, F*
Du Toit, P G (WP) 1981 *NZ* 1, 1982 *S Am* 1,2, 1984 *E* 1,2
Du Toit, P S (WP) 1958 *F* 1,2, 1960 *NZ* 1,2,3,4, *W, I*, 1961 *E, S, F, I, A* 1,2
Duvenhage, F P (GW) 1949 *NZ* 1,3

Edwards, P (NT) 1980 *S Am* 1,2
Ellis, J H (SWA) 1965 *NZ* 1,2,3,4, 1967 *F* 1,2,3,4, 1968 *BI* 1,2,3,4, *F* 1,2, 1969 *A* 1,2,3,4, *S*, 1970 *I, W, NZ* 1,2,3,4, 1971 *F* 1,2, *A* 1,2,3, 1972 *E*, 1974 *BI* 1,2,3,4, *F* 1,2, 1976 *NZ* 1
Ellis, M C (Tvl) 1921 *NZ* 2,3, 1924 *BI* 1,2,3,4
Els, W W (OFS) 1997 *A* 2 (R)
Engelbrecht, J P (WP) 1960 *S, W, I*, 1961 *E, S, F, A* 1,2, 1962 *BI* 2,3,4, 1963 *A* 2,3, 1964 *W, F*, 1965 *I, S, A* 1,2, *NZ* 1,2,3,4, 1967 *F* 1,2,3,4, 1968 *BI* 1,2, *F* 1,2, 1969 *A* 1,2
Erasmus, F S (NT, EP) 1986 *Cv* 3,4, 1989 *Wld* 2
Erasmus, J C (OFS) 1997 *BI* 3, *A* 2, *It, F* 1,2, *S*, 1998 *I* 1,2, *W* 1, *E* 1, *A* 1, *NZ* 2, *A* 2, *S, W* 2, *I* 3, *E* 2
Etlinger, T E (WP) 1896 *BI* 4

Ferreira, C (OFS) 1986 *Cv* 1,2
Ferreira, P S (WP) 1984 *S Am* 1,2
Ferris, H H (Tvl) 1903 *BI* 3
Forbes, H H (Tvl) 1896 *BI* 2
Fourie, C (EP) 1974 *F* 1,2, 1975 *F* 1,2
Fourie, T T (SET) 1974 *BI* 3
Fourie, W L (SWA) 1958 *F* 1,2
Francis, J A J (Tvl) 1912 *S, I, W*, 1913 *E, F*
Frederickson, C A (Tvl) 1974 *BI* 2, 1980 *S Am* 1,2
Frew, A (Tvl) 1903 *BI* 1
Froneman, D C (OFS) 1977 *Wld*
Froneman, I L (Bor) 1933 *A* 1
Fuls, H T (Tvl, EP) 1992 *NZ* (R), 1993 *F* 1,2, *A* 1,2,3, *Arg* 1,2
Fry, S P (WP) 1951 *S, I, W*, 1952 *E, F*, 1953 *A* 1,2,3,4, 1955 *BI* 1,2,3,4
Fyvie, W (N) 1996 *NZ* 4 (t & R), 5 (R), *Arg* 2 (R)

Gage, J H (OFS) 1933 *A* 1
Gainsford, J L (WP) 1960 *S, NZ* 1,2,3,4, *W, I*, 1961 *E, S, F, A* 1,2, 1962 *BI* 1,2,3,4, 1963 *A* 1,2,3,4, 1964 *W, F*, 1965 *I, S, A* 1,2, *NZ* 1,2,3,4, 1967 *F* 1,2,3
Garvey, A C (N) 1996 *Arg* 1,2, *F* 1,2, *W*, 1997 *Tg, BI* 1,2,3 (R), *A* 1 (t), *It, F* 1,2, *E, S*, 1998 *I* 1,2, *W* 1, *E*1, *A* 1, *NZ* 1,2 *A* 2, *W* 2, *S, I* 3, *E* 2
Geel, P J (OFS) 1949 *NZ* 3
Geere, V (Tvl) 1933 *A* 1,2,3,4,5
Geffin, A O (Tvl) 1949 *NZ* 1,2,3,4, 1951 *S, I, W*
Geldenhuys, A (EP) 1992 *NZ, A, F* 1,2
Geldenhuys, S B (NT) 1981 *NZ* 2,3, *US*, 1982 *S Am* 1,2, 1989 *Wld* 1,2
Gentles, T A (WP) 1955 *BI* 1,2,4, 1956 *NZ* 2,3, 1958 *F* 2
Geraghty, E M (Bor) 1949 *NZ* 4
Gerber, D M (EP, WP) 1980 *S Am* 3,4, *F*, 1981 *I* 1,2, *NZ* 1,2,3, *US*, 1982 *S Am* 1,2, 1984 *E* 1,2, *S Am* 1,2, 1986 *Cv* 1,2,3,4, 1992 *NZ, A, F* 1,2, *E*
Gerber, M C (EP) 1958 *F* 1,2, 1960 *S*
Gericke, F W (Tvl) 1960 *S*
Germishuys, J S (OFS, Tvl) 1974 *BI* 2, 1976 *NZ* 1,2,3,4, 1977 *Wld*, 1980 *S Am* 1,2, *BI* 1,2,3,4, *S Am* 3,4, *F*, 1981 *I* 1,2, *NZ* 2,3, *US*
Gibbs, B (GW) 1903 *BI* 2
Goosen, C P (OFS) 1965 *NZ* 2
Gorton, H C (Tvl) 1896 *BI* 1
Gould, R L (N) 1968 *BI* 1,2,3,4
Gray, B G (WP) 1931 *W*, 1932 *E, S*, 1933 *A* 5
Greenwood, C M (WP) 1961 *I*
Greyling, P J F (OFS) 1967 *F* 1,2,3,4, 1968 *BI* 1, *F* 1,2, 1969 *A* 1,2,3,4, *S, E*, 1970 *I, W, NZ* 1,2,3,4, 1971 *F* 1,2, *A* 1,2,3, 1972 *E*
Grobler, C J (OFS) 1974 *BI* 4, 1975 *F* 1,2
Guthrie, F H (WP) 1891 *BI* 1,3, 1896 *BI* 1

Hahn, C H L (Tvl) 1910 *BI* 1,2,3
Hamilton, F (EP) 1891 *BI* 1
Harris, T A (Tvl) 1937 *NZ* 2,3, 1938 *BI* 1,2,3
Hartley, A J (WP) 1891 *BI* 3
Hattingh, H (NT) 1992 *A* (R), *F* 2 (R), *E*, 1994 *Arg* 1,2
Hattingh, L B (OFS) 1933 *A* 2
Heatlie, B H (WP) 1891 *BI* 2,3, 1896 *BI* 1,4, 1903 *BI* 1,3
Hendricks, M (Bol) 1998 *I* 2 (R), *W* 1 (R)
Hendriks, P (Tvl) 1992 *NZ, A*, 1994 *S, W*, 1995 [*A, R, C*], 1996 *A* 1, *NZ* 1, *A* 2, *NZ* 2,3,4,5
Hepburn, T B (WP) 1896 *BI* 4
Heunis, J W (NT) 1981 *NZ* 3 (R), *US*, 1982 *S Am* 1,2, 1984 *E* 1,2, *S Am* 1,2, 1986 *Cv* 1,2,3,4, 1989 *Wld* 1,2
Hill, R A (R) 1960 *W, I*, 1961 *I, A* 1,2, 1962 *BI* 4, 1963 *A* 3
Hills, W G (NT) 1992 *F* 1,2, *E*, 1993 *F* 1,2, *A* 1
Hirsch, J G (EP) 1906 *I*, 1910 *BI* 1
Hobson, T E C (WP) 1903 *BI* 3
Hoffman, R S (Bol) 1953 *A* 3
Holton, D N (EP) 1960 *S*
Honiball, H W (N) 1993 *A* 3 (R), *Arg* 2, 1995 *WS* (R), 1996 *Fj, A* 1, *NZ* 5, *Arg* 1,2, *F* 1,2, *W*, 1997 *Tg, BI* 1,2,3 (R), *NZ* 1 (R), *A* 1 (R), *NZ* 2, *A* 2, *It, F* 1,2, *E*, 1998 *W* 1 (R), *E* 1, *A* 1, *NZ* 1,2, *A* 2, *W* 2, *S, I* 3, *E* 2
Hopwood, D J (WP) 1960 *S, NZ* 3,4, *W*, 1961 *E, S, F, I, A* 1,2, 1962 *BI* 1,2,3,4, 1963 *A* 1,2,4, 1964 *W, F*, 1965 *S, NZ* 3,4
Howe, B F (Bor) 1956 *NZ* 1,4
Howe-Browne, N R F G (WP) 1910 *BI* 1,2,3
Hugo, D P (WP) 1989 *Wld* 1,2

Hurter, M H (NT) 1995 [*R, C*], *W*, 1996 *Fj, A* 1, *NZ* 1,2,3,4,5, 1997 *NZ* 1,2, *A* 2

Immelman, J H (WP) 1913 *F*

Jackson, D C (WP) 1906 *I, W, E*
Jackson, J S (WP) 1903 *BI* 2
Jansen, E (OFS) 1981 *NZ* 1
Jansen, J S (OFS) 1970 *NZ* 1,2,3,4, 1971 *F* 1,2, *A* 1,2,3, 1972 *E*
Jennings, C B (Bor) 1937 *NZ* 1
Johnson, G K (Tvl) 1993 *Arg* 2, 1994 *NZ* 3, *Arg* 1, 1995 *WS*, [*R, C, WS*]
Johnstone, P G A (WP) 1951 *S, I, W*, 1952 *E, F*, 1956 *A* 1, *NZ* 1,2,4
Jones, C H (Tvl) 1903 *NZ* 1
Jones, P S T (WP) 1896 *BI* 1,3,4
Jordaan, R P (NT) 1949 *NZ* 1,2,3,4
Joubert, A J (OFS, N) 1989 *Wld* 1 (R), 1993 *A* 3, *Arg* 1, 1994 *E* 1,2, *NZ* 1,2 (R), 3, *Arg* 2, *S, W*, 1995 [*A, C, WS, F, NZ*], *W, It, E*, 1996 *Fj, A* 1, *NZ* 1,3,4,5, *Arg* 1,2, *F* 1,2, *W*, 1997 *Tg, BI* 1,2, *A* 2
Joubert, S J (WP) 1906 *I, W, E*

Kahts, W J H (NT) 1980 *BI* 1,2,3, *S Am* 3,4, *F*, 1981 *I* 1,2, *NZ* 2, 1982 *S Am* 1,2
Kaminer, J (Tvl) 1958 *F* 2
Kebble, G R (N) 1993 *Arg* 1,2, 1994 *NZ* 1 (R), 2
Kelly, E W (GW) 1896 *BI* 3
Kempson, R (N) 1998 *I* 2 (R), *W* 1, *E* 1, *A* 1, *NZ* 1,2 *A* 2, *W* 2, *S, I* 3, *E* 2
Kenyon, B J (Bor) 1949 *NZ* 4
Kipling, H G (GW) 1931 *W, I*, 1932 *E, S*, 1933 *A* 1,2,3,4,5
Kirkpatrick, A I (GW) 1953 *A* 2, 1956 *NZ* 2, 1958 *F* 1, 1960 *S, NZ* 1,2,3,4, *W, I*, 1961 *E, S, F*
Knight, A S (Tvl) 1912 *S, I, W*, 1913 *E, F*
Knoetze, F (WP) 1989 *Wld* 1,2
Koch, A C (Bol) 1949 *NZ* 2,3,4, 1951 *S, I, W*, 1952 *E, F*, 1953 *A* 1,2,4, 1955 *BI* 1,2,3,4, 1956 *A* 1, *NZ* 2,3, 1958 *F* 1,2, 1960 *NZ* 1,2
Koch, H V (WP) 1949 *NZ* 1,2,3,4
Kotze, G J M (WP) 1967 *F* 1,2,3,4
Krantz, E F W (OFS) 1976 *NZ* 1, 1981 *I* 1,
Krige, J D (WP) 1903 *BI* 1,3, 1906 *S, I, W*
Kritzinger, J L (Tvl) 1974 *BI* 3,4, *F* 1,2, 1975 *F* 1,2, 1976 *NZ* 4
Kroon, C M (EP) 1955 *BI* 1
Kruger, P E (Tvl) 1986 *Cv* 3,4
Kruger, R J (NT) 1993 *Arg* 1,2, 1994 *S, W*, 1995 *WS*, [*A, R, WS, F, NZ*], *W, It, E*, 1996 *Fj, A* 1, *NZ* 1, *A* 2, *NZ* 2,3,4,5, *Arg* 1,2, *F* 1,2, *W*, 1997 *Tg, BI* 1,2, *NZ* 1, *A* 1, *NZ* 2
Kruger, T L (Tvl) 1921 *NZ* 1,2, 1924 *BI* 1,2,3,4, 1928 *NZ* 1,2
Kuhn, S P (Tvl) 1960 *NZ* 3,4, *W, I*, 1961 *E, S, F, I, A* 1,2, 1962 *BI* 1,2,3,4, 1963 *A* 1,2,3, 1965 *I, S*

La Grange, J B (WP) 1924 *BI* 3,4
Larard, A (Tvl) 1896 *BI* 2,4
Lategan, M T (WP) 1949 *NZ* 1,2,3,4, 1951 *S, I, W*, 1952 *E, F*, 1953 *A* 1,2
Laubscher, T G (WP) 1994 *Arg* 1,2, *S, W*, 1995 *It, E*
Lawless, M J (WP) 1964 *F*, 1969 *E* (R), 1970 *I, W*
Ledger, S H (GW) 1912 *S, I*, 1913 *E, F*
Le Roux, A H (OFS, N) 1994 *E* 1, 1998 *I* 1,2, *W* 1 (R), *E* 1 (R), *A* 1 (R), *NZ* 1 (R),2 (R), *A* 2 (R), *W* 2 (R), *S* (R), *I* 3 (R), *E* 2 (t + R)
Le Roux, H P (Tvl) 1993 *F* 1,2, 1994 *E* 1,2, *NZ* 1,2,3, *Arg* 2, *S, W*, 1995 *WS* [*A, R, C* (R), *WS, F, NZ*], *W, It, E*, 1996 *Fj, NZ* 2, *Arg* 1,2, *F* 1,2, *W*
Le Roux, J H S (Tvl) 1994 *E* 2, *NZ* 1,2
Le Roux, M (OFS) 1980 *BI* 1,2,3,4, *S Am* 3,4, *F*, 1981 *I* 1
Le Roux, P A (WP) 1906 *I, W, E*
Little, E M (GW) 1891 *BI* 1,3
Lochner, G P (WP) 1955 *BI* 3, 1956 *A* 1,2, *NZ* 1,2,3,4, 1958 *F* 1,2
Lochner, G P (EP) 1937 *NZ* 3, 1938 *BI* 1,2
Lockyear, R J (GW) 1960 *NZ* 1,2,3,4, 1960 *I*, 1961 *F*
Lombard, A C (EP) 1910 *BI* 2
Lötter, D (Tvl) 1993 *F* 2, *A* 1,2
Lotz, J W (Tvl) 1937 *A* 1,2, *NZ* 1,2,3, 1938 *BI* 1,2,3
Loubser, J A (WP) 1903 *BI* 3, 1906 *S, I, W, E*, 1910 *BI* 1,3

Lourens, M J (NT) 1968 *BI* 2,3,4
Louw, J S (Tvl) 1891 *BI* 1,2,3
Louw, M J (Tvl) 1971 *A* 2,3
Louw, M M (WP) 1928 *NZ* 3,4, 1931 *W, I*, 1932 *E, S*, 1933 *A* 1,2,3,4,5, 1937 *A* 1,2, *NZ* 2,3, 1938 *BI* 1,2,3
Louw, R J (WP) 1980 *S Am* 1,2, *BI* 1,2,3,4 *S Am* 3,4, *F*, 1981 *I* 1,2, *NZ* 1,3, 1982 *S Am* 1,2, 1984 *E* 1,2, *S Am* 1,2
Louw, S C (WP) 1933 *A* 1,2,3,4,5, 1937 *A* 1, *NZ* 1,2,3, 1938 *BI* 1,2,3
Lubbe, E (GW) 1997 *Tg, BI* 1
Luyt, F P (WP) 1910 *BI* 1,2,3, 1912 *S, I, W*, 1913 *E*
Luyt, J D (EP) 1912 *S, W*, 1913 *E, F*
Luyt, R R (WP) 1910 *BI* 2,3, 1912 *S, I, W*, 1913 *E, F*
Lyons, D J (EP) 1896 *BI* 1
Lyster, P J (N) 1933 *A* 2,5, 1937 *NZ* 1

McCallum, I D (WP) 1970 *NZ* 1,2,3,4, 1971 *F* 1,2, *A* 1,2,3, 1974 *BI* 1,2
McCallum, R J (WP) 1974 *BI* 1
McCulloch, J D (GW) 1913 *E, F*
MacDonald, A W (R) 1965 *A* 1, *NZ* 1,2,3,4
Macdonald, D A (WP) 1974 *BI* 2
Macdonald, I (Tvl) 1992 *NZ, A*, 1993 *F* 1, *A* 3, 1994 *E* 2, 1995 *WS* (R)
McDonald, J A J (WP) 1931 *W, I*, 1932 *E, S*
McEwan, W M C (Tvl) 1903 *BI* 1,3
McHardy, E E (OFS) 1912 *S, I, W*, 1913 *E, F*
McKendrick, J A (WP) 1891 *BI* 3
Malan, A S (Tvl) 1960 *NZ* 1,2,3,4, *W, I*, 1961 *E, S, F*, 1962 *BI* 1, 1963 *A* 1,2,3, 1964 *W*, 1965 *I, S*
Malan, A W (NT) 1989 *Wld* 1,2, 1992 *NZ, A*, *F* 1,2, *E*
Malan, E (NT) 1980 *BI* 3 (R), 4
Malan, G F (WP) 1958 *F* 2, 1960 *NZ* 1,3,4, 1961 *E, S, F*, 1962 *BI* 1,2,3, 1963 *A* 1,2,4, 1964 *W*, 1965 *A* 1,2, *NZ* 1,2
Malan, P (Tvl) 1949 *NZ* 4
Mallett, N V H (WP) 1984 *S Am* 1,2
Mans, W J (WP) 1965 *I, S*
Marais, F P (Bol) 1949 *NZ* 1,2, 1951 *S*, 1953 *A* 1,2
Marais, J F K (WP) 1963 *A* 3, 1964 *W, F*, 1965 *I, S, A* 2, 1968 *BI*, 1,2,3,4, *F* 1,2, 1969 *A* 1,2,3,4, *S, E*, 1970 *I, W, NZ* 1,2,3,4, 1971 *F* 1,2, *A* 1,2,3, 1974 *BI* 1,2,3,4, *F* 1,2
Maré, D S (Tvl) 1906 *S*
Marsberg, A F W (GW) 1906 *S, W, E*
Marsberg, P A (GW) 1910 *BI* 1
Martheze, W C (GW) 1903 *BI* 2, 1906 *I, W*
Martin, H J (Tvl) 1937 *A* 2
Mellet, T B (GW) 1896 *BI* 2
Mellish, F W (WP) 1921 *NZ* 1,3, 1924 *BI* 1,2,3,4
Merry, J (EP) 1891 *BI* 1
Metcalf, H D (Bor) 1903 *BI* 2
Meyer, C du P (WP) 1921 *NZ* 1,2,3
Meyer, P J (GW) 1896 *BI* 1
Meyer, W (OFS) 1997 *S* (R)
Michau, J M (Tvl) 1921 *NZ* 1
Michau, J P (WP) 1921 *NZ* 1,2,3
Millar, W A (WP) 1906 *E*, 1910 *BI* 2,3, 1912 *I, W*, 1913 *F*
Mills, W J (WP) 1910 *BI* 2
Moll, T (Tvl) 1910 *BI* 2
Montini, P E (WP) 1956 *A* 1,2
Montgomery, P C (WP) 1997 *BI* 2,3, *NZ* 1, *A* 1, *NZ* 2, *A* 2, *F* 1,2, *E, S*, 1998 *I* 1,2, *W* 1, *E* 1, *A* 1, *NZ* 1,2, *A* 2, *W* 2, *S, I* 3, *E* 2
Moolman, L C (NT) 1977 *Wld*, 1980 *S Am* 1,2, *BI* 1,2,3,4, *S Am* 3,4, *F*, 1981 *I* 1,2, *NZ* 1,2,3, *US*, 1982 *S Am* 1,2, 1984 *S Am* 1,2, 1986 *Cv* 1,2,3,4
Mordt, R H (Z-R, NT) 1980 *S Am* 1,2, *BI* 1,2,3,4, *S Am* 3,4, *F*, 1981 *I* 1,2, *NZ* 1,2,3, *US*, 1982 *S Am* 1,2, 1984 *S Am* 1,2
Morkel, D A (Tvl) 1903 *BI* 1
Morkel, D F T (Tvl) 1906 *I, E*, 1910 *BI* 1,3, 1912 *S, I, W*, 1913 *E, F*
Morkel, H J (WP) 1921 *NZ* 1
Morkel, H W (WP) 1921 *NZ* 1,2
Morkel, J A (WP) 1921 *NZ* 2,3
Morkel, J W H (WP) 1912 *S, I, W*, 1913 *E, F*
Morkel, P G (WP) 1912 *S, I, W*, 1913 *E, F*, 1921 *NZ* 1,2,3
Morkel, P K (WP) 1928 *NZ* 4
Morkel, W H (WP) 1910 *BI* 3, 1912 *S, I, W*, 1913 *E, F*, 1921 *NZ* 1,2,3
Morkel, W S (Tvl) 1906 *S, I, W, E*
Moss, C (N) 1949 *NZ* 1,2,3,4

Mostert, P J (WP) 1921 *NZ* 1,2,3, 1924 *BI* 1,2,4, 1928 *NZ* 1,2,3,4, 1931 *W, I*, 1932 *E, S*
Mulder, J C (Tvl, GL) 1994 *NZ* 2,3, *S, W*, 1995 *WS*, [*A, WS, F, NZ*], *W, It, E*, 1996 *Fj, A* 1, *NZ* 1, *A* 2, *NZ* 2,5, *Arg* 1,2, *F* 1,2, *W*, 1997 *Tg, BI* 1
Muller, G H (WP) 1969 *A* 3,4, *S*, 1970 *W, NZ* 1,2,3,4, 1971 *F* 1,2, 1972 *E*, 1974 *BI* 1,3,4
Muller, H L (OFS) 1986 *Cv* 4 (R), 1989 *Wld* 1 (R)
Muller, H S V (Tvl) 1949 *NZ* 1,2,3,4, 1951 *S, I, W*, 1952 *E, F*, 1953 *A* 1,2,3,4
Muller, L J J (N) 1992 *NZ, A*
Muller, P G (N) 1992 *NZ, A, F* 1,2, *E*, 1993 *F* 1,2, *A* 1,2,3, *Arg* 1,2, 1994 *E* 1,2, *NZ* 1, *S, W*, 1998 *I* 1,2, *W* 1, *E* 1, *A* 1, *NZ* 1,2, *A* 2
Muir, D J (WP) 1997 *It, F* 1,2, *E, S*
Myburgh, F R (EP) 1896 *BI* 1
Myburgh, J L (NT) 1962 *BI* 1, 1963 *A* 4, 1964 *W, F*, 1968 *BI* 1,2,3, *F* 1,2, 1969 *A* 1,2,3,4, *E*, 1970 *I, W, NZ* 3,4
Myburgh, W H (WT) 1924 *BI* 1

Naude, J P (WP) 1963 *A* 4, 1965 *A* 1,2, *NZ* 1,3,4, 1967 *F* 1,2,3,4, 1968 *BI* 1,2,3,4
Neethling, J B (WP) 1967 *F* 1,2,3,4, 1968 *BI* 4, 1969 *S*, 1970 *NZ* 1,2
Nel, J A (Tvl) 1960 *NZ* 1,2, 1963 *A* 1,2, 1965 *A* 2, *NZ* 1,2,3,4, 1970 *NZ* 3,4
Nel, J J (WP) 1956 *A* 1,2, *NZ* 1,2,3,4, 1958 *F* 1,2
Nel, P A R O (Tvl) 1903 *BI* 1,2,3
Nel, P J (N) 1928 *NZ* 1,2,3,4, 1931 *W, I*, 1932 *E, S*, 1933 *A* 1,3,4,5, 1937 *A* 1,2, *NZ* 2,3
Nimb, C F (WP) 1961 *I*
Nomis, S H (Tvl) 1967 *F* 4, 1968 *BI* 1,2,3,4, *F* 1,2, 1969 *A* 1,2,3,4, *S, E*, 1970 *I, W, NZ* 1,2,3,4, 1971 *F* 1,2,4, 1,2,3, 1972 *E*
Nykamp, J L (Tvl) 1933 *A* 2

Ochse, J K (WP) 1951 *I, W*, 1952 *E, F*, 1953 *A* 1,2,4
Oelofse, J S A (Tvl) 1953 *A* 1,2,3,4
Oliver, J F (Tvl) 1928 *NZ* 3,4
Olivier, E (WP) 1967 *F* 1,2,3,4, 1968 *BI* 1,2,3,4, *F* 1,2, 1969 *A* 1,2,3,4, *S, E*
Olivier, J (NT) 1992 *F* 1,2, *E*, 1993 *F* 1,2 *A* 1,2,3, *Arg* 1, 1995 *W, It* (R), *E*, 1996 *Arg* 1,2, *F* 1,2, *W*
Olver, E (EP) 1896 *BI* 1
Oosthuizen, J J (WP) 1974 *BI* 1, *F* 1,2, 1975 *F* 1,2, 1976 *NZ* 1,2,3,4
Oosthuizen, O W (NT, Tvl) 1981 *I* 1 (R), 2, *NZ* 2,3, *US*, 1982 *S Am* 1,2, 1984 *E* 1,2
Osler, B L (WP) 1924 *BI* 1,2,3,4, 1928 *NZ* 1,2,3,4, 1931 *W, I*, 1932 *E, S*, 1933 *A* 1,2,3,4,5
Osler, S G (WP) 1928 *NZ* 1
Otto, K (NT, BB) 1995 [*R, C* (R), *WS* (R)], 1997 *BI* 3, *A* 1, *NZ* 2, *A* 2, *It, F* 1,2, *E, S*, 1998 *I* 1,2, *W* 1, *E* 1, *A* 1, *NZ* 1,2, *A* 2, *W* 2, *S, I* 3, *E* 2
Oxlee, K (N) 1960 *NZ* 1,2,3,4, *W, I*, 1961 *S, A* 1,2, 1962 *BI* 1,2,3,4, 1963 *A* 1,2,4, 1964 *W*, 1965 *NZ* 1,2

Pagel, G L (WP) 1995 [*A* (R), *R, C, NZ* (R)], 1996 *NZ* 5 (R)
Parker, W H (EP) 1965 *A* 1,2
Partridge, J E C (Tvl) 1903 *BI* 1
Payn, C (N) 1924 *BI* 1,2
Pelser, H J M (Tvl) 1958 *F* 1, 1960 *NZ* 1,2,3,4, *W, I*, 1961 *F, I, A* 1,2
Pfaff, B D (WP) 1956 *A* 1
Pickard, J A J (WP) 1953 *A* 3,4, 1956 *NZ* 2, 1958 *F* 2
Pienaar, J F (Tvl) 1993 *F* 1,2, *A* 1,2,3, *Arg* 1,2, 1994 *E* 1,2, *NZ* 2,3, *Arg* 1,2, *F* 1,2, *S, W*, 1995 *WS*, [*A, C, WS, F, NZ*], *W, It, E*, 1996 *Fj, A* 1, *NZ* 1, *A* 2, *NZ* 2
Pienaar, Z M J (OFS) 1980 *S Am* 2 (R), *BI* 1,2,3,4, *S Am* 3,4, *F*, 1981 *I* 1,2, *NZ* 1,2,3
Pitzer, G (NT) 1967 *F* 1,2,3,4, 1968 *BI* 1,2,3,4, *F* 1,2, 1969 *A* 3,4
Pope, C F (WP) 1974 *BI* 1,2,3,4, 1975 *F* 1,2, 1976 *NZ* 2,3,4
Potgieter, H J (OFS) 1928 *NZ* 1,2
Potgieter, H L (OFS) 1977 *Wld*
Powell, A W (GW) 1896 *BI* 3
Powell, J M (GW) 1891 *BI* 2, 1896 *BI* 3, 1903 *BI* 1,2
Prentis, R B (Tvl) 1980 *S Am* 1,2, *BI* 1,2,3,4, *S Am* 3,4, *F*, 1981 *I* 1,2
Pretorius, N F (Tvl) 1928 *NZ* 1,2,3,4
Prinsloo, J (Tvl) 1958 *F* 1,2
Prinsloo, J (NT) 1963 *A* 3

Prinsloo, J P (Tvl) 1928 *NZ* 1
Putter, D J (WT) 1963 *A* 1,2,4

Raaff, J W E (GW) 1903 *BI* 1,2, 1906 *S, W, E*, 1910 *BI* 1
Ras, W J de Wet (OFS) 1976 *NZ* 1 (R), 1980 *S Am* 2 (R)
Reece-Edwards, H (N) 1992 *F* 1,2, 1993 *A* 2
Reid, A (WP) 1903 *BI* 3
Reid, B C (Bor) 1933 *A* 4
Reinach, J (OFS) 1986 *Cv* 1,2,3,4
Rens, I J (Tvl) 1953 *A* 3,4
Retief, D F (NT) 1955 *BI* 1,2,4, 1956 *A* 1,2, *NZ* 1,2,3,4
Reyneke, H J (WP) 1910 *BI* 3
Richards, A R (WP) 1891 *BI* 1,2,3
Richter, A (NT) 1992 *F* 1,2, *E*, 1994 *E* 2, *NZ* 1,2,3, 1995 [*R, C, WS* (R)]
Riley, N M (ET) 1963 *A* 3
Riordan, C A (Tvl) 1910 *BI* 1,2
Robertson, I W (R) 1974 *F* 1,2, 1976 *NZ* 1,2,4
Rodgers, P H (NT, Tvl) 1989 *Wld* 1,2, 1992 *NZ, F* 1,2
Rogers, C D (Tvl) 1984 *E* 1,2, *S Am* 1,2
Roos, G D (WP) 1910 *BI* 2,3
Roos, P J (WP) 1903 *BI* 3, 1906 *I, W, E*
Rosenberg, W (Tvl) 1955 *BI* 2,3,4, 1956 *NZ* 3, 1958 *F* 1
Rossouw, C L C (Tvl) 1995 *WS*, [*R, WS, F, NZ*]
Rossouw, D H (WP) 1953 *A* 3, 4
Rossouw, P W G (WP) 1997 *BI* 2,3, *NZ* 1, *A* 1, *NZ* 2 (R), *A* 2 (R), *It, F* 1,2, *E, S*, 1998 *I* 1,2, *W* 1, *E* 1, *A* 1, *NZ* 1,2, *A* 2, *W* 2, *S, I* 3, *E* 2
Rousseau, W P (WP) 1928 *NZ* 3,4
Roux, F du T (WP) 1960 *W*, 1961 *A* 1,2, 1962 *BI* 1,2,3,4, 1963 *A* 2, 1965 *A* 1,2, *NZ* 1,2,3,4, 1968 *BI* 3,4, *F* 1,2 1969 *A* 1,2,3,4, 1970 *I, NZ* 1,2,3,4
Roux, J P (Tvl) 1994 *E* 2, *NZ* 1,2,3, *Arg* 1, 1995 [*R, C, F* (R)], 1996 *A* 1 (R), *NZ* 1, *A* 2, *NZ* 3
Roux, O A (NT) 1969 *S, E*, 1970 *I, W*, 1972 *E*, 1974 *BI* 3,4

Samuels, T A (GW) 1896 *BI* 2,3,4
Sauermann, J T (Tvl) 1971 *F* 1,2, *A* 1, 1972 *E*, 1974 *BI* 1
Schlebusch, J J J (OFS) 1974 *BI* 3,4, 1975 *F* 2
Schmidt, L U (NT) 1958 *F* 2, 1962 *BI* 2
Schmidt, U L (NT, Tvl) 1986 *Cv* 1,2,3,4, 1989 *Wld* 1,2, 1992 *NZ, A*, 1993 *F* 1,2, *A* 1,2,3, 1994 *Arg* 1,2, *S, W*
Schoeman, J (WP) 1963 *A* 3,4, 1965 *I, S, A* 1, *NZ* 1,2
Scholtz, C P (WP, Tvl) 1994 *Arg* 1, 1995 [*R, C, WS*]
Scholtz, H H (WP) 1921 *NZ* 1,2
Schutte, P J W (Tvl) 1994 *S, W*
Scott, P A (Tvl) 1896 *BI* 1,2,3,4
Sendin, W D (GW) 1921 *NZ* 2
Serfontein, D J (WP) 1980 *BI* 1,2,3,4, *S Am* 3,4, *F*, 1981 *I* 1,2, *NZ* 1,2,3, *US*, 1982 *S Am* 1,2, 1984 *E* 1,2, *S Am* 1,2
Shand, R (GW) 1891 *BI* 2,3
Sheriff, A R (Tvl) 1938 *BI* 1,2,3
Shum, E H (Tvl) 1913 *E*
Sinclair, D J (Tvl) 1955 *BI* 1,2,3,4
Sinclair, J H (Tvl) 1903 *BI* 1
Skene, A L (WP) 1958 *F* 2
Skinstad, R B (WP) 1997 *E* (t), 1998 *W* 1 (R), *E* 1 (t), *NZ* 1 (R),2 (R), *A* 2 (R), *W* 2 (R), *S, I* 3, *E* 2
Slater, J T (EP) 1924 *BI* 3,4, 1928 *NZ* 1
Smal, G P (WP) 1986 *Cv* 1,2,3,4, 1989 *Wld* 1,2
Small, J T (Tvl, N, WP) 1992 *NZ, A, F* 1,2, *E*, 1993 *F* 1,2, *A* 1,2,3, *Arg* 1,2, 1994 *E* 1,2, *NZ* 1,2,3 (t), *Arg* 1, 1995 *WS*, [*A, R, F, NZ*], *W, It, E* (R), 1996 *Fj, A* 1, *NZ* 1, *A* 2, *NZ* 2, *Arg* 1,2, *F* 1,2, *W*, 1997 *Tg, BI* 1, *NZ* 1 (R), *A* 1 (R), *NZ* 2, *A* 2, *It, F* 1,2, *E, S*
Smit, F C (WP) 1992 *E*
Smith, C M (OFS) 1963 *A* 3,4, 1964 *W, F*, 1965 *A* 1,2, *NZ* 2
Smith, C W (GW) 1891 *BI* 2, 1896 *BI* 2,3
Smith, D (GW) 1891 *BI* 2
Smith D J (Z-R) 1980 *BI* 1,2,3,4
Smith, G A C (EP) 1938 *BI* 3
Smith, P F (GW) 1997 *S* (R), 1998 *I* 1 (t),2, *W* 1, *NZ* 1 (R),2 (R), *A* 2 (R), *W* 2
Smollan, F C (Tvl) 1933 *A* 3,4,5
Snedden, R C D (GW) 1891 *BI* 2
Snyman, A H (NT, BB) 1996 *NZ* 3,4, *Arg* 2 (R), *W* (R), 1997 *Tg, BI* 1,2,3, *NZ* 1, *A* 1, *NZ* 2, *A* 2, *It, F* 1,2, *E, S*, 1998 *I* 1,2, *W* 1, *E* 1, *A* 1, *NZ* 1,2, *A* 2, *W* 2, *S, I* 3, *E* 2
Snyman, D S L (WP) 1972 *E*, 1974 *BI* 1,2 (R), *F* 1,2, 1975 *F* 1,2, 1976 *NZ* 2,3, 1977 *Wld*
Snyman, J C P (OFS) 1974 *BI* 2,3,4

Sonnekus, G H H (OFS) 1974 *BI* 3, 1984 *E* 1,2
Spies, J J (NT) 1970 *NZ* 1,2,3,4
Stander, J C J (OFS) 1974 *BI* 4 (R), 1976 *NZ* 1,2,3,4
Stapelberg, W P (NT) 1974 *F* 1,2
Starke, J J (WP) 1956 *NZ* 4
Starke, K T (WP) 1924 *BI* 1,2,3,4
Steenekamp, J G A (Tvl) 1958 *F* 1
Stegmann, A C (WP) 1906 *S, I*
Stegmann, J A (Tvl) 1912 *S, I, W*, 1913 *E, F*
Stewart, C (WP) 1998 *S, I* 3, *E* 2
Stewart, D A (WP) 1960 *S*, 1961 *E, S, F, I*, 1963 *A* 1,3,4, 1964 *W, F*, 1965 *I*
Stofberg, M T S (OFS, NT, WP) 1976 *NZ* 2,3, 1977 *Wld*, 1980 *S Am* 1,2, *BI* 1,2,3,4, *S Am* 3,4, *F*, 1981 *I* 1,2, *NZ* 1,2, *US*, 1982 *S Am* 1,2, 1984 *E* 1,2
Strachan, L C (Tvl) 1932 *E, S*, 1937 *A* 1,2, *NZ* 1,2,3, 1938 *BI* 1,2,3
Stransky, J (N, WP) 1993 *A* 1,2,3, *Arg* 1, 1994 *Arg* 1,2, 1995 *WS*, [*A, R* (t), *C, F, NZ*], *W, It, E*, 1996 *Fj* (R), *NZ* 1, *A* 2, *NZ* 2,3,4,5 (R)
Straeuli, R A W (Tvl) 1994 *NZ* 1, *Arg* 1,2, *S, W*, 1995 *WS*, [*A, WS, NZ* (R)], *E* (R)
Strauss, C P (WP) 1992 *F* 1,2, *E*, 1993 *F* 1,2, *A* 1,2,3, *Arg* 1,2, 1994 *E* 1, *NZ* 1,2, *Arg* 1,2
Strauss, J A (WP) 1984 *S Am* 1
Strauss, J H P (Tvl) 1976 *NZ* 3,4, 1980 *S Am* 1
Strauss, S S F (GW) 1921 *NZ* 3
Strydom, C F (OFS) 1955 *BI* 3, 1956 *A* 1,2, *NZ* 1,4, 1958 *F* 1,
Strydom, J J (Tvl, GL) 1993 *F* 2, *A* 1,2,3, *Arg* 1,2, 1994 *E* 1, 1995 [*A, C, F, NZ*], 1996 *A* 2 (R), *NZ* 2 (R), 3,4, *W* (R), 1997 *Tg*, *BI* 1,2,3, *A* 2
Strydom, L J (NT) 1949 *NZ* 1,2
Styger, J J (OFS) 1992 *NZ* (R), *A, F* 1,2, *E*, 1993 *F* 2 (R), *A* 3 (R)
Suter, M R (N) 1965 *I, S*
Swanepoel, W (OFS) 1997 *BI* 3 (R), *A* 2 (R), *F* 1 (R), 2, *E, S*, 1998 *I* 2 (R), *W* 1 (R), *E* 2 (R)
Swart, J (WP) 1996 *Fj, NZ* 1 (R), *A* 2, *NZ* 2,3,4,5, 1997 *BI* 3 (R), *It, S* (R)
Swart, J J N (SWA) 1955 *BI* 1
Swart, I S (Tvl) 1993 *A* 1,2,3, *Arg* 1, 1994 *E* 1,2, *NZ* 1,3, *Arg* 2 (R), 1995 *WS*, [*A, WS, F, NZ*], *W*, 1996 *A* 2

Taberer, W S (GW) 1896 *BI* 2
Taylor, O B (N) 1962 *BI* 1
Terblanche, C S (Bol) 1998 *I* 1,2, *W* 1, *E* 1, *A* 1, *NZ* 1,2, *A* 2, *W* 2, *S, I* 3, *E* 2
Teichmann, G H (N) 1995 *W*, 1996 *Fj, A* 1, *NZ* 1, *A* 2, *NZ* 2,3,4,5, *Arg* 1,2, *F* 1,2, *W*, 1997 *Tg, BI* 1,2,3, *NZ* 1, *A* 1, *NZ* 2, *A* 2, *It, F* 1,2 *E, S*, 1998 *I* 1,2, *W* 1, *E* 1, *A* 1, *NZ* 1,2, *A* 2, *W* 2, *S, I* 3, *E* 2
Theron, D F (GW) 1996 *A* 2 (R), *NZ* 2 (R), 5, *Arg* 1,2, *F* 1,2, *W*, 1997 *BI* 2 (R), 3, *NZ* 1 (R), *A* 1, *NZ* 2 (R)
Theunissen, D J (GW) 1896 *BI* 3
Thompson, G (WP) 1912 *S, I, W*
Tindall, J C (WP) 1924 *BI* 1, 1928 *NZ* 1,2,3,4
Tobias, E G (SARF, Bol) 1981 *I* 1,2, 1984 *E* 1,2, *S Am* 1,2
Tod, N S (N) 1928 *NZ* 2
Townsend, W H (N) 1921 *NZ* 1
Trenery, W E (GW) 1891 *BI* 2
Tromp, H (NT) 1996 *NZ*3,4, *Arg* 2 (R), *F* 1 (R)
Truter, D R (WP) 1924 *BI* 2,4
Truter, J T (N) 1963 *A* 1, 1964 *F*, 1965 *A* 2
Turner, F G (EP) 1933 *A* 1,2, 1937 *A* 1,2, *NZ* 1,2,3, 1938 *BI* 1,2,3
Twigge, R J (NT) 1960 *S*

Ulyate, C A (Tvl) 1955 *BI* 1,2,3,4, 1956 *NZ* 1,2,3
Uys, P de W (NT) 1960 *W*, 1961 *E, S, I, A* 1,2, 1962 *BI* 1,4, 1963 *A* 1,2, 1969 *A* 1 (R), 2

Van Aswegen, H J (WP) 1981 *NZ* 1, 1982 *S Am* 2 (R)
Van Broeckhuizen, H D (WP) 1896 *BI* 4
Van Buuren, M C (Tvl) 1891 *BI* 1
Van de Vyver, D F (WP) 1937 *A* 2
Van den Berg, D S (N) 1975 *F* 1,2, 1976 *NZ* 1,2
Van den Berg, M A (WP) 1937 *A* 1, *NZ* 1,2,3
Van den Bergh, E (EP) 1994 *Arg* 2 (t & R)
Van der Linde, A (WP) 1995 *It, E*, 1996 *Arg* 1 (R), 2 (R), *F* 1 (R), *W* (R)
Van der Merwe, A J (Bol) 1955 *BI* 2,3,4, 1956 *A* 1,2, *NZ* 1,2,3,4, 1958 *F* 1, 1960 *S, NZ* 2

Van der Merwe, A V (WP) 1931 *W*
Van der Merwe, B S (NT) 1949 *NZ* 1
Van der Merwe, H S (NT) 1960 *NZ* 4, 1963 *A* 2,3,4, 1964 *F*
Van der Merwe, J P (WP) 1970 *W*
Van der Merwe, P R (SWD, WT, GW) 1981 *NZ* 2,3, *US*, 1986 *Cv* 1,2, 1989 *Wld* 1
Vanderplank, B E (N) 1924 *BI* 3,4
Van der Schyff, J H (GW) 1949 *NZ* 1,2,3,4, 1955 *BI* 1
Van der Watt, A E (WP) 1969 *S* (R), *E*, 1970 *I*
Van der Westhuizen, J C (WP) 1928 *NZ* 2,3,4, 1931 *I*
Van der Westhuizen, J H (WP) 1931 *I*, 1932 *E, S*
Van der Westhuizen, J H (NT, BB) 1993 *Arg* 1,2, 1994 *E* 1,2 (R), *Arg* 2, *S, W*, 1995 *WS*, [*A, C* (R), *WS, F, NZ*], *W, It, E*, 1996 *Fj, A* 1,2 (R), *NZ* 2,3 (R), 4,5, *Arg* 1,2, *F* 1,2, *W*, 1997 *Tg, BI* 1,2,3, *NZ* 1, *A* 1, *NZ* 2, *A* 2, *It, F* 1, 1998 *I* 1,2, *W* 1, *E* 1, *A* 1, *NZ* 1,2, *A* 2, *W* 2, *S, I* 3, *E* 2
Van Druten, N J V (Tvl) 1924 *BI* 1,2,3,4, 1928 *NZ* 1,2,3,4
Van Heerden, A J (Tvl) 1921 *NZ* 1,3
Van Heerden, F J (WP) 1994 *E* 1,2 (R), *NZ* 3, 1995 *It, E*, 1996 *NZ* 5 (R), *Arg* 1 (R), 2 (R), 1997 *Tg, BI* 2 (t + R), 3 (R), *NZ* 1 (R), 2 (R)
Van Heerden, J L (NT, Tvl) 1974 *BI* 3,4, *F* 1,2, 1975 *F* 1,2, 1976 *NZ* 1,2,3,4, 1977 *Wld*, 1980 *BI* 1,3,4, *S Am* 3,4, *F*
Van Jaarsveld, C J (Tvl) 1949 *NZ* 1
Van Jaarsveldt, D C (R) 1960 *S*
Van Niekerk, J A (WP) 1928 *NZ* 4
Van Reenen, G L (WP) 1937 *A* 2, *NZ* 1
Van Renen, C G (WP) 1891 *BI* 3, 1896 *BI* 1,4
Van Renen, W (WP) 1903 *BI* 1,3
Van Rensburg, J T J (Tvl) 1992 *NZ, A, E*, 1993 *F* 1,2, *A* 1, 1994 *NZ* 2
Van Rooyen, G W (Tvl) 1921 *NZ* 2,3
Van Ryneveld, R C B (WP) 1910 *BI* 2,3
Van Schalkwyk, D (NT) 1996 *Fj* (R), *NZ* 3,4,5, 1997 *BI* 2,3, *NZ* 1, *A* 1
Van Schoor, R A M (R) 1949 *NZ* 2,3,4, 1951 *S, I, W*, 1952 *E, F*, 1953 *A* 1,2,3,4
Van Vollenhoven, K T (NT) 1955 *BI* 1,2,3,4, 1956 *A* 1,2, *NZ* 3
Van Vuuren, T F (EP) 1912 *S, I, W*, 1913 *E, F*
Van Wyk, C J (Tvl) 1951 *S, I, W*, 1952 *E, F*, 1953 *A* 1,2,3,4, 1955 *BI* 1
Van Wyk, J F B (NT) 1970 *NZ* 1,2,3,4, 1971 *F* 1,2, *A* 1,2,3, 1972 *E*, 1974 *BI* 1,3,4, 1976 *NZ* 3,4
Van Wyk, S P (WP) 1928 *NZ* 1,2
Van Zyl, B P (WP) 1961 *I*
Van Zyl, C G P (OFS) 1965 *NZ* 1,2,3,4
Van Zyl, G H (WP) 1958 *F* 1, 1960 *S, NZ* 1,2,3,4, *W, I*, 1961 *E, S, F, I, A* 1,2, 1962 *BI* 1,3,4
Van Zyl, H J (Tvl) 1960 *NZ* 1,2,3,4, *I*, 1961 *E, S, I, A* 1,2
Van Zyl, P J (Bol) 1961 *I*
Veldsman, P E (WP) 1977 *Wld*
Venter, A G (OFS) 1996 *NZ* 3,4,5, *Arg* 1,2, *F* 1,2, *W*, 1997 *Tg*, 1,2,3, *NZ* 1, *A*, *NZ* 2, *It*, *F* 1,2, *E, S*, 1998 *I* 1,2, *W* 1, *E* 1, *A* 1, *NZ* 1,2, *A* 2, *W* 2, *S* (R), *I* 3 (R), *E* 2 (R)
Venter, B (OFS) 1994 *E* 1,2, *NZ* 1,2,3, *Arg* 1,2, 1995 [*R, C, WS* (R), *NZ* (R)], 1996 *A* 1, *NZ* 1, *A* 2
Venter, F D (Tvl) 1931 *W*, 1932 *S*, 1933 *A* 3
Versfeld, C (WP) 1891 *BI* 3
Versfeld, M (WP) 1891 *BI* 1,2,3
Vigne, J T (Tvl) 1891 *BI* 1,2
Viljoen, J F (GW) 1971 *F* 1,2, *A* 1,2,3, 1972 *E*
Viljoen, J T (N) 1971 *A* 1,2,3
Villet, J V (WP) 1984 *E* 1,2
Visagie, P J (GW) 1967 *F* 1,2,3,4, 1968 *E* 1,2,3,4, *F* 1,2, 1969 *A* 1,2,3,4, *S, E*, 1970 *NZ* 1,2,3,4, 1971 *F* 1,2, *A* 1,2,3
Visagie, R G (OFS, N) 1984 *E* 1,2, *S Am* 1,2, 1993 *F* 1
Visser, J de V (WP) 1981 *NZ* 2, *US*
Visser, M (WP) 1995 *WS* (R)
Visser, P J (Tvl) 1933 *A* 2
Viviers, S S (OFS) 1956 *A* 1,2, *NZ* 2,3,4
Vogel, M L (OFS) 1974 *BI* 2 (R)

Wagenaar, C (NT) 1977 *Wld*
Wahl, J J (WP) 1949 *NZ* 1
Walker, A P (N) 1921 *NZ* 1,3, 1924 *BI* 1,2,3,4
Walker, H N (OFS) 1953 *A* 3, 1956 *A* 2, *NZ* 1,4
Walker, H W (Tvl) 1910 *BI* 1,2,3
Walton, D C (N) 1964 *F*, 1965 *I, S, NZ* 3,4, 1969 *A* 1,2, *E*
Waring, F W (WP) 1931 *I*, 1932 *E*, 1933 *A* 1,2,3,4,5

Wegner, N (WP) 1993 *F* 2, *A* 1,2,3
Wessels, J J (WP) 1896 *BI* 1,2,3
Whipp, P J M (WP) 1974 *BI* 1,2, 1975 *F* 1, 1976 *NZ* 1,3,4, 1980 *S Am* 1,2
White, J (Bor) 1931 *W*, 1933 *A* 1,2,3,4,5, 1937 *A* 1,2, *NZ* 1,2
Wiese, J J (Tvl) 1993 *F* 1, 1995 *WS*, [*R, C, WS, F, NZ*], *W, It, E*, 1996 *NZ* 3 (R), 4 (R), 5, *Arg* 1,2, *F* 1,2, *W*
Williams, A E (GW) 1910 *BI* 1
Williams, A P (WP) 1984 *E* 1,2
Williams, C M (WP) 1993 *Arg* 2, 1994 *E* 1,2, *NZ* 1,2,3, *Arg* 1,2, *S, W*, 1995 *WS*, [*WS, F, NZ*], *It, E*, 1998 *A* 1 (t), *NZ* 1 (t)

Williams, D O (WP) 1937 *A* 1,2, *NZ* 1,2,3, 1938 *BI* 1,2,3
Williams, J G (NT) 1971 *F* 1,2, *A* 1,2,3, 1972 *E*, 1974 *BI* 1,2,4, *F* 1,2, 1976 *NZ* 1,2
Wilson, L G (WP) 1960 *NZ* 3,4, *W, I*, 1961 *E, F, I, A* 1,2, 1962 *BI* 1,2,3,4, 1963 *A* 1,2,3,4, 1964 *W, F*, 1965 *I, S, A* 1,2, *NZ* 1,2,3,4
Wolmarans, B J (OFS) 1977 *Wld*
Wright, G D (EP, Tvl) 1986 *Cv* 3,4, 1989 *Wld* 1,2, 1992 *F* 1,2, *E*
Wyness, M R K (WP) 1962 *BI* 1,2,3,4, 1963 *A* 2

Zeller, W C (N) 1921 *NZ* 2,3
Zimerman, M (WP) 1931 *W, I*, 1932 *E, S*

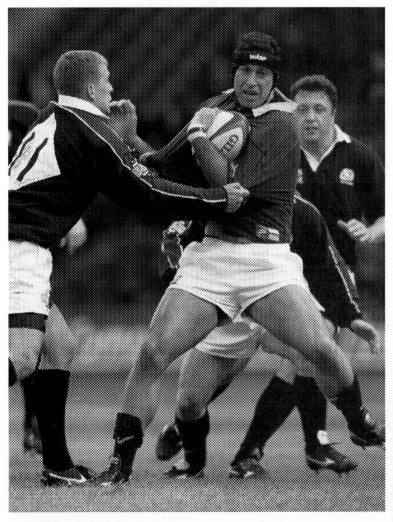

Veteran Springbok lock Mark Andrews takes on the Scotland wing Cameron Murray in South Africa's 35-10 defeat of Scotland at Murrayfield in November.

SOUTH AFRICAN INTERNATIONAL
RECORDS *(up to 30 April 1999)*

MATCH RECORDS

MOST CONSECUTIVE TEST WINS

17 1997 *A* 2, *It*, *F* 1,2, *E*, *S*, 1998 *I* 1,2, *W* 1, *E* 1, *A* 1, *NZ* 1,2, *A* 2, *W* 2, *S*, *I* 3

MOST CONSECUTIVE TESTS WITHOUT DEFEAT

P	W	D	Period
17	17	0	1997–98
16	15	1	1994–96
15	12	3	1960–63

MOST POINTS IN A MATCH
by the team

Pts	Opp	Venue	Year
96	W	Pretoria	1998
74	Tg	Cape Town	1997
68	S	Murrayfield	1997
62	It	Bologna	1997
61	A	Pretoria	1997

by a player

31 by P C Montgomery v Wales at Pretoria 1998
28 by G K Johnson v Western Samoa at Johannesburg 1995
26 by J H de Beer v Australia at Pretoria 1997
26 by P C Montgomery v Scotland at Murrayfield 1997
25 by J T Stransky v Australia at Bloemfontein 1996

MOST TRIES IN A MATCH
by the team

T	Opp	Venue	Year
15	W	Pretoria	1998
12	Tg	Cape Town	1997
10	I	Dublin	1912
10	S	Murrayfield	1997

by a player

4 by C M Williams v Western Samoa at Johannesburg 1995
4 by P W G Rossouw v France at Parc des Princes 1997
4 by C S Terblanche v Ireland at Bloemfontein 1998

MOST CONVERSIONS IN A MATCH
by the team

C	Opp	Venue	Year
9	S	Murrayfield	1997
9	W	Pretoria	1998
7	S	Murrayfield	1951
7	Tg	Cape Town	1997
7	It	Bologna	1997
7	F	Parc des Princes	1997

by a player

9 by P C Montgomery v Wales at Pretoria 1998
8 by P C Montgomery v Scotland at Murrayfield 1997
7 by A Geffin v Scotland at Murrayfield 1951
7 by E Lubbe v Tonga at Cape Town 1997
7 by H W Honiball v Italy at Bologna 1997
7 by H W Honiball v France at Parc des Princes 1997

MOST PENALTY GOALS IN A MATCH
by the team

P	Opp	Venue	Year
7	F	Pretoria	1975
6	A	Bloemfontein	1996
5	several instances		

by a player

6 by G R Bosch v France at Pretoria 1975
6 by J T Stransky v Australia at Bloemfontein 1996
5 by A Geffin v New Zealand at Cape Town 1949
5 by R Blair v World XV at Pretoria 1977
5 by H E Botha v New Zealand at Wellington 1981
5 by J W Heunis v England at Port Elizabeth 1984
5 by H E Botha v New Zealand Cavaliers at Johannesburg 1986
5 by J T J van Rensburg v France at Durban 1993
5 by A J Joubert v England at Pretoria 1994
5 by P C Montgomery v Australia at Johannesburg 1998

331

MOST DROPPED GOALS IN A MATCH
by the team

D	Opp	Venue	Year
3	SAm	Durban	1980
3	I	Durban	1981

by a player

3 by H E Botha v South America at
Durban 1980
3 by H E Botha v Ireland at
Durban 1981
2 by B L Osler v New Zealand at
Durban 1928
2 by H E Botha v New Zealand
Cavaliers at Cape Town 1986
2 by J T Stransky v New Zealand
at Johannesburg 1995

CAREER RECORDS

MOST CAPPED PLAYERS

Caps	Player	Career
53	M G Andrews	1994–98
50	J H van der Westhuizen	1993–98
47	J T Small	1992–97
39	G H Teichmann	1995–98
38	F C H du Preez	1961–71
38	J H Ellis	1965–76
35	J F K Marais	1963–74
34	A J Joubert	1989–97
34	J Dalton	1994–98

MOST CONSECUTIVE TESTS

Tests	Player	Span
38	G H Teichmann	1996–98
25	S H Nomis	1967–72
23	J L Gainsford	1961–67
23	J F K Marais	1968–71
23	P C Montgomery	1997–98

MOST TESTS AS CAPTAIN

Tests	Captain	Span
33	G H Teichmann	1996–98
29	J F Pienaar	1993–96
22	D J de Villiers	1965–70
15	M du Plessis	1975–80
11	J F K Marais	1971–74

MOST TESTS IN INDIVIDUAL POSITIONS

Full-back A J Joubert		34	1989–97
Wing J T Small		43*	1992–97
Centre J L Gainsford		33	1960–67
Fly-half H E Botha		28	1980–92
Scrum-half J H van der Westhuizen		48	1993–98
Prop J F K Marais		35	1963–74
Hooker J Dalton		34	1994–98
Lock M G Andrews		50	1994–98
Flanker J H Ellis		38	1965–76
No. 8 G H Teichmann		39	1995–98

* excludes an appearance as a temporary
replacement

MOST POINTS IN TESTS

Pts	Player	Tests	Career
312	H E Botha	28	1980–92
240	J T Stransky	22	1993–96
169	P C Montgomery	22	1997–98
143	H W Honiball	33	1993–98
130	P J Visagie	25	1967–71

MOST TRIES IN TESTS

Tries	Player	Tests	Career
25	J H van der Westhuizen	50	1993–98
20	J T Small	47	1992–97
19	D M Gerber	24	1980–92
18	P W G Rossouw	23	1997–98
13	C M Williams	18	1993–98

MOST CONVERSIONS IN TESTS

Cons	Player	Tests	Career
50	H E Botha	28	1980–92
36	H W Honiball	33	1993–98
34	P C Montgomery	22	1997–98
30	J T Stransky	22	1993–96
20	P J Visagie	25	1967–71

MOST PENALTY GOALS IN TESTS

Pens	Player	Tests	Career
50	H E Botha	28	1980–92
47	J T Stransky	22	1993–96
23	G R Bosch	9	1974–76
22	H W Honiball	33	1993–98
19	P J Visagie	25	1967–71
17	A J Joubert	34	1989–97
17	P C Montgomery	22	1997–98

MOST DROPPED GOALS IN TESTS

Drops	Player	Tests	Career
18	H E Botha	28	1980–92
5	J D Brewis	10	1949–53
5	P J Visagie	25	1967–71
4	B L Osler	17	1924–33

TRI-NATIONS RECORDS

Record	Detail	Holder	Set
Most points in matches	64	J H de Beer	1997
Most points in season	64	J H de Beer	1997
Most points in match	26	J H de Beer	v Australia (h) 1997
Most tries in matches	3	P C Montgomery	1997–1998
	3	J H van der Westhuizen	1997–1998
Most tries in season	3	P C Montgomery	1997
Most tries in match	2	P C Montgomery	v Australia (h) 1997
Most cons in matches	12	J H de Beer	1997
Most cons in season	12	J H de Beer	1997
Most cons in match	6	J H de Beer	v Australia (h)1997
Most pens in matches	10	J T Stransky	1996
	10	P C Montgomery	1997–1998
Most pens in season	10	J T Stransky	1996
	10	P C Montgomery	1998
Most pens in match	6	J T Stransky	v Australia (h) 1996

SERIES RECORDS

Record	Holder	Detail
Most tries	P W G Rossouw	8 in Europe 1997
Most points	H E Botha	69 v Cavaliers, 1986

MAJOR TOUR RECORDS

Record	Detail	Year	Place
Most team points	753	1937	A & NZ
Most team tries	161	1937	A & NZ
Most individual points	190 by G H Brand	1937	A & NZ
Most individual tries	22 by J A Loubser	1906–07	Europe
Most points in match	38 by A J Joubert	1994 v Swansea	Swansea
Most tries in match	6 by R G Dryburgh	1956 v Queensland	Brisbane

MISCELLANEOUS RECORDS

Record	Holder	Detail
Longest Test career	J M Powell/B H Heatlie/ D M Gerber/ H E Botha	13 seasons, 1891–1903/ 1891–1903/1980–1992/ 1980–1992
Youngest Test cap	A J Hartley	17 yrs 18 days in 1891
Oldest Test cap	W H Morkel	36 yrs 258 days in 1921

SOUTH AFRICAN INTERNATIONAL CAREER RECORDS *(up to 30 April 1999)*

Player	Debut	Caps since last season	Caps	T	C	PG	DG	Pts
A J Joubert	1989 v Wld		34	10	8	17	0	117
P C Montgomery	1997 v BI	1998 *I* 1,2, *W* 1, *E* 1, *A* 1, *NZ* 1,2, *A* 2, *W* 2, *S*, *I* 3, *E* 2	22	10	34	17	0	169
M Hendricks	1998 v I	1998 *I* 2(R), *W* 1(R)	2	1	0	0	0	5
C M Williams	1993 vArg	1998 *A* 1(t), *NZ* 1(t)	18	13	0	0	0	65
C S Terblanche	1998 v I	1998 *I* 1,2, *W* 1, *E* 1, *A* 1, *NZ* 1,2, *A* 2, *W* 2, *S*, *I* 3, *E* 2	12	9	0	0	0	45
P W G Rossouw	1997 v BI	1998 *I* 1,2, *W* 1, *E* 1, *A* 1, *NZ* 1,2, *A* 2, *W* 2, *S*, *I* 3, *E* 2	23	18	0	0	0	90
A H Snyman	1996 v NZ	1998 *I* 1,2, *W* 1, *E* 1, *A* 1, *NZ* 1,2, *A* 2, *W* 2, *S*, *I* 3, *E* 2	29	8	0	0	0	40
C Stewart	1998 v S	1998 *S*, *I* 3, *E* 2	3	0	0	0	0	0
P G Muller	1992 v NZ	1998 *I* 1,2, *W* 1, *E* 1, *A* 1, *NZ* 1,2, *A* 2	25	2	0	0	0	10
H W Honiball	1993 v A	1998 *W* 1(R), *E* 1, *A* 1, *NZ* 1,2, *A* 2, *W* 2, *S*, *I* 3, *E* 2	33	1	36	22	0	143
G S du Toit	1998 v I	1998 *I* 1	1	0	3	2	0	12
P F Smith	1997 v S	1998 *I* 1(t),2, *W* 1, *NZ* 1(R),2(R), *A* 2(R), *W* 2	8	2	2	3	0	23
J H van der Westhuizen	1993 v Arg	1998 *I* 1,2, *W* 1, *E* 1, *A* 1, *NZ* 1,2, *A* 2, *W* 2, *S*, *I* 3, *E* 2	50	25	0	0	0	125
W Swanepoel	1997 v BI	1998 *I* 2(R), *W* 1(R), *E* 2(R)	9	1	0	0	0	5
A E Drotské	1993 vArg	1998 *I* 2(R), *W* 1(R), *I* 3(R)	13	2	0	0	0	10
J Dalton	1994 vArg	1998 *I* 1,2, *W* 1, *E* 1, *A* 1, *NZ* 1,2, *A* 2, *W* 2, *S*, *I* 3, *E* 2	34	5	0	0	0	25
A-H le Roux	1994 v E	1998 *I* 1,2, *W* 1(R), *E* 1(R), *A* 1(R), *NZ* 1(R),2(R), *A* 2(R), *W* 2(R), *S*(R), *I* 3(R), *E* 2(t&R)	13	0	0	0	0	0
R B Kempson	1998 v I	1998 *I* 2(R), *W* 1, *E* 1, *A* 1, *NZ* 1,2, *A* 2, *W* 2, *S*, *I* 3, *E* 2	11	0	0	0	0	0
A C Garvey	1996 vArg	1998 *I* 1,2, *W* 1, *E* 1, *A* 1, *NZ* 1,2, *A* 2, *W* 2, *S*, *I* 3, *E* 2	27	4	0	0	0	20
K Otto	1995 v R	1998 *I* 1,2, *W* 1, *E* 1, *A* 1, *NZ* 1,2, *A* 2, *W* 2, *S*, *I* 3, *E* 2	24	1	0	0	0	5

M G Andrews	1994 v E	1998 *I* 1,2, *W* 1, *E* 1, *A* 1, *NZ* 1,2, *A* 2, *W* 2, *S*, *I* 3, *E* 2	53	9	0	0	0	45
J C Erasmus	1997 v BI	1998 *I* 1,2, *W* 1, *E* 1, *A* 1, *NZ* 2, *A* 2, *W* 2, *I* 3, *E* 2	17	7	0	0	0	35
R B Skinstad	1997 v E	1998 *W* 1(R), *E* 1(t), *NZ* 1(R),2(R), *A* 2(R), *W* 2(R), *S*, *I* 3, *E* 2	10	5	0	0	0	25
A G Venter	1996 v NZ	1998 *I* 1,2, *W* 1, *E* 1, *A* 1, *NZ* 1,2, *A* 2, *W* 2, *S*(R), *I* 3(R), *E* 2(R)	32	6	0	0	0	30
A D Aitken	1997 v F	1998 *I* 2(R), *W* 1(R), *NZ* 1,2(R), *A* 2(R)	7	0	0	0	0	0
G H Teichmann	1995 v W	1998 *I* 1,2, *W* 1, *E* 1, *A* 1, *NZ* 1,2, *A* 2, *W* 2, *S*, *I* 3, *E* 2	39	5	0	0	0	25

South Africa's all-time most capped No. 8 Gary Teichmann, who led his side to the brink of a world record 18 consecutive Test victories.

ONE OF THOSE YEARS

THE 1998 SEASON IN NEW ZEALAND
Donald Cameron *New Zealand Herald*

It must be 40 years since Harold Macmillan offered the cliché about the winds of change blowing through the troubled times in South Africa. New Zealand rugby folk will look at 1998 and pray that there are at least 40 more years ahead before another South African-born gale rips their game to shreds.

In 1997 and before there was an orderly calm about New Zealand rugby. The All Blacks were near as no matter invincible, and that accounted for the Tri-Nations squabble with South Africa and Australia, as well as any other northern pretenders to the southern throne.

Auckland would dominate the Super-12, perhaps allowing someone like Natal to reach the final, and then spend the last third of the home season putting the other first division teams in their places.

Laurie Mains, and then John Hart, demanded the public confidence that they could harness the All Blacks and also keep the busybodies of the New Zealand Rugby Football Union in place.

This serenity, this ordered calm, would be maintained until the All Blacks claimed the 1999 World Cup, which fate (and perhaps an errant Johannesburg waitress) had kept from their grasp in 1991 and 1995.

By the end of 1998 New Zealanders wanted only one Christmas present – the assurance that the horrors of 1998 were a passing aberration, and that the peaceful and prosperous times of All Black success would resume in 1999.

We were not to suspect such stormy discord even at the start, when the All Blacks rather patronisingly dismissed an understrength England side, which gave Hart and company time to try some new players.

Then came the sad face of one of these new men, Taine Randell, taking over as captain from Sean Fitzpatrick, who was heading into television advertising and who later must have regarded his retirement as a masterstroke of good timing. Randell's after-match face grew longer and longer as his ill-organised side suffered two narrow losses to Australia and South Africa, and then were outclassed as Australia took away the Bledisloe Cup.

Then came that final humiliation – South Africa scoring three late tries, two converted, to snatch a brilliant 24-23 victory at Durban, while at Sydney the All Blacks lost their lead and the game, 14-19 to a stunning last-minute try by Matt Burke. Auckland, so long the lord of the manor, let Canterbury in for a flukey try which put the Super-12 trophy in Canterbury's cupboard.

The southern change in New Zealand power was re-emphasised when Otago scored a riotous 49-20 win over Waikato in the national championship first division final – and Auckland, once-mighty Auckland, finished eighth and did not even reach the semi-finals.

The New Zealand public, once sated with success, turned on Hart. In his corporate way Hart had tried to explain that teams and players had to change and New Zealand could not expect to win with senior men like Fitzpatrick and Zinzan Brooke no longer available.

The public reaction was even more bitter when Hart publicly criticised players (he maintained that Andrew Mehrtens, the first five eighth, had made a third of all the All Blacks' mistakes in one loss).

There had been the feeling as far as the NZRFU administration was concerned that what Hart wanted, Hart got. As well as having two fellow selectors and a large support staff, Hart obtained Peter Sloane and Wayne Smith as assistant coaches. After the losses people, and All Blacks, began to complain. Some senior players said that Hart was becoming too over-powering as coach; in modern terms, a control-freak.

The NZRFU acted. Hart was told that he would have to trim his staff. He was left with Gordon Hunter and Sloane as his fellow selectors – Ross Cooper, a former selector, and Smith were regarded as superfluous. Hart buttoned his lip, and seemed to retreat to a deep bunker.

The NZRFU tried to keep the whole game in its own pocket, but was also under fire for appearing to neglect the game at club and lower representative level. So the NZRFU came up with a proposal that would reform the provincial championships. One of the great achievements, apart from Waikato retaining the Ranfurly Shield for the season, was the feat of Taranaki in reaching the first division semi-finals.

Then the NZRFU came up with its new championship plans, which did not even leave Taranaki in the first division, and in fact put them in danger of disappearing as a representative entity.

It was, really, one of *those* years.

NATIONAL CHAMPIONSHIP

Division 1	P	W	D	L	F	A	Bonus	Pts
Otago	9	7	0	2	411	184	7	35
Waikato	9	7	0	2	341	175	5	33
Canterbury	9	6	0	3	335	228	9	33
Taranaki	9	6	0	3	214	171	2	26
Counties/Manukau	9	4	1	4	258	264	7	25
Wellington	9	4	1	4	229	284	3	21
North Harbour	9	4	0	5	203	234	4	20

	P	W	D	L	F	A	Bonus	Pts
Auckland	9	4	0	5	237	261	4	20
Southland	9	2	0	7	127	372	0	8
Northland	9	0	0	9	156	338	5	5

Semi-finals: Waikato 32, Canterbury 13; Otago 61, Taranaki 12
Final: Otago 49, Waikato 20

Division 2	P	W	D	L	F	A	Bonus	Pts
Central Vikings	8	8	0	0	354	88	7	39
Bay of Plenty	8	5	0	3	189	125	2	22
Marlborough	8	4	1	3	185	197	4	22
Nelson Bays	8	4	1	3	162	171	2	20
Thames Valley	8	4	0	4	150	203	3	19
Wanganui	8	4	0	4	140	135	2	18
King Country	8	1	0	7	125	216	4	8
Wairarapa	8	1	0	7	126	287	2	6

Semi-finals: Central Vikings 23, Nelson Bays 20; Bay of Plenty 35, Marlborough 3
Final: Central Vikings 33, Bay of Plenty 18

Division 3	P	W	D	L	F	A	Bonus	Pts
North Otago	8	7	0	1	264	143	5	33
Mid-Canterbury	8	7	0	1	314	112	4	32
South Canterbury	8	5	0	3	143	124	2	22
Horowhenua-Kapiti	8	4	0	4	211	167	6	22
Poverty Bay	8	4	0	4	245	212	5	21
East Coast	8	4	0	4	149	164	4	20
West Coast	8	1	0	7	101	376	2	6
Buller	8	0	0	8	111	249	0	0

Semi-finals: Horowhenua-Kapiti 36, North Otago 26; Mid-Canterbury 52, South Canterbury 17
Final: Mid-Canterbury 18, Horowhenua-Kapiti 13

RANFURLY SHIELD

Waikato 121, Poverty Bay 0; Waikato 76, King Country 0; Waikato 25, Bay of Plenty 18; Waikato 24, Auckland 23; Waikato 95, Southland 7; Waikato 39, North Harbour 22; Waikato 63, Northland 22; Waikato 29, Canterbury 23

NEW ZEALAND MAORI TO SCOTLAND 1998

THE TOURING PARTY

Manager M Blackburn   **Coach** MJ Te Pou   **Assistant Coach** JHM Love
Captain DD Muir

Full-backs: AR Cashmore (Auckland)

Threequarters: TB Reihana (Waikato), NR Berryman (Northland), DPE Gibson (Canterbury), GM Osborne (North Harbour), CS Ralph (Auckland), LR MacDonald (Canterbury), JS Kerr (Canterbury)

Half-backs: RHP MacDonald (Southland), TE Brown (Otago), RJ Duggan (Waikato), AC Flynn (Canterbury)

Forwards: GE Feek (Taranaki), KJ Meeuws (Otago), LARL Lidgard (Counties Manukau), SP McFarland (North Harbour), JF Akurangi (Counties Manukau), NM Maxwell (Canterbury), DAG Waller (Manawatu), JN Coe (Counties Manukau), HATeW Makiri (Counties Manukau), RT Cribb (North Harbour), RB Ford (Canterbury), TV Flavell (North Harbour), G Marsh (Counties Manukau), DD Muir (Waikato)

TOUR RECORD

All matches   Played 3   Won 3   Points for 146   Against 26

SCORING DETAILS

All matches

For:	19T	12C	9PG	=	146pts
Against:	1T		7PG	=	26pts

MATCH DETAILS

1998	OPPONENTS	VENUE	RESULT
11 Nov	Edinburgh Reivers	Hawick	W 69-3
14 Nov	Scotland XV	Murrayfield	W 24-8
18 Nov	Glasgow Caledonians	Perth	W 53-15

MATCH 1   14 November, Mansfield Park, Hawick

Edinburgh Reivers 3 (1PG)   **New Zealand Maori 69** (7G 4T)
Edinburgh Reivers: S Lang; A Common, S Hastings, A Collins, J Kerr; C Chalmers, I Fairley; R McNulty, S Scott, P Wright, D Burns, I Fullarton, A Roxburgh, B Renwick (*capt*), I Sinclair *Substitutions:* G Ross for Chalmers (33 mins); A Watt for McNulty (54 mins); S Nichol for Lang (58 mins); J Hay for Scott (58 mins); G Burns for Fairley (59 mins); G Hayter for Roxburgh (64 mins); C Hogg for Sinclair (64 mins)
Scorer *Penalty Goal:* Chalmers
NZ Maori: Cashmore; Reihana, Berryman, Gibson, Osborne; Brown, Flynn; Feek, McFarland, Meeuws, Maxwell, Coe, Flavell, Muir (*capt*), Marsh *Substitutions:* Ralph for Berryman (50 mins); Duggan for Flynn (50 mins), Waller for Coe (50 mins), Akurangi for McFarland (64 mins), Ford for Marsh (70 mins), L MacDonald for Gibson (70 mins)
Scorers *Tries:* Berryman (2), Feek (2), Cashmore, Reihana, Gibson, Osborne, Meeuws, Duggan, Flavell *Conversions:* Cashmore (7)
Referee B Campsall (England)

MATCH 2   14 November, Murrayfield

Scotland XV 8 (1PG 1T)   **New Zealand Maori 24** (1G 4PG 1T)
Scotland XV: D Lee (London Scottish); A Stanger (Edinburgh Reivers), J Mayer (Edinburgh Reivers), R Shepherd (Glasgow Caledonians), C Murray (Edinburgh Reivers); G Townsend (Brive, France), B Redpath (Edinburgh Reivers)*(capt)*; T Smith (Glasgow Caledonians), G Bulloch (Glasgow Caledonians), P Burnell (London Scottish), S Murray (Bedford), S Grimes (Glasgow Caledonians), R Wainwright (Glasgow Caledonians), E Peters (Bath), A Pountney (Northampton) *Substitutions:* G Weir (Newcastle) for Grimes (57 mins); M Leslie (Edinburgh Reivers) for Wainwright (60 mins); D Hodge (Edinburgh Reivers) for Townsend (60 mins); D Hilton (Bath) for Burnell (67 mins); A Tait (Edinburgh Reivers) for Shepherd (74 mins)
Scorer *Try:* Lee *Penalty Goal:* Lee
NZ Maori: Cashmore; Reihana, Ralph, Gibson, Berryman; Brown, Duggan; Lidgard, McFarland, Meeuws, Maxwell, Coe, Flavell, Muir (*capt*), Marsh
Substitutions: Feek for Lidgard (58 mins); Akurangi for McFarland (58 mins); Cribb for Coe (74 mins); L MacDonald for Gibson (74 mins); Osborne for MacDonald (79 mins); Makiri for Maxwell (79 mins)
Scorers *Tries:* Marsh, Cashmore *Conversion:* Cashmore
Penalty Goals: Cashmore (4)
Referee S Lander (England)

MATCH 3   18 November, McDiarmid Park, Perth

Glasgow Caledonians 15 (4PG 1DG)   **New Zealand Maori 53** (4G 5PG 2T)
Glasgow Caledonians: T Hayes; J Craig, C Simmers, I Jardine (*capt*), A Bulloch; L Smith, C Little; A Kittle, S Scott, G McIlwham, G Perrett, S Campbell, G Flockhart, G McKay, J Shaw *Substitutions:* J Petrie for Flockhart (5 mins); A Collins for Simmers (66 mins); J Manson for Kittle (67 mins); C Paterson for Smith (76 mins)
Scorers *Penalty Goals:* Hayes (4) *Dropped Goal:* Smith
NZ Maori: Cashmore; Osborne, Ralph, Gibson, Kerr; R MacDonald, Duggan; Feek, Akurangi, Meeuws, Waller, Coe, Makiri, Muir (*capt*), Marsh
Substitutions: Lidgard for Feek (40 mins); Berryman for Gibson (52 mins); Flavell for Muir (52 mins); McFarland for Akurangi (68 mins); Reihana for R MacDonald (71 mins); Ford for Coe (75 mins)
Scorers *Tries:* Osborne (2), Meeuws, Muir, Ralph, McFarland
Conversions: Cashmore (4) *Penalty Goals:* Cashmore (5)
Referee J Jutge (France)

The New Zealand Maori team perform the 'haka' before their 24-8 defeat of a Scotland XV at Murrayfield in November.

NEW ZEALAND INTERNATIONAL PLAYERS (*up to 30 April 1999*)

Abbott, H L (Taranaki) 1906 *F*
Aitken, G G (Wellington) 1921 *SA* 1,2
Allen, F R (Auckland) 1946 *A* 1,2, 1947 *A* 1,2, 1949 *A* 1,2
Allen, M R (Taranaki, Manawatu) 1993 *WS* (t), 1996 *S* 2 (t), 1997 *Arg* 1 (R), 2 (R), *SA* 2 (R), *A* 3 (R), *E* 2, *W* (R)
Allen, N H (Counties) 1980 *A* 3, *W*
Alley, G T (Canterbury) 1928 *SA* 1,2,3
Anderson, A (Canterbury) 1983 *S, E*, 1984 *A* 1,2,3, 1987 [*Fj*]
Anderson, B L (Wairarapa-Bush) 1986 *A* 1
Archer, W R (Otago, Southland) 1955 *A* 1,2, 1956 *SA* 1,3
Argus, W G (Canterbury) 1946 *A* 1,2, 1947 *A* 1,2
Arnold, D A (Canterbury) 1963 *I, W*, 1964 *E, F*
Arnold, K D (Waikato) 1947 *A* 1,2
Ashby, D L (Southland) 1958 *A* 2
Asher, A A (Auckland) 1903 *A*
Ashworth, B G (Auckland) 1978 *A* 1,2
Ashworth, J C (Canterbury, Hawke's Bay) 1978 *A* 1,2,3, 1980 *A* 1,2,3, 1981 *SA* 1,2,3, 1982 *A* 1,2, 1983 *BI* 1,2,3,4, *A*, 1984 *F* 1,2, *A* 1,2,3, 1985 *E* 1,2, *A*
Atkinson, H (West Coast) 1913 *A* 1
Avery, H E (Wellington) 1910 *A* 1,2,3

Bachop, G T M (Canterbury) 1989 *W, I*, 1990 *S* 1,2, *A* 1,2,3, *F* 1,2, 1991 *Arg* 1,2, *A* 1,2, [*E, US, C, A, S*], 1992 *Wld* 1, 1994 *SA* 1,2,3, *A*, 1995 *C*, [*I, W, S, E, SA*], 1992
Bachop, S J (Otago) 1994 *F* 2, *SA* 1,2,3, *A*
Badeley, C E O (Auckland) 1921 *SA* 1,2
Baird, J A S (Otago) 1913 *A* 2
Ball, N (Wellington) 1931 *A*, 1932 *A* 2,3, 1935 *W*, 1936 *E*
Barrett, J (Auckland) 1913 *A* 2,3
Barry, E F (Wellington) 1934 *A* 2
Barry, L J (North Harbour) 1995 *F* 2
Batty, G T M (Wellington, Bay of Plenty) 1972 *W, S*, 1973 *E* 1, *I, F, E* 2, 1974 *A* 1,3, *I*, 1975 *S*, 1976 *A* 1,2,3,4, 1977 *BI* 1
Batty, W (Auckland) 1930 *BI* 1,3,4, 1931 *A*
Beatty, G E (Taranaki) 1950 *BI* 1
Bell, R H (Otago) 1951 *A* 3, 1952 *A* 1,2
Bellis, E A (Wanganui) 1921 *SA* 1,2,3
Bennet, R (Otago) 1905 *A*
Berghan, T (Otago) 1938 *A* 1,2,3
Berry, M J (Wairarapa-Bush) 1986 *A* 3 (R)
Berryman, N R (Northland) 1998 *SA* 2 (R)
Bevan, V D (Wellington) 1949 *A* 1,2, 1950 *BI* 1,2,3,4
Birtwistle, W M (Canterbury) 1965 *SA* 1,2,3,4, 1967 *E, W, S*
Black, J E (Canterbury) 1977 *F* 1, 1979 *A*, 1980 *A* 3
Black, N W (Auckland) 1949 *SA* 3
Black, R S (Otago) 1914 *A* 1
Blackadder, T J (Canterbury) 1998 *E* 1 (R),2
Blake, A W (Wairarapa) 1949 *A* 1
Blowers, A F (Auckland) 1996 *SA* 2 (R), 4 (R), 1997 *I, E* 1 (R), *W* (R)
Boggs, E G (Auckland) 1946 *A* 2, 1949 *SA* 1
Bond, J G (Canterbury) 1949 *A* 2
Booth, E E (Otago) 1906 *F*, 1907 *A* 1,3
Boroevich, K G (Wellington) 1986 *F* 1, *A* 1, *F* 3 (R)
Botica, F M (North Harbour) 1986 *F* 1, *A* 1,2,3, *F* 2,3, 1989 *Arg* 1 (R)
Bowden, N J G (Taranaki) 1952 *A* 2
Bowers, R G (Wellington) 1954 *I, F*
Bowman, A W (Hawke's Bay) 1938 *A* 1,2,3
Braid, G J (Bay of Plenty) 1983 *S, E*
Bremner, S G (Auckland, Canterbury) 1952 *A* 2, 1956 *SA* 2
Brewer, M R (Otago, Canterbury) 1986 *F* 1, *A* 1,2,3, *F* 2,3, 1988 *A* 1, 1989 *A, W, I*, 1990 *S* 1,2, *A* 1,2,3, *F* 1,2, 1992 *I* 2, *A*, 1, 1994 *F* 1,2, *SA* 1,2,3, *A*, 1995 *C*, [*I, W, E, SA*], *A* 1,2
Briscoe, K C (Taranaki) 1959 *BI* 2, 1960 *SA* 1,2,3,4, 1963 *I, W*, 1964 *E, S*

Brooke, R M (Auckland) 1992 *I* 2, *A* 1,2,3, *SA*, 1993 *BI* 1,2,3, *A, WS*, 1994 *SA* 2,3, 1995 *C*, [*J, S, E, SA*], *A* 1,2, *It, F* 1,2, 1996 *WS, S* 1, 2, *A* 1, *SA* 1, *A* 2, *SA* 2,3,4,5, 1997 *Fj, Arg* 1,2, *A* 1, *SA* 1, *A* 2, *SA* 2, *A* 3, *I, E* 1, *W, E* 2, 1998 *E* 1,2, *A* 1, *SA* 1, *A* 2, *SA* 2, *A* 3
Brooke, Z V (Auckland) 1987 [*Arg*], 1989 *Arg* 2 (R), 1990 *A* 1,2,3, *F* 1 (R), 1991 *Arg* 2, *A* 1,2, [*E, It, C, A, S*], 1992 *A* 2,3, *SA*, 1993 *BI* 1,2,3 (R), *WS* (R), *S, E*, 1994 *F* 2, *SA* 1,2,3, *A*, 1995 *C*, [*J, S, E, SA*], *A* 1,2, *It, F* 1,2, 1996 *WS, S* 1,2, *A* 1, *SA* 1, *A* 2, *SA* 2,3,4,5, 1997 *Arg* 1,2, *A* 1, *SA* 1, *A* 2, *SA* 2, *A* 3, *I, E* 1, *W, E* 2
Brooke-Cowden, M (Auckland) 1986 *F* 1, *A* 1, 1987 [*W*]
Brown, C (Taranaki) 1913 *A* 2,3
Brown, O M (Auckland) 1992 *I* 2, *A* 1,2,3, *SA*, 1993 *BI* 1,2,3, *A, S, E*, 1994 *F* 1,2, *SA* 1,2,3, *A*, 1995 *C*, [*I, W, S, E, SA*], *A* 1,2, *It, F* 1,2, 1996 *WS, S* 1,2, *A* 1, *SA* 1, *A* 2, *SA* 2,3,4,5, 1997 *Fj, Arg* 1,2, *A* 1, *SA* 1, *A* 2, *SA* 2, *A* 3, *I, E* 1, *W, E* 2, 1998 *E* 1,2, *A* 1, *SA* 1, *A* 2, *SA* 2
Brown, R H (Taranaki) 1955 *A* 3, 1956 *SA* 1,2,3,4, 1957 *A* 1,2, 1958 *A* 1,2,3, 1959 *BI* 1,3, 1961 *F* 1,2,3, 1962 *A* 1
Brownlie, C J (Hawke's Bay) 1924 *W*, 1925 *E, F*
Brownlie, M J (Hawke's Bay) 1924 *I, W*, 1925 *E, F*, 1928 *SA* 1,2,3,4
Bruce, J A (Auckland) 1914 *A* 1,2
Bruce, O D (Canterbury) 1976 *SA* 1,2,4, 1977 *BI* 2,3,4, *F* 1,2, 1978 *A* 1,2, *I, W, E, S*
Bryers, R F (King Country) 1949 *A* 1
Budd, T A (Southland) 1946 *A* 2, 1949 *A* 2
Bullock-Douglas, G A H (Wanganui) 1932 *A* 1,2,3, 1934 *A* 1,2
Bunce, F E (North Harbour) 1992 *Wld* 1,2,3, *I* 1,2, *A* 1,2,3, *SA*, 1993 *BI* 1,2,3, *A, WS, S, E*, 1994 *F* 1,2, *SA* 1,2,3, *A*, 1995 *C*, [*I, W, S, E, SA*], *A* 1,2, *It, F* 1,2, 1996 *WS, S* 1,2, *A*1, *SA* 1, *A* 2, *SA* 2,3,4,5, 1997 *Fj, Arg* 1,2, *A* 1, *SA* 1, *A* 2, *SA* 2, *A* 3, *I, E* 1, *W, E* 2
Burgess, G A J (Auckland) 1981 *SA* 2
Burgess, G F (Southland) 1905 *A*
Burgess, R E (Manawatu) 1971 *BI* 1,2,3, 1972 *A* 3, *W*, 1973 *I, F*
Burke, P S (Taranaki) 1955 *A* 1, 1957 *A* 1,2
Burns, P J (Canterbury) 1908 *AW* 2, 1910 *A* 1,2,3, 1913 *A* 3
Bush, R G (Otago) 1931 *A*
Bush, W K (Canterbury) 1974 *A* 1,2, 1975 *S*, 1976 *I, SA*, 2,4, 1977 *BI* 2,3,4 (R), 1978 *I, W*, 1979 *A*
Buxton, J B (Canterbury) 1955 *A* 3, 1956 *SA* 1

Cain, M J (Taranaki) 1913 *US*, 1914 *A* 1,2,3
Callesen, J A (Manawatu) 1974 *A* 1,2,3, 1975 *S*
Cameron, D (Taranaki) 1908 *AW* 1,2,3
Cameron, L M (Manawatu) 1980 *A* 3, 1981 *SA* 1 (R), 2,3, *R*
Carleton, S R (Canterbury) 1928 *SA* 1,2,3, 1929 *A* 1,2,3
Carrington, K R (Auckland) 1971 *BI* 1,3,4
Carter, M P (Auckland) 1991 *A* 2, [*It, A*], 1997 *Fj* (R), *A* 1 (R), 1998 *E* 2 (R), *A* 2
Casey, S T (Otago) 1905 *S, I, E, W*, 1907 *A* 1,2,3, 1908 *AW* 1
Cashmore, A R (Auckland) 1996 *S2* (R), 1997 *A* 2 (R)
Catley, E H (Waikato) 1946 *A* 1, 1947 *A* 1,2, 1949 *SA* 1,2,3,4
Caughey, T H C (Auckland) 1932 *A* 1,3, 1934 *A* 1,2, 1935 *S, I*, 1936 *E, A* 1, 1937 *SA* 3
Caulton, R W (Wellington) 1959 *BI* 2,3,4, 1960 *SA* 1,4, 1961 *F* 2, 1963 *E* 1,2, *I, W*, 1964 *E, S, F, A* 1,2,3
Cherrington, N P (North Auckland) 1950 *BI* 1
Christian, D L (Auckland) 1949 *SA* 4
Clamp, M (Wellington) 1984 *A* 2,3
Clark, D W (Otago) 1964 *A* 1,2
Clark, W H (Wellington) 1953 *W*, 1954 *I, E, S*, 1955 *A* 1,2, 1956 *SA* 2,3,4
Clarke, A H (Auckland) 1958 *A* 3, 1959 *BI* 4, 1960 *SA* 1
Clarke, D B (Waikato) 1956 *SA* 3,4, 1957 *A* 1,2, 1958 *A* 1,3, 1959 *BI* 1,2,3,4, 1960 *SA* 1,2,3,4, 1961 *F* 1,2,3, 1962 *A* 1,2,3,4,5, 1963 *E* 1,2, *I, W*, 1964 *E, S, F, A* 2,3
Clarke, E (Auckland) 1992 *Wld* 2,3, *I* 1,2, *S* (R), *E*, 1998 *SA* 2, *A* 3

342

Clarke, I J (Waikato) 1953 *W*, 1955 *A* 1,2,3, 1956 *SA* 1,2,3,4, 1957 *A* 1,2, 1958 *A* 1,3, 1959 *BI* 1,2, 1960 *SA* 2,4, 1961 *F* 1,2,3, 1962 *A* 1,2,3, 1963 *E* 1,2
Clarke, R L (Taranaki) 1932 *A* 2,3
Cobden, D G (Canterbury) 1937 *SA* 1
Cockerill, M S (Taranaki) 1951 *A* 1,2,3
Cockroft, E A P (South Canterbury) 1913 *A* 3, 1914 *A* 2,3
Codlin, B W (Counties) 1980 *A* 1,2,3
Collins, A H (Taranaki) 1932 *A* 2,3, 1934 *A* 1
Collins, J L (Poverty Bay) 1964 *A* 1, 1965 *SA* 1,4
Colman, J T H (Taranaki) 1907 *A* 1,2, 1908 *AW* 1,3
Connor, D M (Auckland) 1961 *F* 1,2,3, 1962 *A* 1,2,3,4,5, 1963 *E* 1,2, 1964 *A* 2,3
Conway, R J (Otago, Bay of Plenty) 1959 *BI* 2,3,4, 1960 *SA* 1,3,4, 1965 *SA* 1,2,3,4
Cooke, A E (Auckland, Wellington) 1924 *I, W*, 1925 *E, F*, 1930 *BI* 1,2,3,4
Cooke, R J (Canterbury) 1903 *A*
Cooksley, M S B (Counties, Waikato) 1992 *Wld* 1, 1993 *BI* 2,3 (R), *A*, 1994 *F* 1,2, *SA* 1,2,4
Cooper, G J L (Auckland, Otago) 1986 *F* 1, *A* 1,2, 1992 *Wld* 1,2,3, *I* 1
Cooper, M J A (Waikato) 1992 *I* 2, *SA* (R), 1993 *BI* 1 (R), 3 (t), *WS* (t), *S*, 1994 *F* 1,2
Corner, M M N (Auckland) 1930 *BI* 2,3,4, 1931 *A*, 1934 *A* 1, 1936 *E*
Cossey, R R (Counties) 1958 *A* 1
Cottrell, A I (Canterbury) 1929 *A* 1,2,3, 1930 *BI* 1,2,3,4, 1931 *A*, 1932 *A* 1,2,3
Cottrell, W D (Canterbury) 1968 *A* 1,2, *F* 2,3, 1970 *SA* 1, 1971 *BI* 1,2,3,4
Couch, M B R (Wairarapa) 1947 *A* 1, 1949 *A* 1,2
Coughlan, T D (South Canterbury) 1958 *A* 1
Creighton, J N (Canterbury) 1962 *A* 4
Crichton, S (Wellington) 1983 *S, E*
Cross, T (Canterbury) 1904 *BI*, 1905 *A*
Crowley, K J (Taranaki) 1985 *E* 1,2, *A*, *Arg* 1,2, 1986 *A* 3, *F* 2,3, 1987 *[Arg]*, 1990 *S* 1,2, *A* 1,2,3, *F* 1,2, 1991 *Arg* 1,2, *[A]*
Crowley, P J B (Auckland) 1949 *SA* 3,4, 1950 *BI* 1,2,3,4
Culhane, S D (Southland) 1995 *[J]*, *It, F* 1,2, 1996 *SA* 3,4
Cullen C M (Manawatu, Central Vikings) 1996 *WS, S* 1,2, *A* 1, *SA* 1, *A* 2, *SA* 2,3,4,5, 1997 *Fj, Arg* 1,2, *A* 1, *A* 2, *SA* 2, 3, *I, E* 1, *W, E* 2, 1998 *E* 1,2, *A* 1, *SA* 1, *A* 2, *SA* 2, *A* 3
Cummings, W (Canterbury) 1913 *A* 2,3
Cundy, R T (Wairarapa) 1929 *A* 2 (R)
Cunningham, G R (Auckland) 1979 *A, S, E*, 1980 *A* 1,2
Cunningham, W (Auckland) 1905 *S, I*, 1906 *F*, 1907 *A* 1,2,3, 1908 *AW* 1,2,3
Cupples, L F (Bay of Plenty) 1924 *I, W*
Currie, C J (Canterbury) 1978 *I, W*
Cuthill, J E (Otago) 1913 *A* 1, *US*

Dalley, W C (Canterbury) 1924 *I*, 1928 *SA* 1,2,3,4
Dalton, A G (Counties) 1977 *F* 2, 1978 *A* 1,2,3, *I, W, E, S*, 1979 *F* 1,2, *S*, 1981 *S* 1,2, *SA* 1,2,3, *R, F* 1,2, 1982 *A* 1,2,3, 1983 *BI* 1,2,3,4, *A*, 1984 *F* 1,2, *A* 1,2,3, 1985 *E* 1,2, *A*
Dalton, D (Hawke's Bay) 1935 *I, W*, 1936 *A* 1,2, 1937 *SA* 1,2,3, 1938 *A* 1,2
Dalton, R A (Wellington) 1947 *A* 1,2
Dalzell, G N (Canterbury) 1953 *W*, 1954 *I, E, S, F*
Davie, M G (Canterbury) 1983 *E* (R)
Davies, W A (Auckland, Otago) 1960 *SA* 4, 1962 *A* 4,5
Davis, K (Auckland) 1952 *A* 2, 1953 *W*, 1954 *I, E, S, F*, 1955 *A* 2, 1958 *A* 1,2,3
Davis, L J (Canterbury) 1976 *I*, 1977 *BI* 3,4
Davis, W L (Hawke's Bay) 1967 *A, E, W, F, S*, 1968 *A* 1,2, *F* 1, 1969 *W* 1,2, 1970 *SA* 2
Deans, I B (Canterbury) 1988 *W* 1,2, *A* 1,2,3, 1989 *F* 1,2, *Arg* 1,2, *A*
Deans, R G (Canterbury) 1905 *S, I, E, W*, 1908 *AW* 3
Deans, R M (Canterbury) 1983 *S, E*, 1984 *A* 1 (R), 2,3
Delamore, G W (Wellington) 1949 *SA* 4
Dewar, H (Taranaki) 1913 *A* 1, *US*
Diack, E S (Otago) 1959 *BI* 2
Dick, J (Auckland) 1937 *SA* 1,2, 1938 *A* 3
Dick, M J (Auckland) 1963 *I, W*, 1964 *E, S, F*, 1965 *SA* 3, 1966 *BI* 4, 1967 *A, E, W, F*, 1969 *W* 1,2, 1970 *SA* 1,4
Dixon, M J (Canterbury) 1954 *I, E, S, F*, 1956 *A* 1,2,3,4, 1957 *A* 1,2

Dobson, R L (Auckland) 1949 *A* 1
Dodd, E H (Wellington) 1905 *A*
Donald, A J (Wanganui) 1983 *S, E*, 1984 *F* 1,2, *A* 1,2,3
Donald, J G (Wairarapa) 1921 *SA* 1,2
Donald, Q (Wairarapa) 1924 *I, W*, 1925 *E, F*
Donaldson, M W (Manawatu) 1977 *F* 1,2, 1978 *A* 1,2,3, *I, E, S*, 1979 *F* 1,2, *A, S* (R), 1981 *SA* 3 (R)
Dougan, J P (Wellington) 1972 *A* 1, 1973 *E* 2
Dowd, C W (Auckland) 1993 *BI* 1,2,3, *A, WS, S, E*, 1994 *SA* 1 (R), 1995 *C*, *[I, W, J, E, SA]*, *A* 1,2, *It, F* 1,2, 1996 *WS, S* 1,2, *A* 1, *SA* 1, *A* 2, *SA* 2,3,4,5, 1997 *Fj, Arg* 1,2, *A* 1, *SA* 1, *A* 2, *SA* 2, *A* 3, *I, E* 1, *W*, 1998 *E* 1,2, *A* 1, *SA* 1, *A* 2,3 (R)
Dowd, G W (North Harbour) 1992 *I* 1 (R)
Downing, A J (Auckland) 1913 *A* 1, *US*, 1914 *A* 1,2,3
Drake, J A (Auckland) 1986 *F* 2,3, 1987 *[Fj, Arg, S, W, F]*, *A*
Duff, R H (Canterbury) 1951 *A* 1,2,3, 1952 *A* 1,2, 1955 *A* 2,3, 1956 *SA* 1,2,3,4
Duncan, J (Otago) 1903 *A*
Duncan, M G (Hawke's Bay) 1971 *BI* 3 (R), 4
Duncan, W D (Otago) 1921 *SA* 1,2,3
Dunn, E J (North Auckland) 1979 *S*, 1981 *S* 1
Dunn, I T W (North Auckland) 1983 *BI* 1,4, *A*
Dunn, J M (Auckland) 1946 *A* 1

Earl, A T (Canterbury) 1986 *F* 1, *A* 1, *F* 3 (R), 1987 *[Arg]*, 1989 *W, I*, 1991 *Arg* 1 (R), 2, *A* 1, *[E* (R), *US, S]*, 1992 *A* 2,3 (R)
Eastgate, B P (Canterbury) 1952 *A* 1,2, 1954 *S*
Elliott, K G (Wellington) 1946 *A* 1,2
Ellis, M C G (Otago) 1993 *S, E*, 1995 *C*, *[I* (R), *W, J, S, SA* (R)]
Elsom, A E G (Canterbury) 1952 *A* 1,2, 1953 *W*, 1955 *A* 1,2,3
Elvidge, R R (Otago) 1946 *A* 1,2, 1949 *SA* 1,2,3,4, 1950 *BI* 1,2,3
Erceg, C P (Auckland) 1951 *A* 1,2,3, 1952 *A* 1
Evans, D A (Hawke's Bay) 1910 *A* 2
Eveleigh, K A (Manawatu) 1976 *SA* 2,4, 1977 *BI* 1,2

Fanning, A H N (Canterbury) 1913 *A* 3
Fanning, B J (Canterbury) 1903 *A*, 1904 *BI*
Farrell, C P (Auckland) 1977 *BI* 1,2
Fawcett, C L (Auckland) 1976 *SA* 2,3
Fea, W R (Otago) 1921 *SA* 3
Finlay, B E L (Manawatu) 1959 *BI* 1
Finlay, J (Manawatu) 1946 *A* 1
Finlayson, I (North Auckland) 1928 *SA* 1,2,3,4, 1930 *BI* 1,2
Fitzgerald, J T (Wellington) 1952 *A* 1
Fitzpatrick, B B J (Wellington) 1953 *W*, 1954 *I, F*
Fitzpatrick, S B T (Auckland) 1986 *F* 1, *A* 1, *F* 2,3, 1987 *[It, Fj, Arg, S, W, F]*, *A*, 1988 *W* 1,2, *A* 1,2,3, 1989 *F* 1,2, *Arg* 1,2, *A, W, I*, 1990 *S* 1,2, *A* 1,2,3, *F* 1,2, 1991 *Arg* 1,2, *A* 1,2, *[E, US, It, C, A, S]*, 1992 *Wld* 1,2,3, *I* 1,2, *A* 1,2,3, *SA*, 1993 *BI* 1,2,3, *A, WS, S, E*, 1994 *F* 1,2, *SA* 1,2,3, *A*, 1995 *C*, *[I, W, S, E, SA]*, *A* 1,2, *It, F* 1,2, 1996 *WS, S* 1,2, *A* 1, *SA* 1, *A* 2, *SA* 2,3,4,5, 1997 *Fj, Arg* 1,2, *A* 1, *SA* 1, *A* 2, *SA* 2, *A* 3, *W* (R)
Fleming, J K (Wellington) 1979 *S, E*, 1980 *A* 1,2,3
Fletcher, C J C (North Auckland) 1921 *SA* 3
Fogarty, R (Taranaki) 1921 *SA* 1,3
Ford, B R (Marlborough) 1977 *BI* 3,4, 1978 *I*, 1979 *E*
Forster, S T (Otago) 1993 *S, E*, 1994 *F* 1,2, 1995 *It, F* 1
Fox, G J (Auckland) 1985 *Arg* 1, 1987 *[It, Fj, Arg, S, W, F]*, *A*, 1988 *W* 1,2, *A* 1,2,3, 1989 *F* 1,2, *Arg* 1,2, *A, W, I*, 1990 *S* 1,2, *A* 1,2,3, *F* 1,2, 1991 *Arg* 1,2, *A* 1,2, *[E, It, C, A]*, 1992 *Wld* 1,2 (R), *A* 1,2,3, *SA*, 1993 *BI* 1,2,3, *A, WS*
Francis, A R H (Auckland) 1905 *A*, 1907 *A* 1,2,3, 1908 *AW* 1,2,3, 1910 *A* 1,2,3
Francis, W C (Wellington) 1913 *A* 2,3, 1914 *A* 1,2,3
Fraser, B G (Wellington) 1979 *S, E*, 1980 *A* 3, *W*, 1981 *S* 1,2, *SA* 1,2,3, *R, F* 1,2, 1982 *A* 1,2,3, 1983 *BI* 1,2,3,4, *A, S, E*, 1984 *A* 1
Frazer, H F (Hawke's Bay) 1946 *A* 1,2, 1947 *A* 1,2, 1949 *SA* 2
Fryer, F C (Canterbury) 1907 *A* 1,2,3, 1908 *AW* 2
Fuller, W B (Canterbury) 1910 *A* 1,2
Furlong, B D M (Hawke's Bay) 1970 *SA* 4

Gallagher, J A (Wellington) 1987 *[It, Fj, S, W, F]*, *A*, 1988 *W* 1,2, *A* 1,2,3, 1989 *F* 1,2, *Arg* 1,2, *A, W, I*

343

Gallaher, D (Auckland) 1903 *A*, 1904 *BI*, 1905 *S, E, W,* 1906 *F*
Gard, P C (North Otago) 1971 *BI* 4
Gardiner, A J (Taranaki) 1974 *A* 3
Geddes, J H (Southland) 1929 *A* 1
Geddes, W McK (Auckland) 1913 *A* 2
Gemmell, B McL (Auckland) 1974 *A* 1,2
George, V L (Southland) 1938 *A* 1,2,3
Gilbert, G D M (West Coast) 1935 *S, I, W,* 1936 *E*
Gillespie, C T (Wellington) 1913 *A* 2
Gillespie, W D (Otago) 1958 *A* 3
Gillett, G A (Canterbury, Auckland) 1905 *S, I, E, W,* 1907 *A* 2,3, 1908 *AW* 1,3
Gillies, C C (Otago) 1936 *A* 2
Gilray, C M (Otago) 1905 *A*
Glasgow, F T (Taranaki, Southland) 1905 *S, I, E, W,* 1906 *F*, 1908 *AW* 3
Glenn, W S (Taranaki) 1904 *BI*, 1906 *F*
Goddard, M P (South Canterbury) 1946 *A* 2, 1947 *A* 1,2, 1949 *SA* 3,4
Going, S M (North Auckland) 1967 *A, F*, 1968 *F* 3, 1969 *W* 1,2, 1970 *SA* 1 (R), 4, 1971 *BI* 1,2,3,4, 1972 *A* 1,2,3, *W, S*, 1973 *E* 1, *I, F, E* 2, 1974 *I*, 1975 *S*, 1976 *I* (R), *SA* 1,2,3,4, 1977 *BI* 1,2
Gordon, S B (Waikato) 1993 *S, E*
Graham, D J (Canterbury) 1958 *A* 1,2, 1960 *SA* 2,3, 1961 *F* 1,2,3, 1962 *A* 1,2,3,4,5, 1963 *E* 1,2, *I, W,* 1964 *E, S, F, A* 1,2,3
Graham, J B (Otago) 1913 *US*, 1914 *A* 1,3
Graham, W G (Otago) 1979 *F* 1 (R)
Grant, L A (South Canterbury) 1947 *A* 1,2, 1949 *SA* 1,2
Gray, G D (Canterbury) 1908 *AW* 2, 1913 *A* 1, *US*
Gray, K F (Wellington) 1963 *I, W,* 1964 *E, S, F, A* 1,2,3, 1965 *SA* 1,2,3,4, 1966 *BI* 1,2,3,4, 1967 *W, F, S,* 1968 *A* 1, *F* 2,3, 1969 *W* 1,2
Gray, W N (Bay of Plenty) 1955 *A* 2,3, 1956 *SA* 1,2,3,4
Green, C I (Canterbury) 1983 *S* (R), *E*, 1984 *A* 1,2,3, 1985 *E* 1,2, *A, Arg* 1,2, 1986 *A* 2,3, *F* 2,3, 1987 [*It, Fj, S, W, F*], *A*
Grenside, B A (Hawke's Bay) 1928 *SA* 1,2,3,4, 1929 *A* 2,3
Griffiths, J L (Wellington) 1934 *A* 2, 1935 *S, I, W,* 1936 *A* 1,2, 1938 *A* 3
Guy, R A (North Auckland) 1971 *BI* 1,2,3,4

Haden, A M (Auckland) 1977 *BI* 1,2,3,4, *F* 1,2, 1978 *A* 1,2,3, *I, W, E, S,* 1979 *F* 1,2, *A, S, E,* 1980 *A* 1,2,3, *W,* 1981 *S* 2, *SA* 1,2,3, *R, F* 1,2, 1982 *A* 1,2,3, 1983 *BI* 1,2,3,4, *A,* 1984 *F* 1,2, 1985 *Arg* 1,2
Hadley, S (Auckland) 1928 *SA* 1,2,3,4
Hadley, W E (Auckland) 1934 *A* 1,2, 1935 *S, I, W,* 1936 *E, A* 1,2
Haig, J S (Otago) 1946 *A* 1,2
Haig, L S (Otago) 1950 *BI* 2,3,4, 1951 *A* 1,2,3, 1953 *W,* 1954 *E, S*
Hales, D A (Canterbury) 1972 *A* 1,2,3, *W*
Hamilton, D C (Southland) 1908 *AW* 2
Hammond, I A (Marlborough) 1952 *A* 2
Harper, E T (Canterbury) 1904 *BI*, 1906 *F*
Harris, P C (Manawatu) 1976 *SA* 3
Hart, A H (Taranaki) 1924 *I*
Hart, G F (Canterbury) 1930 *BI* 1,2,3,4, 1931 *A*, 1934 *A* 1, 1935 *S, I, W,* 1936 *A* 1,2
Harvey, B A (Wairarapa-Bush) 1986 *F* 1
Harvey, I H (Wairarapa) 1928 *SA* 4
Harvey, L R (Otago) 1949 *SA* 1,2,3,4, 1950 *BI* 1,2,3,4
Harvey, P (Canterbury) 1904 *BI*
Hasell, E W (Canterbury) 1913 *A* 2,3
Hayward, H O (Auckland) 1908 *AW* 3
Hazlett, E J (Southland) 1966 *BI* 1,2,3,4, 1967 *A, E*
Hazlett, W E (Southland) 1928 *SA* 1,2,3,4, 1930 *BI* 1,2,3,4
Heeps, T R (Wellington) 1962 *A* 1,2,3,4,5
Heke, W R (North Auckland) 1929 *A* 1,2,3
Hemi, R C (Waikato) 1953 *W,* 1954 *I, E, S, F,* 1955 *A* 1,2,3, 1956 *SA* 1,3,4, 1957 *A* 1,2, 1959 *BI* 1,3,4
Henderson, P (Wanganui) 1949 *SA* 1,2,3,4, 1950 *BI* 2,3,4
Henderson, P W (Otago) 1991 *Arg* 1, [*C*], 1992 *Wld* 1,2,3, *I* 1, 1995 [*J*]
Herewini, M A (Auckland) 1962 *A* 5, 1963 *I*, 1964 *S, F,* 1965 *SA* 4, 1966 *BI* 1,2,3,4, 1967 *A*
Hewett, J A (Auckland) 1991 [*It*]

Hewitt, N J (Southland) 1995 [*I* (t), *J*], 1996 *A* 1 (R), 1997 *SA* 1 (R), *I, E* 1, *W, E* 2, 1998 *E* 2 (t + R)
Hewson, A R (Wellington) 1981 *S* 1,2, *SA* 1,2,3, *R, F* 1,2, 1982 *A* 1,2,3, 1983 *BI* 1,2,3,4, *A,* 1984 *F* 1,2, *A* 1
Higginson, G (Canterbury, Hawke's Bay) 1980 *W,* 1981 *S* 1, *SA* 1, 1982 *A* 1,2, 1983 *A*
Hill, S F (Canterbury) 1955 *A* 3, 1956 *SA* 1,3,4, 1957 *A* 1,2, 1958 *A* 3, 1959 *BI* 1,2,3,4
Hines, G R (Waikato) 1980 *A* 3
Hobbs, M J B (Canterbury) 1983 *BI* 1,2,3,4, *A, S, E,* 1984 *F* 1,2, *A* 1,2,3, 1985 *E* 1,2, *A, Arg* 1,2, 1986 *A* 2,3, *F* 2,3
Hoeft, C H (Otago) 1998 *E* 2 (t + R), *A* 2 (R), *SA* 2, *A* 3
Holder, E C (Buller) 1934 *A* 2
Hook, L S (Auckland) 1929 *A* 1,2,3
Hooper, J A (Canterbury) 1937 *SA* 1,2,3
Hopkinson, A E (Canterbury) 1967 *S*, 1968 *A* 2, *F* 1,2,3, 1969 *W* 2, 1970 *SA* 1,2,3
Hore, J (Otago) 1930 *BI* 2,3,4, 1932 *A* 1,2,3, 1934 *A* 1,2, 1935 *S,* 1936 *E*
Horsley, R H (Wellington) 1960 *SA* 2,3,4
Hotop, J (Canterbury) 1952 *A* 1,2, 1955 *A* 3
Howarth, S P (Auckland) 1994 *SA* 1,2,3, *A*
Hughes, A M (Auckland) 1949 *A* 1,2, 1950 *BI* 1,2,3,4
Hughes, E (Southland, Wellington) 1907 *A* 1,2,3, 1908 *AW* 1, 1921 *SA* 1,2
Hunter, B A (Otago) 1971 *BI* 1,2,3
Hunter, J (Taranaki) 1905 *S, I, E, W,* 1906 *F,* 1907 *A* 1,2,3, 1908 *AW* 1,2,3
Hurst, I A (Canterbury) 1973 *I, F, E* 2, 1974 *A* 1,2

Ieremia, A I (Wellington) 1994 *SA* 1,2,3, 1995 [*J*], 1996 *SA* 2 (R), 5 (R), 1997 *A* 1 (R), *SA* 1 (R), *A* 2, *SA* 2, *A* 3, *I, E* 1
Ifwersen, K D (Auckland) 1921 *SA* 3
Innes, C R (Auckland) 1989 *W, I,* 1990 *A* 1,2,3, *F* 1,2, 1991 *Arg* 1,2, *A* 1,2, [*E, US, It, C, A, S*]
Innes, G D (Canterbury) 1932 *A* 2
Irvine, I B (North Auckland) 1952 *A* 1
Irvine, J G (Otago) 1914 *A* 1,2,3
Irvine, W R (Hawke's Bay, Wairarapa) 1924 *I, W,* 1925 *E, F,* 1930 *BI* 1
Irwin, M W (Otago) 1955 *A* 1,2, 1956 *SA* 1, 1958 *A* 2, 1959 *BI* 3,4, 1960 *SA* 1

Jackson, E S (Hawke's Bay) 1936 *A* 1,2, 1937 *SA* 1,2,3, 1938 *A* 3
Jaffray, J L (Otago, South Canterbury) 1972 *A* 2, 1975 *S*, 1976 *I, SA* 1, 1977 *BI* 2, 1979 *F* 1,2
Jarden, R A (Wellington) 1951 *A* 1,2, 1952 *A* 1,2, 1953 *W,* 1954 *I, E, S, F,* 1955 *A* 1,2,3, 1956 *SA* 1,2,3,4
Jefferd, A C R (East Coast) 1981 *S* 1,2, *SA* 1
Jessep, E M (Wellington) 1931 *A*, 1932 *A* 1
Johnson, L M (Wellington) 1928 *SA* 1,2,3,4
Johnston, W (Otago) 1907 *A* 1,2,3
Johnstone, B R (Auckland) 1976 *SA* 2, 1977 *BI* 1,2, *F* 1,2, 1978 *I, W, E, S,* 1979 *F* 1,2, *S, E*
Johnstone, P (Otago) 1949 *SA* 2,4, 1950 *BI* 1,2,3,4, 1951 *A* 1,2,3
Jones, I D (North Auckland, North Harbour) 1990 *S* 1,2, *A* 1,2,3, *F* 1,2, 1991 *Arg* 1,2, *A* 1,2, [*E, US, It, C, A, S*], 1992 *Wld* 1,2,3, *I* 1,2, *A* 1,2,3, *SA*, 1993 *BI* 1,2 (R), 3, *WS, S, E,* 1994 *F* 1,2, *SA* 1,3, *A,* 1995 *C,* [*I, W, S, E, SA*], *A* 1,2, *It, F* 1,2, 1996 *WS, S* 1,2, *A* 1, *SA* 1, *A* 2, *SA* 2,3,4,5, 1997 *Fj, Arg* 1,2, *A* 1, *SA* 1, *A* 2, *SA* 2, *A* 3, *I, E* 1, *W, E* 2, 1998 *E* 1,2, *A* 1, *SA* 1, *A* 2,3 (R)
Jones, M G (North Auckland) 1973 *E* 2
Jones, M N (Auckland) 1987 [*It, Fj, S, F*], *A,* 1988 *W* 1,2, *A* 2,3, 1989 *F* 1,2, *Arg* 1,2, 1990 *F* 1,2, 1991 *Arg* 1,2, *A* 1,2, [*E, US, S*], 1992 *Wld* 1,3, *I* 2, *A* 1,3, *SA,* 1993 *BI* 1,2,3, *A, WS,* 1994 *SA* 3 (R), *A,* 1995 *A* 1 (R), 2, *It, F* 1,2, 1996 *WS, S* 1,2, *A* 1, *SA* 1, *A* 2, *SA* 2,3,4,5, 1997 *Fj,* 1998 *E* 1, *A* 1, *SA* 1, *A* 2
Jones, P F H (North Auckland) 1954 *E, S,* 1955 *A* 1,2, 1956 *SA* 3,4, 1958 *A* 1,2,3, 1959 *BI* 1, 1960 *SA* 1
Joseph, H T (Canterbury) 1971 *BI* 2,3
Joseph, J W (Otago) 1992 *Wld* 2,3 (R), *I* 1, *A* 1 (R), 3, *SA,* 1993 *BI* 1,2,3, *A, WS, S, E,* 1994 *SA* 2 (t), 1995 *C,* [*I, W, J* (R), *S, SA* (R)]

Karam, J F (Wellington, Horowhenua) 1972 *W, S,* 1973 *E* 1, *I, F,* 1974 *A* 1,2,3, *I,* 1975 *S*
Katene, T (Wellington) 1955 *A* 2
Kearney, J C (Otago) 1947 *A* 2, 1949 *SA* 1,2,3

Kelly, J W (Auckland) 1949 *A* 1,2
Kember, G F (Wellington) 1970 *SA* 4
Ketels, R C (Counties) 1980 *W*, 1981 *S* 1,2, *R*, *F* 1
Kiernan, H A D (Auckland) 1903 *A*
Kilby, F D (Wellington) 1932 *A* 1,2,3, 1934 *A* 2
Killeen, B A (Auckland) 1936 *A* 1
King, R R (West Coast) 1934 *A* 2, 1935 *S, I, W*, 1936 *E, A* 1,2, 1937 *SA* 1,2,3, 1938 *A* 1,2,3
Kingstone, C N (Taranaki) 1921 *SA* 1,2,3
Kirk, D E (Auckland) 1985 *E* 1,2, *A, Arg* 1, 1986 *F* 1, *A* 1,2,3, *F* 2,3, 1987 [*It, Fj, Arg, S, W, F*], *A*
Kirkpatrick, I A (Canterbury, Poverty Bay) 1967 *F*, 1968 *A* 1 (R), 2, *F* 1,2,3, 1969 *W* 1,2, 1970 *SA* 1,2,3,4, 1971 *BI* 1,2,3,4, 1972 *A* 1,2,3, *W, S*, 1973 *E* 1, *I, F, E* 2, 1974 *A* 1,2,3, *I* 1975 *S*, 1976 *I, SA* 1,2,3,4, 1977 *BI* 1,2,3,4
Kirton, E W (Otago) 1967 *E, W, F, S*, 1968 *A* 1,2, *F* 1,2,3, 1969 *W* 1,2, 1970 *SA* 2,3
Kirwan, J J (Auckland) 1984 *F* 1,2, 1985 *E* 1,2, *A, Arg* 1,2, 1986 *F* 1, *A* 1,2,3, *F* 2,3, 1987 [*It, Fj, Arg, S, W, F*], *A*, 1988 *W* 1,2, *A* 1,2,3, 1989 *F* 1,2, *Arg* 1,2, *A*, 1990 *S* 1,2, *A* 1,2,3, *F* 1,2, 1991 *Arg* 2, *A* 1,2, [*E, It, C, A, S*], 1992 *Wld* 1,2 (R), 3, *I* 1,2, *A* 1,2,3, *SA*, 1993 *BI* 2,3, *A*, *WS*, 1994 *F* 1,2, *SA* 1,2,3
Kivell, A L (Taranaki) 1929 *A* 2,3
Knight, A (Auckland) 1934 *A* 1
Knight, G A (Manawatu) 1977 *F* 1,2, 1978 *A* 1,2,3, *E, S*, 1979 *F* 1,2, *A*, 1980 *A* 1,2,3, *W*, 1981 *S* 1,2, *SA* 1,3, 1982 *A* 1,2,3, 1983 *BI* 1,2,3,4, *A*, 1984 *F* 1,2, *A* 1,2,3, 1985 *E* 1,2, *A*, 1986 *A* 2,3
Knight, L G (Poverty Bay) 1977 *BI* 1,2,3,4, *F* 1,2
Koteka, T T (Waikato) 1981 *F* 2, 1982 *A* 3
Kreft, A J (Otago) 1968 *A* 2
Kronfeld, J A (Otago) 1995 *C*, [*I, W, S, E, SA*], *A* 1,2 (R) 1996 *WS, S* 1,2, *A* 1, *SA* 1, *A* 2, *SA* 2,3,4,5, 1997 *Fj, Arg* 1,2, *A* 1, *SA* 1, *A* 2, *SA* 2, *A* 3, *I* (R), *E* 1, *W, E* 2, 1998 *E* 1,2, *A* 1, *SA* 1,2 *A* 3

Laidlaw, C R (Otago, Canterbury) 1964 *F, A* 1, 1965 *SA* 1,2,3,4, 1966 *BI* 1,2,3,4, 1967 *E, W, S*, 1968 *A* 1,2, *F* 1,2, 1970 *SA* 1,2,3
Laidlaw, K F (Southland) 1960 *SA* 2,3,4
Lambert, K K (Manawatu) 1972 *S* (R), 1973 *E* 1, *I, F, E* 2, 1974 *I*, 1976 *SA* 1,3,4, 1977 *BI* 1,4
Lambourn, A (Wellington) 1934 *A* 1,2, 1935 *S, I, W*, 1936 *E*, 1937 *SA* 1,2,3, 1938 *A* 3
Larsen, B P (North Harbour) 1992 *Wld* 2,3, *I* 1, 1994 *F* 1,2, *SA* 1,2,3, *A* (t), 1995 [*I, W, J, E*(R)], *It, F* 1, 1996 *S* 2 (t), *SA* 4 (R)
Le Lievre, J M (Canterbury) 1962 *A* 4
Lendrum, R N (Counties) 1973 *E* 2
Leslie, A R (Wellington) 1974 *A* 1,2,3, *I*, 1975 *S*, 1976 *I, SA* 1,2,3,4
Leys, E T (Wellington) 1929 *A* 3
Lilburne, H T (Canterbury, Wellington) 1928 *SA* 3,4, 1929 *A* 1,2,3, 1930 *BI* 1,4, 1931 *A*, 1932 *A* 1, 1934 *A* 2
Lindsay, D F (Otago) 1928 *SA* 1,2,3
Lineen, T R (Auckland) 1957 *A* 1,2, 1958 *A* 1,2,3, 1959 *BI* 1,2,3,4, 1960 *SA* 1,2,3
Lister, T N (South Canterbury) 1968 *A* 1,2, *F* 1, 1969 *W* 1,2, 1970 *SA* 1,4, 1971 *BI* 4
Little, P F (Auckland) 1961 *F* 2,3, 1962 *A* 2,3,5, 1963 *I, W*, 1964 *E, S, F*
Little, W K (North Harbour) 1990 *S* 1,2, *A* 1,2,3, *F* 1,2, 1991 *Arg* 1,2, *A* 1, [*It, S*], 1992 *Wld* 1,2,3, *I* 1,2,3, *SA*, 1993 *BI* 1, *WS* (R), 1994 *SA* 2 (R), *A*, 1995 *C*, [*I, W, S, E, SA*], *A* 1,2, *It, F* 1,2, 1996 *S* 2, *A* 1, *SA* 1, *A* 2, *SA* 2,3,4,5, 1997 *W, E* 2, 1998 *E* 1, *A* 1, *SA* 2, *A* 2
Loader, C J (Wellington) 1954 *I, E, S, F*
Lochore, B J (Wairarapa) 1964 *E, S*, 1965 *SA* 1,2,3,4, 1966 *BI* 1,2,3,4, 1967 *A, E, W, F, S*, 1968 *A* 1, *F* 2,3, 1969 *W* 1,2, 1970 *SA* 1,2,3,4, 1971 *BI* 3
Loe, R W (Waikato, Canterbury) 1987 [*It, Arg*], 1988 *W* 1,2, *A* 1,2,3, 1989 *F* 1,2, *Arg* 1,2, *A, W*, 1990 *S* 1,2, *A* 1,2,3, *F* 1,2, 1991 *Arg* 1,2, *A* 1,2, [*E, It, C, A, S*], 1992 *Wld* 1,2,3, *I* 1, *A* 1,2,3, *SA*, 1994 *F* 1,2, *SA* 1,2,3, *A*, 1995 [*J, S, SA* (R)], *A* 2 (t), *F* 2 (R)
Lomu, J T (Counties) 1994 *F* 1,2, 1995 [*I, W, S, E, SA*], *A* 1,2, *It, F* 1,2, 1996 *WS, S* 1, *A* 1, *SA* 1, *A* 2, 1997 *E* 1, *W, E* 2, 1998 *E* 1,2, *A* 1 (R), *SA* 1, *A* 2, *SA* 2, *A* 3
Long, A J (Auckland) 1903 *A*
Loveridge, D S (Taranaki) 1978 *W*, 1979 *S, E*, 1980 *A* 1,2,3, *W*, 1981 *S* 1,2, *SA* 1,2,3, *R, F* 1,2, 1982 *A* 1,2,3, 1983 *BI* 1,2,3,4, *A*, 1985 *Arg* 2

Lucas, F W (Auckland) 1924 *I*, 1925 *F*, 1928 *SA* 4, 1930 *BI* 1,2,3,4
Lunn, W A (Otago) 1949 *A* 1,2
Lynch, T W (South Canterbury) 1913 *A* 1, 1914 *A* 1,2,3
Lynch, T W (Canterbury) 1951 *A* 1,2,3

McAtamney, F S (Otago) 1956 *SA* 2
McCahill, B J (Auckland) 1987 [*Arg, S* (R), *W* (R)], 1989 *Arg* 1 (R), 2 (R), 1991 *A* 2, [*E, US, C, A*]
McCaw, W A (Southland) 1951 *A* 1,2,3, 1953 *W*, 1954 *F*
McCool, M J (Wairarapa-Bush) 1979 *A*
McCormick, W F (Canterbury) 1965 *SA* 4, 1967 *E, W, F, S*, 1968 *A* 1,2, *F* 1,2,3, 1969 *W* 1,2, 1970 *SA* 1,2,3, 1971 *BI* 1
McCullough, J F (Taranaki) 1959 *BI* 2,3,4
McDonald, A (Otago) 1905 *S, I, E, W*, 1907 *A* 1, 1908 *AW* 1, 1913 *A* 1, *US*
Macdonald, H H (Canterbury, North Auckland) 1972 *W, S*, 1973 *E* 1, *I, F, E* 2, 1974 *I*, 1975 *S*, 1976 *I, SA* 1,2,3
McDowell, S C (Auckland, Bay of Plenty) 1985 *Arg* 1,2, 1986 *A* 2,3, *F* 2,3, 1987 [*It, Fj, S, W, F*], *A*, 1988 *W* 1,2, *A* 1,2,3, 1989 *F* 1,2, *Arg* 1,2, *A, W, I*, 1990 *S* 1,2, *A* 1,2,3, *F* 1,2, 1991 *Arg* 1,2, *A* 1,2, [*E, US, It, C, A, S*], 1992 *I* 1,2
McEldowney, J T (Taranaki) 1977 *BI* 3,4
MacEwan, I N (Wellington) 1956 *SA* 2, 1957 *A* 1,2, 1958 *A* 1,2,3, 1959 *BI* 1,2,3, 1960 *SA* 1,2,3,4, 1961 *F* 1,2,3, 1962 *A* 1,2,3,4
McGrattan, B (Wellington) 1983 *S, E*, 1985 *Arg* 1,2, 1986 *F* 1, *A* 1
McGregor, A J (Auckland) 1913 *A* 1, *US*
McGregor, D (Canterbury, Southland) 1903 *A*, 1904 *BI*, 1905 *E, W*
McGregor, N P (Canterbury) 1924 *W*, 1925 *E*
McGregor, R W (Auckland) 1903 *A*, 1904 *BI*
McHugh, M J (Auckland) 1946 *A* 1,2, 1949 *SA* 3
McIntosh, D N (Wellington) 1956 *SA* 1,2, 1957 *A* 1,2
McKay, D W (Auckland) 1961 *F* 1,2,3, 1963 *E* 1,2
McKechnie, B J (Southland) 1977 *F* 1,2, 1978 *A* 2 (R), 3, *W* (R), *E, S*, 1979 *A*, 1981 *SA* 1 (R), *F* 1
McKellar, G F (Wellington) 1910 *A* 1,2,3
McKenzie, R J (Wellington) 1913 *A* 1, *US*, 1914 *A* 2,3
McKenzie, R McC (Manawatu) 1934 *A* 1, 1935 *S*, 1936 *A* 1, 1937 *SA* 1,2,3, 1938 *A* 1,2,3
McLachlan, J S (Auckland) 1974 *A* 2
McLaren, H C (Waikato) 1952 *A* 1
McLean, A L (Bay of Plenty) 1921 *SA* 2,3
McLean, H F (Wellington, Auckland) 1930 *BI* 3,4, 1932 *A* 1,2,3, 1934 *A* 1, 1935 *I, W*, 1936 *E*
McLean, J K (King Country, Auckland) 1947 *A* 1, 1949 *A* 2
McLeod, B E (Counties) 1964 *A* 1,2,3, 1965 *SA* 1,2,3,4, 1966 *BI* 1,2,3,4, 1967 *E, W, F, S*, 1968 *A* 1,2, *F* 1,2,3, 1969 *W* 1,2, 1970 *SA* 1,2
McLeod, S J (Waikato) 1996 *WS, S* 1, 1997 *Fj* (R), *Arg* 2 (t + R), *I* (R), *E* 1 (R), *W* (t), *E* 2 (R), 1998 *A* 1, *SA* 1 (R)
McMinn, A F (Wairarapa, Manawatu) 1903 *A*, 1905 *A*
McMinn, F A (Manawatu) 1904 *BI*
McMullen, R F (Auckland) 1957 *A* 1,2, 1958 *A* 1,2,3, 1959 *BI* 1,2,3, 1960 *SA* 2,3,4
McNab, J R (Otago) 1949 *SA* 1,2,3, 1950 *BI* 1,2,3
McNaughton, A M (Bay of Plenty) 1971 *BI* 1,2,3
McNeece, J (Southland) 1913 *A* 2,3, 1914 *A* 1,2,3
McPhail, B E (Canterbury) 1959 *BI* 1,4
Macpherson, D G (Otago) 1905 *A*
MacPherson, G L (Otago) 1986 *F* 1
MacRae, I R (Hawke's Bay) 1966 *BI* 1,2,3,4, 1967 *A, E, W, F, S*, 1968 *F* 1,2, 1969 *W* 1,2, 1970 *SA* 1,2,3,4
McRae, J A (Southland) 1946 *A* 1 (R), 2
McWilliams, R G (Auckland) 1928 *SA* 2,3,4, 1929 *A* 1,2,3, 1930 *BI* 1,2,3,4
Mackrell, W H C (Auckland) 1906 *F*
Macky, J V (Auckland) 1913 *A* 2
Maguire, J R (Auckland) 1910 *A* 1,2,3
Mahoney, A (Bush) 1935 *S, I, W*, 1936 *E*
Mains, L W (Otago) 1971 *BI* 2,3,4, 1976 *I*
Major, J (Taranaki) 1967 *A*
Maka, I (Otago) 1998 *E* 2 (R), *A* 1 (R), *SA* 1 (R),2
Manchester, J E (Canterbury) 1932 *A* 1,2,3, 1934 *A* 1,2, 1935 *S, I, W*, 1936 *E*
Mannix, S J (Wellington) 1994 *F* 1

Marshall, J W (Southland, Canterbury) 1995 *F* 2, 1996
WS, S 1,2, *A* 1, *SA* 1, *A* 2, *SA* 2,3,4,5, 1997 *Fj, Arg* 1,2, *A*
1, *SA* 1, *A* 2, *SA* 2, *A* 3, *I, E* 1, *W, E* 2, 1998 *A* 1, *SA* 1, *A*
2, *SA* 2, *A* 3
Mason, D F (Wellington) 1947 *A* 2 (R)
Masters, R R (Canterbury) 1924 *I, W*, 1925 *E, F*
Mataira, H K (Hawke's Bay) 1934 *A* 2
Matheson, J D (Otago) 1972 *A* 1,2,3, *W, S*
Max, D S (Nelson) 1931 *A*, 1934 *A* 1,2
Mayerhofler, M A (Canterbury) 1998 *E* 1,2, *SA* 1, *A* 2,
SA 2, *A* 3
Meads, C E (King Country) 1957 *A* 1,2, 1958 *A* 1,2,3,
1959 *BI* 2,3,4, 1960 *SA* 1,2,3,4, 1961 *F* 1,2,3, 1962 *A*
1,2,3,5, 1963 *E* 1,2, *I, W*, 1964 *E, S, F, A* 1,2,3, 1965 *SA*
1,2,3,4, 1966 *BI* 1,2,3,4, 1967 *A, E, W, F, S*, 1968 *A* 1,2, *F*
1,2,3, 1969 *W* 1,2, 1970 *SA* 3,4, 1971 *BI* 1,2,3,4
Meads, S T (King Country) 1961 *F* 1, 1962 *A* 4,5, 1963
I, 1964 *A* 1,2,3, 1965 *SA* 1,2,3,4, 1966 *BI* 1,2,3,4
Meates, K F (Canterbury) 1952 *A* 1,2
Meates, W A (Otago) 1949 *SA* 2,3,4, 1950 *BI* 1,2,3,4
Meeuws, K J (Otago) 1998 *A* 3
Mehrtens, A P (Canterbury) 1995 *C*, [*I, W, S, E, SA*],
1,2, 1996 *WS, S* 1,2, *A* 1, *SA* 1, *A* 2, *SA* 2,5, 1997 *Fj, SA*
2 (R), *I, E* 1, *W, E* 2, 1998 *E* 1,2, *A* 1, *SA* 1 (R), *A* 2, *SA* 2,
A 3
Metcalfe, T C (Southland) 1931 *A*, 1932 *A* 1
Mexted, G G (Wellington) 1950 *BI* 4
Mexted, M G (Wellington) 1979 *S, E*, 1980 *A* 1,2,3, *W*,
1981 *S* 1,2, *SA* 1,2,3, *R, F* 1,2, 1982 *A* 1,2,3, 1983 *BI*
1,2,3,4, *A, S, E*, 1984 *F* 1,2, *A* 1,2,3, 1985 *E* 1,2, *A, Arg*
1,2
Mill, J J (Hawke's Bay, Wairarapa) 1924 *W*, 1925 *E, F*,
1930 *BI* 1
Milliken, H M (Canterbury) 1938 *A* 1,2,3
Milner, H P (Wanganui) 1970 *SA* 3
Mitchell, N A (Southland, Otago) 1935 *S, I, W*, 1936 *E*,
A 2, 1937 *SA* 3, 1938 *A* 1,2
Mitchell, T W (Canterbury) 1976 *SA* 4 (R)
Mitchell, W J (Canterbury) 1910 *A* 2,3
Mitchinson, F E (Wellington) 1907 *A* 1,2,3, 1908 *AW*
1,2,3, 1910 *A* 1,2,3, 1913 *A* 1 (R), *US*
Moffitt, J E (Wellington) 1921 *SA* 1,2,3
Moore, G J T (Otago) 1949 *A* 1
Moreton, R C (Canterbury) 1962 *A* 3,4, 1964 *A* 1,2,3,
1965 *SA* 2,3
Morgan, J E (North Auckland) 1974 *A* 3, *I*, 1976 *SA*
2,3,4
Morris, T J (Nelson Bays) 1972 *A* 1,2,3
Morrison, T C (South Canterbury) 1938 *A* 1,2,3
Morrison, T G (Otago) 1973 *E* 2 (R)
Morrissey, P J (Canterbury) 1962 *A* 3,4,5
Mourie, G N K (Taranaki) 1977 *BI* 3,4, *F* 1,2, 1978 *I, W,
E, S*, 1979 *F* 1,2, *A, S, E*, 1980 *W*, 1981 *S* 1,2, *F* 1,2, 1982
A 1,2,3
Muller, B L (Taranaki) 1967 *A, E, W, F*, 1968 *A* 1, *F* 1,
1969 *W* 1, 1970 *SA* 1,2,4, 1971 *BI* 1,2,3,4
Mumm, W J (Buller) 1949 *A* 1
Murdoch, K (Otago) 1970 *SA* 4, 1972 *A* 3, *W*
Murdoch, P H (Auckland) 1964 *A* 2,3, 1965 *SA* 1,2,3
Murray, H V (Canterbury) 1913 *A* 1, *US*, 1914 *A* 2,3
Murray, P C (Wanganui) 1908 *AW* 2
Myers, R G (Waikato) 1978 *A* 3
Mynott, H J (Taranaki) 1905 *I, W*, 1906 *F*, 1907 *A* 1,2,3,
1910 *A* 1,3

Nathan, W J (Auckland) 1962 *A* 1,2,3,4,5, 1963 *E* 1,2,
W, 1964 *A*, 1966 *BI* 1,2,3,4, 1967 *A*
Nelson, K A (Otago) 1962 *A* 4,5
Nepia, G (Hawke's Bay, East Coast) 1924 *I, W*, 1925 *E,
F*, 1929 *A* 1, 1930 *BI* 1,2,3,4
Nesbit, S R (Auckland) 1960 *SA* 2,3
Newton, F (Canterbury) 1905 *E, W*, 1906 *F*
Nicholls, H E (Wellington) 1921 *SA* 1
Nicholls, M F (Wellington) 1921 *SA* 1,2,3, 1924 *I, W*,
1925 *E, F*, 1928 *SA* 4, 1930 *BI* 2,3
Nicholson, G W (Auckland) 1903 *A*, 1904 *BI*, 1907 *A*
2,3
Norton, R W (Canterbury) 1971 *BI* 1,2,3,4, 1972 *A*
1,2,3, *W, S*, 1973 *E* 1, *I, F, E* 2, 1974 *A* 1,2,3, *I*, 1975 *S*,
1976 *I, SA* 1,2,3,4, 1977 *BI* 1,2,3,4

O'Brien, J G (Auckland) 1914 *A* 1
O'Callaghan, M W (Manawatu) 1968 *F* 1,2,3
O'Callaghan, T R (Wellington) 1949 *A* 2

O'Donnell, D H (Wellington) 1949 *A* 2
Old, G H (Manawatu) 1981 *SA* 3, *R* (R), 1982 *A* 1 (R)
O'Leary, M J (Auckland) 1910 *A* 1,3, 1913 *A* 2,3
Oliver, A D (Otago) 1997 *Fj* (t), 1998 *E* 1,2, *A* 1, *SA* 1, *A*
2, *SA* 2, *A* 3
Oliver, C J (Canterbury) 1929 *A* 1,2, 1934 *A* 1, 1935 *S, I,
W*, 1936 *E*
Oliver, D J (Wellington) 1930 *BI* 1,2
Oliver, D O (Otago) 1954 *I, F*
Oliver, F J (Southland, Otago, Manawatu) 1976 *SA* 4,
1977 *BI* 1,2,3,4, *F* 1,2, 1978 *A* 1,2,3, *I, W, E, S*, 1979 *F*
1,2, 1981 *SA* 2
Orr, R W (Otago) 1949 *A* 1
Osborne, G M (North Harbour) 1995 *C*, [*I, W, J, E, SA*],
A 1,2, *F* 1 (R), 2, 1996 *SA* 2,3,4,5, 1997 *Arg* 1 (R), *A* 2,3,
I
Osborne, W M (Wanganui) 1975 *S*, 1976 *SA* 2 (R), 4
(R), 1977 *BI* 1,2,3,4, *F* 1 (R), 2, 1978 *I, W, E, S*, 1980 *W*,
1982 *A* 1,3
O'Sullivan, J M (Taranaki) 1905 *S, I, E, W*, 1907 *A* 3
O'Sullivan, T P A (Taranaki) 1960 *SA* 1, 1961 *F* 1, 1962
A 1,2

Page, J R (Wellington) 1931 *A*, 1932 *A* 1,2,3, 1934 *A* 1,2
Palmer, B P (Auckland) 1929 *A* 2, 1932 *A* 2,3
Parker, J H (Canterbury) 1924 *I, W*, 1925 *E*
Parkhill, A A (Otago) 1937 *SA* 1,2,3, 1938 *A* 1,2,3
Parkinson, R M (Poverty Bay) 1972 *A* 1,2,3, *W, S*, 1973
E 1,2
Paterson, A M (Otago) 1908 *AW* 2,3, 1910 *A* 1,2,3
Paton, H (Otago) 1910 *A* 1,3
Pene, A R B (Otago) 1992 *Wld* 1 (R), 2,3, *I* 1,2, *A* 1,2
(R), 1993 *BI* 3, *A, WS, S, E*, 1994 *F* 1,2 (R), *SA* 1 (R)
Phillips, W J (King Country) 1937 *SA* 2, 1938 *A* 1,2
Philpott, S (Canterbury) 1991 [*It* (R), *S* (R)]
Pickering, E A R (Waikato) 1958 *A* 2, 1959 *BI* 1,4
Pierce, M J (Wellington) 1985 *E* 1,2, *A, Arg* 1, 1986 *A*
2,3, *F* 2,3, 1987 [*It, Arg, S, W, F*], *A*, 1988 *W* 1,2, *A* 1,2,3,
1989 *F* 1,2, *Arg* 1,2, *A, W, I*
Pokere, S T (Southland, Auckland) 1981 *SA* 3, 1982 *A*
1,2,3, 1983 *BI* 1,2,3,4, *A, S, E*, 1984 *F* 1,2, *A* 2,3, 1985 *E*
1,2, *A*
Pollock, H R (Wellington) 1932 *A* 1,2,3, 1936 *A* 1,2
Porter, C G (Wellington) 1925 *F*, 1929 *A* 2,3, 1930 *BI*
1,2,3,4
Preston, J P (Canterbury, Wellington) 1991 [*US, S*],
1992 *SA* (R), 1993 *SA* 2,3, *A, WS*, 1996 *SA* 4 (R), 1997 *I*
(R), *E* 1 (R)
Procter, A C (Otago) 1932 *A* 1
Purdue, C A (Southland) 1905 *A*
Purdue, E (Southland) 1905 *A*
Purdue, G B (Southland) 1931 *A*, 1932 *A* 1,2,3
Purvis, G H (Waikato) 1991 [*US*], 1993 *WS*
Purvis, N A (Otago) 1976 *I*

Quaid, C E (Otago) 1938 *A* 1,2

Ralph, C S (Auckland) 1998 *E* 2
Randell, T C (Otago) 1997 *Fj, Arg* 1,2, *A* 1, *SA* 1, *A* 2,
SA 2, *A* 3, *I, E* 1, *W, E* 2, 1998 *E* 1,2, *A* 1, *SA* 1, *A* 2, *SA*
2, *A* 3
Rangi, R E (Auckland) 1964 *A* 2,3, 1965 *A* 1,2,3,4,
1966 *BI* 1,2,3,4
Rankin, J G (Canterbury) 1936 *A* 1,2, 1937 *SA* 2
Reedy, W J (Wellington) 1908 *AW* 2,3
Reid, A R (Waikato) 1952 *A* 1, 1956 *SA* 3,4, 1957 *A* 1,2
Reid, H R (Bay of Plenty) 1980 *A* 1,2, *W*, 1983 *S, E*,
1985 *Arg* 1,2, 1986 *A* 2,3
Reid, K H (Wairarapa) 1929 *A* 1,3
Reid, S T (Hawke's Bay) 1935 *S, I, W*, 1936 *E, A* 1,2,
1937 *SA* 1,2,3
Reside, W B (Wairarapa) 1929 *A* 1
Rhind, P K (Canterbury) 1946 *A* 1,2
Richardson, J (Otago, Southland) 1921 *SA* 1,2,3, 1924 *I,
W*, 1925 *E, F*
Rickit, H (Waikato) 1981 *S* 1,2
Riechelmann, C C (Auckland) 1997 *Fj* (R), *Arg* 1 (R), *A*
1 (R), *SA* 2 (t), *I* (R), *E* 2 (t)
Ridland, A J (Southland) 1910 *A* 1,2,3
Roberts, E J (Wellington) 1914 *A* 1,2,3, 1921 *SA* 2,3
Roberts, F (Wellington) 1905 *S, I, E, W*, 1907 *A* 1,2,3,
1908 *AW* 1,3, 1910 *A* 1,2,3
Roberts, R W (Taranaki) 1913 *A* 1, *US*, 1914 *A* 1,2,3

Robertson, B J (Counties) 1972 *A* 1,3, *S*, 1973 *E* 1, *I*, *F*, 1974 *A* 1,2,3, *I*, 1976 *I*, *SA* 1,2,3,4, 1977 *BI* 1,3,4, *F* 1,2, 1978 *A* 1,2,3, *W*, *E*, *S*, 1979 *F* 1,2, *A*, 1980 *A* 2,3, *W*, 1981 *S* 1,2
Robertson, D J (Otago) 1974 *A* 1,2,3, *I*, 1975 *S*, 1976 *I*, *SA* 1,3,4, 1977 *BI* 1

Robertson, S M (Canterbury) 1998 *A* 2 (R), *SA* 2 (R), *A* 3 (R)
Robilliard, A C C (Canterbury) 1928 *SA* 1,2,3,4
Robinson, C E (Southland) 1951 *A* 1,2,3, 1952 *A* 1,2
Robinson, M D (North Harbour) 1998 *E* 1 (R)
Rollerson, D L (Manawatu) 1980 *W*, 1981 *S* 2, *SA* 1,2,3, *R*, *F* 1 (R), 2
Roper, R A (Taranaki) 1949 *A* 2, 1950 *BI* 1,2,3,4
Rowley, H C B (Wanganui) 1949 *A* 2
Rush, E J (North Harbour) 1995 [*W* (R), *J*], *It*, *F* 1,2, 1996 *S* 1 (R), 2, *A* 1 (t), *SA* 1 (R)
Rush, X J (Auckland) 1998 *A* 3
Rutledge, L M (Southland) 1978 *A* 1,2,3, *I*, *W*, *E*, *S*, 1979 *F* 1,2, *A*, 1980 *A* 1,2,3
Ryan, J (Wellington) 1910 *A* 2, 1914 *A* 1,2,3

Sadler, B S (Wellington) 1935 *S*, *I*, *W*, 1936 *A* 1,2
Salmon, J L B (Wellington) 1981 *R*, *F* 1,2 (R)
Savage, L T (Canterbury) 1949 *SA* 1,2,4
Saxton, C K (South Canterbury) 1938 *A* 1,2,3
Schuler, K J (Manawatu, North Harbour) 1990 *A* 2 (R), 1992 *A* 2, 1995 [*I* (R), *J*]
Schuster, N J (Wellington) 1988 *A* 1,2,3, 1989 *F* 1,2, *Arg* 1,2, *A*, *W*, *I*
Scott, R W H (Auckland) 1946 *A* 1,2, 1947 *A* 1,2, 1949 *SA* 1,2,3,4, 1950 *BI* 1,2,3,4, 1953 *W*, 1954 *I*, *E*, *S*, *F*
Scown, A I (Taranaki) 1972 *A* 1,2,3, *W* (R), *S*
Scrimshaw, G (Canterbury) 1928 *SA* 1
Seear, G A (Otago) 1977 *F* 1,2, 1978 *A* 1,2,3, *I*, *W*, *E*, *S*, 1979 *F* 1,2, *A*
Seeling, C E (Auckland) 1904 *BI*, 1905 *S*, *I*, *E*, *W*, 1906 *F*, 1907 *A* 1,2, 1908 *AW* 1,2,3
Sellars, G M V (Auckland) 1913 *A* 1, *US*
Shaw, M W (Manawatu, Hawke's Bay) 1980 *A* 1,2,3 (R), *W*, 1981 *S* 1,2, *SA* 1,2, *R*, *F* 1,2, 1982 *A* 1,2,3, 1983 *BI* 1,2,3,4, *A*, *S*, *E*, 1984 *F* 1,2, *A* 1, 1985 *E* 1,2, *A*, *Arg* 1,2, 1986 *A* 3
Shelford, F N K (Bay of Plenty) 1981 *SA* 3, *R*, 1984 *A* 2,3
Shelford, W T (North Harbour) 1986 *F* 2,3, 1987 [*It*, *Fj*, *S*, *W*, *F*], *A*, 1988 *W* 1,2, *A* 1,2,3, 1989 *F* 1,2, *Arg* 1,2, *A*, *W*, *I*, 1990 *S* 1,2
Siddells, S K (Wellington) 1921 *SA* 3
Simon, H J (Otago) 1937 *SA* 1,2,3
Simpson, J G (Auckland) 1947 *A* 1,2, 1949 *SA* 1,2,3,4, 1950 *BI* 1,2,3
Simpson, V L J (Canterbury) 1985 *Arg* 1,2
Sims, G S (Otago) 1972 *A* 2
Skeen, J R (Auckland) 1952 *A* 2
Skinner, K L (Otago, Counties) 1949 *SA* 1,2,3,4, 1950 *BI* 1,2,3,4, 1951 *A* 1,2,3, 1952 *A* 1,2, 1953 *W*, 1954 *I*, *E*, *S*, *F*, 1956 *SA* 3,4
Skudder, G R (Waikato) 1969 *W* 2
Sloane, P H (North Auckland) 1979 *E*
Smith, A E (Taranaki) 1969 *W* 1,2, 1970 *SA* 1
Smith, B W (Waikato) 1984 *F* 1,2, *A* 1
Smith, G W (Auckland) 1905 *S*, *I*
Smith, I S T (Otago, North Otago) 1964 *A* 1,2,3, 1965 *SA* 1,2,4, 1966 *BI* 1,2,3
Smith, J B (North Auckland) 1946 *A* 1, 1947 *A* 2, 1949 *A* 1,2
Smith, R M (Canterbury) 1955 *A* 1
Smith, W E (Nelson) 1905 *A*
Smith, W R (Canterbury) 1980 *A* 1, 1982 *A* 1,2,3, 1983 *BI* 2,3, *S*, *E*, 1984 *F* 1,2, *A* 1,2,3, 1985 *E* 1,2, *A*, *Arg* 2
Snow, E M (Nelson) 1929 *A* 1,2,3
Solomon, F (Auckland) 1931 *A*, 1932 *A* 2,3
Sonntag, W T C (Otago) 1929 *A* 1,2,3
Speight, M W (Waikato) 1986 *A* 1
Spencer, C J (Auckland) 1997 *Arg* 1,2, *A* 1, *SA* 1, *A* 2, *SA* 2, *A* 3, *E* 2 (R), 1998 *E* 2 (R), *A* 1 (R), *SA* 1, *A* 3 (R)
Spencer, J C (Wellington) 1905 *A*, 1907 *A* 1 (R)
Spiers, J E (Counties) 1979 *S*, *E*, 1981 *R*, *F* 1,2
Spillane, A P (South Canterbury) 1913 *A* 2,3
Stanley, J T (Auckland) 1986 *F* 1, *A* 1,2,3, *F* 2,3, 1987 [*It*, *Fj*, *Arg*, *S*, *W*, *F*], *A*, 1988 *W* 1,2, *A* 1,2,3, 1989 *F* 1,2, *Arg* 1,2, *A*, *W*, *I*, 1990 *S* 1,2

Stead, J W (Southland) 1904 *BI*, 1905 *S*, *I*, *E*, 1906 *F*, 1908 *AW* 1,3
Steel, A G (Canterbury) 1966 *BI* 1,2,3,4, 1967 *A*, *F*, *S*, 1968 *A* 1,2
Steel, J (West Coast) 1921 *SA* 1,2,3, 1924 *W*, 1925 *E*, *F*
Steele, L B (Wellington) 1951 *A* 1,2,3
Steere, E R G (Hawke's Bay) 1930 *BI* 1,2,3,4, 1931 *A*, 1932 *A* 1
Stensness, L (Auckland) 1993 *BI* 3, *A*, *WS*, 1997 *Fj*, *Arg* 1,2, *A* 1, *SA* 1
Stephens, O G (Wellington) 1968 *F* 3
Stevens, I N (Wellington) 1972 *S*, 1973 *E* 1, 1974 *A* 3
Stewart, A J (Canterbury, South Canterbury) 1963 *E* 1,2, *I*, *W*, 1964 *E*, *S*, *F*, *A* 3
Stewart, J D (Auckland) 1913 *A* 2,3
Stewart, K W (Southland) 1973 *E* 2, 1974 *A* 1,2,3, *I*, 1975 *S*, 1976 *I*, *SA* 1,3, 1979 *S*, *E*, 1981 *SA* 1,2
Stewart, R T (South Canterbury, Canterbury) 1928 *SA* 1,2,3,4, 1930 *BI* 2
Stohr, L B (Taranaki) 1910 *A* 1,2,3
Stone, A M (Waikato, Bay of Plenty) 1981 *F* 1,2, 1983 *BI* 3 (R), 1984 *A* 3, 1986 *F* 1, *A* 1,3, *F* 2,3
Storey, P W (South Canterbury) 1921 *SA* 1,2
Strachan, A D (Auckland, North Harbour) 1992 *Wld* 2,3, *I* 1,2, *A* 1,2,3, *SA*, 1993 *I*, 1995 [*J*, *SA* (t)]
Strahan, S C (Manawatu) 1967 *A*, *E*, *W*, *F*, *S*, 1968 *A* 1,2, *F* 1,2,3, 1970 *SA* 1,2,3, 1972 *A* 1,2,3, 1973 *E* 2
Strang, W A (South Canterbury) 1928 *SA* 1,2, 1930 *BI* 3,4, 1931 *A*
Stringfellow, J C (Wairarapa) 1929 *A* 1 (R), 3
Stuart, K C (Canterbury) 1955 *A* 1
Stuart, R C (Canterbury) 1949 *A* 1,2, 1953 *W*, 1954 *I*, *E*, *S*, *F*
Stuart, R L (Hawke's Bay) 1977 *F* 1 (R)
Sullivan, J L (Taranaki) 1937 *SA* 1,2,3, 1938 *A* 1,2,3
Sutherland, A R (Marlborough) 1970 *SA* 2,4, 1971 *BI* 1, 1972 *A* 1,2,3, *W*, 1973 *E* 1, *I*, *F*
Svenson, K S (Wellington) 1924 *I*, *W*, 1925 *E*, *F*
Swain, J P (Hawke's Bay) 1928 *SA* 1,2,3,4

Tanner, J M (Auckland) 1950 *BI* 4, 1951 *A* 1,2,3, 1953 *W*
Tanner, K J (Canterbury) 1974 *A* 1,2,3, *I*, 1975 *S*, 1976 *I*, *SA* 1
Taylor, G L (Northland) 1996 *SA* 5 (R)
Taylor, H M (Canterbury) 1913 *A* 1, *US*, 1914 *A* 1,2,3
Taylor, J M (Otago) 1937 *SA* 1,2,3, 1938 *A* 1,2,3
Taylor, M B (Waikato) 1979 *F* 1,2, *A*, *S*, *E*, 1980 *A* 1,2
Taylor, N M (Bay of Plenty, Hawke's Bay) 1977 *BI* 2, 4 (R), *F* 1,2, 1978 *A* 1,2,3, *I*, 1982 *A* 2
Taylor, R (Taranaki) 1913 *A* 2,3
Taylor, W T (Canterbury) 1983 *BI* 1,2,3,4, *A*, *S*, 1984 *F* 1,2, *A* 1,2, 1985 *E* 1,2, *A*, *Arg* 1,2, 1986 *A* 2, 1987 [*It*, *Fj*, *S*, *W*, *F*], *A*, 1988 *W* 1,2
Tetzlaff, P L (Auckland) 1947 *A* 1,2
Thimbleby, N W (Hawke's Bay) 1970 *SA* 3
Thomas, B T (Auckland, Wellington) 1962 *A* 5, 1964 *A* 1,2,3
Thomson, H D (Wellington) 1908 *AW* 1
Thorne, G S (Auckland) 1968 *A* 1,2, *F* 1,2,3, 1969 *W* 1, 1970 *SA* 1,2,3,4
Thornton, N H (Auckland) 1947 *A* 1,2, 1949 *SA* 1
Tilyard, J T (Wellington) 1913 *A* 3
Timu, J K R (Otago) 1991 *Arg* 1, *A* 1,2, [*E*, *US*, *C*, *A*], 1992 *Wld* 2, *I* 2, *A* 1,2,3, *SA*, 1993 *BI* 1,2,3, *A*, *WS*, *S*, *E*, 1994 *F* 1,2, *SA* 1,2,3, *A*
Tindill, E W T (Wellington) 1936 *E*
Tonu'u, O F J (Auckland) 1997 *Fj* (R), *A* 3 (R), 1998 *E* 1,2, *SA* 1 (R)
Townsend, L J (Otago) 1955 *A* 1,3
Tremain, K R (Canterbury, Hawke's Bay) 1959 *BI* 2,3,4, 1960 *SA* 1,2,3,4, 1961 *F* 2,3 1962 *A* 1,2,3, 1963 *E* 1,2, *I*, *W*, 1964 *E*, *S*, *F*, *A* 1,2,3, 1965 *SA* 1,2,3,4, 1966 *BI* 1,2,3,4, 1967 *A*, *E*, *W*, *S*, 1968 *A* 1, *F* 1,2,3
Trevathan, D (Otago) 1937 *SA* 1,2,3
Tuck, J M (Waikato) 1929 *A* 1,2,3
Tuigamala, V L (Auckland) 1991 [*US*, *It*, *C*, *S*], 1992 *Wld* 1,2,3, *I* 1, *A* 1,2,3, *SA*, 1993 *BI* 1,2,3, *A*, *WS*, *S*, *E*
Turner, R S (North Harbour) 1992 *Wld* 1,2 (R)
Turtill, H S (Canterbury) 1905 *A*
Twigden, T M (Auckland) 1980 *A* 2,3
Tyler, G A (Auckland) 1903 *A*, 1904 *BI*, 1905 *S*, *I*, *E*, *W*, 1906 *F*

Udy, D K (Wairarapa) 1903 *A*
Umaga, T J F (Wellington) 1997 *Fj, Arg* 1,2, *A* 1, *SA* 1,2
Urbahn, R J (Taranaki) 1959 *BI* 1,3,4
Urlich, R A (Auckland) 1970 *SA* 3,4
Uttley, I N (Wellington) 1963 *E* 1,2

Vidiri, J (Counties Manukau) 1998 *E* 2 (R), *A* 1
Vincent, P B (Canterbury) 1956 *SA* 1,2
Vodanovich, I M H (Wellington) 1955 *A* 1,2,3

Wallace, W J (Wellington) 1903 *A*, 1904 *BI*, 1905 *S, I, E, W*, 1906 *F*, 1907 *A* 1,2,3, 1908 *AW* 2
Walsh, P T (Counties) 1955 *A* 1,2,3, 1956 *SA* 1,2,4, 1957 *A* 1,2, 1958 *A* 1,2,3, 1959 *BI* 1, 1963 *E* 2
Ward, R H (Southland) 1936 *A* 2, 1937 *SA* 1,3
Waterman, A C (North Auckland) 1929 *A* 1,2
Watkins, E L (Wellington) 1905 *A*
Watt, B A (Canterbury) 1962 *A* 1,4, 1963 *E* 1,2, *W*, 1964 *E, S, A* 1
Watt, J M (Otago) 1936 *A* 1,2
Watt, J R (Wellington) 1958 *A* 2, 1960 *SA* 1,2,3,4, 1961 *F* 1,3, 1962 *A* 1,2
Watts, M G (Taranaki) 1979 *F* 1,2, 1980 *A* 1,2,3 (R)
Webb, D S (North Auckland) 1959 *BI* 2
Wells, J (Wellington) 1936 *A* 1,2
West, A H (Taranaki) 1921 *SA* 2,3
Whetton, A J (Auckland) 1984 *A* 1 (R), 3 (R), 1985 *A* (R), *Arg* 1 (R), 1986 *A* 2, 1987 [*It, Fj, Arg, S, W, F*], *A*, 1988 *W* 1,2, *A* 1,2,3, 1989 *F* 1,2, *Arg* 1,2, *A*, 1990 *S* 1,2, *A* 1,2,3, *F* 1,2, 1991 *Arg* 1, [*E, US, It, C, A*]
Whetton, G W (Auckland) 1981 *SA* 3, *R, F* 1,2, 1982 *A* 3, 1983 *BI* 1,2,3,4, 1984 *F* 1,2, *A* 1,2,3, 1985 *E* 1,2, *A, Arg* 2, 1986 *A* 2,3, *F* 2,3, 1987 [*It, Fj, Arg, S, W, F*], *A*, 1988 *W* 1,2, *A* 1,2,3, 1989 *F* 1,2, *Arg* 1,2, *A, W, I*, 1990 *S* 1,2, *A* 1,2,3, *F* 1,2, 1991 *Arg* 1,2, *A* 1,2, [*E, US, It, C, A, S*]
Whineray, W J (Canterbury, Waikato, Auckland) 1957 *A* 1,2, 1958 *A* 1,2,3, 1959 *BI* 1,2,3,4, 1960 *SA* 1,2,3,4, 1961 *F* 1,2,3, 1962 *A* 1,2,3,4,5, 1963 *E* 1,2, *I, W*, 1964 *E, S, F*, 1965 *SA* 1,2,3,4
White, A (Southland) 1921 *SA* 1, 1924 *I*, 1925 *E, F*
White, H L (Auckland) 1954 *I, E, F*, 1955 *A* 3
White, R A (Poverty Bay) 1949 *A* 1,2, 1950 *BI* 1,2,3,4, 1951 *A* 1,2,3, 1952 *A* 1,2, 1953 *W*, 1954 *I, E, S, F*, 1955 *A* 1,2,3, 1956 *SA* 1,2,3,4
White, R M (Wellington) 1946 *A* 1,2, 1947 *A* 1,2

Whiting, G J (King Country) 1972 *A* 1,2, *S*, 1973 *E* 1, *I, F*
Whiting, P J (Auckland) 1971 *BI* 1,2,4, 1972 *A* 1,2,3, *W, S*, 1973 *E* 1, *I, F*, 1974 *A* 1,2,3, *I*, 1976 *I, SA* 1,2,3,4
Williams, B G (Auckland) 1970 *SA* 1,2,3,4, 1971 *BI* 1,2,4, 1972 *A* 1,2,3, *W, S*, 1973 *E* 1, *I, F, E* 2, 1974 *A* 1,2,3, *I*, 1975 *S*, 1976 *I, SA* 1,2,3,4, 1977 *BI* 1,2,3,4, *F* 1, 1978 *A* 1,2,3, *I* (R), *W, E, S*
Williams, G C (Wellington) 1967 *E, W, F, S*, 1968 *A* 2
Williams, P (Otago) 1913 *A* 1
Williment, M (Wellington) 1964 *A* 1, 1965 *SA* 1,2,3, 1966 *BI* 1,2,3,4, 1967 *A*
Willis, R K (Waikato) 1998 *SA* 2, *A* 3
Willocks, C (Otago) 1946 *A* 1,2, 1949 *SA* 1,3,4
Wilson, B W (Otago) 1977 *BI* 3,4, 1978 *A* 1,2,3, 1979 *F* 1,2, *A*
Wilson, D D (Canterbury) 1954 *E, S*
Wilson, H W (Otago) 1949 *A* 1, 1950 *BI* 4, 1951 *A* 1,2,3
Wilson, J W (Otago) 1993 *S, E*, 1994 *A*, 1995 *C*, [*I, J, S, E, SA*], *A* 1,2, *It, F* 1, 1996 *WS, S* 1,2, *A* 1, *SA* 1, *A* 2, *SA* 2,3,4,5, 1997 *Fj, Arg* 1,2, *A* 1, *SA* 1, *A* 2, *SA* 2, *A* 3, *I, E* 1, *W, E* 2, 1998 *E* 1,2, *A* 1, *SA* 1, *A* 2, *SA* 2, *A* 3
Wilson, N A (Wellington) 1908 *AW* 1,2, 1910 *A* 1,2,3, 1913 *A* 2,3, 1914 *A* 1,2,3
Wilson, N L (Otago) 1951 *A* 1,2,3
Wilson, R G (Canterbury) 1979 *S, E*
Wilson, S S (Wellington) 1977 *F* 1,2, 1978 *A* 1,2,3, *I, W, E, S*, 1979 *F* 1,2, *A, S, E*, 1980 *A* 1, *W*, 1981 *S* 1,2, *SA* 1,2,3, *R, F* 1,2, 1982 *A* 1,2,3, 1983 *BI* 1,2,3,4, *A, S, E*
Wolfe, T N (Wellington, Taranaki) 1961 *F* 1,2,3, 1962 *A* 2,3, 1963 *E* 1
Wood, M E (Canterbury, Auckland) 1903 *A*, 1904 *BI*
Woodman, F A (North Auckland) 1981 *SA* 1,2, *F* 2
Wrigley, E (Wairarapa) 1905 *A*
Wright, T J (Auckland) 1986 *F* 1, *A* 1, 1987 [*Arg*], 1988 *W* 1,2, *A* 1,2,3, 1989 *F* 1,2, *Arg* 1,2, *A, W, I*, 1990 *S* 1,2, *A* 1,2,3, *F* 1,2, 1991 *Arg* 1,2, *A* 1,2, [*E, US, It, S*]
Wylie, J T (Auckland) 1913 *A* 1, *US*
Wyllie, A J (Canterbury) 1970 *SA* 2,3, 1971 *BI* 2,3,4, 1972 *W, S*, 1973 *E* 1, *I, F, E* 2

Yates, V M (North Auckland) 1961 *F* 1,2,3
Young, D (Canterbury) 1956 *SA* 2, 1958 *A* 1,2,3, 1960 *SA* 1,2,3,4, 1961 *F* 1,2,3, 1962 *A* 1,2,3,5, 1963 *E* 1,2, *I, W*, 1964 *E, S, F*

NEW ZEALAND INTERNATIONAL RECORDS (*up to 30 April 1999*)

MATCH RECORDS

MOST CONSECUTIVE TEST WINS

17 1965 *SA* 4, 1966 *BI* 1,2,3,4, 1967 *A,E,W,F,S*, 1968 *A* 1,2, *F* 1,2,3, 1969 *W* 1,2

12 1988 *A* 3, 1989 *F* 1,2, *Arg* 1,2, *A,W,I*, 1990 *S* 1,2, *A* 1,2

MOST CONSECUTIVE TESTS WITHOUT DEFEAT

P	W	D	Period
23	22	1	1987–90
17	15	2	1961–64
17	17	0	1965–69

MOST POINTS IN A MATCH
by the team

Pts	Opp	Venue	Year
145	J	Bloemfontein	1995
93	Arg	Wellington	1997
74	Fj	Christchurch	1987
73	C	Auckland	1995
71	Fj	Albany	1997

by a player

45 by S D Culhane v Japan at Bloemfontein 1995
33 by C J Spencer v Argentina at Wellington 1997
33 by A P Mehrtens v Ireland at Dublin 1997
30 by M C G Ellis v Japan at Bloemfontein 1995
28 by A P Mehrtens v Canada at Auckland 1995

MOST TRIES IN A MATCH
by the team

T	Opp	Venue	Year
21	J	Bloemfontein	1995
14	Arg	Wellington	1997
13	US	Berkeley	1913
12	It	Auckland	1987
12	Fj	Christchurch	1987

by a player

6 by M C G Ellis v Japan at Bloemfontein 1995
5 by J W Wilson v Fiji at Albany 1997
4 by D McGregor v England at Crystal Palace 1905

4 by C I Green v Fiji at Christchurch 1987
4 by J A Gallagher v Fiji at Christchurch 1987
4 by J J Kirwan v Wales at Christchurch 1988
4 by J T Lomu v England at Cape Town 1995
4 by C M Cullen v Scotland at Dunedin 1996

MOST CONVERSIONS IN A MATCH
by the team

C	Opp	Venue	Year
20	J	Bloemfontein	1995
10	Fj	Christchurch	1987
10	Arg	Wellington	1997
8	It	Auckland	1987
8	W	Auckland	1988
8	Fj	Albany	1997

by a player

20 by S D Culhane v Japan at Bloemfontein 1995
10 by C J Spencer v Argentina at Wellington 1997
10 by G J Fox v Fiji at Christchurch 1987
8 by G J Fox v Italy at Auckland 1987
8 by G J Fox v Wales at Auckland 1988

MOST PENALTY GOALS IN A MATCH
by the team

P	Opp	Venue	Year
7	WS	Auckland	1993
6	BI	Dunedin	1959
6	E	Christchurch	1985
6	Arg	Wellington	1987
6	S	Christchurch	1987
6	F	Paris	1990
6	SA	Auckland	1994
6	A	Brisbane	1996
6	I	Dublin	1997

by a player

7 by G J Fox v Western Samoa at Auckland 1993
6 by D B Clarke v British Isles at Dunedin 1959
6 by K J Crowley v England at Christchurch 1985

6 by G J Fox v Argentina at
Wellington   1987
6 by G J Fox v Scotland at
Christchurch   1987
6 by G J Fox v France at Paris   1990
6 by S P Howarth v South Africa
at Auckland   1994
6 by A P Mehrtens v Australia at
Brisbane   1996
6 by A P Mehrtens v Ireland at
Dublin   1997

MOST DROPPED GOALS IN A MATCH

by the team

D	Opp	Venue	Year
3	F	Christchurch	1986

by a player

2 by O D Bruce v Ireland at Dublin 1978
2 by F M Botica v France at
Christchurch   1986
2 by A P Mehrtens v Australia at
Auckland   1995

CAREER RECORDS

MOST CAPPED PLAYERS

Caps	Player	Career
92	S B T Fitzpatrick	1986–97
76	I D Jones	1990–98
63	J J Kirwan	1984–94
58	G W Whetton	1981–91
58	Z V Brooke	1987–97
56	O M Brown	1992–98
55	C E Meads	1957–71
55	F E Bunce	1992–97
55	M N Jones	1987–98
51	R M Brooke	1995–98

MOST CONSECUTIVE TESTS

Tests	Player	Span
63	S B T Fitzpatrick	1986–95
40	G W Whetton	1986–91
38	I A Kirkpatrick	1968–77
38	S C McDowell	1987–92
38	R M Brooke	1995–98

MOST TESTS AS CAPTAIN

Tests	Captain	Span
51	S B T Fitzpatrick	1992–97
30	W J Whineray	1958–65
19	G N K Mourie	1977–82
18	B J Lochore	1966–70
17	A G Dalton	1981–85

MOST TESTS IN INDIVIDUAL POSITIONS

Full-back	D B Clarke	31	1956–64
Wing	J J Kirwan	63	1984–94
Centre	F E Bunce	55	1992–97
Fly-half	G J Fox	46	1985–93
Scrum-half	G T M Bachop	31	1989–95
Prop	O M Brown	56	1992–98
Hooker	S B T Fitzpatrick	92	1986–97
Lock	I D Jones	76	1990–98
Flanker	M N Jones	53	1987–98
No. 8	Z V Brooke	52	1987–97

MOST POINTS IN TESTS

Pts	Player	Tests	Career
645	G J Fox	46	1985–93
428	A P Mehrtens	29	1995–98
207	D B Clarke	31	1956–64
201	A R Hewson	19	1981–84
156	C J Spencer	12	1997–98

MOST TRIES IN TESTS

Tries	Player	Tests	Career
35	J J Kirwan	63	1984–94
28	J W Wilson	42	1993–98
25	C M Cullen	29	1996–98
20	F E Bunce	55	1992–97
19	S S Wilson	34	1977–83
19	T J Wright	30	1986–91

MOST CONVERSIONS IN TESTS

Cons	Player	Tests	Career
118	G J Fox	46	1985–93
79	A P Mehrtens	29	1995–98
34	C J Spencer	12	1997–98
33	D B Clarke	31	1956–64
32	S D Culhane	6	1995–96

MOST PENALTY GOALS IN TESTS

Pens	Player	Tests	Career
128	G J Fox	46	1985–93
73	A P Mehrtens	29	1995–98
43	A R Hewson	19	1981–84
38	D B Clarke	31	1956–64
24	W F McCormick	16	1965–71

MOST DROPPED GOALS IN TESTS

Drops	Player	Tests	Career
7	G J Fox	46	1985–93
7	A P Mehrtens	29	1995–98
5	D B Clarke	31	1956–64
5	M A Herewini	10	1962–67
5	O D Bruce	14	1976–78

Trading places. The New Zealand lock Ian Jones wins a lineout ball ahead of England's Dave Sims during the second Test at Eden Park in June 1998. Jones signed for Gloucester the following summer, to succeed one of Kingsholm's favourite sons, Dave Sims.

351

TRI-NATIONS RECORDS

Record	Detail	Holder	Set
Most points in matches	101	A P Mehrtens	1996–98
Most points in season	84	C J Spencer	1997
Most points in match	25	C J Spencer	v S Africa (h) 1997
Most tries in matches	6	C M Cullen	1996–98
Most tries in season	4	C M Cullen	1997
Most tries in match	{ 2	F E Bunce	v S Africa (a) 1997
	{ 2	C M Cullen	v S Africa (h) 1997
Most cons in matches	13	C J Spencer	1997
Most cons in season	13	C J Spencer	1997
Most cons in match	4	C J Spencer	v S Africa (h) 1997
Most pens in matches	27	A P Mehrtens	1996–98
Most pens in season	19	A P Mehrtens	1996
Most pens in match	6	A P Mehrtens	v Australia (a) 1996

SERIES RECORDS

Record	Holder	Detail
Most tries	J J Kirwan	6 v Wales 1988
Most points	A P Mehrtens	78 v Home Unions 1997

MAJOR TOUR RECORDS

Record	Detail	Year	Place
Most team points	976	1905–06	Europe & N Am
Most team tries	243	1905–06	Europe & N Am
Most individual points	246 by W J Wallace	1905–06	Europe & N Am
Most individual tries	44 by J Hunter	1905–06	Europe & N Am
Most points in match	43 by R M Deans	1984 v S Australia	Adelaide
Most tries in match	8 by T R Heeps	1962 v N NSW	Quirindi

MISCELLANEOUS RECORDS

Record	Holder	Detail
Longest Test career	E Hughes/C E Meads	15 seasons, 1907–21/1957–71
Youngest Test cap	J T Lomu	19 yrs 45 days in 1994
Oldest Test cap	E Hughes	40 yrs 123 days in 1921

NEW ZEALAND INTERNATIONAL
CAREER RECORDS (*up to 30 April 1999*)

Player	Debut	Caps since last season	Caps	T	C	PG	DG	Pts
C M Cullen	1996 v WS	1998 *E* 1,2, *A* 1, *SA* 1, *A* 2, *SA* 2, *A* 3	29	25	3	0	0	131
A R Cashmore	1996 v S		2	0	0	0	0	0
J Vidiri	1998 v E	1998 *E* 2(R), *A* 1	2	1	0	0	0	5
J W Wilson	1993 v S	1998 *E* 1,2, *A* 1, *SA* 1, *A* 2, *SA* 2, *A* 3	42	28	1	3	0	151
J T Lomu	1994 v F	1998 *E* 1,2, *A* 1(R), *SA* 1, *A* 2, *SA* 2, *A* 3	27	16	0	0	0	80
M A Mayerhofler	1998 v E	1998 *E* 1,2, *SA* 1, *A* 2, *SA* 2, *A* 3	6	2	0	0	0	10
N R Berryman	1998 v SA	1998 *SA* 2(R)	1	0	0	0	0	0
C S Ralph	1998 v E	1998 *E* 2	1	0	0	0	0	0
E Clarke	1992 v Wd	1998 *SA* 2, *A* 3	10	6	0	0	0	25
S J McLeod	1996 v WS	1998 *A* 1, *SA* 1(R)	10	1	0	0	0	5
W K Little	1990 v S	1998 *E* 1, *A* 1, *SA* 1, *A*2	50	9	0	0	0	44
C J Spencer	1997 v Arg	1998 *E* 2(R), *A* 1(R), *SA* 1, *A* 3(R)	12	5	34	21	0	156
A P Mehrtens	1995 v C	1998 *E* 1,2, *A* 1, *SA* 1(R), *A* 2, *SA* 2, *A* 3	29	6	79	73	7	428
J W Marshall	1995 v F	1998 *A* 1, *SA* 1, *A* 2, *SA* 2, *A* 3	28	12	0	0	0	60
O F J Tonu'u	1997 v Fj	1998 *E* 1,2, *SA* 1(R)	5	0	0	0	0	0
M D Robinson	1998 v E	1998 *E* 1(R)	1	0	0	0	0	0
N J Hewitt	1995 v I	1998 *E* 2(t&R)	9	0	0	0	0	0
A D Oliver	1997 v Fj	1998 *E* 1,2, *A* 1, *SA* 1, *A* 2, *SA* 2, *A* 3	8	0	0	0	0	0
K J Meeuws	1998 v A	1998 *A* 3	1	0	0	0	0	0
C W Dowd	1993 v BL	1998 *E* 1,2, *A* 1, *SA* 1, *A* 2,3(R)	46	2	0	0	0	10
C H Hoeft	1998 v E	1998 *E* 2(t&R), *A* 2(R), *SA* 2, *A* 3	4	0	0	0	0	0
O M Brown	1992 v I	1998 *E* 1,2, *A* 1, *SA* 1, *A* 2, *SA* 2	56	4	0	0	0	20
I D Jones	1990 v S	1998 *E* 1,2, *A* 1, *SA* 1, *A* 2,3(R)	76	9	0	0	0	42
C C Riechelmann	1997 v Fj		6	1	0	0	0	5
R M Brooke	1992 v I	1998 *E* 1,2, *A* 1, *SA* 1, *A*2, *SA* 2, *A* 3	51	4	0	0	0	20
R K Willis	1998 v SA	1998 *SA* 2, *A* 3	2	0	0	0	0	0
M N Jones	1987 v It	1998 *E* 1, *A* 1, *SA* 1, *A* 2	55	13	0	0	0	56
J A Kronfeld	1995 v C	1998 *E* 1,2, *A* 1, *SA* 1,2, *A* 3	36	11	0	0	0	55
M P Carter	1991 v A	1998 *E* 2(R), *A* 2	7	0	0	0	0	0
I Maka	1998 v E	1998 *E* 2(R), *A* 1(R), *SA* 1(R),2	4	1	0	0	0	5
T C Randell	1997 v Fj	1998 *E* 1,2, *A* 1, *SA* 1, *A* 2, *SA* 2, *A* 3	19	9	0	0	0	45

S M Robertson	1998 v A	1998 *A* 2(R), *SA* 2(R), *A* 3(R)	3	0	0	0	0	0
X J Rush	1998 v A	1998 *A* 3	1	0	0	0	0	0
T J Blackadder	1998 v E	1998 *E* 1(R),2	2	0	0	0	0	0

Same old tricks from the maestro. All Black wing Jeff Wilson in familiar pose, breaking through the tackle of England full-back Matt Perry to score his second try during the first Test at Dunedin in June 1998.

FEAST FOLLOWS FAMINE

THE 1998 SEASON IN AUSTRALIA
Peter Jenkins

It was a feast for the Wallabies after four years of famine as the Bledisloe Cup finally made its way back across the Tasman.

With Test matches against the All Blacks always considered the ultimate yardstick for Australian sides, the mid-1990's had been, to not put too fine a point on it, a disaster. Seven successive losses was the sad statistic that confronted the Wallabies as they prepared for the first of three games against New Zealand at the cavernous Melbourne Cricket Ground in early July.

Not since George Gregan pulled off his miraculous tackle at the Sydney Football Stadium in 1994, knocking the ball from the grasp of Jeff Wilson in the throes of a try-scoring dive, had Australia beaten their nearest neighbours. But the MCG was the scene for the first leg of a memorable hat-trick – a clean sweep of three Tests against the All Blacks – that has not been achieved since 1929. When time was blown on a night when more than 75,000 watched from the grandstands, the emotion poured out. Winger Ben Tune leapt into the arms of a trainer, and skipper John Eales called his players into a huddle. He told them to keep a lid on the celebrations, there were still two games to go.

Australia had won the opening Bledisloe Cup match, which also doubled as a Tri-Nations match, by 24-16. New Zealand led 8-0 early but by half-time the Wallabies were in front 15-13. All the second-half points were penalty goals, three of them to Australian full-back Matt Burke, who finished the match as his side's lone scorer.

Round two was slugged out in Christchurch, traditionally a graveyard for the Wallabies. But on this occasion the Australians triumphed 27-23 after leading at one stage by 18 points. Second rower Tom Bowman sidestepped Jonah Lomu on his way to an early try and winger Jason Little was an attacking catalyst, scoring one and having a hand in two others. But the highlight was an inspired ensemble try when the Wallabies kept possession for three minutes and 10 seconds during a passage of play that took in 17 rucks and one maul. Eventually Burke touched down for the try.

So on to Sydney four weeks later for the third Bledisloe encounter, and a 19-14 win. The All Blacks led 11-0 after just 20 minutes and the Australian comeback that followed had legends like former captain Mark Loane singing the praises of a side flourishing under the coaching of Rod Macqueen in his first full season at the helm.

But while the Wallabies were disposing of New Zealand in a

manner they had not managed for 69 years, their record against South Africa was being gnawed at – the Springboks winning both Tri-Nations matches between the two sides to grab the southern hemisphere crown.

A week after beating the All Blacks in Melbourne, the Wallabies were in Perth for the first Test to be played in the West Australian capital, and South Africa won 14-13. It was a case of missed opportunities for the Australians, especially in the final minutes when a field goal option inside the Springboks quarter was never acted upon.

In the second clash, the week before the Wallabies completed their clean sweep of the all Blacks, the South Africans won again, this time 29-15 in Johannesburg. Australia trailed 16-12 at half-time and 16-15 with 25 minutes remaining. But the Springboks came up with the killer blow in the 68th minute when replacement backrower Bobby Skinstad crossed for the second of the home side's two tries.

Either side of the Tri-Nations series, the Wallabies were involved in a hectic season which included 13 Test matches in all. The season kicked off in Brisbane with a sadly under-strength England side mutilated 76-0.

Australian Rugby Union chairman Dick McGruther was appalled when England named a squad minus 14 Test players, saying: 'This is the greatest English sellout since Gallipoli. But we'll welcome them to their fatal landing here. While we wish the English well, unfortunately for them, Australians relish the opportunity to witness a Pommie thrashing and we invite them all to come out and enjoy it.' They did turn up and they witnessed an 11-try whitewash, with Australia scoring their highest ever Test score and their biggest winning margin. Yet the first try was not scored until the 29th minute.

For veteran hooker Phil Kearns, the night was a peak in his career, not because of the result but simply because of his presence. Kearns had not played a Test since 1995 because of serious Achilles tendon and knee injuries. Doctors thought at one stage that he would never play again. Kearns proved them wrong to line up for his 50th international and would go on to play 12 of the 13 Tests in the year.

Two Tests against Scotland followed the English bashing, with the Wallabies winning 45-3 in Sydney and 33-11 in Brisbane. Flanker David Wilson was outstanding throughout the series while Tom Bowman, in the second Test and the third of his career, was man of the match.

After the Tri-Nations series there was the small matter of World Cup qualifiers to contend with in September. Fiji were disposed of 66-20, Tonga were crushed 74-0, and Western Samoa downed

25-13 in a physical encounter in Brisbane.

For the end of season tour to France and England, the Wallabies were missing a string of first-choice selections, including prop Richard Harry, full-back Matt Burke, centre Tim Horan and winger Ben Tune.

For the Test with France in Paris a former Argentine Puma made his debut for the Wallabies, with Patricio Noriega packing into the front row. He would also play against England a week later. Australia defeated the French 32-21, with another rookie emerging as the star of the victory. Inside centre Nathan Grey, deputising for Horan, brought new meaning to midfield authority, hammering the French in defence and attack. Grey plays the game on constant overdrive.

A week later at Twickenham, the Wallabies had to rely on the boot of skipper John Eales to beat England 12-11. Eales landed four penalty goals, the last in the 72nd minute, after a Jeremy Guscott try had helped push England to an 11-9 lead.

On the domestic front, the Super-12 series, played from March to May, had not given the indication that the Wallabies were in for a successful Test season. None of the three Australian teams reached the semi-finals, and the final was an all-New Zealand affair between new champions Canterbury and the dethroned kings from Auckland.

AUSTRALIA TO EUROPE 1998

THE TOURING PARTY

Manager J McKay   **Coach** R Macqueen
Assistant Coaches TA Lane, JS Miller   **Captain** JA Eales
Full-back: CE Latham (Wests & Queensland)

Threequarters: JWC Roff (Canberra & ACT), MD Hardy (ACT), JS Little (Souths
& Queensland), NP Grey (Manly & NSW), DJ Herbert (GPS & Queensland),
SNG Staniforth (Eastwood & NSW)

Half-backs: SJ Larkham (Canberra & ACT), MHM Edmonds (Warringah &
NSW), GM Gregan (Randwick & ACT), CJ Whitaker (Randwick & NSW)

Forwards: PN Kearns (Randwick & NSW), MA Foley (Souths & Queensland),
CD Blades Randwick & NSW), AT Blades (Gordon & NSW), EP Noriega
(Canberra & ACT), GM Panoho (Brothers & Queensland), JP Welborn (Estern
Suburbs & NSW), TM Bowman (Eastern Suburbs & NSW), JA Eales (Brothers &
Queensland), V Ofahengaue (NSW), RST Kefu (Souths & Queensland),
DJ Wilson (Easts & Queensland), BJ Robinson (Souths & ACT), ODA Finegan
(Randwick & ACT), MJ Cockbain (GPS & Queensland)

TOUR RECORD

All matches   Played 3   Won 3   Points for 68   Against 41
International matches   Played 2   Won 2   Points for 44   Against 32

SCORING DETAILS

All matches						International matches					
For:	6T	4C	10PG	=	68pts	For:	3T	1C	9PG	=	44pts
Against:	3T	1C	8PG	=	41pts	Against:	3T	1C	5PG	=	32pts

MATCH DETAILS

1998	OPPONENTS	VENUE	RESULT
15 Nov	France A	Lille	W 24-9
21 Nov	FRANCE	Paris	W 32-21
28 Nov	ENGLAND	Twickenham	W 12-11

MATCH 1   15 November, Stadium du Nord, Lille

France A 9 (3PG)   **Australia XV 24** (3G 1PG)
France A: N Brusque (Pau); J Marlu (Montferrand), R Dourthe (Stade Francais),
F Ribeyrolles (Montferrand), S Kubzik (Perigueux); S Prosper (Agen),
C Laussucq (Stade Francais); R Peillard (Perpignan), O Azam (Montferrand),
S de Besombes (Perpignan), F Belot (Stade Toulousain)(*capt*), J Daude
(Bourgoin-Jallieu), C Moni (Stade Francais), P Raschi (Bourgoin-Jallieu),
A Costes (Montferrand) *Substitutions:* T Mentieres (Pau) for Daude (40 mins);
E Lecomte (Montferrand) for Moni (64 mins)
Scorer *Penalty Goals:* Dourthe (3)
Australia A: Latham; Little, Herbert, Grey, Roff; Larkham, Gregan; Panoho,
Kearns, A Blades, Bowman, Eales (*capt*), Cockbain, Kefu, Wilson *Substitutions:*
Noriega for Panoho (20 mins); Ofahengaue for Kefu (49 mins); Finegan for
Bowman (55 mins); Foley for Kearns (70 mins); Whitaker for Gregan (74 mins);
Hardy for Roff (79 mins)
Scorers *Tries:* Little, Herbert, Gregan *Conversions:* Eales (3) *Penalty Goal:* Eales
Referee DI Ramage (Scotland)

MATCH 2   21 November, Stade de France, Paris   Test Match
FRANCE 21 (1G 3PG 1T)   AUSTRALIA 32 (1G 5PG 2T)

FRANCE: A Gomes (Stade Français); P Bernat-Salles (Biarritz), C Lamaison (Brive), S Glas (Bourgoin-Jallieu), T Lombard (Stade Français); D Aucagne (Pau), P Carbonneau (Brive); S Marconnet (Stade Français), R Ibañez (Perpignan) (*capt*), F Tournaire (Narbonne), O Brouzet (Bègles-Bordeaux), F Pelous (Toulouse), M Lièvremont (Stade Français), T Lièvremont (Stade Français), O Magne (Brive) *Substitution:* R Castel (Bèziers) for M Lièvremont (69 mins)
Scorers *Tries:* Lombard, Carbonneau *Conversion:* Lamaison *Penalty Goals:* Lamaison (3)
AUSTRALIA: Latham; Little, Herbert, Grey, Roff; Larkham, Gregan; Noriega, Kearns, A Blades, Bowman, Eales (*capt*), Cockbain, Kefu, Wilson *Substitutions:* Finegan for Cockbain (56 mins); Ofahengaue for Kefu (58 mins); Foley for Kearns (58 mins)
Scorers *Tries:* Wilson, Bowman, Kefu *Conversion:* Eales *Penalty Goals:* Eales (5)
Referee A Watson (South Africa)

MATCH 3   28 November, Twickenham
Test Match
for the Cook Cup
ENGLAND 11 (2PG 1T)   AUSTRALIA 12 (4PG)

ENGLAND: MB Perry (Bath); T Underwood (Newcastle), PR de Glanville (Bath), JC Guscott (Bath), AS Healey (Leicester); PJ Grayson (Northampton), MJS Dawson (Northampton); J Leonard (Harlequins), R Cockerill (Leicester), DJ Garforth (Leicester), MO Johnson (Leicester), TAK Rodber (Northampton), LBN Dallaglio (Wasps) (*capt*), RA Hill (Saracens), NA Back (Leicester)
Substitution: MJ Catt (Bath) for Grayson (33 mins)
Scorers *Try:* Guscott *Penalty Goals:* Catt (2)
AUSTRALIA: Latham; Little, Herbert, Grey, Roff; Larkham, Gregan; Noriega, Kearns, A Blades, Bowman, Eales (*capt*), Cockbain, Kefu, Wilson *Substitutions:* Foley for Kearns (46 mins); Finegan for Cockbain (50 mins)
Scorer *Penalty Goals:* Eales (4)
Referee PJ Honiss (New Zealand)

The Australian team round off a long season by celebrating their narrow 12-11 victory over England for the Cook Cup at Twickenham in November 1998.

AUSTRALIAN INTERNATIONAL PLAYERS (*up to 30 April 1999*)

N.B. In the summer of 1986, the ARU retrospectively granted full Australian Test status to the five international matches played by the 1927-28 touring team to Europe. In 1988 Test status was extended to all those who played overseas in the 1920s.

Abrahams, A M F (NSW) 1967 *NZ*, 1968 *NZ* 1, 1969 *W*
Adams, N J (NSW) 1955 *NZ* 1
Adamson, R W (NSW) 1912 *US*
Allan, T (NSW) 1946 *NZ* 1, *M*, *NZ* 2, 1947 *NZ* 2, *S, I, W*, 1948 *E, F*, 1949 *M* 1,2,3, *NZ* 1,2
Anlezark, E A (NSW) 1905 *NZ*
Armstrong, A R (NSW) 1923 *NZ* 1,2
Austin, L R (NSW) 1963 *E*

Baker, R L (NSW) 1904 *BI* 1,2
Baker, W H (NSW) 1914 *NZ* 1,2,3
Ballesty, J P (NSW) 1968 *NZ* 1,2, *F, I, S*, 1969 *W, SA* 2,3,4,
Bannon, D P (NSW) 1946 *M*
Bardsley, E J (NSW) 1928 *NZ* 1,3, *M* (R)
Barker, H S (NSW) 1952 *Fj* 1,2, *NZ* 1,2, 1953 *SA* 4, 1954 *Fj* 1,2
Barnett, J T (NSW) 1907 *NZ* 1,2,3, 1908 *W*, 1909 *E*
Barry, M J (Q) 1971 *SA* 3
Barton, R F D (NSW) 1899 *BI* 3
Batch, P G (Q) 1975 *S, W*, 1976 *E, Fj* 1,2,3, *F* 1,2, 1978 *W* 1,2, *NZ* 1,2,3, 1979 *Arg* 2
Batterham, R P (NSW) 1967 *NZ*, 1970 *S*
Battishall, B R (NSW) 1973 *E*
Baxter, A J (NSW) 1949 *M* 1,2,3, *NZ* 1,2, 1951 *NZ* 1,2, 1952 *NZ* 1,2
Baxter, T J (Q) 1958 *NZ* 3
Beith, B McN (NSW) 1914 *NZ* 3
Bell, K R (Q) 1968 *S*
Bell, M D NSW) 1996 *C*
Bennett, W G (NSW) 1931 *M*, 1933 *SA* 1,2,3,
Bermingham, J V (Q) 1934 *NZ* 1,2, 1937 *SA* 1
Berne, J E (NSW) 1975 *S*
Besomo, K S (NSW) 1979 *I* 2
Betts, T N (Q) 1951 *NZ* 2,3, 1954 *Fj* 2
Biilmann, R R (NSW) 1933 *SA* 1,2,3,4
Birt, R (Q) 1914 *NZ* 2
Black, J W (NSW) 1985 *C* 1,2, *NZ, Fj* 1
Blackwood, J G (NSW) 1923 *NZ* 1,2,3, 1925 *NZ*, 1927 *I, W, S*, 1928 *E, F*
Blades, A T (NSW) 1996 *S, I, W* 3, 1997 *NZ* 1 (R), *E* 1 (R), *SA* 1 (R), *NZ* 3, *SA* 2, *Arg* 1,2, *E* 2, *S*, 1998 *E* 1, *S* 1,2, *NZ* 1, *SA* 1, *NZ* 2, *SA* 2, *NZ* 3, *Fj, WS, F, E* 2
Blades, C D (NSW) 1997 *E* 1
Blair, M R (NSW) 1928 *F*, 1931 *M, NZ*
Bland, G V (NSW) 1928 *NZ* 3, *M*, 1932 *NZ* 1,2,3, 1933 *SA* 1,2,4,5
Blomley, J (NSW) 1949 *M* 1,2,3, *NZ* 1,2, 1950 *BI* 1,2
Boland, S B (Q) 1899 *BI* 3,4, 1903 *NZ*
Bond, J H (NSW) 1921 *NZ*
Bonis, E T (Q) 1929 *NZ* 1,2,3, 1930 *BI*, 1931 *M, NZ*, 1932 *NZ* 1,2,3, 1933 *SA* 1,2,3,4,5, 1934 *NZ* 1,2, 1936 *NZ* 1,2, *M*, 1937 *SA* 1, 1938 *NZ* 1
Bosler, J M (NSW) 1953 *SA* 1
Bouffler, R G (NSW) 1899 *BI* 3
Bourke, T K (Q) 1947 *NZ* 2
Bowen, S (NSW) 1993 *SA* 1,2,3, 1995 *[R]*, *NZ* 1,2, 1996 *C, NZ* 1, *SA* 2
Bowers, A J A (NSW) 1923 *NZ* 3, 1925 *NZ*, 1927 *I*
Bowman, T M (NSW) 1998 *E* 1, *S* 1,2, *NZ* 1, *SA* 1, *NZ* 2, *SA* 2, *NZ* 3, *Fj, WS, F, E* 2
Boyce, E S (NSW) 1962 *NZ* 1,2, 1964 *NZ* 1,2,3, 1965 *SA* 1,2, 1966 *W, S*, 1967 *E, I* 1, *F, I* 2
Boyce, J S (NSW) 1962 *NZ* 3,4,5, 1963 *E, SA* 1,2,3,4, 1964 *NZ* 1,3, 1965 *SA* 1,2
Boyd, A (NSW) 1899 *BI* 3
Boyd, A F McC (Q) 1958 *M* 1
Brass, J E (NSW) 1966 *BI* 2, *W, S*, 1967 *E, I* 1, *F, I* 2, *NZ*, 1968 *NZ* 1, *F, I, S*
Breckenridge, J W (NSW) 1927 *I, W, S*, 1928 *E, F*, 1929 *NZ* 1,2,3, 1930 *BI*
Brial, M C (NSW) 1993 *F* 1 (R), 2, 1996 *W* 1 (R), 2, *C, NZ* 1, *SA* 1, *NZ* 2, *SA* 2, *It, I, W* 3, 1997 *NZ* 2

Bridle, O L (V) 1931 *M*, 1932 *NZ* 1,2,3, 1933 *SA* 3,4,5, 1934 *NZ* 1,2, 1936 *NZ* 1,2, *M*
Broad, E G (Q) 1949 *M* 1
Brockhoff, J D (NSW) 1949 *M* 2,3, *NZ* 1,2, 1950 *BI* 1,2, 1951 *NZ* 2,3
Brown, B R (Q) 1972 *NZ* 1,3
Brown, J V (NSW) 1956 *SA* 1,2, 1957 *NZ* 1,2, 1958 *W, I, E, S, F*
Brown, R C (NSW) 1975 *E* 1,2
Brown, S W (NSW) 1953 *SA* 2,3,4
Bryant, H (NSW) 1925 *NZ*
Buchan, A J (NSW) 1946 *NZ* 1,2, 1947 *NZ* 1,2, *S, I, W*, 1948 *E, F*, 1949 *M* 3
Bull, D (NSW) 1928 *M*
Buntine, H (NSW) 1923 *NZ* 1 (R)
Burdon, A (NSW) 1903 *NZ*, 1904 *BI* 1,2, 1905 *NZ*
Burge, A B (NSW) 1907 *NZ* 3, 1908 *W*
Burge, P H (NSW) 1907 *NZ* 1,2,3
Burge, R (NSW) 1928 *NZ* 1,2,3 (R), *M* (R)
Burke, B T (NSW) 1988 *S* (R)
Burke, C T (NSW) 1946 *NZ* 2, 1947 *NZ* 1,2, *S, I, W*, 1948 *E, F*, 1949 *M* 2,3, *NZ* 1,2, 1950 *BI* 1,2, 1951 *NZ* 1,2,3, 1953 *SA* 2,3,4, 1954 *Fj* 1, 1955 *NZ* 1,2,3, 1956 *SA* 1,2,
Burke, M (NSW) 1993 *SA* 3 (R), *F* 1, 1994 *I* 1,2, *It* 1,2, 1995 *[C, R, E]*, *NZ* 1,2, 1996 *W* 1,2, *C, NZ* 1, *SA* 1, *NZ* 2, *SA* 2, *It, S, I, W* 3, 1997 *E* 1, *NZ* 2, 1998 *E* 1, *S* 1,2, *NZ* 1, *SA* 1, *NZ* 2, *SA* 2, *NZ* 3
Burke, M P (NSW) 1984 *E* (R), *I*, 1985 *C* 1,2, *NZ, Fj* 1,2, 1986 *It* (R), *F, Arg* 1,2, *NZ* 1,2,3, 1987 *SK*, *[US, J, I, F, W]*, *NZ, Arg* 1,2
Burnet, D R (NSW) 1972 *F* 1,2, *NZ* 1,2,3, *Fj*
Butler, O F (NSW) 1969 *SA* 1,2, 1970 *S*, 1971 *SA* 2,3, *F* 1,2

Calcraft, W J (NSW) 1985 *C* 1, 1986 *It, Arg* 2
Caldwell, B C (NSW) 1928 *NZ* 3
Cameron, A S (NSW) 1951 *NZ* 1,2,3, 1952 *Fj* 1,2, *NZ* 1,2, 1953 *SA* 1,2,3,4, 1954 *Fj* 1,2, 1955 *NZ* 1,2,3, 1956 *SA* 1,2, 1957 *NZ* 1, 1958 *I*
Campbell, J D (NSW) 1910 *NZ* 1,2,3
Campbell, W A (Q) 1984 *Fj*, 1986 *It, F, Arg* 1,2, *NZ* 1,2,3, 1987 *SK*, *[E, US, J* (R)*, I, F]*, *NZ*, 1988 *E*, 1989 *BI* 1,2,3, *NZ*, 1990 *NZ* 2,3
Campese, D I (ACT, NSW) 1982 *NZ* 1,2,3, 1983 *US, Arg* 1,2, *NZ, It, F* 1,2, 1984 *Fj, NZ* 1,2,3, *E, I, W, S*, 1985 *Fj* 1,2, 1986 *It, F, Arg* 1,2, *NZ* 1,2,3, 1987 *[E, US, J, I, F, W]*, *NZ*, 1988 *E* 1,2, *NZ* 1,2,3, *E, S, It*, 1989 *BI* 1,2,3, *NZ, F* 1,2, 1990 *F* 2,3, *NZ* 1,2,3, 1991 *W, E, NZ* 1,2, *[Arg, WS, W, I, NZ, E]*, 1992 *S* 1,2, *NZ* 1,2,3, *SA, I, W*, 1993 *Tg, NZ, SA* 1,2,3, *C, F* 1,2, 1994 *I* 1,2, *It* 1,2, *WS, NZ*, 1995 *Arg* 1,2, *[SA, C, E]*, *NZ* 2 (R), 1996 *W* 1,2, *C, NZ* 1, *SA* 1, *NZ* 2, *SA* 2, *It, W3*
Canniffe, W D (Q) 1907 *NZ* 2
Caputo, M E (ACT) 1996 *W* 1,2, 1997 *F* 1,2, *NZ* 1
Carberry, C M (NSW, Q) 1973 *Tg* 2, *E*, 1976 *I, US, Fj* 1,2,3, 1981 *F* 1,2, *I, W, S*, 1982 *E*
Cardy, A M (NSW) 1966 *BI* 1,2, *W, S*, 1967 *E, I* 1, *F*, 1968 *NZ* 1,2
Carew, P J (Q) 1899 *BI* 1,2,3,4
Carmichael, P (Q) 1904 *BI* 2, 1907 *NZ* 1, 1908 *W*, 1909 *E*
Carozza, P V (Q) 1990 *F* 1,2,3, *NZ* 2,3, 1992 *S* 1,2, *NZ* 1,2,3, *SA, I, W*, 1993 *Tg, NZ*
Carpenter, M G (V) 1938 *NZ* 1,2,
Carr, E T A (NSW) 1913 *NZ* 1,2,3, 1914 *NZ* 1,2,3
Carr, E W (NSW) 1921 *NZ* 1 (R)
Carroll, D B (NSW) 1908 *W*, 1912 *US*
Carroll, J C (NSW) 1953 *SA* 1
Carroll, J H (NSW) 1958 *M* 2,3, *NZ* 1,2,3, 1959 *BI* 1,2
Carson, J (NSW) 1899 *BI* 1
Carson, P J (NSW) 1979 *NZ*, 1980 *NZ* 3
Carter, D G (NSW) 1988 *E* 1,2, *NZ* 1, 1989 *F* 1,2

Casey, T V (NSW) 1963 *SA* 2,3,4, 1964 *NZ* 1,2,3
Catchpole, K W (NSW) 1961 *Fj* 1,2,3, *SA* 1,2, *F*, 1962 *NZ* 1,2,4, 1963 *SA* 2,3,4, 1964 *NZ* 1,2,3, 1965 *SA* 1,2, 1966 *BI* 1,2, *W*, *S*, 1967 *E*, *I* 1, *F*, *I* 2, *NZ*, 1968 *NZ* 1
Cawsey, R M (NSW) 1949 *M* 1, *NZ* 1,2
Cerutti, W H (NSW) 1928 *NZ* 1,2,3, *M*, 1929 *NZ* 1,2,3, 1930 *BI*, 1931 *M*, *NZ*, 1932 *NZ* 1,2,3, 1933 *SA* 1,2,3,4,5, 1936 *M*, 1937 *SA* 1,2
Challoner, R L (NSW) 1899 *BI* 2
Chapman, G A (NSW) 1962 *NZ* 3,4,5
Clark, J G (Q) 1931 *M*, *NZ*, 1932 *NZ* 1,2, 1933 *SA* 1
Clarken, J C (NSW) 1905 *NZ*, 1910 *NZ* 1,2,3
Cleary, M A (NSW) 1961 *Fj* 1,2,3, *SA* 1,2, *F*
Clements, P (NSW) 1982 *NZ* 3
Clifford, M (NSW) 1938 *NZ* 3
Cobb, W G (NSW) 1899 *BI* 2
Cockbain, M J (Q) 1997 *F* 2 (R), *NZ* 1, *SA* 1,2, 1998 *E* 1, *S* 1,2, *NZ* 1, *SA* 1, *NZ* 2, *SA* 2, *NZ* 3, *Fj*, *Tg* (R), *WS*, *F*, *E* 2
Cocks, M R (NSW, Q) 1972 *F* 1,2, *NZ* 2,3, *Fj*, 1973 *Tg* 1,2, *W*, *E*, 1975 *J* 1
Codey, D (NSW Country, Q) 1983 *Arg* 1, 1984 *E*, *W*, *S*, 1985 *C* 2, *NZ*, 1986 *F*, *Arg* 1, 1987 [*US*, *J*, *F* (R), *W*], *NZ*
Cody, E W (NSW) 1913 *NZ* 1,2,3
Coker, T (Q, ACT) 1987 [*E*, *US*, *F*, *W*], 1991 *NZ* 2, [*Arg*, *WS*, *NZ*, *E*], 1992 *NZ* 1,2,3, *W* (R), 1993 *Tg*, *NZ*, 1995 *Arg* 2, *NZ* 1 (R), 1997 *F* 1 (R), 2, *NZ* 1, *E* 1, *NZ* 2 (R), *SA* 1 (R), *NZ* 3, *SA* 2, *Arg* 1,2
Colbert, R (NSW) 1952 *Fj* 2, *NZ* 1,2, 1953 *SA* 2,3,4
Colton, A J (Q) 1899 *BI* 1,3
Colton, T (Q) 1904 *BI* 1,2
Comrie-Thomson, I R (NSW) 1928 *NZ* 1,2,3 *M*
Connor, D M (Q) 1958 *W*, *I*, *E*, *S*, *F*, *M* 2,3, *NZ* 1,2,3, 1959 *BI* 1,2
Constable, R (Q) 1994 *I* 2 (t & R)
Cook, M T (Q) 1986 *F*, 1987 *SK*, [*J*], 1988 *E* 1,2, *NZ* 1,2,3, *E*, *S*, *It*
Cooke, B P (Q) 1979 *I* 1
Cooke, G M (Q) 1932 *NZ* 1,2,3, 1933 *SA* 1,2,3, 1946 *NZ* 2, 1947 *NZ* 2, *S*, *I*, *W*, 1948 *E*, *F*
Coolican, J E (NSW) 1982 *NZ* 1, 1983 *It*, *F* 1,2
Corfe, A C (Q) 1899 *BI* 2
Cornelsen, G (NSW) 1974 *NZ* 2,3, 1975 *J* 2, *S*, *W*, 1976 *E*, *F* 1,2, 1978 *W* 1,2, *NZ* 1, *NZ* 1,2,3, 1979 *I* 1,2, *NZ*, *Arg* 1,2, 1980 *NZ* 1,2,3, 1981 *I*, *W*, *S*, 1982 *E*
Cornes, J R (Q) 1972 *Fj*
Cornforth, R G W (NSW) 1947 *NZ* 1, 1950 *BI* 2
Cornish, P (ACT) 1990 *F* 2,3, *NZ* 1
Costello, P P S (Q) 1950 *BI* 2
Cottrell, N V (Q) 1949 *M* 1,2,3, *NZ* 1,2, 1950 *BI* 1,2, 1951 *NZ* 1,2,3, 1952 *Fj* 1,2, *NZ* 1,2
Cowper, D L (V) 1931 *NZ*, 1932 *NZ* 1,2,3, 1933 *SA* 1,2,3,4,5
Cox, B P (NSW) 1952 *Fj* 1,2, *NZ* 1,2, 1954 *Fj* 2, 1955 *NZ* 1, 1956 *SA* 2, 1957 *NZ* 1,2
Cox, M H (NSW) 1981 *W*, *S*
Cox, P A (NSW) 1979 *Arg* 1,2, 1980 *Fj*, *NZ* 1,2, 1981 *W* (R), *S*, 1982 *S* 1,2, *NZ* 1,2,3, 1984 *Fj*, *NZ* 1,2,3
Craig, R R (NSW) 1908 *W*
Crakanthorp, J S (NSW) 1923 *NZ* 3
Cremin, J F (NSW) 1946 *NZ* 1,2, 1947 *NZ* 1
Crittle, C P (NSW) 1962 *NZ* 4, 5, 1963 *SA* 2,3,4, 1964 *NZ* 1,2,3, 1965 *SA* 1,2, 1966 *BI* 1,2, *S*, 1967 *E*, *I*
Croft, B H D (NSW) 1928 *M*
Cross, J R (NSW) 1955 *NZ* 1,2,3
Cross, K A (NSW) 1949 *M* 1, *NZ* 1,2, 1950 *BI* 1,2, 1951 *NZ* 2,3, 1952 *NZ* 1, 1953 *SA* 1,2,3,4, 1954 *Fj* 1,2, 1955 *NZ* 3, 1956 *SA* 1,2, 1957 *NZ* 1,2
Crossman, O C (NSW) 1925 *NZ*, 1929 *NZ* 2, 1930 *BI*
Crowe, P J (NSW) 1976 *F* 2, 1978 *W* 1,2, 1979 *I* 2, *NZ*, *Arg* 1
Crowley, D J (Q) 1989 *BI* 1,2,3, 1991 [*WS*], 1992 *I*, *W*, 1993 *C* (R), 1995 *Arg* 1,2, [*SA*, *E*], *NZ* 1, 1996 *W* 2 (R), *C*, *NZ* 1, *SA* 1,2, *I*, *W* 3, 1998 *E* 1 (R), *S* 1 (R),2 (R), *NZ* 1 (R), *SA* 1, *NZ* 2, *SA* 2, *NZ* 3, *Tg*, *WS*
Curley, T G P (NSW) 1957 *NZ* 1,2, 1958 *W*, *I*, *E*, *S*, *F*, *M* 1, *NZ* 1,2,3
Curran, D J (NSW) 1980 *NZ* 3, 1981 *F* 1,2, *W*, 1983 *Arg* 1
Currie, E W (Q) 1899 *BI* 2

Cutler, S A G (NSW) 1982 *NZ* 2 (R), 1984 *NZ* 1,2,3, *E*, *I*, *W*, *S*, 1985 *C* 1,2, *NZ*, *Fj* 1,2, 1986 *It*, *F*, *NZ* 1,2,3, 1987 *SK*, [*E*, *J*, *I*, *F*, *W*], *NZ*, *Arg* 1,2, 1988 *E* 1,2, *NZ* 1,2,3, *E*, *S*, *It*, 1989 *BI* 1,2,3, *NZ*, 1991 [*WS*]

Daly, A J (NSW) 1989 *NZ*, *F* 1,2, 1990 *F* 1,2,3, *US*, *NZ* 1,2,3, 1991 *W*, *E*, *NZ* 1,2, [*Arg*, *W*, *I*, *NZ*, *E*], 1992 *S* 1,2, *NZ* 1,2,3, *SA*, *W* (R), 1993 *Tg*, *NZ*, *SA* 1,2,3, *C*, *F* 1,2, 1994 *I* 1,2, *It* 1,2, *WS*, *NZ*, 1995 [*C*, *R*]
D'Arcy, A M (Q) 1980 *Fj*, *NZ* 3, 1981 *F* 1,2, *I*, *W*, *S*, 1982 *E*, *S* 1,2
Darveniza, P (NSW) 1969 *W*, *SA* 2,3,4
Davidson, R A L (NSW) 1952 *Fj* 1,2, *NZ* 1,2, 1953 *SA* 1, 1957 *NZ* 1,2, 1958 *W*, *I*, *E*, *S*, *F*, *M* 1
Davis, C C (NSW) 1949 *NZ* 1, 1951 *NZ* 1,2,3
Davis, E H (V) 1947 *S*, *W*, 1949 *M* 1,2
Davis, G V (NSW) 1963 *E*, *SA* 1,2,3,4, 1964 *NZ* 1,2,3, 1965 *SA* 1, 1966 *W*, *S*, 1967 *E*, *I* 1, *F*, *I* 2, *NZ*, 1968 *NZ* 1,2,3, *F*, *I*, *S*, 1969 *W*, *SA* 1,2,3,4, 1970 *S*, 1971 *NZ* 1,2,3, *F* 1,2, 1972 *F* 1,2, *NZ* 1,2,3
Davis, G W G (NSW) 1955 *NZ* 2,3
Davis, R A (NSW) 1974 *NZ* 1,2,3
Davis, T S R (NSW) 1921 *NZ*, 1923 *NZ* 1,2,3
Davis, W (NSW) 1899 *BI* 1,3,4
Dawson, W L (NSW) 1946 *NZ* 1,2
Diett, L J (NSW) 1959 *BI* 1,2
Dix, W (NSW) 1907 *NZ* 1,2,3, 1909 *E*
Dixon, E J (Q) 1904 *BI* 3
Donald, K J (Q) 1957 *NZ* 1, 1958 *W*, *I*, *E*, *S*, *M* 2,3, 1959 *BI* 1,2
Dore, E (Q) 1904 *BI* 1
Dore, M J (Q) 1905 *NZ*
Dorr, R W (V) 1936 *M*, 1937 *SA* 1
Douglas, J A (V) 1962 *NZ* 3,4,5
Dowse, J H (NSW) 1961 *Fj* 1,2, *SA* 1,2
Dunbar, A R (NSW) 1910 *NZ* 1,2,3, 1912 *US*
Dunlop, E E (V) 1932 *NZ* 3, 1934 *NZ* 1
Dunn, P K (NSW) 1958 *NZ* 1,2,3, 1959 *BI* 1,2
Dunn, V A (NSW) 1921 *NZ*
Dunworth, D A (Q) 1971 *F* 1,2, 1972 *F* 1,2, 1976 *Fj* 2
Dwyer, L J (NSW) 1910 *NZ* 1,2,3, 1912 *US*, 1913 *NZ* 1, 1914 *NZ* 1,2,3

Eales, J A (Q) 1991 *W*, *E*, *NZ* 1,2, [*Arg*, *WS*, *W*, *I*, *NZ*, *E*], 1992 *S* 1,2, *NZ* 1,2,3, *SA*, *I*, 1994 *I* 1,2, *It* 1,2, *WS*, *NZ*, 1995 *Arg* 1,2, [*SA*, *C*, *R*, *E*], *NZ* 1,2, 1996 *W* 1,2, *C*, *NZ* 1, *SA* 1, *NZ* 2, *SA* 2, *It*, *S*, *I*, 1997 *F* 1,2, *NZ* 1, *E* 1, *NZ* 2, *SA* 1, *Arg* 1,2, *E* 2, *S*, 1998 *E* 1, *S* 1,2, *NZ* 1, *SA* 1, *NZ* 2, *SA* 2, *NZ* 3, *Fj*, *Tg*, *WS*, *F*, *E* 2
Eastes, C C (NSW) 1946 *NZ* 1,2, 1947 *NZ* 1,2, 1949 *M* 1,2
Edmonds, M H M (NSW) 1998 *Tg*
Egerton, R H (NSW) 1991 *W*, *E*, *NZ* 1,2, [*Arg*, *W*, *I*, *NZ*, *E*]
Ella, G A (NSW) 1982 *NZ* 1,2, 1983 *F* 1,2, 1988 *E* 2, *NZ* 1
Ella, G J (NSW) 1982 *S* 1, 1983 *It*, 1985 *C* 2 (R), *Fj* 2
Ella, M G (NSW) 1980 *NZ* 1,2,3, 1981 *F* 2, *S*, 1982 *E*, *S* 1, *NZ* 1,2,3, 1983 *US*, *Arg* 1,2, *NZ*, *It*, *F* 1,2, 1984 *Fj*, *NZ* 1,2,3, *E*, *I*, *W*, *S*
Ellem, M A (NSW) 1976 *Fj* 3 (R)
Elliott, F M (NSW) 1957 *NZ* 1
Elliott, R E (NSW) 1921 *NZ*, 1923 *NZ* 1,2,3
Ellis, C S (NSW) 1899 *BI* 1,2,3,4
Ellis, K J (NSW) 1958 *NZ* 1,2,3, 1959 *BI* 1,2
Ellwood, B J (NSW) 1958 *NZ* 1,2,3, 1961 *Fj* 2,3, *SA* 1, *F*, 1962 *NZ* 1,2,3,4,5, 1963 *SA* 1,2,3,4, 1964 *NZ* 3, 1965 *SA* 1,2, 1966 *BI* 1
Emanuel, D M (NSW) 1957 *NZ* 2, 1958 *W*, *I*, *E*, *S*, *F*, *M* 1,2,3
Emery, N A (NSW) 1947 *NZ* 2, *S*, *I*, *W*, 1948 *E*, *F*, 1949 *M* 2,3, *NZ* 1,2
Erasmus, D J (NSW) 1923 *NZ* 1,2
Erby, A B (NSW) 1923 *NZ* 2,3
Evans, L J (Q) 1903 *NZ*, 1904 *BI* 1,3
Evans, W T (Q) 1899 *BI* 1,2

Fahey, E J (NSW) 1912 *US*, 1913 *NZ* 1, 1914 *NZ* 3
Fairfax, R L (NSW) 1971 *F* 1,2, 1972 *F* 1,2, *NZ* 1, *Fj*, 1973 *W*, *E*
Farmer, E H (Q) 1910 *NZ* 1

Farr-Jones, N C (NSW) 1984 *E, I, W, S*, 1985 *C* 1,2, *NZ, Fj* 1,2, 1986 *It, F, Arg* 1,2, *NZ* 1,2,3, 1987 *SK, [E, I, F, W (R)], NZ, Arg* 2, 1988 *E* 1,2, *NZ* 1,2,3, *E, S, It*, 1989 *BI* 1,2,3, *NZ, F* 1,2, 1990 *F* 1,2,3, *US, NZ* 1,2,3, 1991 *W, E, NZ* 1,2, *[Arg, WS, I, NZ, E]*, 1992 *S* 1,2, *NZ* 1,2,3, *SA*, 1993 *NZ, SA* 1,2,3
Fay, G (NSW) 1971 *SA* 2, 1972 *NZ* 1,2,3, 1973 *Tg* 1,2, *W, E*, 1974 *NZ* 1,2,3, 1975 *E* 1,2, *J* 1, *S, W*, 1976 *I, US*, 1978 *W* 1,2, *NZ* 1,2,3, 1979 *I* 1
Fenwicke, P T (NSW) 1957 *NZ* 1, 1958 *W, I, E*, 1959 *BI* 1,2
Ferguson, R T (NSW) 1923 *NZ* 3
Fihelly, J A (Q) 1907 *NZ* 2
Finau, S F (NSW) 1997 *NZ* 3
Finegan, O D A (ACT) 1996 *W* 1,2, *C, NZ* 1, *SA* 1 (t), *S, W* 3, 1997 *NZ* 3, *SA* 2, *Arg* 1,2, *E* 2, *S*, 1998 *E* 1 (R), *S* 1 (t + R),2 (t + R), *NZ* 1 (R), *SA* 1 (t),2 (R), *NZ* 3 (R), *Fj* (R), *Tg, WS* (t + R), *F* (R), *E* 2 (R)
Finlay, A N (NSW) 1927 *I, W, S*, 1928 *E, F*, 1929 *NZ* 1,2,3, 1930 *BI*
Finley, F G (NSW) 1904 *BI* 3
Finnane, S C (NSW) 1975 *E* 1, *J* 1,2, 1976 *E*, 1978 *W* 1,2
FitzSimons, P (NSW) 1989 *F* 1,2, 1990 *F* 1,2,3, *US, NZ* 1
Flanagan, P (Q) 1907 *NZ* 1,2
Flatley, E J (Q) 1997 *E* 2, *S*
Flett, J A (NSW) 1990 *US, NZ* 2,3, 1991 *[WS]*
Flynn, J P (Q) 1914 *NZ* 1,2
Fogarty, J R (Q) 1949 *M* 2,3
Foley, M A (Q) 1995 *[C (R), R]*, 1996 *W* 2(R), *NZ* 1, *SA* 1, *NZ* 2, *SA* 2, *It, S, I, W* 3, 1997 *NZ* 1 (R), *F* 1, *NZ* 2, *SA* 1, *NZ* 3, *SA* 2, *Arg* 1,2, *E* 2, *S*, 1998 *Tg* (R), *F* (R), *E* 2 (R)
Forbes, C F (Q) 1953 *SA* 2,3,4, 1954 *Fj* 1, 1956 *SA* 1,2
Ford, B (Q) 1957 *NZ* 2
Ford, E E (NSW) 1927 *I, W, S*, 1928 *E, F*, 1929 *NZ* 1,3
Ford, J A (NSW) 1925 *NZ*, 1927 *I, W, S*, 1928 *E*, 1929 *NZ* 1,2,3, 1930 *BI*
Forman, T R (NSW) 1968 *I, S*, 1969 *W, SA* 1,2,3,4
Fox, C L (NSW) 1921 *NZ*, 1928 *F*
Fox, O G (NSW) 1958 *F*
Francis, E (Q) 1914 *NZ* 1,2
Frawley, D (Q, NSW) 1986 *Arg* 2 (R), 1987 *Arg* 1,2, 1988 *E* 1,2, *NZ* 1,2,3, *S, It*
Freedman, J E (NSW) 1962 *NZ* 3,4,5, 1963 *SA* 1
Freeman, E (NSW) 1946 *NZ* 1 (R), *M*
Freney, M E (Q) 1972 *NZ* 1,2,3, 1973 *Tg* 1, *W, E* (R)
Furness, D C (NSW) 1946 *M*
Futter, F C (NSW) 1904 *BI* 3

Gardner, J M (Q) 1987 *Arg* 2, 1988 *E* 1, *NZ* 1, *E*
Gardner, W C (NSW) 1950 *BI* 1
Garner, R L (NSW) 1949 *NZ* 1,2
Gavin, K A (NSW) 1909 *E*
Gavin, T B (NSW) 1988 *NZ* 2,3, *S, It* (R), 1989 *NZ* (R), *F* 1,2, 1990 *F* 1,2,3, *US, NZ* 1,2,3, 1991 *W, E, NZ* 1, 1992 *S* 1,2, *SA, I, W*, 1993 *Tg, NZ, SA* 1,2,3, *C, F* 1,2, 1994 *I* 1,2, *It* 1,2, *WS, NZ*, 1995 *Arg* 1,2, *[SA, C, R, E]*, *NZ* 1,2, 1996 *NZ* 2 (R), *SA* 2, *W* 3
Gelling, A M (Q) 1972 *NZ* 1, *Fj*
George, H W (NSW) 1910 *NZ* 1,2,3, 1912 *US*, 1913 *NZ* 1,3, 1914 *NZ* 1,3
George, W G (NSW) 1923 *NZ* 1,2, 1928 *NZ* 1,2,3, *M*
Gibbons, E de C (NSW) 1936 *NZ* 1,2, *M*
Gibbs, P R (V) 1966 *S*
Giffin, D (ACT) 1996 *W* 3, 1997 *F* 1,2
Gilbert, H (NSW) 1910 *NZ* 1,2,3
Girvan, B (ACT) 1988 *E*
Gordon, G C (NSW) 1929 *NZ* 1
Gordon, K M (NSW) 1950 *BI* 1,2
Gould, R G (Q) 1980 *NZ* 1,2,3, 1981 *I, W, S*, 1982 *S* 2, *NZ* 1,2,3, 1983 *US, Arg* 1, *F* 1,2, 1984 *NZ* 1,2,3, *E, I, W, S*, 1985 *NZ*, 1986 *It*, 1987 *SK, [E]*
Gourley, S R (NSW) 1988 *S, It*, 1989 *BI* 1,2,3
Graham, C S (Q) 1899 *BI* 2
Graham, R (NSW) 1973 *Tg* 1,2, *W, E*, 1974 *NZ* 2,3, 1975 *E* 2, *J* 1,2, *S, W*, 1976 *I, US, Fj* 1,2,3, *F* 1,2
Gralton, A S I (Q) 1899 *BI* 1,4, 1903 *NZ*
Grant, J C (NSW) 1988 *E* 1, *NZ* 2,3, *E*
Graves, R H (NSW) 1907 *NZ* 1 (R)
Greatorex, E N (NSW) 1923 *NZ* 3, 1928 *E, F*

Gregan, G M (ACT) 1994 *It* 1,2, *WS, NZ*, 1995 *Arg* 1,2, *[SA, C (R), R, E]*, 1996 *W* 1, *C* (t), *SA* 1, *NZ* 2, *SA* 2, *It, I, W* 3, 1997 *F* 1,2, *NZ* 1, *E* 1, *NZ* 2, *SA* 1, *NZ* 3, *SA* 2, *Arg* 1,2, *E* 2, *S*, 1998 *E* 1, *S* 1,2, *NZ* 1, *SA* 1, *NZ* 2, *SA* 2, *NZ* 3, *Fj, WS, F, E* 2
Gregory, S C (Q) 1968 *NZ* 3, *F, I, S*, 1969 *SA* 1,3, 1971 *SA* 1,3, *F* 1,2, 1972 *F* 1,2, 1973 *Tg* 1,2, *W, E*
Grey, G O (NSW) 1972 *F* 2 (R), *NZ* 1,2,3, *Fj* (R)
Grey, N P (NSW) 1998 *S* 2 (R), *SA* 2 (R), *Fj* (R), *Tg* (R), *F, E* 2
Griffin, T S (NSW) 1907 *NZ* 1,3, 1908 *W*, 1910 *NZ* 1,2, 1912 *US*
Grigg, P C (Q) 1980 *NZ* 3, 1982 *S* 2, *NZ* 1,2,3, 1983 *Arg* 2, *NZ*, 1984 *Fj, W, S*, 1985 *C* 1,2, *NZ, Fj* 1,2, 1986 *Arg* 1,2, *NZ* 1,2, 1987 *SK, [E, J, I, F, W]*
Grimmond, D N (NSW) 1964 *NZ* 2
Gudsell, K E (NSW) 1951 *NZ* 1,2,3
Guerassimoff, J (Q) 1963 *SA* 2,3,4, 1964 *NZ* 1,2,3, 1965 *SA* 2, 1966 *BI* 1,2, 1967 *E, I, F*
Gunther, W J (NSW) 1957 *NZ* 2

Hall, D (Q) 1980 *Fj, NZ* 1,2,3, 1981 *F* 1,2, 1982 *S* 1,2, *NZ* 1,2, 1983 *US, Arg* 1,2, *NZ, It*
Hamalainen, H A (Q) 1929 *NZ* 1,2,3
Hamilton, B G (NSW) 1946 *M*
Hammand, C A (NSW) 1908 *W*, 1909 *E*
Hammon, J D C (V) 1937 *SA* 2
Handy, C B (Q) 1978 *NZ* 3, 1979 *NZ, Arg* 1,2, 1980 *NZ* 1,2
Hanley, R G (Q) 1983 *US* (R), *It* (R), 1985 *Fj* 2 (R)
Hardcastle, P A (NSW) 1946 *NZ* 1, *M, NZ* 2, 1947 *NZ* 1, 1949 *M* 3
Hardcastle, W R (NSW) 1899 *BI* 4, 1903 *NZ*
Harding, M A (NSW) 1983 *It*
Hardy, M D (ACT) 1997 *F* 1 (t), 2 (R), *NZ* 1 (R), 3 (R), *Arg* 1 (R), 2 (R), 1998 *Tg, WS*
Harry, R L L (NSW) 1996 *W* 1, 2, *NZ* 1, *SA* 1 (t), *NZ* 2, *It, S*, 1997 *NZ* 1,2, *SA* 1, *NZ* 3, *SA* 2, *Arg* 1,2, *E* 2, *S*, 1998 *E* 1, *S* 1,2, *NZ* 1, *Fj*
Hartill, M N (NSW) 1986 *NZ* 1,2,3, 1987 *SK, [J], Arg* 1, 1988 *NZ* 1,2, *E, It*, 1989 *BI* 1 (R), 2,3, *F* 1,2, 1995 *Arg* 1 (R), 2 (R), *[C], NZ* 1,2
Harvey, P B (Q) 1949 *M* 1,2
Harvey, R M (NSW) 1958 *F, M* 3
Hatherell, W I (Q) 1952 *Fj* 1,2
Hauser, R G (Q) 1975 *J* 1 (R), 2, *W* (R), 1976 *E, I, US, Fj* 1,2,3, *F* 1,2, 1978 *W* 1,2, 1979 *I* 1,2
Hawker, M J (NSW) 1980 *Fj, NZ* 1,2,3, 1981 *F* 1,2, *I, W*, 1982 *E, S* 1,2, *NZ* 1,2,3, 1983 *US, Arg* 1,2, *NZ, It, F* 1,2, 1984 *NZ* 1,2,3, 1987 *NZ*
Hawthorne, P F (NSW) 1962 *NZ* 3,4,5, 1963 *E, SA* 1,2,3,4, 1964 *NZ* 1,2,3, 1965 *SA* 1,2, 1966 *BI* 1,2, *W*, 1967 *E, I* 1, *F, I* 2, *NZ*
Hayes, E S (Q) 1934 *NZ* 1,2, 1938 *NZ* 1,2,3
Heath, A (NSW) 1996 *C, SA* 1, *NZ* 2, *SA* 2, *It*, 1997 *NZ* 2, *SA* 1, *E* 2
Heinrich, E L (NSW) 1961 *Fj* 1,2,3, *SA* 2, *F*, 1962 *NZ* 1,2,3, 1963 *E, SA* 1
Heinrich, V W (NSW) 1954 *Fj* 1,2
Heming, R J (NSW) 1961 *Fj* 2,3, *SA* 1,2, *F*, 1962 *NZ* 2,3,4,5, 1963 *SA* 2,3,4, 1964 *NZ* 1,2,3, 1965 *SA* 1,2, 1966 *BI* 1,2, *W*, 1967 *F*
Hemingway, W H (NSW) 1928 *NZ* 2,3, 1931 *M, NZ*, 1932 *NZ* 3
Henry, A R (Q) 1899 *BI* 2
Herbert, A G (Q) 1987 *SK* (R), *[F* (R)], 1990 *F* 1 (R), *US, NZ* 2,3, 1991 *[WS]*, 1992 *NZ* 3 (R), 1993 *NZ* (R), *SA* 2 (R)
Herbert, D J (Q) 1994 *I* 2, *It* 1,2, *WS* (R), 1995 *Arg* 1,2, *[SA, R]*, 1996 *C, SA* 2, *It, S, I*, 1997 *NZ* 1, 1998 *E* 1, *S* 1,2, *NZ* 1, *SA* 1, *NZ* 2, *SA* 2, *Fj, Tg, WS, F, E* 2
Herd, H V (NSW) 1931 *M*
Hickey, J (NSW) 1908 *W*, 1909 *E*
Hillhouse, D W (Q) 1975 *S*, 1976 *E, Fj* 1,2,3, *F* 1,2, 1978 *W* 1,2, 1983 *US, NZ, It, F* 1,2
Hills, E F (V) 1950 *BI* 1,2
Hindmarsh, J A (Q) 1904 *BI* 1
Hindmarsh, J C (NSW) 1975 *J* 2, *S, W*, 1976 *US, Fj* 1,2,3, *F* 1,2
Hipwell, J N B (NSW) 1968 *NZ* 1 (R), 2, *F, I, S*, 1969 *W, SA* 1,2,3,4, 1970 *S*, 1971 *SA* 1,2, *F* 1,2, 1972 *F* 1,2, 1973 *Tg* 1, *W, E*, 1974 *NZ* 1,2,3, 1975 *E* 1,2, *J* 1, *S, W*, 1978 *NZ* 1,2,3, 1981 *F* 1,2, *I, W*, 1982 *E*
Hirschberg, W A (NSW) 1905 *NZ*

Scrum-half George Gregan sets the Wallabies on their way during the narrow 12-11 victory over England at Twickenham in November.

Hodgins, C H (NSW) 1910 *NZ* 1,2,3
Hodgson, A J (NSW) 1933 *SA* 2,3,4, 1934 *NZ* 1, 1936 *NZ* 1,2, *M*, 1937 *SA* 2, 1938 *NZ* 1,2,3
Holbeck, J (ACT) 1997 *NZ* 1 (R), *E* 1, *NZ* 2, *SA* 1, *NZ* 3, *SA* 2
Holt, N C (Q) 1984 *Fj*
Honan, B D (Q) 1968 *NZ* 1 (R), 2, *F, I, S*, 1969 *SA* 1,2,3,4
Honan, R E (Q) 1964 *NZ* 1,2
Horan, T J (Q) 1989 *NZ, F* 1,2, 1990 *F* 1, *NZ* 1,2,3, 1991 *W, E, NZ* 1,2, [*Arg, WS, W, I, NZ, E*], 1992 *S* 1,2, *NZ* 1,2,3, *SA, I, W*, 1993 *Tg, NZ, SA* 1,2,3, *C, F* 1,2, 1995 [*C, R, E*], *NZ* 1,2, 1996 *W* 1,2, *C, NZ* 1, *SA* 1, *It, S, I, W* 3, 1997 *F* 1,2, *NZ* 1, *E* 1, *NZ* 2, *Arg* 1,2, *E* 2, *S*, 1998 *E* 1, *S* 1,2, *NZ* 1, *SA* 1, *NZ* 2, *SA* 2, *NZ* 3, *Fj, Tg, WS*
Horodam, D J (Q) 1913 *NZ* 2
Horsley, G R (Q) 1954 *Fj* 2
Horton, P A (NSW) 1974 *NZ* 1,2,3, 1975 *E* 1,2, *J* 1,2, *S, W*, 1976 *E, F* 1,2, 1978 *W* 1,2, *NZ* 1,2,3, 1979 *NZ, Arg* 1
How, R A (NSW) 1967 *I* 2
Howard, J (Q) 1938 *NZ* 1,2
Howard, J L (NSW) 1970 *S*, 1971 *SA* 1, 1972 *F* 1 (R), *NZ* 2, 1973 *Tg* 1,2, *W*
Howard, P W (Q, ACT) 1993 *NZ*, 1994 *WS, NZ*, 1995 *NZ* 1 (R), 2 (t), 1996 *W* 1,2, *SA* 1, *NZ* 2, *SA* 2, *It, S, W* 3, 1997 *F* 1,2, *NZ* 1, *Arg* 1,2, *E* 2, *S*
Howell, M L (NSW) 1946 *NZ* 1 (R), 1947 *NZ* 1, *S, I, W*
Hughes, B D (NSW) 1913 *NZ* 2,3
Hughes, J C (NSW) 1907 *NZ* 1,3
Hughes, N McL (NSW) 1953 *SA* 1,2,3,4, 1955 *NZ* 1,2,3, 1956 *SA* 1,2, 1958 *W, I, E, S, F*
Humphreys, O W (NSW) 1921 *NZ*
Hutchinson, E E (NSW) 1937 *SA* 1,2
Hutchinson, F E (NSW) 1936 *NZ* 1,2, 1938 *NZ* 1,3

Ide, W P J (Q) 1938 *NZ* 2,3
Ives, W N (NSW) 1929 *NZ* 3

James, P M (Q) 1958 *M* 2,3
James, S L (NSW) 1987 *SK* (R), [*E* (R)], *NZ, Arg* 1,2, 1988 *NZ* 2 (R)
Jessep, E M (V) 1934 *NZ* 1,2
Johnson, A P (NSW) 1946 *NZ* 1, *M*
Johnson, B B (NSW) 1952 *Fj* 1,2, *NZ* 1,2, 1953 *SA* 2,3,4, 1955 *NZ* 1,2
Johnson, P G (NSW) 1959 *BI* 1,2, 1961 *Fj* 1,2,3, *SA* 1,2, *F*, 1962 *NZ* 1,2,3,4,5, 1963 *E, SA* 1,2,3,4, 1964 *NZ* 1,2,3, 1965 *SA* 1,2, 1966 *BI* 1,2, *W, S*, 1967 *E, I* 1, *F, I* 2, *NZ*, 1968 *NZ* 1,2, *F, I, S*, 1970 *S*, 1971 *SA* 1,2, *F* 1,2
Johnstone, B (Q) 1993 *Tg* (R)
Jones, G G (Q) 1952 *Fj* 1,2, 1953 *SA* 1,2,3,4, 1954 *Fj* 1,2, 1955 *NZ* 1,2,3, 1956 *SA* 1
Jones, H (NSW) 1913 *NZ* 1,2,3
Jones, P A (NSW) 1963 *E, SA* 1
Jorgensen, P (NSW) 1992 *S* 1 (R), 2 (R)
Joyce, J E (NSW) 1903 *NZ*
Judd, H A (NSW) 1903 *NZ*, 1904 *BI* 1,2,3, 1905 *NZ*
Judd, P B (NSW) 1925 *NZ*, 1927 *I, W, S*, 1928 *E*, 1931 *M, NZ*
Junee, D K (NSW) 1989 *F* 1 (R), 2 (R), 1994 *WS* (R), *NZ* (R)

Kahl, P R (Q) 1992 *W*
Kassulke, N (Q) 1985 *C* 1,2
Kay, A R (V) 1958 *NZ* 2, 1959 *BI* 2
Kay, P (NSW) 1988 *E* 2
Kearney, K H (NSW) 1947 *NZ* 1,2, *S, I, W*, 1948 *E, F*
Kearns, P N (NSW) 1989 *NZ, F* 1,2, 1990 *F* 1,2,3, *US, NZ* 1,2,3, 1991 *W, E, NZ* 1,2, [*Arg, WS, W, I, NZ, E*], 1992 *S* 1,2, *NZ* 1,2,3, *SA, I, W*, 1993 *Tg, NZ, SA* 1,2,3, *C, F* 1,2, 1994 *I* 1,2, *It* 1,2, *WS, NZ*, 1995 *Arg* 1,2, [*SA, C, E*], *NZ* 1,2, 1998 *E* 1, *S* 1,2, *NZ* 1, *SA* 1, *NZ* 2, *SA* 2, *NZ* 3, *Fj, WS, F, E* 2
Kefu, R S T (Q) 1997 *SA* 2 (R), 1998 *E* 1, *S* 1,2, *NZ* 1, *SA* 1, *NZ* 2, *SA* 2, *NZ* 3, *Fj* (R), *Tg, WS* (R), *F, E* 2
Kelaher, J D (NSW) 1933 *SA* 1,2,3,4,5, 1934 *NZ* 1,2, 1936 *NZ* 1,2, *M*, 1937 *SA* 1,2, 1938 *NZ* 3
Kelaher, T P (NSW) 1992 *NZ* 1, *I* (R), 1993 *NZ*
Kelleher, R J (Q) 1969 *SA* 2,3
Keller, D H (NSW) 1947 *NZ* 1, *S, I, W*, 1948 *E, F*
Kelly, A J (NSW) 1899 *BI* 1
Kelly, R L F (NSW) 1936 *NZ* 1,2, *M*, 1937 *SA* 1,2, 1938 *NZ* 1,2
Kent, A (Q) 1912 *US*

Kerr, F R (V) 1938 *NZ* 1
King, S C (NSW) 1927 *W, S*, 1928 *E, F*, 1929 *NZ* 1,2,3, 1930 *BI*, 1932 *NZ* 1,2
Knight, M (NSW) 1978 *W* 1,2, *NZ* 1
Knight, S O (NSW) 1969 *SA* 2,4, 1970 *S*, 1971 *SA* 1,2,3
Knox, D J (NSW, ACT) 1985 *Fj* 1,2, 1990 *US* (R), 1994 *WS, NZ*, 1996 *It, S, I*, 1997 *SA* 1, *NZ* 3, *SA* 2, *Arg* 1,2
Kraefft, D F (NSW) 1947 *NZ* 2, *S, I, W*, 1948 *E, F*
Kreutzer, S D (Q) 1914 *NZ* 2

Lamb, J S (NSW) 1928 *NZ* 1,2, *M*
Lambie, J K (NSW) 1974 *NZ* 1,2,3, 1975 *W*
Lane, T A (Q) 1985 *C* 1,2, *NZ*
Lang, C W P (V) 1938 *NZ* 2,3
Langford, J F (ACT) 1997 *NZ* 3, *SA* 2, *E* 2, *S*
Larkham, S J (ACT) 1996 *W* 2 (R), 1997 *F* 1,2, *NZ* 2 (R), *SA* 1, *NZ* 3, *SA* 2, *Arg* 1,2, *E* 2, *S*, 1998 *E* 1, *S* 1,2, *NZ* 1, *SA* 1, *NZ* 2, *SA* 2, *NZ* 3, *Fj, Tg* (t), *WS, F, E* 2
Larkin, E R (NSW) 1903 *NZ*
Larkin, K K (Q) 1958 *M* 2,3
Latham, C E (Q) 1998 *F, E* 2
Latimer, N B (NSW) 1957 *NZ* 2
Lawton, R (Q) 1988 *E* 1, *NZ* 2 (R), 3, *S*
Lawton, T (NSW) (Q) 1925 *NZ*, 1927 *I, W, S*, 1928 *E, F*, 1929 *NZ* 1,2,3, 1930 *BI*, 1932 *NZ* 1,2
Lawton, T A (Q) 1983 *F* 1 (R), 2, 1984 *Fj, NZ* 1,2,3, *E, I, W, S*, 1985 *C* 1,2, *NZ, Fj* 1, 1986 *It, F, Arg* 1,2, *NZ* 1,2,3, 1987 *SK*, [*E, US, I, F, W*], *NZ, Arg* 1,2, 1988 *E* 1,2, *NZ* 1,2,3, *E, S, It*, 1989 *BI* 1,2,3
Laycock, W M B (NSW) 1925 *NZ*
Leeds, A J (NSW) 1986 *NZ* 3, 1987 [*US, W*], *NZ, Arg* 1,2, 1988 *E* 1,2, *NZ* 1,2,3, *E, S, It*
Lenehan, J K (NSW) 1958 *W, E, S, F, M* 1,2,3, 1959 *BI* 1,2, 1961 *SA* 1,2, *F*, 1962 *NZ* 2,3,4,5, 1965 *SA* 1,2, 1966 *W, S*, 1967 *E, I* 1, *F, I* 2
L'Estrange, R D (Q) 1971 *F* 1,2, 1972 *NZ* 1,2,3, 1973 *Tg* 1,2, *W, E*, 1974 *NZ* 1,2,3, 1975 *S, W*, 1976 *I, US*
Lewis, L S (Q) 1934 *NZ* 1,2, 1936 *NZ* 2, 1938 *NZ* 1
Lidbury, S (NSW) 1987 *Arg* 1, 1988 *E* 2
Lillicrap, C P (Q) 1985 *Fj* 2, 1987 [*US, I, F, W*], 1989 *BI* 1, 1991 [*WS*]
Lindsay, R T G (Q) 1932 *NZ* 3
Lisle, R J (NSW) 1961 *Fj* 1,2,3, *SA* 1
Little, J S (Q) 1989 *F* 1,2, 1990 *F* 1,2,3, *US*, 1991 *W, E, NZ* 1,2, [*Arg, W, I, NZ, E*], 1992 *NZ* 1,2,3, *SA, I, W*, 1993 *Tg, NZ, SA* 1,2,3, *C, F* 1,2, 1994 *WS, NZ*, 1995 *Arg* 1,2, [*SA, C, E*], *NZ* 1,2, 1996 *It* (R), *I, W* 3, 1997 *F* 1,2, *E* 1, *NZ* 2, *SA* 1, *NZ* 3, *SA* 2, 1998 *E* 1 (R), *S* 2 (R), *NZ* 2, *SA* 2 (R), *NZ* 3, *Fj, Tg, WS, F, E* 2
Livermore, A E (Q) 1946 *NZ* 1, *M*
Loane, M E (Q) 1973 *Tg* 1,2, 1974 *NZ* 1, 1975 *E* 1,2, *J* 1, 1976 *E, I, Fj* 1,2,3, *F* 1,2, 1978 *W* 1,2, 1979 *I* 1,2, *Arg* 1,2, 1981 *F* 1,2, *I, W, S*, 1982 *E, S* 1,2
Logan, D L (NSW) 1958 *M* 1
Loudon, D B (NSW) 1921 *NZ*
Loudon, R B (NSW) 1923 *NZ* 1 (R), 2,3, 1928 *NZ* 1,2,3, *M*, 1929 *NZ* 2, 1933 *SA* 2,3,4,5, 1934 *NZ* 2
Love, E W (NSW) 1932 *NZ* 1,2,3
Lowth, D R (NSW) 1958 *NZ* 1
Lucas, B C (Q) 1905 *NZ*
Lucas, P W (NSW) 1982 *NZ* 1,2,3
Lutge, D (NSW) 1903 *NZ*, 1904 *BI* 1,2,3
Lynagh, M P (Q) 1984 *Fj, E, I, W, S*, 1985 *C* 1,2, *NZ*, 1986 *It, F, Arg* 1,2, *NZ* 1,2,3, 1987 [*E, US, J, I, F, W*], *Arg* 1,2, 1988 *E* 1,2, *NZ* 1,3 (R), *E, S, It*, 1989 *BI* 1,2,3, *NZ, F* 1,2, 1990 *F* 1,2,3, *US, NZ* 1,2,3, 1991 *W, E, NZ*, [*Arg, WS, W, I, NZ, E*], 1992 *S* 1,2, *NZ* 1,2,3, *SA, I*, 1993 *Tg, C, F* 1,2, 1994 *I* 1,2, *It* 1, 1995 *Arg* 1,2, [*SA, C, E*]

McArthur, M (NSW) 1909 *E*
McBain, M I (Q) 1983 *It, F* 1, 1985 *Fj* 2, 1986 *It* (R), 1987 [*J*], 1988 *E* 2 (R), 1989 *BI* 1 (R)
MacBride, J W T (NSW) 1946 *NZ* 1, *M, NZ* 2, 1947 *NZ* 1,2, *S, I, W*, 1948 *E, F*
McCabe, A J M (NSW) 1909 *E*
McCall, R J (Q) 1989 *F* 1,2, 1990 *F* 1,2,3, *US, NZ* 1,2,3, 1991 *W, E, NZ* 1,2, [*Arg, W, I, NZ, E*], 1992 *S* 1,2, *NZ* 1,2,3, *SA, I, W*, 1993 *Tg, NZ, SA* 1,2,3, *C, F* 1,2, 1994 *It* 2, 1995 *Arg* 1,2, [*SA, R, E*]
McCarthy, F J C (Q) 1950 *BI* 1
McCowan, R H (Q) 1899 *BI* 1,2,4
McCue, P A (NSW) 1907 *NZ* 1,3, 1908 *W*, 1909 *E*
McDermott, L C (Q) 1962 *NZ* 1,2
McDonald, B S (NSW) 1969 *SA* 4, 1970 *S*

McDonald, J C (Q) 1938 *NZ* 2,3
Macdougall, D G (NSW) 1961 *Fj* 1, *SA* 1
Macdougall, S G (NSW, ACT) 1971 *SA* 3, 1973 *E*, 1974 *NZ* 1,2,3, 1975 *E* 1,2, 1976 *E*
McGhie, G H (Q) 1929 *NZ* 2,3, 1930 *BI*
McGill, A N (NSW) 1968 *NZ* 1,2, *F*, 1969 *W, SA* 1,2,3,4, 1970 *S*, 1971 *SA* 1,2,3, *F* 1,2, 1972 *F* 1,2, *NZ* 1,2,3, 1973 *Tg* 1,2
McIntyre, A J (Q) 1982 *NZ* 1,2,3, 1983 *F* 1,2, 1984 *Fj, NZ* 1,2,3, *E, I, W, S*, 1985 *C* 1,2, *NZ, Fj* 1,2, 1986 *It, F, Arg* 1,2, 1987 [*E, US, I, F, W*], *NZ, Arg* 2, 1988 *E* 1,2, *NZ* 1,2,3, *E, S, It*, 1989 *NZ*
McKenzie, E J A (NSW, ACT) 1990 *F* 1,2,3, *US, NZ* 1,2,3, 1991 *W, E, NZ* 1,2, [*Arg, W, I, NZ, E*], 1992 *S* 1,2, *NZ* 1,2,3, *SA, I, W*, 1993 *Tg, NZ, SA* 1,2,3, *C, F* 1,2, 1994 *I* 1,2, *It* 1,2, *WS, NZ*, 1995 *Arg* 1,2, [*SA, C* (R), *R, E*], *NZ* 2, 1996 *W* 1,2, 1997 *F* 1,2, *NZ* 1, *E* 1
McKid, W A (NSW) 1976 *E, Fj* 1, 1978 *NZ* 2,3, 1979 *I* 1,2
McKinnon, A (Q) 1904 *BI* 2
McKivat, C H (NSW) 1907 *NZ* 1,3, 1908 *W*, 1909 *E*
McLaughlin, R E M (NSW) 1936 *NZ* 1,2
McLean, A D (Q) 1933 *SA* 1,2,3,4,5, 1934 *NZ* 1,2, 1936 *NZ* 1,2, *M*
McLean, J D (Q) 1904 *BI* 2,3, 1905 *NZ*
McLean, J J (Q) 1971 *SA* 2,3, *F* 1,2, 1972 *F* 1,2, *NZ* 1,2,3, *Fj*, 1973 *W, E*, 1974 *NZ* 1
McLean, P E (Q) 1974 *NZ* 1,2,3, 1975 *J* 1,2, *S, W*, 1976 *E, I, Fj* 1,2,3, *F* 1,2, 1978 *W* 1,2, *NZ* 2, 1979 *I* 1,2, *NZ, Arg* 1,2, 1980 *Fj*, 1981 *F* 1,2, *I, W, S*, 1982 *E, S* 2
McLean, P W (Q) 1978 *NZ* 1,2,3, 1979 *I* 1,2, *NZ, Arg* 1,2, 1980 *Fj* (R), *NZ* 3, 1981 *I, W, S*, 1982 *E, S* 1,2
McLean, R A (NSW) 1971 *SA* 1,2,3, *F* 1,2
McLean, W M (Q) 1946 *NZ* 1, *M, NZ* 2, 1947 *NZ* 1,2
McMahon, M J (Q) 1913 *NZ* 1
McMaster, R E (Q) 1946 *NZ* 1, *M, NZ* 2, 1947 *NZ* 1,2, *I, W*
MacMillan, D I (Q) 1950 *BI* 1,2
McMullen, K V (NSW) 1962 *NZ* 3,5, 1963 *E, SA* 1
McShane, J M S (NSW) 1937 *SA* 1,2
Mackney, W A R (NSW) 1933 *SA* 1,5, 1934 *NZ* 1,2
Magrath, E (NSW) 1961 *Fj* 1, *SA* 2, *F*
Maguire, D J (Q) 1989 *BI* 1,2,3
Malcolm, S J (NSW) 1927 *S*, 1928 *E, F, NZ* 1,2, *M*, 1929 *NZ* 1,2,3, 1930 *BI*, 1931 *NZ*, 1932 *NZ* 1,2,3, 1933 *SA* 4,5, 1934 *NZ* 1,2
Malone, J H (NSW) 1936 *NZ* 1,2, *M*, 1937 *SA* 2
Malouf, B P (NSW) 1982 *NZ* 1
Mandible, E F (NSW) 1907 *NZ* 2,3, 1908 *W*
Manning, J (NSW) 1904 *BI* 2
Manning, R C S (Q) 1967 *NZ*
Mansfield, B W (NSW) 1975 *J* 2
Manu, D T (NSW) 1995 [*R* (t)], *NZ* 1,2, 1996 *W* 1,2 (R), *SA* 1, *NZ* 2, *It, S, I*, 1997 *F* 1, *NZ* 1 (t), *E* 1, *NZ* 2, *SA* 1
Marks, H (NSW) 1899 *BI* 1,2
Marks, R J P (Q) 1962 *NZ* 4,5, 1963 *E, SA* 2,3,4, 1964 *NZ* 1,2,3, 1965 *SA* 1,2, 1966 *W, S*, 1967 *E, I* 1, *F, I* 2
Marrott, W J (NSW) 1923 *NZ* 1,2
Marshall, J S (NSW) 1949 *M* 1
Martin, G J (Q) 1989 *BI* 1,2,3, *NZ, F* 1,2, 1990 *F* 1,3 (R), *NZ* 1
Martin, M C (NSW) 1980 *Fj, NZ* 1,2, 1981 *F* 1,2, *W* (R)
Massey-Westropp, M (NSW) 1914 *NZ* 3
Mathers, M J (NSW) 1980 *Fj, NZ* 2 (R)
Maund, J W (NSW) 1903 *NZ*
Meadows, J E C (V, Q) 1974 *NZ* 1, 1975 *S, W*, 1976 *I, US, Fj* 1,3, *F* 1,2, 1978 *NZ* 1,2,3, 1979 *I* 1,2, 1981 *I, S*, 1982 *E, NZ* 2,3, 1983 *US, Arg* 2, *NZ*
Meadows, R W (NSW) 1958 *M* 1,2,3, *NZ* 1,2,3
Meagher, F W (NSW) 1923 *NZ* 3, 1925 *NZ*, 1927 *I, W*
Meibusch, J H (Q) 1904 *BI* 3
Meibusch, L S (Q) 1912 *US*
Melrose, T C (NSW) 1978 *NZ* 3, 1979 *I* 1,2, *NZ, Arg* 1,2
Merrick, S (NSW) 1995 *NZ* 1,2
Messenger, H H (NSW) 1907 *NZ* 2,3
Middleton, S A (NSW) 1909 *E*, 1910 *NZ* 1,2,3
Miller, A R (NSW) 1952 *Fj* 1,2, *NZ* 1,2, 1953 *SA* 1,2,3,4, 1954 *Fj* 1,2, 1955 *NZ* 1,2,3, 1956 *SA* 1,2, 1957 *NZ* 1,2, 1958 *W, E, S, F, M* 1,2,3, 1959 *BI* 1,2, 1961 *Fj* 1,2,3, *SA* 2, *F*, 1962 *NZ* 1,2, 1966 *BI* 1,2, *W, S*, 1967 *I* 1, *F, I* 2, *NZ* 2
Miller, J M (NSW) 1962 *NZ* 1, 1963 *E, SA* 1, 1966 *W, S*, 1967 *E*

Miller, J S (Q) 1986 *NZ* 2,3, 1987 *SK*, [*US, I, F*], *NZ, Arg* 1,2, 1988 *E* 1,2, *NZ* 2,3, *E, S, It*, 1989 *BI* 1,2,3, *NZ*, 1990 *F* 1,3, 1991 *W*, [*WS, W, I*]
Miller, S W J (NSW) 1899 *BI* 3
Mingey, N (NSW) 1923 *NZ* 1,2
Monaghan, L E (NSW) 1973 *E*, 1974 *NZ* 1,2,3, 1975 *E* 1,2, *S, W*, 1976 *E, I, US, F* 1, 1978 *W* 1,2, *NZ* 1, 1979 *I* 1,2
Monti, C I A (Q) 1938 *NZ* 2
Moon, B J (Q) 1978 *NZ* 2,3, 1979 *I* 1,2, *NZ, Arg* 1,2, 1980 *Fj, NZ* 1,2,3, 1981 *F* 1,2, *I, W, S*, 1982 *E, S* 1,2, 1983 *US, Arg* 1,2, *NZ, It, F* 1,2, 1984 *Fj, NZ* 1,2,3, *E*, 1986 *It, F, Arg* 1,2
Mooney, T P (Q) 1954 *Fj* 1,2
Moran, H M (NSW) 1908 *W*
Morgan, G (Q) 1992 *NZ* 1 (R), 3 (R), *W*, 1993 *Tg, NZ, SA* 1,2,3, *C, F* 1,2, 1994 *I* 1,2, *It* 1, *WS, NZ*, 1996 *W* 1,2, *C, NZ* 1, *SA* 1, *NZ* 2, 1997 *E* 1, *NZ* 2
Morrissey, C V (NSW) 1925 *NZ*
Morrissey, W (Q) 1914 *NZ* 2
Morton, A R (NSW) 1957 *NZ* 1,2, 1958 *F, M* 1,2,3, *NZ* 1,2,3, 1959 *BI* 1,2
Mossop, R P (NSW) 1949 *NZ* 1,2, 1950 *BI* 1,2, 1951 *NZ* 1
Moutray, I E (NSW) 1963 *SA* 2
Munsie, A (NSW) 1928 *NZ* 2
Murdoch, A R (NSW) 1993 *F* 1, 1996 *W* 1
Murphy, P J (Q) 1910 *NZ* 1,2,3, 1913 *NZ* 1,2,3, 1914 *NZ* 1,2,3
Murphy, W (Q) 1912 *US*

Nasser, B P (Q) 1989 *F* 1,2, 1990 *F* 1,2,3, *US, NZ* 2, 1991 [*WS*]
Nicholson, F C (Q) 1904 *BI* 3
Nicholson, F V (Q) 1903 *NZ*, 1904 *BI* 1
Niuqila, A S (NSW) 1988 *S, It*, 1989 *BI* 1
Noriega, E P (ACT) 1998 *F, E* 2
Nothling, O E (NSW) 1921 *NZ*, 1923 *NZ* 1,2,3
Nucifora, D V (Q) 1991 [*Arg* (R)], 1993 *C* (R)

O'Brien, F W H (NSW) 1937 *SA* 2, 1938 *NZ* 3
O'Connor, J A (NSW) 1928 *NZ* 1,2,3, *M*
O'Connor, M (ACT) 1994 *I* 1
O'Connor, M D (ACT, Q) 1979 *Arg* 1,2, 1980 *Fj, NZ* 1,2,3, 1981 *F* 1,2, *I*, 1982 *E, S* 1,2
O'Donnell, C (NSW) 1913 *NZ* 1,2
O'Donnell, I C (NSW) 1899 *BI* 3,4
O'Donnell, J B (NSW) 1928 *NZ* 1,3, *M*
O'Donnell, J M (NSW) 1899 *BI* 4
O'Gorman, J F (NSW) 1961 *Fj* 1, *SA* 1,2, *F*, 1962 *NZ* 2, 1963 *E, SA* 1,2,3,4, 1965 *SA* 1,2, 1966 *W, S*, 1967 *E, I* 1, *F, I* 2
O'Neill, D J (Q) 1964 *NZ* 1,2
O'Neill, J M (Q) 1952 *NZ* 1,2, 1956 *SA* 1,2
Ofahengaue, V (NSW) 1990 *NZ* 1,2,3, 1991 *W, E, NZ* 1,2, [*Arg, W, I, NZ, E*], 1992 *S* 1,2, *SA, I, W*, 1994 *WS, NZ*, 1995 *Arg* 1,2 (R), [*SA, C, E*], *NZ* 1,2, 1997 *Arg* 1 (t + R), 2 (R), *E* 2, *S*, 1998 *E* 1 (R), *S* 2 (R), *NZ* 1 (R), *SA* 1 (R), *NZ* 2 (R), *SA* 2 (R), *NZ* 3 (R), *Fj, WS, F* (R)
Osborne, D H (V) 1975 *E* 1,2, *J* 1
Outterside, R (NSW) 1959 *BI* 1,2
Oxenham, A McE (Q) 1904 *BI* 2, 1907 *NZ* 2
Oxlade, A M (Q) 1904 *BI* 2,3, 1905 *NZ*, 1907 *NZ* 2
Oxlade, B D (Q) 1938 *NZ* 1,2,3

Palfreyman, J R L (NSW) 1929 *NZ* 1, 1930 *BI*, 1931 *NZ*, 1932 *NZ* 3
Panoho, G M (Q) 1998 *SA* 2 (R), *NZ* 3 (R), *Fj* (R), *Tg, WS* (R)
Papworth, B (NSW) 1985 *Fj* 1,2, 1986 *It, Arg* 1,2, *NZ* 1,2,3, 1987 [*E, US, J* (R), *I, F*], *NZ, Arg* 1,2
Parker, A J (Q) 1983 *Arg* 1 (R), 2, *NZ*
Parkinson, C E (Q) 1907 *NZ* 2
Paul, J A (ACT) 1998 *S* 1 (R), *NZ* 1 (R), *SA* 1 (t), *Fj* (R), *Tg*
Pashley, J J (NSW) 1954 *Fj* 1,2, 1958 *M* 1,2,3
Pauling, T P (NSW) 1936 *NZ* 1, 1937 *SA* 1
Payne, S J (NSW) 1996 *W* 2, *C, NZ* 1, *S*, 1997 *F* 1 (t), *NZ* 2 (R), *Arg* 2 (t)
Pearse, G K (NSW) 1975 *W* (R), 1976 *I, US, Fj* 1,2,3, 1978 *NZ* 1,2,3
Penman, A P (NSW) 1905 *NZ*
Perrin, P D (Q) 1962 *NZ* 1
Perrin, T D (NSW) 1931 *M, NZ*

Phelps, R (NSW) 1955 *NZ* 2,3, 1956 *SA* 1,2, 1957 *NZ* 1,2, 1958 *W, I, E, S, F, M* 1, *NZ* 1,2,3, 1961 *Fj* 1,2,3, *SA* 1,2, *F*, 1962 *NZ* 1,2
Phipps, J A (NSW) 1953 *SA* 1,2,3,4, 1954 *Fj* 1,2, 1955 *NZ* 1,2,3, 1956 *SA* 1,2
Phipps, W J (NSW) 1928 *NZ* 2
Pilecki, S J (Q) 1978 *W* 1,2, *NZ* 1,2, 1979 *I* 1,2, *NZ, Arg* 1,2, 1980 *Fj, NZ* 1,2, 1982 *S* 1,2, 1983 *US, Arg* 1,2, *NZ*
Pini, M (Q) 1994 *I* 1, *It* 2, *WS, NZ*, 1995 *Arg* 1,2, [*SA, R* (t)]
Piper, B J C (NSW) 1946 *NZ* 1, *M, NZ* 2, 1947 *NZ* 1, *S, I, W*, 1948 *E, F*, 1949 *M*, 1,2,3
Poidevin, S P (NSW) 1980 *Fj, NZ* 1,2,3, 1981 *F* 1,2, *I, W, S*, 1982 *E, NZ* 1,2,3, 1983 *US, Arg* 1,2, *NZ, It, F* 1,2, 1984 *Fj, NZ* 1,2,3, *E, I, W, S*, 1985 *C* 1,2, *NZ, Fj* 1,2, 1986 *It, F, Arg* 1,2, *NZ* 1,2,3, 1987 *SK,* [*E, J, I, F, W*]*, Arg* 1, 1988 *NZ* 1,2,3, 1989 *NZ*, 1991 *E, NZ* 1,2, [*Arg, W, I, NZ, E*]
Pope, A M (Q) 1968 *NZ* 2 (R)
Potter, R T (Q) 1961 *Fj* 2
Potts, J M (NSW) 1957 *NZ* 1,2, 1958 *W, I*, 1959 *BI* 1
Prentice, C W (NSW) 1914 *NZ* 3
Prentice, W S (NSW) 1908 *W*, 1909 *E*, 1910 *NZ* 1,2,3, 1912 *US*
Price, R A (NSW) 1974 *NZ* 1,2,3, 1975 *E* 1,2, *J* 1,2, 1976 *US*
Primmer, C J (Q) 1951 *NZ* 1,3
Proctor, I J (NSW)) 1967 *NZ*
Prosser, R B (NSW) 1967 *E, I* 1,2, *NZ*, 1968 *NZ* 1,2, *F, I, S*, 1969 *W, SA* 1,2,3,4, 1971 *SA* 1,2,3, *F* 1,2, 1972 *F* 1,2, *NZ* 1,2,3, *Fj*
Pugh, G H (NSW) 1912 *US*
Purcell, M P (Q) 1966 *W, S*, 1967 *I* 2
Purkis, E M (NSW) 1958 *S, M* 1

Ramalli, C (NSW) 1938 *NZ* 2,3
Ramsay, K M (NSW) 1936 *M*, 1937 *SA* 1, 1938 *NZ* 1,3
Rankin, R (NSW) 1936 *NZ* 1,2, *M*, 1937 *SA* 1,2, 1938 *NZ* 1,2
Rathie, D S (Q) 1972 *F* 1,2
Raymond, R L (NSW) 1921 *NZ*
Redwood, C (Q) 1903 *NZ*, 1904 *BI* 1,2,3
Reid, E J (NSW) 1925 *NZ*
Reid, T W (NSW) 1961 *Fj* 1,2,3, *SA* 1, 1962 *NZ* 1
Reilly, N P (Q) 1968 *NZ* 1,2, *F, I, S*, 1969 *W, SA* 1,2,3,4
Reynolds, L J (NSW) 1910 *NZ* 2 (R), 3
Reynolds, R J (NSW) 1984 *Fj, NZ* 1,2,3, 1985 *Fj* 1,2, 1986 *Arg* 1,2, *NZ* 1, 1987 [*J*]
Richards, E W (Q) 1904 *BI* 1,3, 1905 *NZ*, 1907 *NZ* 1 (R), 2
Richards, G (NSW) 1978 *NZ* 2 (R), 3, 1981 *F* 1
Richards, T J (Q) 1908 *W*, 1909 *E*, 1912 *US*
Richards, V S (NSW) 1936 *NZ* 1,2 (R), *M*, 1937 *SA* 1, 1938 *NZ* 1
Richardson, G C (Q) 1971 *SA* 1,2,3, 1972 *NZ* 2,3, *Fj*, 1973 *Tg* 1,2, *W*
Rigney, W A (NSW) 1925 *NZ*
Riley, S A (NSW) 1903 *NZ*
Roberts, B T (NSW) 1956 *SA* 2
Roberts, H F (Q) 1961 *Fj* 1,3, *SA* 2, *F*
Robertson, I J (NSW) 1975 *J* 1,2
Robinson, B J (ACT) 1996 *It* (R), *S* (R), *I* (R), 1997 *F* 1,2, *NZ* 1, *E* 1, *NZ* 2, *SA* 1 (R), *NZ* 3 (R), *SA* 2 (R), *Arg* 1,2, *E* 2, *S*, 1998 *Tg*
Roche, C (Q) 1982 *S* 1,2, *NZ* 1,2,3, 1983 *US, Arg* 1,2, *NZ, It, F* 1,2, 1984 *Fj, NZ* 1,2,3, *I*
Rodriguez, E E (NSW) 1984 *Fj, NZ* 1,2,3, *E, I, W, S*, 1985 *C* 1,2, *NZ, Fj* 1, 1986 *It, F, Arg* 1,2, *NZ* 1,2,3, 1987 *SK,* [*E, J, W* (R)]*, NZ, Arg* 1,2
Roebuck, M C (NSW) 1991 *W, E, NZ* 1,2, [*Arg, WS, W, I, NZ, E*], 1992 *S* 1,2, *NZ* 2,3, *SA, I, W*, 1993 *Tg, SA* 1,2,3, *C, F* 2
Roff, J W (ACT) 1995 [*C, R*]*, NZ* 1,2, 1996 *W* 1,2, *NZ* 1, *SA* 1, *NZ* 2, *SA* 2 (R), *S, I, W* 3, 1997 *F* 1,2, *NZ* 1, *E* 1, *NZ* 2, *SA* 1, *NZ* 3, *SA* 2, *Arg* 1,2, *E* 2, *S*, 1998 *E* 1, *S* 1,2, *NZ* 1, *SA* 1, *NZ* 2, *SA* 2, *Fj, Tg, WS, F, E* 2
Rose, H A (NSW), 1967 *I* 2, *NZ*, 1968 *NZ* 1,2, *F, I, S*, 1969 *W, SA* 1,2,3,4, 1970 *S*
Rosenblum, M E (NSW) 1928 *NZ* 1,2,3, *M*
Rosenblum, R G (NSW) 1969 *SA* 1,3, 1970 *S*
Rosewell, J S H (NSW) 1907 *NZ* 1,3
Ross, A W (NSW) 1927 *I, W, S*, 1928 *E, F*, 1929 *NZ* 1, 1930 *BI*, 1931 *M, NZ*, 1932 *NZ* 2,3, 1933 *SA* 5, 1934 *NZ* 1,2

Ross, W S (Q) 1979 *I* 1,2, *Arg* 2, 1980 *Fj, NZ* 1,2,3, 1982 *S* 1,2, 1983 *US, Arg* 1,2, *NZ*
Rothwell, P R (NSW) 1951 *NZ* 1,2,3, 1952 *Fj* 1
Row, F L (NSW) 1899 *BI* 1,3,4
Row, N E (NSW) 1907 *NZ* 1,3, 1909 *E*, 1910 *NZ* 1,2,3
Rowles, P G (NSW) 1972 *Fj*, 1973 *E*
Roxburgh, J R (NSW) 1968 *NZ* 1,2, *F*, 1969 *W, SA* 1,2,3,4, 1970 *S*
Ruebner, G (NSW) 1966 *BI* 1,2
Russell, C J (NSW) 1907 *NZ* 1,2,3, 1908 *W*, 1909 *E*
Ryan, J R (NSW) 1975 *J* 2, 1976 *I, US, Fj* 1,2,3
Ryan, K J (Q) 1958 *E, M* 1, *NZ* 1,2,3
Ryan, P F (NSW) 1963 *E, SA* 1, 1966 *BI* 1,2

Sampson, J H (NSW) 1899 *BI* 4
Sayle, J L (NSW) 1967 *NZ*
Schulte, B G (Q) 1946 *NZ* 1, *M*
Scott, P R I (NSW) 1962 *NZ* 1,2
Scott-Young, S J (Q) 1990 *F* 2,3 (R), *US, NZ* 3, 1992 *NZ* 1,2,3
Shambrook, G G (Q) 1976 *Fj* 2,3
Shaw, A A (Q) 1973 *W, E*, 1975 *E* 1,2, *J* 2, *S, W*, 1976 *E, I, US, Fj* 1,2,3, *F* 1,2, 1978 *W* 1,2, *NZ* 1,2,3, 1979 *I* 1,2, *NZ, Arg* 1,2, 1980 *Fj, NZ* 1,2,3, 1981 *F* 1,2, *I, W, S*, 1982 *S* 1,2
Shaw, C (NSW) 1925 *NZ* (R)
Shaw, G A (NSW) 1969 *W, SA* 1 (R), 1970 *S*, 1971 *SA* 1,2,3, *F* 1,2, 1973 *W, E*, 1974 *NZ* 1,2,3, 1975 *E* 1,2, *J* 1,2, *W*, 1976 *E, I, US, Fj* 1,2,3, *F* 1,2, 1979 *NZ*
Sheehan, W B J (NSW) 1923 *NZ* 1,2,3, 1927 *W, S*
Shehadie, N M (NSW) 1947 *NZ* 2, 1948 *E, F*, 1949 *M* 1,2,3, *NZ* 1,2, 1950 *BI* 1,2, 1951 *NZ* 1,2,3, 1952 *Fj* 1,2, *NZ* 2, 1953 *SA* 1,2,3,4, 1954 *Fj* 1,2, 1955 *NZ* 1,2,3, 1956 *SA* 1,2, 1957 *NZ* 2, 1958 *W, I*
Sheil, A G R (Q) 1956 *SA* 1
Shepherd, D J (V) 1964 *NZ* 3, 1965 *SA* 1,2, 1966 *BI* 1,2
Simpson, R J (NSW) 1913 *NZ* 2
Skinner, A J (NSW) 1969 *W, SA* 4, 1970 *S*
Slack, A G (Q) 1978 *W* 1,2, *NZ* 1,2, 1979 *NZ, Arg* 1,2, 1980 *Fj*, 1981 *I, W, S*, 1982 *E, S* 1, *NZ* 3, 1983 *US, Arg* 1,2, *NZ, It*, 1984 *Fj, NZ* 1,2,3, *E, I, W, S*, 1986 *It, F, NZ* 1,2,3, 1987 *SK,* [*E, US, J, I, F, W*]
Slater, S H (NSW) 1910 *NZ* 3
Slattery, P J (Q) 1990 *US* (R), 1991 *W* (R), *E* (R), [*WS* (R), *W, I* (R)], 1992 *I, W*, 1993 *Tg, C, F* 1,2, 1994 *I* 1,2, *It* 1 (R), 1995 [*C, R* (R)]
Smairl, A M (NSW) 1928 *NZ* 1,2,3
Smith, B A (Q) 1987 *SK,* [*US, J, I* (R), *W*]*, Arg* 1
Smith, D P (Q) 1993 *SA* 1,2,3, *C, F* 2, 1994 *I* 1,2, *It* 1,2, *WS, NZ*, 1995 *Arg* 1,2, [*SA, R, E*]*, NZ* 1,2, 1998 *SA* 1 (R), *NZ* 3 (R), *Fj*
Smith, F B (NSW) 1905 *NZ*, 1907 *NZ* 1,2,3
Smith, L M (NSW) 1905 *NZ*
Smith, N C (NSW) 1923 *NZ* 1
Smith, P V (NSW) 1967 *NZ*, 1968 *NZ* 1,2, *F, I, S*, 1969 *W, SA* 1
Smith, R A (NSW) 1971 *SA* 1,2, 1972 *F* 1,2, *NZ* 1,2 (R), 3, *Fj*, 1975 *E* 1,2, *J* 1,2, *S, W*, 1976 *E, I, US, Fj* 1,2,3, *F* 1,2
Smith, T S (NSW) 1921 *NZ*, 1925 *NZ*
Snell, H W (NSW) 1928 *NZ* 3
Solomon, H J (NSW) 1949 *M* 3, *NZ* 2, 1950 *BI* 1,2, 1951 *NZ* 1,2, 1952 *Fj* 1,2, *NZ* 1,2, 1953 *SA* 1,2,3, 1955 *NZ* 1
Spragg, S A (NSW) 1899 *BI* 1,2,3,4
Stanley, R G (NSW) 1921 *NZ*, 1923 *NZ* 1,2,3
Stapleton, E T (NSW) 1951 *NZ* 1,2,3, 1952 *Fj* 1,2, *NZ* 1,2, 1953 *SA* 1,2,3,4, 1954 *Fj* 1, 1955 *NZ* 1,2,3, 1958 *NZ* 1
Steggall, J C (Q) 1931 *M, NZ*, 1932 *NZ* 1,2,3, 1933 *SA* 1,2,3,4,5
Stegman, T R (NSW) 1973 *Tg* 1,2
Stephens, O G (NSW) 1973 *Tg* 1,2, *W*, 1974 *NZ* 2,3
Stewart, A A (NSW) 1979 *NZ, Arg* 1,2
Stone, A H (NSW) 1937 *SA* 2, 1938 *NZ* 2,3
Stone, C G (NSW) 1938 *NZ* 1
Stone, J M (NSW) 1946 *M, NZ* 2
Storey, G P (NSW) 1927 *I, W, S*, 1928 *E, F*, 1929 *NZ* 3 (R), 1930 *BI*
Storey, K P (NSW) 1936 *NZ* 2
Storey, N J D (NSW) 1962 *NZ* 1
Strachan, D J (NSW) 1955 *NZ* 2,3
Street, N O (NSW) 1899 *BI* 2
Streeter, S F (NSW) 1978 *NZ* 1
Stuart, R (NSW) 1910 *NZ* 2,3

Stumbles, B D (NSW) 1972 *NZ* 1 (R), 2,3, *Fj*
Sturtridge, G S (V) 1929 *NZ* 2, 1932 *NZ* 1,2,3, 1933 *SA* 1,2,3,4,5
Sullivan, P D (NSW) 1971 *SA* 1,2,3, *F* 1,2, 1972 *F* 1,2, *NZ* 1,2, *Fj*, 1973 *Tg* 1,2, *W*
Summons, A J (NSW) 1958 *W, I, E, S, M* 2, *NZ* 1,2,3, 1959 *BI* 1,2
Suttor, D C (NSW) 1913 *NZ* 1,2,3
Swannell, B I (NSW) 1905 *NZ*
Sweeney, T L (Q) 1953 *SA* 1

Taafe, B S (NSW) 1969 *SA* 1, 1972 *F* 1,2
Tabua, I (Q) 1993 *SA* 2,3, *C, F* 1, 1994 *I* 1,2, *It* 1,2, 1995 [*C, R*]
Tancred, A J (NSW) 1927 *I, W, S*
Tancred, J L (NSW) 1928 *F*
Tanner, W H (Q) 1899 *BI* 1,2
Tasker, W G (NSW) 1913 *NZ* 1,2,3, 1914 *NZ* 1,2,3
Tate, M J (NSW) 1951 *NZ* 3, 1952 *Fj* 1,2, *NZ* 1,2, 1953 *SA* 1, 1954 *Fj* 1,2
Taylor, D A (Q) 1968 *NZ* 1,2, *F, I, S*
Taylor, H C (NSW) 1923 *NZ* 1,2,3
Taylor, J I (NSW) 1971 *SA* 1, 1972 *F* 1,2, *Fj*
Teitzel, R G (Q) 1966 *W, S*, 1967 *E, I* 1, *F, I* 2, *NZ*
Thompson, C E (NSW) 1923 *NZ* 1
Thompson, E G (Q) 1929 *NZ* 1,2,3, 1930 *BI*
Thompson, F (NSW) 1913 *NZ* 1,2,3, 1914 *NZ* 1,2,3
Thompson, J (Q) 1914 *NZ* 1
Thompson, P D (Q) 1950 *BI* 1
Thompson, R J (WA) 1971 *NZ* 3, *F* 2 (R), 1972 *Fj*
Thorn, A M (NSW) 1921 *NZ*
Thorn, E J (NSW) 1923 *NZ* 1,2,3
Thornett, J E (NSW) 1955 *NZ* 1,2,3, 1956 *SA* 1,2, 1958 *W, I, S, F, M* 2,3, *NZ* 2,3, 1959 *BI* 1,2, 1961 *Fj* 2,3, *SA* 1,2, *F*, 1962 *NZ* 2,3,4,5, 1963 *E, SA* 1,2,3,4, 1964 *NZ* 1,2,3, 1965 *SA* 1,2, 1966 *BI* 1,2, 1967 *F*
Thornett, R N (NSW) 1961 *Fj* 1,2,3, *SA* 1,2, *F*, 1962 *NZ* 1,2,3,4,5
Thorpe, A C (NSW) 1929 *NZ* 1 (R)
Timbury, F R V (Q) 1910 *NZ* 1,2,
Tindall, E N (NSW) 1973 *Tg* 2
Toby, A E (NSW) 1925 *NZ*
Tolhurst, H A (NSW) 1931 *M, NZ*
Tombs, R C (NSW) 1992 *S* 1,2, 1994 *I* 2, *It* 1, 1996 *NZ* 2
Tonkin, A E J (NSW) 1947 *S, I, W*, 1948 *E, F*, 1950 *BI* 2
Tooth, R M (NSW) 1951 *NZ* 1,2,3, 1954 *Fj* 1,2, 1955 *NZ* 1,2,3, 1957 *NZ* 1,2
Towers, C H T (NSW) 1927 *I*, 1928 *E, F, NZ* 1,2,3, *M*, 1929 *NZ* 1,3, 1930 *BI*, 1931 *M, NZ*, 1934 *NZ* 1,2, 1937 *SA* 1,2
Trivett, R K (Q) 1966 *BI* 1,2
Tune, B N (Q) 1996 *W* 2, *C, NZ* 1, *SA* 1, *NZ* 2, *SA* 2, 1997 *F* 1,2, *NZ* 1, *E* 1, *NZ* 2, *SA* 1, *NZ* 3, *SA* 2, *Arg*, 1,2, *E* 2, *S*, 1998 *E* 1, *S* 1,2, *NZ* 1, *SA* 1,2, *NZ* 3
Turnbull, A (V) 1961 *Fj* 3
Turnbull, R V (NSW) 1968 *I*
Tuynman, S N (NSW) 1983 *F* 1,2, 1984 *E, I, W, S*, 1985 *C* 1,2, *NZ, Fj* 1,2, 1986 *It, F, Arg* 1,2, *NZ* 1,2,3, 1987 *SK*, [*E, US, J, I, W*], *NZ, Arg* 1 (R), 2, 1988 *E, It*, 1989 *BI* 1,2,3, *NZ*, 1990 *NZ* 1
Tweedale, E (NSW) 1946 *NZ* 1,2, 1947 *NZ* 2, *S, I*, 1948 *E, F*, 1949 *M* 1,2,3

Vaughan, D (NSW) 1983 *US, Arg* 1, *It, F* 1,2
Vaughan, G N (V) 1958 *E, S, F, M* 1,2,3
Verge, A (NSW) 1904 *BI* 1,2

Walden, R J (NSW) 1934 *NZ* 2, 1936 *NZ* 1,2, *M*
Walker, A K (NSW) 1947 *NZ* 1, 1948 *E, F*, 1950 *BI* 1,2

Walker, A S B (NSW) 1912 *US*, 1921 *NZ*
Walker, L F (NSW) 1988 *NZ* 2,3, *S, It*, 1989 *BI* 1,2,3, *NZ*
Walker, L R (NSW) 1982 *NZ* 2,3
Wallace, A C (NSW) 1921 *NZ*, 1927 *I, W, S*, 1928 *E, F*
Wallace, T M (NSW) 1994 *It* 1 (R), 2
Wallach, C (NSW) 1913 *NZ* 1,3, 1914 *NZ* 1,2,3
Walsh, J J (NSW) 1953 *SA* 1,2,3,4
Walsh, P B (NSW) 1904 *BI* 1,2,3
Walsham, K P (NSW) 1962 *NZ* 3, 1963 *E*
Ward, P G (NSW) 1899 *BI* 1,2,3,4
Ward, T (Q) 1899 *BI* 2
Watson, G W (Q) 1907 *NZ* 1
Watson, W T (NSW) 1912 *US*, 1913 *NZ* 1,2,3, 1914 *NZ* 1
Waugh, W W (NSW, ACT) 1993 *SA* 1, 1995 [*C*], *NZ* 1,2, 1996 *S, I*, 1997 *Arg* 1,2
Weatherstone, L J (ACT) 1975 *E* 1,2, *J* 1,2, *S* (R), 1976 *E, I*
Webb, W (NSW) 1899 *BI* 3,4
Welborn, J P (NSW) 1996 *SA* 2, *It*, 1998 *Tg*
Wells, B G (NSW) 1958 *M* 1
Westfield, R E (NSW) 1928 *NZ* 1,2,3, *M*, 1929 *NZ* 2,3
Whitaker, C J (NSW) 1998 *SA* 2 (R), *Fj* (R), *Tg*
White, C J B (NSW) 1899 *BI* 1, 1903 *NZ*, 1904 *BI* 1
White, J M (NSW) 1904 *BI* 3
White, J P L (NSW) 1958 *NZ* 1,2,3, 1961 *Fj* 1,2,3, *SA* 1,2, *F*, 1962 *NZ* 1,2,3,4,5, 1963 *E, SA* 1,2,3,4, 1964 *NZ* 1,2,3, 1965 *SA* 1,2
White, M C (Q) 1931 *M, NZ* 1932 *NZ* 1,2, 1933 *SA* 1,2,3,4,5
White, S W (NSW) 1956 *SA* 1,2, 1958 *I, E, S, M* 2,3
White, W G S (Q) 1933 *SA* 1,2,3,4,5, 1934 *NZ* 1,2, 1936 *NZ* 1,2, *M*
White, W J (NSW) 1928 *NZ* 1, *M*, 1932 *NZ* 1
Wickham, S M (NSW) 1903 *NZ*, 1904 *BI* 1,2,3, 1905 *NZ*
Williams, D (Q) 1913 *NZ* 3, 1914 *NZ* 1,2,3
Williams, I M (NSW) 1987 *Arg* 1,2, 1988 *E* 1,2, *NZ* 1,2,3, 1989 *BI* 2,3, *NZ, F* 1,2, 1990 *F* 1,2,3, *US, NZ* 1
Williams, J L (NSW) 1963 *SA* 1,3,4
Williams, S A (NSW) 1980 *Fj, NZ* 1,2, 1981 *F* 1,2, 1982 *E, NZ* 1,2,3, 1983 *US, Arg* 1 (R), 2, *NZ, It, F* 1,2, 1984 *NZ* 1,2,3, *E, I, W, S*, 1985 *C* 1,2, *NZ, Fj* 1,2
Wilson, B J (NSW) 1949 *NZ* 1,2
Wilson, C R (Q) 1957 *NZ* 1, 1958 *NZ* 1,2,3
Wilson, D J (Q) 1992 *S* 1,2, *NZ* 1,2,3, *SA, I, W*, 1993 *Tg, NZ, SA* 1,2,3, *C, F* 1,2, 1994 *I* 1,2, *It* 1,2, *WS, NZ*, 1995 *Arg* 1,2, [*SA, R, E*], 1996 *W* 1,2, *C, NZ* 1, *SA* 1, *NZ* 2, *SA* 2, *It, S, I, W* 3, 1997 *F* 1,2, *NZ* 1, *E* 1 (t + R), *NZ* 2 (R), *SA* 1, *NZ* 3, *SA* 2, *E* 2 (R), *S* (R), 1998 *E* 1, *S* 1,2, *NZ* 1, *SA* 1, *NZ* 3, *SA* 2, *SA* 2, *NZ* 3, *Fj, WS, F, E* 2
Wilson, V W (Q) 1937 *SA* 1,2, 1938 *NZ* 1,2,3
Windon, C J (NSW) 1946 *NZ* 1,2, 1947 *NZ* 1, *S, I, W*, 1948 *E, F*, 1949 *M* 1,2,3, *NZ* 1,2, 1951 *NZ* 1,2,3, 1952 *Fj* 1,2, *NZ* 1,2
Windon, K S (NSW) 1937 *SA* 1,2, 1946 *M*
Windsor, J C (Q) 1947 *NZ* 2
Winning, K C (Q) 1951 *NZ* 1
Wogan, L W (NSW) 1913 *NZ* 1,2,3, 1914 *NZ* 1,2,3, 1921 *NZ*
Wood, F (NSW) 1907 *NZ* 1,2,3, 1910 *NZ* 1,2,3, 1913 *NZ* 1,2,3, 1914 *NZ* 1,2,3
Wood, R N (Q) 1972 *Fj*
Woods, H F (NSW) 1925 *NZ*, 1927 *I, W, S*, 1928 *E*
Wright, K J (NSW) 1975 *E* 1,2, *J* 1, 1976 *US*, *F* 1,2, 1978 *NZ* 1,2,3

Yanz, K (NSW) 1958 *F*

AUSTRALIAN INTERNATIONAL RECORDS (*up to 30 April 1999*)

MATCH RECORDS

MOST CONSECUTIVE TEST WINS

10 1991 *Arg, WS, W, I, NZ, E*, 1992 *S* 1,2, *NZ* 1,2
9 1993 *F* 2, 1994 *I* 1,2, *It* 1,2, *WS, NZ*, 1995 *Arg* 1,2

MOST CONSECUTIVE TESTS WITHOUT DEFEAT

P	W	D	Period
10	10	0	1991–92
9	9	0	1993–95
7	7	0	1985–86

MOST POINTS IN A MATCH
by the team

Pts	Opp	Venue	Year
76	E	Brisbane	1998
74	C	Brisbane	1996
74	Tg	Canberra	1998
73	WS	Sydney	1994
67	US	Brisbane	1990

by a player

39 by M Burke v Canada at Brisbane — 1996
28 by M P Lynagh v Argentina at Brisbane — 1995
25 by M Burke v Scotland at Sydney — 1998
24 by M P Lynagh v United States at Brisbane — 1990
24 by M P Lynagh v France at Brisbane — 1990
24 by M Burke v New Zealand at Melbourne — 1998

MOST TRIES IN A MATCH
by the team

T	Opp	Venue	Year
13	SK	Brisbane	1987
12	US	Brisbane	1990
12	W	Brisbane	1991
12	Tg	Canberra	1998
11	WS	Sydney	1994
11	E	Brisbane	1998

by a player

4 by G Cornelsen v New Zealand at Auckland — 1978
4 by D I Campese v United States at Sydney — 1983
4 by J S Little v Tonga at Canberra — 1998

MOST CONVERSIONS IN A MATCH
by the team

C	Opp	Venue	Year
9	C	Brisbane	1996
9	Fj	Parramatta	1998
8	It	Rome	1988
8	US	Brisbane	1990
7	C	Sydney	1985
7	Tg	Canberra	1998

by a player

9 by M Burke v Canada at Brisbane — 1996
9 by J A Eales v Fiji at Parramatta — 1998
8 by M P Lynagh v Italy at Rome — 1988
8 by M P Lynagh v United States at Brisbane — 1990
7 by M P Lynagh v Canada at Sydney — 1985

MOST PENALTY GOALS IN A MATCH
by the team

P	Opp	Venue	Year
6	NZ	Sydney	1984
6	F	Sydney	1986
6	E	Brisbane	1988
6	Arg	Buenos Aires	1997
5	several instances		

by a player

6 by M P Lynagh v France at Sydney — 1986
6 by M P Lynagh v England at Brisbane — 1988
6 by D J Knox v Argentina at Buenos Aires — 1997
5 several instances

MOST DROPPED GOALS IN A MATCH

by the team

D	Opp	Venue	Year
3	E	Twickenham	1967
3	I	Dublin	1984
3	Fj	Brisbane	1985

by a player

3 by P F Hawthorne v England at
Twickenham 1967
2 by M G Ella v Ireland at Dublin 1984
2 by D J Knox v Fiji at Brisbane 1985

CAREER RECORDS

MOST CAPPED PLAYERS

Caps	Player	Career
101	D I Campese	1982–96
72	M P Lynagh	1984–95
67	T J Horan	1989–98
64	J A Eales	1991–98
63	N C Farr Jones	1984–93
61	P N Kearns	1989–98
60	D J Wilson	1992–98
59	S P Poidevin	1980–91
58	J S Little	1989–98
51	E J A McKenzie	1990–97

MOST CONSECUTIVE TESTS

Tests	Player	Span
46	P N Kearns	1989–95
42	D I Campese	1990–95
37	P G Johnson	1959–68
34	M P Lynagh	1988–92

MOST TESTS AS CAPTAIN

Tests	Captain	Span
36	N C Farr Jones	1988–92
33	J A Eales	1996–98
19	A G Slack	1984–87
16	J E Thornett	1962–67
16	G V Davis	1969–72

MOST TESTS IN INDIVIDUAL POSITIONS

Full-back M Burke		29	1993–98
Wing D I Campese		85	1982–96
Centre T J Horan		60	1989–98
Fly-half M P Lynagh		64	1984–95

Scrum-half N C Farr Jones		62	1984–93
Prop E J A McKenzie		51	1990–97
Hooker P N Kearns		61	1989–98
Lock J A Eales		62	1991–98
Flanker { S P Poidevin		59	1980–91
{ D J Wilson		59	1992–98
No. 8 T B Gavin		43	1988–96

MOST POINTS IN TESTS

Pts	Player	Tests	Career
911	M P Lynagh	72	1984–95
354	M Burke	32	1993–98
315	D I Campese	101	1982–96
260	P E McLean	30	1974–82
239	M Burke	24	1993–97
165	J A Eales	64	1991–98

MOST TRIES IN TESTS

Tries	Player	Tests	Career
64	D I Campese	101	1982–96
26	T J Horan	67	1989–98
19	J S Little	58	1989–98
17	M P Lynagh	72	1984–95
16	M Burke	32	1993–98
16	B N Tune	25	1996–98

MOST CONVERSIONS IN TESTS

Cons	Player	Tests	Career
140	M P Lynagh	72	1984–95
44	M Burke	32	1993–98
30	J A Eales	64	1991–98
27	P E McLean	30	1974–82
19	D J Knox	13	1985–97

MOST PENALTY GOALS IN TESTS

Pens	Player	Tests	Career
177	M P Lynagh	72	1984–95
62	P E McLean	30	1974–82
62	M Burke	32	1993–98
32	J A Eales	64	1991–98
23	M C Roebuck	23	1991–93

MOST DROPPED GOALS IN TESTS

Drops	Player	Tests	Career
9	P F Hawthorne	21	1962–67
9	M P Lynagh	72	1984–95
8	M G Ella	25	1980–84
4	P E McLean	30	1974–82

TRI-NATIONS RECORDS

Record	Detail	Holder	Set
Most points in matches	98	M Burke	1996 to 1998
Most points in season	50	M Burke	1998
Most points in match	24	M Burke	v N Zealand (h) 1998
Most tries in matches	5	B N Tune	1996 to 1998
Most tries in season	3	B N Tune	1997
	3	M Burke	1998
Most tries in match	2	B N Tune	v S Africa (h) 1997
	2	M Burke	v N Zealand (h) 1998
Most cons in matches	7	D J Knox	1997
Most cons in season	7	D J Knox	1997
Most cons in match	3	D J Knox	v S Africa (h) 1997
Most pens in matches	24	M Burke	1996 to 1998
Most pens in season	11	M Burke	1996 and 1998
Most pens in match	5	M Burke	v S Africa (a) 1998
	5	M Burke	v N Zealand (h) 1996

SERIES RECORDS

Record	Holder	Detail
Most tries	D I Campese	6 in Europe 1988
Most points	M Burke	74 in Europe 1996

MAJOR TOUR RECORDS

Record	Detail	Year	Place
Most team points	500	1947–48	Europe
Most team tries	115	1947–48	Europe
Most individual points	154 by P E McLean	1975–76	Britain & Ireland
Most individual tries	23 by C J Russell	1908–09	Britain
Most points in match	26 by A J Leeds	1986 v Buller (NZ)	Westport
	26 by M C Roebuck	1993 v Fr Barbarians	Clermont Ferrand
Most tries in match	6 by J S Boyce	1962 v Wairarapa (NZ)	Masterton

MISCELLANEOUS RECORDS

Record	Holder	Detail
Longest Test career	G M Cooke/A R Miller	16 seasons, 1932–1947–48/1952–67
Youngest Test cap	B W Ford	18 yrs 90 days in 1957
Oldest Test cap	A R Miller	38 yrs 113 days in 1967

AUSTRALIAN INTERNATIONAL CAREER RECORDS (*up to 30 April 1999*)

Player	Debut	Caps since last season	Caps	T	C	PG	DG	Pts
M Burke	1993 v SA	1998 *E* 1, *S* 1,2, *NZ* 1, *SA* 1, *NZ* 2, *SA* 2, *NZ* 3	32	16	44	62	0	354
C E Latham	1998 v F	1998 *F, E*2	2	0	0	0	0	0
M D Hardy	1997 v F	1998 *Tg, WS*	8	2	0	0	0	10
J W Roff	1995 v C	1998 *E*1, *S* 1,2, *NZ* 1, *SA* 1, *NZ* 2, *SA* 2, *NZ* 3, *Fj, Tg, WS, F, E* 2	38	11	2	3	0	68
B N Tune	1996 v W	1998 *E* 1, *S* 1,2, *NZ* 1, *SA* 1,2, *NZ* 3	25	16	0	0	0	80
D P Smith	1993 v SA	1998 *SA* 1(R), *NZ* 3(R), *Fj*	21	10	0	0	0	50
N P Grey	1998 v S	1998 *S* 2(R), *SA* 2(R), *Fj*(R), *Tg*(R), *F, E*2	6	2	0	0	0	10
J S Little	1989 v F	1998 *E* 1(R), *S* 2(R), *NZ* 2, *SA* 2(R), *NZ* 3, *Fj, Tg, WS, F, E*2	58	19	0	0	0	92
S N G Staniforth	None		0	0	0	0	0	0
D J Herbert	1994 v I	1998 *E*1, *S* 1,2, *NZ* 1, *SA* 1, *NZ* 2, *SA* 2, *Fj, Tg, WS, F,E*2	26	5	0	0	0	25
T J Horan	1989 v NZ	1998 *E* 1, *S* 1,2, *NZ* 1, *SA* 1, *NZ* 2, *SA* 2, *NZ* 3, *Fj, Tg, WS*	67	26	0	0	0	120
S J Larkham	1996 v W	1998 *E* 1, *S* 1,2, *NZ* 1, *SA* 1, *NZ* 2, *SA* 2, *NZ* 3, *Fj, Tg*(t), *WS, F, E* 2	25	12	2	0	0	64
M H M Edmonds	1998 v Tg	1998 *Tg*	1	2	5	0	0	20
G M Gregan	1994 v It	1998 *E* 1, *S* 1,2, *NZ* 1, *SA* 1, *NZ* 2, *SA* 2, *NZ* 3, *Fj, WS, F, E* 2	42	8	0	0	0	40
C J Whitaker	1998 v SA	1998 *SA* 2(R), *Fj*(R), *Tg*	3	1	0	0	0	5
J A Paul	1998 v S	1998 *S* 1(R), *NZ* 1(R), *SA* 1(t), *Fj*(R), *Tg*	5	2	0	0	0	10
P N Kearns	1989 v NZ	1998 *E*1, *S* 1,2, *NZ* 1, *SA* 1, *NZ* 2, *SA* 2, *NZ* 3, *Fj, WS, F, E* 2	61	8	0	0	0	34
M A Foley	1995 v C	1998 *Tg*(R), *F*(R), *E* 2(R)	24	3	0	0	0	15
E P Noriega★	1998 v F	1998 *F, E*2	2	0	0	0	0	0
R L L Harry	1996 v W	1998 *E* 1, *S* 1,2, *NZ* 1, *Fj*	23	1	0	0	0	5
D J Crowley	1989 v BL	1998 *E* 1(R), *S* 1(R),2(R), *NZ* 1(R), *SA* 1, *NZ* 2, *SA* 2, *NZ* 3, *Tg, WS*	29	1	0	0	0	5
A T Blades	1996 v S	1998 *E* 1, *S* 1,2, *NZ* 1, *SA* 1, *NZ* 2, *SA* 2, *NZ* 3, *Fj, WS, F,E* 2	24	0	0	0	0	0

C D Blades	1997 v E		1	0	0	0	0	0
G M Panoho	1998 v SA	1998 *SA* 2(R), *NZ* 3(R), *Fj*(R), *Tg*, *WS*(R)	5	0	0	0	0	0
J P Welborn	1996 v SA	1998 *Tg*	3	0	0	0	0	0
T M Bowman	1998 v E	1998 *E* 1, *S* 1,2, *NZ* 1, *SA* 1, *NZ* 2, *SA* 2, *NZ* 3, *Fj*, *WS*, *F*, *E* 2	12	2	0	0	0	10
J F Langford	1997 v NZ		4	0	0	0	0	0
M J Cockbain	1997 v F	1998 *E* 1, *S* 1,2, *NZ* 1, *SA* 1, *NZ* 2, *SA* 2, *NZ* 3, *Fj*, *Tg*(R), *WS*, *F*, *E* 2	17	0	0	0	0	0
J A Eales	1991 v W	1998 *E* 1, *S* 1,2, *NZ* 1, *SA* 1, *NZ* 2, *SA* 2, *NZ* 3, *Fj*, *Tg*, *WS*, *F*, *E* 2	64	2	30	32	0	165
D J Wilson	1992 v S	1998 *E* 1, *S* 1,2, *NZ* 1, *SA* 1, *NZ* 2, *SA* 2, *NZ* 3, *Fj*, *WS*, *F*, *E* 2	60	11	0	0	0	55
B J Robinson	1996 v It	1998 *Tg*	16	1	0	0	0	5
O D A Finegan	1996 v W	1998 *E* 1(R), *S* 1(t&R),2 (t&R), *NZ* 1(R), *SA* 1(t),2(R), *NZ* 3(R), *Fj*(R), *Tg*, *WS*(t&R), *F*(R), *E*2(R)	26	5	0	0	0	25
V Ofahengaue	1990 v NZ	1998 *E* 1(R), *S* 1(R),2(R), *NZ* 1(R), *SA* 1(R), *NZ* 2(R), *SA* 2(R), *NZ* 3(R), *Fj*, *WS*, *F*(R)	41	11	0	0	0	51
S F Finau	1997 v NZ		1	0	0	0	0	0
R S T Kefu	1997 v SA	1998 *E* 1, *S* 1,2, *NZ* 1, *SA* 1, *NZ* 2, *SA* 2, *NZ* 3, *Fj*(R), *Tg*, *WS*(R), *F*, *E* 2	14	2	0	0	0	10

* *Noriega was capped 22 times by Argentina.*

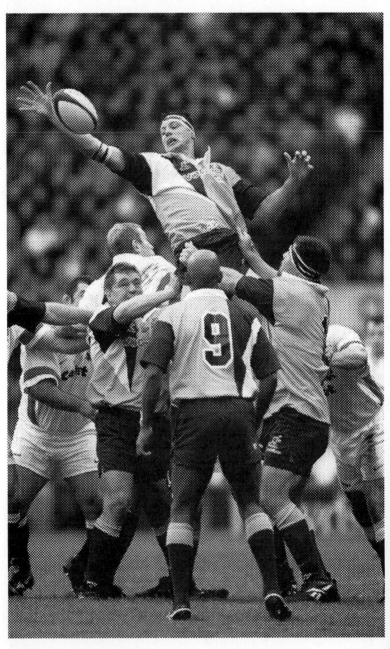

Matt Cockbain stretches to win the lineout during the Cook Cup match against England at Twickenham in November 1998.

RESULTS OF INTERNATIONAL MATCHES (*up to 30 April 1999*)

Cap matches only.
Years for Five Nations matches are for the second half of the season: eg 1972 means season 1971-72. Years for matches against touring teams from the Southern Hemisphere refer to the actual year of the match.
  Points-scoring was first introduced in 1886, when an International Board was formed by Scotland, Ireland and Wales. Points values varied between countries until 1890, when England agreed to join the Board, and uniform values were adopted.

Northern Hemisphere seasons	Try	Conversion	Penalty goal	Dropped goal	Goal from mark
1890-91	1	2	2	3	3
1891-92 to 1892-93	2	3	3	4	4
1893-94 to 1904-05	3	2	3	4	4
1905-06 to 1947-48	3	2	3	4	3
1948-49 to 1970-71	3	2	3	3	3
1971-72 to 1991-92	4	2	3	3	3*
1992-93 onwards	5	2	3	3	–

*The goal from mark ceased to exist when the free-kick clause was introduced, 1977-78.
  WC indicates a fixture played during the Rugby World Cup finals. LC indicates a fixture played in the Latin Cup. TN indicates a fixture played in the Tri-Nations.

ENGLAND v SCOTLAND
Played 116   England won 60, Scotland won 39, Drawn 17
Highest scores England 41-13 in 1997, Scotland 33-6 in 1986
Biggest wins England 41-13 in 1997, Scotland 33-6 in 1986

1871 Raeburn Place (Edinburgh) **Scotland** 1G 1T to 1T
1872 The Oval (London) **England** 1G 1DG 2T to 1DG
1873 Glasgow **Drawn** no score
1874 The Oval **England** 1DG to 1T
1875 Raeburn Place **Drawn** no score
1876 The Oval **England** 1G 1T to 0
1877 Raeburn Place **Scotland** 1 DG to 0
1878 The Oval **Drawn** no score
1879 Raeburn Place **Drawn** Scotland 1DG England 1G
1880 Manchester **England** 2G 3T to 1G
1881 Raeburn Place **Drawn** Scotland 1G 1T England 1DG 1T
1882 Manchester **Scotland** 2T to 0
1883 Raeburn Place **England** 2T to 1T
1884 Blackheath (London) **England** 1G to 1T
1885 No Match
1886 Raeburn Place **Drawn** no score
1887 Manchester **Drawn** 1T each
1888 No Match
1889 No Match
1890 Raeburn Place **England** 1G 1T to 0
1891 Richmond (London) **Scotland** 9-3
1892 Raeburn Place **England** 5-0
1893 Leeds **Scotland** 8-0
1894 Raeburn Place **Scotland** 6-0
1895 Richmond **Scotland** 6-3
1896 Glasgow **Scotland** 11-0
1897 Manchester **England** 12-3
1898 Powderhall (Edinburgh) **Drawn** 3-3
1899 Blackheath **Scotland** 5-0
1900 Inverleith (Edinburgh) **Drawn** 0-0
1901 Blackheath **Scotland** 18-3
1902 Inverleith **England** 6-3
1903 Richmond **Scotland** 10-6
1904 Inverleith **Scotland** 6-3
1905 Richmond **Scotland** 8-0
1906 Inverleith **England** 9-3
1907 Blackheath **Scotland** 8-3
1908 Inverleith **Scotland** 16-10
1909 Richmond **Scotland** 18-8
1910 Inverleith **England** 14-5
1911 Twickenham **England** 13-8
1912 Inverleith **Scotland** 8-3
1913 Twickenham **England** 3-0
1914 Inverleith **England** 16-15
1920 Twickenham **England** 13-4
1921 Inverleith **England** 18-0
1922 Twickenham **England** 11-5
1923 Inverleith **England** 8-6
1924 Twickenham **England** 19-0
1925 Murrayfield **Scotland** 14-11
1926 Twickenham **Scotland** 17-9
1927 Murrayfield **Scotland** 21-13
1928 Twickenham **England** 6-0
1929 Murrayfield **Scotland** 12-6

1930 Twickenham **Drawn** 0-0
1931 Murrayfield **Scotland** 28-19
1932 Twickenham **England** 16-3
1933 Murrayfield **Scotland** 3-0
1934 Twickenham **England** 6-3
1935 Murrayfield **Scotland** 10-7
1936 Twickenham **England** 9-8
1937 Murrayfield **England** 6-3
1938 Twickenham **Scotland** 21-16
1939 Murrayfield **England** 9-6
1947 Twickenham **England** 24-5
1948 Murrayfield **Scotland** 6-3
1949 Twickenham **England** 19-3
1950 Murrayfield **Scotland** 13-11
1951 Twickenham **England** 5-3
1952 Murrayfield **England** 19-3
1953 Twickenham **England** 26-8
1954 Murrayfield **England** 13-3
1955 Twickenham **England** 9-6
1956 Murrayfield **England** 11-6
1957 Twickenham **England** 16-3
1958 Murrayfield **Drawn** 3-3
1959 Twickenham **Drawn** 3-3
1960 Murrayfield **England** 21-12
1961 Twickenham **England** 6-0
1962 Murrayfield **Drawn** 3-3
1963 Twickenham **England** 10-8
1964 Murrayfield **Scotland** 15-6
1965 Twickenham **Drawn** 3-3
1966 Murrayfield **Scotland** 6-3
1967 Twickenham **England** 27-14
1968 Murrayfield **England** 8-6
1969 Twickenham **England** 8-3

1970 Murrayfield **Scotland** 14-5
1971 Twickenham **Scotland** 16-15
1971 Murrayfield **Scotland** 26-6
Special centenary match – non-championship
1972 Murrayfield **Scotland** 23-9
1973 Twickenham **England** 20-13
1974 Murrayfield **Scotland** 16-14
1975 Twickenham **England** 7-6
1976 Murrayfield **Scotland** 22-12
1977 Twickenham **England** 26-6
1978 Murrayfield **England** 15-0
1979 Twickenham **Drawn** 7-7
1980 Murrayfield **England** 30-18
1981 Twickenham **England** 23-17
1982 Murrayfield **Drawn** 9-9
1983 Twickenham **Scotland** 22-12
1984 Murrayfield **Scotland** 18-6
1985 Twickenham **England** 10-7
1986 Murrayfield **Scotland** 33-6
1987 Twickenham **England** 21-12
1988 Murrayfield **England** 9-6
1989 Twickenham **Drawn** 12-12
1990 Murrayfield **Scotland** 13-7
1991 Twickenham **England** 21-12
1991 Murrayfield *WC* **England** 9-6
1992 Murrayfield **England** 25-7
1993 Twickenham **England** 26-12
1994 Murrayfield **England** 15-14
1995 Twickenham **England** 24-12
1996 Murrayfield **England** 18-9
1997 Twickenham **England** 41-13
1998 Murrayfield **England** 34-20
1999 Twickenham **England** 24-21

ENGLAND v IRELAND
Played 112   England won 66, Ireland won 38, Drawn 8
Highest scores England 46-6 in 1997, Ireland 26-21 in 1974
Biggest wins England 46-6 in 1997, Ireland 22-0 in 1947

1875 The Oval (London) **England** 1G 1DG
    1T to 0
1876 Dublin **England** 1G 1T to 0
1877 The Oval **England** 2G 2T to 0
1878 Dublin **England** 2G 1T to 0
1879 The Oval **England** 2G 1DG 2T to 0
1880 Dublin **England** 1G 1T to 1T
1881 Manchester **England** 2G 2T to 0
1882 Dublin **Drawn** 2T each
1883 Manchester **England** 1G 3T to 1T
1884 Dublin **England** 1G to 0
1885 Manchester **England** 2T to 1T
1886 Dublin **England** 1T to 0
1887 Dublin **Ireland** 2G to 0
1888 No Match
1889 No Match
1890 Blackheath (London) **England** 3T to 0
1891 Dublin **England** 9-0
1892 Manchester **England** 7-0
1893 Dublin **England** 4-0
1894 Blackheath **Ireland** 7-5
1895 Dublin **England** 6-3
1896 Leeds **Ireland** 10-4

1897 Dublin **Ireland** 13-9
1898 Richmond (London) **Ireland** 9-6
1899 Dublin **Ireland** 6-0
1900 Richmond **England** 15-4
1901 Dublin **Ireland** 10-6
1902 Leicester **England** 6-3
1903 Dublin **Ireland** 6-0
1904 Blackheath **England** 19-0
1905 Cork **Ireland** 17-3
1906 Leicester **Ireland** 16-6
1907 Dublin **Ireland** 17-9
1908 Richmond **England** 13-3
1909 Dublin **England** 11-5
1910 Twickenham **Drawn** 0-0
1911 Dublin **Ireland** 3-0
1912 Twickenham **England** 15-0
1913 Dublin **England** 15-4
1914 Twickenham **England** 17-12
1920 Dublin **England** 14-11
1921 Twickenham **England** 15-0
1922 Dublin **England** 12-3
1923 Leicester **England** 23-5
1924 Belfast **England** 14-3

1925 Twickenham **Drawn** 6-6
1926 Dublin **Ireland** 19-15
1927 Twickenham **England** 8-6
1928 Dublin **England** 7-6
1929 Twickenham **Ireland** 6-5
1930 Dublin **Ireland** 4-3
1931 Twickenham **Ireland** 6-5
1932 Dublin **England** 11-8
1933 Twickenham **England** 17-6
1934 Dublin **England** 13-3
1935 Twickenham **England** 14-3
1936 Dublin **Ireland** 6-3
1937 Twickenham **England** 9-8
1938 Dublin **England** 36-14
1939 Twickenham **Ireland** 5-0
1947 Dublin **Ireland** 22-0
1948 Twickenham **Ireland** 11-10
1949 Dublin **Ireland** 14-5
1950 Twickenham **England** 3-0
1951 Dublin **Ireland** 3-0
1952 Twickenham **England** 3-0
1953 Dublin **Drawn** 9-9
1954 Twickenham **England** 14-3
1955 Dublin **Drawn** 6-6
1956 Twickenham **England** 20-0
1957 Dublin **England** 6-0
1958 Twickenham **England** 6-0
1959 Dublin **England** 3-0
1960 Twickenham **England** 8-5
1961 Dublin **Ireland** 11-8
1962 Twickenham **England** 16-0
1963 Dublin **Drawn** 0-0
1964 Twickenham **Ireland** 18-5
1965 Dublin **Ireland** 5-0
1966 Twickenham **Drawn** 6-6

1967 Dublin **England** 8-3
1968 Twickenham **Drawn** 9-9
1969 Dublin **Ireland** 17-15
1970 Twickenham **England** 9-3
1971 Dublin **England** 9-6
1972 Twickenham **Ireland** 16-12
1973 Dublin **Ireland** 18-9
1974 Twickenham **Ireland** 26-21
1975 Dublin **Ireland** 12-9
1976 Twickenham **Ireland** 13-12
1977 Dublin **England** 4-0
1978 Twickenham **England** 15-9
1979 Dublin **Ireland** 12-7
1980 Twickenham **England** 24-9
1981 Dublin **England** 10-6
1982 Twickenham **Ireland** 16-15
1983 Dublin **Ireland** 25-15
1984 Twickenham **England** 12-9
1985 Dublin **Ireland** 13-10
1986 Twickenham **England** 25-20
1987 Dublin **Ireland** 17-0
1988 Twickenham **England** 35-3
1988 Dublin **England** 21-10
  Non-championship match
1989 Dublin **England** 16-3
1990 Twickenham **England** 23-0
1991 Dublin **England** 16-7
1992 Twickenham **England** 38-9
1993 Dublin **Ireland** 17-3
1994 Twickenham **Ireland** 13-12
1995 Dublin **England** 20-8
1996 Twickenham **England** 28-15
1997 Dublin **England** 46-6
1998 Twickenham **England** 35-17
1999 Dublin **England** 27-15

ENGLAND v WALES
Played 105   England won 44, Wales won 49, Drawn 12
Highest scores England 60-26 in 1998, Wales 34-21 in 1967
Biggest wins England 60-26 in 1998, Wales 25-0 in 1905

1881 Blackheath (London) **England** 7G
  1DG 6T to 0
1882 No Match
1883 Swansea **England** 2G 4T to 0
1884 Leeds **England** 1G 2T to 1G
1885 Swansea **England** 1G 4T to 1G 1T
1886 Blackheath **England** 1GM 2T to 1G
1887 Llanelli **Drawn** no score
1888 No Match
1889 No Match
1890 Dewsbury **Wales** 1T to 0
1891 Newport **England** 7-3
1892 Blackheath **England** 17-0
1893 Cardiff **Wales** 12-11
1894 Birkenhead **England** 24-3
1895 Swansea **England** 14-6
1896 Blackheath **England** 25-0
1897 Newport **Wales** 11-0
1898 Blackheath **England** 14-7
1899 Swansea **Wales** 26-3
1900 Gloucester **Wales** 13-3

1901 Cardiff **Wales** 13-0
1902 Blackheath **Wales** 9-8
1903 Swansea **Wales** 21-5
1904 Leicester **Drawn** 14-14
1905 Cardiff **Wales** 25-0
1906 Richmond (London) **Wales** 16-3
1907 Swansea **Wales** 22-0
1908 Bristol **Wales** 28-18
1909 Cardiff **Wales** 8-0
1910 Twickenham **England** 11-6
1911 Swansea **Wales** 15-11
1912 Twickenham **England** 8-0
1913 Cardiff **England** 12-0
1914 Twickenham **England** 10-9
1920 Swansea **Wales** 19-5
1921 Twickenham **England** 18-3
1922 Cardiff **Wales** 28-6
1923 Twickenham **England** 7-3
1924 Swansea **England** 17-9
1925 Twickenham **England** 12-6
1926 Cardiff **Drawn** 3-3

377

1927 Twickenham **England** 11-9
1928 Swansea **England** 10-8
1929 Twickenham **England** 8-3
1930 Cardiff **England** 11-3
1931 Twickenham **Drawn** 11-11
1932 Swansea **Wales** 12-5
1933 Twickenham **Wales** 7-3
1934 Cardiff **England** 9-0
1935 Twickenham **Drawn** 3-3
1936 Swansea **Drawn** 0-0
1937 Twickenham **England** 4-3
1938 Cardiff **Wales** 14-8
1939 Twickenham **England** 3-0
1947 Cardiff **England** 9-6
1948 Twickenham **Drawn** 3-3
1949 Cardiff **Wales** 9-3
1950 Twickenham **Wales** 11-5
1951 Swansea **Wales** 23-5
1952 Twickenham **Wales** 8-6
1953 Cardiff **England** 8-3
1954 Twickenham **England** 9-6
1955 Cardiff **Wales** 3-0
1956 Twickenham **Wales** 8-3
1957 Cardiff **England** 3-0
1958 Twickenham **Drawn** 3-3
1959 Cardiff **Wales** 5-0
1960 Twickenham **England** 14-6
1961 Cardiff **Wales** 6-3
1962 Twickenham **Drawn** 0-0
1963 Cardiff **England** 13-6
1964 Twickenham **Drawn** 6-6
1965 Cardiff **Wales** 14-3
1966 Twickenham **Wales** 11-6
1967 Cardiff **Wales** 34-21

1968 Twickenham **Drawn** 11-11
1969 Cardiff **Wales** 30-9
1970 Twickenham **Wales** 17-13
1971 Cardiff **Wales** 22-6
1972 Twickenham **Wales** 12-3
1973 Cardiff **Wales** 25-9
1974 Twickenham **England** 16-12
1975 Cardiff **Wales** 20-4
1976 Twickenham **Wales** 21-9
1977 Cardiff **Wales** 14-9
1978 Twickenham **Wales** 9-6
1979 Cardiff **Wales** 27-3
1980 Twickenham **England** 9-8
1981 Cardiff **Wales** 21-19
1982 Twickenham **England** 17-7
1983 Cardiff **Drawn** 13-13
1984 Twickenham **Wales** 24-15
1985 Cardiff **Wales** 24-15
1986 Twickenham **England** 21-18
1987 Cardiff **Wales** 19-12
1987 Brisbane *WC* **Wales** 16-3
1988 Twickenham **Wales** 11-3
1989 Cardiff **Wales** 12-9
1990 Twickenham **England** 34-6
1991 Cardiff **England** 25-6
1992 Twickenham **England** 24-0
1993 Cardiff **Wales** 10-9
1994 Twickenham **England** 15-8
1995 Cardiff **England** 23-9
1996 Twickenham **England** 21-15
1997 Cardiff **England** 34-13
1998 Twickenham **England** 60-26
1999 Wembley **Wales** 32-31

ENGLAND v FRANCE

Played 76   England won 41, France won 28, Drawn 7
Highest scores England 41-13 in 1907, France 37-12 in 1972
Biggest wins England 37-0 in 1911, France 37-12 in 1972

1906 Paris **England** 35-8
1907 Richmond (London) **England** 41-13
1908 Paris **England** 19-0
1909 Leicester **England** 22-0
1910 Paris **England** 11-3
1911 Twickenham **England** 37-0
1912 Paris **England** 18-8
1913 Twickenham **England** 20-0
1914 Paris **England** 39-13
1920 Twickenham **England** 8-3
1921 Paris **England** 10-6
1922 Twickenham **Drawn** 11-11
1923 Paris **England** 12-3
1924 Twickenham **England** 19-7
1925 Paris **England** 13-11
1926 Twickenham **England** 11-0
1927 Paris **France** 3-0
1928 Twickenham **England** 18-8
1929 Paris **England** 16-6
1930 Twickenham **England** 11-5
1931 Paris **France** 14-13
1947 Twickenham **England** 6-3

1948 Paris **France** 15-0
1949 Twickenham **England** 8-3
1950 Paris **France** 6-3
1951 Twickenham **France** 11-3
1952 Paris **England** 6-3
1953 Twickenham **England** 11-0
1954 Paris **France** 11-3
1955 Twickenham **France** 16-9
1956 Paris **France** 14-9
1957 Twickenham **England** 9-5
1958 Paris **England** 14-0
1959 Twickenham **Drawn** 3-3
1960 Paris **Drawn** 3-3
1961 Twickenham **Drawn** 5-5
1962 Paris **France** 13-0
1963 Twickenham **England** 6-5
1964 Paris **England** 6-3
1965 Twickenham **England** 9-6
1966 Paris **France** 13-0
1967 Twickenham **France** 16-12
1968 Paris **France** 14-9
1969 Twickenham **England** 22-8

1970 Paris **France** 35-13	1986 Paris **France** 29-10
1971 Twickenham **Drawn** 14-14	1987 Twickenham **France** 19-15
1972 Paris **France** 37-12	1988 Paris **France** 10-9
1973 Twickenham **England** 14-6	1989 Twickenham **England** 11-0
1974 Paris **Drawn** 12-12	1990 Paris **England** 26-7
1975 Twickenham **France** 27-20	1991 Twickenham **England** 21-19
1976 Paris **France** 30-9	1991 Paris *WC* **England** 19-10
1977 Twickenham **France** 4-3	1992 Paris **England** 31-13
1978 Paris **France** 15-6	1993 Twickenham **England** 16-15
1979 Twickenham **England** 7-6	1994 Paris **England** 18-14
1980 Paris **England** 17-13	1995 Twickenham **England** 31-10
1981 Twickenham **France** 16-12	1995 Pretoria *WC* **France** 19-9
1982 Paris **England** 27-15	1996 Paris **France** 15-12
1983 Twickenham **France** 19-15	1997 Twickenham **France** 23-20
1984 Paris **France** 32-18	1998 Paris **France** 24-17
1985 Twickenham **Drawn** 9-9	1999 Twickenham **England** 21-10

ENGLAND v NEW ZEALAND
Played 22   England won 4, New Zealand won 17, Drawn 1
Highest scores England 29-45 in 1995, New Zealand 64-22 in 1998
Biggest wins England 13-0 in 1936, New Zealand 64-22 in 1998

1905 Crystal Palace (London) **New Zealand** 15-0	1983 Twickenham **England** 15-9
1925 Twickenham **New Zealand** 17-11	1985 *1* Christchurch **New Zealand** 18-13
1936 Twickenham **England** 13-0	*2* Wellington **New Zealand** 42-15
1954 Twickenham **New Zealand** 5-0	*New Zealand won series 2-0*
1963 *1* Auckland **New Zealand** 21-11	1991 Twickenham *WC* **New Zealand** 18-12
2 Christchurch **New Zealand** 9-6	1993 Twickenham **England** 15-9
New Zealand won series 2-0	1995 Cape Town *WC* **New Zealand** 45-29
1964 Twickenham **New Zealand** 14-0	1997 *1* Manchester **New Zealand** 25-8
1967 Twickenham **New Zealand** 23-11	*2* Twickenham **Drawn** 26-26
1973 Twickenham **New Zealand** 9-0	*New Zealand won series 1-0, with 1 draw*
1973 Auckland **England** 16-10	1998 *1* Dunedin **New Zealand** 64-22
1978 Twickenham **New Zealand** 16-6	*2* Auckland **New Zealand** 40-10
1979 Twickenham **New Zealand** 10-9	*New Zealand won series 2-0*

ENGLAND v SOUTH AFRICA
Played 16   England won 5, South Africa won 10, Drawn 1
Highest scores England 33-16 in 1992, South Africa 35-9 in 1984
Biggest wins England 33-16 in 1992 & 32-15 in 1994, South Africa 35-9 in 1984

1906 Crystal Palace (London) **Drawn** 3-3	1992 Twickenham **England** 33-16
1913 Twickenham **South Africa** 9-3	1994 *1* Pretoria **England** 32-15
1932 Twickenham **South Africa** 7-0	*2* Cape Town **South Africa** 27-9
1952 Twickenham **South Africa** 8-3	*Series drawn 1-1*
1961 Twickenham **South Africa** 5-0	1995 Twickenham **South Africa** 24-14
1969 Twickenham **England** 11-8	1997 Twickenham **South Africa** 29-11
1972 Johannesburg **England** 18-9	1998 Cape Town **South Africa** 18-0
1984 *1* Port Elizabeth **South Africa** 33-15	1998 Twickenham **England** 13-7
2 Johannesburg **South Africa** 35-9	
South Africa won series 2-0	

ENGLAND v AUSTRALIA
Played 23   England won 7, Australia won 15, Drawn 1
Highest scores England 28-19 in 1988, Australia 76-0 in 1998
Biggest wins England 20-3 in 1973 & 23-6 in 1976, Australia 76-0 in 1998

1909 Blackheath (London) **Australia** 9-3	1928 Twickenham **England** 18-11

1948 Twickenham **Australia** 11-0
1958 Twickenham **England** 9-6
1963 Sydney **Australia** 18-9
1967 Twickenham **Australia** 23-11
1973 Twickenham **England** 20-3
1975 *1* Sydney **Australia** 16-9
    2 Brisbane **Australia** 30-21
    Australia won series 2-0
1976 Twickenham **England** 23-6
1982 Twickenham **England** 15-11
1984 Twickenham **Australia** 19-3
1987 Sydney *WC* **Australia** 19-6
1988 *1* Brisbane **Australia** 22-16

    2 Sydney **Australia** 28-8
    Australia won series 2-0
1988 Twickenham **England** 28-19
1991 Sydney **Australia** 40-15
1991 Twickenham *WC* **Australia** 12-6
1995 Cape Town *WC* **England** 25-22
1997 *1* Sydney **Australia** 25-6
    2 Twickenham **Drawn** 15-15
    Australia won series 1-0, with 1 draw
1998 *1* Brisbane **Australia** 76-0
    2 Twickenham **Australia** 12-11
    Australia won series 2-0

ENGLAND v NEW ZEALAND NATIVES
Played 1　England won 1
Highest score England 7-0 in 1889, NZ Natives 0-7 in 1889
Biggest win England 7-0 in 1889, NZ Natives no win

1889 Blackheath **England** 1G 4T to 0

ENGLAND v RFU PRESIDENT'S XV
Played 1　President's XV won 1
Highest score England 11-28 in 1971, RFU President's XV 28-11 in 1971
Biggest win RFU President's XV 28-11 in 1971

1971 Twickenham **President's XV** 28-11

ENGLAND v ARGENTINA
Played 9　England won 6, Argentina won 2, Drawn 1
Highest scores England 51-0 in 1990, Argentina 33-13 in 1997
Biggest wins England 51-0 in 1990, Argentina 33-13 in 1997

1981 *1* Buenos Aires **Drawn** 19-19
    2 Buenos Aires **England** 12-6
    England won series 1-0 with 1 draw
1990 *1* Buenos Aires **England** 25-12
    2 Buenos Aires **Argentina** 15-13
    Series drawn 1-1

1990 Twickenham **England** 51-0
1995 Durban *WC* **England** 24-18
1996 Twickenham **England** 20-18
1997 *1* Buenos Aires **England** 46-20
    2 Buenos Aires **Argentina** 33-13
    Series drawn 1-1

ENGLAND v ROMANIA
Played 3　England won 3
Highest scores England 58-3 in 1989, Romania 15-22 in 1985
Biggest win England 58-3 in 1989, Romania no win

1985 Twickenham **England** 22-15
1989 Bucharest **England** 58-3

1994 Twickenham **England** 54-3

ENGLAND v JAPAN
Played 1　England won 1
Highest score England 60-7 in 1987, Japan 7-60 in 1987
Biggest win England 60-7 in 1987, Japan no win

1987 Sydney *WC* **England** 60-7

ENGLAND v UNITED STATES
Played 2   England won 2
Highest scores England 37-9 in 1991, United States 9-37 in 1991
Biggest win England 37-9 in 1991, United States no win

1987 Sydney *WC* **England** 34-6   1991 Twickenham *WC* **England** 37-9

ENGLAND v FIJI
Played 3   England won 3
Highest scores England 58-23 in 1989, Fiji 23-58 in 1989
Biggest win England 58-23 in 1989, Fiji no win

1988 Suva **England** 25-12   1991 Suva **England** 28-12
1989 Twickenham **England** 58-23

ENGLAND v ITALY
Played 4   England won 4
Highest scores England 54-21 in 1996, Italy 21-54 in 1996
Biggest win England 54-21 in 1996, Italy no win

1991 Twickenham *WC* **England** 36-6   1996 Twickenham **England** 54-21
1995 Durban *WC* **England** 27-20   1998 Huddersfield **England** 23-15

ENGLAND v CANADA
Played 2   England won 2
Highest scores England 60-19 in 1994, Canada 19-60 in 1994
Biggest win England 60-19 in 1994, Canada no win

1992 Wembley **England** 26-13   1994 Twickenham **England** 60-19

ENGLAND v WESTERN SAMOA
Played 2   England won 2
Highest scores England 44-22 in 1995, Western Samoa 22-44 in 1995
Biggest win England 44-22 in 1995, Western Samoa no win

1995 Durban *WC* **England** 44-22   1995 Twickenham **England** 27-9

ENGLAND v THE NETHERLANDS
Played 1   England won 1
Highest scores England 110-0 in 1998, The Netherlands 0-110 in 1998
Biggest win England 110-0 in 1998, The Netherlands no win

1998 Huddersfield **England** 110-0

SCOTLAND v IRELAND
Played 111   Scotland won 60, Ireland won 45, Drawn 5, Abandoned 1
Highest scores Scotland 38-10 in 1997, Ireland 26-8 in 1953
Biggest wins Scotland 38-10 in 1997, Ireland 21-0 in 1950

1877 Belfast **Scotland** 4G 2DG 2T to 0   1882 Glasgow **Scotland** 2T to 0
1878 No Match   1883 Belfast **Scotland** 1G 1T to 0
1879 Belfast **Scotland** 1G 1DG 1T to 0   1884 Raeburn Place (Edinburgh) **Scotland**
1880 Glasgow **Scotland** 1G 2DG 2T to 0   2G 2T to 1T
1881 Belfast **Ireland** 1DG to 1T

1885 Belfast **Abandoned** Ireland 0 Scotland 1T
1885 Raeburn Place **Scotland** 1G 2T to 0
1886 Raeburn Place **Scotland** 3G 1DG 2T to 0
1887 Belfast **Scotland** 1G 1GM 2T to 0
1888 Raeburn Place **Scotland** 1G to 0
1889 Belfast **Scotland** 1DG to 0
1890 Raeburn Place **Scotland** 1DG 1T to 0
1891 Belfast **Scotland** 14-0
1892 Raeburn Place **Scotland** 2-0
1893 Belfast **Drawn** 0-0
1894 Dublin **Ireland** 5-0
1895 Raeburn Place **Scotland** 6-0
1896 Dublin **Drawn** 0-0
1897 Powderhall (Edinburgh) **Scotland** 8-3
1898 Belfast **Scotland** 8-0
1899 Inverleith (Edinburgh) **Ireland** 9-3
1900 Dublin **Drawn** 0-0
1901 Inverleith **Scotland** 9-5
1902 Belfast **Ireland** 5-0
1903 Inverleith **Scotland** 3-0
1904 Dublin **Scotland** 19-3
1905 Inverleith **Ireland** 11-5
1906 Dublin **Scotland** 13-6
1907 Inverleith **Scotland** 15-3
1908 Dublin **Ireland** 16-11
1909 Inverleith **Scotland** 9-3
1910 Belfast **Scotland** 14-0
1911 Inverleith **Ireland** 16-10
1912 Dublin **Ireland** 10-8
1913 Inverleith **Scotland** 29-14
1914 Dublin **Ireland** 6-0
1920 Inverleith **Scotland** 19-0
1921 Dublin **Ireland** 9-8
1922 Inverleith **Scotland** 6-3
1923 Dublin **Scotland** 13-3
1924 Inverleith **Scotland** 13-8
1925 Dublin **Scotland** 14-8
1926 Murrayfield **Ireland** 3-0
1927 Dublin **Ireland** 6-0
1928 Murrayfield **Ireland** 13-5
1929 Dublin **Scotland** 16-7
1930 Murrayfield **Ireland** 14-11
1931 Dublin **Ireland** 8-5
1932 Murrayfield **Ireland** 20-8
1933 Dublin **Scotland** 8-6
1934 Murrayfield **Scotland** 16-9
1935 Dublin **Ireland** 12-5
1936 Murrayfield **Ireland** 10-4
1937 Dublin **Ireland** 11-4
1938 Murrayfield **Scotland** 23-14
1939 Dublin **Ireland** 12-3
1947 Murrayfield **Ireland** 3-0

1948 Dublin **Ireland** 6-0
1949 Murrayfield **Ireland** 13-3
1950 Dublin **Ireland** 21-0
1951 Murrayfield **Ireland** 6-5
1952 Dublin **Ireland** 12-8
1953 Murrayfield **Ireland** 26-8
1954 Belfast **Ireland** 6-0
1955 Murrayfield **Scotland** 12-3
1956 Dublin **Ireland** 14-10
1957 Murrayfield **Ireland** 5-3
1958 Dublin **Ireland** 12-6
1959 Murrayfield **Ireland** 8-3
1960 Dublin **Scotland** 6-5
1961 Murrayfield **Scotland** 16-8
1962 Dublin **Scotland** 20-6
1963 Murrayfield **Scotland** 3-0
1964 Dublin **Scotland** 6-3
1965 Murrayfield **Ireland** 16-6
1966 Dublin **Scotland** 11-3
1967 Murrayfield **Ireland** 5-3
1968 Dublin **Ireland** 14-6
1969 Murrayfield **Ireland** 16-0
1970 Dublin **Ireland** 16-11
1971 Murrayfield **Ireland** 17-5
1972 No Match
1973 Murrayfield **Scotland** 19-14
1974 Dublin **Ireland** 9-6
1975 Murrayfield **Scotland** 20-13
1976 Dublin **Scotland** 15-6
1977 Murrayfield **Scotland** 21-18
1978 Dublin **Ireland** 12-9
1979 Murrayfield **Drawn** 11-11
1980 Dublin **Ireland** 22-15
1981 Murrayfield **Scotland** 10-9
1982 Dublin **Ireland** 21-12
1983 Murrayfield **Ireland** 15-13
1984 Dublin **Scotland** 32-9
1985 Murrayfield **Ireland** 18-15
1986 Dublin **Scotland** 10-9
1987 Murrayfield **Scotland** 16-12
1988 Dublin **Ireland** 22-18
1989 Murrayfield **Scotland** 37-21
1990 Dublin **Scotland** 13-10
1991 Murrayfield **Scotland** 28-25
1991 Murrayfield *WC* **Scotland** 24-15
1992 Dublin **Scotland** 18-10
1993 Murrayfield **Scotland** 15-3
1994 Dublin **Drawn** 6-6
1995 Murrayfield **Scotland** 26-13
1996 Dublin **Scotland** 16-10
1997 Murrayfield **Scotland** 38-10
1998 Dublin **Scotland** 17-16
1999 Murrayfield **Scotland** 30-13

SCOTLAND v WALES

Played 103   Scotland won 45, Wales won 56, Drawn 2
Highest scores Scotland 35-10 in 1924, Wales 35-12 in 1972
Biggest wins Scotland 35-10 in 1924, Wales 35-12 in 1972 & 29-6 in 1994

1883 Raeburn Place (Edinburgh) **Scotland** 3G to 1G

1884 Newport **Scotland** 1DG 1T to 0
1885 Glasgow **Drawn** no score

1886 Cardiff **Scotland** 2G 8T to 0	1949 Murrayfield **Scotland** 6-5
1887 Raeburn Place **Scotland** 4G 8T to 0	1950 Swansea **Wales** 12-0
1888 Newport **Wales** 1T to 0	1951 Murrayfield **Scotland** 19-0
1889 Raeburn Place **Scotland** 2T to 0	1952 Cardiff **Wales** 11-0
1890 Cardiff **Scotland** 1G 2T to 1T	1953 Murrayfield **Wales** 12-0
1891 Raeburn Place **Scotland** 15-0	1954 Swansea **Wales** 15-3
1892 Swansea **Scotland** 7-2	1955 Murrayfield **Scotland** 14-8
1893 Raeburn Place **Wales** 9-0	1956 Cardiff **Wales** 9-3
1894 Newport **Wales** 7-0	1957 Murrayfield **Scotland** 9-6
1895 Raeburn Place **Scotland** 5-4	1958 Cardiff **Wales** 8-3
1896 Cardiff **Wales** 6-0	1959 Murrayfield **Scotland** 6-5
1897 No Match	1960 Cardiff **Wales** 8-0
1898 No Match	1961 Murrayfield **Scotland** 3-0
1899 Inverleith (Edinburgh) **Scotland** 21-10	1962 Cardiff **Scotland** 8-3
1900 Swansea **Wales** 12-3	1963 Murrayfield **Wales** 6-0
1901 Inverleith **Scotland** 18-8	1964 Cardiff **Wales** 11-3
1902 Cardiff **Wales** 14-5	1965 Murrayfield **Wales** 14-12
1903 Inverleith **Scotland** 6-0	1966 Cardiff **Wales** 8-3
1904 Swansea **Wales** 21-3	1967 Murrayfield **Scotland** 11-5
1905 Inverleith **Wales** 6-3	1968 Cardiff **Wales** 5-0
1906 Cardiff **Wales** 9-3	1969 Murrayfield **Wales** 17-3
1907 Inverleith **Scotland** 6-3	1970 Cardiff **Wales** 18-9
1908 Swansea **Wales** 6-5	1971 Murrayfield **Wales** 19-18
1909 Inverleith **Wales** 5-3	1972 Cardiff **Wales** 35-12
1910 Cardiff **Wales** 14-0	1973 Murrayfield **Scotland** 10-9
1911 Inverleith **Wales** 32-10	1974 Cardiff **Wales** 6-0
1912 Swansea **Wales** 21-6	1975 Murrayfield **Scotland** 12-10
1913 Inverleith **Wales** 8-0	1976 Cardiff **Wales** 28-6
1914 Cardiff **Wales** 24-5	1977 Murrayfield **Wales** 18-9
1920 Inverleith **Scotland** 9-5	1978 Cardiff **Wales** 22-14
1921 Swansea **Scotland** 14-8	1979 Murrayfield **Wales** 19-13
1922 Inverleith **Drawn** 9-9	1980 Cardiff **Wales** 17-6
1923 Cardiff **Scotland** 11-8	1981 Murrayfield **Scotland** 15-6
1924 Inverleith **Scotland** 35-10	1982 Cardiff **Scotland** 34-18
1925 Swansea **Scotland** 24-14	1983 Murrayfield **Wales** 19-15
1926 Murrayfield **Scotland** 8-5	1984 Cardiff **Scotland** 15-9
1927 Cardiff **Scotland** 5-0	1985 Murrayfield **Wales** 25-21
1928 Murrayfield **Wales** 13-0	1986 Cardiff **Wales** 22-15
1929 Swansea **Wales** 14-7	1987 Murrayfield **Scotland** 21-15
1930 Murrayfield **Scotland** 12-9	1988 Cardiff **Wales** 25-20
1931 Cardiff **Wales** 13-8	1989 Murrayfield **Scotland** 23-7
1932 Murrayfield **Wales** 6-0	1990 Cardiff **Scotland** 13-9
1933 Swansea **Scotland** 11-3	1991 Murrayfield **Scotland** 32-12
1934 Murrayfield **Wales** 13-6	1992 Cardiff **Wales** 15-12
1935 Cardiff **Wales** 10-6	1993 Murrayfield **Scotland** 20-0
1936 Murrayfield **Wales** 13-3	1994 Cardiff **Wales** 29-6
1937 Swansea **Scotland** 13-6	1995 Murrayfield **Scotland** 26-13
1938 Murrayfield **Scotland** 8-6	1996 Cardiff **Scotland** 16-14
1939 Cardiff **Wales** 11-3	1997 Murrayfield **Wales** 34-19
1947 Murrayfield **Wales** 22-8	1998 Wembley **Wales** 19-13
1948 Cardiff **Wales** 14-0	1999 Murrayfield **Scotland** 33-20

SCOTLAND v FRANCE
Played 71   Scotland won 33, France won 35, Drawn 3
Highest scores Scotland 36-22 in 1999, France 51-16 in 1998
Biggest wins Scotland 31-3 in 1912, France 51-16 in 1998

1910 Inverleith (Edinburgh) **Scotland** 27-0	1920 Paris **Scotland** 5-0
1911 Paris **France** 16-15	1921 Inverleith **France** 3-0
1912 Inverleith **Scotland** 31-3	1922 Paris **Drawn** 3-3
1913 Paris **Scotland** 21-3	1923 Inverleith **Scotland** 16-3
1914 No Match	1924 Paris **France** 12-10

1925 Inverleith **Scotland** 25-4		1971 Paris **France** 13-8
1926 Paris **Scotland** 20-6		1972 Murrayfield **Scotland** 20-9
1927 Murrayfield **Scotland** 23-6		1973 Paris **France** 16-13
1928 Paris **Scotland** 15-6		1974 Murrayfield **Scotland** 19-6
1929 Murrayfield **Scotland** 6-3		1975 Paris **France** 10-9
1930 Paris **France** 7-3		1976 Murrayfield **France** 13-6
1931 Murrayfield **Scotland** 6-4		1977 Paris **France** 23-3
1947 Paris **France** 8-3		1978 Murrayfield **France** 19-16
1948 Murrayfield **Scotland** 9-8		1979 Paris **France** 21-17
1949 Paris **Scotland** 8-0		1980 Murrayfield **Scotland** 22-14
1950 Murrayfield **Scotland** 8-5		1981 Paris **France** 16-9
1951 Paris **France** 14-12		1982 Murrayfield **Scotland** 16-7
1952 Murrayfield **France** 13-11		1983 Paris **France** 19-15
1953 Paris **France** 11-5		1984 Murrayfield **Scotland** 21-12
1954 Murrayfield **France** 3-0		1985 Paris **France** 11-3
1955 Paris **France** 15-0		1986 Murrayfield **Scotland** 18-17
1956 Murrayfield **Scotland** 12-0		1987 Paris **France** 28-22
1957 Paris **Scotland** 6-0		1987 Christchurch *WC* **Drawn** 20-20
1958 Murrayfield **Scotland** 11-9		1988 Murrayfield **Scotland** 23-12
1959 Paris **France** 9-0		1989 Paris **France** 19-3
1960 Murrayfield **France** 13-11		1990 Murrayfield **Scotland** 21-0
1961 Paris **France** 11-0		1991 Paris **France** 15-9
1962 Murrayfield **France** 11-3		1992 Murrayfield **Scotland** 10-6
1963 Paris **Scotland** 11-6		1993 Paris **France** 11-3
1964 Murrayfield **Scotland** 10-0		1994 Murrayfield **France** 20-12
1965 Paris **France** 16-8		1995 Paris **Scotland** 23-21
1966 Murrayfield **Drawn** 3-3		1995 Pretoria *WC* **France** 22-19
1967 Paris **Scotland** 9-8		1996 Murrayfield **Scotland** 19-14
1968 Murrayfield **France** 8-6		1997 Paris **France** 47-20
1969 Paris **Scotland** 6-3		1998 Murrayfield **France** 51-16
1970 Murrayfield **France** 11-9		1999 Paris **Scotland** 36-22

SCOTLAND v NEW ZEALAND
Played 20   Scotland won 0, New Zealand won 18, Drawn 2
Highest scores Scotland 31-62 in 1996, New Zealand 62-31 in 1996
Biggest wins Scotland no win, New Zealand 51-15 in 1993

1905 Inverleith (Edinburgh) **New Zealand** 12-7	1983 Murrayfield **Drawn** 25-25
1935 Murrayfield **New Zealand** 18-8	1987 Christchurch *WC* **New Zealand** 30-3
1954 Murrayfield **New Zealand** 3-0	1990 *1* Dunedin **New Zealand** 31-16
1964 Murrayfield **Drawn** 0-0	*2* Auckland **New Zealand** 21-18
1967 Murrayfield **New Zealand** 14-3	*New Zealand won series 2-0*
1972 Murrayfield **New Zealand** 14-9	1991 Cardiff *WC* **New Zealand** 13-6
1975 Auckland **New Zealand** 24-0	1993 Murrayfield **New Zealand** 51-15
1978 Murrayfield **New Zealand** 18-9	1995 Pretoria *WC* **New Zealand** 48-30
1979 Murrayfield **New Zealand** 20-6	1996 *1* Dunedin **New Zealand** 62-31
1981 *1* Dunedin **New Zealand** 11-4	*2* Auckland **New Zealand** 36-12
2 Auckland **New Zealand** 40-15	*New Zealand won series 2-0*
New Zealand won series 2-0	

SCOTLAND v SOUTH AFRICA
Played 11   Scotland won 3, South Africa won 8, Drawn 0
Highest scores Scotland 10-18 in 1960 & 10-34 in 1994 & 10-68 in 1997 & 10-35 in 1998, South Africa 68-10 in 1997
Biggest wins Scotland 6-0 in 1906, South Africa 68-10 in 1997

1906 Glasgow **Scotland** 6-0	1951 Murrayfield **South Africa** 44-0
1912 Inverleith **South Africa** 16-0	1960 Port Elizabeth **South Africa** 18-10
1932 Murrayfield **South Africa** 6-3	1961 Murrayfield **South Africa** 12-5

1965 Murrayfield **Scotland** 8-5
1969 Murrayfield **Scotland** 6-3
1994 Murrayfield **South Africa** 34-10

1997 Murrayfield **South Africa** 68-10
1998 Murrayfield **South Africa** 35-10

SCOTLAND v AUSTRALIA
Played 18   Scotland won 7, Australia won 11, Drawn 0
Highest scores Scotland 24-15 in 1981, Australia 45-3 in 1998
Biggest wins Scotland 24-15 in 1981, Australia 45-3 in 1998

1927 Murrayfield **Scotland** 10-8
1947 Murrayfield **Australia** 16-7
1958 Murrayfield **Scotland** 12-8
1966 Murrayfield **Scotland** 11-5
1968 Murrayfield **Scotland** 9-3
1970 Sydney **Australia** 23-3
1975 Murrayfield **Scotland** 10-3
1981 Murrayfield **Scotland** 24-15
1982 *1* Brisbane **Scotland** 12-7
   2 Sydney **Australia** 33-9
   Series drawn 1-1

1984 Murrayfield **Australia** 37-12
1988 Murrayfield **Australia** 32-13
1992 *1* Sydney **Australia** 27-12
   2 Brisbane **Australia** 37-13
   Australia won series 2-0
1996 Murrayfield **Australia** 29-19
1997 Murrayfield **Australia** 37-8
1998 *1* Sydney **Australia** 45-3
   2 Brisbane **Australia** 33-11
   Australia won series 2-0

SCOTLAND v SRU PRESIDENT'S XV
Played 1   Scotland won 1
Highest scores Scotland 27-16 in 1972, SRU President's XV 16-27 in 1973
Biggest win Scotland 27-16 in 1973, SRU President's XV no win

1973 Murrayfield **Scotland** 27-16

SCOTLAND v ROMANIA
Played 7   Scotland won 5, Romania won 2, Drawn 0
Highest scores Scotland 55-28 in 1987, Romania 28-55 in 1987 & 28-22 in 1984
Biggest wins Scotland 49-16 in 1995, Romania 28-22 in 1984 & 18-12 in 1991

1981 Murrayfield **Scotland** 12-6
1984 Bucharest **Romania** 28-22
1986 Bucharest **Scotland** 33-18
1987 Dunedin *WC* **Scotland** 55-28

1989 Murrayfield **Scotland** 32-0
1991 Bucharest **Romania** 18-12
1995 Murrayfield **Scotland** 49-16

SCOTLAND v ZIMBABWE
Played 2   Scotland won 2
Highest scores Scotland 60-21 in 1987, Zimbabwe 21-60 in 1987
Biggest win Scotland 60-21 in 1987 & 51-12 in 1991, Zimbabwe no win

1987 Wellington *WC* **Scotland** 60-21

1991 Murrayfield *WC* **Scotland** 51-12

SCOTLAND v FIJI
Played 2   Scotland won 1, Fiji won 1
Highest scores Scotland 38-17 in 1989, Fiji 51-26 in 1998
Biggest win Scotland 38-17 in 1989, Fiji 51-26 in 1998

1989 Murrayfield **Scotland** 38-17

1998 Suva **Fiji** 51-26

SCOTLAND v ARGENTINA
Played 3   Scotland won 1, Argentina won 2, Drawn 0
Highest scores Scotland 49-3 in 1990, Argentina 19-17 in 1994
Biggest wins Scotland 49-3 in 1990, Argentina 19-17 in 1994

1990 Murrayfield **Scotland** 49-3
1994 *1* Buenos Aires **Argentina** 16-15

2 Buenos Aires **Argentina** 19-17
Argentina won series 2-0

SCOTLAND v JAPAN
Played 1   Scotland won 1
Highest scores Scotland 47-9 in 1991, Japan 9-47 in 1991
Biggest win Scotland 47-9 in 1991, Japan no win

1991 Murrayfield *WC* **Scotland** 47-9

SCOTLAND v WESTERN SAMOA
Played 2   Scotland won 1, Drawn 1
Highest scores Scotland 28-6 in 1991, Western Samoa 15-15 in 1995
Biggest win Scotland 28-6 in 1991, Western Samoa no win

1991 Murrayfield *WC* **Scotland** 28-6

1995 Murrayfield **Drawn** 15-15

SCOTLAND v CANADA
Played 1   Scotland won 1
Highest scores Scotland 22-6 in 1995, Canada 6-22 in 1995
Biggest win Scotland 22-6 in 1995, Canada no win

1995 Murrayfield **Scotland** 22-6

SCOTLAND v IVORY COAST
Played 1   Scotland won 1
Highest scores Scotland 89-0 in 1995, Ivory Coast 0-89 in 1995
Biggest win Scotland 89-0 in 1995, Ivory Coast no win

1995 Rustenburg *WC* **Scotland** 89-0

SCOTLAND v TONGA
Played 1   Scotland won 1
Highest scores Scotland 41-5 in 1995, Tonga 5-41 in 1995
Biggest win Scotland 41-5 in 1995, Tonga no win

1995 Pretoria *WC* **Scotland** 41-5

SCOTLAND v ITALY
Played 3   Scotland won 2, Italy won 1
Highest scores Scotland 30-12 in 1999, Italy 25-21 in 1998
Biggest wins Scotland 30-12 in 1999, Italy 25-21 in 1998

1996 Murrayfield **Scotland** 29-22
1998 Treviso **Italy** 25-21

1999 Murrayfield **Scotland** 30-12

IRELAND v WALES

Played 103   Ireland won 38, Wales won 59, Drawn 6
Highest scores Ireland 30-17 in 1996, Wales 34-9 in 1976
Biggest wins Ireland 19-3 in 1925, Wales 29-0 in 1907

1882 Dublin **Wales** 2G 2T to 0	1948 Belfast **Ireland** 6-3
1883 No Match	1949 Swansea **Ireland** 5-0
1884 Cardiff **Wales** 1DG 2T to 0	1950 Belfast **Wales** 6-3
1885 No Match	1951 Cardiff **Drawn** 3-3
1886 No Match	1952 Dublin **Wales** 14-3
1887 Birkenhead **Wales** 1DG 1T to 3T	1953 Swansea **Wales** 5-3
1888 Dublin **Ireland** 1G 1DG 1T to 0	1954 Dublin **Wales** 12-9
1889 Swansea **Ireland** 2T to 0	1955 Cardiff **Wales** 21-3
1890 Dublin **Drawn** 1G each	1956 Dublin **Ireland** 11-3
1891 Llanelli **Wales** 6-4	1957 Cardiff **Wales** 6-5
1892 Dublin **Ireland** 9-0	1958 Dublin **Wales** 9-6
1893 Llanelli **Wales** 2-0	1959 Cardiff **Wales** 8-6
1894 Belfast **Ireland** 3-0	1960 Dublin **Wales** 10-9
1895 Cardiff **Wales** 5-3	1961 Cardiff **Wales** 9-0
1896 Dublin **Ireland** 8-4	1962 Dublin **Drawn** 3-3
1897 No Match	1963 Cardiff **Ireland** 14-6
1898 Limerick **Wales** 11-3	1964 Dublin **Wales** 15-6
1899 Cardiff **Ireland** 3-0	1965 Cardiff **Wales** 14-8
1900 Belfast **Wales** 3-0	1966 Dublin **Ireland** 9-6
1901 Swansea **Wales** 10-9	1967 Cardiff **Ireland** 3-0
1902 Dublin **Wales** 15-0	1968 Dublin **Ireland** 9-6
1903 Cardiff **Wales** 18-0	1969 Cardiff **Wales** 24-11
1904 Belfast **Ireland** 14-12	1970 Dublin **Ireland** 14-0
1905 Swansea **Wales** 10-3	1971 Cardiff **Wales** 23-9
1906 Belfast **Ireland** 11-6	1972 No Match
1907 Cardiff **Wales** 29-0	1973 Cardiff **Wales** 16-12
1908 Belfast **Wales** 11-5	1974 Dublin **Drawn** 9-9
1909 Swansea **Wales** 18-5	1975 Cardiff **Wales** 32-4
1910 Dublin **Wales** 19-3	1976 Dublin **Wales** 34-9
1911 Cardiff **Wales** 16-0	1977 Cardiff **Wales** 25-9
1912 Belfast **Ireland** 12-5	1978 Dublin **Wales** 20-16
1913 Swansea **Wales** 16-13	1979 Cardiff **Wales** 24-21
1914 Belfast **Wales** 11-3	1980 Dublin **Ireland** 21-7
1920 Cardiff **Wales** 28-4	1981 Cardiff **Wales** 9-8
1921 Belfast **Wales** 6-0	1982 Dublin **Ireland** 20-12
1922 Swansea **Wales** 11-5	1983 Cardiff **Wales** 23-9
1923 Dublin **Ireland** 5-4	1984 Dublin **Wales** 18-9
1924 Cardiff **Ireland** 13-10	1985 Cardiff **Ireland** 21-9
1925 Belfast **Ireland** 19-3	1986 Dublin **Wales** 19-12
1926 Swansea **Wales** 11-8	1987 Cardiff **Ireland** 15-11
1927 Dublin **Ireland** 19-9	1987 Wellington *WC* **Wales** 13-6
1928 Cardiff **Ireland** 13-10	1988 Dublin **Wales** 12-9
1929 Belfast **Drawn** 5-5	1989 Cardiff **Ireland** 19-13
1930 Swansea **Wales** 12-7	1990 Dublin **Ireland** 14-8
1931 Belfast **Wales** 15-3	1991 Cardiff **Drawn** 21-21
1932 Cardiff **Ireland** 12-10	1992 Dublin **Wales** 16-15
1933 Belfast **Ireland** 10-5	1993 Cardiff **Ireland** 19-14
1934 Swansea **Wales** 13-0	1994 Dublin **Wales** 17-15
1935 Belfast **Ireland** 9-3	1995 Cardiff **Ireland** 16-12
1936 Cardiff **Wales** 3-0	1995 Johannesburg *WC* **Ireland** 24-23
1937 Belfast **Ireland** 5-3	1996 Dublin **Ireland** 30-17
1938 Swansea **Wales** 11-5	1997 Cardiff **Ireland** 26-25
1939 Belfast **Wales** 7-0	1998 Dublin **Wales** 30-21
1947 Swansea **Wales** 6-0	1999 Wembley **Ireland** 29-23

Conor McGuinness (Ireland) is closed down by Phillippe Benetton (France) during the Five Nations match at Lansdowne Road in February 1999.

IRELAND v FRANCE

Played 73   Ireland won 25, France won 43, Drawn 5
Highest scores Ireland 25-5 in 1911 & 25-6 in 1975, France 45-10 in 1996
Biggest wins Ireland 24-0 in 1913, France 45-10 in 1996

1909 Dublin **Ireland** 19-8	1966 Paris **France** 11-6
1910 Paris **Ireland** 8-3	1967 Dublin **France** 11-6
1911 Cork **Ireland** 25-5	1968 Paris **France** 16-6
1912 Paris **Ireland** 11-6	1969 Dublin **Ireland** 17-9
1913 Cork **Ireland** 24-0	1970 Paris **France** 8-0
1914 Paris **Ireland** 8-6	1971 Dublin **Drawn** 9-9
1920 Dublin **France** 15-7	1972 Paris **Ireland** 14-9
1921 Paris **France** 20-10	1972 Dublin **Ireland** 24-14
1922 Dublin **Ireland** 8-3	*Non-championship match*
1923 Paris **France** 14-8	1973 Dublin **Ireland** 6-4
1924 Dublin **Ireland** 6-0	1974 Paris **France** 9-6
1925 Paris **Ireland** 9-3	1975 Dublin **Ireland** 25-6
1926 Belfast **Ireland** 11-0	1976 Paris **France** 26-3
1927 Paris **Ireland** 8-3	1977 Dublin **France** 15-6
1928 Belfast **Ireland** 12-8	1978 Paris **France** 10-9
1929 Paris **Ireland** 6-0	1979 Dublin **Drawn** 9-9
1930 Belfast **France** 5-0	1980 Paris **France** 19-18
1931 Paris **France** 3-0	1981 Dublin **France** 19-13
1947 Dublin **France** 12-8	1982 Paris **France** 22-9
1948 Paris **Ireland** 13-6	1983 Dublin **Ireland** 22-16
1949 Dublin **France** 16-9	1984 Paris **France** 25-12
1950 Paris **Drawn** 3-3	1985 Dublin **Drawn** 15-15
1951 Dublin **Ireland** 9-8	1986 Paris **France** 29-9
1952 Paris **Ireland** 11-8	1987 Dublin **France** 19-13
1953 Belfast **Ireland** 16-3	1988 Paris **France** 25-6
1954 Paris **France** 8-0	1989 Dublin **France** 26-21
1955 Dublin **France** 5-3	1990 Paris **France** 31-12
1956 Paris **France** 14-8	1991 Dublin **France** 21-13
1957 Dublin **Ireland** 11-6	1992 Paris **France** 44-12
1958 Paris **France** 11-6	1993 Dublin **France** 21-6
1959 Dublin **Ireland** 9-5	1994 Paris **France** 35-15
1960 Paris **France** 23-6	1995 Dublin **France** 25-7
1961 Dublin **France** 15-3	1995 Durban *WC* **France** 36-12
1962 Paris **France** 11-0	1996 Paris **France** 45-10
1963 Dublin **France** 24-5	1997 Dublin **France** 32-15
1964 Paris **France** 27-6	1998 Paris **France** 18-16
1965 Dublin **Drawn** 3-3	1999 Dublin **France** 10-9

IRELAND v NEW ZEALAND

Played 14   Ireland won 0, New Zealand won 13, Drawn 1
Highest scores Ireland 21-24 in 1992, New Zealand 63-15 in 1997
Biggest win Ireland no win, New Zealand 59-6 in 1992

1905 Dublin **New Zealand** 15-0	1978 Dublin **New Zealand** 10-6
1924 Dublin **New Zealand** 6-0	1989 Dublin **New Zealand** 23-6
1935 Dublin **New Zealand** 17-9	1992 *1* Dunedin **New Zealand** 24-21
1954 Dublin **New Zealand** 14-3	*2* Wellington **New Zealand** 59-6
1963 Dublin **New Zealand** 6-5	*New Zealand won series 2-0*
1973 Dublin **Drawn** 10-10	1995 Johannesburg *WC* **New Zealand** 43-19
1974 Dublin **New Zealand** 15-6	1997 Dublin **New Zealand** 63-15
1976 Wellington **New Zealand** 11-3	

IRELAND v SOUTH AFRICA
Played 13   Ireland won 1, South Africa won 11, Drawn 1
Highest scores Ireland 15-23 in 1981, South Africa 38-0 in 1912
Biggest wins Ireland 9-6 in 1965, South Africa 38-0 in 1912

1906 Belfast **South Africa** 15-12
1912 Dublin **South Africa** 38-0
1931 Dublin **South Africa** 8-3
1951 Dublin **South Africa** 17-5
1960 Dublin **South Africa** 8-3
1961 Cape Town **South Africa** 24-8
1965 Dublin **Ireland** 9-6
1970 Dublin **Drawn** 8-8

1981 *1* Cape Town **South Africa** 23-15
    2 Durban **South Africa** 12-10
    South Africa won series 2-0
1998 *1* Bloemfontein **South Africa** 37-13
    2 Pretoria **South Africa** 33-0
    South Africa won series 2-0
1998 Dublin **South Africa** 27-13

IRELAND v AUSTRALIA
Played 17   Ireland won 6, Australia won 11, Drawn 0
Highest scores Ireland 27-12 in 1979, Australia 42-17 in 1992
Biggest wins Ireland 27-12 in 1979, Australia 42-17 in 1992

1927 Dublin **Australia** 5-3
1947 Dublin **Australia** 16-3
1958 Dublin **Ireland** 9-6
1967 Dublin **Ireland** 15-8
1967 Sydney **Ireland** 11-5
1968 Dublin **Ireland** 10-3
1976 Dublin **Australia** 20-10
1979 *1* Brisbane **Ireland** 27-12
    2 Sydney **Ireland** 9-3
    Ireland won series 2-0

1981 Dublin **Australia** 16-12
1984 Dublin **Australia** 16-9
1987 Sydney *WC* **Australia** 33-15
1991 Dublin *WC* **Australia** 19-18
1992 Dublin **Australia** 42-17
1994 *1* Brisbane **Australia** 33-13
    2 Sydney **Australia** 32-18
    Australia won series 2-0
1996 Dublin **Australia** 22-12

IRELAND v NEW ZEALAND NATIVES
Played 1   New Zealand Natives won 1
Highest scores Ireland 4-13 in 1888, Zew Zealand Natives 13-4 in 1888
Biggest win Ireland no win, New Zealand Natives 13-4 in 1888

1888 Dublin **New Zealand Natives**
    4G 1T to 1G 1T

IRELAND v IRU PRESIDENT'S XV
Played 1   Drawn 1
Highest scores Ireland 18-18 in 1974, IRFU President's XV 18-18 in 1974

1974 Dublin **Drawn** 18-18

IRELAND v ROMANIA
Played 3   Ireland won 3
Highest scores Ireland 60-0 in 1986, Romania 35-53 in 1998
Biggest win Ireland 60-0 in 1986, Romania no win

1986 Dublin **Ireland** 60-0
1993 Dublin **Ireland** 25-3

1998 Dublin **Ireland** 53-35

IRELAND v CANADA
Played 2   Ireland won 2
Highest scores Ireland 46-19 in 1987, Canada 19-46 in 1987
Biggest win Ireland 46-19 in 1987, Canada no win

1987 Dunedin *WC* **Ireland** 46-19   1997 Dublin **Ireland** 33-11

IRELAND v TONGA
Played 1   Ireland won 1
Highest scores Ireland 32-9 in 1987, Tonga 9-32 in 1987
Biggest win Ireland 32-9 in 1987, Tonga no win

1987 Brisbane *WC* **Ireland** 32-9

IRELAND v WESTERN SAMOA
Played 2   Ireland won 1, Western Samoa won 1, Drawn 0
Highest scores Ireland 49-22 in 1988, Western Samoa 40-25 in 1996
Biggest wins Ireland 49-22 in 1988, Western Samoa 40-25 in 1996

1988 Dublin **Ireland** 49-22   1996 Dublin **Western Samoa** 40-25

IRELAND v ITALY
Played 5   Ireland won 2, Italy won 3, Drawn 0
Highest scores Ireland 39-30 in 1999, Italy 37-29 in 1997 & 37-22 in 1997
Biggest wins Ireland 31-15 in 1988, Italy 37-22 in 1997

1988 Dublin **Ireland** 31-15   1997 Bologna **Italy** 37-22
1995 Treviso **Italy** 22-12   1999 Dublin **Ireland** 39-30
1997 Dublin **Italy** 37-29

IRELAND v ARGENTINA
Played 1   Ireland won 1
Highest scores Ireland 20-18 in 1990, Argentina 18-20 in 1990
Biggest win Ireland 20-18 in 1990, Argentina no win

1990 Dublin **Ireland** 20-18

IRELAND v NAMIBIA
Played 2   Namibia won 2
Highest scores Ireland 15-26 in 1991, Namibia 26-15 in 1991
Biggest win Ireland no win, Namibia 26-15 in 1991

1991 *1* Windhoek **Namibia** 15-6   *2* Windhoek **Namibia** 26-15
                                            Namibia won series 2-0

IRELAND v ZIMBABWE
Played 1   Ireland won 1
Highest scores Ireland 55-11 in 1991, Zimbabwe 11-55 in 1991
Biggest win Ireland 55-11 in 1991, Zimbabwe no win

1991 Dublin *WC* **Ireland** 55-11

391

IRELAND v JAPAN
Played 2   Ireland won 2
Highest scores Ireland 50-28 in 1995, Japan 28-50 in 1995
Biggest win Ireland 50-28 in 1995, Japan no win

1991 Dublin *WC* **Ireland** 32-16	1995 Bloemfontein *WC* **Ireland** 50-28

IRELAND v UNITED STATES
Played 2   Ireland won 2
Highest scores Ireland 26-15 in 1994, United States 18-25 in 1996
Biggest win Ireland 26-15 in 1994, United States no win

1994 Dublin **Ireland** 26-15	1996 Atlanta **Ireland** 25-18

IRELAND v FIJI
Played 1   Ireland won 1
Highest scores Ireland 44-8 in 1995, Fiji 8-44 in 1995
Biggest win Ireland 44-8 in 1995, Fiji no win

1995 Dublin **Ireland** 44-8

IRELAND v GEORGIA
Played 1   Ireland won 1
Highest scores Ireland 70-0 in 1998, Georgia 0-70 in 1998
Biggest win Ireland 70-0 in 1998, Georgia no win

1998 Dublin **Ireland** 70-0

WALES v FRANCE
Played 74   Wales won 39, France won 32, Drawn 3
Highest scores Wales 49-14 in 1910, France 51-0 in 1998
Biggest wins Wales 47-5 in 1909, France 51-0 in 1998

1908 Cardiff **Wales** 36-4	1951 Paris **France** 8-3
1909 Paris **Wales** 47-5	1952 Swansea **Wales** 9-5
1910 Swansea **Wales** 49-14	1953 Paris **Wales** 6-3
1911 Paris **Wales** 15-0	1954 Cardiff **Wales** 19-13
1912 Newport **Wales** 14-8	1955 Paris **Wales** 16-11
1913 Paris **Wales** 11-8	1956 Cardiff **Wales** 5-3
1914 Swansea **Wales** 31-0	1957 Paris **Wales** 19-13
1920 Paris **Wales** 6-5	1958 Cardiff **France** 16-6
1921 Cardiff **Wales** 12-4	1959 Paris **France** 11-3
1922 Paris **Wales** 11-3	1960 Cardiff **France** 16-8
1923 Swansea **Wales** 16-8	1961 Paris **France** 8-6
1924 Paris **Wales** 10-6	1962 Cardiff **Wales** 3-0
1925 Cardiff **Wales** 11-5	1963 Paris **France** 5-3
1926 Paris **Wales** 7-5	1964 Cardiff **Drawn** 11-11
1927 Swansea **Wales** 25-7	1965 Paris **France** 22-13
1928 Paris **France** 8-3	1966 Cardiff **Wales** 9-8
1929 Cardiff **Wales** 8-3	1967 Paris **France** 20-14
1930 Paris **Wales** 11-0	1968 Cardiff **France** 14-9
1931 Swansea **Wales** 35-3	1969 Paris **Drawn** 8-8
1947 Paris **Wales** 3-0	1970 Cardiff **Wales** 11-6
1948 Swansea **France** 11-3	1971 Paris **Wales** 9-5
1949 Paris **France** 5-3	1972 Cardiff **Wales** 20-6
1950 Cardiff **Wales** 21-0	1973 Paris **France** 12-3

1974 Cardiff **Drawn** 16-16
1975 Paris **Wales** 25-10
1976 Cardiff **Wales** 19-13
1977 Paris **France** 16-9
1978 Cardiff **Wales** 16-7
1979 Paris **France** 14-13
1980 Cardiff **Wales** 18-9
1981 Paris **France** 19-15
1982 Cardiff **Wales** 22-12
1983 Paris **France** 16-9
1984 Cardiff **France** 21-16
1985 Paris **France** 14-3
1986 Cardiff **France** 23-15
1987 Paris **France** 16-9
1988 Cardiff **France** 10-9

1989 Paris **France** 31-12
1990 Cardiff **France** 29-19
1991 Paris **France** 36-3
1991 Cardiff **France** 22-9
Non-championship match
1992 Cardiff **France** 12-9
1993 Paris **France** 26-10
1994 Cardiff **Wales** 24-15
1995 Paris **France** 21-9
1996 Cardiff **Wales** 16-15
1996 Cardiff **France** 40-33
Non-championship match
1997 Paris **France** 27-22
1998 Wembley **France** 51-0
1999 Paris **Wales** 34-33

WALES v NEW ZEALAND
Played 17   Wales won 3, New Zealand won 14, Drawn 0
Highest scores Wales 16-19 in 1972, New Zealand 54-9 in 1988
Biggest wins Wales 13-8 in 1953, New Zealand 52-3 in 1988

1905 Cardiff **Wales** 3-0
1924 Swansea **New Zealand** 19-0
1935 Cardiff **Wales** 13-12
1953 Cardiff **Wales** 13-8
1963 Cardiff **New Zealand** 6-0
1967 Cardiff **New Zealand** 13-6
1969 *1* Christchurch **New Zealand** 19-0
    2 Auckland **New Zealand** 33-12
    New Zealand won series 2-0
1972 Cardiff **New Zealand** 19-16

1978 Cardiff **New Zealand** 13-12
1980 Cardiff **New Zealand** 23-3
1987 Brisbane *WC* **New Zealand** 49-6
1988 *1* Christchurch **New Zealand** 52-3
    2 Auckland **New Zealand** 54-9
    New Zealand won series 2-0
1989 Cardiff **New Zealand** 34-9
1995 Johannesburg *WC* **New Zealand** 34-9
1997 Wembley **New Zealand** 42-7

WALES v SOUTH AFRICA
Played 12   Wales won 0, South Africa won 11, Drawn 1
Highest scores Wales 20-37 in 1996 & 20-28 in 1998, South Africa 96-13 in 1998
Biggest win Wales no win, South Africa 96-13 in 1998

1906 Swansea **South Africa** 11-0
1912 Cardiff **South Africa** 3-0
1931 Swansea **South Africa** 8-3
1951 Cardiff **South Africa** 6-3
1960 Cardiff **South Africa** 3-0
1964 Durban **South Africa** 24-3

1970 Cardiff **Drawn** 6-6
1994 Cardiff **South Africa** 20-12
1995 Johannesburg **South Africa** 40-11
1996 Cardiff **South Africa** 37-20
1998 Pretoria **South Africa** 96-13
1998 Wembley **South Africa** 28-20

WALES v AUSTRALIA
Played 19   Wales won 8, Australia won 11, Drawn 0
Highest scores Wales 28-3 in 1975, Australia 63-6 in 1991
Biggest wins Wales 28-3 in 1975, Australia 63-6 in 1991

1908 Cardiff **Wales** 9-6
1927 Cardiff **Australia** 18-8
1947 Cardiff **Wales** 6-0
1958 Cardiff **Wales** 9-3
1966 Cardiff **Australia** 14-11
1969 Sydney **Wales** 19-16
1973 Cardiff **Wales** 24-0
1975 Cardiff **Wales** 28-3

1978 *1* Brisbane **Australia** 18-8
    2 Sydney **Australia** 19-17
    Australia won series 2-0
1981 Cardiff **Wales** 18-13
1984 Cardiff **Australia** 28-9
1987 Rotorua *WC* **Wales** 22-21
1991 Brisbane **Australia** 63-6

1991 Cardiff *WC* **Australia** 38-3	*2* Sydney **Australia** 42-3
1992 Cardiff **Australia** 23-6	*Australia won series 2-0*
1996 *1* Brisbane **Australia** 56-25	1996 Cardiff **Australia** 28-19

WALES v NEW ZEALAND NATIVES
Played 1   Wales won 1
Highest scores Wales 5-0 in 1888, New Zealand Natives 0-5 in 1888
Biggest win Wales 5-0 in 1888, New Zealand Natives no win

1888 Swansea **Wales** 1G 2T to 0

WALES v NEW ZEALAND ARMY
Played 1   New Zealand Army won 1
Highest scores Wales 3-6 in 1919, New Zealand Army 6-3 in 1919
Biggest win Wales no win, New Zealand Army 6-3 in 1919

1919 Swansea **New Zealand Army** 6-3

WALES v ROMANIA
Played 4   Wales won 2, Romania won 2
Highest scores Wales 70-21 in 1997, Romania 24-6 in 1983
Biggest wins Wales 70-21 in 1997, Romania 24-6 in 1983

1983 Bucharest **Romania** 24-6	1994 Bucharest **Wales** 16-9
1988 Cardiff **Romania** 15-9	1997 Wrexham **Wales** 70-21

WALES v FIJI
Played 4   Wales won 4
Highest scores Wales 40-3 in 1985, Fiji 15-22 in 1986 & 15-19 in 1995
Biggest win Wales 40-3 in 1985, Fiji no win

1985 Cardiff **Wales** 40-3	1994 Suva **Wales** 23-8
1986 Suva **Wales** 22-15	1995 Cardiff **Wales** 19-15

WALES v TONGA
Played 4   Wales won 4
Highest scores Wales 46-12 in 1997, Tonga 16-29 in 1987
Biggest win Wales 46-12 in 1997, Tonga no win

1986 Nuku'Alofa **Wales** 15-7	1994 Nuku'Alofa **Wales** 18-9
1987 Palmerston North *WC* **Wales** 29-16	1997 Swansea **Wales** 46-12

WALES v WESTERN SAMOA
Played 4   Wales won 2, Western Samoa won 2, Drawn 0
Highest scores Wales 32-14 in 1986, Western Samoa 34-9 in 1994
Biggest wins Wales 28-6 in 1988, Western Samoa 34-9 in 1994

1986 Apia **Wales** 32-14	1991 Cardiff *WC* **Western Samoa** 16-13
1988 Cardiff **Wales** 28-6	1994 Moamoa **Western Samoa** 34-9

WALES v CANADA
Played 4   Wales won 3, Canada won 1, Drawn 0
Highest scores Wales 40-9 in 1987, Canada 26-24 in 1993
Biggest wins Wales 40-9 in 1987, Canada 26-24 in 1993

1987 Invercargill *WC* **Wales** 40-9
1993 Cardiff **Canada** 26-24

1994 Toronto **Wales** 33-15
1997 Toronto **Wales** 28-25

WALES v UNITED STATES
Played 4   Wales won 4
Highest scores Wales 46-0 in 1987, United States 23-28 in 1997
Biggest win Wales 46-0 in 1987, United States no win

1987 Cardiff **Wales** 46-0
1997 Cardiff **Wales** 34-14
1997 *1* Wilmington **Wales** 30-20

2 San Francisco **Wales** 28-23
Wales won series 2-0

WALES v NAMIBIA
Played 3   Wales won 3
Highest scores Wales 38-23 in 1993, Namibia 30-34 in 1990
Biggest win Wales 38-23 in 1993, Namibia no win

1990 *1* Windhoek **Wales** 18-9
    2 Windhoek **Wales** 34-30
    Wales won series 2-0

1993 Windhoek **Wales** 38-23

WALES v BARBARIANS
Played 2   Wales won 1, Barbarians won 1
Highest scores Wales 31-10 in 1996, Barbarians 31-24 in 1990
Biggest wins Wales 31-10 in 1996, Barbarians 31-24 in 1990

1990 Cardiff **Barbarians** 31-24

1996 Cardiff **Wales** 31-10

WALES v ARGENTINA
Played 2   Wales won 2
Highest scores Wales 43-30 in 1998, Argentina 30-43 in 1998
Biggest win Wales 43-30 in 1998, Argentina no win

1991 Cardiff *WC* **Wales** 16-7

1998 Llanelli **Wales** 43-30

WALES v ZIMBABWE
Played 3   Wales won 3
Highest scores Wales 49-11 in 1998, Zimbabwe 14-35 in 1993
Biggest win Wales 49-11 in 1998, Zimbabwe no win

1993 *1* Bulawayo **Wales** 35-14
    2 Harare **Wales** 42-13
    Wales won series 2-0

1998 Harare **Wales** 49-11

WALES v JAPAN
Played 2   Wales won 2
Highest scores Wales 57-10 in 1995, Japan 10-57 in 1995
Biggest win Wales 55-5 in 1993, Japan no win

1993 Cardiff **Wales 55-5**   1995 Bloemfontein *WC* **Wales** 57-10

WALES v PORTUGAL
Played 1   Wales won 1
Highest scores Wales 102-11 in 1994, Portugal 11-102 in 1994
Biggest win Wales 102-11 in 1994, Portugal no win

1994 Lisbon **Wales** 102-11

WALES v SPAIN
Played 1   Wales won 1
Highest scores Wales 54-0 in 1994, Spain 0-54 in 1994
Bigegst win Wales 54-0 in 1994, Spain no win

1994 Madrid **Wales** 54-0

WALES v ITALY
Played 5   Wales won 5
Highest scores Wales 60-21 in 1999, Italy 26-31 in 1996
Biggest win Wales 60-21 in 1999, Italy no win

1994 Cardiff **Wales** 29-19   1998 Llanelli **Wales** 23-20
1996 Cardiff **Wales** 31-26   1999 Treviso **Wales** 60-21
1996 Rome **Wales** 31-22

FRANCE v NEW ZEALAND
Played 32   France won 8, New Zealand won 24, Drawn 0
Highest scores France 24-19 in 1979, New Zealand 38-8 in 1906
Biggest wins France 22-8 in 1994, New Zealand 38-8 in 1906

1906 Paris **New Zealand** 38-8
1925 Toulouse **New Zealand** 30-6
1954 Paris **France** 3-0
1961 *1* Auckland **New Zealand** 13-6
    2 Wellington **New Zealand** 5-3
    3 Christchurch **New Zealand** 32-3
    New Zealand won series 3-0
1964 Paris **New Zealand** 12-3
1967 Paris **New Zealand** 21-15
1968 *1* Christchurch **New Zealand** 12-9
    2 Wellington **New Zealand** 9-3
    3 Auckland **New Zealand** 19-12
    New Zealand won series 3-0
1973 Paris **France** 13-6
1977 *1* Toulouse **France** 18-13
    2 Paris **New Zealand** 15-3
    Series drawn 1-1
1979 *1* Christchurch **New Zealand** 23-9
    2 Auckland **France** 24-19
    Series drawn 1-1
1981 *1* Toulouse **New Zealand** 13-9

    2 Paris **New Zealand** 18-6
    New Zealand won series 2-0
1984 *1* Christchurch **New Zealand** 10-9
    2 Auckland **New Zealand** 31-18
    New Zealand won series 2-0
1986 Christchurch **New Zealand** 18-9
1986 *1* Toulouse **New Zealand** 19-7
    2 Nantes **France** 16-3
    Series drawn 1-1
1987 Auckland *WC* **New Zealand** 29-9
1989 *1* Christchurch **New Zealand** 25-17
    2 Auckland **New Zealand** 34-20
    New Zealand won series 2-0
1990 *1* Nantes **New Zealand** 24-3
    2 Paris **New Zealand** 30-12
    New Zealand won series 2-0
1994 *1* Christchurch **France** 22-8
    2 Auckland **France** 23-20
    France won series 2-0
1995 *1* Toulouse **France** 22-15

2 Paris **New Zealand** 37-12
Series drawn 1-1

FRANCE v SOUTH AFRICA

Played 28   France won 5, South Africa won 18, Drawn 5
Highest scores France 32-36 in 1997, South Africa 52-10 in 1997
Biggest wins France 29-16 in 1992, South Africa 52-10 in 1997

1913 Bordeaux **South Africa** 38-5
1952 Paris **South Africa** 25-3
1958 *1* Cape Town **Drawn** 3-3
    2 Johannesburg **France** 9-5
    France won series 1-0, with 1 draw
1961 Paris **Drawn** 0-0
1964 Springs (SA) **France** 8-6
1967 *1* Durban **South Africa** 26-3
    2 Bloemfontein **South Africa** 16-3
    3 Johannesburg **France** 19-14
    4 Cape Town **Drawn** 6-6
    South Africa won series 2-1, with 1 draw
1968 *1* Bordeaux **South Africa** 12-9
    2 Paris **South Africa** 16-11
    South Africa won series 2-0
1971 *1* Bloemfontein **South Africa** 22-9
    2 Durban **Drawn** 8-8
    South Africa won series 1-0, with 1 draw
1974 *1* Toulouse **South Africa** 13-4

    2 Paris **South Africa** 10-8
    South Africa won series 2-0
1975 *1* Bloemfontein **South Africa** 38-25
    2 Pretoria **South Africa** 33-18
    South Africa won series 2-0
1980 Pretoria **South Africa** 37-15
1992 *1* Lyons **South Africa** 20-15
    2 Paris **France** 29-16
    Series drawn 1-1
1993 *1* Durban **Drawn** 20-20
    2 Johannesburg **France** 18-17
    France won series 1-0, with 1 draw
1995 Durban *WC* **South Africa** 19-15
1996 *1* Bordeaux **South Africa** 22-12
    2 Paris **South Africa** 13-12
    South Africa won series 2-0
1997 *1* Lyons **South Africa** 36-32
    2 Paris **South Africa** 52-10
    South Africa won series 2-0

FRANCE v AUSTRALIA

Played 28   France won 13, Australia won 13, Drawn 2
Highest scores France 34-6 in 1976, Australia 48-31 in 1990
Biggest wins France 34-6 in 1976, Australia 24-3 in 1993

1928 Paris **Australia** 11-8
1948 Paris **France** 13-6
1958 Paris **France** 19-0
1961 Sydney **France** 15-8
1967 Paris **France** 20-14
1968 Sydney **Australia** 11-10
1971 *1* Toulouse **Australia** 13-11
    2 Paris **France** 18-9
    Series drawn 1-1
1972 *1* Sydney **Drawn** 14-14
    2 Brisbane **France** 16-15
    France won series 1-0, with 1 draw
1976 *1* Bordeaux **France** 18-15
    2 Paris **France** 34-6
    France won series 2-0
1981 *1* Brisbane **Australia** 17-15
    2 Sydney **Australia** 24-14
    Australia won series 2-0
1983 *1* Clermont-Ferrand **Drawn** 15-15

    2 Paris **France** 15-6
    France won series 1-0, with 1 draw
1986 Sydney **Australia** 27-14
1987 Sydney *WC* **France** 30-24
1989 *1* Strasbourg **Australia** 32-15
    2 Lille **France** 25-19
    Series drawn 1-1
1990 *1* Sydney **Australia** 21-9
    2 Brisbane **Australia** 48-31
    3 Sydney **France** 28-19
    Australia won series 2-1
1993 *1* Bordeaux **France** 16-13
    2 Paris **Australia** 24-3
    Series drawn 1-1
1997 *1* Sydney **Australia** 29-15
    2 Brisbane **Australia** 26-19
    Australia won series 2-0
1998 Paris **Australia** 32-21

FRANCE v UNITED STATES

Played 5   France won 4, United States won 1, Drawn 0
Highest scores France 41-9 in 1991, United States 17-3 in 1924
Biggest wins France 41-9 in 1991, United States 17-3 in 1924

1920 Paris **France** 14-5

1924 Paris **United States** 17-3

1976 Chicago **France** 33-14
1991 *1* Denver **France** 41-9

2 Colorado Springs **France** 10-3★
★Abandoned after 43 mins
France won series 2-0

FRANCE v ROMANIA
Played 45   France won 35, Romania won 8, Drawn 2
Highest scores France 64-12 in 1996, Romania 21-33 in 1991
Biggest wins France 59-3 in 1924, Romania 15-0 in 1980

1924 Paris **France** 59-3
1938 Bucharest **France** 11-8
1957 Bucharest **France** 18-15
1957 Bordeaux **France** 39-0
1960 Bucharest **Romania** 11-5
1961 Bayonne **Drawn** 5-5
1962 Bucharest **Romania** 3-0
1963 Toulouse **Drawn** 6-6
1964 Bucharest **France** 9-6
1965 Lyons **France** 8-3
1966 Bucharest **France** 9-3
1967 Nantes **France** 11-3
1968 Bucharest **Romania** 15-14
1969 Tarbes **France** 14-9
1970 Bucharest **France** 14-3
1971 Béziers **France** 31-12
1972 Constanza **France** 15-6
1973 Valence **France** 7-6
1974 Bucharest **Romania** 15-10
1975 Bordeaux **France** 36-12
1976 Bucharest **Romania** 15-12
1977 Clermont-Ferrand **France** 9-6
1978 Bucharest **France** 9-6

1979 Montauban **France** 30-12
1980 Bucharest **Romania** 15-0
1981 Narbonne **France** 17-9
1982 Bucharest **Romania** 13-9
1983 Toulouse **France** 26-15
1984 Bucharest **France** 18-3
1986 Lille **France** 25-13
1986 Bucharest **France** 20-3
1987 Wellington *WC* **France** 55-12
1987 Agen **France** 49-3
1988 Bucharest **France** 16-12
1990 Auch **Romania** 12-6
1991 Bucharest **France** 33-21
1991 Béziers *WC* **France** 30-3
1992 Le Havre **France** 25-6
1993 Bucharest **France** 37-20
1993 Brive **France** 51-0
1995 Bucharest **France** 24-15
1995 Tucumán *LC* **France** 52-8
1996 Aurillac **France** 64-12
1997 Bucharest **France** 51-20
1997 Lourdes *LC* **France** 39-3

FRANCE v NEW ZEALAND MAORIS
Played 1   New Zealand Maoris won 1
Highest scores France 3-12 in 1926, New Zealand Maoris 12-3 in 1926
Biggest win France no win, New Zealand Maoris 12-3 in 1926

1926 Paris **New Zealand Maoris** 12-3

FRANCE v GERMANY
Played 15   France won 13, Germany won 2, Drawn 0
Highest scores France 38-17 in 1933, Germany 17-16 in 1927 & 17-38 in 1933
Biggest wins France 34-0 in 1931, Germany 3-0 in 1938

1927 Paris **France** 30-5
1927 Frankfurt **Germany** 17-16
1928 Hanover **France** 14-3
1929 Paris **France** 24-0
1930 Berlin **France** 31-0
1931 Paris **France** 34-0
1932 Frankfurt **France** 20-4
1933 Paris **France** 38-17

1934 Hanover **France** 13-9
1935 Paris **France** 18-3
1936 *1* Berlin **France** 19-14
    2 Hanover **France** 6-3
    France won series 2-0
1937 Paris **France** 27-6
1938 Frankfurt **Germany** 3-0
1938 Bucharest **France** 8-5

FRANCE v ITALY

Played 20   France won 19, Italy won 1, Drawn 0
Highest scores France 60-13 in 1967, Italy 40-32 in 1997
Biggest wins France 60-13 in 1967, Italy 40-32 in 1997

1937 Paris **France** 43-5	1961 Chambéry **France** 17-0
1952 Milan **France** 17-8	1962 Brescia **France** 6-3
1953 Lyons **France** 22-8	1963 Grenoble **France** 14-12
1954 Rome **France** 39-12	1964 Parma **France** 12-3
1955 Grenoble **France** 24-0	1965 Pau **France** 21-0
1956 Padua **France** 16-3	1966 Naples **France** 21-0
1957 Agen **France** 38-6	1967 Toulon **France** 60-13
1958 Naples **France** 11-3	1995 Buenos Aires *LC* **France** 34-22
1959 Nantes **France** 22-0	1997 Grenoble **Italy** 40-32
1960 Treviso **France** 26-0	1997 Auch *LC* **France** 30-19

FRANCE v BRITISH XVs

Played 5   France won 2, British XVs won 3, Drawn 0
Highest scores France 27-29 in 1989, British XV 36-3 in 1940
Biggest wins France 21-9 in 1945, British XV 36-3 in 1940

1940 Paris **British XV** 36-3	1946 Paris **France** 10-0
1945 Paris **France** 21-9	1989 Paris **British XV** 29-27
1945 Richmond **British XV** 27-6	

FRANCE v NEW ZEALAND ARMY

Played 1   New Zealand Army won 1
Highest scores France 9-14 in 1946, New Zealand Army 14-9 in 1946
Biggest win France no win, New Zealand Army 14-9 in 1946

1946 Paris **New Zealand Army** 14-9

FRANCE v ARGENTINA

Played 33   France won 28, Argentina won 4, Drawn 1
Highest scores France 47-12 in 1995, Argentina 27-31 in 1974 & 27-34 in 1996 & 27-32 in 1997
Biggest wins France 47-12 in 1995, Argentina 18-6 in 1988

1949 *1* Buenos Aires **France** 5-0	*2* Paris **France** 13-6
2 Buenos Aires **France** 12-3	*France won series 2-0*
France won series 2-0	1985 *1* Buenos Aires **Argentina** 24-16
1954 *1* Buenos Aires **France** 22-8	*2* Buenos Aires **France** 23-15
2 Buenos Aires **France** 30-3	*Series drawn 1-1*
France won series 2-0	1986 *1* Buenos Aires **Argentina** 15-13
1960 *1* Buenos Aires **France** 37-3	*2* Buenos Aires **France** 22-9
2 Buenos Aires **France** 12-3	*Series drawn 1-1*
3 Buenos Aires **France** 29-6	1988 *1* Buenos Aires **France** 18-15
France won series 3-0	*2* Buenos Aires **Argentina** 18-6
1974 *1* Buenos Aires **France** 20-15	*Series drawn 1-1*
2 Buenos Aires **France** 31-27	1988 *1* Nantes **France** 29-9
France won series 2-0	*2* Lille **France** 28-18
1975 *1* Lyons **France** 29-6	*France won series 2-0*
2 Paris **France** 36-21	1992 *1* Buenos Aires **France** 27-12
France won series 2-0	*2* Buenos Aires **France** 33-9
1977 *1* Buenos Aires **France** 26-3	*France won series 2-0*
2 Buenos Aires **Drawn** 18-18	1992 Nantes **Argentina** 24-20
France won series 1-0, with 1 draw	1995 Buenos Aires *LC* **France** 47-12
1982 *1* Toulouse **France** 25-12	1996 *1* Buenos Aires **France** 34-27

2 Buenos Aires **France** 34-15
France won series 2-0
1997 Tarbes *LC* **France** 32-27
1998 *1* Buenos Aires **France** 35-18

2 Buenos Aires **France** 37-12
France won series 2-0
1998 Nantes **France** 34-14

FRANCE v CZECHOSLOVAKIA
Played 2   France won 2
Highest scores France 28-3 in 1956, Czechoslovakia 6-19 in 1968
Biggest win France 28-3 in 1956, Czechoslovakia no win

1956 Toulouse **France** 28-3

1968 Prague **France** 19-6

FRANCE v FIJI
Played 4   France won 4
Highest scores France 34-9 in 1998, Fiji 16-31 in 1987
Biggest win France 34-9 in 1998, Fiji no win

1964 Paris **France** 21-3
1987 Auckland *WC* **France** 31-16

1991 Grenoble *WC* **France** 33-9
1998 Suva **France** 34-9

FRANCE v JAPAN
Played 1   France won 1
Highest scores France 30-18 in 1973, Japan 18-30 in 1973
Biggest win France 30-18 in 1973, Japan no win

1973 Bordeaux **France** 30-18

FRANCE v ZIMBABWE
Played 1   France won 1
Highest scores France 70-12 in 1987, Zimbabwe 12-70 in 1987
Biggest win France 70-12 in 1987, Zimbabwe no win

1987 Auckland *WC* **France** 70-12

FRANCE v CANADA
Played 3   France won 2, Canada won 1, Drawn 0
Highest scores France 28-9 in 1994, Canada 18-16 in 1994
Biggest wins France 28-9 in 1994, Canada 18-16 in 1994

1991 Agen *WC* **France** 19-13
1994 Nepean **Canada** 18-16

1994 Besançon **France** 28-9

FRANCE v TONGA
Played 1   France won 1
Highest scores France 38-10 in 1995, Tonga 10-38 in 1995
Biggest win France 38-10 in 1995, Tonga no win

1995 Pretoria *WC* **France** 38-10

FRANCE v IVORY COAST
Played 1   France won 1
Highest scores France 54-18 in 1995, Ivory Coast 18-54 in 1995
Biggest win France 54-18 in 1995, Ivory Coast no win

1995 Rustenburg *WC* **France** 54-18

NEW ZEALAND v SOUTH AFRICA
Played 51   New Zealand won 24, South Africa won 24, Drawn 3
Highest scores New Zealand 55-35 in 1997, South Africa 35-55 in 1997
Biggest wins New Zealand 55-35 in 1997, South Africa 17-0 in 1928

1921 *1* Dunedin **New Zealand** 13-5
    2 Auckland **South Africa** 9-5
    3 Wellington **Drawn** 0-0
    Series drawn 1-1, with 1 draw
1928 *1* Durban **South Africa** 17-0
    2 Johannesburg **New Zealand** 7-6
    3 Port Elizabeth **South Africa** 11-6
    4 Cape Town **New Zealand** 13-5
    Series drawn 2-2
1937 *1* Wellington **New Zealand** 13-7
    2 Christchurch **South Africa** 13-6
    3 Auckland **South Africa** 17-6
    South Africa won series 2-1
1949 *1* Cape Town **South Africa** 15-11
    2 Johannesburg **South Africa** 12-6
    3 Durban **South Africa** 9-3
    4 Port Elizabeth **South Africa** 11-8
    South Africa won series 4-0
1956 *1* Dunedin **New Zealand** 10-6
    2 Wellington **South Africa** 8-3
    3 Christchurch **New Zealand** 17-10
    4 Auckland **New Zealand** 11-5
    New Zealand won series 3-1
1960 *1* Johannesburg **South Africa** 13-0
    2 Cape Town **New Zealand** 11-3
    3 Bloemfontein **Drawn** 11-11
    4 Port Elizabeth **South Africa** 8-3
    South Africa won series 2-1, with 1 draw
1965 *1* Wellington **New Zealand** 6-3
    2 Dunedin **New Zealand** 13-0
    3 Christchurch **South Africa** 19-16

    4 Auckland **New Zealand** 20-3
    New Zealand won series 3-1
1970 *1* Pretoria **South Africa** 17-6
    2 Cape Town **New Zealand** 9-8
    3 Port Elizabeth **South Africa** 14-3
    4 Johannesburg **South Africa** 20-17
    South Africa won series 3-1
1976 *1* Durban **South Africa** 16-7
    2 Bloemfontein **New Zealand** 15-9
    3 Cape Town **South Africa** 15-10
    4 Johannesburg **South Africa** 15-14
    South Africa won series 3-1
1981 *1* Christchurch **New Zealand** 14-9
    2 Wellington **South Africa** 24-12
    3 Auckland **New Zealand** 25-22
    New Zealand won series 2-1
1992 Johannesburg **New Zealand** 27-24
1994 *1* Dunedin **New Zealand** 22-14
    2 Wellington **New Zealand** 13-9
    3 Auckland **Drawn** 18-18
    New Zealand won series 2-0, with 1 draw
1995 Johannesburg *WC* **South Africa** 15-12
    (*aet*)
1996 Christchurch *TN* **New Zealand** 15-11
1996 Cape Town *TN* **New Zealand** 29-18
1996 *1* Durban **New Zealand** 23-19
    2 Pretoria **New Zealand** 33-26
    3 Johannesburg **South Africa** 32-22
    New Zealand won series 2-1
1997 Johannesbury *TN* **New Zealand** 35-32
1997 Auckland *TN* **New Zealand** 55-35
1998 Wellington *TN* **South Africa** 13-3
1998 Durban *TN* **South Africa** 24-23

NEW ZEALAND v AUSTRALIA
Played 108   New Zealand won 73, Australia won 30, Drawn 5
Highest scores New Zealand 43-6 in 1996, Australia 30-16 in 1978
Biggest wins New Zealand 43-6 in 1996, Australia 26-10 in 1980

1903 Sydney **New Zealand** 22-3
1905 Dunedin **New Zealand** 14-3
1907 *1* Sydney **New Zealand** 26-6
    2 Brisbane **New Zealand** 14-5
    3 Sydney **Drawn** 5-5
    New Zealand won series 2-0, with 1 draw
1910 *1* Sydney **New Zealand** 6-0
    2 Sydney **Australia** 11-0

    3 Sydney **New Zealand** 28-13
    New Zealand won series 2-1
1913 *1* Wellington **New Zealand** 30-5
    2 Dunedin **New Zealand** 25-13
    3 Christchurch **Australia** 16-5
    New Zealand won series 2-1
1914 *1* Sydney **New Zealand** 5-0
    2 Brisbane **New Zealand** 17-0

3 Sydney **New Zealand** 22-7
New Zealand won series 3-0
1929 *1* Sydney **Australia** 9-8
    2 Brisbane **Australia** 17-9
    3 Sydney **Australia** 15-13
    Australia won series 3-0
1931 Auckland **New Zealand** 20-13
1932 *1* Sydney **Australia** 22-17
    2 Brisbane **New Zealand** 21-3
    3 Sydney **New Zealand** 21-13
    New Zealand won series 2-1
1934 *1* Sydney **Australia** 25-11
    2 Sydney **Drawn** 3-3
    Australia won series 1-0, with 1 draw
1936 *1* Wellington **New Zealand** 11-6
    2 Dunedin **New Zealand** 38-13
    New Zealand won series 2-0
1938 *1* Sydney **New Zealand** 24-9
    2 Brisbane **New Zealand** 20-14
    3 Sydney **New Zealand** 14-6
    New Zealand won series 3-0
1946 *1* Dunedin **New Zealand** 31-8
    2 Auckland **New Zealand** 14-10
    New Zealand won series 2-0
1947 *1* Brisbane **New Zealand** 13-5
    2 Sydney **New Zealand** 27-14
    New Zealand won series 2-0
1949 *1* Wellington **Australia** 11-6
    2 Auckland **Australia** 16-9
    Australia won series 2-0
1951 *1* Sydney **New Zealand** 8-0
    2 Sydney **New Zealand** 17-11
    3 Brisbane **New Zealand** 16-6
    New Zealand won series 3-0
1952 *1* Christchurch **Australia** 14-9
    2 Wellington **New Zealand** 15-8
    Series drawn 1-1
1955 *1* Wellington **New Zealand** 16-8
    2 Dunedin **New Zealand** 8-0
    3 Auckland **Australia** 8-3
    New Zealand won series 2-1
1957 *1* Sydney **New Zealand** 25-11
    2 Brisbane **New Zealand** 22-9
    New Zealand won series 2-0
1958 *1* Wellington **New Zealand** 25-3
    2 Christchurch **Australia** 6-3
    3 Auckland **New Zealand** 17-8
    New Zealand won series 2-1
1962 *1* Brisbane **New Zealand** 20-6
    2 Sydney **New Zealand** 14-5
    New Zealand won series 2-0
1962 *1* Wellington **Drawn** 9-9
    2 Dunedin **New Zealand** 3-0
    3 Auckland **New Zealand** 16-8
    New Zealand won series 2-0, with1 draw
1964 *1* Dunedin **New Zealand** 14-9
    2 Christchurch **New Zealand** 18-3
    3 Wellington **Australia** 20-5
    New Zealand won series 2-1
1967 Wellington **New Zealand** 29-9
1968 *1* Sydney **New Zealand** 27-11
    2 Brisbane **New Zealand** 19-18
    New Zealand won series 2-0

1972 *1* Wellington **New Zealand** 29-6
    2 Christchurch **New Zealand** 30-17
    3 Auckland **New Zealand** 38-3
    New Zealand won series 3-0
1974 *1* Sydney **New Zealand** 11-6
    2 Brisbane **Drawn** 16-16
    3 Sydney **New Zealand** 16-6
    New Zealand won series 2-0, with 1 draw
1978 *1* Wellington **New Zealand** 13-12
    2 Christchurch **New Zealand** 22-6
    3 Auckland **Australia** 30-16
    New Zealand won series 2-1
1979 Sydney **Australia** 12-6
1980 *1* Sydney **Australia** 13-9
    2 Brisbane **New Zealand** 12-9
    3 Sydney **Australia** 26-10
    Australia won series 2-1
1982 *1* Christchurch **New Zealand** 23-16
    2 Wellington **Australia** 19-16
    3 Auckland **New Zealand** 33-18
    New Zealand won series 2-1
1983 Sydney **New Zealand** 18-8
1984 *1* Sydney **Australia** 16-9
    2 Brisbane **New Zealand** 19-15
    3 Sydney **New Zealand** 25-24
    New Zealand won series 2-1
1985 Auckland **New Zealand** 10-9
1986 *1* Wellington **Australia** 13-12
    2 Dunedin **New Zealand** 13-12
    3 Auckland **Australia** 22-9
    Australia won series 2-1
1987 Sydney **New Zealand** 30-16
1988 *1* Sydney **New Zealand** 32-7
    2 Brisbane **Drawn** 19-19
    3 Sydney **New Zealand** 30-9
    New Zealand won series 2-0, with 1 draw
1989 Auckland **New Zealand** 24-12
1990 *1* Christchurch **New Zealand** 21-6
    2 Auckland **New Zealand** 27-17
    3 Wellington **Australia** 21-9
    New Zealand won series 2-1
1991 *1* Sydney **Australia** 21-12
    2 Auckland **New Zealand** 6-3
1991 Dublin *WC* **Australia** 16-6
1992 *1* Sydney **Australia** 16-15
    2 Brisbane **Australia** 19-17
    3 Sydney **New Zealand** 26-23
    Australia won series 2-1
1993 Dunedin **New Zealand** 25-10
1994 Sydney **Australia** 20-16
1995 Auckland **New Zealand** 28-16
1995 Sydney **New Zealand** 34-23
1996 Wellington *TN* **New Zealand** 43-6
1996 Brisbane *TN* **New Zealand** 32-25
    New Zealand won series 2-0
1997 Christchurch *TN* **New Zealand** 30-13
1997 Melbourne *TN* **New Zealand** 33-18
1997 Dunedin *TN* **New Zealand** 36-24
    New Zealand won series 3-0
1998 Melbourne *TN* **Australia** 24-16
1998 Christchurch *TN* **Australia** 27-23
1998 Sydney **Australia** 19-14
    Australia won series 3-0

NEW ZEALAND v UNITED STATES

Played 2   New Zealand won 2
Highest scores New Zealand 51-3 in 1913, United States 6-46 in 1991
Biggest win New Zealand 51-3 in 1913, United States no win

1913 Berkeley **New Zealand** 51-3   1991 Gloucester *WC* **New Zealand** 46-6

NEW ZEALAND v ROMANIA

Played 1   New Zealand won 1
Highest score New Zealand 14-6 in 1981, Romania 6-14 in 1981
Biggest win New Zealand 14-6 in 1981, Romania no win

1981 Bucharest **New Zealand** 14-6

NEW ZEALAND v ARGENTINA

Played 9   New Zealand won 8, Drawn 1
Highest scores New Zealand 93-8 in 1997, Argentina 21-21 in 1985
Biggest win New Zealand 93-8 in 1997, Argentina no win

1985 *1* Buenos Aires **New Zealand** 33-20   1991 *1* Buenos Aires **New Zealand** 28-14
    2 Buenos Aires **Drawn** 21-21   *2* Buenos Aires **New Zealand** 36-6
    New Zealand won series 1-0, with 1 draw   *New Zealand won series 2-0*
1987 Wellington *WC* **New Zealand** 46-15   1997 *1* Wellington **New Zealand** 93-8
1989 *1* Dunedin **New Zealand** 60-9   *2* Hamilton **New Zealand** 62-10
    2 Wellington **New Zealand** 49-12   *New Zealand won series 2-0*
    New Zealand won series 2-0

NEW ZEALAND v ITALY

Played 3   New Zealand won 3
Highest scores New Zealand 70-6 in 1987 & 70-6 in 1995, Italy 21-31 in 1991
Biggest win New Zealand 70-6 in 1987 & 70-6 in 1995, Italy no win

1987 Auckland *WC* **New Zealand** 70-6   1995 Bologna **New Zealand** 70-6
1991 Leicester *WC* **New Zealand** 31-21

NEW ZEALAND v FIJI

Played 2   New Zealand won 2
Highest scores New Zealand 74-13 in 1987, Fiji 13-74 in 1987
Biggest win New Zealand 71-5 in 1997, Fiji no win

1987 Christchurch *WC* **New Zealand** 74-13   1997 Albany **New Zealand** 71-5

NEW ZEALAND v CANADA

Played 2   New Zealand won 2
Highest scores New Zealand 73-7 in 1995, Canada 13-29 in 1991
Biggest win New Zealand 73-7 in 1995, Canada no win

1991 Lille *WC* **New Zealand** 29-13   1995 Auckland **New Zealand** 73-7

NEW ZEALAND v WORLD XVs

Played 3   New Zealand won 2, World XV won 1, Drawn 0
Highest scores New Zealand 54-26 in 1992, World XV 28-14 in 1992
Biggest wins New Zealand 54-26 in 1992, World XV 28-14 in 1992

1992 *1* Christchurch **World XV** 28-14   *3* Auckland **New Zealand** 26-15
    2 Wellington **New Zealand** 54-26   *New Zealand won series 2-1*

NEW ZEALAND v WESTERN SAMOA

Played 2   New Zealand won 2
Highest scores New Zealand 51-10 in 1996, Western Samoa 13-35 in 1993
Biggest win New Zealand 51-10 in 1996, Western Samoa no win

1993 Auckland **New Zealand** 35-13   1996 Napier **New Zealand** 51-10

NEW ZEALAND v JAPAN

Played 1   New Zealand won 1
Highest scores New Zealand 145-17 in 1995, Japan 17-145 in 1995
Biggest win New Zealand 145-17 in 1995, Japan no win

1995 Bloemfontein *WC* **New Zealand**
    145-17

SOUTH AFRICA v AUSTRALIA

Played 39   South Africa won 27, Australia won 12, Drawn 0
Highest scores South Africa 61-22 in 1997, Australia 32-20 in 1997
Biggest wins South Africa 61-22 in 1997, Australia 26-3 in 1992

1933 *1* Cape Town **South Africa** 17-3   1965 *1* Sydney **Australia** 18-11
    2 Durban **Australia** 21-6   *2* Brisbane **Australia** 12-8
    3 Johannesburg **South Africa** 12-3   *Australia won series 2-0*
    4 Port Elizabeth **South Africa** 11-0   1969 *1* Johannesburg **South Africa** 30-11
    5 Bloemfontein **Australia** 15-4   *2* Durban **South Africa** 16-9
    South Africa won series 3-2   *3* Cape Town **South Africa** 11-3
1937 *1* Sydney **South Africa** 9-5   *4* Bloemfontein **South Africa** 19-8
    2 Sydney **South Africa** 26-17   *South Africa won series 4-0*
    South Africa won series 2-0   1971 *1* Sydney **South Africa** 19-11
1953 *1* Johannesburg **South Africa** 25-3   *2* Brisbane **South Africa** 14-6
    2 Cape Town **Australia** 18-14   *3* Sydney **South Africa** 18-6
    3 Durban **South Africa** 18-8   *South Africa won series 3-0*
    4 Port Elizabeth **South Africa** 22-9   1992 Cape Town **Australia** 26-3
    South Africa won series 3-1   1993 *1* Sydney **South Africa** 19-12
1956 *1* Sydney **South Africa** 9-0   *2* Brisbane **Australia** 28-20
    2 Brisbane **South Africa** 9-0   *3* Sydney **Australia** 19-12
    South Africa won series 2-0   *Australia won series 2-1*
1961 *1* Johannesburg **South Africa** 28-3   1995 Cape Town *WC* **South Africa** 27-18
    2 Port Elizabeth **South Africa** 23-11 1996 Sydney *TN* **Australia** 21-16
    South Africa won series 2-0   1996 Bloemfontein *TN* **South Africa** 25-19
1963 *1* Pretoria **South Africa** 14-3   1997 Brisbane *TN* **Australia** 32-20
    2 Cape Town **Australia** 9-5   1997 Pretoria *TN* **South Africa** 61-22
    3 Johannesburg **Australia** 11-9   1998 Perth *TN* **South Africa** 14-13
    4 Port Elizabeth **South Africa** 22-6   1998 Johannesburg *TN* **South Africa** 29-15
    Series drawn 2-2

SOUTH AFRICA v WORLD XVs

Played 3   South Africa won 3
Highest scores South Africa 45-24 in 1977, World XV 24-45 in 1977
Biggest win South Africa 45-24 in 1977, World XV no win

1977 Pretoria **South Africa** 45-24	2 Johannesburg **South Africa** 22-16
1989 *1* Cape Town **South Africa** 20-19	*South Africa won series 2-0*

SOUTH AFRICA v SOUTH AMERICA

Played 8   South Africa won 7, South America won 1, Drawn 0
Highest scores South Africa 50-18 in 1982, South America 21-12 in 1982
Biggest wins South Africa 50-18 in 1982, South America 21-12 in 1982

1980 *1* Johannesburg **South Africa** 24-9	1982 *1* Pretoria **South Africa** 50-18
2 Durban **South Africa** 18-9	2 Bloemfontein **South America** 21-12
South Africa won series 2-0	*Series drawn 1-1*
1980 *1* Montevideo **South Africa** 22-13	1984 *1* Pretoria **South Africa** 32-15
2 Santiago **South Africa** 30-16	2 Cape Town **South Africa** 22-13
South Africa won series 2-0	*South Africa won series 2-0*

SOUTH AFRICA v UNITED STATES

Played 1   South Africa won 1
Highest scores South Africa 38-7 in 1981, United States 7-38 in 1981
Biggest win South Africa 38-7 in 1981, United States no win

1981 Glenville **South Africa** 38-7

SOUTH AFRICA v NEW ZEALAND CAVALIERS

Played 4   South Africa won 3, New Zealand Cavaliers won 1, Drawn 0
Highest scores South Africa 33-18 in 1986, New Zealand Cavaliers 19-18 in 1986
Biggest wins South Africa 33-18 in 1986, New Zealand Cavaliers 19-18 in 1986

1986 *1* Cape Town **South Africa** 21-15	4 Johannesburg **South Africa** 24-10
2 Durban **New Zealand Cavaliers** 19-18	*South Africa won series 3-1*
3 Pretoria **South Africa** 33-18	

SOUTH AFRICA v ARGENTINA

Played 6   South Africa won 6
Highest scores South Africa 52-23 in 1993, Argentina 26-29 in 1993 & 26-46 in 1994
Biggest wins South Africa 46-15 in 1996, Argentina no win

1993 *1* Buenos Aires **South Africa** 29-26	2 Johannesburg **South Africa** 46-26
2 Buenos Aires **South Africa** 52-23	*South Africa won series 2-0*
South Africa won series 2-0	1996 *1* Buenos Aires **South Africa** 46-15
1994 *1* Port Elizabeth **South Africa** 42-22	2 Buenos Aires **South Africa** 44-21
	South Africa win series 2-0

SOUTH AFRICA v WESTERN SAMOA

Played 2   South Africa won 2
Highest scores South Africa 60-8 in 1995, Western Samoa 14-42 in 1995
Biggest win South Africa 60-8 in 1995, Western Samoa no win

1995 Johannesburg **South Africa** 60-8	1995 Johannesburg *WC* **South Africa** 42-14

SOUTH AFRICA v ROMANIA
Played 1   South Africa won 1
Highest score South Africa 21-8 in 1995, Romania 8-21 in 1995
Biggest win South Africa 21-8 in 1995, Romania no win

1995 Cape Town *WC* **South Africa** 21-8

SOUTH AFRICA v CANADA
Played 1   South Africa won 1
Highest scores South Africa 20-0 in 1995, Canada 0-20 in 1995
Biggest win South Africa 20-0 in 1995, Canada no win

1995 Port Elizabeth *WC* **South Africa** 20-0

SOUTH AFRICA v ITALY
Played 2   South Africa won 2
Highest scores South Africa 62-31 in 1997, Italy 31-62 in 1997
Biggest win South Africa 62-31 in 1997, Italy no win

1995 Rome **South Africa** 40-21   1997 Bologna **South Africa** 62-31

SOUTH AFRICA v FIJI
Played 1   South Africa won 1
Highest scores South Africa 43-18 in 1996, Fiji 18-43 in 1996
Biggest win South Africa 43-18 in 1996, Fiji no win

1996 Pretoria **South Africa** 43-18

SOUTH AFRICA v TONGA
Played 1   South Africa won 1
Higest scores South Africa 74-10 in 1997, Tonga 10-74 in 1997
Biggest win South Africa 74-10 in 1997, Tonga no win

1997 Cape Town **South Africa** 74-10

AUSTRALIA v UNITED STATES
Played 5   Australia won 5
Highest scores Australia 67-9 in 1990, United States 12-24 in 1976 & 12-47 in 1987
Biggest win Australia 67-9 in 1990, United States no win

1912 Berkeley **Australia** 12-8   1987 Brisbane *WC* **Australia** 47-12
1976 Los Angeles **Australia** 24-12   1990 Brisbane **Australia** 67-9
1983 Sydney **Australia** 49-3

AUSTRALIA v NEW ZEALAND MAORIS
Played 10   Australia won 4, New Zealand Maoris won 4, Drawn 2
Highest scores Australia 31-6 in 1936, New Zealand Maoris 20-0 in 1946
Biggest wins Australia 31-6 in 1936, New Zealand Maoris 20-0 in 1946

1928 Wellington **New Zealand Maoris** 9-8   1949 *1* Sydney **New Zealand Maoris** 12-3
1931 Palmerston North **Australia** 14-3   *2* Brisbane **Drawn** 8-8
1936 Palmerston North **Australia** 31-6   *3* Sydney **Australia** 18-3
1946 Hamilton **New Zealand Maoris** 20-0   *Series drawn 1-1, with 1 draw*

1958 *1* Brisbane **Australia** 15-14
    2 Sydney **Drawn** 3-3

3 Melbourne **New Zealand Maoris**
   13-6
Series drawn 1-1, with 1 draw

AUSTRALIA v FIJI
Played 16   Australia won 13, Fiji won 2, Drawn 1
Highest scores Australia 66-20 in 1998, Fiji 28-52 in 1985
Biggest wins Australia 66-20 in 1998, Fiji 17-15 in 1952 & 18-16 in 1954

1952 *1* Sydney **Australia** 15-9
    2 Sydney **Fiji** 17-15
    Series drawn 1-1
1954 *1* Brisbane **Australia** 22-19
    2 Sydney **Fiji** 18-16
    Series drawn 1-1
1961 *1* Brisbane **Australia** 24-6
    2 Sydney **Australia** 20-14
    3 Melbourne **Drawn** 3-3
    Australia won series 2-0, with 1 draw
1972 Suva **Australia** 21-19

1976 *1* Sydney **Australia** 22-6
    2 Brisbane **Australia** 21-9
    3 Sydney **Australia** 27-17
    Australia won series 3-0
1980 Suva **Australia** 22-9
1984 Suva **Australia** 16-3
1985 *1* Brisbane **Australia** 52-28
    2 Sydney **Australia** 31-9
    Australia won series 2-0
1998 Sydney **Australia** 66-20

AUSTRALIA v TONGA
Played 4   Australia won 3, Tonga won 1, Drawn 0
Highest scores Australia 74-0 in 1998, Tonga 16-11 in 1973
Biggest wins Australia 74-0 in 1998, Tonga 16-11 in 1973

1973 *1* Sydney **Australia** 30-12
    2 Brisbane **Tonga** 16-11
    Series drawn 1-1

1993 Brisbane **Australia** 52-14
1998 Canberra **Australia** 74-0

AUSTRALIA v JAPAN
Played 3   Australia won 3
Highest scores Australia 50-25 in 1975, Japan 25-50 in 1973
Biggest win Australia 50-25 in 1975, Japan no win

1975 *1* Sydney **Australia** 37-7
    2 Brisbane **Australia** 50-25
    Australia won series 2-0

1987 Sydney *WC* **Australia** 42-23

AUSTRALIA v ARGENTINA
Played 13   Australia won 8, Argentina won 4, Drawn 1
Highest scores Australia 53-7 in 1995, Argentina 27-19 in 1987
Biggest wins Australia 53-7 in 1995, Argentina 18-3 in 1983

1979 *1* Buenos Aires **Argentina** 24-13
    2 Buenos Aires **Australia** 17-12
    Series drawn 1-1
1983 *1* Brisbane **Argentina** 18-3
    2 Sydney **Australia** 29-13
    Series drawn 1-1
1986 *1* Brisbane **Australia** 39-19
    2 Sydney **Australia** 26-0
    Australia won series 2-0
1987 *1* Buenos Aires **Drawn** 19-19

    2 Buenos Aires **Argentina** 27-19
    Argentina won series 1-0, with 1 draw
1991 Llanelli *WC* **Australia** 32-19
1995 *1* Brisbane **Australia** 53-7
    2 Sydney **Australia** 30-13
    Australia won series 2-0
1997 *1* Buenos Aires **Australia** 23-15
    2 Buenos Aires **Argentina** 18-16
    Series drawn 1-1

AUSTRALIA v WESTERN SAMOA

Played 3   Australia won 3
Highest scores Australia 73-3 in 1994, Western Samoa 13-25 in 1998
Biggest win Australia 73-3 in 1994, Western Samoa no win

1991 Pontypool *WC* **Australia** 9-3   1998 Brisbane **Australia** 25-13
1994 Sydney **Australia** 73-3

AUSTRALIA v ITALY

Played 6   Australia won 6
Highest scores Australia 55-6 in 1988, Italy 20-23 in 1994
Biggest win Australia 55-6 in 1988, Italy no win

1983 Rovigo **Australia** 29-7   *2* Melbourne **Australia** 20-7
1986 Brisbane **Australia** 39-18   *Australia won series 2-0*
1988 Rome **Australia** 55-6   1996 Padua **Australia** 40-18
1994 *1* Brisbane **Australia** 23-20

AUSTRALIA v CANADA

Played 5   Australia won 5
Highest scores Australia 74-9 in 1996, Canada 16-43 in 1993
Biggest win Australia 74-9 in 1996, Canada no win

1985 *1* Sydney **Australia** 59-3   1993 Calgary **Australia** 43-16
    2 Brisbane **Australia** 43-15   1995 Port Elizabeth *WC* **Australia** 27-11
    Australia won series 2-0   1996 Brisbane **Australia** 74-9

AUSTRALIA v KOREA

Played 1   Australia won 1
Highest scores Australia 65-18 in 1987, Korea 18-65 in 1987
Biggest win Australia 65-18 in 1987, Korea no win

1987 Brisbane **Australia** 65-18

AUSTRALIA v ROMANIA

Played 1   Australia won 1
highest scores Australia 42-3 in 1995, Romania 3-42 in 1995
Biggest win Australia 42-3 in 1995, Romania no win

1995 Stellenbosch *WC* **Australia** 42-3

INTERNATIONAL HONOURS

WORLD CUP WINNERS
New Zealand once: 1987
Australia once: 1991
South Africa once: 1995

GRAND SLAM WINNERS
England 11 times: 1913, 1914, 1921, 1923, 1924, 1928, 1957, 1980, 1991, 1992, 1995.
Wales 8 times: 1908, 1909, 1911, 1950, 1952, 1971, 1976, 1978. **France** 6 times: 1968, 1977, 1981, 1987, 1997, 1998. **Scotland** 3 times; 1925, 1984, 1990. **Ireland** once: 1948.

TRIPLE CROWN WINNERS
England 21 times: 1883, 1884, 1892, 1913, 1914, 1921, 1923, 1924, 1928, 1934, 1937, 1954, 1957, 1960, 1980, 1991, 1992, 1995, 1996, 1997, 1998. **Wales** 17 times: 1893, 1900, 1902, 1905, 1908, 1909, 1911, 1950, 1952, 1965, 1969, 1971, 1976, 1977, 1978, 1979, 1988.
Scotland 10 times: 1891, 1895, 1901, 1903, 1907, 1925, 1933, 1938, 1984, 1990.
Ireland 6 times: 1894, 1899, 1948, 1949, 1982, 1985.

INTERNATIONAL CHAMPIONSHIP WINNERS

Year	Winner	Year	Winner	Year	Winner	Year	Winner
1883	England	1912	{ England / Ireland	1947	{ Wales / England	1972*	—
1884	England	1913	England	1948	Ireland	1973	Quintuple tie
1885*	—	1914	England	1949	Ireland	1974	Ireland
1886	{ England / Scotland	1920	{ England / Scotland / Wales	1950	Wales	1975	Wales
1887	Scotland			1951	Ireland	1976	Wales
1888*	—			1952	Wales	1977	France
1889*	—	1921	England	1953	England	1978	Wales
1890	{ England / Scotland	1922	Wales	1954	{ England / France / Wales	1979	Wales
1891	Scotland	1923	England			1980	England
1892	England	1924	England	1955	{ France / Wales / Wales	1981	France
1893	Wales	1925	Scotland			1982	Ireland
1894	Ireland	1926	{ Scotland / Ireland	1956	Wales	1983	{ France / Ireland
1895	Scotland	1927	{ Scotland / Ireland	1957	England	1984	Scotland
1896	Ireland			1958	England	1985	Ireland
1897*	—	1928	England	1959	France	1986	{ France / Scotland
1898*	—	1929	Scotland	1960	{ France / England	1987	France
1899	Ireland	1930	England	1961	France	1988	{ Wales / France
1900	Wales	1931	Wales	1962	France	1989	France
1901	Scotland	1932	{ England / Wales / Ireland	1963	England	1990	Scotland
1902	Wales			1964	{ Scotland / Wales	1991	England
1903	Scotland	1933	Scotland	1965	Wales	1992	England
1904	Scotland	1934	England	1966	Wales	1993	France
1905	Wales	1935	Ireland	1967	France	1994**	Wales
1906	{ Ireland / Wales	1936	Wales	1968	France	1995	England
1907	Scotland	1937	England	1969	Wales	1996**	England
1908	Wales	1938	Scotland	1970	{ France / Wales	1997	France
1909	Wales	1939	{ England / Wales / Ireland	1971	Wales	1998	France
1910	England					1999**	Scotland
1911	Wales						

*Matches not completed, for various reasons
** Indicates winners of the Five Nations Trophy (introduced 1993) on points difference

Wales and England have won the title outright 22 times each; Scotland 14 times; France 12 and Ireland 10.

LATIN CUP WINNERS
France twice: 1995, 1997

TRI-NATIONS WINNERS
New Zealand twice: 1996, 1997
South Africa once: 1998

INTERNATIONAL REFEREES 1998-99

Leading Referees

Up to 30 April 1999, in major international matches. These include all matches for which senior members of the International Board have awarded caps, and also all matches played in the World Cup final stages.

15 or more internationals

W D Bevan	Wales	37	A E Freethy	Wales	18
J M Fleming	Scotland	32	R C Quittenton	England	18
C Norling	Wales	25	J R West	Ireland	18
D J Bishop	New Zealand	24	J B Anderson	Scotland	18
E F Morrison	England	24	R Hourquet	France	18
K D Kelleher	Ireland	23	D P D'Arcy	Ireland	17
D G Walters	Wales	23	F Palmade	France	17
M Joseph	Wales	22	S R Hilditch	Ireland	17
R C Williams	Ireland	21	B S Cumberlege	England	16
K V J Fitzgerald	Australia	21	O E Doyle	Ireland	16
F A Howard	England	20	C J Hawke	New Zealand	16
A M Hosie	Scotland	19	D I H Burnett	Ireland	15
Capt M J Dowling	Ireland	18	C H Gadney	England	15

Major International Match Appearances 1997-98

Matches controlled between 1 May 1998 and 30 April 1999

1998

Fj v S	*P J Honiss (New Zealand)
A v E	A Watson (South Africa)
Z v W	J Meuwesen (Namibia)
A v S	A Watson (South Africa)
SA v I	E F Morrison (England)
Arg v F	*S R Walsh (New Zealand)
NZ v E	W J Erickson (Australia)
A v S	B Campsall (England)
SA v I	J Dumé (France)
Arg v F	P J Honiss (New Zealand))
Fj v F	*A Cole (Australia)
NZ v E	P Marshall (Australia)
SA v W	P D O'Brien (New Zealand)
SA v E	C J Hawke (New Zealand)
A v NZ	C Thomas (Wales)
A v SA	C J Hawke (New Zealand)
NZ v SA	E F Morrison (England)
NZ v A	W D Bevan (Wales)
SA v NZ	P Marshall (Australia)
SA v A	J M Fleming (Scotland)
A v NZ	D T M McHugh (Ireland)
A v Fj	*A Lewis (Ireland)
A v Tg	S R Walsh (New Zealand)
A v WS	P J Honiss (New Zealand))
E v H	*R Duhau (France)

I v Gg	R G Davies (Wales)
W v SA	*S Dickinson (Australia)
F v Arg	A Cole (Australia)
F v A	A Watson (South Africa)
S v SA	*C White (England)
I v R	P J Honiss (New Zealand)
W v Arg	A Lewis (Ireland)
E v It	D Mené (France)
E v A	P J Honiss (New Zealand)
I v SA	C Thomas (Wales)
E v SA	P D O'Brien (New Zealand)

1999

I v F	P Marshall (Australia)
S v W	E F Morrison (England)
E v S	D T M McHugh (Ireland)
W v I	*S Young (Australia)
F v W	J M Fleming (Scotland)
I v E	P D O'Brien (New Zealand)
S v It	R G Davies (Wales)
It v W	*R Dickson (Scotland)
E v F	C J Hawke (New Zealand) rep by J M Fleming (Scotland)
S v I	W D Bevan (Wales)
F v S	C Thomas (Wales)
I v It	D Gillet (France)
W v E	A Watson (South Africa)

* Denotes debut in a major international

Replacement Referees in Major Internationals *(up to 30 April 1999)*

F Gardiner (Ireland)	Replaced	**J Tulloch** (Scotland)	I v SA 1912
B Marie (France)	Replaced	**R W Gilliland** (Ireland)	F v W 1965
A R Taylor (N Zealand)	Replaced	**J P Murphy** (N Zealand)	NZ v SA 1965
R F Johnson (England)	Replaced	**R Calmet** (France)	E v W 1970
F Palmade (France)	Replaced	**K A Pattinson** (England)	F v S 1973
J M Fleming (Scotland)	Replaced	**J B Anderson** (Scotland)	Arg v WS *1991
J M Fleming (Scotland)	Replaced	**C J Hawke** (N Zealand)	E v F 1999

* Match in World Cup final stages

Dismissals in Major International Matches *(up to 30 April 1999)*

A E Freethy	sent off	C J Brownlie (NZ)	E v NZ	1925
K D Kelleher	sent off	C E Meads (NZ)	S v NZ	1967
R T Burnett	sent off	M A Burton (E)	A v E	1975
W M Cooney	sent off	J Sovau (Fj)	A v Fj	1976
N R Sanson	sent off	G A D Wheel (W)	W v I	1977
N R Sanson	sent off	W P Duggan (I)	W v I	1977
D I H Burnett	sent off	P Ringer (W)	E v W	1980
C Norling	sent off	J-P Garuet (F)	F v I	1984
K V J Fitzgerald	sent off	H D Richards (W)	NZ v W	*1987
F A Howard	sent off	D Codey (A)	A v W	*1987
K V J Fitzgerald	sent off	M Taga (Fj)	Fj v E	1988
O E Doyle	sent off	A Lorieux (F)	Arg v F	1988
B W Stirling	sent off	T Vonolagi (Fj)	E v Fj	1989
B W Stirling	sent off	N Nadruku (Fj)	E v Fj	1989
F A Howard	sent off	K Moseley (W)	W v F	1990
F A Howard	sent off	A Carminati (F)	S v F	1990
F A Howard	sent off	A Stoop (Nm)	Nm v W	1990
A J Spreadbury	sent off	A Benazzi (F)	A v F	1990
C Norling	sent off	P Gallart (F)	A v F	1990
C J Hawke	sent off	F E Mendez (Arg)	E v Arg	1990
E F Morrison	sent off	C Cojocariu (R)	R v F	1991
J M Fleming	sent off	P L Sporleder (Arg)	WS v Arg	*1991
J M Fleming	sent off	M G Keenan (WS)	WS v Arg	*1991
S R Hilditch	sent off	G Lascubé (F)	F v E	1992
S R Hilditch	sent off	V Moscato (F)	F v E	1992
D J Bishop	sent off	O Roumat (Wld)	NZ v Wld	1992
E F Morrison	sent off	J T Small (SA)	A v SA	1993
I Rogers	sent off	M E Cardinal (C)	C v F	1994
I Rogers	sent off	P Sella (F)	C v F	1994
D Mené	sent off	J D Davies (W)	W v E	1995
S Lander	sent off	F Mahoni (Tg)	F v Tg	*1995
D T M McHugh	sent off	J Dalton (SA)	SA v C	*1995
D T M McHugh	sent off	R G A Snow (C)	SA v C	*1995
D T M McHugh	sent off	G L Rees (C)	SA v C	*1995
J Dumé	sent off	G R Jenkins (W)	SA v W	1995
W J Erickson	sent off	V B Cavubati (Fj)	NZ v Fj	1997
W D Bevan	sent off	A G Venter (SA)	NZ v SA	1997
C Giacomel	sent off	R Travaglini (Arg)	F v Arg	1997
W J Erickson	sent off	D J Grewcock (E)	NZ v E	1998
S R Walsh	sent off	J Sitoa (Tg)	A v Tg	1998
R G Davies	sent off	M Giovanelli (It)	S v It	1999

* Matches in World Cup final stages

WORLD INTERNATIONAL RECORDS

Both match and career records are for official cap matches played by senior members of the International Board, up to 30 April 1999. Figures include Test performances for the Lions (shown in brackets).

MATCH RECORDS

MOST CONSECUTIVE TEST WINS

17 by N Zealand 1965 *SA* 4, 1966 *BI* 1,2,3,4, 1967 *A, E, W, F, S,* 1968 *A* 1,2, *F* 1,2,3, 1969 *W* 1,2

17 by S Africa 1997 *A* 2, *It, F* 1,2, *E, S,* 1998 *I* 1,2, *W* 1, *E* 1, *A* 1, *NZ* 1,2, *A* 2, *W* 2, *S, I* 3

MOST CONSECUTIVE TESTS WITHOUT DEFEAT

P	W	D	Period
23 by NZ	22	1	1987–90
17 by NZ	15	2	1961–64
17 by NZ	17	0	1965–69
17 by SA	17	0	1997–98

MOST POINTS IN A MATCH
by the team

Pts	Opps	Venue	Year
145 by NZ	J	Bloemfontein	1995
110 by E	H	Huddersfield	1998
102 by W	Pt	Lisbon	1994
96 by SA	W	Pretoria	1998
93 by NZ	Arg	Wellington	1997
89 by S	Iv	Rustenburg	1995

by a player

45 by S D Culhane, New Zealand v Japan at Bloemfontein — 1995

44 by A G Hastings, Scotland v Ivory Coast at Rustenburg — 1995

39 by M Burke, Australia v Canada at Brisbane — 1996

33 by C J Spencer, New Zealand v Argentina at Wellington — 1997

33 by A P Mehrtens, New Zealand v Ireland at Dublin — 1997

31 by A G Hastings, Scotland v Tonga at Pretoria — 1995

31 by P C Montgomery, S Africa v Wales at Pretoria — 1998

MOST TRIES IN A MATCH
by the team

Tries	Opps	Venue	Year
21 by NZ	J	Bloemfontein	1995
16 by W	Pt	Lisbon	1994
16 by E	H	Huddersfield	1998

15 by SA	W	Pretoria	1998
14 by NZ	Arg	Wellington	1997

by a player

6 by M C G Ellis, New Zealand v Japan at Bloemfontein — 1995

5 by G C Lindsay, Scotland v Wales at Raeburn Place — 1887

5 by D Lambert, England v France at Richmond — 1907

5 by R Underwood, England v Fiji at Twickenham — 1989

5 by J W Wilson, New Zealand v Fiji at Albany — 1997

MOST CONVERSIONS IN A MATCH
by the team

Cons	Opps	Venue	Year
20 by NZ	J	Bloemfontein	1995
15 by E	H	Huddersfield	1998
11 by W	Pt	Lisbon	1994
10 by NZ	Fj	Christchurch	1987
10 by NZ	Arg	Wellington	1997
10 by I	Gg	Dublin	1998

by a player

20 by S D Culhane, New Zealand v Japan at Bloemfontein — 1995

15 by P J Grayson, England v Holland at Huddersfield — 1998

11 by N R Jenkins, Wales v Portugal at Lisbon — 1994

10 by G J Fox, New Zealand v Fiji at Christchurch — 1987

10 by C J Spencer, New Zealand v Argentina at Wellington — 1997

10 by E P Elwood, Ireland v Georgia at Dublin — 1998

MOST PENALTY GOALS IN A MATCH
by the team

Penalties	Opps	Venue	Year
8 by W	C	Cardiff	1993
8 by S	Tg	Pretoria	1995
8 by F	I	Durban	1995
8 by I	It	Dublin	1997

by a player

8 by N R Jenkins, Wales v Canada at Cardiff — 1993

8 by A G Hastings, Scotland v
Tonga at Pretoria 1995
8 by T Lacroix, France v Ireland at
Durban 1995
8 by P A Burke, Ireland v Italy at
Dublin 1997

MOST DROPPED GOALS IN A MATCH

by the team

Drops	Opps	Venue	Year
3 by F	I	Paris	1960
3 by A	E	Twickenham	1967
3 by S	I	Murrayfield	1973
3 by SA	SAm	Durban	1980
3 by SA	I	Durban	1981
3 by A	I	Dublin	1984
3 by F	E	Twickenham	1985
3 by A	Fj	Brisbane	1985
3 by F	NZ	Christchurch	1986
3 by NZ	F	Christchurch	1986
3 by F	A	Sydney	1990
3 by F	S	Paris	1991
3 by F	NZ	Christchurch	1994

by a player

3 by P Albaladejo, France v
Ireland at Paris 1960
3 by P F Hawthorne, Australia v
England at Twickenham 1967
3 by H E Botha, South Africa v
S America at Durban 1980
3 by H E Botha, South Africa v
Ireland at Durban 1981
3 by J-P Lescarboura, France v
England at Twickenham 1985
3 by J-P Lescarboura, France v
New Zealand at Christchurch 1986
3 by D Camberabero, France v
Australia at Sydney 1990

CAREER RECORDS

MOST CAPPED PLAYERS

Caps	Player	Career
111	P Sella (France)	1982–95
101	D I Campese (Australia)	1982–96
93	S Blanco (France)	1980–91
92	S B T Fitzpatrick (New Zealand)	1986–97
91 (6)	R Underwood (England/Lions)	1984–96
81(12)	C M H Gibson (Ireland/Lions)	1964–79
80(17)	W J McBride (Ireland/Lions)	1962–75
79 (7)	I C Evans (Wales/Lions)	1987–98
76 (5)	C R Andrew (England/Lions)	1985–97
76	I D Jones (New Zealand)	1990–98
74 (3)	J Leonard (England/Lions)	1990–99
73 (1)	W D C Carling (England/Lions)	1988–97
72	M P Lynagh (Australia)	1984–95

MOST CONSECUTIVE TESTS

Tests	Player	Span
63	S B T Fitzpatrick (New Zealand)	1986–95
53	G O Edwards (Wales)	1967–78
52	W J McBride (Ireland)	1964–75
49	A B Carmichael (Scotland)	1967–78
49	P A Orr (Ireland)	1976–86

MOST TESTS AS CAPTAIN

Tests	Captain	Span
59	W D C Carling (England)	1988–96
51	S B T Fitzpatrick (New Zealand)	1992–97
36	N C Farr-Jones (Australia)	1988–92
34	J-P Rives (France)	1978–84

The boot is on the other foot. Welsh fly-half Neil Jenkins recovered from a poor season the year before to help resurrect his country's fortunes. Jenkins now trails only Australia's Michael Lynagh as the highest points-scorer in Test history.

34	P Saint-André (France)	1994-97
33	J A Eales (Australia)	1991-98
33	G H Teichmann (South Africa)	1996-98
30	W J Whineray (New Zealand)	1958-65

MOST TESTS IN INDIVIDUAL POSITIONS

Full-back S Blanco (France)	81	1980-91
Wing R Underwood (England/Lions)	91 (6)	1984-96

Centre P Sella (France)		104	1982–95
Fly-half C R Andrew (England/Lions)		75 (5)	1985–97
Scrum-half G O Edwards (Wales/Lions)		63(10)	1967–78
Prop J Leonard (England/Lions)		74 (3)	1990–99
Hooker S B T Fitzpatrick (New Zealand)		92	1986–97
Lock W J McBride (Ireland/Lions)		80(17)	1962–75
Flanker ⌠ J F Slattery (Ireland/Lions)		65 (4)	1970–84
⌡ P J Winterbottom (England/Lions)		65 (7)	1982–93
No 8 D Richards (England/Lions)		53*(6)	1986–96

* excludes an appearance as a temporary replacement

MOST POINTS IN TESTS

Points	Player	Tests	Career
911	M P Lynagh (Australia)	72	1984–95
767 (41)	N R Jenkins (Wales/Lions)	67(3)	1991–99
733 (66)	A G Hastings (Scotland/Lions)	67(6)	1986–95
645	G J Fox (New Zealand)	46	1985–93
428	A P Mehrtens (New Zealand)	29	1995–98

MOST TRIES IN TESTS

Tries	Player	Tests	Career
64	D I Campese (Australia)	101	1982–96
50(1)	R Underwood (England/Lions)	91(6)	1984–96
38	S Blanco (France)	93	1980–91
35	J J Kirwan (N Zealand)	63	1984–94
34(1)	I C Evans (Wales/Lions)	79(7)	1987–98

MOST CONVERSIONS IN TESTS

Cons	Player	Tests	Career
140	M P Lynagh (Australia)	72	1984–95
118	G J Fox (N Zealand)	46	1985–93
94(1)	N R Jenkins (Wales/Lions)	67(3)	1991–99
87(1)	A G Hastings (Scotland/Lions)	67(6)	1986–95
79	A P Mehrtens (New Zealand)	29	1995–98
68	A P Mehrtens (N Zealand)	22	1995–97
50	H E Botha (S Africa)	28	1980–92

MOST PENALTY GOALS IN TESTS

Penalties	Player	Tests	Career
177	M P Lynagh (Australia)	72	1984–95
177(13)	N R Jenkins (Wales/Lions)	67(3)	1991–99
160(20)	A G Hastings (Scotland/Lions)	67(6)	1986–95
128	G J Fox (N Zealand)	46	1985–93
89	T Lacroix (France)	38	1989–97
87 (1)	C R Andrew (England/Lions)	76(5)	1985–97

MOST DROPPED GOALS IN TESTS

Drops	Player	Tests	Career
23(2)	C R Andrew (England/Lions)	76(5)	1985–97
18	H E Botha (S Africa)	28	1980–92
15	J-P Lescarboura (France)	28	1982–90
13	J Davies (Wales)	32	1985–97
12	P Albaladejo (France)	30	1954–64
12(0)	J Y Rutherford (Scotland/Lions)	43(1)	1979–87

INTERNATIONAL CHAMPIONSHIP RECORDS

Record	Detail		Set
Most points in season	146 by England	in four matches	1998
Most tries in season	21 by Wales	in four matches	1910
Highest Score	60 by England	60-26 v Wales	1998
Biggest win	51 by France	51-0 v Wales	1998
Most appearances	56 for Ireland	C M H Gibson	1964–79
Most points in matches	288 for Scotland	A G Hastings	1986–95
Most points in season	67 for England	J M Webb	1992
Most points in match	24 for France	S Viars	v Ireland, 1992
	24 for England	C R Andrew	v Scotland, 1995
	24 for France	C Lamaison	v Scotland, 1997
Most tries in matches	24 for Scotland	I S Smith	1924–1933
Most tries in season	8 for England	C N Lowe	1914
	8 for Scotland	I S Smith	1925
Tries in all four games	For England	H C Catcheside	1924
	For Scotland	A C Wallace	1925
	For France	P Estève	1983
	For France	P Sella	1986
	For Scotland	G P J Townsend	1999
Most tries in match	5 for Scotland	G C Lindsay	v Wales, 1887
Most cons in matches	32 for Wales	J Bancroft	1909–14
Most cons in season	14 for England	P J Grayson	1998
Most cons in match	8 for Wales	J Bancroft	v France, 1910
Most pens in matches	77 for Scotland	A G Hastings	1986–95
Most pens in season	18 for England	S D Hodgkinson	1991
Most pens in match	7 for England	S D Hodgkinson	v Wales, 1991
	7 for England	C R Andrew	v Scotland, 1995
	7 for England	J P Wilkinson	v France, 1999
Most drops in matches	9 for France	J-P Lescarboura	1982–88
	9 for England	C R Andrew	1985–97
Most drops in season	5 for France	G Camberabero	1967
Drops in all four games	For France	J-P Lescarboura	1984
Most drops in match	3 for France	P Albaladejo	v Ireland, 1960
	3 for France	J-P Lescarboura	v England, 1985

PARTNERSHIP RECORDS

Position	Holders	Detail	Span
Centre threequarters	W D C Carling & J C Guscott	45(1) for England/ Lions	1989–96
Half-backs	M P Lynagh & N C Farr-Jones	47 for Australia	1985–92
Front row	A J Daly, P N Kearns & E J A McKenzie	37 for Australia	1990–95
Second row	I D Jones & R M Brooke	46 for N Zealand	1992–98
Back row	J Matheu, G Basquet & J Prat	22 for France	1945–51

OTHER MAJOR TEST RECORDS

Record	Holder	Detail
Fastest to 100 points	A P Mehrtens	in his 5th Test for N Zealand
	S D Culhane	in his 5th Test for N Zealand
	C J Spencer	in his 5th Test for N Zealand
Fastest to ten tries	M C G Ellis	in his 6th Test for N Zealand

MAJOR TOUR RECORDS

Record	Detail	Year	Place
Most team points	976 by NZ	1905–06	Europe & NAm
Most team tries	243 by NZ	1905–06	Europe & NAm
Biggest win	117-6 by NZ	1974 v S Australia	Adelaide
Most individual points	246 by W J Wallace	1905–06 for NZ	Europe & NAm
Most individual tries	44 by J Hunter	1905–06 for NZ	Europe & NAm
Most points in match	43 by R M Deans	1984 v S Australia for NZ	Adelaide
Most tries in match	8 by T R Heeps	1962 v Northern NSW for NZ	Quirindi

OTHER INTERNATIONAL MATCH RECORDS

Up to 15 May 1999. These are included for comparison and cover performances since 1971 by teams and players in Test matches for nations which are not senior members of the International Board.

Most points in a match
By a team
164 Hong Kong v Singapore 1994 Kuala Lumpar
By a player
50 A Billington Hong Kong v Singapore 1994 Kuala Lumpar

Most tries in a match
By a team
26 Hong Kong v Singapore 1994 Kuala Lumpar
By a player
10 A Billington Hong Kong v Singapore 1994 Kuala Lumpar

Most conversions in a match
By a team
17 Hong Kong v Singapore 1994 Kuala Lumpar
By a player
17 J McKee Hong Kong v Singapore 1994 Kuala Lumpar

Most penalty goals in a match
By a team
9 Japan v Tonga 1999 Tokyo
By a player
9 K Hirose Japan v Tonga 1999 Tokyo

Most dropped goals in a match
By a team
3 Argentina v SA Gazelles 1971 Pretoria
3 Argentina v Australia 1979 Buenos Aires
3 Argentina v New Zealand 1985 Buenos Aires
3 Romania v France 1995 Bucharest

By a player
3 T A Harris-Smith Argentina v SA Gazelles 1971
3 H Porta Argentina v Australia 1979
3 H Porta Argentina v New Zealand 1985
3 N Nichitean Romania v France 1995

Most points in matches
687 D Dominguez (Italy)
530 H Porta (Argentina/S America)
483 S Bettarello (Italy)

Most tries in matches
25 Marcello Cuttitta (Italy)

Most conversions in matches
95 D Dominguez (Italy)
54 H Porta (Argentina/S America)
46 S Bettarello (Italy)

Most penalty goals in matches
144 D Dominguez (Italy)
109 H Porta (Argentina/S America)
104 S Bettarello (Italy)

Most dropped goals in matches
25 H Porta (Argentina/S America)
17 S Bettarello (Italy)

Most matches as captain
43 H Porta (Argentina/S America)

Biggest win on a major tour
128-0 W Samoa v Marlborough (New Zealand) 1993 Blenheim

BAABAAS ENJOY UNBEATEN SEASON

THE BARBARIANS 1998-99
Geoff Windsor-Lewis

In a highly successful season the BaaBaas won all their matches, beat league champions Leicester on two occasions and initiated the Scottish Amicable Trophy.

Combined Services provided the first opposition of the season in the Remembrance match at Portsmouth, a match in which Gareth Wyatt, the Pontypridd wing, scored four tries, showing all his elusive qualities. Pool-Jones, over from Stade Français, Tuamalolo, the Tonga fly-half, and Trevor Walsh all had their moments and the crowd was treated to some spectacular running rugby.

Leicester at Christmas proved that not everything has changed in the rugby world and a marvellous crowd of nearly 15,000 gave their support. Scott Hastings gave an inspired team talk, the team stuck to the task and, coming back from an early setback, managed a fine victory. Scully and Chalmers directed play with all their experience and a formidable back row of Giovanelli, Eric Miller and Jan Machacek was too much for the home side.

In January the club took part in the Argentine Centenary Sevens at Mar del Plata. The BaaBaas were the only club side invited, bar the local hosts, and the competition was as tough as expected with the BaaBaas group consisting of Argentina, FIRA and Brazil. In the quarter-finals they drew FIRA again but lost the match.

The BaaBaas then enjoyed a runaway victory at Northampton against East Midlands with a final score of 51-19. The higher pace and all-round ability of the visitors, well led by Rob Wainwright, gave them an opportunity to show their attacking talents. Harvey Thorneycroft scored two tries and Gregori Kacala was the outstanding forward.

In the final match of the season Premiership Champions Leicester found a star-studded Barbarian team too much for them. Captained by Francois Pienaar, the BaaBaas scored nine tries, in a match of many memorable movements.

The club were pleased to initiate the Scottish Amicable Trophy match – their sponsors have now generously given £108,000 to the four Home Unions' Youth Charitable Trusts, and the relationship grows every year.

RESULTS 1998-99 (up to 23 May 1999)

Played 4 Won 4 Lost 0 Points for 195 (16G 1PG 16T) **Points against** 96 (9G 1PG 6T)

10 Nov 1998	**Beat Combined Services** at Portsmouth (The Remembrance Match) 51 (3G 6T) to 20 (1G 1PG 2T)
29 Dec	**Beat Leicester Tigers** at Welford Road 38 (5G 1PG) to 24 (2G 2T)
8 and 9 Jan 1999	**Quarter-finalists** Argentine Centenary Sevens at Mar del Plata
3 March	**Beat East Midlands** at Franklins Gardens 51 (3G 6T) to 19 (2G 1T)
23 May	**Beat Leicester Tigers** at Twickenham (The Scottish Amicable Trophy Match) 55 (5G 4T) to 33 (4G 1T)

PLAYERS 1998/1999 (up to 23 May 1999)

Abbreviations: *CS* – Combined Services; *L* – Leicester; *EM* – East Midlands; *SAT* – Scottish Amicable Trophy Match v. Leicester at Twickenham; *ACS* – Argentina Centenary Sevens (Squad and results listed separately); (R) = Replacement; * – New Barbarian

Full-backs: J Thomas (Cardiff & Wales) *CS*; * L Criscuolo (Coventry & Argentina *L*; * JSD Moffatt (Loughborough University & Rotheram *EM*; A Joubert (Natal & South Africa) *SAT*; * G Osborne (North Harbour & New Zealand) *SAT*(R).

Wings: * G Wyatt (Pontypridd) *CS*; H Thorneycroft (Northampton) *CS, L, EM*; D Stark (Glasgow & Scotland) *L*; * L Scrase (Wasps) *EM*; * P Davies (Henley) *L*(R), *EM*(R), *ACS*; * P Bernat-Salles (Biarritz & France) *SAT*; * J Small (Western Province & South Africa) *SAT*.

Centres: * T Walsh (Henley) *CS, EM*; *W Ruane (Galwegians) *CS*; * W Little (North Harbour & New Zealand) *SAT*; L Arbizu (Brive & Argentina) *SAT*(R); S Hastings (Edinburgh & Scotland) *L*; * L Martin (Begles & Bordeaux) *L*; * L Colceriu (Edinburgh Academicals & Romania) *EM*; * F Bunce (North Harbour & New Zealand) *SAT*; * C Stoica (Narbonne & Italy) *SAT*(R).

Fly-halves: S Tuamalolo (Ebbw Vale & Tonga) *CS*; * T Jensen (Rosslyn Park) *CS*(R); C Chalmers (Glasgow & Scotland) *L*; * T Castaignede (Castres & France) *SAT*; L Criscuolo (Coventry & Argentina) *EM*.

Scrum-halves: D Scully (Rotherham) *CS, L*; * I Sanders (Gloucester) *CS*(R); * M Friday (Wasps) *EM*; G Peacocke (Cambridge University *EM*(R), *ACS*; A Pichot (Richmond & Argentina) *SAT*.

Forwards: * E Byrne (St Mary's College) *CS*; * S Byrne (Blackrock) *CS*; J Phillips (Northampton) *CS*; * K Whitley (Coventry & Canada) *CS, EM*; * P Williams (Cardiff) *CS, EM, ACS*; R Pool-Jones (Stade Français & England) *CS*; * M Venner (Henley) *CS, L*(R); * R Baxter (Exeter) *CS*(R); W Bullock (Coventry) *CS, EM*(R); J Duffy (Galwegians) *CS*(R); M Cuttitta (Calvisano & Italy) *L*; * J Evans (Bristol) *L*; T Murphy (Harlequins) *L*(R), *EM*(R); * J Mallett (Bath) *L*; * J Chandler (Northampton) *L*; * S Grimes (Glasgow & Scotland) *L*; * E Miller (Tenerure College & Ireland) *L*; J Machacek (Sale & Czech Republic) *L*; * M Giovanelli (Narbonne & Italy) *L, SAT*; * M Foulds (Cambridge University) *EM*; * K McKenzie (Glasgow University & Scotland) *EM*; S Cronk (Newport) *EM*; * M McVie (Watsonians) *EM*; * D Craddock (Manchester) *EM*(R); R Wainwright (Watsonians & Scotland) *EM*; * G Kacala (Cardiff & Poland) *EM*; * T Burgon (Manchester) *EM*(R); JP Du Randt (Free State & South Africa) *SAT*; * R Ibanez (Perpignan & France) *SAT*; * M Scelzo (Hindu & Argentina) *SAT*; * A Benazzi (Agen & France) *SAT*; J Langford (ACT & Australia) *SAT*; * Z Brooke (Harlequins & New Zealand) *SAT*; * F Pienaar (Saracens, Transvaal & South Africa) *SAT*; D Hilton (Bath & Scotland) *SAT*(R); D Weir (Newcastle & Scotland) *SAT*(R); * W Fyvie (Natal & South Africa) *SAT*(R).

Argentina Centenary Sevens Squad: P Davies (Henley); * C Stephens (Leeds); S Foale (Northampton); P Williams (Cardiff); * G Peacocke (Cambridge University); M Denny (Cambridge University); * H Whitford (Cambridge University); * P Jorgensen (Australia); S Nawavu (Fiji); * V Satala (Fiji).

HONOURS FOR CORK, SWANSEA AND CAMBRIDGE

UNIVERSITY RUGBY 1998-99

European Students Cup

30 January, 1999, Donnybrook, Dublin
University College Cork 14 (2PG 1DG 1T)
Grenoble University 10 (2T)

January 30th will go down as All-Ireland day when the history of European Rugby competitions is written. For apart from Ulster beating Colomiers to secure the European Cup, UC Cork won the handsome glass trophy that is the prize for the corresponding Universities' tournament.

Two tries in the opening quarter of the match seemed to set up a victory for the French students. Rénaud Cartillier went over from a tapped penalty in the eighth minute and his second-row partner David Dussert ploughed over from a lineout to make it 10-0 a dozen minutes later. But the tenacity of the Irish was never better illustrated than in this match. Colin Healy kicked a penalty on the half-hour and, with their lineout play improving, Niall Kenneally brought Cork back to 8-10 in the ninth minute of the second half with a try. Aidan O'Shea edged his side ahead with a 60th-minute drop goal and Brian O'Mahony's penalty five minutes from time sealed victory on the day Irish rugby will remember for years.

UC Cork: C Healy; N Kenneally, P Barry, A O'Shea (*capt*), D Holt; B O'Mahony, P Stringer, A McSweeney, G Flannery, M Ross, J Fitzgerald, M O'Driscoll, B Cahill, D Lane, T Cahill *Substitutions:* A Hickie for B Cahill (44 mins); L Twomey for Kenneally (58 mins)
Scorers *Try:* Kenneally *Penalty Goals:* Healy, O'Mahony *Dropped Goal:* O'Shea
Grenoble University: F Boyet; Y Largyet, J Mazille, S Hauw, S Beyret; T Bonnefoy, A Maldera; G Chatel, T Algret, S Viac, D Dussert, R Cartillier, J-E Bahoken, F Degalbert, G Olliver *Substitutions:* R Gerbier for Bahoken (66 mins); R Bernachon for Hauw (66 mins)
Scorers *Tries:* Cartillier, Dussert
Referee B Campsall (England)
Previous winner: 1998 Paul Sabatier (Toulouse) University

BUSA Trophy

24 March 1999, Twickenham
University of Wales Swansea 35 (3G 3PG 1T)
St Mary's University College 15 (1G 1PG 1T)

Swansea retained their 1998 British Universities' title with style, despite trailing by three points at the interval. Their second-half display brought the neutrals among the 7,500 spectators to their feet and the try scored by James Baker in injury-time was one of the best seen in a University final for many years.

The Welsh side fielded nine of their previous season's successful XV and, slightly against the run of play, opened the scoring after 22 minutes when skipper Ben Martin finished off a move initiated by Ben Davies and Baker. A try by Dominic Little and a Simon Amor penalty made it 8-5 to the Englishmen before half-time.

Ed Lewsey, the former Watford GS pupil whose brother Josh played for England in 1998, took the game by the scruff of the neck in the second half and, with his partner Cerith Rees, had a hand in three tries. Rees and Lewsey both touched down to take Swansea clear and in stoppage time at the end of the match the scrum-half caught St Mary's napping when he launched a counter attack from his own 22. After breaching the defence he unleashed the speedy Baker who sprinted 60 metres for a spectacular score.

University of Wales Swansea: D Kendrick; B Davies, O Jones, J Baker, A Cox; C Rees, E Lewsey; N Hennessy, S James, J Meredith, P Langley, T Radbourne, B Martin (*capt*), G Roberts, R Griffiths
Scorers *Tries:* Martin, Rees, Lewsey, Baker *Conversions:* Rees (3) *Penalty Goals:* Rees (3)
St Mary's University College: C Trace; S Price, J Stebbings, K Mullen, B Shelbourne; S Amor, M Percival; J Smith, R McGee, D Little, J Pettemerides, J Winterbottom, T Booth (*capt*), R Salisbury, D Blaney *Substitutions:* R Carr for Salisbury (temp 3-7 mins) and for Booth (78 mins); M Jackson for Little (78 mins)
Scorers *Tries:* Little, penalty try *Conversion:* Amor *Penalty Goal:* Amor
Referee S Savage (Warwickshire)
Previous winners: Loughborough have won the title 25 times; Swansea nine; Durham eight; Liverpool seven; Bristol five; Cardiff and Manchester four; Bangor, Brunel and UWIST twice; Aberystwyth, Birmingham, Leeds, Newcastle, Northumbria and UWIC once each.

The Bowring Bowl

8 December 1998, Twickenham
Cambridge University 16 (2PG 2T)
Oxford University 12 (1G 1T)

Cambridge won the Bowring Bowl for the fifth year running, equalling the series record set by their predecessors of 1972-76 and 1980-84. Their Auckland fly-half Paul Moran was the architect of the victory. His tactical nous was invaluable to the Light Blues and in a game in which there was little to choose between two well-matched packs, his kicking out of the hand time and again repelled Oxford's brave efforts to attack.

On a sodden pitch Oxford took an early lead when Nick Booth capitalised on a Cambridge handling error to score a try. Mark Denney squared the match five minutes before half-time when he turned

The Innes brothers celebrate Cambridge's record-equalling fifth successive victory over Oxford in the Varsity match at Twickenham in December 1998.

Oxford's defence inside out for a lovely solo score. Early in the second half Stefan Rodgers, son of Tony the Cambridge coach and guru, put them ahead for the first time with a battling run to the tryline and two Moran penalties gave Cambridge an invaluable 11-point cushion before Nick Humphries sneaked over on the blind side for a try that Booth converted. That score gave Oxford hope with 10 minutes to go, but Cambridge refused to slacken their stranglehold on an undistinguished match and, in the end, the margin of victory was an accurate reflection of the afternoon's events.

'They were clever in their play while we simply made too many mistakes,' summed up David Kelaher, Oxford's captain. For Cambridge, a beaming Tony Rodgers said afterwards, 'This was a very satisfying win given that we were underdogs.'

Cambridge University: R J Morrow; A R Bidwell, M P Robinson,
M C A Denney, S J Lippiett; P D Moran, G M Peacocke; M T Foulds *(capt)*,
S K Rodgers, C P Hart, H J Innes, A R Innes, O J Slack, H M Whitford,
M W D Haslett *Substitution:* T H Mouton for Slack (temp 6-10 mins)
Scorers *Tries:* Denney, Rodgers *Penalty Goals:* Moran (2)
Oxford University: R J Woodfine; N J Booth, N W Ashley, K D Shuman,
N C Humphries; R M Governey, S J Barry; A S Collins, P B O'Connor,
A Reuben, A J Roberts, M B Challender, N Celliers, T Miuchi, D J Kelaher *(capt)*
Substitution: R Heaslip for Kelaher (temp 46-75 mins)
Scorers *Tries:* Booth, Humphries *Conversion:* Booth
Referee E F Morrison (England)

VARSITY MATCH RESULTS

117 Matches played   Oxford 48 wins   Cambridge 56 wins   13 Draws

*Match played at Oxford 1871-72; Cambridge 1872-73; The Oval 1873-74 to 1879-80; Blackheath 1880-81 to 1886-87; Queen's Club 1887-88 to 1920-21; then Twickenham. *At this date no match could be won unless a goal was scored.* † Penalty try.*

1871-72	**Oxford**	1G 1T to 0
1872-73	**Cambridge**	1G 2T to 0
1873-74	Drawn	1T each
1874-75*	Drawn	Oxford 2T to 0
1875-76	**Oxford**	1T to 0
1876-77	**Cambridge**	1G 2T to 0
1877-78	**Oxford**	2T to 0
1878-79	Drawn	No score
1879-80	**Cambridge**	1G 1DG to 1DG
1880-81	Drawn	1T each
1881-82	**Oxford**	2G 1T to 1G
1882-83	**Oxford**	1T to 0
1883-84	**Oxford**	3G 4T to 1G
1884-85	**Oxford**	3G 1T to 1T
1885-86	**Cambridge**	2T to 0
1886-87	**Cambridge**	3T to 0
1887-88	**Cambridge**	1DG 2T to 0
1888-89	**Cambridge**	1G 2T to 0
1889-90	**Oxford**	1G 1T to 0
1890-91	Drawn	1G each
1891-92	**Cambridge**	2T to 0
1892-93	Drawn	No score
1893-94	**Oxford**	1T to 0
1894-95	Drawn	1G each
1895-96	**Cambridge**	1G to 0
1896-97	**Oxford**	1G 1DG to 1G 1T
1897-98	**Oxford**	2T to 0
1898-99	**Cambridge**	1G 2T to 0
1899-1900	**Cambridge**	2G 4T to 0
1900-01	**Oxford**	2G to 1G 1T
1901-02	**Oxford**	1G 1T to 0
1902-03	Drawn	1G 1T each
1903-04	**Oxford**	3G 1T to 2G 1T
1904-05	**Cambridge**	3G to 2G
1905-06	**Cambridge**	3G (15) to 2G 1T (13)
1906-07	**Oxford**	4T (12) to 1G 1T (8)
1907-08	**Oxford**	1G 4T (17) to 0
1908-09	Drawn	1G (5) each
1909-10	**Oxford**	4G 5T (35) to 1T (3)
1910-11	**Oxford**	4G 1T (23) to 3G 1T (18)
1911-12	**Oxford**	2G 3T (19) to 0
1912-13	**Cambridge**	2G (10) to 1T (3)
1913-14	**Cambridge**	1DG 3T (13) to 1T (3)
1914-18	*No matches*	
1919-20	**Cambridge**	1PG 1DG (7) to 1G (5)
1920-21	**Cambridge**	1G 4T (17) to 1G 3T (14)
1921-22	**Oxford**	1G 2T (11) to 1G (5)
1922-23	**Cambridge**	3G 2T (21) to 1G 1T (8)
1923-24	**Oxford**	3G 2T (21) to 1G 1PG 2T (14)
1924-25	**Oxford**	1G 2T (11) to 2T (6)
1925-26	**Cambridge**	3G 6T (33) to 1T (3)
1926-27	**Cambridge**	3G 5T (30) to 1G (5)
1927-28	**Cambridge**	2G 2PG 2T (22) to 1G 3T (14)
1928-29	**Cambridge**	1G 3T (14) to 1PG 1DG 1T (10)
1929-30	**Oxford**	1G 1DG (9) to 0
1930-31	Drawn	Oxford 1PG (3) Cambridge 1T (3)
1931-32	**Oxford**	1DG 2T (10) to 1T (3)
1932-33	**Oxford**	1G 1T (8) to 1T (3)
1933-34	**Oxford**	1G (5) to 1T (3)
1934-35	**Cambridge**	2G 1PG 1DG 4T (29) to 1DG (4)
1935-36	Drawn	No score
1936-37	**Cambridge**	2T (6) to 1G (5)
1937-38	**Oxford**	1G 4T (17) to 1DG (4)
1938-39	**Cambridge**	1G 1PG (8) to 2PG (6)
1939-45	*War-time series*	
1945-46	**Cambridge**	1G 2T (11) to 1G 1PG (8)
1946-47	**Oxford**	1G 1DG 2T (15) to 1G (5)
1947-48	**Cambridge**	2PG (6) to 0
1948-49	**Oxford**	1G 1DG 2T (14) to 1G 1PG (8)
1949-50	**Oxford**	1T (3) to 0
1950-51	**Oxford**	1G 1PG (8) to 0
1951-52	**Oxford**	2G 1T (13) to 0
1952-53	**Cambridge**	1PG 1T (6) to 1G (5)
1953-54	Drawn	Oxford 1PG 1T (6) Cambridge 2PG (6)
1954-55	**Cambridge**	1PG (3) to 0
1955-56	**Oxford**	1PG 2T (9) to 1G (5)
1956-57	**Cambridge**	1G 1PG 1DG 1T (14) to 2PG 1T (9)
1957-58	**Oxford**	1T (3) to 0
1958-59	**Cambridge**	1G 1PG 3T (17) to 1PG 1T (6)
1959-60	**Oxford**	3PG (9) to 1PG (3)
1960-61	**Cambridge**	2G 1T (13) to 0
1961-62	**Cambridge**	1DG 2T (9) to 1DG (3)
1962-63	**Cambridge**	1G 1PG 1DG 1T (14) to 0
1963-64	**Cambridge**	2G 1PG 2T (19) to 1G 1PG 1DG (11)
1964-65	**Oxford**	2G 1PG 2T (19) to 1PG 1GM (6)
1965-66	Drawn	1G (5) each
1966-67	**Oxford**	1G 1T (8) to 1DG 1T (6)
1967-68	**Cambridge**	1T 1PG (6) to 0
1968-69	**Cambridge**	1T 1PG 1DG (9) to 2T (6)
1969-70	**Oxford**	3PG (9) to 2PG (6)
1970-71	**Oxford**	1G 1DG 2T (14) to 1PG (3)
1971-72	**Oxford**	3PG 3T (21) to 1PG (3)
1972-73	**Cambridge**	1G 1PG 1DG 1T (16) to 2PG (6)
1973-74	**Cambridge**	1PG 1DG 2T (14) to 1G 2PG (12)
1974-75	**Cambridge**	1G 2PG 1T (16) to 5PG (15)
1975-76	**Cambridge**	2G 5PG 1DG 1T (34) to 3PG 1DG (12)
1976-77	**Cambridge**	1G 3PG (15) to 0
1977-78	**Oxford**	4PG 1T (16) to 2PG 1T (10)
1978-79	**Cambridge**	2G 3PG 1T (25) to 1PG 1T (7)
1979-80	**Oxford**	2PG 1DG (9) to 1PG (3)
1980-81	**Cambridge**	3PG 1T (13) to 3PG (9)
1981-82	**Cambridge**	3PG (9) to 2PG (6)
1982-83	**Cambridge**	3PG 1DG 2T (20) to 1G 1PG 1T (13)
1983-84	**Cambridge**	4PG 2T (20) to 3PG (9)
1984-85	**Cambridge**	4G 3T (32) to 2PG (6)
1985-86	**Oxford**	1PG 1T (7) to 2PG (6)
1986-87	**Oxford**	3PG 2DG (15) to 1PG 1DG 1T (10)
1987-88	**Cambridge**	1DG 3T (15) to 2PG 1T (10)
1988-89	**Oxford**	2G 1DG 3T (27) to 1DG 1T (7)
1989-90	**Cambridge**	2G 2PG 1T (22) to 1G 1PG 1T (13)
1990-91	**Oxford**	2G 2PG 1DG (21) to 1G 2PG (12)
1991-92	**Cambridge**	2PG 1DG 2T (17) to 1DG 2T (11)
1992-93	**Cambridge**	1G 2PG 2DG (19) to 1PG 1DG 1T (11)
1993-94	**Oxford**	3PG 2DG 1T (20) to 1DG 1T (8)
1994-95	**Cambridge**	1G 1PG 2DG 2T (26) to 1G 2PG 1DG (21)
1995-96	**Cambridge**	1G† 3PG 1T (21) to 1G 3PG 1DG (19)
1996-97	**Cambridge**	2G 2PG 1DG (23) to 1G (7)
1997-98	**Cambridge**	3G 1PG 1T (29) to 2G 1PG (17)
1998-99	**Cambridge**	2PG 2T (16) to 1G 1T (12)

CALL FOR CLUB CORNWALL

TETLEY'S BITTER COUNTY CHAMPIONSHIP

22 May 1999, Twickenham
Cornwall 24 (1G 4PG 1T) **Gloucestershire 15** (5PG)

Talk after Cornwall's triumph was of their forming a club to compete in the senior divisions of the RFU League structure. The reality, of course, is that such a club would have to work its way through the league structure to reach the highest echelons, though a Club Cornwall could attempt a buyout of a Premiership outfit.

For the moment they are the county champions, having beaten old rivals Gloucestershire in the first-ever final involving two sides from the south-west. But the 22,000 Cornish supporters who enjoyed a fifth day out at Twickenham in a decade had to endure a tense finish before celebrating only their third success in the competition.

The first half was a tight one in which the only try scored was by Jimmy Tucker in the 16th minute after Cornwall's powerful Fijian wing Nat Saumi had made a sizzling break. Penalty goals accounted for the rest of the points in the 14-12 half-time scoreline and, after two more penalties in the 10th and 15th minutes of the second half, Cornwall still held a precarious two-point lead as the game entered its last quarter. At the death Cornwall made the title theirs when fly-half Stewart Whitworth crossed in the fifth minute of injury time.

Cornwall: A Birkett (Launceston); N Saumi (Penzance-Newlyn), J Tucker (Launceston), C Laity (Exeter), S Larkins (Redruth); S Whitworth (Redruth), M Roderick (Penzance-Newlyn); P Risdon (Launceston), N Grigg (Launceston), J Thomas (Penzance-Newlyn), G Hutchings (Launceston), K Moseley (Penzance-Newlyn), J Atkinson (Penzance-Newlyn), D Shipton (Launceston) *(capt)*, M Addinall (Penryn) *Substitutions* E Nancekivell (Launceston) for Larkins (39 mins); S Rush (Launceston) for Thomas (62 mins); B Lucas (Launceston) for Grigg (77 mins); L Mruk (Penzance-Newlyn) for Hutchings (81 mins); P Gadsdon (Penzance-Newlyn) for Roderick (85 mins)
Scorers *Tries:* Tucker, Whitworth *Conversion:* Saumi *Penalty Goals:* Larkins (3), Saumi
Gloucestershire: S Morgan (Gloucester); J Perrins (Stroud), D Edwards (Cinderford), L Osborne (Lydney), C Dunlop (Lydney); S Thompson (Stroud), J Davis (Lydney); A Martin (Cinderford), N Nelmes (Lydney) *(capt)*, A Powles (Gloucester), B Guy (Ashley Down & Bristol), A Adams (Clifton), R York (Cheltenham), M Nicholls (Lydney), A Tarplee (Cheltenham) *Substitutions:* S Ward (Gloucester) for Thompson (61 mins); J Roberts (Lydney) for Guy (61 mins); G Williams (Lydney) for Martin (69 mins); P Knight (Sale) for Davis (71 mins); R James (Matson) for Nicholls (77 mins); N Matthews (Matson) for Nelmes (81 mins)
Scorer *Penalty Goals:* Osborne (5)
Referee N Yates (Manchester)

Lancashire and Gloucestershire have won the title 16 times each, Yorkshire 12, Warwickshire 10, Middlesex 8, Durham 8 (twice jointly), Devon 7 (once jointly), Kent 3 times, Cheshire 3, Cornwall 3, Hampshire, East Midlands, Northumberland, Cumbria (formerly Cumberland) twice each, Surrey twice (once jointly), and Midlands, Somerset, Leicestershire, Staffordshire and North Midlands once each.

LEICESTER OUTCLASSED

SCOTTISH AMICABLE TROPHY 1999

23 May 1999, Twickenham
Barbarians 55 (5G 4T) **Leicester 33** (4G 1T)

The match involving the English club champions and a World XV had previously been sponsored by Sanyo. Scottish Amicable stepped in to support the match in 1999 and were happy to bring their World XV under the umbrella of the Barbarians. Bob Dwyer, the former Australia and Leicester supremo, again coached the scratch side and must have taken considerable pleasure in seeing his charges demolish his former club.

The Tigers, for their part, took this end-of-term match seriously and fielded a side that was a mix of youth and experience. Yet they never really recovered from conceding two early converted tries to André Joubert and Jason Little and were forced to play catch-up rugby for the entire game. Thomas Castaignède, Glen Osborne and Joubert, among the galaxy of stars in the Barbarians' colours, were eager to run the ball from all quarters. At 35, Joubert showed that he had lost neither his pace nor relish for counterattack. Osborne's elusive running had the experts scratching their heads at why he is unable to command an All Black place while Castaignède was . . . well, simply Castaignède and earned the man-of-the-match award.

Barbarians: A J Joubert (South Africa); P Bernat-Salles (France), F E Bunce (New Zealand), W K Little (New Zealand), J T Small (South Africa); T Castaignède (France), A Pichot (Argentina); J P du Randt (South Africa), R Ibañez (France), M Scelzo (Argentina), A Benazzi (France), J F Langford (Australia), M Giovanelli (Italy), Z V Brooke (New Zealand), J F Pienaar (South Africa) (*capt*) *Substitutions:* W Fyvie (South Africa) for Pienaar (51 mins); A-C Stoica (Italy) for Bunce (51 mins); G M Osborne (New Zealand) for Joubert (57 mins); G W Weir (Scotland) for Giovanelli (61 mins); M Caputo (Australia) for Ibañez (60 mins); L Arbizu (Argentina) for Little (65 mins); D I W Hilton (Scotland) for du Randt (65 mins)
Scorers *Tries:* Joubert (2), Osborne (2), Little, Brooke, Small, Castaignède, Bernat-Salles *Conversions:* Castaignède (5)
Leicester: G Murphy; J Ferris, C Joiner, J Stuart, D Lougheed; P Howard, J Hamilton; D Jelley, R Cockerill, D Garforth, M Johnson (*capt*), F van Heerden, L Moody, M Corry, P Gustard *Substitutions:* M Meenan for Howard (51 mins); G Becconsall for Hamilton (51 mins); G Rowntree for Jelley (59 mins); D West for Cockerill (59 mins); T Stimpson for Murphy (72 mins); P Howard for Joiner (72 mins); A Balding for Corry (72 mins)
Scorers *Tries:* Moody (2), Ferris, Rowntree, West *Conversions:* Murphy (3), Stimpson
Referee C White (England)
Previous Results **1996** Leicester 31, World XV 40 **1997** Wasps 31, World XV 52 **1998** Newcastle 47, World XV 41

A CHANGING GAME

SEVENS RUGBY IN 1998-99

There was a time when sevens rugby competitions signalled the beginning of the end of the season in Britain. The Scottish circuit started in early April and the curtain came down on the rugby year at the end of the same month with the traditional Middlesex event at Twickenham. The abbreviated game, moreover, was virtually unheard of outside the Home Unions. How things have changed.

An international tournament featuring the world's eight leading rugby nations was staged in 1973 as part of the SRU centenary celebrations and in 1976 the Hong Kong Sevens was launched. Now the game has its own World Cup and the annual Hong Kong competition on the last weekend of March has become one of the highlights of international rugby's calendar.

The game evolved a little further last season with rugby featuring for the first time at the Commonwealth Games staged in Kuala Lumpur in September. New Zealand, bolstered by the power of Jonah Lomu and the guile of Christian Cullen, carried off the gold medal beating Fiji, the reigning world champions, 21-12 in front of a capacity crowd of 12,000 at the Petaling Jaya Stadium.

The tables were turned in March at the Hong Kong tournament when the same sides contested the final. New Zealand seemed to be heading for another victory when they went 12-7 ahead in the first half, but the inventive Fijians, inspired by Waisale Serevi and the powerful Marika Vunibaka, stormed back to take a record ninth title with a 21-12 victory.

The International Rugby Board (IRB), the game's ruling body, have announced that with effect from December 1999 there will be an annual World Rugby Sevens Series staged over a six/seven-month period. The original plan was for there to be a series of regional tournaments culminating in finals to be held in Hong Kong in June. Organisers of the Hong Kong tournament, though, were unwilling to move the date of their extravaganza by three months, citing bad weather as the reason for their reluctance. Final details of the schedule were awaited as this publication went to press.

One sevens tournament, however, has become a victim of the shortened game's expansion: the Middlesex Sevens, which have run without interruption since 1926, have been staged for the last time in Twickenham's traditional late-season slot. Waisale Serevi, the undisputed king of seven-a-side rugby, masterminded a victory for the Penguins against Saracens in a high-scoring final played on a wet pitch. The Watford club went behind for the only time in the match when Taniela Qauqau scored in the 35th second of sudden-death extra-time. But despite the excitement of the final the occasion was a mere shadow of its former self, the rival attraction of the Air France Paris Sevens (won by New Zealand) having proved a greater draw for players and spectators. From the year 2000, the Middlesex event will be held as a pipe-opener to the new season in England.

COMMONWEALTH GAMES Kuala Lumpur 12-14 September 1998
Semi-finals: New Zealand 19, Samoa 14; Fiji 28, Australia 14
Play-off: Australia 33, Samoa 12
Final: New Zealand 21, Fiji 12

HONG KONG SEVENS 26-28 March 1999
Semi-finals: Fiji 45, Australia 5; New Zealand 12, Samoa 7
Final: Fiji 21, New Zealand 12

PARIS SEVENS 29-30 May 1999
Semi-finals: France 21, South Africa 0; New Zealand 19, Fiji 14
Final: New Zealand 36, France 26

MIDDLESEX SEVENS 29 May 1999
First round: Saracens 34, London Welsh 7; Newcastle 26, Exeter University 5; Richmond 12, Gloucester 14; Harlow 21, Boland 42; San Isidro 45, Westcombe Park 12; Leicester 21, Wasps 12; Bath 7, Harlequins 34; Sale 0, Penguins 47
Second round: Saracens 21, Newcastle 12; Boland 41, Gloucester 5; San Isidro 22, Leicester 12; Penguins 28, Harlequins 12
Semi-finals: Saracens 15, Boland 7; Penguins 28, San Isidro 7
Final: Penguins 40, Saracens 35

Teams in the Middlesex final
Penguins: T Seru, T Quaqua, W Serevi (*capt*), J Forster; N Humphries, N Sailosi, K Izatt *Substitutions:* C Newby, D W O'Mahony
Scorers *Tries:* Quaqua (3), Serevi, O'Mahony, Seru *Conversions:* Serevi (5)
Saracens: B Daniel, M Singer, A Penaud, M Powell; K Sorrell, M Cairns, B Johnston *Substitution:* S Ravenscroft
Scorers *Tries:* Singer (2), Sorrell, Johnston, Powell *Conversions:* Singer (5)
Referee J Burtenshaw (London Society)

Harlequins have won the title 13 times, Richmond 9 (including one win by their second VII), London Welsh 8, London Scottish 7, St Mary's Hospital and Loughborough Colleges 5 each, Rosslyn Park and Wasps 4 each, Barbarians 3, Blackheath and St Luke's College (now Exeter University) twice, Sale, Met Police, Cardiff, Cambridge University, Notts (now Nottingham), Heriot's FP, Stewart's-Melville, Western Samoa, Bath, Leicester, Wigan (RL) and the Penguins once each.

HAT-TRICK FOR THE ARMY

WILLIS CORROON INTER-SERVICES TOURNAMENT 1999

The Army retained the Willis Corroon Trophy with a clean sweep of victories for the second year running. In doing so, they secured a hat-trick of titles and remained unbeaten in inter-service matches since March 1996 when they lost 9-6 (all penalties) against the Royal Navy.

As in the previous season, the organisers took the matches on the road and broke new ground by staging a game in Wales for the first time. At Sardis Road, home of the Pontypridd club, the Army gave notice of their strength with a convincing seven tries to one demolition of the Royal Air Force. The airmen had no answer to an Army pack that was bolstered by the presence of internationals Rob Wainwright and Tim Rodber, both of whom scored tries.

A fortnight later, England discard Spencer Brown staked a claim for a place in Clive Woodward's summer tour squad when he broke away for two first-half tries to give the Royal Navy a 21-7 half-time lead against the Royal Air Force at Gloucester. Evergreen Rory Underwood turned out for his 32nd inter-services match and enjoyed himself playing in the centre. But the Navy's big pack was too strong for the airmen and forced the only score of the second half with a late try from a drive at a tapped penalty.

That set up a Twickenham showdown for the title between the two unbeaten sides. A crowd of 26,000 turned out to see the Army surge ahead 14-3 in the first quarter of an hour, thanks to tries by Gloucester threequarters Rory Greenslade-Jones and Brian Johnson. Hard though the Navy pack laboured after that, their inability to retain possession, especially from the lineout, was the main cause of their downfall.

RESULTS
31 March, Pontypridd Army 43, Royal Air Force 8
14 April, Gloucester Royal Navy 28, Royal Air Force 7
24 April, Twickenham Army 24, Royal Navy 13

FINAL TABLE

	P	W	D	L	F	A	Pts
Army	2	2	0	0	67	21	4
Navy	2	1	0	1	41	31	2
RAF	2	0	0	2	15	71	0

The Army have won the Inter-Services tournament 31 times, the Royal Navy 17 times and the Royal Air Force 14 times. The Army and the Royal Air Force have shared it on two occasions and there have been ten triple ties.

DAY OF THE MINNOWS

NPI CUP & TETLEY'S BITTER VASE 1998-99

The Junior clubs' day out at Twickenham turned into a triumph for the minnows. Aldwinians, coached by former Lancashire and Sale stalwart Mike Kenrick, started as rank outsiders against Dudley Kingswinford whose league status two divisions higher should, or so it was thought, have given them a clear advantage on the field.

A disappointing match came briefly to life in the first ten minutes of the second half. Aldwinians were 6-3 ahead at the interval but conceded a try to lock Gavin Tipper three minutes into the second half. But Dean Schofield's two tries in the next seven minutes and Kenrick's arrival as a substitute took the side from North-West One into a lead that was never remotely threatened in the last half-hour.

Billericay had a more convincing 19-3 win in the Vase final with fly-half Kevin Harman contributing 14 goal points.

17 April 1999, Twickenham
Aldwinians 21 (1G 3PG 1T) **Dudley Kingswinford 10** (1G 1PG)

Aldwinians: T.Crossman; J Hampson, N Hyde, M Woodward, R Skaife; M Jackson, J Openshaw; H Stelmaszek, S Graham, P Donbavand, P Kenrick, D Schofield, C Rushworth, S Brown, C Jackson (*capt*) *Substitution:* M Kenrick for Brown (47 mins)
Scorers *Tries:* Schofield (2) *Conversion:* M Jackson *Penalty Goals:* M Jackson (3)
Dudley Kingswinford: A Grosvenor; W Port, P Whiting, A Hart, P Baker; E Smith, S Perry; C Evans, M Davies (*capt*), M Lockley, J MacRae, G Tipper, N Shillingford, B Connett, I Langford *Substitutions:* R Port for Baker (40 mins); M Wilson for Whiting (52 mins); M Halstead for Grosvenor (58 mins); W Millard for MacRae (65 mins); R Smith for Davies (73 mins); A Atterbury for Evans (78 mins)
Scorers *Try:* Tipper *Conversion:* Smith *Penalty Goal:* Smith
Referee J Barnard

17 April 1999, Twickenham
Billericay 19 (1G 4PG) **Silhillians 3** (1PG)

Billericay : J Stevens; M Coxford, R Schofield, N Glister, A Collings; K Harman, G Smith; G Pearmain, P Daly (*capt*), T Bond, S Clow, R Holdgate, M Green, J Hayter, J Bailey *Substitutions* W Hallett for Pearmain (33 mins); A White for Green (temp 61 to 69 mins); M Hughes for Green (71 mins); A Hudson for Glister (71 mins); A White for Hayter (75 mins); J Wicks for Stevens (78 mins); J Brown for Bond (78 mins)
Scorers *Try:* Bailey *Conversion:* Harman *Penalty Goals:* Harman (4)
Silhillians: A Waight; S Liggins, G Atkinson, A Tapper, P Short; S Rutter, E Dawes; A Wiles, K Lane, G Webb, I Hateley, R Lazenby, A Clutterbuck (*capt*), D Stanley, A Brown *Substitutions:* J Brierley for Dawes (temp 37-40 mins) and for Waight (71 mins); N Savage for Lazenby (40 mins); A Durrant for Brown (54 mins); A Dent for Stanley (60 mins); M Mallett for Wiles (75 mins); S Mair for Atkinson (77 mins);
Scorer *Penalty Goal:* Rutter
Referee J Burtenshaw

OBITUARY 1998-99 *(up to 30 April 1999)*

Robert Dunlop AGAR (Malone), whose death at the age of 78 was reported during the summer of 1998, was a forward in the only Ireland side to date to win the Grand Slam, in 1948, and featured in the side that won the Triple Crown in 1949.

Trevor BERGHAN (Otago) broke into the 1938 All Black party for the tour to Australia and appeared in all three of the Test matches as a five-eighth, New Zealand making a clean sweep of the series. The outbreak of War a year later effectively ended a promising rugby career. Died in Auckland on 23 September aged 84.

Ronald Winston BOON (Cardiff, London Welsh) was the hero of Wales's first Twickenham win, in 1933, scoring a try and dropping a goal in a 7-3 victory. An elusive wing, he won the first of 12 Welsh caps in 1930 and remained an automatic choice in the side for four seasons. He excelled at cricket (for Glamorgan), represented Wales at athletics and served London Welsh as secretary when the club became one of the best playing sides of the 1960s. He had recently emigrated to New Zealand where he died at Waikupurah on 3 August. He was 89.

Roy BURNETT (Newport) was the challenger to Cliff Morgan's fly-half reign in the Welsh sides of the early 1950s. A jinking runner of rare pace, he captained Newport in 1952-53, the season he finally displaced Cliff to win his only Welsh cap, against England at Cardiff. A subsequent switch to the wing extended his career with Newport until 1959 when he finally retired after making 373 appearances for the club. Died suddenly on 30 July at the age of 71.

Philippe Sidney de Quetteville CABOT (South Canterbury, Otago), who died in Totnes, Devon, at the age of 98 on 12 December, had been the oldest surviving All Black since 1994. His outstanding season as a wing forward was in 1921 when he made his only New Zealand appearance against New South Wales at Christchurch.

David Hardie CHISHOLM (Melrose), who died on 27 July aged 61, was the flying half of an effective partnership with Alex Hastie that served Melrose and Scotland so effectively during the 1960s. Dave Chisholm followed his brother Robin into the Scottish side for the first of 14 internationals in 1964. A clever tactician, he played ten times with his club consort before tasting defeat in a Scotland jersey. The run was ended by the 1967 All Blacks in the game where Chisholm was the target of a kick by Colin Meads that led to the dismissal of the famous All Black.

Dr Henry COCKBURN MC (St Mary's Hospital, Richmond), the former medical superintendent of St Mary's Hospital in Paddington, died on 4 December at the age of 84. In the 1930s he formed a noted half-back pairing with England fly-half Tommy Kemp, first for St Mary's when the hospital side was one of the best in England, and later for Richmond.

Right Rev Francis William COCKS CB (Cambridge University, Wasps), the former Bishop of Shrewsbury and Chaplain-in-Chief of the RAF who died on 20 August aged 84, was a useful forward in his youth. He won his Cambridge Blue in the scoreless draw of 1935 and played county rugby for Hampshire.

Leonard John CUNNINGHAM (Aberavon), who propped 14 times for Wales between 1960 and 1964, died on 20 July in Bridgend. He was 67. In an Aberavon career that spanned more than decade Len Cunningham captained the club twice, in 1958-59 and 1962-63, and was an integral part of the pack during the Wizards' championship season of 1961.

John Thomas DOYLE (Bective Rangers), a noted bloodstock agent whose purchases included the Gold Cup winner, Mill House, won his only cap for Ireland on the wing against Wales in Belfast in 1935. Ireland's win was achieved by a team that played with only 14 men for most of the match. Jack Doyle died at the age of 83 on 3 October.

Tom ELLIOT MBE (Gala) was nearly 30 when he gained his first Scottish cap in 1955. That was the celebrated occasion when Scotland beat Wales to bring to an end a record run of 17 consecutive Test defeats stretching back to 1951. He went on to win 14 caps up to 1958 and toured South Africa with the 1955 Lions. A farmer, he died on 3 May aged 72.

431

Ivan FRANCESCATO (Tarvisium, Treviso) died suddenly on 18 January aged 31. One of four brothers who played international rugby for Italy, he was a versatile player who won caps at scrum-half and centre. He made the first of his 38 appearances in a 29-21 win against Romania in 1990 scoring a try on debut, and by 1991 typified the growing determination and skills of Italian rugby players. His career coincided with Italy's coming of age as a rugby-playing nation and his loss will be greatly felt, for he was an inspiring presence who would have played a part in both the forthcoming World Cup and Italy's entry to the Six Nations.

Colin Marius GREENWOOD (Western Province) scored two tries in his only Test for South Africa against Ireland in Cape Town in 1961. He switched codes soon after the match joining Wakefield Trinity and was told that he would not be allowed to sail to England until his Springbok blazer was returned. During his league career he won two Challenge Cup medals with Trinity and did stints with clubs in Sydney and Canterbury. Died suddenly at the wheel of his car on 3 October near George. He was 63.

Ian Arthur HAMMOND (Marlborough) was a mobile hooker who forced his way into the All Black squad that toured Australia in 1951. He played in seven matches on that visit, scoring the only try of his first-class career against Central West. Although he failed to break into the Test side on tour, he gained his cap the next season in the 15-8 defeat of Australia at Wellington. A farmer, he died at Blenheim on 20 May at the age of 72.

Donald James HAYWARD (Newbridge) played 15 times for Wales between 1949 and 1952 and toured Australasia with the 1950 Lions, appearing in three Tests. He was at the heart of the Welsh packs which paved the way for two Grand Slams, in 1950 (as a lock) and 1952 (after successfully converting to prop), but was lost to the Union code soon after when he joined Wigan RL. Later emigrated to New Zealand. He died in Wellington on 16 February aged 73.

Jack HEATON (Liverpool University, Waterloo), whose death aged 86 was reported in November, was one of England's most forceful threequarters before and after World War II. He won nine caps between 1935 and 1947 as a centre and wing, kicked seven goals in internationals and captained successful England and Lancashire teams after the war.

Aaron Remana HOPA (Waikato) died at sea during a scuba diving course near Slipper Island on 8 December. Only 27, he was regarded as a strong contender for one of the back-row places in the New Zealand 1999 World Cup squad. A relative latecomer to first-class rugby, he made his provincial debut for Waikato in 1995 and was a mainstay of their Ranfurly Shield and National Championship triumphs in 1998. That year he toured England as a rookie with the All Blacks, scoring a try in the match against the English Rugby Partnership XV.

Alister Ernest HOPKINSON (South Canterbury, Canterbury), the 1967-70 All Black who propped in nine Tests, died in Christchurch on 17 January aged 57. He won his spurs on the 1967 tour to Britain making his Test debut against Scotland. For three years he was the unsung hero of an unbeaten New Zealand front row, his career at this level lasting until defeats in South Africa in 1970 put an end to a record-winning streak.

James Cecil Harding IRELAND (Glasgow HSFP), the last surviving member of the first Scotland side to carry off the Grand Slam, died at Polmont on 25 October at the age of 94. He won 11 consecutive caps from 1925, when he appeared in the inaugural international at Murrayfield where Scotland beat England to carry off the Grand Slam, to 1927. Scotland won or shared the Championship title in all three of his seasons in the international XV. He became a first-class referee, officiating at five internationals just before World War II, and later, in 1950-51, served the SRU as president.

Myrddin JONES, president of the WRU in 1988-89, died on 16 January aged 82. A former Gorseinon player, he gave 20 years' service to the Union and accompanied the national side on its tour of New Zealand during his year of presidency.

Rowley JONES (London Welsh, Ebbw Vale, Pontypool), whose death in Hertfordshire at the age of 83 was reported in November, was a highly respected WRU administrator who helped organise the first Welsh Secondary Schools tour, to South Africa in 1956. He was president of the Union when, in 1977-78, Wales won their last Grand Slam to date.

Trevor JONES, the Welsh referee who was in charge of six Five Nations matches between 1947 and 1951, died in December aged 85.

William James KENYON JONES MBE (Oxford University, London Welsh), who as K W J Jones won Oxford Blues as a forward in 1931 and 1932, died in London on 16 December at the age of 87. His only cap for Wales was in 1934 against England when he was one of 13 new caps in a side beaten 9-0 at Cardiff.

James Charles KEARNEY (Otago, Canterbury, Ashburton) played for the 1945-46 touring Kiwis whose brand of attacking play won them many friends in the Home Unions and France. Although his tour was cut short by injury, he returned home to become one of the best New Zealand five-eighths of the 1940s. He played in four Tests, scoring a try on debut against Australia in 1947 and dropped goals in the first two Tests of the ill-starred tour of South Africa in 1949. Died at Ranfurly on 1 October aged 78.

Orton Wallace KNIGHT (Auckland, Manawatu, RNZAF), who died in Auckland on 23 March aged 86, appeared in a wartime international for England against Wales in 1942 while on a posting to Britain with the RNZAF. His son, Michael, played for New Zealand in 1968.

Durbar LAWRIE, who died on 7 March aged 84, just hours after Wales's one-point win against France in Paris, was for 42 years Bridgend's 'Mr Rugby'. He served the club as secretary and president and was its most loyal supporter.

Denzil McLeod Murray LLOYD, a leading WRU referee in the 1970s when he took control of two Five Nations matches and officiated at the 1976 WRU Cup final, died on 8 September. In 1989, he managed the Wales B party that toured Canada.

Keith OXLEE (Natal), who died on 31 August aged 63, won 19 caps as South Africa's fly-half from 1960 to 1965. Often he was the match-winner, either kicking a tie-breaking penalty or scoring a decisive try. He retired with 88 Test points to his name, a then Springbok record, and scored more than 200 points in all matches for South Africa. His 102 matches for Natal spanned 16 years and included the famous six-all draw in which he scored a try against Wilson Whineray's 1960 All Blacks.

William Michael PATTERSON (Sale, Wasps) was uncapped when called to New Zealand as a tour replacement for the Lions in 1959. He played in nine matches including the second Test before winning two England caps as a centre in 1961. Bill Patterson's death at the age of 62 was reported in December.

Captain Michael Alan PEAREY (Gosforth, Royal Navy), who died in October at the age of 65, was a talented centre in his playing days. He came close to winning England honours in 1959 after appearing in the first English trial at Birkenhead and was for several seasons the mainstay of the Royal Navy's threequarter line in the Services' tournament. Later he was a valued committee member of the RFU and enjoyed a happy year as its president in 1990-91 when England achieved the Grand Slam for the first time for 11 years.

Brian Desmond PFAFF (Western Province), who died in Johannesburg on 8 May aged 68, toured New Zealand and Australia with the 1956 Springboks. His only Test was as fly-half against Australia in the opening international of that tour, injuries restricting him to only three appearances on the New Zealand leg of the visit. Later the same year he led the South African Universities on their successful tour of Britain.

Jan Albertus Jacobus PICKARD (Western Province) played four Tests for South Africa between 1953 and 1958, toured Europe in 1951-52 and visited New Zealand with the 1956 side. He was best known as a robust captain of Western Province and later served on the executive of both the South African Rugby Board and the IRB. Died aged 70 on 30 May.

Alexander William RAMSAY (Oxford University) was a flanker in the 1952 Oxford side and captained the Blues in the drawn match of 1953. He was later a distinguished RFU committee member and was elected president of the Union in 1979-80 when England won the Grand Slam. His death at the age of 67 was reported in February.

Arthur Morgan REES CBE (Cambridge University, Met Police, London Welsh), the former Chief Constable of Staffordshire who died on 13 May aged 85, was an intelligent loose forward in the Welsh sides of the 1930s. Tough and fast, he enjoyed his finest hour in December 1935 when, at the tender age of 22, he led the Welsh pack that paved the way for a famous 13-12 win over the Third All Blacks. His leadership that afternoon in a typical tough, physical battle with the New Zealanders was a significant factor in Wales's triumph, for he knew how to restrain his pack when tempers threatened to boil over. He won Cambridge Blues in 1933 and 1934 and went on to gain 13 caps for Wales. After the War he was a well-known London referee.

Ian ROGERS, South Africa's leading referee, died of cancer on 26 November in Pietermaritzburg. He was 41. His refereeing career took off in 1984 when he was promoted to the provincial list and in 1993 he controlled his first international. At the 1995 World Cup he was in charge of the Ireland-Wales group match and he was due to take control of further World Cup qualifying games before his untimely death deprived rugby of one its foremost officials.

Louis Ulrich SCHMIDT (Northern Transvaal) was South Africa's flanker in two Tests between 1958 and 1962. Easily recognised by his handlebar moustache, he was known as the original Blue Bull after a caricature depicted him as such in *Die Vaderland* in 1963. He died in Pretoria on 23 January aged 62. His son Uli was South Africa's hooker in the 1990s.

Johannes Petrus Jacobus SCHOEMAN (South-Western Districts), who refereed the third Test of the 1968 series between the Springboks and Lions, died on 10 October aged 75.

Dr Douglas William Cumming SMITH OBE (London Scottish, Army) won eight caps for Scotland as a wing between 1949 and 1953 and played in one Test for the 1950 Lions against Australia. But it was as the charismatic manager of the outstanding 1971 Lions that he will be remembered in rugby circles. The side beat the All Blacks 2-1 with one match drawn to become the only Lions tourists to date to take a series off New Zealand. Smith was an Essex GP who upheld the tradition that former players put something back into the game. Apart from his success as Lions manager he was for many seasons a committee member at London Scottish and served the SRU as president in 1986-87. He died on 22 September at Midhurst. He was 73.

Wilson SMITH (Halifax), who died on his 94th birthday (17 November), played centre for Yorkshire against the 1924 All Blacks and was thought to be the last surviving player of those who had appeared against that famous invincible side. He made 11 appearances for the county before turning professional with Halifax RL club.

Charles Edward Bell STEWART (Kelso), one of Scottish rugby's most faithful servants, died in Kelso on 29 November. He was 61. A one-club player, he served Kelso as a dynamic loose forward for the best part of a decade. He gained two caps in 1960 and 1961 and toured South Africa in 1960 when Scotland became the first Home Union to make an overseas Test visit. After a successful stint as club coach he turned to administration rising to the presidency of the SRU in 1990-91.

Erdam Albert STRASHEIM, who died in Pretoria on 11 June at the age of 81, refereed eight South African Tests between 1958 and 1968. His first appointment was the famous second Test of 1958 when France became the first overseas side to take a home series off the Springboks this century.

Neville Henry THORNTON (King Country, Auckland) died at Auckland on 12 September aged 79. One of the first New Zealand players to understand the role of the modern number eight position, he featured prominently in the 1945-46 Kiwis side to the Home Unions and France and was an automatic choice for the All Blacks tour to Australia in 1947 playing in both of the Tests and heading the list of try scorers. Two years later he lost his Test place after a disappointing first international at Cape Town and he retired from first-class rugby at the end of the tour.

Basil Holmes TRAVERS OBE (Oxford University, Harlequins, New South Wales), who died in Sydney on 18 December aged 79, won Blues in 1946 and 1947, when he was captain. As a back-row forward Jika Travers gained six England caps between 1947 and 1949 before returning to Australia where he captained New South Wales to a 17-12 victory over the 1950 Lions. Later a distinguished Sydney headmaster.

William TRAVERS (Pill Harriers, Newport), who died on 4 June at the age of 84, was one of the select band of players capped by Wales before and after World War II. Bill Travers was a hooker whose father George had hooked for Wales in the famous victory over the 1905 All Blacks. Travers junior came into the Welsh side in 1937 and originally retired in 1946 after taking part in war-time and 'Victory' internationals. But in 1949, aged 35, he came out of retirement to return to the Welsh front row for all four of that year's Five Nations matches, bringing his cap tally to 12. As tough as teak, he also appeared in 20 of the 23 matches played by the 1938 Lions in South Africa including two of the Tests.

Lord Justice George Stanley WALLER PC (Cambridge University), the High Court judge who died on 5 February aged 84, won a Blue as a forward in the 1932 Varsity match.

Graham Alexander WILSON (Oxford University), whose death was reported in May at the age of 75, won Oxford Blues in 1946 and 1948, when he skippered a winning XV from the second row, before winning three Scotland caps in 1949. Gullie Wilson was nominated to be Scotland's place-kicker that season as a result of an informal goal-kicking competition held just before the French match. He was given the job, he later claimed, because he had missed the goal by the least margin.

We also record with regret the deaths of several of the game's journalists and writers during the past year: Michael Melford, the first rugby correspondent to the Sunday Telegraph; *Colin Price of the* Daily Mirror; *Christopher Wordsworth, late of the* Observer; *freelance Doug Ibbotson; and Quintus van Rooyen, who for more than 25 years edited the* South African Annual.

FIXTURES 1999-2000

*Venues and fixtures are subject to alteration. At the time of going to press, only the **weekends** for which League and European Cup matches had been scheduled were known. See press for details on which days during weekends those matches will be played.*

Saturday 21 August

ENGLAND v USA (Twickenham)
SCOTLAND v ARGENTINA (Murrayfield)
WALES v CANADA (Cardiff)

Saturday 28 August

ENGLAND v CANADA (Twickenham)
SCOTLAND v ROMANIA (Hampden Park)
IRELAND v ARGENTINA (Lansdowne Road)
WALES v FRANCE (Cardiff)

RFU Tetley's Bitter Cup *Preliminary round*

Saturday 4 September

SRU Premiership
Hawick v Watsonians
Heriot's FP v Currie
Jed-Forest v Glasgow Hawks
Melrose v Gala
West of Scotland v Kelso

WRU Premiership
Bridgend v Swansea
Caerphilly v Edinburgh
Dunvant v Neath
Glasgow v Pontypridd
Llanelli v Ebbw Vale
Newport v Cardiff

Tuesday 7 September

EFDR XV v England (Liverpool FC)

RFU Allied Dunbar Leagues
Division 2
Exeter v Waterloo
Henley v London Welsh
Manchester v Worcester
Moseley v West Hartlepool
Orrell v Leeds
Rugby v Coventry
Wakefield v Rotherham

Saturday 11 September

RFU Allied Dunbar Leagues
Division 1
Bristol v Bedford
Gloucester v Newcastle
Harlequins v Bath
Northampton v Leicester
Sale v Wasps
Saracens v London Irish

Division 2
Coventry v Henley
Leeds v Exeter
London Welsh v Rotherham
Orrell v Wakefield
Waterloo v Moseley
West Hartlepool v Manchester
Worcester v Rugby

SRU Premiership
Currie v Melrose
Gala v Hawick
Glasgow Hawks v Heriot's FP
Kelso v Jed-Forest
Watsonians v West of Scotland

WRU Premiership
Bridgend v Cardiff
Ebbw Vale v Caerphilly
Edinburgh v Glasgow
Neath v Newport
Pontypridd v Dunvant
Swansea v Llanelli

Saturday 18 September

EFDR XV v England (Twickenham)

RFU Allied Dunbar Leagues
Division 2
Exeter v Orrell
Henley v Worcester
Manchester v Waterloo
Moseley v Leeds
Rotherham v Coventry
Rugby v West Hartlepool
Wakefield v London Welsh

RFU Tetley's Bitter Cup *First round*

SRU Premiership
Hawick v Currie
Jed-Forest v Heriot's FP
Kelso v Watsonians
Melrose v Glasgow Hawks
West of Scotland v Gala

WRU Premiership
Caerphilly v Swansea
Dunvant v Edinburgh
Glasgow v Ebbw Vale
Llanelli v Bridgend
Neath v Cardiff
Newport v Pontypridd

Saturday 25 September

RFU Allied Dunbar Leagues
Division 1
Bath v Northampton
Bedford v London Irish
Harlequins v Saracens
Leicester v Sale
Newcastle v Bristol
Wasps v Gloucester

Division 2
Coventry v London Welsh
Exeter v Wakefield
Leeds v Manchester
Orrell v Moseley
Waterloo v Rugby
West Hartlepool v Henley
Worcester v Rotherham

SRU Premiership
Currie v West of Scotland
Gala v Kelso
Glasgow Hawks v Hawick
Heriot's FP v Melrose
Watsonians v Jed-Forest

WRU Premiership
Bridgend v Caerphilly
Ebbw Vale v Dunvant
Edinburgh v Newport
Llanelli v Cardiff
Pontypridd v Neath
Swansea v Glasgow

WRU SWALEC Cup *First round*

Friday 1 October
WORLD CUP
WALES v ARGENTINA (Cardiff)

FIJI v NAMIBIA (Béziers)

SRU Premiership
Hawick v Heriot's FP
Jed-Forest v Melrose
Kelso v Currie
Watsonians v Gala

Saturday 2 October

WORLD CUP
ENGLAND v ITALY (Twickenham)
FRANCE v CANADA (Béziers)
IRELAND v USA (Lansdowne Road)
SPAIN v URUGUAY (Gala)

RFU Allied Dunbar Leagues
Division 1
Bristol v Wasps
Gloucester v Leicester
London Irish v Newcastle
Northampton v Harlequins
Sale v Bath
Saracens v Bedford

Division 2
Henley v Waterloo
London Welsh v Worcester
Manchester v Orrell
Moseley v Exeter
Rotherham v West Hartlepool
Rugby v Leeds
Wakefield v Coventry

SRU Premiership
West of Scotland v Glasgow Hawks

WRU Premiership
Caerphilly v Llanelli
Cardiff v Pontypridd
Dunvant v Swansea
Glasgow v Bridgend
Neath v Edinburgh
Newport v Ebbw Vale

Sunday 3 October
WORLD CUP
AUSTRALIA v ROMANIA (Belfast)
NEW ZEALAND v TONGA (Bristol)
SAMOA v JAPAN (Wrexham)
SCOTLAND v SOUTH AFRICA
    (Murrayfield)

437

Friday 8 October

WORLD CUP
FRANCE v NAMIBIA (Bordeaux)
SCOTLAND v URUGUAY
 (Murrayfield)

Saturday 9 October

WORLD CUP
ENGLAND v NEW ZEALAND
 (Twickenham)
FIJI v CANADA (Bordeaux)
USA v ROMANIA (Lansdowne Road)
WALES v JAPAN (Cardiff)

RFU Allied Dunbar Leagues
Division 1
Bath v Gloucester
Harlequins v Sale
Leicester v Bristol
Newcastle v Bedford
Northampton v Saracens
Wasps v London Irish

Division 2
Exeter v Manchester
Leeds v Henley
Moseley v Wakefield
Orrell v Rugby
Waterloo v Rotherham
West Hartlepool v London Welsh
Worcester v Coventry

SRU Premiership
Currie v Watsonians
Gala v Jed-Forest
Glasgow Hawks v Kelso
Heriot's FP v West of Scotland
Melrose v Hawick

WRU Premiership
Caerphilly v Cardiff
Bridgend v Dunvant
Ebbw Vale v Neath
Glasgow v Llanelli
Pontypridd v Edinburgh
Swansea v Newport

Sunday 10 October

WORLD CUP
ARGENTINA v SAMOA (Llanelli)
IRELAND v AUSTRALIA (Lansdowne Road)
ITALY v TONGA (Leicester)

SOUTH AFRICA v SPAIN
 (Murrayfield)

Thursday 14 October

WORLD CUP
AUSTRALIA v USA (Limerick)
CANADA v NAMIBIA (Toulouse)
NEW ZEALAND v ITALY
 (Huddersfield)
WALES v SAMOA (Cardiff)

Friday 15 October

WORLD CUP
ENGLAND v TONGA (Twickenham)
IRELAND v ROMANIA (Lansdowne Road)
SOUTH AFRICA v URUGUAY
 (Murrayfield)

Saturday 16 October

WORLD CUP
ARGENTINA v JAPAN (Cardiff)
FRANCE v FIJI (Toulouse)
SCOTLAND v SPAIN (Murrayfield)

RFU Allied Dunbar Leagues
Division 1
Bedford v Wasps
Bristol v Bath
Gloucester v Harlequins
London Irish v Leicester
Sale v Northampton
Saracens v Newcastle

Division 2
Coventry v West Hartlepool
Henley v Orrell
London Welsh v Waterloo
Manchester v Moseley
Rotherham v Leeds
Rugby v Exeter
Wakefield v Worcester

RFU Tetley's Bitter Cup *Second round*

WRU Premiership
Cardiff v Edinburgh
Dunvant v Llanelli
Glasgow v Caerphilly
Neath v Swansea
Newport v Bridgend
Pontypridd v Ebbw Vale

Sunday 17 October

SRU Premiership
Gala v Currie
Jed-Forest v Hawick
Kelso v Heriot's FP
Watsonians v Glasgow Hawks
West of Scotland v Melrose

Wednesday 20 October

WORLD CUP *Quarter-final play-offs*

Saturday 23 October

WORLD CUP *Quarter-final*

RFU Allied Dunbar Leagues
Division 2
Exeter v Henley
Leeds v London Welsh
Manchester v Wakefield
Moseley v Rugby
Orrell v Rotherham
Waterloo v Coventry
West Hartlepool v Worcester

SRU Premiership
Glasgow Hawks v Gala
Hawick v West of Scotland
Heriot's FP v Watsonians
Jed-Forest v Currie
Melrose v Kelso

WRU Premiership
Bridgend v Neath
Caerphilly v Dunvant
Ebbw Vale v Edinburgh
Glasgow v Cardiff
Llanelli v Newport
Swansea v Pontypridd

WRU SWALEC Cup *Second round*

Sunday 24 October

WORLD CUP *Quarter-finals*

Saturday 30 October

WORLD CUP *First semi-final*
(Twickenham)

RFU Allied Dunbar Leagues
Division 1
Bath v London Irish
Harlequins v Bristol
Leicester v Bedford

Northampton v Gloucester
Sale v Saracens
Wasps v Newcastle

WRU Premiership
Dunvant v Glasgow
Ebbw Vale v Cardiff
Edinburgh v Swansea
Neath v Llanelli
Newport v Caerphilly
Pontypridd v Bridgend

Sunday 31 October

WORLD CUP *Second semi-final*
(Twickenham)

Wed 3, Thur 4 or Fri 5 November

WRU Premiership
Bridgend v Edinburgh
Caerphilly v Neath
Cardiff v Dunvant
Glasgow v Newport
Llanelli v Pontypridd
Swansea v Ebbw Vale

Thursday 4 November

WORLD CUP *Third place play-off*
(Cardiff)

Saturday 6 November

WORLD CUP FINAL (Cardiff)

RFU Allied Dunbar Leagues
Division 1
Bedford v Bath
Bristol v Northampton
Gloucester v Sale
London Irish v Harlequins
Newcastle v Leicester
Saracens v Wasps

Saturday 13 November

RFU Allied Dunbar Leagues
Division 1
Bath v Newcastle
Gloucester v Saracens
Harlequins v Bedford
Leicester v Wasps
Northampton v London Irish
Sale v Bristol

RFU Tetley's Bitter Cup *Third round*

WRU Premiership
Dunvant v Newport
Ebbw Vale v Bridgend
Glasgow v Neath
Llanelli v Edinburgh
Pontypridd v Caerphilly
Swansea v Cardiff

Fri 19, Sat 20 or Sun 21 November

European Cup *First round*
Bath v Toulouse
Bourgoin v Ulster
Cardiff v Harlequins
Colomiers v Saracens
Edinburgh v Grenoble
Leinster v Leicester
Munster v Pontypridd
Northampton v Neath
Stade Français v Glasgow
Swansea v Padua
Treviso v Montferrand
Wasps v Llanelli

European Shield *First round*

Saturday 20 November

RFU Allied Dunbar Leagues
Division 2
Coventry v Leeds
Henley v Moseley
London Welsh v Orrell
Rotherham v Exeter
Rugby v Manchester
Wakefield v West Hartlepool
Worcester v Waterloo

SRU Premiership
Currie v Glasgow Hawks
Gala v Heriot's FP
Kelso v Hawick
Watsonians v Melrose
West of Scotland v Jed-Forest

WRU SWALEC Cup *Third round*

Fri 26, Sat 27 or Sun 28 November

European Cup *Second round*
Glasgow v Leinster
Grenoble v Northampton
Harlequins v Treviso
Leicester v Stade Français
Llanelli v Bourgoin
Montferrand v Cardiff

Neath v Edinburgh
Padua v Bath
Pontypridd v Colomiers
Saracens v Munster
Toulouse v Swansea
Ulster v Wasps

European Shield *Second round*

Saturday 27 November

RFU Allied Dunbar Leagues
Division 2
Exeter v London Welsh
Leeds v Worcester
Manchester v Henley
Moseley v Rotherham
Orrell v Coventry
Rugby v Wakefield
Waterloo v West Hartlepool

SRU Premiership
Currie v Heriot's FP
Gala v Melrose
Glasgow Hawks v Jed-Forest
Kelso v West of Scotland
Watsonians v Hawick

Saturday 4 December

RFU Allied Dunbar Leagues
Division 1
Bedford v Northampton
Bristol v Gloucester
London Irish v Sale
Newcastle v Harlequins
Saracens v Leicester
Wasps v Bath

Division 2
Coventry v Exeter
Henley v Rugby
London Welsh v Moseley
Rotherham v Manchester
Wakefield v Waterloo
West Hartlepool v Leeds
Worcester v Orrell

SRU Premiership
Hawick v Gala
Heriot's FP v Glasgow Hawks
Jed-Forest v Kelso
Melrose v Currie
West of Scotland v Watsonians

IRFU League
Division 1
Ballymena v DLSP
Buccaneers v Cork Const
Dungannon v St Mary's Coll
Garryowen v Terenure Coll
Lansdowne v Shannon
Young Munster v Clontarf

WRU Premiership
Cardiff v Newport
Ebbw Vale v Llanelli
Edinburgh v Caerphilly
Neath v Dunvant
Pontypridd v Glasgow
Swansea v Bridgend

Tuesday 7 December

**Oxford University v Cambridge
University** (Twickenham)

Fri 10, Sat 11 or Sun 12 December

European Cup *Third round*
Bourgoin v Wasps
Cardiff v Treviso
Colomiers v Munster
Glasgow v Leicester
Harlequins v Montferrand
Neath v Grenoble
Northampton v Edinburgh
Padua v Toulouse
Saracens v Pontypridd
Stade Français v Leinster
Swansea v Bath
Ulster v Llanelli

European Shield *Third round*

Saturday 11 December

RFU Allied Dunbar Leagues
Division 2
Exeter v Worcester
Henley v Wakefield
Leeds v Waterloo
Manchester v London Welsh
Moseley v Coventry
Orrell v West Hartlepool
Rugby v Rotherham

SRU Premiership
Currie v Hawick
Gala v West of Scotland
Glasgow Hawks v Melrose

Heriot's FP v Jed-Forest
Watsonians v Kelso

Fri 17, Sat 18 or Sun 19 December

European Cup *Fourth round*
Bath v Swansea
Edinburgh v Northampton
Grenoble v Neath
Leicester v Glasgow
Leinster v Stade Français
Llanelli v Ulster
Montferrand v Harlequins
Munster v Colomiers
Pontypridd v Saracens
Toulouse v Padua
Treviso v Cardiff
Wasps v Bourgoin

European Shield *Fourth round*

Saturday 18 December

RFU Allied Dunbar Leagues
Division 2
Coventry v Manchester
London Welsh v Rugby
Rotherham v Henley
Wakefield v Leeds
Waterloo v Orrell
West Hartlepool v Exeter
Worcester v Moseley

WRU SWALEC Cup *Fourth round*

Sunday 26 December

RFU Allied Dunbar Leagues
Division 1
Bath v Leicester
Bristol v Saracens
Gloucester v London Irish
Harlequins v Wasps
Northampton v Newcastle
Sale v Bedford

Mon 27 or Tues 28 December

WRU Premiership
Caerphilly v Ebbw Vale
Cardiff v Bridgend
Dunvant v Pontypridd
Glasgow v Edinburgh
Llanelli v Swansea
Newport v Neath

Tuesday 28 December

IRFU League
Division 1
Clontarf v Dungannon
Cork Const v Garryowen
DLSP v Lansdowne
St Mary's Coll v Buccaneers
Shannon v Young Munster
Terenure Coll v Ballymena

Wednesday 29 December

RFU Allied Dunbar Leagues
Division 1
Bedford v Gloucester
Leicester v Harlequins
London Irish v Bristol
Newcastle v Sale
Saracens v Bath
Wasps v Northampton

Sunday 2 January 1999

RFU Tetley's Bitter Cup *Fourth round*

Monday 3 January

WRU Premiership
Bridgend v Llanelli
Cardiff v Neath
Ebbw Vale v Glasgow
Edinburgh v Dunvant
Pontypridd v Newport
Swansea v Caerphilly

Fri 7, Sat 8 or Sun 9 January

European Cup *Fifth round*
Bath v Padua
Bourgoin v Llanelli
Cardiff v Montferrand
Colomiers v Pontypridd
Edinburgh v Neath
Leinster v Glasgow
Munster v Saracens
Northampton v Grenoble
Stade Français v Leicester
Swansea v Toulouse
Treviso v Harlequins
Wasps v Ulster

European Shield *Fifth round*

Saturday 8 January

RFU Allied Dunbar Leagues
Division 2
Coventry v Orrell
Henley v Manchester
London Welsh v Exeter
Rotherham v Moseley
Wakefield v Rugby
West Hartlepool v Waterloo
Worcester v Leeds

Fri 14, Sat 15 or Sun 16 January

European Cup *Sixth round*
Glasgow v Stade Français
Grenoble v Edinburgh
Harlequins v Cardiff
Leicester v Leinster
Llanelli v Wasps
Montferrand v Treviso
Neath v Northampton
Padua v Swansea
Pontypridd v Munster
Saracens v Colomiers
Toulouse v Bath
Ulster v Bourgoin

European Shield *Sixth round*

Saturday 15 January

RFU Allied Dunbar Leagues
Division 2
Exeter v Coventry
Leeds v West Hartlepool
Manchester v Rotherham
Moseley v London Welsh
Orrell v Worcester
Rugby v Henley
Waterloo v Wakefield

SRU Premiership
Hawick v Glasgow Hawks
Jed-Forest v Watsonians
Kelso v Gala
Melrose v Heriot's FP
West of Scotland v Currie

Saturday 22 January

RFU Allied Dunbar Leagues
Division 1
Bath v Wasps
Gloucester v Bristol
Harlequins v Newcastle

Leicester v Saracens
Northampton v Bedford
Sale v London Irish

Division 2
Exeter v Rotherham
Leeds v Coventry
Manchester v Rugby
Moseley v Henley
Orrell v London Welsh
Waterloo v Worcester
West Hartlepool v Wakefield

SRU Premiership
Currie v Kelso
Gala v Watsonians
Glasgow Hawks v West of Scotland
Heriot's FP v Hawick
Melrose v Jed-Forest

IRFU League
Division 1
Ballymena v Clontarf
Buccaneers v Shannon
Dungannon v Cork Const
Garryowen v St Mary's Coll
Lansdowne v Terenure Coll
Young Munster v DLSP

WRU SWALEC Cup *Fifth round*

Tuesday 25 January

RFU Allied Dunbar Leagues
Division 1
Bedford v Harlequins
Bristol v Sale
London Irish v Northampton
Newcastle v Bath
Saracens v Gloucester
Wasps v Leicester

Saturday 29 January

RFU Tetley's Bitter Cup *Fifth round*

SRU Premiership
Hawick v Melrose
Jed-Forest v Gala
Kelso v Glasgow Hawks
Watsonians v Currie
West of Scotland v Heriot's FP

IRFU League
Division 1
Clontarf v Lansdowne

Cork Const v Young Munster
DLSP v Garryowen
St Mary's Coll v Ballymena
Shannon v Dungannon

WRU Premiership
Caerphilly v Bridgend
Cardiff v Llanelli
Dunvant v Ebbw Vale
Glasgow v Swansea
Neath v Pontypridd
Newport v Edinburgh

Sunday 30 January

IRFU League
Division 1
Terenure Coll v Buccaneers

Friday 4 February

England A v Ireland A
Wales A v France A (Wrexham RFC)
Italy A v Scotland A

Saturday 5 February

ENGLAND v IRELAND
    (Twickenham)
WALES v FRANCE (Cardiff)
ITALY v SCOTLAND (Rome)

Wednesday 9 February

IRFU League
Division 1
Lansdowne v St Mary's Coll

Saturday 12 February

RFU Allied Dunbar Leagues
Division 1
Bath v Bedford
Harlequins v London Irish
Leicester v Newcastle
Northampton v Bristol
Sale v Gloucester
Wasps v Saracens

Division 2
Coventry v Waterloo
Henley v Exeter
London Welsh v Leeds
Rotherham v Orrell
Rugby v Moseley
Wakefield v Manchester
Worcester v West Hartlepool

443

IRFU League
Division 1
Ballymena v Cork Const
Buccaneers v Clontarf
Dungannon v DLSP
Young Munster v Terenure Coll

WRU Premiership
Bridgend v Glasgow
Ebbw Vale v Newport
Edinburgh v Neath
Llanelli v Caerphilly
Pontypridd v Cardiff
Swansea v Dunvant

Sunday 13 February

IRFU League
Division 1
Garryowen v Shannon

Friday 18 February

France A v England A
Ireland A v Scotland A
Wales A v Italy A (Ebbw Vale)

Saturday 19 February

FRANCE v ENGLAND (Paris)
IRELAND v SCOTLAND (Lansdowne Road)
WALES v ITALY (Cardiff)

Saturday 26 February

RFU Tetley's Bitter Cup *Quarter-Finals*

RFU Allied Dunbar Leagues
Division 2
Exeter v Rugby
Leeds v Rotherham
Moseley v Manchester
Orrell v Henley
Waterloo v London Welsh
West Hartlepool v Coventry
Worcester v Wakefield

SRU Premiership
Currie v Gala
Glasgow Hawks v Watsonians
Hawick v Jed-Forest
Heriot's FP v Kelso
Melrose v West of Scotland

IRFU League
Division 1
Clontarf v Garryowen
Cork Const v Lansdowne
DLSP v Buccaneers
St Mary's Coll v Young Munster
Shannon v Ballymena
Terenure Coll v Dungannon

WRU SWALEC Cup *Sixth round*

Friday 3 March

England A v Wales A
Scotland A v France A
Ireland A v Italy A

Saturday 4 March

ENGLAND v WALES (Twickenham)
SCOTLAND v FRANCE (Murrayfield)
IRELAND v ITALY (Lansdowne Road)

Saturday 11 March

RFU Allied Dunbar Leagues
Division 1
Bedford v Leicester
Bristol v Harlequins
Gloucester v Northampton
London Irish v Bath
Newcastle v Wasps
Saracens v Sale

Division 2
Coventry v Worcester
Henley v Leeds
London Welsh v West Hartlepool
Manchester v Exeter
Rotherham v Waterloo
Rugby v Orrell
Wakefield v Moseley

SRU Premiership
Currie v Jed-Forest
Gala v Glasgow Hawks
Kelso v Melrose
Watsonians v Heriot's FP
West of Scotland v Hawick

IRFU League
Division 1
Ballymena v Young Munster
DLSP v Cork Const
Dungannon v Lansdowne

Garryowen v Buccaneers
Terenure Coll v Shannon

WRU Premiership
Cardiff v Caerphilly
Dunvant v Bridgend
Edinburgh v Pontypridd
Llanelli v Glasgow
Neath v Ebbw Vale
Newport v Swansea

Sunday 12 March

IRFU League
Division 1
St Mary's Coll v Clontarf

Friday 17 March

Wales A v Scotland A (Bridgend)
Italy A v England A
France A v Ireland A

Saturday 18 March

WALES v SCOTLAND (Cardiff)
ITALY v ENGLAND (Rome)

Sunday 19 March

FRANCE v IRELAND (Paris)

Wednesday 22 March

BUSA Halifax Final (Twickenham)

Fri 24, Sat 25 or Sun 26 March

Hong Kong Sevens

Saturday 25 March

RFU Allied Dunbar Leagues
Division 1
Bath v Bristol
Harlequins v Gloucester
Leicester v London Irish
Newcastle v Saracens
Northampton v Sale
Wasps v Bedford

Division 2
Coventry v Wakefield
Exeter v Moseley
Leeds v Rugby
Orrell v Manchester
Waterloo v Henley
West Hartlepool v Rotherham
Worcester v London Welsh

SRU Premiership
Glasgow Hawks v Currie
Hawick v Kelso
Heriot's FP v Gala
Jed-Forest v West of Scotland
Melrose v Watsonians

IRFU League
Division 1
Buccaneers v Ballymena
Clontarf v DLSP
Cork Const v Terenure Coll
Shannon v St Mary's Coll
Young Munster v Dungannon

WRU SWALEC Cup *Quarter-finals*

Friday 31 March

Ireland A v Wales A

Saturday 1 April

IRELAND v WALES (Lansdowne
  Road)
FRANCE v ITALY
Scotland A v England A (Edinburgh)

Sunday 2 April

SCOTLAND v ENGLAND
  (Murrayfield)

Saturday 8 April

RFU Tetley's Bitter Cup *Semi-Finals*

RFU Allied Dunbar Leagues
Division 1
Bedford v Newcastle
Bristol v Leicester
Gloucester v Bath
London Irish v Wasps
Sale v Harlequins
Saracens v Northampton

Division 2
Henley v West Hartlepool
London Welsh v Coventry
Manchester v Leeds
Moseley v Orrell
Rotherham v Worcester
Rugby v Waterloo
Wakefield v Exeter

IRFU League
Division 1
Ballymena v Dungannon
Clontarf v Terenure Coll
Lansdowne v Buccaneers
St Mary's Coll v DLSP
Shannon v Cork Const

WRU Premiership
Bridgend v Newport
Caerphilly v Glasgow
Ebbw Vale v Pontypridd
Edinburgh v Cardiff
Llanelli v Dunvant
Swansea v Neath

Sunday 9 April

IRFU League
Division 1
Garryowen v Young Munster

Saturday 15 April

European Cup *Quarter-finals*

European Shield *Quarter-finals*

RFU Allied Dunbar Leagues
Division 2
Coventry v Rotherham
Leeds v Moseley
London Welsh v Wakefield
Orrell v Exeter
Waterloo v Manchester
West Hartlepool v Rugby
Worcester v Henley

IRFU League
Division 1
Lansdowne v Garryowen

Tuesday 18 April

RFU Allied Dunbar Leagues
Division 1
Bath v Sale
Bedford v Saracens
Harlequins v Northampton
Leicester v Gloucester
Newcastle v London Irish
Wasps v Bristol

Wednesday 19 April

Royal Navy v Royal Air Force

Saturday 22 April

RFU Allied Dunbar Leagues
Division 1
Bristol v Newcastle
Gloucester v Wasps
London Irish v Bedford
Northampton v Bath
Sale v Leicester
Saracens v Harlequins

Division 2
Exeter v Leeds
Henley v Coventry
Manchester v West Hartlepool
Moseley v Waterloo
Rotherham v London Welsh
Rugby v Worcester
Wakefield v Orrell

SRU Cup Final (Murrayfield)

IRFU League
Division 1
Ballymena v Lansdowne
Cork Const v Clontarf
DLSP v Shannon
Dungannon v Garryowen
Terenure Coll v St Mary's Coll
Young Munster v Buccaneers

WRU SWALEC Cup *Semi-finals*

Tue 25 or Wed 26 April

WRU Premiership
Cardiff v Glasgow
Dunvant v Caerphilly
Edinburgh v Ebbw Vale
Neath v Bridgend
Newport v Llanelli
Pontypridd v Swansea

Saturday 29 April

RFU Allied Dunbar Leagues
Division 1
Bath v Harlequins
Bedford v Bristol
Leicester v Northampton
London Irish v Saracens
Newcastle v Gloucester
Wasps v Sale

Division 2
Coventry v Rugby
Leeds v Orrell

London Welsh v Henley
Rotherham v Wakefield
Waterloo v Exeter
West Hartlepool v Moseley
Worcester v Manchester

IRFU League
Division 1
Buccaneers v Dungannon
DLSP v Terenure Coll
Garryowen v Ballymena
Lansdowne v Young Munster
St Mary's Coll v Cork Const
Shannon v Clontarf

WRU Premiership
Bridgend v Pontypridd
Caerphilly v Newport
Cardiff v Ebbw Vale
Glasgow v Dunvant
Llanelli v Neath
Swansea v Edinburgh

Saturday 6 May
European Cup *Semi-finals*

European Shield *Semi-finals*

Army v Royal Navy (Twickenham)

RFU Allied Dunbar Leagues
Division 1
Bath v Saracens
Bristol v London Irish
Gloucester v Bedford
Harlequins v Leicester
Northampton v Wasps
Sale v Newcastle

Division 2
Exeter v West Hartlepool
Henley v Rotherham
Leeds v Wakefield
Manchester v Coventry
Moseley v Worcester
Orrell v Waterloo
Rugby v London Welsh

WRU Premiership
Dunvant v Cardiff

Ebbw Vale v Swansea
Edinburgh v Bridgend
Neath v Caerphilly
Newport v Glasgow
Pontypridd v Llanelli

Saturday 13 May
RFU Tetley's Bitter Cup Final
  (Twickenham)

RFU Allied Dunbar Leagues
Division 2
Coventry v Moseley
London Welsh v Manchester
Rotherham v Rugby
Wakefield v Henley
Waterloo v Leeds
West Hartlepool v Orrell
Worcester v Exeter

WRU Premiership
Bridgend v Ebbw Vale
Caerphilly v Pontypridd
Cardiff v Swansea
Edinburgh v Llanelli
Neath v Glasgow
Newport v Dunvant

Saturday 20 May
WRU SWALEC Cup Final (Cardiff)

RFU Allied Dunbar Leagues
Division 1
Bedford v Sale
Leicester v Bath
London Irish v Gloucester
Newcastle v Northampton
Saracens v Bristol
Wasps v Harlequins

Saturday 27 May
European Cup Final

European Shield Final

Saturday 8 July
French Club Championship Final
  (Paris)

If you enjoyed this book here is a selection of other bestselling sports titles from Headline

ROTHMANS RUGBY LEAGUE YEARBOOK 1999	Raymond Fletcher	£17.99 ☐
ROTHMANS FOOTBALL YEARBOOK 1999-2000	Glenda Rollin and Jack Rollin	£18.99 ☐
A LOT OF HARD YAKKA	Simon Hughes	£6.99 ☐
DARK TRADE	Donald McRae	£7.99 ☐
TO WIN JUST ONCE	Sean Magee	£6.99 ☐
ATHERS	David Norrie	£6.99 ☐
LEFT FOOT FORWARD	Garry Nelson	£5.99 ☐
FERGIE	Stephen F. Kelly	£6.99 ☐
DERBY DAYS	Dougie and Eddy Brimson	£6.99 ☐
MY TOUR DIARIES	Angus Fraser	£6.99 ☐
MANCHESTER UNITED RUINED MY LIFE	Colin Shindler	£5.99 ☐

Headline books are available at your local bookshop or newsagent. Alternatively, books can be ordered direct from the publisher. Just tick the titles you want and fill in the form below. Prices and availability subject to change without notice.

Buy four books from the selection above and get free postage and packaging and delivery within 48 hours. Just send a cheque or postal order made payable to Bookpoint Ltd to the value of the total cover price of the four books. Alternatively, if you wish to buy fewer than four books the following postage and packaging applies:

UK and BFPO: £4.30 for one book; £6.30 for two books; £8.30 for three books.

Overseas and Eire: £4.80 for one book; £7.10 for 2 or 3 books (surface mail).

Please enclose a cheque or postal order made payable to *Bookpoint Limited*, and send to: Headline Publishing Ltd, 39 Milton Park, Abingdon, OXON OX14 4TD, UK.
Email Address: orders@bookpoint.co.uk

If you would prefer to pay by credit card, our call team would be delighted to take your order by telephone. Our direct line is 01235 400 414 (lines open 9.00 am–6.00 pm Monday to Saturday 24 hour message answering service). Alternatively you can send a fax on 01235 400 454.

Name ....

Address ....

....

....

If you would prefer to pay by credit card, please complete:
Please debit my Visa/Access/Diner's Card/American Express (delete as applicable) card number:

Signature .... Expiry Date ....